Psychology

To the researchers, past
and present, whose work
embodies psychology
today, and to the students
who will follow in their
footsteps to shape the
psychology of tomorrow.

Douglas A. Bernstein

Edward J. Roy

Thomas K. Srull

Christopher D. Wickens

University of Illinois at Urbana-Champaign

Psychology

HOUGHTON MIFFLIN COMPANY   **Boston**
Dallas   **Geneva, Illinois**   **Palo Alto**   **Princeton**

Cover photograph by James Scherer

Anatomical illustrations by Joel Ito

Charts and Graphs by Boston Graphics, Inc.

Illustrations by Paul Schulenburg on pages 33, 53, 84, 94, 133, 140, 156, 179, 185, 194, 199, 246, 252, 256, 265, 274, 312, 325, 337, 338, 353, 451, 454, 457

Photo Credits

Table of contents: **p. vii:** © Yoav/Phototake; **p. viii:** © Andrew Brilliant; **p. ix:** © Andrew Brilliant; **p. x:** © Chuck O'Rear/Woodfin Camp & Associates; **p. xi:** © Carlos Vergara/Nawrocki Stock Photo; **p. xii:** © Elizabeth Crews; **p. xiii:** © Jeff Cadge/The Image Bank; **p. xiv:** © J. Guichard/Sygma; **p. xv:** © Owen Franken/Sygma; **p. xvi:** © Tom Grill/Comstock Inc.; **p. xvii:** © Jim Pickerell/Click, Chicago; **p. xviii:** © Julie Houck/Stock, Boston.

(Photo credits continue following subject index.)

Printed in the U.S.A.

Library of Congress Catalog Card Number: 87-80237

ISBN: 0-395-35506-0

DEFGHIJ-VH-9543210

Brief Contents

Contents

3   BIOLOGICAL BASES OF BEHAVIOR   80

Contents

4   SENSATION   118

5 PERCEPTION   162

6 CONSCIOUSNESS   204

7

LEARNING   242

8
MEMORY   280

9
THOUGHT AND LANGUAGE   320

10 MENTAL ABILITIES   366

13   STRESS AND COPING   472

14   PERSONALITY   504

16

TREATMENT OF PSYCHOLOGICAL DISORDERS

Preface

To explain psychology well, a teacher must serve both the discipline of psychology itself and the students who are seeking to learn about it. The discipline is vast, covering virtually all of human behavior and much of animal behavior as well. The time allotted to explain the discipline at the introductory level is usually so short as to be measured in mere weeks. Nevertheless, our years of teaching, as well as many discussions with other teachers, have convinced us that the introductory course *can* do justice to psychology, communicating the substance and complexity of our science to a remarkable degree without leaving students bewildered or bored.

When we set out to write this text, we sought to achieve that same objective. More specifically, we had several goals in mind:

To explore the full range of psychology, from cell to society, in an eclectic manner as free as possible from theoretical bias.

To balance our need to explain the content of psychology with an emphasis on the *doing* of psychology, through a blend of conceptual discussion and description of research studies.

To foster scientific attitudes and to help our readers learn to think critically by examining the ways that psychologists have solved, or failed to solve, fascinating puzzles of behavior and mental processes.

To produce a text that, without oversimplifying psychology, is clear, accessible, and enjoyable for students to read—even spiced now and again with a touch of humor.

To demonstrate that, in spite of its diversity, psychology is a notably integrated discipline in which each subfield is linked to other subfields by common interests and overarching research questions. The productive cross-fertilization among social, clinical, and biological psychologists in researching health and illness is just one recent example of how different types of psychologists benefit from and build on one another's work.

Such a wide range of goals offered a formidable challenge. Indeed, we joined the ranks of teachers who constantly rework the introductory course trying to find the most intellectually satisfying, pragmatic, and stimulating approach possible. In numerous discussions we reminded each other that no introductory psychology text (at least none that is portable) can cover every topic, concept, research finding, or application that every instructor might consider important.

Authors make many decisions about what to include in a text, and however great their aspirations, compromises must always be made. We believe we have made the right ones. Some details we had hoped to present had to be excluded for the sake of space. Nevertheless, the text acknowledges that psychology is a rich, complex structure of theory and research. In attempting to capture that richness and complexity, we have striven to make each of our chapters comprehensive, detailed, and current.

In addition to covering classic studies and established topics, we include research on fascinating topics of recent importance, such as metamemory, artificial intelligence, top-down and bottom-up processing, and the pruning of neurons after adolescence. Our Chapter 15, on abnormal psychology, is based on the new DSM-III-R diagnostic system.

We also have striven to present research findings as conclusions drawn from studies that are not infallible. Part of teaching students to think critically is to have them examine the limitations and flaws in the studies presented to them by authorities, and on this point we did not compromise.

We have, however, retained the features that make the text easier to comprehend. Each chapter begins with an anecdote or case history. Abundant examples make clear psychology's relevance to everyday life. We have included a wealth of visual material to capture the student's interest and explicate the subject at hand (for example, forty full-color illustrations lead the reader through otherwise complex anatomical structures).

We have also taken pains to draw attention to ethical considerations in the practice of psychology, melding the discussion into the body of the text, rather than consigning it to an isolated section where it might be ignored. One such example occurs in Chapter 16, Therapy, where we discuss patients' rights.

We have incorporated in the text frequent references to practical applications of psychological research. In Chapter 5, on perception, we discuss psychology's contribution to aviation safety. In Chapter 7, we use the discussion of observational learning to cast light on the effects of television violence. Chapter 8, Memory, proved to be an appropriate context for the discussion of courtroom behavior as well as an opportunity for students to improve their exam-taking techniques.

Finally, we have tried to place our discussion of historical events and trends into the context where they are relevant, again choosing not to deal with them in isolation.

Knowing we could not please everyone, we nevertheless tried to create a text with a structure and features that would be compatible with a wide range of faculty goals and priorities.

ORGANIZATION AND SPECIAL FEATURES

Perhaps the greatest hurdle in teaching this complex field is that no consensus exists on what chapter sequence will present psychology to students in the most logical and comprehensible manner. Like other teachers, we have a preferred outline, and it is reflected in our table of contents.

We begin in Chapter 1 with an overview of the nature of psychology, a summary of the research and other activities associated with the various subfields within psychology, and a description of some of the research methods psychologists use. Then, to begin surveying the field, we move to Chapter 2, Human Development, where we show the reader how the principles and processes studied in each subfield come together across the human being's lifespan.

Other notable features of our table of contents:

Unlike some other texts, we devote separate chapters to motivation, emotion, and stress and coping (Chapters 11, 12, and 13). This enables us to cover these areas in the depth they deserve and, in particular, to present a detailed discussion of stress, one of the major subjects of psychological research during the past decade.

We devote two separate but related chapters to social psychology (Chapters 17 and 18).

We cover the methods of psychological research initially in Chapter 1, and we deepen that coverage with a statistics appendix that covers inferential as well as descriptive statistics. The appendix facilitates the learning of difficult concepts by focusing on a single research study throughout.

Nevertheless, we have refrained from grouping the chapters into sections and thereby imposing our sequence on your teaching. Indeed, we designed each chapter to be a freestanding unit so that you may assign chapters in any order you wish.

We have also built into the book an integrating tool, called *Linkages,* which highlights some of the relationships among the various subfields in psychology. This tool consists of two parts, one that occurs at the beginning of each chapter and another near the end. In the first few pages of each chapter, a linkage diagram (*Linkages: An Overview*) illustrates ways that the chapter sheds light on questions arising in other chapters and how material in other chapters helps illuminate questions raised in the current one. Each diagram carries an extended caption that discusses some of these linkages. Color coding in each diagram, combined with a key placed near the end of the book, directs the student to pages that carry further discussion of each linkage question. One such discussion always appears at the end of the chapter, where a corresponding linkage box (*Linkages: An Example*) addresses at length a question previously raised in that chapter's linkage diagram. By establishing ties with chapters that precede or follow a given chapter, the linkage diagrams and linkage boxes combine with the text narrative to highlight the network of relationships among psychology's subareas. The linkage program does not require that you follow our text's chapter sequence.

The linkage tool is our sole use of boxed material. When we have chosen to emphasize a special topic, we have placed it in a *Highlight,* a section that follows logically and directly from the narrative. These Highlights, analogous to a magnifying glass placed over particular topics in each chapter, allow the reader to examine selected topics in detail without being distracted from the chapter's narrative flow.

Each chapter concludes with *Future Directions,* a section intended to excite and inform students about new trends. Here we offer our views on the directions that theory, research, and applications will take in future years. We also suggest courses that an interested student could take in psychology and other disciplines to learn more about the chapter's topic.

ANCILLARY PACKAGE

Accompanying this book are, among other ancillaries, an *Instructor's Manual,* a *Test Bank,* and a *Study Guide.* Because these items were prepared by the lead author and his colleagues in the University of Illinois psychology department, you will find an especially high level of coordination between the textbook and these supplements. Each supplement contains unique features not found in the supplements available with competing books.

Instructor's Manual (by Sandra S. Goss and Douglas A. Bernstein)

The *Instructor's Manual* contains a complete set of lecture outlines, supplemented by handouts, references, and suggestions for classroom demonstrations.

It also contains other material that will be useful to teachers of large introductory courses, such as a section on classroom management and administration of large multisection courses. Another section in the Instructor's Manual examines careers in psychology, and instructors may find they want to distribute it to students. This section was written by John P. Fiore, Director of the University of Illinois Undergraduate Advising Office and Associate Department Head for Undergraduate Study.

Study Guide (by Bridget Schoppert and Douglas A. Bernstein)

The *Study Guide* employs numerous techniques that help students to learn. Each chapter contains a detailed outline, a key terms section that includes examples and aids to remembering, a list of learning objectives, and a "Concepts and Exercises" section that shows students how to apply their knowledge of psychology to everyday issues and concerns. In addition, each chapter concludes with a two-part self-quiz consisting of thirty multiple-choice questions. An answer key tells the student not only which response is correct but also why each of the other choices is wrong.

Test Bank (edited by Sandra S. Goss and Douglas A. Bernstein)

The *Test Bank* contains one hundred multiple-choice items and three to five essay questions for each chapter of the text. Many questions have already been class-tested and, where this information is available, are accompanied by graphs indicating the question's discriminative power, level of difficulty, the percentage of students who chose each response, and the relationship between students' performance on a given item and their overall performance on the test in which the item appeared.

Other Ancillaries Available on Adoption

The *Instructor's Manual, Test Bank,* and *Study Guide* are also available to adopters on disk for use on microcomputers. The detailed lecture outlines that appear in the *Instructor's Manual* are also available on disk in a generic ASCII-code version known as *LectureBank*; this format allows instructors to use standard word-processing software to integrate their own lecture notes and ideas into the text lectures. The *Study Guide* is an interactive program under the title *Microstudy Plus*, which gives students feedback on incorrect as well as on correct answers. *Microtest* allows instructors to generate exams and to integrate their own test items with those on the disk. Also included in the ancillary package is *GPA: Grade Performance Analyzer,* which allows instructors to construct rosters for each course section and to monitor and analyze student performance throughout the term. In addition, a set of *computer simulations* that illustrate intriguing phenomena in psychology is available.

Also offered to adopters of the text are two noncomputer teaching aids. A set of more than 100 images, most in full color, have been rendered in *transparency or slide form.* Labels on these images are presented in large-scale type to enable them to be viewed more easily in the classroom. Finally, a *videocassette* containing several short films on topics in psychology supplements the material covered in the text.

ACKNOWLEDGMENTS

We are very aware of and grateful to many people who provided the help, criticism, and encouragement that made it possible to transform the idea of this book into the object you now hold in your hands.

We first wish to thank Alison Clarke-Stewart (University of California, Irvine), a leading scholar in her field, for writing Chapter 2 on human development. Professor Clarke-Stewart's skills as a writer are evident throughout the chapter, as is her command of the important themes and issues in development.

Thanks are also due to the Department of Psychology at the University of Illinois at Urbana-Champaign, especially to its head, Emanuel Donchin, who provided us with a firm base of support throughout the writing of the book. We are especially grateful to Diane Weidner for coordinating communication between the authors and Houghton Mifflin. Her unselfish devotion to helping us assumed heroic proportions at times; we thank you very much, Diane. Thanks also go to Helen Bryan and Pattsie Petrie, of the Susan Stout Memorial Library, for their unfailing help and endless patience in response to our many complex and obscure requests for references. Cathy Stein contributed material on psychological testing to the chapter on mental abilities, and we appreciate her help.

We owe a special debt to the colleagues listed below, who read and evaluated all or part of the manuscript as it was being developed. Their advice and suggestions for improvements were responsible for many of the good qualities you will find in the book. If you have any criticisms, they probably involve areas these people warned us about.

Paul Abramson, University of California, Los Angeles
Elizabeth Allgeier, Bowling Green State University
Craig A. Anderson, Rice University
Ruth L. Ault, Davidson College
James R. Averill, University of Massachusetts, Amherst
Lewis M. Barker, Baylor University
Deborah Belle, Boston University
Michael Best, Southern Methodist University
Robert C. Bolles, University of Washington
Nathan Brody, Wesleyan University
Rosalind Dymond Cartwright, Rush Medical College
Charles Cofer, University of North Carolina, Chapel Hill
Ellen Marie Cooper, Pennsylvania State University, University Park
Paul Cornwell, Pennsylvania State University, University Park
Xenia Coulter, Empire State College
Richard B. Day, McMaster University
Frank DaPolito, University of Dayton
Randy L. Diehl, University of Texas, Austin
Halford H. Fairchild, Association of Black Psychologists
J. Gregor Fetterman, Arizona State University
Jeffrey D. Fisher, University of Connecticut, Storrs
Randy D. Fisher, University of Central Florida
Robert A. Frank, University of Cincinnati
Irene Hanson Frieze, University of Pittsburgh
Adrienne Gans, New York University
Don Gawley, Indiana University, Bloomington
Richard A. Griggs, University of Florida

Carlos V. Grijalva, University of California, Los Angeles
Sandra S. Goss, University of Illinois, Urbana
Robert W. Grossman, Kalamazoo College
Ruben C. Gur, University of Pennsylvania
Anne Harris, Arizona State University
Robert B. Hays, George Washington University
Steven R. Heyman, University of Wyoming
Deborah L. Holmes, Loyola University of Chicago
Ralph W. Hood, Jr., University of Tennessee, Chattanooga
Jeffrey A. Howard, Eckerd College
Earl Hunt, University of Washington
Janet Shibley Hyde, University of Wisconsin, Madison
Cynthia E. Jayne, Temple University School of Medicine
James D. Kestenbaum, Rochester Institute of Technology
David L. Kohfield, Southern Illinois University, Edwardsville
Marcy Lansman, University of North Carolina, Chapel Hill
Arnold A. Lazarus, Rutgers, The State University
Richard L. Leavy, Ohio Wesleyan University
Marc S. Lewis, University of Texas, Austin
Lewis R. Lieberman, Columbus College
Sanford Lopater, Christopher Newport College
Steven Lopez, University of Southern California
James Luginbuhl, North Carolina State University
Joseph G. Malpeli, University of Illinois, Urbana
Margaret W. Matlin, State University of New York, Geneseo
Donald H. McBurney, University of Pittsburgh
Gerald A. Mendelsohn, University of California, Berkeley
Donald H. Mershon, North Carolina State University
Lawrence S. Meyers, California State University, Sacramento
Peter M. Milner, McGill University
James S. Nairne, University of Texas, Arlington
Patricia Parmelee, Philadelphia Geriatric Center
Anne C. Petersen, Pennsylvania State University, University Park
Terry F. Pettijohn, The Ohio State University, Marion
James O. Prochaska, University of Rhode Island
Kathryn Quina, University of Rhode Island
Stephen K. Reed, Florida Atlantic University
Janet Morgan Riggs, Gettysburg College
Richard J. Sanders, University of North Carolina, Wilmington
Timothy Schallert, University of Texas, Austin
Janet Ward Schofield, University of Pittsburgh
Bridget Schoppert, University of Illinois, Urbana
David A. Schroeder, University of Arkansas, Fayetteville
Marian Schwartz, University of Wisconsin, Madison
Michael B. Sewall, Mohawk Valley Community College
Michael D. Spiegler, Providence College
Charles D. Spielberger, University of South Florida
Valerie N. Stratton, Pennsylvania State University, Altoona
Thomas K. Tutko, San Jose State University
Ryan D. Tweney, Bowling Green State University
Benjamin Wallace, Cleveland State University
Michael J. Watkins, Rice University
Paul J. Wellman, Texas A & M University
Ben A. Williams, University of Southern California

Sharon Wolf, California State University, Long Beach
William R. Wooten, Brown University

We also want to thank Katie Steele, who got this project off the ground by encouraging us to stop talking about this book and start writing it. We were consistently delighted by the caring, the enthusiasm, and the professionalism of everyone we had dealings with in Houghton Mifflin's College Division. The debt of gratitude we owe for their unwavering support and their commitment to this project can never be repaid.

Finally, we want to express our deepest appreciation to our families and friends. Their love saw us through an exhilarating but demanding period of our lives. They endured our hours at the computer, missed meals, postponed vacations, and occasional irritability. Their faith in us was more important than they realize, and it will be cherished forever.

Left to right: Christopher D. Wickens, Edward J. Roy, Thomas K. Srull, Douglas A. Bernstein

Psychology

*C*an hypnosis help eyewitnesses recall forgotten details of a crime? Are infants harmed by day care? Does watching violent television programs make a person more aggressive? Can electroshock therapy help the mentally ill? We will discuss all of these questions in this book, because they all relate to psychology.

Psychology is the science of behavior and mental processes. This means that psychologists use the methods of science to investigate all kinds of behavior and mental processes, from the activity of a single nerve cell to the social conflicts in a complex society, from the development of language in childhood to the adjustments required in old age. In this opening chapter, we offer an overview of the field, including a description of what subfields and approaches psychology encompasses, what psychologists do, and how psychologists go about their work. In later chapters, we will focus on the results of psychological research and how those results are being applied to improve the quality of life for many people.

FROM CELL TO SOCIETY: THE SCOPE OF PSYCHOLOGY

As an illustration of the scope of psychology, consider the case of Jack Montgomery. Jack is a 47-year-old father of five and leader of a youth group at the East Side YMCA. For the last twenty-five years, he has smoked more than two packs of unfiltered cigarettes a day. This pattern of behavior has not been kind to him. Jack has already lost one lung to emphysema, and his doctors have warned him that he will soon die unless he quits smoking. When he brings children from the Y to a day camp and begins chopping firewood, he can make only two or three ax strokes before his breathing becomes heavy wheezes. One of the young campers is naive enough to tell him he should stop smoking. "Son," says Jack, "I've tried to quit, but I would rather die than live without cigarettes."

Is smoking a learned habit, a nicotine addiction maintained by biological forces, or a combination of the two? Do different people smoke for different reasons, and do those reasons determine how difficult it will be for them to quit? Why do people start smoking in the first place? Health warnings have dramatically reduced the prevalence of smoking over the last two decades, but nearly one-third of American adults still smoke; some of them began using tobacco before they entered high school (Gallup, 1986). Why don't smokers heed warnings about the grave dangers of smoking? What can be done to motivate smokers to quit? These are just a few of the questions that a psychologist might ask about smoking. There are lists at least as long for other phenomena. Which questions particular psychologists choose to address and where they look for the answers depend on their area of specialization and on the psychological approach they prefer.

2

1

The World of Psychology

Subfields of Psychology

In 1879, in Leipzig, Germany, Wilhelm Wundt—a physician and physiologist who hoped to identify the basic elements of human consciousness—established the first formal psychology laboratory. We will have more to say about the history of psychology in Chapter 6. For now, suffice it to say that psychology has expanded greatly since the founding of Wundt's laboratory. Like other sciences, psychology has developed numerous subfields, or areas of specialization (see Table 1.1). These subfields approach behavior and mental processes in somewhat different ways.

Biological psychology   Psychologists who analyze the biological factors in behavior and mental processes are called **biological** or **physiological psychologists.** They might analyze, for example, the relationship between how a smoker smokes (the rate of puffs) and how much deadly carbon monoxide reaches the brain.

Some biological psychologists explore the chemical interactions within and between nerve cells, especially in the brain and spinal cord. Understanding these interactions is vital to understanding behavior and mental life because experiences, perceptions, actions, and emotions all depend on how nerve cells communicate. Some researchers explore the relationships between brain activity and behavior. For example, they might map the parts of the brain that become activated when people solve problems or confront unexpected events.

TABLE 1.1 _____

Subfields of Psychology
Researchers in each of psychology's subfields approach their work from a characteristic perspective. These perspectives are reflected in the following sample of general questions and issues typically of interest to psychologists in each subfield.

Specialty	Some Common Questions
Biological psychology	How do the electrical and chemical activities in nerve cells influence behavior? Which parts of the brain control which kinds of behavior? What happens in the brain when we think or become emotional?
Experimental and cognitive psychology	What rules govern what we perceive, how we learn, what we remember, and what we forget? How are thought processes organized? How are judgments and decisions made?
Personality psychology	How do people differ psychologically? How can personality differences be measured? Is personality inherited or learned? Can it be changed?
Social psychology	How and to what extent can a person or a group influence the attitudes, actions, emotions, and mental processes of other people? What determines whether two people will be attracted to one another?
Clinical psychology	In what ways do behavior and mental processes become abnormal? How can various forms of abnormality be measured and distinguished? What causes such abnormality, and how can it be treated?
Developmental psychology	How do such attributes as thinking, social skills, intelligence, language, and personality grow over time? What factors facilitate or distort this growth? How can this knowledge be used to improve child-rearing practices?
Quantitative psychology	What mathematical tools can measure and predict personality, intelligence, judgment, and emotions? How can research data best be analyzed?

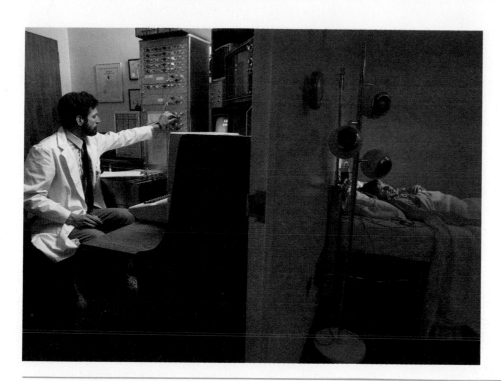

Monitoring brain activity during sleep. The relationship between dreams and brain functions is just one of the many research topics pursued by biological psychologists.

Other biological psychologists look for clues to how hormones influence emotion and behavior. Still others painstakingly unravel the puzzle of how certain groups of nerve cells allow people to translate energy from the outside world into the experiences of sight and hearing.

Experimental and cognitive psychology Many smokers say that cigarettes help them to concentrate and to perform various mental tasks more efficiently. Is this self-delusion, or does smoking change mental efficiency?

This is the type of question that experimental and cognitive psychologists might ask. They have found, for example, that giving nicotine to rats can impair the rats' ability to recall tasks they learned just twenty-four hours earlier (Gilliam & Schlesinger, 1985). But researchers have also found that male smokers do better at detecting rapidly presented stimuli on a televison screen after being allowed to smoke than after twelve hours of cigarette deprivation (Edwards et al., 1985).

Experimental psychology once *was* psychology. This was the area in which Wilhelm Wundt, William James, Edward Titchener, and other early psychologists worked. They used the term *experimental* to distinguish their experiments on human perception, learning, and memory from the endeavors of philosophers and others who thought hard about such phenomena but performed no experiments. The scientific methods of experimental psychology are now evident in research in every subfield of psychology.

Today, **experimental psychologists** continue to conduct experiments aimed at better understanding learning, memory, and other basic behavioral and mental processes in both animals and humans. Research on human learning has helped curriculum planners and teachers in everything from deciding how much new material should be presented in one lesson to advising students on how to study. You may find some of the research described in Chapter 8, on memory, especially valuable as you prepare for tests.

In recent years, many experimental psychologists have begun to shift their research toward ever more detailed analysis of the mental processes involved

Research by cognitive psychologists on how people perceive and process information has resulted in the design of less confusing, more informative control systems for nuclear power plants, airplanes, automobiles, and other equipment.

in learning, memory, and perception. They explore the processes underlying judgment, decision making, problem solving, imagination, and other aspects of complex human thought, or *cognition*. Those who focus on these processes have come to be known as **cognitive psychologists.**

Cognitive psychologists also study people with learning problems—people like Phil, a grade-school student with the learning disability known as *dyslexia*. Like other dyslexics, Phil has normal intellectual abilities and a perfect understanding of speech; but somewhere in the process of translating printed symbols into meanings in his head, something goes wrong. When Phil reads, he often leaves out words or confuses the letters *b* and *d* or *o* and *c*. Where, why, and how these disruptions occur are some of the questions being asked by psychologists who study how the mind perceives each letter, how letters are grouped into words, how words are grouped into sentences, and how sentences are grouped into ideas. As they find answers to such questions, psychologists and other professionals can begin to correct the problems of dyslexia and other learning disabilities.

One of the many places where cognitive and experimental psychology come together is engineering. For example, the safety of commercial aviation is in part due to psychological studies of how people perceive the world around them and how much information they can handle at once. This research has allowed cognitive psychologists to advise engineers about how to arrange an airliner's vast array of instruments and warning lights so that the pilot can quickly understand and act on them. *Engineering psychologists* are becoming increasingly prominent in the design of everything from telephone equipment and computer keyboards to control panels for nuclear power plants.

Personality psychology Whereas experimental and cognitive psychologists seek laws that govern the behavior of people in general, **personality psychologists** focus on the characteristics that make us unique. They also try to identify the specific ways in which people differ and to explore the relationships between people's personalities and their tendency to think, act, and feel in certain ways. For example, personality researchers have found that some

Some people love risky activities; others avoid them. Individual differences of this kind are one of the topics studied by personality psychologists.

people tend to attribute success or failure to external forces, such as good or bad luck; other people believe that success or failure is controlled largely by personal effort. As we will see in Chapter 14, on personality, such differences have been linked to a variety of behaviors, from the tendency to smoke cigarettes to the tendency to become depressed.

Social psychology   Junior high school students do not simply wake up one morning and decide to start smoking cigarettes. Social influences over time shape their behavior. They may see their parents, and especially their friends, smoking. They cannot help seeing magazine ads that portray the glamour supposedly associated with smoking. Influences like these are the special interest of **social psychologists.** They study how people influence one another, especially in groups of two or more.

Some social psychology research focuses on how people influence one another's attitudes. For example, studies of prejudice show that children learn negative attitudes and biased behavior toward certain racial or ethnic groups by listening to bigoted parents or friends. Other research focuses on group behavior—asking, for example, how the personality of a group's leader affects its ability to solve problems, make decisions, or maintain a pleasant social atmosphere. *Industrial-organizational psychologists* often conduct or apply research on such questions in the business world. They might help select the people most likely to work well in various settings, improve supervisors' leadership skills, create groups that function at maximum efficiency, and suggest other research-based steps to increase both productivity and satisfaction.

Clinical psychology   Whereas most psychologists explore normal behavior and mental processes, **clinical psychologists** seek to understand and correct abnormal functioning. Using tests, interviews, and observations, they conduct research on the causes and symptoms of mental disorders. In the consulting room, they use similar methods to pinpoint individuals' problems and offer therapy to help solve those problems.

A counseling session in a battered women's shelter. Working with troubled people to prevent today's problems from getting worse is part of the work of community psychologists. Community psychologists have also created walk-in crisis clinics and other programs aimed at reaching out to people in need of help.

Preventing disorders is another concern of clinical psychologists, especially those called *community psychologists.* Their emphasis on prevention has inspired programs to head off psychological problems among teenage parents, people under heavy stress, and others who may be at high risk for developing mental disorders.

Developmental psychology Behavior and mental processes change constantly over the course of a lifetime. **Developmental psychologists** have set themselves the task of describing those changes, trying to understand their causes, and exploring their effects. They have conducted research on the stress of adolescence, the challenges of adulthood, and the changes associated with old age. But because changes in language, thinking, social skills, and personality occur most rapidly and dramatically in infancy and childhood, much developmental research has focused on those early stages of life.

Research by developmental psychologists has increased the understanding of how childhood experiences are related to subsequent behavior and thought. Early work by René Spitz showed, for example, that orphaned infants placed in an institution where they had basic care, but no chance to form a close attachment to an adult, typically became socially and emotionally disordered. Orphans placed in homes where conditions were quite bad, but where they could develop a close relationship with a caregiver, did far better emotionally. Other research has helped launch special educational programs for underprivileged preschoolers who appear likely to be at a disadvantage when they start school.

Quantitative psychology The rules of science require that the topic studied—whether chemical reactions, planetary movements, or memory—be accurately measured and carefully analyzed so that the results of research will be as free from error as possible. All psychologists therefore face the task of measuring and analyzing the phenomena they choose to study. Many of these phenomena—heart activity, learning, emotions, mental disorders, social development, or any of a thousand other behaviors or mental processes—are particularly difficult to translate into quantitative form and are not easy to analyze using conventional mathematical tools.

Suppose, for example, that you want to analyze smoking behavior. You could ask subjects to fill out a questionnaire summarizing their smoking over the past six months; you could ask them to keep track of their smoking over the next two weeks by recording in a daily diary the time and place of each cigarette. You could also observe the subjects as they smoke, recording the number and duration of puffs. Whatever the approach, you need a method of summarizing and analyzing the data you have collected, in order to compare one subject with the next and perhaps even to identify groups of subjects with similar smoking styles. Figure 1.1 illustrates both the difficulty of dealing with such data and one method that quantitative psychologists have developed to analyze and present them.

Quantitative, or *measurement,* **psychologists** devote much of their energy to developing and applying mathematical methods for summarizing and analyzing data from virtually every area of psychology. For example, they have helped biological psychologists find precise mathematical ways of describing the changes in a subject's heart rate, blood pressure, or brain waves when certain stimuli are presented. Some of these methods, known collectively as **statistical analyses,** are discussed in the Appendix.

Quantitative psychologists are also involved in constructing and evaluating paper-and-pencil tests used to measure traits, attitudes, mental capacity, and mental disorders. These tests are used every day to help diagnose people's problems and to select individuals for admission to everything from college to jobs in the military and the space program.

In other studies, quantitative psychologists attempt to create mathematical formulas, or *models,* to describe and even predict such complex behavior as judgment and decision making. In diagnosing a patient's physical problems, for example, doctors use information from physical examinations, medical histories, blood tests, brain scans, and many other sources. How is all this information combined to reach a diagnosis? A quantitative psychologist might

Figure 1.1
Spectral Analysis of Smoking Behavior
Section a shows the time intervals between cigarettes for one person over a two-week period. The variability and apparent disorder in the data make the data difficult to summarize and certainly difficult to compare mathematically with data for another smoker. Section b shows how to bring order to the data through the use of a special technique called spectral analysis (Gottman, 1981). The single peak in the curve suggests that this particular smoker tends to show a regular sequence of progressively longer, then progressively shorter intervals between light-up times. Other smokers may show far less regularity (Emmons & Bernstein, 1987). The meaning of such patterns and of differences in patterns between smokers is still not clear, but the patterns would not even have been noticed if quantitative psychologists had not developed analytic techniques capable of detecting them.

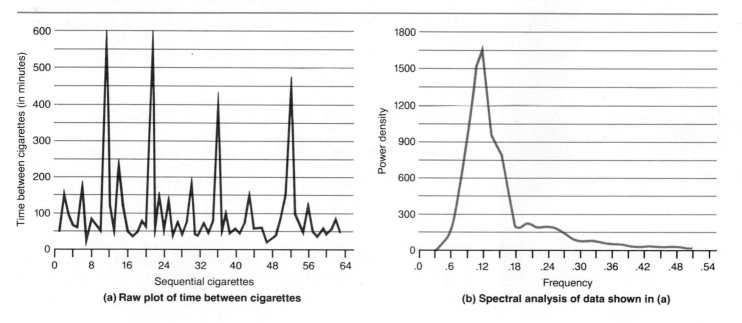

(a) Raw plot of time between cigarettes

(b) Spectral analysis of data shown in (a)

try to describe the process in mathematical terms, creating a model to predict other doctors' diagnoses in future experiments and, by implication, in actual medical situations.

Psychological Approaches

Suppose you were a psychologist trying to understand why a certain group of people had failed when they tried to quit smoking. Where would you look for an answer? Would you search for environmental stressors that might have prompted relapse? Would you blame the physical discomfort created by quitting?

Many such approaches are possible and useful. The one you would choose would most likely depend on your assumptions about the most important factors causing, maintaining, and altering behavior and mental processes in general and cigarette smoking in particular. These assumptions would lead you to prefer different theoretical approaches. The most influential approaches in psychology today are generally labeled biological, psychodynamic, behavioral, humanistic, and cognitive.

The biological approach   One way to understand smoking is to explore how and why smokers need or become addicted to nicotine. This reflects the *biological approach*. It begins with the assumption that biological factors, such as genetics, electrical and chemical activity in the brain, and the actions of hormones are the most important determinants of behavior and mental processes. Those who adopt this approach study emotions, mental disorders, memory, thinking, and other psychological phenomena by seeking out and learning about their biological components.

The behavioral approach to psychology emphasizes the idea that much human behavior is learned, often on the basis of watching others. Advertisers capitalize on learning principles by associating their products with sexuality, status, and other rewards.

The psychodynamic approach   The psychodynamic approach was founded by Sigmund Freud, the famous Viennese physician whose interest in "neurotics" (people with physical symptoms with no physical causes) led him to develop, late in the nineteenth century, a theory of personality, mental disorder, and therapy known as *psychoanalysis*. The *psychodynamic approach* presumes that behavior and mental processes reflect constant, dynamic, and often unconscious struggles within each person. These struggles are varied and complex, but they usually involve conflict between the impulse to satisfy instincts or wishes (for food, sex, or aggression, for example) and the restrictions imposed by society.

Viewed from this perspective, abnormal or problematic behavior reflects either an unsatisfactory resolution of conflicts or an outright failure to resolve them. Smoking might thus be but one symptom of an unconscious conflict between wanting to remain a pampered infant and wanting to be an independent adult; inhaling a cigarette might symbolize sucking on a bottle. A psychodynamic psychologist would expect therapy aimed at resolving inner conflicts to greatly enhance a person's ability to quit smoking permanently.

The behavioral approach   At about the same time that Freud was developing his psychodynamic approach, a young American, John Watson, was urging psychologists to study only what they could observe directly, and not unobservable mental events. By focusing on observable actions alone, said Watson, psychologists would not have to rely on people's possibly distorted reports about mental processes and could begin to understand behavior whether it occurs in adults, children, the mentally ill, or animals.

Watson's views gave birth to the *behavioral approach* to psychology. According to this approach, the pattern of rewards and punishments that each person has experienced determines most behaviors and ways of thinking. Biological factors provide the raw material on which these rewards, punishments, and other learning experiences act to mold each of us.

Few behaviorists endorse a version of the behavioral approach as radical as Watson's, but they do suggest that most problematic behaviors can be changed by helping people to unlearn old habits and develop new and better ones. Thus, smoking might be viewed as a habit learned by watching others and maintained because the smoker associates cigarettes with pleasant social occasions, relief from stress, or other rewards. People might break the habit if they learn to develop rewarding alternative responses in situations previously associated with smoking.

The humanistic approach   So far, the approaches we have described focus on how a person is acted upon, whether by biological forces, inner conflicts, or environmental stimuli. In contrast, a fundamental assumption of the *humanistic approach* is that people control themselves. Furthermore, according to this approach, each person has an innate tendency to grow toward his or her own potential, although the environment (including other people) may block this growth.

According to the humanistic perspective, behavior is determined primarily by each person's capacity to *choose* how to think and act. These choices are dictated, say humanistic psychologists, by each individual's unique perception of the world. If you perceive the world as a supportive, friendly place, you are likely to feel happy and secure. If you view it as dangerous and hostile, you will probably be defensive and anxious. Humanistic psychologists view even severe depression not as mental illness but as a sign of a person's pessimistic perceptions and attitudes. Seen from the humanistic perspective, the decision to smoke or not, or to quit or not, depends primarily on how a person perceives the benefits and the dangers involved. Unless the smoker decides to quit, any effort prompted by someone else is likely to fail.

The potential for joyful growth as a basic part of each individual is emphasized by the humanistic approach to psychology. Whether that potential is realized, however, depends upon our perceptions of the world and on how we choose to behave based on those perceptions.

The cognitive approach   In the last fifteen years or so, another perspective—the cognitive approach—has become particularly influential. More than any of the other approaches we have discussed, the *cognitive approach* emphasizes the importance of thoughts and other mental processes. This perspective focuses directly on mental processes—that is, on how the brain takes in information; uses its functions of perception, memory, thought, judgment, decision making, and the like to process that information; and generates integrated patterns of behavior.

For example, the cognitive perspective would hold that a person continues to smoke or tries to quit because of what that person recalls about the dangers of smoking, how that person perceives those dangers (are they personally threatening?), and how he or she judges the effects of quitting (would it reduce the risks significantly?). Similarly, since severe behavior disorders reflect some disorganization in the processing of information, effective treatment might range from drugs to training that would help a person think in more organized or rational ways.

The question of which of these approaches is the "right" one can never be answered, simply because "rightness" or "wrongness" is not at issue. Nor does each psychologist have to choose and adhere once and for all to just one approach. In studying smoking, for example, one might want to consider biological, cognitive, and behavioral variables; indeed, this is exactly what many smoking researchers do. Each approach to psychology emphasizes a particular set of factors that tells part of the story of behavior and mental processes. We will see throughout this book that each approach has made its own contribution to psychological theory, research, and applications. A full understanding of psychology is unlikely to develop without appreciating these diverse contributions.

Unity Within Diversity

Psychology's many subfields and approaches have led psychologists into a wide variety of interests and activities. These activities include conducting research and applying the results to solve and prevent human problems, as well as teaching and writing about research findings and psychological knowledge. In spite of this diversity, however, at least two factors unify psychologists' varied interests, activities, and values.

First, because they are all interested in behavior and mental processes, psychologists in every subfield constantly draw on and contribute to knowledge from all the other subfields. For example, the biological psychologist's finding that chemical imbalances in the brain can produce disordered thinking may provide the clinical psychologist with clues to the cause of certain mental disorders. Similarly, research in developmental psychology may help the cognitive psychologist better understand how the ability to use language, solve problems, or think logically is built up over time.

Second, because psychology is a science, all of its subfields emphasize *empirical research*—the collection and analysis of information about topics of interest. Psychologists not only speculate about certain phenomena, such as smoking behavior, but also gather information, or *data,* about it. Even psychologists who do not themselves conduct research depend heavily on research discoveries to teach or write knowledgeably, provide up-to-date treatment, and solve the endless variety of problems they confront every day. Indeed, most of the facts, theories, and applications that make up today's psychological knowledge originated in or were stimulated by research.

Without this research base, psychology might merge with philosophy, or psychologists might issue proclamations with no more credibility than those of astrologers or the *National Enquirer.* To make it easier to appreciate and evaluate the research described in later chapters, we turn now to a general review of the goals of scientific research and of the rules and methods that help psychologists make progress toward those goals. More detailed coverage of data analysis is offered in the Appendix.

THE GOALS OF RESEARCH

There is a country and western song called "Can't Stop Smokin' That Cigarette." On hearing that song over twenty years ago, a psychologist we know became curious about why so many people find it so hard to quit smoking. He has been doing research on smoking ever since. His story is not unusual. The research adventure in psychology, as in all other sciences, often begins simply enough—with curiosity.

Curiosity frequently provokes very interesting, very stimulating questions, but often these questions are phrased in terms that are too general to be investigated scientifically. After agonizing over the glacial slowness with which a group of friends chooses a restaurant or movie, for example, you might notice the same phenomenon in other groups and begin to ask such questions as: How do groups make decisions? What would help them work more efficiently? The scientist must be more specific—asking: What kinds of groups and what kinds of decisions are involved? (The decision-making process

Supportive therapy in a nursing home. Psychology's many subspecialties offer a remarkably wide range of opportunities for careers in research and service relating to all stages of the lifespan and to all aspects of behavior.

among prisoners planning an escape might be different from that used by children choosing a game.) What is meant by *efficiency?* (Ratings of efficiency by group members and ratings by an outside observer might tell very different stories.)

If you are trained as a psychologist, you would begin to ask these more precise questions. The new questions might be less interesting than those you first posed, but you are more likely to be able to answer them with some confidence. It is only by putting together the answers to many smaller questions that researchers begin to see answers to some of the larger ones.

To find these answers, psychologists, like other scientists, depend on the accumulation of knowledge over many years by many people. They also rely on several levels of research guided by four basic goals: description, prediction, control, and explanation.

Description

In order to answer any research question, the scientist must first describe the phenomenon of interest. If, for example, you decided to use jury deliberations at criminal trials as the source of data for studying group decision making, you would first have to gather detailed information about trials and jury deliberations. How are criminal trials conducted? What are the characteristics of the defendants, the witnesses, the attorneys, and the evidence? What do jurors say to each other about the evidence? Do they vote secretly or publicly?

These are just a few of the characteristics of decision making in the courtroom that you would measure and summarize before aiming for more ambitious goals, such as predicting the outcome of a trial. Such descriptive data are usually collected through surveys, case studies, and observations, each of which we will describe shortly.

Prediction

As you examine your data, you would probably begin to see some interesting patterns. It might appear, for example, that six-person juries reach verdicts more slowly than twelve-member juries or that witnesses who wear suits or dresses impress jurors more than those who wear blue jeans. Noticing these apparent relationships, you might aim for a more ambitious research goal: prediction. You might, for example, predict that if defense witnesses are well dressed, then the jury is likely to acquit the defendants. When a prediction is stated as a specific, testable proposition about a phenomenon, it is called a **hypothesis.**

To test your hypothesis, you would gather additional data, looking not only for evidence that supports the hypothesis but also for evidence that *refutes* it. In research aimed at prediction, one typically tests hypotheses by analyzing descriptive data in order to detect relationships between **variables,** which are specific factors or characteristics that can vary in some way. Witnesses' clothing, for example, can vary from cutoffs to formal wear, and verdicts can vary from guilty to not guilty.

The relationships detected in prediction-oriented research usually appear as correlations. **Correlation** means just what it says: "co-relation," the degree to which one variable is related to another. For example, you could test the hypothesis that small juries make slower decisions than large juries by analyzing descriptive data to see whether jury size and decision time are correlated, or related to one another. If jury size and decision time are related, then knowing the size of the jury in a given trial would allow you to predict something about how long that jury took to reach its verdict.

To confirm a hypothesis, however, you need to know more than the simple fact that two variables are correlated. You also need to know how strong the correlation is and what its direction is. The correlation may be so weak that knowing something about one variable tells you very little about the other. Or the *direction* of the correlation may differ from the predicted relationship; it may turn out that smaller juries tend to make faster rather than slower decisions.

The strength and direction of correlations can be summarized precisely by calculating a statistic called the **correlation coefficient.** We will not discuss the mathematics of the procedure here, but understanding its underlying logic will clarify the meaning of many research findings.

HIGHLIGHT

Correlation: The Foundation of Prediction

The correlation coefficient, or *r* for short, can vary from 0 to +1.00 or −1.00. Thus, the coefficient includes both an absolute value (0, .20, .50, and so on) and a sign (plus or minus).

The absolute value of *r* indicates the strength of the relationship. An *r* of 0 between people's hat size and the age of their cars, for example, indicates that there is no correlation between the variables. A correlation of +1.00 or −1.00 indicates a perfect correlation, which means that if you know the value of one variable, you can predict the value of the other variable with certainty. An *r* of +.50 or −.50 suggests a relationship of intermediate strength.

The sign of a correlation coefficient indicates its direction. A plus sign means that the relationship between variables is *positive;* that is, as one variable changes, the other variable changes in the same direction. For example, the correlation between the cost of a gasoline purchase and the number of gallons pumped is positive; as gallons increase or decrease, so does the cost. A minus sign in the correlation coefficient indicates that the relationship is *negative,* which means that, as one variable increases or decreases, the other changes in the opposite direction. For example, as the amount of money spent on a shopping trip increases, the amount remaining decreases (see Figure 1.2).

Statistical significance The variables of interest in psychology are seldom perfectly correlated or totally uncorrelated. In testing your earlier hypothesis on jury size you might find the correlation between jury size and decision time to be +.60. This coefficient suggests that there is a reasonably strong, but imperfect, relationship between the variables. As a result, knowing the size of a jury would allow you to make predictions about decision time better than you could by random guessing. However, the predictions would not be perfectly accurate.

Notice that, in this case, even though the correlation is high, it actually weakens your hypothesis, because the correlation is positive. It indicates that larger juries have longer decision times, exactly the opposite of what you predicted. A coefficient of −.60 (the smaller the jury, the longer its decision times) would have supported the hypothesis.

How high or low does a correlation have to be to support or undermine a researcher's hypothesis? As we discuss in the Appendix, the answer depends on the probability that the correlation could have resulted simply by chance and on certain conventional rules. When a correlation is higher than would be expected by chance alone, it is said to be **statistically significant.**

The limits of correlational research Researchers often claim to find meaning in nonsignificant coefficients, and even significant coefficients may sometimes be rather low. To many psychologists this openness to interpretation is a major weakness of correlational research.

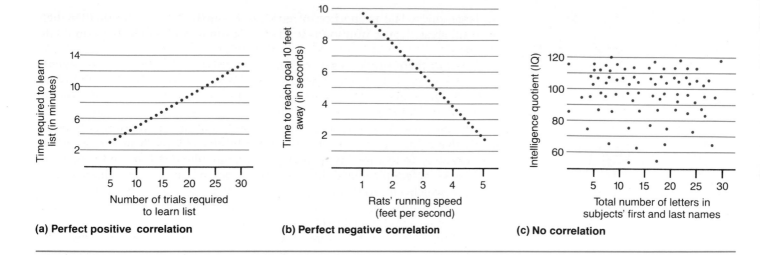

(a) Perfect positive correlation **(b) Perfect negative correlation** **(c) No correlation**

Figure 1.2
Three Scatterplots
The strength and direction of the correlation between variables can be pictured in a graph called a scatterplot. Here are three examples. In section a, we have plotted the number of 30-second trials subjects took to learn a list of meaningless words against the number of minutes the subjects were in the experiment. Since time in the lab and the number of trials are positively and perfectly correlated, the scatterplot appears as a straight line; one can predict the value of either variable once the value of the other is known. In section b is the scatterplot representing the perfect negative correlation between rats' running speeds and the time it took them to reach a goal ten feet away. The higher the animals' speeds, the lower their running times; again, one variable can be predicted perfectly from the other. Section c illustrates the scatterplot of the zero correlation (no relationship) between IQ and the length of people's names. The shape of the "cloud" of data points gives clues to the size and direction of the correlation it reflects. Higher and higher correlations create ever tighter scatters that begin to approximate straight lines.

Correlations have other weaknesses as well. Although a correlation indicates the *degree* of relationship between two variables, it does not indicate *why* they are related. You can easily observe the strong positive correlation between the amount of alcohol consumed and the intensity of the hangover the next morning, but the strength and direction of the relationship give no information about the biochemical processes driving the relationship.

Moreover, the fact that two variables are correlated cannot tell you whether there is a *cause-and-effect* relationship between them, such that one variable actually influences the other. For example, in some English towns, there is a high positive correlation between the number of storks nesting in chimneys and the number of infants born in the town that year. There are also data that show a high negative correlation between the proportion of licensed gun owners in an area and the annual crime rate there. Does this mean that storks are delivering English babies or that the crime rate would drop if more people bought guns? Chances are good that the answer is no (about storks, the answer is definitely no).

Arguing that storks or guns are the causes of higher birth rates or lower crime rates fails to take into account other factors that may influence both variables at the same time. These other factors provide alternative hypotheses that can account for the observed correlation. It may turn out that conditions favoring the survival of storks in England also support agricultural production, tourism, and other activities that directly and indirectly strengthen the British economy; this increased prosperity may prompt more people to decide to have children. Similarly, the relationship between rates of crime and of gun ownership may occur, not because gun ownership reduces crime, but because both rates are influenced by another factor: the environment. High crime rates are usually associated with poverty, drug abuse, and other problems common to large cities. The proportion of gun owners in those cities is smaller than in rural areas, where hunting is a favorite pastime (and where the crime rate is low).

Despite their limitations, correlational methods are important components of psychological research. They greatly enhance psychologists' ability to describe and predict phenomena; they help in the evaluation of existing hypotheses; and they often lead to new hypotheses. In some situations, they are the only methods available. For example, suppose a psychologist hypothesizes that fighting between parents causes children to develop mental disorders. An ideal way to test this hypothesis might be to take one hundred newborns, put some in conflict-filled homes and others in conflict-free homes, and observe which children develop problems. If those in conflict-filled homes show significantly more mental disorders, then the hypothesis that there is a cause-and-effect relationship between conflict and disorders would be strengthened. But because this manipulation of families would be unethical, the investigator must instead test the hypothesis by using sophisticated correlational methods. ◾

Control

Suppose that, after observing smokers in many situations, a psychologist finds a high positive correlation between the amount of stress in a situation and the number of cigarettes consumed per hour in that situation. The psychologist hypothesizes that smokers use tobacco to cope with stress. This makes intuitive sense, but there are other plausible hypotheses. Perhaps the people in high-stress situations all happen to be heavier smokers. Perhaps some of the low-stress observations took place in no-smoking areas. Perhaps some of the smokers observed in low-stress conditions were out of cigarettes or were trying to quit.

A researcher trying to describe or predict smoking, using only correlational methods, might find it difficult to choose among these hypotheses. To rule out rival hypotheses, the psychologist might aim for a more ambitious goal: control. He or she would try to establish a situation in which factors that might interfere with an understanding of the cause-effect relationship are eliminated. Instead of merely observing smokers who happen to come into view, the experimenter might ask some smokers to serve as volunteers for a study in which they perform high- or low-stress tasks in the same laboratory setting. The experimenter would be careful to vary the stressfulness of the situation while keeping everything else constant—the age, sex, and health history of the smokers, how much they typically smoke per day, and so on. Under these controlled conditions, if more smoking occurred in the high- than in the low-stress situations, the researcher would have strong evidence that stress can produce changes in smoking behavior.

When a researcher can manipulate one variable and observe its effect on another variable, we call the result *controlled research.* Controlled research involves *experimental methods,* which we will discuss shortly. In our smoking example, the need to exert control over many aspects of the environment forced the experimenter to work in a laboratory setting, but controlled experiments can also be conducted in the "real world" if proper precautions are taken against unwanted external influences.

Explanation

After examining data from descriptive, predictive, or controlled research (usually all three), scientists can begin to suggest explanations. For example, you might explain the finding that larger juries reach decisions more slowly by suggesting that it takes longer for all members to be heard. Explanations often include or lead to the formation of general rules about certain categories of behavior or mental processes, such as that larger groups take more time to do anything.

Sometimes these general rules are organized into a **theory**, which is an integrated set of principles that can be used to account for, predict, and even control certain phenomena. In devising his theory of evolution, for example, Charles Darwin formed a set of principles that accounts for the development of all life on earth from ancient fossils to living creatures, explains why there is so much variability in animal life, and allows predictions about the future of our planet. Sigmund Freud's theory of psychoanalysis provides an example of a psychological theory whose scope is almost as broad; it seeks to explain virtually all aspects of why people behave as they do. Other psychological theories focus on explaining narrower phenomena, such as color vision, memory, and sleep. Theories are tentative explanations that must be evaluated scientifically.

Predictions flowing from a theory proposed by one psychologist will be tested in correlational and experimental research by many other psychologists. If research supports a theory, that theory usually expands to become a more prominent explanation of some aspect of psychology. If not, the theory is revised or, sometimes, abandoned. Some explanations in science are so well established by constant reconfirmation and fit so consistently and well into everything else we know that they become known as *laws*.

The constant formulation, evaluation, reformulation, and abandonment of psychological theories results in many explanations of behavior and mental processes. In later chapters, we will present several competing theories for many psychological phenomena—which may give you the impression that psychology is in a state of confusion. Actually, *ferment* is a better word for the situation. The existence of conflicting theories helps motivate psychologists to expand their knowledge through more creative research.

There is no fixed sequence in the relationships among description, prediction, control, and explanation. Sometimes explanatory theories spark the curiosity that begins new research projects and guides researchers in their choice of which variables to explore. Psychoanalytic theory, for example, influences some researchers to look at people's dreams for clues to the causes of human problems. Sometimes psychological research begins with observation of, say, children playing together and leads to predictions or explanations that foster the development of a new theory of human relations. Figure 1.3 shows

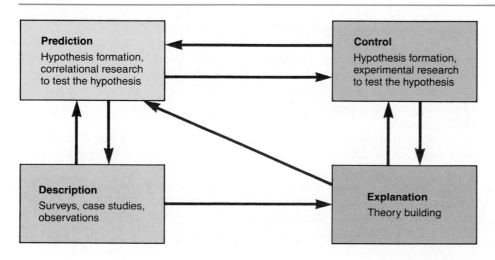

Figure 1.3
Goals and Methods of Psychological Research
Note that all four research goals interact. Predictions lead not only to collection of additional descriptive data, but also to the conduct of controlled experiments, all of which help to confirm or disconfirm the predictions. In turn, controlled research leads to explanatory theories, which themselves generate new predictions about behavior and mental processes. This cycle is endless and endlessly productive in terms of expanding psychological knowledge.

how, as in other sciences, the goals, methods, and data sources of psychology interact constantly. Without descriptive, predictive, and experimental data, there would be nothing to explain; without explanatory theories, the data might never be organized in a coherent and usable way. This continuing interaction of theory and data lies at the heart of the research process that has created the massive amount of knowledge generated in psychology over the past century.

SOME RESEARCH METHODS

Now that we have briefly reviewed the goals of psychological research, we will consider the specific methods used to conduct this research. These methods include surveys, case studies, naturalistic observations, and experiments.

Surveys

Survey methods involve giving people *questionnaires,* or special interviews designed to obtain descriptions of their behavior, attitudes, beliefs, opinions, and intentions. For example, surveys in psychological research have helped clarify differences in the ways people from different social classes discipline their children (lower-class families tend to be more strict). They have also revealed that sexual acts once thought to be quite unusual (such as homosexuality) or shameful (such as masturbation) are relatively common and that the frequency of behaviors such as premarital sex has increased dramatically over a period of years (Hunt, 1974; Kinsey et al., 1953).

To conduct a useful survey, researchers must phrase the questions and select the respondents very carefully. Consider a survey conducted several years ago by Abigail ("Dear Abby") Van Buren. She asked her female readers whether they would prefer to have sexual relations with their partners or just to be held and cuddled. The results showed a preference for cuddling. Does this mean that sex is going out of style? Very unlikely. There are several other possible explanations. Perhaps the preference for cuddling emerged because the question was phrased in "either-or" terms, leaving no room for the respondent to indicate that she liked both cuddling and sex. Or perhaps the women who answered the question were not representative of the population as a whole; perhaps only those with insensitive or overly demanding partners bothered to respond. A totally different picture might have emerged if a different set of women had been asked a more carefully thought-out question.

Other problems that may lurk within the survey method are more difficult to avoid. People may be reluctant to admit undesirable or embarrassing things about themselves. A person may be too proud to admit to earning a below-poverty-level salary or too abashed to reveal a preference for unusual sexual practices. People may say what they feel they should say about an issue, particularly if a survey assesses beliefs about which there are socially "acceptable" and "unacceptable" answers. For example, people may be reluctant to admit negative attitudes toward minorities or may understate the strengths of those attitudes.

In spite of these problems, surveys provide an excellent way of gathering large amounts of data from a large number of people at relatively low cost. Without them, psychologists (and the rest of the population as well) would be far less aware of basic patterns and changes in the behaviors and mental processes that they study. Usually, survey data lead psychologists to formulate predictions and testable hypotheses and to test those hypotheses through additional correlational and experimental research.

Psychologists use surveys to gather information about the attitudes and behaviors of large numbers of people. Careful analysis of data collected through the survey method can provide useful descriptions of behavior patterns, not to mention valuable predictions about the outcome of an election.

Case Studies

The close-up view provided by a case study is sometimes more helpful than the broad portrait given by a survey. A **case study** is an intensive examination of some phenomenon in a particular individual, group, or situation. Case studies are especially useful when a phenomenon is very complex or relatively rare.

The use of case studies has a particularly long tradition in clinical psychology. Freud's development of psychoanalysis, for example, was based on case studies of "neurotics" whose paralysis or other physical symptoms disappeared when they were hypnotized or asleep. In general, the earliest stages of descriptive research on a mental disorder or method of treatment involve case studies of a few patients.

Case studies have also played a special role in *neuropsychology*, the study of the relationships among brain activity, thinking, and behavior. Consider, for example, the case of Dr. P, *The Man Who Mistook His Wife for a Hat* (Sacks, 1985). A distinguished musician with superior intelligence, Dr. P began to display such odd symptoms as the inability to recognize the faces of familiar people and a failure to distinguish between people and inanimate objects. During a visit to a neurologist, Dr. P mistook his foot for his shoe. When he rose to leave, he tried to lift off his wife's head and put it, like a hat, on his own. He could not name even the most common objects when he looked at them, although he could describe them. When handed a glove, for example, he said, "A continuous surface, infolded on itself. It appears to have . . . five outpouchings, if this is the word. . . . A container of some sort." Only later, when he put it on his hand, did he exclaim, "My God, it's a glove!" (Sacks, 1985, p. 13)

Using case studies like this one, pioneers of neuropsychological diagnosis, such as Ward Halstead, Ralph Reitan, and Alexander Luria, carefully noted the specific mental and behavioral deficits appearing in people with particular kinds of brain damage or disease. The exact nature of the damage or disease was often established through autopsies. Eventually, neuropsychologists developed a careful classification of the kinds of brain disorders that result from injuries, malformations, tumors, poisoning, and other causes. (The cause of Dr. P's symptoms was apparently a large brain tumor).

Case studies have one major limitation, however: cases are not necessarily representative samples. Just as visitors from another galaxy would err wildly if they tried to describe the typical Earthling after meeting Rodney Dangerfield, Phyllis Diller, and Joan Rivers, psychologists can be led astray if they do not have access to a representative sample of humans. Furthermore, the reasons for behavior in one case may not apply in all others. Some brain-damaged patients, for example, may suffer psychological as well as physical traumas, so that some of their behavior may be unrelated to their brain injury.

Still, like surveys, case studies provide raw material for psychological research. They can be interesting and valuable sources of information about particular people, and they serve as the testing ground for new treatments, training programs, and other applications of research.

Naturalistic Observation

Sometimes the best way to gather descriptive data about a psychological phenomenon is to observe it as it occurs in the natural environment. This is especially true when other approaches are likely to be disruptive or misleading. For example, if you studied animals only by observing them in laboratory experiments, you would not be likely to see how cues in their natural environment normally affect their behavior, and you might conclude that

The research of ethologist Konrad Lorenz helped demonstrate the automatic nature of much animal behavior. Here, he shows that baby geese will follow the first creature, including him, from whom they hear mother goose sounds.

learning alone determines most of their behavior. In contrast, **ethologists,** scientists who study animal behavior in its natural environment, have found that much of the behavior of lower animals consists of inherited patterns that are very predictable, stereotyped, and triggered automatically by environmental events.

Konrad Lorenz, one of the founders of ethology, provided many demonstrations of the inborn, but environmentally triggered, nature of animal behavior. One of the most delightful showed that baby geese follow their mother because her movement and honking provide signals that are naturally attractive. To prove that any moving, honking object would provide the same "follow me" signal, Lorenz squatted and made mother goose noises in front of newborn geese whose real mother was not present. Soon the goslings were following him wherever he went, much to the amusement of his neighbors.

By carefully observing people in natural settings, psychologists often uncover behaviors that suggest personality differences and enduring patterns of social interaction. John Gottman, for example, began his research on differences between popular and unpopular schoolchildren by observing children's play groups and watching how newcomers attempted to join in. Popular children, he found, tended to blend gradually into the flow of activities; unpopular youngsters typically entered by disrupting the group in some way (Gottman, 1987; Putallaz & Gottman, 1981).

Sometimes, clinical psychologists use naturalistic observation to gather information about a person's problematic behavior in preparation for changing it. Similarly, industrial-organizational and engineering psychologists observe how groups or equipment function before they suggest changes. For example, to help computer programmers design a better word-processing system, a psychologist might first observe how people use the systems already in existence.

Experiments

Suppose a psychologist observes a positive correlation between entering a treatment program and quitting smoking. Is quitting *caused* by the treatment? Neither surveys, case studies, nor naturalistic observations are likely to give a satisfactory answer. To determine whether a cause-and-effect relationship exists, a psychologist would want to conduct an experiment.

Experiments are arrangements in which the researcher manipulates or controls one variable and then observes the effect of that manipulation on another variable. The variable controlled by the experimenter is called the **independent variable.** The variable to be observed is called the **dependent variable** because it is affected by, or *depends on,* the independent variable.

The structure of experiments   To illustrate the basic structure of experiments, consider an experiment designed to determine whether a treatment program of group discussions and antismoking tips causes smokers to quit. As illustrated in Figure 1.4, a psychologist could conduct an experiment in which both treated and untreated smokers try to quit. The experimenter controls whether or not treatment is administered to each smoker, so the presence or absence of treatment is the independent variable. How many cigarettes the subjects smoke after treatment—the variable to be observed—is the dependent variable. More complicated experimental designs may compare the effects of three or more amounts or levels of the independent variable on more than one dependent variable.

The group that receives the experimental treatment is called, naturally enough, the **experimental group.** The people who receive no treatment are

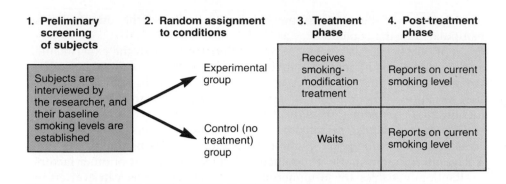

Figure 1.4
Design of a Simple Treatment Versus No-Treatment Experiment
Ideally, the only difference between treated and untreated subjects in such experiments is whether or not they actually get the treatment whose effects the researcher wishes to evaluate. Under such ideal circumstances, any difference in the results should be attributable to the treatment.

called the **control group;** control groups provide baselines against which to compare the performance of people in other conditions. In this case, we have a no-treatment control group that allows the experimenter to measure how much change in smoking behavior can be expected even without treatment. If everything about the two groups is exactly the same except for the exposure to treatment, then any difference in smoking behavior should be caused by (not merely correlated with) that treatment.

Selecting the subjects The process of selecting subjects for any experiment (or survey, for that matter) is called **sampling.** Sampling should not be taken lightly. If the subjects chosen come from a particular subgroup in the population (say, left-handed male construction workers), the results of the experiment might apply, or *generalize,* only to people like them.

Ideally, in order for an experiment's results to reveal something about people in general, the researcher chooses subjects who are representative of people in general. When every member of the population has an equal chance of being chosen for study, the individuals selected constitute a **random sample.** If not everyone in a population has an equal chance of being selected, the sample is said to be a **biased sample.**

It is important to understand that a random sample of the entire population is not always necessary or even desirable. For example, if you *want* to learn about the behavior of left-handed male construction workers, all the subjects should be randomly selected from that group. Furthermore, you might begin by conducting experiments on a particular subgroup, such as college students, and then repeat those experiments on broader, more representative samples to determine if the same results appear again. If research has shown that results are fairly consistent, regardless of the subjects' age, sex, social status, intelligence, and the like, then you could confidently draw your next sample from whatever willing group is at hand.

Flaws in experimental control Once the independent and dependent variables have been identified, the subjects selected, and the experiment conducted, the results can be collected and summarized. For our example, the data show that almost all treated subjects quit smoking completely and that no control subjects did so (Bernstein, 1970). At this point, you might be ready to believe that the treatment caused the difference in quitting rates. But before coming to that conclusion, it is essential to consider other factors that might account for the results, especially confounding variables.

Confounding variables confuse, or *confound,* interpretation of an experiment's results. Any factor that might have affected the dependent variable, along with or instead of the independent variable, may be a confounding variable. When confounding variables are present, the investigator cannot

Using the experimental method to evaluate the effects of a smoking cessation program involves, at minimum, a comparison of the quitting rate among smokers who received the treatment program with that of a group receiving no treatment.

know which variable was responsible for the results—the one that was manipulated or the confound.

In an ideal research world, the only difference between the experimental and the control conditions would involve different amounts of the independent variable, such as the presence or absence of treatment. In reality, however, there are always other differences, especially in **random variables.** These are uncontrolled, sometimes uncontrollable, factors such as differences in the subjects' backgrounds, personalities, physical health, and vulnerability to stress, as well as differences in the experimental conditions due to the time of day, interruptions, noise, experimenter fatigue, and a host of other factors.

Random variables are so numerous that no experimenter can ever create groups that are equivalent on all of them. The next best thing is to distribute their effects equally across groups. It is standard practice to flip a coin or use some other random process to assign each subject to either the experimental or the control group. The idea is to distribute random variables tied to the subjects randomly, so that, for example, the number of smokers who have the most trouble quitting is about equal in each group. Similarly, experimenters usually schedule people in experimental and control groups so that about an equal number from each group participates in the experiment on any given day or part of a day. Procedures like these balance out and minimize the effects of uncontrolled variables on the results of an experiment.

Results can also be confounded by the basic design of an experiment. To take just one example, suppose that the experimental and control groups in a study of antismoking treatments experienced different amounts of contact with the experimenter. The experimental group saw the experimenter for three weekly sessions; people in the control group had no contact with the experimenter from the time they filled out a questionnaire at the beginning of the study until they reported on their smoking at the end of the experiment. Would the people in the control group have done better if they had spent more time with the experimenter? Was the difference in the groups' quitting rates due to the treatment itself or to some combination of treatment and the opportunity to gain confidence from the experimenter or to feel more involved in the experiment? The latter is entirely possible.

This possibility illustrates a third source of confounding: differences in what subjects think about the experimental situation. A famous example comes from a group of industrial psychologists who conducted an experiment in a General Electric plant in Hawthorne, Illinois, to determine how to increase the workers' productivity (Roethlisberger & Dickson, 1939). Eight assembly line workers were studied. In the first experiment, the lighting in the room (the independent variable) was gradually increased, and the effect on productivity (the dependent variable) was observed. Productivity improved as lighting was increased. Then a new schedule of rest breaks was introduced, which increased productivity further. You might think that the researchers had found some simple ways to improve productivity. But when the lighting levels were reduced in the plant, the researchers again found increases in productivity. In fact, no matter what was done to the job environment, productivity rose. Why did this happen? It appeared that the subjects recognized the special attention they were receiving and that this recognition motivated them to work harder and better. Their response is called the *Hawthorne effect.*

When medical and psychological treatments are evaluated, improvements stemming solely from the subjects' knowledge and perceptions of those treatments is usually called the *placebo effect.* A **placebo** (pronounced "pla-see-bow") is a treatment that contains no active ingredient but nevertheless produces an effect because a person *believes* it will have that effect. Patients may improve after they are given a new drug, not because the drug contains an effective treatment for their illness, but because they believe that the drug will help them.

How can researchers determine the extent to which an experimental result is caused by the independent variable or by a placebo effect? Often they include a special control group that receives only a placebo. The placebo must appear exactly the same as the experimental treatment. If the experimental group received an injection, people in the placebo group would receive one as well but it would contain only a saline solution or some other inactive substance. Then the experimenter can compare the experimental group, the placebo group, and those receiving no treatment.

A fourth potential confound comes from **experimenter bias,** the unintentional effect that experimenters may exert on results. Robert Rosenthal demonstrated the power of experimenter bias more than twenty years ago (1966). His subjects were laboratory assistants who were asked to run rats in a maze. In one study, Rosenthal told some of the assistants that their rats were bred to be particularly "maze-bright"; he told the others that their rats were "maze-dull." In fact, both groups of rats were randomly drawn from the same population and had equal maze-learning capabilities. But the maze-bright animals learned the maze significantly faster than the maze-dull rats. How was this possible? Rosenthal concluded that the result had nothing to do with the rats and everything to do with the experimenters. He suggested that the assistants' knowledge of their rats' supposedly superior (or inferior) capabilities caused them to subtly bias or alter their training techniques, which in turn speeded or slowed the animals' learning. Similarly, if an experiment is examining the effectiveness of a treatment for smoking, the researcher might inadvertently bias the results by communicating greater confidence when giving the treatments he or she expects to be most helpful and conveying somewhat less enthusiasm when administering the placebo.

To prevent experimenter bias from confounding results, experimenters use a **double-blind design,** in which both the subjects and those giving the treatments are unaware of, or "blind" to, who is receiving a placebo. Only the director of the study—a person with no direct contact with the subjects— knows who is in the experimental group and who is in the placebo group.

In short, experiments are vital tools for examining cause-effect relationships between variables, but like the other methods we have described, they are vulnerable to error. Scientists maximize the value of experimental methods by designing experiments to eliminate as many confounds as possible, repeating their studies to ensure consistent results, then tempering their interpretation of the results to take into account the limitations or problems that remain. Psychologists' research designs are also limited by the need to consider the welfare of their human or animal subjects.

HIGHLIGHT

Ethical Standards for Psychologists

A researcher might study severe anxiety by putting a gun to people's heads. Or a researcher might measure the influence of heredity on intelligence by taking newborn children away from intelligent and not-so-intelligent parents and randomly assigning half of each group to live in intellectually barren homes. They *might* do these things, but such potentially harmful methods are unethical and therefore are not used by psychologists.

In each of these examples, the ethical course of action is obvious: the psychologist must find another way to conduct the research. Psychologists often face more complex ethical questions, in which they must decide how to balance conflicting values. Many experiments reflect a compromise between the need to protect subjects from harm and the need to know about the unknown. In finding ways to help people cope with anxiety, for example, researchers may ask them to try new coping skills while enduring an anxiety-provoking situation.

When research does involve some discomfort for the subjects, the researcher must determine that the potential benefits of the work in terms of new knowledge and human welfare outweigh any risks or discomfort to the subjects and minimize the discomfort and risk involved. When people are the research subjects, the researcher must also inform them about everything in the study that might influence their decision to participate and ensure that their involvement is voluntary. If the researcher deceives people about an experiment because full disclosure beforehand would bias their behavior in some way, the researcher must also reveal and justify the deception afterward. Whether or not deception is involved, all researchers must act to prevent subjects from suffering any long-term negative consequences of their participation.

These responsibilities form just one aspect of the ethical guidelines for psychologists that have been formulated by the American Psychological Association (APA). The latest edition of these standards begins as follows:

> Psychologists respect the dignity and worth of the individual and strive for the preservation and protection of fundamental human rights. They are committed to increasing knowledge of human behavior and of people's understanding of themselves and others and to the utilization of such knowledge for the promotion of human welfare. . . . They use their skills only for purposes consistent with these values and do not knowingly permit their misuse by others. (APA, 1981, p. 633.)

The APA then spells out the implications of this statement in several specific areas. For example, as teachers, psychologists should strive to give students a complete, accurate, and up-to-date view of each topic rather than a narrow, biased point of view. Psychologists should perform only those services and use those techniques for which they are adequately trained; a biological psychologist untrained in clinical methods should not try to offer psychotherapy. Psychologists should also be careful to explain their qualifications accurately and should not exaggerate the effectiveness of their services. Except in the most unusual circumstances (to be discussed in Chapter 16, on psychotherapy), they should not reveal information obtained from clients or students. And they should avoid situations in which a conflict of interest might impair their judgment or harm someone else. They should not, for example, have sexual relations with their clients or with the students or employees they supervise.

The vast majority of psychologists adhere scrupulously to the ethical principles of the APA. But as we will see in later chapters, doubt is likely to arise in some cases about whether, for example, the benefits of a certain method outweigh its potential risks to the subjects or whether certain kinds of treatments offered by psychotherapists are valuable. Indeed, ethical principles for psychologists continue to evolve as psychologists face new and more complex ethical issues in their work. ◼

FUTURE DIRECTIONS

Before you begin what we hope will be an exciting tour of the discipline called psychology, we would like to point out a few things about how this book is organized and why. We will move next to a chapter on developmental psychology, describing how a single cell develops into the complex and fascinating organism known as a human being. Examining developmental psychology first provides both a preview of the many aspects of behavior and mental processes to be discussed in later chapters and a portrait of the human being as a unified whole—a creature who can act and react, feel and think, plan and imagine, learn and remember, and above all, be consciously aware of the world and communicate with it through language. Through the rest of the book, we will examine in more detail each of the major components of behavior and mental processes that ultimately come together in the developed human being.

This process of piecing together behavior and mental processes begins with cells and other biological structures. Thus, in Chapter 3 we will examine the biological bases of behavior, showing how nerve cells communicate with one another to create behavior and mental activity. Next, in Chapter 4, on sensation, we will consider how special groups of cells detect sound, light, and other forms of energy and how they convert this energy into the sensations of hearing, vision, taste, smell, and touch. How we organize, interpret, and attend to these sensations is the subject of Chapter 5, on perception. The analysis of how we experience the world is continued in Chapter 6, where we will focus on consciousness and how it is affected by sleep, hypnosis, meditation, and drugs.

Having brought the complexities of consciousness into the picture, we will next consider learning, memory, decision making, thinking, and the use of language, all of which are covered in Chapters 7 through 9. Of course, some people are better at these processes than others; in Chapter 10, we will discuss such individual differences in mental ability.

Because psychology involves not only the study of what people do but also why they do it, we will turn to the topic of motivation in Chapter 11. Few motivated behaviors occur in a neutral state. Most are accompanied by anger, joy, fear, hope, desperation, or any number of other emotions, the topic of Chapter 12.

At that point, we will be ready to begin looking at how all the behavioral and mental processes considered so far are integrated in functioning individuals and how those individuals relate to their environments. We will begin this phase of study by considering in Chapter 13 how people react to, cope with, and may be harmed by various kinds of stress. We will see that there are clear individual differences in people's responses to stress and that some of these differences seem to be related to their personality, the topic of Chapter 14. There we will consider what personality is and how it relates to behavior and mental processes. In Chapter 15 we will review some of the many ways in which human behavior and mental processes can go awry and some of the factors that may create these problems. In Chapter 16 we will describe the major approaches and methods used in treating psychological problems. Finally, in Chapters 17 and 18 we will examine social psychology—the ways in which one person's actions, thoughts, attitudes, emotions, and other processes influence and are influenced by other people.

In each of these chapters, you will see that research in each specialized area of psychology draws on and contributes to work in other psychological subfields. We will illustrate just a few of these linkages at the beginning of each chapter with a special "Linkages" diagram. By examining the diagram, you can see both how the topic of the chapter is related to other fields of psychology and how the chapter is related to what you have studied or will study in other chapters in the book. One of these relationships is given special attention at the end of the chapter in a "Linkages" box. In each chapter, you will also see that psychological research has led to applications that have helped people in a multitude of ways.

SUMMARY

1. Psychology is the science of behavior and mental processes. The topics included in this field range from the study of nerve cell activity to the interaction of people in families and other groups.

2. Because the subject matter of psychology is so diverse, most psychologists have chosen to work in particular subfields within the discipline. Biological, or physiological, psychologists study such topics as the ways in which nerve cells communicate with one another and the role played by the nervous system in regulating and controlling behavior. Experimental psychologists focus their research efforts on basic psychological processes such as learning, memory, and perception in both animals and humans. Cognitive psychologists focus on studying such complex phenomena as thinking, judgment, decision making, problem solving, language, and imagination. Personality psychologists focus on the unique characteristics that determine individuals' behavior. Social psychology focuses on questions of how people influence one another, especially in groups of two or more. Clinical psychologists provide direct service to troubled people and conduct research on abnormal behavior. Developmental psychology specializes in describing and attempting to understand the development of behavior and mental processes over a lifetime. Quantitative psychology focuses on ways of measuring and analyzing many of the behavioral and mental processes being explored by psychologists in other subfields.

3. Psychologists also differ in their theoretical approaches. Those adopting a biological approach tend to view behavior and mental processes as the result of complex physiological processes. The psychodynamic perspective sees behavior and mental processes as a struggle to resolve conflicts between impulses and the demands made by society to control those impulses. Behavioral psychologists see behavior as determined primarily by learning based on past experiences with rewards and punishments. The humanistic approach views behavior as controlled by the decisions that people make about their lives based on their perceptions of the world. The cognitive approach advocates the idea that behavior cannot be understood until we understand the basic mental processes that underlie it.

4. In spite of the diversity of its subfields and theoretical approaches, psychology is unified both by constant interaction and sharing of knowledge among researchers in every subfield and by their research orientation.

5. Research in psychology, as in other sciences, focuses on four main goals: description, prediction, control, and explanation. Description involves the careful recording of mental and behavioral processes and a search for relationships among them. Prediction is initially sought by research designed to evaluate the strength and direction of correlations between the variables found in descriptive research. To test various hypotheses about whether the relationships between correlated variables reflect cause and effect, some measure of control must be introduced. The goal of control is sought through experimental research. The goal of explanation is approached by building on descriptive, predictive, and controlled research to create theories of behavior and mental processes. These theories drive an endless cycle of research as they generate additional descriptions and hypotheses, prompt predictions, and suggest new experiments.

6. Psychologists employ numerous research methods in their work. Most prominent among these are surveys, case studies, naturalistic observations, and experiments. Surveys are used to collect large amounts of information from many people at relatively low cost. They also may reveal issues and phenomena to be investigated by other research methods. To be most useful, surveys should be based on a large and representative sample of the people one wishes to study.

7. Case studies are also valuable sources of information, but they focus on a single case or event. Researchers must be careful not to depend too heavily on case study data, because they typically do not reflect the behavior and mental processes of people in general.

8. Naturalistic observation, outside of a laboratory setting, is a way of gathering data about behavior without altering that behavior.

9. In an experiment, an investigator purposely manipulates one variable (the independent variable) and watches for an effect of that manipulation on a second, dependent, variable. The main advantage of experiments is that they allow the researcher to systematically eliminate factors that might be causing some phenomenon and ultimately to establish with reasonable certainty what factor is the main cause. The interpretation of experimental results can be damaged in several ways, especially by the action of random, uncontrolled variables, flaws in the basic design of the experiment; subjects' perceptions of the experiment (placebo effects); and bias on the part of the experimenter.

10. In doing research, teaching, therapy, writing, consulting, or other tasks, psychologists are bound by the ethical standards of the American Psychological Association.

KEY TERMS

Definitions of terms appear on the pages shown in parentheses.

biased sample (21)
biological psychologist (4)
case study (19)
clinical psychologist (7)
cognitive psychologist (6)
confounding variable (21)
control group (21)
correlation (13)
correlation coefficient (14)
dependent variable (20)
developmental psychologist (8)
double-blind design (23)
ethologist (20)
experiment (20)
experimental group (20)
experimental psychologist (5)
experimenter bias (23)
hypothesis (13)
independent variable (20)
personality psychologist (6)
physiological psychologist (4)
placebo (22)
psychology (2)
quantitative psychologist (9)
random sample (21)
random variable (22)
sampling (21)
social psychologist (7)
statistical analysis (9)
statistically significant (14)
survey (18)
theory (17)
variable (13)

RECOMMENDED READINGS

American Psychological Association (1967). *Casebook on ethical standards of psychologists*. Washington, D.C.: APA. This booklet contains a set of cases in which psychologists' behavior came to the attention of the APA committee on professional and ethical standards. These cases illustrate the kinds of problems that led to the development of the APA's ethical standards. The committee's judgment about each case, along with the resulting penalty, if any, is also included.

Keith-Spiegel, P., & Koocher, G. P. (1985). *Ethics in psychology: Professional standards and cases*. New York: Random House. An updated treatment of ethics in psychology and the cases that help fine-tune ethical standards.

Stanovich, K. E. (1986). *How to think straight about psychology*. Glenview, Ill.: Scott, Foresman. A highly readable paperback that is designed to help students evaluate and think critically about psychological theories and phenomena, including such sensationalized topics as parapsychology.

F or several years in the late 1700s, people living in and around the Caune Woods of Aveyron, France, reported sighting a wild boy running naked with the animals. After repeated attempts, hunters were able to capture the boy, who had been lost or abandoned by his parents at a very early age and had grown to the age of about eleven with only animals as his family. This Wild Boy of Aveyron was sent to Paris. Scientists there expected to observe a human in a pure state of nature—what philosopher Jean-Jacques Rousseau had termed the "noble savage." After all, here was a human being who had grown up unencumbered and uncontaminated by the evils and arbitrary rules of society. The scientists also expected that, after a year or so of intense education, the boy would be able to tell them about his life in the wild and about the activities of animals in their natural environment.

What the researchers found was a dirty, frightened creature who crawled and trotted like a wild animal, who would eat the filthiest of garbage, and who preferred raw to cooked meat. He spent most of his time silently rocking back and forth and would snarl and attack anyone who tried to touch him.

Though Jean-Marc-Gaspard Itard and other scientists worked with the boy for more than ten years, they were able to produce only minor changes in his behavior. He never learned to speak and his social behavior remained so backward that he was never able to live unguarded among other people. A dramatized account of Itard's work is presented in François Truffaut's fascinating film *The Wild Child.*

Unfortunately, there have been other, more recent examples similar to that of the Wild Boy. Children have been rescued after having been confined for years in closets and other cruelly restricted environments that cut them off from interaction with other people. Invariably, these children find it extremely difficult to interact with others. Often they are unable to learn language, and they display other social and mental difficulties that remain with them for life. Such cases highlight the importance of early social contacts with other people for normal human development. They also underscore the need to know as much as possible about early development and what can facilitate or retard it.

Psychologists have contributed greatly to our understanding of the effects of early experience on development. A study by Harold Skeels (1966), for example, showed that mentally retarded orphans showed far greater social and emotional progress if they were given warm, individualized attention by a particular caregiver than if they received only routine care. **Developmental psychology** is the psychological specialty that documents the course of such social, emotional, moral, and intellectual development and explores how development in different domains fits together, is affected by experience, and relates to other areas of psychology (see Linkages diagram).

Developmental psychologists study when certain skills first appear, how they change with age, and whether they change in a sudden spurt or gradually. They want to know if everyone develops skills at the same rate or if slow starters sometimes end up ahead. They are interested in the *processes* of

2

**Human
Development**

LINKAGES
an overview

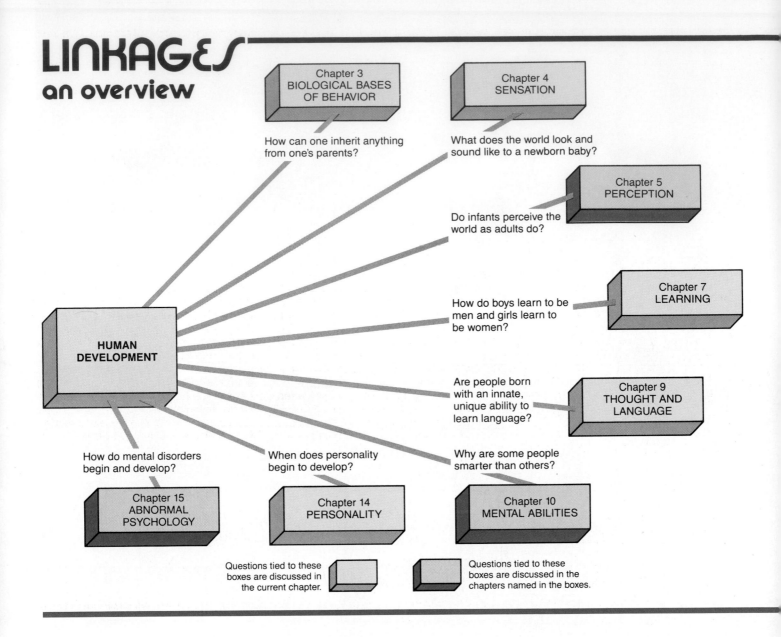

Chapter 3
BIOLOGICAL BASES
OF BEHAVIOR

How can one inherit anything
from one's parents?

Chapter 4
SENSATION

What does the world look and
sound like to a newborn baby?

Chapter 5
PERCEPTION

Do infants perceive the
world as adults do?

Chapter 7
LEARNING

How do boys learn to be
men and girls learn to
be women?

**HUMAN
DEVELOPMENT**

Are people born
with an innate,
unique ability to
learn language?

Chapter 9
THOUGHT AND
LANGUAGE

How do mental disorders
begin and develop?

When does personality
begin to develop?

Why are some people
smarter than others?

Chapter 15
ABNORMAL
PSYCHOLOGY

Chapter 14
PERSONALITY

Chapter 10
MENTAL ABILITIES

Questions tied to these
boxes are discussed in
the current chapter.

Questions tied to these
boxes are discussed in the
chapters named in the boxes.

development. How do transitions from lower to higher levels of ability occur? How much of development is determined by children's inheritance of abilities from their parents? How much can the environment permanently alter development?

In this chapter, you will read about how a person develops from a fertilized egg into a mature adult and how adults, too, change with time. You will learn about the milestones of growth in sensation, emotion, thinking, social behavior, and many of the other domains that are taken up in detail in the rest of the book. We begin by considering the study of human development; then we will review development in different domains, from the moment of conception on.

THE STUDY OF DEVELOPMENT

Today infants and children are cherished, nurtured, taught, and studied; but it was not always so. In most Western cultures, no special allowances were made for youth's fragility or limitations until the nineteenth century. Today

HUMAN DEVELOPMENT AND PSYCHOLOGY

In order to understand a phenomenon, people often look to its origins. In physics, cosmologists try to decipher how the universe began and evolved. In biology, paleontologists try to uncover and understand the varied forms that life has taken over the ages. So, too, do developmental psychologists study the changes that are likely to occur with age in each domain of psychology: sensation, perception, memory, thought, language, intelligence, personality, and social relations.

The study of developmental psychology is interesting in its own right, but it also illuminates other specific areas of psychology, as this diagram suggests. Sometimes research in developmental psychology has upset long-held beliefs. Ideas about intelligence are one example. Many people have believed that intelligence is a single factor that is given to people at birth and remains fixed for life until it somehow decays with age. Through research on everything from the effects of lead on a fetus to the varied abilities of the elderly, developmental psychologists have outlined a far different, far more complicated view of mental abilities.

The questions in this diagram, like those in similar diagrams in other chapters, illustrate just a few of the ways in which this chapter's topic is linked with other subareas of psychology. The questions linked to the yellow boxes are discussed in the current chapter; the other questions are addressed in the chapters named in the blue boxes. At the back of the book, the section entitled "Answers to Linkages Diagram Questions" lists where you can find those discussions. At the end of each chapter, we discuss one linkage in detail.

parents await children's advances—the first tooth, the first step, the first word—with bated breath. Before the nineteenth century, such milestones were scorned or ignored. Crawling, for example, was regarded as animallike. As soon as they could stand, children were put into clothes stiff with iron and whalebone, so that they would be held erect and made more like adults. Children were neither encouraged nor expected to be happy, cheerful, or playful. Instead, parents tried to integrate their offspring as quickly as possible into the adult world of hard work and serious pursuits.

What happened to bring us to our current fondness for children and, at the same time, to the rise of developmental psychology? Much like the history of an individual, this change in thinking involved many influences.

Philosophical Roots

One influence was the philosophers of the seventeenth and eighteenth centuries. In essays first published in the 1690s, John Locke suggested that what happens during childhood has a profound and permanent impact on the individual. He proposed that the newborn infant is like a blank slate, or *tabula rasa,* on which experience writes its story. If parents take advantage of infancy to reason with and teach their children desirable habits, he believed, they will reap benefits as the children grow into rational and responsible members of society.

Some seventy years later, Rousseau went even further in suggesting that childhood is a unique period of life. But, in his view, children are to be understood and valued for what they are, rather than for what they will become. Rousseau believed children to be capable of discovering how the world operates without adult teaching, so he argued that they should be allowed to grow as nature dictates, with little guidance or pressure from parents.

These two philosophers raised issues that have motivated the study of development to this day. Two central questions grew out of those issues. First, how much of a person's development is attributable to *nurture*—to teaching and other influences from the external environment—and how much comes from within the individual's *nature,* or genetic makeup? Second, does development occur in distinct stages over the lifespan? Rousseau suggested that childhood is a stage that is qualitatively different from later life, and psychologists since his time have generally agreed that there are orderly sequences in development from infancy to adulthood. But do the changes occur gradually and smoothly, or is there a series of distinct stages? According to those who advocate a "stage" theory of development, children's abilities and behaviors at one stage are *qualitatively* different from those at other stages. Each stage builds on the preceding stages, and all children go through the stages in the same order. Both the question of whether such stages exist and can be identified and the question of the relative importance of nature and nurture remain very important issues for developmental psychologists.

Scientific Observation

The issues of developmental psychology may be rooted in philosophy, but its methods are grounded in science. The first person to treat the study of development systematically and scientifically was G. Stanley Hall. From 1890 to 1910, Hall explored children's and adolescents' intellectual development, using the survey method. Other psychologists preferred techniques based on more precise measurements, including the first intelligence test, developed by Alfred Binet and Theophile Simon in France. This test, the forerunner of today's IQ tests, was given and scored in a standardized form, thus providing a quantitative yardstick of children's mental development.

Arnold Lucius Gesell, a developmental psychologist of the early twentieth century, advocated using observation to study development. He designed the first observation room, a dome-shaped structure in which he could observe and photograph children without disturbing them. To determine milestones of normal development, he also collected file cabinets full of detailed observations of what children can do at different ages.

Gesell used these observations to support his theory that development is simply the natural unfolding of abilities with age. He demonstrated, for example, that motor skills, such as standing and walking, picking up a cube, and throwing a ball, develop in a fixed sequence in all children, as Figure 2.1 illustrates. Their order and the age at which they develop, Gesell believed, is determined by nature and is relatively unaffected by nurture. Only under extreme environmental conditions—such as famine, war, or poverty—are children thrown off this biologically programmed timetable. This type of natural growth or change, which unfolds in a fixed sequence relatively independent of the environment, is called **maturation.**

Observation of children as they explore their environment and interact with others has provided psychologists with a rich source of data for understanding human development.

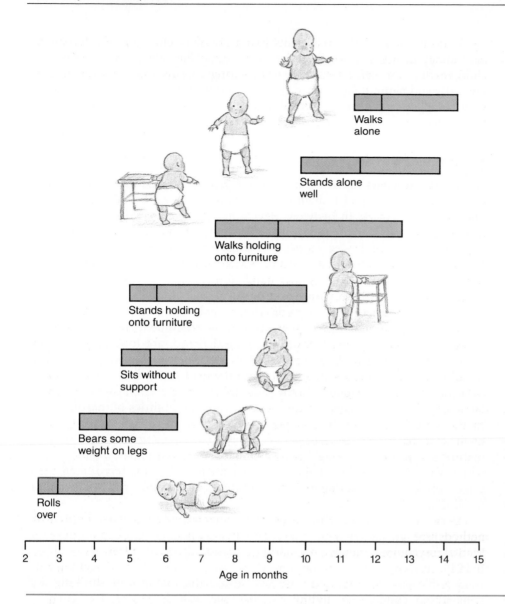

Figure 2.1
Motor Development: An Example of Maturation
The left end of each bar indicates the age at which 25 percent of the infants tested were able to perform the stated behavior; 50 percent of the babies were performing the behavior at the age indicated by the vertical line in the bars; and the right end indicates the age at which 90 percent could do so (Frankenberg & Dodds, 1967). Although different infants achieve milestones of motor development at slightly different ages, all infants—regardless of their ethnicity, social class, or temperament—achieve them in the same order. Thus, motor development during infancy is maturational.

Bars labeled (top to bottom): Walks alone; Stands alone well; Walks holding onto furniture; Stands holding onto furniture; Sits without support; Bears some weight on legs; Rolls over. Horizontal axis: Age in months, 2 3 4 5 6 7 8 9 10 11 12 13 14 15.

While Gesell was observing children, John B. Watson sent the field of developmental psychology in another direction through his emphasis on _behaviorism,_ the learning-oriented approach to psychology described in the previous chapter. In 1918 Watson began doing laboratory experiments with children, showing that childhood learning experiences can have lasting effects. For example, in one experiment he first showed that nine-month-old Albert was not afraid of a white rat, a rabbit, and other white objects. Then Watson banged a steel bar near Albert's head every time a white rat appeared. After several bangs, Albert began to draw back at the sight of the rat, cry, and try to crawl away. He reacted similarly when Watson showed him other white objects. Watson had demonstrated that an infant could learn to fear a previously innocuous object and that this fear would generalize to similar objects.

From his experiments, Watson inferred that children learn everything, from skills to phobias. "Give me one dozen healthy infants," he wrote, "well formed, and my own specified world to bring them up in . . . and I'll guarantee to take any one at random and train him to become any type of specialist I might select" (Watson, 1930, p. 104). We will return to this theory later, in Chapter 14, on personality, and Chapter 16, on therapy.

Watson's ideas and experiments had a powerful effect on developmental psychology in America for the next forty years. They also had an impact on child rearing, for while Gesell was reassuring parents that children mature normally and naturally given enough time and love, Watson burdened parents with complete responsibility for influencing, through learning, all their children's behavior.

Theories of Development

Quite different views of nature and nurture were expressed in the first explicit theories of the *stages* of human development. Sigmund Freud proposed the first of these theories. In his view, development was not simply the result of benign growth toward maturity, as Gesell posited; nor was it due solely to environmental experiences, as Watson suggested. Instead, said Freud, it was the product of both internal (indeed, sexual) urges and external conditions, particularly how mother and father handled their child's sexual impulses. His theory incorporated both nature and nurture.

It was also a theory based on developmental stages, because according to Freud, as children grow older, their sexual urges become focused on different zones of the body. Infants' sexual urges, said Freud, are located in the *oral* zone, their mouths, and are expressed in the intense pleasure of sucking. Toddlers feel sexual urges connected with the *anal* zone, as they gain control over their bowel movements. In the preschool years, children's sexual feelings come from the *phallic* zone, as they discover the possibilities of masturbation. In the school years, children experience a period of *latency,* during which explicit sexual urges are suspended. Finally, adolescents begin to express mature sexual urges through *genital* contact. Freud's *psychodynamic theory,* which we will discuss in Chapter 14, on personality, intimately linked these stages of sexual development with children's emotional and psychological development.

Between 1930 and 1960, most developmental psychologists adopted the approach of Gesell, Watson, or Freud. The next major influence on developmental psychology came from another master theorist, Swiss psychologist Jean Piaget, whose thinking dominated the field in the 1970s. Piaget used his remarkable observational skills to investigate the nuances of thinking and behavior in children, including his own son and daughters. He wove his observations and inferences into the most comprehensive and influential theory yet formulated of how thought and knowledge develop from infancy to adulthood.

Piaget suggested that the influences of nature and nurture are inseparable and interactive. As children actively manipulate and explore their surroundings, *mental images* of objects and actions guide them; experience in turn modifies these images. For example, the infant's image of a ball becomes complete only after experience has shown that a ball can be held, rolled, or bounced. Having this image lets the infant know what to do with a red ball, a big ball, or a small ball and suggests something to try out on oranges and eggs. According to Piaget, different types of mental images appear in an unvarying sequence and contribute to distinct developmental stages characterized by increasingly sophisticated modes of thought. We will describe these stages later in this chapter.

Nature and Nurture Today

In the 1980s, we accept as given Piaget's notion that both heredity and environment contribute to development. The question that interests developmental psychologists now is not one of either-or, but of *how much* and *how*

An environment full of new and interesting stimuli provides the ideal circumstances for the fullest development of a child's inherited intellectual potential.

each influence contributes. Some characteristics, such as physical size and appearance, are under such strong genetic control that only extreme environmental conditions can affect their expression. Others, such as intelligence and sociability, are more easily affected by environmental forces.

Developmental psychologists now realize that the contributions of nature and nurture can affect one another. The environment affects whether or not an inherited characteristic will be expressed: a stimulating environment encourages the expression of an individual's genetic potential, and a sterile environment suppresses it. For example, children are more likely to develop their fullest inherited intellectual capacities when they are given plenty of stimulation, rather than being isolated and ignored. At the same time, individuals' inherited characteristics can affect environments. For example, some of the qualities children have inherited evoke particular responses from their environments. An active, happy baby evokes more social reactions than an expressionless, passive one; an interested, intelligent child evokes more attention and teaching than a dull one. Also, especially as children get older, they actively seek the environments they find most compatible with their natural interests: the musical child learns to play the flute, the verbal one studies languages.

Documenting and probing the complex mutual influences of nature and nurture are important parts of the work of developmental psychologists. The reason is not simply academic. For example, based on their research, developmental psychologists have helped encourage the replacement of large, impersonal orphanages and child asylums with small group and foster homes. They have also helped establish educational programs, such as Project Head Start for preschool children. And they have drawn attention to how children are affected by insensitive day care, divorce, gender stereotypes, and televised violence.

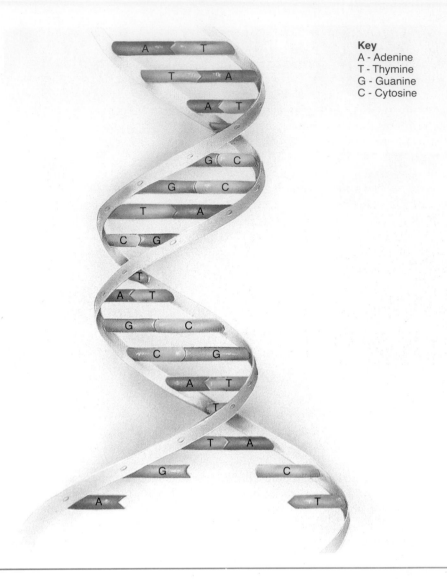

Key
A - Adenine
T - Thymine
G - Guanine
C - Cytosine

Figure 2.2
The Structure of DNA
Two strands of molecules intertwine to form a double spiral, the structure of the DNA molecule. The sides of the spiral are made up of sugar and phosphate. Each "step" in the spiral is composed of two of four nitrogen-containing molecules: adenine, thymine, guanine, and cytosine. The particular sequence of the molecules on the steps varies, to constitute a code that ultimately directs how a cell behaves. The two strands of the spiral can "unzip"; then each of the single strands draws on molecules floating in the cell to synthesize a complementary strand, forming a new, but identical, double spiral. In this way, the DNA molecule makes a copy of itself, so that the genetic code can be passed on to new cells (Watson, 1976).

BEGINNINGS

Nowhere are the joint contributions of heredity and environment clearer than in development during the eventful nine months before birth. How does a single fertilized egg become a functioning newborn? For centuries, it was thought that a miniature human being was carried, preformed, in one parent or the other. This idea persisted until 1759, when a medical student named Caspar Friedrich Wolff made two startling, but sound, suggestions. He said, first, that the infant is not preformed at conception but is assembled out of small structures, and second, that mother and father contribute equally to their offspring. Since Wolff's time, increasingly sophisticated technical advances have permitted us to discover and record how conception and prenatal development occur.

Genetic Building Blocks

Life for the new human being begins when a sperm from the father-to-be penetrates, or *fertilizes,* the ovum of the mother-to-be and forms a brand new cell. This new cell carries a heritage from both mother and father through structures known as chromosomes.

The **chromosomes** are long, thin structures within each cell and are made up of more than a thousand genes strung out like a chain. The genes are made of molecules of **deoxyribonucleic acid (DNA),** each of which consists of two strands of sugar, phosphate, and nitrogen-containing molecules twisted around each other in a double spiral (see Figure 2.2). The particular order in which the nitrogen-containing molecules are arranged in DNA determines which protein the gene will produce; proteins, in turn, direct a cell's activities. Thus, DNA within the chromosomes provides the individual's genetic code, a blueprint for constructing the entire human being, including eye color, height, blood type, inherited disorders, and the like.

How is the message in this code maintained through the years, as we grow and age, and from generation to generation? New cells are produced by the division of existing cells. In most human cells, there are twenty-three *pairs* of chromosomes that carry the genetic code, and when cells divide, the chromosomes duplicate themselves, so that each of the new cells also contains twenty-three pairs of chromosomes. However, the sperm and ova that join to produce a new human being are an exception. When sperm and ova are produced by cell division, the chromosome pairs are split and rearranged, leaving each sperm and ovum cell with just one member of each pair of chromosomes, or twenty-three *single* chromosomes. (Figure 2.3 shows how this process works.) Then, when sperm and ovum unite at conception to form a new cell, that cell has twenty-three pairs of chromosomes, half from the mother and half from the father.

These forty-six chromosomes contain the individual's **genotype,** the set of genes inherited from both parents. How the individual actually looks and acts is his or her **phenotype. Dominant** genes in the genotype are those that are expressed in the phenotype whenever they are present; **recessive** genes

Figure 2.3
Cell Division and the Genetic Code
Cell division in the sperm and ova is called meiosis. Shown here is a simplified view of meiosis in a hypothetical cell with only two pairs of chromosomes. When meiosis begins, the chromosomes in each cell line up in pairs. The pairs are made of homologous chromosomes, which means that the chromosome from the father and the one from the mother contain alternate genes for the same trait. Next, the chromosomes double, then separate and separate again. The process has two especially significant results. First, in humans it produces cells that have only twenty-three chromosomes each. Second, it reshuffles genes and chromosomes, resulting in the infinite variation in characteristics seen from one individual to the next.

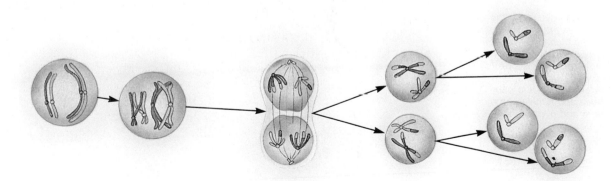

During the first stage of meiosis pairs of homologous chromosomes line up together and double. Homologous chromosomes exchange segments, thus creating new combinations of genes.

The paired chromosomes separate randomly, moving to opposite ends of the cell.

The cell divides. The resulting cells then go through several stages and divide again.

The result is four daughter cells, each of which has only half as many chromosomes as the original cell.

are expressed outwardly only when they are paired with a similar gene from the other parent. For example, a single dominant gene for brown eyes from either parent will create a brown-eyed child, but it would take two recessive genes for blue eyes to create a blue-eyed child. Most traits in which heredity plays a role, such as intelligence and emotionality, are affected by more than one gene; in other words, they are **polygenic.** The phenotype reflects the influence of both the genotype (nature) and the environment in which the person lives and grows (nurture).

Prenatal Development

The union of sperm and ovum takes place in the woman's fallopian tube; Figure 2.4 describes this process of conception. The new cell, called a **zygote,** then begins the rapid process of cell division that some nine months later will result in a multimillion-celled infant.

Germinal stage   The first two weeks after fertilization are called the *germinal stage*. During this time, the zygote divides rapidly. By sixty hours after conception, there are twelve to sixteen cells forming a mulberrylike sphere. Up to this point, all the cells have been identical, but now they begin to differentiate as the tiny mass of cells moves slowly down the fallopian tube, dividing all the while. When it arrives in the uterine cavity, some four days after fertilization, the mass has become a hollow, fluid-filled sphere of over a hundred cells. Within another two days, the cells have separated into sections that will become the **embryo** (the developing individual), the *placenta* (which transmits nutrients and carries away wastes), the *amnion* (or "bag of waters" surrounding the embryo), and the *yolk sac* (which will produce blood). This little ball of cells floats freely for a day or two, then on about the seventh day after fertilization, it starts to attach itself to the lining of the uterine wall.

Embryonic stage   When attachment is complete, by about the fourteenth day after fertilization, the second, or *embryonic, stage* of prenatal development begins. During this time, which continues through about the eighth week, the basic plan for the body emerges, and all the organs are created. The placenta begins to "breathe," digest, and excrete for the embryo. It is connected to the

Figure 2.4
Conception
First, the ovary releases an ovum into the abdominal cavity (a). Then the movements of millions of cilia on the feathery flaps projecting from the fallopian tube draw the ovum toward its funnel (b). Once inside (c), the ovum continues meiosis. Then sperm penetrate the ovum, stimulating it to complete meiosis (d). Male and female chromosomes from the sperm and ovum mingle (e). The fertilized ovum, or zygote, divides repeatedly as it moves through the fallopian tube (f–i). On about the seventh day, the sphere of cells attaches to the uterine wall (j) (Grobstein, 1979).

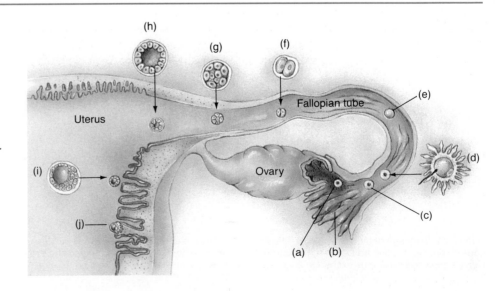

embryo by the umbilical cord, which brings in oxygen, carbohydrates, fats, proteins, and mineral salts and removes carbon dioxide and urea to be disposed of by the mother's lungs and kidneys. The placenta is selective, allowing in beneficial materials, such as nutrients and antibodies, and screening out many potentially harmful substances, including most bacteria. But this screening is imperfect. Gases, viruses, nicotine, alcohol, and other drugs can pass through to the embryo.

By the end of the first month after fertilization, the foundation for the brain, eyes, and nervous system has been laid. The embryo's heart is beating, and a digestive system has begun to form. By the end of the second month, the translucent embryo looks decidedly human. Its eyes, ears, and nose have assumed their proper positions on the face; its jaw, mouth, and lips have formed. The tiny arms have elbows, hands, and stubby fingers; the legs have knees, ankles, and toes. The inch-long embryo, weighing less than one-tenth of an ounce, has a heart, nervous system, stomach, esophagus, and ovaries or testes (see Figure 2.5).

The embryonic stage is known as a **critical period,** an interval during which certain kinds of growth must occur if development is to proceed normally. Specific physical developments must take place during the embryonic stage, or they never will. If the heart, eyes, ears, hands, and feet do not appear in the embryonic period, they cannot form later on. And if they form incorrectly, the defects will be permanent. During this period, environmental effects can be especially devastating. A baby whose mother has rubella (German measles) during the third or fourth week after conception, for example, has a 50 percent chance of being blind, deaf, or mentally retarded or of having a heart malformation. A baby whose mother has rubella in the second month of pregnancy has a 22 percent chance of having one of these congenital defects. If the mother has rubella later on in the pregnancy, the likelihood that the baby will have one of these defects is substantially less.

Severe damage can also occur if the baby's mother takes certain drugs during the embryonic period. This was demonstrated most dramatically in 1961, when ten thousand babies, most of them in Germany and England, were born without arms and legs, a condition called *phocomelia* ("seal limbs"). It turned out that their mothers had taken the drug thalidomide to prevent morning sickness, which often occurs in the first trimester of pregnancy.

Fetal stage   The embryo becomes a **fetus** in the third prenatal stage, when the cartilage in the bones starts to harden. In this *fetal* stage, which extends until birth, systems become integrated, the various organs grow and function more efficiently, and some finishing touches (such as fingerprints) are added.

By the end of the third month after conception, the fetus can kick its legs, curl its toes, twist its feet, make a fist, turn its head, frown, open its mouth, swallow, and take a few practice "breaths" of amniotic fluid. By the end of the fifth month, the fetus is a foot long and weighs a pound. In the sixth month, the eyelids, which have been sealed, open. The fetus now has a well-developed grasp and abundant taste buds and can breathe regularly for as long as twenty-four hours at a time. This ability gives the fetus some chance of surviving in an incubator if born prematurely.

By the end of the seventh month, the fetus weighs about two pounds and, if born prematurely, has a 50-50 chance of survival. Its organ systems are all functional. In the eighth and ninth months, the fetus becomes rounder and heavier. It is sensitive to a variety of outside sounds and responds to light and touch. It can lift its head, and it may even be able to learn. In one study done many years ago (Spelt, 1948), a loud noise was paired with vibrations on the mother's abdomen. At first, the vibrations did not cause any reaction

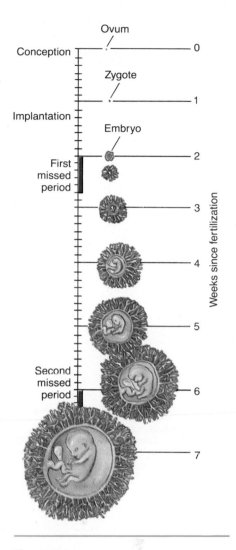

Figure 2.5
Prenatal Development: The First Weeks
These drawings show the ovum, zygote, and embryo only slightly smaller than their actual sizes during the first seven weeks of life (Patten, 1968).

in the fetus, but eventually the vibrations alone caused it to startle. Unfortunately, it was not possible in this study to separate the fetus's reaction from the mother's. The two have been separated in more recent studies. Anthony DeCasper demonstrated that infants whose mothers repeatedly read them a Dr. Seuss story before they were born preferred the sound of this story to other sounds after they were born (Spence & DeCasper, 1982).

During the fetal stage of development, the environment provided by the mother continues to affect the baby's development, but the effects are on size, behavior, intelligence, and health, rather than on the formation of organs and limbs. Table 2.1 lists some of the conditions that most often endanger the child. The mother's physical condition, health, and age, her nutrition before and during pregnancy, the emotional stresses she undergoes, and the drugs, nicotine, and alcohol she consumes all make a difference in the behavior and condition of the infant. Of particular concern is the effect of these factors on brain development. Babies born to women who are alcoholics, for example, have a 44 percent chance of suffering from **fetal alcohol syndrome,** a pattern of defects that includes physical malformations of the face and mental retardation (Jones, Smith, Ulleland & Streissguth, 1973). Fetal alcohol syndrome is linked to heavy drinking, but even moderate drinking can cause less severe effects on infants' intellectual functioning (Hanson, 1977).

The likelihood that these potentially harmful factors in the environment will affect any particular infant depends on three things: the infant's inherited

A fetus at twelve weeks. At this point of prenatal development, the fetus can kick its legs, make a fist, turn its head, squint, open its mouth, swallow, and take a few ''breaths'' of amniotic fluid.

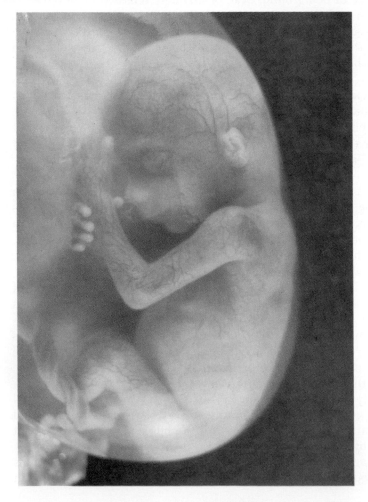

Mother's Condition or Behavior	Possible Effect on Embryo, Fetus, or Newborn
Incompatibility of maternal and fetal blood	Jaundice, anemia, death
Any viral infection: rubella, mumps, hepatitis, influenza	Malformations, fetal death, prematurity, retarded fetal growth, disorders, and infection in the newborn
Malnutrition	Retarded fetal growth, malformations, less-developed brain, greater vulnerability to disease
Excessive use of vitamin A	Cleft palate, congenital anomalies
Use of analgesics	Respiratory depression
Use of aspirin in large doses	Respiratory depression, bleeding
Use of anesthetics or barbiturates	Respiratory depression
Narcotic addiction	Growth deficiency, withdrawal syndrome, respiratory depression, death
Heavy smoking	Retarded fetal growth, increased fetal heart rate, prematurity
Daily use of alcohol	Growth deficiency, developmental lag
Exposure to X rays	Malformations, cancer

TABLE 2.1

Some Maternal Conditions Endangering the Child

A mother's physical condition or choice of actions can have direct and dangerous consequences for her unborn child.

SOURCE: Adapted from C. L. Blair and E. M. Salerno, *The Expanding Family: Childbearing*, 1976. Reprinted by permission of Little, Brown and Company.

constitution, the stage of prenatal development during which the infant is exposed, and the intensity of the factor. A strong dose of a damaging factor during a critical period in a genetically susceptible infant is most likely to cause malformations or deficiencies. Nevertheless, mechanisms built into the human organism maintain normal development under all but the most adverse conditions. Mental or physical problems resulting from all harmful factors affect fewer than 5 percent of the babies born in this country (Heinonen, Slone & Shapiro, 1976). The vast majority of fetuses arrive at the end of their nine-month gestation period averaging a healthy seven pounds and ready to continue a normal course of development in the outside world. In the sections to follow, we discuss the process of birth and trace the newborn's growing capacity to perceive, interact with, and think about the world.

INFANCY

Birth

Today, the birth of an infant may take place at home, in a hospital delivery room or birthing room, or on an operating table. It may involve anesthesia, pain-killing drugs, Lamaze training, doctors, family, and friends. The options are many; there is no one right way to have a baby.

The current wisdom is that the birth experience is better for both mother and infant if drugs and anesthesia are kept to a minimum and if both parents are active participants. Drugs and anesthesia decrease the vigor of the infant's sucking and breathing, thereby increasing the risk that the baby will suffer from oxygen deprivation. They also decrease the infant's attentiveness. These effects may last for some time and may lead to poorer vision and retarded muscular and neural development (Brackbill, 1979; Lester, Als & Brazelton,

1982). Having the father participate, it is believed, helps the mother through the pain of labor and delivery and involves the father emotionally with his infant from the very beginning.

Frederick Leboyer (1975) advocated other procedures—darkening the room, muffling loud sounds, waiting to cut the umbilical cord until it has stopped pulsing, and then easing the baby into a warm bath. Whether or not one takes such measures is a matter of personal taste. They do reduce the infant's bodily tensions and increase its quiet alertness, but the effects are apparently limited to the first few hours or minutes after birth (Sorrells-Jones, 1983).

Capacities of the Newborn

Regardless of the birth procedure, the baby does arrive. What happens then is extremely important. In the United States, the infant mortality rate is among the lowest in the world, but one out of every hundred babies still does not make it through the critical first month. In fact, more deaths occur during the first month after birth than at any other time except old age. Some infants have organic defects that lead to death. Some fail at one of the four tasks that must be accomplished in the first few hours after birth: breathing, circulating blood and stabilizing blood pressure, controlling body temperature, and ingesting food and excreting waste.

For those infants that do succeed at these tasks, the first few weeks are spent in a simple cycle of states. About 70 percent of the time, newborns are asleep. When they are not sleeping, newborns are drowsy, crying, awake and active, or awake and inactive. It is when they are in this last state, which occurs infrequently in segments only a few minutes long, that infants observe their surroundings and seem most capable of learning.

What can newborn infants see and hear? This question has provided an intriguing challenge, because newborns are extremely difficult to study. If they are held upright, their heads fall forward or backward; if they are lying down, they are likely to fall asleep. If the lights are too bright, they shut their eyes; if the lights are too dim, back to sleep they go. The most a researcher can hope for is about six minutes of an infant's attention.

Nevertheless, psychologists persevere in their attempts to capture infants' interest and attention. One thing they do is to show infants objects or pictures and watch where they look and for how long. More sophisticated technology is used to film infants' eye movements as they scan objects or pictures. Psychologists also record changes in infants' heart rates, sucking rates, brain waves, movements, and skin conductance (a measure of perspiration associated with emotion) when objects are shown or sounds are made. From research using all these techniques, researchers have gleaned a fair picture of what infants can see and hear at birth and soon after.

Vision   At birth, the infant's vision is quite limited. A very rough estimate is that the newborn has 20:600 sight; that is, an object 20 feet away looks as clear as it would if it were viewed from 600 feet away by an adult with normal vision. This limitation in what infants can see is the result of several immaturities in the visual system. The newborn's eye does not have a distinct fovea (the area in the adult eye on which central images are formed), and cells in the visual area of the infant's brain are not fully developed. Further, eye movements are slow and jerky, and the infant cannot change focus when objects move closer or farther away.

Although their vision is seriously limited, infants are by no means blind. The visual contrast between a mother's hair and face, for instance, is visible to the young infant, and although infants cannot see small objects on the other side of the room, they can see large objects close up—the distance at which most interaction with parents takes place. Infants particularly seem to enjoy looking at faces. It is now generally thought that this is not because faces have an innate attractiveness for infants, but because they contain attractive elements, such as contour, contrast, complexity, and movement (Olson & Sherman, 1983). Infants, it seems, look longest at what they can see best: patterns with the largest visible elements, the most movement, and the greatest amount of contrast (Banks & Salapatek, 1983).

Hearing   What can the newborn hear? At birth, hearing is somewhat impaired by amniotic fluid left in the ear. But this fluid is soon gone, and at two or three days of age, newborns can hear soft voices and can notice the difference between tones about one note apart on the musical scale (Schulman-Galambos & Galambos, 1979; Starr et al., 1977; Weir, 1979). By two weeks of age, infants respond to the difference between a human voice and other sounds, such as that of a bell. At four weeks, they can hear the difference between sounds as similar as "bah" and "pah" (Eimas et al., 1971). Newborn infants can also locate sounds (Muir & Field, 1979).

Smell and taste   Newborns are equipped with a good sense of smell. They will turn away from a noxious odor like ammonia and toward a sweet smell like flowers. Within a few days after birth, breast-fed babies prefer the odor of their own mother's milk to that of another mother's (Russell, 1976). Newborns can also taste the difference between water, sugar water, salt water, and milk, and they react differently depending on the concentration of sweet, salty, and bitter solutions (Ganchrow, Steiner & Daher, 1983). They suck longer and slower, pause for shorter periods, and smile and lick their upper lips when given a sweet solution (Ganchrow et al., 1983; Lipsitt et al., 1976).

Reflexes   In the first few weeks and months of life, babies' actions are dominated by involuntary, unlearned reactions called **reflexes.** These are swift, automatic movements in response to external stimuli; Figure 2.6 shows an example of the *grasping reflex*. More than twenty other reflexes have been observed in newborn infants. For example, the *rooting reflex* causes the infant to turn its mouth toward a finger or nipple that touches its cheek. The *sucking reflex* makes the newborn suck on anything that touches its lips. Most reflexes disappear within three or four months; their failure to disappear may signal problems in brain development.

Figure 2.6
Reflexes in the Newborn
When a finger is pressed into the newborn's palm, the palmar grasp reflex *causes the infant to hold on tightly enough to suspend its entire weight. The* Moro reflex *is a response to an abrupt loud noise or the sensation of falling: the arms and legs are flung to the sides, hands open and fingers spread, then the arms are brought in toward the body in a hugging motion, hands now fisted, back arched, and legs fully extended. Other reflexes include the* stepping, *or* automatic walking, *reflex and the* swimming reflex.

Sensorimotor Development

The fascinating journey from the simple reflexes of the newborn to the cognitive understanding of the two-year-old was most carefully charted by Piaget. Piaget (1952) called the first stage of cognitive development the **sensorimotor period,** because rather than exhibiting any understanding of or reflection about the world, the infant's mental activity is confined to sensory perceptions and motor skills. Even so, the infant gradually develops more complex schemes. According to Piaget, a **scheme** is a basic unit of knowledge, which may be a pattern of action, a mental image of an object, or a complex idea. At first, the infant's schemes are simple sensory and motor functions, such as looking and grasping. Piaget called these simple behaviors *object-action schemes*. As motor skills develop and voluntary actions come to replace reflexes, babies elaborate simple schemes into complex ones; they begin to wave or shake and later to insert or build.

The elaboration of schemes   The elaboration of object-action schemes occurs, according to Piaget, in a fixed sequence. For the first month or so, infants simply look, listen, and practice basic reflexes. During the next three months, they repeat actions for the sheer pleasure of it. From about four to eight months of age, infants repeat actions because they bring some interesting response. From eight to twelve months, babies begin to use their schemes to get a toy that is out of reach, to put two objects together, or to achieve other goals. From twelve to eighteen months, they begin to experiment with their schemes, repeating and modifying actions to see the effects of different actions. The toddler picks up a spoon full of grape jelly. She holds it flat, she tips it one way, she tips it the other way, she slowly turns it upside down. She stirs the jelly on the tray. She smears it on her hands, in her hair, and on everything else within reach.

Two processes guide this development of schemes: *organization,* which is the combination and integration of separate simple schemes into more complex patterns, and *adaptation,* which consists of assimilation and accommodation. In **assimilation,** infants take in new information about objects by trying out existing schemes on objects that fit those schemes. Suppose, for example, that a baby boy is given a new rattle. He examines it, sucks on it, waves it, and throws it—discovering that this rattle, like others, is suckable, waveable, and throwable. In **accommodation,** schemes are modified as the infant tries out familiar schemes on objects that do not fit them. The baby is given a cup. He examines it, sucks on it, waves it, and throws it. But this time, he discovers that, to suck on it, he can put only the edge in his mouth; to wave it, he must hold onto the handle; and throwing it will not work at all, because Mother removes the cup from his playpen.

The concept of object permanence   During the sensorimotor period, according to Piaget, while infants are experimenting with objects and actions, they come to form *mental representations* of those objects and actions. By the time they are about two years old, infants do not have to look at, touch, or suck an object to know that it exists. Piaget called this knowledge **object permanence,** and said that it, too, occurs in stages.

The first evidence that object permanence is developing, according to Piaget, appears when infants are four to eight months old. At this age, for the first time, they are able to recognize a familiar object even if part of it is covered by a blanket or otherwise hidden from view. This shows that infants have some primitive mental representation of objects. But, if an object is completely hidden, they will not search for it; out of sight, said Piaget, is literally out of mind for infants at this stage.

From eight to twelve months, infants will search briefly for a hidden object, but their search is haphazard and ineffective. Even if the infant watches someone move an object from one hiding place to another, he or she may search for it in the first place it was hidden. From twelve to eighteen months, infants look for a hidden object where it was last hidden, as long as they have seen it being moved. Otherwise, they cannot find it.

Not until eighteen to twenty-four months do infants apparently become able to picture and follow events in their minds. Now they can figure out sequential movements of objects even if they have not seen them. They look for the object in places other than where they saw it last, sometimes in completely new places. They have a mental representation of the object that is completely separate from their immediate perception of it. Their concept of objects as permanent, according to Piaget, is now fully developed.

An update on object permanence   Other researchers have challenged Piaget's account of the development of object permanence. When his tests of object permanence have been changed slightly, infants' responses have changed, too. For example, if toys are hidden under smaller, lighter covers than Piaget used, infants are more likely to remove the covers to find the hidden toys (Rader, Spiro & Firestone, 1979). And if the experimenter simply turns the light out and does not use a cover to hide the object, infants as young as five months old have reached for the object in the dark (Bower & Wishart, 1972).

Why do these results differ from Piaget's? As Paul Harris (1974) pointed out, finding a hidden object requires two things: (1) mentally representing the hidden object and (2) figuring out where it might be. Piaget's tests did not allow for the possibility that an infant might know that an object exists but not have adequate strategies for finding it. Other researchers have found that even infants under one year old can recall some past experiences and events, such as peekaboo, pattycake, and bedtime and mealtime routines, and they can find familiar household objects and toys at home (Ashmead & Perlmutter, 1980).

The general consensus among developmental psychologists now seems to be that infants develop mental representations earlier than Piaget's demonstrations suggested. What is important, however, is not the age at which infants develop this ability, but the fact that they do, a fact first pointed out by Piaget and first illustrated by his ingenious, if not completely controlled, experiments.

Early Social Interactions

Life for the infant is more than learning about physical objects. In the first months of life, infants are attracted by the faces, voices, and actions of people. And most babies are immensely attractive creatures themselves, with their tiny bodies, large eyes, chubby cheeks, rosebud mouths, and soft gurgles. These qualities exert a powerful pull on people around them, especially parents.

Parent-infant interaction   From the very beginning and increasingly thereafter, mothers are eager to engage their infants in social interaction. And in their limited ways, infants participate in these interactions. Even in the early months, infants are sensitive to their parents' overt expressions of emotion. In one study (Cohn & Tronick, 1983) researchers tested the ability of three-month-olds to respond to emotional cues from their mothers. Some mothers acted normally, whereas others were asked to act depressed. Babies of the "depressed" mothers spent more time protesting, reacting warily, looking away, or giving only fleeting smiles.

These reactions do not mean that the infants *recognized* the emotions that their mothers conveyed. Other researchers showed four-month-old infants various kinds of faces, as in Figure 2.7 (p. 46). The infants did seem to have a built-in predisposition to smile at *noticeable* facial expressions—like toothy smiles—but were not generally able to distinguish among subtle facial expressions of emotion (Oster, 1981; Oster & Ewy, 1980). This ability begins to develop later in infancy, as we will see in Chapter 12, on emotion.

By the time infants are three months old, they engage in mutual gazing with their mothers for up to 20 seconds at a stretch (Peery & Stern, 1976). Mothers look at the baby, open their eyes wide, make exaggerated faces, and baby-talk in high voices. The infants smile, and smiling has a spiraling effect. The more the infant smiles, the more the mother stays nearby and responds to these smiles, usually with a return smile (Brackbill, 1958; Clarke-Stewart, 1973). Infants also draw their mothers into interaction by crying. A mother's heart beats faster when she watches a videotape of an infant, especially her own, crying (Donovan, Leavitt & Balling, 1978; Wiesenfeld & Klorman,

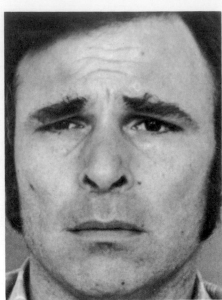

Figure 2.7
Infants and Emotions
Do young infants react to the emotions expressed in faces or to facial features alone? The faces pictured here were part of an experiment on this question. One group saw a sad face and a close-mouthed smile; another group saw a sad face and an open-mouthed, toothy smile; a third saw the sad face and the toothy smile upside down. Infants looked longer at the upright toothy grin than at the sad face, but they did not look at the upside-down toothy grin or at the closed-mouth smile longer than at the sad face. Thus, it appears that, at four months of age, infants respond more to faces than to the emotions those faces convey.
(Unmasking the Face, Reprint Edition, Consulting Psychologists Press, Palo Alto, CA, 1984. Copyright Paul Ekman and Wallace V. Friesen.)

1978). But although crying produces an automatic physiological reaction, it does not lead to automatic soothing. In our culture, even well-intentioned mothers sometimes let their babies cry.

Capitalizing on the infant's social behaviors, such as gazing, smiling, and vocalizing, mothers can have "dialogues" with their babies. At first, these dialogues are really pseudodialogues, in which the baby acts and the mother fills in the pauses as if the baby has taken a turn (Trevarthen, 1977):

Mother: Aren't you my cutie?
Pause
Imagined response from baby: Yes.
Mother: You sure are!

By the end of the first year, after countless pseudodialogues, most mother-infant pairs have evolved exquisitely coordinated dialogues, and infants are taking their turns in the "conversations" (Newson, 1977):

Baby: (Looks at a toy)
Mother: Do you like that?
Baby: Da!
Mother: Yes, it's a nice toy, isn't it?
Baby: Da Da!

The infant grows attached   While the mother becomes more attached to the infant and the two become more coordinated social partners, the infant begins to form a deep and enduring tie to her. It is the infant's first love affair, with all the joy of togetherness and pain of separation of love affairs at any age.

Mary Ainsworth (1973) described this relationship as developing in phases. At first, the newborn infant responds to anyone; all faces are beautiful, all arms can give comfort. This phase lasts only a few weeks or months and ends when the infant can discriminate among people and pick out parents from the crowd. In the second phase, infants respond differently to familiar and unfamiliar people, smiling or vocalizing to those whom they recognize, crying when they leave, and finding comfort in their soothing. The third phase begins sometime around six or seven months, when the baby shows evidence of forming a true **attachment**—an affectionate, close, and enduring relationship with the single person with whom the baby has shared many experiences. The baby actively seeks proximity and physical contact with this person— usually the mother—crawling after her, calling her, embracing her, clambering up into her lap, or protesting when she leaves. This phase continues through the second and third years.

In 1976 a book called *Maternal-Infant Bonding* was published. It changed the way that newborn infants are treated from the moment of birth. The authors, pediatricians Marshall Klaus and John Kennell, had observed mothers and their newborns and found that, during the first hour or so after birth, babies are usually awake and will gaze at the mother's face while the mother gazes at and touches the infant. The importance of this early contact was demonstrated by Klaus and Kennell's experiments on the effect of leaving mothers and newborns together for the hour after birth or giving them extra opportunities to be together during their hospital stay. They found that women who were given early and extended contact with their babies were later more emotionally attached to them than mothers given only the routine contact allowed by usual hospital procedures. Further, mothers given early and extended contact with their infants felt more competent and were more reluctant to leave their infants with another person. They stayed closer to their infants, often gazing into their eyes, touching and soothing them, and fondling and kissing them. This difference occurred in the hospital and lasted for a year or more (Hales et al., 1977; Kennell et al., 1974).

Klaus and Kennell advocated a change in hospital procedures, so that infants would not be separated from their mothers at birth or stay apart from them in a newborn nursery. Their findings fueled dramatic reform of hospital policy across the country. Today, a little more than a decade later, nearly all hospitals in this country allow mothers to keep their babies with them after delivery.

But, as it turns out, subsequent research did not support expectations that mother-infant contact in the first hours after birth would guarantee a good mother-child relationship and that lack of it would hamper that relationship. The mothers in Klaus and Kennell's studies were young and poor. In families that are psychologically prepared for and eagerly await an infant's birth, early contact does not seem to make a difference (Svejda, Pannabecker & Emde, 1982). Psychologists now believe that the mother's emotional bond to her infant develops slowly over the first three months and is affected by the infant's increasing responsiveness—not just by what happens in the first hour after birth.

Do infants develop attachments to fathers? Despite fathers' expressed interest in sharing child care, the actual amount of father-infant interaction in most American families is still surprisingly limited. Not only is father-infant interaction less frequent than mother-infant interaction; most studies show that it has a somewhat different nature. Mothers tend to feed, bathe, dress, cuddle, and talk to their infants, whereas fathers are more likely to play with, jiggle, and toss them, especially sons (Clarke-Stewart, 1978, 1980; Lamb, 1977). Fathers are usually just as sensitive and responsive to their infant's expressions while things are going well; but when the baby gets bored or distressed, fathers may not do as well as mothers (Frodi et al., 1978; Power & Parke, 1983). Nevertheless, infants do form attachments to fathers as well as to mothers, though often a little later (Cohen & Campos, 1974; Kotelchuck, 1976; Lamb, 1976a). After the attachment has formed, the father often becomes the toddler's preferred play partner (Clarke-Stewart, 1980; Lynn & Cross, 1974).

Mutual eye contact, exaggerated facial expressions, and shared baby talk are an important part of the early social interactions that promote an enduring bond of attachment between parent and child.

HIGHLIGHT

Variations in Attachment

The amount of closeness that human infants seek depends on the experience they have with their particular caregiver. An infant whose mother has been absent, aloof, or unresponsive is likely to need more closeness than one whose mother has been accessible and responsive. Infants who are ill or tired may require more closeness. For infants with a **secure attachment,** the urge to be close is balanced by an urge to explore the environment. The infant uses the mother as a home base, sallying forth to explore and play, but returning to her periodically for comfort and contact. Securely attached children can tolerate brief separations from their mother, but they are always happy to see her return and always receptive to her overtures of contact.

The majority of infants studied in this country (66 percent in research by Ainsworth, Blehar, Waters, and Wall in 1978, for example) have this type of secure relationship with their mothers. Other infants have an **insecure avoidant attachment;** they avoid or ignore the mother when she approaches them or returns after a brief separation and seem to be just as satisfied with comfort from another person. Still other infants have an **insecure ambivalent attachment.** They are very upset when their mother leaves, but when she returns, they act angry and reject her efforts at contact; when picked up, they squirm to get down.

The security of their child's attachment is of great importance to parents. But the nature of this attachment has more far-reaching implications. Compared with children who are insecurely attached, children who are securely attached to their mothers tend to be more socially and emotionally competent; more cooperative, enthusiastic, and persistent; better at solving problems; more compliant and controlled; and more popular and playful (Cassidy & Main, 1984; Jacobson & Wille, 1986; Lutkenhaus, 1984; Schneider-Rosen & Cicchetti, 1984; Thompson & Lamb, 1983; Waters, Wippman & Sroufe, 1979; Weston & Richardson, 1985).

Researchers in one study found that securely attached one-year-old boys had fewer psychological problems as six-year-olds than insecurely attached boys (Lewis et al., 1984). But the study also showed that attachment is just one of a number of factors—including stressful events and family characteristics—that affect the course of children's social and psychological development. Although attachment is important in a child's psychological development, a secure attachment does not guarantee confidence and competence, and an insecure attachment does not ensure pathology.

Differences in children's attachment relationships stem largely from the fact that the person to whom the baby develops an attachment not only must provide care and feeding but also must be loving, helpful, sensitive, and responsive (Ainsworth, 1973; Arend, Gove & Sroufe, 1979; Clarke-Stewart, 1973; Pastor, 1981; Rutter, 1974). Mothers who are critical, rejecting, interfering, abusive, unresponsive, or neglectful are likely to foster insecure attachments in their infants (Ainsworth, 1973; Beckwith, 1972; Egeland & Sroufe, 1981). This is especially true if those infants are ill or have other inborn characteristics that make them especially needy. Here again we see the interaction of nature and nurture.

Concern has recently been expressed about how the daily separations experienced by infants in day care will affect their attachment to their mothers. It is true that separation from the mother is painful for young children. If the separation lasts a week or more, young children who have formed an attachment to their mothers protest, then become apathetic and mournful, and finally seem to lose interest in the missing mother (Robertson & Robertson, 1971). But day care does not involve a lasting separation. Most researchers studying day care have found no apparent negative effects on the quality of children's attachments (Clarke-Stewart & Fein, 1983). Although infants in day care may become fond of or feel comfort and security with a day care provider, they still prefer their mothers. The relationship with the provider does not have the same emotional intensity or level of involvement as the attachment to their mothers.

Available studies have tended to focus on good day care, however. In two studies of less-than-optimal day care (Schwartz, 1983; Vaughn et al., 1979), a greater number of day care infants (compared to those at home with their mothers) avoided or ignored their mothers after a brief separation. Whether this reflected a reasonable and realistic adaptation to their daily separations, a reaction to less affectionate behavior from their mothers at home, or a pathological response to the whole situation is still an open question. The effects of infant day care require careful research, as more mothers of younger infants take on full-time employment. ◼

Individual Temperament

From the moment they are born, infants show their individuality, and these individual characteristics affect the kinds of relationships parents and infants form. Some infants are active and vigorous; they splash, thrash, and wriggle. Others lie still most of the time. Some infants approach a new object with enthusiasm; others turn away or fuss. Some are acutely aware of every sight

The fact that babies' temperaments differ is apparent quite early and can significantly influence the way their parents react to them.

and sound; others are oblivious to loud noises or wet diapers. Some infants whimper; others kick, scream, and wail. These characteristics make up the infant's **temperament,** which is the basic, natural disposition of an individual.

In some of the most extensive research ever done on infant temperament, Alexander Thomas and Stella Chess (1977) found three main temperament patterns. *Easy babies,* the most common kind, get hungry and sleepy at predictable times, react to new situations cheerfully, and seldom fuss. *Difficult babies* are the opposite: irregular and irritable. The third group is *slow-to-warm-up,* reacting warily to new situations but eventually coming to enjoy them.

Temperament is the beginning of an individual's identity or personality. But not every difficult baby becomes an elderly curmudgeon, nor does each easy baby develop into Miss Congeniality. In temperament, too, nature interacts with nurture. Many events take place between infancy and adulthood to shift the individual's development in one direction or another.

One possibly influential factor is the "goodness of fit," or match, between the infant's temperament and the parents' expectations, desires, and personal styles. When a mother believes she is responsible for her infant's behavior, an easy child might reassure her. If the mother is looking for signs of assertiveness, perhaps because she herself was victimized as a child and needs reassurance that her baby is "tough," a difficult child might prove welcome. If parent and infant are in tune, chances increase that temperamental qualities will be stable.

Consider, for example, Chinese and Caucasian children. At birth, Chinese infants are calmer, less changeable, less perturbable, and more easily consoled when upset than Caucasian infants, suggesting that there may be an inherited predisposition toward self-control in the Chinese. This inherited tendency is then powerfully reinforced by the Chinese culture. Compared with Caucasian-American parents, Chinese-American parents are less likely to reward and stimulate babbling and smiling, and more likely to maintain close control of their young children (Kagan, Kearsley & Zelazo, 1978; Kriger & Kroes, 1972; Smith & Freedman, 1983). The children, in turn, are more dependent on their mothers and less likely to play by themselves; they are less vocal, noisy, and active than Caucasian-American children (Kagan et al., 1978; Smith & Freedman, 1983). These temperamental differences between children in different ethnic groups illustrate the combined contributions of nature and nurture.

Learning to Talk: First Words

From the time they are born, infants can hear the sounds of speech. Newborns have lower thresholds for sounds that are in the range of speech than for other sounds (Eisenberg, 1976; Hoversten & Moncur, 1969). When they hear speech, babies open their eyes wider, look around for the sound, grimace, cry, or stop crying (Eisenberg, 1976). Researchers have concluded, judging from where infants look or how fast they suck in order to hear recordings of different voices, that infants also prefer certain *kinds* of speech. They like rising tones, spoken by women or children (Sullivan & Horowitz, 1983). They also like speech that is high-pitched, exaggerated, and expressive (Lieberman, 1967; Turnure, 1971). In short, they like to hear the *baby talk* used by nearly all adults talking to babies (Fernald, 1981; Glenn & Cunningham, 1983).

Babblings are the first sounds infants make that resemble speech. These repetitions of syllables ("bababa," "mamama," "dadada") begin at about four months of age and, although meaningless to the baby, are a delight to parents. During much of the first year, infants the world over make the same babbling sounds. At about nine months, however, babies who hear only English start to lose their German gutterals and French nasals. Beginning at this time, too, they begin to shorten some of their vocalizations to "da," "duh," and "ma." These sounds, which soon replace babbling, seem very much like language. Babies use them in specific contexts and with obvious purpose (Dore, 1978). Accompanied by appropriate gestures, they may be used to express joy ("oohwow") or anger ("uh-uh-uh"), to get something that is out of reach ("engh-engh"), or to point out something interesting ("Dah!").

At the same time, infants notice the gestures that adults use to communicate. Mothers often claim of their year-old infants, "She doesn't talk, but she understands everything I say." This is not quite true. The twelve-month-old may understand some of the mother's words, but she is likely to rely on cues other than words to figure out what the mother means. Mother may be pointing to the ball while she says, "Where is the ball?" Or the ball itself may serve as a cue if the mother says, "Roll the ball to me."

Without using gestures or other cues, Janellen Huttenlocher (1974) asked children to locate objects and perform actions. She established that ten- to twelve-month-olds can understand a few words—certainly more words than they can say. Proper names and object words are among the first words they understand. Often the very first word they understand is a pet's name.

Proper names and object words—words like *cookie, doggie, shoe, truck,* and *mama*—are also among the first words children are likely to say when, at around twelve to eighteen months of age, they begin to talk. Nouns for simple object categories *(dog, flower)* are acquired first, rather than either more general nouns *(animal, plant)* or more specific names *(collie, rose)* (Rosch et al., 1976).

Of course, these early words do not sound exactly like adult language. Babies usually reduce them to a shorter, easier form, like "duh" for *duck* or "mih" for *milk*. Children make themselves understood, however, by using gestures, intonations, facial expressions, and interminable repetitions. If they have a word for an object, they "overextend" it to cover more ground. Thus they might use *fly* for all insects and perhaps for other small things like raisins and M&Ms; they might use *dog* for cats, bears, and horses (Clark & Clark, 1977; Rosch, 1975). Children make these "errors" because their vocabularies are limited, not because they fail to notice the difference between dogs and cats or because they want to eat a fly (Fremgen & Fay, 1980; Rescorla, 1981). Until they can say the conventional words for objects, they overextend the words they have, use all-purpose sounds (like "dat" or "dis"), and coin new words (like *pepping* for "shaking the pepper shaker").

This **one-word stage** lasts for about six months. During this period, children build up their vocabularies a word at a time and tend to use words one at a time. We will discuss the subsequent development of language when we examine language in detail, in Chapter 9.

COGNITIVE DEVELOPMENT IN CHILDHOOD

Children make major advances in language and thought between infancy and adolescence. The child progresses from a toddler who can barely put two words together to a logical and articulate creature who can speak and write paragraphs, do mathematical calculations, and recite the batting averages of the New York Yankees. How and why do these changes occur? The primary explanation lies in the child's growing ability to think. We are now ready to take a closer look at this *cognitive* development, beginning with Piaget's description and then considering some alternative views.

Logical Thought

According to Piaget, the ability to form mental representations marks the end of the sensorimotor period and the beginning of the second major stage of cognitive development, called the preoperational period (Piaget, 1962). This stage lasts from the ages of about two to seven. At the age of about seven, the child enters a third period, the concrete operational stage, which lasts until about the age of eleven. Table 2.2 summarizes the characteristics of these and other stages of cognitive development.

The preoperational period   The second stage of cognitive development is called the **preoperational period** because it precedes the time when children can perform mental operations, such as counting, adding, and subtracting. During this stage, however, children begin to understand, create, and use symbols to represent things that are not present.

This ability to symbolize opens up vast new domains for two- to four-year-olds. Pretending, drawing, and talking are all modes of symbolic repre-

TABLE 2.2 _____

Piaget's Periods of Cognitive Development

According to Piaget, each period of children's cognitive development is characterized by a predictable set of features.

Period	Activities and Achievements
Sensorimotor *Birth to two years*	Infants discover aspects of the world through their sensory impressions, motor activities, and coordination of the two.
	They learn to differentiate themselves from the external world. They learn that objects exist even when they are not visible and that they are independent of the infant's own actions. They gain some appreciation of cause and effect.
Preoperational *Two to seven years*	Children cannot yet manipulate and transform information in logical ways, but they now can think in images and symbols.
	They become able to represent something with something else, acquire language, and play games of pretend. Intelligence at this stage is said to be intuitive, because children cannot make general, logical statements.
Concrete operational *Seven to eleven years*	Children can understand logical principles that apply to concrete external objects.
	They can appreciate that certain properties of an object remain the same, despite changes in appearance, and sort objects into categories. They can appreciate the perspective of another viewer. They can think about two concepts, such as longer and shorter, at the same time.
Formal operational *Over eleven years*	Adolescents and adults can think logically about abstractions, can speculate, and can consider what might or what ought to be.
	They can work in probabilities and possibilities. They can imagine other worlds, especially ideal ones.
	They can reason about purely verbal or logical statements. They can relate any element or statement to any other, manipulate variables in a scientific experiment, and deal with proportions and analogies. They reflect on their own activity of thinking.

Figure 2.8
A Test of Egocentrism
In Piaget's three-mountain task, the model on the table shows mountains of varying heights and colors. The experimenter asks the child to choose photographs that depict how the scene appears to the doll, which the experimenter seats in different positions around the table (Piaget & Inhelder, 1967). Children younger than about eight years do not usually succeed on this task; they often choose the photo showing their own view, not the doll's.

sentation that these children enjoy. A two-year-old might use a scarf as a pillow, use a finger for a horse, or pretend to be Mommy or Daddy. At the age of three or four, children symbolize intricate roles and events as they play school, house, doctor, and Star Wars.

In the second half of the preoperational stage, from ages four to seven, children's thinking is still characterized by intuition, not yet by logic. They know many things about people, toys, animals, vehicles, and food. But their reasoning is often wrong or even bizarre by adult standards. They assume, for instance, that dreams are real, originating and taking place outside of themselves. Dreams are "pictures on the window," "a circus in the room," or "something from the sky." Children of this age, Piaget found, also believe that inanimate objects are alive and have intentions, feelings, and consciousness. The clouds go slowly because they have no paws or legs. Flowers grow because they want to.

According to Piaget, children at this age are not only intuitive, but also *egocentric*. They cannot understand that other people have different perspectives from their own. When their eyes are closed, they think that no one can see them. They assume that others see, hear, feel, and think exactly what they do. They believe that rivers are for them to swim in. The clouds do not just bring rain; they bring rain to their own garden. With his "three-mountain" experiment, shown in Figure 2.8, Piaget became the first researcher to study preschoolers' egocentric perspective.

Children's use of intuition rather than logic in the preoperational period can be illustrated by showing them two rows of different numbers of objects, say, straws and glasses, and asking them to match an equal number of straws and glasses. They will usually be unable to do so. Instead of matching them by placing one straw in front of one glass, the children lengthen the row of straws so that the two sets cover equal amounts of space and give the appearance of being equal. If preschool children watch equal amounts of juice being poured into a tall, thin glass and a short, wide one and are then asked which contains more, they will usually guess the taller one. They do not have the ability to *conserve* number or amount. **Conservation** is the ability to

Type of conservation	First display	Second display	Child is asked
Length	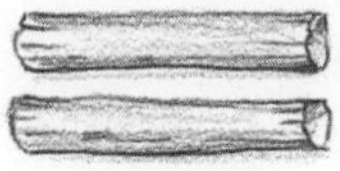 The child sees two sticks of equal length and agrees that they are of equal length.	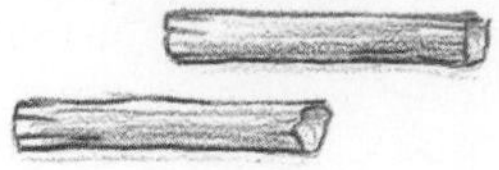 The experimenter moves one stick over.	Which stick is longer? Preconserving child will say that one of the sticks is longer. Conserving child will say that they are both the same length.
Liquid quantity	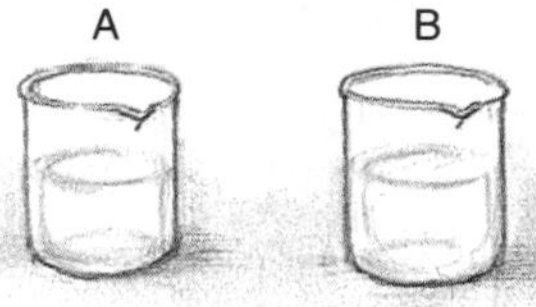 The child sees two beakers filled with water and says that they both contain the same amount of water.	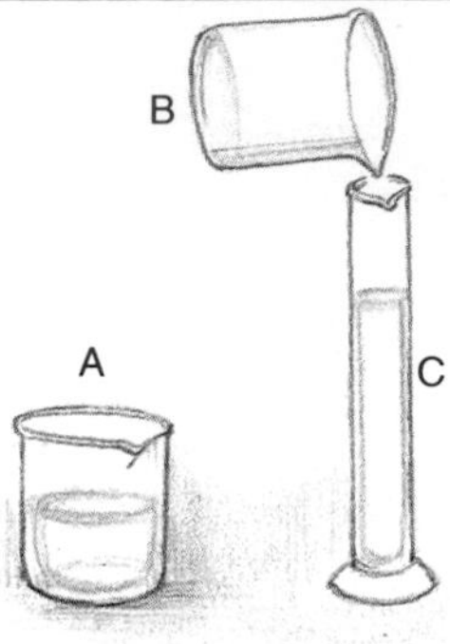 The experimenter pours water from B into a tall, thin beaker C, so that water level in C is higher than in A.	Which beaker has more water? Preconserving child will say that C has more water: "See, it's higher." Conserving child will say that they have the same amount of water: "You only poured it!"
Substance amount	The child sees two identical clay balls and acknowledges that the two have equal amounts of clay.	 The experimenter rolls out one of the balls.	Do the two pieces have the same amount of clay? Preconserving child will say that the long piece has more clay. Conserving child will say that the two pieces have the same amount of clay.

Figure 2.9
Conservation
Here are some of the procedures that have been used to test children's ability to conserve length, liquid quantity, and substance amount. Conservation of area and conservation of volume may be tested in a similar way. The ability to conserve makes it possible for children to begin thinking logically about the world and to mentally manipulate numbers and other objects.

recognize that important properties of a substance—such as number, volume, or weight—remain constant despite changes in shape, length, or position (see Figure 2.9).

Concrete operations Sometime around age six or seven, when children do develop the ability to conserve number and amount, they enter what Piaget called the stage of **concrete operations,** which lasts until adolescence. Now they can count, measure, add, and subtract; their thinking is no longer dominated by visual appearances. They can use simple logic and perform simple mental manipulations and operations.

For example, children can now arrange objects into classes (such as tools, fruit, and vehicles) or series (such as largest to smallest) by systematic searching and ordering. They realize that if A is larger than B and B is larger than C, then A is larger than C. In the preoperational period, if children are shown a picture of eight tulips and four daisies and are asked, "Are there more tulips or more flowers?" they will answer, "More tulips." They are apparently unable to think beyond the fact that there are more tulips than daisies. In the concrete operational period, however, children have outgrown this difficulty in understanding classes and subclasses.

Criticisms of Piaget's theory Piaget's observations and demonstrations of children's cognitive development are vivid and fascinating, but not all developmental psychologists are convinced by his interpretations. For example, some have questioned whether Piaget's three-mountain experiment really proves that children in the preoperational period are egocentric. It turns out that children at this age are quite capable of taking another person's perspective when they are given simpler tests, such as identifying the doll's view of a simpler display consisting of more familiar objects (Borke, 1975), or have the display covered while they say what it looks like to the doll (Hardwick, McIntyre & Pick, 1976).

Developmental psychologists have also questioned Piaget's tests of children's understanding of classes and subclasses. They have found that children correctly answer questions about classes and subclasses earlier than Piaget reported—if the questions are phrased to emphasize the general class rather than the subclass. For example, preschool children can correctly answer such questions as "Are there more tulips or more of all the flowers?" (Siegel et al., 1978) or "Which is more, the tulips or the whole bouquet of flowers?"

Criticism of Piaget's theory has also come from researchers who have demonstrated that, even when they use Piaget's tests, they can get children to succeed at younger ages than Piaget did by first giving them some relevant training. For example, preschool children have succeeded at tests of concrete operations after being trained to focus on relevant dimensions, such as number, height, and width (Gelman, 1969), or after hearing higher-level arguments from older children (Silverman & Stone, 1972).

These serious criticisms make it clear that there are weaknesses in Piaget's explanations of development; indeed, his work alone may not be sufficient to explain all of cognitive development. Still, there are substantial differences in the thinking of two-year-olds and four-year-olds, six-year-olds and eleven-year-olds, and Piaget's work helps to predict and consider these differences. His theory is the most comprehensive and complex available. Still, it is not as comprehensive and complex as cognitive development itself, and other developmental psychologists have offered alternative perspectives.

Learning Theory and Information Processing

One alternative perspective is the behavioral, or *learning theory,* approach. Some learning theorists have explained the development of children's thought in terms of the consequences of performing particular behaviors (Bijou & Baer, 1961). They suggest that, if children are rewarded for speaking in long sentences, for learning the alphabet, or for saying that tulips are flowers, they will be more inclined to repeat those behaviors and will thus learn cognitive skills.

Most psychologists do not find this explanation of cognitive development particularly satisfying. For one thing, learning is not always tied to the obvious consequences of behavior. Children will imitate others' actions without receiving any reward for doing so, particularly if those people are powerful and affectionate (Bandura & Huston, 1961). So, although we will see in later chapters that learning theory has value for understanding and changing many aspects of behavior, most American developmental psychologists have become interested in a different approach.

That approach, which dominates cognitive psychology today, involves describing children's cognitive activities in terms of **information processing,** examining how information is taken in, remembered or forgotten, and used. Developmental psychologists taking this approach attempt to describe the processes that go on inside the child's head. Their research focuses on quantitative changes in children's mental capacities, rather than on qualitative advances or stages, as Piaget's did. They do not follow the learning theorists' emphasis on children's overt behavior and its consequences. Rather, information-processing researchers try to understand the mental operations children use as they take in and organize information so that it can be stored in memory and put to use later on. This type of research has shown that children gradually get better at doing these things as they get older.

For one thing, children's attention spans lengthen with age. Very young infants pay attention to their surroundings for only short periods. Toddlers can pay attention for longer periods but are easily distracted. By school age, children can work, watch, or listen for long periods. By adulthood, concentration can become so intense that a person may be oblivious to distractions.

As their attention spans increase, so do the speeds with which children can take in sensory images and the efficiency with which they change their focus of attention (Manis, Keating & Morrison, 1980). With age, children's exploration of the world also becomes more selective; they learn to focus on the relevant parts of incoming information and ignore the rest. This allows children to select round pegs to put into round holes, regardless of the pegs' color or length. Children also improve in their ability to perceive relationships among things and differences between them (rough versus smooth, spherical versus cubical)—in more complex forms and more complicated backgrounds. In short, for the first five or six years, children's ability to absorb information improves.

There are also marked improvements in memory. Preschoolers can hold only two or three pieces, or *chunks,* of information in their immediate memories; five-year-olds, only four; seven-year-olds, only five (Miller, 1956; Morrison, Holmes & Haith, 1974; Pascual-Leone, 1970). Older children can hold about seven pieces of information. More important, they become better at remembering more complex and abstract chunks of information, such as the gist of what several different people have said during a conversation. Their memories also become more accurate, extensive, and well organized.

There are at least three reasons for these improvements in memory. First, during the school years, children learn strategies for remembering and studying. For example, they learn to rehearse or repeat information over and over to help fix it in memory. Second, children's metamemories are improving. (*Metamemory* is an awareness of what memory itself is, what situations call for deliberate memorization, and what factors affect memory.) Third, much improvement is due to the knowledge children accumulate over the school years. A larger knowledge base allows them to draw more inferences and to integrate new information into a more complete network.

Variations in the Pace of Cognitive Development

We have seen that children get better at looking, listening, talking, reading, and remembering over the years from two to twelve. Within this general trend, however, there are large individual differences; some children are mentally precocious, while others lag behind their peers. As we will see in Chapter 10, on mental abilities, cognitive and clinical psychologists have focused considerable attention on measuring and understanding the biological, psychological, and environmental causes of individual differences in mental ability. Developmental psychologists have also done so. Their interest is not entirely academic; many have sought to improve cognitive skills and to speed up and ultimately raise children's cognitive functioning to higher levels.

These psychologists have studied children's cognitive development in a range of environments. They have found that children in especially barren

As cognitive development advances, children can explore and interact with their world in ever more complex ways.

residential institutions, who are deprived of the everyday sights, sounds, and feelings provided by conversation and loving interaction, by pictures and books, even by television and radio, develop more slowly than children in normal family environments (Dennis, 1960, 1973). Such severe deprivation can impair intellectual development by as much as 50 IQ points by the time children are two or three years old, and if the deprivation continues, it may result in permanently lower levels of cognitive functioning.

At home, too, children's cognitive development has been related to various aspects of their surroundings (Clarke-Stewart & Apfel, 1979; Wachs & Gruen, 1982). Children do best when exposed to a variety of interesting materials and experiences, but not so many that they are overwhelmed. The presence of a supportive and stimulating adult is also important. Children need to know that their actions have predictable consequences. They learn this from parents who smile at their smiles, respond to their cries, and pay attention to their gestures. They can benefit from parents who read and talk to them, who encourage and actively help them to explore, and who teach them.

To improve the cognitive skills of children who lack these advantages, developmental psychologists have provided some children with extra lessons, stimulating materials, and educational contact with sensitive adults. The most substantial effort to provide this kind of help is Project Head Start, a preschool program for poor children, which currently serves some 400,000 youngsters every year. This and numerous smaller projects have significantly increased children's scores on intelligence tests (Lazar et al., 1982; Ramey & Haskins, 1981).

Such preschool programs can have enduring effects, including such indirect benefits as improved self-esteem and more positive feelings about school. Still, children clearly need continued support and stimulation if gains in cognitive development are to continue. IQ gains usually last only one to two years after a special program ends and then begin to diminish.

The early years of childhood are special and profoundly important for cognitive development. But they are not absolutely critical in the same way that the embryonic period of prenatal development is critical for organ formation. The effects of negative or positive early experience on cognitive development are, to a large extent, reversible (Clarke & Clarke, 1976; Kagan, 1985).

SOCIAL AND EMOTIONAL DEVELOPMENT IN CHILDHOOD

The saga of social development over the years of childhood is the story of an enlarging social world, which comes to include brothers and sisters, playmates and classmates, and teachers and strangers. Social relationships with these people become based on common interests and feelings, not just security or proximity. The child develops a growing understanding of social rules and roles and of emotional situations and signals. The child hones skills for playing with others or working alone, for making friends and keeping them, for knowing how to act like a girl or a boy. How and why do these social developments and socialization occur?

Relationships with Parents and Siblings

From the age of two on, as children seek more autonomy, the nature of their relationship with their parents changes. From two to four years, children emerge from a dependent relationship with their parents to become more self-

Though relationships with siblings may not always be cordial, they are often among the closest and most positive in a child's life.

reliant individuals (Mahler, Pine & Bergman, 1975). They are no longer distressed by brief separations from parents, and they are willing to tolerate being farther away (Rheingold & Eckerman, 1971). They assert their independence by turning their backs, literally and figuratively, through noncompliance with parental wishes. Still, the emotional bond between parent and child remains intense (Clarke-Stewart & Hevey, 1981; Maccoby & Feldman, 1972).

By age two, children may also become closer to their brothers and sisters, spending as much time with them as with their mothers and much more time than with their fathers (Lawson & Ingleby, 1974). By the time they are five, siblings spend twice as much time together as they spend with both parents combined (Bank & Kahn, 1975). During this time, they talk, play, and imitate one another. And even though they may often fight (Dale, 1983; Dunn & Kendrick, 1982a; Pepler, Corter & Abramovitch, 1982), they also have strong positive feelings for one another (Dunn & Kendrick, 1982b).

Relationships with Peers

Children also interact and make friends with their peers, to whom they are attracted through common interests and skills (Bronson, 1975; Ross & Goldman, 1977; Rubenstein & Howes, 1976). These childhood peer relationships and the social skills learned within them, help provide the foundation for the ability to interact with others throughout life.

Changing play patterns For preschool children, interactions with other children usually involve toys. For two-year-olds, it is the toy itself, not the other child, that is the focus of the child's interest (Mueller & Lucas, 1975). Two-year-olds spend most of their play time simply watching their peers play with toys, taking toys away from their peers, or playing alongside them in *parallel play*, that is, using the same toys but not interacting (Mueller & Vandell, 1979; Parten, 1932, 1933).

For three-year-olds, toys are no longer ends in themselves, but serve as mediators of interaction, which help children elicit responses from their peers. This is the age when children also begin to use objects symbolically and to make believe, alone and in their play with peers. By age four, children begin to converse about their common activities and to borrow and lend toys in what is called *associative play* (Parten, 1932, 1933). This play is still an egocentric, "me-first" affair, however. By the end of the preschool period, play reaches a new level of maturity. Children begin to cooperate, to divide roles, and to share goals (Parten, 1932, 1933).

In the school years, peer interaction becomes more complex and structured. School children play games with rules, such as marbles, jacks, and Simon Says. They play on teams. They tutor each other. They continue to cooperate in achieving goals, but they also begin to compete—sometimes at the expense of cooperation.

Conformity and friendship Even though they are often competitors, school children still try hard to be like their peers. They are influenced by peers' opinions, advice, interests, dress, and lifestyles. Between third and ninth grade, children increasingly prefer to be with their peers rather than with their parents, and they become more and more influenced by peers' opinions, evaluations, and actions.

Indeed, it is in the school years that friends become important and friendships become long-lasting. Children begin to understand that feelings, not things, keep friends together. By early adolescence, most children have formed intimate, mutually shared friendships that can survive minor disputes because they are based on commitment, trust, and underlying loyalty (Berndt, 1978a; Selman, 1981).

Social Skills and Understanding

The dramatic changes in peer relationships over the years from two to twelve can be traced in part to increasing social competence. As children get older, they are less apt to stare, cry, point, suck their thumbs, or flee; they play, smile, and laugh more (Blurton-Jones, 1972; Mueller, 1972; Smith & Connolly, 1972). They become better able to follow social rules and more capable of acting in harmony in groups. They grow increasingly sensitive to the rights of minorities (Selman et al., 1983). They learn more elaborate and appropriate ways of helping and comforting each other (Zahn-Waxler, Iannotti & Chapman, 1982).

Interpreting situations and signals   Children's increased social competence is due in part to their growing ability to detect and interpret emotional signals and social situations. At three or four, children can name typical facial expressions of happiness, sadness, anger, and fear (Camras, 1977). As they get older, they learn to recognize a wider range of emotions and to predict how a person will feel in emotion-provoking situations. In one study, for example, Helene Borke (1971) read children a series of short stories about children who ate a favorite snack, lost a toy, got lost in the woods, or were made to go to bed. The subjects were then asked to say how the children in the stories felt. Three- and four-year-olds were good at identifying happiness. Six-year-olds were also able to say when characters might feel fear and sadness. Seven- and eight-year-olds could identify the emotion of anger as well.

Over the school years, childrens' understanding of people gradually becomes more psychological. For one thing, they learn that people do not always express what they feel (Gnepp, 1983; Selman, 1980). They also come to realize that individuals have abiding personal dispositions, or personalities. By the end of elementary school, they begin to describe people in terms of inferred, stable psychological attributes, such as "really conceited; he thinks he's great," or "real sensitive, a lot more than most people" (Barenboim, 1981; Livesley & Bromley, 1973; Rholes & Ruble, 1984).

Social rules and roles   As they develop, children learn not only the meaning of social signals and situations but also the rules that govern social interactions and society at large. For example, they learn to be polite. By six years of age, children begin to say "Can I swing?" or "Please may I swing?" instead of the peremptory "Let me swing" (Bates, 1976; Garvey, 1975). Children also learn to control the expression of emotions to conform to social norms (Ekman, 1980); they smile when greeting Grandmother and try not to cry when hurt or angry. They learn all sorts of other social conventions: manners, rules of dress and grooming, and regulations for play, including when, where, how, and with what (for example, "boys should not play with dolls"). Through the school years, children become aware of subtle distinctions between types of rules and become more flexible in complying with arbitrary ones.

Knowledge of adult roles in society also increases during childhood. The toddler first pretends to perform some imaginary act, such as bathing the baby or hosing the fire, but is not aware that the act is part of a social role. Later, the child begins to understand that certain actions are part of social roles: that parents buy things, make phone calls, and clean house; that doctors wear white coats, ask to look at your tongue, and give injections. At age four, the child understands how two or three roles fit together and can play family. By age six, children understand whole networks of roles, such as teachers, students, principal, and janitor, allowing them to play school (Watson, 1981).

HIGHLIGHT

Gender Roles

Many of the roles children learn about are linked to gender. In Western civilization, some roles, like firefighter, have traditionally been masculine, whereas others, like nurse, have traditionally been feminine. Such specific vocational traditions are not nearly as strong as they once were, but there are still **gender roles** in our society. These are the general patterns of work, appearance, and behavior that are associated with being male or female. They persist because their biological and social roots are deep.

Even before children are able to learn gender roles, there are many differences between the sexes. From conception there are physical differences between boys and girls. Girls are, on the average, physically more mature than boys and less susceptible to environmental assaults. Girls also suffer less from speech, learning, and behavior disorders; mental retardation; emotional problems; and sleep disorders (Shepherd-Look, 1982). As a group, they tend to have greater sensitivity to others' speech patterns and greater verbal ability (they speak and write earlier and more fluently). At the same time, girls have less visual-spatial ability (they are less skilled at manipulating objects, constructing three-dimensional forms, and mentally manipulating figures and pictures). Girls are also less physically aggressive, are less inclined to hit an obstacle or a person, and tend to be more nurturant and emotionally empathic (Hoffman, 1977; Maccoby & Jacklin, 1974; Restak, 1979). Boys play in larger groups and spaces, enjoying noisier, more strenuous physical games like soccer and football. All-boy play tends to be vigorous; all-girl play tends to be more orderly (DiPietro, 1981). Girls form smaller groups (often pairs), play in smaller spaces, and spend their time exploring and refining social rules and roles. They enjoy the social aspects of interaction and develop relationships that are intimate and intense.

These differences between boys and girls have a foundation in biology, but biological factors do not tell the whole story. Many of the differences in boys and girls also stem from socialization. Through **socialization,** parents, teachers, and other authorities (including influential figures on television) teach children the skills and social norms necessary to be well-functioning members of society. In doing so, these teachers consciously or inadvertently pass on their ideas about "appropriate" behaviors for boys and girls.

This teaching tends to bolster and amplify any biological predisposition toward spatial superiority or physical aggressiveness in males and verbal skill or nurturance in females. Boys prefer and are given cars, trucks, balls, and guns. Girls like and are given dolls, irons, flowers, and pretty clothes. Boys are encouraged to achieve, compete, control their feelings, act independent, and assume personal responsibility. Girls are encouraged to be expressive, nurturant, reflective, dependent, obedient, and unselfish (Block, 1983; Hoffman, 1977; Shepherd-Look, 1982; Tudiver, 1979).

Children also pick up notions of what is appropriate behavior simply by watching what peers and adults do. Especially around the age of five or six, after they have figured out that they are either boys or girls and are beginning to realize that sex is based on anatomy and cannot be changed, children watch, prefer, and imitate people of their own sex (Bryan & Luria, 1978; Slaby & Frey, 1975). They also subscribe most rigidly to gender stereotypes around this age, stating confidently that women can't be firefighters, men are

Socialization by parents and others typically encourages interests and activities traditionally associated with a child's own gender.

never nurses, boys don't play with dolls, and girls don't like trucks (Marantz & Mansfield, 1977).

The mixture of biological makeup (nature) and social conditioning (nurture) makes it virtually impossible to say that gender roles are either inherited or learned. Still, parents can, if they wish, avoid obvious gender typing. They can push girls to be independent by being firm and demanding. They can model nurturance for sons by being responsive and warm (Baumrind, 1979). In fact, a study by Eleanor Maccoby and Carol Jacklin (Turkington, 1984) suggests that many parents today take a less rigid approach to gender role socialization than did parents a decade ago. Nevertheless, teachers, neighbors, casual acquaintances, even strangers typically react to children on the basis of their sex (Frisch, 1977), and gender stereotypes are still rampant in textbooks and on television. ■

Socialization

Through the process of socialization, children learn not only gender roles but also other rules about appropriate social and emotional behavior.

Socialization styles   Parents differ in the outcomes they value most for their children and in the methods they use to convey their values. These differences are related to the adults' personalities, their financial and psychological circumstances, their levels of education, and their occupations.

In American society, parents with lower levels of education and less-skilled occupations are more likely to value conformity to rules and authority. They are usually more strict and more likely to enforce their rules about room cleaning or "talking back" with spankings or other punishments. Parents with higher levels of education, higher status, and professional occupations are more likely to encourage self-direction in their children. They do so by being more permissive, letting children make more of their own decisions about, say, how their rooms look, and expressing willingness to seriously consider, if not always accept, their children's ideas and wishes. Such parents tend to request that clothes be picked up and to explain why rather than to set down arbitrary rules.

These differences in socialization style may be rooted in the different living and working conditions of the two groups (Kohn, 1977). Educated parents tend to presume that their children will be educated as well, so they are more likely to try to prepare them to make decisions for themselves. Less-privileged adults, who usually have to follow someone else's orders, tend to prepare their youngsters to do the same. External stress is important as well. Financial difficulties, lack of job security, and the like can make parents more neglectful or more likely to punish their children (Patterson, 1982).

Finally, socialization styles are shaped by the children themselves and the temperaments they are born with. Mothers of very active children tend to get into power struggles with them and have difficulty controlling them (Buss, 1981). Mothers of difficult children do more controlling, warning, prohibiting, and removing of objects than mothers of children with easy dispositions (Bates, 1980). Difficult children persist in their troublesome actions longer and ignore, protest, or fuss at their mothers' attempts to control them.

Together, all these factors create complex socialization patterns in different families. Although each family is unique, the patterns can be grouped into broad categories. Using a sample of parents in Berkeley, California, Diana Baumrind found three distinct patterns (Baumrind, 1971, 1975, 1979; Baumrind & Black, 1967). **Authoritarian parents** were firm, punitive, and unsympathetic. They valued obedience from their children and authority for themselves. They tried to shape their children's behavior to meet a set standard and to curb the children's's wills. They did not encourage independence. They were detached and seldom praised their youngsters. In contrast, **permissive parents** gave their children complete freedom, and their discipline was lax. The third group, **authoritative parents,** reasoned with their children, encouraging give and take. They allowed children increasing responsibility as they got older and better at making decisions. They were firm, but also understanding. They set limits, but also encouraged independence. Their demands were reasonable, rational, and consistent.

Socialization outcomes   Baumrind found that these three socialization styles were consistently related to children's behavior. Authoritarian parents had children who were unfriendly, distrustful, and withdrawn. The children of permissive parents were immature, dependent, and unhappy; their lack of self-reliance and self-control was evident in their tendency to have tantrums or to seek parental help when encountering even slight difficulties. Children raised by authoritative parents were friendly, cooperative, self-reliant, and socially responsible—an ideal combination of social skills.

Baumrind's study, along with others, provides suggestive evidence that socialization patterns can affect children's social and emotional development (Clarke-Stewart, Friedman & Koch, 1985). Strict, heavy-handed discipline is associated with well-controlled behavior. But such children are also fearful, dependent, and submissive, their exploration and intellectual striving dulled. Extreme permissiveness, on the other hand, appears to foster outgoing, sociable behavior and intellectual striving, but it may make children less persistent and more aggressive. How affectionate the parents are has much to do with the effects of their discipline. A restrictive but affectionate parent, for example, is more likely to raise a child who is polite, obedient, and dependent. A restrictive and hostile parent may raise a withdrawn, neurotic, quarrelsome child.

Socialization styles have also been related to children's moral and altruistic behavior. Children who are given orders, threats, and punishments are more likely to cheat and less likely to experience guilt or to accept blame after doing something wrong (Hoffman, 1970). Children are more likely to behave morally and generously when their parents are authoritative. Such parents create an atmosphere of warm approval, praise, sympathy, and acceptance, and within that atmosphere, prohibit immoral actions and explain why the child should act in particular ways. This kind of discipline helps children integrate their capacity for empathy with a more sophisticated knowledge of how their behavior affects others.

ADOLESCENCE

Generally, the years of middle childhood pass smoothly, as children busy themselves with schoolwork, hobbies, friends, and clubs. Adolescence changes things drastically. All adolescents undergo significant changes in their physical size, shape, and capacities. In our society, many adolescents also experience substantial changes in their social activities, relationships, and responsibilities; in their abilities to think and reason; and in their views of themselves. These psychological changes are the result of both nature (physical changes) and nurture (the change in settings and expectations to which our culture exposes adolescents).

The Big Shakeup

The first and most visible sign that adolescence has begun is a sudden spurt in physical growth. Beginning at about 10½ for girls and about 12 for boys, weight and height increase dramatically (see Figure 2.10). Quite suddenly, adolescents find themselves in new bodies, which, because arms and legs lengthen at different rates, are often gawky and awkward. At the end of the growth spurt, menstruation begins in females and live sperm are produced in males. **Puberty**—the condition of being able for the first time to reproduce—is also characterized by fuller breasts and rounder curves in females, broad shoulders and narrow hips in males. Facial, underarm, and pubic hair grows. Voices deepen, and acne appears.

There are psychological changes as well. Young adolescents begin to realize that they are no longer children; yet they are far from adult. In Western cultures, early adolescence, from twelve to sixteen or so, is fraught with ups and downs. Moods swing wildly from one extreme to the other: from elation at a girlfriend's kiss to dejection at a failed exam (Csikszentmihalyi & Larson, 1984). Sexual interest stirs and there are opportunities to smoke, drink alcohol, and take drugs. All of this can be very disorienting. Adolescents must cope and adjust, often without enough accurate information about what they are facing and certainly without enough experience to guide them. This is their first big shakeup; it changes how they act, how they feel, and how they think.

Early adolescence presents a challenge to self-esteem, especially if it is accompanied by other stresses, as often happens on the American scene. For example, self-esteem usually drops among girls who reach puberty, begin dating, and shift from elementary to junior high school all at the same time (Simmons, Rosenberg & Rosenberg, 1973). They suffer from combined uncertainties about their bodies, boys, and books. Uncertainty about their physical appearance is particularly devastating to adolescents. They desperately want to be attractive, and their self-esteem depends in large measure on whether they think they are. Some of them, especially girls who already have shaky self-esteem, develop eating disorders, such as bulimia (dieting, binging,

Figure 2.10
Adolescent Growth
At about age 10½, girls begin their growth spurt and are temporarily taller than their male peers. When boys, at about age 12, begin their growth spurt, they usually grow faster and for a longer period of time than girls. Adolescents may grow as much as 5 inches a year.
(Adapted from "Standards from birth to maturity for height, weight, height velocity: British children" by Tanner, J. M., Whitehouse, R. H., and Takaishi, M. *Archives of Diseases in Childhood*, 1966, *41*, 454–471.)

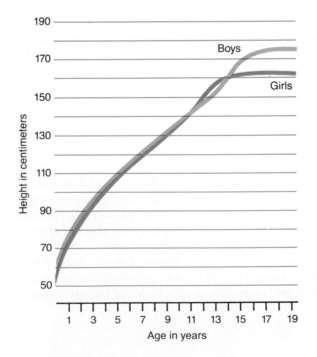

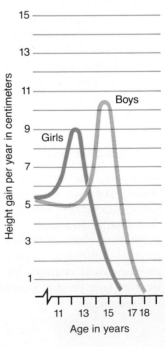

Adolescence tends to be a time of emotional highs and lows as the teenager matures physically, discovers the opposite sex, and worries about being accepted by a peer group.

and purging) and anorexia nervosa (self-starvation), ostensibly to improve their appearance.

Still another factor affecting self-esteem is physical maturity. Boys, and to some extent girls, who go through puberty early are accepted by their peers and teachers as mature; they have higher status, become leaders, and tend to be poised and relaxed. Those who reach puberty late feel rejected, dependent, and dominated by others. These differences between early and late maturers may persist into adulthood (Duke et al., 1982; Faust, 1960; Greif & Ulman, 1982; Jones, 1957; Jones & Bayley, 1950; Mussen & Jones, 1957).

Social Relationships with Parents and Peers

Though many teenagers maintain placid and satisfying relationships with their families, their struggle with all the changes and pressures of adolescence is often reflected in family conflicts, especially with parents. Teenagers express the need to experience life on their own terms; they are no longer content to accept all their parents' rules and values. This can lead to bickering over everything from taking out the garbage to who left the gallon of milk on top of the refrigerator. In one study, college students described the typical relationship between parent and adolescent as most like that between guard and prisoner (Wish, Deutsch & Kaplan, 1976). As one observer noted, adolescents and their parents are in conflict in all families some of the time and in some families all of the time (Montemayor, 1983). Serious conflicts often lead to serious problems, including running away, pregnancy, stealing, even suicide (Montemayor, 1983). Fortunately, conflicts are less severe than this in most families and usually diminish by late adolescence, particularly if the adolescent leaves home (Sullivan & Sullivan, 1980).

In early adolescence, conflict with families or a desire for the company of people with common interests leads many teenagers to seek and "hang out" with other teenagers. Adolescents influence each other to look and act alike in many ways, from musical tastes and dancing to smoking and skipping school (Condry & Siman, 1974; Krosnick & Judd, 1982). By ninth grade, adolescents say that their relationships with their peers are closer than those with their parents (Bowerman & Kinch, 1956; Hunter & Youniss, 1982).

Identity

In many modern Third World cultures and in our own in earlier times, the end of early adolescence, around the age of sixteen, marked the beginning of adulthood: work, parenting, and grown-up responsibilities. In modern America, the transition from childhood to adulthood is more drawn out, often lasting into the early twenties. Adolescents spend a substantial amount of time being students, trainees, and apprentices, unable by law to drink or to vote.

This lengthened period of adolescence has created special problems—among them, finding or forming an identity. The rough journey through early adolescence behind them, adolescents' major psychological task is to answer the critical question: Who am I? Most adolescents have not thought about this before. As young children, their concepts of themselves were based on fleeting, sometimes inaccurate, perceptions. For example, when preschool children are asked to describe themselves, they often do so in terms of some favorite or habitual activity: "I watch TV," "I walk to school," or "I do the dishes" (Keller, Ford & Meacham, 1978). At eight or nine, children identify themselves in terms of such facts as their sex, age, name, physical appearance, likes, and dislikes. They may still describe themselves in terms of what they do, but they now include how well they do it compared with other children (Secord & Peevers, 1974). By age eleven, many children, especially girls, begin to describe themselves in terms of social relationships and personality characteristics. A sense of a unique self develops gradually over the years of middle childhood, then erupts during adolescence in the form of dramatically increased self-consciousness and self-awareness. Adolescents begin to think of themselves in terms of general, stable psychological characteristics (Damon & Hart, 1982).

The issue of identity formation in adolescence is a central one in the theory of development proposed by Erik Erikson (1968). In his theory, there are eight stages of psychosocial development over the lifespan; they are outlined in Table 2.3. Each stage focuses on one issue or crisis that is especially important at that particular time of life. How the person resolves these issues is reflected in his or her personality and social relationships. If an issue is resolved positively, Erikson claimed, this will be reflected in positive characteristics, such as trust, autonomy, initiative, and industry. If the crisis is not resolved positively, the person will be psychologically troubled and cope less effectively with subsequent crises.

Events of late adolescence—graduating from high school, going to college, and forging new relationships—challenge the adolescent's self-concept and precipitate what Erikson called an **identity crisis.** In this crisis, the adolescent must develop an integrated image of himself or herself as a unique person. This is done by pulling together self-knowledge acquired during childhood. If infancy and childhood brought trust, admiration, and autonomy, according to Erikson, the adolescent will resolve the identity crisis positively, feeling self-confident and competent. If infancy and childhood resulted in feelings of mistrust, shame, guilt, and inferiority, the adolescent will be confused about his or her identity and goals.

There is some limited empirical support for Erikson's ideas about the identity crisis. In this phase of adolescence, young people do consider alternative identities (Waterman, 1982). They "try out" being rebellious, studious, or detached, as they think about and try to resolve questions they may have about sexuality, self-worth, industriousness, and independence. By the time they are twenty-one, researchers suggest, most adolescents have resolved the identity crisis in a way that is consistent with their self-image and the historical era in which they are living. They are ready to enter adulthood with self-confidence. Basically the same people who entered adolescence, they have

TABLE 2.3
Erikson's Stages of Psychosocial Development
Each of Erikson's stages of development is characterized by one of two primary outcomes.

Age	Central Psychological Issue or Crisis
First year	**Trust versus mistrust** Infants learn to trust or mistrust that their needs will be met by the world, especially by the mother.
Second year	**Autonomy versus shame and doubt** Children learn to exercise will, to make choices, and to control themselves, or they become uncertain and doubt that they can do things by themselves.
Third to fifth year	**Initiative versus guilt** Children learn to initiate activities and enjoy their accomplishments, acquiring direction and purpose. If they are not allowed initiative, they feel guilty for their attempts at independence.
Sixth year through puberty	**Industry versus inferiority** Children develop a sense of industry and curiosity and are eager to learn, or they feel inferior and lose interest in the tasks before them.
Adolescence	**Identity versus role confusion** Adolescents come to see themselves as unique and integrated persons with an ideology, or they become confused about what they want out of life.
Early adulthood	**Intimacy versus isolation** Young people become able to commit themselves to another person, or they develop a sense of isolation and feel they have no one in the world but themselves.
Middle age	**Generativity versus stagnation** Adults are willing to have and care for children and to devote themselves to their work and the common good, or they become self-centered and inactive.
Old age	**Integrity versus despair** Older people enter a period of reflection, becoming assured that their lives have been meaningful and ready to face death with acceptance and dignity. Or they are in despair for their unaccomplished goals, failures, and ill-spent lives.

more mature attitudes and behavior, more consistent goals and values, and a clearer idea of who they are (Adams & Jones, 1983; Dusek & Flaherty, 1981; Savin-Williams & Demo, 1984; Waterman, Geary & Waterman, 1974).

Abstract Thought

One reason that adolescents can develop a conscious identity is that they can now think and reason about abstract concepts. As shown in Table 2.2, adolescence begins a stage of cognitive development that Piaget called the **formal operational period,** a stage marked by the ability to engage in hypothetical thinking, including the imagination of logical consequences. For example, adolescents can consider various strategies for finding a part-time job and recognize that some methods are more likely to lead to success than others. They are also able to form general concepts and to understand the impact of the past on the present and the present on the future. They can question social institutions; think about the world as it might be and ought to be; and consider the ramifications of love, morality, work, politics, philosophy, and religion. They can think logically and systematically about symbols and propositions, regardless of whether the propositions are true. For example, "Suppose there were no money in the world" might become an idea about which they could think logically to reach a set of possible consequences. They can reflect on and analyze their own mental processes, recognizing that, for example, they tend to be too optimistic or trusting. They can focus on form and symbolism in art and literature, going beyond the content of a painting or a book to see what the artist or author was trying to say about the world.

HIGHLIGHT

Moral Reasoning and Moral Action

One particular domain in which adolescents apply their advanced level of reasoning is morality. The formal study of moral reasoning in childhood and adolescence began with Piaget's watching children play marbles (Piaget, 1932). He noticed that, as children got older, their marble games and the nature of the rules changed, as did the children's willingness to follow the rules. These changes, Piaget believed, reflected children's underlying moral thought about fairness (who goes first), reciprocity (taking turns), and justice (giving up a marble when one loses).

Piaget saw children's moral development as occurring in two stages. In the first, from five to ten years, children operate within a system of *external morality*, in which rules are perceived as sacred and unalterable, as absolute extensions of the dictates of parents and other authority figures. After about age ten, children enter the second stage, in which they begin to operate according to a system of *internal morality*. They recognize that rules can be changed if everyone consents and that rules are made up through reasoning and discussion among equals.

Kohlberg's stages of moral reasoning   Piaget's work on moral reasoning was the starting point for Lawrence Kohlberg, who exploited one of Piaget's methods: interviewing subjects about hypothetical moral dilemmas. Perhaps the most famous of these was the "Heinz dilemma":

> In Europe, a woman was near death from a special kind of cancer. There was one drug that the doctors thought might save her. It was a form of radium that a druggist in the same town had recently discovered. The drug was expensive to make, but the druggist was charging ten times what the drug cost him to make. He paid $200 for the radium and charged $2000 for a small dose of the drug. The sick woman's husband, Heinz, went to everyone he knew to borrow the money, but could only get together about $1000, which was half of what it cost. He told the druggist that his wife was dying and asked him to sell it cheaper or let him pay later. But the druggist said, "No, I discovered the drug and I'm going to make money from it." So Heinz got desperate and considered breaking into the man's store to steal the drug for his wife. Should Heinz steal the radium? (Kohlberg & Gilligan, 1971, pp. 1072–1073).

Kohlberg was far more interested in the reasons children gave for their answers than in the answers themselves. He found that their reasons changed systematically and consistently as they got older and could be divided into six stages.

Stage 1   Judgments are based on avoiding punishment from a superior authority. A child in this stage might feel that Heinz should not steal the drug because he will be jailed.

Stage 2 What is right involves a fair exchange. A Stage 2 child might feel that Heinz should steal the drug because his wife will repay him later. Stage 1 and Stage 2 moral judgments are basically selfish.

Stage 3 What should be done depends on how others will feel about the action. In this stage, children (or adolescents) want to please others and get their approval. Many Stage 3 individuals feel that Heinz should steal the drug because he loves his wife and because she and the rest of the family will approve.

Stage 4 Moral action means doing one's duty; rules and social order are respected for their own sake. A Stage 4 person might reason that the husband should steal the drug for his wife because he has a duty to care for her, or that he should not steal the drug because stealing is illegal.

Stage 5 Moral decisions depend on personal standards, not on the dictates of authority figures or society. In this stage, people view rules and laws as arbitrary but respect them because they protect human welfare. They support laws but believe that individual rights can sometimes supersede these laws if the laws become destructive. For example, they might decide that life is more important than property. This stage is not attained until adolescence or later.

Stage 6 Judgments of morality are based on universal ethical principles, such as justice, reciprocity, equality, and respect for human life and rights. In this stage, people might support stealing the drug based on the principle of preserving and respecting life. (Kohlberg also proposed a seventh stage, which extends this idea to include reasoning on the basis of even more general cosmic or spiritual principles of morality.)

Not all individuals achieve the highest of Kohlberg's levels, however. Only about 20 percent of the adults tested reached Stage 5, and none reached Stage 6. Kohlberg considered Stages 6 and 7 to be theoretical ideals, seen only rarely in extraordinary individuals, such as Mahatma Gandhi and Martin Luther King, Jr.

Socialization into a gender role may affect moral reasoning. Carol Gilligan (1982) has suggested that, for girls and women, the moral ideal is based on caring and relationships, not on the abstract concept of justice that Kohlberg documented in his male subjects. For example, when one girl, Amy, was asked whether Heinz should steal the drug, she replied:

> Well, I don't think so. . . . he really shouldn't steal the drug—but his wife shouldn't die either. If he stole the drug, he might save his wife then, but if he did, he might have to go to jail, and then his wife might get sicker again, and he couldn't get more of the drug. . . . So, they should really just talk it out and find some other way to make the money. (Gilligan, 1982, p. 28)

In Amy's eyes, the central issue in determining what is moral is not the rules that prevail in a world of people standing alone, but the need to protect enduring relationships and fulfill human needs. Gilligan suggested that the ideal of morality based on justice is a masculine notion of morality.

Moral action How is a person's level of moral reasoning related to the way he or she actually behaves? In one study, 120 junior high school students were given the opportunity to cheat on tests and games (Krebs & Kohlberg, 1973). Of the children whose reasoning was at Stage 1 or 2, 75 percent cheated at least once. Of those who reasoned at Stage 3 or 4, 65 percent cheated. Of those who had reached Stage 5, only 20 percent cheated.

These results suggest that there is indeed a relationship between moral reasoning and moral behavior. In another study, however, higher scores on the moral dilemmas were tied to less cheating *only* if the subjects were asked about the dilemmas before they were tempted to cheat. If they were interviewed

Mother Theresa. Kohlberg suggested that the very highest stages of moral development may only be reached by a few remarkable individuals.

after the temptation tests, higher moral reasoning seemed to be associated with less resistance to temptation (Krebs, 1967). It may be that interviewing people about their moral judgments before a temptation test made those with higher moral reasoning (and more cognitive awareness) suspicious about the situation.

Thus, the relationship between moral reasoning and moral action is not a simple one. Any decision, moral or otherwise, involves not only knowing what one ought to do, but also knowing the probability that one will get caught, the gains one can make, the level of one's ambition, and the difficulty of carrying out the action. Research has shown that whether or not a person behaves morally in any particular situation depends on how stressful the situation is, how much the person has to give up in order to act morally, and whether the person has effective coping strategies, such as being able to size up the situation accurately and figure out whether possible solutions are practical (Haan, Aerts & Cooper, 1985). The development of moral action as well as moral reasoning, these researchers suggest, has to involve more than cognitive knowledge. It cannot be facilitated by ordinary school instruction, such as having a teacher direct an abstract discussion about hypothetical moral dilemmas. Children and adolescents need to have vivid emotional experiences in solving the real moral problems that confront them. They can be encouraged in this by arguing issues out with each other, without adult control. ◼

ADULTHOOD

Development does not end with adolescence. Adults, too, go through developmental periods and transitions and experience physical and cognitive changes. Because researchers are just beginning to investigate development in adulthood, our discussion of this age period is relatively brief.

Physical Changes

In adulthood, physical growth continues. Shoulder width, height, and chest size increase until people are in their forties or fifties, when they begin to decrease (Rossman, 1977). Around this time, body shape changes as muscle decreases and fat increases, especially around the midriff. The sensitivity of the senses begins to decline (Fozard et al., 1977). After middle age (around forty-five), people become less sensitive to light, less accurate at perceiving differences in distance, and slower and less acute at seeing details. Increased farsightedness begins around age forty, often making reading glasses necessary. Some hearing loss begins as early as age twenty-five (Rockstein & Sussman, 1979), so that by their mid-thirties, nearly everyone shows some hearing impairment. With age, people become more susceptible to disease.

Cognitive Changes

Like physical changes, cognitive changes through middle adulthood are generally improvements. During this period, adults show improving performance on tests of vocabulary, comprehension, and general knowledge, especially if they use these abilities in their daily lives or engage in enriching activities such as travel or reading (Botwinick, 1977; Eichorn et al., 1981). The nature of their thought may also change. Psychologists have suggested that adult thinking is more complex and adaptive than adolescent thinking (Labouvie-Vief, 1982). They have found a stage of problem-finding that comes after the problem-solving level of Piaget's formal operational period. The rules of logic that are intellectual toys for adolescents become, in this stage, tools to be applied to the real world (Arlin, 1980). Further, adults can understand, as adolescents cannot, the contradictions inherent in thinking. They see the possibilities and problems in every course of action (Riegel, 1975).

It is not until late in adulthood—after sixty-five or so—that a number of intellectual abilities decline in some people. For example, in one long-term study, reasoning, mathematical ability, and verbal comprehension began to decline after age sixty-seven (Schaie, 1979; Schaie & Labouvie-Vief, 1974). This is also the time when the brain may begin to register new information at a slower speed (Kline & Szafran, 1975). Like young children, older adults are more likely to be distracted (Hoyer & Plude, 1980). If they are asked to do something they know how to do well—naming familiar objects, for example—older adults do just as well as younger ones (Poon & Fozard, 1978). They are slower and less effective, however, when asked to do something they are not used to doing or to solve a complex problem they have not seen before (Craik & Rabinowitz, 1984). They can still do such tasks but need more time, some instructions, and a little help. In one study, for example, older adults trying to decide if strings of letters were words did better when the strings were shown in sentences (Cohen & Faulkner, 1983).

Memory also declines with age. For a few unfortunate people, this decline is dramatically hastened and intensified by Alzheimer's disease or other organic brain disorders, but in most cases, the loss is slower and need not produce severe senility. Thus, most older adults remain able to repeat information they have just heard, though they may not do as well if they must think about the information as well as remember it. For example, it is difficult for many older people to repeat a series of numbers backwards or to do a mathematical calculation in their heads (Fozard, 1980). It is also more difficult for them to remember or understand events and stories, especially complicated ones (Cohen & Faulkner, 1981). But, again, if they are given enough time, enough instruction (for example, "Write down the key words"), and enough support and structure, they can do as well as younger adults.

Although remembering verbal material and solving cognitive problems become more difficult in old age, the picture is not entirely bleak. Just as physical exercise can maintain a fit body, continued mental exercise can help people think and remember effectively and creatively. This fact is exemplified by historians and philosophers whose continuing mental activity reaches a peak of creative production when they are in their sixties, by poets who produce their best work while in their eighties, and by composers in their seventies who continue to write beautiful music (Lehman, 1968). Similarly, Supreme Court justices may be at the height of their mental abilities in their seventies. As one researcher put it, "Use it or lose it." Most older adults in our society "use it" and live out their last years as functionally intelligent as when they were younger. We will say more about the cognitive changes that occur with age in Chapter 10, on mental abilities.

Social and Psychological Changes

Early adulthood   In their twenties, men and women enter the adult world. They decide on an occupation, or at least take a job, and often become preoccupied with their careers (Levinson, 1978; Vaillant, 1977). The other major aspect of life at this time is love; most young adults become capable of making a meaningful, enduring, intimate commitment to another person. Having resolved their identity crisis, they develop a capacity for and concern with real intimacy (Erikson, 1968; Vaillant, 1977), appreciating more fully the uniqueness and separateness of others. This intimacy may include sexual intimacy, friendship, or mutual intellectual stimulation.

All this comes at a time when, having separated from their parents and become more financially and psychologically independent, young adults may be experiencing isolation and loneliness. They may view the future with a mixture of anticipation, fear, and insecurity (Levinson, 1978). This is the time when and some of the reasons why many people marry.

Another important reason for marriage during these years is the desire to keep in step with peers. Many milestones that mark a person's progress through life are expected to occur within particular age ranges. Bernice Neugarten (1968) called this the **social clock.** Its markers include completing school, leaving home, getting married, having a child, and becoming a grandparent. The actual age range for these events depends to some extent on the individual's class and culture. In lower-class, tradition-based groups, such events tend to occur earlier than in middle-class, "sophisticated" groups (Olsen, 1969). Whatever age is considered normal, being "on time" in achieving these milestones, as in achieving physical maturity in adolescence, is perceived as easier and less stressful (Neugarten & Hagestad, 1976). For one thing, it avoids endless questions from relatives about when one is going to get married or have children. In spite of these pressures in some segments of American society, in general less emphasis is placed on the ticking of the social clock today than in past decades (Neugarten, 1979).

In the thirties, adults settle down and decide what is important in life (Levinson, 1978). This, according to Erikson, is when people become concerned with producing something that will outlast them, usually through parenthood

A growing capacity to form enduring and committed relationships with another person, combined with insecurity about the future, makes young adulthood a common time to marry.

or job achievements. Erikson called this concern the **crisis of generativity.** If people do not resolve it, he suggested, they stagnate.

For most American adults, however, tension occurs not between generativity and stagnation, but between two types of generativity—parenthood versus achievement. Especially for women, the demands of children and career often pull in opposite directions. Devotion to one's job may lead to guilt about depriving one's children of attention; too much emphasis on home life can impair work productivity. This stressful, some say impossible, balancing act can lead to anxiety, frustration, and conflicts at home and on the job, leaving some parents feeling and performing below par in both locations. Being an adult in today's world, with all its appealing options, is still hard work.

Middle adulthood   Sometime around age forty, between early and middle adulthood, people experience a **midlife transition.** During this transition, they reappraise and may modify their lives and relationships. They may shift away from their earlier emphasis on a career or switch to a new career. Some feel invigorated and liberated; others may feel upset and have a midlife crisis (Levinson, 1978; Vaillant, 1977).

No one knows how many people experience an actual crisis during the midlife transition. For men, midlife crises may be connected to such physical factors as being overweight or having high blood pressure, but it is how an individual *feels* about health or virility that is particularly important. Similarly, the physiological changes of menopause can create problems, but most of its symptoms are likely to be less significant than the social and psychological problems of midlife transition. Women who have chosen a career over a family now hear the biological clock ticking out their last childbearing years. The

Middle adulthood tends to be a time during which people become deeply committed to building personal monuments, either by raising children or through occupational achievements.

HUMAN DEVELOPMENT AND LANGUAGE

Are people born with an innate, unique ability to learn language?

The debate over the degree to which people's abilities are inherited or developed through learning continues, sometimes heatedly. To understand the roles of nature and nurture, we often need to look at what specialists have learned about the nature of specific abilities. Consider language. Does the child's ability to learn language reflect an innate ability unique to humans?

Some researchers have examined this question by trying to teach nonhuman species to use language. They have typically used chimpanzees and gorillas as subjects, because at maturity these primates are estimated to have the intelligence of two- or three-year-old children, who are usually well on their way to learning language. Hence, if these animals cannot learn language, their intelligence cannot be blamed. Instead, failure would be attributed to the absence of an appropriate genetic makeup.

Can nonhuman primates learn to use language? This question is not simple, for at least two reasons. First, language is more than just communication, but defining just when animals are exhibiting that "something more" is a source of debate. Most higher animals communicate in some way or another, by gestures, grunts, chirps, or cries; even bees have a fairly elaborate system of communication to direct other bees to sources of nectar. But what sets language apart from these communications is grammar, a set of formal rules for combining words. Because of these rules, people can take a relatively small number of words and use them to create an almost infinite number of unique sentences. Second, because

of their muscular structures, nonhuman primates will never be able to "speak" in the same way that humans do. To test chimps' ability to learn language, investigators therefore must devise novel ways for them to communicate.

David and Ann Premack taught their chimp, Sarah, to communicate by placing different-shaped plastic chips, symbolizing words, on a magnetic board (Premack, 1971). Lana, a chimpanzee studied by Duane Rumbaugh (1977), learned to communicate by pressing keys on a specially designed computer. Probably the most successful medium, however, has been American Sign Language (ASL), the language of the deaf based on hand gestures. It was used by Beatrice and Allen Gardner with the chimp Washoe and her friends, by Herbert Terrace with a chimp named Nim, and by Penny Patterson with a gorilla named Koko.

All five of these studies produced certain common findings. First, Washoe, Lana, Sarah, Nim, and Koko all mastered from 130 up to 500 words (a fairly extensive vocabulary, although modest in comparison to the at least 2,000-word vocabulary of the average three-year-old human). Their vocabulary included names for concrete objects, such as *apple* or *me;* verbs, such as *tickle* and *eat;* adjectives, such as *happy* and *big;* and adverbs, such as *again.* Second, the animals combined the words in sentences, expressing desires and wishes like "You tickle me" or "If Sarah good, then apple." Finally, all these animals seemed to enjoy their communication tools and used them spontaneously to interact with their caretakers whenever possible.

contrast between youth and middle age may be especially upsetting for men who matured earlier in adolescence and were sociable and athletic rather than intellectual (Block, 1971).

For both men and women, the emerging sexuality of their teenage children or the emptiness of the nest as those children leave home may precipitate a crisis. The declining health or death of an elderly parent may also precipitate a crisis. People in the midlife transition may feel caught between the preceding and following generations, pressured by the expenses of college on one side and of nursing homes on the other.

After the midlife transition, the middle years of adulthood are often a time of satisfaction and happiness. Most people feel the pleasure of progress,

In spite of these findings, controversy still surrounds the most critical issue: Did these animals really learn language? The Gardners, who have spent years observing not only Washoe but also several of her companions, concluded that the chimps made humanlike efforts to communicate with each other and, more importantly, combined words in systematic order. For example, if Washoe wanted to be tickled, she would gesture, "You tickle Washoe." But if she wanted to do the tickling, she would gesture, "Washoe tickle you." The correct placement of object and subject in these sentences suggested that Washoe was following a set of rules for word combination; in other words, a grammar (Gardner & Gardner, 1978). The Premacks and Patterson drew similar conclusions regarding the language skills of their apes, Sarah and Koko (Patterson, 1978; Premack, 1971).

Indeed, for a time, many felt that there really was not much that is unique or qualitatively different about humans' language skills. But this line of thinking was challenged by the conclusions of Terrace and his colleagues in their investigation of Nim (Terrace et al., 1979). Terrace noticed many subtle characteristics of Nim's communications that seemed quite different from a child's use of language, and he argued that chimps in other studies demonstrated these same characteristics.

First consider the size of sentences. A child begins with single-word utterances, then goes through a stage of two-word "sentences" ("Me hungry," "Nice kitty"), and then gradually produces longer and longer utterances. Nim, in contrast, started with the ability to combine gestures into strings of two or three but never used longer strings that conveyed more elaborate and sophisticated messages. Thus, the ape was never able to say anything equivalent to a three-year-old child's "I want to go to Wendy's for a hamburger. OK?"

Second, children use language spontaneously and creatively. They use it not only to communicate their wishes but also to express ideas and to guide their own activities. Terrace questioned whether the animals' use of language demonstrated these characteristics. A large number of the sentences spoken by chimps were requests for food, tickling, baths, pets, and other things that had been experienced as pleasurable. In this sense, is such behavior by chimps qualitatively different from the behavior of rats, who can run a maze to get food, or of dolphins at Sea World, who can learn to string together a series of actions to obtain a desired goal? The apes are certainly intelligent, and their ability to string gestures together is impressive. But, argued Terrace, they lack the tendency to communicate in the spontaneous and expanding fashion of the two- or three-year-old child.

Finally, Terrace questioned whether experimenter bias influenced the reports of the chimps' communications. Chimps may string together many words that are related to a given topic (the wish for food, the appearance of a pet, and so forth). But, consciously or not, experimenters who hope to conclude that chimps learn language might tend to ignore strings that violate grammatical order or to reinterpret ambiguous strings so that they make grammatical sense. If Nim sees someone holding a banana and signs "Nim banana," the experimenter might assume the word order is correct and means "Nim wants the banana." But perhaps the animal is trying instead to say, "That banana belongs to Nim," in which case the word order would be wrong. Furthermore, although the reports of the experiments indicate that the chimps formed sentences spontaneously, Terrace argued that careful observation of videotapes revealed that the chimps may have been responding to subtle prompts and gestures from the experimenters.

So where does this leave our original question about the role of genetics in human language abilities? Psychologists are still not in full agreement about whether chimps can or cannot learn language. Two things are clear, however. First, whatever the chimp and gorilla do learn is a much more primitive and limited form of communication than that learned by children. And second, in chimps, unlike humans, the level of communication does not do justice to their overall level of intelligence; that is, these animals are smarter than their "language" productions suggest. The evidence to date therefore favors the view that genetics provides humans with language abilities that are unique.

embodied in grandchildren, career promotions, regained privacy, and the opportunity to pursue personally gratifying interests.

Late adulthood   From fifty-five to seventy-five, most people think of themselves as middle-aged, not old (Neugarten, 1974). Only about one-quarter of these "young-old" people have health problems. Most of the men and more than half of the women are married, and they see their children frequently. Many have a living parent. They are active and influential politically and socially; they often are physically vigorous. Men and women who have been employed usually retire from their jobs in this period. Those with an adequate income, good health, and little investment in their work retire with joyful

The simultaneous demands placed on middle-aged adults by the needs of college-aged children and elderly parents can be a source of considerable strain, but most people cope successfully with these pressures and go on to enjoy their own later years.

anticipation of good times at leisure. Those forced to retire with insufficient funds face it with dread. Still others retire in name only and go right on working. A person's adjustment to retirement seems best predicted by whether or not he or she views it as a choice (Neugarten, Havighurst & Tobin, 1968).

During this period, people make psychological as well as social changes. Although their basic personalities remain stable (McCrae & Costa, 1982; Thomae, 1980), people generally become more inward looking, cautious, and conforming (Neugarten, 1977; Reedy, 1983). Many men and women also become more *androgynous,* showing some of the characteristics of the other sex as well as of their own. Women become more assertive, men more nurturant, especially if they are grandparents (Fiske, 1980; Hyde & Phillis, 1979).

With the onset of old age, people also become aware that death is approaching. They watch as their friends disappear. They feel their health deteriorating, their strength waning, and their intellectual capabilities declining. The awareness of one's impending death brings about the last psychological crisis, according to Erikson, in which people evaluate their lives and accomplishments and affirm them as meaningful or meaningless. In old age, people also tend to become more philosophical and reflective. They attempt to put their lives into perspective. They reminisce, resolve past conflicts, and integrate past events. They may also become more interested in the religious and spiritual side of life (Butler, 1963). This "life review" may trigger anxiety, guilt, and despair, or it may allow people to face their own death and the deaths of friends and relatives with a feeling of peace and acceptance (Butler, 1975; Erikson, 1968; Lieberman & Tobin, 1983).

Even the actual confrontation with death does not have to bring despair and depression. The elderly can be helped to feel better physically and psychologically if they continue to be socially active and useful. For example, old people who are given parties, plants, or pets are happier and more alert and do not die as soon as those who receive less attention (Kastenbaum, 1965; Rodin & Langer, 1977). When death finally is imminent, old people strive for a death with dignity, love, affection, physical contact, and no pain (Schulz, 1978).

FUTURE DIRECTIONS

We have traced the journey of human development from conception to death. It is a complex and convoluted journey with gentle slopes and winding paths, sharp curves and critical turning points, many roads not taken and occasional wrong turns. It is a journey that differs for different people, depending on how well equipped they are for the trip, where they want to go, how fast they want to get there, and how much support they get along the way.

Much research over the past eighty years has charted this developmental journey and its infinite variations. We know what newborns can see and hear, when babies start to walk and talk, whether preschoolers can run and read, what changes puberty brings, and which mental faculties are the first to fail. We are getting better at predicting the direction that an individual will take on the developmental journey: whether he or she will do well in school, cheat on tests, feel insecure in a strange situation, or beat up the teacher. We are learning more and more about the processes of development, about how people learn new habits, incorporate new information, form new relationships, and about how these depend on inherited traits and past experiences.

Still, there is much to learn. Future developmental psychologists will be less content to describe the developmental landscape and more concerned with explaining what underlies it. They will probe beneath the surface with the help of better methods, more precise measures, more refined theories, and increased knowledge gained both from other areas of psychology and from other fields, such as genetics, physiology, neurology, and anthropology. They will probe the connections between brain and behavior, inheritance and intelligence, culture and child rearing. They will push back the frontiers of knowledge about the beginnings and ends of life, peering at prenatal learning and assessing the abilities of the elderly. They will search for evidence to support such theoretical constructs as the identity crisis, the social clock, and the life review. In their search for developmental continuities, they will integrate knowledge across different domains of development and emphasize development across the entire lifespan. They will use their findings to design better treatments for people with disabilities and better procedures for hospitals, schools, homes, and day care centers. They will continue to test the limits of environmental intervention.

You will be able to follow the progress of research in this fascinating and fertile field by taking courses in infancy, child development, adolescence, lifespan development, language acquisition, cognitive development, or social development.

SUMMARY

1. Developmental psychologists study the processes of development: how skills, mental abilities, and other human attributes appear and change with age.

2. A central question in developmental psychology is the relative influences of nature and nurture, a theme that had its origins in the philosophies of John Locke and Jean-Jacques Rousseau. Another question is whether skills and abilities develop gradually or in distinct stages.

3. In the early part of the twentieth century, Arnold Gesell stressed nature in his theory of development, proposing that development is maturational—the natural unfolding of abilities with age. John Watson took the opposite view, claiming that development is learning—shaped by the external environment. Sigmund Freud began to bring nature and nurture together by suggesting that development depends on both internal forces (children's sexual urges) and external conditions (how parents handle the children's sexual urges). Jean Piaget fully integrated the influences of nature and nurture in his theory of cognitive development. Today we accept as given the notion that both heredity and environment affect development and ask, not whether, but how much and how each contributes.

4. Life begins with the union of an ovum and a sperm. Each contains twenty-three chromosomes, made up of genes of DNA, which transmit the genetic code from parent to offspring. There are three stages of prenatal development: the germinal, embryonic, and fetal stages. The germinal stage encompasses the first two weeks after conception. The embryonic stage is a critical period, a time when certain organs must develop properly, or they never will. Development of organs at this stage is markedly and irrevocably affected by drugs, disease, and alcohol. During the fetal stage, adverse conditions may harm the infant's size, behavior, intelligence, or health.

5. Newborn infants have limited vision, hearing, and other sensory abilities. Motor behavior in the first few months of life is dominated by reflexes: swift, automatic responses to external stimuli.

6. During their first two years, infants progress from simple reflexive actions to complex mental schemes that integrate voluntary actions and physical objects. According to Piaget, cognitive development occurs in a fixed sequence of stages, and he called this first stage the sensorimotor period. In later stages, the child can develop mental representations of objects and shows object permanence: the ability to recognize that objects continue to exist even when they are hidden from view.

7. The first social relationship for the infant is usually with the mother. Over the first months of the baby's life, the mother becomes attached to her infant, and

the infant becomes attached to her. Fathers, too, form close relationships with infants. Infants' attachment with parents may be secure or insecure, depending to a large extent on whether the parents are rejecting or responsive and loving.

8. The nature of the attachment also depends on the infant's temperament. Most infants can be classified as having easy, difficult, or slow-to-warm-up temperaments. Whether they retain these traits depends on the mesh of the traits with the parents' expectations and demands.

9. Infants begin to talk by babbling, making syllabic sounds that resemble speech. At twelve to eighteen months, they utter single words and build up their vocabularies one word at a time.

10. Piaget called the stage of cognitive development from about two to seven years the preoperational period. During this time, children come to use symbols, but they do not have the ability to think logically and rationally. Their understanding of the world is intuitive and often egocentric. Sometime around age six or seven, they develop the ability to think logically about concrete objects, entering, according to Piaget, the concrete operational period. They can solve simple problems and begin to show conservation by recognizing that, for example, the amount of a substance does not change even when its shape changes.

11. Psychologists who take an information-processing approach have documented age-related improvements in children's attention span, their ability to explore and focus on features of the environment, and their memory. How fast children develop cognitive abilities depends to a certain extent on how stimulating and supportive their environments are.

12. From age two on, children seek more autonomy from their parents. They also spend time with, imitate, learn from, love, and fight with their siblings. Over the childhood years, interactions with peers increase in cooperation, competition, and conformity. Children increasingly base their friendships on feelings, not things.

13. The changes in children's social relationships grow in part from their increasing social competence. They learn to interpret and understand social situations and emotional signals. They learn social rules and roles, including those related to gender. Gender roles are based on both biological differences between the sexes and, to a larger extent, on implicit and explicit socialization by parents, teachers, peers, and the media. Parents usually use one of three styles of teaching social rules and values to their children: authoritarian, permissive, or authoritative. Authoritative parents tend to have more competent and cooperative children.

14. Puberty brings about physical changes that lead to psychological changes. Early adolescence is a period of wide mood swings, shaky self-esteem, conflict with parents, and closeness to friends. Later adolescence focuses on finding an answer to the question: Who am I? Formal abstract reasoning now becomes more sophisticated, and principled moral judgment becomes possible for the first time.

15. In early and middle adulthood, physical and cognitive changes are generally positive, including increased physical size and advanced reasoning ability. In late adulthood, physical, sensory, and intellectual abilities generally decline. This is particularly true for tasks that are unfamiliar, complex, or difficult.

16. In their twenties, young adults make occupational choices and form intimate commitments. In their thirties, they settle down, get serious, and decide what is important. Sometime around age forty, adults experience a midlife transition, which may or may not be a crisis. The forties and fifties are often times of satisfaction. In their sixties, people contend with the issue of retirement. They generally become more inward looking, cautious, and conforming. In their seventies and eighties, people confront their own mortality. They may become more philosophical and reflective as they review their lives.

KEY TERMS

Definitions of terms appear on the pages shown in parentheses.

accommodation (44)
assimilation (44)
attachment (47)
authoritarian parent (62)
authoritative parent (63)
babbling (50)
chromosome (37)
concrete operations (54)
conservation (53)
crisis of generativity (73)
critical period (39)
deoxyribonucleic acid (DNA) (37)
developmental psychology (28)
dominant (37)
embryo (38)
fetal alcohol syndrome (40)
fetus (39)
formal operational period (67)
gender role (61)
genotype (37)
identity crisis (66)

information processing (55)
insecure ambivalent attachment (48)
insecure avoidant attachment (48)
maturation (32)
midlife transition (73)
object permanence (44)
one-word stage (51)
permissive parent (63)
phenotype (37)
polygenic (38)
preoperational period (52)
puberty (64)
recessive (37)
reflex (43)
scheme (43)
secure attachment (48)
sensorimotor period (43)
social clock (72)
socialization (61)
temperament (50)
zygote (38)

RECOMMENDED READINGS

Annis, L. F. (1978). *The child before birth*. Ithaca, N.Y.: Cornell University Press. A thorough and clearly written presentation of the prenatal development of the child, with explanations of Rh disease and other possible prenatal complications.

Blythe, R. (1979). *The view in winter: Reflections on old age*. New York: Harcourt Brace Jovanovich. How people see themselves as they age, in their own words.

Clarke, A. M., and Clarke, A. D. B. (Eds.). (1976). *Early experience: Myth and evidence*. New York: Free Press. A collection of articles demonstrating the remarkable resiliency of children who recover from extremely depriving and depressing early experiences. This book takes the position that early childhood is *not* a critical period for intellectual and social development.

Erikson, E. (1968). *Identity, youth, and crisis*. New York: W. W. Norton. An elucidation of Erikson's theory of adolescence as a crucial stage in the life cycle that demands resolution of earlier crises.

Gilligan, C. (1982). *In a different voice: Psychological theory and women's development*. Cambridge, Mass.: Harvard University Press. An original theory of moral development in girls and women, contrasting their moral and psychological orientation with those of boys and men and supported by data gathered in extensive interviews.

Levinson, D. (1978). *The seasons of a man's life*. New York: Knopf. One of the first modern developmental studies of adulthood. It is often criticized for focusing on well-educated males, but it remains important.

Parke, R. D. (1977). *Fathers*. Cambridge, Mass.: Harvard University Press. A comprehensive, but readable presentation that reviews research on the roles of fathers, how they differ from those of mothers, and what effects they have on children's development.

Piaget, J. (1962). *Play, dreams, and imitation in childhood*. New York: W. W. Norton. One of the major classics written by Piaget, weaving together his theoretical framework with wonderful examples from children's lives.

Stern, D. (1977). *The first relationship*. Cambridge, Mass.: Harvard University Press. A most readable account of what has been learned through close analysis of videotapes of early mother-infant interactions.

Tavris, C., and Offir, C. (1977). *The longest war: Sex differences in perspective*. New York: Harcourt Brace Jovanovich. An entertaining and comprehensive review of research on sex and gender differences, discussed from the perspectives of psychologists, biologists, sociologists, psychoanalysts, and anthropologists.

*O*ne evening in 1983, a man we will call MD had a mild stroke. A stroke is a disruption of blood flow to part of the brain; the resulting tissue damage can cause death. If damage is less severe, part of the stroke victim's brain does not work the way it should. Many stroke victims are paralyzed or unable to remember things. Some experience more specific problems, such as inability to recognize faces, name colors, or use numbers. MD was exceptional because his brain damage resulted in a particularly narrow loss; namely, the inability to name fruits and vegetables. His verbal abilities and memory for other things were perfectly normal. In fact, he could name an abacus or a sphinx, objects many normal people might have difficulty identifying, but when presented with an apple or an orange, MD was dumfounded. On the other hand, he could read the word *apple,* then pick one out of a group of other objects and describe what it was like. His problem seemed to be only with gaining access to the proper words for fruits and vegetables. MD's condition must have been exasperating, but it was not debilitating; he has returned to work at a federal agency (fortunately, not the Department of Agriculture).

The story of MD vividly illustrates the fact that normal behavior depends on normal brain functioning. Indeed, no behavior or mental process could take place were it not for the many physical structures and biological processes that define our bodies and keep us alive. **Biological,** or **physiological, psychology** takes center stage at this level of cells and organs. Researchers in this area ask questions about the nature and location of the physical and chemical changes that occur when, for example, people learn, forget, see, think, become emotional, or fall asleep. They also try to identify the specific biological mechanisms that cause and are influenced by those changes.

This search for an understanding of biological factors in behavior and mental processes is important to research in virtually every area of psychology, as the Linkages diagram suggests. In fact, a full understanding of psychology demands at least some familiarity with basic biological structures and mechanisms. In this chapter, we provide an introduction to some of the most important of those structures and mechanisms.

But we should begin at the beginning. The development of a human being from a single cell into a complex, functioning individual occurs in part because various cells in the body specialize to become skin, bones, muscles, hair, and so on. For psychology, the most interesting specializations are those that allow cells to communicate with one another. When cells communicate, a body becomes an integrated whole that not only can detect what is in the world but also can respond to that world. The body contains several systems that are specialized for communication. Foremost among them is the nervous system.

3

Biological Bases
of Behavior

LINKAGES
an overview

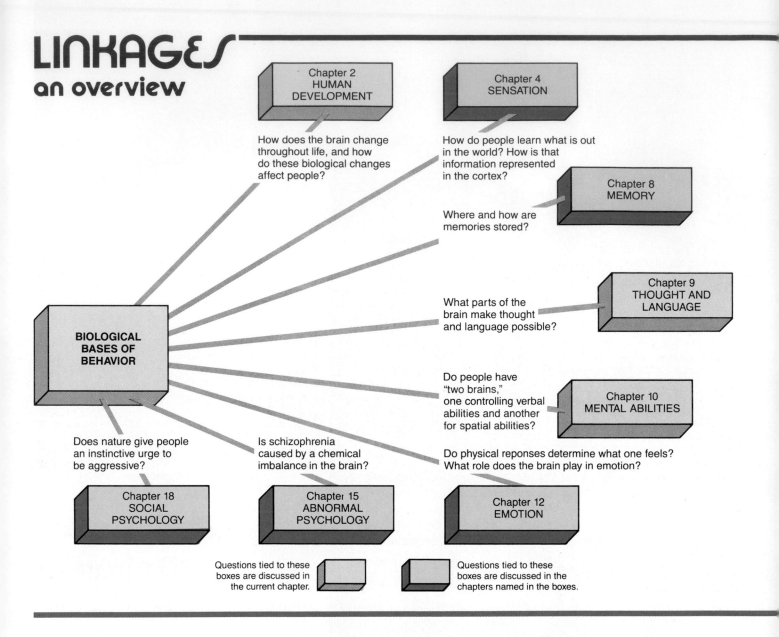

Chapter 2
HUMAN
DEVELOPMENT

How does the brain change throughout life, and how do these biological changes affect people?

Chapter 4
SENSATION

How do people learn what is out in the world? How is that information represented in the cortex?

Chapter 8
MEMORY

Where and how are memories stored?

Chapter 9
THOUGHT AND LANGUAGE

What parts of the brain make thought and language possible?

BIOLOGICAL BASES OF BEHAVIOR

Do people have "two brains," one controlling verbal abilities and another for spatial abilities?

Chapter 10
MENTAL ABILITIES

Does nature give people an instinctive urge to be aggressive?

Is schizophrenia caused by a chemical imbalance in the brain?

Do physical reponses determine what one feels? What role does the brain play in emotion?

Chapter 18
SOCIAL PSYCHOLOGY

Chapter 15
ABNORMAL PSYCHOLOGY

Chapter 12
EMOTION

Questions tied to these boxes are discussed in the current chapter.

Questions tied to these boxes are discussed in the chapters named in the boxes.

THE NERVOUS SYSTEM: AN OVERVIEW

The **nervous system** is a complex combination of cells whose primary function is to allow an organism to gain information about what is going on inside and outside the body and to respond appropriately. The parts of the nervous system that provide information about the environment are known as senses, or **sensory systems.** These include hearing, vision, taste, smell, and touch, each of which we will describe in the next chapter. Other parts of the nervous system are called **motor systems;** they influence muscles and other organs to respond to the environment in some way.

Figure 3.1 (p. 84) illustrates the three basic functions of the nervous system: receiving information, or "input"; integrating it with previous information to generate choices and decisions; and guiding actions, or "output." In this example, light reflected from an object stimulates the eyes to communicate signals to the brain by way of nerve cells. Other nerve cells in the brain interpret this input, based on previous experience, as either an

BIOLOGICAL BASES OF BEHAVIOR AND PSYCHOLOGY

All thoughts, feelings, and actions take place in and through the physical body, making biological structures and processes important to all aspects of psychology. Whether we are examining the bond between a mother and child or the distress of a person suffering from a psychological disorder, it is useful to ask what part is played by chemicals in the blood, by parts of the brain, or by other biological phenomena.

One specific approach to such questions is to ask whether a particular part of the brain controls a certain psychological process. In the 1920s, for example, an outstanding research psychologist named Karl Lashley was sure that memories were concentrated, or localized in certain parts of the brain. To test this idea, he taught rats to perform a certain task, then removed part of their brains. Much to Lashley's dismay, the rats continued to remember how to do the task, even after large segments of their brains had been removed, and it did not seem to matter which parts were gone. Lashley eventually gave up looking for the location of memories, concluding in exasperation that they must be stored diffusely throughout the brain (Lashley, 1929).

Subsequent research revealed that Lashley was both right and wrong. As we describe in the chapter on memory, large parts of the brain are involved in creating memories, but when the appropriate parts of the brain are removed, specific memories can be disrupted. To go beyond Lashley's research to reach this understanding, however, scientists had to develop both new techniques and better information about the brain's architecture and how it works. In this chapter, we discuss some of what they have learned, introducing some basic facts about the biological structures and processes that underlie behavior and mental processes. In later chapters, we will build on this information to examine more specifically how biological factors shape psychological processes.

appealing snack or a dog treat. The brain decides which it is, then sends signals to the arm and hand muscles to either grasp the object or wave it away.

Either way, information has been taken in, processed, and acted on. This sequence might remind you of the functions of a computer, which, like the nervous system, has input and output functions and a central processor. As this and other chapters will show, however, the nervous system not only is much more complex and flexible in its functioning than any computer yet constructed, but also has capacities for creativity, analysis, and judgment that today's computers do not have. The nervous system has two major units: the central nervous system and the peripheral nervous system (see Figure 3.2, p. 84). All of its parts are connected throughout the body and function together.

The **central nervous system (CNS)** is the part encased in bone. It includes the brain, which is inside the skull, and the spinal cord, which is in the spinal column (or backbone). The CNS is the central executive of the body; most information about the environment is sent to it to be processed and acted on.

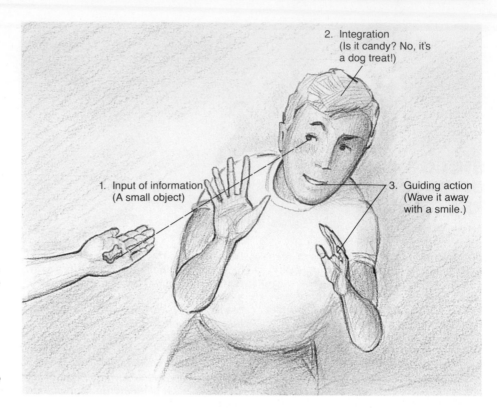

2. Integration
(Is it candy? No, it's
a dog treat!)

1. Input of information
(A small object)

3. Guiding action
(Wave it away
with a smile.)

Figure 3.1
Three Functions of the Nervous System
The nervous system's three main functions involve receiving information, integrating or processing that information, and guiding actions. Here, the visual information received—a small object offered by a friend—is integrated with what the person knows about the appearance of hors d'oeuvres and dog treats and about whether the friend is a practical joker. The result of this information processing will be a decision to either refuse the object or to reach out for it while preparing the mouth and stomach to receive food.

The **peripheral nervous system** includes all of the nervous system that is not housed in bone. It has two main subsystems. The first is the **somatic nervous system,** which transmits information from the senses to the CNS and carries signals from the CNS to the muscles that move the skeleton. The somatic nervous system is involved, for example, in relaying from the hand the sensations of warm sand and in passing on to the arm the brain's message about moving the hand around in that sand. The second subsystem is the **autonomic nervous system (ANS);** it carries messages back and forth between the CNS and the heart, lungs, and other organs and glands in the body. These messages increase, decrease, or otherwise regulate the activity of

Figure 3.2
Organization of the Nervous System
The bone-encased **central nervous system** (CNS) is made up of the brain and spinal cord and acts as the body's central information processor, decision maker, and director of actions. The peripheral nervous system includes all nerves not housed in bone and functions mainly to carry messages. The somatic subsystem of the peripheral nervous system transmits sensory information to the CNS from the outside world and conveys instructions from the CNS to the muscles. The autonomic subsystem conveys messages from the CNS that alter the activity of organs and glands and sends information about that activity back to the brain.

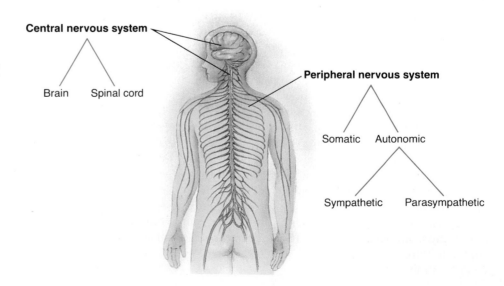

Central nervous system

Brain   Spinal cord

Peripheral nervous system

Somatic   Autonomic

Sympathetic   Parasympathetic

these organs and glands to meet varying demands placed on the body and also provide information to the brain about that activity.

The autonomic nervous system itself has two divisions, known as the *sympathetic* and *parasympathetic* branches, which often create opposite effects. For example, the sympathetic nervous system can make the heart beat faster, whereas the parasympathetic nervous system can slow it down. These systems are described in more detail in Chapter 12, on emotion. For now, we will consider how these and other components of the nervous system communicate with one another and with the rest of the body.

COMMUNICATION IN THE NERVOUS SYSTEM

The hallmark of the nervous system is its role in carrying messages from one part of the body to another. This is possible because the fundamental units of the nervous system are special cells called nerve cells, or **neurons,** which have the remarkable ability to communicate with one another.

Neurons: The Basic Unit of the Nervous System

Neurons share characteristics with every other kind of cell in the body. First, as Figure 3.3 illustrates, they have an *outer membrane,* which, like a fine screen, lets some substances pass in and out while blocking others. Second, each neuron has a *cell body,* which contains a **nucleus.** The nucleus carries the genetic information that determines whether the cell will be a liver cell, a brain cell, or whatever, and acts to direct that cell's functioning. Third, neurons contain structures called *mitochondria,* which turn oxygen and glucose

Figure 3.3
The Neuron
(a) The cell body of a neuron, enlarged from one of the whole neurons shown in (b). The cell body has typical cell elements, including an outer membrane and mitochondria. (b) Some of the shapes neurons can take, highlighting the fibers extending outward from each cell body. These fibers, the axons and dendrites, are among the features that make neurons unique.

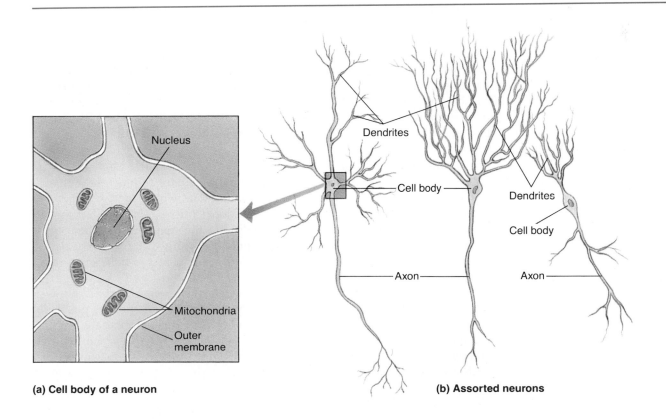

(a) Cell body of a neuron

(b) Assorted neurons

into usable energy. This process is especially vital to brain cells, because although the brain accounts for only 2 percent of the body's weight, it consumes more than 20 percent of the body's oxygen (Sokoloff, 1981).

But the characteristics that make neurons special are even more interesting. Unlike other types of cells, they can transmit signals, both within themselves and to other neurons. Three types of physical specializations enable nerve cells to perform this feat. The first is their *structure*. Although neurons come in a wide variety of shapes and sizes, all have long, thin fibers that extend outward from the cell body (see Figure 3.3). When these fibers get close to other neurons, communication between the cells can take place. The second specialization is the *excitable surface membrane* of some of these fibers, which allows a signal to be sent from one end of the neuron to the other. The third specialization involves the minute gaps, or *synapses,* between nerve cells, where one neuron receives signals from another.

The structure of neurons: Axons and dendrites

The fibers extending from a neuron's cell body fall into just two categories: axons and dendrites. **Axons** are the fibers that carry signals from the cell body out to where communication occurs with other nerve cells. Each nerve cell generally has only one axon leaving the cell body, but that one axon may have many branches. Axons can be very short, or like the axon that sends signals from the spinal cord all the way down to the big toe, they can be several feet long. **Dendrites** are the fibers that receive signals from the axons of other neurons and carry those signals to the cell body. A neuron can have dozens, hundreds, or thousands of dendrites. Usually dendrites have many branches (*dendrite* means literally "of a tree" in Greek).

Occasionally axons carry signals to other axons and to the cell bodies of other neurons. But, as a general rule, the axon delivers these signals from the cell body of one cell to the dendrites of another cell; those dendrites in turn transmit the signal to their cell body, which may relay the signal down its axon and thus on to a third cell, and so on. Thus *axons* carry signals *away* from the cell body, whereas *dendrites detect* those signals.

Axons and dendrites allow neurons to influence anywhere from 1,000 to 100,000 other nerve cells (Guroff, 1980), some of which may be quite far away. These intercell communication patterns permit the brain to conduct extremely complex information processing. But, like the cables connecting parts of a computer, axons and dendrites are not of much use unless a signal can be sent from one end and received at the other. Such signals can occur in the nervous system thanks to the two other special features of neurons: the membrane of their axons and the synapses between neurons.

Membranes and action potentials

To understand these signals in the nervous system, you first need to know something about cell membranes. The outer membrane of all cells is *selectively permeable,* which means that it lets some chemical molecules pass through yet blocks others. Some molecules can cross the membrane any time, anywhere along the membrane. Others must be carried across. Still others can pass only by going through channels, or holes, in the membrane. These channels have *gates* that can be opened to let certain molecules through.

Many molecules carry a positive or a negative electrical charge. If, because of the selective permeability of the membrane, the distribution of positively and negatively charged molecules inside and outside the membrane is uneven, the membrane is said to be *polarized*. In fact, the inside of the membrane in all body cells is slightly negative compared with the outside. Because molecules with a positive charge are attracted to those with a negative charge, a force

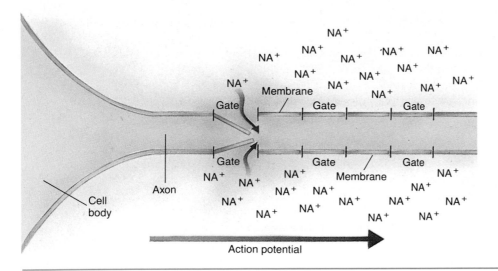

Figure 3.4
The Beginning of an Action Potential
This very diagrammatic view of a polarized nerve cell axon shows the normally closed sodium gates in the cell membrane. If stimulation of the cell causes depolarization near a particular gate, that gate may swing open, allowing sodium to rush into the axon, stimulating the next gate to open, and so on down the axon. This spread of depolarization and the consequent progressive entry of sodium into the cell is called an action potential; when it occurs, the cell is said to have fired. The action potential fired by one cell may subsequently stimulate other cells to fire.

(called an *electrical potential*) drives positively charged molecules toward the inside of the cell, but many of them are kept outside by the membrane.

For communication in the nervous system, the most important of these "excluded" molecules is sodium (the same sodium in table salt); when it is positively charged, sodium is symbolized Na⁺. Sodium is highly concentrated on the outside of the cell. Though strongly attracted to negatively charged chlorine molecules inside the cell, it can pass through the membrane only by going through channels, or *sodium gates,* which are distributed all along the axon. Normally the sodium gates are closed, but sometimes the membrane around a particular sodium gate becomes less polarized, or *depolarized,* causing the gate to open, as shown in Figure 3.4. Sodium then rushes into the cell through the open gate, changing the potential at a neighboring gate, which causes that gate to open. This sequence continues, and the change in potential spreads like a wild rumor all the way down the axon.

This abrupt change in the potential of an axon is called an **action potential,** and its contagious nature is referred to as its *self-propagating* property. When the neuron shoots an action potential down its axon, the neuron is said to have *fired.* This kind of nerve communication is of an "all-or-none" variety; the cell either fires at full strength or does not fire at all. The speed of the action potential as it moves down an axon is constant for a given cell, but in different cells the speed ranges from 0.2 meters per second to 120 meters per second (about 260 miles per hour; McGeer, Eccles & McGeer, 1978). The speed depends on the diameter of the axon (larger ones are faster) and on whether myelin is present. **Myelin** is a fatty substance that wraps around some axons and speeds action potentials. Larger, myelinated cells are usually found in the parts of the nervous system that carry the most urgently needed information. For example, in the somatic nervous system, fast-acting sensory, or *afferent,* neurons receive information from the environment about onrushing trains, hot irons, and other dangers, whereas high-speed motor, or *efferent,* neurons carry messages that prompt immediate protective actions in the appropriate muscles. *Afferent* means "coming toward"; *efferent* means "going away." Where more and more connecting nerves, called *interneurons,* come between sensory and motor neurons, the system slows down somewhat.

Although each neuron fires or does not fire, in an "all-or-none" fashion, the neuron's *rate* of firing varies. It can fire over and over, because the sodium gates open only briefly, allowing polarization to build up again after they

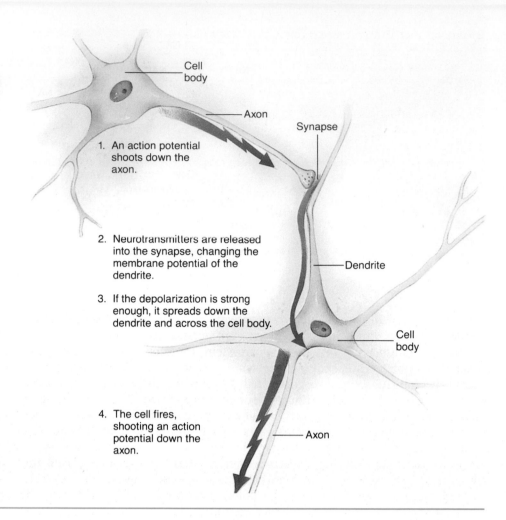

1. An action potential shoots down the axon.

2. Neurotransmitters are released into the synapse, changing the membrane potential of the dendrite.

3. If the depolarization is strong enough, it spreads down the dendrite and across the cell body.

4. The cell fires, shooting an action potential down the axon.

Figure 3.5
Communication Between Neurons
When a neuron fires, a self-propagating action potential shoots to the end of its axon, triggering the release of a neurotransmitter into the synapse. This stimulates neighboring cells. One type of stimulation is excitatory, causing depolarization of the neighboring cells, which may be strong enough to fire their action potentials.

Figure 3.6
Integration of Neural Signals
The signals that a neuron receives can arrive at its dendrites or at its cell body. These signals, which typically come from many neighboring cells, can be conflicting. Some are excitatory, stimulating the cell to fire; other, inhibitory signals tell the cell not to fire. Whether the cell actually fires or not at any given moment depends on a number of factors, including whether excitatory or inhibitory messages predominate at the junction of the cell body and the axon.

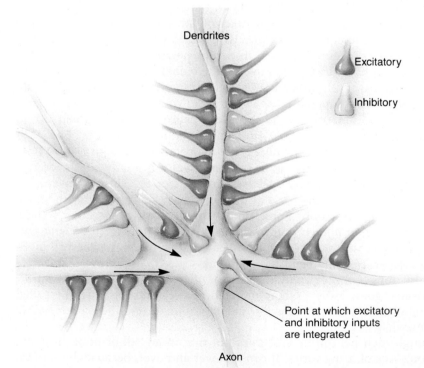

close. Between firings, there is a rest, or **refractory period,** while the membrane becomes polarized again. Because the refractory period is quite short, a neuron can send action potentials down its axon at rates of up to one thousand per second. The pattern of repeated action potentials amounts to a coded message.

Synapses and communication between cells   How does the action potential in one neuron have an effect on the next neuron? For communication to occur *between* cells, the signal must somehow be transferred across the gap, or **synapse,** between neurons, usually between one neuron's axon and the dendrites of another (see Figure 3.5).

The transfer is accomplished by a type of chemical called a **neurotransmitter;** as we shall see, there are many different neurotransmitters, each of which is used by a particular set of neurons. When an action potential reaches a synapse, the axon releases neurotransmitters. These neurotransmitters spread across the synapse to reach the next, or *postsynaptic,* cell. There the neurotransmitters trigger a change in the membrane potential of the postsynaptic cell, thus creating an electrical signal. This signal is either *excitatory,* making the postsynaptic cell more likely to fire, or *inhibitory,* making the cell less likely to fire. If the signal is excitatory, a wave of depolarization in the membrane of the postsynaptic cell's dendrite begins to move toward its cell body. However, unlike the action potential in an axon, which remains at a constant strength, this signal fades as it goes along. Only if the signal is strong enough to begin with will it pass through the next cell body and trigger a new action potential. Because a neuron may have synapses with thousands of other neurons, it may receive a conflicting pattern of excitatory ("fire") and inhibitory ("don't fire") signals (see Figure 3.6). Whether or not the neuron fires and how rapidly it fires depend on which kind of signal predominates from moment to moment at the junction of the cell body and the axon.

Neurotransmitters and Receptors

The predominating signal itself depends both on the types of neurotransmitters that reach the postsynaptic cell and on where they wash ashore. We have represented part of a synapse in Figure 3.7 (p. 90). Note that the axon is enlarged at its tip and that this presynaptic area contains many little bags called *vesicles.* These vesicles are made of membrane material and contain the neurotransmitters that are released into the synapse.

The neurotransmitters can stimulate the postsynaptic neuron only at specialized sites, called **receptors,** on the surface of the postsynaptic cell. Receptors are usually located on the dendrites, sometimes on the cell body. These receptors "recognize" only one type of neurotransmitter. Like a jigsaw puzzle piece fitting perfectly into its proper place, a given neurotransmitter fits snugly into its own receptors but not into receptors for other neurotransmitters (see Figure 3.8, p. 90). Only when a neurotransmitter fits precisely into a receptor does it trigger the chemical response that changes the membrane potential and passes on a signal from one neuron to another.

What that signal will be depends in part on what type of receptor the neurotransmitter contacts. Stimulation of *excitatory receptors* makes the cell more likely to fire. Stimulation of *inhibitory receptors,* on the other hand, makes the cell less likely to fire. Though each receptor recognizes only one type of neurotransmitter, a given neurotransmitter can stimulate both types of receptors. As a result, the same neurotransmitter may produce both excitatory and inhibitory effects in different locations.

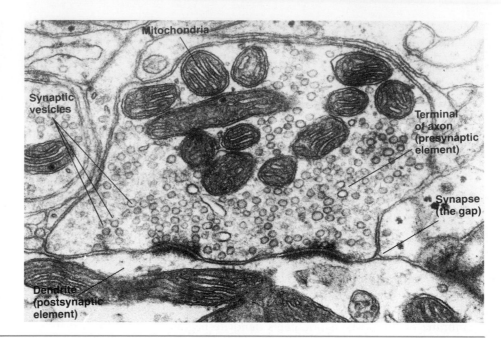

Figure 3.7
Part of a Synapse
A photo taken through an electron micro-scope shows part of a neural synapse mag-nified 50,000 times. Clearly visible are the mitochondria and the neurotransmit-ter-containing vesicles in the ending of the presynaptic cell's axon, the narrow gap between the cells, and the dendrite of the postsynaptic cell.
(Micrograph produced by John E. Heuser of Wash-ington University School of Medicine, St. Louis, MO.)

The neurotransmitter stays at the receptor site for only a brief time. It must be removed from the synapse after interacting with its receptor, or it will continue to stimulate receptors indefinitely. The removal occurs in one of two ways. An enzyme at the synapse can break down the neurotransmitter. Or, more commonly, the neurotransmitter can be transported back into its presynaptic area; this process is called *reuptake*.

Figure 3.8
The Relationship Between Neurotransmitters and Receptors
Neurotransmitters influence postsynaptic cells by stimulating special receptors on the surface of those cells' membranes. Each type of receptor receives only one type of neurotransmitter, the two fitting together like puzzle pieces or like a key in a lock. Stimu-lation of these receptors by their neurotrans-mitter causes them, in turn, to either help or hinder the generation of a wave of depolari-zation in their cell's dendrites. As noted ear-lier, only if this wave is strong enough will it pass through the cell body to trigger an action potential.

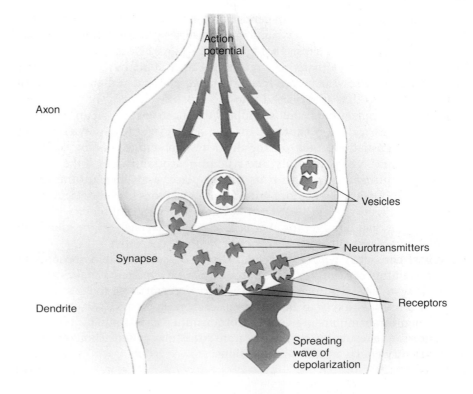

Pathways and Nuclei

Nerve cells are not lined up neatly like computer circuits or carefully laid-out streets. In fact, the nervous system looks more like Boston, with distinct neighborhoods, winding back streets, and multilaned expressways.

The nervous system's "neighborhoods" are collections of cell bodies called **nuclei.** The nervous system's "highways" are made up of axons that travel together in bundles called **fiber tracts.** The fiber tracts are also known as *pathways.* Like a freeway ramp, the axon from a given cell may merge with and leave fiber tracts, and it may send branches into other tracts.

In learning your way around these structures, there is no substitute for memorizing some descriptive terms. Most of the terms provide a description of the appearance or location of a structure. For example, an area of the brain now known to be important in memory was named the *hippocampus,* Greek for "seahorse," and another area was called the *mammillary bodies,* because they resemble breasts. Table 3.1 contains translations of some of the directional terms used in anatomy. Like *northwest* or *southeast,* these terms can be combined to form words like *anterior-medial* (the front part of the middle of a structure) or *ventromedial* (the bottom part of the middle of a structure). In describing pathways in the nervous system, an *o* is often used to indicate "from this to that." For example, the spin*o*thalamic tract carries information from the spine to the thalamus.

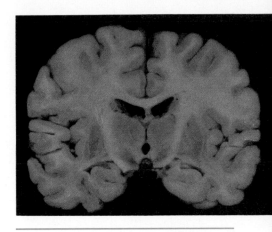

Many major nuclei and fiber tracts in the nervous system are visible to the naked eye. The cell bodies in this slice of brain tissue, for example, appear gray and are referred to as "gray matter." Bundles of axons are known as fiber tracts, or "white matter." They appear white because larger axons are coated with fatty myelin.

STRUCTURES AND FUNCTIONS OF THE CENTRAL NERVOUS SYSTEM

The structure and functioning of these collections of neurons are impressive in themselves, but when they blend into larger, more complex combinations to form the central nervous system their role in human behavior becomes clearest. The central nervous system, or CNS, allows us to walk and talk, to breathe and sigh, to play the piano or the horses, to read books, and best of all, to think about them. The link between the brain and behavior is vital and fragile. A stroke or other malfunction in the central nervous system can leave a person with deficits in sensation, movement, language, recognition of the world, and countless other aspects of behavior and mental processing that most of us take for granted. If the damage or disorder is severe enough, the central nervous system may even lose its ability to maintain breathing, the heartbeat—in other words, life itself.

In this section, we review the structures of the central nervous system and consider their role in the creation and coordination of behavior and mental processes. Later we will discuss some of the chemical processes that underlie the functioning of the CNS. Our exploration begins at the spinal cord and progresses upward, toward the skull (see Figure 3.9, p. 92).

The Spinal Cord

The **spinal cord** receives signals from peripheral senses, such as touch, and relays them upward to the brain through fibers within the cord. Neurons in the spinal cord also carry signals downward. For example, axons from neurons in the brain stimulate cells in the spinal cord that, in turn, cause muscles to contract and move the body.

Some simple behaviors are organized completely within the spinal cord. These behaviors are called **reflexes** because the response to an incoming signal is directly "reflected" back out. They are controlled by a *reflex pathway*

TABLE 3.1

Directional Terms Used to Describe the Nervous System
The seemingly complex terms used to refer to structures in the nervous system are actually quite informative. As the table shows, each term describes some aspect of where a structure is located. Often these terms are combined, as in ventromedial ("lower middle"), to create more precise designations.

Term	Direction
Ventral	Lower; toward the belly in animals
Dorsal	Upper; toward the back in animals
Anterior	Toward the front
Posterior	Toward the rear
Medial	Toward the middle
Lateral	Toward the side; away from the middle
Basal	Toward the base or bottom
Rostral	Toward the nose
Caudal	Toward the tail

Forebrain—including cerebral cortex, striatum, limbic system, thalamus, and hypothalamus

Midbrain (hidden by forebrain)

Hindbrain—including cerebellum and medulla

Spinal cord

Figure 3.9
An Overview of the Central Nervous System
The central nervous system is beautifully adapted to its functions, but it was not the work of a city planner. Its anatomy reflects the fact that it evolved over millions of years. Newer structures that handle higher mental functions (such as the cerebral cortex) were built on older ones (like the medulla) that coordinate more basic processes, such as heart rate and breathing.

Smooth movements require the coordination of neural activity in both the brain and the spinal cord. Without this coordination, walking would be far more difficult and would require assistance similar to the system shown here. This system uses computer control and electrical stimulation of muscles to help paralyzed people walk.

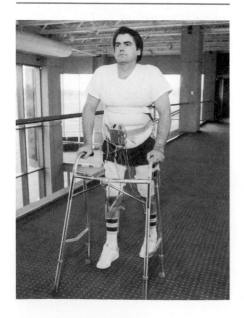

(sometimes called a *reflex arc*), which consists of a sensory, or *afferent,* neuron; a minimal number of connecting neurons, or *interneurons;* and a motor, or *efferent* neuron (see Figure 3.10).

For example, suppose you sleepily reach for a pot of hot water to make your morning coffee and touch the hot burner instead. The incoming nerve impulses from sensory, or afferent, neurons in your hand quickly stimulate the fibers that operate your arm muscles, and you withdraw your hand. This is called the *withdrawal reflex,* and it occurs entirely within the spinal cord. The pain stimulus does go on to the brain for analysis, but because of the reflex, your muscles respond without waiting for instructions from the brain. Because the brain is not involved in spinal reflexes, they are considered involuntary. They are very fast, because they involve few time-consuming synapses.

Four principles of central nervous system functioning   Although the spinal cord is far simpler than the brain, its functioning demonstrates the principles that govern the whole central nervous system. The first principle of CNS functioning is central coordination of opposing actions. For example, when a simple spinal reflex set off by touching a hot burner causes one set of arm muscles to contract, that contraction causes another reflex that makes an opposing set of muscles relax. If this did not happen, the arm would go rigid. Second, the central nervous system coordinates the creation of complicated behaviors from simpler ones. Thus, the complex movements involved in walking are built up of reflexes that not only prompt repeated contraction-relaxation cycles in the muscles of each arm and leg, but also time these cycles so that the left arm and right leg move forward while the right arm and left leg swing or push backward.

The third principle of CNS activity is that smooth functioning depends on feedback systems. In a **feedback system,** information about the consequences of an action is returned to the source of the action, so that adjustments can be made. A thermostat is the classic example of feedback. You set the thermostat to the desired temperature and the furnace generates heat, while the thermostat monitors the room temperature. When the desired temperature has been reached, the thermostat feeds that information back to the furnace, which turns off. When the temperature drops below the desired level, the furnace goes on again. When feedback keeps a bodily function such as body temperature within a steady range, it is called **homeostasis.** The spinal cord does not have a thermostat, but muscles have stretch receptors that send impulses to the spinal cord to let it know how extended they are; a reflex pathway then adjusts the muscle contraction. This feedback tends to stabilize the position of the body and allows smooth movements. This reflexive feedback is also what causes the classic knee-jerk response when the knee is tapped (through a feedback system, the tapping causes the thigh muscle to stretch and reflexively contract), as Figure 3.10 shows.

Fourth, normal behavior results from the coordination of several levels of central nervous system organization. Consider again the act of walking. When you walk, the brain directs your movements, but rather than override the reflex connections already present in the spinal cord, it works right along with them.

Studying the Brain

Much of what psychologists have learned about the brain has come from studies with animals. Another major source of knowledge comes from studying deficits in victims of strokes and other localized brain damage. Examining

Figure 3.10
An Example of a Reflex Pathway
A tap on the knee sets off an almost instantaneous sequence of events, beginning with the stimulation of sensory neurons. When those neurons fire, their axons, which end within the spinal cord, cause connecting neurons, or interneurons, to fire. This in turn stimulates the firing of motor neurons with axons ending in the thigh muscles. The result is a contraction of the thigh muscles and a kicking of the lower leg and foot. Information about the knee tap and about what the leg has done also ascends to the cerebral cortex, but the sensorimotor reflex is completed without waiting for guidance from the brain.

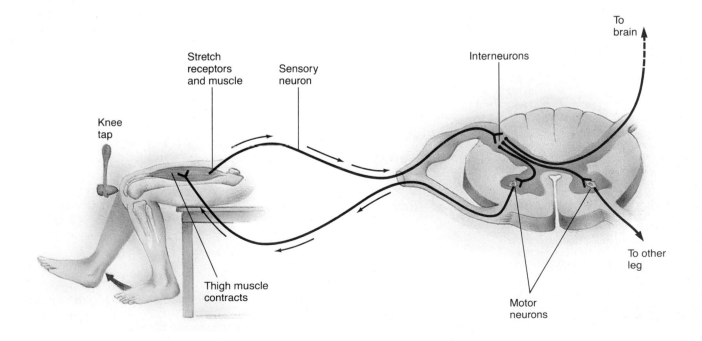

these patients and sometimes studying their brains after death can reveal a relationship between damage to a specific part of the brain and loss of particular behavior or mental activity.

New technologies have also allowed psychologists to view the brain's functioning more directly: to eavesdrop on and take "snapshots" of its activity. These techniques have helped reveal that some complex mental functions appear to be handled in one particular area of the brain and that others are not as localized. We will describe some of the details later. However, the brain is so complex that it is difficult to make simple statements about specific regions and kinds of behavior. Damage to one region can lead to malfunctioning of other parts that are far removed.

HIGHLIGHT

Monitoring the Brain

The most basic methods for studying the living brain employ special devices that can detect and amplify the brain's electrical activity. The microphones of these devices can be so small and sensitive that, in experiments with animals, they can be surgically implanted in or near a single neuron to record its firing. This single-unit recording lets researchers "listen to" the signals that nerve cells send to each other and lets them try to decipher the codes that the nervous system uses. (We will describe some of these codes in Chapter 4, on sensation.)

The collective electrical activity of the brain's many nerve cells generates signals strong enough to be measured by recording electrodes attached to the surface of the skull. The recordings that result are called **electroencephalograms,** or **EEGs.** Though it is very difficult to make any sense of the activity of millions of neurons firing at once, special electronic filters, high-speed computers, and other technological advances have made it possible to look for EEG patterns that may be related to brain damage, certain mental disorders, and even particular thought processes (see Figure 3.11).

Another important method of brain research takes advantage of the fact that electrical stimulation of a set of neurons will cause action potentials to travel down their axons and release a neurotransmitter, just as if they were stimulated by other neurons. Patients who need brain surgery sometimes volunteer to have a stimulating electrode lowered into their brain during the operation, so that specific effects can be observed when neurons in specific areas are made to fire. This painless electrical stimulation can cause the patient to move a particular body part or report a sound, smell, or other sensory experience.

Figure 3.11
Eavesdropping on the Brain
One way to gather clues about what happens in the brain during various kinds of mental activity involves recording EEG, or brain wave, tracings. (a) The EEG pattern summarized by a computer as a subject watches stimuli that occur in an expected and predictable way. (b) The brain wave pattern that typically appears when the subject encounters unexpected and surprising stimuli. The large drop in the EEG tracing usually occurs about 0.3 seconds after an unexpected stimulus.

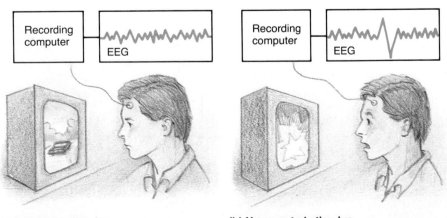

(a) **Expected stimulus**   (b) **Unexpected stimulus**

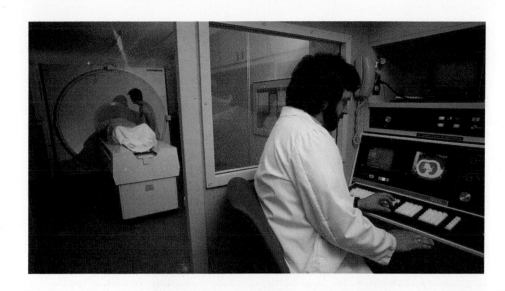

CT and PET scanning exemplify the advancing technology that is making it possible to obtain increasingly detailed images of the structure and functioning of the brain.

Recently, more sophisticated techniques have been developed to localize functions and to monitor brain activity without surgery. Most of these involve picking up signals from deep within the brain and feeding them to computers that can construct a two- or three-dimensional picture of the brain. In general, the techniques are similar to computer-assisted tomography, or CT scanning. CT scans are like X rays, however, in revealing only the *structure* of the brain. The newer techniques can also reveal the *activity* of particular brain regions.

These techniques measure the signals arising from the intense activity in neurons when their action potentials fire. Actively firing neurons must increase their oxygen and glucose (sugar) consumption, and they need an increased supply of blood to do so. The location of these areas of increased brain activity can be detected by marking blood, oxygen, or glucose with radioactive substances and then measuring, from outside the skull, where the radioactivity becomes concentrated. The location of brain activity can be especially precise when *positron*-emitting radioactive isotopes are used, because positron radio-activity emits simultaneous signals in two exactly opposite directions. Thus, by placing a person's head at the center of an array of radiation detectors, it is possible to take a radiation "picture" of a cross-section of the brain (or any other organ). The procedure is called *positron emission tomography,* or PET scanning.

PET scans have great value in allowing us to see which parts of the brain are involved in specific normal functions, as well as the activity associated with abnormal conditions. For example, Figure 3.12 (p. 96) shows PET scans of glucose utilization in a person suffering from cycles of deep depression and wild elation (Baxter et al., 1985). (These cycles are associated with a behavior pattern described in Chapter 15 as bipolar disorder.) PET scans and related techniques are now being used along with traditional psychological techniques to diagnose mental and behavioral disorders.

Another technique that shows great promise for nonsurgical diagnosis of brain activity is *magnetic resonance imaging,* or *MRI.* This technique does not use radioactive isotopes; instead, it detects the magnetic fields that surround the atoms in brain tissue. Though still in its infancy, MRI has already improved on CT scans by producing clearer pictures of brain structures and providing much more information about them. It has further assisted in the process of detecting abnormalities in the brains of people who display depression, schizophrenia, and other mental disorders (Rangel-Guerra et al., 1983; Smith et al., 1984). ∎

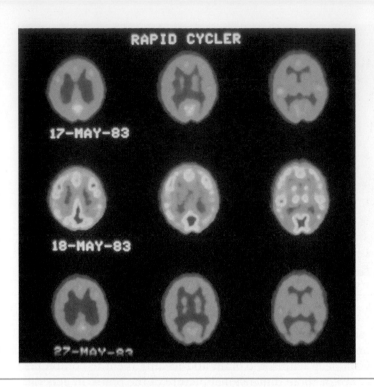

Figure 3.12
PET Scans of a Patient Prone to Dramatic Mood Changes
The three sets of ovals represent overhead views of what was going on at three different levels of the patient's brain on three different days. Glucose consumption associated with increased brain activity shows up red on these scans. There was an abnormally low amount of activity on the seventeenth and the twenty-seventh of May, when the patient was depressed, but the scan shows about a 40 percent increase in activity (essentially normal) on the eighteenth, when the patient was in a more upbeat, almost elated, mood. Scans like these help not only to detect abnormal brain activity, but also to begin to trace its location.
(L. R. Baxter et al., *Archives of General Psychiatry*, 1985, volume 42, page 444. Copyright 1985, American Medical Association.)

The Structure of the Brain

As shown in Figures 3.9 and 3.13, the brain has three major subdivisions: the hindbrain, midbrain, and forebrain. On opening the skull one sees the outer surface of part of the forebrain, a wrinkled surface called the *cerebral cortex* (*cortex* means "bark"). Beneath the forebrain is the midbrain, and under that, near the spinal cord, lies the hindbrain, where we begin our exploration.

The hindbrain   As you can see in Figure 3.13, the **hindbrain** is an extension of the spinal cord, but inside the skull. Blood pressure, heart rate, breathing, and many other vital functions are controlled by nuclei in the hindbrain, particularly in an area called the **medulla.** As in the spinal cord, reflexes and feedback systems are important to the functioning of the hindbrain. For example, if blood pressure drops, heart action increases reflexively to compensate for that drop. When one stands up very quickly, there is sometimes

Figure 3.13
Major Structures of the Brain: The Hindbrain, Midbrain, and Forebrain
This view from the side of a section cut down the middle of the brain reveals the hindbrain, which includes the cerebellum, the medulla, the reticular formation, and other areas. The midbrain lies between the hindbrain and the forebrain. Many of these subdivisions do not have clear-cut borders, since they are all interconnected by fiber tracts.

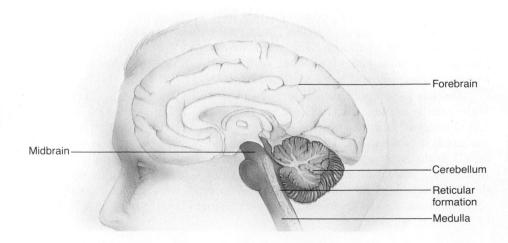

such a sudden drop in blood pressure that it produces some temporary lightheadedness until the hindbrain reflex "catches up."

The **cerebellum** is also part of the hindbrain. Its primary function is to control finely coordinated movements, such as threading a needle. Recent research has shown that the cerebellum is also a place where certain types of learned associations that involve movement are stored (McCormick & Thompson, 1984). This appears to be where well-rehearsed movements, such as those associated with ballet, piano playing, and athletics, reside.

The midbrain   As its name implies, the **midbrain** lies between the hindbrain and the forebrain. It is a small structure in humans, but it serves some very important functions. Information from the eyes, ears, and skin is relayed through the midbrain, and certain types of automatic behaviors are controlled there. For example, when a loud noise causes you to reflexively turn your head and look in the direction of the sound, your midbrain circuits are at work.

One vital midbrain nucleus is the blackish *substantia nigra* (meaning literally "black stuff"). This small area is necessary for the smooth initiation of movement. Without it, you would find it difficult, if not impossible, to get up out of a chair or lift your hand to swat a fly.

The reticular formation   Threading throughout the hindbrain and midbrain is a collection of nuclei and fibers composed of cells that are not arranged in any well-defined form (see Figure 3.13). Because they look like a network, they are called the **reticular formation** (*reticular* means "netlike"). This network is very important in altering the activity of the rest of the brain. It is involved, for example, in arousal and attention; stimulating an animal's reticular formation will arouse the animal from sleep.

The forebrain   The **forebrain** is the most highly developed part of the brain. It is responsible for the most complex aspects of behavior and mental life. As shown in Figure 3.14, the forebrain is composed of two main structures: the *diencephalon* and the *telencephalon*. Two structures in the diencephalon, the **hypothalamus** and the **thalamus**, are involved in emotion, basic drives, and sensation.

Hunger, thirst, and sex drives, for example, are regulated, in part, by the hypothalamus, a structure with many connections to and from the autonomic nervous system, as well as to other parts of the brain. Damage to the hypothalamus can disrupt these drives. Destruction of one section of the

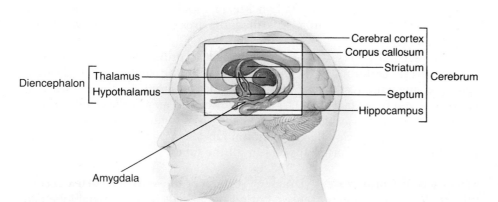

Figure 3.14
Some Structures of the Forebrain
The forebrain is divided into the telencephalon, or cerebrum, and the diencephalon. Many of the structures of the cerebrum are covered by the outer "bark" of the cerebral cortex. Here we see some of the structures that lie deep within the cerebrum, including the striatum, the hippocampus, and the septum. The diencephalon includes the hypothalamus and the thalamus.

hypothalamus results in an overwhelming urge to eat, imbalances in the regulation of blood sugar, and consequent obesity. Damage to another area of the male's hypothalamus causes the sex organs to degenerate and the sex drive to disappear. We will discuss these functions of the hypothalamus in more detail in the chapters on motivation and emotion.

As suggested by its name, the hypothalamus lies underneath the thalamus (*hypo-* means "under"). The thalamus relays signals from the eyes and other sense organs to upper levels in the brain, and it plays an important role in processing and making sense out of this information.

The largest part of the forebrain is the *telencephalon,* meaning "front end of the brain," where it is located. It is also called the **cerebrum.** The outermost part of the cerebrum appears rather round or spherical and has right and left halves that are similar in appearance. These halves are called the **cerebral hemispheres.**

The *striatum* is one of several structures in the cerebrum. Its name, which means "striped," comes from the fiber tracts that pass through the structure, giving it a striped appearance. Along with the substantia nigra, the striatum is responsible for smooth initiation of movement. Thus, damage or dysfunction in these areas can keep a person from voluntarily taking a step or beginning some other practiced movement. If someone helps the person get started, however, these movements can be flawlessly coordinated as long as the cerebellum is intact.

The cerebrum also contains several parts of the **limbic system,** a set of structures that includes the **hippocampus** and the **septum.** Other parts of the limbic system, such as the hypothalamus, are actually in the diencephalon. The limbic system is a "system" because its components have major interconnections and because they influence related functions. For example, the limbic system plays an important role in regulating emotion, as well as in memory and some thought processes. Damage to the hippocampus results in the inability to remember recent events for very long. In one case, a patient's hippocampus was surgically removed in an attempt to control epileptic seizures. Although his IQ actually improved after the surgery and he could recall old memories, he was almost totally unable to form new memories (Milner, Corkin & Teuber, 1968).

The Cerebral Cortex

The outer surface of the cerebral hemispheres, the **cerebral cortex,** has a surface area of one to two square feet—an area that is larger than it looks because of the folds, or *convolutions,* that allow the cortex to fit compactly inside the skull. The convolutions give the surface of the human brain its wrinkled appearance, its ridges and valleys. The ridges are called *gyri* and the valleys, *sulci* or *fissures.* As you can see in Figure 3.15, several deep sulci divide the cortex into four areas called the *frontal, parietal, occipital,* and *temporal lobes.*

The cerebral cortex can also be divided according to the functions its various areas perform. These functions—including higher-order thought, complex integration and analysis of information from all the senses, and control of voluntary movements—are performed in areas called *motor cortex, sensory cortex,* and *association cortex.* As shown in Figure 3.15, sensory cortex lies in the parietal, occipital, and temporal lobes; motor cortex is in the frontal lobe; and association cortex appears in all the lobes.

Sensory and motor cortex   Different regions of the **sensory cortex** receive information about different senses. For example, cells in the parietal lobe take

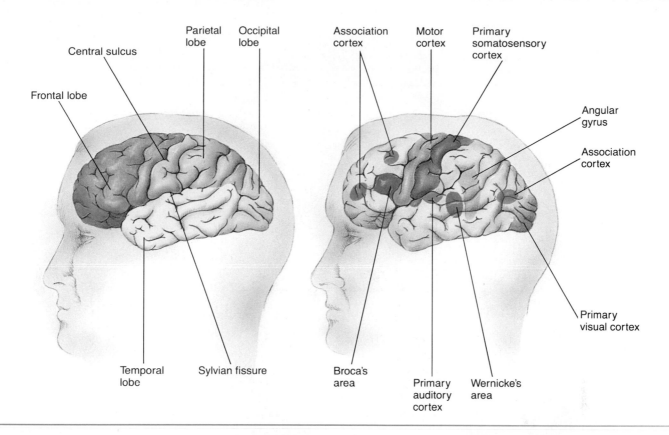

Figure 3.15
The Cerebral Cortex (viewed from the left side)
The ridges (gyri) and valleys (sulci) are landmarks that divide the cortex into four lobes: the frontal, the parietal, the occipital, and the temporal. These terms describe anatomical regions, but the cortex is also divided in terms of function. These functional areas include motor cortex (which controls movement), sensory cortex (which receives information from the senses), and association cortex (which integrates information). Also illustrated are Wernicke's area, which is involved in the interpretation of speech, and Broca's area, a region vital to the production of speech. (These two areas are only found on the left side of the cortex.)

in information from the skin about touch, pain, and temperature, whereas cells in the occipital lobe receive visual information from the thalamus to analyze what we see. Stimuli from the ears reach cells in the temporal lobe near areas of cortex that are involved in understanding language.

In the *somatosensory cortex,* skin sensations from neighboring parts of the body are represented in neighboring parts of cortex, as Figure 3.16 (p. 100) illustrates. It is as if the outline of a tiny person, dangling upside down, determined the location of the sensory and motor areas. This pattern is called the *homunculus,* which means "little man."

The motor cortex follows the same pattern. Neurons in specific areas of the **motor cortex** initiate voluntary movements in specific parts of the body, some controlling movement of the hand, others stimulating movement of the foot, the knee, the head, and so on. The motor cortex is arranged in a way that mirrors the somatosensory cortex. For example, as you can see in Figure 3.16, the parts of the motor cortex that control the hands are near parts of the sensory cortex that receive sensory information from the hands.

Association cortex   Parts of the cerebral cortex that are not directly involved with receiving specific sensory information or initiating movement are called **association cortex.** The term *association* is appropriate because these areas receive information from more than one sense or combine sensory and motor information. These are the areas that perform such complex cognitive tasks as associating words with images and other abstract thinking.

As you might expect, association areas form a large part of the cerebral cortex in human beings. This is one reason why damage to association areas can create severe deficits in all kinds of mental abilities. One of the most devastating, called *aphasia,* involves difficulty in producing or understanding speech.

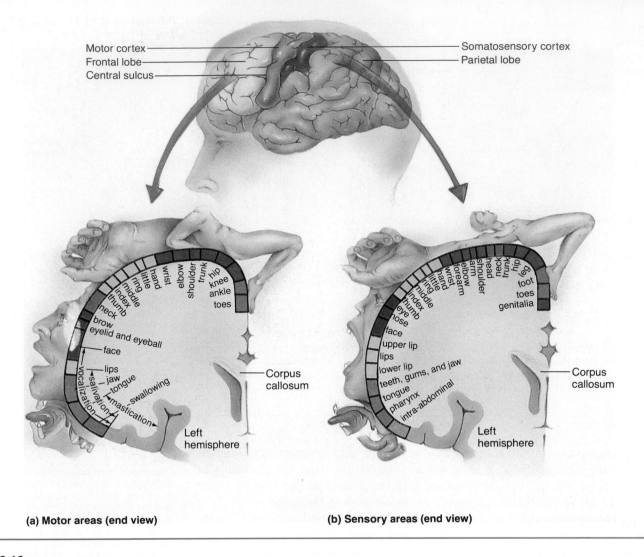

(a) Motor areas (end view)   (b) Sensory areas (end view)

Figure 3.16
Motor and Somatosensory Cortex
The areas of cortex that move parts of the body (motor cortex) and receive sensory input from body parts (somatosensory cortex) occupy neighboring regions on each side of the central sulcus. These regions appear in both hemispheres; here we show only those on the left side, looking from the back of the brain toward the front. The cross-sections also show how areas controlling movement of neighboring parts of the body, like the foot and leg, occupy neighboring parts of motor cortex. Areas receiving input from neighboring body parts, like the lips and tongue, are near one another in the sensory cortex.
(Reprinted with permission of Macmillan Publishing Company from *The Cerebral Cortex of Man* by Wilder Penfield and Theodore Rasmussen. Copyright © 1950 by Macmillan Publishing Company, renewed 1978 by Theodore Rasmussen.)

Damage to association cortex in the frontal lobe near motor areas that control facial muscles can cause problems in the production of speech. This part of the cortex on the left side of the brain is called *Broca's area* (see Figure 3.15). It was named after Paul Broca, who in the 1860s described the speech difficulties that result from damage to the region. Damage to Broca's area causes the mental organization of speech to suffer. A person can still sing with ease but has great difficulty speaking, and what the person says is often grammatically incorrect. Each word comes slowly. One patient who was asked about a dental appointment said haltingly, "Yes . . . Monday . . . Dad and Dick . . . Wednesday 9 o'clock . . . 10 o'clock . . . doctors . . . and . . . teeth" (Geschwind, 1979). The ideas—dentists and teeth—are right, but the fluency is gone.

Damage to a different association area can leave fluency intact but disrupt the ability to understand the meaning of words. *Wernicke's area*, described in the 1870s by Carl Wernicke, is also on the left side, in the temporal lobe, near the primary receiving area in the cortex for hearing, as Figure 3.15 shows. Wernicke's area is involved in the interpretation of speech and, because it also receives input from the visual cortex, is also involved in interpreting written words. Damage to Wernicke's area produces complicated symptoms. A person with Wernicke's aphasia may have difficulty comprehending speech and may also produce speech that is fluent but difficult to comprehend. For example, a patient asked to describe a picture of two boys stealing cookies behind a woman's back said, "Mother is away here working her work to get her better, but when she's looking the two boys looking in the other part. She's working another time" (Geschwind, 1979).

Based on the symptoms of damage to brain areas, combined with anatomical evidence of connections among these areas, Wernicke and, later, Norman Geschwind proposed a model of how language is understood and produced. According to this model, language information reaches Wernicke's area from either the auditory cortex for spoken language or from the visual cortex for written language. In Wernicke's area, the words are interpreted and the structure of a verbal response is formed. The output from Wernicke's area goes to Broca's area, where a detailed program for vocalization is formed. This program is relayed to adjacent areas of the motor cortex to produce speech. The neural structures involved in transforming the output into writing are not known.

HIGHLIGHT

Recovery from Brain Damage

Analysis of the consequences of brain damage has greatly increased understanding of how the brain works, but it is often a study of tragedy. There are heroic recoveries from brain damage, but more often the victim of a stroke or other damage is permanently enfeebled in some way. Why is recovery so rare and difficult? If a damaged arm heals itself, why doesn't a damaged brain?

There are several reasons. First, the brain of an adult animal cannot make new neural cells. During development, brain cells divide and multiply as other cells do, but in maturity the brain cells stop dividing and cannot produce more cells in response to injury. *Glial cells,* which provide support for neurons, continue to divide; neurons do not. A second problem arises because the brain's axons and dendrites form a dense network, with interwoven fibers making connections near and far. Even if new neurons could be grown, their axons and dendrites would have to reestablish all their former communication links. This is almost impossible, because glial cells "clean up" after brain damage, not only by consuming injured neurons, but also by forming a barrier to new connections.

Nevertheless, the brain does try to heal itself. Undamaged tissue tries to take over for lost tissue, partly by changing its function and partly by sprouting new axons and dendrites to make new connections. For example, if Broca's area is damaged, unaffected nearby areas can take on some language functions, and some speech ability can be regained. Unfortunately, these compensatory changes rarely result in total restoration of lost functions.

Nerves in the peripheral nervous system are much better at reestablishing communication links. This is so because the glial cells of the peripheral nervous system (called *Schwann cells*) form "tunnels" that guide the growth of the axons. Scientists are now trying to devise ways of guiding newly sprouted axons in the central nervous system. There are also growth factors that help stimulate and guide the growth of axons, and there is a great deal of interest in learning how they work.

Another approach to improving the brain's ability to regain lost functions is to replace lost tissue with tissue transplanted from another brain. So far, scientists have made amazing progress in animal studies, by transplanting a portion of tissue from a still-developing fetal brain into the brain of an adult animal. If the receiving animal does not reject the graft, the graft will send axons out into the brain and make some functional connections. A variety of behavioral deficits from brain damage have been reversed by brain grafts in experimental animals. For example, a rat with damage to its hippocampus has difficulty learning new tasks; after receiving a graft of septal tissue from a fetal rat (septal tissue normally sends fibers to the hippocampus), the adult rat's learning ability improved (Low et al., 1982). An animal model of Parkinson's disease suggests that damage to certain cells of the substantia nigra results in impaired movement systems. Grafting substantia nigra tissue from a fetal animal into a brain-damaged adult resulted in normal movement abilities (Freed, 1983).

Yet another prospect is that the brain might be stimulated to reestablish its ability to produce new neurons. Recently, scientists studying the brains of birds discovered a part of the brain where cell division does take place in the adult (Nottebohm, 1985). The male canary learns a new repertoire of songs every year and forgets many of the songs at the end of the breeding season. Each year, a part of the brain related to the learning of songs actually grows by the process of cell division. Later the cells die, and the cycle repeats. Fernando Nottebohm, whose lab made the discovery, has suggested that future research be aimed at discovering whether the formation of new neurons might be possible in adult humans and, if not, why not.

Even if new neurons did form, however, they would still be faced with the problem mentioned earlier: namely, setting up the correct lines of communication with other, preexisting neurons. Thus, this approach would have to be combined with techniques that allow new connections to be formed.

All of these approaches to helping the brain to recover from damage form an exciting research area, and there are encouraging signs that we may someday be able to help the brain to heal itself. ■

The Divided Brain in a Unified Self

A striking idea emerged from observations of people with brain damage. Damage to limited areas of the left hemisphere causes some loss of the ability to use or comprehend language; damage to corresponding parts of the right hemisphere usually does not. Perhaps, then, the right and left halves of the brain serve different functions.

This is not an entirely new concept. It had long been understood, for example, that most pathways to sensory organs or muscles cross over as they enter or leave the brain. As a result, the left hemisphere receives information from and controls movements of the right side of the body, whereas the right hemisphere receives input from and controls the left side of the body. But these functions, although divided, are performed by both sides of the brain. By the nineteenth century, it was apparent that language centers, such as Broca's area and Wernicke's area, are almost exclusively on the left side of the brain. This suggested that one hemisphere is specialized for a function with which the other side seems not to be involved at all. During the 1960s, studies by Roger Sperry, Michael Gazzaniga, and their colleagues firmly established that there are indeed some differences between the hemispheres.

Split-brain studies   The people Sperry studied had such severe epilepsy that their seizures began in one hemisphere, then spread to engulf the whole brain. As a last resort, the two hemispheres in these people were isolated from each other by an operation that severed the **corpus callosum,** a massive bundle of more than a million fibers that connects the two hemispheres (see Figure 3.17).

Using a special apparatus, the researchers presented visual images to only *one* side of these patients' split brains and found that severing the tie between the hemispheres had dramatically affected the way these people were able to

Corpus
callosum

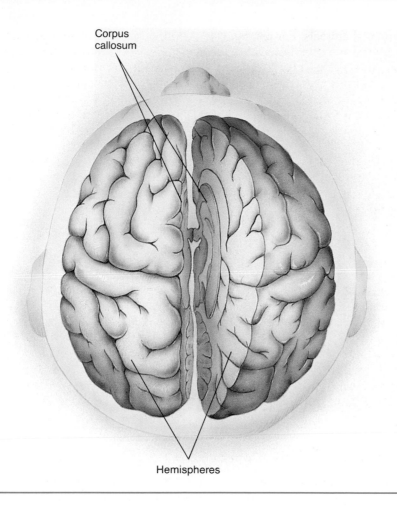

Hemispheres

Figure 3.17
The Brain's Left and Right Hemispheres
*Joined by a core bundle of nerve fibers
known as the corpus callosum, the two cerebral hemispheres look nearly the same but
perform somewhat different tasks. For one
thing, the left hemisphere receives sensory
input from and controls movement on the
right side of the body. The right hemisphere
senses and controls the left side of the
body.*

think and deal with the world. For example, when the image of a spoon was presented to the left, or language-oriented, side of patient NG's brain, she could say what the spoon was. But she could not describe the spoon in words when it was presented to the right side of her brain. Her right hemisphere knew what the object was, however. Using her left hand (controlled by the right hemisphere), NG could pick out the spoon from a group of other objects by its shape. When asked what she had just grasped, she replied, "A pencil." In other tests, the image of a nude woman was presented to NG's right hemisphere. The right hemisphere recognized the picture (NG blushed and giggled), but the patient could not describe it because the left (language) half of her brain did not see it (Sperry, 1968).

The language specializations of the left hemisphere are sometimes described as resulting in uniquely human capabilities that other animals do not possess. There are controversies about whether nonhuman animals have language abilities, but it is worth noting that monkeys' left hemispheres are specialized to recognize sounds made by other monkeys (Heffner & Heffner, 1984). Damage to the left temporal lobe results in a loss of the ability to distinguish different vocal noises, coos, made by other monkeys, but damage to the right temporal cortex has no effect on this ability. Therefore, even though primates may not be capable of language as such, it does appear they have an analog to Wernicke's area in humans.

Though the right hemisphere has no control over spoken language in most people, it does have some language ability. A split-brain patient's right hemisphere can guide the left hand in spelling out words with Scrabble tiles

Figure 3.18
Lateralization of the Cerebral Hemispheres: Evidence from PET Scans
These PET scans show overhead views of a section of a person's brain that was receiving different kinds of stimulation. At the upper left, the subject was resting, with eyes open and ears plugged. Note that the greatest brain activity, as indicated by the brighter color, is in the visual cortex, which is receiving input from the eyes. As shown at the lower left, when the subject listened to spoken language, the left (more language oriented) side of the brain, especially the auditory cortex in the temporal lobe, became more active, but the right temporal lobe did not; the visual and frontal areas were also active. However, when listening to music (lower right), there is intense activity in the right temporal lobe, but little in the left. When the subject heard both words and music, temporal cortex on both sides of the brain became activated. Here is visual evidence of the involvement of each side of the brain in processing different kinds of information.

(Courtesy of Drs. J. C. Mazziotta and M. E. Phelps, UCLA School of Medicine. Reprinted from *Neurology* with permission, Vol. 32, No. 9, pp. 921–937, September 1982. Copyright 1982 by Harcourt Brace Jovanovich, Inc.)

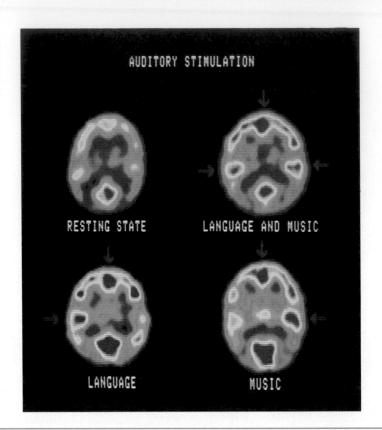

(Gazzaniga & LeDoux, 1978). Communicating in this way, the right hemisphere has revealed that it has self-awareness and normal learning abilities. In fact, the right hemisphere is superior to the left on tasks dealing with spatial relations, especially drawing three-dimensional shapes. The right hemisphere is also much better than the left at recognizing human faces.

Lateralization of normal brains   Sperry concluded from his studies that each hemisphere in the split-brain patient has its own "private sensations, perceptions, thought, and ideas all of which are cut off from the corresponding experiences in the opposite hemisphere. . . . In many respects each disconnected hemisphere appears to have a separate mind of its own" (Sperry, 1974). But when the hemispheres are *not* disconnected, are their functions different? Are certain functions, such as mathematical reasoning or language skills, **lateralized,** or performed more efficiently by one hemisphere than by the other?

To find out, researchers have presented images to just one hemisphere of people with normal brains and then measured lateralization by assessing how fast they could analyze information. If information is presented to one side of the brain and that side is specialized to analyze that type of information, a subject's responses will be faster than if the information must first be transferred to the other hemisphere for analysis. These studies have confirmed that the left hemisphere has better logical and language abilities than the right, whereas the right hemisphere has better spatial, artistic, and musical abilities (Springer & Deutsch, 1985). PET scans of normal people receiving varying kinds of auditory stimulation also demonstrate these asymmetries of function (see Figure 3.18).

The precise nature and degree of lateralization vary quite a bit among individuals. For example, among about a third of left-handed people, either the right hemisphere or both hemispheres control language functions (Springer

& Deutsch, 1985). Only about 5 percent of right-handed people have language controlled by the right hemisphere. Surprisingly, left-handed people are also more likely to be brilliant mathematicians, be nearsighted, suffer allergies, stutter, and have reading difficulties.

Although the two hemispheres are somewhat specialized, the differences between them should not be exaggerated. People are not left-brained or right-brained in the same way that they are left- or right-handed. Normally the corpus callosum integrates the functions of the two hemispheres so that people are not aware of their "two brains." The hemispheres work so closely together, and each makes up so well for whatever lack of ability the other may have, that people are normally unaware that their brains are made up of two partially independent, somewhat specialized halves. In fact, even if the activity of one hemisphere is dominant, the effect is usually detectable only as differences in certain mental abilities or cognitive styles. For example, a person with a dominant right hemisphere may lean toward musical rather than foreign language studies. As we will see in later chapters, lateralization may also produce effects on the expression and suppression of emotion.

THE CHEMISTRY OF PSYCHOLOGY

So far, we have seen that the cells of the nervous system communicate by releasing neurotransmitters at their synapses. And we have outlined some of the basic structures of the nervous system and their functions. Now we need to pull these topics together, by examining which neurotransmitters occur in these structures and describing how these chemicals affect our behavior and mental processes.

Recall that different sets of neurons use different neurotransmitters. A group of neurons that communicates using the same neurotransmitter is called a **neurotransmitter system.** Usually the suffix *-ergic* is added to the name of a neurotransmitter to make it an adjective. Thus, for example, a group of neurons using the chemical dopamine as a neurotransmitter is called a *dopaminergic system.*

Neurotransmitters became interesting to biological psychologists when it became apparent that certain neurotransmitter systems might be related to particular behaviors and disorders. There is good evidence, for example, that one neurotransmitter system plays a role in some types of senility, whereas another system has been tied to some types of depression. Keep in mind, though, that a neurotransmitter can fit into more than one type of receptor in different parts of the brain or even in different parts of the same cell. As a result, a neurotransmitter can serve multiple functions, sometimes stimulating the firing of neurons in one area of the brain while at the same time inhibiting firing in another.

Brain research suggests that the left cerebral hemisphere tends to be dominant in verbal skills such as writing, while the right hemisphere tends to dominate in artistic or other spatial skills. However, the hemispheres work together so closely that people are normally unaware of these specializations. Shown above are artist Raymond Saunders and writer Margaret Atwood.

Five Neurotransmitters

At least fifty chemicals are known to act as neurotransmitters, and new ones are being discovered every year. Five of the most important and most intensely studied are acetylcholine, norepinephrine, serotonin, dopamine, and GABA.

Acetylcholine   The first compound to be established as a neurotransmitter was **acetylcholine** (pronounced "a-set-ill-coal-ene"). Neurons that communicate by using acetylcholine are called *cholinergic.* These neurons occur in both the peripheral and the central nervous systems. At the junctions of neurons and muscles, cholinergic neurons control the contraction of muscles. In the brain, cholinergic neurons are especially plentiful in the striatum (part of the forebrain), where they occur in circuits that are important for movement. Axons of cholinergic neurons also make up major pathways in the limbic system and other areas of the cerebrum that are involved in memory (Bartus et al., 1982; see Figure 3.19).

Indeed, cholinergic neurons may hold the key to Alzheimer's disease, a severe brain disorder which causes a progressive and devastating loss of memory and degeneration of personality. Some estimates suggest that as many as 5 percent of people over the age of sixty-five have Alzheimer's disease (Coyle, Price & DeLong, 1983). The problem seems to stem from a nearly complete loss of cholinergic neurons from a nucleus in the basal forebrain that sends fibers to the cerebral cortex (Whitehouse et al., 1983). Activating cholinergic neurons, usually with drugs that act as acetylcholine would, can facilitate memory processes somewhat. At present there is no effective way to reverse the effects of Alzheimer's disease, but research is currently active.

Norepinephrine   Like acetylcholine, **norepinephrine** occurs in both the central and the peripheral nervous systems. Collections of neurons that use norepinephrine or its close relative *epinephrine* are called *adrenergic* systems. The name makes sense because norepinephrine is also called *noradrenaline*, and epinephrine is also known as *adrenaline*. Approximately half of the norepinephrine in the brain is contained in cells located in the *locus coeruleus* ("blue spot") near the reticular formation in the hindbrain (see Figure 3.13). There are only about 3,000 cells in the locus coeruleus, but each sends out an axon that branches so extensively that it makes contact with as many as 100,000 other cells (Moore & Bloom, 1979; Swanson, 1976).

Because adrenergic systems cover a lot of territory, it is logical that norepinephrine shapes several broad categories of behavior. Indeed, there is good evidence that norepinephrine is involved in the appearance of wakefulness and sleep, in the process of learning, and in the regulation of mood, including depression and elation. For example, compared with others, depressed people have lower levels of norepinephrine or its metabolites (Bunney, Goodwin & Murphy, 1972; Crow et al., 1984), but researchers have not yet determined whether these low levels are a cause or an effect of depression.

Serotonin   The neurotransmitter **serotonin** is similar to norepinephrine in several ways: (1) most of the cells that use it as a neurotransmitter occur in a restricted region along the midline of the hindbrain; (2) serotonergic axons send branches throughout the forebrain, including the hypothalamus, the

Figure 3.19
Examples of Neurotransmitter Pathways
Neurons that release a certain neurotransmitter may be concentrated in one particular region (indicated by dots) and send fibers into other regions, to which they communicate across synapses (arrows). Examples are shown here for (a) acetylcholine, (b) norepinephrine, (c) serotonin, and (d) dopamine.

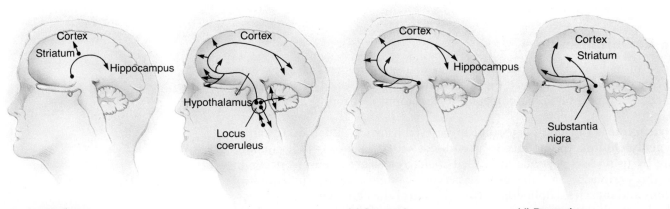

(a) **Acetylcholine**   (b) **Norepinephrine**   (c) **Serotonin**   (d) **Dopamine**

Loss of neurons that use the neurotransmitter acetylcholine appears to be the cause of Alzheimer's disease, a brain disorder in which lively, active people gradually become withdrawn, insecure, and often hostile as their ability to work or perform routine tasks diminishes and their need for supervision increases.

hippocampus, and the cerebral cortex; and (3) serotonin affects sleep and moods. Serotonin is also active in the neural circuits that descend from the brain to help block pain sensations.

Serotonin differs from norepinephrine, however, in that one of the substances from which it is made, tryptophan, can be used by the brain directly from the food a person eats. This is one way in which dietary factors may affect mood or drowsiness. For example, compared with a high-protein meal, a meal high in carbohydrates produces increased levels of serotonin and, at least in women, drowsiness. In men, the reported mood change is "calmness" (Spring et al., 1982–1983).

Dopamine The neurons that use **dopamine** as a neurotransmitter are more restricted than those that use norepinephrine or serotonin, and their axons do not branch as extensively. The functions of dopaminergic neurons are also more restricted.

Some neurons that release dopamine are involved in movement; their degeneration is the cause of *Parkinson's disease,* which produces shakiness and extreme difficulty in initiating movements. Like Alzheimer's disease, Parkinson's is most common in elderly people. The neurons that degenerate have their cell bodies in the substantia nigra of the midbrain; their axons travel in a very organized way to the striatum, by way of the *nigrostriatal pathway.* Other dopaminergic systems send axons from the midbrain to the forebrain, including the cerebral cortex. Malfunctioning of these dopaminergic neurons may be responsible for *schizophrenia,* a psychological disorder in which there are severe distortions in perception, movement, emotional expression, and thought. People diagnosed as schizophrenic may see or hear imaginary things and may act or think very strangely.

GABA The major inhibitory neurotransmittor is **GABA,** which stands for "gamma-amino butyric acid." GABA reduces the likelihood that the postsynaptic neuron will fire an action potential. It is used by neurons in widespread regions of the brain.

For example, when you fall asleep, neurons that use GABA deserve part of the credit. Dysfunctions in GABA systems may be related to the appearance of severe anxiety. In fact, GABA has been implicated in a variety of behavioral disorders, including Huntington's disease and epilepsy. *Huntington's disease* is an inherited disorder that results in the loss of many GABA-activated neurons in the striatum. Normally these GABA systems inhibit dopamine systems. When they are lost in Huntington's disease, the dopamine systems may run wild, with effects that are in some ways the opposite of those of Parkinson's disease. Instead of facing an inability to begin movements, the victim is plagued by uncontrollable movement of the arms and legs, along with a progressive loss of cognitive abilities. *Epilepsy* is a brain disorder that produces intense repetitive electrical discharges, known as *seizures,* along with convulsive movements. Repeated or sustained seizures can result in permanent brain damage; fortunately, drug treatments can reduce their frequency or severity. Because epilepsy results from wildly spreading excitation through large populations of neurons, it is logical that a deficiency of GABA, the major inhibitory neurotransmitter, could be part of the problem.

Drugs, Neurotransmitters, and Behavior

Like naturally occurring neurotransmitters, **psychoactive drugs** are chemicals that may affect behavior, mental processes, and conscious experience. Included among these drugs are those, like cocaine, that are used mainly for pleasure or escape and those that are used to treat mental disorders. The study of psychoactive drugs and their effects is called **psychopharmacology.**

Most psychoactive drugs act by altering neurotransmission in at least one of four ways: (1) by *altering the amount* of neurotransmitter released by a neuron; (2) by *mimicking* the neurotransmitter at the receptor site; (3) by *blocking* receptors for certain neurotransmitters; or (4) by *blocking reuptake* of the neurotransmitter from the synapse. Because a single drug often produces more than one of these effects, it can be difficult to determine how the drug creates some observed result. We will consider each of these mechanisms.

Altering the amount of neurotransmitter released The treatment for Parkinson's disease illustrates how a drug may act by altering the amount of neutrotransmitter available to be released. Recall that Parkinson's disease involves the death of many dopamine cells in the nigrostriatal system, making movement very difficult. The search for a drug to combat the disease began with the assumption that, if the amount of dopamine in the remaining nigrostriatal neurons could be increased, those neurons might partially compensate for the lost cells. To devise a way of increasing the amount of dopamine available, researchers used the knowledge that dopamine is made in the brain from a compound called *L-dopa;* once L-dopa is in the brain, dopaminergic neurons take it up and convert it to dopamine.

Giving L-dopa to victims of Parkinson's disease turned out to be an effective treatment, but for some unknown reason, the treatment is effective only for several years. Something about the dopaminergic system adjusts, so that L-dopa no longer relieves Parkinsonian symptoms. Because this adjustment is related to the length of treatment, physicians try to delay using L-dopa for as long as possible.

Other drugs cause more neurotransmitter to be released from the presynaptic endings. For example, the stimulant amphetamine releases such neurotransmitters as norepinephrine and dopamine, which normally activate large parts of the brain. This creates signals to the affected neurons that are similar to those that would occur if rapidly firing neurons were flooding the synapses with a neurotransmitter. Like L-dopa, amphetamine changes the neurotransmitter system if the drug is used regularly. With amphetamine, one result is the appearance of mental disturbances similar to one type of schizophrenia.

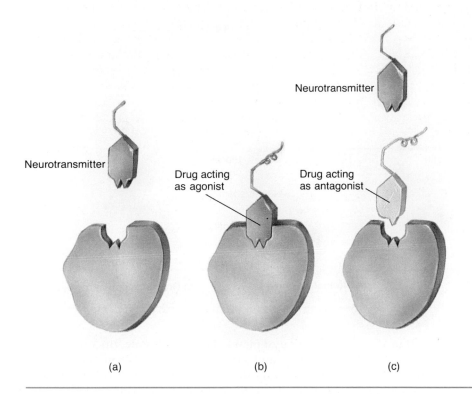

Neurotransmitter

Neurotransmitter

Drug acting
as agonist

Drug acting
as antagonist

(a)   (b)   (c)

Figure 3.20
Agonists and Antagonists
(a) A molecule of neurotransmitter approaches a receptor on a nerve cell's dendrites. Note that it will fit into the receptor and stimulate it. (b) If a drug molecule or other substance is similar enough to the neurotransmitter that normally stimulates the receptor, it will act as an agonist, changing the receptor's membrane potential in the same way the neurotransmitter would. (c) An antagonist, a drug molecule that is similar enough to occupy a receptor site, but not similar enough to stimulate it. The drug blocks the natural neurotransmitter from reaching and acting on the receptor. Certain snake venoms, for example, paralyze prey by blocking acetylcholine receptors in the peripheral nervous system that normally produce muscle movement.

Mimicking neurotransmitters If a molecule is very similar to a certain neurotransmitter, it may fool that transmitter's receptors and occupy them itself. Many drugs, called **agonists,** mimic neurotransmitters in this way, fitting snugly into the receptors and changing a cell's membrane potential just as the neurotransmitter would (see Figure 3.20). For example, *ephedrine* is a drug that mimics norepinephrine and therefore has arousing properties. It is used clinically to treat *narcolepsy,* a disease in which a person falls asleep abruptly and unpredictably during the day (Goodman, Goodman & Gilman, 1980). The drugs mentioned earlier that may improve memory in Alzheimer's disease by acting like acetylcholine are also agonists.

Blocking receptors Some drugs are similar enough to a neurotransmitter to occupy its receptor sites on nerve cells, but not similar enough to fit snugly and change those cells' membrane potential. These drugs are called **antagonists** (see Figure 3.20). As long as they are attached to receptors, they compete with and block neurotransmitters from occupying and acting on the receptors.

One prominent application of antagonists is in the treatment of schizophrenia. No one has a "cure" for schizophrenia, but the drugs that partially relieve its symptoms have one feature in common: they are all antagonists that occupy dopamine receptors and prevent dopamine from producing its normal effects. Dopamine antagonists may relieve schizophrenic symptoms by blocking dopaminergic activity in neurons that send axons to the frontal lobes of the cerebral cortex. There, it is hypothesized, excess dopamine may disrupt thought, producing schizophrenic symptoms.

Unfortunately, the drugs that relieve these symptoms also prevent dopamine from reaching its receptors in other parts of the brain. As noted earlier, too little dopamine in the nigrostriatal tract produces inability to initiate certain movements and other symptoms resembling those of Parkinson's disease. Furthermore, as the brain adapts to prolonged use of dopamine-blocking drugs, even more serious, often irreversible, movement disorders

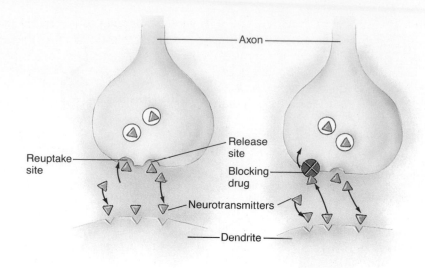

Figure 3.21
Drug Effects on Reuptake
Neurotransmitters normally remain in the synapse for only a short time; most are reabsorbed by the axons that secreted them (a). However, drugs like cocaine, which block the sites on the axon where this reuptake takes place (b), can slow or temporarily stop the process, thereby intensifying the effects of the neurotransmitter.

(a) Normal reuptake   **(b) Drug blocking reuptake**

may appear. For example, *tardive dyskinesia* causes grotesque, uncontrollable, repetitive movements of the body and face. In Chapter 16, on therapy, we will discuss the difficulties of weighing these problems against the benefits of using dopamine-antagonist drugs in the treatment of mental disorders.

Blocking reuptake   Many drugs interfere with the removal, or reuptake, of a neurotransmitter from synapses. The result is that the concentration of neurotransmitter remaining in a synapse increases, and the normal actions of the neurotransmitter are enhanced (see Figure 3.21). Many drugs that are used to treat depression, for example, seem to work by blocking the reuptake of norepinephrine and serotonin, thus making more of these chemicals available and in turn improving mood. The mechanism by which these drugs relieve depression is still not entirely clear, however, because some drugs that block the removal of norepinephrine do not combat depression. Cocaine, for example, blocks the removal of norepinephrine, increases arousal, and lifts one's mood, but it does not relieve severe depression.

Other drugs block the deactivation of acetylcholine in synapses between neurons and at the junctions of neurons and muscles. The result is excessive contraction of all muscles, leading to death. Insecticides that are vital to modern agriculture, for example, act by blocking the removal of acetylcholine. Because nerve gas also works in this way, military agencies have been very interested in cholinergic neurochemistry.

HIGHLIGHT

**Opiates,
Endorphins, and
the Placebo
Effect**

The study of psychopharmacology has led not only to the development of drugs useful in treating brain disorders, but also to a better understanding of how the normal brain operates. For one thing, the analysis of drug action has led to the discovery of some new neurotransmitters (Snyder & Childers, 1979).

Endorphins are one important example. They were discovered in the 1970s by scientists who were interested in how *opiates,* such as morphine and heroin, affect the brain. These powerful drugs are derived from poppy flowers and can relieve pain, produce euphoria, and in high doses, bring on sleep. After marking morphine with a radioactive substance, researchers traced where it became concentrated in the brain. They found that opiates became bound to nerve cell receptors that were not associated with any then-known neurotransmitter. Since it was extremely unlikely that the brain had developed opiate receptors just in case a person might want to use morphine or heroin, researchers reasoned that the body must contain a substance that is similar to opiates and that its receptors can be "fooled" by them.

This hypothesis led to the search for a naturally occurring, or endogenous, morphine, which was called *endorphin* for short. It turned out that there were, not one, but many such natural-opiate compounds. Thus the term **endorphin** actually refers to any neurotransmitter that can bind to the same receptors that opiates bind to and that produces the same behavioral effects. As we will describe in Chapter 4, on sensation, neurons in several parts of the brain use endorphins, including pathways that adjust how much pain gets to the brain.

More was learned about how endorphins work after researchers developed a substance that can block the actions of both opiates and endorphins. This antagonist is called *naloxone*. It binds to opiate receptors, where its blocking action has proved valuable in saving the lives of people who have taken overdoses of heroin. It has also revealed some fascinating clues to the puzzling phenomenon called the *placebo effect*. As noted in Chapter 1, a placebo is a substance or treatment that contains no active ingredient but creates an effect because people receiving the placebo expect the effect to occur. For example, one-third of those who received a placebo could tolerate as much electrical current applied to a tooth before they felt any pain as people who were given painkilling morphine. This placebo effect had been found before. However, the truly remarkable result occurred when the people were given naloxone. Those who were less sensitive to pain after receiving a placebo became more sensitive when they were given both the placebo and naloxone (Levine, Gordon & Fields, 1979). Naloxone had reversed the placebo effect.

Thus, people's *belief* that they are getting an effective drug may activate the endorphin system, releasing the body's own painkillers; when naloxone blocks the endogenous opiates, no relief occurs. If supported by further research, this hypothesis would have important implications for helping people to cope with pain and other problems without drugs. It has already stimulated research on the mechanism by which expectations might stimulate the endorphin system. ◣

ENDOCRINE SYSTEMS

Neurons are not the only cells that can communicate with one another in ways that affect behavior and mental processes. Another class of cells that can do this is found in **endocrine systems.** The cells in these systems group together in special organs, called *glands,* which communicate, much as neurons do, by secreting chemicals. In this case, the chemicals are called **hormones.** Obviously, hormones are similar to neurotransmitters. In fact, some chemicals, such as adrenaline, act both as hormones and as neurotransmitters. But, whereas neurons secrete neurotransmitters into synapses, glands put their chemicals into the bloodstream, which carries them throughout the body. In this way, glands can stimulate remote cells to which they have no direct connection. Thus, neural communication is rather like the telephone, through which information is given out over wires to particular people. Endocrine communication is more like a newspaper, which circulates information to a large number of people.

Figure 3.22 (p. 112) shows the location and functions of some of the major endocrine organs. Hormones from these organs stimulate cells in both

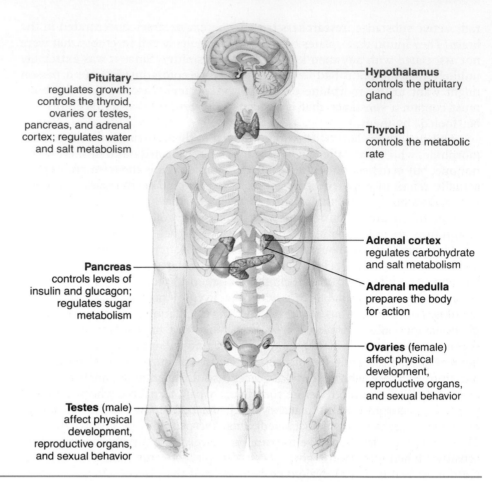

Pituitary
regulates growth; controls the thyroid, ovaries or testes, pancreas, and adrenal cortex; regulates water and salt metabolism

Hypothalamus
controls the pituitary gland

Thyroid
controls the metabolic rate

Pancreas
controls levels of insulin and glucagon; regulates sugar metabolism

Adrenal cortex
regulates carbohydrate and salt metabolism

Adrenal medulla
prepares the body for action

Ovaries (female)
affect physical development, reproductive organs, and sexual behavior

Testes (male)
affect physical development, reproductive organs, and sexual behavior

Figure 3.22
Some Major Glands of the Endocrine System
Each of the glands shown releases its hormones into the bloodstream. Even the hypothalamus, a part of the brain, regulates the adjacent pituitary gland by secreting hormones. Each hormone acts on many organs, including the brain, producing coordinated effects (such as the fight-or-flight syndrome) throughout the body.

the peripheral and the central nervous systems. Usually they affect the growth and metabolism of various tissues and produce very general changes in behavior and mental processes. Some hormones affect general energy levels, arousal, and learning. Others regulate such basic behaviors as hunger and eating, thirst, aggression, and sexual behavior. The secretion of almost all hormones is affected by psychological processes, especially stress.

Just as neurotransmitters have their own receptors, there are *target tissues,* or *target organs,* whose cells have receptors that respond to particular hormones. The target organs for a hormone typically form a coordinated system. For example, when the sex hormones estrogen and progesterone begin to be secreted by a woman's ovaries, they travel through the bloodstream, activating her reproductive system. They cause the uterus to grow in preparation for nurturing an embryo; they enlarge the breasts to prepare them for their feeding function; and at the same time, they stimulate the brain and pituitary gland to cause a mature egg to be released for fertilization.

The action of adrenal hormones provides another example of a coordinated endocrine system. When the brain interprets a situation as threatening, it causes the adrenal glands to release adrenaline into the bloodstream. This produces a coordinated set of responses called the **fight-or-flight syndrome,** which prepares the animal or person for action in response to danger: the heart beats faster, the liver releases glucose into the bloodstream, and the organism is generally placed in a state of high arousal.

The fight-or-flight syndrome illustrates the fact that, like so many other systems we have described, endocrine systems are set up in feedback loops, which both are controlled by and act on the brain. Actually, a chain of several hormones is usually involved, each of which causes the secretion of another hormone. The chain begins with the brain, which, as the body's executive, is active in both the nervous system and the endocrine system. For instance, the brain controls the pituitary gland by releasing hormones from the hypothalamus into the bloodstream. The pituitary secretes many different hormones, some of which stimulate other glands to secrete their hormones. These hormones then act on cells in the body, as well as feed back to the brain and pituitary. As with a thermostat and furnace, this feedback may cause the brain and pituitary to provide more stimulation or to reduce the stimulation. If the output of the final gland falls below some level, feedback causes the brain and pituitary to stimulate increased secretion. This system tends to keep the output of hormones within a certain range.

FUTURE DIRECTIONS

In trying to understand behavior and mental processes, some psychologists have paid little attention to biological factors, preferring to look at humans and animals as "black boxes" that receive stimuli from the outside world and generate responses. For them, the study of the biological and mental processes that go on inside the box is not of great concern. However, the desire to better understand these processes drives much current psychological research.

Today, knowledge of these biological systems is increasing at an explosive rate. Scientists are far from understanding the details of brain functions and how those functions translate into what people experience as the mind, but impressive progress is being made. People from a wide variety of scientific disciplines are applying their techniques to understanding the nervous system. Medical researchers, anatomists, biochemists, physiologists, and psychologists are all beginning to see themselves as neuroscientists.

Neuroscience is now in an era in which technical breakthroughs have allowed a tremendous amount of information to be gathered in a short time. Radioactive compounds have been used only in the last couple of decades; PET scans have been in use only for a few years. Other techniques, such as those of molecular biology, are even more recent. Advances in computer technology greatly aid all of these approaches to understanding the biological bases of behavior, because they allow scientists to gather more and more details of basic biological processes.

Specific biological factors in such disease processes as Alzheimer's disease and schizophrenia will be found and will lead to improved treatment and possibly even prevention. Genetic markers will be identified that will help determine who might be susceptible to certain kinds of disorders, such as alcoholism, making it possible to offer help long before the problem becomes extreme. Progress will be made in reversing some degenerative diseases, perhaps by aiding the body's own restorative powers. If scientists succeed in transplanting brain tissue, so that damaged tissue can be replaced and lost functions regained, they will face an obvious ethical and practical dilemma: Who gives up the brain tissue to be transplanted? One possibility is to use tissue from spontaneously or medically aborted fetuses, but this would not be acceptable to some people. Another alternative is a cross-species transplant. Scientists have already successfully transplanted tissue from a mouse into a rat (Bjorklund et al., 1982).

In the case of Parkinson's disease, a person can be both donor and recipient of transplanted tissue. This is because cells of the adrenal gland, which have neuronlike properties, become neurons when placed in the brain. Since a person can live with just one adrenal gland, the other adrenal gland can be grafted into the caudate nucleus. This procedure has been done in humans

BIOLOGICAL BASES OF BEHAVIOR AND HUMAN DEVELOPMENT

How does the brain change throughout life, and how do these biological changes affect people?

We have seen in this chapter how certain pathological changes in the brain produce severe disorders, such as Parkinsonism and Alzheimer's disease. But even in the absence of disease, the brain changes throughout life. What are these changes, and what are their effects? How are they related to developments in sensory and motor capabilities, in personality, in mental ability, and in other characteristics that we described in Chapter 2?

PET scans are one technique that researchers have used to begin to answer these questions. They have uncovered some interesting correlations between changes in neural activity and the behavior of human newborns and young infants. Among newborns, activity is relatively high in the thalamus but low in the striatum. This pattern may be related to the way newborns move: they make non-purposeful, sweeping movements of the arms and legs, much like patients with Huntington's disease, who have a hyperactive thalamus and a degenerated striatum (Chugani & Phelps, 1986). During the second and third months of life, activity increases in many cortical regions, a change that correlates with the loss of subcortically controlled reflexes, such as the grasping reflex. When infants are around eight or nine months old, PET scans show increased activity in the frontal cortex, a development that correlates

well with the apparent beginnings of cognitive activity in infants (Chugani & Phelps, 1986).

These changes do not reflect the appearance of new cells: all the neurons the brain will ever have are present at birth. What does increase after birth is the number of dendrites and synapses. In fact, by the time children are six or seven years old, their brains have more dendrites and use twice as much metabolic fuel as those of adults (Chugani & Phelps, 1986; Huttenlocher, 1979). In early adolescence, there is actually a reduction in the number of dendrites and neural connections, so that the adult level is reached by about the age of fourteen (see Figure A).

This general pattern is found not only in humans but in all animals: the brain overproduces neural connections, establishes the usefulness of certain connections, and then "prunes" the extra connections (Cowan, 1979). Thus, we cannot determine mental ability simply by counting the number of dendrites and synapses. One possibility is that, when there are many neural connections, development can take many paths. Some scientists believe that the pruning of connections may reflect a process whereby those connections that are used survive, while the others die. As we saw in Chapter 2, it is during these same adolescent

with encouraging, even spectacular, results. Two Parkinson's patients who received this graft dramatically improved in their ability to walk and produce fine movements, such as handwriting (Madrazo et al., 1987).

It is also likely that a molecular basis for learning and memory will be found, and it will probably relate to a variety of changes in the nervous system. The ways that complex neural networks allow the brain to sense information and solve complicated problems will be unraveled, and perhaps the principles derived from such work will be applied to the creation of computers that can more efficiently solve problems too complex even for the human brain.

Future technologies will surely be added to those already used to study the brain and other biological structures. Currently, PET scans and electrical recordings are limited in how much information they can glean from the brain or how quickly they can trace changes in activity. New techniques, many using the latest supercomputers, will allow more rapid, more detailed, monitoring of brain activity. As these techniques are developed and shown to be safe, more research on how the brain works will be conducted with normal people instead of laboratory animals or medical patients.

years that people develop the capacity for more abstract thinking and more concentrated problem solving.

Even as dendrites are pruned, the brain retains the ability to "rewire" itself, to form new connections, throughout life. The genes apparently determine the basic pattern of growth and the major lines of connection, the "highways" of the brain and its general architecture. But the details seem to depend on such extragenetic factors as the complexity and interest of the environment. For example, researchers have compared the brains of rats raised in individual cages with only a boring view of the side of the cage (and no intellectually stimulating reading material) and the brains of rats raised in an environment filled with interesting toys and stimulating playmates. The cerebral cortex of those from the enriched environment had more and longer dendrites and more synapses than the cortexes of animals from barren, individual housing (Turner & Greenough, 1985; Volkmar & Greenough, 1972). Furthermore, increases in the number of cortical synapses also occurred when old animals who had always lived in the boring individual cages were moved to an enriched environment (Green, Greenough & Schlumpf, 1983). Researchers have not yet determined whether an enriched environment stimulates the development of

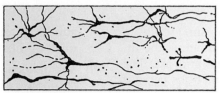

(a) At birth

(b) Six years old

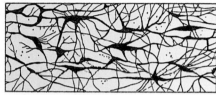

(c) Fourteen years old

Figure A
Changes in Neurons of the Cerebral Cortex During Development
Neurons generate an overabundance of dendrites during childhood. During adolescence, extra dendrites are "pruned" until they reach a level characteristic of the adult. (From J. L. Conel, *The Postnatal Development of the Human Cerebral Cortex*, Vols. I, VIII, Harvard University Press, 1939, 1967. Reprinted by permission.)

new connections or slows down normal pruning, or whether animals will lose synaptic complexity if they are moved from an enriched to a barren environment.

In any event, this line of research highlights the interaction of environmental and genetic factors. Within constraints set by genetics, interactions with the world appear to mold the brain itself. And to the extent that these research findings apply to humans, they hold obvious implications for how people raise children and treat the elderly. These findings may someday help explain why, as noted in Chapter 2, children raised in stimulating environments tend to show faster and more extensive cognitive development than those from more barren backgrounds.

The larger question of how the nervous system is responsible for the mind will be more difficult to answer. How do all the details fit together? More information than any individual can master is being generated about such questions. It will take some great minds, probably working with great computers, to synthesize this information into a vision of how the inside of the "black box" generates experience and behavior.

If you are interested in taking part in this collective adventure, either as a participant scientist or as an informed spectator, you can prepare yourself by learning more about both physical and psychological sciences. Relevant courses offered by most psychology departments include physiological psychology, sensation and perception, learning and memory, motivation and emotion, and abnormal psychology. Many departments now offer courses in drugs and behavior. Courses in other departments are also relevant; take as much chemistry, physiology, anatomy, and computer science as you can. Studying the relationships between body and mind is an interdisciplinary adventure, so having a broad background will help you greatly in many different areas of life.

SUMMARY

1. The nervous system allows an organism to take in information from the environment, integrate the information with previous experiences, and act. The nervous system can perform these functions because its basic unit, cells called neurons, can communicate with one another. The major parts of the nervous system are the central nervous system, which consists of the spinal cord and the brain, and the peripheral nervous system, which consists of sensory and motor nerves and the autonomic nervous system.

2. Signals in the nervous system are transmitted from one end of a neuron to the other end and from one neuron to another. The characteristics of the neurons that permit this communication include their structure of fibers, the excitable surface of some of these fibers, and the synapses, or gaps, between cells.

3. Neurons have cell bodies and two types of fibers, called axons and dendrites. Axons carry signals away from the cell body; dendrites carry signals to the cell body. Because these fibers have many branches, each neuron can contact thousands of other neurons.

4. Like other cells, neurons have selectively permeable membranes. Because the distribution of electrically charged molecules is uneven between the inside of cells and the outside, an electrical force called a potential is created. The membrane surface of the axon can transmit a disturbance in the potential, called an action potential, from one end of the axon to the other. This occurs when gates in the membrane are briefly opened, allowing sodium to rush in.

5. Action potentials are the language of neurons; neurons influence one another by transmitting signals that make it more or less likely for an action potential to be fired. They do this through chemicals called neurotransmitters. When an action potential reaches the end of an axon, the axon releases a neurotransmitter. The neurotransmitter crosses the synapse and interacts with receptors on the dendrites or the cell body of the next cell. This interaction creates a signal that can make that cell either more or less likely to fire its action potential. Each neuron constantly integrates signals received at its many synapses; the result of this integration determines how often the neuron will fire an action potential.

6. Groups of neuron cell bodies are called nuclei. A collection of axons is called a fiber tract or pathway. Areas of cell bodies are gray matter, and areas of myelinated fiber tracts are white matter.

7. Throughout the central nervous system, opposing actions are coordinated; complex systems can be built up from simple components, such as reflexes; feedback adjusts output; and behavior results from the coordination of several levels of organization.

8. Technologies such as the electroencephalogram, CT scanning, PET scanning, and magnetic resonance imaging, have allowed researchers to study the functioning of the human brain in ever-increasing detail.

9. The brain's major subdivisions are the hindbrain, midbrain, and forebrain. The forebrain is the largest part; its outer surface is the cerebral cortex. Major structures of the brain below the surface include the medulla and cerebellum of the hindbrain; the reticular formation; the hypothalamus and thalamus of the forebrain; and the structures of the limbic system.

10. The cerebral cortex is responsible for much of the higher functions of the brain, such as speech and reasoning. The cortex has sensory areas, motor areas, and association areas. Specific functions, such as language production and comprehension, are coordinated by particular regions within these areas.

11. The right and left hemispheres of the cerebral cortex are specialized to some degree in their functions. In most people, the left hemisphere is more active in linguistic and logical tasks; the right hemisphere, in spatial, musical, and artistic tasks. The hemispheres are connected and coordinated through the corpus callosum, allowing the two hemispheres to operate in a coordinated fashion.

12. Neurons that use the same neurotransmitter form a neurotransmitter system. Acetylcholine systems in the brain influence memory processes and movement. Norepinephrine is released by a small number of neurons with axons that spread widely throughout the brain; it is involved in arousal, mood, and learning. Serotonin is another pervasive neurotransmitter; it is active in systems regulating mood, attention, and pain control, among other processes. Dopamine has a more restricted distribution. Its systems are involved in movement and higher cognitive activities; Parkinson's disease and schizophrenia both involve a disturbance of dopaminergic function. GABA is an inhibitory neurotransmitter.

13. Many drugs affect behavior and mental processes by altering neurotransmission, especially by competing for neurotransmitter receptors. Because neurotransmitter systems adjust to pharmacological influences, the long-term responses to continuing drug treatments are difficult to predict.

14. Experiments with drugs have led to the discovery of new neurotransmitters. For example, endorphins, a family of neurotransmitters with painkilling effects,

were discovered when it appeared that the body has neuronal receptors especially tailored to receive morphine and other opiates.

15. Like nervous system cells, cells of the endocrine system communicate by releasing a chemical that is a signal to other cells. However, the chemicals of the endocrine system, called hormones, are carried by the bloodstream to remote target organs. The target organs often produce a coordinated response to hormonal stimulation. One of these is the flight-or-fight syndrome, which is set off by adrenal hormones that prepare for action in times of stress. Feedback processes are involved in the control of most endocrine systems. The brain is the main controller; through the hypothalamus, it controls the pituitary gland, which in turn controls endocrine organs in the body. The brain is also a target organ for most endocrine systems.

KEY TERMS

Definitions of terms appear on the pages shown in parentheses.

acetylcholine (105)
action potential (87)
agonist (109)
antagonist (109)
association cortex (99)
autonomic nervous system (ANS) (84)
axon (86)
biological (physiological) psychology (80)
central nervous system (CNS) (83)
cerebellum (97)
cerebral cortex (98)
cerebral hemisphere (98)
cerebrum (98)
corpus callosum (102)

dendrite (86)
dopamine (107)
electroencephalogram (EEG) (94)
endocrine system (111)
endorphin (111)
feedback system (92)
fiber tract (91)
fight-or-flight syndrome (112)
forebrain (97)
GABA (107)
hindbrain (96)
hippocampus (98)
homeostasis (93)
hormone (111)
hypothalamus (97)

lateralization (104)
limbic system (98)
medulla (96)
midbrain (97)
motor cortex (99)
motor system (82)
myelin (87)
nervous system (82)
neuron (85)
neurotransmitter (89)
neurotransmitter system (105)
norepinephrine (106)
nucleus (85, 91)
peripheral nervous system (84)

psychoactive drug (108)
psychopharmacology (108)
receptor (89)
reflex (91)
refractory period (89)
reticular formation (97)
sensory system (82)
sensory cortex (98)
septum (98)
serotonin (106)
somatic nervous system (84)
spinal cord (91)
synapse (89)
thalamus (97)

RECOMMENDED READINGS

The brain: A Scientific American book (1979). San Francisco: W. H. Freeman. The September 1979 issue of *Scientific American* was devoted to the brain. These articles were published as a book, *The brain*. The articles are all excellent, written at a high level but digestible if you spend some time on them. The subjects span everything from single neurons to brain disorders.

Cooper, J. R., Bloom, F. E., and Roth, R. H. (1986). *The biochemical basis of neuropharmacology* (5th ed.). New York: Oxford. This is the standard introductory text covering neurotransmitters and how psychoactive drugs affect neurotransmitters.

Gazzaniga, M. S., and LeDoux, J. E. (1978). *The integrated mind.* New York: Plenum. An interesting treatment of split-brain research.

Snyder, S. (1980). *Biological aspects of mental disorder.* New York: Oxford. An excellent discussion of the biological contributions to such disorders as depression, schizophrenia, and anxiety.

G eorge H. sees and hears things that other people do not. This is not because he has especially good vision and hearing, but because he suffers from schizophrenia, a severe form of mental disorder described in Chapter 15. George sees and hears things that are not really there, but the accusing voices he hears and the stern faces he sees on the walls are real to him. In fact, he has been in a mental hospital for nearly thirty years, in part because he cannot ignore his version of reality long enough to hold a job, let alone a normal conversation. George's case highlights the fact that, in order to get along in human society, one must hold a view of reality that is similar to that held by others.

But what is reality, and how do people recognize it? Philosophers have debated this deceptively simple question for centuries. The seventeenth-century British philosopher John Locke held that, whatever reality is, people can gain knowledge about the outside world only through the senses. This *empirical,* or data-based, approach has become the basis for the scientific study of psychology. It presumes that contact with reality and knowledge of the world come to us—as they come to George—only through the senses.

A **sense** is a system that translates data from outside the nervous system into neural activity, giving the nervous system, especially the brain, information about the world. For example, vision is the system through which the eyes convert light into neural activity that tells the brain something about the source of the light (for example, that it is bright) or about objects from which it is reflected (for example, that a round, red object is out there). These messages from the senses are called **sensations** and comprise the raw information that affects many kinds of behavior and mental processes (see Linkages diagram, pp. 120–121).

Traditionally, psychologists have distinguished between sensation—the initial message from the senses—and *perception,* or the way the message is interpreted and given meaning in terms of previous experiences. Thus, you do not actually "sense" a cat lying on the sofa; you see shapes and colors—visual sensations. But, because of your previous knowledge of the world, you interpret, or perceive, these sensations as a cat. However, recent research has made it more and more difficult to draw a clear line between sensation and perception. That research has shown that the process of interpreting sensations takes place at many levels, beginning in the sense organs themselves and continuing into the brain. Even previous experience can shape what people sense, causing you not to notice, for example, the familiar chiming of the living room clock, but leaving you very sensitive to the slightest sound when you walk down a dark alley at midnight.

In this chapter, we cover the earlier parts of the sensation-perception process, examining the ways in which the senses pick up information and convert it into forms the brain can use. In the next chapter, we will discuss the later segments of the sensation-perception process, along with *psychophysics,* the laws that govern how physical energy is converted into psychological experience. Together, these chapters will illustrate how human beings

4

Sensation

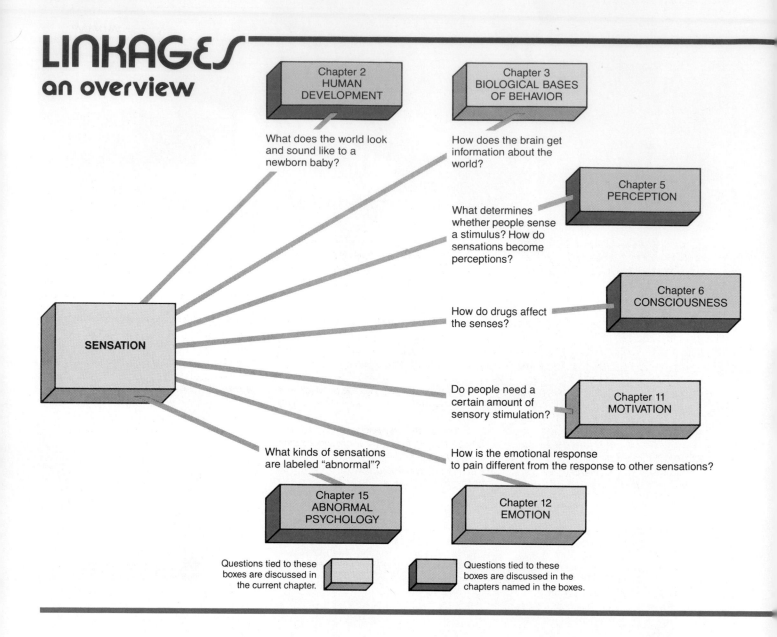

LINKAGES
an overview

Chapter 2
HUMAN
DEVELOPMENT

What does the world look
and sound like to a
newborn baby?

Chapter 3
BIOLOGICAL BASES
OF BEHAVIOR

How does the brain get
information about the
world?

Chapter 5
PERCEPTION

What determines
whether people sense
a stimulus? How do
sensations become
perceptions?

Chapter 6
CONSCIOUSNESS

How do drugs affect
the senses?

SENSATION

Do people need a
certain amount of
sensory stimulation?

Chapter 11
MOTIVATION

What kinds of sensations
are labeled "abnormal"?

How is the emotional response
to pain different from the response to other sensations?

Chapter 15
ABNORMAL
PSYCHOLOGY

Chapter 12
EMOTION

Questions tied to these
boxes are discussed in
the current chapter.

Questions tied to these
boxes are discussed in the
chapters named in the boxes.

create, with the sense organs and the brain, their own worlds and their
own realities.

SENSORY SYSTEMS

The senses gather information about the world through the various forms of
energy they can detect, such as sound, light, heat, and physical pressure. For
example, the eyes detect light energy, the ears detect the energy of sound,
and the skin detects the energy of heat and pressure. These sensory systems
are far from perfect, though. For one thing, they cannot detect such energy
sources as X rays and microwaves. Further, there are limits to how much
energy they can deal with at the same time. Humans depend primarily on
vision, hearing, and the skin senses to gain information about the world; they
depend less than other animals on smell and taste. There are also senses that
provide information to the brain from the rest of the body. All of these senses
must detect stimuli, encode them into neural activity, and transfer this coded
information to the brain.

SENSATION AND PSYCHOLOGY

There is a special type of cell in the nervous system, which we did not describe in the previous chapter: the receptor cell. Receptor cells are the starting point for the subject of this chapter, sensation, which is closely linked to the topics discussed in the previous chapter. Consider pain. In Chapter 3, we described chemicals in the brain that can relieve pain; in this chapter, we see how information about pain reaches your brain in the first place. To do so, we discuss many of the structures and processes introduced in Chapter 3, but our focus now is on the senses, which provide the link between the self and the reality of the world beyond the brain.

When this link works improperly, the consequences can be devastating. For example, what to you is a normal amount of sensory stimulation may constitute an overload for children suffering from the severe disorder known as autism. Autistic children appear to deal with that overload by withdrawing (Zentall & Zentall, 1983). A normal child prefers to look at an interesting, varied visual stimulus, such as a face, but an autistic child will instead look at a blank face or even a blank screen. Autism may be a way of turning off sensory overload, with the unfortunate result that the whole world is turned off.

Even a normal person filters out many stimuli. In fact, so much information about the world is available to the very sensitive senses that most of it must be ignored. Somehow people must filter out

most incoming information and shape the information that does get through. That filtering and shaping depend on perception, consciousness, and the mental processes described in Chapters 7 through 9. Thus, in studying sensation, we examine the biological equipment that brings in data about the world. In the chapters that follow, we will explore the other processes that determine how people transform that data into knowledge and the experience of reality.

Steps in Sensation

Figure 4.1 (p. 122) illustrates the basic steps in sensation. At each step, information is processed in some way. In some sensory systems, the first step in sensation involves **accessory structures,** which modify the stimulus. The lens of the eye is an accessory structure that changes incoming light by focusing it; the outer part of the ear is an accessory structure that collects sound. The second step in sensation is **transduction,** the process of converting incoming energy into neural activity. Just as a radio receives energy and transduces it into sounds, the ears receive sound energy and transduce it into neural activity that people recognize as voices, music, and other auditory experiences. Transduction takes place at structures called **receptors,** cells that are specialized to detect certain forms of energy. Next, sensory nerves transfer the receptors' activity to the brain. For all the senses but smell, the information is taken first to the thalamus, which relays it to the cerebral cortex.

Each nerve cell that carries sensory information responds to only a small part of the incoming energy. This portion of the world that affects a given neuron is its **receptive field.** For example, in the visual system, one neuron

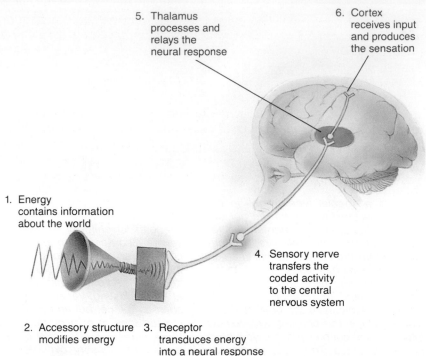

5. Thalamus processes and relays the neural response

6. Cortex receives input and produces the sensation

1. Energy contains information about the world

4. Sensory nerve transfers the coded activity to the central nervous system

2. Accessory structure modifies energy

3. Receptor transduces energy into a neural response

Figure 4.1
Elements of a Sensory System
The different sensory systems have many features in common. Objects in the world generate energy that is focused by accessory structures and detected by sensory receptors, which convert the energy into neural signals. As the signals are transferred through parts of the brain, information is extracted and analyzed. In the cerebral cortex, the information is further analyzed and compared with sensory experiences stored in memory.

might respond to light that is in a small area at the top of whatever you look at; this area is the receptive field for that neuron.

The Problem of Coding

When receptors transduce energy, they must somehow code the physical properties of the stimulus into firing patterns that, when organized by the brain, allow one to make sense of the stimulus; to tell, for example, whether you are looking at a dog or a cat. Each psychological dimension of a sensation, such as the brightness or color of light, must have a corresponding physical dimension that is coded by sensory receptors.

As a way of thinking about the problem of coding, suppose that, for your birthday, you are given a Pet Brain, a new product inspired by the people who brought us Pet Rocks and Cabbage Patch dolls. Your Pet Brain is definitely alive (the guarantee says so), but it does not seem to respond when you talk to it. You show it an ice cream sundae; no response. You show it pictures of other highly attractive brains; no response. You are about to deposit your Pet Brain in the garbage disposal when you suddenly realize that you are not talking the same language. You should be buzzing the brain's sensory nerves with action potentials to send it messages and recording from its motor nerves to discern its responses.

After having this brilliant insight and setting up a little electric shocker, you are faced with an even more awesome problem. How do you describe an ice cream sundae in terms of action potentials? This is the problem of coding. **Coding** is the translation of a stimulus's physical properties into a pattern of neural activity that specifically identifies those physical properties. Now you realize that, if you want the brain to see the sundae, you should probably stimulate its optic nerve (the nerve from the eye to the brain) rather than its auditory nerve (the nerve from the ear to the brain). This idea is based on the doctrine of **specific nerve energies:** stimulation of a particular sensory nerve provides codes for that one sense, no matter how the stimulation takes place. For example, if you close your eyes and apply gentle pressure to your eyeball, you will produce activity in the optic nerve. You will sense this activity as a light stimulus and see little spots of light. Similarly, electrical stimulation of the optic nerve is coded and sensed as light; electrical stimulation of the auditory nerve is coded and sensed as sound.

Having chosen the optic nerve to convey visual information, you must next code the specific attributes of the sundae stimulus: the soft white curves of the vanilla ice cream, the dark richness of the chocolate, the bright redness of the cherry on top. These dimensions must be coded in the language of neural activity. As described in the previous chapter, this language is made up of membrane potentials in dendrites and cell bodies and action potentials in axons.

Some attributes are coded fairly simply. For example, stimulus intensity is often coded by a neuron's rate of firing. A bright light will cause some neurons in the visual system to fire faster than will a dim light. The codes can be very complex, and information can be recoded at each of several relay points as it makes its way through the brain. Sensory psychologists are still working on deciphering the codes that the brain uses; your Pet Brain may have to wait a while to appreciate the beauty of an ice cream sundae.

Representing Stimuli in the Brain

As sensory systems transfer information to the brain, they also organize that information. This organized information is called a *representation*. If you have read Chapter 3, you are already familiar with some characteristics of sensory representations. In humans, representations in the cerebral cortex of vision, hearing, and the skin senses share the following features:

1. A primary area of sensory cortex receives information through the thalamus from each of these senses. (Figure 3.15 shows where these areas of the brain are.)

2. The representation of the sensory world in the cortex is *contralateral* to the part of the world being sensed. Thus, for example, the left side of the primary visual cortex "sees" the right side of the world, and the right side of the somatosensory cortex "feels" the left side of the body. This happens because nerve fibers from each side of the body cross on their way to the thalamus. As noted in Chapter 3, the same thing happens in the motor cortex, so that the left side of the brain controls the right side of the body and vice versa.

3. The primary cortex contains a map, or **topographical representation,** of each sense. This means that any two points that are next to each other in the stimulus will be represented next to each other in the brain. The proportions on the sensory map may be distorted, but the relationships among the various points are maintained.

4. The density of nerve fibers at any given part of a sense organ determines the extent of its representation in the cortex. For example, your fingertips, which have many receptors for touch, have a larger area of cortex representing them than does the skin on your back.

5. Each region of primary sensory cortex is divided into columns of cells that have similar properties. For example, one column of cells in the visual cortex might respond most to diagonal lines; another column might respond most to edges.

6. For each of the senses, regions of cortex other than the primary areas do more complex processing of sensory information. Called **association cortex,** some of these areas contain representations of more than one sense; others provide additional representation areas for a given sense. Hearing, for example, is represented in several association areas.

In short, sensory systems convert some form of energy into neural activity. Often the energy is first modified by accessory structures; then a sensory receptor converts the energy to neural activity. The pattern of neural activity codes physical properties of the energy. The codes are modified as the information is transferred to the brain and processed further.

In the rest of this chapter, we describe individual sensory systems. We will consider (1) the form of energy that is detected by the sense; (2) the accessory stuctures and receptors that transduce the energy; (3) the coding and information processing that occurs at the receptor; and (4) the transfer of information from the receptor to the brain.

HEARING

When Neil Armstrong stepped onto the moon in 1969, he proclaimed, "That's one small step for a man, one giant leap for mankind." Many people on earth heard him because the words were transferred back to earth by radio. But if Armstrong had taken off his space helmet, thrown it high over his head, and shouted, "Whoo-ee! I can moonwalk!" not even an astronaut standing nearby could have heard him. Why? Because he would have been speaking into airless, empty space. **Sound** is a repetitive fluctuation in the pressure of a medium like air, and it cannot exist in a place like the moon, which has almost no atmosphere.

Sounds

The fluctuations in pressure that constitute sound are produced by the vibrations of an object. Each time the object moves outward, its energy increases the pressure in the medium immediately around it. As the object moves back, the pressure drops. In speech, for example, the vibrating object is the vocal cords, and the medium is air. When you speak, your vocal cords vibrate, producing fluctuations in air pressure that spread as waves. A *wave* is a repetitive variation in pressure that spreads out in three dimensions. The wave can move great distances, but the air itself barely moves (if the air were moving, your vocal cords would create a breeze, not sound). Imagine a jam-packed line of people waiting for a movie. If someone at the rear of the line violently shoves the next person, a wave of people jostling against people may spread all the way to the front of the line, but the person who shoved is still no closer to getting into the theater.

The physical characteristics of sound   We can represent sound graphically as a **waveform,** as in Figure 4.2. The waveform represents in two dimensions the wave that moves through the air in three dimensions.

Three characteristics of the waveform are important in understanding sounds. First, the difference in the air pressure of the peak and of the trough is the **amplitude** of the sound. Second, the distance from one peak to the next is the **wavelength.** And third, **frequency** is the number of complete waves, or cycles, that pass by a given point in space every second. Frequency is described in hertz, abbreviated Hz (for Heinrich Hertz, a nineteenth-century physicist who studied energy waves). One cycle per second is 1 hertz. Because the speed of sound is constant, frequency and wavelength are inversely related;

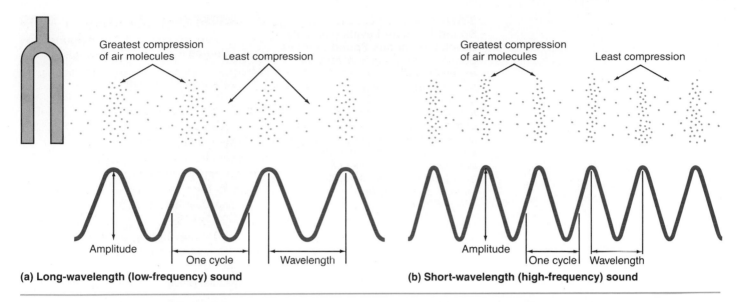

(a) Long-wavelength (low-frequency) sound   (b) Short-wavelength (high-frequency) sound

that is, the longer the wavelength, the lower the frequency. Likewise, high-frequency sound is short-wavelength sound.

The simplest waveform has just one frequency and can be represented by what is known in mathematics as a *sine wave;* the waveform in Figure 4.2 is an example. A sound that can be represented by a perfect sine wave is called a *pure tone.* In contrast, most sounds are mixtures of a large number of frequencies and amplitudes and correspond to complex waveforms.

Psychological dimensions of sound   The frequency and amplitude of sound waves determine the sounds that you hear. These *physical* characteristics of the waves produce the *psychological* dimensions of sound known as pitch, loudness, and timbre.

Pitch—how high or low a tone is—is the psychological dimension determined by the frequency of sound waves. High-frequency waves are sensed as sounds of high pitch. The highest note on a piano has a frequency of about 4,000 hertz; the lowest note has a frequency of about 50 hertz. Humans can

Figure 4.2
Waveforms, a Representation of Sound Waves
The molecules of air around a sound source are unevenly distributed. Regions of greater compression of air molecules alternate with regions of lesser compression because of the to-and-fro vibrations of the object generating the sound. The variations in air molecule compression can be represented as a waveform of pressure across time, with greater pressure indicated by the peak in the curve. The point where the air is compressed the most is the peak of the graph. The lowest point, or trough, is where the air pressure is lowest.

A musical synthesizer can produce the sounds of different instruments—say, a piano and a trumpet—by combining sine waves in various ways. The auditory system takes the opposite approach: it can analyze the mixture that makes up a sound into its component sine waves.

TABLE 4.1 _____
Sound Pressure Levels (Intensity Levels) of Various Sound Sources
Sound intensity varies across an extremely wide range, so the scale used to describe sounds is logarithmic. Every increase of 20 decibels reflects a tenfold multiplication of the amplitude of the sound waves. A whisper is 10 times as intense as a barely audible sound (which is, by definition, 0 decibels), and the noise of a subway train (100 decibels) is 10,000 times as intense as a whisper.

Source	Sound Level (dB)
Manned spacecraft launch (from 45 m)	180
Loudest rock band on record	160
Pain threshold (approximate)	140
Large jet motor (at 22 m)	120
Loudest human shout on record	111
Heavy auto traffic	100
Conversation (at about 1 m)	60
Quiet office	40
Soft whisper	20
Threshold of hearing	0

SOURCE: M. W. Levine and J. M. Shefner, *Fundamentals of Sensation and Perception,* 1981. Reprinted by permission of M. W. Levine.

hear sounds from about 20 hertz to about 20,000 hertz. **Loudness** is determined by the amplitude of the sound wave; waves with greater amplitude produce sensations of louder sounds. Loudness is described in units called *decibels,* abbreviated dB. Table 4.1 gives examples of the loudness of some common sounds, expressed in decibels. By definition, 0 decibels is the minimal detectable sound for normal hearing. **Timbre** is the quality of sound that identifies it, so that, for example, a middle C played on the piano is clearly distinguishable from a middle C played on a trumpet. The timbre depends on the mixture of frequencies and amplitudes that make up the sound.

Figure 4.3 illustrates how one basic sine wave is apparent in a musical note from a piano, with other waves added onto the basic shape. The basic sine wave is called the *fundamental frequency;* the other waves give the tone its timbre. Because the added waves are multiples of the fundamental frequency of the note, the result does not sound out of tune. The regularities of the wave make it sound musical. In contrast, a **noise** does not have such regularities. Instead, it is a random sum of waveforms that are not related to one another in any regular way, as Figure 4.3 shows.

The Ear

The ear converts sound into neural activity through its accessory structures and a fascinating series of transduction mechanisms. This transduction begins the process that allows us to experience the world of sound.

Auditory accessory structures   Sound waves are collected in the outer ear, beginning with the **pinna,** the crumpled, oddly shaped part of the ear on the side of the head. The pinna funnels sound down through the ear canal (see Figure 4.4, p. 128). At the bottom of the ear canal, the sound waves reach the middle ear where they strike a tightly stretched membrane known as the

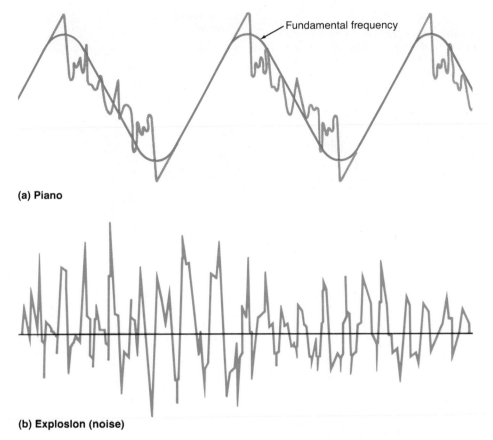

(a) Piano

(b) Explosion (noise)

Figure 4.3
Timbre
Even when playing a single note, musical instruments produce complex waveforms. (a) The waveform produced by a piano playing one note, C below middle C. The fundamental frequency is 130 hertz, but multiples of this fundamental frequency also contribute to the sound. Because the components of the complex wave have a simple relationship to the fundamental frequency, the sound is musical. (b) The waveform produced by an explosion. Explosions are normally considered noise rather than music, because their waveforms are very irregular, rather than repeating.
(Part a from *Speech and Hearing* (revised ed.), by Harvey Fletcher, D. Van Nostrand Company, Inc., 1952. Part b reprinted by permission of John Wiley and Sons, Inc. From E. G. Boring et al., *Foundations of Psychology*. Copyright © 1948.)

eardrum, or **tympanic membrane.** The waves set up vibrations in the tympanic membrane that match the sound waves.

These vibrations are transferred through a chain of three tiny bones named for their shapes: the **malleus** (**"hammer"**), the **incus** (**"anvil"**), and the **stapes** (**"stirrup"**) (see Figure 4.4). Each passes on whatever vibration it receives to its nearest neighbor. At the end of this chain of bones is another membrane, the **oval window.** The bones focus the movements of the tympanic membrane onto the smaller oval window, thereby amplifying the changes in pressure produced by the original sound waves. *Conduction deafness* occurs if the junctions between these bones fuse, reducing or preventing accurate reproduction of vibrations. A hearing aid that amplifies the input to the eardrum or surgery to loosen the bones can sometimes combat conduction deafness.

Auditory transduction When the sound vibrations pass from the stapes through the oval window, they enter the inner ear, a world of fluid-filled spirals. They are now in the **cochlea,** the structure in which transduction actually occurs.

The cochlea is wrapped into a coiled spiral (*cochlea* is derived from the Greek word for "snail"). If you unwrapped it, you would see that a fluid-filled duct runs down its length. The **basilar membrane** forms the floor of this long duct (see Figure 4.5, p. 128). The sound waves pass through the fluid in the cochlea just as they traveled through the air. Whenever a wave passes through the fluid in the duct, it moves the basilar membrane, and this movement deforms **hair cells** that touch the membrane.

The hair cells are exquisitely sensitive to any change in their shape, and they make connections with fibers from the **auditory nerve,** which sends its

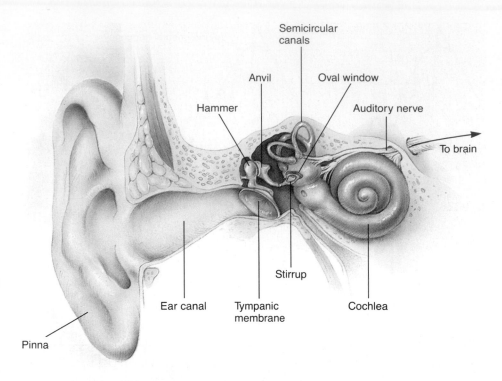

Figure 4.4
Structures of the Ear
The outer ear (pinna and ear canal) channel sound waves into the middle ear, where the vibrations of the tympanic membrane are amplified by the delicate bones that stimulate the cochlea. In the cochlea of the inner ear, the vibrations are transduced into neural activity changes, which are sent along the auditory nerve to the brain.

axons into the brain. If either the auditory nerve or the hair cells are damaged, an irreversible impairment called *nerve deafness* may result. This condition cannot be improved by conventional hearing aids, though it can be alleviated to some extent in some patients by *cochlear implants*. These sophisticated electronic devices can translate sounds gathered by a tiny microphone into electronic signals that reach the brain by way of an electrode implanted in the cochlea.

The mechanical deformation of hair cells causes a change in the electrical activity of the auditory nerve. In the following sections, we will show how this activity codes information about the amplitude and frequency of sound waves, allowing people to sense the loudness and pitch of sounds.

Figure 4.5
The Cochlea
The vibrations of the stapes, or stirrup, set up vibrations in the fluid inside the cochlea. The coils of the cochlea are unfolded in this illustration to show the path of the fluid waves along the basilar membrane. Movements of the basilar membrane stimulate the hair cells, which finally transduce the vibrations into changes in neural firing patterns.

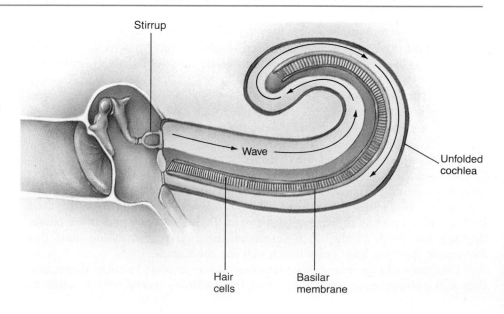

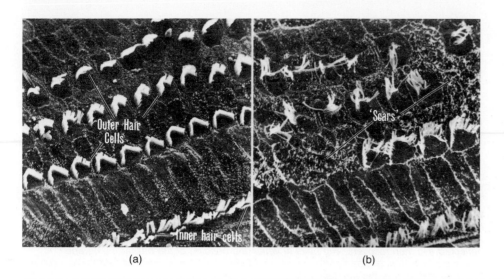

(a)   (b)

High intensity sounds are one cause of nerve deafness. They can actually rip off the hair cells normally attached to the basilar membrane. Generally, any sound that is loud enough to produce a ringing sensation in the ears causes some damage. Small amounts of damage can accumulate over many years to produce a significant hearing loss. These scanning electron micrographs illustrate the effect of intense sound on the inner ear. (a) Cochlea of a normal guinea pig, showing three rows of outer hair cells and one row of inner hair cells. (b) Cochlea of a guinea pig after twenty-four-hour exposure to a sound level approached by loud rock music (2000 hertz at 120 decibels).

The Coding of Intensity

The auditory system can respond to a wide range of sound intensities. On the low end, the faintest sound that can be heard moves the hair cells less than the diameter of a single hydrogen atom (Hudspeth, 1983). On the high end, sounds more than a trillion times more intense can also be heard; sounds this intense can be sensed even by the skin. Between these extremes, the auditory system codes intensity in a generally straightforward way: the more intense the sound, the more rapid the firing of a given neuron. Some cells may increase their firing rate as the intensity increases, up to a point; then they decrease their firing rate as the intensity increases further. And sometimes the firing rate of individual neurons in the auditory nerve depends on both the frequency and the intensity of the stimulus.

Frequency Coding

How do people tell the difference between one note and another? Recall that the pitch of a sound depends on its frequency. Differences in frequency appear to be coded in two ways, which are described by place theory and the volley theory.

Place theory   Georg von Békésy did some pioneering, but gruesome experiments to figure out how frequency is coded. He opened the skulls of human cadavers, exposed the cochlea, and made a hole in the cochlear wall to observe the basilar membrane. He then presented his "volunteers" with sounds of different frequencies by mechanically vibrating a rubber membrane that was installed in place of the oval window. With sensitive optical instruments, von Békésy observed ripples of waves moving down the basilar membrane. He also noticed something very important. The outline of the waves, called the *envelope,* grows and reaches a peak; then it quickly tapers off to smaller and smaller fluctuations, much like an ocean wave that crests and then dissolves. Figure 4.6 (p. 130) illustrates this traveling wave. Its critical feature is that the distance along the basilar membrane to the peak of the wave envelope depends on the frequency of the sound. High-frequency sounds produce a wave that peaks soon after it starts down the basilar membrane. Lower-frequency sounds produce a wave that peaks farther along the basilar membrane, farther from the stirrup.

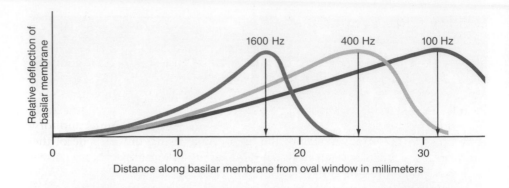

Figure 4.6
Movements of the Basilar Membrane That Support the Place Theory of Frequency Coding
As vibrations of the cochlear fluid spread along the basilar membrane, the membrane is deflected and then recovers. The point at which the bending of the basilar membrane reaches a maximum is different for each sound frequency. The arrows indicate the location of hair cells that receive the greatest stimulation for sounds of differing frequencies.
(Adapted from *Experiments in Hearing* by G. von Békésy. Copyright © 1960. Reprinted with permission of McGraw-Hill Book Company. From G. L. Rasmussen and W. F. Windle, *Neural Mechanisms of the Auditory and Vestibular Systems,* 1960. Courtesy of Charles C Thomas, Publisher, Springfield, Illinois.)

What do these differences in peak points mean? According to **place theory** (also called the *traveling wave theory*), the peak of the wave represents the greatest response by hair cells. In other words, hair cells at a particular place on the basilar membrane respond most to a particular frequency of sound. Thus, if exposed to a very loud, damaging noise of a particular frequency, a person loses hair cells at one spot on the basilar membrane, as well as the ability to hear sounds of that frequency. Place theory is also supported by studies showing that each neuron in the auditory nerve is most sensitive to a specific frequency, which is called its **characteristic frequency** (see Figure 4.7).

Figure 4.7
Determination of Characteristic Frequencies
Each curve, representing different nerve fibers, is generated by determining the minimum intensity of a sound at each frequency needed to stimulate the nerve. The bottom point on each curve corresponds to the frequency to which the nerve is most sensitive; even a very faint sound at that frequency will cause that fiber to fire. The characteristic frequency of one fiber is about 3,000 hertz, whereas the characteristic frequency of the other fiber is about 10,000 hertz.

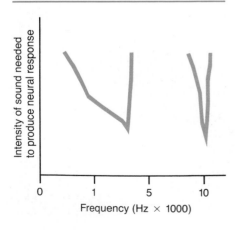

Frequency matching: The volley theory Though place theory accounts for a great deal of experimental data on hearing, it cannot provide a complete explanation of how frequency is coded. In particular, it cannot account for the coding of very low frequencies, such as that of a deep bass note, because there are no auditory nerve fibers that have very low characteristic frequencies. But, since humans can hear frequencies as low as 20 hertz, they must be coded somehow. How?

Frequency matching seems to be the answer. **Frequency matching** means that the firing rate of a neuron matches the frequency of a sound wave. For example, one neuron might fire at every peak of a wave. Thus, a sound of 20 hertz could be coded by a neuron that fires twenty times per second.

Since no neuron can fire faster than one thousand times per second, clearly no neuron can match frequencies of, say, 10,000 hertz. However, the summed activity of a group of neurons can match sounds of *moderate* frequencies; each neuron in the group might fire at every other wave peak or at every fifth peak, for example. Because a group of neurons fires in a sort of volley, the frequency-matching theory is sometimes called the **volley theory** of frequency coding.

In summary, the nervous system apparently uses more than one way to code the full range of audible frequencies. The lowest frequencies are coded by matching the frequency with the firing rate of auditory nerve fibers (frequency coding). Low to moderate frequencies are coded by both frequency matching and the place on the basilar membrane where the traveling wave peaks. And high frequencies are coded exclusively by the place where the traveling wave peaks.

Auditory Pathways and the Auditory Cortex

Before we can hear sounds, the information coded in the activity of auditory nerve fibers must be conveyed to the brain and processed further. The auditory nerve, which makes one or two synapses before reaching the thalamus, brings the information to the brain. From the thalamus, the information is relayed to the auditory cortex. On their way to the thalamus, the fibers of the auditory nerve cross to the opposite side of the brain. As a result, the left side of the auditory cortex receives input from the right ear, and the right auditory cortex receives sounds reaching the left ear.

The first cells in the cortex to receive information about sounds are called **primary auditory cortex.** This area, in the temporal lobe, is connected to areas of the brain involved in language perception and production. Cells in the auditory cortex have preferred frequencies, just as neurons in the auditory nerve do. Neighboring cells in the cortex have similar preferred frequencies; thus, the auditory cortex provides a map of sound frequencies. This arrangement is called a **tonotopic organization.**

The cortex is not just a passive warehouse of information coded by the nervous system; it must further process the information if we are to hear. For example, although we noted in Figure 4.7 that each neuron in the auditory nerve has a "favorite," or characteristic, frequency, each responds to some extent to a range of frequencies. Therefore, the nervous system must examine the pattern of activity of a number of neurons in order to determine the frequency of a given sound.

VISION

Fatal automobile accidents are much more likely to occur at night than in the daytime, even though people drive far fewer miles after dark. Fatigue and alcohol certainly contribute to this phenomenon. However, another important reason is that people tend to drive as fast and as confidently at night as they do in the daytime, in spite of the fact that their ability to see deteriorates dangerously as illumination falls (Leibowitz & Owens, 1986). In other words, most people do not understand the limitations of the visual system. The visual system is one of the most remarkable senses, with its ability to transduce light energy into neural activity that, when processed in the brain, results in the precious experience of sight.

Light

What we call light is a form of energy known as *electromagnetic radiation.* Unlike sound, light does not need a medium to pass through; it has some of the properties of waves and some of the properties of particles. Light waves are like particles that pass through space, but they vibrate with a certain wavelength. Therefore, it is correct to refer to light as either *light waves* or *light rays.* Most electromagnetic radiation, including X rays, radio waves, television signals, and radar, passes through space undetected by the human eye. As Figure 4.8 (p. 132) shows, **visible light** is electromagnetic radiation that has a wavelength from about 400 nanometers to about 700 nanometers. (A *nanometer* is one-billionth of a meter.)

Our sensations of light depend on two physical dimensions of light waves: intensity and wavelength. **Light intensity** refers to how much energy the light contains; it determines the brightness of light. What color we sense depends mainly on **light wavelength.** At a given intensity, different wavelengths produce sensations of different colors. For instance, 440-nanometer light appears violet-blue, and 600-nanometer light appears orangish-red.

Even with the aid of modern high beam headlights, limitations of the human visual system dangerously reduce drivers' ability to see road hazards at night or in other low-light situations.

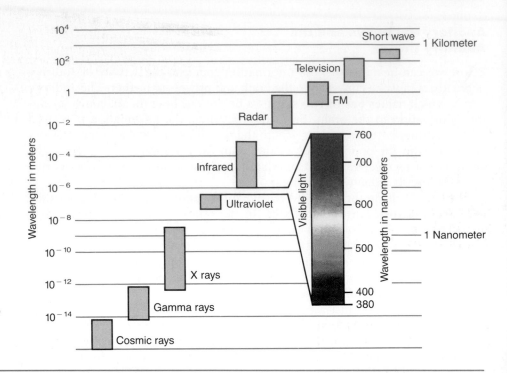

Figure 4.8
The Spectrum of Electromagnetic Energy
The eye is sensitive to a very limited range of wavelengths. Electronic instruments have detectors for other ranges of wavelengths and, in effect, "see" their own kind of light, just as the eye sees visible light.

Focusing Light: Accessory Structures of the Eye

Light energy is transduced into neural activity in the eye. But first, the accessory structures of the eye get more information from the light by focusing light rays into a sharp image. Figure 4.9 shows the structures that detect and focus light. First the light rays enter the eye by passing through the curved, transparent protective layer called the **cornea.** Then the light passes through the **pupil,** the opening just behind the cornea. The **iris,** which gives the eyes their color, adjusts the amount of light allowed into the eye by constricting to reduce the size of the pupil or relaxing to enlarge it. Directly behind the pupil is the **lens.** Like the cornea and like the lens in a camera, the lens of the eye is curved so that it bends light rays, focusing them on the surface at the back of the eye, called the **retina.**

Figure 4.10 illustrates how the lens bends light rays from a point source so that they meet at a point on the retina. If the rays meet either in front of the retina or behind it, the image will be out of focus. The muscles that hold the lens adjust its shape so that either near or far objects can be focused on the retina. If you peer at something very close, for example, your muscles must tighten the lens, making it more curved, to obtain a focused image. This ability to change the shape of the lens to bend light rays so that objects are in focus is called **accommodation.** With age, the lens loses some of its flexibility, and accommodation becomes more difficult. This is why most older people need reading glasses.

Converting Light into Images: Visual Transduction

The retina, the structure where visual transduction takes place, is actually an intricate network of cells. Before transduction can occur, light rays must pass through several layers in this network to reach photoreceptor cells. The **photoreceptors** in the retina code light energy into neural activity. First we

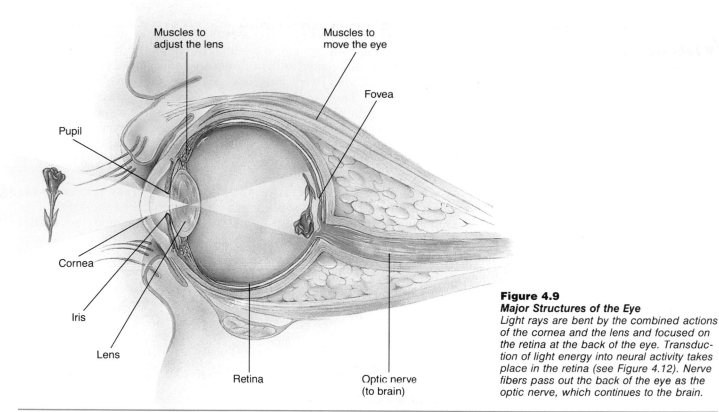

Figure 4.9
Major Structures of the Eye
Light rays are bent by the combined actions of the cornea and the lens and focused on the retina at the back of the eye. Transduction of light energy into neural activity takes place in the retina (see Figure 4.12). Nerve fibers pass out the back of the eye as the optic nerve, which continues to the brain.

will consider the photoreceptors and how they work; then we will describe how other cells in the retina operate.

Photoreceptors Photoreceptors can change light into neural activity because they are specialized nerve cells that have **photopigments**, or chemicals that respond to light. When light strikes a photopigment, the photopigment breaks apart, changing the membrane potential of the photoreceptor cell. As we noted in Chapter 3, this change in membrane potential provides a signal that can be transferred to the brain.

The retina has two basic types of photoreceptors: **rods** and **cones.** As their names imply, these cells differ in shape, but there are other important differences as well. For one thing, the photopigment in rods includes a substance called *rhodopsin,* whereas the photopigment in cones includes one

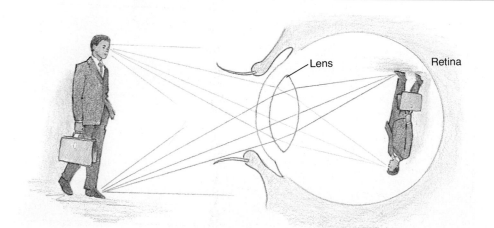

Figure 4.10
The Lens and the Retinal Image
Objects in the world can be thought of as consisting of many point sources of light. Light rays from the top of an object are focused at the bottom of the image on the retinal surface. Similarly, rays from the right side of the object end up on the left side of the retinal image. The brain rearranges this upside down and reversed image so that we see it as it is. To be in focus, rays from each point of the object must meet at a single point on the retinal surface.

of three varieties of *iodopsin*. The fact that there are three different pigments in cones allows the cone system to distinguish colors. Rods and cones also respond somewhat differently to light. Rods are more sensitive to light than cones; but because they have only one pigment, the rods are unable to discriminate colors. Thus, rods allow us to see even when there is very little light, as on a moonlit night. But if you have trouble trying to match a pair of socks in a darkened bedroom, you now know the reason: because the light is dim, you are seeing with your rods, which cannot discriminate colors. At higher light intensities, the cones, with their ability to detect colors, become most active in vision.

The rods and cones also differ in their distribution in the eye. Cones are very concentrated in the center of the retina, a region called the **fovea.** This concentration of photoreceptors makes spatial discrimination, or **acuity,** greatest in the fovea. Indeed, the fovea is precisely where the eye focuses the light coming from objects you look at. There are no rods in the fovea. With increasing distance from the fovea, however, the number of cones gradually decreases, and the proportion of rods gradually increases. Thus, if you are trying to detect a small amount of light, such as that from a faint star, it is better to look slightly away from where you expect to see it. This focuses the weak light on the very light sensitive rods outside the fovea. Because cones do not work well in low light, looking directly at the star will make it seem to disappear.

Dark adaptation   After a photopigment has broken down in response to light, new photopigment molecules are put together. This takes a little time, however. When you first come from bright sunshine into a dark place like a theater, you cannot see because your photoreceptors, especially your rods, do not yet have enough photopigment. In the dark, your photoreceptors synthesize more photopigments, and your ability to see gradually increases. This increasing ability to see in the dark as time passes is called **dark adaptation.**

The different properties of rods and cones shape the course of dark adaptation, as Figure 4.11 illustrates. Cones adapt to the dark more quickly than rods; but even when they are completely dark-adapted, the cones are not nearly as sensitive to light. The rods take about 45 minutes to adapt completely to darkness. Thus, when you enter a dark theater, there is some immediate

Cone cells in the retina allow us to see color, but they do not operate well in low-light conditions. This is why it is so difficult to see colors in dim light.

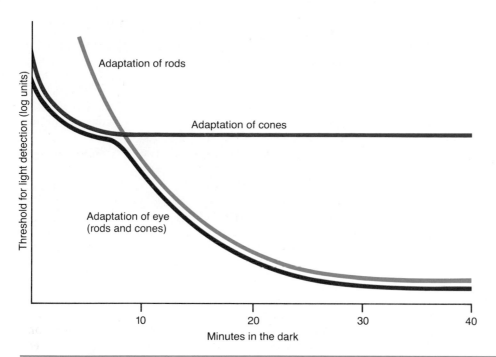

Adaptation of rods

Adaptation of cones

Adaptation of eye
(rods and cones)

Threshold for light detection (log units)

10   20   30   40

Minutes in the dark

Figure 4.11
Dark Adaptation
The eye becomes more sensitive to dim light the longer it is in darkness. We can quantify the process of dark adaptation by determining the visual threshold, which is the intensity of the faintest detectable light. This graph shows how the threshold declines (which means that sensitivity increases) for rods, for cones, and for vision overall, with time spent in the dark. Notice that the change occurs in two phases because of the two types of photoreceptors. This pattern reflects the combined contributions of rods and cones and the differences in how they adapt to darkness. Cones, represented by the reddish line, adapt rapidly; their increase in sensitivity is represented by the first drop in the curve. However, even when completely dark-adapted, cones are not nearly as sensitive to light as rods are. Rods, represented by the blue line, adapt more slowly but are more sensitive than cones after a period of dark adaptation. The threshold for the eye as a whole, represented by the purple line, drops rapidly, slows down, then drops again.

increase in sensitivity to light as your cones adapt; then sensitivity rises more slowly as your rods adapt. Overall, your sensitivity to light increases some ten thousandfold after an hour or so in a darkened room. This is too slow to avoid tripping over someone in a theater, but helps immensely if you are working for a long time in a darkroom.

Interactions of cells in the retina   The eye actually sharpens visual images, so that they are clearer than the light image that strikes the retina. To explain how the eye does this, we need to describe the interactions among the cells that make up the retina. Figure 4.12 (p. 136) illustrates some of the cells in various layers of the retina. The most direct connections from the photoreceptor cells to the brain go first to **bipolar cells** and then to ganglion cells; the axons of ganglion cells form the optic nerve that extends out of the eye and into the brain. However, the path is often far more complicated.

Two complications are especially important. First, most bipolar cells receive input from many photoreceptors, as illustrated in the top portion of Figure 4.13 (p. 137); this arrangement is called **convergence.** Second, photoreceptor cells make connections to other types of cells in the retina, including *horizontal cells* and *amacrine cells,* which make *lateral* connections between bipolar cells. Through these connections, the response to light by a cell at one point on the retina can excite or inhibit the response of a neighboring cell. The bottom portion of Figure 4.13, for example, illustrates **lateral inhibition;** here the stimulation of one cell is producing a signal that makes it seem as if there is less light at another cell than there really is.

Together, these interactions enhance our sensation of *contrast,* and they influence the sensitivity and acuity of our vision. First consider a case of lateral inhibition. Most of the time, the light reaching one of two photoreceptors will be slightly greater than that reaching the other one. As Figure 4.13 illustrates, the photoreceptor receiving more light will suppress the eventual output to the brain from the photoreceptor receiving less light. Therefore, the output to the brain is a comparison of the light hitting two neighboring points. Whatever difference exists between the light reaching the two photoreceptors is exaggerated.

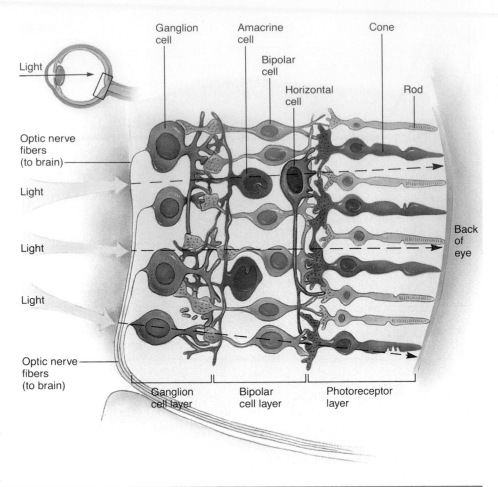

Figure 4.12
Organization of Cells in the Retina
Light rays actually pass through several layers of cells before striking the photoreceptive rods and cones. Signals generated by the rods and cones then go back toward the surface of the retina, passing through the bipolar cells and on to the ganglion cells. Axons from the ganglion cells form the optic nerve that sends signals to the brain. Interconnections among the horizontal cells, the amacrine cells, the bipolar cells, and the ganglion cells allow the eye to begin analyzing visual information even before that information leaves the retina. In effect, the cells of the retina are outposts of the brain.

This exaggeration is important, because differences in amounts of incoming light are created by specific features of objects. For example, the visual image of the edge of an object contains a transition from a lighter region to a darker region. Lateral inhibition in the retina enhances this difference, creating contrast that sharpens the edge and makes it more noticeable. Convergence of input from photoreceptors to bipolar cells (as shown in Figure 4.13) also enhances contrast by allowing bipolar cells to compare the amount of light on larger regions of the retina. Thus, convergence and lateral connections combine to increase the eye's sensitivity to differences in the amount of light falling on different parts of the retina.

The degree of convergence also influences the sensitivity and acuity of cells. Convergence increases the sensitivity of each bipolar cell, because light striking any of the photoreceptors to which it is connected will stimulate it. It should come as no surprise, therefore, that there is a great deal of convergence in areas surrounding the fovea, where the light-sensitive rods predominate. However, convergence "confuses" bipolar cells, making it difficult for them to tell which photoreceptor was actually hit by light. This reduces the accuracy, or acuity, of rod vision.

In the fovea, however, there is much less convergence. One cone tends to excite just one bipolar cell, making the area less light sensitive, but far better able to detect tiny details.

Ganglion cells and their receptive fields   Photoreceptors, bipolar cells, and horizontal cells communicate through the release of neurotransmitters. But,

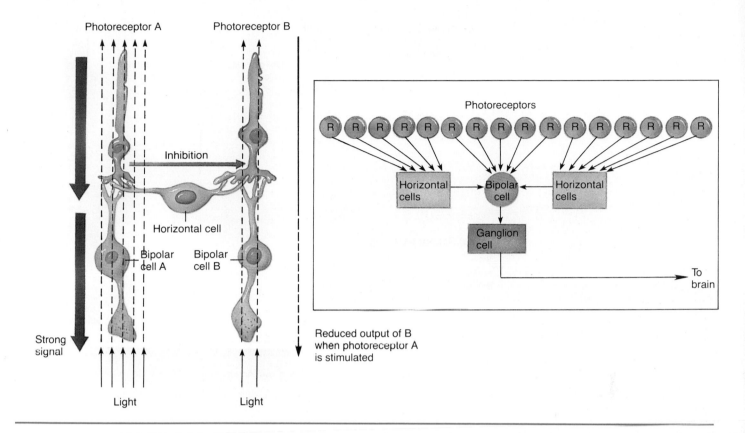

as we noted in Chapter 3, neurotransmitters cause only small, graded changes in the next cell's membrane potential, which may not be strong enough to produce a sequence of action potentials that will reach the brain. **Ganglion cells** are the cells in the retina that generate these action potentials. As shown in Figure 4.12, they are stimulated by bipolar cells, and their axons extend out of the retina and travel to the brain.

What message do ganglion cells send on to the brain? To find out, we could theoretically place an electrode in the axon of one of your ganglion cells, record the signal it sends to your brain when we present various visual stimuli, and thus determine what this one cell "sees." In other words, we could determine the ganglion cell's **receptive field,** which is that part of the retina and the corresponding part of the visual world to which that cell responds. What we would find is that most ganglion cells have what is called a *center-surround receptive field.* That is, most ganglion cells in effect compare the amount of light stimulating rods and cones in the center of their receptive fields with that stimulating the rods and cones in the surrounding area. As Figure 4.14 (p. 138) illustrates, some center-surround ganglion cells are activated by darkness in the center of the field and by light in the regions surrounding the dark center. Their activity is inhibited by light in the center of the field and by dark spots in the surrounding area. Other center-surround ganglion cells work in just the opposite way. They are activated by light in the center and darkness in the surrounding area.

The result of the center-surround receptive fields, as Figure 4.14 illustrates, is to optimize the detection of variations, such as edges and small spots of light or dark. In fact, as Figure 4.15 (p. 139) demonstrates, people see a sharper contrast between darker and lighter areas than actually exists. By enhancing people's sensation of edges and other important features, the retina is reporting to the brain an "improved" version of the visual world.

Figure 4.13
Convergence and Lateral Inhibition Among Retinal Cells
Right: Input from many photoreceptors converges onto bipolar cells in the retina. Many receptors feed directly into a given bipolar cell, and many receptors have indirect input to bipolar cells by influencing horizontal cells. As shown at left, the input from horizontal cells to bipolar cells is often inhibitory. The bipolar cell of photoreceptor A makes a connection to a horizontal cell that synapses on the bipolar cell of photoreceptor B. When A is stimulated, it excites the horizontal cell, which inhibits the bipolar cell of B. Thus, light shining on photoreceptor A actually inhibits the signal that photoreceptor B sends to the brain. Light striking photoreceptor A both sends a signal to the brain that there is light at point A and makes it appear as if there is less light at point B than there really is.

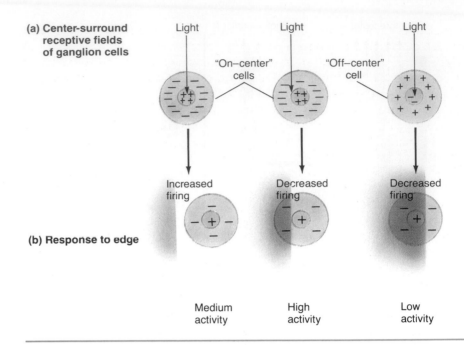

(a) Center-surround receptive fields of ganglion cells

"On–center" cells

"Off–center" cell

Light   Light   Light

Increased firing   Decreased firing   Decreased firing

(b) Response to edge

Medium activity   High activity   Low activity

Figure 4.14
Lateral Inhibition and the Center-Surround Arrangement Allows Ganglion Cells to Act as Edge Detectors
(a) Light falling on photoreceptors in the center of the receptive field of an "on-center" ganglion cell increases its firing activity, whereas light falling on photoreceptors in the area surrounding the center (the "surround"), decreases that activity. The arrangement is just the opposite in an "off-center" ganglion cell, where light falling on photoreceptors in the center of the receptive field decreases the activity of the cell. (b) An edge is a region of light next to a region of relative darkness. If, as shown at left, an edge is outside the receptive field of an on-center ganglion cell, there will be a uniform amount of light on both the excitatory center and the inhibitory surround, thus creating a moderate amount of activity. If, as shown in the middle, the dark side of an edge covers a large portion of the inhibitory surround but leaves light on the excitatory center, the output of the cell will be high, signaling an edge in its receptive field. When, as shown at right, the dark area covers both the center and the surround of the ganglion cell, its activity will be lower, because neither segment of the cell's receptive field is receiving much stimulation.

The many colors of the rainbow are created as sunlight passes through water droplets in the air and is separated into light of different wavelengths.

Color Vision

Perhaps the most salient feature of visual sensation is color. An advertising agent might tell you about the impact of color on buying preferences, a poet might tell you about the beauty of color, but we will tell you about how it works—which is itself a thing of elegance and beauty.

Wavelengths and color sensations   We noted earlier that, at a given intensity, each wavelength of light is sensed as a certain color (look again at Figure 4.8). Sunlight is a mixture of all wavelengths of light. When this full spectrum of white light shines on grass, the grass absorbs most of the wavelengths and reflects a combination of wavelengths that appears green. When sunlight passes through a droplet of water, the different wavelengths of light are bent to different degrees, thus separating into a colorful rainbow.

The spectrum of color found in the rainbow illustrates an important concept: the sensation produced by a mixture of different wavelengths of light is not the same as those produced by separate wavelengths. Further, there are three separate aspects of the sensation of color: hue, saturation, and brightness. These are *psychological* dimensions that correspond roughly to the physical properties of light. **Hue** is the essential "color," determined by the dominant wavelength of the light. Black, white, and gray are not considered hues because no wavelength predominates in them. **Saturation** is related to the purity of a color. A color is more saturated and more pure if a single wavelength is relatively more intense than other wavelengths. If we add a broad variety of wavelengths to a pure hue, the color is said to be *desaturated*. For example, pastels are colors that have been desaturated by the addition of whiteness. **Brightness** corresponds to the overall intensity of all of the wavelengths making up light. However, as we will discuss in Chapter 5, on perception, our experience of the brightness of a particular color also depends on the brightness and hue of stimuli in other parts of the visual field.

The color circle shown in Figure 4.16 is made up of hues arranged according to their perceived similarities. If you mix light of two different wavelengths but equal intensity, you produce the color that is at the midpoint of a line drawn between the two original colors on the color circle. You are probably familiar with a different form of color mixing in which paints are combined. Like other physical objects, paints of different colors reflect certain wavelengths and absorb all others. As a result, mixing paints is *subtractive color mixing*; the two paints absorb, or subtract, more wavelengths of light than either one does alone. Because of this subtraction, mixing two paints usually produces a darker color. Thus, if you keep combining different colored paints, all of the wavelengths will eventually be subtracted, resulting in black (you usually get a disgusting mud color on the way to black). In contrast, mixing two lights of different wavelengths is *additive color mixing*, because the effects of the wavelengths from each light are added together, stimulating more cones. Mixing lights usually produces a lighter color. Thus, if you keep

Figure 4.15
Visual Effects Caused by Lateral Inhibition
Lateral inhibition among retinal cells produces a number of visual effects, including the appearance of dark spots at the intersections of the black boxes in this figure called the Hermann grid. When you look directly at a given intersection, the dark spot disappears, because ganglion cells in the fovea have smaller receptive fields than those elsewhere in the retina. The receptive fields of two ganglion cells projected onto the pattern show how, at the intersection, the ganglion cell on the left has more whiteness shining on the inhibitory surround. Thus, the output of the cell is reduced compared to that of the one on the right, and the spot on the left appears "darker."

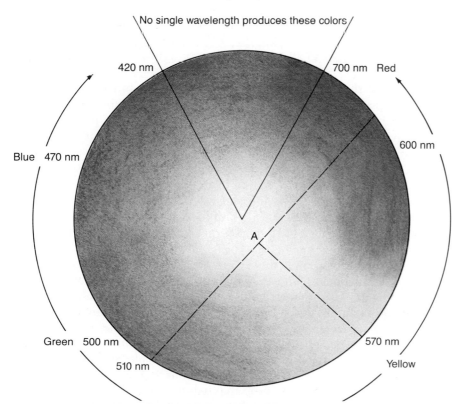

Non-Spectral Hues

No single wavelength produces these colors

420 nm   700 nm   Red

Blue   470 nm   600 nm

A

Green   500 nm   570 nm

510 nm   Yellow

These colors produced by either a single wavelength or a mixture

Spectral Hues

Figure 4.16
The Color Circle
Ordering the colors according to their psychological similarities results in a circle that reveals some interesting things about color vision. For example, although there are pure wavelengths that are sensed as red or green, there is no single wavelength that corresponds to purple. The color circle also allows one to predict the result of additive mixing of two colored lights. The resulting color will be on a line between the two starting colors, the exact location on the line depending on the relative proportions of the two colors. For example, mixing equal amounts of pure green and pure red will produce yellow, the color that lies at the midpoint of the line connecting red and green. This circle also reveals how purple can be generated: by mixing red and blue light.

Figure 4.17
Matching a Color by Mixing Lights of Pure Wavelengths
Experiments like this generated the information that led Young to propose the trichromatic theory of color vision. The subject is presented with a target color on the left side of the display; the subject's task is to adjust the intensity of the different pure-wavelength lights until the resultant mixture looks exactly like the target. A large number of colors can be matched with just two mixing lights, but Young found that any color can be matched by mixing three pure wavelength lights.

Color to be matched

Knob to adjust intensity

Mixture of many wavelengths

Each projector produces one pure wavelength color

The discovery of three types of cones, and how their activity can combine, made color television possible. Color television screens have microscopic dots, or elements, that are either red, green, or blue. The television broadcast excites these elements to varying degrees, thus mixing their colors to produce many other colors. We see these color mixtures rather than patterns of red, green, and blue because the element dots are too small and close together to be seen individually.

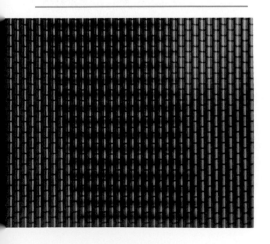

adding different colored lights, you eventually get white (the combined color of all wavelengths).

By mixing lights of just a few wavelengths, you can produce different color sensations. How many wavelengths are needed to create any color? Figure 4.17 illustrates an experiment that addresses this question. The answer has helped lead scientists to an important theory of how we sense color.

The trichromatic theory of color vision Early in the nineteenth century, Thomas Young and, later, Hermann von Helmholtz established through experimentation that any color could be matched by mixing pure lights of just three wavelengths of light. For example, by mixing blue light (about 440 nanometers), green (about 510 nanometers), and red (about 600 nanometers) in different ratios, you can produce any other color. Based on this evidence, Young and Helmholtz postulated that there are three types of visual elements, each of which is most sensitive to different wavelengths, and that information from these three elements combines to produce the sensation of color. This theory of color vision is called the *Young-Helmholtz theory,* or the **trichromatic theory.**

Support for the trichromatic theory has come from modern recordings of the responses of individual photoreceptors to light of a particular wavelength. As shown in Figure 4.18, this research reveals that there are three types of cones. Although each type responds to a broad range of wavelengths, each is most sensitive to particular wavelengths. *Short-wavelength cones* respond most to light of 440 nanometers (a shade of blue). *Medium-wavelength cones* are most sensitive to light of about 530 nanometers (a shade of green). Finally, *long-wavelength cones* respond best to light of about 560 nanometers (reddish yellow). Recently, scientists have found the basis for this differential sensitivity in the form of genes that direct different cones to produce pigments sensitive to blue, green, or yellow-red (Nathans et al., 1986; Nathans, Thomas & Hogness, 1986).

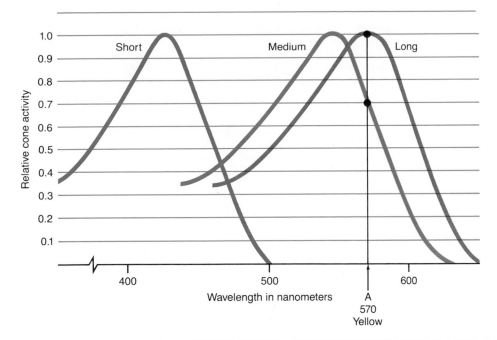

Figure 4.18
Relative Responses of Three Cone Types to Different Wavelengths of Light
Each type of cone responds to a range of wavelengths, but responds more to some wavelengths than to others. Because each cone type responds to a range of wavelengths, it is possible to generate the same pattern of output of cones—and hence the same sensation of color—by more than one combination of wavelengths. For example, a pure light of 570 nanometers (A in the figure) stimulates long-wavelength cones at 1.0 relative units and medium-wavelength cones at 0.7 relative units. This ratio of cone activity (1/0.7 = 1.4) yields the sensation of yellow. Any combination of wavelengths at the proper intensity that generates the same ratio of activity in these cone types will produce the sensation of yellow.

Note that no single cone, by itself, can signal the color of a light. The *ratio* of the activities of the three types of cones indicates what color will be sensed. Color vision is therefore coded by the pattern of activity of the different cones. For example, you will sense a light as yellow if it has a pure wavelength of 570 nanometers; this light stimulates both medium- and long-wavelength cones, as illustrated by arrow A in Figure 4.18. But you will sense the same color when the same two cone types are stimulated by mixtures of other lights that stimulate the same pattern of activity in these two types of cones.

Figure 4.19
Afterimages Produced by the Opponent-Process Nature of Color Vision
Stare at the dot in the figure for at least 30 seconds, then fixate on the dot in the white space below it.

The opponent-process theory of color vision   Some aspects of color vision cannot be explained by the trichromatic theory in its simplest form. For example, it cannot account for color afterimages. If you stare at Figure 4.19 for 30 seconds and then look at the blank white space below it, you will see an afterimage. What was yellow in the original image will be blue in the afterimage, and what was green before will appear red.

This type of observation led Ewald Hering to offer an alternative to the trichromatic theory, called the **opponent-process theory.** It holds that the visual elements sensitive to color are grouped into three pairs and that the members of each pair oppose, or inhibit, each other. The three pairs are a red-green element, a blue-yellow element, and a black-white element. Each element signals one color or the other—red or green, for example—but never both. This explains why certain colors, such as greenish red or yellowish blue, never occur, even though it is quite possible to see bluish green or reddish yellow. Hering's opponent-process theory also explains color afterimages. It proposes that, when one part of an opponent pair is no longer stimulated, the other is automatically activated. Thus, if the original image you looked at were green, the afterimage would be red (see Figure 4.19).

The opponent-process theory is also consistent with characteristics of the color circle. Every color on the circle has a complementary color. Two colors are **complementary** if gray results when lights of the two colors are mixed together. On the color circle (Figure 4.16), complementary colors are roughly opposite. Red and green are complementary, as are yellow and blue. Notice

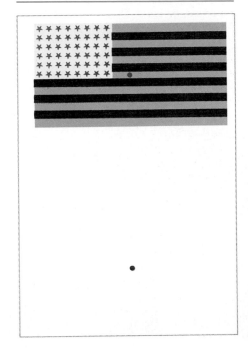

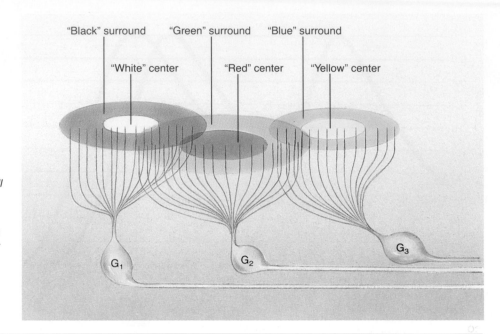

Figure 4.20
Color Coding and the Ganglion Cells
The center and surround of the ganglion cell receptive fields form the anatomical basis for opponent colors. Some ganglion cells, like G2, have a center whose photoreceptors respond best to red wavelengths and a surround that responds best to green wavelengths. Other ganglion cells pair blue and yellow. Some ganglion cells have receptive fields that are not particular about color; they receive input from all types of photoreceptors. The receptive fields of some ganglion cells overlap.

that complementary colors are *opponent* colors in Hering's theory. According to opponent-process theory, complementary colors stimulate the same visual element (for example, red-green) in opposite directions, canceling each other out. Thus, the theory helps explain why mixing complementary colors produces gray. The opponent-process theory also explains why colors such as purple appear on the color circle, but not in the spectrum of visible light (see Figure 4.8). Purple is actually a product of stimulating the blue element and the red element in the visual system.

A synthesis   The trichromatic and opponent-process theories seem quite different, but both are correct to some extent, and together, they can explain most of what we now know about color vision. Electrical recordings made from different types of cells in the retina paved the way for a synthesis of the two theories.

At the level of the photoreceptors, the trichromatic theory is right: as we said, there are three types of cones. However, we also noted that output from many photoreceptors feeds into each ganglion cell, and the output from the ganglion cell goes to the brain. Recall that the receptive fields of most ganglion cells are arranged in center-surround patterns. The center and the surround are color coded, as illustrated in Figure 4.20. The center responds best to one color, and the surround responds best to a different color. This color coding arises because varying proportions of the three cone types feed into the center and surround of the ganglion cell.

When either the center or the surround of the ganglion cell is stimulated, the other is inhibited. In other words, the colors to which the center versus the surround of a given ganglion cell are most responsive are opponent colors. Recordings from many ganglion cells show that three very common pairs of opponent colors are those predicted by Hering's opponent-process theory: red-green, blue-yellow, and white-black. White-black cells receive input from all types of cones, so it does not matter what color stimulates them. Stimulating both the center and the surround cancels the effects of either light, producing gray. This is the basis for complementary colors. In dim light, cones are not responsive, but rods are, and all ganglion cells lose the color-coding aspect of their center-surround properties.

In summary, color vision is possible because three types of cones have different sensitivities to different wavelengths, as the trichromatic theory suggests. The sensation of different colors results from stimulating the three cone types in different ratios. Because there are three types of cones, any color can be produced by mixing three different wavelengths of light. But the story does not end there. The output from cones is fed into ganglion cells; the center and surround of the ganglion cells respond to different colors and inhibit each other. This activity provides the basis for the phenomena of complementary colors and afterimages. Therefore, the trichromatic theory embodies the properties of the photoreceptors, while Hering's opponent-process theory embodies the properties of the other layers of the retina. Both theories are needed to account for the complexity of visual sensations of color.

Color blindness What kind of color vision would a person have if he or she had cones containing only two of the three color-sensitive pigments mentioned earlier? Many people have this condition, and they are described as *color blind*. They are not actually blind to all color; they simply discriminate fewer colors than other people.

The most common form of color blindness involves red and green. To people with red-green color blindness, red and green look the same; they probably appear much like brown does to people with normal vision. Examine Figure 4.21 to determine whether you might be color blind. If you have three types of cone pigments, you should be able to see a 48 embedded in the figure; if you are red-green color blind, the 48 will not be apparent.

Visual Pathways to the Brain

In addition to all the retinal visual processing that we have described, even more elaborate processing takes place within the brain. Information is brought there by axons from ganglion cells. These axons, which are several inches long, leave the eye as a bundle of fibers called the **optic nerve.** The axons from all of the ganglion cells converge and exit the eyeball at one point (see Figures 4.9 and 4.12). This exit point has no photoreceptors and is therefore insensitive to light, creating a **blind spot,** as Figure 4.22 demonstrates.

Figure 4.21
A Test for Red-Green Color Blindness
Because people with red-green color blindness do not discriminate red from green, they do not see the red 48 embedded in the green dots. However, they are still able to discriminate red from blue.
(Dvorine Color Vision Test. Copyright 1944, 1953, 1958 by The Psychological Corporation. Reproduced by permission. All rights reserved.)

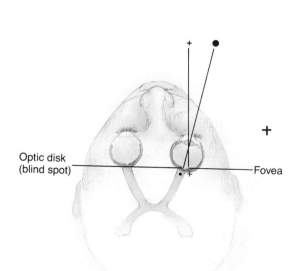

Optic disk (blind spot) — Fovea

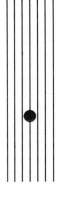

Figure 4.22
The Blind Spot
The blind spot occurs in the region of the retina where the axons from the ganglion cells leave the eye as the optic nerve; the area is devoid of photoreceptors. To "see" your blind spot, cover your left eye and stare at the cross. Move the page closer and farther away, and at some point (less than 1 foot from your face), the dot to the right should disappear from view. When this happens, the vertical lines around the dot will probably look like they are continuous, since the brain tends to fill in visual information at the blind spot. We are not normally aware of the blind spot, because the blind spot of one eye is in the normal visual field of the other eye.

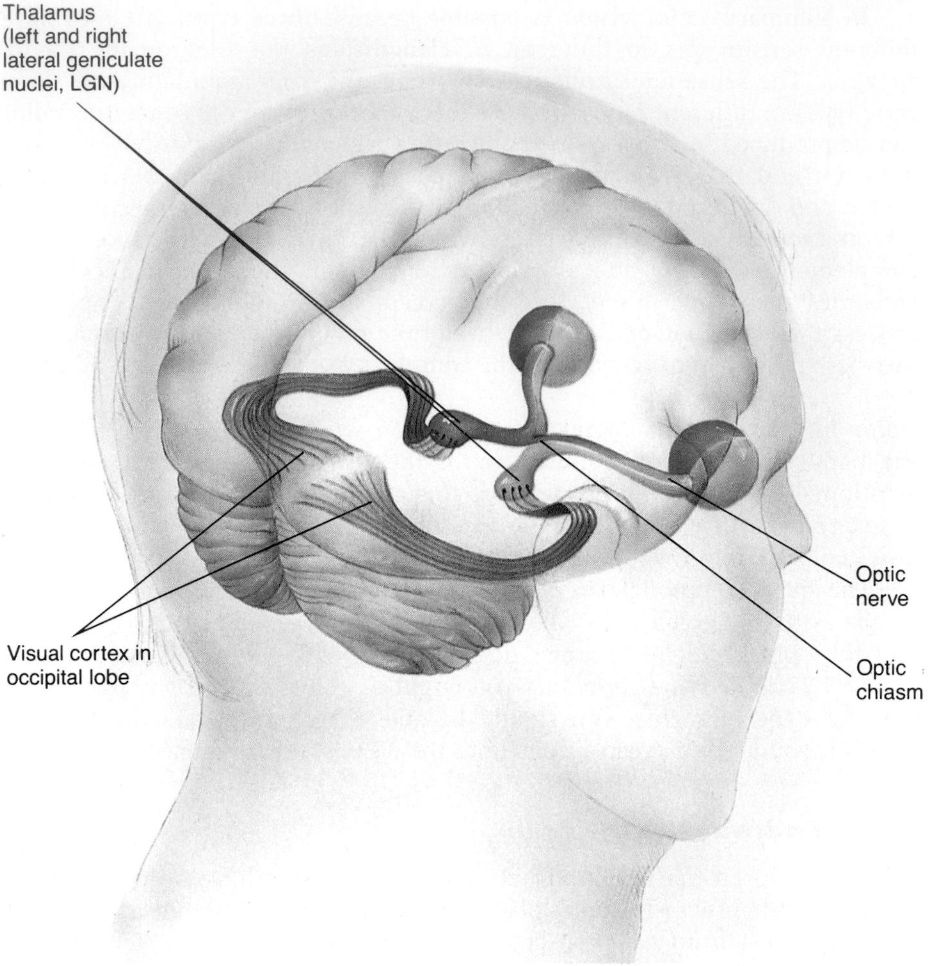

Thalamus
(left and right
lateral geniculate
nuclei, LGN)

Figure 4.23
Pathways from the Ganglion Cells into the Brain
Light rays from the right side of the visual field (everything on the right side of what you are looking at) end up on the left half of the retina. In order to unite both eyes' information about the right visual field in the same part of the brain, one of the pathways must cross over to the other side of the brain. From the right eye, the axons from the nasal side of the retina (the side nearer the nose, which receives input from the right visual field) cross over the midline and travel with those fibers from the left eye, which also receive input from the right side of the visual world. A similar arrangement unites left visual field information from both eyes in the right side of the brain. Fibers from the nasal side of the left eye's retina cross the midline, while fibers from the part of it toward the ear remain uncrossed. The axons have a synapse in the thalamus, in the lateral geniculate nucleus. From there, neurons send axons to the visual cortex in the occipital lobe.

Optic
nerve

Optic
chiasm

Visual cortex in
occipital lobe

After leaving the retina, about half the fibers of the optic nerve cross over to the opposite side of the brain at a structure called the **optic chiasm** (*chiasm* means "cross"). Whether a fiber crosses over depends on the location of its receptive field. Fibers from the inside half of each eye, nearest to the nose, cross over; fibers from the outside half of each eye do not. This arrangement makes sense when you realize that the same half of each eye is looking at the same part of the visual field, as Figure 4.23 shows. Thus, the crossing at the optic chiasm brings all the visual information about the right half of the visual world to the left hemisphere of the brain and information from the left half to the right hemisphere of the brain.

The optic chiasm is part of the bottom surface of the brain; beyond the chiasm, the fibers ascend into the brain itself. The axons from most of the ganglion cells in the retina finally end and form synapses in the thalamus, in a specific region called the **lateral geniculate nucleus (LGN),** as Figure 4.23 shows. Neurons in the LGN then relay the visual input to the **primary visual cortex,** which lies in the occipital lobe at the back of the brain. The most complex processing of visual information occurs in the visual cortex. There sensations finally become conscious. Two important characteristics of the visual cortex that influence these sensations are the receptive fields of the cortical cells and the organization of the cortex.

Feature detectors   Unlike the cells of the retina or the LGN, few cells in the cortex have center-surround receptive fields. They respond instead to certain

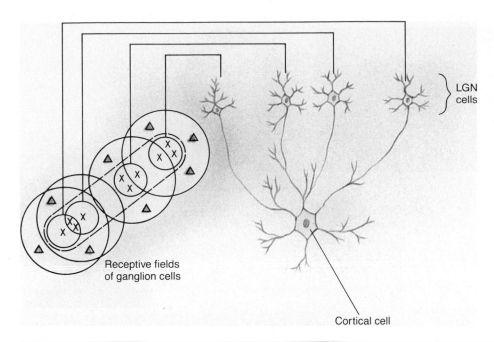

Receptive fields
of ganglion cells

Cortical cell

Figure 4.24
Construction of a Feature Detector
The cortical cell in this case responds best to a bar-shaped light stimulus. The output from several ganglion cells that have receptive fields in a row and have excitatory centers goes to the lateral geniculate nucleus (LGN). The output from those LGN cells feeds into one cell in the cortex. This cortical cell responds best when all of the LGN cells are excited, and the LGN cells are excited when light falls on the center of the receptive fields of the ganglion cells; in other words, when a bar-shaped light is oriented so that it stimulates the centers of the receptive fields. Rotating the bar to a different orientation would no longer stimulate this particular cortical cell.
(From Hubel, D. H., and Wiesel, T. N., 1962, 1965; redrawn by Kuffler, S. W., and Nicholls, A., 1976, *From Neuron to Brain,* Sinauer Associates, Inc.)

features of objects in the visual field (Hubel & Wiesel, 1979). For example, a specific cell in the cortex might respond only to vertical edges. No matter where in the receptive field a vertical edge is presented, this cell increases its firing rate. Another class of cells might respond only to moving objects; a third might respond only to objects with corners. These cells in the cortex that respond to specific features of objects are called **feature detectors.** How do they work? Feature detectors might function by combining the input from a number of center-surround ganglion cells, as illustrated in Figure 4.24.

One theory of how the cortex puts together information from the ganglion cells to produce feature detectors is called the *hierarchical feature-detection model.* This model holds that any object seen is a compilation of features and that complex feature detectors are built up out of more and more complex connections of simpler feature detectors (Hubel & Wiesel, 1979). For example, several center-surround cells might feed into one cell that is a line detector, and several line detectors might feed into one cell that responds to a particular spatial orientation, such as the vertical. With further connections, a more complex detector, such as a "box detector," might be built from the simpler line and corner detectors.

The problem with using this model to explain how people see patterns and objects is that they would need a high-order feature detector corresponding to each recognized object. An example of such a high-order feature detector would be a "grandmother cell," a cell that fires whenever you see your grandmother, from any angle, no matter what she is wearing. Although a hierarchical feature-detection model has a certain simplicity, the question of whether we actually have the immense number of specific feature detectors needed to sense each of the vast array of visual stimuli is still unanswered.

Spatial
Frequency
Analysis

One alternative to the feature-detection model is the *spatial frequency filter model.* According to this model, the brain analyzes patterns, not by putting together information about lines, edges, and other features, but by analyzing gradual changes in brightness over broad areas. Compared with the feature-detection model, this

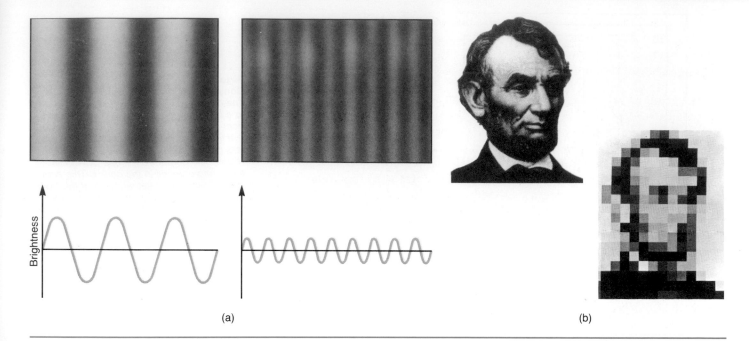

(a)   (b)

Figure 4.25
Spatial Frequency
The visual system has detectors for different spatial frequencies. (a) These gratings illustrate two different "pure" spatial frequencies, analogous to two pure tones. The one on the left is of low spatial frequency and high amplitude; the one on the right is of higher spatial frequency and low amplitude. By adding together appropriate sine waves representing pure spatial frequencies, it is possible to represent images that do not initially appear anything like sine waves. (b) An illustration of how the visual system can extract information based on a spatial frequency analysis of a visual pattern. The image on the bottom was generated by a computer, which took an average of the light-dark level within each block of the figure on the top. The blocks are therefore a low spatial frequency analysis of the figure, but the edges of the blocks are a high spatial frequency component that interferes with "seeing" the figure. To see just the low spatial frequency components, take off your glasses (if you wear them), and blur your vision by squinting. The figure on the bottom will now look as much like Lincoln as the one on the top, and much more so than the blocked figure viewed normally.

(Part a: From *Fundamentals of Sensation and Perception* by M. W. Levine and J. M. Shefner, Addison-Wesley, 1981. Part b: Leon B. Harmon and Bela Julesz, *Science,* 180: 1194–97 (1973). Copyright 1973 by the AAAs.)

view is much more difficult to appreciate intuitively, but it does not require a specific cell for every type of visual sensation.

The spatial frequency model points out, first, that any pattern, no matter how complex, can theoretically be decomposed into component regions of light and dark, which can be represented by sine waves, just as any sound can be synthesized by combining sound waves of many different amplitudes and frequencies. Look at Figure 4.25a, which shows how a pattern of light and dark bars can be represented by a sine wave. The pattern of bars is called a *sine-wave grating.* Narrow areas of light and dark are represented by a high-frequency sine wave, and broader areas of light and dark are represented by a lower-frequency sine wave.

If you combined many gratings like those in Figure 4.25a with different frequencies and orientations, you would end up with a complex pattern. The spatial frequency filter model suggests that the brain does the opposite. It holds that the brain analyzes the visual world by reducing it to patterns of alternating light and dark of different frequencies. It says that your brain, in effect, can analyze waveforms using complex Fourier analysis (pronounced "for-yay"). *Fourier analysis* decomposes a complicated waveform into the simple sine waves that created it (see Figure 4.25b). Even if a pattern of light and dark did not start out as sine waves, it can be *represented* in the brain as a collection of many sine waves.

What evidence is there that your visual cortex might do this complicated kind of mathematics? If you shine a series of sine-wave gratings (like those in Figure 4.25a) on the retina and record the activity of cells in the visual cortex, you find that each neuron responds best to a bar-and-space grating with a particular frequency. You can take a specific cell and find its preferred sine wave; the same cell will also have a preferred bar stimulus.

There is another clue that the visual system might work according to the spatial frequency filter model. If there were specific feature detectors for each object or shape in a particular cortical location, removing one part of the visual cortex should eliminate the ability to see a certain type of object. But removing part of the cortex does not have this effect. This suggests that a large part of the visual cortex might participate, through Fourier analysis, in sensing each object.

This description of spatial frequency analysis should demonstrate that there is a great deal to learn about the way the brain makes use of its sensory input. The mysteries are by no means solved, and there is evidence to support at least two drastically different theories of how people see things. ◼

Organization of cortex   If you poked around in the visual cortex with an electrode, recording the activity of cells while presenting a variety of visual stimuli, you would discover that the retina's topographical map of the visual world is maintained all the way to the brain. That is, neighboring points in the retina are represented in neighboring cells in the cortex. The map is a distorted one, however. A larger area of cortex is devoted to the areas of the retina that have many photoreceptors. For example, the fovea, which is densely packed with photoreceptors, is represented in an especially large segment of cortex.

If you explored the surface of the cortex with an electrode, you would also find that there is more than one complete map of the retina. In fact, there are more than ten complete representations of the visual world on primates' visual cortex (Merzenich & Kaas, 1980). Other senses also have multiple representations; the large number for vision may reflect its special importance, but no one yet knows for sure.

Another thing you would notice about the visual cortex is that each point on the topographical map is made up of functional columns of cells that share a common property, such as responding to one type of visual stimulus. These columns are arranged perpendicular to the surface of the cortex. For example, if we locate a cell that responds to diagonal lines in a particular spot in the visual field, most of the cells in a column above and below it will also respond to diagonal lines. Other properties are represented by whole columns of cells, so that we could record the activity of a column in which all of the cells are most sensitive to a particular color.

THE CHEMICAL SENSES: SMELL AND TASTE

There are animals without vision, and there are animals without hearing, but there are no animals without some form of chemical sense; that is, without some sense that arises from the interaction of chemicals and receptors. Smell, or **olfaction,** detects chemicals that are airborne, or *volatile.* Taste, or **gustation,** is the sense that detects chemicals in solution that come into contact with receptors inside the mouth.

Olfaction

All animals use olfaction, the sense of smell, along with taste, to detect and select things to eat. For many animals, olfaction also plays an important role in communication and other social behavior. Chemicals called **pheromones** can be released by one animal, detected by another, and then shape that second animal's behavior or physiology. Often, though not always, the pheromone is detected by the olfactory system. For example, many male animals determine whether a potential partner is ready for sex partly on the basis of the other animal's odor. Smells can also create readiness for mating in females.

There is no solid evidence that people give off or can smell pheromones that act as sexual attractants. But humans can still use olfactory information from other individuals. For example, after just a few hours of contact, mothers can usually identify their newborn babies by the infants' smell or the smell of

Substances that have similar chemical structures generally tend to have similar odors, but how olfactory receptors in the nose discriminate various smells and code them in ways the brain can interpret is still unknown.

their clothing (Porter et al., 1983). Adults can also tell males from females on the basis of smell, although the discrimination is based mainly on the strength of the odor rather than on a specific smell (Doty, 1981). And males generally claim to prefer the odor of their regular sex partner to the odors of unfamiliar females, although they make this assertion even when the odors have been switched (Schleidt, Hold & Attili, 1981).

For humans, however, the role of olfaction is quite different from its role for dogs and other animals. Humans tend to form a learned association between certain odors and sexual activity, which may enhance their readiness for sex but does not drive them to it. Manufacturers of perfumes, colognes, and aftershaves have certainly capitalized on these learned associations in an attempt to increase their sales.

We sense odors in the upper part of the nose (see Figure 4.26). Receptors there detect molecules that pass from the air into the moisture of the lining of the nose. Molecules can reach these receptors either through the nose or through an opening in the palate at the back of the mouth. Thus, the olfactory sense is a dual sense: unlike the other senses, it detects objects that are either internal (in the mouth) or external (Rozin, 1982).

In any event, olfaction is the only sense that does not send its messages to the thalamus. The axons from the nose pass a short distance, through a bony plate, directly into the brain, where they synapse in a structure called the **olfactory bulb.** Connections from the olfactory bulb spread diffusely through the brain, but they are especially plentiful in the amygdala, a part of the brain involved in emotional experience. This anatomical fact is consistent with the psychological fact that smells are emotionally powerful.

Not all smells affect everyone equally, since almost everyone is incapable of sensing certain odors. For example, about 33 percent of people are unable to smell cineole, the odor of camphor, and about 3 percent cannot detect sweat. People in these categories may count themselves lucky, but for sewer

Figure 4.26
The Olfactory System: The Nose and the Rose
Airborne chemicals from the rose reach the olfactory area through the nostrils and through the back of the mouth. Fibers pass directly from the olfactory area to the olfactory bulb in the brain, and from there signals pass to areas such as the hypothalamus and amygdala that are involved in emotion.

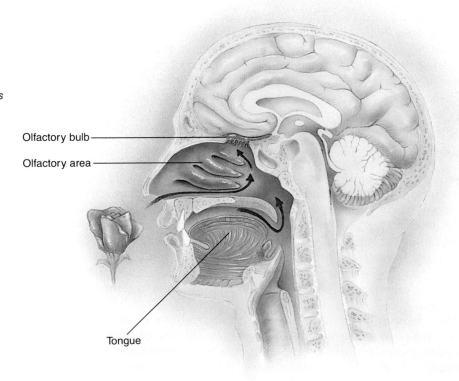

workers unable to smell deadly hydrogen cyanide gas, such "odor blindness" can be dangerous.

Gustation

The chemical sense system in the mouth is gustation, or taste. The receptors for taste are in the taste buds, which are grouped together in structures called **papillae** on the tongue. There are about ten thousand taste buds in the normal person's mouth, most of them on the tongue. Others are located at the back of the throat.

Our taste system detects only a very few elementary sensations: sweet, sour, bitter, and salty. Each taste bud responds best to one or two of these categories, but it also responds weakly to other categories. The sensation of a particular substance results from the coded *pattern* of responses by many taste buds, none of which is completely specific for a given taste. However, different regions of the tongue are more sensitive to different tastes. For example, the back of the tongue is most sensitive to bitterness, and the front of the tongue is most sensitive to sweetness.

HIGHLIGHT

Taste Receptors and Sugar Substitutes

Scientists are still trying to determine the properties that allow chemicals to stimulate specific types of taste receptors. Among the facts they do know is that sweetness is signaled when a chemical fits into receptor sites at three points (Raloff, 1985). This knowledge has allowed chemists to design new chemicals that fit receptors just that way, making a substance taste sweet. If the new chemical is also safe and has few calories, it is bound to be a popular and profitable artificial sweetener.

For a time, it was thought that saccharin was such a chemical. It is a very potent stimulator of sweetness receptors, but, because it appears to cause cancer, saccharin has now been largely replaced by aspartame (marketed as NutraSweet).

NutraSweet is described by its manufacturer (Searle) as safe and the most thoroughly tested compound ever marketed. Its use was approved by the Food and Drug Administration (FDA). Nevertheless, there is some controversy about whether aspartame causes problems in the central nervous system. Most of the concern has focused on the phenylalanine in aspartame. Phenylalanine is a precursor, or preliminary form, of several neurotransmitters (substances that allow communication between neurons), and it competes for entry into the brain with other neurotransmitter precursors. The amount of a precursor in the brain can alter the amount of neurotransmitter in the brain, and this, in turn, can alter a person's behavior or mood. Some people have claimed that aspartame causes sleep problems, headaches, and can even increase appetite by affecting the neurotransmitter serotonin. But the FDA has judged that the changes are not significant enough to cause the problems that aspartame's critics attribute to it.

Another artificial sweetener on the horizon, called RTI-001, does not contain phenylalanine (Raloff, 1985). It has passed initial safety tests, but it must undergo years of testing before it is ready for the market.

There is another way to produce sweet sensations without sugar: use chemicals to modify the taste receptors so that they will send coded signals for sweetness to the brain. For example, "miracle fruit," native to Africa, contains a substance that modifies sweetness receptors so that they respond to acids like vinegar, which normally taste sour (Bartoshuk et al., 1974). If you first eat miracle fruit, anything that normally tastes sour will instead taste sweet. ■

The blending of smell and taste is usually referred to as flavor. Because smell and taste are so easily confused, most people are unaware of how much the flavor of food is due to its smell. Yet, if you close your eyes and hold your nose, thus preventing odors from reaching olfactory receptors, you will probably be unable to tell whether you are eating a potato or an apple. This is why the nasal congestion that accompanies a common cold makes food seem tasteless.

Smell, Taste, and Flavor

There are some reasons to consider smell and taste as two components of just one sensoriperceptual system, **flavor** (Rozin, 1982). Most of the properties that make food taste good are actually odors detected by the olfactory system, not activities of the taste system. And there is some evidence that the olfactory and gustatory pathways converge in some areas of the brain (Van Buskirk & Erickson, 1977). Still, no one knows yet how smell and taste come to seem like one sensation.

Flavor is also affected by the temperature of food. When the temperature is high, the chemicals in food become more volatile, releasing aromas that rise from the mouth into the nose and create better taste sensations. This is why many people find hot pizza delicious and cold pizza disgusting. Even the texture of food can alter its flavor. The texture and the heat of food are sensed through nerve endings in the mouth that are sensitive to temperature, pressure, touch, and pain—sensations that we examine in the next section.

SOMATIC SENSES AND THE VESTIBULAR SYSTEM

Some senses are not located in a specific organ, such as the eye or the ear. These are the **somatic senses,** also called **somatosensory systems,** which are spread throughout the body. The somatic senses include the skin senses of touch, temperature, and pain, and kinesthesia, the sense that tells the brain where the parts of the body are. Even though it is not strictly a somatosensory system, the vestibular system will also be considered in this section because its function—telling the brain about the position and movements of the head—is closely related to kinesthesia.

Touch and Temperature

Touch is vitally important. Blind people survive and prosper, as do deaf people and people without taste. But a person without touch would have difficulty surviving. Without a sense of touch, you could not even swallow food.

The stimulus and receptors for touch   The energy detected and transduced into neural activity by the sense of touch is a mechanical deformation of tissue, generally the skin, frequently by stimulation of the hairs on the skin. Hairs do not sense anything directly (an observation you must have made, gratefully, when you got your first haircut), but when hairs are bent, they deform the skin beneath them.

Presumably, the receptors that respond to this deformation are in or somewhere near the skin. The skin covers nearly two square yards of surface, weighs more than twenty pounds, and includes many nerve endings that are candidates for the role of touch receptor. Some nerves that enter the skin from the spinal cord simply end; these are called *free nerve endings.* Many other nerves end in a variety of elaborate, specialized structures. However, there is no relationship between the type of nerve ending and the type of sensory information carried by the nerve. Our best information at present suggests that there are no specialized receptors for touch. Instead, many types of nerve endings respond to mechanical stimuli, but the exact process through which they transduce mechanical energy is still unknown.

People do more than just passively respond to whatever happens to come in contact with their bodies; jellyfish can do that much. For humans, touch can also be an active sense that is used to get specific information. Much as you can look as well as just see, you can also touch as well as feel. When people are involved in active sensing, they usually use the part of the sensory apparatus that has the greatest resolution, or sensitivity. For vision, this part is the fovea; for touch, the fingertips have the greatest sensitivity and accuracy. (The area of primary sensory cortex devoted to the fingertips is correspondingly large, as you can see in Figure 3.16.) Fingertip touch is the main way we explore the textures of surfaces. It can be extremely sensitive, as is evident not only in sensual caresses but also in the speed with which blind people can read Braille. The mouth, especially the lips, also has many touch receptors (one reason why kissing is so popular). You probably no longer depend on your lips to explore the world, but for infants and young children, who have not developed the ability to coordinate hand movements, the sense of touch in the mouth is an important way of learning about the world.

Adaptation of touch receptors   Constant input from all the touch nerves would provide an abundance of unnecessary information. Once you get dressed, for example, you do not need to be constantly reminded that you are wearing clothes and in fact do not continue to feel your clothes against your skin. *Changes* in touch (for example, that your jeans have suddenly dropped to your knees) constitute the most important sensory information.

The touch sense emphasizes changes and filters out excess information through **adaptation,** the process through which responsiveness to a constant stimulus decreases over time. Typically, a touch nerve responds with a burst of firing when a stimulus is applied, then quickly returns to baseline firing rates, even though the stimulus may still be in contact with the skin. If the touch pressure increases, the nerve again responds with an increase in firing rate, but then it again slows down. A much smaller number of nerves adapts more slowly, continuing to fire at an elevated rate as long as pressure is applied to the skin.

The coding of touch information   The sense of touch codes information about three aspects of an object in contact with the skin: How heavy is it? Is it vibrating? and Where is it? The *intensity* of the stimulus—how heavy it is— is coded by both the firing rate of individual nerves and the number of nerves stimulated. A heavy object produces a higher rate of firing and stimulates more nerves than a light object. *Vibrations* are simply rapid fluctuations in pressure, and information about them is also coded by changes in the firing rate. *Location* is coded much as it is for vision: by the organization of the information.

In the sense of touch, this organization is called **somatotopic** (*somato-* means "body," and *topos* means "place"). Basically, the information is organized so that signals from neighboring points on the skin stay next to each other, even as they ascend from the skin through the spinal cord to the thalamus and on to the cortex. Consequently, just as there is a topographical map of the visual field in the brain, the area of cortex, called *somatosensory cortex,* that receives touch information resembles a map of the surface of the body. (To confirm this, look again at Figure 3.16.) For example, the cells in the cortex that receive input from the wrist and the hand are close to each other, because the wrist and hand are close to each other on the surface of the skin. As with the other senses, these representations are contralateral; input from the left hand and wrist goes mainly to the right side of the brain.

Temperature   When you lie on a beach in the summer and dig your toes in the sand, you experience a pleasant stimulation, part of which comes from the sensation of the warmth of the sand. But are touch and temperature separate senses? To some extent they are. Electrical recordings made from

The sense of touch was vital to Helen Keller, as it is to other blind people who "read" the raised dots of Braille with their fingers.

sensory nerves on the skin show that some of them clearly respond to a change in temperature, but not to simple contact by a thermally neutral stimulus. There are "warm fibers" that increase their firing rates when the temperature changes in the range of about 95° to 115° F (35° to 47° C). Temperatures above this range are painful and stimulate different fibers. Other fibers are "cold fibers"; they respond to a broad range of cool temperatures.

Still, many of the fibers that respond to temperature also respond to touch. Even free nerve endings in the skin can convey touch, temperature, or pain. Different patterns of activity in a single nerve fiber can code different stimuli. For example, in one nerve a brief, smooth increase in firing might signal touch; a sustained, regular increase in the same nerve might signal warmth; and variable, high-frequency activity could signal pain (Wall & Cronly-Dillon, 1960). But because no one knows how the different stimuli set up different patterns of firing, scientists have so far been unable to resolve whether each of the various skin senses has a separate existence or whether they are just aspects of the touch sense. Because the same nerves sometimes respond to both touch and temperature, you might expect that these sensations sometimes interact. This does, in fact, happen. For example, either warm or cold objects feel much heavier than thermally neutral objects—up to 250 percent heavier (Stevens, 1982).

Pain

The skin senses can convey a great deal of pleasure, but a change in the intensity of the same kind of stimulation can create a distinctly different sensation: pain. Pain provides you with information about the impact of the world on your body; it can tell you, "You have just crushed your left thumb with a hammer." Pain also has a distinctly aversive emotional component. Researchers trying to understand pain have focused on the information-carrying aspects of pain, its emotional components, and the various ways that the brain can adjust the amount of pain that reaches consciousness.

Pain as an information sense   If we consider just the information-carrying aspect of pain, it is very similar to touch and temperature. The receptors for pain are free nerve endings, but no one knows how the free nerve endings that signal pain differ from other free nerve endings. Much is still unknown about just how pain is created, but it appears that painful stimuli damage tissue and cause the release of *bradykinin,* a chemical that fits into specialized receptors in pain nerves, causing them to fire.

Two types of nerve fibers carry pain signals from the skin to the spinal cord. *A-delta fibers* carry sharp pain, and *C fibers* carry several types of pain, including chronic, dull aches. These same C fibers also respond to nonpainful touch, but with a different pattern of firing. Both A-delta and C fibers carry the pain impulses into the spinal cord, where they form synapses with neurons that carry the pain signals to the thalamus and other parts of the brain (see Figure 4.27).

Emotional aspects of pain   All senses can have emotional components, most of which are learned responses. For example, the smell of baking cookies may make you feel happy because it has been associated with happy childhood times. The emotional response to pain is more direct. Specific pathways carry an emotional component of the painful stimulus to areas of the medulla and reticular formation (see Figure 4.27), activating aversion.

Nevertheless, the overall emotional response to pain depends greatly on cognitive factors. For example, experimenters have compared two groups' responses to a precise, painful stimulus. The two groups involved (1) people

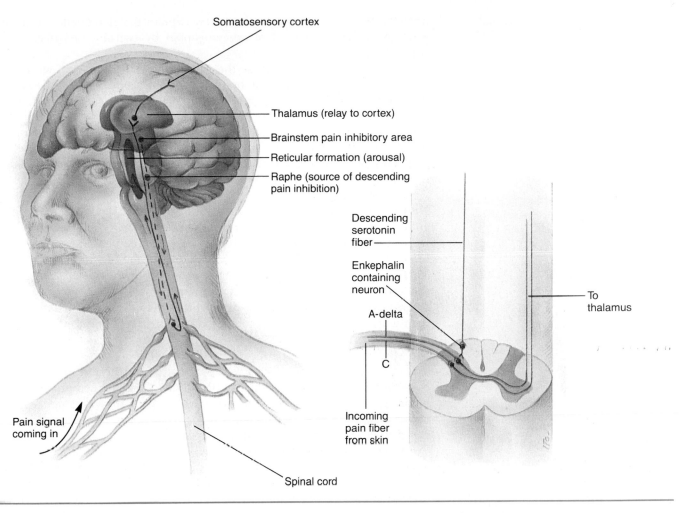

Somatosensory cortex

Thalamus (relay to cortex)

Brainstem pain inhibitory area

Reticular formation (arousal)

Raphe (source of descending pain inhibition)

Descending serotonin fiber

Enkephalin containing neuron

A-delta

C

To thalamus

Incoming pain fiber from skin

Pain signal coming in

Spinal cord

who were informed about the nature of the stimulus and when to expect it and (2) people who were not informed. Knowing about pain seemed to make it less aversive, even though the sensation was reported to be just as intense (Mayer & Price, 1982). Just how cognitive factors influence what people perceive and feel will be explored in the chapters on perception, emotion, and stress.

Modulation of pain: The gate theory   Pain is an extremely useful sense, because in the long run, it protects a person from harm. However, there are times when enough is enough. Fortunately, the nervous system has several mechanisms for controlling the experience of pain. One explanation of how the nervous system controls the amount of pain that reaches the brain is the **gate theory** (Melzack & Wall, 1965). It holds that there is a functional "gate" in the spinal cord that either lets pain impulses travel upward to the brain or blocks their progress. According to the theory, this gate can be closed by two mechanisms.

First, input from other skin senses can come into the spinal cord at the same time the pain gets there and can "take over" the pathways that the pain impulses would have used. Thus, nonpainful and painful sensations coming into the spinal cord in effect compete for pathways to the brain. This appears to be why rubbing the skin around a wound reduces the pain you feel, why electrical stimulation of the skin around a painful spot relieves the pain, and why scratching relieves itching. (Itching is actually low-level activity in pain

Figure 4.27
Pain Pathways
Pain messages are carried from the periphery to the brain by way of the spinal cord. A-delta fibers are myelinated (that is, coated with the fatty substance myelin) and carry information about sharp pain. As noted in Chapter 3, impulses travel faster on myelinated fibers, so it makes sense that these fibers carry the sharp pains that come from punctures and other life-threatening stimuli. C fibers are unmyelinated fibers that carry several types of pain, including chronic, dull aches. Pain fibers make synapses in the reticular formation, causing arousal. They also project to the thalamus and from there to the cortex. Incoming pain messages can be "gated," or blocked in several ways, including by signals that descend from the brain to the spinal cord. Some of these gating neurons in the spinal cord use enkephalin, a natural opioid, as their neurotransmitter.

fibers.) This mechanism may also partly explain the effectiveness of acupuncture, the Oriental method of relieving pain by twirling fine needles in the skin.

Second, the brain can close the gate by sending signals down the spinal cord. These messages from the brain block pain signals when they synapse in the spinal cord. The result is **analgesia,** the absence of the sensation of pain in the presence of a normally painful stimulus. Support for this aspect of the gate theory has come from the discovery that electrical stimulation of certain parts of the brain produces analgesia (Reynolds, 1969). For example, if part of a rat's brainstem is electrically stimulated, the pain signal generated by heating the tip of the animal's tail never reaches the brain.

Natural analgesics   How messages from the brain block pain signals is not entirely clear, but two classes of substances seem to play a role: (1) the neurotransmitter *serotonin,* which is released by nerves descending from the brain, and (2) natural opiates called *endorphins, enkephalins,* and *dynorphins.* These natural painkillers act at many levels of the pain pathway, including the spinal cord, where they block the synapses of the fibers that carry pain signals from the skin and other parts of the body. Natural opiates also relieve pain when the adrenal and pituitary glands secrete them into the bloodstream as hormones.

Most of the time, the endorphin system is not active as an analgesic. This makes sense; chronic analgesia would defeat the purpose of pain, which is to cause you to escape or avoid damaging stimuli. Constant activity of the natural opiate system would not solve the problem of pain anyway, since, as with the opiate drugs discussed in Chapter 6, on consciousness, tolerance and addiction can also develop with endorphins.

What conditions cause the body to ease its own pain? Again, we do not have all the answers, but we do know that certain physiological conditions can activate natural analgesic systems. For example, there is evidence that a hormonal endorphin system operates during the late stages of pregnancy to reduce the mother's labor pains somewhat and create an apparent state of bliss in the fetus (Pert, 1979). Further, as we saw in Chapter 3, an endorphin system is activated when people *believe* they are receiving a painkiller, even when they get only a placebo. We also know that physical or psychological stress can activate natural analgesic systems. Different types of stress apparently bring different analgesic systems into action (Watkins & Mayer, 1982). For example, ridiculous as it may seem, shocking a rat's front feet activates a different system than shocking its hind feet. Stress-induced release of endorphins may account for instances in which severely injured soldiers and athletes continue to perform with no apparent pain.

If biological psychologists can determine how natural analgesic systems are brought into action, perhaps it will be possible to activate them in an alternating sequence, to relieve pain without producing tolerance and addiction (Watkins & Mayer, 1982). There is certainly a great need for this. Despite modern drugs, the pain of arthritis, migraine headaches, back pain, cancer, and other physical disorders imposes a heavy burden, causing suffering and disability to millions and costing more than $70 billion a year in medical costs, lost working days, and compensation (Bonica, 1984).

Proprioception

Most sensory systems receive information from the external world, such as the light reflected off green grass or the feeling of cool water washing over your feet. But as far as the brain is concerned, the rest of the body is "out there" too, and we know about where we are and what each part of our body is doing only because sensory systems provide this information to the brain. These sensory systems are called **proprioceptive** ("received from one's own").

Kinesthesia   The sense that tells you where the parts of your body are with respect to each other is **kinesthesia.** You probably do not think much about kinesthetic information, but you definitely use it. For example, even with your eyes closed, you can usually do a decent job of touching two fingers together in front of you. To do this, you must know where each finger is with respect to your body. You also depend on kinesthetic information to guide all your movements. Otherwise, it would be impossible to develop or improve any motor skill, from basic walking to complex athletic movements. These movement patterns become simple and fluid because, with practice, the brain uses kinesthetic information automatically.

Kinesthesia also plays an important role in a person's sense of self. Consider the case of Christina, the "disembodied woman." Christina has a rare neurological disease that, for unknown reasons, causes degeneration of the spinal nerves that provide kinesthetic information (Sacks, 1984). At first, Christina had difficulty holding onto objects; she would either grab them too tightly or let them slip out of her hands. Then she had trouble moving; she would rise from bed and flop onto the ground like a rag doll. Soon she began to feel she was losing her body; she was becoming disembodied, like a ghost. Once she became annoyed at her roommate for tapping her fingers on a table top. Then Christina saw that it was not her roommate, but Christina herself who was tapping. Her limbs were on their own, and her body was doing things she did not know about. The disease progressed until Christina had no sense of where her body was or what it was doing, even though all of her other senses were intact. If she looked at her hand and concentrated very hard, she could guide its movements. But she had a permanent loss of her sense of self. Today she still feels separated from herself, a stranger in her own body.

Normally, kinesthetic information comes from both muscles and joints. Receptors in muscle fibers send information to the brain about the stretching of muscles, although their main role is to control muscle contraction (McCloskey, 1978). The primary source of kinesthetic information comes from *joint receptors.* These are nerve endings similar to those in the skin, but they are located where two bones meet, and they respond to deflections of the joint. When the position of the bones changes, joint receptors transduce this mechanical energy into neural activity, providing information about both the rate of change and the angle of the bones. This coded information goes to the spinal cord and is sent from there to the thalamus along with sensory information from the skin. Eventually it goes to the somatosensory cortex and to the cerebellum (see Figure 3.13), which is involved in the coordination of movements.

Vestibular sense   Whereas kinesthesia tells the brain about where body parts are in relation to one another, the **vestibular sense** tells about the position of the body in space and about its general movements. It is often thought of as the sense of balance. We usually become aware of the vestibular sense only when we overstimulate it and become dizzy.

Two vestibular sacs and three semicircular canals which are part of the inner ear are the organs for the vestibular sense. (You can see the semicircular canals in Figure 4.4; the vestibular sacs connect these canals and the cochlea.) The *vestibular sacs* are filled with fluid and contain small crystals called *otoliths* ("ear stones") that rest on hair endings. Because gravity pulls the otoliths toward the earth, they shift when the head tilts, stimulating the hair endings and providing information to the brain about the position of the head with

LINKAGES

an example

SENSATION AND MOTIVATION

Do people need a certain amount of sensory stimulation?

So far, we have focused on particular types of sensation—sights and sounds, smells and tastes, and so on—but the overall level of sensory stimulation is also significant. Prisoners in dark, solitary confinement, for example, commonly say that the lack of sensory stimulation is in itself extremely unpleasant. In the laboratory, psychologists have found that *sensory deprivation,* a prolonged reduction in exposure to sensory stimuli, has wide-ranging effects.

One of the first experiments on sensory deprivation took place in the early 1950s at McGill University. Student volunteers were told that they would be paid the equivalent of about one hundred of today's U.S. dollars for every day they remained in a small room that was sound-proofed and dimly lighted (Bexton, Heron & Scott, 1954). Food, water, and toilet facilities were available on request, but the subjects spent most of their time on a cot (see Figure A). They wore translucent goggles, which blurred their vision, as well as gloves and padded tubes around their arms, which prevented any distinct experience of touch. An air conditioner provided a constant, dull noise in the background. How did the students react? The first day was usually easy; they slept most of the time. But it did not take long for the volunteers to become extremely bored and restless; many experienced irritability and dramatic mood shifts. In spite of the large monetary incentive, few students remained in sensory deprivation for more than two or three days.

Subjects in similar experiments almost always terminate sensory deprivation sooner than they think they will (Goldberger, 1982). An extended period of sensory deprivation seems temporarily to impair some people's ability to react quickly to visual or auditory signals, to solve mental problems efficiently, and to perform other complex tasks (Suedfeld, 1980; Zubek, 1969). As a result, special care is now taken to ensure that people likely to experience some degree of sensory

Figure A
A Sensory Deprivation Chamber
Subjects in early sensory deprivation experiments were asked to lie for days at a time on a soft cot, while wearing translucent, vision-blurring goggles and gloves and padded arm tubes that minimized touch sensations. Their heads were surrounded by U-shaped pillows and an air conditioner provided constant, dull background noise.

respect to the earth. Astronauts beyond the pull of the earth's gravity do not receive this information, which may contribute to "space sickness."

The *semicircular canals* give information that is independent of the earth. They are fluid-filled, arc-shaped tubes that are oriented in three different planes. Tiny hairs extend into the fluid in the canals. Whenever the head moves or changes its rate of movement, in any direction, the fluid in at least one of the canals moves, bending the hairs. This bending stimulates neurons that travel with the auditory nerve, signaling to the brain the amount and direction of head movement.

The vestibular system has neural connections to the cerebellum, to the part of the autonomic nervous system that affects the digestive system, and to the muscles of the eyes. The connections to the cerebellum help coordinate bodily movements. The connections to the eye muscles create vestibular-ocular reflexes. For example, when your head moves in one direction, your eyes reflexively move in the opposite direction. This allows your eyes to fixate on a point in space even when the head is moving around. You can demonstrate this reflex by having a friend spin you around on a bar stool for a while; when you stop, try to fix your gaze on one point in the room. You will be unable to do so, because the excitation of the vestibular system will cause your eyes to repeatedly move in the direction opposite to that in which you were spinning.

deprivation—airline pilots on long night-time flights, astronauts living for days in small space capsules, and people working in isolated weather stations, for example—receive stimulation through task variety, work breaks, and the like (Rasmussen, 1973). Some people seem to react to sensory deprivation by creating their own internally generated sensations in the form of imagined sights and sounds (Heron, 1957; Suedfeld, 1980; Zubek et al., 1961). Indeed, while they are deprived of normal levels of sensory stimulation, subjects seem to be motivated to obtain any kind of stimulation they can get. Deprived subjects will gladly listen to a monotonous recording of old stock market price reports; they will even ask that it be played repeatedly (Bexton, 1953).

These findings regarding the effects of sensory deprivation suggest that everyone is motivated to obtain at least some sensory stimulation most of the time. Why? Sensory stimulation produces not only specific information about stimuli but also an increase in *arousal,* which is general activation of physiological systems. According to one prominent theory of motivation, discussed in Chapter 11, people are motivated to behave in ways that keep the level of arousal within an optimal range. When arousal is too high,

people seek to reduce it; when arousal is too low, they seek to increase it.

Thus, too much sensory input, as well as the deprivation of sensory stimulation, may be aversive. Too much stimulation may produce overarousal, which, like underarousal, creates discomfort and can interfere with the ability to perform physical or mental tasks. In fact, a form of sensory deprivation known as restricted environmental stimulation (REST) has been used to reduce overarousal and some of the problems it may cause. Many people find REST pleasant and relaxing, especially when it consists of floating for a time in a large, dark, soundproof tank of body-temperature water (Suedfeld, 1980). More specifically, for some people periods of REST appear to create long-term reductions in high blood pressure and other stress-related problems (Fine & Turner, 1982; Kristeller, Schwartz & Black, 1982; Suedfeld, 1980; Suedfeld, Roy & Landon, 1982), but it is still unclear whether these effects stem from reduced sensory input, from placebo effects, or from some combination of the two.

How much stimulation is enough, and how much is too much? Research on motivation and on the links between sensation and motivation indicate that the answer varies from person to person.

People differ in their optimal level of arousal. (The consequences of these differences are discussed in the chapter on motivation.) Furthermore, there are individual differences in sensitivity to sensory stimulation; the same sensory input therefore produces different levels of arousal in different people. People whose nervous systems are particularly sensitive to sensory stimulation may find that it does not take much input to keep their arousal at an optimal level, so they usually prefer relatively quiet, solitary activities.

In short, people do seem to need some sensory stimulation, but the amount varies from person to person, and this difference helps shape motivation. Whether people are motivated to increase stimulation through social contacts or sky diving or to reduce stimulation by seeking solitude, quiet activities, or rest depends to some extent on their optimal level of arousal and their sensitivity to sensory stimulation. Thus, the constant regulation of arousal and the stimulation underlying it helps account for the endless decisions that people make about how to spend their time.

(Artwork adapted from "The Pathology of Boredom" by Woodburn Horon. Copyright © 1957 by Scientific American. All rights reserved.)

Experienced dancers can spin with a minimum of dizziness by holding their heads still and focusing their eyes on one spot as long as possible during each rotation.

The vestibular-ocular reflexes allow remarkable feats of coordination. Consider, for example, a professional baseball player chasing a fly ball. Despite the fact that his body and eyes are moving up and down as he runs, he can continue to fixate on the ball (which is also moving) well enough to judge its exact trajectory and intercept it.

FUTURE DIRECTIONS

In this chapter, you have seen how sensory systems allow people to make contact with the outside world as well as with what is going on within their own bodies. The study of these systems has been somewhat unusual. On one hand, it is tied up with very abstract issues, with questions at the core of philosophy, such as: What is reality? How can we know what it is? On the other hand, the study of sensory systems has led to some of the most concrete, down-to-earth research in psychology. This work focuses on learning more about just how sensory systems detect energy, transduce it, and send it to the brain in a usable form. As we will describe in the next chapter, there has also been intense research on how people interpret sensations to build reality.

Psychologists have accumulated a tremendous body of knowledge in these areas, but much remains unknown or poorly understood, and the research goes on. For some senses, such as olfaction, we still need to learn more about transduction. For other senses, the major questions relate to how the brain processes the information it receives. When it comes to the transition from sensation to perception, to how the pathways and connections give rise to perception and subjective reality, we still know very little. For the major senses, the task is to learn what the relevant "features" are—if the brain indeed codes features—and to describe how connections in the cortex generate feature detectors. This task has practical applications: researchers in the field of artificial intelligence would like to build computers that can see and recognize objects, for both industrial and military purposes. But building a computer

Figure 4.28
The McCollough Effect
The McCollough effect is a visual phenomenon that cannot yet be adequately explained. To see the effect, first adapt to (a) the red-and-black and green-and-black gratings by staring at them as described in the text. Then inspect (b) the black-and-white star pattern. The white horizontal bars will appear a subtle, pale, but distinct pink, and the vertical white bars will appear pale green.
(From Fundamentals of *Sensation and Perception* by M. W. Levine and J. M. Shefner, Addison-Wesley, 1981.)

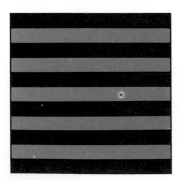
(a)

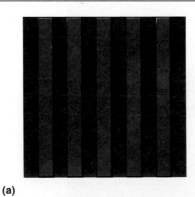

(b)

that can extract the relevant features of an image and recognize objects from any angle has turned out to be more difficult than many scientists thought (Waldrop, 1984). If we knew how the brain does it, perhaps we could construct computers that could do it.

There are still some peculiarities of color vision that scientists do not fully understand. One visual aftereffect is particularly bizarre because it lasts for a very long time. To experience this effect, first stare at the pair of grating patterns in Figure 4.28a for five to ten minutes, alternating between the two in ten-second fixations (rigid fixation is not necessary and may even reduce the effect we wish to demonstrate). When you then look at the black and white bars in Figure 4.28b, you will see pale green where the vertical bars are and pale pink where the horizontal bars are. This is known as the *McCollough effect,* a type of color-contingent aftereffect (McCollough, 1965). Such contingent aftereffects have been known to persist for days or even months (Hurvich, 1981), though they are not permanent or damaging to the visual system. Variations of this aftereffect are often reported by people who use personal computers and word processors, including your authors. The scrolling green and black horizontal bars on many computer screens can set up aftereffects of pinkness when a white object is inspected (especially when surrounded by a black background), and the effects can last for weeks. In contrast to most afterimages, which result from retinal responses, these longer aftereffects are thought to reflect the way images are processed in the brain. We do not understand how.

These are just a few of the as-yet-unsolved mysteries of sensation. For more detailed information on sensory systems and how they work, consider taking courses on sensation and perception, biological psychology, vision, or speech and hearing.

SUMMARY

1. Sensory systems convert energy from the external environment and from the rest of the body into neural activity, so that the nervous system, particularly the brain, can gain information about the world.

2. Sensory systems have many features in common. For some senses, such as vision and hearing, accessory structures modify the incoming energy; receptors transduce the energy into neural activity; the neural activity codes physical properties of the energy; and the coded neural activity goes to the central nervous system for further processing. The representations of sensory information in the central nervous system maintain the topographical relationships of the stimuli. There are also several common features to the way information from most senses is represented in the cerebral cortex. Information from the left side of the sensory world is represented in the right side of the cerebral cortex, and vice versa. There are multiple topographical representations of the sensory world, as well as areas of cortex that integrate information from more than one sense.

3. Sound is a repetitive fluctuation in the pressure of a medium like air. Frequency and amplitude are roughly related to the psychological dimensions of pitch and loudness, respectively. Timbre, or the quality of sound, is related to the complexity of the mixture of waveforms, of amplitude and frequency patterns.

4. The energy from sound waves is collected and transmitted through a series of accessory structures (the pinna, tympanic membrane, malleus, incus, stapes, and oval window) to the cochlea. Transduction occurs when sound energy stimulates hair cells in the basilar membrane of the cochlea, which in turn stimulate the auditory nerve. Intensity is coded by the firing rate of auditory neurons. Some frequencies, especially high frequencies, are coded by the place on the basilar membrane where the wave envelope peaks. Very low frequencies are coded by frequency matching, which means that the firing rate of a neuron matches the frequency of a sound wave. Low to moderate frequencies are coded through a combination of both methods.

5. Auditory information is relayed through the thalamus to the auditory cortex. The representation of information there is tonotopic; that is, sounds of similar frequency activate neighboring cells in the cortex.

6. Visible light is electromagnetic radiation with a wavelength from about 400 to about 700 nanometers. The amount of energy in the light determines its intensity, or brightness. Lights of different wavelengths are sensed as different colors.

7. Accessory structures of the eye include the cornea, the pupil, the iris, and the lens. These structures focus light rays on the retina, the netlike structure that contains the photoreceptors.

8. The photoreceptors—cones and rods—have photopigments that transduce light into neural activity. Rods and cones differ in their shape, their sensitivity to light, their ability to discriminate colors, and their distribution across the retina. The fovea, the area of highest acuity, has only cones, which are color-sensitive. Rods are more sensitive to light, but do not discriminate colors; they are distributed in retinal areas around the fovea.

9. From the photoreceptors, energy transduced from light is transferred to bipolar cells and to ganglion cells, with horizontal cells and other cells making lateral connections among the bipolar and ganglion cells. As a result of these interactions, most ganglion cells in effect compare the amount of light falling on the center of their receptive fields with that falling on the surrounding area. The result is that the retina enhances the contrast between dark and light areas.

10. Color vision is based on variations in the wavelengths of light. The color of an object depends on which of the wavelengths striking it are absorbed and which are reflected. Hue is determined by the dominant wavelength; saturation, by the relative intensity of a single wavelength; and brightness, by the overall intensity of all the wavelengths. Two major theories of color vision include the Young-Helmholtz, or trichromatic, theory (based on three types of cones that are sensitive to short, medium, or long wavelengths) and the Hering opponent-process theory. The latter emphasizes color opponents, or complementary colors, which cancel and produce gray when mixed together. Hering postulated red-green, blue-yellow, and black-white visual elements, based on color afterimages and complementary colors.

11. After retinal processing of visual information, ganglion cells send action potentials to the brain. Their axons travel through the optic chiasm and terminate in the lateral geniculate nucleus (LGN) of the thalamus. Neurons in the LGN send visual information on to the visual cortex, where cells detect and respond to such features as lines, edges, certain orientations, certain colors, and so on. One theory about this aspect of vision suggests that more and more complex feature detectors are hierarchically built out of simpler feature detectors. Another theory suggests that the visual system analyzes input into spatial frequencies of light and dark.

12. The senses of smell (olfaction) and taste (gustation) both detect chemicals, and the two senses interact. Olfaction detects volatile chemicals that come into contact with olfactory receptors in the nose. Olfactory signals are sent to the olfactory bulb in the brain without passing through the thalamus. Gustation detects chemicals that come into contact with taste receptors on the tongue and in other parts of the mouth. Taste sensations are limited to sweet, sour, bitter, and salty, but taste in combination with smell generates flavor.

13. The skin senses include touch, temperature, and pain. Nerve endings in the skin generate touch sensations when they are mechanically stimulated. Some nerve endings are sensitive to temperature. Some nerves respond to both temperature and touch. In the cerebral cortex, touch and temperature information maintains a somatotopic organization, with a larger part of cortex devoted to regions of the skin that have many nerve endings for touch.

14. Pain protects the body from damaging stimuli. Sharp pain and dull, chronic pain are carried by different fibers. The emotional response to pain depends on how the painful stimulus is interpreted. Pain can also be modulated by competition from other skin senses, as well as by messages descending from the brain through the spinal cord. In addition, the body has natural analgesic systems that help reduce pain, especially when the pain is prolonged.

15. Proprioceptive senses provide the brain with information about the body. Kinesthesia provides information about the positions of body parts with respect to each other, and the vestibular sense provides the brain with information about the position of the body in space.

KEY TERMS

Definitions of terms appear on the pages shown in parentheses.

accessory structure (121)	blind spot (143)
accommodation (132)	brightness (139)
acuity (134)	characteristic frequency
adaptation (151)	(130)
amplitude (124)	cochlea (127)
analgesia (154)	coding (122)
anvil (127)	complementary colors (141)
association cortex (124)	cones (133)
auditory nerve (127)	convergence (135)
basilar membrane (127)	cornea (132)
bipolar cell (135)	dark adaptation (134)

RECOMMENDED READINGS

Cornsweet, T. N. (1970). *Visual perception.* New York: Academic Press. A classic text on all aspects of vision.

Hubel, D. H., & Wiesel, T. N. (1979). Brain mechanisms of vision. *Scientific American, 241,* 150–162. As a *Scientific American* article, this fairly short piece summarizes for general readers the history of the pioneering work that led to the hierarchical model of brain mechanisms of vision.

Levine, M. W., & Shefner, J. M. (1981). *Fundamentals of sensation and perception.* Reading, Mass.: Addison-Wesley. This is a highly readable but thorough treatment of both sensation and perception in vision and audition.

Schiffman, H. R. (1982). *Sensation and perception: An integrated approach.* New York: Wiley. This is a good source of additional details about all of the senses covered in this chapter.

A pilot making an approach to an airport must perceive very accurately how far away the runway is and the angle of approach in order to control the plane's speed and altitude for a touchdown at the end of the runway. For the pilots of four Boeing 727s in 1966, this perception failed disastrously, causing plane crashes in Chicago, Salt Lake City, Cincinnati, and Tokyo. The four incidents had three factors in common. First, they all took place on clear nights, with the runway well in sight; the pilots did not have to rely on instruments. Second, they involved approaches over dark water toward runways lying on a background of upward-sloping city lights in the distance. Third, all of the planes crashed short of the runway.

Conrad Kraft, an engineering psychologist at Boeing Aircraft Corporation, gathered these findings. Kraft believed that the absence of altitude cues from the dark water below the aircraft, in combination with an upward-sloping, lighted terrain, led the pilots to misperceive their altitude. He suggested that the pilots assumed that the airport and city lights lay on a flat rather than an upward-sloping surface, believed they were flying at a higher altitude than they actually were (higher than they should be), and therefore tried to "correct" their altitudes, bringing the planes down too low and crashing.

In fact, this was exactly what happened. But how did Kraft reach his correct diagnosis? The principles of sensation that we described in the previous chapter—how receptors in the eyes, ears, and other senses receive light, sound, and other types of energy and convert them into signals that are sent to the brain —could not by themselves provide the answers. Sensations provide raw information about the environment but do not give much meaning to that information. It was Kraft's knowledge of the basic principles of perception that led him to a correct diagnosis.

Perception is the process through which raw sensations from the environment are interpreted, using knowledge and understanding of the world, so that they become meaningful experiences. Perception is related to many other areas of psychology (see Linkages diagram) and, as we will see, is critical to a wide range of actions, from flying an airplane safely to reading a book.

The first thing to understand about perception is that it is not a passive process of simply absorbing and decoding incoming sensations. If it were, people's understanding of the environment would be poor indeed. The visual scene, for example, would be a constantly changing, confusing mosaic of lights and color. The auditory world would be a din of buzzing, humming, and shrieking. Instead, human brains take the sensory stimuli that bombard everyone and actively create from them the coherent world that is perceived. People fill in missing information and draw on past experiences to give meaning to what they see, hear, or touch. For example, the raw sensations coming from the stimuli in Figure 5.1 (p. 164) inform you only that there are four straight lines that contact one another at ninety-degree angles. Yet you instantly see this pattern as a meaningful object: a square.

Later in this chapter, we will describe many other examples of how perception creates people's experience of the world as an organized, recog-

162

5

Perception

LINKAGES
an overview

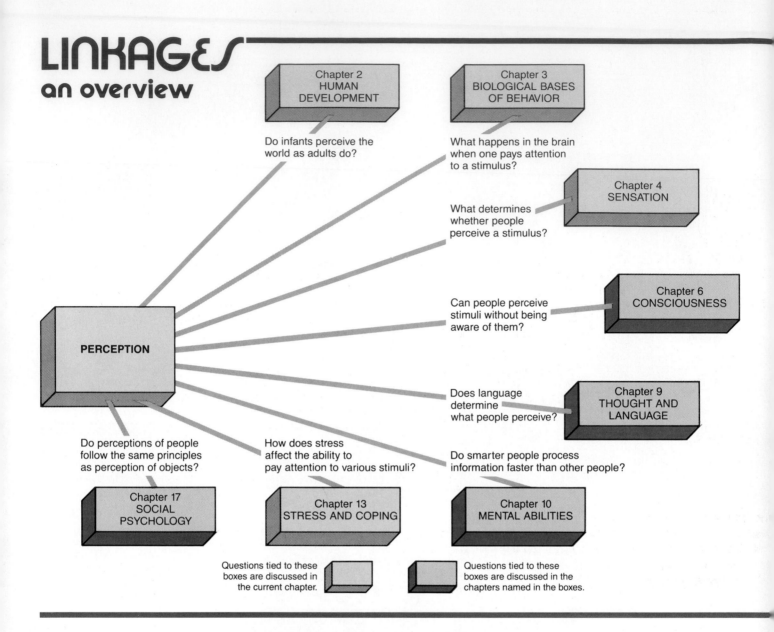

Chapter 2 HUMAN DEVELOPMENT

Do infants perceive the world as adults do?

Chapter 3 BIOLOGICAL BASES OF BEHAVIOR

What happens in the brain when one pays attention to a stimulus?

Chapter 4 SENSATION

What determines whether people perceive a stimulus?

PERCEPTION

Chapter 6 CONSCIOUSNESS

Can people perceive stimuli without being aware of them?

Chapter 9 THOUGHT AND LANGUAGE

Does language determine what people perceive?

Do perceptions of people follow the same principles as perception of objects?

How does stress affect the ability to pay attention to various stimuli?

Do smarter people process information faster than other people?

Chapter 17 SOCIAL PSYCHOLOGY

Chapter 13 STRESS AND COPING

Chapter 10 MENTAL ABILITIES

Questions tied to these boxes are discussed in the current chapter.

Questions tied to these boxes are discussed in the chapters named in the boxes.

Figure 5.1
What Do You See?

nizable place. We will discuss the various ways in which perceptual processes interpret incoming sensations. We will answer such questions as How do people know what is out there in the physical world? How do they recognize familiar objects and understand their size, shape, and color? How do people know where things are in space? We will illustrate some perceptual illusions, the fascinating mistakes that even the most sophisticated perceiver can make under certain circumstances. We will consider the complex process of attention, because part of perception involves attending to some things and ignoring others. We will see that people make such choices about what to notice based partly on what they already know and hope will happen. Finally, we will look at some applications of research on perception.

FROM SENSATION TO PERCEPTION: AN OVERVIEW

Whereas the senses create a physical code from a stimulus, perception's job is to go beyond this code and draw on knowledge of the world to interpret what is out there. Suppose, for example, that your retinas transmit signals to

PERCEPTION AND PSYCHOLOGY

In order to behave, think, and reason about the world, people must first perceive the information received through the senses. For example, your choice of how to respond to what you hear someone say depends on your perception of what the spoken words mean.

As modern psychology developed at the end of the nineteenth century, many of its pioneers believed that, much as chemical compounds are formed by a combination of chemical elements, perceptions are formed by combining raw sensory stimulus elements. In fact, however, perception turns out to be much more complicated, as when you can

perceive a person behind a picket fence even though the raw sensory stimuli reaching your eyes do not portray the entire person. Attempts to explain perception must also take individual differences into account. A skilled and experienced radiologist is much more likely than a novice to perceive that an X ray shows a leg fracture, even though both sense the same visual stimuli. But if the patient has been complaining about great pain in the leg, even the inexperienced doctor is likely to perceive the fracture, because he or she will expect to see it. Knowledge and expectancy, as well as sensations, shape what one perceives.

In this chapter, we describe some of the ways they exert this influence; in later chapters we will examine other processes important to the formation of knowledge and expectancies.

your brain indicating that a stimulus below and just in front of you is brown in color and long, narrow, and wavy in shape. Is the stimulus a snake or a rope? The answer, in the form of an interpretation of the stimulus by your perceptual apparatus, will prompt you to ignore the object, run from it, or pick it up.

Some Features of Perception

This example helps illustrate six characteristics of perception that we will refer to repeatedly. First, perception is generally *knowledge based*. If you do not know what snakes or ropes look like, especially if you do not know how to tell the difference between them, your chances of surviving in the woods are poor.

Second, perception is often *inferential*. People do not always have complete sensory information at hand, but the perceptual system uses people's knowledge to make inferences about what they may not be able to hear, see, or feel. Thus, if you know what a snake looks like, you will perceive it as a snake even though the underbrush conceals the last few inches of the stimulus. You would not say, "Wow, if that thing had a tail, I'd swear it was a snake." Or consider the blind spot that we discussed in the chapter on sensation. The blind spot has no light receptors, but people do not perceive the resulting "hole" in the visual world, because their perceptual apparatus fills it in.

Third, perception is *categorical;* it allows people to place apparently different sensations in the same category based on some common features. Thus, you may not know exactly what *kind* of snake you are looking at, but it has enough "snakey" characteristics (long, round, scales, tapered tail, forked tongue, beady little eyes) for you to place the stimulus in the snake category. Similarly, people can instantly place certain sounds in a category called "human voice," even if they sound unlike any other voice they have ever heard.

Fourth, perception is *relational.* You perceive a stimulus pattern as a snake, not only because it has snakey features, but also because these features are related to one another in a coherent and consistent way. The tapered tail appears at the end of the body, not in the middle; there is a beady little eye on each side of the head, which is at the end opposite the tail. In the same way, your ability to perceive that someone is unusually tall requires that you see him or her in relation to more normally proportioned people.

Fifth, perception is *adaptive,* allowing people to focus on the most important information for handling a particular situation. For example, peripheral vision is very sensitive to moving stimuli. This is adaptive in that it allows people to react quickly to potentially threatening motions across a wide range of space. Further, your perceptual apparatus focuses first on whether the stimulus you suddenly encounter is a snake or a rope, not on whether it is a king snake or a python. The details will be filled in later, perhaps from a safer distance. On the other hand, if you worked at the zoo and were told to feed the boa constrictor, species identification would be very adaptive indeed, especially if you wanted to keep your job. This aspect of perception helps us to quickly identify stimuli associated with food or other desirable goals, as well as those that are likely to be dangerous.

Finally, many perceptual processes operate *automatically.* You do not have to stop and consciously ask yourself, "Is that a rope or a snake?" The question is asked and answered much more quickly—so quickly, in fact, that you are unaware of having done it.

Relating Sensation and Perception

As noted in the previous chapter, sensation and perception overlap somewhat. The sensory processes do not register everything in the outside world with equal emphasis; they highlight certain features. Thus, interpretation of a stimulus begins even before information about the stimulus reaches the brain. For example, the cells of the retina emphasize edges and changes, so that you see more contrast than the physical stimulus actually contains. When you look at the sky on a rainy day, the stimuli reaching your eyes actually include several different wavelengths of light; but your eyes themselves combine data about those wavelengths, and the eyes "tell" the brain that it is seeing one color: gray. Thus, perception appears to add additional information, based on prior knowledge, to what comes into the sensory systems. In this sense, perception may be a primitive version of the knowledge-based processes that we will discuss in Chapter 9, on thought and language. These processes allow people to learn concepts, make judgments, and reach decisions.

How perception actually does work and which of its six features are therefore most important are still matters of considerable debate. On one side of the question are researchers like Peter Lindsay and Donald Norman (1977), who emphasize the knowledge-based, inferential characteristics of perception. Called **constructionists,** they argue that the perceptual system must often

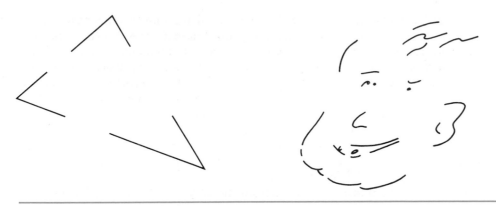

Figure 5.2
The Constructionist View of Perception
These stimuli demonstrate the construction-ist view of perception: when you look at them, you perceive more than is actually in the sensory information.

construct an image of reality from fragments of sensory information, much as an archaeologist reconstructs an entire dinosaur from a few bits of bone. This, they suggest, is how the mind can perceive the images in Figure 5.2 as a triangle and a face, even though much of the sensory information is incomplete.

On the other side are those, such as James Gibson, who stress the adaptive and automatic properties of perception. Gibson (1979) argued that most of the cues humans need in order to get along in the natural world are available from the stimuli themselves and are usually registered *directly* by the senses. Because of his emphasis on the rich sources of information available in the natural environment, Gibson's approach to perception is often called **ecological.** In his view, stimuli that need reconstruction, like those in Figure 5.2, occur only in the artificial world of the psychologist's laboratory. When people perceive depth, for example, they do not first perceive stimuli as two-dimensional and then construct a three-dimensional version of the world. Instead, as Figure 5.3 illustrates, the stimuli that reach the eye tell people automatically about depth.

The debate over these opposing points of view remains unresolved, partly because, as so often happens in psychology, both have value. Constructionist

Figure 5.3
The Ecological View of Perception
People see textured surfaces everywhere. Seen in three dimensions, the texture of this surface appears rougher up close and finer as it recedes into the distance. The ecological approach to perception suggests that the visual system has adapted so that this change in texture, known as a textural gradient, automatically cues people to distance and depth, with no inferential reasoning required.
(Photo © Kryn Taconis/Magnum.)

principles often hold for the process of recognizing objects—the "What is it?" aspect of perception. This recognition must often be performed in fleeting glances, when sensory evidence is incomplete. Yet the ecological view seems to describe accurately and precisely the way people perceive their own movement through the world, as well as the specific properties of objects, such as their distance from the viewer and their color, shape, and orientation —the "What kind?" and "Where?" of perception.

PSYCHOPHYSICS

Human perceptual processes range from the very simple, such as listening for a faint sound in a quiet house, to the very complex, such as evaluating and appreciating an architect's design. The most basic perceptual processes— assessing whether a stimulus is present and, if present, how strong or intense it is—might appear to belong in the chapter on sensation, but there is an important reason for covering them here. As you will see, even deciding whether a stimulus is present depends on what people know about the world, what they expect, and even what they want to perceive.

Absolute Thresholds: Is Something Out There?

The simplest perceptual categorization involves deciding whether a stimulus is present. This process begins with and depends on the sensory receptors and raw sensations. Indeed, the receptors' sensitivity to small amounts of energy can be a matter of life and death. If you are lost in the woods on a dark night, your safety may depend on detecting a faint glimmer of light or hearing the distant call of a search party.

Determining thresholds The minimum detectable amount of light, sound, pressure, or other physical energy is called the *absolute threshold.* This threshold can be amazingly low. Normal human vision, for example, can detect the light equivalent to a single candle flame burning on a dark night thirty miles away! Table 5.1 presents values of the absolute thresholds for vision, hearing, taste, smell, and touch.

The information in Table 5.1 was derived from careful experiments by psychologists whose specialty is **psychophysics,** an area that focuses on the relationship between the *physical* energy of environmental stimuli and the conscious *psychological* experience those stimuli produce. Psychophysical research involves not only finding absolute thresholds for the senses but also determining how sensitive people are to changes in the intensity or other qualities of those stimuli. These very basic questions get at the foundation of how people make contact with and become conscious of the world; it is not surprising that the earliest psychologists concerned themselves primarily with psychophysical research.

To get an idea of how psychophysical research is done, consider a typical experiment on the absolute threshold for vision. A subject is brought into a laboratory, and the lights are turned out. After the subject's eyes have adapted to the darkness, many brief flashes of light are presented one at a time at varying intensities, from less than that of a candle burning thirty miles away to levels considerably higher. Each time, the subject is asked if the stimulus was seen. The pattern of yes or no responses to the varying light intensities usually forms a curve similar to that shown in Figure 5.4. As you can see, the absolute threshold is actually not absolute. Sometimes a stimulus of a particular intensity will be perceived, and at other times, it will not. Because of this

TABLE 5.1 _____
Value of the Absolute Threshold
Examples of stimuli at the absolute threshold for five primary senses.

Sense	Absolute Threshold
Vision	A candle flame seen at thirty miles on a dark, clear night.
Hearing	The tick of a watch under quiet conditions at twenty feet.
Taste	One teaspoon of sugar in two gallons of water.
Smell	One drop of perfume diffused into the entire volume of a six-room apartment.
Touch	The wing of a fly falling on your cheek from a distance of one centimeter.

SOURCE: Galanter, E. (1962). Contemporary psychophysics. In R. Brown (Ed.). *New Directions in Psychology.* New York: Holt, Rinehart & Winston.

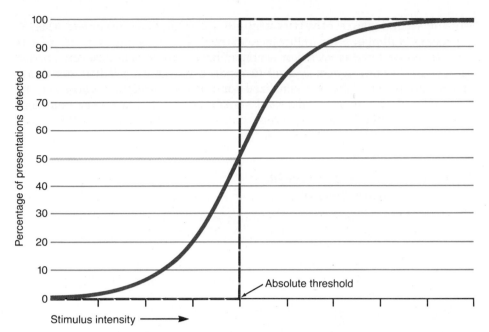

Figure 5.4
The Absolute Threshold
This graph shows the relationship between the percentage of times that a signal is detected and the intensity of that stimulus as measured in physical units. If the absolute threshold were indeed absolute, a signal of a particular intensity would always be detected, and any signal below that intensity would never be detected. In that case, the graph would show the relationship indicated by the dashed line, with no reports when the stimulus is below the threshold and 100 percent of the reports above it. Instead, the absolute threshold is defined by the horizontal line, which intersects the curve at the intensity at which the signal is detected with 50 percent accuracy.

variability, the *exact* amount of energy corresponding to any particular person's absolute threshold cannot actually be determined. To get around this problem, psychophysicists have redefined the **absolute threshold** as the minimum amount of energy that can be detected 50 percent of the time.

Sources of threshold variation   Why should there be variability in an "absolute" threshold? Psychologists have long been aware of two reasons: internal noise and response bias.

Internal noise is the spontaneous, random firing of nerve cells. It occurs because the nervous system is never inactive. Thus, a person trying to detect a faint ray of light in an otherwise dark environment or trying to hear a soft sound in an otherwise quiet place does so against a background of the spontaneous firing of nerve cells of varying intensity. Sometimes this firing occurs in the brain's sensory areas or in receptor cells of the eye, ear, or other sense organs. It is a little like "snow" on a television screen or static on the radio. If the level of internal noise happens to be high at a particular moment, it may be mistaken for an external light or sound. If the level of internal noise is extremely low, the energy added by a faint light or sound may not create enough neural activity to make that stimulus noticeable (see Figure 5.5).

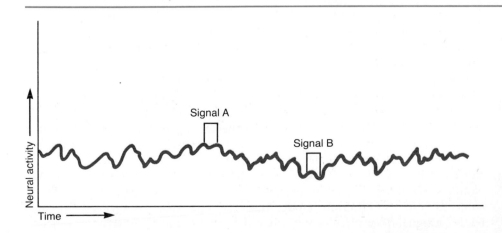

Figure 5.5
Neural Noise and Its Effects
This graph shows an example of the randomly changing neural noise in the part of the brain where detection of, say, sound takes place and the added energy caused by two signals, marked A and B. Because the random activity is already high when signal A occurs, the signal and noise together generate enough total activity to stand out from the average activity level; therefore, signal A will probably be detected. But signal B occurs when the noise happens to be low, and the total energy of the signal plus noise is no greater than the average noise level alone. Thus, signal B will probably not be detected.

The second source of variation in absolute threshold, **response bias,** is a person's willingness or reluctance to respond to a stimulus. It reflects motivation and expectancies. For example, people being paid for every correct detection of a faint light may tend to report seeing it even if it is not there. In contrast, people who are penalized for every incorrect detection may be cautious and fail to report detected signals unless they are very confident about them. Similarly, a person who *expects* a stimulus to occur will be more likely to detect it than one who does not.

Going Beyond the Threshold: Signal Detection Theory

Obviously, then, perception of a stimulus is not determined by the intensity or other characteristics of the stimulus alone. Since neural noise and response bias can never be entirely eliminated, researchers in psychophysics have gone beyond trying to determine thresholds and have turned to signal detection theory (Green & Swets, 1965) to understand how sources of variation affect perception.

Signal detection theory is a formal mathematical model of what determines people's reports that a near-threshold stimulus has or has not occurred. It permits psychologists to identify the effects of response bias. It also allows them to compare different people's ability to detect sensory stimuli even when circumstances create different response biases and thus different patterns of stimulus reporting. The theory begins by doing away with the notion of an absolute threshold. Instead, it assumes that perception of a stimulus depends on two factors: sensitivity and the response criterion. **Sensitivity** refers to the ability to detect a stimulus; it is influenced by neural noise and by the intensity of the stimulus, as well as by the capacity of the sensory system. The **response criterion** is the amount of energy necessary for a person to justify reporting that a signal has occurred. It is the internal rule a person uses to decide whether or not to report a stimulus, and it reflects the person's motivation and expectations.

To separate the effects of these two factors so that each can be measured, signal detection theory provides a special set of methods. The researcher presents stimuli on some trials but nothing on others. The no-stimulus trials are called *catch trials,* because they are designed to catch the subject's tendency to respond (perhaps because of sensory noise or bias) when nothing is there. Instead of letting the response bias vary in unknown ways, which would interfere with measuring sensitivity, signal detection theorists *alter* the bias, either by offering money or by changing the person's expectations. Then they look at what happens to the person's responses. To alter a subject's expectancy that a stimulus will occur, for example, the researcher might change the percentage of trials on which it actually does occur.

Figure 5.6a shows the possible outcomes when the signal detection method is used. When a stimulus is presented and the subject detects it, the response is called a *hit.* If the subject fails to detect the signal, the error is called a *miss.* A *false alarm* occurs when no stimulus is presented, but the subject reports one anyway. Reporting no stimulus when none is given is called a *correct rejection.*

Suppose a stimulus is presented on 50 percent of the trials, and the subject responds as in Figure 5.6b, with 60 percent hits and 40 percent false alarms. The same subject might then be given trials on which he or she is told that signals will occur, say, 90 percent of the time (Figure 5.6c). This change would *increase* the subject's expectancy of a stimulus, which would *lower* the subject's response criterion. Under these circumstances, subjects report detecting a signal more often—even when they are unsure about its occurrence—

Figure 5.6
Signal Detection
(a) The possible outcomes of signal trials and catch trials. (b) Outcome percentages when a stimulus is presented 50 percent of the time. (c) Outcomes when a stimulus is presented 90 percent of the time.

		Stimulus presented?	
		Yes	No
Subject's response	Yes	Hit	False alarm
	No	Miss	Correct rejection

(a) Possible outcomes

		Stimulus presented?	
		Yes	No
Subject's response	Yes	Hit 60%	False alarm 40%
	No	Miss 40%	Correct rejection 60%

(b) Stimulus presented on 50% of the trials

		Stimulus presented?	
		Yes	No
Subject's response	Yes	Hit 90%	False alarm 50%
	No	Miss 10%	Correct rejection 50%

(c) Stimulus presented on 90% of the trials

than in trials on which the signal occurs only rarely. Thus, the percentage of hits goes up, but so too will the percentage of false alarms.

Researchers estimate subjects' sensitivity by examining the overall pattern of hits and false alarms that occurs as the experimenter manipulates the response criterion by changing the percentage of catch trials or altering the rewards offered. Figure 5.7 shows examples. The resulting curve is known as a **receiver operating characteristic (ROC) curve,** and its shape provides a measure of a subject's sensitivity. The more bowed the curve, the greater the sensitivity. Sensitivity in signal detection theory is measured in units called d' (d prime).

Consider the case in Figure 5.7a. The ROC curve shows that increasing the percentage of trials with a signal increased the subject's hit rate faster than the false-alarm rate. That means that the person discriminated between trials with the signal and trials without the signal; in other words, the subject was sensitive to the difference between the two kinds of trials. Thus, we would conclude that this person is quite sensitive to the stimulus. Certainly he or she is more sensitive than the person whose data are plotted in Figure 5.7b, where increasing the percentage of trials on which the signal occurred increased the false-alarm rate about as fast as it increased the hit rate—perhaps indicating that the person was merely guessing. Here, $d' = 0$.

Sensitivity, and thus the shape of the ROC curve, depends not only on a person's capacity to detect stimuli but also on stimulus intensity. Thus, the shape of the curve will change if the stimulus changes, as Figure 5.8 illustrates. For a particular stimulus, however, differences in ROC curves indicate differences in people's ability to detect stimuli.

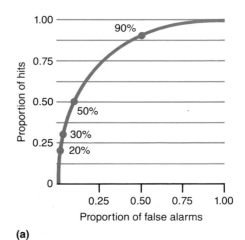

(a)

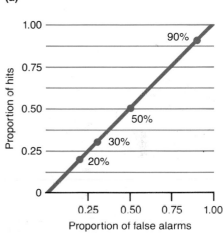

(b)

Figure 5.7
Receiver Operating Characteristics (ROC) Curves
Here we see the proportion of hits and false alarms that occur as the expectancy for a stimulus is changed by changing the percentage of trials on which a target stimulus is presented. (a) The bowed shape of the ROC curve indicates that the subject is quite sensitive to the signal. (b) The sensitivity (d') here is 0.

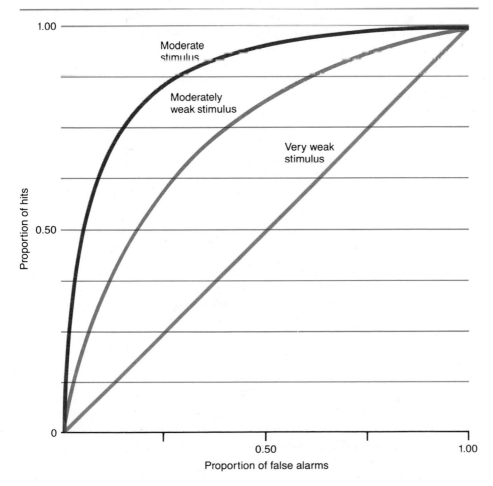

Figure 5.8
ROC Curves and Stimulus Intensity
When a person detects a moderate sound, hits increase much faster than false alarms as the percentage of stimulus trials increases, as the top curve shows. The curve for a quieter sound might show less sensitivity (middle curve), and for an extremely soft sound, it might look like the straight diagonal line. The d' value for the diagonal line is 0, and d' increases for the more bowed ROC curves. Note: A very loud sound would always show hits, and never show false alarms, and d' would be infinite.

HIGHLIGHT

Some Applications of Signal Detection Theory

Signal detection theory is important not only because it allows psychologists to separate the contributions of sensitivity and response criteria to perceptual performance, but also because it can help them analyze why people sometimes fail to detect important signals.

Consider an airport security guard looking for images of bombs or weapons on a video display showing X rays of passenger luggage. Why might the guard sometimes fail in this important task? The problem might be inadequate sensitivity. After hours on duty, the guard might nod off briefly just as a signal occurs (a miss) or, on suddenly jerking awake, misperceive a hair dryer as a gun (a false alarm). A second possibility relates to response criteria. Perhaps the guard's airport is particularly quiet, and no one has ever tried to conceal a weapon there; knowing this, the guard's expectancy level is low. Or perhaps the guard wants to avoid a false alarm that might unnecessarily upset the terminal crowd. In either case, the guard's response criterion is high; another way of saying this is that the guard has a *conservative response bias*. The result is that mildly weaponlike images on the screen are not likely to provoke a warning from the guard.

Recognition of these possibilities has led psychologists to make a variety of recommendations to help those working at signal detection tasks maintain vigilance and an optimal response criterion (Warm, 1984; Wickens, 1984a). Some of their recommendations are quite simple. For example, people driving long distances are advised to take breaks every so often in order to combat fatigue and boredom. On tasks offering monotonous stimulation, such as truck driving or inspecting parts as they move down an assembly line, detection accuracy may be maintained by having workers engage in mild physical exercise, listen to music, or receive other varied sensory input. Psychologists also recommend setting the pace and complexity of a detection task so that it provides enough challenge to keep workers alert without overwhelming them. One Japanese bottling plant, for example, improved its inspectors' accuracy simply by slowing the rate at which bottles moved by. Finally, giving workers information about their performance in the form of feedback about hits and false alarms can lengthen the duration of detection accuracy. This can be done in many ways, including purposely presenting defective parts, phony target signals, or other critical stimuli from time to random time. This occasional feedback, plus knowledge that performance is being monitored, may help minimize signal detection errors.

Some psychologists have applied signal detection theory to situations involving the recognition of events in memory, in particular to eyewitness testimony. For example, when a crime witness tries to identify a suspect in a police lineup, the interests of justice demand that the detection process be as sensitive as possible, producing the fewest possible misses (failures to identify the suspect) and false alarms (erroneously identifying an innocent person). Typically, a lineup consists of people similar in appearance to the suspect, so that none will be automatically ruled out. But even when this precaution is taken, several factors can distort a witness's response to a lineup, producing either misses or false alarms.

As in any other detection task, witnesses bring with them a response bias. Some witnesses' fear of seeing an innocent person tried or punished may create a very high response criterion, making them unlikely to identify an alleged criminal. Other witnesses may want to see someone, anyone, convicted when a crime has been committed; their response criterion may be so low that they will very likely identify someone in any lineup as the criminal. These people have what is called a *risky bias*.

On the basis of signal detection theory, psychologists have recommended that officers remind witnesses that the criminal they saw at the scene of the crime might *not* actually be in the lineup. This reminder tends to lower the witness's expectation of seeing the criminal and, in turn, raises the response criterion. Researchers also argue that the suspect and others in the lineup should look equally dissimilar from each other to reduce the chance that the suspect will be chosen by guessing (Ellison & Buckhout, 1981).

These and other applications of signal detection theory alert people to problems related to perception in legal, medical, industrial, and other settings. They also suggest ways of combating those problems. ■

Judging Differences Between Stimuli: Weber's Law

Often people must not only detect the presence or absence of a stimulus but also determine whether two stimuli are the same or different. For example, when tuning up, musicians must determine if notes played by two instruments have the same pitch; when repainting part of a wall, you may need to determine if the new paint matches the old.

It turns out that people's ability to judge changes or differences in the amount of a stimulus depends on how much of that stimulus there is to begin with. More specifically, the ability to detect differences declines as the magnitude of the stimulus increases. When comparing the weights of two envelopes, you will be able to detect a difference of as little as an ounce, but when comparing two boxes weighing around fifty pounds, you may not notice a difference unless it is a pound or more.

This relationship between the initial intensity of a stimulus and ability to detect a change in its magnitude is described by Weber's law, one of the oldest in psychology. Named after the nineteenth-century German physiologist Ernst Weber (pronounced "vayber"), **Weber's law** describes the smallest detectable difference in stimulus energy, a quantity known as the **just-noticeable difference (JND).** It states that the just-noticeable difference is a constant fraction of the intensity of the stimulus. The constant fraction, labeled K, is different for each sensory system and for different aspects of sensation within those systems. In algebraic terms, Weber's law is $JND = KI$, where I is the amount, or intensity, of the stimulus. For example, the value of K for weight is 0.02. If an object weighed 25 pounds (I), the JND would be only half a pound (25 pounds $\times$ 0.02 = 0.5 pounds). In other words, for 25 pounds of luggage, barbell, or other liftable object, a half-pound increase is necessary before one can detect a change.

The value of K represents the ability to detect differences. The smaller the value of K, the more sensitive a sense is to stimulus differences. For example, K for vision is 0.017, which indicates a high degree of sensitivity; only a small change in the intensity of light is needed to notice a difference in its brightness. Table 5.2 lists the value of K for a variety of sense modalities and reveals the variability in people's ability to judge differences in stimuli. Weber's law is found to be valid over a wide range of stimulus amplitudes, but it does not hold when stimuli are either very intense or very weak.

The fact that the judgment of differences follows Weber's law illustrates the adaptive nature of perception: the ability to discriminate differences generally matches the need to discriminate these differences in everyday life. For example, people rarely need to exercise fine discriminations between large quantities (such as the brightness of a flashbulb versus that of a spotlight), but such judgments are often required between small quantities, such as the subtle differences in the shading of an X ray that might indicate a tumor. The

When a stereo is playing very softly, it takes only a very small increase in volume to notice the change. If the music is already blaring, it takes a much larger increase in volume before the music sounds louder. This relationship between the initial amount of a stimulus and the amount of energy that must be added to notice a change has been described by Weber's law.

TABLE 5.2
Weber Constants (*K*) for Different Sense Modalities
The value of Weber's constant fraction differs from one sense to another; senses that are most important for survival tend to be the most sensitive.

Pitch	.003
Brightness	.017
Weight	.020
Loudness	.100
Pressure on skin	.140
Saltiness of taste	.200

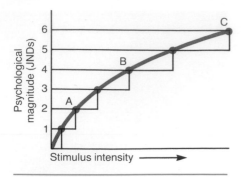

Figure 5.9
*Fechner's Law Applied
to a Visual Stimulus*
*Larger and larger increases in physical en-
ergy (the horizontal axis) are required to
produce equal increases in psychological
perception (JNDs, on the vertical axis).
Thus, points A and B are perceived as
equally different from each other, as are
points B and C. Note that the increase in
energy required to make a light appear two
JNDs brighter is much greater when going
from the fourth to the sixth JND (point B to
point C) than from the second to the fourth
JND (point A to point B). Another way of
saying this is that, as our perceptual experience increases arithmetically (from 1 to 2 to
3 to 4), the stimulus energy involved increases geometrically (from, say, 1 to 4 to 9
to 16). The purple line shows what this function looks like.*

Figure 5.10
Stevens's Power Law
*Stevens's power law is $S = KI^b$, where S is
the perceived magnitude of the stimulus, K
is the constant, I is the physical intensity of
the stimulus, and b is a variable that
changes from one type of stimulus to another. Note that Stevens's power law generates equally accurate descriptions of the relationships between stimulus intensity and
psychological perception for brightness
(which follows Fechner's law) and for shock
(which does not).*

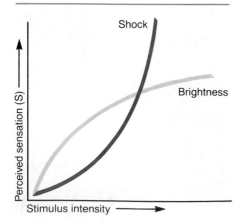

adaptive nature of perception is also illustrated by the senses' different
sensitivities to change (see Table 5.2). Humans depend on vision far more
than they do on the sense of taste; so it is sensible that K is smaller, and
sensitivity greater, for vision than for taste.

Weber's law also applies to more complex stimuli. You might be concerned
about a twenty-cent increase in a forty-cent bus fare; this 50 percent increase
(20/40) is well above the JND for noticing changes in cost. But the same
twenty-cent increase in your monthly rent would be less than a JND and thus
unlikely to cause notice, let alone concern.

Judging Stimulus Magnitude:
Fechner's and Stevens's Laws

Weber's law describes the fact that the more there is of some stimulus to
begin with, the more the amount must change in order for any change to be
noticed. In 1860 Gustav Fechner proposed that Weber's law could also be
used to understand the psychological experience, or perception, of stimulus
magnitude. That is, it could help answer such questions as how much brighter
a lightbulb must be to appear twice as bright as a 100-watt bulb.

Fechner reasoned that, since the JND is the smallest detectable *change* in
the subjective magnitude of a stimulus, then the total subjective magnitude
or intensity of any stimulus should be related to the number of JNDs by which
that stimulus differs from zero. That is, one should be able to measure
subjective magnitude by adding JNDs. Furthermore, since JNDs become
progressively larger—that is, require more stimulus energy—as a stimulus
grows more intense, larger and larger increases in physical energy will be
necessary to obtain equal changes in subjective intensity when stimuli are of
greater magnitude. In other words, constant increases in physical energy will
produce progressively smaller increases in subjective magnitude. More precisely, **Fechner's law** states that the perceived magnitude of a stimulus is the
product of K for the particular sensory system involved and the logarithm of
the stimulus intensity. Figure 5.9 depicts this relationship for a visual stimulus.

Although Fechner's law describes fairly well how people judge the loudness
of sounds, the brightness of lights, and the intensity of many other sensations,
it does not apply to some stimuli. For example, contrary to Fechner's law,
each successive increase in the perceived intensity of electric shock takes *less
and less* of an increase in physical energy.

S. S. Stevens found a way around this problem. By asking subjects to
estimate the relative magnitude of stimuli of varying intensities, he found that
their responses followed a formula that became known as **Stevens's power
law** (Stevens, 1957). It is somewhat more complex than Fechner's law, but it
also works better. Figure 5.10 contains the formula and an example of how
it generates accurate functions relating energy to subjective intensity for almost
any kind of stimulus. To better understand the everyday importance of
Fechner's or Stevens's law, consider the problem of designing the volume
control for a radio. How do you make the knob turn so that each angle of
rotation of the dial will cause the same subjective increase in loudness to the
listener? The answer is provided by the power law for sound. Starting from
zero, each constant angle of rotation marked on the dial should produce an
increasing amount of stimulus energy, and the amount of this increase is
given by the power law.

Important as it is, the detection of faint amounts of energy and of relative
magnitudes of pure stimuli are only tiny components of the perceptual
activities that most people perform every day. Perception also involves
organizing all the sensations coming from the world. It is to this organizational
aspect of perception that we now turn.

ORGANIZING THE PERCEPTUAL WORLD

Suppose for a moment that you are driving down a busy road while searching for Barney's Diner, an unfamiliar restaurant where you are to meet a friend. The roadside is crammed with signs of all shapes and colors, some moving, some rotating, and some standing still. If you are ever to recognize the one sign that says "Barney's Diner," you must impose some sort of organization on this overwhelming cafeteria of visual information.

Most people do this sort of thing all the time, but how? How do you know where one sign ends and another begins? How do you distinguish between signs and the background against which you perceive them? How do you realize that a sign remains the same size as you approach it, even though its image on your retina gets larger as the sign gets closer? In this section, we will describe some of the organizational processes that allow people to understand the jumble of lights and sounds in the world.

Principles of Perceptual Organization

You finally recognize the "Barney's Diner" sign because the sign's letters match the pattern of letters that you have stored in your memory. Before this match can take place, however, your perceptual system must first separate those letters from the larger background of lights, colors, letters, and other competing stimuli. Two basic principles of perceptual organization—*figure-ground perception* and *grouping*—guide this initial organization.

Figure and ground   When you look at a complex visual scene or listen to a noisy environment, your perceptual apparatus automatically picks out certain objects or sounds to be *figures* (that is, the features to be emphasized) and relegates others to be *ground* (that is, background). For example, as you drive up to an intersection, a stop sign becomes a figure, standing out clearly against the background of trees, houses, and cars. A **figure** is the part of the visual field that has meaning, stands in front of the rest, and always seems to include the contours or borders that separate it from the relatively meaningless background (Rubin, 1915).

The relationship between figure and ground is usually, but not always, clear cut. Consider Figure 5.11. What do you see? The fact that you can now look at Figure 5.11 and repeatedly reverse figure and ground to see faces, then a vase, then faces again clearly illustrates that perception involves an active interpretation of stimuli. Figure 5.11 also illustrates a second point: as we noted earlier, perception is categorical. That is, when people perceive sensory evidence, they usually assign it to one category or another, rarely to both or to something in between. You cannot, for instance, easily perceive Figure 5.11 as both a vase and two faces at the same time.

Grouping   Why is it that certain parts of the perceptual world become figure and others become background, even when nothing in particular stands out in the physical pattern that falls on the retina? The answer is that certain inherent features of stimuli lead people to group them together, more or less automatically, into coherent objects or sounds.

Early in this century, a group of German psychologists described the principles behind this grouping of stimuli. They argued that people perceive sights and sounds as organized wholes. These wholes, they said, are different from and more than just the sum of the individual sensations, much as water becomes something more than just an assortment of hydrogen and oxygen atoms. Because the German word meaning roughly "whole figure" is *Gestalt*, these researchers became known as **Gestalt psychologists.** They proposed

Figure 5.11
Figure-Ground Perception
What do you see? At first, you may perceive two faces staring at each other. If so, the space between the two faces is the **ground**—*the meaningless, contourless background behind the faces that form the figure. But look again. You may also perceive the figure as a vase or candle holder. Now the spaces on each side, which formerly had been meaningful figures, take on the meaningless properties of ground.*

Figure 5.12
Gestalt Principles of Perceptual Grouping
You probably perceive a as being made up of two groups of two dots plus two single dots, rather than as three groups of two dots or some other arrangement. In b, you see two columns of X's and two columns of O's, rather than four rows of XOXO, illustrating the principle of similarity. You see the symbol in c as being made out of two continuous lines—one straight and one curved—not one of the other discontinuous forms shown in the figure. You immediately perceive the disconnected line segments of d as a triangle and a circle. In e, the different orientation of the lines in one quadrant of the square makes that quadrant stand out from the others. In f, both figures are the same three-dimensional cube viewed from different angles, but the one on the left is normally perceived as a two-dimensional hexagon with lines running through it; the other, as a three-dimensional cube.

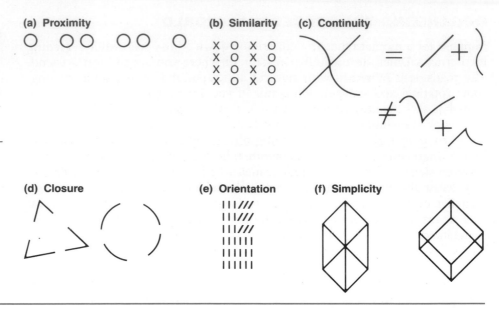

The fact that you perceive a cat behind the railing and a tree outside the window—even though neither object can be seen in its entirety—illustrates the perceptual tendency known as closure. Without it, the world would appear to be a confusing array of fragmented images.

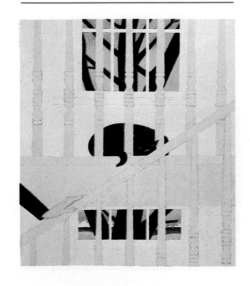

six principles or properties that lead the perceptual system to "glue" raw sensations together in particular ways, organizing stimuli into a world of shapes and patterns. These principles, which are illustrated in Figure 5.12, are

1. **Proximity** The closer objects are to one another, the more likely they are to be perceived as belonging together, as in Figure 5.12a.

2. **Similarity** Similar elements are perceived to be part of a group, as in Figure 5.12b. People wearing the same school colors at a stadium will be perceived as belonging together even if they are not seated close together.

3. **Continuity** Sensations that appear to create a continuous form are perceived as belonging together, as in Figure 5.12c.

4. **Closure** People tend to fill in missing contours to form a complete object, as in Figure 5.12d.

5. **Orientation** When basic features of stimuli have the same orientation (such as horizontal, vertical, or at an angle), people tend to group those stimuli together (Beck, 1966; Olson & Attneave, 1970). Thus, you group the vertical lines of a grove of standing trees together and see those trees separately from their fallen neighbors in the undergrowth. Figure 5.12e provides another example. The feature-detecting cells in the visual cortex, which we described in Chapter 4, appear to be responsible for this aspect of perceptual grouping.

6. **Simplicity** People tend to group stimulus features in a way that provides the simplest interpretation of the world (Hochberg & McAlister, 1955), as in Figure 5.12f. Consider what it takes to describe each pattern. To describe the figure on the left in two dimensions, you need only say that it is a hexagon with six radii of equal lengths. To describe it as a three-dimensional figure, you would have to say that it is a cube with sides of equal length, which is being viewed from a certain unusual angle. The simpler, more economical, two-dimensional perception will prevail. For the second figure, on the other hand, the two-dimensional interpretation is not nearly as simple to describe, because the shape is no longer a simple hexagon. You would have to describe it as "two overlapping squares with lines connecting their corresponding corners." The three-dimensional interpretation (a cube) is now simpler and more naturally perceived.

Having considered some of the ways people organize sensations into perceptions, consider some of the things these perceptions convey about the environment.

Perceptual Constancy

Suppose that, one sunny day, you are watching a friend walking toward you along a tree-lined sidewalk. The raw sensations generated by this movement are actually rather bizarre. For one thing, the size of the image on your retinas keeps getting larger as your friend gets closer. To demonstrate this effect to yourself, look at a distant person and hold your hand out at arm's length in front of your eyes. The image of your hand will completely block your view of the person, because the retinal image of the person is so small. Try the same thing when the person is three feet away. Your retinal image of the person will now be so much larger that your hand can no longer cover all of it. But you perceive the person as being closer now, not bigger. Similarly, as your friend walks along, passing from bright sunshine through the dark shadows of trees, the sensations reaching your eyes would suggest that your friend becomes darker in color, then lighter, then darker again. But instead you perceive an individual whose coloring remains the same.

This example illustrates **perceptual constancy,** the perception of objects as constant in size, shape, color, and other properties despite changes in their retinal image. Without this aspect of perception, the world would be an Alice-in-Wonderland kind of place in which objects continuously changed their properties.

Size constancy   Why does the perceived size of objects stay more or less constant, no matter what changes occur in the size of their retinal image? Part of the reason is that perception is knowledge based, and experience tells us that most objects (aside from balloons) do not spontaneously change size. However, familiarity is not the only source of size constancy. Years ago, people in an experiment were asked to estimate the size of an unfamiliar object viewed at varying distances by adjusting a disk of light until the light disk seemed to be the same size as the object. If lack of familiarity with the objects had eliminated size constancy, the estimated sizes should have been similar to the size of the retinal image, and closer objects would have been judged to be larger. In fact, the people came quite close to an accurate perception of the unfamiliar objects' true size (Holway & Boring, 1941).

What produced this accurate perception of size? As objects move closer or farther away, the brain perceives the change in distance and automatically adjusts the perception. The formula describing this adjustment is

$$\text{Perceived size} = \text{retinal image} \times \text{perceived distance}$$

In other words, the perceived size of an object is equal to the size of the retinal image multiplied by the perceived distance (Holway & Boring, 1941). Here again, we see that perception is relational: the retinal image is interpreted in relation to perceived distance. As an object moves closer, its retinal image increases, but the perceived distance decreases at the same rate, and the perceived size remains constant. If, instead, a balloon is inflated in front of your eyes, the retinal image increases, but perceived distance remains constant, and the perceived size (correctly) increases.

As another example, hold the retinal image constant by fixing your eyes on a bar of light (a bright fluorescent light is a good choice) and stare at it for thirty seconds or so, in order to form a good afterimage. This afterimage represents a retinal image of a constant size. Now shift your gaze from the light to a distant wall. The perceived size of the afterimage will now be larger because the retinal image is now being multiplied by a larger perceived distance.

The relationships in the perceptual system among retinal size, perceived size, and perceived distance do not always produce desirable effects. People may perceive objects with smaller retinal images to be farther away than those with larger images, even when the distance is in fact the same. One experiment suggested that this error may be responsible for the higher accident rate among drivers of small cars (Eberts & MacMillan, 1985). A small car produces a smaller retinal image at a given distance than a larger one, possibly causing the driver of a following vehicle to *overestimate* the distance to the small car and therefore fail to brake in time to avoid a rear-end collision.

Although the perceptual system usually produces size constancy correctly and automatically, it can sometimes fail. Figure 5.13 illustrates one such case. Why is size constancy violated in this figure? The answer will be clear when we consider depth perception a bit later.

Shape constancy   The principles of shape constancy are closely related to those of size constancy. To see shape constancy at work, remember what page you are on, close this book, and tilt it toward and away from you several times. The book will continue to look rectangular, even though the shape of its retinal image changed dramatically as you moved it. The brain automatically integrates information about retinal images and distance as movement occurs. In this case, the distance information involved the difference in distance between the near and the far edges of the book.

Brightness constancy   No matter how the amount of light striking an object changes, its perceived brightness remains constant. You could demonstrate this constancy by watching a friend walk by a leafy tree on a sunny day or by placing a lump of coal in sunlight and a piece of white paper in some shade next to it. The coal still looks very dark and the paper still looks very bright, even though a light meter would reveal much more light energy reflected to the eyes from the sun-bathed coal than from the shaded paper.

Of course, one reason why the coal continues to look dark, no matter what the illumination, is that you know that coal is black, illustrating once again the knowledge-based property of perception. Another reason is that the coal is still the darkest object *relative to* its background in the sunlight, and the paper is the brightest object *relative to* its background in the shade. The brightness of an object is perceived in relation to its background.

Constancy and the nature of perception   All of these perceptual constancies demonstrate the characteristics of perception that we described at the beginning of this chapter. Perception, we have noted, is both knowledge based and relative. For example, we have shown how the size of an object is perceived in relation to distance and its brightness in relation to its background. Figure 5.14 shows how sometimes the relational nature of perception can trick one into misperceiving the world.

Nevertheless, perceptual constancies also demonstrate the adaptive nature of perception. Thanks to the constancies of perception, people perceive constant, stable objects. Imagine trying to deal with a world in which objects changed their form as constantly as their images changed on your retinas. Perceptual constancy also demonstrates the principle of simplicity at work. The world is far simpler if one can assume that objects are constant and that distances and lighting change, rather than assuming that the objects themselves change.

Depth Perception: Experiencing the Third Dimension

You have seen how one of the most important factors underlying size and shape constancy is perceived distance. Perception of distance, or **depth**

Figure 5.13
A Violation of Size Constancy
The two baseball players in the picture appear to be of very different sizes, even though you know that their heights are probably much the same. For an explanation of why constancy is violated here, read on to the section on depth perception.
(Wide World Photos)

If you were to trace the outline of this floating object, you would see that its image is oval-shaped. However, the perceptual principle of shape constancy causes you to perceive it as the perfectly circular life ring that it is.

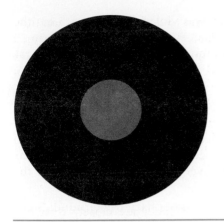 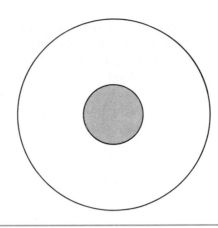

Figure 5.14
Brightness Constancy
You probably perceive the inner ring on the left to be brighter than the inner ring on the right. But, if you carefully examine the inner circles alone, by covering the surround, you will see that the two are of equal intensity. The brighter surround in the right-hand ring leads you to perceive its inner ring as relatively darker. Here is an example of how the tendency to perceive stimulus properties in relation to their surroundings can create illusions.

perception, also allows people to experience the world in three-dimensional depth, not as a two-dimensional movie. How can this be, when all visual information comes through a set of two-dimensional retinas? There are two reasons. The first involves a wide variety of cues provided by the environment. The second is a set of properties of the visual system itself.

Stimulus cues   To some extent, people perceive depth through the same cues that an artist uses to create the impression of depth and distance on a two-dimensional canvas. These cues are actually specific characteristics of visual stimuli. Figure 5.15 illustrates several of them.

> Look first at the two men at the far left of the picture. They illustrate the principle of **relative size:** objects producing larger images on the retina are perceived as closer than those producing smaller ones.
>
> Another cue comes from height in the visual field: more distant objects are usually higher in the visual field than those nearby. The woman near the man at the front of Figure 5.15 therefore appears to be farther away.

Figure 5.15
Stimulus Cues for Depth Perception

Parallel lines seem to converge as they extend into the distance. This illusion provides linear perspective cues for distance; objects near where the lines "meet" are perceived as farther away than those located where the lines appear farther apart.

(By the way, this is why size constancy was violated in Figure 5.13; the more distant ballplayer is lower, not higher in the visual field.)

The woman standing by the car in the middle of the picture illustrates another depth cue called **interposition.** Closer objects block one's view of things farther away.

The figure at the far right of the picture is seen as still farther away, in part because she is standing near a point in the road where its edges, like all parallel lines that recede into the distance, appear to converge toward a single point. This apparent convergence provides a cue called **linear perspective.** The closer together two converging lines are, the greater the perceived distance.

Finally, the road in the picture disappears into a hazy background. Since greater distances usually produce less clarity, **reduced clarity** is interpreted as a cue for greater distance. The effect of clarity on perceived distance explains why a mountain viewed on a hazy day appears to loom larger than the same mountain on a clear day. The haze acts as a cue for greater distance, but the size of the mountain's retinal image is unchanged. The same retinal image accompanied by a greater perceived distance produces a larger perceived size.

Two additional stimulus cues for depth come from **gradients,** which are continuous changes across the visual field. A **textural gradient** is a graduated change in the texture, or "grain," of the visual field. (It was illustrated in Figure 5.3, as an example of Gibson's ecological approach to perception.) Texture appears finer and less detailed as distance increases; so as texture changes across the retinal image, as in the fields illustrated in Figures 5.3 and 5.15, people perceive a change in distance.

The second gradient cue is the **movement gradient,** which is the graduated difference in the apparent movement of objects. Faster relative movement across the visual field indicates less distance. The next time you are riding in a car in an open area, look out the side window at an object of intermediate distance (for example, a house). The telephone poles and other objects closest to you will appear to fly across your visual field at a rapid rate; in contrast, distant trees may seem motionless or even appear to move along with you. It is this difference in relative movement that provides cues to the difference in distance.

Cues based on properties of the visual system   Because each eye is located at a slightly different spot on the head, each receives a slightly different view of the world, as Figure 5.16 illustrates. The difference between the two retinal images of an object is called **binocular disparity** and is responsible for creating the experience of a solid, three-dimensional object. For any particular object, this disparity decreases with increasing distance. Nevertheless, with both eyes open, the brain combines the two images, processes information about the amount of disparity and the distance, and generates the impression of a single object having its correct depth, as well as height and width. Binocular disparity is one of the strongest cues of depth perception.

In the late nineteenth century, an understanding of binocular disparity was used to produce the *stereoscope,* a hand-held device that creates the appearance of depth by displaying to each eye a separate photograph of an object or scene, each taken from a slightly different angle. The same principle is used today to create the impression of three dimensions in Viewmaster slide viewers and in 3-D movies.

A second consequence of having two eyes located at slightly different places is that the eyes must converge, or rotate inward, in order to project

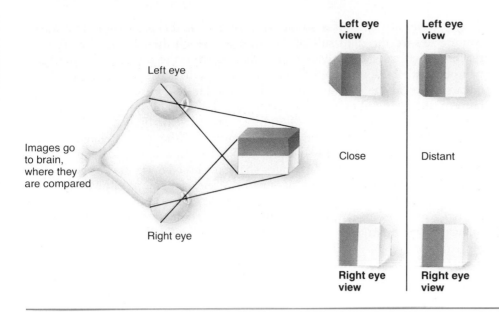

Left eye view | **Left eye view**

Close | Distant

Right eye view | **Right eye view**

Figure 5.16
Binocular Disparity
Each eye has a slightly different view of the cube. The difference between views is greater when the cube is close than when it is far away. For a quick demonstration, hold a pencil up vertically about six inches in front of you. Close one eye and take note of where the pencil is relative to the objects in the background. Now open that eye and close the other one. Notice how the pencil seems to shift slightly and how it obscures slightly different parts of the background. These are the two views your eyes have of that pencil. If you now hold the pencil at arm's length or look at some other narrow vertical object some distance away, there is less difference in the angles at which the two eyes see the object, and the amount of disparity (or shift) decreases.

the image of an object on each retina. This **convergence** provides another cue to depth. As Figure 5.17 shows, the closer the object is, the more "cross-eyed" the viewer must become in order to achieve a focused image. The brain receives and processes information from the eye muscles about the amount of muscular activity; the greater the activity, the closer the object is perceived to be.

What binocular disparity does for depth perception, the placement of the ears does for sound localization, that is, determining the directions from which sounds arise. The cues that are used to locate sounds depend on the fact that

Close view   Distant view

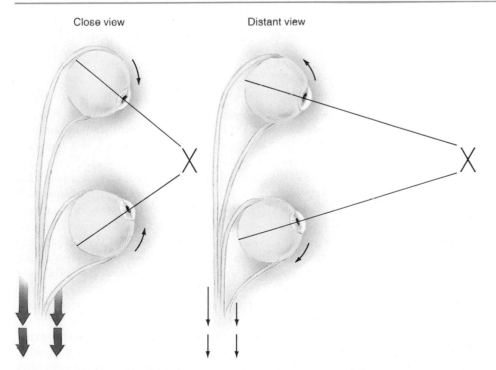

Proprioceptive information

Figure 5.17
Convergence
The arrows along the nerve fibers coming from the eyeballs represent the strength of proprioceptive information about muscle activity.

people have two ears. If a sound is continuous, the peak of sound waves coming toward the right side of the head will reach the right ear before they reach the left ear. Similarly, a sound coming from the right side of the head will be a little bit louder to the right ear than to the left ear, because the head blocks some of the sound from the left ear. Thus, the nervous system uses both timing cues and intensity to locate sounds. This ability to localize sounds requires sophisticated analysis of auditory input by the brain.

The final depth cue based on the anatomy of the eye is related to facts we noted in the chapter on sensation. To bring an image into focus on the retina, the lens of the eyeball changes shape, or *accommodates*. To accomplish this feat, muscles surrounding the lens must either tighten, to make the lens more curved for focusing on close objects, or relax, to flatten the lens for focusing on more distant objects. Information about the muscles' activity is relayed to the brain, and this accommodation cue helps create the perception of distance.

Watching the World Go By: The Perception of Motion

As a tennis player brings her racket back to return a shot, the most important thing she must perceive about the ball is not its size or shape or even its precise location and distance. The critical property is its *motion*: how fast it is going and where it is heading.

The perception of motion usually occurs as visual patterns move across the surface of the retina. Like distance perception, it requires that one somehow translate this two-dimensional retinal image into a three-dimensional experience. People make this translation automatically by using both visual cues and information about the movement of parts of the body.

Consistent with his ecological theory, Gibson (1966) argued that information indicating motion occurs in the visual stimulus itself. The movement gradient we discussed earlier provides a good example. Imagine you are riding in a car that is moving forward toward the horizon. When you are looking forward in the moving car, objects in your visual field appear to diverge from a single point, the point where the road disappears into the horizon, and move progressively faster as they move away from this vanishing point. This pattern is automatically perceived as the forward movement of your own body toward and past unmoving objects.

Looming, which is a rapid expansion in the size of an image so that it fills the available space on the retina, provides another cue to motion. As noted earlier, when an image looms, there is an automatic tendency to perceive it as an approaching stimulus, not an expanding object viewed at a constant distance.

Although the movement of light across the retina is normally associated with motion, it is not always sufficient to create the perception of motion. If movement of the retinal image were the only factor necessary for motion perception, then when you swing your head around, or even rotate your eyeballs from side to side, you should perceive everything in the visual field to be moving in the opposite direction. This is not the case, because as we discussed in the chapter on sensation, the brain also receives and processes information about the motion of the eye and head. If the brain determines that all of the movement of light on the retina is due to such bodily movement, the outside world is perceived as stable, not moving.

Sensations of head and eye movement can actually compensate for external motion, slowing down and smoothing out the perception of moving objects. For example, by moving your head and eyes, you can perceive a speeding race car as a focused, smoothly moving object. But if you hold your head and eyes still as the car goes by, you will perceive it as a much more rapidly moving blur.

Perceptual Illusions

The perceptual cues we have described constantly and automatically convey precise information about the features of a multitude of objects and surfaces. As a result, you can walk down stairs, toss a wad of paper into a distant trashcan, avoid collisions while driving, and accomplish a thousand other everyday acts with little hesitation and without a second thought. In fact, you are unlikely to become aware of perceptual cues at all unless you read about them or unless they create an inaccurate or distorted view of reality. In Chapter 6, on consciousness, we will describe how distorted perceptions can come about through sleep, hypnosis, drugs, and other circumstances; here we are concerned with those distortions of reality known as *perceptual illusions.*

Illusions of motion   One such illusion is *stroboscopic motion,* the perception of motion produced when snapshot images, each slightly different from the next, are presented one after the other. This is the principle behind the motion picture, which produces perceptions of motion from a series of still shots.

The "moving" neon lights seen on advertising signs are an application of another type of stroboscopic motion, an illusion called the *phi phenomenon.* If the timing is right, a series of lights flashing on and off sequentially at slightly different locations is perceived as just one light moving from one point to the next. Movement is perceived even though nothing is actually moving.

The perception of movement in these cases is consistent with the principle of simplicity. It is simpler to assume that there is one object moving in space rather than several stationary objects, each of which turns on and off in sequence.

Illusory movement may also occur if you adopt the wrong frame of reference or the wrong hypothesis. Normally, when there is relative movement between figure and ground, the figure is more likely to be perceived as moving and the background as stable. If you therefore perceive a figure to be moving when it is not, the illusion is called *induced motion.* You may experience this effect when you sit in a stationary car in a parking lot, and the vehicle next to you begins to move slowly backward. You are likely to perceive your own car as drifting forward—even though cues from the vestibular senses tell you that you are not moving, and your kinesthetic senses say that your foot is planted firmly on the brake.

Why are these vestibular and kinesthetic cues temporarily ignored? The answer lies in a phenomenon known as **visual dominance.** When information received by the visual system conflicts with information coming from other sensory modalities, the sense of vision normally wins the battle and is perceived as accurate (Posner, Nissen & Klein, 1976).

Illusions of shape, size, and depth   Figure 5.18 (p. 184) presents five other perceptual illusions. The first three (a through c) involve distortions of shape; they support the Gestalt principle that the whole is different from the sum of its parts. Sections d and e show illusions of size and depth.

The *Ebbinghaus illusion* is shown in Figure 5.18d. Look at the circles in the center of each pattern. The one on the left probably looks smaller to you than the one on the right, though both are in fact the same size. This illusion illustrates again that perceptual judgments take place *relative to* some context. In the left-hand pattern, the context (or background) for the center, which

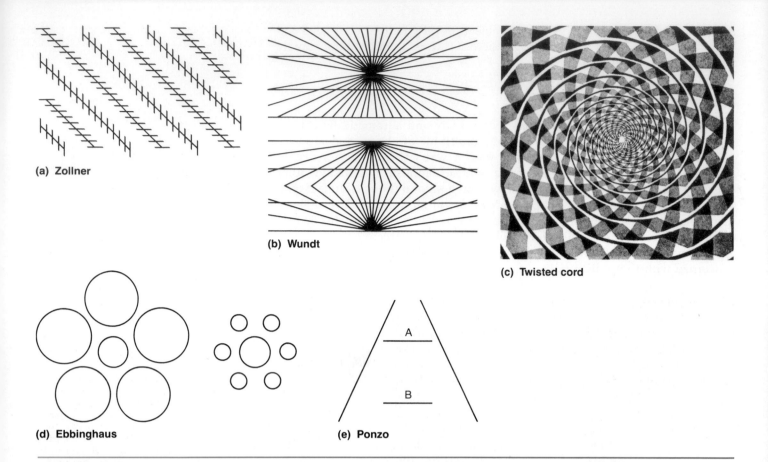

(a) Zollner

(b) Wundt

(c) Twisted cord

(d) Ebbinghaus

(e) Ponzo

Figure 5.18
Five Perceptual Illusions
(a) In the Zollner illusion, you can focus attention directly on a pair of parallel lines to establish that they are in fact parallel, but if you draw back to consider the entire figure, you get the clear impression that they are not parallel. (b) The lines in the Wundt illusion are actually parallel, and (c) the twisted cord is actually made up of concentric circles. (d) The Ebbinghaus illusion is a direct analogy to the misjudgment of brightness shown in Figure 5.14. (e) The Ponzo illusion uses converging lines to create the impression that the top horizontal line is at a greater distance than the bottom one. This greater perceived distance, multiplied by the top line's retinal size, gives it a larger perceived size (length) than the bottom line, even though the two are identical.

consists of larger objects, creates the perception that the center circle is relatively small. The right-hand center circle appears in a context of smaller objects, making you perceive it as larger. Dieters should keep this in mind: a small meal looks more substantial if served on a small plate. Diet-food advertisers use this fact to make their products look more filling.

Other illusions involving size result from the way in which the perceptual system automatically "grabs onto" any cue to depth in order to provide a three-dimensional interpretation of a stimulus. The *Ponzo illusion* (Figure 5.18e) is a perfect example. Line segment A looks longer than segment B, yet they are the same length. You misperceive their lengths because the perceptual system uses the converging lines as its primary depth cue (recall linear perspective, on page 180). Thus, you view the region where the lines are closer together as more distant. Then the principle of relative size takes over: recall that when two objects have retinal images of the same size, the one perceived as farther away is seen as larger. As a result, the line seen as more distant here is also seen as longer.

Perceptions of size constancy and distance also seem to interact in the *moon illusion,* the perception that the moon is much larger when it is near the horizon than when it is high in the night sky, even though the size of the retinal image of the moon stays the same. Lloyd Kaufman and Irvin Rock (1962) have argued that when one looks at the moon on the horizon, the intervening space is filled with objects (houses, trees, or mountains) that convey a sense of greater distance than when one looks straight up and sees nothing but the moon (see Figure 5.19). The greater perceived distance apparently makes the moon on the horizon look larger.

Figure 5.19
Example of the Moon Illusion
Experiments show that the moon illusion is destroyed when subjects look at paper cutout moons placed on a laboratory horizon where no intervening terrain can be seen. Also, when mirrors are used to give people the impression of intervening terrain stretching toward the highest point in the sky and to make the view toward the horizon look empty, the illusion is reversed: the horizon moon then looks smaller.

Probably the best-known and most studied perceptual illusion is the *Müller-Lyer illusion,* shown in Figure 5.20a (p. 186). Of the two arrow shafts in the figure, the one on the left seems shorter, despite the fact that the two are of equal length. Richard Gregory (1968, 1973) has argued that this illusion, like the Ponzo illusion, represents a misapplication of the depth cue of linear perspective. The convergence of the arrowheads on each side of the shaft on the left makes the shaft appear to be the closest part of the scene (like the outside corner of the house in Figure 5.20b), whereas the divergence of the arrowheads on the right makes that shaft seem to be toward the back. By the logic applied to the Ponzo and moon illusions, the more "distant" shaft appears to be larger.

The idea that depth cues underlie the Müller-Lyer illusion has been supported by investigations showing that the illusion is stronger among subjects who have more experience making depth and distance judgments using parallel lines and corners (Gregory, 1968; Segall et al., 1963). In addition, increasing the amount of three-dimensional information in the drawing increases the magnitude of the illusion (Liebowitz et al., 1969).

Attractive and simple as the depth perception theory of the Müller-Lyer illusion may seem, it cannot account for some phenomena. A striking example is shown in Figure 5.20c. In this figure, there are no converging lines to suggest distance, and the figure does not give a feeling of three-dimensionality; yet it does create a misjudgment of distance like that in the Müller-Lyer illusion. Why? One proposed explanation is that the perceived length of an

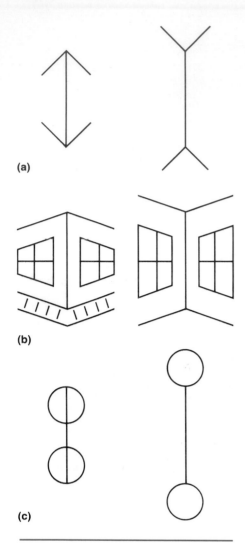

Figure 5.20
Variations on the Müller-Lyer Illusion
(a) The Müller-Lyer illusion. (b) The Müller-Lyer illusion in a three-dimensional context, in which the vertical line is used to form the outside corner of a house and the inside corner of a room. The inside corner looks taller. (c) A demonstration of the illusion that does not only involve perception of three dimensions.

object is based on the "frame" of which it is a part. When the frame is perceived as larger, as it is in the right side of Figure 5.20c, so is the line segment included within it (Rock, 1978).

This example shows that explanations of some perceptual illusions remain incomplete. Perhaps the best conclusion to offer at this point is that illusions such as the Müller-Lyer are multiply determined. After all, since perception is based on many principles, it seems reasonable that illusions could reflect the violation of more than one of them.

Distortions of perception may also be created, not by cues provided by the environment, but by the same factors that create response bias in detecting stimuli: motivation, experience, bias, and expectancy. In one classic study, children were asked to estimate the size of poker chips by adjusting a disk of light to match a displayed chip. Children who had been told they could use the poker chip to buy candy estimated the chip to be significantly larger than other children did, a result suggesting that objects that are more important may be perceived as larger (Lambert, Solomon & Watson, 1949). You will see in the next section that the motivational and other individual-difference factors highlighted in our discussion of signal detection theory can also affect the speed and accuracy with which people are able to recognize objects in the world.

RECOGNIZING THE PERCEPTUAL WORLD

In discussing how people organize the perceptual world by segregating it into figure and ground and then assessing the properties of objects, we have so far ignored one vital question: How do people recognize what the object is? If you are driving in search of Barney's Diner, exactly what happens when your eyes finally locate the pattern of light that spells out "Barney's Diner"? How do you recognize it as the place you are seeking?

Basically, the brain must analyze the incoming pattern of light and compare that pattern to what is stored in memory. If it finds a match, recognition takes place. Thus, recognition depends on the stimuli, sensations, and memory. But the factors that create response bias in the detection of stimuli—motivation and expectancy—also influence recognition. If you desperately want to see the sign, perhaps because a long-lost lover waits at the diner, you will see it sooner than if you are going to meet some unexciting person. And you will recognize the sign more easily if it appears precisely at the corner where your map says you should expect it rather than a block earlier.

Once you recognize a stimulus, your perception of it may never be the same. Look at Figure 5.21. Do you see anything familiar? If not, turn to Figure 5.22 (p. 188). Now look at Figure 5.21 again. You should now see it in an entirely new light; in fact, you may never again be able to perceive the figure as you did at first. The difference between your "before" and "after" experience of Figure 5.21 is the difference between the sensory world before and after a perceptual match occurs and recognition takes place.

These examples illustrate the two types of processing that appear to be involved in recognition. Those aspects of recognition that begin at the "top," guided by higher-level cognitive processes and by psychological factors like expectations and motivation, are called **top-down processing** (Lindsay & Norman, 1977). Other aspects of recognition depend first on the information about the stimulus that comes "up" to the brain from the sensory receptors; this is called **bottom-up processing.** First, how does bottom-up processing work?

Figure 5.21
Perceptual Categorization
For the identity of this figure, turn the page.
(Photo by Ronald C. James)

Feature Analysis

Some psychologists have suggested that recognition occurs through the firing of a particular set of neurons in the brain that become active only when they find their match in the perceptual world (Lindsay & Norman, 1977), much as only one fork in a row of tuning forks will vibrate when its matching pitch is played. We described this view, the hierarchical feature-detection model, in the chapter on sensation.

As we noted there, one problem with this model is that you would need a different feature detector for every one of the seemingly infinite number of specific sights, sounds, smells, and other stimuli that you recognize. (We also noted that the spatial frequency model may provide another description of how the brain analyzes patterns; this is not yet confirmed.) Nevertheless, there are specific feature detectors in the visual cortex that respond to particular lines, edges, corners, angles, and other features of stimuli (Hubel & Wiesel, 1979). And there are cells that fire only in response to features corresponding to different pitches, loudnesses, and timbres of sounds.

This evidence that cells of the brain respond to specific features of stimuli supports the view that recognition occurs by means of **feature analysis.** According to this view, any stimulus can be described as a combination of features. The letter *A,* for example, can be described as consisting of one horizontal and two angular lines, connected at an acute angle. The sensory system analyzes a stimulus into a set of such features. Then the brain compares this set against the lists of features or perhaps prototypes of objects in memory to find the best match. If there is a match, recognition occurs.

Feature analysis not only explains how people recognize stimuli that are exactly like familiar ones, but also provides a plausible explanation for the fact that different stimuli can be given the same interpretation. When you look at, say, a dachshund, Saint Bernard, or poodle, you recognize each animal as a dog, because each presents a pattern of features that corresponds to a stored category you know as *dog*. But what happens when a combination of features comes close to, but does not quite match, a stored perceptual category, as when you see a three-legged dog? Here, the recognition process places the stimulus in the closest category, while also noting the features that do not fit

Figure 5.22
Another Version of Figure 5.21
Now that you can identify the figure clearly, look back to the previous figure, which should now be much easier to recognize.

Figure 5.23
Limitations of Bottom-up Processing
Because the same physical stimulus can be recognized in different ways from time to time, perceptual processing must depend in part on internal factors, not just on the nature of the stimulus itself.

that category. Thus, you say, "That's a dog with three legs"; you do not say, "That's a milking stool."

Feature analysis can nicely explain how a set of diverse stimuli (a dachshund and a Saint Bernard, for example) can be assigned to one category as long as the stimuli share many of the same features. But feature analysis cannot easily explain how people handle ambiguous stimuli, assigning a stimulus sometimes to one category and sometimes to another. In Figure 5.11, for example, you could recognize the stimulus sometimes as a vase and sometimes as two faces. And in Figure 5.23, one stimulus pattern can be recognized as the number 13 or the letter *B;* another can be perceived as a lowercase *b* or as a baseball cap. Since these shifting recognitions are based on the same stimulus pattern, the differences in perception cannot be attributed to feature analysis or some other bottom-up processing.

Top-down Processing

The differences in your perception of the patterns in Figure 5.23 must have something to do with the *context* in which these stimuli are embedded. The ambiguous patterns are likely to be perceived in relation to what is around them: they are perceived as a number when next to other numbers, as a letter when accompanied by other letters, as a hat when on top of a head. The context creates an *expectancy* about what will be perceived. Along with motivation—wants and needs—expectancy is a major factor that influences perception through top-down processing.

Expectancy Look at Figure 5.24a. How old is the woman you see? Look again, because like the vase-face example in Figure 5.11, this is an ambiguous figure. Some people immediately see an attractive young woman wearing a feathered hat and turning her head away. Others see an old hag with a large nose and a protruding chin (Boring, 1930).

Which one you recognize first can be influenced by what you expect to see. If you spent last summer working among high-fashion models, you might be more likely to see the young woman than if you had been working in a nursing home. The effect of expectancy was demonstrated in the laboratory by Robert Leeper (1935) who showed people either Figure 5.24b, in which the young woman is strongly emphasized, or Figure 5.24c, which makes the old woman stand out. Then he showed Figure 5.24a, the ambiguous drawing, to everyone. Most of those who had first seen the version emphasizing the young woman continued to see her in the ambiguous figure, whereas the old woman was identified first by those who had seen the version emphasizing her.

Thus, past experience, like context, can create a certain expectancy, biasing perception toward one recognition or another under different circumstances. In other words, expectancy creates a **perceptual set,** a readiness or predisposition to perceive a stimulus in a certain way. This effect of expectancy applies to sounds as well as to sights. The raw sound "eye screem" takes on two very different meanings when heard in the context of "I scream whenever I am angry" as opposed to "I love ice cream."

The expectancy created by a familiar context can help people recognize objects. For example, in one experiment, people were shown a familiar scene, like a kitchen. Then they were given a very brief glimpse of an object that would be expected in that context (for example, a loaf of bread) or one that would be unexpected (for example, a mailbox). Although the two objects were roughly the same size and shape, the subjects more readily recognized the object that fit the context than the object that did not (Palmer, 1975). Similarly, in another experiment, people had a more difficult time recognizing objects when certain expected properties were violated (Biederman et al., 1981). For example, in scenes like those in Figure 5.25, the fire hydrant was more easily perceived when it was on the ground than when it was on the mailbox; the car was recognized more readily on the street than floating inside a house.

Motivation Suppose you are very hungry as you drive down the street of an unfamiliar city. You don't care if you find Barney's Diner or not; you'll eat anywhere. In this state of mind, you are likely to show many false alarms, slamming on the brakes and salivating at the sight of "Eaton's Furniture," "Burger's Body Shop," "Cherry Hill Estates," or any other sign that even hints at food.

Many motives besides hunger can alter perceptions. If you have ever watched an athletic contest, you probably remember a time when an obviously

(a)

(b)   **(c)**

Figure 5.24
An Ambiguous Figure
(a) Which face do you see? (b)–(c) Unambiguous portraits of the young and old women, respectively.

Figure 5.25
Context and Recognition
These are examples of stimuli used by Biederman et al. (1981). On the left, the fire hydrant is harder to perceive because it is in the wrong location and unsupported. On the right, the car is harder to see because of its inappropriate size and location.
(From *Human Factors*, 1981, *23*, 152–163. Copyright 1981, by the Human Factors Society, Inc. and reproduced by permission.)

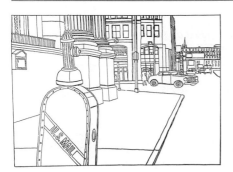

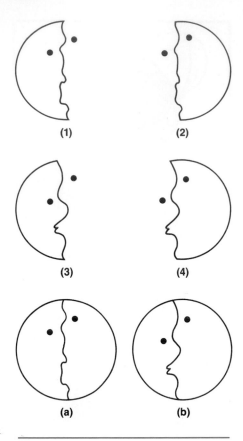

Figure 5.26
Motivation and Recognition
Schafer and Murphy (1943) trained people to associate names with profiles 1, 2, 3, and 4. The people received money when two of the profiles were presented and lost money when the other two appeared. After training, the people were shown brief glimpses of ambiguous figures created by combining one rewarded and one punished profile (sections A and B) and were asked to name the face they perceived. The people reported seeing the rewarded face significantly more than half the time.

blind or demented referee incorrectly called a foul on the team you wanted to win. You knew the call was wrong because you clearly saw the other team's player at fault. But suppose you had been cheering for the other team. The chances are good that you would have seen the same call as the right one. The effect of motivation on the categorization of ambiguous stimuli was also demonstrated in a classic laboratory study (Schafer & Murphy, 1943). Figure 5.26 explains the experiment. The results indicated that people are biased toward recognizing stimuli that fall in a category that is associated with reward.

Top-down and Bottom-up Processes Together

Though we have discussed them separately, bottom-up and top-down processing work together in a constant interaction that creates the experience of a recognizable world. In fact, one kind of processing will "fill in" when the other becomes impaired. We described this phenomenon as closure when we discussed the perception of objects. In Figure 5.12d, for example, top-down processing took over to allow recognition of an object, even though the poor stimulus quality of an incomplete drawing made bottom-up processing difficult.

For word recognition, too, top-down processing can compensate for an ambiguous stimulus that could not by itself promote good bottom-up processing. In fact, reading illustrates the interaction of bottom-up and top-down processing beautifully. Even when the quality of the raw stimulus on the printed page becomes quite poor, as in Figure 5.27, top-down processes compensate to make continued reading possible. They allow you to fill in where words are not well perceived and processed, thus giving a general idea of the meaning of the text. Even though the middle character in the words THE and CAT may be of poor quality, the letters surrounding it provide a context that allows a top-down process to tell you it is an *H* in the first case and an *A* in the second. This sort of thing would not work if the world were not *redundant,* giving multiple clues about what is going on. If you lose or miss one stimulus in a pattern, others can fill in the gaps so that you can still recognize the total pattern. There is so much redundancy in written language, for example, that many of the words and letters you see are not needed. Fo- ex-mp-e y-u c-n r-ad -hi- se-te-ce -it- ev-ry -hi-d l-tt-r m-ss-ng.

For the spoken word, too, top-down processing can compensate for ambiguous stimuli, a fact that was nicely illustrated in a laboratory experiment in which subjects heard strings of five words, such as "wet brought who socks some," read in a background that was so noisy that an average of only 75 percent of the words could be recognized (Miller, Heise & Lichten, 1951). Under these conditions, "bottom-up" processing was difficult, because the quality of the raw stimuli was poor. But when the same words, presented

Figure 5.27
Interaction of Top-down and Bottom-up Processing
Top-down processing assists in reading the obscured text on the top line. However, in the bottom line, the words are not coherently related, so top-down processing cannot operate.

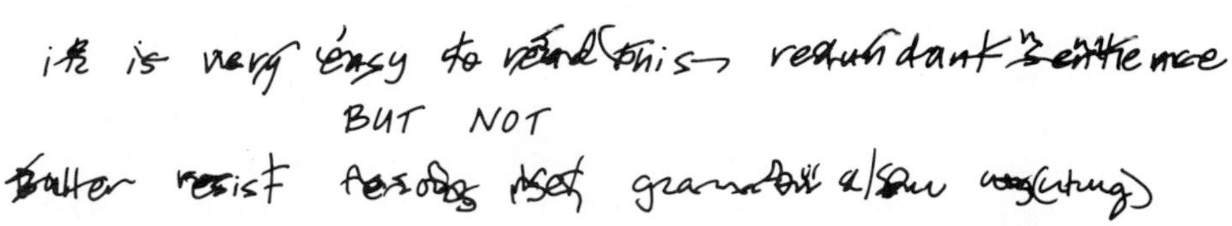

it is very easy to read this redundant sentence
BUT NOT
better resist reading that grammar class wording

under the same noisy conditions, were reordered to make a meaningful sentence (for example, "who brought some wet socks"), a second group of subjects was able to recognize almost every word. In fact, in order to reduce their performance to that of the first group, the noise level had to be doubled! Why? When the words were in meaningless order, only bottom-up processing was available, and recognizing one word was no help in identifying the next. The meaningful sentence provided a more familiar context, allowing for some top-down processing in which hearing one word helped the listener make a reasonable guess (based on knowledge and experience) about the others.

Research on the effects of top-down processing also shows how much truth there is in such sayings as "beauty is in the eye of the beholder." Indeed, the reality that people perceive and often assume is just like everyone else's is actually somewhat different for each person. This is not only important in understanding perceptual processes, but also, as we will discuss in Chapters 14 and 15, helpful in understanding the basis of individual personalities and behavior disorders.

ATTENTION

Believe it or not, you still haven't found Barney's Diner. As you continue driving, you turn on the radio and catch a particularly interesting story about aliens who have landed in the parking lot of a Columbus, Ohio, shopping center. After listening intently to the story, you realize that you have not been paying attention to your search for Barney's. Did you miss it? The fact that you are not sure demonstrates that it is often necessary to pay attention to something in order to perceive it.

Attention is the process of directing and focusing certain psychological resources, usually by voluntary control, to enhance information processing, performance, and mental experience. For example, in order to read this page, you focused a psychological resource when you shifted your attention from the television, the newspaper, or whatever else you were paying attention to earlier. And you will do it again, should you shift from reading to listening to a nearby conversation (even though your eyes may remain fixed on the book).

Selective Attention

Part of the reason why everyone experiences a somewhat different reality is that everyone pays attention to somewhat different aspects of the environment. Like a spotlight on a dark night, the beam of attention is too narrow to illuminate the entire world at once (Wachtel, 1967). As a result, you may be hard pressed to perform more than a few actions at one time or to listen to more than one voice at a time. The attentional spotlight must scan the environment sequentially. In other words, attention is *selective,* focusing on some stimuli while ignoring others. This selectivity can sometimes be a blessing, allowing you, for example, to "tune out" a boring lecture and focus attention on something more enjoyable.

What determines where the attentional spotlight moves, which things are attended to, and which are not? For one thing, stimuli that have certain properties tend to attract attention. Characteristics of stimuli that may attract attention include large size, high intensity, contrast, and novelty. Advertisers use these characteristics all the time, creating ads containing large, bright, colorful images; high volume levels; lots of novelty; and unexpected contrasts.

BLUE   GREEN

GREEN   ORANGE

PURPLE   ORANGE

GREEN   BLUE

RED   RED

GRAY   GRAY

RED   BLUE

BLUE   PURPLE

Figure 5.28
Stroop Task
*The task here is to say the color of the ink in
which each word is printed.*

However, after our discussion of signal detection theory, you should not be surprised that the focus of attention is also determined by motivation and expectancy. Thus, compared with someone who has just eaten, a hungry person's attention will be more readily attracted to the smell of food or a food advertisement.

Focused and Divided Attention

Look at the list of words in Figure 5.28. Now read the list and say aloud, as fast as you can, the color of the ink in which each word is printed.

You probably went through a good deal of fumbling and confusion as you performed this exercise, known as the *Stroop task* (Keele, 1973; Stroop, 1935). Why? You were trying to keep your attention focused on one aspect of the stimuli (color) when another very powerful aspect (the meaning of the words) was competing for your attention. Further, these two aspects of the stimuli called for *incompatible* responses (for example, saying "red" when reading the word *green*).

This simple task illustrates two facts about attention. First, it is all too easy to lose the *focus* of attention on one particular stimulus or stimulus aspect when another aspect is also attention getting. In this case, two competing stimulus aspects are color and the meaning of a single word. Second, it may be very easy to *divide* attention between two stimuli or aspects of stimuli, especially if they are physically close or similar. Thus, the difficulty of the Stroop task lies in the fact that you are perceiving both the meaning of the word and its color at the same time, but must try to ignore one stimulus aspect. Whereas attention may be divided between two aspects of a single stimulus, it is not so easy to divide attention between very different stimuli or between different tasks. This limitation can be inconvenient, as when you try to watch television and have a conversation at the same time.

The limitations on the capacity to divide attention were demonstrated years ago by Colin Cherry (1953), who asked subjects to perform a **dichotic listening** task, which is a task in which different messages are played into each ear. To force the subjects to attend to only one of the messages, Cherry asked them to *shadow* one of the messages; that is, to repeat immediately, word for word, everything heard in one ear. After performing this task for a while, the people could say almost nothing about what had been presented to the nonattended ear. They not only failed to understand the meaning of a prose message played to that ear, but could not even report if the message had remained in English, had been replaced by a string of foreign language words, or had become a string of nonsense syllables.

The ability to divide attention between visual events is also limited. In one experiment, for example, people watched a screen on which two video games were superimposed. When they were told to focus attention on the stimuli in one of the games, they became totally unaware of events in the other game (Neisser & Becklan, 1975). The beam of attention was not wide enough to capture two visual stories taking place at the same location.

The ability to divide attention is not entirely fixed. It depends in part on how much people practice doing it, what kind of simultaneous stimuli are present, and the amount of stress involved.

Practice   People who are experienced at dividing their attention do better at it than novices. Experience helps because extensive practice allows a person to process and act on perceptual information so automatically that the practiced task requires little attention. This makes it possible for other tasks to be carried out at the same time, with no loss in performance (Schneider & Shiffrin, 1977). For example, skilled typists can transcribe a written message and perform an auditory shadowing task simultaneously just as well as they can perform either task alone (Shaffer, 1975). Obviously, it is easier to divide attention between two sets of stimuli when one of them no longer requires much attention in order to be perceived and processed.

Nature of the stimuli In general, the closer together two stimuli are, the more easily they can be perceived at the same time. Dividing attention is also easier when the stimuli do not compete for attention through the same sensory system, because the human brain appears to have more than one pool of attentional resources and more than one spotlight of attention (Navon & Gopher, 1979; Wickens, 1984a). Having different attentional resources is a little like having an extra person available to help out when there is more than one job to do at the same time. However, each spotlight of attention tends to focus on a particular sensory channel. Thus, if two sets of stimuli (say, a light and a sound) involve different senses, people can more easily perceive them at the same time than if both are visual or auditory and thus have to compete for the same resources.

This is one reason why skilled secretaries can type and shadow efficiently at the same time: typing requires visual perception (and movement of the fingers and hands), whereas shadowing requires auditory perception and vocal responses (Shaffer, 1975). Somewhat different attentional resources are used in each task (Wickens, Sandry & Vidulich, 1983). This notion of different attentional resource pools also helps explain a driver's ability to listen to the radio while steering safely. It also accounts for laws that allow cars to have radios, but not televisions, in the front seat.

Stress Suppose your job is to operate the controls of a modern, very automated power plant. You face a vast visual array of dials, meters, graphs, charts, and warning lights. Should a serious problem occur, all of these stimuli will urgently compete for your attention. To perceive all of them correctly, it is critical that your beam of attention be divided as widely as possible. But the stress of emergency situations tends to narrow attention, not broaden it (Easterbrook, 1959; Hockey, 1984).

This effect was clearly demonstrated in the 1979 accident at the Three Mile Island nuclear power plant. A loss of coolant flowing to one of the reactors threatened to expose the radioactive fuel core and trigger a meltdown. During the first few minutes of coolant loss, the plant operators paid attention only to certain indicators, which, as it turned out, gave them incorrect information. These faulty indicators suggested that the coolant pressure was too high, not too low. Under the stress of the emergency, the operators' attention was not wide enough to perceive information from other displays, which were showing the true status of the reactor. As a result, the operators shut off a pump that would have restored badly needed coolant, an error that made the situation far worse than it might have been (Rubinstein & Mason, 1979; Wickens, 1984b).

Exactly why the ability to divide attention is reduced under stress is not fully understood, but awareness of the problem has led engineering psychologists who aid in the improvement of instrumentation systems for, say, nuclear power plant control rooms, to recommend steps to counteract it. They have suggested that various instrument displays be better integrated physically so that, as attention narrows, critical pieces of information are less likely to be ignored (Goodstein, 1981). At the same time, other psychologists are pursuing, at the biological level, clues about the basis of attentional narrowing and many other aspects of attention.

HIGHLIGHT

Attention and the Brain

Unlike the visual cortex, neurotransmitters, and other brain structures and chemicals, attention cannot be seen. We can only observe its effects on various kinds of performance. However, psychologists have begun to learn more about attention and how it is used by looking at physiological changes that occur as people focus and divide their attention in many different kinds of tasks.

For example, subjects in one study were asked to hold a series of digits in memory while their pupil diameters were measured (Kahneman, Beatty & Pollack, 1967). Pupil enlargement usually accompanies stress, excitement, and other emotions. The results showed that, as the subjects attempted to place each new digit in memory, their pupils grew larger and larger. As the subjects "emptied" their memory by recalling the items they had been holding, their pupils gradually returned to their original diameter. Thus, this study suggests that pupil diameter can serve as a measure of how much attentional resources are being mobilized as a person performs a task.

Some general clues about where these resources are coming from have been provided by the electroencephalograph (EEG), which measures the electrical activity of the brain. (For more on the EEG, see page 94.) One EEG measure, the evoked brain potential, provides a rather precise measure of where a person's attention is being directed from moment to moment. The **evoked potential,** or **EP,** is a small, temporary change in EEG voltage that is evoked by some stimulus. One of these changes is called the *P300* because it is a positive swing in electrical voltage that occurs about 300 milliseconds after a stimulus. The P300 appears to register faithfully whether a particular stimulus is attended to or not (Donchin, Kramer & Wickens, 1986; Pritchard, 1981). By measuring P300s, psychologists can determine, for example, whether a person reading a book is being distracted by sounds in the room. One experiment (Squires et al., 1977) found that, when subjects were engrossed in a book, a series of clicking sounds occurring about every 2 seconds evoked no P300; if attention was directed away from the book to the clicks, the P300s were large (see Figure 5.29).

The allocation of attention in a more complex visual environment was monitored through EPs in another experiment, in which subjects viewed a display similar to what air traffic controllers see on their radar screens (Wickens et al., 1980). The subjects were told that half of the aircraft on the screen were important and must be monitored; these appeared on the screen as squares. They were told that the other aircraft, represented by circles, were

Figure 5.29
The P300 and Attention
Note the larger P300 when attention is focused on the tones (b) than when it is absorbed in a book (a).

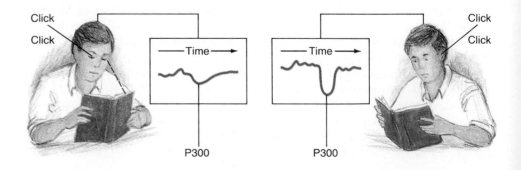

not their responsibility and could be ignored. They were also told that they should be careful to notice when an "important" aircraft began to flash on the screen. Clear P300s occurred only when "important" aircraft flashed. Later, after a simple instruction to switch attention to the circles, the EP pattern was reversed completely: P300s occurred only when the previously "unimportant" aircraft flashed.

Although neither pupil size, EEG, nor EPs can take experimenters inside the head to show exactly what attention is, these measures have brought psychologists a step closer to identifying attention as something that might actually be measured apart from the performance that it generates. Indeed, experiments using these measures have raised the suggestion that air traffic controllers, power plant operators, and others who work with complex systems might someday have their attention monitored by computers that can record EPs and make certain that important warnings are not ignored. However, this step is not likely to be taken very soon, if at all. In addition to the ethical question of whether it is acceptable to expose employees' brain waves to scrutiny by computers and managers, there are many technological problems in recording and understanding EPs outside the laboratory. Nevertheless, as we discuss in the next section, the occasional disasters that result from failures of attention make the idea of computer-based monitoring worthy of some consideration. ◼

SOME APPLICATIONS OF RESEARCH ON PERCEPTION

Throughout this chapter, we have alluded to some of the ways in which the nature of the human perceptual system relates to people's ability (or inability) to handle a variety of tasks, from recognizing restaurant signs to detecting weapons at an airport security checkpoint. In this section, we focus more closely on the application of perception research to just two areas in which perception is particularly important: aviation and reading.

Aviation Psychology

Perception is particularly vital in aviation because of the number of lives riding on it. Indeed, much of the impetus for research on perception in aviation has come from tragic incidents that resulted in part from failures of perception (Hurst, 1984; Wiener, 1977). As we noted at the opening of this chapter, four Boeing 727 crashes in 1966 resulted from pilots' misperceptions of their altitude and an inappropriate correction to reduce altitude. Conrad Kraft (1978) hypothesized that these misperceptions occurred because the night was clear and the pilots ignored correct information on their instruments. To test this hypothesis, Kraft designed an aircraft simulator that could recreate the conditions surrounding the crashes. He found that eleven out of twelve experienced Boeing flight instructors made the same errors of judgment while "flying" the simulator and, had they been flying a real aircraft, would have crashed.

Kraft's research showed dramatically that estimation of size and distance can sometimes be distorted when the physical world does not conform to people's expectations and assumptions. In this case, the pilots' expectations were that the airport terrain and city lights lay on a flat rather than an upward-sloping surface. The research led to the simple, but effective, recommendation that pilots rely on their instruments extensively during night flight, even in

The pilot of a modern commercial jetliner is faced with a potentially overwhelming array of visual and auditory signals that must be correctly perceived and interpreted to ensure a safe landing.

clear weather, and recognize the extent to which the human perceptual system can be tricked.

Illusory movement   Another example of a misperception involves a particular illusion of movement known as the **autokinetic effect.** This effect occurs when one looks at a single point of light in an otherwise dark environment. In the absence of other cues that could provide reference points, the light may seem to move. Consider the possible effect on a military pilot flying in formation near other aircraft at night, using only the light of a wingtip to judge the next plane's relative position. Even when that plane's relative position remains fixed, the autokinetic effect can lead the pilot to believe that the plane has moved away somewhat. The pilot may then try to close the apparently growing gap and instead collide with the other plane.

Research has shown that the autokinetic effect occurs mainly when there is a single, continuous light source against a dark background. Psychologists have used this research to help aircraft designers minimize the illusion, advising them to create reference markers on airplanes that are illuminated either by two adjacent lights or by flashing lights.

Divided attention   Nowhere have the limits of the ability to divide attention under stress been more clearly and tragically demonstrated than just prior to the crash of an Eastern Airlines L1011 into the Florida Everglades in 1972 (Wiener, 1977). The plane was approaching Miami's airport at night, when the crew became aware of a warning light indicating that the landing gear was malfunctioning. Concerned about the possible failure, they set the autopilot for level flight and then directed their attention to diagnosing the cause of the warning light. Somehow the autopilot setting was moved so that it produced a gradual descent. As the plane came closer to the ground, air traffic controllers, as well as auditory and visual signals in the cockpit, warned the crew of their situation. But their attention was so intently focused on the landing gear problem that they did not pay attention to these signals until it was too late to avoid disaster.

Even in less stressful circumstances, the severe restrictions on the ability to divide attention between two visual events can present a major problem to pilots. Often they must watch both their instruments and the world outside the plane, a feat requiring that they constantly shift head and eyes from the instrument panel to a window and back again. A bit of technology known as the *head-up display* is intended to make simultaneous observation possible. It projects an image of the instrument panel onto the window of the cockpit, allowing the pilot to see the outside world while continuing to watch the flight instruments.

Does it work? Research has indicated that the limits of divided attention can erase the apparent advantages of the head-up display. In a simulation experiment, pilots were actually slower and less accurate in detecting another aircraft on the runway when they were using the head-up display than when they flew without it (Fischer, Haines & Price, 1980). In short, just because two visual stimuli are in the same location in space (and thus on the retina), there is no guarantee that both will be perceived. This research has warned aircraft designers that the head-up display is not a cure-all for the problem of divided visual attention.

Reading

Few would disagree that reading is one of the most important abilities in the human repertoire. But the vital role of visual perception in making this skill possible is less often appreciated unless perceptual problems interfere with reading speed or accuracy.

From letters to text   Normally when you read, your eyes scan across the page, stopping to fixate at various points, then making short jumps from one position to the next. These jumps are called **saccadic** (pronounced "sack-attic") **movements.** Two factors place physical limits on how fast you can read coherent text: (1) how rapidly you can shift from one fixation to the next (that is, the minimum time you can spend on one fixation before moving on) and (2) how much print you can take in at a single fixation.

The minimum time you can spend on one fixation is fairly well defined at around 250 milliseconds, meaning that humans can make no more than about four fixations per second. The amount you can perceive during one fixation has also been defined with some accuracy. The maximum visual "window" perceived while reading is roughly ten characters to the left and right of the fixation point for each eye.

If we assume that people can make no more than four eye fixations per second, that they have a twenty-character window, and that twenty characters is roughly three words, the maximum possible reading speed would be somewhere around seven hundred words per minute. Actually, this estimate is probably somewhat optimistic, because fixations are usually longer than 250 milliseconds whenever words are less familiar. Also, successive fixations often overlap, so that people rarely if ever move their eyes a full twenty characters. In any event, a normal reader typically reads far less than this maximum—only about three hundred words per minute, although there is great variation among individuals and among different kinds of reading material (most of us read novels faster than technical journal articles).

Speed reading and reading problems   To read any faster than six to seven hundred words per minute, you must *skim,* skipping some letters and words altogether. Teaching people to skim is exactly how speed reading courses attempt to fulfill their promise of reading rates in excess of one thousand words per minute. The fact that these courses work to some extent is

PERCEPTION AND HUMAN DEVELOPMENT
Do infants perceive the world as adults do?

We have said that perception is knowledge based, and we have seen the important role that knowledge plays in recognition. But what evidence is there that knowledge, or experience with the world, is in fact necessary for basic aspects of perception, such as perceptual constancy? If perception is knowledge based, does that mean that heredity is not important or that infants perceive the world much differently from adults? Philosophers have long debated whether babies are born with perceptual abilities or whether they acquire them by seeing, hearing, smelling, and touching things. Develop-

mental psychologists have provided some answers, thereby also shaping understanding of the nature of perception.

Researchers have focused special attention on whether infants can perceive depth, distance, and size constancy. One of the most popular techniques for studying infants' depth perception involves the *visual cliff,* a glass-topped table shown in Figure A. A pattern is placed beneath the table in a way that makes just one side of the table seem to be a deep cliff. A ten-month-old infant placed in the middle of the apparatus will calmly crawl across the shallow side to reach the parent but will hesitate and cry rather than crawl over what appears to be a cliff (Gibson & Walk, 1960). This behavior does not tell us whether depth perception is innate, however, because infants old enough to crawl have already had considerable experience with the visual world. They may have learned to perceive depth after birth but before participating in visual-cliff research. Other researchers therefore placed even younger infants on the deep side of a visual cliff and compared their behavior and heart rates to the same measures taken while they were on the shallow side (Campos, Langer &

Figure A
The Visual Cliff
The infant readily crosses the shallow side of the test apparatus but hesitates to crawl over what appears to be a cliff.
(© Enrico Ferorelli/DOT)

attributable to the redundancy of language and the top-down processing we discussed earlier.

Still, compared to normal reading, skimming techniques must inevitably disrupt comprehension, especially if the material is difficult and its information content is high (that is, not very redundant). This is not to suggest that skimming and speed reading are bad habits. In fact, one of the most important reading skills is **adaptive reading** (Anderson, 1979), in which the reader speeds up and slows down according to the information content of the material and the level of comprehension that is required.

Just as the speed of reading with full comprehension cannot be greatly increased by skimming techniques, there is strong evidence that slow readers' speeds are not limited by inefficient scanning of the material (Carver, 1972; Wickelgren, 1979). Their limited speed often relates instead to problems in comprehending and integrating word meaning.

An extreme example of these problems is **dyslexia,** a condition in which a person with normal intelligence and full comprehension of spoken words has difficulty understanding written words. A dyslexic child could follow your spoken instruction to "Go over to the table and take the apples out of the bag" but might be mystified by the same request made in writing. This disruption in the perceptual process of translating letters on the page into meaningful interpretations can obviously create major obstacles to learning.

Figure B
*The development of linear
perspective cues.*
(a) The trapezoid window used by Kaufmann et al. (1981) looks as though it is slanted away from you even though it is a full front view—that is, both ends are the same distance away. (b) A five-month-old reaches for the side of the display that is physically closer, even though it was the side that linear cues would indicate—to older children and adults—is farther away. (From Kaufmann, R., Maland, J., and Yonas, A. "A sensitivity of 5 and 7 month old infants to pictorial depth information." *Journal of Experimental Child Psychology,* 1981, *32,* 162–168.)

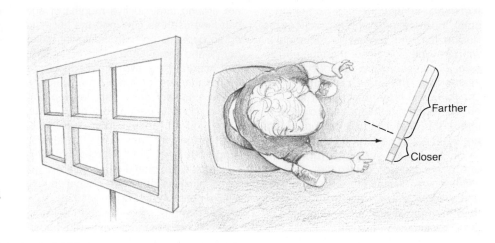

Krowitz, 1970). On the deep side, the infants' heart rates slowed significantly, they cried less, and they were more attentive to what was below them.

These results suggest that even very young babies perceived the depth beneath them, but that they were not frightened by it. Here is a fascinating interaction of nature and nurture. It appears that depth perception is present at birth, but that fear and avoidance of the danger sometimes associated with depth do not develop until an infant is old enough to crawl into trouble.

We have seen that adults use many cues to perceive depth. Which ones do infants use? The use of motion cues to discriminate depth appears to develop as early as three months, but size constancy seems to be learned (Yonas & Arterberry, in press). Unlike adults, very young infants seem not to perceive smaller objects as farther away than larger ones. Only at around six months do infants begin to use size constancy from stimulus cues for depth and distance perception.

Can infants use linear perspective and recognize that the place where two straight lines appear to converge is farther away? To find out, one study used a trapezoid window like the one shown at the top of Figure B (Kaufmann, Maland & Yonas, 1981). When adults look at such a window with one eye closed (so that binocular depth cues are not avail-
(continued)

Despite intense study, psychologists are not sure what causes dyslexia. One possible factor involves *sensory memory,* which, as discussed in Chapter 8, on memory, is the extremely brief impression that sensory information makes before it is transferred to the perceptual centers of the brain for further processing. The sensory memory for visual stimuli appears to persist *longer* for dyslexic people than for normal readers (DiLollo et al., 1983; Stanley & Hall, 1973). As a result, for dyslexic people, one eye fixation's physical images of letters or words may not disappear quickly enough to avoid interfering with the perception of images in the next fixation.

Although research in dyslexia and other reading disabilities is growing, the questions about them still far outnumber the answers. This is another area, like many others to be discussed later in this book, in which psychologists continue to be challenged to conduct research that will address and ultimately solve a significant problem.

FUTURE DIRECTIONS

You have seen how perception translates raw sensations into information that is meaningful and useful to the perceiver. The process is elaborate, involving numerous components and operations, many of which depend on both bottom-

able), the trapezoidal shape produces the illusion that the window is rectangular, with the wide side closer than the narrow side. The researchers reasoned that, if infants have the same perception, they should reveal it by reaching for the side of the window that appears closest to them—the wide side (see bottom of Figure B). A patch was placed over one eye (babies are notoriously poor at keeping one eye closed on command), and the window was displayed so that the wide end was actually farther from the baby than the narrow end. Five-month-old infants reached for the narrow (actually closer) end of the window, suggesting that linear perspective cues were not controlling their perception. But seven-month-olds consistently reached for the wider (actually more distant) end of the window. Linear perspective cues caused them, like adults, to perceive it as closer.

Other research has outlined the development of the ability to use binocular disparity—the difference between the images seen by each eye—to perceive depth and distance. Only when infants

are around three to five months of age can they use this cue, and the ability to do so depends on both biological maturation and experience. The brain cells that integrate the two images to create the experience of three-dimensionality, called *binocular cells,* can develop only during a critical period very early in life. If they do not appear then, they never will. Further, for these cells to develop (and, with them, depth perception) each eye must focus on the same object at the same time during the critical period (Blakemore & Van Slayters, 1974).

Before this critical period for binocular cell development was well understood, children born with *strabismus,* a weakness in the eye muscles that prevents coordinated focusing of both eyes on the same point, often failed to develop binocular cues for depth and distance. By the time corrective surgery was performed (usually at age eight or nine), the critical period for the development of binocular cells had passed, and these children had to depend on linear perspective and other distance and depth cues. Today, ophthalmologists realize that

the earlier they operate on children with strabismus, the greater the likelihood that these children will develop normal depth perception.

In summary, there is little doubt that some of the basic building blocks of perception are present at birth or within the first few months of life, thus making it possible for infants to perceive many aspects of their surroundings in ways that approximate adult perception. These building blocks include such organ-based depth cues as accommodation, convergence, and binocular disparity, as well as the stimulus cue of relative motion. But these cues alone are not enough to produce full perceptual capabilities. Experience with the world is necessary to acquire most stimulus cues, such as linear perspective, and to learn to *interpret* cues: to know which objects are closer and which are farther away, to know that falls of greater distance are more dangerous, and to use depth and distance cues to move effectively through the world. Like so many aspects of human psychology, perception is the result of a blending of heredity and environment.

up and top-down processing. Because perception is one of the oldest specialties in psychology, dating back over a hundred years to the psychophysical research of Weber and Fechner, knowledge about perception is extensive.

Yet questions and debates remain. One of the most important controversies, mentioned at the beginning of the chapter, involves the conflict between the constructionist view that perception involves mainly knowledge-based inferences about fragmentary sensations and the ecological view that much of perception results from processing well-developed and rich sensations offered by the natural world.

The ecological position has stimulated a growing amount of research. This work has begun to identify cues in the natural environment that are important to the perception of complex events and actions. One recent trend, for example, involves focusing on the visual cues that lead to perception of whole-body motions, such as walking and running (Johansson et al., 1980). A still photograph of twelve points of light attached to the hands, elbows, shoulders, ankles, knees, and hips of a person in a dark room cannot be recognized as a human form. However, the moment these same points of light are viewed in a movie of the person walking or jogging, they are instantly recognized as human movement; even the sex of the figure can be identified (Johansson et al., 1980). Exactly how this is done is an emerging area of research in perception. At the same time, research on the stimulus features that contribute to bottom-up processing has become closely linked to studies of sensation and neurophysiology. Such research involves trying to determine both the importance to perception of cells that are line and angle detectors and the role of spatial frequency analysis.

Still other intriguing questions remain. For example, exactly what is attention? How does it relate to the functioning of different parts of the brain? What more can evoked potentials tell researchers about attention? When and why do sensory systems cooperate and compete with one another?

Some of the most compelling demonstrations of the complexity of perception have resulted from attempts to develop computers that can hear and see. Programming a computer to imitate even the simplest perceptual processes—such as understanding words or recognizing a cup on a cluttered desk—often requires an enormous amount of computer power and results in a process that takes far more time than human perception. More complex, but still commonplace, processes—such as understanding the continuous flow of rapid speech, reading messy handwriting, or recognizing a cup being tossed in the air—are beyond the capabilities of today's computers. Perhaps this is because the computer programs are not focused on the most appropriate stimuli or do not have the appropriate knowledge for top-down processing. It may be that, until researchers more fully understand perception, the methods for teaching a computer to perceive may be too inefficient and cumbersome even for supercomputers. Better understanding of basic perceptual processes might lead to programs that will allow computers to perceive the world as easily as people do. However, it is also possible that the problem is not in the programs, but in the machines. It may turn out that no machine will ever be able to perceive as smoothly and automatically as humans do.

If you want to learn more about these and other aspects of perception, consider taking the basic course in the area, which is usually called sensation and perception. It often includes a laboratory in which you will gain first-hand experience with perceptual principles and illusions. Many departments also offer more advanced courses in perception. If the idea of programming computers to perceive intrigues you, look for courses in the area of artificial intelligence; they are commonly offered by computer science departments.

SUMMARY

1. Perception is the active process through which people use their knowledge and understanding of the world to interpret raw sensations as meaningful experiences.

2. Perception has six main characteristics. First, it is knowledge based; it develops through experience with the world. Second, it is inferential; it allows people to fill in information that may be missing from raw sensations. Third, it is categorical; it helps people decide what general type of stimulus they are encountering. Fourth, perception is relational; it compares each stimulus with those around it. Fifth, perception is adaptive, allowing people to focus on the most important aspects of a stimulus while ignoring others. Sixth, perceptual processes often operate automatically, without awareness.

3. The constructionist view of perception suggests that the perceptual system constructs the experience of reality by interpreting raw sensations on the basis of what people have learned. The ecological approach emphasizes the automatic and adaptive features of perception, suggesting that the cues people use to form perceptions lie, not in the knowledge base, but in the stimuli themselves.

4. Psychophysics is the study of the relationship between stimulus energy and the psychological experience of that energy. It has traditionally been concerned with matters such as determining absolute thresholds for the detection of stimuli. Signal detection theory has been applied to the measurement of absolute thresholds in a way that separates the effects of sensitivity from those of the response criterion.

5. Psychophysics is also concerned with the ability to detect changes in stimulus intensity and the experience of stimulus magnitude. Weber's law states that

the minimum detectable amount of change in a stimulus increases in proportion to the initial amount, or intensity, of the stimulus. The less the initial stimulation, the smaller the change needs to be. Fechner's and Stevens's laws relate the perceived magnitude of a stimulus to its physical intensity, by either a logarithmic function (Fechner's law) or a power function (Stevens's power law).

6. When people perceive objects or sounds, they automatically discriminate figure from background. In addition, the perceptual system automatically groups objects or sounds together on the basis of the Gestalt principles of proximity, similarity, continuity, closure, orientation, and simplicity.

7. The brightness, size, and shape of objects are seen as constant, even though the sensations that the eyes receive from those objects may change. Size and shape constancy depend on the relationship between the retinal image of the object and the knowledge-based perception of its distance. Brightness constancy depends on the perceived relationship between the brightness of an object and its background.

8. The perception of distance, or depth perception, depends partly on cues from the outside world and partly on the physical structure of the visual system. Some of the cues from the environment are relative size, height, interposition, linear perspective, clarity, and gradients. Cues based on the structure of the visual system include binocular disparity (the fact that the eyes are set slightly apart), convergence of the eyes (the fact that the eyes must move to focus on the same object), and accommodation (the change in the shape of the lenses as objects are brought into focus).

9. The perception of motion results, in part, from the movement of stimuli across the retina. However, this sensation is interpreted along with information about movement of the head, eyes, and other parts of the body. In this way, retinal stimulation resulting from one's own movement can be discriminated from motion resulting from the movement of external objects.

10. Perceptual illusions are distortions of reality that result when principles of perception are applied inappropriately. For example, an illusion of motion called the phi phenomenon results when stimuli appear to be at different positions at different times. Induced motion results when our perceptual system misinterprets which parts of the environment are stable and which are moving. Many illusions involve the misinterpretation of shape, size, and depth. They are caused by misreading three-dimensional distance cues and by evaluating stimuli in the context of their surroundings.

11. The ability to recognize objects in the world is based on finding a match between the pattern of sensations organized by the perceptual system and a known pattern already stored in memory.

12. The ability to recognize what an object or sound is depends in part on bottom-up processing, which is the analysis of the sensory information coming from the basic features of the stimulus. Recognition also depends on top-down processing, which is influenced by expectancy, memories, and motivation. Bottom-up and top-down processing commonly work together to create recognition of stimulus patterns. Top-down processing can fill in missing gaps in the physical stimuli, in part because verbal material is often redundant.

13. Attention is the (usually voluntary) process of focusing psychological resources to selectively enhance information processing. Stimuli that attract attention (or distract it from other stimuli) tend to be those high in intensity, novelty, and contrast. People are also more likely to attend to stimuli in which they are especially interested.

14. People can sometimes attend to two sets of stimuli at once, especially with practice or if different sensory modalities are involved. However, as with computers shared by two or more users, there are limits to how well people can perform divided attention tasks. These limits are particularly great under stressful conditions, because the focus of attention tends to narrow. The allocation of attentional resources during all sorts of divided attention tasks can be monitored in the laboratory by observing changes in subjects' pupillary dilation and brain wave patterns. These patterns may indicate the kind of task to which attention is devoted and can suggest which environmental stimuli are being attended to or ignored.

15. Research on human perception has numerous practical applications. In aviation, accurate size and distance judgments, knowledge of visual illusions, and attention are all important to safety. In reading, the length of eye fixations and the number of letters or words perceived during a fixation put physical limitations on reading speed. So do other factors such as practice and the complexity of the text. Together, these limits suggest that speed reading usually results in some loss of comprehension. Reading problems such as dyslexia can result from failure to perceive letters accurately.

KEY TERMS

Definitions of terms appear on the pages shown in parentheses.

absolute threshold (169)
adaptive reading (198)
attention (191)
autokinetic effect (196)
binocular disparity (180)
bottom-up processing (186)
closure (176)
constructionist (166)
continuity (176)
convergence (181)
depth perception (178)
dichotic listening (192)
dyslexia (198)
ecological view (167)
evoked potential (EP) (194)
feature analysis (187)
Fechner's law (174)
figure (175)
Gestalt psychologist (175)
gradient (180)
internal noise (169)
interposition (180)
just-noticeable difference (JND) (173)
linear perspective (180)
looming (182)
movement gradient (180)
orientation (176)
perception (162)
perceptual constancy (177)
perceptual set (189)
proximity (176)
psychophysics (168)
receiver operating characteristic (ROC) curve (171)
reduced clarity (180)
relative size (179)
response bias (170)
response criterion (170)
saccadic movement (197)
sensitivity (170)
signal detection theory (170)
similarity (176)
simplicity (176)
Stevens's power law (174)
textural gradient (180)
top-down processing (186)
visual dominance (183)
Weber's law (173)

RECOMMENDED READINGS

Dember, W. N., & Warm, J. S. (1979). *Psychology of perception* (2nd ed.). New York: Holt, Rinehart & Winston. Contains a more in-depth treatment of many of the topics covered in this chapter.

Gregory, R. *Eye and brain.* (1977). New York: McGraw-Hill. A classic treatment of visual perception.

Kahneman, D. *Attention.* (1973). New York: Prentice-Hall. An excellent source of information on attention.

Lindsay, P., & Norman, D. (1977). *Human information processing: An introduction to psychology.* New York: Academic Press. A very readable discussion of the recognition of objects and words.

Rock, I. (1975). *An introduction to perception.* New York: Macmillan. Contains excellent discussion of theories of optical illusions.

Rock, I. (1986). The description and analysis of object and event perception. In K. Boff, K. Kaufman & J. Thomas (Eds.), *Handbook of perception and performance.* New York: Wiley. Another fine discussion of theories of visual illusion.

P eople with a rare brain disorder known as *prosopagnosia* are perfectly normal in every way except one: they cannot recognize familiar faces, including those of their family and closest friends. They do not even recognize themselves in a mirror. The disorder appears to be related to a specific and unusual pattern of brain damage, which may be brought on by a stroke or by herpes-related encephalitis. In spite of their disability, prosopagnosics show a much stronger emotional response (in the form of increased sweating, or skin conductance) when they see familiar rather than unfamiliar faces (Tranel & Damasio, 1985). It is as if these people's autonomic nervous systems recognize familiar faces, but that this is not paralleled by a reportable experience. The puzzle of how part of these people's perceptual apparatus can recognize stimuli that another part knows nothing about illustrates the complexity of human mental processes—especially the complexity of human consciousness.

Exactly what is *consciousness?* The concept is familiar, but elusive. William James, one of psychology's founders, once wrote of consciousness: "Its meaning we know as long as no one asks us to define it." Definition is indeed difficult, but the term **consciousness** is usually used in two ways. First, consciousness is awareness of external stimuli and of internal mental activity (Natsoulas, 1978, 1983). As an illustration of this definition, consider that you are now conscious of reading this book. You may also be conscious of a noise outside, of feeling sleepy or hungry, or of thinking about what you will be doing later. If consciousness involved nothing other than that of which people are aware, however, the phenomenon, though certainly remarkable, might not be so puzzling. Most psychologists think of consciousness more broadly, defining it as also including mental processes of which people are unaware—such as prosopagnosics' partial and nonverbally expressed recognition of familiar faces. The complexity of consciousness is fundamental to humans' psychological makeup and is manifested not only in aberrations such as prosopagnosia, but in many everyday mental phenomena as well.

Ironically, the study of consciousness sometimes gets lost in the shuffle, as psychologists focus their attention on perception, memory, thinking, and other more specific aspects of mental life. But, like a melody playing softly in the background, consciousness remains at the heart of psychology (see Linkages diagram). In this chapter, we review its role in the history of psychology, consider several varieties of consciousness, and discuss what happens when consciousness is altered by sleep, hypnosis, meditation, and drugs.

The early history of psychology is actually the history of the study of consciousness. Wilhelm Wundt, the man whose research at the University of Leipzig founded European psychology in the 1870s, sought to understand the *structure* of consciousness. To do so, he carefully observed conscious experience to find its basic sensations and other mental building blocks. Since no one can directly observe anyone else's conscious experiences, Wundt, E. B. Titchener, and other early **structuralist** psychologists examined their own mental activity through a method called *introspection*. They presented a

204

6

Consciousness

LINKAGES
an overview

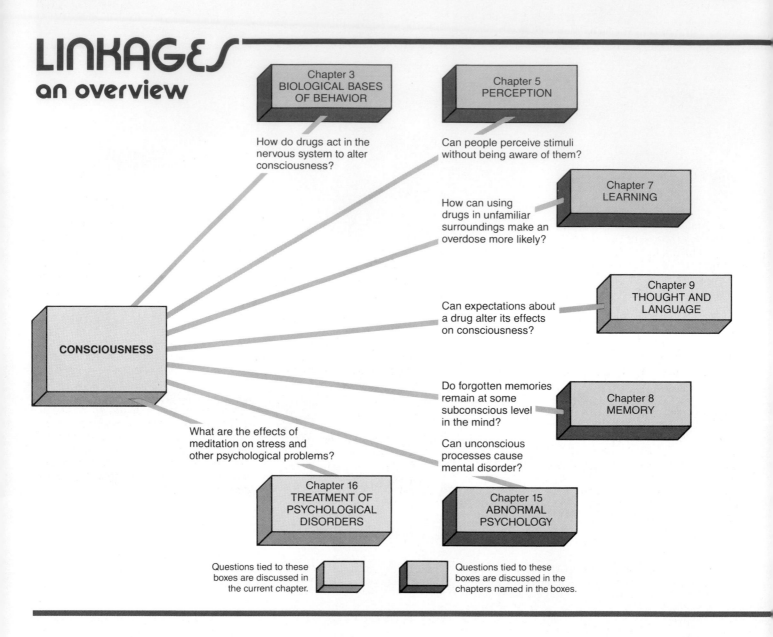

Chapter 3
BIOLOGICAL BASES OF BEHAVIOR

How do drugs act in the nervous system to alter consciousness?

Chapter 5
PERCEPTION

Can people perceive stimuli without being aware of them?

Chapter 7
LEARNING

How can using drugs in unfamiliar surroundings make an overdose more likely?

CONSCIOUSNESS

Chapter 9
THOUGHT AND LANGUAGE

Can expectations about a drug alter its effects on consciousness?

Do forgotten memories remain at some subconscious level in the mind?

Chapter 8
MEMORY

What are the effects of meditation on stress and other psychological problems?

Can unconscious processes cause mental disorder?

Chapter 16
TREATMENT OF PSYCHOLOGICAL DISORDERS

Chapter 15
ABNORMAL PSYCHOLOGY

Questions tied to these boxes are discussed in the current chapter.

Questions tied to these boxes are discussed in the chapters named in the boxes.

stimulus—say, a bright red object—to themselves and then attempted to identify the individual sensations, such as redness or brightness, that combined to create the total conscious experience of the stimulus.

Also during the 1870s, William James, an American, began research that ultimately went beyond structuralism. James was interested not only in the building blocks of consciousness, but also in how consciousness *functions* to help people adapt to their environments (James, 1890, 1892). James's approach, which became known as **functionalism,** focused on the ongoing "stream" of consciousness—the ever-changing pattern of images, sensations, memories, and other mental events. He wanted to know how the whole process works. Why, for example, do people remember recent events better than things that happened in the distant past? To answer his questions, James and his followers (Angell, 1907) supplemented introspection with observation of other people during experiments on such functions as learning and memory.

Functionalism was soon displaced in America by **behaviorism,** an approach that focused on studying behavior itself. Led by John B. Watson early in this century, behaviorists argued that consciousness is an inherently private concept

CONSCIOUSNESS AND PSYCHOLOGY

The links between the concept of consciousness and various subspecialties in psychology are particularly numerous because of the history of psychology. Interest in consciousness was primarily responsible for the emergence of psychology as a field. Early psychologists, such as Wilhelm Wundt and E. B. Titchener, were interested in analyzing the basic elements of conscious awareness of the world, much as chemists do with physical materials. Others, such as William James, focused their research on how consciousness functions to help people adapt to and get along in the world. These initial efforts to understand the structure or function of consciousness were overshadowed for several decades by American behaviorism, which emphasized the study of overt, directly observable behaviors, not covert mental processes. However, the last twenty years or so have witnessed the reemergence of consciousness as a central target of study in psychology.

This focus on consciousness is evident primarily in psychologists' preference for the cognitive approach to research on many aspects of human behavior. This approach studies not just stimulus-response relationships but also the mental events that link them. For example, many psychologists interested in hypnosis are attempting to go beyond describing how hypnotized subjects behave, instead focusing on the changes that take place in the subjects' conscious experience, in their information-processing capacities, and even in their brain activity. In one study, hypnotized subjects were given suggestions that colored grids presented on a television screen would be especially bright and interesting, especially drab and boring, or hidden from view behind a cardboard box (Spiegel et al., 1985). The results included not only overt behavioral responses to these hypnotic suggestions but also the brain activity that would be expected if the stimuli actually had the suggested characteristics. In the perception chapter, we gave another example of the focus on consciousness in modern psychology, when we discussed humans' ability to process perceptual information even though they are not always aware of doing so. Indeed, the modern study of consciousness leads into virtually every psychological subspecialty. As you read in later chapters about psychologists' research on learning, memory, information processing, mental abilities, and other mental processes and problems, keep in mind that they are pursuing in updated form the venerable tradition of exploring consciousness.

that neither introspection nor any other method can penetrate scientifically. Therefore, they urged psychologists to turn away from the study of conscious experience, away from examining what people think or feel. Instead, said the behaviorists, analyze how behavior is related to its environment, how stimuli bring about responses.

From the 1920s through the 1960s, American psychology became the science of behavior, and psychologists became less inclined to ask people what they thought or felt. Nevertheless, many psychologists continued to do research on the then-taboo topics of consciousness and mental activity. For example, Gestalt psychologists showed that people do not just passively detect and automatically react to stimuli. They emphasized instead how, as we discussed in the chapter on perception, people's ability to organize and think about stimuli determines, in large measure, the way they will react to those stimuli.

By the 1960s, some researchers in virtually every area of psychology considered strict behaviorism to be incomplete. Research evidence and their own experience told them that such mental activities as imagining, attending, thinking, and anticipating are intimately involved in the development and

Wilhelm Wundt founded the first European psychology laboratory at the University of Leipzig in 1879. His structuralist approach used introspection to identify the basic sensations that underlie conscious experiences.

John B. Watson founded behaviorism, an approach to psychology that abandoned the study of conscious experience and focused instead on analyzing observable behavior and its relationship to the environment.

regulation of behavior. The resurgence of interest in these *cognitive* variables continued during the 1970s, and now research on cognition and other aspects of consciousness has become the mainstream in most areas of psychology. As a result, psychology today is not just the science of behavior, but the science of behavior *and mental processes.*

Psychologists who study consciousness approach their task from varying perspectives. For example, some focus directly on the mental processes that underlie and affect consciousness. Others investigate how consciousness functions as a "central executive," the coordinated set of mental processes that, for example, decides what is perceived, directs moment-to-moment behavior, and plans future behavior.

VARIETIES OF CONSCIOUSNESS

Earlier we noted that consciousness includes not only awareness but also mental processes that are outside of awareness. This two-part definition suggests that mental activities take place simultaneously at several *levels* of consciousness. As an illustration, focus for a moment on the way your tongue feels as it rests or moves around inside your mouth. You are now probably much more aware of the sensations in your tongue than you were a few minutes ago. But where were those sensations before you focused on them? They were there all the time, but they were outside your awareness, presumably at a **level of consciousness,** or segment of mental activity, to which you were directing little or no attention.

Levels of Consciousness

The mental activities of which people are aware from moment to moment are said to be at the **conscious level.** Tongue sensations and everything else of which people are not currently conscious, but of which people can easily *become* conscious, are at the **preconscious level.** The amount of material at this level far surpasses what is present at the conscious level at any given moment. For example, in a trivia game, your ability to come up with obscure information (which, perhaps, you did not even know you knew) stems from the fact that a large part of your storehouse of memories is at the preconscious level.

In addition to memories, many of the basic assumptions and inferences people make about the world appear to operate at the preconscious level. For example, consider the following sentence: "When the bell rang, Jim waited until the others had left before he approached the professor." You can easily understand the sentence and picture the situation, because you presume or infer the following: "Professors teach classes," "Jim is a male's name," "Students leave the room at the end of classes," and "Students may talk to professors after class."

With a little effort, most people can bring preconscious perceptions and inferences into awareness, but there are some processes that cannot normally be experienced consciously. Trying to focus your attention on physiological processes such as blood pressure or liver functioning still leaves you unable to feel them. They occur at the **nonconscious level,** meaning that they are totally inaccessible to conscious experience.

Learning about nonconscious events usually requires special methods. In **biofeedback,** for example, a person connected to a special measuring device can watch a meter that keeps track of such nonconscious events as blood pressure or muscle tension in the forehead. Having this information allows

The correct answers to trivia questions, along with a vast amount of other more important information, reside at a preconscious level of consciousness where it can be retrieved when needed.

some individuals to control the nonconscious process enough to relieve such problems as high blood pressure and tension headaches.

Can perceptions, memories, ideas, impulses, wishes, feelings, and other important mental processes exist where we cannot easily get at them? Sigmund Freud, the famous Viennese physician who founded psychoanalysis, said yes. He suggested that there is an **unconscious level** of consciousness, which contains sexual, aggressive, and other impulses, as well as once-conscious but unacceptable thoughts and feelings. (We will examine these ideas in Chapter 14, on personality.) Those who do not accept Freud's theory use the term **subconscious level** to describe the mental level at which important, but normally inaccessible, mental processes take place.

HIGHLIGHT

Are People of Two Minds?

At one time or another, you have probably tried to recall a name that you could not quite remember, even though it was on the tip of your tongue. After giving up and going on to think of other things, the name may suddenly have occurred to you "out of the blue," as though your brain had continued to search for it while your conscious attention was directed elsewhere.

Another familiar illustration of people's apparent ability to process information at a subconscious level is the *cocktail party phenomenon*. While paying close attention to a conversation with someone in a noisy, crowded room, you might suddenly be distracted by something—perhaps your name or an obscene word—in another conversation. Though you are not consciously focused on that other discussion, your brain perceives something significant and redirects your attention to it (Moray, 1960).

Other examples of the ability to process information at a subconscious level, without conscious attention, come from the laboratory. One experiment (Von Wright, Anderson & Stenman, 1975) taught people to fear certain words by repeatedly pairing those words with a mild electric shock. Fear was detected through the galvanic skin response (GSR), which provides an indication of

Research evidence suggests that surgery patients may be able to hear and later comply with instructions or suggestions given while they are under anesthesia and of which they have no memory.

increased sweat gland activity in the skin. After this fear response was well established, the subjects were asked to listen to and immediately repeat each word of a message that came into only one side of a pair of headphones. While this task was taking up all the subjects' conscious attention, a series of words was presented to the other, nonattending ear. Some of these words had no emotional significance; others were the words that the subjects had learned to fear or synonyms for them (for example, *chilly* instead of *cold*). As shown in Figure 6.1, these fear-related words prompted a GSR, indicating that the subjects must have perceived and recognized the words' meanings even though they did not consciously pay attention to them.

The advertising industry is anxious to quell rumors that it uses subliminal stimuli to try altering consumers' buying behavior. Consumers need not worry about it, because research has shown the effects of such stimuli to range from trivial and short-lived to nonexistent.

PEOPLE HAVE BEEN TRYING TO FIND THE BREASTS IN THESE ICE CUBES SINCE 1957.

The advertising industry is sometimes charged with sneaking seductive little pictures into ads.

Supposedly, these pictures can get you to buy a product without your even seeing them.

Consider the photograph above. According to some people, there's a pair of female breasts hidden in the patterns of light refracted by the ice cubes.

Well, if you really searched you probably *could* see the breasts. For that matter, you could also see Millard Fillmore, a stuffed pork chop and a 1946 Dodge.

The point is that so-called "subliminal advertising" simply doesn't exist. Overactive imaginations, however, most certainly do.

So if anyone claims to see breasts in that drink up there, they aren't in the ice cubes.

They're in the eye of the beholder.

ADVERTISING
ANOTHER WORD FOR FREEDOM OF CHOICE.
American Association of Advertising Agencies

There is also evidence that subconscious perception and information processing can affect conscious judgments and reactions. For example, Sheldon Bach and George Klein (1957) showed slides of people's faces, along with slides of the word *happy* or *sad*. The words were presented *subliminally*, that is, in flashes so brief that those watching are not aware of having seen them. Yet when these people were asked to describe the faces, they described those that had been associated with the word *sad* as sadder than those that had been paired with *happy*.

In the 1950s, some advertisers tried using subliminal messages to influence consumers to buy certain products. Moviegoers were exposed to the subliminal message "buy popcorn" and supermarket owners blended imperceptible commercials for certain items into their stores' usual background music. The effects of subconscious perceptions have been found to be relatively short-lived and probably incapable of controlling very much behavior for very long (Cherry, 1953; Vokey & Read, 1985). Yet the fact that information processing can go on at a subconscious level provides important clues to understanding many aspects of human behavior.

A different notion of "two minds" arises from the division of the brain's cerebral cortex into two sides, or hemispheres. As we discussed in the chapter on biological psychology, each hemisphere of the brain tends to perform certain tasks more quickly and easily than the other. Furthermore, each hemisphere receives information coming mainly from the opposite side of the body. When something goes wrong with the relationship between the two hemispheres, the consequences for consciousness can be dramatic. For example, people suffering damage to certain parts of the right parietal lobe may become unaware of everything in the left half of the world, as Figure 6.2 illustrates. But normally the two hemispheres work so closely together, integrating their functions, that the "two minds" become one (Levy, 1985). ■

States of Consciousness

Mental activity is constantly changing. The characteristics of consciousness at any particular moment—for example, what reaches awareness, what levels of mental activity are most prominent, and how efficiently a person is functioning—are usually referred to as the **state of consciousness.**

Imagine for a moment that you know everything that is going on in an airplane en route from New York to Los Angeles. In the cockpit, the pilot calmly scans the instruments while talking to an air traffic center on the ground. In seat 37B, a sales representative has just polished off her second scotch as she works on plans for the next day's sales meeting. Nearby, a young mother gazes out the window, daydreaming, while her small son sleeps in her lap, dreaming dreams of his own.

Each of these people is experiencing a different state of consciousness. Notice first that possible states of consciousness range from deep sleep to alert wakefulness, with many gradations in between. Second, there are both *passive* and *active* states of consciousness (Hilgard, 1980). The daydreaming mother is simply letting her mind wander, *passively* observing the images, memories, and other mental events that come unbidden to mind. In contrast, the sales representative is *actively* manipulating her mental activity, considering various courses of action and speculating about their likely outcomes. Third, some states of consciousness (such as sleep) are brought on by natural processes such as fatigue or relaxation, whereas others (such as concentration or being "high") come about by choice; that is, through practiced mental efforts or the chemical action of drugs.

Though most people spend most of their time in what is called the normal waking state, the mental processes in that familiar condition can be quite

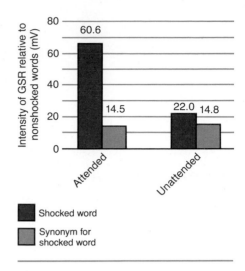

Figure 6.1
Conditioning Without Awareness
In an experiment by Von Wright, Anderson, and Stenman (1975), the largest physical reaction to words previously associated with shock occurred when the subject was paying attention to them. However, a substantial response also occurred when these words or their synonyms were presented while the subject was not attending to them. This provides just one illustration that mental processing can occur outside of immediate awareness.

Figure 6.2
Brain Hemispheres and Consciousness
A person with damage to the right parietal lobe was asked to look at a clock and draw it. The drawing shows his lack of awareness of the left side of the world; all the clock's numerals are on the right side. People with this type of brain damage may wash or dress only the right side of their bodies.
(From Mountcastle, V. B., "The world around us: Neutral command functions for selective attention." *Neurosciences Research Program Bulletin*, 1976, 14, Suppl., 1–47. Copyright © 1976 MIT Press.)

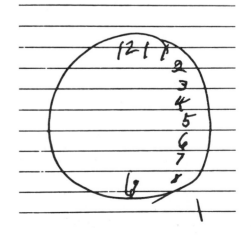

variable. Some of the variations are quantitative, a matter of degree. For example, you may notice yourself becoming more alert when danger threatens or more mentally relaxed after completing a tough assignment. Other variations alter the kind or quality of mental processes. A drunk's mistaken judgment that it is safe to drive home is a good example.

When quantitative and qualitative changes in mental processes are extensive enough that the person or objective observers notice significant differences in psychological and behavioral functioning, that person is said to have entered an **altered,** or **alternate, state of consciousness** (Ludwig, 1969; Zinberg, 1974). Though the borderline between normal and altered states of consciousness is not always clear, altered states tend to have a few general characteristics (Martindale, 1981).

1. Cognitive processes may become shallow, careless, or uncritical. Many hypnotized subjects, for example, readily accept the truth of a statement like "You are an English sheepdog." Drugs or alcohol can lead to states in which wandering attention and impaired judgment can result in anything from a fatal automobile accident to poor business decisions.

2. There may be changes in self-perceptions and perceptions of the world. Dreams, drugs, hypnosis, and meditation, for example, may make people see, hear, smell, taste, or feel things that are not really there; become more intensely aware of what *is* there; or misperceive reality in strange or frightening ways.

3. Normal inhibitions or self-control may weaken or disappear. A hypnotized person may not only believe that he or she is a sheepdog, but also begin acting like one.

In the sections that follow, we take a look at some of the most interesting and important altered states of consciousness. Our coverage begins with the most common and natural states and progresses to others that are perhaps less familiar and certainly more artificially induced.

DAYDREAMING

Daydreaming is the altered state of consciousness closest to the normal waking state. In normal waking consciousness, attention shifts constantly back and forth between the external world and thoughts, memories, and other events of the internal world. Usually these shifts are biased toward the external world and toward experiencing it in a clear, organized, and realistic way. But, in **daydreams,** this balance of attention is reversed, shifting away from external stimuli to dwell on internal events, sometimes in a fantasy-oriented, unrealistic way (Marsh, 1977; Singer, 1976).

Most people slip in and out of daydreams with great ease, often imagining past or future events. For example, faced with the choice of a college major, a student might begin imagining all the problems that could result from choosing the "wrong" one or all the benefits of finding success. Daydreaming can interfere with daily living, but usually it is harmless and may even be helpful. Daydreams can offer relief from mental work or from unpleasant or boring situations. Because the mind may wander freely during daydreams, they sometimes stimulate creative ideas.

Why do people daydream? No one knows for sure. Freud suggested that daydreams, like night dreams, provide a way of expressing unconscious feelings, wishes, and impulses. Or perhaps daydreaming is a constant part of mental life, a part that is usually obscured by more dominant processes but that appears when pressing demands for mental activity subside. Daydreaming may even maintain mental activity at some desirable level when the outside world offers too little stimulation.

Evidence for these last two notions comes from an experiment in which the mental demands on subjects were reduced. They spent forty-five to sixty minutes of their day lying on a bed in a dimly lit room, relaxed but fully awake (Foulkes & Fleisher, 1975). At six randomly selected times, an experimenter asked them to describe their current mental experience. Only 38 percent of the responses suggested that the subjects were in full waking consciousness. The rest indicated some degree of daydreaming, from "mind wandering" and lack of awareness of the laboratory to uncontrolled thoughts and the perception of imaginary sights and sounds. Just over half of the subjects reported at least one visual or auditory hallucination, an experience not unlike those of subjects, mentioned in the chapter on sensation, who were placed in sensory deprivation chambers.

Research of this type demonstrates that the boundaries between states of consciousness are not sharply defined. In daydreams, mental activities associated with the waking state and with sleep sometimes appear together. Even when people are not daydreaming, fragments from one state may appear when they are least expected. In the middle of a busy day, perfectly normal people might think that they see or hear something that is not really there or, during a nightmare, have a thought like "I'm sure glad this is only a dream."

SLEEP AND DREAMING

According to ancient myths, to sleep is to take leave of your senses, to lose control, and to flirt with death by letting the soul wander freely. Early psychologists thought of sleep as a time during which most mental activity appeared to stop (Cartwright, 1978). During the last sixty years, however, research has revealed that sleep is actually a very active, complex state.

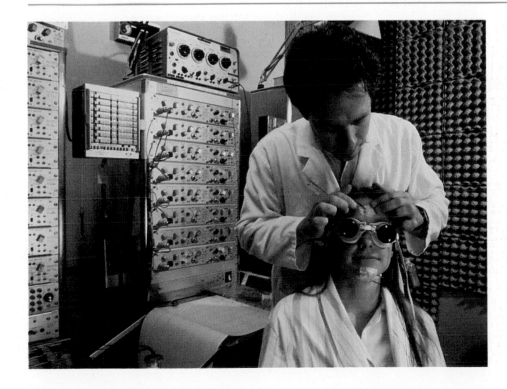

The electroencephalogram (EEG) allows scientists to record brain activity through electrodes attached to the skull. The advent of this technology opened the door to the scientific study of sleep. This subject's brain waves will be monitored throughout the night in a sleep laboratory.

Stages of Sleep

Probably the most important technological step toward expanding scientific research on sleep came in 1919 when Hans Berger, a German psychiatrist, developed the *electroencephalogram,* or *EEG,* mentioned in previous chapters. When researchers used EEGs to measure human brain activity during sleep, they found, not a wasteland of inactivity, but several distinctive patterns of "brain waves" (Loomis, Harvey & Hobart, 1937). The height (or amplitude) and speed (or frequency) of these waves changed systematically throughout the night.

William Dement and Nathaniel Kleitman (1957) used these systematic changes to identify four stages of sleep, plus stage 0, which precedes sleep. During stage 0, a person is relaxed, with eyes closed, but awake. As you can see in Figure 6.3, the EEG at this stage shows a mixture of brain waves, including some alpha waves. **Alpha waves** are very rhythmic waves that occur at a speed of about 8 to 12 cycles per second. During stage 0, there may be considerable tension in the body, and the eyes move normally. The next stages, stages 1 through 4, have been called **quiet sleep,** because all of them are accompanied by slow, deep breathing; a calm, regular heartbeat; and reduced blood pressure.

Quiet sleep   As people drift from stage 0 into stage 1 sleep, their eyes move more slowly and begin to roll. The EEG frequency becomes irregular, and the alpha waves begin to disappear (see Figure 6.3). This pattern is actually very similar to that shown by a person who is fully awake and mentally active. After a few minutes in stage 1, a person enters stage 2 sleep. In this stage, the EEG has sharply pointed waves called *sleep spindles.* There are also occasional *K complexes,* which are special waves with high peaks and deep valleys. As the person gradually enters stage 3 sleep, spindles and K complexes continue to appear, but they are now mixed with much slower (0.5 to 0.3 cycles per second), much higher amplitude patterns known as **delta waves.** When delta waves occur more than 50 percent of the time, the person has entered stage 4, the deepest level of sleep, from which it is most difficult to be roused. It takes about half an hour to reach stage 4 from stage 1 sleep.

Figure 6.3
Sleep EEGs
Electroencephalograms recorded during relaxed wakefulness (stage 0) and the four main stages of sleep. Notice the regular patterns of alpha waves in stage 0, the sleep spindles and K complexes in stage 2, and the slower delta waves in stages 3 and 4.
(Reprinted with permission of Macmillan Publishing Company from *Sleep: An Experimental Approach* by W. B. Webb. Copyright © 1968 by Wilse B. Webb.)

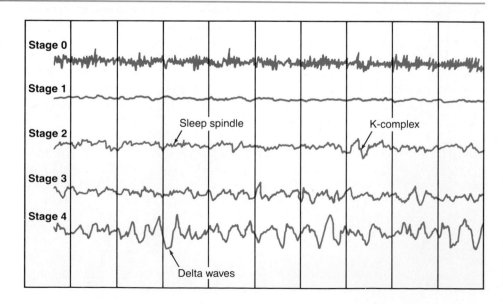

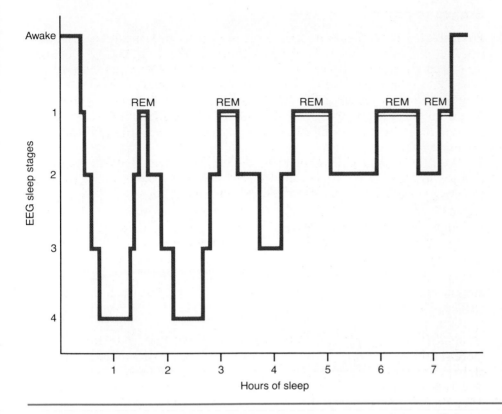

Figure 6.4
A Night's Sleep
The sequence of EEG stages during a typical night. Notice that sleep is deepest during the first part of the night and more shallow later on, when REM sleep becomes more prominent.
(Adapted from Cartwright, *A Primer of Sleep and Dreaming*. Reading, Mass.: Addison-Wesley, 1978.)

REM sleep   After thirty to forty minutes in stage 4, the sleeper begins to retrace the journey, returning through stages 3 and 2 to stage 1. Then the person enters an extraordinary stage known as **active sleep** or **REM** (for rapid-eye-movement) **sleep.** As in stage 1, the EEG during REM resembles that of someone who is active and awake; but now the heart rate, respiration, blood pressure, and other physiological patterns are also very much like those occurring during the day. At the same time, the sleeper begins rapid eye movements beneath closed lids (Aserinsky & Kleitman, 1953). Paradoxically, while the brain waves and other measures resemble those of a person awake, muscle tone decreases to the point of virtual paralysis. Sudden, twitchy spasms appear, especially in the face and hands.

What is going on during this *paradoxical sleep?* Because rapid eye movements make a person appear to be scanning some private, internal world, researchers began waking people up during REM. In about 80 percent of these awakenings, the people said they had been dreaming.[1] In contrast, reports of dreams occurred only 7 percent of the time when non-REM sleep was interrupted (Dement & Kleitman, 1957).

A night's sleep   During the night, people travel up and down through these stages of sleep four to six times. Each complete circuit takes about ninety minutes and has a somewhat different itinerary, as Figure 6.4 shows. During the first half of the night most of the time is spent in deeper sleep (stages 3 and 4) and only a few minutes in REM. The last half of the night is dominated by stage 2 and REM sleep, from which people finally wake up.

---

[1]The fact that people often dream while in a partially paralyzed state may help explain why dreams sometimes contain the unpleasant feeling of being unable to move. On the other hand, immobility while dreaming may protect people from acting out their dreams or falling out of bed.

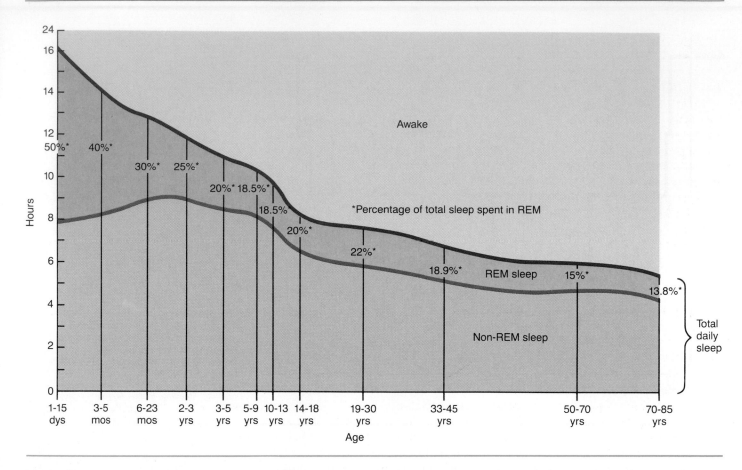

Figure 6.5
Sleep and Dreaming over the Lifespan
The typical changes that occur in total daily sleep, non-REM sleep, REM sleep, and percentage of REM sleep from infancy to old age. Notice first that people tend to sleep less as they get older. Note also the sharp reduction in the percentage of REM sleep, from about eight hours per day in infancy to less than an hour per day by age seventy. Non-REM sleep time also decreases somewhat but, compared to the drop in REM, remains relatively stable. After age twenty, however, non-REM sleep contains less and less of the deepest, or stage 4, sleep.
("Ontogenetic Development of the Human Sleep Dream Cycle," H. P. Roffwarg et al., *Science*, Vol. 152, #3722, p. 608, April 29, 1966. Reprinted with permission of The American Association for the Advancement of Science.)

Over the years, the pattern of sleep undergoes some predictable changes. An average infant spends about sixteen hours a day asleep; after age seventy, the average person sleeps only about six hours a day (Roffwarg, Muzio & Dement, 1966). Most of the decrease in total sleeping time comes out of REM sleep. As Figure 6.5 illustrates, REM accounts for half of total sleep at birth, but less than 15 percent in later life. Non-REM sleep also decreases, but much more slowly. On the average, young adults spend about 25 percent of the night in REM, about 50 percent in stage 2, about 20 percent in stages 3 and 4, and the rest in non-REM stage 1.

Of course, each sleeper may deviate from this pattern in many ways. There are light sleepers and deep sleepers, as well as long sleepers (who sleep for nine or ten hours a night, even more on weekends) and short sleepers (who average only five or six hours). Good sleepers fall asleep within ten minutes of getting into bed and remain asleep until morning; poor sleepers may take an hour or more to get to sleep and usually wake up at least once during the night. In other words, most people develop their own style of sleep which, barring such conditions as stress, does not vary much from one night to the next (Clausen, Sersen & Lidsky, 1974).

The Rhythm of Sleep

The cycle of waking and sleeping is known as a **circadian rhythm** because it repeats about once every twenty-four hours (*circadian* means "about a day"). Usually the environment provides many external signals about when to sleep and when to wake up. But even when volunteers live for weeks or months without these external cues, a daily rhythm of sleep and wakefulness continues. The rhythm does not coincide with the twenty-four-hour cycle of the sun; instead, most people settle down to something approximating a twenty-five-hour *lunar day* (the time it takes the moon to go around the earth). Still, the continued existence of the circadian rhythm in the absence of external signals suggests that there must be internal signals from a built-in biological clock.

These signals appear to come from the more primitive parts of the brain, especially the hindbrain (see Figure 3.13). If surgery or drugs disrupt the normal activity of this part of the brain, an animal either almost never sleeps or sleeps almost all the time (Bloom, Lazerson & Hofstadter, 1985). Further, a specific area in the hypothalamus (called the *suprachiasmatic nuclei*) seems to regulate the timing of sleep (Ibuka, Inouye & Kawamura, 1977).

Disruption of the circadian rhythm can create significant problems. One is *jet lag*—the fatigue, irritability, and sleeping problems that often follow a long airplane trip. While travelers' bodies are preparing for the night's sleep they would be getting if they were home, the clock at their new location says it is time for lunch. Related problems plague nurses, air traffic controllers, police officers, and others who must frequently change their work shifts, and thus their sleeping hours, from daytime to all night to evening. For several days after moving to a new shift, many have a hard time getting to sleep and feel tired and grouchy. They do not work at top efficiency. This condition can become constant if shift changes occur frequently and randomly. The effects may not only hurt a company's profits but also endanger the worker and others. The accident at the Three Mile Island nuclear power plant (described on page 193) appears to have been caused in part by inattention and confusion among employees, all of whom had just been put on the night shift (Moore-Ede, Sulzman & Fuller, 1982).

In an experiment designed to minimize disruptions of the sleep cycle, workers at a chemical plant in Utah remained on the same shift for three weeks, after which they moved to the next shift; that is, from day to evening, then from evening to night. This systematic pattern of change made it easier for them to adjust, and they had to adjust less often. Workers reported fewer problems, absenteeism and turnover were reduced; and productivity increased (Czeisler, Moore-Ede & Coleman, 1982). More recently, researchers have also tried to reset people's biological clocks by exposing them to intense light or giving them carefully timed doses of sleep medication (Czeisler et al., 1986; Turek & Losee-Olson, 1986). ◼

Sleep Disorders

Almost everyone sometimes has trouble sleeping, especially during times of stress. Sleep disorders can be a temporary annoyance or a long-term, even life-threatening, problem. The most common sleeping problem is **insomnia,** a general term for conditions in which a person feels tired during the day because of trouble falling or staying asleep (see Figure 6.6, p. 218). About 25 to 30 million Americans are chronic insomniacs (Coates & Thoreson, 1977).

Sleeping pills or alcohol may relieve insomnia temporarily, but they can also be dangerous, especially if taken together. Several psychological approaches—including biofeedback, relaxation training, stress management, and psychotherapy, which we will describe in later chapters—can help (Bootzin & Nicassio, 1978; Woolfolk & McNulty, 1983). Insomniacs may also find that they can alleviate their problem by going to bed only when they are sleepy and getting out of bed whenever they cannot sleep (Lacks et al., 1983). This helps them associate being in bed with sleeping rather than with wakefulness. Such associations are described in more detail in Chapter 7, on learning.

Sleeping too much can be a problem, too. People suffering from **hyper-somnia** not only sleep longer than most people at night, but also feel tired

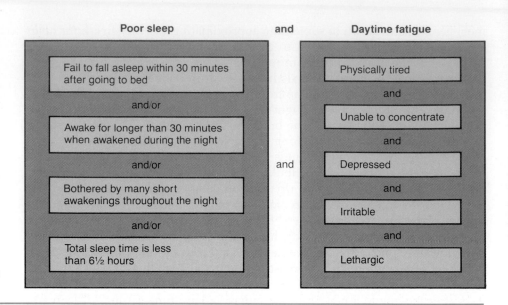

Figure 6.6
Criteria for Insomnia
One authoritative book (Coates & Thoreson, 1977) offers the following advice. Do not consider yourself an insomniac unless you experience poor sleep and daytime fatigue. Be sure your daytime fatigue is caused by poor sleep and not by something else, such as boredom or personal problems. Even if your sleep is poor (in other words, short or disturbed), you do not have a sleep problem if it does not bother you during the day. (Adapted from Coates and Thoresen, 1977. *How to Sleep Better*.)

and take one or more naps during the daytime. More disturbing, however, is a daytime disorder called **narcolepsy.** Its victims switch abruptly and without warning from an active, often emotional waking state into several minutes of REM sleep. In most cases, the muscle paralysis associated with REM causes the narcoleptic to collapse on the spot and remain briefly immobilized even after awakening. These attacks are usually more embarrassing and frightening than harmful, unless the person is doing something dangerous. The causes of hypersomnia and narcolepsy are unknown. Stimulants can be used to treat these problems, but the drugs can be dangerous. Scheduling one or two naps a day may help minimize the problem.

Other less dangerous, though very upsetting, sleep disorders include nightmares and night terrors. **Nightmares** are frightening, sometimes recurring dreams that take place during REM sleep. **Night terrors** involve a rapid shift from stage 4 to REM sleep, often accompanied by a horrific dream that makes the dreamer sit up staring, let out a bloodcurdling scream, and abruptly awaken into a state of intense fear that may last up to half an hour. This phenomenon is especially common in children, but milder versions occur among adults as well.

Like night terrors, **sleepwalking** starts primarily in non-REM sleep, especially in stage 4, and is most common during childhood (Jacobson, Kales & Kales, 1969). In the morning, sleepwalkers usually have no memory of their travels. Sleepwalking itself is not dangerous, but accidents can happen. And, contrary to popular belief, awakening a sleepwalker is not harmful. Drugs are sometimes used to treat sleepwalking, but parents can simply protect most children from the dangers of sleepwalking until they outgrow the problem. One adult sleepwalker (whose activities included handling loaded guns) was cured by his wife, who blew a whistle whenever her husband began one of his nocturnal strolls (Meyer, 1975).

Why Do People Sleep?

No one knows exactly why people sleep, but there are a number of tantalizing clues. One possibility is that sleep, especially non-REM sleep, may provide a period during which the body can rest and restore itself for future activity (Adam & Oswald, 1977). This notion is supported by the facts that the amount of non-REM sleep remains fairly stable over the lifespan and that both short and long sleepers get their deep, non-REM sleep first and in about the same amounts (Hartmann, Baekeland & Zwilling, 1972).

In spite of the apparent importance of non-REM sleep, people who go without sleep for as long as a week usually display no serious ill effects. They do, of course, become very sleepy, and they may become irritable or report not being alert. But their ability to perform a variety of interesting tasks is not impaired very much (Webb, 1975); only boring tasks suffer. And they do not make up all the sleep they lost, hour for hour. Instead, they get about twice a normal night's sleep; then they wake up with no notable aftereffects.

In contrast, if people are awakened every time an EEG shows them entering a REM stage, so that they are deprived only of REM sleep, they compensate for the loss more directly. Dement (1960) found that the more nights subjects were kept from REM sleep, the more they tended to enter it. Eventually, instead of having the usual five or six REM episodes each night, they had dozens. Further, when they were allowed to sleep normally on subsequent nights, they tended to "rebound" by spending about twice the normal amount of time in REM, apparently recovering much of what they had lost.

If people rest, grow, and recover during non-REM sleep, why should they have such a strong need for REM sleep? One theory claims that REM time is spent developing, checking, and expanding nerve connections in the brain (Roffwarg, Muzio & Dement, 1966). The fact that people get much more REM sleep during infancy and childhood, when the brain is still developing relatively rapidly, is consistent with this view. Before birth, when their brains are growing fastest, babies spend over 80 percent of their time in REM sleep. In contrast, animals whose brains and behavior patterns are already well developed at birth (such as the guinea pig) spend very little of their early sleep in REM (Cartwright, 1978).

A related function of REM sleep may be to help imprint what people have learned during the day. Thus, there may be more REM sleep in the early years because every day is crammed with new experiences to assimilate. REM may also increase temporarily after intense mental efforts. Animals spend an unusually long time in REM sleep after sessions of maze learning, but as Figure 6.7 illustrates, they go back to their normal time in REM once they have mastered the task (Block, Hennevin & LeConte, 1977). REM sleep may also be a time of thinking about and adjusting to the day's events or problems. For example, when people in an experiment wore glasses that distorted or restricted their vision, their amount of REM sleep increased at first. But once they became accustomed to their new view of the world, the amount of REM sleep returned to normal (Herman & Roffwarg, 1983; Luce, 1971).

Dreams and Dreaming

Most sleep researchers agree that the mind continues to engage in various activities during all stages of sleep. When aroused from even the deepest non-REM sleep, for example, people commonly report having had isolated thoughts or feelings quite similar to what they experience while awake ("I was thinking about a car I used to drive"). **Dreams** occur mainly during REM sleep (though they may take place at other times) and are distinguished from other cognitive processes during sleep by being more storylike sequences of images, sensations, and perceptions that last anywhere from several seconds to many minutes.

Evidence that sleep does not involve a total loss of consciousness or mental functioning comes from reports of **lucid dreaming,** in which the sleeper is aware of dreaming *while a dream is happening* (Laberge et al., 1981).

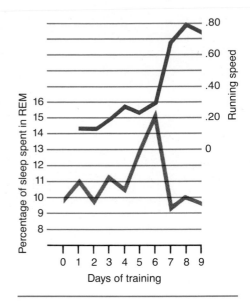

Figure 6.7
REM Sleep and Learning
The upper curve shows rats' average running speed as they learned their way around a maze over a period of days. The lower curve shows the average percentage of REM sleep during spontaneous sleep episodes occurring in the two hours following the practice session. Notice that the REM increase was maximum when learning was in progress. When the learning plateau was reached, REM sleep returned to the pre-learning level.
(Adapted from V. Bloch et al, "Interaction between post-trial reticular stimulation and subsequent paradoxical sleep in memory consolidation processes." In R. R. Drucker-Colin and J. L. McGlaugh (Eds.), *Neurobiology of sleep and memory.* With permission of Academic Press.)

In one experiment, people were asked to press a hand-held switch whenever they were dreaming (Brown & Cartwright, 1977). Not only were they able to do so, but when they were awakened after giving the signal, the percentage of dream reports was even higher than when experimenters awakened them on the basis of physiological signs of REM.

Dreams may be organized or chaotic, realistic or bizarre, and contain anything from a boring replay of yesterday's trip to the laundromat to a dazzling journey through a world of pure fantasy. Sometimes they even provide creative solutions to perplexing problems. For example, after racking his brain for two days in an effort to come up with a story about good and evil in the same person, author Robert Louis Stevenson had a dream in which a man drank a substance that turned him into a monster (Hill, 1968). The dream inspired the book called *The Strange Case of Dr. Jekyll and Mr. Hyde.* The history of science is full of similar examples; the double-helix shape of the DNA molecule (shown in Figure 2.2) apparently also came to its discoverer in a dream.

Research has left little doubt that everyone dreams during every night of normal sleep. Whether you remember a dream depends in part on the general principles of memory (discussed in Chapter 8) and in part on how you sleep and wake up (Cartwright, 1978). For example, just as you are most likely to recall the first and last items on a grocery list, you are also most likely to recall in the morning the first dreams of the night and especially the ones that occurred just before you woke up. Further, the fewer dreams you have and the more vivid or emotional they are, the easier they are to recall. Perhaps because memory is poor for events during very deep sleep, dreams that occur during the lighter sleep stages and REM are recalled best. This is why lighter sleepers tend to remember more dreams. Recall is also more likely if you wake up abruptly and lie quietly while writing or tape-recording your recollections.

Why Do People Dream?

Over thousands of years of speculation, dreams have been characterized as supernatural, psychological, or physiological events. Dreams have been considered messages from the gods, the dead, or other spiritual sources that convey instructions, advice, or glimpses into the dreamer's future (Lewin, 1983). As you might expect, psychologists tend to view dreams as psychological events that contain information about the dreamer's mental processes. Freud (1900) called dreams the "royal road to a knowledge of the unconscious mind." He theorized that, when people sleep, their psychological defenses relax somewhat, allowing normally unconscious impulses and wishes to appear in dreams, usually in disguised form. As we will discuss in Chapter 16, on therapy, some therapists have used the interpretation of dreams to understand and treat mental disorders.

Some more recent research suggests that dreams are better understood as physiological than as psychological events. The *activation-synthesis* hypothesis holds, for example, that dreams represent efforts by the cerebral cortex to make sense out of the random signals that reach it during sleep from a "dream-state generator," which may lie somewhere in the hindbrain (Hobson & McCarley, 1977). Another view attributes dreams to changes in norepinephrine, serotonin, and other neurotransmitters in the brain (Hartmann, 1982; see Chapter 3). Biologist Francis Crick has argued that dreams result when the brain "erases" memories and random associations that it does not need for efficient functioning (Crick & Mitchison, 1983). This notion is compatible with the idea mentioned earlier that REM sleep serves to "tidy up" the mind and memory. Christopher Evans (1983) proposed that, like a computer running a test of its programs, the brain must regularly check its neural circuits when the system is "down" or "off line"—that is, asleep. Dreams, he said, are the byproduct of that process—a temporary, perhaps accidental, glimpse into the material that the brain is scanning, sorting, and reorganizing.

Do these theories mean that dreams have no psychological significance? Not at all. For one thing, the evidence gathered for physiological explanations of dreaming is still tentative. For another, whatever the physiological explanation for dreams, psychological factors may still be important. For example, one group of researchers found that, compared with happily married women, those getting divorced (or recently divorced) had dreams that contained more negative emotions and fewer images of themselves as wives (Cartwright et al., 1984). Thus, even if the raw material of dreams comes strictly from physiological activity and has no inherent meaning, the mental style or current concerns of the dreamer may still determine how that activity is organized and recalled.

HYPNOSIS

Of all the altered states of consciousness, none provokes more speculation and wonder than hypnosis. Its name comes from the Greek word *hypnos,* which means "sleep," but though hypnotized people often appear to be in a sleeplike state in which they can hear and speak, they are not truly asleep. **Hypnosis** is commonly defined as an altered state of consciousness brought on by special induction techniques and characterized by varying degrees of responsiveness to suggestions for changes in experience and behavior (Orne, 1977, 1980).

What does it feel like to be hypnotized? The only way to know for sure is to try it; people often report that their bodies feel "asleep" while their minds remain active and alert. Many are fully aware of being hypnotized. Some report not-unpleasant sensations of spinning, floating, dizziness, or apparent changes in the size of their bodies. Most hypnotized people do not feel forced to follow the hypnotist's instructions; they simply see no reason to refuse (Gill & Brenman, 1959; Hilgard, 1965).

Standing-room-only audiences love to watch hypnotized people forget their own names or act like chickens. Few leave these demonstrations disappointed; but many leave with questions about what hypnosis is, who is susceptible to it and why, and what it can accomplish. Although there are still no final answers to these questions, there are some useful theories and research.

Hypnotic Behavior

Franz Anton Mesmer, a late eighteenth-century Austrian physician, popularized *mesmerism*—what we now call hypnosis—in order to cure patients of paralysis and other disorders. He hypnotized his patients by bringing them in contact with magnetized objects and substances that supposedly redistributed a magnetic fluid in their bodies. Over the years, Mesmer and then others discovered other methods for inducing hypnosis. In the nineteenth century, James Braid, an English physician, demonstrated that people could be induced to enter a hypnotic trance merely by having them stare at a shiny object. Around 1860, A. A. Liebeault, director of a French medical clinic, began to induce hypnosis by suggesting to his subjects that they were relaxed and sleepy; this is the procedure that is most common today.

Hypnosis may also be induced by telling a person to watch his or her hand rise slowly into the air and to go to sleep when it reaches the face, or to listen to his or her own breathing. Whatever the specifics, all procedures

Mesmerism, a forerunner of hypnosis, was once used to cure all sorts of physical disorders. Patients would touch afflicted body parts to magnetized metal rods extending from a tub of water. Upon being touched by Mesmer, the patients would then fall into a curative "crisis" or trance, sometimes accompanied by convulsions.

Figure 6.8
Behavioral Differences During Hypnotic Age Regression
Here are the signatures of a male and female before hypnotically induced age regression (top) and while age-regressed (bottom). Notice that the lower signatures look less mature; one is even printed rather than written. In spite of such apparent changes in overt behavior, the things people "recall" during age regression are not especially accurate and are subject to the usual distortions associated with attempts to retrieve old memories (Nash et al., 1986). (From *Hypnotic Susceptibility* by Ernest R. Hilgard, copyright © 1965 by Harcourt Brace Jovanovich, Inc. Reprinted by permission of the publisher.)

for inducing hypnosis focus people's attention on a restricted, often monotonous set of stimuli (usually including the hypnotist's voice) while asking them to shut out everything else as they imagine certain feelings.

The results can be fascinating. Hypnotized people may show changes in movement, sensation, perception, memory, motivation, emotion, thinking, and other dimensions. For example, people told that their eyes will not open may struggle fruitlessly to open them. They can be made to appear deaf, blind, or unable to smell; they may become less sensitive to pain. They may perceive a disgusting smell as perfume, an empty chair as being occupied by a nonexistent cat. Feelings of happiness or sadness can be made to appear and disappear. Hypnotized people may forget their own telephone numbers; sometimes they can recall forgotten memories. Some people even appear to display **age regression,** in which they not only recall but seem to reenact behaviors from childhood. (Figure 6.8 provides an example.) For some subjects, the influence of hypnosis can sometimes be extended for hours or days by **posthypnotic suggestions**—instructions about experiences or behavior to take place after hypnosis has been terminated (say, whistling "Dixie" whenever someone coughs).

Hilgard (1965) has summarized the changes that people undergo when they are hypnotized, noting that some people display them more than others.

1. Hypnotized people show *reduced planfulness.* In other words, they tend not to initiate actions on their own, preferring to wait for the hypnotist's instructions. One subject said, "At one point I was trying to decide if my legs were crossed, but I couldn't tell, and didn't quite have the initiative to move to find out" (Hilgard, 1965, p. 6).

2. Hypnotized people ignore everything except the hypnotist's voice and whatever it points out; their *attention is redistributed.* One subject described the experience this way: "Your voice came in my ear and *filled* my head" (Hilgard, 1965, p. 13). This is an extreme form of selective attention, described in the chapter on perception.

3. The ability to *fantasize* is enhanced, so that people can easily put themselves into various scenes or vividly relive old memories.

4. Hypnotized people are more willing to accept apparent distortions of reality. This willingness is part of *reduced reality testing,* a tendency not to question whether stated facts are true. Thus, a person might begin to shiver in a very warm room because the hypnotist says it has just begun to snow.

5. People under hypnosis appear to be especially good at *role taking,* easily and convincingly behaving as if they are, say, a different age or a member of the opposite sex.

6. Many hypnotized people experience **posthypnotic amnesia.** That is, they cannot remember what happened while they were hypnotized. For some, recall fails even when they are told what went on.

Who Can Be Hypnotized?

Researchers have developed special tests to measure hypnotic **susceptibility,** the degree to which people comply with and become involved in hypnosis and hypnotic suggestions. Examples include the Stanford Hypnotic Susceptibility Scales (SHSS; Weitzenhoffer & Hilgard, 1959, 1962) and the Harvard Group Scale of Hypnotic Susceptibility (Shor & Orne, 1963). These tests begin with a standard hypnotic induction, followed by suggestions that the person cannot speak or that the person's arm is rigid; points are awarded for each suggestion followed. These tests show that about 10 to 15 percent of adults are excellent hypnotic subjects. Another 10 percent or so are difficult or impossible to hypnotize and display few, if any, hypnotic behaviors. Most people fall somewhere between these extremes (Hilgard, 1965, 1982).

Does this mean that some people possess a trait or ability that allows them to be hypnotized more easily than others? Or does susceptibility depend on situational variables, such as the hypnotist, where and when the hypnosis takes place, and so on? Both individual ability and situational factors appear to influence susceptibility. At any particular time, a person's *willingness* to be hypnotized may be more important than general hypnotic susceptibility in determining responsiveness. The idea that one person can hypnotize another against his or her will is a myth. The effect of attitudes and past experiences also suggests that hypnotic susceptibility may come about, in part, through learning. In fact, people can improve their susceptibility by learning to think

We now know that hypnosis can be induced by staring at an object or in other ways that are much simpler than Mesmer's elaborate rituals.

more favorably about hypnosis and to accept hypnotic suggestions, by watching what good hypnotic subjects do, or by practicing (DeVoge & Sachs, 1973; Diamond, 1974; Gfeller, Lynn & Pribble, 1987; Gorassini & Spanos, 1986).

There is little or no scientific evidence, however, that susceptible subjects share a constellation of personality traits, such as a tendency to be especially suggestible or compliant or desirous of pleasing others. About the only traits that set the susceptible apart from other people are a tendency to have a more active imagination (Tellegren & Atkinson, 1974; Wilson & Barber, 1978); an ability to concentrate on a single activity for a long time (Graham & Evans, 1977); and an ability to leave reality easily by becoming deeply absorbed in activities like books or movies (J. R. Hilgard, 1979; Lynn & Rhue, 1986). Some evidence suggests that the right cerebral hemisphere in susceptible people is more active than the left, but why this should be or how it relates to susceptibility is unclear (McLeod-Morgan & Lack, 1982).

Explaining Hypnosis

Hypnotized people often look and act differently from those who are not hypnotized (Hilgard, 1965), but do the differences signal an altered state of consciousness? According to the **state theory** of hypnosis, hypnosis does indeed create an altered state of consciousness; role theory offers a different explanation.

Role theory   According to **role theory,** hypnotized subjects merely act in accordance with a special social role, which demands compliance (Barber, 1969; Sarbin, 1950). The procedures for inducing hypnosis, this theory suggests, provide a socially acceptable reason to follow the hypnotist's suggestions, much the same way that a nurse's uniform or the title of doctor provide good reasons for medical patients to remove all of their clothing on command. Support for role theory comes from observations that people will behave in the unusual, even bizarre fashion normally associated with hypnosis even when they are not hypnotized. On television game shows, you will see apparently normal, certainly unhypnotized individuals scream, jump around, hug and kiss total strangers, and generally make fools of themselves. In the laboratory, virtually every hypnotic phenomenon, from arm rigidity, to pain tolerance, to age regression can be duplicated by a motivated, but unhypnotized, volunteer (Barber, 1969; Orne, 1970; Orne & Evans, 1965).

There is also more direct evidence that hypnotized people engage in a certain amount of role taking. In one experiment decades ago, Frank Pattie (1935) demonstrated that people whom hypnosis had made deaf or insensitive to touch could actually hear and feel, in spite of the fact that they otherwise behaved (and believed) that they could not. Figure 6.9 illustrates how Pattie

Figure 6.9
Can Hypnosis Produce Blindness?
The top row in this figure looks like gibberish, but it can be read as the numbers and letters in the lower row if viewed through special glasses and with one eye closed. Frank Pattie (1935) found that hypnotized subjects who had been given suggestions for blindness in one eye were unable to read the numbers and letters while wearing the special glasses, indicating that both eyes were in fact working normally.
(From Pattie, F. A. "A report of attempts to produce uniocular blindness by hypnotic suggestion," *British Journal of Medical Psychology,* 1935, *15,* 236, Figure 1.)

demonstrated that one person who thought she was blind while hypnotized could in fact see. In another study, hypnotized subjects were asked to immerse their hands in ice-cold water after being told that they would feel no pain (Hilgard, Morgan & MacDonald, 1975). Indeed, the subjects' oral reports indicated almost no pain, as Figure 6.10 shows. However, a very different story was told by the subjects' nonimmersed hands, which were asked to press a key to indicate if "any part of you" experiences pain. It has been suggested that a "hidden observer" reports on pain that is reaching the person but has somehow been separated, or *dissociated,* from conscious awareness (Hilgard, 1977). This hidden observer's report may itself reflect role taking, since the amount of pain reported nonverbally often depends on what the hypnotist tells the subject to expect (Spanos & Hewitt, 1980; Spanos, Gwynn & Stam, 1983).

State theory   Does all this mean that hypnosis involves nothing more than providing a good reason to do things that we might have done for other reasons? State theorists say no. They point to subtle differences between hypnotized and nonhypnotized people, usually in the *way* they carry out suggestions. For example, in an experiment on posthypnotic behavior, hypnotized people and people who had been asked to simulate hypnosis were told that they would run their hands through their hair whenever they heard the word *experiment* (Orne, Sheehan & Evans, 1968). Simulators did so only when the hypnotist said the cue word; hypnotized subjects complied no matter who said it. After being given a posthypnotic suggestion to forget a word list, highly susceptible subjects recall some words, but in random order. Less susceptible people and nonhypnotized subjects tend to recall the words roughly in the order they were originally presented (Kihlstrom & Evans, 1976; Spanos & Bodorik, 1977).

State theorists hold that these differences between hypnotized and nonhypnotized people indicate that hypnotized people are not just role playing; they are experiencing a special state of consciousness. In their view, even if subjects enter hypnosis in response to the demands of a social role or other external influences, once hypnotized they display significant changes in basic mental processes, changes that do not appear in unhypnotized people (Orne, 1980).

Dissociation theory   To explain these changes in mental processes, Ernest Hilgard (1977, 1979) proposes a blending of role and state theories. He suggests that hypnosis is not a single specific state, but a general condition, in which people allow themselves to reorganize the ways in which their behavior is controlled.

Hilgard argues that the ego, or self, usually determines what people pay attention to, what they perceive and remember, how they act, and so on. But, says Hilgard, hypnosis creates a *dissociation,* a partial and temporary breakup of this central control. Dissociation allows body movements that are normally under voluntary control, for example, to take place on their own, and it allows normally involuntary processes, such as overt reactions to sound or pain, to become voluntary and controllable. This, he says, is the basis for the hidden-observer effect mentioned earlier. Dissociation may also give people greater control over memory and perception, allowing hypnotized individuals to, say, temporarily blot out some events (as in posthypnotic amnesia). Dissociation also occurs outside of hypnosis when, for example, two or more thoughts or perceptions take place simultaneously and independently, even though the person may be aware of only one (Hilgard, 1979).

According to Hilgard's **dissociation theory** of hypnosis, the relaxation of central control within the hypnotized person is accompanied by a *social*

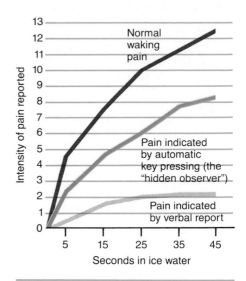

Figure 6.10
Reports of Pain in Hypnosis
Nonverbal behavior sometimes contradicts verbal reports of analgesia (reduced pain) by hypnotized subjects. Here, average reports of pain during immersion of a hand in ice water are compared for nonhypnotized subjects, subjects given hypnotic suggestions for analgesia, and hypnotized subjects given the same suggestions but asked to indicate by pressing a key if "any part of them" feels pain. Nonverbal reports by this so-called hidden observer suggest that pain is being experienced but not reported directly because of the social demands of the experimental situation.
(From *Divided Consciousness: Multiple Controls in Human Thought and Action* by E. R. Hilgard. Copyright © 1977 John Wiley and Sons, Inc. Reprinted by permission of John Wiley and Sons, Inc.)

agreement to share some of that control with the hypnotist. For a time, the hypnotist is allowed to determine what the subject will experience and do. Thus, from Hilgard's point of view, hypnosis becomes a socially agreed-upon opportunity to display one's ability to let mental functions become dissociated. If only a limited degree of dissociation of mental functions occurs in a hypnotic situation, the person may not experience a change in consciousness; if more profound dissociation takes place, he or she may enter an altered state of consciousness. According to Hilgard, then, compliance with a social role may account for part of the story, but hypnosis also creates significant changes in mental processes.

Dissociation theory is not universally accepted (Spanos, Radtke & Bertrand, 1985), but continuing research relating to it should enhance understanding not only of hypnosis but also of how people influence one another and how the brain processes information and organizes behavior (Wilson & Kihlstrom, 1986).

Some Uses of Hypnosis

Debate over what hypnosis is has not diminished its application to human problems. For example, some therapists have had moderate success in helping clients stop using cigarettes, alcohol, or drugs by offering posthypnotic suggestions that those substances will create nausea or disgust. Much better results have been reported in the hypnotic control of pain; hypnosis appears to be the only anesthetic some people need to protect them from the pain of dental work, childbirth, burns, abdominal surgery, and painful procedures such as spinal taps (Finer, 1980). Other people find hypnotic relief from the chronic pain of arthritis, nerve damage, migraine headaches, and cancer (Hilgard, 1980; Long, 1986). Hypnotic suggestion can reduce the nausea and vomiting sometimes associated with cancer chemotherapy (Redd, 1984) and has even helped minimize bleeding during surgery (Gerschman, Reade & Burrows, 1980).

Other applications of hypnosis are very controversial, especially when it has been used to try to uncover events from a person's past or to improve a crime witness's memory. Age regression, for example, certainly involves something other than actually becoming younger; it probably combines actual recall or reconstruction of early memories with imagining and acting out past actions (Foenander & Burrows, 1980). And there is evidence that recall does not become more accurate during hypnosis. Instead, people's confidence in hypnosis may prompt them to unintentionally distort information or inaccurately reconstruct events (Loftus & Loftus, 1980; Orne, 1979). Concern over these problems has led the American Medical Association and the American Psychological Association to oppose the use of hypnosis in obtaining crime reports from victims and witnesses. Courts in several states disqualify testimony from people who have been hypnotized.

MEDITATION

Separation of mind and body, a sense of timelessness, a feeling of oneness with the universe, increased self-knowledge, ecstasy—all these effects some-times accompany deep hypnosis (Hilgard, 1979; Tart, 1969). Similar effects can be sought more directly, through **meditation,** a set of techniques designed to create an altered state of consciousness characterized by inner peace and tranquility (Shapiro & Walsh, 1984). Many people believe that, just as you can see the bottom of a deep lake when its waters are calm, the peaceful state

Sufi "whirling dervishes" enter a meditative state through a wild, ecstatic dance ritual.

reached through meditation helps them to see into their own inner depths. Meditation, they claim, helps them gain awareness of their relationship to the world and the universe; understand themselves more clearly, thereby achieving greater self-esteem and growth; decrease stress and anxiety; and even improve performance in everything from work to tennis.

Meditation Methods

There is no single "right" way to create a meditative state. Methods developed over the years range from sitting quietly with closed eyes to the ecstatic dancing of Sufi "whirling dervishes." Some meditation procedures involve *opening up* attention by calmly pausing to take in as much of what is going on in the outside world as possible (Ornstein, 1977). Far more popular are *focusing* methods. They aim at narrowing attention to just one thing—a word, a sound, or an object—long enough for the meditator to stop thinking about *anything* and to experience nothing but pure awareness. Nevertheless, most methods of meditating share a few basic components. They all call for the meditator to (1) find a quiet environment, (2) assume a comfortable position, (3) use a mental device to organize attention, and (4) take a passive attitude (Benson, 1975).

What the meditator focuses on is far less important than doing so with a passive attitude. To organize attention, meditators may, for example, inwardly name every sound or thought that reaches consciousness; focus on the sound of their own breathing or on a candle flame; or slowly repeat a *mantra,* which is a soothing word or phrase such as *om* (meaning "I am"). At first, there is a natural tendency to think about the object of attention or to evaluate what is going on. When attention begins to wander, the person may try to refocus it. But these active efforts prevent the person from entering a meditative state (Shapiro, 1980).

To learn a passive attitude, new meditators are encouraged to observe the distractions that occur but to make no effort to get rid of them. The goal is to allow rational, analytical thoughts to fall away on their own and to let attention return peacefully to the object of focus. In other words, you achieve a passive attitude by not trying to achieve it. Learning to adopt this attitude may require weeks or even months. It may take years to learn to reach the most profound meditative states.

The Effects of Meditation

During a typical meditation session, respiration, heart rate, muscle tension, blood pressure, and oxygen consumption decrease (Shapiro & Giber, 1978; Wallace & Benson, 1972). Most forms of meditation are also accompanied by a considerable amount of alpha wave activity, the brain wave pattern commonly found during a relaxed, eyes-closed, waking state (see Figure 6.3). Meditators commonly report feeling deep relaxation and inner peace. They may also experience significant decreases in such problems as general anxiety, high blood pressure, alcoholism, drug addiction, insomnia, and other stress-related problems (Smith, 1975). More generally, meditators' scores on personality tests indicate increases in general mental health, self-esteem, and social openness (Shapiro & Giber, 1978).

Exactly how meditation produces its effects is unclear. A great deal of research is needed to pinpoint the mechanisms involved. What we do know now is that meditation seems to help some people, but not others, depending on who they are and what their goals or problems are. Meditation appears most helpful to basically "normal" people who wish to enhance their personal growth or deal with problems of moderate intensity. It should be used in moderation, however. Meditating for very long periods may produce dizziness, anxiety, confusion, depression, and restlessness (Otis, 1984), not to mention its interfering with work and other activities.

Most of meditation's effects can be achieved through many other means, including biofeedback, hypnosis, and just relaxing (Holmes, 1984; Shapiro, 1984). This was well illustrated in an experiment on public-speaking anxiety (Kirsch & Henry, 1979). After only three weeks of meditation, clients who had had a strong fear of public speaking showed significant increases in confidence, significant reductions in anxiety, and greatly improved performance while giving a speech. They did significantly better than a second group of people, who received no treatment for their fear of public speaking. But their gains were matched by a third group, who received different forms of therapy (specifically, progressive relaxation training and systematic desensitization, which we will describe in later chapters).

In spite of findings like these, proponents of meditation claim that it can have unique results. They argue that other methods do not create the same uplifting altered state that can lead to true enlightenment (Deikman, 1982). A final evaluation of this argument must await advances in the ability to measure people's subjective experience, especially through the EEG, evoked potentials, and other tools (discussed in Chapter 3) that allow researchers to monitor what is going on in different parts of the brain during various experiences.

PSYCHOACTIVE DRUGS

Alterations in consciousness are frequently brought about by **psychoactive drugs**, chemical substances that act on the brain to create psychological effects. As mentioned in Chapter 3, these effects usually result when the drug competes with or alters the availability of neurotransmitters. Some psychoactive drugs—particularly caffeine, nicotine, and alcohol—are so much a part of

Americans' lives that they may not think of them as drugs or as changing their states of consciousness. But they are and they do.

Table 6.1 (p. 230) provides a summary of psychoactive drugs. Their enjoyable or medically beneficial effects are often marred by undesirable side effects stemming from overuse or abuse. As Table 6.1 shows, abuse of some drugs can lead to *physical dependence,* or *addiction,* as the abuser's body develops a physical need for the drug. Addiction also tends to create *tolerance,* meaning that larger and larger amounts of the drug are needed to obtain the same effects. Addicts who try to discontinue use of the drug typically experience very unpleasant, often dangerous, *withdrawal symptoms.* Other drugs may lead to *psychological dependence,* a condition in which the abuser, though not physically addicted, comes to depend on the chemical to function efficiently. These aspects of drug abuse are discussed in Chapter 15, on abnormal psychology; in this section, we focus on the effects on consciousness of some of the best-known, most commonly used psychoactive drugs.

Caffeine is a psychoactive drug that appears in so many forms that people are not always aware of consuming it.

Depressants

Depressants are a class of drugs whose action depresses central nervous system functioning. The most familiar of these are alcohol, barbiturates, and tranquilizers.

Alcohol Alcohol is one of the oldest, and certainly the most widely used, drugs in the world. In the United States alone, over 100 million people drink it in an endless variety of beverages. Like those of other depressants (see Table 6.1), alcohol's depressant effects on consciousness depend on the amount reaching the brain. Since alcohol is broken down, or *metabolized,* by the liver at the rate of about one ounce per hour, it has little effect on the brain if consumed that slowly. Most people drink faster.

About two ounces of alcohol usually bring feelings of relaxation, happiness, and well-being. They also begin to *depress,* or temporarily knock out, areas of the cerebral cortex that normally keep people from doing things they know they should not do. As the dose of alcohol increases, more and more of the brain's activity is depressed or impaired, resulting in confused or disorganized thinking, slurred speech, disruptions in coordination and balance, and, finally, sleep. Rapid consumption of more than thirty ounces of alcohol numbs the medulla and other brain centers that control breathing and heart action, until sleep becomes death.

Counting ounces can be misleading, however, because the actual amount of alcohol in the blood, and the resulting level of drunkenness, depends not only on how fast a person drinks, but also on what a person drinks and how rapidly it is absorbed. For example, straight whiskey and other cocktails that are high in alcohol content generally have stronger effects than wine or beer, which contain lower concentrations of alcohol. Alcohol also enters the bloodstream more rapidly if the drinker's stomach is empty and more slowly if the stomach is full. But filling up on food before drinking only delays the effects of excessive drinking. It does not prevent them. And nothing developed so far can protect the overindulgent drinker from the next morning's hangover, which is actually the result of alcohol poisoning.

The specific effects of alcohol vary considerably from person to person. As social inhibitions weaken, some drinkers begin talking too loud, acting silly, or telling others exactly what they think of them. Those who have been inhibiting aggression may become unpredictably impulsive or even physically violent (Steele, 1986). Emotional reactions range from euphoria to deep sadness. As discussed in this chapter's Linkages box, people's responses to alcohol may be influenced to some extent by what they expect.

TABLE 6.1 _____

Major Classes of Psychoactive Drugs
There is a wide range of psychoactive drugs, each class of which has its own set of characteristic effects and uses. One particular class, the antipsychotics, will be discussed again in Chapter 16, on the treatment of psychological disorders.

Drugs	Trade Names	Street Names
Depressants		
Alcohol	Ethyl alcohol	Booze
Barbiturates (phenobarbital, amobarbital, pentobarbital, pentothal)	Luminal, Amytal, Seconal, Nembutal, Thiopental	Downers, yellow jackets, blue devils, barbs
Nonbarbiturate hypnotics (e.g., glutethimide, methaqualone)	Doriden, Quaalude	Ludes
Tranquilizers (meprobamate, chlordiazepoxide, diazepam)	Miltown, Equanil, Librium, Valium	Tranks
Stimulants		
Amphetamines	Benzedrine, Dexedrine, Methedrine	Speed, uppers, pep pills, bennies, dexies
Antidepressants	Parnate, Tofranil, Elavil	
Cocaine		Coke, snow, flake
Convulsants (e.g., strychnine)	Metrazol, Picrotoxin	
Caffeine		
Nicotine		
Narcotic opiates		
Opium		
Morphine	Percodan, Demerol	M
Heroin		Horse, smack, junk
Codeine	Tylenol 3	
Antipsychotics		
Phenothiazines, reserpine, butyrophenones	Thorazine, Serpasil, Haldol, Inapsine	
Lithium		
Psychedelics and Hallucinogens		
LSD (lysergic acid diethylamine)		Acid
Mescaline		Mesc
Psilocybin		
Amphetamine variants	MDA, STP	
Phencyclidine		PCP, angel dust
Cannabis		Pot, dope, reefer, grass

Main Effects Sought by User	Potential for Physical Dependence (Addiction)	Potential for Psychological Dependence
Relaxation, anxiety reduction, sleep	High	High
Relaxation, anxiety reduction, sleep	High	High
Relaxation, anxiety reduction, sleep	High	High
Relaxation, anxiety reduction, sleep	Moderate to high	High
Alertness, euphoria	Some	High
Relief from depression	Low	Moderate
Alertness, euphoria	Moderate to high*	High
Alertness, euphoria	Low	Low
Alertness	Low	Moderate
Alertness, calmness, sociability	Moderate**	High
Euphoria	High	High
Euphoria, pain control	High	High
Euphoria, pain control	High	High
Euphoria, cough and pain control	High	High
Moderation of psychotic symptoms	Low	Low
Control of mania and depression	Low	Low
Mind expansion, hallucinations, exhilaration	Low	Low
Mind expansion, hallucinations, exhilaration	Low	Low
Mind expansion, hallucinations, exhilaration	Low	Low
Mind expansion, hallucinations, exhilaration	Unknown	Unknown
Mind expansion, hallucinations, exhilaration	Unknown	High
Euphoria, relaxation	Low	Moderate

* The degree to which cocaine use can lead to physical addiction is still a matter of debate and intense research.

** The question of whether nicotine leads to physical as well as psychological dependence is still not settled.

Barbiturates Sometimes called "downers" or sleeping pills, *barbiturates* form a group of central nervous system depressants which, like alcohol, can create physical dependence. They carry trade names such as Seconal, Tuinal, and Nembutal. (Methaqualone, or Quaalude, has effects similar to those of barbiturates.) These drugs were originally developed and prescribed to promote sleep and relaxation in agitated patients. Small doses produce relaxation and mild euphoria but can also disrupt muscle coordination, mental concentration, and the ability to work. They also bring very deep sleep; overdoses can be fatal. Addicts who try to give up barbiturates may experience withdrawal symptoms more severe than those created by any other drug. The symptoms may include restlessness, violent outbursts, convulsions, hallucinations, and even sudden death.

Tranquilizers As their name suggests, *tranquilizers* are prescribed by physicians to help patients relax and, perhaps most important, feel free from anxiety. The first tranquilizer, meprobamate, was introduced in the 1950s and sold as Miltown or Equanil. It can be taken in small daily doses for anxiety, but its effects resemble those of barbiturates; overdoses can bring on sleep or even death. In the 1960s, a new group of tranquilizers called *benzodiazepines* appeared, under such trade names as Librium and Valium. These drugs retain the antianxiety effects of barbiturates and meprobamate, but they do not create as much sleepiness or depressed breathing. It is very difficult to commit suicide by taking an overdose of these tranquilizers.

The widespread use of tranquilizers (over 100 million prescriptions per year in the United States alone) has led to misuse. Too often, doctors prescribe these drugs routinely, for years at a time, without enough concern for what is making the patient anxious. Patients become psychologically, if not physically, dependent on their chemical crutch. Many long-term users experience confusion, disorientation, uncontrolled anger, and other undesirable symptoms. Worse still, some people combine alcohol with tranquilizers. The effects of this combination on mental functioning and motor coordination can be fatal, especially if a person is foolish enough to drive a car under its influence.

Stimulants

Stimulants are chemicals that have the ability to increase behavioral activity. Those to be discussed here, *amphetamines* and *cocaine,* do so primarily by augmenting the action of the neurotransmitter norepinephrine.

Amphetamines Benzedrine, Dexedrine, and Methadrine are some of the trade names for *amphetamines*. These stimulants, or "uppers," were first synthesized to relieve asthma and nasal congestion. They stimulate the brain as well as the sympathetic branch of the autonomic nervous system. Arousal of the sympathetic nervous system produces increased heart rate and blood pressure, constriction of blood vessels and shrinking of mucus membranes (thus relieving stuffy noses), suppression of appetite, and alertness.

The desire to lose weight, to stay awake, or to experience the "high" associated with greatly increased energy and arousal has led many people to abuse or become addicted to amphetamines. Continued use can produce severe restlessness, sleeplessness, heart problems, mental confusion, suspiciousness, nonstop talking, and in extreme cases, symptoms similar to those of paranoid schizophrenia—such as false beliefs about being watched or persecuted by hostile forces.

Cocaine   The leaves of the coca plant are the source of cocaine. Like many other now-outlawed drugs, cocaine was once sold legally as medicine; Sigmund Freud once recommended it for relieving depression. It even appeared in the original recipe for Coca-Cola. It reduces pain and stimulates self-confidence, well-being, and optimism.

Continued abuse of cocaine can lead to nausea, overactivity, sleeplessness, paranoid thinking, a sudden depressive "crash," and hallucinations. Overdoses, especially of the purified and potent form of cocaine called "crack," can be fatal (Kozel, Grider & Adams, 1982). Even small doses can result in death, as was tragically illustrated in the well-publicized cocaine-related deaths of stellar athletes Len Bias and Don Rogers in 1986. Many abusers become so preoccupied with obtaining and using the drug that their lives are ruined. There is also evidence that cocaine can lead to physical addiction as well as strong psychological dependence (Jones, 1984).

Narcotics

Narcotics—particularly opium, morphine, and heroin—are a class of drugs distinguished by their sleep-inducing and pain-relieving effects (Julien, 1981). The poppy plant yields a substance called *opium,* which means "plant of joy." Raw opium can relieve pain while bringing on feelings of well-being and dreamy relaxation. One of the most active ingredients in opium is *morphine,* a drug isolated in the early 1800s and since used throughout the world for the relief of pain. *Heroin* is derived from morphine but is three times more powerful, producing a particularly intense pleasurable reaction, or "rush."

The effects of narcotics, or *opiates,* on consciousness are quite complex. Drowsy, cloudy feelings occur because the opiates, somewhat like alcohol and barbiturates, depress the activity of some parts of the cerebral cortex. But they can also create excitation in other parts, causing some users to experience euphoria (Wise & Bozarth, 1984). Recent evidence suggests that they kill pain because they are chemically similar to the body's own "natural opiates" (discussed in Chapters 3 and 4). As a result, opiates can occupy the brain's receptors for these natural painkillers and mimic their effects, blocking pain from reaching the brain or reducing the person's awareness of it (Julien, 1981).

Until the early part of this century, opium and morphine were as available as aspirin is today. Stores sold them for pain, diarrhea, coughs, and many other physical ills. But because they are highly addictive, narcotics have been outlawed for nonprescription use in the United States since 1914. Still, heroin addicts number in the hundreds of thousands, risking death through overdoses, contaminated drugs, or AIDS (acquired immune deficiency syndrome) contracted through the sharing of drug-injection needles.

Psychedelics and Hallucinogens

Psychedelic, or "mind-expanding," drugs alter consciousness by producing a temporary loss of contact with reality and changes in emotion, perception, and thought. These changes often include gross distortions in body image (one may feel gigantic or very tiny), loss of identity (confusion about who you are), dreamlike fantasies, and hallucinations. Psychedelics are, in some superficial ways at least, similar to the psychotic forms of mental illness described in Chapter 15. For this reason, psychedelic drugs are also sometimes called *hallucinogens* or *psychotomimetics* (mimicking psychosis). Some, including mescaline and psilocybin, which occur in certain mushrooms and cacti,

Cocaine produces feelings of well-being, but its users run a high risk of ruining their lives by becoming psychologically or physically dependent on the drug.

have been used for many centuries, usually in connection with native Americans' magical or religious rituals.

LSD   *Lysergic acid diethylamide (LSD)* is one of the most powerful and by far the best-known of psychedelics. It was first synthesized in 1938 by Swiss chemist Albert Hofmann as one of several compounds derived from a fungus growing on rye grain. One day he accidentally ingested a miniscule amount of the substance and experienced some strange effects. To observe the effects more carefully, he tried another dose and later described the experience:

> I lost all count of time. . . . everything appeared deformed as in a faulty mirror. Space and time became more and more disorganized and I was overcome by a fear that I was going out of my mind. The worst part of it being that I was clearly aware of my condition. . . . Occasionally, I felt as if I were out of my body. I thought I had died. My ego seemed suspended somewhere in space, from where I saw my dead body lying on the sofa. . . . Acoustic perceptions, such as the noise of water gushing from a tap or the spoken word, were transformed into optical illusions. (Quoted in Julien, 1981, p. 155)

Some of the effects of LSD have been attributed to its ability to occupy and block receptors that are normally used by the neurotransmitter serotonin. This appears to make the brain's reticular formation (shown in Figure 3.13) more sensitive, thus amplifying and otherwise distorting incoming sensory stimuli (Julien, 1981).

The exact effects of LSD on each person's consciousness, like the effects of alcohol, may vary considerably, depending on who takes it and why, where it is taken, and who else is present. "Bad trips" can produce anything from merely unpleasant reactions to psychotic episodes, especially in unstable people. Sometimes "flashbacks" occur, in which the person is suddenly and unpredictably returned to an LSD-like state of consciousness weeks or months after using the drug. Other ill effects attributed to taking LSD include brain damage, chromosome breakage, or mental disorder. Although none of these problems has yet been definitely linked to the moderate use of LSD, the possible linkage is certainly reason for caution. Fortunately, LSD does not normally produce either psychological or physical dependence.

PCP   Phencyclidine is a surgical anesthetic, which became known in the late 1960s as the *"PeaCe Pill"* or *PCP*. It is well known by the street name "angel dust." Its side effects when swallowed, smoked, or snorted include agitated excitement, disorientation, and hallucinations. It is very dangerous. Small doses create insensitivity to pain, psychological separation from the world and from one's own body, rigidity, a blank stare, and an inability to speak. Higher doses bring stupor and mental confusion that may last from a few hours to a few days. In some cases, a drug-induced psychosis appears and continues for months. PCP users have been known to jump off buildings or get hurt in other ways because they do not recognize danger or feel pain. Worse, the drug can cause the user to injure or kill others. Overdoses can be fatal.

Marijuana   A mixture of crushed leaves, flowers, and stems from the hemp plant (*Cannabis sativa*) makes up marijuana. The active ingredient is tetra-hydrocannabinol, or THC, which usually makes up about 1 to 5 percent of the drug (some strains of marijuana may contain even more). When inhaled from a marijuana cigarette, or "joint," THC enters the bloodstream through the lungs and reaches peak concentrations within ten to thirty minutes. It is absorbed by many organs, including the brain, where it continues to affect consciousness for two to three hours. Absorption through the stomach and intestines is slower; so when marijuana is eaten (usually in cookies or brownies), its effects do not peak for at least an hour and may last for several hours. The action of THC, unlike that of, say, LSD, has not been tied to any particular neurotransmitter system.

At low or moderate doses, marijuana produces relaxation and reduces anxiety. According to a government report,

> At low, usual "social" doses, the individual may experience an increased sense of well-being: initial restlessness and hilarity followed by a dreamy, carefree state of relaxation; alteration of sensory perceptions including expansion of space and time; and a more vivid sense of touch, sight, smell, tastes and sound; a feeling of hunger, especially a craving for sweets; and subtle changes in thought formation and expression. (National Commission on Marijuana and Drug Abuse, 1972, p. 68)

Marijuana may also interfere with the ability to remember what happened just a few seconds ago, making it difficult to carry out complex mental or physical tasks (Jaffe, 1975). These effects become more intense at larger doses (the equivalent of several joints); at very high levels, a person may occasionally experience vivid phenomena similar to those associated with LSD. Unlike depressants, such as alcohol or barbiturates, excessive doses of marijuana do not produce the downward spiral to anesthesia, coma, or death.

Since the late 1800s, marijuana has been controversial. On one side are those who see it as a recreational drug that is not addictive and has fewer harmful effects than alcohol. It ranks second in popularity among young drug users, surpassed only by alcohol (see Figure 6.11). On the other side are critics who see marijuana as a menace that leads to abuse of more dangerous drugs and to criminal behavior. Currently, the laws (though not always the facts) reflect the second view; growing, selling, or possessing marijuana has been outlawed in most states since the 1930s and has been illegal under federal law since 1970. Numerous government commissions and task forces

Figure 6.11
Drug Use Among College-Age Students
The green bars represent the percentage of students reporting using a given drug during 1980. The gold bars show the figures for 1985. These data and other, more recent figures show that the use of most drugs other than alcohol among the young is decreasing somewhat in the 1980s. The notable exception has been cocaine, whose use (and consequent death toll) continues to rise
(From Russell, C, "One-third of College Students Try Cocaine, Survey Finds." *The Washington Post*, Tuesday, July 8, 1986, p. A3.)

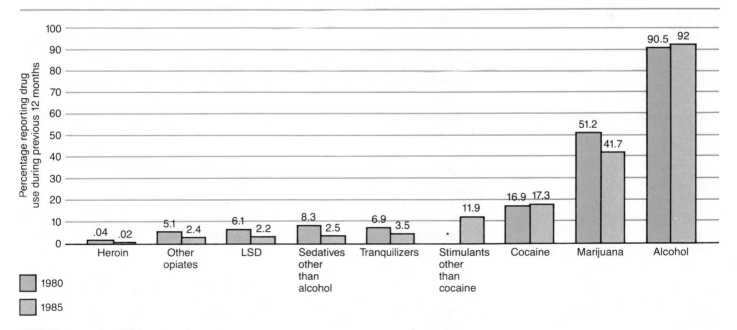

1980

1985

*1980 Figures not available

CONSCIOUSNESS AND THOUGHT

Can Expectations About a Drug Alter Its Effects on Consciousness?

If you wanted to predict how marijuana or some other drug would alter a friend's consciousness or behavior, you would want to know about more than the biochemical effects of the drug. Consider the aggressiveness many people display when they are drunk (Critchlow, 1986). In one study, male social drinkers were given either tonic water or a vodka-and-tonic mixture in which the alcohol could not be tasted (Lang et al., 1975). The vodka mixture brought the drinkers' blood-alcohol content to 0.1 percent, the level at which most states define a person as legally drunk. Half the people drinking each beverage were told what they were drinking. The other half were misinformed; they thought either that they were drinking alcohol when they were not or that they were consuming no alcohol when they were. Then a research assistant, posing as an obnoxious fellow subject, angered the subjects. Later they were allowed to hurt him by administering electric shocks as part of an experiment. (The assistant appeared to be shocked, but no electricity actually reached him.)

What happened? Aggressiveness, as measured by the strength of the shocks, depended not on whether the people were drunk or sober, but on their expectations. Legally drunk subjects who did not think they had been drinking did not perceive themselves as drunk and tended to be less aggressive than sober people who perceived themselves to be drunk, as Figure A shows.

In another study using the same design, people who were told that they had consumed alcohol laughed more at comedy records than those who were told that they had drunk only tonic water (Vuchinich, Tucker & Sobell, 1979). Whether or not they had actually had alcohol made no difference. Obviously, how people expect alcohol to affect them may be just as important as chemistry in its diverse effects on consciousness.

The same can be said about other drugs. For example, volunteers in one study who expressed the most worry about the effects of taking psilocybin, a psychedelic drug similar to LSD, tended to report the most anxiety, nausea, and other negative symptoms while under the drug's influence. Those with the most positive expectations experienced the fewest negative effects (Metzner, Litwin & Weil, 1965). Similarly, marijuana's effects depend in part on what each person expects them to be (Jones, 1971).

Studies like these reveal that drugs of all kinds work in at least two ways. Their *specific* effects are brought on by the chemicals themselves, whereas their *nonspecific,* or *placebo,* effects are produced by what a person *thinks* the drug will do (Shapiro & Morris, 1978). For example, most of the specific effects of alcohol, such as its ability to disrupt muscular coordination, balance, speech, and thought, tend to occur whether or not the drinker expects them (Vuchinich & Sobell, 1978). Other, nonspecific effects, such as happiness, sadness, adventurousness, or anger, appear to depend on both the biological consequences of the drug and what a person has learned to expect (Keane, Lisman & Kreutzer, 1980; Marlatt & Rohsenow, 1980).

The expectations themselves depend on the operation of several pro-

that have summarized research on marijuana have reached remarkably similar conclusions (Commission of Inquiry into the Non-medical Use of Drugs, 1970, 1972, 1973; *Marijuana and Health,* 1980; National Academy of Sciences, 1982; National Commission on Marijuana and Drug Abuse, 1972; *Report of the British Advisory Committee on Drug Dependence,* 1968). They can be summarized as follows:

1. In and of itself, marijuana use does not cause aggressiveness, juvenile delinquency, or violent crime. Indeed, criminal behavior by marijuana users is more likely due to their abuse of alcohol, amphetamines, or opiates.

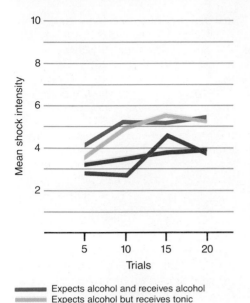

Figure A
The Role of Expectancy in Alcohol's Effects on Aggressiveness
In this experiment, aggression was measured by the intensity of shocks that subjects delivered to another person over several experimental trials. Shocks given by people who thought they had been drinking were significantly more intense, whether the subjects actually had alcohol or not, than those given by subjects who were sober or at least thought they were. Thus, aggression was influenced more by the subjects' expectancies than by alcohol itself.
(From "Effects of Alcohol on Aggression in Males," A. R. Lang, D. J. Goeckner, V. J. Adesso & G. A. Marlett, *Journal of Abnormal Psychology*, #84, pp. 508–516. Copyright 1975 by the American Psychological Association. Adapted by permission of the author.)

cesses. To form expectations about the effects of a drug (or anything else), a person must be able to *store* and later *recall* memories of how it feels to consume the drug and must have *learned* that doing so leads to the same effects. Above all, the person must be able to *think* about these memories and learnings in an integrated way. This integrated thinking usually involves elaborated versions of the schemes, or basic units of knowledge, discussed in the development chapter. These elaborations are clusters of knowledge; they allow people to form an image, mental model, or prediction relating to some aspect of the world—in this case, the consequences of drug use. We will see in Chapter 9 that predictions and other integrated thoughts often take the form of *propositions*, such as "I am now ingesting a drug and therefore will probably soon feel the same way I felt the last time I used it."

The link between expectations and the effects of drugs on consciousness illustrates the influence that higher mental processes can have on all aspects of behavior, including those supposedly controlled by chemicals.

2. Marijuana is the least potent of all psychoactive drugs. Moderate use presents few, if any, significant health hazards. However, like all psychoactive drugs, it easily reaches a developing fetus and thus should not be used by pregnant women.

3. Marijuana's interference with muscular coordination is a significant contributor to automobile accidents. People should not drive after using it.

4. Marijuana may have medical as well as recreational uses. Because it expands breathing passages, reduces the pressure of fluid within the eye, and inhibits nausea and epileptic seizures, it is sometimes helpful in

Marijuana is a popular, but illegal, psychoactive drug whose potential for harm is still a matter of uncertainty and debate.

treating asthma, glaucoma, epilepsy, and the nausea brought on by cancer chemotherapy.

5. Significant hazards may be associated with smoking large amounts of marijuana for long periods of time. These include (a) closing, rather than opening, of breathing passages, thus, like cigarette smoking, creating a risk of bronchitis and asthma; (b) suppression of the body's immune system, possibly leaving it unusually vulnerable to infection; (c) possible reductions in the male sex hormone testosterone and a corresponding reduction in sperm count; and (d) stress on the heart, especially in persons with cardiovascular problems.

So is marijuana a simple pleasure that should be legalized, or a menace to be stamped out? The evidence available so far tells a reasonably comforting story, but the dangers of marijuana, like the hazards of tobacco and alcohol, might take many years to detect. Perhaps it is best for now to echo Julien's (1981) reminder of what Saint Thomas Aquinas said five centuries ago: "Nothing is intrinsically good or evil, but its manner of usage may make it so."

FUTURE DIRECTIONS

The most influential psychological theories today view human behavior as guided by conscious and subconscious mental events and processes, not just by the external consequences of behavior. As a result, the study of consciousness now pervades most researchers' work and provides a kind of conceptual meeting place for ideas and findings from many areas of psychology. For example, both those studying decision making and those exploring brain activity realize that their research is related to consciousness. Recognizing this common ground, each group of researchers may become more aware of the importance of the other's work. The result may be research on the role of biological factors such as hemispheric laterality in determining the speed of decision making and studies of the EEGs that accompany efforts to make decisions.

This blending of different perspectives and methods is bound to create research aimed at broad questions about consciousness and the interaction of its component processes. In fact, this mutual intellectual stimulation has gone beyond the borders of psychology. Investigators from disciplines as diverse as biology, psychology, linguistics, electrical engineering, and computer science— all interested in the broad field called *cognitive science*—work together in special research settings and interdisciplinary programs to pursue the common goal of better understanding human consciousness.

Because consciousness is so central to psychology, the future of research on one is the future of research on the other. To cite just one example, a major aspect of the study of consciousness is sure to be how the two cerebral hemispheres work together as they perform various mental operations. Psychologists have already begun to understand some of the basic principles that determine hemispheric cooperation (Levy, 1985), and the next several years should see this basic understanding expand dramatically.

The same can be said of research in attention, perception, memory, and subconscious processes, as well as sleep, hypnosis, and other altered states of consciousness. As research continues, in psychology and elsewhere, on the mental experiences, processes, and functions associated with consciousness, there will be new discoveries, new theories, and new possibilities. Some already show promise for immediate and obvious benefits. For example, knowledge of the characteristic effects of particular drugs on brain wave patterns has led to the development of an EEG-like test known as ADMIT (Alcohol Drug Motorsensory Impairment Test); it may be capable of objectively measuring drug impaired behavior and determining what drug is involved (see Figure 6.12). Such a tool may improve emergency room treatment of unconscious overdose victims by telling physicians what substance caused the coma. It may also allow police to detect and remove from the highways motorists whose driving is impaired by any drug, not just alcohol.

Other, more controversial studies point to the possibility of undiscovered potential in the many states and levels of human consciousness. For example, the ability of peaceful mental images to block the perception of pain (Elton, Burrows & Stanley, 1980; Turk, 1978) has led to experiments in which cancer

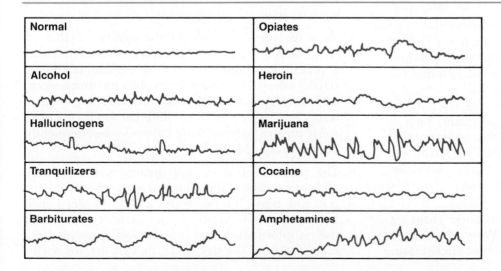

Normal	Opiates
Alcohol	Heroin
Hallucinogens	Marijuana
Tranquilizers	Cocaine
Barbiturates	Amphetamines

Figure 6.12
The Electronystagmograph
A test called ADMIT uses the electronystagmograph to measure the specific effects of drugs on EEG patterns. Here are brain waves of people who had used one of the psychoactive drugs discussed earlier in this chapter. Notice that the patterns not only differ markedly from those in a nondrug EEG, but each has its own individual characteristics. If ADMIT proves itself valid, these drug "fingerprints" on the EEG may help doctors determine, for example, what class of drugs an overdose victim has used. (Copyright © 1985 by The New York Times Company. Reprinted by permission.)

patients are encouraged to help cure themselves by vividly imagining radiation or chemotherapy breaking up their tumor and carrying it off. This imagery is sometimes associated with greater-than-expected improvement (Simonton & Simonton, 1975); no one knows why. Perhaps these patients would have improved anyway, but some interpret the data to mean that the conscious or subconscious mental processes that can alter blood pressure, heart rate, and muscle tension through biofeedback may be capable of fighting diseases as well. These are controversial, if not fanciful, ideas, and careful psychological research is needed to find out if any of them amount to more than wishful thinking or sensational speculation.

We have barely scratched the surface of the study of consciousness. For more detailed information and broader reading, consider taking courses in cognitive psychology, psychopharmacology, and sleep. Also look for courses that offer lectures and direct experience with meditation and hypnosis.

SUMMARY

1. Consciousness is an elusive concept whose definition includes not only awareness—of oneself, the world, and mental processes—but also a wide range of mental activities occurring outside of awareness.

2. Consciousness has been a major focus of research and theory in psychology since the field first took shape in the late 1800s. Early psychologists were interested in trying to understand the structure of consciousness: the basic sensations and other mental building blocks that create mental life. These structuralists were later overshadowed by functionalist researchers, who focused on how consciousness functioned to help people adapt to their environment. Later still, the functionalist view was superseded by behaviorists, who focused on studying only overt behavior. Today, the study of consciousness has made a stunning comeback. Instead of focusing just on observable behavior, psychological research now tends to focus on such cognitive activities as imagining, attending, thinking, deciding, and anticipating.

3. There are several levels of consciousness. That of which people are immediately aware is the conscious level. That which people happen to be ignoring but can easily become aware of (like the ticking of a clock) is said to be at the preconscious level. At the nonconscious level are all those processes, such as the activity of the liver or kidneys, that people cannot bring into awareness. The subconscious, or unconscious, level appears to contain thoughts, memories, and mental activities that go on without awareness, but that may nonetheless affect behavior.

4. The state of consciousness is constantly changing, like the varying flow of a stream. When the changes are particularly noticeable, we call them altered states of consciousness. Some of these altered states occur naturally, as in daydreaming or sleep; others are brought on by special means, such as hypnosis, meditation, or drugs.

5. Daydreaming is the altered state of consciousness closest to the waking state. When daydreaming, attention tends to shift from its normal focus on external stimuli to dwell more on internal events, including fantasy. Daydreaming may "take over" as a substitute when the outside world offers too little stimulation.

6. Sleep normally occurs each night as part of the body's natural circadian rhythm and is comprised of several stages, beginning with the lightest (stage 1 sleep) and progressing gradually to the deepest (stage 4 sleep). People progress up and down through these stages several times each night, gradually spending more time at the lighter stages, particularly in a special stage called rapid-eye-movement (REM) sleep. This is where most dreaming occurs.

7. Sleep disorders can disrupt the natural rhythm of sleep. Among the most common is insomnia, in which a person feels tired because of trouble falling or staying asleep. Hypersomnia involves too much sleep, and narcolepsy is sudden daytime sleeping. Nightmares and night terrors are different kinds of frightening dreams; sleepwalking happens most frequently during childhood.

8. The purpose of sleep and dreams is not entirely understood. Non-REM sleep may provide a time for rest and repair of the body, and REM sleep may function to let the brain "check its circuits," eliminate useless information, and "imprint" what people have learned during the day. Even though dreams them-

selves may be no more than the meaningless by-products of all this brain activity, the way people recall and organize them may still tell us something about their mental style and current concerns.

9. Hypnosis is a well-known, but still poorly understood phenomenon. Hypnotized people tend to focus all their attention on the hypnotist and then to passively follow his or her instructions and suggestions. They also become very good at fantasy or role taking, often acting as if unlikely or impossible events have taken place. Some people are excellent hypnotic subjects, whereas some cannot be hypnotized; most people fall somewhere in between.

10. Hypnotic phenomena have been explained in two main ways: as the result of playing a special social role that gives people permission to act in unusual ways, and as the result of entering a special state of consciousness. The debate over which of these views is more accurate continues, and some theorists have tried to combine aspects of both. For example, Hilgard's dissociation theory suggests that people sometimes allow normally well-integrated mental processes to become disorganized, or dissociated. Hilgard says that hypnotic subjects enter into an implicit social contract with the hypnotist, in which they agree to allow this dissociation and to share control over their mental processes. From this perspective, hypnosis does involve social role taking, but if enough dissociation takes place, there is an altered state of consciousness as well.

11. Meditation involves a number of mental techniques that bring about an altered state of consciousness characterized by feelings of inner peace and tranquility. Meditation has become popular as a means of promoting self-understanding and personal growth. The meditative state is normally reached either by paying attention as widely as possible to everything that is going on in the environment or by focusing attention very narrowly on a specific thought or object. Meditation usually requires a quiet place, a comfortable position, a device for organizing attention, and a passive attitude that allows a meditative state to occur. Proponents emphasize the numerous physical, psychological, and behavioral benefits of meditation, but exactly how it works is unclear.

12. Psychoactive drugs bring about a wide variety of changes in consciousness, from relaxation and drowsiness to confident optimism, wild excitement, or flights of bizarre fantasy. These drugs fall into several major categories, including depressants (such as alcohol, barbiturates, and tranquilizers), stimulants (such as amphetamines and cocaine), narcotics (such as opium, morphine, and heroin), and psychedelics (such as LSD, PCP, and marijuana).

KEY TERMS

Definitions of terms appear on the pages shown in parentheses.

active sleep (REM sleep) (215)
age regression (222)
alpha wave (214)
altered (alternate) state of consciousness (212)
behaviorism (206)
biofeedback (208)
circadian rhythm (216)
conscious level (208)
consciousness (204)
daydream (212)
delta wave (214)
depressant (229)
dissociation theory (225)
dream (219)
functionalism (206)
hypersomnia (217)
hypnosis (221)
insomnia (217)
level of consciousness (208)
lucid dreaming (219)
meditation (226)
narcolepsy (218)
narcotic (233)
nightmare (218)
night terrors (218)
nonconscious level (208)
posthypnotic amnesia (223)
posthypnotic suggestion (222)
preconscious level (208)
psychedelic (233)
psychoactive drug (228)
quiet sleep (214)
role theory (224)
sleepwalking (218)
state of consciousness (211)
state theory (224)
stimulant (232)
structuralism (204)
subconscious level (209)
susceptibility (223)
unconscious level (209)

RECOMMENDED READINGS

Cartwright, R. D. (1978). *A primer on sleep and dreaming.* Reading, Mass.: Addison-Wesley. A good basic introduction to the methods and results of sleep research.

Davis, M., Eshelman, E. R., & McKay, M. (1982). *The relaxation and stress reduction workbook.* Oakland, Calif.: New Harbinger Publications. A "workbook" containing clear and basic descriptions of progressive relaxation, meditation, self-hypnosis, and other antistress methods.

Evans, C. (1983). *Landscapes of the night: How and why we dream.* New York: Viking. A good overview of dream theories, past and present.

Hilgard, E. R. (1987). *History of psychology in America.* San Diego, Calif.: Harcourt, Brace, Jovanovich. A comprehensive view of the people, theories, methods, and issues prominent in American psychology over the last century. Hilgard, an expert on hypnosis, covers the scientific exploration of consciousness particularly well.

Julien, R. M. (1981). *A primer of drug action* (3rd ed.). San Francisco: W. H. Freeman. An excellent introductory volume that contains authoritative information about the background, mechanisms of action, and effects of a wide variety of psychoactive drugs.

Shapiro, D. H., & Walsh, R. N. (Eds.). (1984). *Meditation: Classic and contemporary perspectives.* New York: Aldine. A good collection of writings covering theories, research results, and applications of numerous meditative techniques.

Wallace, B., & Fisher, L. E. (1987). *Consciousness and behavior* (2nd ed.). Boston: Allyn & Bacon. A thorough overview of the psychology of consciousness, including all the topics covered in this chapter.

C harles Darwin's theory of evolution (1859) is based on the idea that many behavior patterns are not learned by each animal but instead develop slowly, through genetic inheritance, over millions of years. Survivors—those individuals in a species who most clearly display patterns of action and appearance that allow them to elude predators, withstand the elements, find food, and successfully mate—live to produce offspring with similar characteristics. Other, less adaptive attributes die out of the species along with the unfortunate creatures who carry them. This evolutionary principle of *natural selection,* or survival of the fittest among varying individuals, has maintained an endlessly diverse range of life forms on earth.

Examples of these genetically inherited, or *instinctual,* behavior patterns abound in the animal world. The size, shape, and location of birds' nests vary greatly from species to species. Different types of spiders spin webs with characteristic shapes, and different types of hummingbirds offer unique aerial displays to attract mates. Individual animals confirm the instinctual nature of these and many other complex, but highly predictable, behavior patterns by performing them successfully, often perfectly, the first time. Even when separated from their species at birth, many animals display behavior patterns characteristic of their kind without ever having seen them. Ethologists—scientists who study animal behavior in its natural habitat—refer to such instinctual behavior patterns as *species-specific.*

Scientists have also found environmental signals called *sign stimuli* that trigger automatic behavior patterns. For example, if a male stickleback fish swims too close to the nest of another male, he will be warned off and possibly attacked; the sign stimulus for the attack is a red area on the belly that males develop during mating season. Ethologist Niko Tinbergen (1953) demonstrated the power of this sign stimulus when male sticklebacks in his aquarium attacked model fish with a red spot painted on their bellies; they ignored models without the red spot.

Instinctual responses and rigidly stimulus-controlled behavior are adaptive under many circumstances, but they change only very slowly, from one generation to the next. This slow rate of species adaptation may not allow individual organisms to survive large and sudden environmental changes—a habitat-destroying volcanic eruption, for example—unless those individuals also have the capacity to rapidly adjust their behavior through *learning.* In humans, the organism whose behavior is the least controlled by instincts, the ability to learn has reached a remarkably high level. This ability and the principles underlying it are the topics of this chapter.

Psychologists have traditionally defined learning as any relatively permanent change in behavior that results from past experience. But because learned responses are not always performed, some psychologists now prefer to define **learning** as any relatively permanent change in the *organism* that results from past experience. Learning, for example, allows people to radically change their "nest-building" behavior, producing sprawling, airy ranch homes or peaked-roof bungalows, depending on whether they decide to live in Hawaii or Alaska.

7

Learning

LINKAGES
an overview

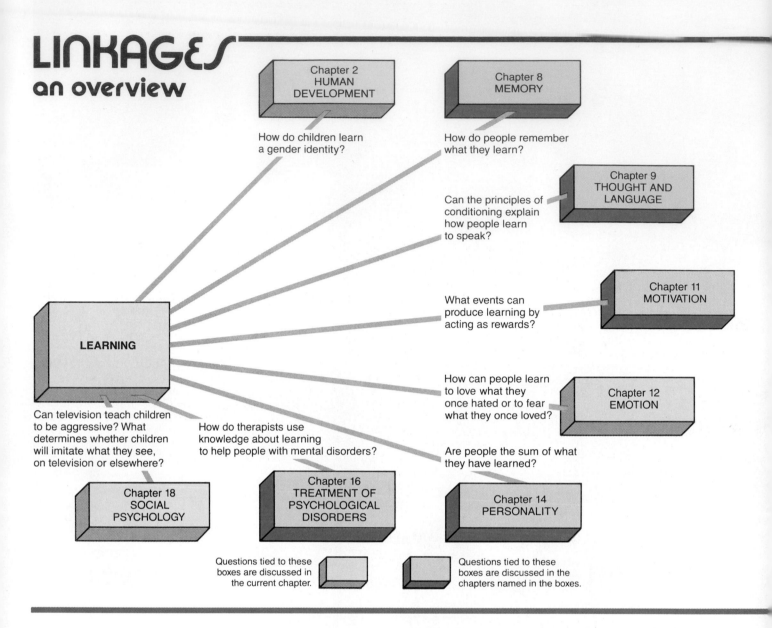

Chapter 2
HUMAN DEVELOPMENT

Chapter 8
MEMORY

Chapter 9
THOUGHT AND LANGUAGE

Chapter 11
MOTIVATION

Chapter 12
EMOTION

LEARNING

Chapter 18
SOCIAL PSYCHOLOGY

Chapter 16
TREATMENT OF PSYCHOLOGICAL DISORDERS

Chapter 14
PERSONALITY

How do children learn a gender identity?

How do people remember what they learn?

Can the principles of conditioning explain how people learn to speak?

What events can produce learning by acting as rewards?

How can people learn to love what they once hated or to fear what they once loved?

Can television teach children to be aggressive? What determines whether children will imitate what they see, on television or elsewhere?

How do therapists use knowledge about learning to help people with mental disorders?

Are people the sum of what they have learned?

Questions tied to these boxes are discussed in the current chapter.

Questions tied to these boxes are discussed in the chapters named in the boxes.

If you want to understand the importance of learning, ask someone who is fifty or sixty years older than you what the world was like when he or she was your age. The person will almost certainly tell you that family life, work, school, even cooking has changed dramatically and that they have learned to adapt to those changes. Indeed, learning is central to being human. The Linkages diagram shows just a few of the ways in which learning plays a role in other areas of psychology.

People learn primarily by identifying relationships between events and noting the regularity in the world around them. When two things occur together regularly, you can predict the occurrence of one from knowledge of the other. For example, people learn from personal experience that a clear blue sky means dry weather and that too little sleep makes them irritable. Relationships can also be learned from observing other people. Most people learn how to hail a cab, play chess, or smoke a cigarette primarily from watching others.

Which relationships do people identify, and how do they do it? What determines whether and how people learn? More experimental research has been conducted on the topic of learning than on any other topic in psychology.

LEARNING AND PSYCHOLOGY

Learning involves relatively permanent changes in any organism, changes that are due to experience rather than to, say, physical development or instincts. Because these changes can appear in so many areas of life—people must learn to read, talk, play games, work, and get along with others—the principles of learning are related to and important in understanding many areas of psychology.

Most of the research described in this chapter has to do with the learning of relatively simple responses. This is so because experimenters often prefer to work in a laboratory, where responses can be precisely measured and where the influences on those responses can

be identified and controlled far more than in the natural environment. However, more general and more complex patterns of responses are also acquired and modified on the basis of the learning principles discussed in this chapter.

Edith N is one example. She visited a psychotherapist when she was sixty-four years old because of a strong, irrational fear of thunderstorms. Her problem had begun when she was about five years old and had caused her embarrassment and suffering ever since. After hearing a stormy forecast or seeing ominous clouds, her palms would sweat, her heart palpitated, and she would run indoors. Edith's therapist carefully explored her problem and her background.

It turned out that, when she was small, her parents had constantly warned of the dangers of lightning and had refused to go outside when a thunderstorm was predicted. This, the psychologist suggested, created a link in Edith's mind between the sights and sounds of thunderstorms and the possibility of death. Her fear, in other words, had been learned.

Many psychologists depend on basic research on the principles of learning to help them understand and treat problems like Edith's. In this chapter, we describe these principles and point out some of the other ways in which they relate to the understanding and beneficial alteration of human and animal behavior.

Much of this work was guided by the behaviorist approach to psychology introduced in Chapter 1. It was inspired by the hope that all behavior could be explained by a few basic principles of learning and by the idea that all learning amounted to the automatic formation of associations. As research has accumulated, the concept of learning has become more complicated. But, to begin, we will consider two models of how associations can be learned; these models are called classical and instrumental conditioning.

CLASSICAL CONDITIONING

At the opening bars of the national anthem, a young ballplayer's heart may begin pounding; those sounds tell him that the game is about to begin. A small flashing light on a control panel may make an airplane pilot's adrenaline flow, because it means that something has gone seriously wrong. These people were not born with these reactions; they learned them from associations between stimuli. The experimental study of this kind of learning was begun early in this century, almost by accident, by Ivan Petrovich Pavlov.

Pavlov's Discovery

Pavlov is one of the best-known figures in psychology, but he was not a psychologist. A Russian physiologist, Pavlov won a Nobel Prize in 1904 for his work on the physiology of dogs' digestive systems. During his research, Pavlov noticed a strange phenomenon: his dogs sometimes salivated when no food was present—for example, when they saw the assistant who normally brought their food. Pavlov reasoned that some mechanism in the brain must be the cause of this "psychic secretion," and he devoted the rest of his life to research aimed at understanding that mechanism.

The initial experiment   Pavlov devised a very simple experiment to determine how salivation could occur in the absence of an obvious physical cause. First he performed an operation to divert a dog's saliva into a container, so that the amount secreted could be measured precisely. He then confined the dog in the apparatus shown in Figure 7.1. The experiment itself had three phases.

In the first phase, Pavlov confirmed that, when meat powder was placed on the dog's tongue, the dog salivated, but that it did not salivate in response to the sound of a buzzer. Thus Pavlov established the existence of the two basic components for his experiment: a natural reflex (the dog's salivation when food was placed on its tongue) and a neutral stimulus (the sound of the buzzer). Recall that a *reflex* is an automatic reaction to a stimulus, such as shivering in the cold or jumping when you are jabbed with a needle. A *neutral stimulus* is one that initially does not elicit the reflex being studied. However, when it is first presented, a neutral stimulus may elicit a response called an *orienting reflex*. For example, when the buzzer was first sounded in Pavlov's experiment, the dog did not salivate; but it did pick up its ears, turn toward the sound, and sniff around.

In the second phase of the experiment, Pavlov sounded the buzzer and then quickly placed meat powder in the dog's mouth. The dog then salivated. This *pairing* sequence—the buzzer followed immediately by meat powder—was repeated several times. In the final phase of the experiment, the buzzer

Figure 7.1
Apparatus Used in Pavlov's Experiments
Dogs were surgically prepared and then restrained in the harness. Saliva flowed into a tube inserted in the dog's cheek. The amount of saliva secreted was then recorded by a pen attached to a slowly moving drum of paper.

Pen recording on cylinder

Phase I: Before conditioning has occurred

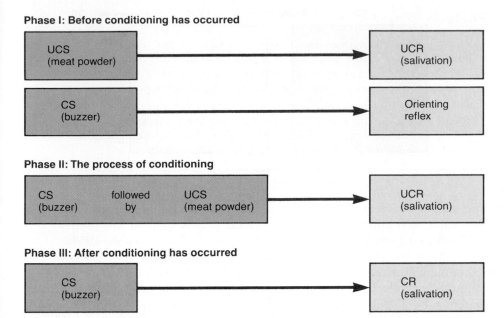

| UCS (meat powder) | → | UCR (salivation) |

| CS (buzzer) | → | Orienting reflex |

Phase II: The process of conditioning

| CS (buzzer)   followed by   UCS (meat powder) | → | UCR (salivation) |

Phase III: After conditioning has occurred

| CS (buzzer) | → | CR (salivation) |

Figure 7.2
Classical Conditioning
Before classical conditioning has occurred, meat powder on a dog's tongue produces salivation, but the sound of a buzzer does not. During the process of conditioning, the buzzer is paired on numerous trials with the meat powder. After classical conditioning has taken place, the sound of the buzzer alone produces a salivation response.

was sounded, and the dog salivated, even though no meat powder was presented. In other words, the buzzer by itself now elicited salivation.

The elements of classical conditioning Pavlov's experiment was the first demonstration of what today is called **classical conditioning**—a procedure in which a neutral stimulus is paired with a stimulus that elicits a reflex or other response until the neutral stimulus alone comes to elicit a similar response. Figure 7.2 shows the basic elements of classical conditioning. The stimulus that elicits a response without conditioning, like the meat powder in Pavlov's experiment, is called the **unconditioned stimulus,** or **UCS.** The automatic, or unlearned, reaction to this stimulus is called the **unconditioned response,** or **UCR.** The neutral stimulus that is paired with the unconditioned stimulus is called the **conditioned stimulus (CS),** and the response it comes to elicit is called a **conditioned response (CR).**

We described one example of classical conditioning in the chapter on human development. When John Watson paired a loud noise with a rat, so that Little Albert came to fear furry animals, he was using classical conditioning to create a new response—fear—to the previously neutral animal.

Establishing a Conditioned Response

The process through which a conditioned stimulus begins to produce a conditioned response is called **acquisition.** Some conditioned responses are easier to acquire than others, and responses can vary in strength. For example, a toddler might develop a conditioned fear response to the sight of doctors (CS), if doctors have been consistently paired with the pain of an injection (UCS). The child's conditioned response to doctors might range from mild agitation to intense fear. How easily a conditioned response is acquired and how strong it is depend on both what the conditioned and unconditioned stimuli are and how they are paired.

The intensity and relevance of stimuli As the intensity of the unconditioned stimulus increases, so does the strength of the conditioned response and the

Associating the sight of a small animal with a sudden noise or other unpleasant stimulus can create a classically conditioned fear of that animal. But pairing unfamiliar animals or other novel stimuli with pleasant experiences can, as this youngster has found, also help create a liking for them.

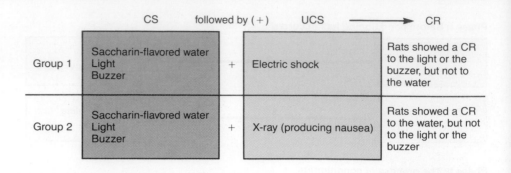

	CS	followed by (+)	UCS	→	CR
Group 1	Saccharin-flavored water Light Buzzer	+	Electric shock		Rats showed a CR to the light or the buzzer, but not to the water
Group 2	Saccharin-flavored water Light Buzzer	+	X-ray (producing nausea)		Rats showed a CR to the water, but not to the light or the buzzer

Figure 7.3
Selective Classical Conditioning
Electric-shock aversion was more easily conditioned to a light or sound than to the taste of water. However, radiation-caused nausea was more easily conditioned to the taste of flavored water than to either a light or a buzzer.

speed with which it appears. For example, in a case like Pavlov's study of salivation, conditioning is faster if several pellets of food are used as the unconditioned stimulus than if only one is used (Wagner et al., 1964).

Some CS-UCS associations are formed especially easily. Consider the experiment illustrated in Figure 7.3 (Garcia & Koelling, 1966). The conditioned stimulus actually consisted of three stimuli: the taste of saccharin-flavored water, a light, and a loud buzzer. For one group of rats, this three-part conditioned stimulus was paired with electric shock (UCS). These rats showed an aversion (CR) to either the light *or* the buzzer, but not to the water. For another group, however, the unconditioned stimulus was mild radiation that produced nausea. These rats later showed a strong aversion to the saccharin-flavored water, but no response at all to the light or the sound of the buzzer.

These results suggest that responses may not become conditioned to just *any* neutral stimulus. In fact, organisms may be biologically "prepared" to learn some associations more readily than others. People, for example, are much more likely to develop a conditioned fear of, say, rats or snakes than doorknobs or stereos. Similarly, in the natural environment, nausea is more likely to be produced by something that is eaten or drunk than by an external stimulus like noise. Perhaps for this reason, nausea is more likely to become a conditioned response to an internal stimulus, such as a saccharin flavor, than to an external stimulus, such as a sound. This experiment and others like it suggest that animals are particularly prone to learn the type of associations that are most common in, or relevant to, their environment (Best, Best & Henggeler, 1977; Rozin & Kalat, 1971).

The pairing of stimuli The strength of the conditioned response also tends to increase as the number of CS-UCS pairings increases. However, this is true only up to a point. After a critical number of pairings, the strength of the conditioned response stays about the same.

The arrangement of these pairings need not precisely duplicate the sequence of Pavlov's original experiment in order to produce conditioning; the stimuli may be paired in several ways, as Figure 7.4 illustrates. In *simultaneous conditioning,* the conditioned and the unconditioned stimulus are presented and terminated at the same time. In *trace conditioning,* the conditioned stimulus begins and ends before the unconditioned stimulus is presented. You might turn on a buzzer for two seconds, let a few seconds pass, and then deliver a shock. In *backward conditioning,* the conditioned stimulus is presented after the unconditioned stimulus is terminated.

The most effective method of producing a strong conditioned response is to present the conditioned stimulus, leave it on while presenting the unconditioned stimulus, and then terminate both at the same time. This arrangement is called **delayed conditioning.** For example, for efficient conditioning of fear (CR) to the sound of a buzzer (CS), the buzzer should be sounded for a

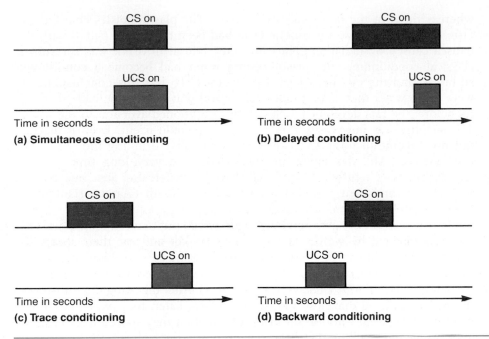

Figure 7.4
Stimulus Onset and Offset in Various Types of Classical Conditioning
(a) In simultaneous conditioning, the CS and the UCS come on and go off at the same time. (b) In delayed conditioning, the CS comes on before the UCS, but both go off at the same time. (c) In trace conditioning, the CS comes on and goes off before the UCS comes on. (d) In backward conditioning, the UCS comes on first and, just as it is terminated, the CS comes on.

total of, say, four seconds. Two seconds after the buzzer is turned on, shock (UCS) would begin and continue for two seconds; then both the buzzer and the shock should be turned off at the same time.

Whichever sequence is used, the time between the stimuli may be critical. The optimal interval between the onset of the conditioned stimulus and the onset of the unconditioned stimulus is very short, typically between one-half and one second (Ross & Ross, 1971). As this interval increases, the conditioned response usually weakens. In general, a conditioned response will not develop if the delay between the conditioned and the unconditioned stimulus is more than several seconds. But this rule does not apply in one case: the learning of aversions to certain tastes.

HIGHLIGHT

The Special Case of Taste-Aversion Learning

In a strange twist of history, the study of taste aversion began with the advent of the atomic bomb. Once the bomb had become a reality, scientists in many disciplines began trying to understand the effects of prolonged exposure to radiation. Psychologist John Garcia was one of them. While investigating the effects of radiation, he discovered a phenomenon that led directly to the study of taste-aversion learning.

In one of Garcia's studies, rats were exposed to radiation once a week for about eight hours (Garcia et al., 1956). The radiation caused nausea in the rats. As the weeks passed, the rats drank almost no water inside the radiation chamber, but they drank their normal amount as soon as they were returned to their home cage. Why? The most obvious hypothesis was that something about the radiation was leading the rats to drink less. To test this idea, the animals were placed inside the radiation chamber, but no radiation was administered. They still refused to drink.

The researchers began to understand the cause of the rats' behavior when they noticed that the water bottles in the radiation chamber were plastic, whereas those in the home cage were glass. The plastic bottles changed the taste of the water, and this unique taste had been repeatedly paired with the nausea caused by radiation. Thus, the rats' refusal to drink was a result of classical conditioning: the plastic-tasting water had become a conditioned stimulus, and the rats had learned to avoid it. To test this conclusion, rats were given water that had a unique flavor and that eventually made them ill. As before, the rats developed a classically conditioned aversion to the water. The surprise was how easily this conditioning could occur. Even if the rats did not become ill until seven or eight hours after drinking the water, the taste aversion still developed and persisted for a very long time. In one experiment, rats refused to drink salt-flavored water after just one pairing with illness, and their aversion persisted for a month (Garcia, Hankins & Rusiniak, 1974).

The power of taste-aversion learning has been put to work to help western ranchers plagued by wolves and coyotes that kill and eat their sheep. To alleviate this problem without killing the wolves and coyotes, chopped mutton laced with a small dose of lithium chloride was given to wolves (Garcia, Rusiniak & Brett, 1977; Gustavson et al., 1974). After digesting this substance, the wolves suffered dizziness and severe nausea. Later, they were placed in a pen with live sheep (mutton on the hoof). At first they started to attack, but after biting and smelling the sheep several times, the wolves withdrew. Later, the doors of the pen were opened, and a dramatic role reversal occurred: the wolves were literally chased away by the sheep! Now ranchers often lace a carcass with enough lithium chloride to make wolves and coyotes ill and prevent them from killing sheep.

People, too, develop classically conditioned taste aversions, as Ilene Bernstein (1978) demonstrated. She gave one group of cancer patients a unique flavor of ice cream, Mapletoff, one hour before they received chemotherapy, which produces nausea as a side effect. A second group was given the same ice cream on days they did not receive chemotherapy. A third group was not given any ice cream. Approximately five months later, all three groups were asked to taste several flavors of ice cream and select their favorite. Two groups chose the Mapletoff: those who had not previously tasted it and those who had eaten it when they did not receive chemotherapy. In contrast, those who had eaten Mapletoff before receiving chemotherapy found the flavor very distasteful. Similarly, people who experience food poisoning may never again eat the type of food that made them so ill—even though they may not feel the effects of the poisoning until hours after eating the food. ■

Predictive value   No one knows for sure why taste aversion can be conditioned when there is a very long delay between the conditioned and the unconditioned stimulus. One hypothesis is that taste aversion represents a qualitatively different, "prepared" type of learning (Seligman, 1970). Another hypothesis is that the time interval between the conditioned and unconditioned stimulus is not as critical as the **predictive value** of the conditioned stimulus; that is, its ability to predict or signal the unconditioned stimulus.

The predictive value of a conditioned stimulus is closely related to the regularity of its association with a particular unconditioned stimulus. In the Garcia study *every time* the rats drank the water, they became ill; in the Bernstein study the *only* time the cancer patients ate the ice cream, they became ill. Thus, taste-aversion learning in these experiments may have occurred despite long delays between the unconditioned and the conditioned. stimulus, because the conditioned stimulus was an extremely powerful predictor of the unconditioned stimulus (Revusky, 1971, 1977). To investigate the effect of predictive value on conditioning, Robert Rescorla (1968) gave

	Phase 1	Phase 2	Test phase	Result
Group 1	(no treatment)	CS = light and noise UCS = shock	light ⟶ CR? noise ⟶ CR?	Yes Yes
Group 2	CS = noise UCS = shock	CS = light and noise UCS = shock	noise ⟶ CR? light ⟶ CR?	Yes No

Figure 7.5
Blocking
One group of rats learned a fear response to both light and noise; they later showed a conditioned fear response to either the light or the noise. A second group of rats first learned a fear response to noise; then the light was included as an additional CS. Even though the light was repeatedly paired with shock, these rats later showed no fear response to the light. The training with one CS apparently prevented, or blocked, the rats from learning another CS that was subsequently added.

several groups of rats the same *number* of pairings of a buzzer with electric shocks, but some of the rats were also given shocks when they did *not* hear the buzzer. For that group, the conditioned stimulus did not have high predictive value, and compared with the other rats, these animals developed much weaker conditioned responses to the buzzer. Even though the number of CS-UCS pairings was identical, the strength of the conditioned response dropped as predictive value decreased.

But there is still another possibility to consider: even if a conditioned stimulus occurs every time an unconditioned stimulus occurs, it may not be a very *useful* predictor of an unconditioned stimulus. Suppose, for example, that a conditioned stimulus always occurs along with an unconditioned stimulus, but that, after some period of time, so does another conditioned stimulus. Will the new conditioned stimulus come to elicit a conditioned response?

In an experiment by Leon Kamin (1969), the answer was no. He used the procedure illustrated in Figure 7.5. You would be in much the same situation as his rats if, after you learned that the sight of your Aunt Mabel predicted long, boring conversations, she later developed the habit of whistling the theme from *Star Wars*. It is unlikely that you would come to associate that music with boredom. Usually, once a conditioned stimulus is linked to an unconditioned stimulus, pairing a second conditioned stimulus with that unconditioned stimulus will not create a conditioned response to the new conditioned stimulus; additional learning under these conditions seems to be **blocked.**

What Is Learned in Classical Conditioning?

Pavlov believed that, during classical conditioning, the conditioned and unconditioned stimuli are associated because of their *contiguity,* or close proximity in time and space. Early researchers also thought that just about any association could be created through classical conditioning. We have seen that this is an oversimplified picture of classical conditioning. Kamin's study and research on taste-aversion learning indicate that stimulus contiguity is not necessary or sufficient to produce classical conditioning. What is learned in classical conditioning seems to be whether the unconditioned stimulus can be predicted by the conditioned stimulus (Dickinson & Mackintosh, 1978; Rescorla, 1978). Furthermore, Garcia's work has shown that classically

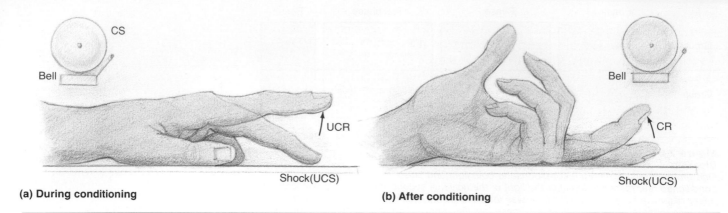

(a) During conditioning   (b) After conditioning

Figure 7.6
The Conditioned Response
Delos Wickens was one of the first to dem-
onstrate that the CR and UCR are not nec-
essarily identical. In his experiment, sub-
jects were conditioned (a) to remove a
finger from an electrode at the sound of a
bell. When the shock and the bell were
paired during conditioning, the subject
moved the finger away from the palm; this
was the UCR. (b) After conditioning, the
subject's hand was placed so that removing
the finger required moving it toward the
palm; this was the CR. The effect was the
same (the subject escaped or avoided
shock), but the CR and UCR involved differ-
ent muscles (Wickens, 1938).

conditioned responses are much more likely to form when certain types of conditioned and unconditioned stimuli (such as taste and nausea or light and shock) are paired.

There is yet another way in which Pavlov's view of classical conditioning has been revised. He thought that, through conditioning, the conditioned stimulus comes to substitute for the unconditioned stimulus. If this were so, the conditioned response ought to be identical to the unconditioned response. In fact, the two responses are often not the same, as Figure 7.6 illustrates. They can, in fact, be dramatically different.

In some cases, the conditioned and unconditioned responses may even be opposite physiological reactions. For example, when a person is given insulin (UCS), the typical reaction is lowered blood sugar (UCR). If a buzzer is sounded immediately before the injections, classical conditioning will occur. The buzzer becomes a conditioned stimulus, but the conditioned response elicited by the sound of the buzzer is an *increase* in blood sugar—the opposite of the unconditioned response (Flaherty et al., 1980). The buzzer seems to act as a signal to the body to prepare for the insulin, and the body begins to produce more blood sugar to counteract the drop in blood sugar that insulin has produced in the past. Obviously, classical conditioning involves learning, but it does not merely promote the substitution of the conditioned stimulus for the unconditioned stimulus or the conditioned response for the unconditioned response.

HIGHLIGHT

The Conditioned Response and Drug Abuse

The relationship between the conditioned and the unconditioned response may help explain what happens in drug addiction and some drug overdoses. If a person uses an addictive drug repeatedly, he or she will need increasingly larger doses of the drug to produce the same effect. For example, people use morphine to reduce pain, but over time, larger and larger doses of morphine may be required to maintain its painkilling effect. Why?

Classical conditioning may provide at least part of the answer (Baker & Tiffany, 1985). The features of the room in which the injection is usually given, the sight of the needle, or other environmental stimuli may become conditioned stimuli that elicit a conditioned response. But just like the conditioned response to insulin, this response is the *opposite* of the unconditioned response; thus, the conditioned stimulus elicits an *increase* in pain (Siegel & Ellsworth, 1986). Thus, as the conditioned responses are developed, larger and larger doses are needed to reduce pain. An experienced drug user is likely to develop other conditioned responses to environmental cues as well. For example, before a heroin addict "shoots up," his or her breathing rate may increase in anticipation of the drug's tendency to depress breathing.

Such conditioning may make experienced drug users especially vulnerable to accidental overdoses. Each year, about 1 percent of all heroin addicts die from overdoses (Maurer & Vogel, 1973). A strange aspect of these deaths is the fact that the fatal dosage is often no greater than that tolerated many times in the past (Reed, 1980). How can this be? To find out, Siegel (1984) interviewed heroin addicts who had received emergency treatment for overdoses. He found that 70 percent of them had *not* taken an unusually large dose, but they *had* injected themselves in unfamiliar surroundings when the overdose occurred. In other words, they had injected themselves in surroundings that did not provide the conditioned stimuli that had come to elicit conditioned responses opposite to those produced by the drug. As a result, they were not physiologically "ready" for the drug, and it had stronger effects than usual, becoming in some cases a fatal overdose. ■

Conditioned Responses over Time

Developing a classically conditioned response is usually functional; that is, it has some adaptive value. The rat that learns to avoid salt-flavored water after becoming violently ill, for example, is adapting to its environment. But environmental conditions change, and it is important to learn to react differently when they do. In this section, we look at how conditioned responses change over time.

Stimulus generalization and discrimination   Once a conditioned response develops, stimuli that are similar but not identical to the conditioned stimulus will also elicit it. This phenomenon is called **stimulus generalization.** Usually the greater the similarity between a new stimulus and the conditioned stimulus, the stronger the conditioned response will be. Figure 7.7 shows an example. Stimulus generalization has obvious advantages. It would be adaptive, for example, for a person who became sick after drinking sour-smelling milk to avoid other dairy products that give off an odor resembling, though not necessarily identical to, that originally associated with illness. However, generalization would be dangerous if it had no limits. Most people would be frightened to see a real lion in their home, but imagine the inconvenience if you became fearful every time you saw a cat or a picture of a lion.

Stimulus generalization does not run amok like this, because it is balanced by a complementary process called **stimulus discrimination.** Through stimulus discrimination, people learn to differentiate among similar stimuli. An infant's crying commonly becomes a conditioned stimulus for its mother, whose conditioned response might include waking out of a deep sleep at the baby's slightest fussing. Yet the same mother might sleep soundly while someone else's baby cries.

Extinction   In general, a conditioned stimulus continues to elicit the conditioned response only if the unconditioned stimulus continues to appear, at least periodically. For example, dogs in one experiment were conditioned to salivate at the sound of a bell (Pavlov, 1927). Then the bell was repeatedly sounded, but no meat powder was presented. As the conditioned stimulus was presented repeatedly *without* the unconditioned stimulus, the strength of the conditioned response began to decrease. As Figure 7.8 shows, salivation was almost completely eliminated by the sixth trial. This gradual disappearance of a conditioned response by eliminating the association between conditioned and unconditioned stimuli is called **extinction.**

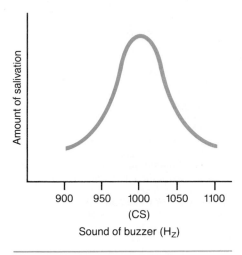

Figure 7.7
Stimulus Generalization
The strength of a response is greatest when a new stimulus closely resembles the CS. Here, the CS is the sound of a buzzer at 1,000 hertz, and the CR is salivation. As the new stimulus becomes less similar to the CS, or farther away from 1,000 hertz, the strength of the CR—in this case, amount of salivation—is reduced.

Figure 7.8
Extinction
Pavlov found that the amount of saliva secreted in response to a buzzer decreased steadily as the number of unreinforced trials increased. Eventually the dog no longer showed a CR to the buzzer at all. Extinction had taken place.

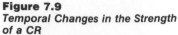

Figure 7.9
Temporal Changes in the Strength of a CR
The strength of the CR increases during conditioning trials. During extinction, the strength of the CR is reduced as more trials occur in which the CS is presented without the UCS; eventually the CR disappears completely. However, after a brief delay, the CR reappears. In general, the longer the delay before the new presentation of the CS, the more pronounced spontaneous recovery is (that is, the stronger the CR is).

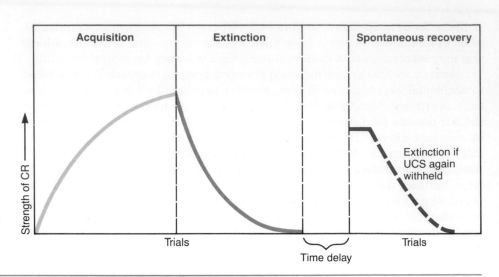

Extinction does not simply erase learning, however. If the conditioned stimulus and the unconditioned stimulus are again paired after the conditioned response has been extinguished, the conditioned response returns to its original strength very quickly, often after only one or two trials. This quick relearning of a conditioned response after extinction is called **reconditioning.** Because reconditioning takes much less time than the original conditioning, we know that some change in the organism persists even after extinction.

Additional evidence for this conclusion comes from the phenomenon illustrated in Figure 7.9. Suppose that, after extinction, the conditioned stimulus does not appear for a while and then again recurs without the unconditioned stimulus. What will happen? As Figure 7.9 shows, the conditioned response will temporarily reappear under these conditions. This reappearance of the conditioned response after extinction (and without further CS-UCS pairings) is called **spontaneous recovery.** In general, the longer the time between extinction and the reappearance of the conditioned stimulus, the stronger the recovered conditioned response. However, unless the unconditioned stimulus is again paired with the conditioned stimulus, extinction rapidly occurs again.

Classical Conditioning of Human Behavior

Several decades ago, Watson and other behaviorists believed that all behavior could be explained by the principles of classical conditioning. Their faith was misplaced, but these principles do operate in many domains of both human and animal behavior. Classical conditioning of emotional reactions has received the most study, because these quick physiological reactions are the easiest unconditioned responses to analyze. The following are just a few applications of classical conditioning to emotions and to physical and mental health.

Phobias and anxiety **Phobias** are strong fears of objects or situations that are either not objectively dangerous—public speaking, for example—or are less dangerous than the phobic person's anxiety reaction would suggest. Many situation-specific fears are the result of classical conditioning (Kalish, 1981). For example, the childhood experience of being frightened by a large dog can produce a dog phobia that is so intense and generalized that a person might refuse to go near *any* dog. Being in a truly dangerous or traumatic situation can also result in classical conditioning of very long-lasting fears. In one study, military veterans showed elevated galvanic skin responses (GSRs) to simulated battle sounds fifteen years after combat (Edwards & Acker, 1972).

Can classical conditioning also produce a general state of anxiety or more severe psychological disorders? Pavlov thought so. He studied the development of such disturbances in animals, hoping that the results might apply to fear-related disorders in human beings. In one famous discrimination experiment, he taught a dog to salivate in response to a circle but not in response to an ellipse. Then he put the dog through a long series of trials in which the ellipse was changed to look more and more like a circle. As the discrimination became more and more difficult, the dog did not know how to respond. The animal began to make mistakes; its behavior became very erratic and unpredictable; it began to bark and snarl; and it tried to escape. Pavlov called the dog's behavior an *experimental neurosis*. In general, such "neuroses" seem to result whenever an animal is placed in conflict. If animals are exposed to such conflicts long enough, their life expectancy is greatly reduced (Liddell, 1950).

Are there human parallels to these neurotic animals? Possibly; as described in Chapter 13, on stress, continued work at difficult tasks, internal conflicts, and an inability to control the environment appear to have potentially harmful, even life-threatening, consequences for human beings' health.

Hypertension Even when conflicts do not produce anxiety comparable to the experimental neuroses created by Pavlov, they are a source of stress that can create physical problems, such as hypertension (high blood pressure in particular). Chronic, or continued, hypertension has been called the "silent killer," because people are often unaware that they suffer from it until they experience a stroke or heart attack.

Classical conditioning may play a role in hypertension. Research indicates that high blood pressure is easily conditioned to stressful events, such as an electric shock. If an environmental cue is present each time the shock is received, a person's blood pressure will increase in response to that cue even if the shock is eliminated. Similarly, a person who experiences many stressful events at home or at work may show an increase in blood pressure simply by walking into that environment. Other symptoms of continued stress may include headaches, ulcers, skin rashes, and so on.

Promoting health and treating illness Fortunately, the stress, anxiety, fears, and other difficulties sometimes created or intensified by classical conditioning can also be relieved by the procedures of classical conditioning.

Joseph Wolpe (1958) pioneered the development of these procedures. Using techniques he had found successful in treating experimental neuroses in laboratory animals, Wolpe showed that irrational fears could be relieved by *systematic desensitization,* a treatment procedure that associates a feared stimulus with a new response, such as relaxation. For Edith N, the woman with a thunderstorm phobia, who is described in this chapter's Linkages diagram, desensitization took thirteen treatment sessions. Her therapist first helped Edith learn to relax deeply and then to associate that relaxation with gradually more intense sights and sounds of thunderstorms (presented on videotape). In the end, Edith could calmly go on with her life indoors even when a thunderstorm raged outdoors. Desensitization is discussed in more detail in Chapter 16, on therapy.

Researchers are constantly looking for new medical applications of classical conditioning. Its principles are now being used to ease patients' reactions to hay fever and other allergies (Russell et al., 1984; Sampson & Jolie, 1984). Of course, there are drugs that control allergic reactions, but the drugs usually

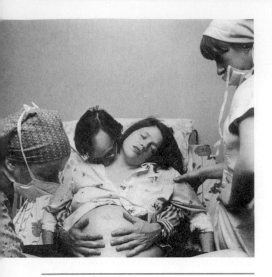

Classical conditioning is a key to the Lamaze childbirth procedure. At sessions held during pregnancy, the expectant mother relaxes and breathes slowly and deeply while her partner holds her and speaks to her. During the actual delivery, the partner holds the woman in the same way and utters the same phrases; these have become conditioned stimuli, and they elicit the same slow, deep pattern of breathing. This procedure has been very successful in helping some women give birth drug free and with a minimum of pain.

have such unwanted side effects as severe drowsiness. By pairing a drug with a unique stimulus, such as a strange odor, researchers have tried to teach people a conditioned response that will, by itself, alleviate the allergic reaction. The results of this line of research are still only preliminary, but they suggest that, after a series of such trials, a response that reduces allergy symptoms can be conditioned.

INSTRUMENTAL CONDITIONING

Much of what people learn cannot be described as classical conditioning. In classical conditioning, conditioned and unconditioned stimuli are paired, and an association occurs between them such that a previously neutral conditioned stimulus now elicits a conditioned response. Notice that both stimuli occur prior to or along with the conditioned response. But people can also learn associations between responses and the stimuli that *follow* them—in other words, between behavior and its consequences. A child learns to say "please" in order to get a piece of candy; a headache sufferer learns to take a pill in order to escape pain; a dog learns to shake hands in order to get a treat. All of these responses are *instrumental* in obtaining something rewarding for the person or animal. **Instrumental conditioning** is a procedure in which responses are learned that help produce some rewarding or desired effect.

From the Puzzle Box to the Skinner Box

At just about the time that Pavlov was conducting his experiments in Russia, American psychologist Edward L. Thorndike was discovering the principles of instrumental learning. To study whether animals can "think" and reason, Thorndike devised an elaborate cage called a *puzzle box* (see Figure 7.10). An animal, usually a hungry cat, was placed in the puzzle box and had to learn some response—say, stepping on a small lever—in order to unlock the door

Figure 7.10
Thorndike's Puzzle Box
A sample "puzzle box," as used in Thorndike's research. Because a rope is connected to both the door latch and the pedal, a cat can open the door by pressing down on the lever.

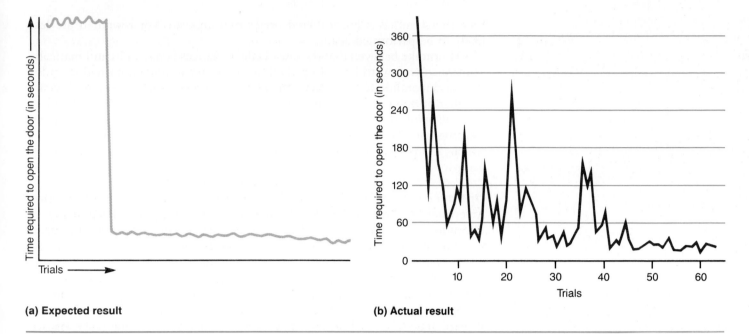

(a) Expected result

(b) Actual result

Figure 7.11
Learning in a Puzzle Box
*Did Thorndike's cats come to "understand"
the puzzle box? If they did, the time required to open the door should have decreased sharply at some point, as shown in
(a). However, the actual results (b) showed
a very gradual decrease in the time required to open the door.*

and get out. When the cat succeeded, it was rewarded with food and then
placed back inside the box. After several trials, the cat walked calmly over
to the lever, pushed it down with its paw, strolled through the opened door,
and ate.

It is clear that cats in this situation learned something, because, over the
course of the trials, it took them less time to get out of the cage. But did they
really understand the task? Thorndike found that, during the first few trials,
cats took a long time to discover the secret of opening the door. Then, he
thought, at some point a cat would suddenly understand, or gain **insight**
about, what was necessary and perform the response very quickly. In fact,
however, as Figure 7.11 shows, Thorndike (1898) found no such quick
change. Instead, the amount of time a cat took to open the door declined very
gradually over the trials; in some cases, a cat actually took longer on one trial
than it did on the previous trial. In other words, there was no evidence that
the cats suddenly understood the task.

The law of effect   What, then, were Thorndike's cats learning? On the first
few trials, the cats performed a great many responses, almost at random. They
might run back and forth, scratch at the bars, meow, rub their faces, and so
on. Eventually, they stepped on the lever, and the door opened. Thorndike
argued that stimulus-response bonds were formed between the stimuli of the
cage and all of these responses. However, any response (for example, scratching
the bars) that did not produce a rewarding effect (opening the door) became
weaker over time, and any response that did have the rewarding effect became
stronger over time, so that eventually the cat required less time to open the
door.

What was happening, said Thorndike, was analogous to Darwin's law of
natural selection. Much as Darwin found that, over generations, those
characteristics of species that best fit the environment ultimately survive, so
too it appeared that those responses of individuals that best fit the environment
survive. Learning, said Thorndike, is governed by the **law of effect**. According
to this law, if a response made in the presence of a particular stimulus is
followed by a reward, that same response is more likely to be made the next

time the stimulus is encountered. Responses that are not rewarded are less likely to be performed again.

Thorndike believed that the law of effect changes behavior as automatically as plants turn toward light. Like the links between an unconditioned stimulus and an unconditioned response, the effect of a reward on a response occurs whether or not a person or an animal understands the relationship. The mere *association* of stimuli, responses, and effects, Thorndike argued, produces learning. He also believed that, even though people may reason in ways in which animals do not, the law of effect still applies to much of human behavior.

Operant conditioning   Decades after Thorndike published his work, another American psychologist, B. F. Skinner, extended and formalized many of Thorndike's ideas. Skinner emphasized that, during instrumental conditioning, an organism learns a response by *operating on* the environment. Therefore, he called the process of learning these responses **operant conditioning,** a synonym for instrumental conditioning. Skinner's primary aim was to analyze how behavior is changed by its consequences.

To study operant conditioning, Skinner devised some new tools. One was an experimental chamber that, much to his chagrin, has come to be known as the *Skinner box.* The experimenter can control it completely. Usually it is soundproof, lightproof, and kept at a constant temperature. It contains a device that the animal can operate in order to get a reward. For example, rats are usually placed in a box like the one displayed in Figure 7.12, which has a lever; when the lever is pressed, a food pellet drops through a thin tube. Skinner also developed the *cumulative recorder,* a device that monitors the rate at which a particular response is given, producing a graph like the one in Figure 7.13. The graph shows both the total number of relevant responses (for example, the number of times the rat pressed the lever) and when each response occurred. Thus, it provides a precise picture of how the rate of some action changes over time.

Figure 7.12
Skinner Boxes
(a) A rat presses a bar to obtain water from a tube. (b) A pigeon pecks a plastic key; this briefly opens a door that gives the pigeon access to a tray of food.
(Photo a: Courtesy Pfizer, Inc. Photo b: Courtesy of Peter J. Urcuioli.)

(a)   (b)

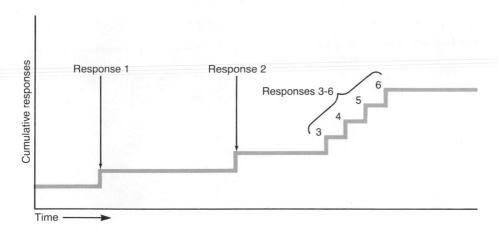

Figure 7.13
A Cumulative Record
Such records reflect how much time elapses between one response and the next. For example, responses 1 and 2 were separated by a considerable amount of time. But little time passed between responses 3, 4, 5, and 6.

Basic Components of Instrumental Conditioning

The tools Skinner devised allowed him and other researchers to choose an arbitrary response, arrange various relationships between that response and its consequences, and then analyze how those consequences affected behavior. They found that the basic phenomena of classical conditioning—stimulus generalization, stimulus discrimination, extinction, and spontaneous recovery—also occur in instrumental conditioning. However, the basic components of instrumental conditioning are known as operants, reinforcers, and discriminative stimuli.

Operants and reinforcers   Skinner introduced the term *operant* or *operant response* to distinguish the responses in instrumental conditioning from those in classical conditioning. Recall that, in classical conditioning, the conditioned response is automatically elicited in response to a given stimulus but does not affect whether or when the stimulus occurs. Pavlov's dogs salivated when a buzzer rang, but the salivation had no effect on the buzzer or on whether food was presented. In contrast, an **operant** is a response that has some effect on the world; it is a response that *operates on* the environment in some way. For example, when a child says, "Momma, I'm hungry" and is then fed, the child has emitted an operant response that determines when a particular stimulus (in this case, food) will appear. Similarly, touching a hot barbecue grill is an operant that results in a painful burn.

A **reinforcer** is a stimulus event that increases the probability that the operant, or response, that immediately preceded it will occur again. There are two main types of reinforcers: positive and negative. **Positive reinforcers** are stimuli that strengthen a response if they follow that response. They are roughly equivalent to rewards. The food given to a hungry pigeon every time it pecks a key is a positive reinforcer; its presentation increases the pigeon's key pecking. Smiles, food, money, and many other desirable outcomes act as positive reinforcers for people. Presenting a positive reinforcer after a response is called *positive reinforcement*. **Negative reinforcers** are unpleasant stimuli, such as pain, boredom, or too much heat or cold. Removal of a negative reinforcer following some response will strengthen that response's probability of recurring. For example, if the response of taking aspirin is followed by the removal of headache pain, aspirin taking is likely to occur when similar pain appears again. The process of strengthening behavior by following it with the removal of a negative reinforcer is called *negative reinforcement*.

A touch, a smile, and a look of love are among the many social stimuli that can serve as positive reinforcers for humans.

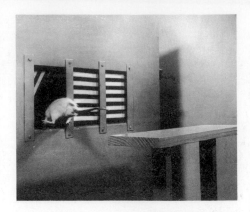

Figure 7.14
Stimulus Discrimination
In this experiment, the rat could jump from the stand through any one of the three doors, but it was reinforced only if it jumped through the door that differed from the other two. As you can see, the rat learned to do this quite well. For example, in the left-hand panel, it learned to discriminate diagonal from horizontal stripes, and in the middle panel, it learned to discriminate vertical from horizontal stripes.
(Frank Lotz Miller/Black Star.)

Just as breaking the link between a conditioned and an unconditioned stimulus weakens a conditioned response, ending the relationship between a response and its consequences weakens the response. In other words, failure to reinforce a response *extinguishes* that response; that is, the rate at which the response is made decreases, and eventually the response may disappear. If bar pressing no longer brings food, a rat stops pressing; if repeated knocking on your friend's door brings nothing but silence, you eventually stop knocking. The process of weakening behavior simply by not reinforcing it is called *extinction*.

Discriminative stimuli and stimulus control   Even if you have been reinforced in the past for telling jokes at parties, you are not likely to do so at funerals. Pigeons show similar wisdom. If they have been repeatedly reinforced for pecking a key when a red light is on but were not reinforced for pecking when a green light was on, they will eventually peck only when they see a red light. Their behavior demonstrates the effect of **discriminative stimuli,** which are stimuli that signal whether reinforcement is available if a certain response is made. When an organism learns to make a particular response in the presence of one stimulus but not another, *stimulus discrimination* has occurred (see Figure 7.14). Another way to say this is that the response is now under *stimulus control*. In general, stimulus discrimination allows people or animals to learn what is appropriate (reinforced) and inappropriate (not reinforced) in a particular situation.

Stimulus *generalization* also occurs in instrumental conditioning; that is, organisms often perform a response in the presence of a stimulus that is similar, but not identical, to the one that previously signaled the availability of reinforcement. And, as in classical conditioning, the more similar the new stimulus is to the old, the more likely it is that the response will be performed.

Forming and Strengthening Operants

Daily life is full of examples of instrumental conditioning. People go to movies, parties, classes, and jobs primarily because doing so brings immediate or eventual positive reinforcers. Their behavior may seem far removed from that of key-pecking pigeons, door-opening cats, and lever-pressing rats. But by studying simple animal behaviors, psychologists have painstakingly described how various contingencies can govern certain human actions, establish new behaviors, and alter the frequency of others. They have addressed such questions as: What is the effect of the type or timing of a reinforcer? How are established behaviors eliminated? How can new responses be established through instrumental conditioning?

Shaping   Imagine that you want to train your dog, Eugene, to sit and to shake hands. The basic method using positive reinforcement is obvious: every time Eugene sits and shakes hands, you give him a dog treat. But the problem is also obvious: smart as Eugene is, he may never perform the desired behavior in the first place, so you will never be able to give the reward. Instead of your teaching and Eugene's learning, the two of you will just stare at each other indefinitely. The way around this problem is to shape Eugene's behavior. **Shaping** is accomplished by reinforcing **successive approximations**—that is, responses that come successively closer to the desired response. For example, you might first give Eugene a dog treat whenever he sits down. Then you might reward him only when he sits and partially lifts a paw. Next, you might reward more complete paw lifting. Eventually, you would require that Eugene perform the entire sit-lift-shake sequence before offering the reward. Shaping is an extremely powerful, widely used tool. Animal trainers have used it to teach wild beasts to roller-skate and jump through hoops.

Many human skills are acquired through shaping. For example, bike-riding skills often begin with merely learning to steer and pedal a three-wheeler; later, balance is shaped by riding a two-wheeler whose training wheels are gradually raised.

Delay and size of reinforcement   Much of human behavior is learned and maintained because it is regularly reinforced. But many people overeat, smoke, drink too much, or procrastinate, even though they know these behaviors are bad for them and even though they may honestly want to eliminate them. They just cannot seem to change; they seem to lack "self-control." If behavior is controlled by its consequences, why do people perform acts that are ultimately self-defeating?

The answer lies in the timing of reinforcers. The good feelings (positive reinforcers) that follow, say, drinking too much are immediate; a hangover or other negative consequences are usually delayed. You saw that, in classical conditioning, a delay between the conditioned stimulus and the unconditioned stimulus produces only a weak conditioned response. Similarly, operant conditioning is stronger when the delay in receiving a reinforcer is short (Kalish, 1981). Immediate consequences of a behavior will affect the behavior more strongly than delayed consequences. Thus, under some conditions, delaying reward for even a few seconds can decrease the effectiveness of positive reinforcement.

The size of a reinforcer is also important. In general, conditioning proceeds more quickly when a reinforcer is large than when it is small. For example, hungry animals given larger food pellets will learn a new task faster than those given smaller pellets (Meltzer & Brahlek, 1968).

Schedules of reinforcement   So far, we have talked as if a reinforcer is delivered every time a particular response occurs. Sometimes it is, and this arrangement is called a **continuous reinforcement schedule.** But very often reinforcement is administered only some of the time; the result is called a **partial,** or **intermittent, reinforcement schedule.**

We can classify most intermittent schedules according to (1) whether the delivery of reinforcers is determined by the number of responses the organism has made or by the time that has elapsed since the last reinforcer, and (2) whether the delivery schedule is fixed or variable. This way of classifying schedules produces four basic types of intermittent reinforcement.

1. **Fixed ratio (FR) schedules** provide reinforcement following a fixed number of responses. A rat might receive food after every tenth bar press (FR 10) or after every twentieth one (FR 20); a factory worker might be paid ten dollars for every ten widgets he or she assembles.

2. **Variable ratio (VR) schedules** also call for reinforcement after a given number of responses, but that number varies from one reinforcement to the next. On a VR 30 schedule, a rat might sometimes be reinforced after ten bar presses, sometimes after fifty bar presses; but an *average* of thirty responses would occur before reinforcement was given.

3. **Fixed interval (FI) schedules** provide reinforcement for the first response that occurs after some fixed time has passed since the last reward. For example, on an FI 60 schedule, the first response after sixty seconds have passed will be rewarded.

4. **Variable interval (VI) schedules** reinforce the first response after some period of time, but the amount of time varies. In a VI 60 schedule, for example, the first response to occur after an *average* of one minute would be reinforced, but the actual time between reinforcements could vary from, say, 1 second to 120 seconds.

Numerous experiments on partial reinforcement schedules have shown that different schedules of reinforcement produce very different patterns of responding, as Figure 7.15 illustrates (Skinner, 1961). For example, on a fixed ratio schedule, rewards come only after a particular number of responses, resulting in a high rate of responding. The appearance of many responses in a short time on fixed ratio schedules helps explain why production workers are often paid on a *piecework* basis; that is, according to the number of items they produce.

Figure 7.15
Schedules of Reinforcement
The curves' steepness indicates the rate of responding. In general, the rate of responding is higher under ratio schedules than under interval schedules. It is also higher under fixed schedules than under variable schedules.
(From "Teaching Machines" by B. F. Skinner. Copyright © 1961 by Scientific American, Inc. All rights reserved.)

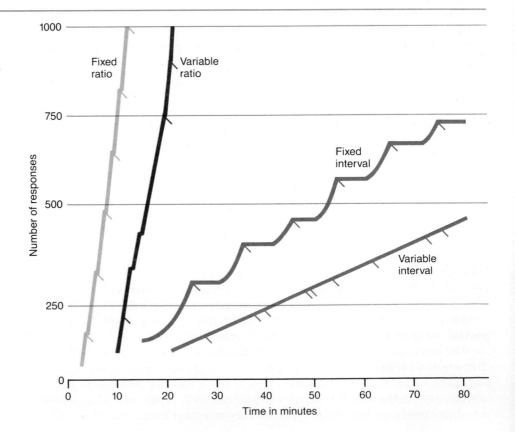

Variable ratio schedules, which provide occasional and unpredictable reinforcement, also generate a high rate of responding. The best example of behavior that operates according to a variable ratio schedule is gambling. Golf and bowling also provide variable ratio reinforcement that keeps even mediocre, often frustrated, players "hooked" for years.

When a fixed interval schedule is in effect, it does not matter how many responses are performed during the time between rewards. As a result, the rate of responding typically drops steeply immediately after reinforcement and then increases as the time for another reward approaches. Thus, fixed interval schedules usually produce the "scallop" effect shown in Figure 7.15. Each scallop will be much wider if the time interval is long (for example, one hour) than if it is short (for example, one minute). Behavior resulting from a variable interval schedule looks quite different. The unpredictable timing of rewards typically generates a slow, but steady rate of responding. Intentionally or not, teachers often place their students on interval schedules. When they schedule only one midterm and a final, they create a fixed interval schedule; students often respond by studying little most of the time and then increasing their studying just before each exam.

Schedules and extinction   The intense or steady patterns of response typically created by variable reinforcement schedules are especially difficult to eliminate through extinction. Consider the parents of a toddler who cries and screams after being put to bed for the night. They could extinguish the crying by consistently ignoring it. In one case, parents put their child to bed each night and did not return until the next morning (Williams, 1959). The child cried for forty-five minutes the first night, cried a little less each night thereafter, and after ten days of continuous nonreinforcement, began sleeping peacefully every night. The crying had extinguished. But ignoring a wailing child is not easy. If parents finally cuddle their child after he or she has cried for many minutes, they are reinforcing the child's prolonged crying on a partial (VI or VR) reinforcement schedule. The child's crying might then be even more difficult to control.

In general, behaviors learned under a partial reinforcement schedule are far more difficult to extinguish than those learned on a continuous reinforcement schedule. This phenomenon—called the **partial reinforcement extinction effect**—is easy to understand if you imagine yourself in a hotel lobby with a broken candy machine and a broken slot machine. If you deposit money in the broken candy machine, you will probably extinguish (stop putting money in) very quickly. Because the machine usually delivers its goodies on a continuous reinforcement schedule, it is easy to tell that it is not going to provide a reinforcer. But slot machines offer an intermittent and unpredictable schedule. You might put in coin after coin because it is difficult to determine whether the machine is broken or is simply not paying off at the moment.

In short, distinguishing between partial reinforcement and extinction is more difficult than distinguishing between continuous reinforcement and extinction. As a result, responses previously maintained on a partial schedule are likely to continue longer under extinction than those maintained on a continuous reinforcement schedule. The more unpredictable (variable) the reinforcement has been, the longer it usually takes for extinction to occur. For example, animals that received reinforcement on every other trial extinguish faster than those that received reinforcement on a random selection of half the trials (Capaldi, 1967).

Secondary reinforcement   If food is presented to a hungry animal following some behavior, the probability of that behavior's occurrence will almost always

Social approval is an important secondary reinforcer for human beings.

be strengthened. This result is due to food's status as a **primary reinforcer,** something that meets an organism's most basic needs. Water, air, and moderate temperatures are other examples. Like an unconditioned stimulus, the power of a primary reinforcer is automatic. If primary reinforcers, such as food, were the only effective reinforcers, however, instrumental learning would be very limited. Parents would have to carry around food, soft drinks, and other basic reinforcers, in order to reward their children's appropriate behavior.

Fortunately, there are other, far more conveniently dispensed rewards that can acquire reinforcing power through their past association with primary reinforcers. Called **secondary reinforcers,** these are rewards that people and animals *learn* to like. For example, in one study, chimpanzees were taught to insert poker chips in a vending machine to obtain pieces of fruit. Later, the chimpanzees learned to do a number of other tasks, not for food, but for poker chips (Cowles, 1937). Through their association with the primary reinforcer (food), the chips had become secondary reinforcers. For humans, money is the most obvious secondary reinforcer; some people will do anything for it, even though it tastes terrible. Its reinforcing power lies in its association with the many rewards it can buy. Smiles and other forms of social approval are also important examples of secondary reinforcers for human beings.

Negative Reinforcement

Positive reinforcement alone, whether based on food, love, money, or even Superbowl tickets, does not make the world go around. Often, people are more interested in acting to escape or prevent some unpleasantness than in obtaining something pleasant. In other words, behavior is often molded by negative reinforcement.

The effects of negative reinforcement can be studied through either escape conditioning or avoidance conditioning. **Escape conditioning** takes place when an organism learns to make a particular response in order to terminate an aversive stimulus. Dogs learn to jump over the barrier in a shuttle box to escape shock (see Figure 7.16). Similarly, parents often learn to give in to (and thus inadvertently strengthen) children's obnoxious demands for candy, because doing so temporarily terminates whining. In general, the speed of learning rises as the magnitude of the aversive stimulus increases. For example,

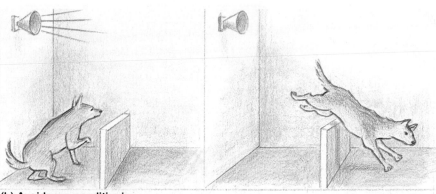

(a) Escape conditioning   **(b) Avoidance conditioning**

animals will learn to escape a strong shock much more quickly than a weak shock (Campbell & Kraeling, 1953). Learning also proceeds more quickly if the aversive stimulus ends immediately after the response, rather than after some delay (Tarpy & Sawabini, 1974).

Now imagine that some signal—say, a buzzer or blinking light—occurs just a few seconds before the grid in one side of a shuttle box is electrified. If the animal jumps over the barrier very quickly after hearing or seeing the signal, it can avoid the shock altogether. When an animal responds to a signal in a way that avoids exposure to an aversive stimulus, **avoidance conditioning** has occurred. Along with positive reinforcement, avoidance conditioning is one of the most important influences on everyday behavior. Most people go to work or school even when they would rather stay in bed, and they stop at red lights even when they are in a hurry. Each of these behaviors reflects avoidance conditioning, because each behavior allows people to avoid a negative consequence, such as getting a traffic ticket or going on welfare. Unfortunately, avoidance conditioning may prevent people from learning new, more desirable behaviors. Some people with limited social skills may fear doing something embarrassing and learn to shy away from social situations.

Avoidance is a very difficult habit to break. In one demonstration of its persistence, dogs were trained to jump over the barrier of a shuttle box when a shock signal was given. After just ten trials, the shock was permanently shut off. However, the dogs continued to jump over the barrier whenever the signal was given, for the next five hundred trials, at which time the experiment was terminated (Solomon, Kamin & Wynne, 1953). Such "irrational" behavior persists because the avoidance response prevents an animal or human from learning that an alternative behavior may in fact be easier or more adaptive. Phobias are often preserved in the same way. The person whose fear of elevators prompts avoidance of them will never discover that they are safe and comfortable.

Figure 7.16
A Shuttle Box
Studies of negative reinforcement frequently use a shuttle box. It has two compartments, usually separated by a barrier, and its floor is an electric grid. Shock can be administered through the grid to each compartment independently. In (a) escape conditioning, the animal can escape shock by jumping over the barrier to the next compartment. In (b) avoidance conditioning, a buzzer signals the onset of shock; the animal can thus avoid the shock entirely if it jumps quickly enough after the buzzer sounds.
(From *The Psychology of Learning and Memory* by Douglas L. Hintzman. Copyright 1978 W. H. Freeman and Company. Used by permission.)

Punishment

Both positive and negative reinforcement *increase* the frequency of a response. In contrast, **punishment** involves the presentation of an aversive stimulus or the removal of a pleasant stimulus; it *decreases* the frequency of the immediately preceding response. Shouting "No!" and swatting your dog when it begins chewing on the rug is an example of punishment that presents a negative stimulus following a response. Confiscating a teenager's rock concert tickets because of rude behavior is an example of punishment that removes a positive reinforcer.

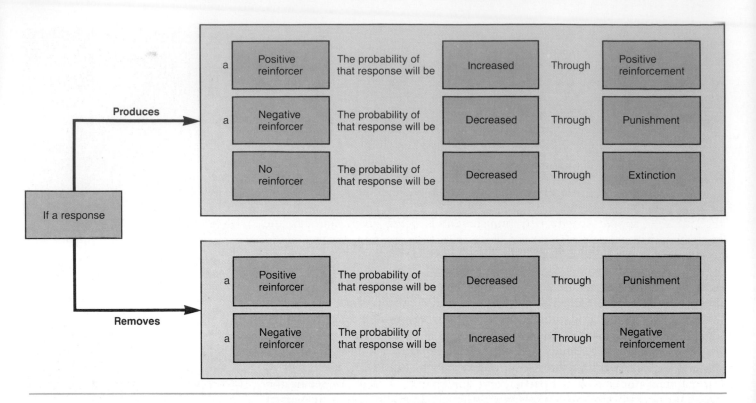

Figure 7.17
Reinforcement Contingencies
The future probability that a response will appear is a function of whether the response produces or removes various types of reinforcers.

Punishment and negative reinforcement are often confused, but as shown in Figure 7.17, they are quite different. Reinforcement *strengthens* behavior; punishment *weakens* it. If shock is *turned off* when a rat presses a lever, that is negative reinforcement; it increases the probability that the rat will press the lever when shock occurs again. But if shock is *turned on* when the rat presses the lever, that is punishment; the rat will be less likely to press the lever again.

The use of punishment to control behavior has had a long and controversial history in psychology. Many people object to using punishment because it seems cruel. Others advocate punishment because it works. Both views are only partly correct. If misused or overused, punishment can be cruel; when used properly and within limits, it can be very effective.

Consider, for example, the baby boy pictured in Figure 7.18. He suffered from chronic ruminative disorder, a condition that made him regurgitate all of his food, producing severe malnutrition. This disorder dramatically lowers resistance to disease and results in death in about 20 percent of cases. Drugs, surgery, and physical restraints had all failed to help the boy. He was literally starving to death when two psychologists were consulted. As a last resort, they suggested punishment. An intense electric shock was administered to the boy's leg at the first sign of after-meal vomiting, and the shock was continued at one-second intervals until the signs of vomiting had stopped. After six treatments, the vomiting response to food was eliminated (Lang & Melamed, 1969). Punishment had saved the boy's life.

Although punishment can change behavior, it has several drawbacks. First, it often produces undesirable side effects. For example, if a parent punishes a child for saying a vulgar word, the child may associate the punisher with the punishment and end up fearing the parent. Second, punishment is often ineffective, especially with animals or young children, unless it is administered immediately after the response and each time the response is made. Third, even when punishment is effective, it is often situation-specific, working only in a very particular environment. In other words, punishment may suppress behavior, but it does not necessarily eliminate it altogether. Thus, after punishment, a child might stop using a particular word in front of a parent—but continue using it in the presence of other people. Punishment may even produce misunderstanding. A child asks his mother at breakfast to "pass the damn milk over here." She slaps him, whereupon he says, "Okay, okay, can I have the damn butter?"

For these reasons, punishment is most effective when several guidelines are followed. First, to prevent development of a general fear of the punisher, the punisher should specify why punishment is being given and that the *behavior* is being punished, not the *person*. Second, the punishment should be immediate and sufficiently severe to eliminate the response. Mild words of annoyance may actually reinforce a child's pranks. Finally, more appropriate responses should be identified and positively reinforced. As the frequency of appropriate behavior increases through reinforcement, the frequency of the undesirable response decreases, as does the need for punishment. When these guidelines are not followed, the beneficial effects of punishment are wiped out or may be only temporary. American prisons provide one of the most obvious examples. Prisons are notoriously ineffective at producing long-term improvements in criminals' behavior. For example, of 537 prisoners released from Illinois jails during a three-month period in 1983, nearly half were arrested again within twenty months, and about one-third were jailed again (Illinois Criminal Justice Information Authority, 1985).

Applications of Instrumental Conditioning

The study of instrumental conditioning has led to numerous procedures for developing or shaping behavior. The careful use of rewards for appropriate behaviors and extinction (or mild punishment) for inappropriate behaviors has helped countless mental patients, mentally retarded individuals, and hard-to-manage children to develop the behavior patterns they need to live happier and more productive lives. Some of these procedures are discussed in Chapter 16, on therapy. Instrumental conditioning is also used in schools and by people trying to change their own behavior.

Programmed instruction is one classroom application of instrumental conditioning, in which new material is presented in small, planned steps. After reading each segment of material, the student is immediately questioned about it. Paying attention and giving correct responses bring positive reinforcement (usually in the form of information that the answer is correct) and the opportunity to go on to the next step. After incorrect answers, the student is told the right answer and either tries again or goes back to the previous step to be sure more basic information is learned. The general idea behind programmed instruction is to provide immediate rewards for correct responses, thus strengthening those responses while letting the student proceed at his or her own pace until the material has been mastered. Today, programmed instruction is often given by computers (see Figure 7.19, p. 268).

Other applications of instrumental conditioning use the power of discriminative stimuli. This approach is often useful if you want to change a behavior but cannot do anything about its consequences. Those who lack the self-control not to overeat, for example, might concentrate on altering environmental stimuli that cause overeating. Often this means replacing cues for eating with cues for other behaviors. For example, many overeaters tend to sit at the dinner table long after finishing a meal. During this time, they may

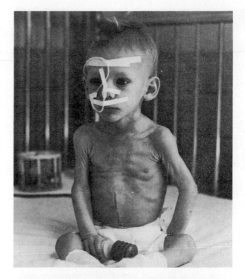

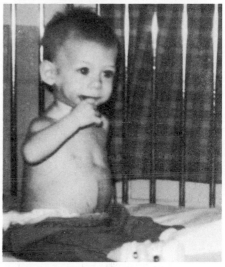

Figure 7.18
The Uses of Punishment
This infant boy suffered from chronic ruminative disorder, a relatively common condition in which an infant regurgitates all food. The picture on the top was taken when the boy was approximately one year old and had been vomiting for four months. The picture on the bottom is the same boy thirteen days after punishment with electric shock had eliminated the vomiting response. His body weight increased 26 percent in two weeks. He also displayed normal physical and psychological health when tested six months, one year, and two years later (Lang & Melamed, 1969). The use of punishment has become a common treatment for this type of case, but when the danger of starvation is not so severe, electric shock may be replaced with some milder punishment, such as squirting lemon juice into an infant's mouth (Sajwaj, Libet & Agras, 1974).
(Lang, P. and Melamed, B., "Case report: Avoidance conditioning of an infant with chronic ruminative vomiting." *Journal of Abnormal Psychology, 74* 1–8. Copyright 1969 by the American Psychological Association. Reprinted by permission of the author.)

Figure 7.19
Programmed Instruction by Computer
With programmed instruction, students can proceed at their own pace. Because information is presented in very small units, attentive students can often complete an entire unit without making any mistakes. When computers are used in programmed instruction, the process can become very flexible. For example, if a student makes several mistakes on the same unit, the computer can branch off into a remedial lesson that breaks the material down at an even more basic level. Thus, misunderstandings can be detected early and not allowed to interfere with the learning of later material.
(© Michael Siluk/EKM-Nepenthe.)

munch on candies and dessert. By leaving the table immediately after a meal and taking a walk, a significant amount of excessive eating can be eliminated. Similarly, people trying to quit smoking often find initial abstinence easier if they stay away from bars and other places that contain discriminative stimuli for smoking.

Stimulus control can also help insomniacs (Bootzin & Nicassio, 1978). The key is to associate the stimulus of the bed or bedroom with sleeping—not with the frustration of insomnia or with other behaviors. Much more so than average, insomniacs tend to use their beds for such nonsleeping activities as watching television, eating, writing letters, reading magazines, worrying, and so on. Soon the bedroom becomes a signal, or discriminative stimulus, for so many activities that relaxation and sleep become less and less likely. But if insomniacs begin to use their beds only for sleeping and perform other activities elsewhere, there is a good chance that their insomnia can be eliminated (Hill, 1982).

HIGHLIGHT

Learning to Control the Environment

Perhaps one of the most important things for an organism to learn is that it has some control over its environment. When this learning does not occur, the typical response is to stop trying. This phenomenon has been called **learned helplessness** (Seligman, 1975).

An experiment with dogs provided one of the most powerful demonstrations of learned helplessness. Each dog stood in a harness over an electric grid. At random intervals, a strong electric shock was administered. The dogs in group A could maintain some control over their environment, because the shock was turned off whenever they pushed a button with their nose. Each dog in group B was paired with one in group A. Group B animals could not themselves control the shock; whenever it came on, they had to wait until their partner pushed the button to shut it off. Thus both groups received an identical amount of shock. The only difference was that those in group A could control it and those in group B could not.

An interesting thing happened when these dogs were moved to a new environment: a shuttle box similar to that in Figure 7.16. A signal was given and, after a ten-second interval, one side of the box was electrified. The dogs in group A quickly learned to jump over the barrier into the safe compartment. The dogs in group B behaved very differently. At first they barked and cried, but then they simply stood still and endured whatever shock was administered. Even though there was an obvious way to avoid the shock, these dogs never tried to find it. Because of their prior experience with uncontrollable shock, they had learned to be helpless (Mineka & Hendersen, 1985; Seligman & Maier, 1967).

Does similar learning take place in people? In one experiment, people were given a set of problems to solve. There were no correct solutions, so no matter how hard they tried, these people were doomed to failure. Later, when these same people were given a new set of problems that could be solved quite easily, they failed again—this time because they did not *try* to find the correct solutions. Apparently they did not try because they believed that the task was beyond their abilities (Dweck & Reppucci, 1973).

These results appear to reflect a general phenomenon. When people begin to *believe* that there is nothing they can do to change their lives and that control of their own destiny is impossible, they generally stop trying to improve their lot (Dweck & Licht, 1980). Instead, they tend to endure painful situations passively (Seligman, Klein & Miller, 1976). If there is physical pain involved, it may be eased by *stress-induced analgesia,* triggered by endorphins and other internal painkilling mechanisms discussed in Chapters 3 and 4 (Maier, Laudenslager & Ryan, 1984). But, especially in humans, helplessness often results in severe depression and other stress-related problems described in Chapter 13 (Mandler, 1984; Peterson & Seligman, 1984). ■

SOCIAL LEARNING

Most human learning takes place when people are with other people. And much of it follows the principles of instrumental and classical conditioning. But, according to traditional accounts of conditioning, an organism must have direct, personal experience with stimulus pairings or the consequences of responses in order for learning to occur. **Social learning** theorists argue that people also learn from the experience of others, through processes known as vicarious conditioning and observational learning.

Vicarious Conditioning

A child who sees a friend sent to the principal's office for throwing mud will learn something important; so will the child who sees a playmate rewarded after picking up scattered toys. In both cases, associations are learned, even though the events are happening to other people and the conditioning is thus **vicarious.** Through vicarious classical conditioning, for example, an emotional reaction to some stimulus can be learned on the basis of someone else's behavior. It works like this. Another person's delight or disgust with, say, a particular politician, may act as an unconditioned stimulus that triggers a similar emotion (UCR) in you. Because the politician's name is paired with the unconditioned stimulus, it may become for you a conditioned stimulus. Even though you have never encountered the politician yourself, his or her name may elicit an emotional reaction (CR) from you (Kravetz, 1974; Venn & Short, 1973).

Vicarious instrumental conditioning can also take place. A series of experiments by Albert Bandura and his colleagues provided dramatic demonstrations of this and other aspects of social learning. In one study, they showed nursery school children a short film starring an adult and a large, inflatable, bottom-heavy "Bobo" doll (Bandura, 1965). The adult in the film punched the Bobo doll in the nose, kicked it, threw objects at it, and hit its head with a hammer while saying things like "Sockeroo!" There were different endings to the film. Some children saw an ending in which the aggressive adult was called a "champion" by a second adult and rewarded with candy and soft drinks; some saw the aggressor scolded, spanked, and called a "bad person"; some saw an ending in which there was neither reward nor punishment. After the film, each child was allowed to play alone with a Bobo doll. In this and similar studies, Bandura found that imitation of the aggressive model was greatest among those children who had seen the model rewarded. Thus, the reinforcement that the children saw in the film—but did not directly experience—influenced their behavior.

Observational Learning

Bandura's Bobo doll studies supported the idea that learning can occur not only through direct conditioning, but also through vicarious conditioning. His research highlighted other interesting phenomena as well, including **observational learning,** the ability to learn new behaviors by watching the behavior of others. In the experiment just described, for example, children who had seen the adult punished for Bobo abuse played with the doll much less than

Figure 7.20
Observational Learning
After children have observed a model, they often reproduce many of the model's acts precisely.
(Bandura, A., Ross, D., and Ross, S. A. "Imitation of film-mediated aggressive models." *Journal of Abnormal and Social Psychology, 66,* 3–11. Copyright 1963 by the American Psychological Association. Reprinted by permission of the author.)

any other group. However, when the researcher offered these children a piece of candy for every behavior from the film that they could perform, they performed just as many aggressive behaviors as the other children (Bandura, 1965). Seeing the adult punished had produced a tendency not to *perform* what was learned, but it did not result in a failure to *learn* what was seen. Thus, learning may occur even when there is no immediate change in performance.

Bandura also showed that children will learn and imitate an adult's behavior even when no vicarious reward is involved. In one study, preschool children watched films in which adults either sat quietly beside a Bobo doll or viciously attacked it. Later, the children were left in a room with the same doll. Those who had seen aggressive behavior were the most aggressive. Furthermore, as Figure 7.20 shows, these children often imitated the adult's attack blow for blow and kick for kick (Bandura, Ross & Ross, 1963). Learning, said Bandura, may occur even though *neither* model nor observer is reinforced.

Observational learning seems to be a powerful source of the subtle socialization we mentioned in the chapter on human development. For example, experiments show that children are more willing to help and share after seeing a demonstration by a warm, powerful model—even after some months have elapsed (Bryan, 1975; Mussen & Eisenberg, 1977). They are even more likely to imitate a dishonest act than to behave honestly (Stein, 1967).

HIGHLIGHT

Observational Learning and Television Violence

If observational learning is important, then surely television—and televised violence—must teach American children a great deal. It is estimated that the average child in the United States has spent more time watching television than attending school (Liebert & Poulos, 1975). By the time the average American child reaches fifteen, he or she will have watched approximately 24,000 televised shootings (Greene, 1985).

To investigate the effects of televised violence, researchers have used many methods, including laboratory experiments in which children watch brief films or full-length movies, longitudinal field studies—a form of naturalistic observation in which children's at-home viewing habits are analyzed—and interventions in which children are exposed for long periods to carefully controlled types of television programs. The evidence from all these studies suggests that exposure to large amounts of violent activity on television results in more aggressive behavior (Huesmann, Laperspetz & Eron, 1984; Leyens et al., 1975; Parke et al., 1977). For example, compared with children who watch an equal number of nonviolent movies, children who are exposed to several violent movies become more aggressive in their interactions with other children (Leyens et al., 1975).

There is now convincing evidence that such effects of watching violence are long-lasting. For example, one study tracked people from the age of eight (in 1960) until thirty (in 1982). Those who watched more television violence as children were much more likely to be convicted of violent crimes as adults. Moreover, these same people were more likely to rely on physical punishment of their own children, and their children tended to be much more aggressive than average. These results were found in the United States, Israel, Finland, Australia, Poland, and the Netherlands. Television violence can thus have a profound effect on children, even in countries such as Finland in which the number of violent shows is very small (National Coalition on Television Violence, 1984). Of course, not every viewer is equally affected by televised violence; the influence of parents, peers, and others may lessen or amplify the basic effect. Still, the relationship between watching violence and displaying it is powerful.

How does televised aggression affect viewers' aggressiveness? One strong possibility is that television provides information about how to express aggression or take risks along with plenty of specific illustrations. Children have poked each other's eyes out after watching the Three Stooges appear to do so on television. Several children have jumped off buildings after telling their friends they were Batman or Superman (Associated Press, 1984). A wave of teenage suicides followed the 1984 broadcast of a show depicting a suicide pact between two depressed high school students.

Television may also have more subtle effects, and they may be more widespread. In one study, for example, children who watched more than twenty-five hours of television per week were compared with those who watched four hours or less per week. The children's galvanic skin responses (GSRs) were monitored while they watched a violent boxing match. (Recall that GSRs provide a measure of physiological arousal.) The GSRs of the children who watched very little television were highly elevated during the boxing match; those of the children who were heavy television viewers were not (Cline, Croft & Courrier, 1973). These results suggest that longer or more intense exposure to television violence may numb or even eliminate the emotional reactions that people normally experience when they see others suffer. If this is so, then the relationship between watching televised violence and behaving aggressively may occur because the viewer has been *desensitized* to signs of suffering in other people.

Is television an unusually powerful source of observational learning? For some children it is, because they watch so much of it. And for society at large, television is a special source of observational learning, because millions of people view the same models. But there is nothing at all unusual about the processes by which people learn from television. Children pick up slang by hearing it used by others; adolescents learn to dance by watching others; adults do everything from buying designer clothes to picking stocks as a result of what they have learned by watching others. Observational learning in these situations is more difficult to identify and analyze than learning from television, but these sources of learning are certainly no less common. ■

According to Bandura, four requirements must be met if observational learning is to occur (Bandura, 1977). The first is *attention*. You cannot learn unless you pay reasonably close attention to what is happening around you. Second, observational learning requires *retention*. You must not only attend to the observed behavior but also remember it at some later time. Third, you must be able to *reproduce* the behavior; that is, you must be capable of performing the act. The fourth factor is *motivation*. In general, you will only perform the act if there is some motivation or reason to do so.

Television provides a rich source of observational learning. Its programs can help children to acquire many desirable behaviors, but it can also teach the specifics of violent behavior.

COGNITIVE PROCESSES IN LEARNING

Pioneers in the study of conditioning hoped to explain all learning by the principle of reinforcement and the automatic, unthinking formation of simple associations. We have seen that studies of social learning have challenged the view that all learning requires reinforcement. Bandura and other social learning theorists have also contested the view that all learning consists simply of establishing associations. Children, for example, must learn to produce sentences they have never heard before. That is, they must acquire the ability to generate new sentences as well as to reproduce old ones. Similarly, if you learn a foreign language, you need to learn not only a chain of associations, but also a set of abstract rules that reflect the structure of the language. This kind of learning requires the use of symbols. It requires thinking, ideas, images, and other forms of mental representation described in the chapters on development and thought. In other words, *cognitive processes*— how people represent, store, and use information—play an important role in learning.

Much as the Gestalt psychologists argued that, in perception, the whole is greater than the sum of its parts, cognitive views of learning hold that learning is more than the sum of stimulus-response associations. And much as we saw in Chapter 5 that perception may involve top-down as well as bottom-up processing and may depend on the meaning attached to sensations, so, too, some forms of learning require higher mental processes and depend on how the learner attaches meaning to events. In Chapters 8 and 9, we will examine memory, language, and other cognitive processes in some detail; here we will look at just two cognitive processes that seem to be important to learning.

Insight

Wolfgang Köhler was a Gestalt psychologist whose work on learning happened almost by accident. A German, he was visiting the island of Tenerife when World War I broke out. The British confined Köhler to the island for the duration of the war, and he devoted his time there to studying a colony of chimpanzees. In 1925 he published his findings in *The Mentality of Apes,* a book that remains a classic treatise on cognitive processes in learning.

Köhler began his work only a decade or so after Thorndike published his research on how cats learn in a puzzle box. Recall that Thorndike's results supported the view that associations form the bedrock of learning—a view disputed by Gestalt psychologists like Köhler. Köhler argued that the problem Thorndike set for his cats determined the type of learning they demonstrated. Thorndike's puzzle box, he said, forced animals to use a trial-and-error strategy in which they had to happen on an answer through associations. Perhaps pushing a lever would open the door, but how could the cat possibly know in advance? Even a Nobel laureate put in such a puzzle box would have to start pushing and pulling things until he or she discovered what worked.

Köhler's approach was quite different. He put a chimpanzee in a cage and placed a piece of fruit so that it was visible but out of the animal's reach. He sometimes hung the fruit from a string too high to reach, sometimes on the ground, but too far outside the cage to be retrieved. Many of the chimps overcame these obstacles easily. For example, if the fruit was on the ground outside the cage, the animal might thrust its arm through the cage. When this strategy was unsuccessful, some chimps looked around the cage and, finding a long stick, used it to rake in the banana. Surprised that the chimpanzees could solve these problems, Köhler tried more difficult tasks. But again the chimps proved very adept. Figures 7.21 and 7.22 show examples of their surprising ability to devise methods to reach the fruit. Even when a chimpanzee had to use a very short stick to retrieve a slightly longer stick, in order to rake in a longer stick to obtain yet another stick long enough to retrieve fruit, the chimp succeeded easily.

Were the chimps simply demonstrating the results of previously formed associations? Köhler thought not, and three observations buttressed his claim that something more than automatic associations was involved. First, once a chimpanzee solved a particular problem, it would immediately do the same thing if faced with a similar situation. In other words, it acted as if it understood the problem precisely. Second, Köhler's chimpanzees rarely tried a solution

Figure 7.21
A "Multiple-Stick" Problem
Though it appears rather complicated, some chimpanzees solved this problem easily.
(Yerkes Regional Primate Research Center of Emory University.)

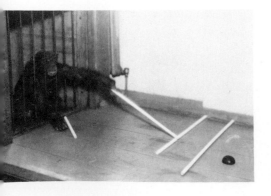

(a)   (b)   (c)

Figure 7.22
Cognitive Processes in Learning
(a) A chimpanzee has taken a fifteen-foot pole, fixed it in the ground, climbed all the way to the top, and falls to the ground after grabbing the fruit. (b) A subject that retrieved two wooden boxes from different areas of the compound, stacked them on top of one another, climbed to the top with a long pole, and then knocked down the fruit. (c) A subject that stacked three boxes on top of one another and climbed to the top of all three to reach the fruit.
(Kohler, W. 1976. *The Mentality of Apes.* London: Routledge and Kegan Paul Plc.)

that did not work. Third, they often reached a solution quite suddenly. When confronted with a piece of fruit hanging from a string, for example, a chimp might jump for it several times. Then it would stop jumping, look up, and pace back and forth. Finally it would run over to one of the wooden crates, place it directly under the banana, and climb on top of it to reach the fruit.

Thus, Köhler's chimpanzees behaved quite differently from Thorndike's cats. The chimps seemed to understand the principle involved in solving a problem. For example, Köhler once took an animal into a room where a banana hung from a string. This chimp had already learned to solve the same problem using a box, but there were no boxes—or any other objects—in the room. After looking confused for several minutes, the animal went over to Köhler, dragged him by the arm until he stood beneath the banana, and then started climbing up his back!

Köhler believed that the only explanation for these results was that the chimpanzees suddenly saw new relationships that were never learned in the past; in other words, they had *insight* into the problem as a whole, not just specific stimulus-response associations between its specific elements. The chimpanzees, he argued, perceived the global organization of the problem and used whatever specifics were available in order to solve it.

Latent Learning and Cognitive Maps

Edward Tolman's research on rats' ability to find their way through a maze also shed light on cognitive factors in learning. When he began his investigations in the 1920s, hundreds of experiments had already been conducted in which rats were placed in mazes like the one shown in Figure 7.23 (p. 274). The rats' task was to go from the start box to the goal box, where they were rewarded with food. The standard finding was that the rats were likely to take many wrong turns, but that over the course of many trials, they would make successively fewer mistakes. The standard interpretation was that the rats learned a long chain of turning responses that were reinforced by the food. Tolman disagreed and offered evidence for an alternative interpretation.

In one of his studies, for example, three groups of rats were placed in the same maze once a day for twelve consecutive days (Tolman & Honzik, 1930). For group A, food was placed in the goal box on each trial. These rats gradually improved their performance so that, by the end of the experiment, they made

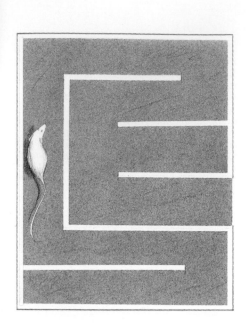

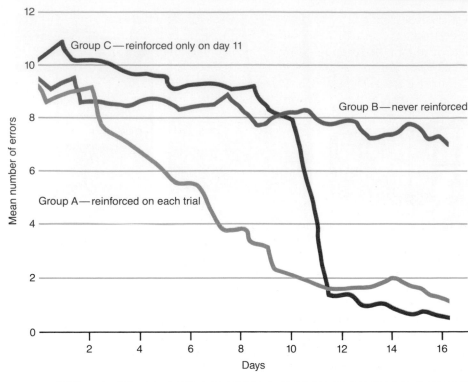

Figure 7.23
Latent Learning
When rats are put in the same maze for several days, they make many wrong turns if no reinforcement is provided for correct turns. However, as the performance of group C indicates, performance improves dramatically once reinforcement is provided. Results like this led Edward Tolman to argue that animals can learn a maze and develop a cognitive map of it even in the absence of reward. He claimed that the later reinforcement—not the original learning—was responsible for animals' performance of what they had learned.
(Tolman & Honzik, 1930)

only one or two mistakes as they ran through the maze (see Figure 7.23). Group B also ran the maze once a day, but there was never any food in their goal box. These animals continued to make many errors throughout the experiment. Neither of these results is surprising, and each is consistent with a reinforcement view of learning.

The third group of rats, group C, was the critical one. For the first ten days, they received no reinforcement for running the maze and continued to make many mistakes. But on day 11, food was placed in their goal box for the first time. Then a very surprising thing happened: on the day after receiving reinforcement, these rats made almost no mistakes. In fact, their performance was just as good as that of the rats who had been reinforced every day. In other words, the single reinforcement trial on day 11 produced a dramatic change in their performance the next day.

Tolman argued that these results supported two conclusions. First, notice that the rats in group C improved their performance the *first* time they ran the maze after being reinforced. The reinforcement on day 11 could not have affected the rats' learning of the maze itself; it simply changed their subsequent performance. They must have learned the maze earlier. Therefore, the rats (like the children in Bandura's experiment who did not imitate the model until they were rewarded for doing so) demonstrated **latent learning**—learning that is not demonstrated when it occurs. Second, because the rats' performance changed immediately after the first reinforcement trial, Tolman argued that the results he obtained could occur only if the rats had earlier developed a **cognitive map**—that is, the mental representation of the particular spatial arrangement of the maze. Tolman concluded that cognitive maps are developed naturally through experience, even in the absence of any response or reinforcement. Research on learning in the natural environment has supported these views. Humans develop mental maps of shopping malls and city streets, even when they receive no direct reinforcement or reward for doing so.

FUTURE DIRECTIONS

Because learning is so basic to human life, it has been the subject of intense research interest in psychology for over a hundred years. As a result, many important laws of learning were discovered during that time. Especially during the 1960s and 1970s, however, a notion prevailed that psychologists had uncovered about all there was to know about learning, and the pace of research in the area slackened. Indeed, the field appeared to have lost some of its perspective. Researchers focused on the learning of relatively simple overt behaviors, and animals were the primary subjects. Very little attention was paid to the more complex knowledge that people acquire through everyday experience.

Today, researchers seek to expand on earlier work, which outlined the basic principles governing learning. Some of the most exciting work in this area suggests, for example, that decreases in the body's immune response—the cellular and physiological activity described in Chapter 13 as protecting the body from infection—can be classically conditioned (Ader & Cohen, 1985). If this immunosuppression can be made to occur in relation to external signals, perhaps *increases* in the immune response can also be conditioned, thus someday making it possible to fight disease with less medication and fewer harmful side effects.

Researchers also recognize that some human learning involves automatic associations, that some involves rational thought, and that most requires a blending of the two. They have been working to determine the similarities of and differences between the most automatic, stimulus-bound, often subconscious learning and learning that involves interpretation, reasoning, insight, and other cognitive processes. One result is that research on learning has become more closely related to studies of the thinking, reasoning, and problem-solving processes covered in Chapter 9.

Today, even classical and instrumental conditioning are thought to involve cognitive processes. Some theorists speculate that what may be learned during conditioning is actually a cognitive expectancy. That is, in classical conditioning, the presence of the conditioned stimulus leads the organism to expect the unconditioned stimulus; in instrumental conditioning, the organism comes to expect that a given response will be followed by a reinforcer. As we saw in the case of learned helplessness, the examination of the specific role that cognitive processes might play in learning has produced innovative theories that can have important applications.

The relationship between learning and memory has also inspired new study. In fact, learning and memory may be so intertwined that it is impossible to study one without the other. Whenever the performance of a new response is delayed until some time after it is learned, some representation of the original experience must have been stored in memory. For example, Skinner (1950) trained a pigeon to peck at a key whenever the key was illuminated

LINKAGES
an example

LEARNING AND HUMAN DEVELOPMENT
How Do Children Learn a Gender Identity?

As we discussed in Chapter 2, the very foundation of people's identities as men and women is strongly influenced by what they learn as children about gender roles. Children tend to develop a *gender identity* by the age of two or three. That is, they begin to comprehend that they are a boy or a girl and that they are different from children of the opposite sex (Thompson, 1975). Both boys and girls at this age believe that girls "like to play with dolls," "talk a lot," and the like. Boys are described by both sexes as preferring to play with cars, help their fathers, build

As children grow, the combination of modeling and reinforcement by parents, peers, and others tends to create an environment that shapes behaviors and preferences traditionally associated with either a male or a female gender identity.

things, and so on (Kuhn, Nash & Brucken, 1978). Moreover, the differences that exist at age two or three become even more pronounced as time goes on. Behavioral differences are evident by the third year, and sex-typed choices in toys and play activities become more and more apparent as children grow.

Parents are the most important socializing agents during these early years, and their role is central to children's learning of gender identity. This influence seems to begin with the way parents view their newborn children. There is evidence that parents think of newborn boys and girls differently, probably because their own gender-role learning has led them to expect different behavior from boys and girls. Newborn boys and girls are virtually indistinguishable, yet adults who

with a particular pattern. Four years later, the same pigeon was placed in front of the key. It did nothing. But when the key was lit with the pattern used earlier, the pigeon began pecking immediately. Obviously, the original training experience had been stored in memory for at least four years. Researchers are now exploring questions such as how computer operators remember to use procedures that were learned weeks or even months earlier (Ross, 1984).

Because psychologists have turned away from the assumption that all learning can be explained by the formation of new associations, the acquisition of specific skills has also drawn new attention. Psychologists have begun to examine complex, everyday learning tasks, such as how people learn to solve arithmetic problems (Greeno, Riley & Gelman, 1984; Stigler, 1984; Wilkinson, 1984), understand stories (Myers et al., 1984), recognize music (Bharucha, 1984; Pollard-Gott, 1983), use computer programs (Ross, 1984), analyze X rays (Lesgold, 1984), and recognize partially hidden objects (Kellman & Spelke, 1983). For example, college students must learn the spatial relationships among the various buildings on campus. Usually they do so very easily, but only recently have psychologists begun to understand how this is possible (Hirtle & Jonides, 1985). Future research on learning is bound to include detailed examinations of how people acquire such complex skills in the natural environment.

To learn more about the field of learning, consider taking a course or two in the area. Some learning courses include laboratory sections that allow you to gain first-hand experience with the principles of human and animal learning.

think they are looking at a boy tend to describe the child as strong, robust, and active; those who think they are looking at a girl tend to describe the child as soft, delicate, and passive (Luria & Rubin, 1974). Similarly, adults who see an infant jump in response to a jack-in-the-box tend to label the reaction as anger when they think the child is a boy, but as fear when they think the baby is a girl (Condry & Condry, 1976).

Not surprisingly, parents also treat boys and girls differently. They tend to show a pattern of labeling and reinforcement that is likely to increase the probability of one set of behaviors in girls and another in boys. From infancy on, parents dress boys and girls differently and provide them with different toys. Observational studies indicate that parents tend to encourage independence, achievement, and competition in boys and sensitivity, empathy, and trustworthiness in girls (Block, 1980). In general, both mothers and fathers reinforce sons for being physical, engaging in independent acts, and playing with objects. Daughters are reinforced for both helping and requesting help from others (Huston, 1983).

Behaviors not consistent with the child's gender role often tend to be discouraged, though the range of acceptable behaviors for girls tends to be somewhat wider than that for boys. For example, parents seem to be more tolerant when a daughter engages in masculine behaviors than when a son engages in feminine ones. The same is true of peers in nursery school and kindergarten; girls tend not to chastise other girls who play with "boys'" toys or engage in other masculine behaviors, but boys often make disparaging remarks to other boys who play with "girls'" toys or otherwise display feminine actions (Langlois & Downs, 1980). In one study, five-year-old boys played with hair ribbons, dolls, and other "girls'" toys more often when alone than when an adult or another boy was present. However, the presence of an observer tended not to change the play activities of five-year-old girls (Hartrup & Moore, 1963; Kobasigawa, Arikaki & Awiguni, 1966). Thus, it appears that boys are subject to stronger sanctions against sex-inappropriate behaviors than are girls.

Once children begin to form a gender identity, they look for appropriate models (Kohlberg, 1966). The most obvious models are, of course, their parents. Children's books and television also offer gender-role models. Content analyses of written material for children indicate that females in these media are often fearful, frequently give up easily, and ask others for help. Males are portrayed as active and goal oriented. A similar pattern of differences appears in television programming (Sternglanz & Serbin, 1974). It is not surprising that children who watch the most television also have the most rigid assumptions about what is appropriate behavior for each gender (Greer, 1980).

In short, no matter how one may feel about the desirability of differential gender roles, there is no denying the importance of learning in creating them.

SUMMARY

1. Individuals adapt to changes in the environment through the process of learning. Historically, learning has been defined as any relatively permanent change in behavior that results from past experience. However, because learned responses are not always performed, some psychologists now prefer to define learning as any relatively permanent change in the organism that results from past experience.

2. One form of learning is classical conditioning. This occurs when a conditioned stimulus (such as a buzzer) is repeatedly paired with an unconditioned stimulus (such as meat powder on a dog's tongue). Eventually the conditioned stimulus will elicit a conditioned response (such as salivation) even when the unconditioned stimulus is not presented.

3. Acquisition is the process through which a conditioned stimulus begins to produce a conditioned response. The most important factors determining the strength of a conditioned response are the intensity of the unconditioned stimulus, the relevance of the conditioned stimulus, the number of CS-UCS pairings, and the time interval between the conditioned and the unconditioned stimulus. In general, a conditioned response will fail to develop if the time interval between the conditioned and the unconditioned stimulus is more than several seconds. One exception to this rule, however, is taste-aversion learning. This type of conditioning can occur even when the interval between the conditioned and the unconditioned stimulus is as long as ten to twelve hours. Studies of taste-aversion learning demonstrate that contiguity in time between the conditioned and the unconditioned stimulus is not a necessary condition for learning. The phenomenon of blocking indicates that contiguous presentations of the conditioned and the unconditioned stimulus are also not sufficient for conditioning to occur. Recently, theorists have suggested that classical conditioning occurs whenever a conditioned stimulus can be used to predict an unconditioned stimulus.

4. Several pieces of evidence indicate that the conditioned response is not identical to the unconditioned

response; in fact, in some cases, it appears to be exactly the opposite. Stimulus generalization leads conditioned responses to occur following stimuli that are similar, but not identical to, a conditioned stimulus. Stimulus discrimination limits generalization, prompting conditioned responses to some stimuli, but not others.

5. Several powerful phenomena occur in classical conditioning. If the unconditioned stimulus is no longer paired with the conditioned stimulus, the conditioned response will weaken and eventually disappear completely; this is the phenomenon of extinction. After extinction has occurred, the conditioned response often reappears if the conditioned stimulus is presented after some period of time; this is the phenomenon of spontaneous recovery. In addition, the conditioned response will revert to its original strength if the conditioned and unconditioned stimuli are paired only one or two times after extinction has occurred; this is the phenomenon of reconditioning.

6. Classical conditioning appears to play a role in emotional disturbances, hypertension, certain illnesses, situation-specific fears, and some cases of drug overdose. On the other hand, classical conditioning principles also underlie therapeutic techniques developed to treat cases of fear, anxiety, allergies, and other common problems.

7. Instrumental conditioning is the process through which an organism learns to emit a response in order to obtain a reward or avoid an aversive stimulus. The law of effect, named by Edward Thorndike, holds that any response that produces the desired effect becomes more likely over time. Similarly, any response that does not produce the desired effect becomes less likely over time. Skinner prefers the term *operant conditioning* to *instrumental conditioning*, because the organism is learning to *operate on* the environment. Today the two terms are often used interchangeably.

8. Any event that increases the probability of the immediately preceding response recurring is called a positive reinforcer. Any event whose removal increases the probability of the immediately preceding response recurring is called a negative reinforcer.

9. Complex responses can be learned through shaping; this process involves reinforcing closer and closer approximations to the desired response. In general, instrumental conditioning proceeds more quickly when the delay in receiving reinforcement is short than when it is long, and when the reinforcement is large than when it is small. A continuous reinforcement schedule is one in which the response is reinforced each time it occurs. In addition, there are four basic types of partial reinforcement schedules: fixed ratio, variable ratio, fixed interval, and variable interval.

Extinction, spontaneous recovery, and the development of secondary reinforcers are all common phenomena in instrumental conditioning.

10. Negative reinforcement is responsible for the phenomena of escape conditioning and avoidance conditioning. Punishment also plays an important role in instrumental conditioning. It involves the presentation of an aversive stimulus or the removal of a pleasant stimulus, and it decreases the frequency of the immediately preceding response.

11. The principles of instrumental conditioning have been used in many spheres of life. For example, punishment is very successful in treating cases of chronic ruminative disorder. Programmed instruction, a highly successful educational technique, is based on reinforcing correct responses. Overeating and insomnia can also be treated with instrumental conditioning principles.

12. Studies of social learning indicate that (a) both classical and instrumental conditioning occur in the natural social environment; (b) both classical and instrumental learning can occur vicariously; and (c) humans often engage in observational learning, in which they learn by watching others, even though they are not directly reinforced.

13. Observational learning depends on attention, retention, reproduction, and motivation. Much research on observational learning concerns the effects of television violence on aggression. Both experimental and field studies suggest that those who watch large amounts of violent programming become more aggressive themselves. Recent research suggests that these effects may be quite long-lasting.

14. Experiments on insight and latent learning suggest that cognitive processes also play an important role in learning. For example, both humans and animals form cognitive maps of their environments, even in the absence of any reinforcement.

KEY TERMS

Definitions of terms appear on the pages shown in parentheses.

acquisition (247)
avoidance conditioning (265)
blocking (251)
classical conditioning (247)
cognitive map (275)
conditioned response (CR) (247)
conditioned stimulus (CS) (247)
continuous reinforcement schedule (261)

delayed conditioning (248)
discriminative stimuli (260)
escape conditioning (264)
extinction (253)
fixed interval (FI) schedule (262)
fixed ratio (FR) schedule (262)
insight (257)
instrumental conditioning (256)

RECOMMENDED READINGS

Bower, G. H., & Hilgard, E. R. (1981). *Theories of learning* (5th ed.). Englewood Cliffs, N.J.: Prentice Hall. A classic textbook that presents specific theories of learning and evaluates the evidence pertaining to each.

Flaherty, C. F. (1985). *Animal learning and cognition.* New York: Knopf. Covers various topics in animal learning. A brief historical introduction is provided for each, and many contemporary controversies are discussed. Both biological and cognitive factors in learning are highlighted.

Hill, W. F. (1982). *Principles of learning: A handbook of applications.* Palo Alto, Calif.: Mayfield. An excellent discussion of how the principles of learning apply to everyday life.

Hill, W. F. (1985). *Learning: A survey of psychological interpretations* (4th ed.). New York: Harper & Row. An excellent introduction to the study of learning for the new student. Considerable emphasis given to how learning relates to memory and motivation.

Kalish, H. I. (1981). *From behavioral science to behavior modification.* New York: McGraw-Hill. The author discusses how experimental work in learning led to the development of various behavior modification techniques. Numerous examples are provided, and all aspects of behavior are covered.

*T*here is a scene in the film *On Golden Pond* in which an elderly Henry Fonda strolls away from the cabin he has shared with his wife every summer for decades and, after having gone some distance, suddenly becomes disoriented. He can neither remember where the cabin is nor recall how to get to town. Panicked, he begins to run and eventually gets safely back home, but is badly shaken. Experiences like this, which can plague older people, highlight dramatically the importance of that indispensable mental capacity called *memory*. Memory allows people to learn and to survive. Without memory, you would not know how to shut off the alarm, take a shower, get dressed, or find *your* way home. You would be unable to communicate with other people, because you would not remember what words mean or even what you had just said. You would be unaware of your own likes and dislikes, and you would have no idea of who you were in any meaningful sense.

Yet memory is full of paradoxes. It is not unusual, for example, for people to remember the name of their first-grade teacher, but not the name of someone they met just a minute ago. In other words, remarkable as it is, the human memory system is far from perfect. Like perception, memory is selective; people retain some information and lose some. And what people recall can be shaped by a surprisingly large number of factors, including the tendency to embellish or simplify what they report.

In this chapter, we describe what is known about both memory and forgetting. Some of the material here may be of immediate use to you in studying for exams and recalling what you have learned.

THE SCOPE OF THE MEMORY SYSTEM

Mathematician John Griffith has estimated that, by the time the average person dies, he or she will have stored five hundred times as much information as can be found in the *Encyclopedia Britannica* (Hunt, 1982). In your own encyclopedia of memories you could include the meanings of thousands of words. You could fill a volume simply by describing your personal experiences. You could also fill a volume with such procedures as how to play checkers, wind a watch, tie a shoelace, and so on. And this list does not even begin to exhaust the inventory of an average person's memory (Taylor, 1981).

The impressive capacity of human memory reveals a complex mental system. Our exploration of this system begins with a look at the kinds of information it can handle. Then we describe the mental processes involved in memory and the stages through which information passes in order to become permanent memories.

Three Types of Memory

In which hand does the Statue of Liberty hold her torch? When was the last time you spent cash for something? What part of speech is used to modify a

8

Memory

LINKAGES
an overview

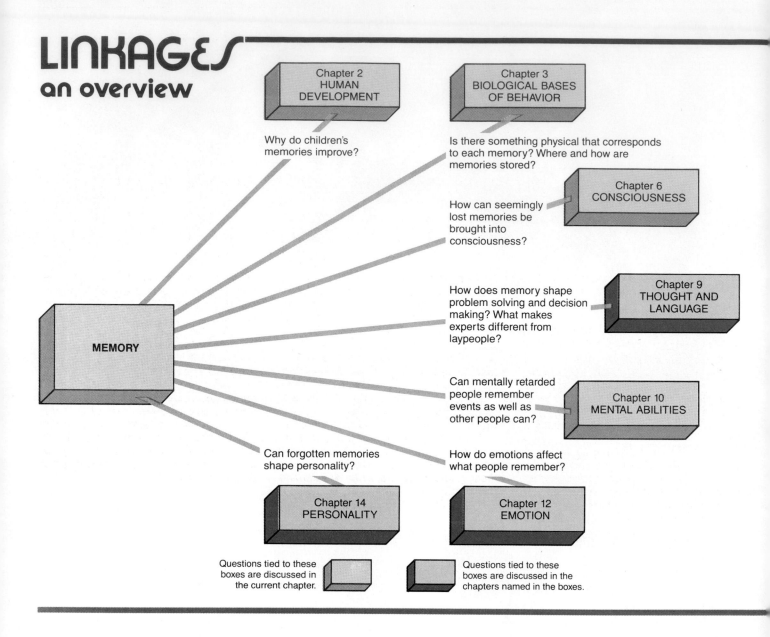

Chapter 2
HUMAN DEVELOPMENT

Why do children's memories improve?

Chapter 3
BIOLOGICAL BASES OF BEHAVIOR

Is there something physical that corresponds to each memory? Where and how are memories stored?

Chapter 6
CONSCIOUSNESS

How can seemingly lost memories be brought into consciousness?

Chapter 9
THOUGHT AND LANGUAGE

How does memory shape problem solving and decision making? What makes experts different from laypeople?

Chapter 10
MENTAL ABILITIES

Can mentally retarded people remember events as well as other people can?

MEMORY

Can forgotten memories shape personality?

How do emotions affect what people remember?

Chapter 14
PERSONALITY

Chapter 12
EMOTION

Questions tied to these boxes are discussed in the current chapter.

Questions tied to these boxes are discussed in the chapters named in the boxes.

---

noun? The first question is likely to elicit a visual image; to answer the second, you must recall a particular event in your life; and the third requires general knowledge unlikely to be tied to a specific event. Some theorists argue that answering each of these questions requires a different type of memory (Brewer & Pani, 1984). How many types of memory are there? No one is sure, but most research suggests that there are at least three basic types. Each is named for the kind of information it handles: episodic, semantic, and procedural (Tulving, 1985).

Any memory of a specific event that happened while you were present is an **episodic memory**—what you had for dinner yesterday or where you were last Friday night. More research has been devoted to episodic memory than to any other type. **Semantic memory** contains generalized knowledge of the world that does not involve memory of a specific event, or episode. For example, most people can answer questions like: Who was the first president of the United States? Are wrenches pets or tools? Most people know that wrenches are tools without remembering any specific episode in which they learned that fact. As a general rule, people convey episodic memories by

MEMORY AND PSYCHOLOGY

Much of what people commonly call "learning" was not discussed in our chapter on learning. How, for example, did you learn the meanings of the types of conditioning discussed in that chapter? Obviously, you had to use your memory. How people learn such facts is a central topic of this chapter, because much research on memory has looked at how people remember verbal material. But clearly, memory shapes behavior, not only in the classroom, but throughout life.

Take the case of Anna O, who was treated by Joseph Breuer, a close colleague of Freud. Anna suffered from paralysis, coughing, and insensitivity in her elbows, but none of these symptoms

had a physical cause. Breuer found that, when he hypnotized Anna, she could recall an unpleasant memory and express the emotions she felt at the time; then a symptom related to that memory would disappear. Later, in place of hypnosis, Freud used free association as a tool for eliciting memories. During free association, clients say whatever comes to mind; in the process, they often unearth long-buried memories. Why should the revival of a memory be tied to the disappearance of paralysis? Is the repression of memories a key to explaining behavior? We will discuss questions like these in later chapters, when we examine personality and abnormal psychology. But how forgetting occurs, how events

are encoded in memory, and how ideas may become associated are all pieces of the puzzle of memory that we consider in this chapter.

To answer these questions, psychologists draw on ideas that we encountered in the study of perception, on research in what children of various ages can remember, and on insights into how the brain works. The resulting view of memory provides one part of a larger picture, a picture of how the mind works. Thus, the study of memory is very closely linked with the examination of how people think and speak, topics discussed in Chapters 9 and 10.

saying, "I remember when . . . ," whereas they convey semantic memories by saying, "I know that . . ." (Tulving, 1972, 1982). **Procedural memory,** also called *skill memory,* involves how to do things. Knowing how to ride a bicycle, read a map, swim—these and thousands of other examples are types of procedural memory. Often, stored procedures involve complicated sequences of movements that cannot be described adequately in words. A gymnast, for example, might find it impossible to describe the exact motions required for a particular routine; an automobile mechanic might not be able to say exactly how to set an engine's timing correctly.

Many activities require all three types of memory. Consider a game of tennis. Knowing the rules of the game or how many sets are needed to win a match involves semantic memory. Remembering the score or which side served last requires episodic memory. Knowing how to lob or volley involves procedural memory. Some theorists argue that no distinction among types of memory is necessary, because all three are represented and retrieved in the same way (Anderson, 1976). No matter how the controversy is resolved, however, the three types remain useful labels for the contents of memory.

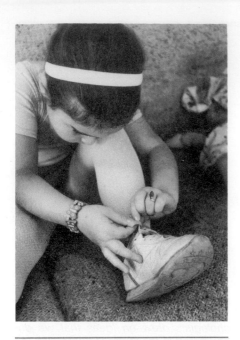

Procedural memories involve skills that can usually be learned only through repetition. This is why parents not only tell children how to tie a shoe, but also show them the steps and then let them practice.

Basic Memory Processes

Most people have a favorite story about forgetfulness. For example, one of the authors sometimes drives to work and sometimes walks. On one occasion, he drove, forgot that he had driven, and walked home. When he failed to find his car in its normal spot the next morning, he called the police to report the car stolen. After about twenty-four hours, the police called to let him know that they had found the car parked next to the psychology building on campus and that it had been towed to a storage area. When he went to retrieve the car, it was embarrassing enough for the author to explain that he had made a mistake, but particularly so when he realized that he was once again stranded because he had forgotten to bring his car keys. What went wrong? There are several possibilities, because remembering the contents of episodic, semantic, or procedural memory requires the flawless operation of three fundamental processes—encoding, storage, and retrieval—outlined in Figure 8.1. A breakdown of any one of these processes will produce some degree of forgetting (Melton, 1963).

First, information must be put into memory, a step that requires **encoding**. Just as incoming sensory information must be coded so that it can be communicated to the brain, information to be remembered must be put in a form that the memory system can accept and use. In the memory system, sensory information is put into various memory codes, or mental representations of physical stimuli. As discussed in Chapter 9, on thought, mental representations can take many forms. For example, people sometimes put information into **acoustic codes,** which represent information as sequences of sounds. **Visual codes** represent stimuli as pictures. **Semantic codes** represent an experience by its general meaning. Thus, if you see a billboard that reads "Huey's Going Out of Business Sale—50% Off Everything in Stock," you might encode the sound of the words as if they had been spoken (acoustic coding), the image of the letters as they were arranged on the sign (visual coding), or the fact that you saw an ad for Huey's (semantic coding). The way stimuli are coded can influence what is remembered. For example, semantic coding might allow you to clearly remember seeing a car parked in your neighbors' driveway just before their house was robbed, but because there was little or no other coding, you might not be able to remember the make, model, or color (Bahrick & Boucher, 1968).

The second basic memory process is **storage,** which simply means maintaining information in the system over time. Episodic, semantic, and procedural memories can be stored for a very long time. When you find it possible to use a pogo stick or perform some other "rusty" skill or to recall facts and events from many years ago, you are depending on your memory's storage capacity.

Figure 8.1
Basic Memory Processes
Successfully remembering something requires three basic processes. First, the item must be encoded, or put in a form that can be placed in, memory. Second, it must be stored, or maintained, in memory. Finally, it must be retrieved, or recovered, from memory. If any of these processes fails to operate properly, forgetting will occur.

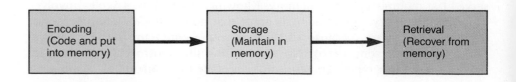

Encoding (Code and put into memory) → Storage (Maintain in memory) → Retrieval (Recover from memory)

The human memory system allows us to encode, store, and retrieve a lifetime of experiences. Without it, we would have no sense of who we are.

Retrieval is the process of finding information stored in memory and bringing it into consciousness. Retrieving stored information like your address or telephone number is usually so fast and effortless as to seem automatic. Only when you try to retrieve other kinds of information—such as the answer to a quiz question that you know but cannot quite recall—do you become aware of the searching process.

Encoding, storage, and retrieval are all vital links in the memory chain. The author's forgetfulness might thus be traced to information about his car's location being (a) never properly encoded, (b) encoded but never stored, or (c) stored but never retrieved.

Three Stages of Memory

As noted in the sensation and perception chapters, a great deal of information reaches people, but only a fraction of it is perceived. Similarly, people remember some incoming information far better and far longer than other information. For example, suppose your friends throw a surprise party for you. On entering the room, you might barely notice, and later fail to recall, the flash from a camera. And you might forget in a few seconds the name of a person you met at the party. But if you live to be a hundred, you will never forget where the party took place or how surprised and pleased you were. Why do some stimuli leave no more than a fleeting impression and others remain in memory forever? There are a number of factors to consider, the most important of which involves how extensively incoming information is processed. The most influential theories of memory suggest that, in order for information to become firmly embedded in memory, it must pass through three stages of processing: sensory memory, short-term memory, and long-term memory (Atkinson & Shiffrin, 1968; see Figure 8.2, p. 286).

In the first, *sensory memory* stage, *sensory registers* hold information from the senses—sights or sounds, for example—for a fraction of a second. Information in the sensory registers may be attended to, analyzed, and encoded as a meaningful pattern; as we described in Chapter 5, this process is known as *perception*. If the information in sensory memory is perceived, it can enter

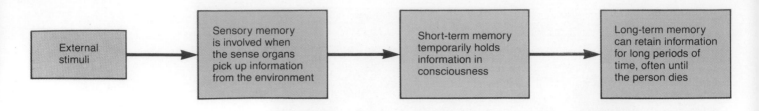

Figure 8.2
The Three Stages of Memory
Here is a very basic overview of the human memory system. In the first memory stage, the eyes, ears, or other sense organs pick up visual, auditory, and other information from the environment. The second stage involves the detection and brief holding in consciousness of distinct patterns of energy, such as recognizable images or understandable words. The third stage allows information to be retained for use hours, days, or even years later.

the second, or *short-term memory,* stage where, if nothing further is done, it will disappear in twenty seconds or so. If you further process the information in short-term memory, it may be encoded into *long-term memory,* where it may remain indefinitely.

Your reading this sentence is an example of all three stages of memory. As you read, light energy reflected from the page is converted to neural activity and registered in sensory memory. If you pay attention to these stimuli, your perception of the patterns of light can be held in short-term memory. While you read, you are constantly recognizing words by matching your perceptions of them with the patterns and meanings you have stored in long-term memory. In addition, you are also holding the early parts of the sentence in short-term memory, so that they can be integrated and understood as you read the rest of the sentence. Thus, all three memory stages are necessary for you to understand a sentence.

In the following sections, we describe the three stages of memory one by one, along with the encoding, storage, and retrieval processes associated with each one. Some of the words and methods we use may seem to suggest that each stage of memory is a box that passively receives information from the preceding stage. But the memory system is not a chain of fancy recorders that passively collect what the world presents. Instead, memory (like perception) is an active process in which the three stages interact. As shown in the example of reading a sentence, encoding new information usually requires retrieving information already stored in memory and linking the new information to the old. Thus, what is already in long-term memory constantly influences how new experiences are encoded.

To see how information stored in long-term memory affects your own encoding of new information, read the passage in Figure 8.3, then turn away

Figure 8.3
The Role of Memory in Comprehension
What is already stored in long-term memory affects the ability to comprehend and remember new information.
(From "Contextual Prerequisites for Understanding: Some Investigations of Comprehension and Recall" by Bransford and Johnson. *Journal of Verbal Learning and Verbal Behavior, 61,* pp. 717–726, 1972. With permission of Academic Press.)

The procedure is actually quite simple. First you arrange items into different groups. Of course one pile may be sufficient depending on how much there is to do. If you have to go somewhere else due to lack of facilities that is the next step; otherwise, you are pretty well set. It is important not to overdo things. That is, it is better to do too few things at once than too many. In the short run this may not seem important but complications can easily arise. A mistake can be expensive as well. At first, the whole procedure will seem complicated. Soon, however, it will become just another facet of life. It is difficult to foresee any end to the necessity for this task in the immediate future, but then, one never can tell. After the procedure is completed one arranges the materials into different groups again. Then they can be put into their appropriate places. Eventually they will be used once more and the whole cycle will then have to be repeated. However, that is part of life.

and try to recall as much of it as possible. To find out the title of the paragraph, read the footnote at the bottom of the next page;[1] then read the passage again. During this second reading, the passage should make a lot more sense and be much easier to remember (Bransford & Johnson, 1972). Reading the title of the passage allowed you to retrieve from long-term memory your knowledge about the topic. On the second reading, this knowledge created new expectations about the passage, which allowed you to process the passage more efficiently. In general, as you gain more knowledge in an area, it becomes easier and easier to remember new things about it.

SENSORY MEMORY

We have said that, in order to recognize incoming stimuli, the brain must analyze them and compare them to what is already stored in long-term memory. This process is nearly, but not quite, instantaneous. As a result, the impression that stimuli make on the senses must be maintained for a short time. This is the job of the sensory registers, as Figure 8.2 shows. The **sensory registers** hold incoming information long enough for it to be processed further. This type of memory, called **sensory memory**, is very primitive and very, very brief, but it lasts long enough to connect one impression to the next, so that people experience a smooth flow of information.

Capacity of the Sensory Registers

Most of what we know about sensory memory comes from studies of the sensory register for visual information. For many years, researchers puzzled over how much information this register could hold and for how long. Several answers came out of experiments on how the eyes look at the world. When you look around, it seems as if your eyes are moving slowly but smoothly, like a movie camera scanning a scene. In fact, they are not. As noted in the perception chapter, your eyes fixate at one point for about one-fourth of a second and then rapidly jump to a new position. This rapid jumping from one fixation point to another is called *saccadic eye movement.*

How much information can a person glean from just one eye fixation? Several experiments addressed this question by showing people a display that included from one letter to twelve different letters arranged in rows. Each display was presented for such a short time (for example, one-tenth of a second) that the subjects did not have a chance to move their eyes while it was visible; they saw it in only one fixation. Then, with the display removed, they were asked to report as many letters as possible (McDougall, 1904). People typically reported only about four or five items, even when the display included more than five. In other words, it appeared that there is a limit to how much information people can glean in a single fixation and that the limit is about four or five items. This limit is called the *span of apprehension.*

George Sperling (1960) was working on his doctoral dissertation when he noticed something very important about these experiments. The subjects often claimed that, although they could report only about four or five items, they had in fact *seen* the entire display. Why was this important? If the subjects were correct, then the span of apprehension indicated, not a limit on how much they could *see,* but a limit on how much they could *remember and report.*

How could these two types of limitations be disentangled? Recall that the subjects were shown a display for a very brief time and then were asked to report all of the letters in the display; this is called the *whole-report procedure.* Sperling devised a *partial-report procedure,* outlined in Figure 8.4 (p. 288). A

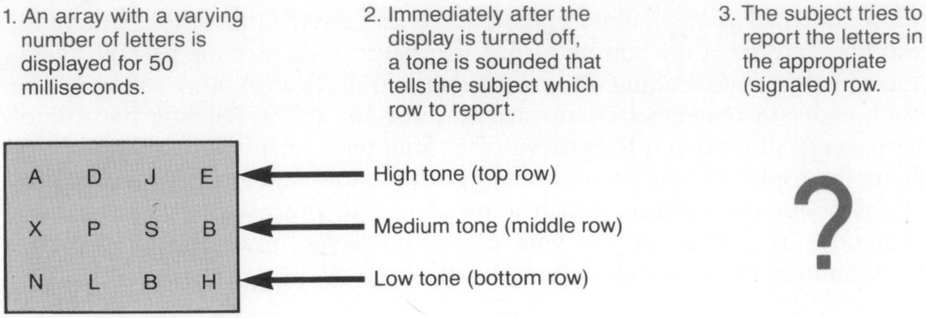

1. An array with a varying number of letters is displayed for 50 milliseconds.

2. Immediately after the display is turned off, a tone is sounded that tells the subject which row to report.

3. The subject tries to report the letters in the appropriate (signaled) row.

A	D	J	E
X	P	S	B
N	L	B	H

◄—— High tone (top row)

◄—— Medium tone (middle row)

◄—— Low tone (bottom row)

?

Figure 8.4
Studying Sensory Memory with the Partial-Report Procedure
Subjects are presented with an array of from three to twelve letters for fifty milliseconds (or one-twentieth of a second) and are then asked to report some of what they saw. Because they do not know which row they are to recall until after the display has disappeared, they must keep all the letters in memory to successfully complete the task.
(From *Human Memory: The Processing of Information* by G. R. Loftus and E. F. Loftus. Copyright © 1976 by Lawrence Erlbaum Associates, Inc.)

person was shown a display of three rows of letters and, just after it was shut off, heard a tone. If the tone was high pitched, the subject was supposed to report only the top row of letters. If the tone was medium pitched, only the middle row was to be reported. And if the subjects heard a low-pitched tone, only the lowest row was to be reported. Notice that the subjects did not know which row was supposed to be reported until after the display had been shut off. As a result, they had to pay attention to the entire display and then retrieve the requested items from memory.

With this procedure, Sperling believed he could distinguish limitations on what people can see from limitations on what they can remember. To understand why, consider the trials in which subjects were shown twelve letters, as in Figure 8.4. How many letters must a person have available in memory in order to report all four letters in any row, regardless of which tone is sounded? Since subjects did not know which tone would sound until after the display was removed, perfect performance could occur only if the person had all twelve letters stored in memory.

By using the partial-report procedure in this way, Sperling estimated the number of items that were both seen and available in memory. Figure 8.5 shows the results. Clearly, many more items were available in people's memory than had been thought. Why, then, could subjects *report* only four or five letters? By increasing the time between the presentation of the letters and the tone, Sperling found that subjects' memory of the display faded continuously and decayed completely after about one second. Thus, by the time the subjects in the whole-report condition could report four or five items, the memory of the other items had *decayed,* or faded. In other words, what subjects had been claiming all along was correct: they were able to see more items than they could report. The span of apprehension reflected a limit, not on how much they could see, but on how long information could be held in the sensory register.

Properties of Sensory Memory

Experiments like Sperling's helped establish the fact that the sensory registers retain mental representations of visual images only for a very brief time. These representations are called **icons,** and the sensory register for them is called

[1]The title of the passage on page 286 is "Washing Clothes."

iconic memory. Most icons last no more than one second, but there are conditions in which an icon can last a bit longer. The major determinant of how long an icon lasts is the strength of the visual stimulus (for example, its brightness). The stronger the visual stimulus, the more slowly the icon fades (Long & Beaton, 1982). As we noted in the chapter on perception, unusual persistence of an icon may play a role in the reading disorder known as dyslexia.

Thanks to iconic memory, people do not notice their saccadic eye movements, and the flow of information does not stop with every blink. The image from each fixation lasts long enough to give one the perception of a smooth flow of visual information. Thus, iconic memory allows people to see a smooth flow of images when watching a movie (Loftus, 1983) or when one object passes in front of another (Mace & Turvey, 1983). Another interesting property of iconic memory is that it can lay one image on top of another, so that information is *summed,* as in Figure 8.6 (p. 290).

Psychologists believe that each of the other senses has its own type of sensory register; among them, only echoic memory has received much study so far. **Echoic memory** is the sensory register for auditory sensations; an **echo** in this context is the mental representation of a sound in sensory memory. Experiments like Sperling's indicate that iconic and echoic memory have essentially the same properties, with one exception. Unlike an icon, an echo characteristically lasts up to several seconds, probably because of the physiology of the ear. For both the echo and the icon, research suggests that encoding is minimal. Both icons and echoes are very faithful reproductions of the physical stimulus, virtual copies of the information provided by the senses (Sakitt & Long, 1979).

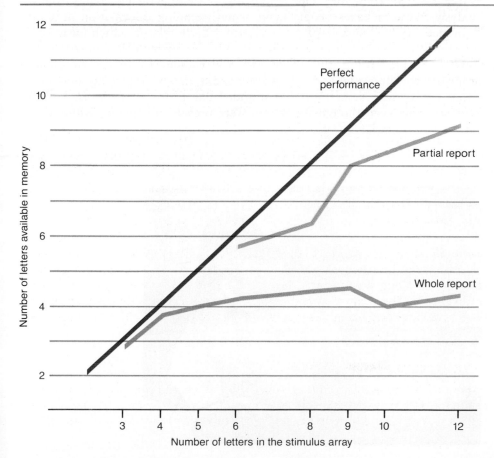

Figure 8.5
Results of a Sensory Memory Experiment
By using the partial-report procedure, Sperling found that subjects can retain nine or ten letters out of a twelve-letter display. However, because forgetting is extremely rapid, usually taking place within a second or two, performance is poor in the whole-report procedure. In the time it took people to report about four letters, they had already forgotten the rest.
(From G. Sperling, "The Information Available in Brief Visual Presentation," 74, pp. 1–29, Psychological Monographs. Copyright © 1960 by the American Psychological Association. Adapted by permission of the author.)

Figure 8.6
***Summation of Information in
Iconic Memory***
*Researchers showed subjects the top panel
for six milliseconds, shut it off, and then
presented the middle panel for six milliseconds. Subjects were able to identify the
nonsense syllable (VOH) because the two
iconic images, or mental representations,
became superimposed. The superimposed
image is shown in the lower panel.*
(From "Some Temporal Characteristics of Visual
Pattern Perception" by Ericksen and Collins, *Journal of Experimental Psychology*, 74, pp. 476–484.
Copyright © 1967 by the American Psychological
Association. Adapted by permission of the authors.)

Without further processing, icons, echoes, and other sensory memories
simply fade away. The process controlling what information in sensory memory
will be captured is called *selective attention,* which is described in the chapter
on perception. Thus, perception itself processes and captures the elusive
impressions of sensory memory, transferring them to short-term memory.

SHORT-TERM MEMORY

Whereas sensory registers typically store information for only a second or so,
the information in **short-term,** or **working, memory** can last from one second
to more than a minute. When you look up a phone number and then dial the
phone or check your *TV Guide* and then change the channel, you are using
short-term memory. In fact, you might say that people *live* in short-term
memory, because it provides much of their consciousness of the present. As
its name implies, however, short-term memory can be fragile. For instance,
you might forget the number you just looked up before you can dial it. In
the following sections, we discuss how information in short-term memory is
encoded, stored, and retrieved.

Encoding

If you attend to and perceive a stimulus, it enters short-term memory.
Information is much more elaborately encoded in short-term memory than in
the sensory registers. Various types of memory codes can be used, but research
suggests that much of the information in short-term memory—particularly
verbal information—is represented by an acoustic code.

How do we know this? One convincing piece of evidence comes from an
analysis of the mistakes people make when encoding information in short-
term memory. The mistakes tend to be *acoustically related,* which means that
they involve the substitution of similar sounds. For example, R. Conrad (1964)
showed people strings of letters and asked them to repeat the letters
immediately. The mistakes they made tended to involve replacing the correct
letter, say, *C,* with something that sounded like it, for example, *D, P,* or *T.*
This was true even though the letters were presented visually, without any
sound.

*Information such as a new phone number is
placed in short term, or* working, *memory
where, as we shall see, it tends to
disappear rapidly unless we take steps to
prevent its loss.*

9 2 5	G M N
8 6 4 2	S L R R
3 7 6 5 4	V O E P G
6 2 7 4 1 8	X W D X Q O
0 4 0 1 4 7 3	E P H H J A E
1 9 2 2 3 5 3 0	Z D O F W D S V
4 8 6 8 5 4 3 3 2	D T Y N R H E H Q
2 5 3 1 9 7 1 7 6 8	K H W D A G R O F Z
8 5 1 2 9 6 1 9 4 5 0	U D F F W H D Q D G E
9 1 8 5 4 6 9 4 2 9 3 7	Q M R H X Z D P R R E H

CAT BOAT RUG

RUN BEACH PLANT LIGHT

SUIT WATCH CUT STAIRS CAR

JUNK LONE GAME CALL WOOD HEART

FRAME PATCH CROSS DRUG DESK HORSE LAW

CLOTHES CHOOSE GIFT DRIVE BOOK TREE HAIR THIS

DRESS CLERK FILM BASE SPEND SERVE BOOK LOW TIME

STONE ALL NAIL DOOR HOPE EARL FEEL BUY COPE GRAPE

AGE SOFT FALL STORE PUT TRUE SMALL FREE CHECK MAIL LEAF

LOG DAY TIME CHESS LAKE CUT BIRD SHEET YOUR SEE STREET WHEEL

Storage

You can easily determine the capacity of short-term memory by conducting a simple experiment designed by Darlene Howard (1983) and shown in Figure 8.7. The maximum number of items you can recall perfectly after one presentation is called the **immediate memory span.** If your memory span is like most people's, you can repeat about six or seven items from the test in Figure 8.7. The interesting thing is that you should come up with about the same number whether you estimate your immediate memory span with digits, letters, words, or virtually any type of unit (Hayes, 1952; Pollack, 1953). When George Miller (1956) noticed that studies of a wide variety of tasks showed the same limit on the ability to process information, he pointed out that the limit seems to be a "magic number" of 7 plus or minus 2. This is the capacity of short-term memory; it applies, not to a certain number of discrete elements, but to the number of *meaningful groupings* of information, called **chunks.**

The capacity of short-term memory is almost always between five and nine chunks. For example, read the following letters to a friend, pausing at each dash: FB-ITW-AC-IAI-BMB-MW. The chances are very good that your friend will not be able to repeat this string of letters perfectly. Why? There are fifteen letters, which is more than most people's immediate memory span. But if you pause when you read the letters, so that they are grouped as FBI-TWA-CIA-IBM-BMW, the chances are very good that your friend will be able to repeat the string back easily (Bower, 1975). They are the same fifteen

Figure 8.7
Capacity of Short-Term Memory
These materials can be used to test your immediate, or short-term, memory span. Have a friend read the items in the top row at the rate of about one per second; then try to repeat them back in exactly the same order. If you are able to do this perfectly, have your friend read the next row. Each row contains one additional item. Continue until you make a mistake. Most people are perfect at this task until they reach six or seven items. The maximum number of items you can repeat back perfectly is your immediate memory span.
(Adapted with permission of Macmillan Publishing Company from *Cognitive Psychology: Memory, Language, and Thought* by Darlene V. Howard. Copyright © 1983 by Darlene V. Howard.)

letters, but they will be processed, not as fifteen separate letters, but as five meaningful chunks of information.

Chunks of information can become very complex. For example, if someone read to you, "The boy in the red shirt kicked his mother in the shin," you could probably repeat the sentence very easily. Yet it contains twelve separate words and forty-three individual letters. How can you repeat the sentence so effortlessly? The answer is that people can build bigger and bigger chunks of information (Simon, 1974). In this case, you might represent "the boy in the red shirt" as one chunk of information rather than as six words or nineteen letters. Similarly, "kicked his mother" and "in the shin" represent separate chunks of information.

Notice that chunking in this way also demonstrates the interaction of short-term and long-term memory. You cannot come up with a meaningful grouping of information if you do no more than passively take it in. Chunking requires that you relate the information being encoded in short-term memory to information already in long-term memory.

HIGHLIGHT

The Power of Chunking

Learning to use bigger and bigger chunks of information can noticeably improve the amount of information held in short-term memory. For example, as noted in the chapter on development, children's memories improve in part because they gradually become able to hold as many as seven chunks in memory, but also because they become better able to group information into chunks.

A notable demonstration of the power of chunking comes from an experiment with a college student of average intelligence, with no unusual memory skills (Chase & Ericsson, 1979). At the beginning of the experiment, his immediate memory span was seven digits. The experimenters began by presenting a small number of digits and asking the student to repeat them in the same order. If he was correct, they increased the number of items on the list by one and repeated the procedure. Whenever the student made a mistake, the number of items was decreased by one and the procedure was repeated. He received a new random set of digits on each trial. This procedure was continued for one hour a day, approximately four days a week. After six months, the student's immediate memory span had increased to thirty-eight items (Ericsson, Chase & Faloon, 1980). After two years, it had increased to approximately two hundred items (Chase & Ericsson, 1981).

Other people's increased memory abilities are not restricted to strings of random numbers. Many cocktail waitresses, for example, can remember a much longer list of drinks than the average person (Bennett, 1983). One waiter taught himself to remember up to sixteen complete dinner orders without taking notes (Chase & Ericsson, 1981). All of these people owe their remarkable abilities to continued practice with some useful method of grouping items—such as drinks or meals—into larger and larger chunks. For example, because the student in Chase and Ericsson's (1979) experiment was a runner, he encoded long sequences of digits as times in a race. If the first four digits were 3-2-7-8, he encoded them as the chunk 3:27.8 and thought of it as "3 minutes, 27.8 seconds, close to a world's record for the mile." In short, although the capacity of short-term memory is more or less constant, at seven plus or minus two chunks of meaningful information, the size of those chunks can vary. Learn to group more items into a meaningful chunk, and you can greatly increase your memory span.

Notice, however, that memory improvement takes many hours of practice and requires not only elaborate chunking, but also encoding and organizing new information in terms of knowledge already stored in long-term memory.

In other words, though chunking alone can improve short-term memory, it is most effective when combined with strategies for relating short-term memory chunks to information in long-term memory. Learning to move information rapidly back and forth between short-term and long-term memory is also particularly effective. One simple example is companies' use of meaningful, and thus memorable, chunks in such toll-free customer-assistance numbers as 1-800-REACH US or CALL GTE. And renowned chess masters, who have been known to play and win several games at once, even when blindfolded, have learned to chunk visual images of each game's layout and use prior knowledge to encode new information quickly and efficiently into both short-term and long-term memory. We discuss some of these more elaborate memory improvement methods later in the chapter. ◼

Duration By **rehearsing** information, repeating it to yourself, you can maintain it in short-term memory for as long as you want. But people usually forget information in short-term memory quickly unless they continue to rehearse it. You have undoubtedly experienced this yourself. In order to hold a telephone number in short-term memory while you walk across the room to dial the phone, you must rehearse the number over and over. If a friend comes in and interrupts you, even for a few seconds, you may forget the number. But this limitation of short-term memory is actually useful. Imagine what life would be like if you kept remembering every phone number you ever dialed or every conversation you ever heard.

How long does unrehearsed information stay in short-term memory? To answer this question, researchers needed a way to prevent rehearsal. In two famous experiments published almost simultaneously, John Brown (1958) in England and Lloyd and Margaret Peterson (1959) in the United States devised a method for doing so, which is called the **Brown-Peterson procedure.** A subject is presented with a group of three letters, such as GRB. Then the subject counts backward by threes from an arbitrarily selected number until a signal is given. Counting prevents the subject from rehearsing the letters. On the signal, the subject stops counting and tries to recall the letters. By varying the number of seconds the subject counts backward, the experimenter can determine how much forgetting takes place over a given amount of time.

As you can see in Figure 8.8, forgetting of information in short-term memory happens gradually but quite rapidly; after eighteen seconds, subjects can remember almost nothing (Peterson & Peterson, 1959). This is a striking demonstration of the importance of rehearsal for keeping information in short-term memory. Evidence from these and other experiments suggests that *unrehearsed* information can be maintained in short-term memory for no more than about twenty seconds. As noted earlier, although this can be a blessing, it can sometimes be dangerous. For example, on May 17, 1986, an air traffic controller at Chicago's O'Hare Field forgot that he had just instructed an aircraft to land on one runway and allowed another plane to take off on an intersecting runway. The two aircraft missed each other by only twenty feet.

Causes of forgetting Why do people forget information in short-term memory so rapidly? Researchers have found that either of two processes may be the cause (Reitman, 1971, 1974; Shiffrin, 1973). One process is *decay*. The mental representation of a stimulus may simply disappear gradually from the system, much as letters on a piece of steel are eaten away by rust and become less distinct over time. Forgetting also occurs because of *interference* from other information. For example, the appearance of new information in short-term memory can result in the *displacement* of information already there. Like a workbench, short-term memory can hold only a limited number of items; when additional items are added, the old ones tend to "fall off" (Klatzky,

Figure 8.8
Forgetting in Short-Term Memory
The graph shows the percentage of non-sense syllables recalled after various intervals during which rehearsal was prevented. Note that there was virtually complete forgetting after a delay of eighteen seconds.
(From "Short Term Retention of Individual Verbal Items" by Peterson and Peterson, *Journal of Experimental Psychology, 58,* pp.193–198. Copyright © 1959 by the American Psychological Association. Adapted by permission of the authors.)

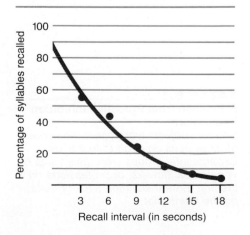

1980). This is one reason why the phone number you just looked up is likely to drop out of short-term memory if you read another number before dialing. Rehearsal prevents displacement by reentering the same information into short-term memory.

Displacement is an example of **retroactive interference,** in which new information placed in memory interferes with the ability to recall information already in memory. There can also be **proactive interference,** in which previously learned information, now residing in long-term memory, interferes with the ability to remember new information. Mistakenly saying the English word *window* instead of the German equivalent that you just learned is an example of proactive interference. It is easier to keep the two types of interference straight if you remember that *pro*active interference operates forward in time (the past interferes with the present), whereas *retro*active interference operates backward in time (the present interferes with the past).

What is stored? You have seen that information is usually encoded into short-term memory acoustically (by how it sounds); that how much is remembered depends on how the information is grouped; and that, unless it is rehearsed, information is very quickly forgotten. There is yet another question to consider about the storage of information in short-term memory: How is the information represented mentally when it is stored?

To find out, Delos Wickens (1973) used a variation of the Brown-Peterson procedure and came up with a surprising answer. Each of four groups of subjects was given four recall trials. Table 8.1 lists the types of items given to each group. One, called the "fruit group," was given the names of three kinds of fruit on each trial. The vegetable group was to remember the names of three vegetables on the first three trials, but on the fourth trial, they were given the names of three fruits. As Table 8.1 shows, the type of words given on the fourth trial was also shifted for the flower and the profession groups.

The results are shown in Figure 8.9. The performance of the fruit group declined steadily across trials because of increasing proactive interference. The other groups showed a similar decline across the first three trials. However, their performance improved on the fourth trial, when the category of the words they tried to remember was shifted. This improvement, caused by changing the category of information to be remembered, is called a *release from proactive interference.* Notice that there were different amounts of release from proactive interference, depending on the degree of similarity between word categories. When the words to be learned shifted from vegetables to fruits, the improvement was quite small. Improvement was intermediate for the shift from flowers to fruits and very large for the shift from professions to fruits. Why?

One possibility is that the words were represented in memory, not as single units, but as collections of attributes or *features,* such as what the item looks like, what it tastes like, where one finds it, and so on. Because fruits

TABLE 8.1

A Release from Proactive Inhibition Experiment

Control subjects were given the names of three fruits on each of four trials. Experimental groups were given lists of vegetables, flowers, or professions on the first three trials, then a list of fruits on the fourth trial.

Group	Trial 1	Trial 2	Trial 3	Trial 4
Fruit (control)	Fruits	Fruits	Fruits	Fruits
Vegetable	Vegetables	Vegetables	Vegetables	Fruits
Flower	Flowers	Flowers	Flowers	Fruits
Profession	Professions	Professions	Professions	Fruits

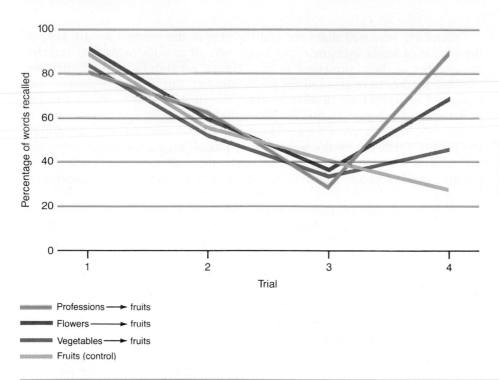

Figure 8.9
Release from Proactive Interference
Control subjects showed a steady decline in performance over four trials in which lists of fruits were to be recalled. This reflects a buildup of proactive interference from one list of fruit to the next. The other groups showed a release from proactive interference when—after three trials with lists of vegetables, flowers, or professions—they were to recall a list of fruits. The release effect on trial 4 was complete when the change in category was from professions to fruits, because professions share virtually no features with fruits. Thus, subjects recalled the fruit list on trial 4 as well as they had recalled the professions on the first trial.
(From "Some Characteristics of Word Encoding" by Wickens. *Memory and Cognition, 1*, pp. 485–490. Copyright 1973 Psychonomic Society Publications.)

and vegetables have many features in common, one category still interferes a great deal with the other, and the amount of release from proactive interference is quite small. However, fruits and professions have virtually nothing in common, so the shift in this case creates almost complete release from proactive interference (Wickens, 1972). In other words, old information interferes less with new information if the new information is very different from the old. Thus, your old phone number might interfere with your recall of a new phone number, but it would not interfere with your remembering the name of a new friend.

The idea that words are represented in short-term memory, not as single units, but as bundles of multiple features is very important, and we will return to it later in this chapter.

Retrieval

Imagine that you are holding certain information in short-term memory—for example, the digits 4-2-6. When asked for this information, you can give it, but the process is not as instantaneous as it may seem. Your ability to report what is in short-term memory depends on a process of search and retrieval.

How does retrieval work? Saul Sternberg (1966, 1969) looked at two theoretical possibilities, known as parallel search and serial search. In a **parallel search,** all of the information in short-term memory is examined in parallel, or all at once. In a **serial search,** information is examined serially, or one piece at a time. To determine which type of search is used, Sternberg gave people several digits to remember and then gave them a probe number. The subjects' task was to determine whether the probe number had been part of the original set of digits. In order to answer, subjects had to compare the probe number to the numbers in memory. People can perform this task very rapidly, and they almost never make a mistake. But do they scan the digits in memory all at once or one by one?

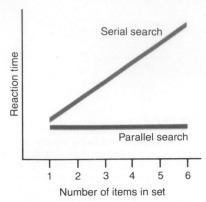

(a) Predicted outcomes

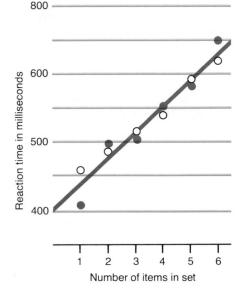

○ Negative responses
● Positive responses

(b) Actual outcome

Figure 8.10
Short-Term Memory Scanning
How does the time needed to retrieve an item from short-term memory change as a function of the number of items? Predictions for a serial search model and a parallel search model are shown in (a). Typical empirical data are shown in (b); researchers have concluded from results like these that the search process in short-term memory is serial.
(From "High Speed Scanning in Human Memory" by S. Sternberg, *Science*, Vol. 153, #3736, pp. 652–654, August 5, 1966. Copyright 1966 by the American Association for the Advancement of Science.)

Sternberg reasoned that time and the size of the number set are keys to the puzzle. If items in memory are examined all at once (a parallel search), the number of digits presented in the original set should have no effect on the time it takes to respond to the probe number. But if items in memory are examined one at a time (a serial search), the time needed to respond to the probe should increase as the length of the original list increases. Some of Sternberg's findings are shown in Figure 8.10. As you can see, they follow the pattern predicted by the serial search model: for each item added to the list, there is a corresponding increase in the time taken for the search. To be precise, it takes about ⅟₂₅ of a second to scan a single item in short-term memory.

Sternberg found another interesting result by comparing the time taken for yes and no responses. Obviously, a person would need to search all the items in the set in order to determine that the probe number was not in the set. But you would think that, in order to say yes, subjects would have to search only long enough to find the probe number; this should take less time. This is not what happens. People took the same amount of time to make a positive or a negative response. In other words, the search does not stop when a match to the probe number is found. Instead, the search continues through the entire set. In short, the evidence indicates that people retrieve information from short-term memory through an *exhaustive serial search*. Figure 8.11 summarizes much of what we have said about short-term, or working, memory.

LONG-TERM MEMORY

Table 8.2 contrasts the characteristics of short-term memory with those of sensory and long-term memory. Since long-term memory and short-term memory interact constantly, should they be considered two storage systems or one?

Distinguishing Between Short-Term and Long-Term Memory

Psychologists studying memory have distinguished short-term from long-term memory because the two appear to be governed by different scientific laws and therefore seem to be qualitatively different. For one thing, as Table 8.2 shows, there are good reasons for believing that both the encoding and storage processes in long-term memory differ from those of short-term memory. (We will describe these differences shortly.) Evidence that information is transferred from short-term memory to another type of storage also supports the view that short- and long-term memory should be considered distinct. This evidence comes from experiments on recall and from research on the biology of memory.

Serial-position curves   Look at the following list of words for thirty seconds, then look away and try to recall as many words as you can, in any order: bed, rest, quilt, dream, sheet, artichoke, mattress, pillow, night, snore, pajamas. Which words you recall depends in part on their *serial position;* that is, on where the words were in the list, as Figure 8.12 (p. 298) shows. Figure 8.12 is a *serial-position curve,* which is a plot of the chances of recalling the words in each position in a list. For the first two or three words in a list, recall is very good, a characteristic that is called the **primacy effect.** The probability of recall decreases for words in the middle of the list and then rises dramatically for the last few words. The ease of recalling words near the end of a list is called the **recency effect.**

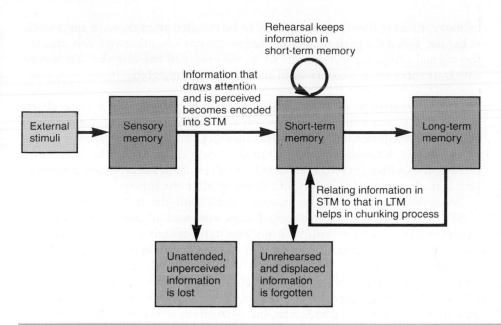

Figure 8.11
Another View of the Memory System
We have now seen that information that is attended to and perceived is encoded into short-term memory. If it is not rehearsed or is displaced by new information, this information will be lost. Chunking, aided by information already in long-term memory, can help hold more information in short-term memory.

The primacy effect occurs because the words at the beginning of a list are rehearsed much more often than any of the other words on the list (Rundus, 1971). But why does the recency effect occur? If short-term and long-term memory are indeed distinct, then one possibility is that, when the test is given immediately after the list is read, the last four or five words in the list are still in short-term memory and thus are easily recalled. On the other hand, the beginning and the middle of the list must be retrieved from long-term memory.

To test this hypothesis, Murray Glanzer and Anita Cunitz (1966) gave a list of words to two groups of people. They asked one group to recall the list immediately after it was given. The second group was given a list, immediately performed a mental arithmetic task for thirty seconds, and then tried to recall as many words as possible. As Figure 8.13 (p. 298) shows, no recency effect occurred among those in the second group. Performing the arithmetic task before recalling the list displaced the last several words from short-term

TABLE 8.2
The Three Stages of Memory
Encoding, storage, and retrieval processes have somewhat different characteristics at each stage of memory.

Stage of Memory	Encoding	Storage	Retrieval
Sensory memory	Minimal; has a pure sensory quality	Great capacity, but decays after a second or so	Automatic
Short-term memory	Primarily acoustic coding	Capacity limited to 7 ± 2 chunks; duration about 20 seconds unless rehearsed	Serial search
Long-term memory	Primarily semantic coding	Appears to have no capacity or duration limitations	Strongly affected by how well the information is integrated with existing knowledge

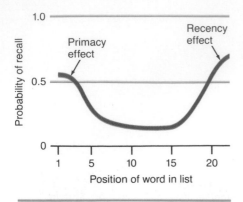

Figure 8.12
A Serial-Position Curve
The probability of recalling an item is plotted as a function of its serial position on a list of items. Generally, the first several items are likely to be recalled (the primacy effect); items in the middle of the list are much less likely to be recalled; and the last several items are recalled very well (the recency effect).

Figure 8.13
Separating Short-Term from Long-Term Memory
The serial-position curve shows both a primacy and a recency effect when subjects recall the list immediately after the last item is presented. It appears that the recency effect is based on retrieving the last several items from short-term memory, because when subjects perform an arithmetic task after hearing the last item, the recency effect disappears. The arithmetic task apparently displaces the words in short-term memory, leaving only those in long-term memory available for retrieval.
(From "Two Storage Mechanisms in Free Recall," by M. Glanzer and A. R. Cunitz. In *Journal of Verbal Learning and Verbal Behavior,* 1966, 5, 351–360 Copyright 1966 by Academic Press, Inc., Reprinted by permission.)

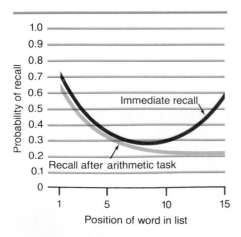

memory, making them no more likely to be recalled than those in the middle of the list. Since the performance of the two groups was otherwise very similar, the normal recency effect appears to be the result of keeping the last several words in short-term memory until the test is administered.

Biological research Evidence that information is transferred from short-term memory to another, distinct system also comes from observations of how certain brain injuries and drugs affect memory. For example, damage to the hippocampus, which is part of the limbic system described in the chapter on biological psychology (see Figure 3.14), often results in **anterograde amnesia,** or a loss of memory for any event occurring after the injury.

A striking example is the case of a man with the initials HM (Milner, 1966). Part of his hippocampus had been removed in order to end severe epileptic seizures. Afterward, both his long-term memory and his short-term memory appeared normal, but he had a severe problem. He had had the operation when he was twenty-seven years old. Two years later, he still believed that he was twenty-seven. When his family moved into a new house, HM could not remember the new address or even how to get there. When he was told that his uncle had died, he grieved in a normal way. But soon afterward, he began to ask why his uncle had not visited him. Each time he was told of his uncle's death, HM became just as upset as when he was first told. In short, the surgery had apparently destroyed the mechanism that transfers information from short-term to long-term memory. HM could not learn anything new.

Another condition, **retrograde amnesia,** involves a loss of memory for events *prior to* some critical injury. Often, a person with this condition is unable to remember anything that took place in the months, or even years, before the injury. In most cases, the memories return gradually. The most distant events are recalled first, and the person gradually has better and better memory for events leading up to the injury. But recovery is seldom complete, and the person may never remember the last few seconds before the injury. For example, one man received a severe blow to the head after being thrown from his motorcycle. After regaining consciousness, he claimed that he was eleven years old. Over the next three months, he gradually recalled more and more of his life. He remembered when he was twelve, thirteen, and so on— right up until the time he was riding his motorcycle the day of the accident. But he was never able to remember what happened just before the accident (Baddeley, 1982). Those final events must have been encoded into short-term memory, but apparently they were never successfully transferred into long-term memory.

Drugs, too, can disrupt the transfer of information from short-term to long-term memory. Smoking marijuana, for example, does not appear to affect the retrieval of information from short-term memory (Darley et al., 1973a). Nor does it affect retrieval from long-term memory (Darley et al., 1973b). But marijuana does inhibit the transfer of information from short-term to long-term memory.

The damage to memory in all these cases is consistent with the view that short-term and long-term memory are distinct systems; the problems are tied to an inability to transfer information from one system to the other. But psychologists do not yet know exactly how, physiologically, this transfer occurs. One view is that it involves *trace consolidation.* In other words, some physiological trace that codes the experience must be gradually transformed, fixed, and consolidated if the memory is to endure.

It seems likely that the primary mechanism for trace consolidation is the movement of electrical impulses within clusters of neurons in the brain. For

People with conditions similar to HM's, or who, like this man, have Alzheimer's disease, learn to cope with them in many creative ways. One woman wrote a detailed schedule of what she is to do during every fifteen minutes of each day (including when to eat and when to write the next day's schedule). She then checked each item off as it happened so that she would remember to do it once, but not twice. When she travels, she sends herself twenty postcards a day so that she will have a written "memory" of the trip.

example, information in short-term memory is erased by any event that suppresses neural activity in the brain. Physical blows to the head, anesthetics, and various types of poisoning—such as that from carbon monoxide—all suppress neural activity, and all erase information from short-term memory. Similarly, information in short-term memory is erased by events that usually cause strong but random sets of electrical impulses, such as the electroshock treatments described in Chapter 16, on therapy. The information being transferred from short-term to long-term memory seems to be vulnerable to destruction for only a minute or so (Chorover, 1965).

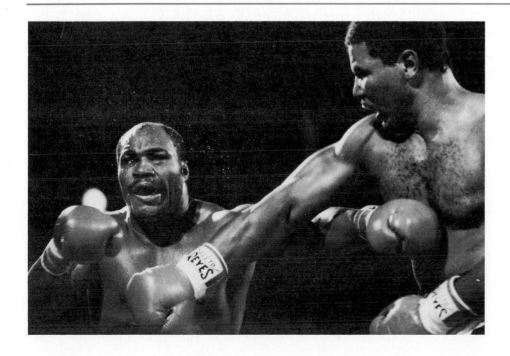

A severe blow to the head can wipe out information held in short-term memory or prevent its transfer to long-term storage. Thus, after the fight, this boxer may not recall the punch that knocked him out.

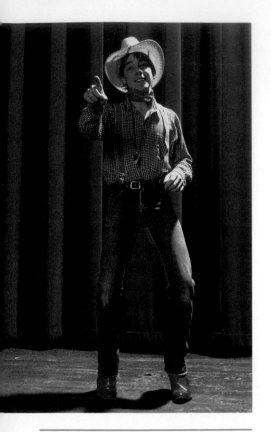

Learning one's part in a play or memorizing other material is greatly facilitated by elaborative rehearsal, a procedure through which new information is not merely repeated but also related to what is already stored in long-term memory.

Encoding

Despite uncertainty about the physiological details of consolidation, psychologists have learned a good deal about how people encode information into long-term memory. Much information appears to be encoded automatically, with little or no effort. This is particularly true for tasks that are well practiced. People learn and remember many things while driving, reading, or walking down the street, for example, even though they do not consciously attempt to memorize them. At other times, however, encoding is more effortful. As noted earlier, one of the primary mechanisms used to intentionally remember things is rehearsal. The importance of rehearsal was demonstrated by Hermann Ebbinghaus, a German psychologist who began the experimental study of long-term memory about a hundred years ago.

The early investigations of Ebbinghaus   Today, Ebbinghaus's methods seem rather quaint. He used only himself as a subject. To time his experiments, he used a metronome, a mechanical device that makes a sound at constant intervals. His aim was to study memory in its "pure" form, uncontaminated by emotional reactions and other preexisting associations between what was already in memory and new material. To eliminate such associations, Ebbinghaus created the *nonsense syllable*, a meaningless set of two consonants and a vowel. POF, XEM, and QAL are examples. Ebbinghaus read aloud, to the beat of the metronome, a list of nonsense syllables. Then he tried to recall the syllables. He measured how difficult it was to learn a list by determining how many trials (repetitions through the list) were needed before he could repeat the entire list without making any errors. On just one trial, he could learn a seven-item list (the capacity of short-term memory). But as the number of items increased slightly, three to four times as many repetitions were required for perfect recall.

Rehearsal   Ebbinghaus learned his lists by rehearsing them, but his attempts to study memory uncontaminated by associations limited the type of rehearsal he could use. There appear to be two basic types of rehearsal: maintenance and elaborative. **Maintenance rehearsal** involves repeating an item over and over, as you might do to use a new phone number. This method can keep an item active in short-term memory, but it is very ineffective for encoding information into long-term memory. Far more effective is **elaborative rehearsal**, which involves thinking about how new material relates to information already stored in long-term memory.

Many of the most common failures of memory result from ineffective rehearsal strategies. For example, just repeating a new person's name to yourself when you are introduced is not a very effective strategy for memorizing it. Instead, if you have difficulty remembering new names, try thinking for a moment about how the new person and the new name are related to things you already know. Children's memories improve during their school years in part because they learn to rehearse, not just by repeating words, but by organizing items according to consistent concepts or meanings (Bach & Underwood, 1970) or by associating them through mental pictures or rhymes.

HIGHLIGHT

Rehearsal and Levels of Processing

Table 8.2 summarized considerable research evidence suggesting that sensory, short-term, and long-term memory can be distinguished not only by differences in their durations and capacities, but also by differences in their characteristic encoding processes. Some psychologists have suggested, however, that this research does not necessarily prove that there are three stages of memory. Fergus Craik and Robert Lockhart (1972), for example, have proposed an alternative view, which holds that differences in how well something is remembered reflects a single dimension: the degree or depth to which incoming information is mentally processed. From the perspective of this increasingly influential **level-of-processing model,** most incoming information immediately disappears from memory because it is not attended to or processed enough to create anything more than a brief impression. According to this view, the icons, echoes, and other representations of information selected by attention and perception for further processing tend to be encoded better and thus to stay in memory longer. How long depends on how elaborate the mental processing and encoding becomes—how much it is thought about, organized, and related to existing knowledge.

Much of the research on rehearsal's role in memory has been conducted within the framework of level-of-processing theory. In one experiment, college students were allowed to look for one minute at a picture of a living room. One group was told that several small x's had been embedded in the picture and that they were to try to locate them by scanning the picture vertically and horizontally. This is a relatively shallow level of processing, because the subjects could complete the task without ever thinking about the objects in the room. A second group was told that the x's had been placed at the edges of objects in the picture and that they should direct their attention to the contours of the objects. A third group was told to look at the picture and to think about what they would do with the various objects if they owned them. As a result, they had to relate the new information in the picture to other information stored in long-term memory. Following this relatively deep level of processing, these people recalled about thirty objects from the picture— roughly eight times as many as the other two groups (Bransford, Nitsch & Franks, 1977).

The most important conclusion to be drawn from research conducted within the level-of-processing framework is that memory is much more strongly determined by internal than by external factors. External factors, such as how the information is displayed and how long a person is exposed to it, are not nearly as important as how the person thinks about it in relation to existing knowledge. For example, noticing *distinctive features*—attributes of new information that are noticeably different from what you already know or expect—make that information more memorable (Graesser & Nakamura, 1982). The importance of distinctiveness was illustrated earlier when you probably recalled the unusual and nonsleep-related word *artichoke* from the list on page 296, even though, on the basis of its position in the middle of the sequence, you might normally have forgotten it. You might also have done particularly well at memorizing that list by thinking about most of the items as being related to something you already know about: sleep. ◼

Semantic coding The successful encoding of information into long-term memory is the result of a relatively deep level of processing that tends to "imprint" the information. However, in doing this deep processing, people tend to ignore physical features and other details about the information and to concentrate on its underlying meaning. Thus, whereas short-term memory involves primarily an acoustic coding of information, long-term memory normally involves *semantic* coding. In other words, people encode general meanings or general ideas and not many of the specifics.

The dominance of semantic coding in long-term memory is highlighted by the errors that people make in recall. We have seen that the most common recall mistakes in short-term memory are acoustic; a person may incorrectly report something that *sounds like* the correct word. In contrast, mistakes in recall from long-term memory tend to involve substitutions that mean the same as the correct word. For example, a subject who has processed into long-term memory the list "watch, coffee, car, school" probably encoded four general ideas. Thus, errors in recall might appear as "watch, coffee, *automobile*, school." You might have made this type of semantic error yourself if, in trying to remember the list on page 296, you recalled seeing the word *sleep*. It was not there, but its meaning was closely related to those of the words that were.

The loss of detail that comes with semantic coding was demonstrated in a classic study by Jacqueline Sachs (1967), in which people first listened to tape-recorded passages. Then Sachs gave the subjects sentences and asked them whether each exact sentence had been in the taped passage. People did very well when they were tested immediately (using mainly short-term memory). But after only twenty-seven seconds, at which point the information had to be retrieved from long-term memory, they could not determine which of two sentences they had heard if both sentences expressed the same meaning. For example, they could not determine whether they had heard "He sent a letter about it to Galileo, the great Italian scientist" or "A letter about it was sent to Galileo, the great Italian scientist." In other words, they remembered the general meaning of what they had heard, but not the exact wording.

Counterfeiters count on the fact that people encode the general meaning of visual stimuli. For example, most people shown the display in Figure 8.14 are unable to choose the correct penny (Nickerson & Adams, 1979).

People are clearly capable of encoding images, as well as general meaning, into long-term memory. In one study, for example, people viewed 2,500 pictures. (It took sixteen hours just to present the stimuli!) Still, the subjects later correctly recognized more than 90 percent of the pictures tested (Standing, Conezio & Haber, 1970). One reason why pictures are remembered so well is that they have many distinctive features, which are likely to attract attention and to be perceived and encoded. Another reason is that such stimuli may be represented in terms of both a visual code and a semantic code. Such a *dual coding theory* suggests that information is better remembered when it is represented in both codes than in only one (Paivio, 1978).

Figure 8.14
Long-Term Memory for a Penny
Most subjects were unable to correctly identify from a display like this the correct image of a penny. The answer is A.
(From "Long-term memory for a common object" by R. S. Nickerson and M. J. Adams. *Cognitive Psychology*, 1979, 11, 287–307.)

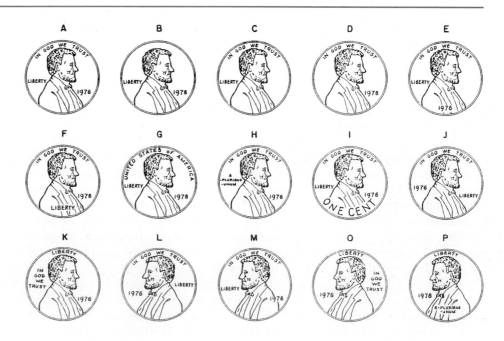

Individuals with **eidetic imagery,** commonly called *photographic memory,* go far beyond recognizing recently seen pictures; they have automatic, long-term, detailed, and vivid images of virtually everything they have seen. About 5 percent of all school-age children have eidetic imagery, but almost no adults have it (Haber, 1979; Leask, Haber & Haber, 1969; Merritt, 1979). Why the ability to store detailed images disappears with age is not known.

Storage

Whereas the capacity of short-term memory is quite limited, there is reason to believe that long-term memory has an unlimited, or at least an undetermined, capacity (Tulving, 1974). Evidence for this conclusion comes from studies on how and why people forget.

The course of forgetting   The systematic study of forgetting was also begun by Ebbinghaus. To measure forgetting, he devised the *method of savings,* which involves computing the difference between the number of repetitions needed to learn a list of words and the number of repetitions needed to relearn it after some time has elapsed. This difference is called the **savings.** If it took Ebbinghaus ten trials to learn a list and ten more trials to relearn it, there would be no savings, and forgetting would have been complete. If it took him ten trials to learn the list and only five trials to relearn it, there would be a savings of 50 percent. As you can see in Figure 8.15, Ebbinghaus found that some savings existed even thirty-one days after the original learning. In general, savings declines (and forgetting increases) as time passes. However, the most dramatic drop in what people retain in long-term memory occurs during the first nine hours, especially in the first hour. After this initial decline, the rate of forgetting slows down considerably.

Ebbinghaus's use of nonsense syllables has been criticized by contemporary psychologists, who have substituted real words, sentences, and even stories. However, Ebbinghaus's curve of forgetting has been repeatedly confirmed. Although people remember sensible stories better than nonsense syllables, the

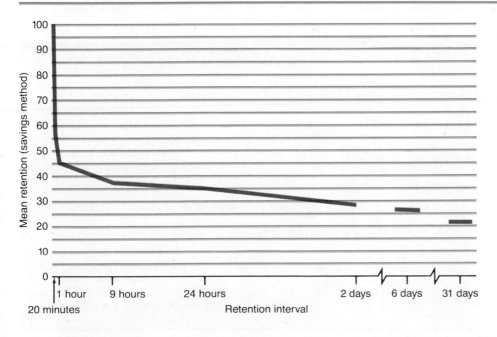

Figure 8.15
Ebbinghaus's Curve of Forgetting
Ebbinghaus found that most forgetting occurs during the first nine hours after learning, especially during the first hour. After that, forgetting continues, but at a much slower rate (Ebbinghaus, 1885).

This man has not used a pogo stick since he was ten, but because his memory of how to do it is not entirely gone, he will take less time to relearn the skill than when he originally acquired it. In other words, his memory will display some savings.

shape of the forgetting curve is the same no matter what material is involved (Davis & Moore, 1935). There is virtually always a strong initial drop in memory, followed by a much more moderate decrease over time (Slamecka & McElree, 1983).

Savings can be very long-lasting. You may well forget something you have learned if you do not use the information, but it is very easy to relearn the material if the need arises. This is true of virtually everything—from meaningless passages in a foreign language, to motor skills like riding a bicycle, to academic subjects like physics.

Causes of forgetting   Whatever the benefits of long-term savings, you are more likely to be aware of the frustrations of forgetting. Drama critic and humorist Robert Benchley offered an extreme, if facetious, example. He claimed that when, several years after graduating, he tried to recall everything he had learned in college, he came up with just thirty-nine items. They included statements like "Charlemagne either died or was born or did something with the Holy Roman Empire in 800" and "Marcus Aurelius had a son who turned out to be a bad boy." Is that all he learned in four years? Not at all. The typical college student will learn literally thousands of things, and many of them will be represented in memory until death. But people do forget. Why?

In our discussion of short-term memory, we noted the two main causes of forgetting: decay and interference. **Decay theory** suggests that, if people do not use information in long-term memory, it gradually fades until it is lost completely. In contrast, **interference theory** holds that forgetting information in long-term memory is due to the influence of other learning. As noted earlier, one way it can occur is through retroactive interference, in which learning new information interferes with the ability to remember old information. The person given something to learn and then tested on it after various delay intervals remembers less and less as the delays become longer. But is this due to decay or to interference? It is not easy to tell, because longer delays produce not only more decay but also more retroactive interference, because the subject is exposed to further information while waiting.

Karl Dallenbach thought that he could determine the cause of forgetting by creating a situation in which time passed but there was no accompanying interference. Evidence of forgetting in such a situation would suggest that

TABLE 8.3

Procedures for Studying Interference
Proactive interference occurs when previously learned material interferes with the learning of new material. Retroactive interference occurs when learning new information inhibits the recall of previously learned information.

Proactive Interference				
Group	**Time 1**	**Time 2**	**Time 3**	**Result**
Experimental	Learn list A	Learn list B	Recall list B	The experimental group will suffer from proactive interference, and the control group will be able to recall more material from list B.
Control	Nothing	Learn list B	Recall list B	

Retroactive Interference				
Group	**Time 1**	**Time 2**	**Time 3**	**Result**
Experimental	Learn list A	Learn list B	Recall list A	The experimental group will suffer from retroactive interference, and the control group will be able to recall more of the material from List A.
Control	Learn list A	Nothing	Recall list A	

decay, not interference, was operating. The subjects in one such experiment were, of all things, cockroaches (Minimi & Dallenbach, 1946). These creatures have a natural tendency to avoid light, but the researchers conditioned them to avoid a dark area of their cage by shocking them there. After learning to stay in the light, some of the roaches were returned to their normal laboratory environment. Members of another group were placed individually in small cotton-lined boxes, in which they could breathe but not move. The researchers reasoned that this group would not experience the interference associated with normal physical activity.

Later, the researchers calculated savings scores as each group of cockroaches again learned to avoid the dark area. Figure 8.16a shows the results. The performance of the two groups was very similar when reconditioning was done after only a half-hour's delay, but as the delay lengthened, the difference between the groups grew. Savings declined only slightly for the immobilized cockroaches but dropped dramatically for those that had been normally active. These results strongly support the notion that forgetting, at least in this situation, was due to interference, not to decay.

So much for cockroaches. What about humans? In another of Dallenbach's experiments, college students learned a list of nonsense syllables and then either continued with their waking routine or were sheltered from interference by going to sleep. Again, while the delay (and thus the decay) was held constant for both groups, the greater interference associated with being awake produced much more forgetting, as Figure 8.16b shows (Jenkins & Dallenbach, 1924). Results like these suggest that interference is the key to forgetting. As we have seen, the interference can be retroactive, in which new information interferes with recall of older information, or proactive, in which old information interferes with learning new information. Table 8.3 outlines the types of experiments used to study the influence of each form of interference on long-term memory.

Retrieval

A great deal of research indicates that interference produces forgetting mainly by creating failures of retrieval. In one study, for example, people were presented with different numbers of word lists. Each list contained words from six semantic categories, such as types of buildings (hut, cottage, tent, hotel) and earth formations (cliff, river, hill, volcano). Some people learned a list and then recalled as many of the words as possible. Other groups learned the first list and then learned different numbers of other lists before trying to recall the first one. The results were dramatic. As the number of intervening lists increased, the number of words that people could recall from the original list declined consistently (Tulving & Psotka, 1971). These results reflected strong retroactive interference. Then the researchers gave a second test, in which they provided people with a cue by telling them the category of the words (such as types of buildings) to be recalled. Now the number of intervening lists had almost no effect on the number of words recalled from the original list, as Figure 8.17 (p. 306) shows.

This result indicated that the words were still represented in long-term memory, but that people were unable to retrieve them without appropriate cues. In other words, the original forgetting was due to a failure in retrieval. Findings like these have led some theorists to conclude that all forgetting from long-term memory is due to some form of retrieval failure (Eysenck, 1977; Raaijmakers & Shiffrin, 1981; Tulving, 1974). Does this mean that everything in long-term memory remains there until death, even if we cannot always, or ever, recall it? Some theorists say yes, others say no, arguing that

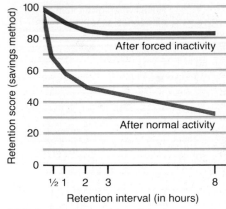

(a) **Retention by cockroaches**

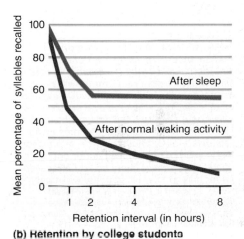

(b) **Retention by college students**

Figure 8.16
Retention of Memory over Time
Forgetting occurs much more rapidly over time if (a) cockroaches or (b) college students engage in normal activity after learning than if the interval before recall is spent quietly. These results suggest that interference is much more important in forgetting than is the passage of time.
(© 1946 by the Board of Trustees of the University of Illinois.)

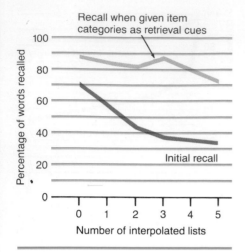

Figure 8.17
Retrieval from Long-Term Memory
Performance at recalling a list of items is strongly influenced by the number of other lists learned before recalling the initial list; this reflects the effect of retroactive interference. However, when retrieval cues are provided on a second recall test for the original list, the interfering effect of the intervening lists disappears. In other words, information that could not be retrieved under one set of conditions (without cues) could be recalled under different circumstances (with cues).
(From "Retroactive Inhibition in Free Recall: Inaccessibility of Information Available in the Memory Store" by Tulving and Psotka. *Journal of Experimental Psychology, 87,* pp. 1–8, 1971. Copyright © 1971 by the American Psychological Association. Adapted by permission of the authors.)

interference may also cause information to be displaced from long-term memory. No one yet knows for sure. What we do know is that a great deal of information remains in the system for years or even decades.

Retrieval cues Stimuli like the category cues given in the Tulving & Psotka (1971) experiment can help people retrieve information from long-term memory. These stimuli, called **retrieval cues,** allow people to recall things that were once forgotten and help them to recognize information stored in memory. In general, recognition tasks are easier than recall tasks because they contain more retrieval cues. For example, most students find it easier to recognize the correct alternative on a multiple-choice exam than to recall material "cold" on an essay test.

Which cues are most effective at aiding retrieval depends on the degree to which they tap into information that was encoded at the time of original learning (Tulving, 1979; Tulving & Thomson, 1973). This is known as the **encoding specificity principle.** Because long-term memories are often encoded semantically, cues that evoke the meaning of the stored information tend to work best. For example, imagine people learning a long list of sentences, one of which is either (1) "The man lifted the piano" or (2) "The man tuned the piano." Giving the cue "something heavy" during a recall test will help subjects remember the first sentence, because they probably encoded something about the weight of a piano. "Something heavy" would probably not help in recalling the second sentence, however, because the subjects probably encoded something about the piano's sound rather than its weight. The cue "makes nice sounds" would be likely to help subjects recall the second sentence, but not the first (Barclay et al., 1974).

Context and state dependence In general, people remember more when their efforts at recall take place in the same environment in which they learned, because they tend to encode features of the environment where the learning took place. These features later act as effective retrieval cues. Members of a university diving club provided one demonstration of this principle. They learned lists of words while either on shore or submerged twenty feet underwater. Then they tried to recall as many of the words as possible, again either on shore or underwater. Those who originally learned underwater scored much better when they were tested underwater than when they were tested on shore. Similarly, those who had learned the words on shore did better when tested on shore (Godden & Baddeley, 1975).

When memory can be helped or hindered by such similarities in context, it is called *context-dependent.* For example, one study found that students remember better when tested in the classroom in which they learned material than when tested in a very different classroom (Smith, Glenberg & Bjork, 1978). This context dependency effect is not always strong (Saufley, Otaka & Bavaresco, 1985), but some students do find it helpful to study for a test in the classroom where the test will be given.

Like the external environment, your internal psychological environment can be encoded when you learn, and it, too, can act as a retrieval cue. When a person's internal state can aid or impede retrieval, memory is called *state-dependent.* For example, if people learn new material while under the influence of marijuana, they tend to recall it better if they are also tested under the influence of marijuana (Eich et al., 1975). Similar effects have been found with alcohol (Cowan, 1976), with various other drugs (Eich, 1980), and with positive or negative mood states. College students remember more positive incidents from their diaries and more positive events from early childhood when they are in a positive mood at the time of recall. More negative events tend to be recalled when people are in a negative mood (Bower, 1981).

State-dependent memory effects are particularly noticeable in people with bipolar disorder, a condition characterized by dramatic changes in mood, which was once known as manic-depression. These people recall information learned in the manic state much better when they are in another manic state than when they are depressed. And information learned in a depressed state is recalled best when the person is again in a depressed state (Henry, Weingartner & Murphy, 1973).

The retrieval of incomplete knowledge   One final and important characteristic of long-term memory retrieval is exemplified by the *feeling-of-knowing experience* (Hart, 1965, 1967; Nelson et al., 1982; Nelson & Narens, 1980). In a typical experiment, subjects are asked trivia questions. When subjects cannot answer a question, they are asked to estimate the probability that they could recognize the correct answer if they were given several options. People are surprisingly accurate at this task; the correlation between their predictions and their actual ability to recognize the items is as high as .70. Apparently people have incomplete knowledge of some answers—they know that they know the answer but simply cannot recall it.

In another example of incomplete knowledge, dictionary definitions of certain words were read to people (Brown & McNeill, 1966). If they could not recall a defined word, they were asked whether they could identify particular features of the word such as how many syllables it has, what letter it begins with, or what words it rhymes with. Again, people proved to be quite good at this task.

How is it possible to have incomplete knowledge? Earlier we described research that suggests that information in short-term memory is represented as unique bundles of features. Similarly, it seems that individual words, as well as answers to trivia questions and other information, are represented in long-term memory as unique collections of features. Often people can retrieve some of the features (how many syllables a word has, what it rhymes with, and so on) but not enough features to identify the word.

Figure 8.18 summarizes much of the material we have covered on long-term memory and other aspects of the human memory system.

Figure 8.18
A Final Overview of the Memory System
You have now seen how sensory memory, short-term memory, and long-term memory relate to one another to create a complex, yet highly organized system for encoding, storing, and retrieving information.

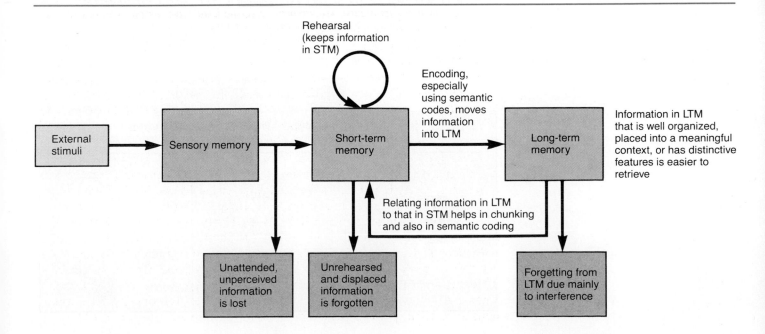

CONSTRUCTING MEMORY

We have now described how information is encoded, stored, and retrieved through sensory, short-term, and long-term memory processes. As noted earlier, this remarkable memory system is not just an automatic record-and-playback machine. You saw, for example, that what gets encoded, stored, and retrieved can be affected by factors such as what information is already in the system. Among the other factors affecting memory are how people perceive and think about incoming information. In other words, to some extent people construct their memories.

Memory is constantly affected by the generalized knowledge about the world that each person has stored in long-term semantic memory. Much of this knowledge is represented in terms of *schemas,* or organized clusters of information about objects, events, or people. For example, simply hearing the words *baseball game* or *sexually transmitted disease* is likely to activate whole clusters of information in long-term memory. As noted in the next chapter, this generalized knowledge provides a basis for making inferences about incoming information during the encoding stage.

As shown in Figure 8.19, generalized knowledge also affects the way information is recalled. Another example is provided by an experiment in which researchers had undergraduates wait for several minutes in the small, cluttered office of a graduate student (Brewer & Treyens, 1981). When later asked to recall everything that was in the office, most of the students mistakenly "remembered" that books were present, even though there were none. Apparently, the general knowledge that graduate students read many books influenced the subjects' memory of what was in the room.

People must organize new information as they receive it. However, they use their existing knowledge to fill in gaps in that information. In this way, memories are constructed. To study this process, Rebecca Sulin and D. James Dooling (1974) asked their subjects to read a long passage about a dictator. In one case, the dictator was a fictitious character named Gerald Martin; in

Figure 8.19
Reconstructive Memory
Carmichael, Hogan, and Walter (1932) showed people figures like these, along with various labels. In the first case, for example, the experimenter might comment, "This tends to resemble eyeglasses [or a dumbbell]." When the subjects were later asked to reproduce the figures, their drawings were likely to resemble the items mentioned by the experimenter. In other words, the labels given to ambiguous items altered the subjects' memory of them.

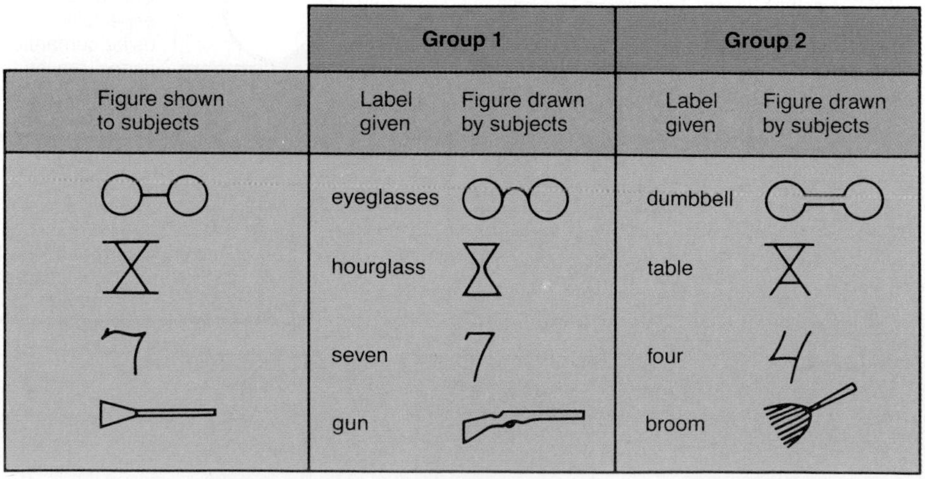

Figure shown to subjects	Group 1		Group 2	
	Label given	Figure drawn by subjects	Label given	Figure drawn by subjects
○—○	eyeglasses	○○	dumbbell	○—○
X	hourglass	X	table	X
7	seven	7	four	4
⊳—	gun	(rifle)	broom	(broom)

another, Adolph Hitler. Later, subjects were asked if the passage contained the statement "He hated the Jews particularly and so persecuted them." This statement was not in the passage, but those who had been told that they were reading about Hitler "remembered" the statement more often than subjects who had read about Gerald Martin.

The concept of constructive memory suggests that what we remember is determined in part by our perceptual biases and by what we find convenient or comfortable to remember.

HIGHLIGHT

Memory and the Courts

Distortions of memory become a matter of special concern in criminal courts. Often witnesses to a crime were emotionally aroused when they saw or heard the events they must describe in court. And there is reason to believe that the memory of events that occurred under emotional circumstances may be different from the memory of events commonly studied in the laboratory (Loftus & Burns, 1982). For example, in 1985 two Vietnamese men happened to be held in the same Georgia jail. One was about to be tried for murder, and the other had been arrested for theft. Unfortunately, the wrong man was taken to the murder trial. For days, he sat in the courtroom, claiming that a mistake had been made, but the trial proceeded and two eyewitnesses testified under oath that he was the murderer. Only an alert jailer and a fingerprint check prevented a miscarriage of justice.

There is also evidence that the form of a question can alter a witness's memory. For example, if a witness is asked, "How fast was the blue car going when it slammed into the truck?" he or she is likely to recall a higher speed than if asked "How fast was the blue car going when it hit the truck?"

There are still other concerns about how memory works in the courtroom. For example, how do jurors take in and remember the contradictory facts presented during a trial (Hastie, Penrod & Pennington, 1983)? Very little is understood about this. Little is known, too, about how jurors use the judge's instructions during their deliberations (Hastie, Penrod & Pennington, 1983). They are usually not permitted to take written notes. And many of the instructions that are read to juries in criminal trials are very difficult to remember, because they are filled with unfamiliar legal jargon (Charrow & Charrow, 1979). Consider the following instruction to a jury:

> You must not consider as evidence any statement of counsel made during the trial; however, if counsel for both parties have stipulated to any fact, or any fact has been admitted by counsel, you will regard that fact as being conclusively proven as to the party or parties making the stipulation or admission. As to any

question to which an objection was sustained, you must not speculate as to what the answer might have been or as to the reason for the objection. You must not consider for any purpose any offer of evidence that was rejected or any evidence that was stricken out by the court; such matter is to be treated as though you had never known of it. (Reed, 1982)

Now consider a set of modified instructions that includes the same content written in more or less everyday language:

As I mentioned earlier, it is your job to decide from the evidence what the facts are. Here are . . . rules that will help you decide what is, and what is not, evidence.

1. *Lawyer's statement*   Ordinarily, any statement made by the lawyers in this case is not evidence. However, if all the lawyers agree that some particular thing is true, you must accept it as truth.

2. *Rejected evidence*   At times during this trial, items or testimony were offered as evidence, but I did not allow them to become evidence. Since they never became evidence, you must not consider them.

3. *Stricken evidence*   At times, I ordered some piece of evidence to be stricken, or thrown out. Since that is no longer evidence, you must ignore it, also. (Reed, 1982)

When the modified instructions were used, jurors' recall improved nearly 50 percent. Obviously, jurors can follow the judge's instructions only if they can recall the basic content (Reed, 1982). ■

IMPROVING YOUR MEMORY

In psychology, as in medicine, physics, and other sciences, practical progress does not always require theoretical certainty. Even though some basic questions about what memory is and how it works resist final answers, psychologists know a great deal about how memory changes over the years and how people can improve their memories. The two keys are metamemory and mnemonics (pronounced "knee-monics").

Metamemory

How people try to remember something, and consequently how well they perform, is shaped to a great extent by what they know about memory. **Metamemory** is the name for knowledge about how your own memory works. It consists of three types of knowledge (Flavell, 1985; Flavell & Wellman, 1977).

First, metamemory involves understanding the abilities and weaknesses of your own memory. Preschool children are notoriously weak in this kind of understanding. They know that the way people look does not affect their memory, that noise interferes with remembering, and that it is harder to remember many items than a few. But in their self-confident naiveté, they deny that they ever forget anything and claim that they can remember quantities of information beyond their own (or anyone else's) capacity (Flavell, Friedrichs & Hoyt, 1970). Only in the school years do children learn the limits—and the strengths—of their memories. This knowledge obviously influences how a person goes about learning something. You might, for instance, be comfortable memorizing a list of directions; another person might write the directions down immediately.

Second, metamemory involves knowledge about different types of tasks. For example, children learn to use different strategies for memorization when they know they will face a short-answer test, which requires recall, rather than a multiple-choice test, which for the most part requires only recognition (Horowitz & Horowitz, 1975).

Third, metamemory involves knowledge of what types of strategies are most effective in remembering new information. This is the aspect of metamemory that is most likely to change dramatically with age and experience (Fabricius & Wellman, 1983). Consider the use of the rehearsal strategy—repeating information until it is fixed in memory. Children as young as five *may* rehearse items when they are asked to remember something (Flavell, Beach & Chinsky, 1966; Istomina, 1975; Keeney, Cannizzo & Flavell, 1967). But most five-year-olds do not use rehearsal to help them remember. They learn to rehearse in elementary school, and they refine their rehearsal strategies over the school years.

For example, suppose two groups of children, one consisting of five-year-olds and one of ten-year-olds, are asked to memorize lists of words. The two groups will probably do equally well if the word lists are short, but the older group will do much better than the younger on a long list. Why? Rote rehearsal, the younger children's main strategy, is very effective for recalling short lists. But when the older children are given a long list, they tend to combine rote rehearsal with more elaborate strategies, such as stringing the words into meaningful sentences or fitting them into different categories. Young children do not realize that rote rehearsal is no longer effective with a longer list, and they continue to use it. In this sense, their metamemory is not as good as that of older children; as a result, their performance is much poorer. This difference can be largely eliminated by teaching younger children to use a different strategy. We therefore know that the difference in performance is due, not to ability, but to the strategy used (Brown, 1975).

Investigations of metamemory hold great promise for furthering the understanding of various types of memory deficits. The difficulties of retarded children are one example. Investigations of metamemory have pointed out differences between retarded and normal children that are similar to those between younger and older normal children. For example, normal ten-year-olds use rote rehearsal to remember a short list of items, but elaborative rehearsal when given a long list. Retarded ten-year-olds, however, like normal five-year-olds, tend to use rote rehearsal regardless of the length of the list. Again, the difference between groups can be eliminated or substantially reduced by teaching retarded children to use a more effective strategy (Butterfield, Wambold & Belmont, 1973; Campione & Brown, 1977; Resnick & Glaser, 1976). Teaching them to do so, however, is difficult, as we will describe when we discuss mental retardation in Chapter 10.

Mnemonics

Mnemonics are strategies for placing information in an organized context in order to remember it. For example, to remember the names of the Great Lakes, you can simply remember the mnemonic HOMES, and the lake names will follow easily: Huron, Ontario, Michigan, Erie, and Superior. Verbal organization is the basis for many other mnemonics. For example, you can link items by weaving them into a story, or you can create a sentence or a rhyme. To remember the spelling of arithmetic, some children learn "A rat in Tom's house might eat Tom's ice cream."

Classical mnemonics   Two very simple but powerful methods that can be used to remember almost anything are the peg-word system and the method of loci. The first step in using the *peg-word system* is to learn a list of words

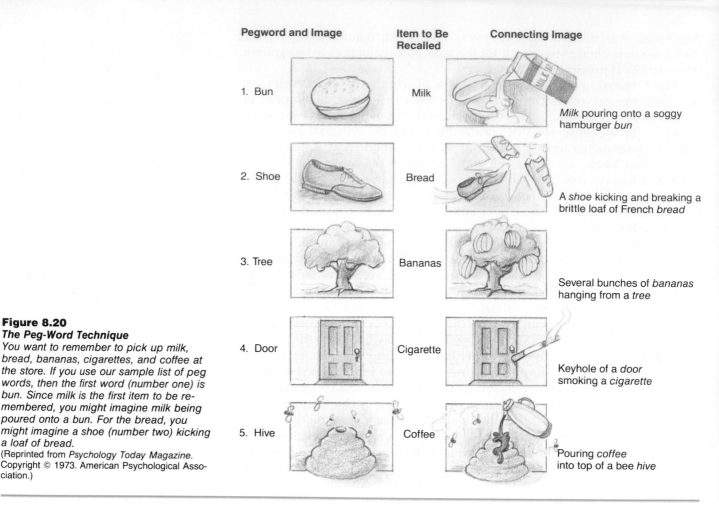

Pegword and Image	Item to Be Recalled	Connecting Image

1. Bun — Milk — *Milk* pouring onto a soggy hamburger *bun*

2. Shoe — Bread — A *shoe* kicking and breaking a brittle loaf of French *bread*

3. Tree — Bananas — Several bunches of *bananas* hanging from a *tree*

4. Door — Cigarette — Keyhole of a *door* smoking a *cigarette*

5. Hive — Coffee — Pouring *coffee* into top of a bee *hive*

Figure 8.20
The Peg-Word Technique
You want to remember to pick up milk, bread, bananas, cigarettes, and coffee at the store. If you use our sample list of peg words, then the first word (number one) is bun. Since milk is the first item to be remembered, you might imagine milk being poured onto a bun. For the bread, you might imagine a shoe (number two) kicking a loaf of bread.
(Reprinted from *Psychology Today Magazine.* Copyright © 1973. American Psychological Association.)

to serve as memory pegs. One of the most popular of these lists is: one is a bun, two is a shoe, three is a tree, four is a door, five is a hive, six is a stick, seven is heaven, eight is a gate, nine is a line, and ten is a hen. Once you learn such a list, you can use it to help you remember anything. For each item to be remembered, create an image or association between it and the previously learned peg word. Figure 8.20 illustrates an example suggested by Gordon Bower (1973). In general, the more novel and vivid you make the images and the better they interrelate the objects involved, the more effective they will be.

One of the authors was introduced as a college student to another popular mnemonic. His roommate, who was known to brag a bit, said that he could remember any one hundred words if he had enough time to think about them. A bet of $100 was made, the words were read, and the author lost. It was, as they say, a real learning experience. The author's friend had used a powerful and ancient mnemonic called the *method of loci* (pronounced "low-sigh"), or the method of places. The first step in this method is to think about a set of familiar geographic locations. For example, if you use your home, you might imagine walking along the sidewalk, up the steps, through the front door, around all four corners of the living room, and through each of the other rooms. Step two is to imagine each item to be remembered in one of these locations. Whenever you want to remember a list, you use the same locations, in the same order. As with the peg-word system, particularly vivid images seem to be particularly effective (Bower, 1970). For example, tomatoes smashed against the front door or bananas hanging from the bedroom ceiling might be helpful in recalling items from a grocery list.

These and other mnemonic systems share one characteristic: each requires that you have a well-learned body of knowledge (such as peg words or geographical locations) that can be used to provide a *context* for organizing incoming information. Thus, the success of these strategies provides yet another demonstration of the importance of relating new information to knowledge already stored in memory.

Remembering textbook material   Most of the procedures discussed so far were devised for remembering arbitrary lists. When you want to remember more organized material, such as a chapter in a textbook, the same principles apply. In other words, you should create a context in which to organize the information.

More specific advice comes from a study that examined how successful and unsuccessful college students approach their reading (Whimbey, 1976). Unsuccessful students tend to read the material straight through; they do not slow down when they reach a difficult section; and they keep going even when they do not understand what is being said. In contrast, successful college students monitor their own performance, reread difficult sections, and periodically stop to review what they have learned before going on. In short, effective learners engage in a very deep level of processing. They are active learners, thinking of each new fact in relation to other material. As a result, they not only learn to see similarities and differences among facts and ideas, but also create a context in which many new facts can be organized effectively. You can create a context for new knowledge by, for instance, taking the role of an instructor and trying to explain to a friend the information you are learning. His or her questions will not only reveal any gaps in your memory

The differences between success and failure in college may reflect strategy, not ability. Even previously unsuccessful students can learn how to learn by adopting a more efficient style or strategy for studying.

MEMORY AND BIOLOGICAL BASES OF BEHAVIOR

Where and How Are Memories Stored?

All of our tips for improving memory will not do very much for victims of Alzheimer's disease or other people suffering from severe biological disturbance of the memory system. To understand their problems, we need to supplement the study of mental processes with a different level of analysis—an analysis of the physiological basis of memory. In other words, we need to understand the physical changes that take place in the brain when people encode, store, and retrieve information.

Psychologists assume that each new experience leaves in the brain a unique physical representation, often called an *engram* or a *memory trace*. Little is known about these theoretical memory traces. But scientists have uncovered much information about changes that seem to occur in brain cells when memories are formed and about groups of cells that play a part in memory.

Recall from Chapter 3 that chemical communication in brain cells takes place at the synapses between axons and dendrites. At the synaptic level, is a memory embodied by new synaptic connections or by improved communication at preexisting connections? There is evidence for both. In the brains of animals that have been exposed to a complicated environment or required to learn a new motor task, neurons in certain parts of the brain develop more synapses and have longer dendrites to receive the new synapses (Rosenzweig, Bennett & Diamond, 1972; Turner & Greenough, 1985). It is likely that the new synapses are involved in the storage of new memories.

Evidence that communication at existing synapses is improved when a memory is stored comes from a different kind of experiment. For example, the nervous systems of simple marine snails, such as *Aplysia* and *Hermissenda,* are so rudimentary that the same individual neurons can be identified from animal to animal; yet even these animals can learn and have memory. By studying individual synapses in such animals while a memory is being formed, scientists discovered that activating two inputs to a synapse simultaneously makes it easier for a signal to cross the synapse later. The signal across the synapse is strengthened because of changes in the flow of ions in presynaptic and postsynaptic neurons (Farley & Alkon, 1985; Goelet et al., 1986). Scientists are now investigating the brains of mammals to determine whether similar types of changes occur when a memory is formed in more complicated brains (Thompson, 1986).

Where in the brain do changes related to memory occur? Do synapses develop and grow stronger only in special brain regions that store memories, or are memories spread throughout the entire brain? In Chapters 3 and 4, we described how different sensory systems are represented in different anatomical regions; specific aspects of an experience are probably stored in these areas of cortex. But a memory involves more than one sensory system. For example, even in the simple case of a rat remembering a maze it has learned, the experience of the maze involves visual experience, olfactory experience, specific movements, and the like. Thus, memories are localized in the sense that certain brain areas store specific aspects of each remembered event, and memories are distributed in the sense that many brain systems are involved in experiencing a whole event (Squire, 1986).

In the formation of new memories, several brain regions are vital, including the hippocampus and nearby parts of cortex, the amygdala, and the thalamus (see Figure A). These areas connect to regions of cortex where the memories are probably stored. Damage to these subcortical areas results in anterograde amnesia, the inability to form new memories, as we described in the case of HM, who had damage in the hippocampus and surrounding areas. It is clear that the hippocampus does not actually store the memories, however, since HM retained most of his memories from the years before part of his hippocampus had been removed. Another patient, RB, was studied after a stroke impaired his memory. He could no longer form new memories, but his IQ was above normal (111). When he died and his brain was examined, it was discovered that the damage was restricted almost entirely to the hippocampus (Squire, 1986). In monkeys, too, injury to the hippocampus impairs memory formation, but more severe memory impairments result from the combination of damage to the hippocampus and amygdala, especially when the memories involve more than one sensory system (Murray & Mishkin, 1985).

Interestingly, although patients cannot form new memories of events following hippocampal damage, they can learn *how* to do things. For example, people with hippocampal damage can learn the new skill of reading words backwards in a mirror, but they do not remember the practice sessions. This suggests that various brain regions may play different roles in the formation of episodic and procedural memory.

for the material, but the lecture you create will establish an outline or framework into which you can place new information.

Based on what is known about memory, we can suggest two specific guidelines for reading a textbook. First, make sure that you understand what you are reading before moving on. Second, use the SQ3R method, which is one of the most successful strategies for remembering textbook material (Anderson, 1978; Frase, 1975; Rickards, 1976; Thomas & Robinson, 1972).

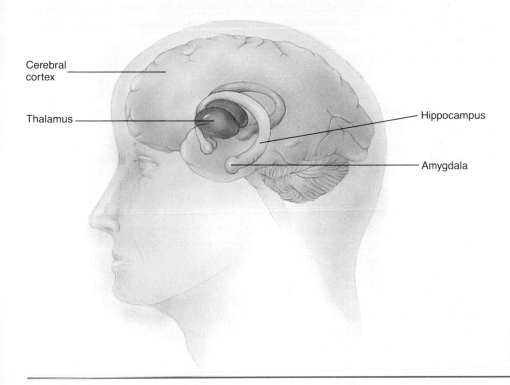

Cerebral cortex

Thalamus

Hippocampus

Amygdala

Figure A
Some Brain Structures Involved in Memory

The thalamus is also important in the early stages of the formation of new memories, although this area is less well understood than the hippocampus. One patient, NA, had very restricted damage to part of the thalamus because of a bizarre accident in his dormitory room at an Air Force flight school. His roommate was practicing fencing with a miniature foil when NA accidentally stepped into the path of one of his thrusts. The foil entered his right nostril and went straight into his brain. After the accident, NA no longer had any ability to form verbal memories, but there was no impairment in his formation of visual memories (Squire, 1986). Thus, it appears that memory involves both widespread storage of the memory trace and specialized regions for memory formation. Some regions may even be specialized for specific types of memories.

Certain neurotransmitters (substances released at synapses) are also critically important in the formation of memories. As we described in Chapter 3, the brain is organized not only by the anatomy of its structures but also by the neurotransmitter systems used by neurons within anatomical regions. No single neurotransmitter is responsible for memory, but several neurotransmitters play prominent roles. As we mentioned in Chapter 3, the importance of acetylcholine in memory is demonstrated by Alzheimer's patients; their memory problems appear related to a deficiency in acetylcholine neurons that send fibers to the hippocampus and the cortex (Coyle, Price & DeLong, 1983). Drugs that interfere with acetylcholine neurotransmission impair memory, and drugs or dietary supplements that enhance acetylcholine function sometimes improve memory in aging experimental animals and humans (Bartus et al., 1982). But improving cholinergic function is by no means a certain way to improve memory. Intense research is now in progress to better understand cholinergic systems and their relationship to memory.

The more we learn about the physiology of memory, the more we see that no single explanation will account for all types of memory. No single structure or neurotransmitter is exclusively involved in memory formation or storage, but studies of the hippocampus and of acetylcholine have provided an encouraging beginning.

SQ3R stands for the five activities that should be followed when you read a chapter: survey, question, read, recite, and review. These activities are designed to increase the depth to which you process the information you read.

1. *Survey*   One of the best ways to begin a new chapter is by *not* reading it. Instead, take a few minutes to skim the chapter. Look at the section headings and any boldface or italicized terms. Obtain a general idea of

what material will be discussed, how it is organized, and how its topics relate to one another and to what you already know. Some people find it useful to survey the entire chapter once and then survey each major section in a little more detail before reading it.

2. *Question*   Before reading each section, stop and ask yourself what content will be covered and what information should be extracted from it.

3. *Read*   Read the text, but think about the material as you read. Are the questions you raised earlier being answered? Do you see the connections between the topics?

4. *Recite*   At the end of each section, stop and recite the major points. Resist the temptation to be passive by mumbling something like, "Oh, I remember that." Put the ideas into your own words.

5. *Review*   Finally, at the end of the chapter, review all the material. You should see connections not only within a section, but also among the sections. The objective is to see how the author has organized the material. Once you grasp the organization, the individual facts will be far easier to remember as well.

Is there anything to add to all of this? Yes. At the end, take a break. Relax. Approach each chapter fresh. There is nothing to be gained from cramming. Following these procedures will not only allow you to learn and remember the material better, but also save you considerable time.

Lecture notes   Lectures are very common in colleges and universities, but they are far from an ideal method for conveying information. Important details in lectures are usually remembered no better than unimportant ones (Goolkasian, Terry & Park, 1979). In fact, jokes and parenthetical remarks in a lecture seem to be remembered far better than major topic statements (Kintsch & Bates, 1977).

Taking notes does help people remember what was said in a lecture (Peper & Meyer, 1978). Unfortunately, effective note taking is not an easily acquired skill. The major difficulty is that the learner has no control over the pace of the lecture. But by using what you know about memory, you can devise some simple strategies for taking and using notes effectively. A first step is to realize that, in note taking, more is not necessarily better; it may be worse. Taking detailed notes of everything requires that you pay attention to everything that is said—the unimportant as well as the important—and leaves little time for thinking about the material. In fact, the thinking involved in note taking is often more important than the writing, because it provides a framework for the facts. (This is why borrowing notes from other people is not nearly as effective as taking your own. It is very difficult to read notes if you do not have the general framework of the lecture already stored in memory.) Note takers who concentrate on expressing the major ideas in relatively few words remember more than those who try to catch every detail (Howe, 1970). In short, the best way to take notes is to think about what is being said, draw connections with other material in the lecture, and then summarize the major points clearly and concisely.

Once you have a set of lecture notes, what should you do with them? Review the notes as soon as possible after the lecture so that you can fill in missing details and decipher your scribbles. Do not wait until a few days before an exam. As you saw earlier, most forgetting from long-term memory occurs within the first few hours after learning.

When the time comes for serious study, resist the urge to read your notes passively. Use them actively, as if they were a chapter in a textbook. Look for the "big picture." Write a detailed outline. Think about how various points are related to one another and how the topics themselves are interrelated. Once you have organized the material, the details will make more sense and will be much easier to remember. Go slowly and do it well. In the end, you will save yourself considerable time by being organized and efficient the first time you go through your notes.

FUTURE DIRECTIONS

Our understanding of memory has advanced considerably since Ebbinghaus began experimental investigations of the topic a hundred years ago. Many of the laws that govern sensory memory, short-term memory, and long-term memory have been discovered; and a great deal is known about how information is encoded, stored, and retrieved from each of these memory systems.

During the next decade, prominent topics of debate and research are likely to include the controversy about how many types of memory there are, the value of levels-of-processing theory, and questions about how memory works in everyday life. The study of how memory functions in eyewitness testimony during criminal trials is one specific example. Another is the examination of the role that sensory memory plays in the processing of complex information from the natural environment (Adelson, 1983; Coltheart, 1980, 1983; Finke, 1983; Finke & Freyd, 1985; Klatzky, 1983).

Researchers are also investigating the causes and consequences of becoming an expert. For example, how do physicians learn radiological anatomy—the science of the relationships between anatomical structure and the patterns seen on X ray plates (Lesgold, 1984; Lesgold et al., 1981)? Whereas true experts store huge bodies of organized information in memory and can read X rays easily, students tend to make certain systematic and predictable errors. Why? In this and other areas of expertise, experts' mental representations of information in their field tends to change over the course of several years. Individual facts are integrated with one another, and the entire body of knowledge is organized more effectively. As a result, experts suffer less than nonexperts from both proactive and retroactive interference (Reder & Anderson, 1980; Smith, Adams & Schorr, 1978). Exactly how this improvement occurs remains something of a mystery. In the next chapter, we will look more closely at the thought processes of experts, as well as at efforts to "teach" computers to perform like experts.

Finally, there is enormous excitement about relating what is known about normal and abnormal memory. For example, if patients suffering from anterograde amnesia (the inability to remember anything after some traumatic event, such as a head injury) play a complicated game, they later have no recollection of having played the game. But some of them play the game better the next time, improving their performance at the same rate as one would expect from a person with normal memory. One interpretation is that, although these patients have no *episodic memory* of ever having played the game, their *semantic knowledge* of the game has increased. Another possibility is that whatever caused the amnesia leaves the procedural memory system unaffected, even though it is divorced from any episodic memory. How the episodic experience is translated into semantic or procedural knowledge, and how they can become completely disassociated in memory, are unanswered questions.

There are, of course, many other unresolved issues. Courses on learning and memory provide an excellent starting place for learning more about the latest research, as well as for studying the basic principles of memory in more detail. Other relevant courses include cognitive psychology and experimental psychology.

SUMMARY

1. Most psychologists agree that there are at least three basic types of memory. Episodic memory contains information about specific events in one's life. Semantic memory contains generalized knowledge about the world. Procedural, or skill, memory contains information about how to do various things.

2. There are three basic memory processes. Encoding occurs when one transforms stimulus information in the environment into some type of mental representation. Storage pertains to maintaining information in the memory system over time. Retrieval is the process of accessing previously stored information from memory.

3. The sensory memory system holds incoming stimulus information in sensory registers for a very brief period of time. At this stage, encoding is minimal, and sensory memories are relatively faithful representations of external stimuli. Icons, in iconic memory, typically fade after about one second, whereas echoes, in echoic memory, can last up to three or four seconds.

4. Information is encoded in short-term, or working, memory primarily through the use of an acoustic code. The capacity of short-term memory is roughly seven chunks, or meaningful groupings of information. However, information appears to decay within twenty seconds or fall prey to interference if it is not rehearsed. The retrieval of information from short-term memory appears to involve an exhaustive serial search of what is stored. Nevertheless, retrieval is extremely fast. For example, it takes about $\frac{1}{25}$ of a second to retrieve a single letter from short-term memory.

5. Several pieces of evidence suggest that short-term and long-term memory represent distinct systems. For example, although serial-position curves show both primacy and recency effects after immediate recall, the recency effect is eliminated if a brief distracting task is administered just before recall. There is also biological evidence for this distinction. For example, although people who have had part of their hippocampus surgically removed maintain both short-term and long-term memory, they are unable to learn any new information. In addition, marijuana does not appear to affect retrieval from either short-term or long-term memory, but it does inhibit the transfer of information from short-term to long-term memory.

6. Hermann Ebbinghaus began investigating long-term memory about a hundred years ago. Two of his major discoveries were: (1) the rate of forgetting from long-term memory is fastest during the first several hours and then slows down considerably, and (2) adding just a few items to a list drastically increases the amount of time needed to learn it.

7. A major finding of long-term memory research is that people store the general meaning of events and not the specific details of what they learn. According to the levels-of-processing model, how well one can remember information depends on how "deeply" it is processed. A deep level of processing requires that the person think about the new information in relation to existing knowledge and discover how it is distinct from what is already known. Thus, long-term memory normally involves semantic coding of general meanings or ideas.

8. Long-term memory appears to have an unlimited capacity. Research suggests that most, if not all, forgetting from long-term memory is due to interference, or an inability to retrieve what has already been stored because of the influence of other learning. Retroactive interference occurs when new material interferes with the ability to remember information that was learned at an earlier time.

9. Much prior knowledge is represented in terms of schemas, or organized clusters of information about objects, events, or people. These schemas affect the processing of new information in two major ways. First, they provide a basis for making inferences at the time of encoding. Second, they affect the way specific events are recalled at some later time.

10. Metamemory is the name for knowledge people have about their own memory system. This knowledge often determines the strategies people use for remembering new information. Many observed differences in memory performance (such as those between young and old children or between normal and retarded children) are due to the strategies people use rather than to inherent differences in ability. With training, many of these differences can be eliminated.

11. Mnemonics are devices that are used to remember things better. Two of the simplest but most powerful mnemonics are the peg-word system and the method of loci. Their usefulness lies in the fact that they provide a context for organizing material more effectively.

12. The key to remembering textbook material is to read actively rather than passively. One of the most effective

ways to do this is to follow the SQ3R method: survey, question, read, recite, and review. Lecture note taking is also most beneficial when it is done actively rather than passively. Taking good notes requires that you think about how each main point relates to the others. Studying from lecture notes is most effective when one can identify the larger structure of the lecture.

KEY TERMS

Definitions of terms appear on the pages shown in parentheses.

acoustic code (284)
anterograde amnesia (298)
Brown-Peterson procedure (293)
chunk (291)
decay theory (304)
echo (289)
echoic memory (289)
eidetic imagery (303)
elaborative rehearsal (300)
encoding (284)
encoding specificity principle (306)
episodic memory (282)
icon (288)
iconic memory (289)
immediate memory span (291)
interference theory (304)
level-of-processing model (301)
maintenance rehearsal (300)

metamemory (310)
mnemonic (311)
parallel research (295)
primacy effect (296)
proactive interference (294)
procedural memory (283)
recency effect (296)
rehearsing (293)
retrieval (285)
retrieval cue (306)
retroactive interference (294)
retrograde amnesia (298)
savings (303)
semantic code (284)
semantic memory (282)
sensory memory (287)
sensory register (287)
serial search (295)
short-term (working) memory (290)
storage (284)
visual code (284)

RECOMMENDED READINGS

Bransford, J. D. (1979). *Human cognition: Learning, understanding, and remembering.* Belmont, Calif.: Wadsworth. Oriented around the role that memory plays in complex learning. Particular attention is paid to school-related activities.

Ellis, H. C., & Hunt, R. R. (1983). *Fundamentals of human memory and cognition* (3rd ed.). Dubuque, Iowa: William C. Brown. A short and basic introduction to memory which is excellent for beginning students. The role that semantic memory plays in the processing of new information is highlighted.

Higbee, K. L. (1977). *Your memory: How it works and how to improve it.* Englewood Cliffs, N.J.: Prentice-Hall. One of the most popular texts on how to develop better memory. Many different mnemonics are presented.

Klatzky, R. L. (1980). *Human memory: Structures and processes* (2nd ed.). San Francisco: Freeman. A basic text that might be used in an introductory course on human memory. Many of the complexities of studying human memory are discussed, but the writing is clear and easy to understand.

Stern, L. (1985). *The structures and strategies of human memory.* Homewood, Ill.: Dorsey Press. An introductory text with an emphasis on applications. Deals with the role of memory in thinking, decision making, and problem solving in detail.

Wingfield, A., & Byrnes, D. L. (1981). *The psychology of human memory.* New York: Academic Press. An excellent introduction to all aspects of memory. Emphasis is given to the classical theories of memory, and each is critically evaluated.

Zechmeister, E. B., & Nyberg, S. E. (1982). *Human memory: An introduction to research and theory.* Monterey, Calif.: Brooks/Cole. An excellent book for the serious student. In addition to explaining basic memory phenomena, the authors provide the materials and procedures for many experiments.

*D*r. Joyce Wallace, a New York City internist, was having trouble figuring out what was the matter with "Laura McBride," a forty-three-year-old woman who reported pains in her stomach and abdomen, aching muscles, irritability, occasional dizzy spells, and general tiredness (Roueché, 1986). The doctor's initial hypothesis was iron-deficiency anemia, a condition in which the level of oxygen-carrying hemoglobin in the blood is too low. There was some evidence to support that hypothesis. A physical examination revealed that Laura's spleen was somewhat enlarged, and blood tests showed low hemoglobin and high red blood cell production, suggesting that her body was attempting to compensate for the loss of hemoglobin. However, other tests revealed normal iron levels. Perhaps she was losing blood through internal bleeding, but a stool test ruled that out. Had Laura been vomiting blood? She said no. Blood in the urine? No. How about abnormally heavy menstrual flow? Nothing unusual there. During the next week, Dr. Wallace puzzled over the problem, while additional tests showed a worsening hemoglobin situation and Laura reported more intense pain, now accompanied by cramps, shortness of breath, and severe loss of energy. Clearly, this woman's blood was becoming less and less capable of sustaining her, but if it was not actually being lost, what was happening to it? Finally, the doctor decided to look at a smear of Laura's blood on a microscope slide. What she saw—a condition called *basophilic stippling*—indicated that some kind of poison was destroying Laura's red blood cells. But what could be poisoning her? Laura spent most of her time at home, repairing and restoring paintings, but it could not be anything there because none of her teenage daughters was affected at all. Or *was* something poisoning her? Dr. Wallace asked herself, "What does Laura do that the girls do not?" Well, she works with paintings. Paint. Lead! She might be suffering from lead poisoning! When the next blood test showed a lead level seven times higher than normal, Dr. Wallace knew she was right at last.

To solve this medical mystery—and prescribe the appropriate treatment—Dr. Wallace relied on her ability to think, solve problems, and make judgments and decisions. She employed these higher mental processes to weigh the pros and cons of contrasting hypotheses and to reach decisions about what tests to order and how to interpret them. These same high-level mental processes also played a central role in other aspects of the case, as Dr. Wallace consulted with the patient and other physicians using that uniquely human capability known as language.

The work of a physician is but one example of the thinking, judging, decision-making, problem-solving, and linguistic communication that occur in an unending stream in every human being all the time. These processes are involved in everything from a restaurant customer's choice between shrimp and roast beef to a national leader's decisions about actions that could lead to nuclear war. How good are human judgments and decisions? What factors can interfere with or influence them? How are thoughts transformed into language? Psychologists have been studying these questions for many years. In this chapter, we introduce some of their findings and highlight the importance of their research (see Linkages diagram, p. 322).

9

Thought and
Language

LINKAGES
an overview

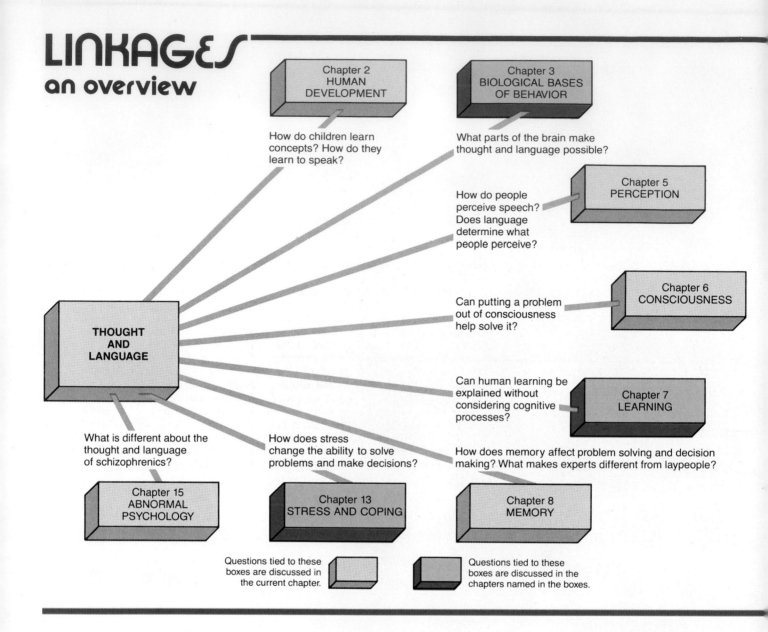

**Chapter 2
HUMAN DEVELOPMENT**

How do children learn concepts? How do they learn to speak?

**Chapter 3
BIOLOGICAL BASES OF BEHAVIOR**

What parts of the brain make thought and language possible?

**Chapter 5
PERCEPTION**

How do people perceive speech? Does language determine what people perceive?

**Chapter 6
CONSCIOUSNESS**

Can putting a problem out of consciousness help solve it?

**Chapter 7
LEARNING**

Can human learning be explained without considering cognitive processes?

THOUGHT AND LANGUAGE

What is different about the thought and language of schizophrenics?

How does stress change the ability to solve problems and make decisions?

How does memory affect problem solving and decision making? What makes experts different from laypeople?

**Chapter 15
ABNORMAL PSYCHOLOGY**

**Chapter 13
STRESS AND COPING**

**Chapter 8
MEMORY**

Questions tied to these boxes are discussed in the current chapter.

Questions tied to these boxes are discussed in the chapters named in the boxes.

FROM STIMULUS TO ACTION: AN OVERVIEW

If you think that Dr. Wallace had a difficult time diagnosing Laura's illness, consider the situation faced by the astronauts on Apollo 13. As they approached the moon on April 17, 1970, they heard an explosion. An oxygen tank had ruptured. Faced with potential catastrophe, the crew had to take immediate action and answer some crucial questions. Was the damage so extensive that the mission should be aborted? Which systems still operated normally? How would the damage affect the crew's ability to return to earth? The crew needed to figure out how to survive with the depleted oxygen supply and how to navigate despite the damage. To solve these problems, they relied on extensive communication with ground control. As it turned out, the moon landing had to be scrubbed, but ways were found to conserve enough oxygen to sustain the crew until they could get back to earth.

The physician's task may appear far removed from the concerns of astronauts, but the mental processes involved are surprisingly similar. In both

THOUGHT, LANGUAGE, AND PSYCHOLOGY

To solve a complex problem, you must be able to think. But before you can think about the problem, you must often call on some of the more basic mental skills discussed in other chapters. For example, you must attend to the problem, sensing and perceiving all its elements. In doing so, you may remember other possible solutions that have worked for you in the past, or you may try out different approaches that you have recently learned.

The relationship between thought and learning is a particularly important one. Children must learn to solve problems and, more generally, to think, understand, and reason. In Chapter 2, we discussed the development of these processes. The expert problem solver or decision maker learns mental strategies that distinguish him or her from the novice. When people fail to develop or learn efficient thinking strategies, various kinds of problems result. As we will see in the chapter on mental abilities, for example, mentally retarded people often do not learn or remember the cognitive strategies needed to deal with complex mental tasks. A different problem appears in mental disorders such as schizophrenia (discussed in Chapter 15), in which mental capacity is not diminished, but there are nevertheless severe disruptions in the ability to think logically and rationally.

Just as the study of thinking requires an understanding of other areas of psychology, so too does the study of language, which forms the basis for much of human thought and expression. For example, it is important to know that the biological basis of language appears to be localized in certain parts of the cerebral cortex and that there are many ways in which the perception and understanding of speech is similar to the perception and understanding of the visual world. These and many other links between thought, language, and various psychological specialty areas will be apparent throughout this chapter.

situations, people have to perceive a complex pattern of incoming stimuli, much of it in the form of language; evaluate that pattern; and make decisions about it. Often these processes occur so quickly and appear so complicated that the task of analyzing them may seem like trying to nail Jell-O to a tree. To describe and begin to understand what happens between the presentation of stimuli and the execution of responses, many psychologists in recent years have considered people mainly as information-processing systems.

The Human Information-Processing System

Any **information-processing system** receives information, represents information with symbols, and manipulates those representations. According to this model, information from a stimulus is passed through several stages before a response is made, and at each stage, the information is transformed (Wickens, 1984). Figure 9.1 (p. 324) shows these stages.

We have examined the first two stages in previous chapters. In the first stage, information about the stimulus reaches the brain by way of the sensory

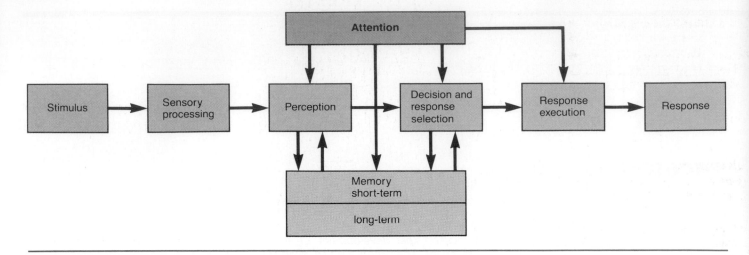

Figure 9.1
An Information-Processing Model
Information is transformed or changed by different operations or stages of information processing, each requiring some minimum amount of time for execution. Certain of these stages require heavy dependence on both short-term and long-term memory. And certain of the stages compete with short-term memory for attention, that limited supply of mental energy that is required for information processing to be carried out efficiently.

receptors. This stage does not require attention. In the second stage, the information must be perceived and recognized, a process involving the memory systems discussed in Chapter 8. Recall that, to recognize a stimulus, people match the perceived pattern to a pattern in long-term memory. In addition, various kinds of encoding are used to hold new information in memory; thus, information is further transformed at this stage. It demands relatively little attention. In the third stage, once the stimulus has been recognized, it is necessary to decide what to do with it. The information may simply be stored in memory. But if the decision is to take some action, then a response must also be selected before the fourth stage—execution of the response—can occur. This third stage demands more attention than does perception. To begin exploring how information is processed during this third, decision-making stage, consider a relatively simple example: a case in which a decision is made so quickly that you may not be conscious of thinking about it.

High-Speed Decision Making

Imagine that, as you are speeding down a road late at night, the green traffic light you are approaching suddenly turns yellow. In an instant you must decide whether to apply the brakes or floor the accelerator. Here is a situation in which a stimulus is presented, a *decision* must be made under extreme time pressure, and then the decision must be translated into action.

Reaction times   Psychologists have studied how people make decisions like this by examining **reaction time,** the elapsed time between the presentation of a physical stimulus and an overt response. Reaction time is the total time needed for all the stages shown in Figure 9.1. In fact, the study of reaction time helped generate the information-processing approach. If cognition involves distinct stages, as the information-processing approach holds, then each stage must take some time. Therefore, one should be able to infer what stages or substages exist by examining changes in **mental chronometry,** the timing of mental events (Posner, 1978).

In a typical reaction-time task in the laboratory, a subject must rapidly say a particular word or push a certain button in response to a stimulus. Even in such simple situations, several factors influence reaction times. First, the reaction time to *intense stimuli,* such as bright lights or loud sounds, is shorter than to weaker stimuli. Second, the easier it is to *discriminate* between two or more stimuli, or the greater the difference between them, the shorter the reaction time will be.

A quarterback routinely makes split-second decisions about whether to run, pass the ball (and to whom), or throw it away.

A third factor is the *complexity* of the decision; that is, the larger the number of possible actions that might be carried out in response to a set of stimuli, the longer the reaction time. Suppose that, having cleared the yellow light, you are now scanning road signs for a turnoff to the town of Savoy. If you know that the turnoff is to the right and that the sign will say simply, "Savoy," there is only one possible stimulus-response combination, your decision will be simple, and your reaction time will be short. In contrast, if you do not know how the Savoy turnoff will be marked or in which direction the town lies, your choice will be more complex, and your reaction time will be longer.

Reaction time is also influenced by *stimulus-response compatibility*. If the relationship between a set of possible stimuli and possible responses is a natural or compatible one, then reaction time will be fast. If it is not, then reaction time will be slow. Figure 9.2 illustrates compatible and incompatible relationships.

Expectancy, too, affects reaction time. As we noted in the chapter on perception, expected stimuli are perceived more quickly than those that are surprising. Expectancy has the same effect on response time: people respond faster to stimuli that they anticipate and slower to those that surprise them.

Finally, in any reaction-time task there is a *speed-accuracy tradeoff.* If you try to respond quickly, errors increase; if you try for an error-free performance, reaction time increases (Pachella, 1974).

Knowing that these factors influence reaction time has expanded understanding of decision making under time pressure. To generate quick decisions

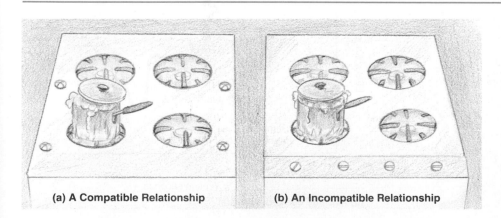

(a) A Compatible Relationship   **(b) An Incompatible Relationship**

Figure 9.2
Stimulus-Response Compatibility
Suppose a cook is standing in front of the stove when a pot starts to boil over (a stimulus). The cook must rapidly adjust the appropriate dial to reduce the heat (the response). How fast the cook reacts may depend in part on the design of the stove. In the stove shown in (a), the dials are placed next to the burners, and there is a clear and visually compatible association that determines which stimulus belongs to which response. In (b), however, this compatibility does not exist, and reaction time will be much slower.

by other drivers when an ambulance approaches, for example, designers of the warning systems on ambulances use light and sound stimuli that are not only very intense, but also very discriminable from any others that occur in normal traffic.

Important as reaction times are, however, they cannot directly measure what is going on between the presentation of a stimulus and the execution of a response. Reaction times alone, for example, cannot tell us how long it takes for response selection to begin, although there have been many ingenious efforts to make inferences about such things (Donders, 1969; Pachella, 1974). To analyze mental events and their timing more directly, psychologists have turned to other methods, such as the use of evoked brain potentials.

Evoked brain potentials   Recall that the **evoked brain potential** is the small temporary change in voltage that occurs in response to discrete stimuli. By recording a series of responses to the same stimuli, researchers can determine the **average evoked potential.** Figure 9.3 shows an example. Each peak reflects the firing of large groups of neurons, within different regions of the brain, at different times during the information-processing sequence. Thus, the pattern of the peaks provides information that is more precise than overall reaction time.

The first negative peak, called N100, occurs around 100 milliseconds after the stimulus. It reflects initial sensory processing, and its voltage comes directly from the primary sensory cortex (shown in Figure 3.15) that processes the stimulus. Thus, N100s produced by auditory stimuli are different from

Figure 9.3
Evoked Potentials
(a) The EEG tracing produced when a subject's name is presented. The box indicates what is happening just after the name is presented. Although it is difficult for the untrained eye to see, there is a small temporary change in the voltage pattern. If several of these evoked potentials were averaged so that the random variations in the EEG tracings were eliminated, the result would appear as in (b), with a negative peak (N100) followed by a large positive peak (P300).

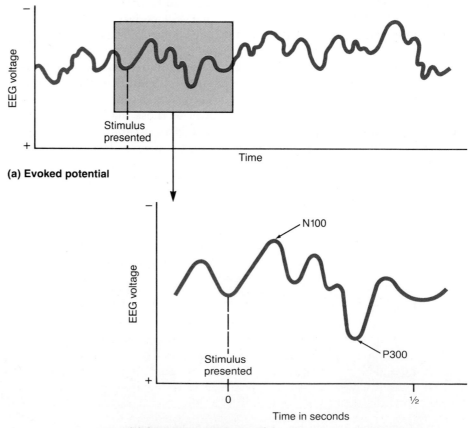

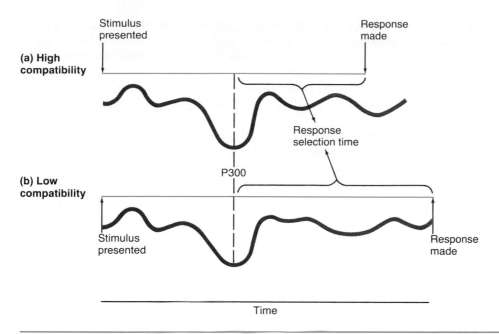

Figure 9.4
Effects of Stimulus-Response Compatibility
McCarthy and Donchin (1981) gave people two buttons and then presented the word right or left. Sometimes the subjects were told to give a compatible response, pressing the right button in response to the word right and the left button in response to the word left. At other times, the assignment was incompatible: to press the left button to the word right and vice versa. Here is a schematic picture of the results of McCarthy and Donchin's experiment. As you might expect, variation in compatibility had a strong effect on reaction time, but it did not affect the timing of the P300. Therefore, the researchers concluded that stimulus-response compatibility does not affect perceptual processing. When incompatibility lengthens reaction time, it does so by producing a delay in selecting the response.

those produced by visual stimuli. Stimuli that are in the focus of attention produce larger N100s than those that are ignored (Hillyard, Picton & Regan, 1978).

Of particular interest is the positive peak called P300; as we described in the chapter on perception, it occurs roughly 300 to 500 milliseconds after a stimulus. It seems to signal the time at which perception of a stimulus is completed and the significance of that stimulus has been evaluated. Stimuli that are quite surprising, and therefore significant, produce large P300s compared to stimuli that are routine and expected (Donchin, 1981; Pritchard, 1981).

Once researchers had established the meaning of the P300, they could use it to study the timing of mental events. For example, Figure 9.4 describes an experiment on the effects of stimulus-response compatibility which shows that compatibility alters the speed of response selection but does not seem to alter the timing of perception.

Evoked potentials have also been used to determine the mental capabilities of patients who cannot communicate normally and to determine precisely what region of the brain has been damaged by a disease, accident, or poison.

Cognitive Processes

Reaction times and evoked potentials yield clues about what is going on when you decide to stop or speed through that yellow traffic light, but they do not tell how you do it. Moreover, day after day you make decisions more complicated and more time consuming than those made in reaction-time tasks. You consider your situation, imagine what might happen, reminisce, and daydream. In short, you think. How?

Decades ago, American behaviorist John Watson argued that thought is nothing more than covert speech. But if thought and speech are identical, why do people often have such a difficult time translating their thoughts into words? This intuitive case against Watson's view was bolstered in 1947 by a rather heroic experiment by Scott Smith (Smith et al., 1947). If Watson's view were correct, Smith reasoned that paralyzing the speech muscles should disrupt thinking. Smith took a dose of curare, a potentially lethal drug that temporarily paralyzes the peripheral nervous system, including the vocal apparatus. The paralysis was so complete that Smith needed respirators to help him breathe but, despite the drug's devastating effect on the speech system, Smith reported that he had lucid thoughts and could perform mental arithmetic and understand what was going on around him just as well as before taking the drug. This and other experiments have made a convincing case that thought is more than covert speech.

Another way of looking at thought is to consider it as part of the information-processing model. In this view, cognitive processes involve a transformation and manipulation of information that has been encoded and stored in short-term and especially in long-term memory. **Thinking** thus can be defined as the manipulation of mental representations. Sometimes people perform these manipulations consciously, in order to reason, understand a situation, solve a problem, or make a decision. At other times, such as when people daydream, the manipulations are less goal directed. In the next section, we look at what is meant by mental representations and how people manipulate them in thought.

THINKING

What do people have in mind—what do they manipulate—when they think? A definitive answer has eluded both philosophers and psychologists, in part because of the inherent difficulty of pinning down such an abstract notion as thinking, let alone the contents of thought. Further, thought may take different forms at different times and in different people. In spite of its ephemeral nature, thinking does appear to be based largely on the ability to form, manipulate, and relate *concepts*. We therefore begin our discussion of thinking by considering concepts and concept formation. Later we consider how concepts are related to each other by propositions, how they are represented, and how these representations are used in thinking.

Concepts

The basic ingredients of mental activity, the building blocks of thought, are **concepts**—classes or categories of objects, events, or ideas with common properties. Concepts may be concrete and visual, such as the concepts *round* or *red,* but they may also be abstract, such as the concepts *truth* and *justice.* To have a concept is to recognize the set of properties or relationships that are shared by and define members of the category. For example, the concept *bird* includes such properties as having feathers, laying eggs, and being able to fly. Most birds have all of these properties, but even those, like penguins, that cannot fly are still birds, because they possess enough other bird properties (feathers, wings, and the like). But having just one bird property is not enough; snakes lay eggs and bats can fly, but neither are birds. It is usually the *combination* of properties that defines a concept.

Concepts are vital to thought, because they allow you to address each object or event you encounter, not as something new and unique, but as an example of a category that is already known. This makes logical thought possible. You can decide whether a whale is a bird without having either creature in the room with you. The concepts *whale* and *bird* are enough to let you follow the rules of logic to reach a correct answer.

Artificial and natural concepts For years, psychologists focused their research on what are now called **artificial concepts.** These are concepts that can be clearly defined by a set of rules or properties, so that each member of

Both a space shuttle and a hot air balloon are examples of the natural concept "aircraft," but most people would probably think of the space shuttle, with its wings, as the better example. A prototype of the concept is probably an airplane.

the concept has all of the defining properties and no nonmember does. For example, the concept *square* can be defined as "a shape with four equal sides and four right-angle corners." Any object that does not contain all of these features simply is not a square.

In contrast, try to define the concept *home* or *game*. These are examples of **natural concepts**, concepts that have no fixed set of *defining* features but instead share a set of *characteristic* features. Members of a natural concept need not possess all of the characteristic features. One characteristic feature of the natural concept *bird*, for example, is the ability to fly; but an ostrich is a bird even though it cannot fly. Outside the laboratory, most of the concepts people use seem to be natural, rather than artificial.

The boundaries of a natural concept are fuzzy, and some members of the concept are better examples of the concept than others. The more characteristic features a particular example shares, the greater its degree of belongingness to the concept (Rosch, 1975). A robin, a chicken, an ostrich, and a penguin are all birds. But a robin is a better example than the other three, because a robin can fly and is closer to the size and proportion of what most people, through common and frequent experience, think of as a typical bird. A member of a natural concept that possesses all or most of its characteristic features is called a **prototype** or is said to be *prototypical*. Thus, the robin is a prototypical bird.

Learning concepts   Prototypes play a role in one of the most important cognitive tasks a child faces: learning the concepts he or she will need in order to think as an adult. The task is not easy, and it takes time. Even adults continue to refine and elaborate concepts through experience. For example, the dimensions of the concepts *right* and *wrong*, which begin as so clear and simple, later become quite complex as moral development progresses. As we suggested in the chapter on development, people learn that it is sometimes wrong to follow orders and that disobedience in the face of injustice is sometimes right.

(a) Concept defined by Affirmation Rule: large

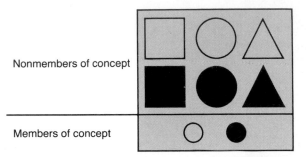

(b) Concept defined by Conjunctive Rule: small _and_ round

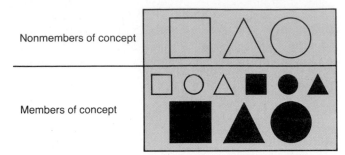

(c) Concept defined by Disjunctive Rule: small _or_ black

Figure 9.5
Stimuli for a Concept-Learning
Experiment
Membership in a concept may be defined by many different rules which relate to one or more attributes or features. Sections a, b, and c illustrate three examples of these rules.

Some natural concepts are learned by identifying prototypes and then adding less typical examples as one learns more about the breadth of the concept. The importance of this prototype-matching strategy is reflected in the illustrations in most books for very young children. The concept _house,_ for example, is usually accompanied by a drawing of a square structure with windows and a chimney. An igloo is also a house, but it will take some time and experience for children to learn that. Concepts may also be learned by forming and testing hypotheses about the rules defining them. Children are constantly forming and testing hypotheses about concepts. For example, a child who sees a small, square grocery store might, on the basis of its size and shape, hypothesize that it is a house. This hypothesis will be disproven when he or she calls it a house and is corrected by a parent who explains the differences between houses and stores.

To study concept learning in the laboratory, psychologists often use artificial concepts, such as _square,_ because the members of the concept can be neatly defined (Trabasso & Bower, 1968). For example, a researcher might use the sort of stimuli shown in Figure 9.5. Each of the objects has three _properties,_ or _attributes_—size, shape, and color—and concepts can be defined easily by establishing rules about these attributes. One rule, for example, might be that a member of the concept must be small and triangular. A researcher might show subjects a series of stimuli, some of which follow this rule and some of which do not. As each stimulus is presented, the subjects say whether they think it is a member of the concept or not and, on the basis of feedback about the correctness of their responses, make and test hypotheses about the rule that defines the concept.

Generally, how easily artificial concepts are learned depends on the _number of attributes_ that must be taken into account and on the _rule_ regarding the combination of features. Knowing which attributes are relevant in defining a concept is important and can be difficult. The fewer the attributes that must be considered, the easier a concept is to learn. For example, _extraterrestrial_ is an easy concept to learn, because one must consider only one attribute: hailing from someplace other than Earth. In contrast, a concept such as _tax-deductible_ is difficult to learn, because it is defined by a large number of attributes that may change from year to year.

The ease of concept learning can be predicted in part by the kind of rule that is used to bind the attributes together (Bourne, 1967). The simplest classification rule is called the **affirmation,** or **one-feature, rule.** For Figure 9.5a, an affirmation rule would be "all large objects are members of the concept, and all small objects are not members." The next easiest classification rule to learn is the **conjunctive rule,** which is based on two or more attributes and requires that all of them be present (see Figure 9.5b). For example, a club might allow entry only to those who are over eighteen and owners of Jaguar automobiles. The **disjunctive rule** is slightly more difficult to learn. It holds that members of a concept must have one feature *or* another (see Figure 9.5c). For example, club membership might be restricted to those who are either over eighteen or know the manager.

Mental Representations of Concepts

How are concepts represented in the mind? Our discussion of memory suggested one possibility. Recall that people encode into memory, especially long-term memory, not just individual pieces of information, such as words or pictures, but lists of the features or attributes of those items. Recall also that the more distinctive or unusual those features are, the easier the information is to remember. As people learn concepts, it may be the concepts' defining features that are mentally represented and encoded into long-term memory. This would help explain why artificial concepts, such as *square,* with their relatively few and usually distinctive features, tend to be easier to learn and remember than natural concepts, such as *game,* which are fuzzier, because they do not have a fixed set of defining features.

The notion that concepts are mentally represented as lists of features would also help explain research results like those of one particular reaction-time experiment (Smith, Shoben & Rips, 1973). In the study, people were asked to say whether sentences like "A robin is a bird" and "An ostrich is a bird" are true or false. Reaction times to correctly answer such questions were much faster when the sentence used prototypical examples of a concept ("A robin is a bird") than when the examples were not prototypical. Presumably this was because the prototypical examples shared more easily identifiable features with the stored concept than did nonprototypical examples.

Concepts may also be mentally represented by visual images. Thinking of concepts such as *beautiful, tranquil,* or *violent* might instantly bring to mind mental pictures, or visual prototypes, of these concepts. Individual differences in how people tend to represent concepts and the kinds of concepts that tend to be represented as features or images are not well understood. Nor are we sure that there are not other still-undiscovered ways of mentally representing concepts.

Concepts are closely related to the idea of *schemas,* discussed in the chapter on memory. As we mentioned there, a schema is a mental representation of information about a class of events or things. Schemas preserve the average characteristics of several specific examples or cases, without retaining the specific details of any of them. In their ability to encapsulate the general characteristics of a large number of specific examples, schemas provide a very efficient way of representing and thinking about events and objects in the world.

Whether concepts are represented as features, as images, as schemas, or in other ways, humans appear to combine them to form *propositions* and *mental models.*

Propositions   Concepts represent important building blocks of mental experience and essential components of the ability to think. Part of thinking involves relating various concepts to one another, and these relationships are usually represented by propositions. A **proposition** is the smallest unit of knowledge that can stand as a separate assertion. Usually taking the form of a sentence, propositions may be true or false. Propositions may represent the relationship between a concept and a property of that concept ("Birds have wings" or "Turtles cannot sing") or they may relate two or more concepts to each other ("Dogs chase cats" or "Rob cheated on the test").

Mental models   Recently, some psychologists have focused their attention on how concepts involving physical processes and mechanical or computational devices might be represented as mental models. **Mental models** are essentially large clusters of propositions that represent people's understanding of how things work and guide their interaction with those things (Gentner & Stevens, 1983; Johnson-Laird, 1983). For example, a mental model might describe a person's understanding of an electric wall switch (Brown, 1981), or a computer (Carey, 1982). Understanding people's mental models of, say, personal computers can be very important in teaching people to use them. If the teacher knows that the new student has an incorrect model (perhaps thinking of the machine's memory as impossible to erase), it is easier to understand and prevent the kinds of mistakes he or she is likely to make.

Propositions and mental models are abstract terms, which in conscious thought translate into the specific words and images people work with every day. For example, in solving a math problem about how long it would take three people to do a job, if you know how long it takes two people to do it, you might find yourself silently restating in words the problem's concepts and their interrelationships. Here is a case of using words to represent concepts. In other cases, thinking involves the manipulation of images, as when you think about how an acquaintance would look in glasses.

We will save our discussion of thinking with words until the end of the chapter, when we look at language in some detail. Here, we look at the other modes of thought: images and cognitive maps.

Images and Cognitive Maps

Operations on images   To get a better visual image of an object, you might move closer to examine its details or use binoculars or a zoom lens. Do people do the same thing with mental images, and if so, how are mental images manipulated? In the last twenty years, some very clever investigations have addressed this question. For example, Steven Kosslyn (1976) asked people to form a mental image of an object such as a cat and then asked questions about it, such as "Does it have a head?" and "Does it have claws?" The smaller the detail in question, the longer people took to answer the question, as if they were indeed zooming in to the level of detail necessary to answer the question. The finer the detail required by the question, the greater the zoom and the longer the response time.

Roger Shepard and Jacqueline Metzler (1971) found evidence that people can imagine the rotation of objects in their minds. In their experiments, subjects viewed pairs of objects like those shown in Figure 9.6. Their task was to decide if the two objects were identical or mirror images of each other. Shepard and Metzler found that each added degree of difference in the orientation of the two objects added a constant amount of time to the decision. Thus, it looked as if the subjects imagined the rotation of one of the objects at a constant rate until it was lined up in the same orientation as the other.

Figure 9.6
Imagining the Rotation of Objects
Subjects are to decide if the two objects in each pair are identical or not. To do this, they must imagine the rotation of one of the objects so that it will be in the same orientation as the other. The objects in (a) are identical; those in (b) are different. The time needed to decide about each pair increases with the amount of rotation that subjects must imagine.
(From "Mental Rotation of Three-Dimensional Objects," R. Shepard et al., *Science,* Vol. 171, #3972, pp. 701–703, figure on page 702, 19 February 1971. Copyright 1971 by the American Association for the Advancement of Science.)

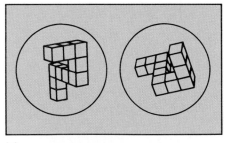
(a)

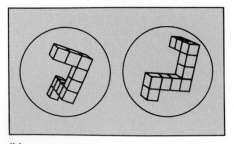
(b)

Though we cannot yet say exactly what goes on when people think by manipulating images, the information obtained so far suggests that, like other mental events, imagining involves its own systematic chronometry. Moreover, the manipulations performed on images are very similar to those that would be performed on the objects themselves.

Maps and spatial cognition   Even people who do not usually use images in most of their thinking may employ them to navigate through a particular environment. Especially when that environment is new, people tend to imagine specific objects and landmarks as they try to go from one place to another. Finally, after gaining a lot of experience in the environment, people acquire an overall *cognitive map* of it.

Useful as they are, cognitive maps are not accurate copies of the environment; they include systematic distortions. One distortion results from *rectangular bias,* a tendency to impose a rectangular north-south-east-west grid on the environment. For those who live in flat midwestern cities, this represents no distortion at all, since these cities actually conform to that grid. But people's cognitive maps tend to distort the subtle twists and turns in many environments. For example, when asked to draw a map of Paris, most Parisians straighten out the bends of the Seine River in an effort to make it conform more closely to a north-south flow (Milgram & Jodelet, 1976).

The rectangular bias also distorts the sense of relative locations. If you were asked where Reno, Nevada, is with respect to San Diego, California, you would probably answer, with little hesitation, northeast (Stevens & Coupe, 1978). After all, Nevada is east of California, and Reno is north of San Diego. But because California "bends" to the east, Reno is in fact northwest of San Diego.

In other words, people tend to simplify complex material in the world. Most of the time, this simplification is efficient and useful. But the costs humans must pay are certain systematic biases, such as false perceptions guided by top-down processes and expectancies, distortions of memory, and, as we have seen here, distortions of spatial cognition.

Reasoning and Heuristics

Whatever the units of thought are, the degree to which people achieve the goals of thinking depends on how they manipulate those units. If they manipulate them to reach a valid conclusion, then they are said to be rational. If someone tells you that negotiating with terrorists only leads to more terrorism, would you agree? To determine your response, you would want to collect some evidence, but you would also need to exercise your powers of reasoning. **Reasoning** is the process by which you evaluate and generate arguments and reach conclusions. The procedures that yield a valid conclusion are known as **logic.**

At the core of the study of logic lie the rules for evaluating **syllogisms,** which are arguments made up of two propositions, called **premises,** and a conclusion based on those premises. For example, if all people on welfare are poor and if all lazy bums are poor, does it follow that all people on welfare are lazy bums? No. The rules of logic indicate that, whatever the empirical truth or falsity of each of the propositions, the conclusion drawn from this line of reasoning is not logically sound, or *valid.* Another example: All gun owners are people. All criminals are people. Therefore, all gun owners are criminals. These logically incorrect syllogisms illustrate a general principle of logic, namely, that if "All A's are B" and "All C's are B," it does *not* follow that "All A's are C."

Scholars have also defined rules for determining the probability of events, and procedures for determining which of several possible decisions will yield the result most satisfying to the decision maker. Consider now how well these rules for reaching rational conclusions and decisions actually describe how people think.

Beliefs, wishes, and logic   Consider the following syllogism:

> All psychologists are brilliant. The authors of this text are psychologists. Therefore, the authors of this text are brilliant.

Do you agree? If you are like most people, you probably find yourself of two minds. On the one hand, the conclusion does follow logically from the preceding statements; the argument is *valid*. On the other hand, you probably are a little uncertain about our brilliance. Probably you reason that, although the logic of these statements is impeccable, the conclusion remains at odds with your general knowledge of the world, because the first statement is probably false. Obviously, reasoning depends on both knowledge of the world and an understanding of what is logical. If the premises are false, one should reject a conclusion flowing from them as invalid, even if the logic of the argument is sound.

Psychologists have found, however, that people often accept a syllogistic argument as valid even when it is not, if the conclusion agrees with their attitudes. For example, consider the following syllogism:

> America is a free country. In a free country, all people have equal opportunity. Therefore, in America all people have equal opportunity.

William McGuire (1960) found that people's belief in the validity of conclusions like this was based only in part on logical thinking. To a large extent, their reaction was influenced by the degree to which they believed that the conclusion was true, independent of the truth of the premises or the logic that followed from those premises. This tendency is sometimes demonstrated in the courtroom, when the defendant is a member of the clergy or a sweet, elderly

"No woman can be a good vice president; Geraldine Ferraro is a woman, therefore, she should not be vice president." The logic of this syllogism is correct, but because the first premise is wrong, voters basing their choice on this logic alone will reach an erroneous conclusion.

woman. The jury may remain unpersuaded by the prosecution's logically sound arguments based on true premises, because the logical conclusion (that the sweet, old woman poisoned her sister) is at odds with the jury's beliefs about how the world operates. In other words, the conclusions that people reach are based on both logical and wishful thinking.

Heuristics and biases   The idea that wishful thinking may sometimes overrule rational thinking could simply mean that people reason according to the laws of formal logic, probability, and rational choice, except when their thinking is marred by specific wishes or needs. But research has begun to show that the laws of logic and probability do not always provide a good description of how people actually think. However intelligent, expert, or objective people are, they sometimes tend to violate these laws in their everyday thinking. Much thinking seems to be based instead on **heuristics,** which are mental shortcuts or rules of thumb (Kahneman, Slovic & Tversky, 1982; Tversky & Kahneman, 1974).

Suppose, for example, that you are about to leave home in the morning but cannot find your watch. You might search for the watch in every possible location, room by room. This approach involves using an **algorithm,** which is a systematic procedure that cannot fail to produce a solution. But to obtain the same outcome more quickly, you are likely to search first in the places where your past experience suggests the watch might be; this approach is a heuristic. Similarly, in deciding which political candidates to vote for, your rule of thumb might be to support all those in a particular party rather than researching the views of each individual. People use heuristics like these because they are easy and frequently work well. But heuristics can also bias cognitive processes and cause errors. For example, many of those who vote for everyone on a particular party's election ticket may later be chagrined to discover that they got the president they wanted, but they also got a local sheriff whose views they despise.

Other heuristics guide people's judgment about what events are probable or what hypotheses are likely to be true. Amos Tversky and Daniel Kahneman have described three heuristics that people seem to use intuitively to make many of these judgments (Kahneman, Slovic & Tversky, 1982).

The anchoring heuristic   People use the **anchoring heuristic** when they estimate an event's probability by adjusting a preliminary estimate. In other words, people judge how likely it is that, say, they will be mugged in a given city by using new information to alter whatever initial impression they might have had. This sounds like a reasonable strategy, but the preliminary, starting value biases the final estimate. Once people have fixed a starting point, their adjustments of the initial judgment tend to be inadequate. It is as if they drop a mental anchor at one hypothesis or estimate and then cannot move very far from that original judgment. Thus, if a person assumes that the probability of being mugged in New York is 90 percent and then receives information about how improbable such events actually are, he or she may reduce the estimate to only 80 percent.

The representativeness heuristic   The **representativeness heuristic** involves judging the probability that a hypothesis is true or that an example belongs to a certain class of items by first focusing on the similarities between the example and a larger class of events or items, and then determining whether the particular example represents essential features of the larger class. For example, suppose you encounter a man who is tidy, small in stature, wears glasses, speaks quietly, and is somewhat shy. If asked whether this person is likely to be a librarian or a farmer, what would you say? Tversky and Kahneman (1974) found that most of their subjects chose *librarian.* But the chances are that this answer would be wrong. It is true that the description is more similar to or representative of the prototypical librarian than the prototypical farmer, but the fact that there are many more farmers in the world than librarians means that there are probably more farmers than librarians who match this particular physical description. Therefore, logic would dictate that a man matching this description is more likely to be a farmer than a librarian. When using the representativeness heuristic, people tend to ignore the overall probabilities, the **base-rate frequency,** and focus instead on what is representative or typical of the available evidence. Base-rate logic would suggest that almost any set of male physical features is more likely to belong to a farmer than a librarian.

The availability heuristic   Even when people use base-rate probability information to help them judge group membership or assess the truthfulness of a hypothesis, they may employ a third heuristic that can bias their probability judgment. The **availability heuristic** involves judging the frequency or probability of an event or hypothesis by how easily the hypothesis or examples of the event can be brought to mind. Thus, people tend to choose the hypothesis or alternative that is most mentally "available," much as you might choose which sweater to wear on the basis of which is on top in the drawer. This shortcut tends to work well because, among other reasons, what we remember most easily *are* very frequent events or hypotheses. But the availability heuristic can lead to biased judgments, especially when mental availability and actual frequency fail to correspond. For example, television news reports showing the grisly aftermath of gangland shootings and airline crashes may make these relatively rare events so memorable that people avoid certain cities or refuse to fly because they come to overestimate the frequency of crime or the probability of a crash (Slovic, 1984).

These heuristics represent only some of the strategies that people use intuitively, and they create only some of the biases and limitations evident in our reasoning. We will see others in the following sections, as we take a closer look at two common goals of thinking: problem solving and decision making.

PROBLEM SOLVING

Four characteristics describe problem solving: (1) where you are (the problem) is not where you would like to be (the solution); (2) the path between the problem and its solution is not obvious; (3) often you must spend considerable effort to understand, or *diagnose,* the problem; and (4) to diagnose or eliminate the problem, you may need to form several hypotheses about which path is correct and then test those hypotheses. To diagnose the problem when a patient has an unfamiliar combination of symptoms, for example, a physician must relate the available information—that is, the symptoms—to knowledge of the patient's medical history and of a variety of possible diseases. The physician might generate hypotheses about the patient's illness, review test results, try various treatments, and observe the effects on the patient. The many unnecessary tests performed in hospitals and the all-too-frequent cases of misdiagnosis testify to the fact that people's problem-solving skills often leave much to be desired.

Problems in Problem Solving

Problem solving involves understanding the problem (diagnosis), devising a plan to solve the problem, executing the plan, and evaluating the results (Polya, 1957). Many problem-solving difficulties occur at the start, with diagnosis. Proposing and testing hypotheses systematically is often an efficient, effective method of diagnosis, but it can lead to dead ends and frustrations that sometimes push people into trying to solve problems through blind trial and error. The frustration comes from five main sources.

Multiple hypotheses Often, people begin to solve a problem with only a vague notion of which hypothesis to test. For example, there may be a dozen reasons why a car will not start. Which hypotheses should be tested and in what order?

People seem to have a difficult time entertaining more than two or three hypotheses at one time (Mehle, 1982). The limited capacity of short-term memory, discussed in Chapter 8, may be part of the reason. As a result, the correct hypothesis is often neglected. Which hypothesis one chooses to consider may depend, not on which is most likely, but on the availability heuristic. In other words, the particular hypothesis that is considered may be one that is remembered most readily, which may not be the best hypothesis at all. Several characteristics make particular hypotheses easier to remember—for example, their simplicity, their emotional content, and how recently they have been experienced (Tversky & Kahneman, 1974). Thus, the auto mechanic troubleshooting your car might diagnose the problem as being identical to one encountered the day before, simply because this hypothesis is most easily brought to mind.

Mental sets Sometimes people are so blinded by one hypothesis or strategy that they continue to apply it even when better alternatives should be obvious (a clear case of the anchoring heuristic at work). An example devised by Abraham Luchins (1942) is shown in Figure 9.7. The object of each problem in the figure is to use three jars with specified capacities to obtain a certain amount of liquid. For example, in the first problem you are to obtain 21 quarts by using three jars that have capacities of 8, 35, and 3 quarts, respectively. The solution is to fill jar B to its capacity, 35 quarts, and then use its contents to fill jar A to its capacity of 8 quarts, leaving 27 quarts in jar B. Then pour liquid from jar B to fill jar C to its capacity twice, leaving 21 quarts in jar B [$27 - (2 \times 3) = 21$]. In other words, the solution is to apply the equation $B - A - 2C$. Now solve the remaining problems.

If you went through the problems in Figure 9.7, you found that a similar solution worked each time. But what happened with problem 7? If you are like most people, you did not notice that it has a simpler solution (namely, $A + C$). Instead, you succumbed to a **mental set,** the tendency for old patterns of problem solving to persist (Sweller & Gee, 1978). In the Luchins jar problem, the mental set consists of a tendency to stick with a strategy or solution that worked in the past. Figure 9.8 shows that a mental set may also restrict your perception of the problem itself. Figure 9.9 (p. 338) shows two ways of going beyond constraints to solve the nine-dot problem.

Yet another restriction on problem solving may come from experience with objects. Once people become accustomed to using an object for one type of function, they may be blinded to other ways of using it. Thus, experience may produce **functional fixedness,** a tendency to avoid using familiar objects in creative, but useful ways. Figure 9.10 (p. 338) illustrates an experiment that provided an excellent example of functional fixedness (Maier, 1930).

The confirmation bias Anyone who has suffered through a series of medical tests knows that diagnosis is not a one-shot decision. Instead, the physician chooses an initial hypothesis on the basis of observed symptoms and then orders further tests or evaluates additional symptoms to confirm or refute the

Problem: Measure out the following quantities by using jars with the stated capacities:	Jar A (quarts)	Jar B (quarts)	Jar C (quarts)
1 21 quarts	8	35	3
2 10 quarts	6	18	1
3 19 quarts	5	32	4
4 21 quarts	20	57	8
5 18 quarts	8	40	7
6 6 quarts	7	17	2
7 15 quarts	12	33	3

Figure 9.7
The Luchins Jar Problem
The problem is to obtain the volume of liquid shown in the first column by filling jars with the capacities shown in the next three columns. Each line represents a different problem. Such problems have been used to show that people often fall prey to mental sets that prevent them from using the most efficient solution.

Figure 9.8
The Nine-Dot Problem
The task is to draw no more than four lines that run through all nine dots on the page without lifting your pencil from the paper. Many people find such puzzles difficult because they fail to break out of mental sets that create artificial constraints on the range of solutions: drawing within the frame laid out by the dots and drawing through the middle of each dot.

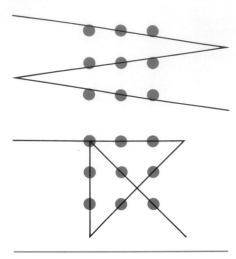

Figure 9.9
Two Creative Solutions to the Nine-Dot Problem

hypothesis. The problem is that humans have a strong bias to confirm rather than to refute the hypothesis they have chosen, even in the face of strong evidence against that hypothesis. People are quite willing to perceive and interpret data that support a hypothesis, but they tend to ignore factors that are inconsistent with it (Levine, 1966). Thus, the confirmation bias may be seen as a form of anchoring, in that it involves reluctance to abandon an initial hypothesis.

The 1979 accident at Three Mile Island provides a dramatic example of confirmation bias (Rubenstein & Mason, 1979; Wickens, 1984). As noted in Chapter 5, the control room operators could have formed either of two hypotheses about what might have been wrong inside the nuclear reactor. Either the water pressure in the reactor core was too high, creating the danger of an explosion, or it was too low, a condition that could lead to a meltdown. Several symptoms supported the correct hypothesis (the pressure was indeed low), but one defective meter indicated that the pressure was too high. Because the supervisors had used that meter to establish their original hypothesis of high pressure, they failed to appreciate other symptoms of the actual low pressure until after they had implemented the disastrous decision to shut down an emergency pump.

An experiment conducted by David Rosenhan (1973) provided a rather alarming example of the confirmation bias. Rosenhan and nine confederates presented themselves at ten different mental hospitals and complained of the same faked symptom: hearing a voice that said "dull," "empty," and "thud." Otherwise, they reported only truthful facts about their very normal lives. Nevertheless, all were admitted, and most were diagnosed as schizophrenic, a severe condition described in Chapter 15, on abnormal psychology. Once in the hospital, these "patients" behaved normally and reported no further symptoms, but even their normal actions were interpreted as symptoms of mental illness—evidence confirming the original, incorrect hypothesis that they were schizophrenic. For example, the "patients" took notes about their experiences in the hospital. In at least one case, the staff described this "writing behavior" as a symptom. Another "patient" accurately stated that he had a

Figure 9.10

An Example of Functional Fixedness
People were asked to fasten together two strings hanging from the ceiling but out of reach of each other. Several tools were available in the room. The solution was to take a heavy tool, such as a pair of pliers, attach it to one of the strings, and swing it like a pendulum until that string could be reached while holding the other. The solution is not easily arrived at, however, because most people fixate on the usual function of the pliers as a hand tool rather than hypothesizing their role as a pendulum weight. Moreover, the people in the experiment were more likely to hit on the solution and use the pliers if the tools were scattered around the room than if they were neatly contained in a tool box. Apparently, when the pliers were in a tool box, their function as a tool was emphasized, and the mental set became nearly impossible to break.

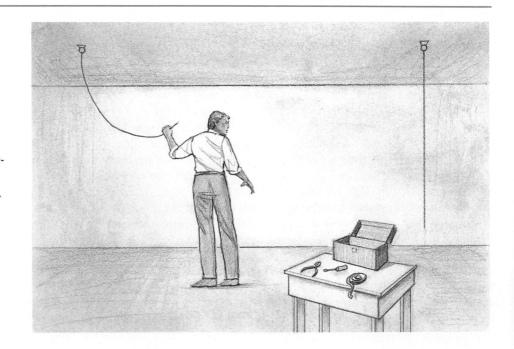

good family life, even though he sometimes had arguments with his wife and occasionally had to spank his children. This rather normal pattern was described in staff notes as follows: "his attempts to control emotionality with his wife and children are punctuated by angry outbursts and, in the case of the children, spankings."

What is the source of confirmation bias? One possibility is that mental effort is required to abandon old hypotheses and construct new ones and that people tend to avoid complex mental operations (Rasmussen, 1981; Shugan, 1980). This *cognitive laziness* may discourage attention to alternative hypotheses. Furthermore, to admit that one is wrong may threaten self-esteem. This *cognitive conceit* (Fischoff, 1977) may lead people to search for and find confirming evidence and ignore contradictory evidence.

Ignoring negative evidence   Often, what does not happen can be as important as what does happen. For example, when troubleshooting a car, a symptom of headlight failure might lead you to hypothesize that the battery is low. Yet, if this were the case, other battery-powered equipment should also have failed. The fact that these symptoms are not present is important in disconfirming your original hypothesis. The absence of symptoms can provide important evidence for or against a hypothesis. Compared with symptoms that are present, however, people are less likely to notice and observe symptoms that do not occur (Hunt & Rouse, 1981). People have a difficult time using the absence of symptoms to help eliminate hypotheses from consideration.

Ignoring base-rate information   Hypothesis testing can also be impaired by the representativeness heuristic—the strategy of ignoring probability and focusing instead on what is most representative. For example, when a medical diagnosis is made, two variables should influence the choice of the hypothesis: the evidence, or how closely the symptoms match those of the disease being considered, and the base rate, or how frequently the disease occurs. If a patient shows symptoms that match the textbook description of two diseases, call them *afacitis* and *carlosis*, but carlosis occurs 100 times more often, the physician's best choice is to diagnose carlosis. In fact, the base rate may make carlosis the best diagnosis even if the symptoms look a bit more like afacitis. However, when confronted with a situation like this, people tend to ignore base-rate information (Christenssen-Szalanski & Bushyhead, 1981). It seems that the capacity of short-term memory is exceeded when new evidence and base-rate information must be combined. What is sacrificed is the more abstract, less visible base rate.

Improving Problem-Solving Skills

How can you improve your ability to solve problems? Are there any easily taught techniques or methods that will give you the problem-solving skill of an expert? In the following sections, we try to answer these questions.

Avoiding the pitfalls   Perhaps the most obvious step that you can take to improve your problem solving is to avoid errors of syllogistic reasoning. Imagery can help. The pictures shown in Figure 9.11 (p. 340), called *Venn diagrams,* are one example. To solve a syllogism, you can draw the Venn representation of the two premises and see whether the conclusion is consistent with both. Less formally, you can imagine a scene that includes the elements in the syllogism (Johnson-Laird & Steedman, 1978).

Other weaknesses in problem solving are more difficult to remedy. Psychologists have reasoned that it should be possible to train people not to

Figure 9.11
Venn Diagrams

These diagrams represent three different, but logically correct interpretations of the statement "Some A's are not B's." This statement is an equally valid description of "Some Democrats are not New Yorkers," which is represented by (a); "Some federal employees are not senators," which is represented by (b); or "Some Albanians are not Chinese," which is represented by (c). Typically, however, people assume that only a diagram like (a) represents the statement and therefore assume that the statement also implies "Some B's are not A's."

Syllogism 1	**Syllogism 2**	**Syllogism 3**
Premise 1　Some A's are not B's.	Some A's are not B's.	Some A's are not B's.
Premise 2　Some B's are not A's.	No B's are not A's.	All B's are not A's.
Conclusion　Therefore no A's are B's.	Therefore all B's are A's.	Therefore some A's are B's.
(false)	(true)	(false)

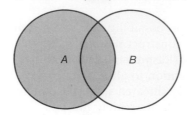 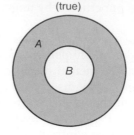 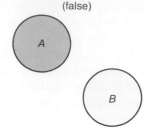

fall prey to the biases that impair problem solving—to *debias* people, as Baruch Fischoff (1982) put it. Attempts to do this have produced some modest improvements in problem solving. For example, in one study, cautioning people against their tendency to anchor on a hypothesis reduced the magnitude of the confirmation bias and increased their openness to alternative evidence (Lopes, 1982).

Many anecdotal reports over the years have suggested that a technique called *incubation* may improve problem-solving ability. **Incubation** involves putting the problem aside for a while and turning to some other mental activity while the problem "incubates," perhaps at a subconscious level, as described in the chapter on consciousness. For example, French mathematician J. H. Poincaré claimed that his insights into Fuchsian functions occurred suddenly as he was stepping onto a bus (Poincaré, 1913). However, it appears that incubation aids problem solving only if the incubation period is preceded by a lengthy period of preparation (Silviera, 1971). Incubation may aid problem solving mainly by allowing mental sets and other biases to dissipate somewhat, engendering a fresh approach.

A heuristic known as decomposition may also help solve problems. **Decomposition** consists of breaking a problem into smaller elements by working backward from the final goal. Decomposition can be effective at

Life is full of problems, but the chances of solving them efficiently improve when people adopt systematic and logical approaches.

breaking down even a large, seemingly unmanageable problem (such as writing a long term paper) into a series of smaller, more manageable subproblems (such as finding appropriate references, writing an outline, creating a first draft, and so on).

Imitating the expert   Scientists, engineers, physicians, maintenance technicians, auto mechanics, and labor negotiators, to name just a few, are well-paid professionals, presumably because of their expertise in solving problems. What do these experts bring to a situation that a novice cannot? Experience and knowledge, for one thing. As a result, experts frequently proceed by looking for similarities and analogies between current and past problems. More than novices, they can relate new information and new experiences to past experiences and existing knowledge. This produces one of the most important general differences between the expert and the novice: the ability to use existing knowledge to organize new information into chunks, as we described in the chapter on memory.

Experts appear to have the ability to visualize problems more clearly and efficiently than novices, by using their past knowledge and experience to chunk a large number of problem elements into a smaller number of more meaningful units. One result is that experts seem to suffer less than nonexperts from the interference problems described in the chapter on memory. Psychologists do not yet know why this is so. Another result is that experts may not need to decompose a problem into subproblems. Once experts understand a problem, they can immediately bring to mind all of the steps from the problem to the goal, as if these were a single mental chunk.

Expertise also carries a danger: using analogies to past experience can lead to the traps of functional fixedness and mental sets. As a Zen proverb says, "In the mind of the beginner there are many possibilities; in the mind of the expert, few." Top-down, knowledge-driven processes, described in Chapter 5, bias people toward seeing what they expect or want to see. Thus, they can prevent people from seeing a problem in different ways. Indeed, there is a thin line between using past experience well and being trapped by it.

The benefits of experience may also be limited because feedback about a solution is delayed (Brehmer, 1981). Often, experts receive information about the correctness of a proposed solution only long after they have forgotten how they came to that answer. As a result, they cannot use the feedback to improve their problem-solving methods. Furthermore, the confirmation bias may prevent them from seeing that a proposed solution was incorrect (Fischoff & Slovic, 1980).

In short, experience alone does not ensure excellence at problem solving, and practice may not make perfect. A book by Christopher Cerf (1984) gives further reason for skepticism; it details fantastically erroneous predictions by experts. Table 9.1 (p. 342) shows a few of them.

Teaching the novice   Despite the pitfalls and failures of expertise, it is fair to say that, for the most part, experts are better than novices in their area of expertise. This conclusion leads to an intriguing question: Are there shortcuts to achieving expertise?

After carefully reviewing the literature, Richard Mayer (1983) concluded that claims of "instant" shortcuts to expertise must be viewed with some skepticism. The most important characteristic of any expert problem solver, he noted, is extensive knowledge in the problem area. For example, in one study, teaching students to use general strategies, such as diagrams, did improve their ability to solve mathematical problems, but only after the students had already mastered a good deal of mathematical knowledge (Schoenfeld, 1979). Knowledge allows the expert to perceive the elements of

TABLE 9.1

Some Expert Opinions

Experts typically have a larger store of knowledge about things falling within their realm of expertise, but even confidently stated opinions based on this knowledge can turn out to be incorrect, as these examples from Christopher Cerf's The Experts Speak *(1984) clearly show.*

On the possibility of painless surgery through anesthesia:
" 'Knife' and 'pain' are two words in surgery that must forever be associated. . . . To this compulsory combination we shall have to adjust ourselves." (Dr. Alfred Velpeau, professor of surgery, Paris Faculty of Medicine, 1839)

On the hazards of cigarette smoking:
"If excessive smoking actually plays a role in the production of lung cancer, it seems to be a minor one." (Dr. W. C. Heuper, National Cancer Institute, 1954)

On the stock market (one week before the disastrous 1929 crash that wiped out over $50 billion in investments):
"Stocks have reached what looks like a permanently high plateau." (Irving Fisher, professor of economics, Yale University, 1929)

On the prospects of war with Japan (three years before the December 1941 Japanese attack on Pearl Harbor):
"A Japanese attack on Pearl Harbor is a strategic impossibility." (Major George F. Eliot, military science writer, 1938)

On the value of personal computers:
"There is no reason for any individual to have a computer in their home." (Ken Olson, president, Digital Equipment Corporation, 1977)

On the concept of the airplane:
"Heavier-than-air flying machines are impossible." (Lord Kelvin, mathematician, physicist, and president of the British Royal Society, 1895)

a problem as a chunk, to understand the correlations between problem elements, and to draw on past analogies. In short, there seems to be no substitute for putting in the hard work needed to acquire knowledge. Once you possess this knowledge, however, you can learn shortcuts that will allow you to take maximum advantage of it.

HIGHLIGHT

Artificial Intelligence

The possibility of teaching expertise holds special interest for those who work in **artificial intelligence,** the field that studies how to program computers to imitate the products of human perception, understanding, and thought. To reach this goal, it is not necessary for the computer to imitate the processes of the brain, any more than airplanes must mimic a bird's wing flapping. Nevertheless, just as aircraft have been improved by imitating some characteristics of birds in flight so, too, progress in artificial intelligence may depend on the careful study of human cognitive processes.

Research in artificial intelligence has concentrated on imitating human perception, speech comprehension, and problem solving. A problem-solving computer needs to be supplied with two basic elements: (1) an extensive knowledge base about the area in which problems are to be solved; and (2) an *inference engine,* a set of procedures for using the facts in the knowledge base to solve problems. Computers, like people, can use two main types of procedures for problem solving: algorithms and heuristics. As noted earlier, algorithms are precise, step-by-step statements of logical and computational operations that guarantee a solution. Heuristics, as we have seen, are mental rules of thumb or shortcuts that *often* work, but do not always.

Computers are good at following algorithms, because algorithms do not require much flexibility. Indeed, many problems, like solving differential equations or computing statistical tests, are best handled by algorithms, and therefore by computers. But algorithms are not terribly efficient. For example, an algorithm for a chess-playing computer might consider all possible moves, then all possible countermoves by the opponent, then all possible counter-countermoves, and so on, until the "best" move is determined. After each move by the opponent, the computer could determine which move would produce a sequence of moves that would result in victory the greatest number of times, and in loss the fewest possible times. The problem is that this algorithm is impossibly complex even for the fastest supercomputer; it would need to consider around 10^{120} possible sequences of moves, an astronomically large number that could occupy much of the world's computer power for years (Solso, 1979).

Many researchers working in artificial intelligence have concluded that the most effective procedures for problem solving are humanlike heuristics. A heuristic for problem solving might specify the most logical place to start looking for a solution, or the rules under which different strategies or algorithms should be used, or the most relevant kind of information about a problem. For chess playing, for example, a heuristic might immediately eliminate a number of potentially absurd moves, such as moving one's queen to a position where it will be taken.

Attempts to use computers for problem solving have had some success in the case of **expert systems,** computer programs that help people solve problems in a fairly restricted, specific area. For example, the expert system MYCIN helps physicians diagnose disease and prescribe antibiotics (Shortliffe, 1983). MYCIN has incorporated a large and growing knowledge base from several expert physicians, and it has the capacity to ask important questions. Much like Dr. Wallace in the beginning of this chapter, MYCIN begins by reviewing the patient's symptoms and medical history, then uses this information to reason backward to establish the most likely cause of the symptoms. When MYCIN needs additional information, it searches its own knowledge base and, if the search is not successful, requests the information from a

"Expert systems," a form of artificial intelligence technology that uses the knowledge and logic of experts to guide the diagnosis and solution of problems, are helping service technicians more efficiently diagnose and correct malfunctions in customers' automobiles.
(Reproduced courtesy of General Motors Corporation.)

consulting physician. The program is also able to explain the precise reasoning behind a suggested diagnosis and treatment. Other expert systems are being used in chemistry, industry, and business. One key to their success lies in the fact that they are used only in one specific area, for which a large knowledge base has been compiled. The difficulties encountered in developing these systems have highlighted critical ways in which human thought goes well beyond readily programmable heuristics and algorithms. Here are three of the most important problems.

1. *Storing the knowledge base*   Human experts have the knowledge that must be coded into the expert system, but often they cannot easily verbalize it in a way that can be coded by a programming language. Even when experts can articulate the facts, another problem remains: how the information is stored. Like a good library or like long-term memory, the knowledge base must be more than a warehouse of facts; it must have organization, cross-referencing, and careful tagging and labeling.

2. *Building in common sense*   Analysis of a problem sometimes brings you to conclusions that you know are wrong; they just do not make sense. Typically, you reject these conclusions and start again. But most expert computer systems will forge ahead single-mindedly.

3. *Using wider knowledge*   Expert systems typically store a great deal of knowledge about one specific area, but people often reach solutions by looking at a problem from different perspectives and borrowing knowledge or analogies from other domains. It is often impossible to know what domains of knowledge will be useful until after the expert system has been used, and incorporating all potentially useful domains would make the computer program impossibly large. Fortunately, as the MYCIN program illustrates, expert systems can be programmed to request information that they need but do not have.

Obviously, artificial intelligence has come a long way since the first algorithms were developed for arithmetic calculators in the sixteenth century. But it will be a very long time before anyone can create truly intelligent robots like C3PO of *Star Wars* or HAL of *2001*. There is an irony in the development of artificial intelligence. The more powerful computers and computer programs have become, the more psychologists have been forced to realize how much they do not yet know about human perception, understanding, and thought (Dreyfus & Dreyfus, 1979). ■

RISKY DECISION MAKING

The ability to solve problems often overlaps with another critical skill: decision making. When you solve a problem, you must make decisions about what to consider. Even after you have correctly diagnosed a problem, you may be left with a difficult decision. For example, after a doctor determines that a patient's problem is cancer, someone must still make the crucial decision of whether to risk operating.

Earlier we looked at high-speed decisions—fairly simple decisions made when time is of the essence. In making these types of decisions, people generally err only when they try to respond too quickly. In contrast, many decisions, like those of jurors and physicians, take more time, are more complex, and are vulnerable to several types of errors. Sometimes a decision is difficult because each alternative has several characteristics. Often, the main problem is that the world itself is unpredictable and uncertain. Your decision to buy one car instead of another, for example, may be an error if the car turns out to be a lemon. But if there was no evidence that the car was faulty, you would chalk up the error to random factors in the world, not to a failure of your own decision making. You cannot see the future. Thus, decisions made in the face of the world's uncertainty are called *risky*.

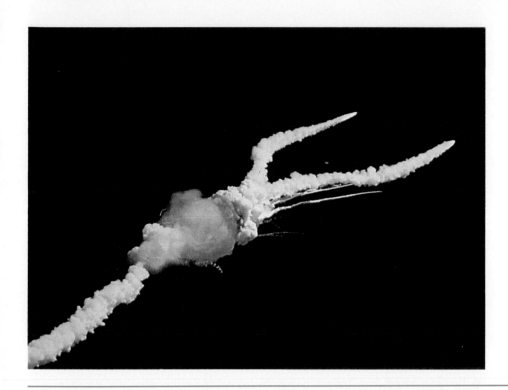

The disastrous decision to launch the space shuttle Challenger in thirty-eight-degree weather exemplifies a risky decision apparently flawed by biases in the decision-makers' processing of information about the pros and cons of the "go" and "no-go" options.

Although many incorrect decisions result from the world's uncertainty, it is also true that people often make poor decisions because of limits, biases, and fallacies in information processing. For example, even if we discount the advantages of hindsight, it is probably fair to say that the decision not to more carefully protect the American fleet at Pearl Harbor was a poor one. In the following pages, we consider some techniques for making good decisions and some of the biases or limitations that influence decisions.

Rational Decision Making

Whenever you make a major decision, such as where to attend college or whether to accept a job offer, you consider several important characteristics, or *attributes,* of the alternatives. In choosing a college, for example, the attributes might be tuition costs, closeness to home, social life, quality of the faculty, and so on. Unfortunately, people often fail to choose the alternative that in the long run satisfies most of their important values.

One reason for such failure appears to be that, as in hypothesis testing, the limited capacity of short-term memory prevents people from keeping in mind and considering all of the attributes in their relative order of importance (Edwards, 1977). Instead, a decision may be guided by the availability heuristic, so that the choice is influenced only by the most available attribute, which is often the most salient characteristic. For example, you might choose the highest-paying job without fully weighing the fact that it is also farthest from home and offers the least independence (Tversky, 1977). To escape the frailties of short-term memory, you might use the technique shown in Table 9.2 (p. 346), based on *multiattribute utility theory* (Edwards, 1977). Whether you are trying to select an apartment or choose a site for an airport, this procedure can help you make a good choice (Edwards, 1977; Fischoff, Slovic & Lichtenstein, 1977; Wickens & Kramer, 1985). But the procedure assumes that the alternatives and attributes are all *certain;* it does not allow for the uncertainty about outcomes that complicates many decisions.

TABLE 9.2
Problem Solving Using Multiattribute Utility Theory

(2) Attributes	Importance	(3) College 1	College 2	College 3	College 4
		(1) *Alternatives*			
At₁ (cost)	3	4	1	3	2
At₂ (academics)	2	1	2	3	4
At₃ (social)	1	1	3	2	4
(4) **Computing the products**		3 × 4 + 2 × 1 + 1 × 1	3 × 1 + 2 × 2 + 1 × 3	3 × 3 + 2 × 3 + 1 × 2	3 × 2 + 2 × 4 + 1 × 4
(5) **Summing the products**		15	10	17	18

(6)

To choose between colleges,

(1) List all the alternatives (colleges) across the columns and all attributes that might possibly matter down the rows, in order of their importance.

(2) Assign numerical weights to each attribute, giving 1 to the least important, 2 to the next, and so on.

(3) Give each alternative a score for each attribute, with 1 again indicating the lowest score (such as most expensive, poorest academics).

(4) Multiply the score in each cell by the importance weight for that row.

(5) Add the products down each column.

(6) Compare the columns. The column with the highest total is the winner and should be chosen.

Figure 9.12 shows how choices made under uncertainty can be analyzed. Suppose the choice is whether to buy a new car or fix the old one. The steps for analyzing the situation and reaching a rational decision are:

1. List each possible action.

2. Define the possible outcomes of each action.

3. Assign a *value* to each outcome. Sometimes the value of the outcome might be simply its monetary cost, but often the value must instead be *judged*. Any subjective measure of value is called the **utility** of the alternative. For example, repairing the car would involve a significant cost in both time and money. If the repairs succeed, their cost might be more than compensated for by the utility of having a usable car, so a

Figure 9.12
Application of Expected Utility Theory to Risky Decision Making
Following the steps described in the text, the action of repairing one's car is found to have a higher expected utility (is less negative) than the action of buying a new car. Hence the rational decision maker should choose to repair the car.

Possible actions	Possible outcomes		Expected utility:
Repair car	**Repairs will succeed** Utility: +50 Probability of outcome: 0.20 Expected utility: (+50) (0.20) = +10.00	**Repairs will fail** Utility: −200 Probability of outcome: 0.80 Expected utility: (−200) (0.80) = −160.00	Of repairing the car: (+10.00) + (−160.00) = −150
Buy new car	**New car will work** Utility: −200 Probability of outcome: 0.90 Expected utility: (−200) (0.90) = −180.00	**New car will not work** Utility: −500 Probability of outcome: 0.10 Expected utility: (−500) (0.10) = −50.00	Of buying a new car: (−180.00) + (−50.00) = −230

utility of +50 is assigned. If the repairs fail, the continued anxiety, frustration, and cost of having to seek further repairs must be considered; hence the utility of this outcome is large and negative. The exact numbers assigned for the various outcomes are arbitrary; their *relative* size and direction are significant in making a decision.

4. Note the *probability* of each outcome. For example, you might estimate that, in view of your car's condition, there is only a 20 percent chance that repairs will be successful. (The probabilities in each row must add up to 1.00.)

5. Multiply the probability in each column of the table by the utility value in each cell. This product is the **expected utility** of each outcome.

6. Add the expected utilities for the possible outcomes of each action; this sum represents the expected utility for each action. The action with the highest total (the most positive or least negative) is the one that should be chosen. It is the rational choice, given this kind of systematic analysis of costs, benefits, and risks.

This procedure is so straightforward that it may seem surprising that people often make bad decisions. But a closer look at steps 3 and 4—the assignment of value and probability—will show that making decisions is far from simple.

Perceptions of Value

When people consider various alternatives, their preferences depend, not on simple differences between costs and benefits, but on how they judge the utility of outcomes and on whether each outcome is seen as risky or a sure thing. Numerous experiments have shown that people tend to have certain biases in making these evaluations (Tversky & Kahneman, 1981). Figure 9.13 (p. 348) shows the relationship between the objective value of an outcome and its judged utility. Equal changes in value do not give equal changes in utility, for several reasons (Edwards et al., 1965; Tversky & Kahneman, 1981).

First, the utility of a specific gain depends, not on the absolute increase in value, but on what the starting point was. Suppose you can take some action to receive a coupon for a free dinner worth $10. Does this gain have the same utility as having an extra $10 added to a dividend check? The amount is the same, but as Figure 9.13 shows, people behave as if the difference in utility between $0 and $10 (+U1 in the figure) is much greater than the difference between $100 and $110 (+U2). This calls to mind Weber's law of psychophysics discussed in the chapter on perception. How much a difference in value means depends on how much you already have (Edwards, Lindman & Phillips, 1965).

Second, gains and losses are perceived quite differently, as you can see by comparing −U1 and +U1 in Figure 9.13, each of which is the result of a ten-dollar difference in value. Gaining a certain value has less utility than avoiding a loss of the same value (Tversky & Kahneman, 1981). In other words, the pleasure of winning a certain amount is less than the pain of losing the same amount.

In addition, your preference among decision alternatives depends on whether the outcomes associated with them are risky or sure things. The reaction to risk depends on whether you are contemplating a loss or a gain. Suppose you are offered a choice between receiving one dollar for sure and gambling that dollar with a 50-50 chance of either winning two dollars or getting nothing. Which would you choose? The expected value of the outcome is the same for each option, but most people choose the smaller, but certain gain (Tversky & Kahneman, 1981). When people are faced with a choice

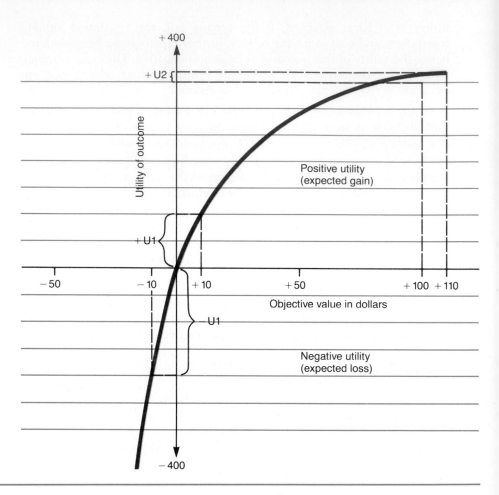

Figure 9.13
The Relationship Between Value and Utility
Notice that increases in value produce differing increases in utility, depending on the initial amount of value. For example, equal increases in value produce smaller increases in utility at higher initial values. Notice also that a $10 loss in value produces a much greater change in utility than does a $10 gain.

between two gains of the same expected value—one risky and one a sure thing—they generally choose the sure thing.

Now suppose you are forced to make the unpleasant choice between losing one dollar and accepting a gamble with a 50-50 chance of breaking even or losing two dollars. For either choice, the expected loss (outcome probability times outcome value) is one dollar. Most people accept the risky gamble. Thus, when offered the choice between risky losses and certain losses that have the same negative expected value, risk aversion vanishes, and people are more likely to select the risky rather than the sure alternative.

Because evaluation of an outcome is shaped by whether it is a gain or a loss, a risky or a sure thing, people can respond very differently to a decision, depending on how it is framed (Tversky & Kahneman, 1981). For example, a person might view the removal of a leg very negatively (as an expected loss) if it is contrasted with keeping the leg, but as an expected gain if the surgery prevents certain death.

Perceptions of Probability

Differences between value and utility do not explain why people gamble. In reality, gambling involves choosing an expected loss instead of the sure thing of not gambling. (If gambling yielded an expected gain for the gambler, Las Vegas and Atlantic City casinos would reap no profits.) The explanation for gambling seems to come from a second element of risky decision making: people's perception of the probability that events will occur.

One way in which people's perception of probability differs from reality is called the **gambler's fallacy.** People believe that events in a random process will correct themselves. This belief is false. For example, if you flip a coin and it comes up heads ten times in a row, the chance that it will come up heads on the eleventh try is still 50 percent.

A second departure from reality results because people consistently *overestimate the probability of very rare events and underestimate the probability of very frequent ones* (Erlick, 1961; Tversky & Kahneman, 1981). In gambling or lotteries, the probability of a payoff is actually very rare (say, 1 percent). But if you perceive that your chances of winning are instead 5 percent, then the expected value of playing is artificially inflated and will be greater than the cost of entering. With this biased value, the decision to enter the gamble has a positive expected value.

There is one important exception to the tendency to underestimate frequent events, however. When the event being estimated is the probability that one's own forecast or belief is correct, people tend to overestimate the probability, expressing overconfidence in their own predictions. Baruch Fischoff and Donald MacGregor (1982) used an ingenious approach to study this bias. They asked people whether they believed that a certain event would occur—for example, that a certain sports team would win—and how confident they were about this prediction. After the events, the accuracy of the forecasts was computed and compared with the confidence ratings assigned to the predictions. Sure enough, the confidence was consistently greater than the accuracy. That is, people tend to believe, more than they should, that they are going to be right.

This inflated confidence in prediction holds true even when people make predictions concerning the accuracy of their own memory. For example, Fischoff (1980) asked people questions based on general knowledge, such as: Which of the following causes the most deaths in the United States: appendicitis, abortion, or childbirth? (The correct answer is appendicitis.) The people were also to indicate how confident they were that their answers were correct. Again, confidence was high, even though the answers were wrong more often than they were right.

Can *debiasing* eliminate this overconfidence? When Asher Koriat and his colleagues explicitly asked forecasters to list why their forecasts might be wrong, the forecasters offered forecasts that were less excessively optimistic (Koriat et al., 1980). They were able to reduce, but not eliminate, the tendency toward overconfidence. In short, be wary when people express confidence that a forecast is correct. They will be wrong more often than they think.

The gambler's fallacy leads people to continue putting money into a slot machine on the assumption that it is "due" to pay off. However, the probability of hitting the jackpot is unaffected by previous outcomes and remains equally low on every play.

Decision Making and the Law

Decision making is especially critical in legal matters (Loftus, 1979). Decisions by an eyewitness that a suspect is or is not the culprit, by a judge to hand down a long or short sentence, or by a jury to decide guilt or innocence—all can have monumental consequences for a defendant. In Chapters 5 and 8, we showed some of the ways in which perception and memory influence courtroom procedures. Psychologists have also examined decision making in the criminal justice system, particularly decision making by jurors.

It is evident that the jury should pay attention to the credibility or estimated reliability of an eyewitness in reaching a judgment of guilt or innocence. For example, if two witnesses of low credibility provide testimony that implies guilt, and one witness of impeccable credentials implies innocence, the jury should favor the one credible witness over the two unreliable ones when they weigh the evidence (Schum, 1975). But experiments suggest that juries do not always act this way. In several experiments, investigators have staged crimes viewed by subjects who act as witnesses. The witnesses then report details of the crime and their confidence in the accuracy of their report. A frequent finding, reminiscent of the overconfidence of forecasters, is that witnesses' expressions of confidence are much greater than the accuracy of their reports (Hosch & Cooper, 1982). In fact, a witness's asserted confidence is often unrelated to accuracy, particularly where violent incidents are involved (Clifford & Hollin, 1981). When a situation is violent, the overall accuracy of the testimony is also reduced.

Can jurors detect differences in eyewitness reliability, and are they swayed by assertions of confidence? R. C. Lindsey, Gary Wells, and Carolyne Rumpel (1981) staged crimes and divided their witnesses into three groups. Each group watched the crime in varying amounts of light, so that the visibility of the crime was different for each group, and the reports varied in accuracy. As in other experiments, the witnesses who were very confident of their reports were just as likely to be wrong as the witnesses who were more cautious. When mock juries later heard the witnesses' testimony, the juries could not discriminate those witnesses within a group whose reports were accurate from those who were not. The juries did discriminate somewhat among the three groups of witnesses; they believed those for whom the crime was very visible more than those who had a poor view of the crime. But the juries believed the testimony of those who had a poor view to a much greater degree than was warranted, since those witnesses could recall the details only poorly. Witnesses' inflated confidence in the accuracy of their own testimony often gets passed along to juries.

Jurors may also misjudge witnesses because of their reaction to the witnesses' attention to detail. Gary Wells and Michael Leippe (1981), for example, found that mock juries were impressed by and more likely to believe witnesses who could accurately report trivial details about the crime. It was as if the jurors took this ability as evidence that the witnesses had a good memory of the crime. At first, this conclusion might sound reasonable; but as we saw in the chapter on perception, the ability to divide attention is limited. As a result, a witness who views a violent crime might focus attention on the crime and the criminal, or on surrounding details, but probably not on both. Hence, it is not surprising that Wells and Leippe (1981) also found that a witness who very accurately remembers the unimportant details at a crime scene is likely to be poor at recalling facial features, stature, and other important details about the criminal.

Together these investigations suggest that juries do not pay as much attention as they should to the credibility of eyewitness testimony. The message seems to be more important than the messenger. Elizabeth Loftus (1979) suggested that these biases might be reduced by having juries listen to testimony by psychologists about the biases and failures of eyewitnesses. But, at least for now, these biases will exert influences of unknown magnitude on our legal system. ◼

LANGUAGE

So far, our discussion of thinking has assumed that people have a crucial skill: the ability to use language. This ability provides both a vehicle for the mind's communication with itself and the most important means of communicating with others. Other animals can communicate, but none appears to have the means to do so with the systematic rules, precision, and infinite range that human language allows. And only humans can pass communication through the ages, so that generation after generation can learn from and enjoy the heritage of its ancestors.

The Elements of Language

A **language** has two basic elements: symbols, such as words, and a set of rules, called **grammar,** for combining those symbols. These two components allow human language to be at once rule-bound and creative. With a vocabulary of no more than 50,000 to 100,000 words (the vocabulary of the typical college student), humans can create and understand an infinite number of sentences. All of the sentences ever articulated are created from just a few dozen categories of sounds. The power of language comes from the way these rather unimpressive raw materials are organized according to rules. This organization occurs at several levels.

From sounds to sentences   Organization occurs first at the level of sounds. A **phoneme** is the smallest unit of sound that affects the meaning of speech. Changing a phoneme changes the meaning of a word, much as changing a letter in a printed word changes its meaning. *Tea* has a meaning different from *sea,* and *sight* is different from *sit.*

Each spoken language consists of roughly thirty to fifty phonemes. English has twenty-six letters, but it has about forty phonemes. The *a* in *cat* and the *a* in *cake,* for example, are different English phonemes. Many of the letter sounds are phonemes (including "ell," "aitch," and "em"), but so are the sounds "th" and "sh." Sounds that we consider different phonemes may be considered just one phoneme in another language, and sounds that are considered one phoneme in English are distinguished as different phonemes in other languages. For example, to English speakers the *p* in *pin* and the *p* in *dip* are one phoneme, but in the Thai language, they are two phonemes. In the Thai language, the "p" sound in *pin* combined with "-ay" gives a word

Words and grammatical rules about how they are combined comprise language, the most important way through which people communicate with one another and with themselves.

Certain gifted speakers have used language so effectively that the messages they communicate are stored forever in the memories of their audiences.

meaning "danger"; the "p" sound in *dip* combined with "-ay" creates a word meaning "to go."

Although changing a phoneme affects meaning, phonemes themselves are not meaningful. They are combined to form the second level of organization: morphemes. A **morpheme** is the smallest unit of language that has meaning. Word stems like *dog* and *run* are morphemes, but so are prefixes like *un-* and suffixes like *-ed,* because they have meaning even though they cannot stand alone. **Words** are made up of one or more morphemes. Words, in turn, are combined to form phrases and sentences according to a set of rules called **syntax.** Compare the following sentences:

> Fatal accidents deter careful drivers.
> Snows sudden floods melting cause.

The first sentence makes perfect sense, but the second sentence violates English syntax. If the words were reordered, however, they would produce the perfectly acceptable sentence "Melting snows cause sudden floods" (Marks & Miller, 1964).

Even if you use English phonemes combined in proper ways to form morphemes strung together according to the laws of English syntax, you may not end up with an acceptable English sentence. Consider the sentence "Rapid bouquets deter sudden neighbors." It somehow sounds right, but it is nonsense. Why? It has syntax, but it ignores the set of rules, called **semantics,** that govern the meaning of words and sentences.

Surface structure and deep structure   So far, we have discussed elements of language that are apparent in the sentences people produce. These elements were the focus of study for linguists and *psycholinguists* (psychologists who deal with language) for many decades. Then, in 1957, linguist Noam Chomsky started a revolution in the study of language. He argued that, if linguists studied only the language that people produced, they would never uncover the principles that account for all the sentences that people create. They could not explain, for example, how one articulated sentence, such as "This is my old friend" has more than one meaning (*old* can mean "aged" or "long-standing"). And by looking only at sentences produced, linguists could not account for the very close relationships between the meanings of such apparently different sentences as "Don't give up just because things look bad" and "The opera ain't over 'til the fat lady sings."

To take these aspects of language into account, Chomsky proposed a more abstract level of analysis. Behind the word strings that people produce, called **surface structures,** there is, he said, a **deep structure,** an abstract representation of the relationships expressed in a sentence. For example, the surface structure "The shooting of the psychologist was terrible" may represent either of two deep structures: (1) that the psychologist had terrible aim, or (2) that it was terrible that someone shot the psychologist. Chomsky developed rules for transforming deep structures into surface structures and for relating sentences to each other.

Since Chomsky proposed his first analysis of deep and surface structures, he and others have proposed many revisions of those ideas. The debates go well beyond what we can consider here. For our purposes, what is important about Chomsky's ideas is that they encouraged psychologists to analyze not just people's verbal behavior or the rules of grammar, but also the possible mental representations that verbal behavior reflects.

Communicating Through Language

When you speak, you have an idea or proposition to be conveyed, but sounds are transmitted. How is your idea translated into those sounds? If your communication is successful, your listener ends up, not simply with the sounds you transmitted, but with an idea or proposition that matches, or approximates, the one with which you began. How? Figure 9.14 illustrates an analysis of these processes. The speaker starts with an idea, which is translated,

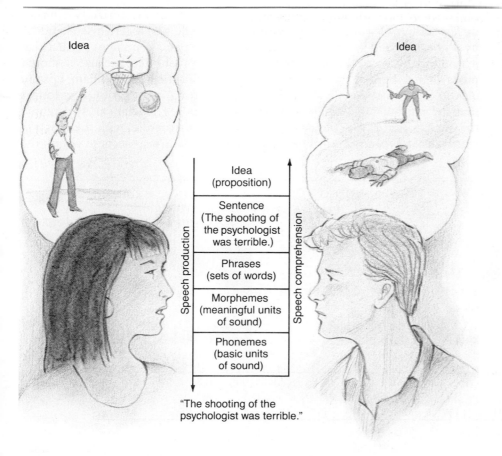

Figure 9.14
Producing and Comprehending Speech
The listener on the right has interpreted the speaker's message in a way that differs from the speaker's intended deep structure. Obviously, identical surface structures can correspond to distinctly different deep structures.

modified, and elaborated into a specific string of words, which are encoded into sounds by mechanisms of the throat and mouth. The listener must take this string of sounds and go through the reverse process in order to "decode" the message. If the encoding and decoding processes are error free, the ideas of speaker and listeners will match, and the communication will be successful. The specific words, however, may soon be forgotten. As we saw in the chapter on memory, it is the underlying meaning, not the specific word string, that the listener is likely to encode and remember. Now consider how the decoding process occurs from the point of view of the listener.

Perceiving words   When you listen to someone speak, what you perceive is a series of words. It sounds as if there is a distinct pause between each word, while the phonemes within a word are heard as a continuous string. But this is not the case, as Figure 9.15 demonstrates. A **speech spectrograph,** as shown in the figure, is a visual representation of the frequencies of speech as they unfold over time. The spectrograph shows that breaks occur, not between words, but within the words. You hear the breaks between, instead of within, words because of the top-down processing that we discussed in the chapter on perception. Because you know what the word should sound like, you recognize the sounds when they occur, and you perceive them as separate units, even if the physical stimuli are not separated. The top-down processing of speech also explains why speech in a language you do not understand sounds like a continuous stream and seems to be uttered at a much faster rate than speech in your own language. Because your brain does not know where each word in an unfamiliar language starts and stops, you do not hear the gaps between words; the gaps, after all, are not physically there. And because you do not perceive gaps between words, the sounds run together at what seems to be a faster-than-normal rate.

Understanding sentences   Suppose you are asked to memorize two meaningless strings of words: "Haky deeb um flut recile pav togert disen" and "A hyaky deeb reciled the dison togently um flutests pav." You might predict that it would be easier to learn the first string, which is shorter, because it should put a lighter burden on short-term memory. Surprisingly, William Epstein (1961) found that people learned the second string more easily. It is longer than the first, but it is also more sentencelike and more grammatical. Apparently, the organization of the sounds into a sentencelike structure, with the function words *the* and *a* and endings like *-ed,* allowed Epstein's subjects to chunk the

Figure 9.15
A Speech Spectrograph
This is the visual representation of the speech sounds in the phrase "Speech we may see." The vertical axis shows the frequencies of the speech sounds; the horizontal axis shows the passage of time. You would hear the phrase as four distinct words. But notice that the pauses actually occur, not between the words, but between the "p" and "ee" in speech *and again between "ee" and "ch" in the same word.*
(From *Cognitive Psychology and Information Processing* by Lachman/Lachman/Butterfield, page 513, figure 13.4. Copyright © 1979 Lawrence Erlbaum Associates.)

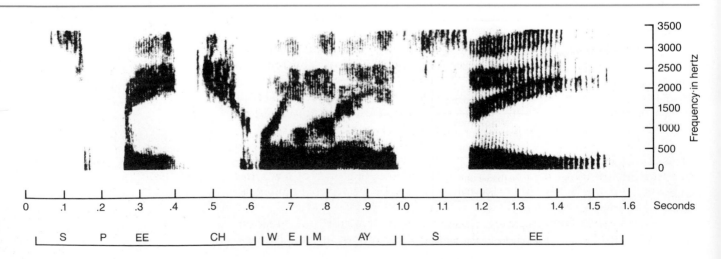

sounds into more easily memorized units. Thus, the extra sounds added to the second sentence actually reduced the burden on short-term memory.

Experiments like Epstein's have demonstrated that syntax, the pattern of word order, plays a very important role in the comprehension of sentences. Instead of simply decoding speech word by word, researchers have found that people treat grammatical constituents, such as phrases, as separate units or chunks (Fodor, Bever & Garrett, 1974).

Although both syntax and word meanings are important to comprehension, they still do not tell the whole story. For example, knowing the meaning of words and proper word order does not explain why people understand that only one of the phrases "Ruth eats fruit" and "fruit eats Ruth" is semantically correct. For this understanding, people also rely on knowledge of the world. Although both phrases are syntactically correct, you should have greater trouble reading the second string. Or if you read the strings in a hurry, your mind would probably automatically "reorganize" the second sentence to another form, such as "the fruit was eaten by Ruth" (Fillenbaum, 1974). In other words, through top-down processing, people use their vast store of knowledge to find and impose meaning and organization, as well as grammatical structure, on words.

Understanding conversations   Suppose we have been able to program a computer with all the rules and knowledge we have discussed so far—with rules for decoding spoken phonemes and written letters into words, rules of syntax, a dictionary of the meanings of words, and an encyclopedia of knowledge of the world. Now we ask our unfortunate computer to make sense of the following conversation:

A: You goin' to the gym today to work out?
B: Well I *am* flabby, but only if I can hook a ride with Jim. It's a long way.
A: I'm afraid I heard his transmission's conked out, and it's at the shop
B: Oh [pause] then I guess it won't work out.

You probably had little trouble understanding this conversation, but the computer would be at a loss. The first problem is that the grammar is not complete. For example, the fact that the first sentence is a question would be indicated only by a rising tone of voice. Second, because both participants understand the general gist of the dialogue, certain ambiguous terms take on different meanings in different sentences (for example, *it* in lines 2, 3, and 4; *work out* in lines 1 and 4; and *gym* versus *Jim* in lines 1 and 2). Third, having the gist allows you to understand the meaning of words or phrases like *hook, I'm afraid,* and *conked out,* and to know that the transmission is actually part of Jim's car, not a part of Jim. These are things that the computer could not easily "understand."

In general, difficulties in programming a computer to understand conversations arise because the use of language is knowledge-driven and relies on the *context* in which words are spoken or written. This use of context creates one of the greatest challenges in the development of artificial intelligence for speech recognition. As we noted in Chapter 5, people use context to interpret and impose meaning on stimuli—including language. A statement like "Wow are you smart!" can be interpreted as "I think you're an idiot" depending on the context (perhaps the tone of voice). Thus, understanding language involves constructing meaning out of sounds, just as recalling stored memories sometimes involves constructing information based partly on the context in which that information is encoded or retrieved.

The context for understanding language may be created by the situation. Richard Mayer (1983) reported seeing a sign in a laundromat in Santa Barbara,

California, that said, "Not responsible for clothes you may have stolen." The words themselves could easily mean "The owner is not responsible if you steal someone else's clothes." But, from the context created by the situation, it is obvious that the sign was meant to warn people not to leave their belongings unattended.

An individual's personal history also forms part of the context of a situation. Thus, people's educational and cultural backgrounds help shape their understanding of a communication. As an example, read the following ambiguous passage:

> Every Saturday night, four good friends get together. When Jerry, Mike, and Pat arrived, Karen was sitting in her living room writing some notes. She quickly gathered the cards and stood up to greet her friends at the door. They followed her into the living room but as usual they couldn't agree on exactly what to play. Jerry eventually took a stand and set things up. Finally, they began to play. Karen's recorder filled the room with soft and pleasant music. Early in the evening, Mike noticed Pat's hand and the many diamonds. As the night progressed the tempo of play increased. Finally, a lull in the activities occurred. Taking advantage of this, Jerry pondered the arrangement in front of him. Mike interrupted Jerry's reverie and said, "Let's hear the score." They listened carefully and commented on their performance. When the comments were all heard, exhausted but happy, Karen's friends went home. (Anderson et al., 1977)

In a laboratory study, music majors tended to interpret this passage as describing a music practice session, whereas students in other fields typically read it as the description of a friendly card game (Anderson et al., 1977).

Stages of Language Development

Once people have learned to speak, they use the many rules of language naturally and automatically to generate correct sentences and to reject incorrect ones, even though most people would have a difficult time stating the rules. For example, in an instant you know that the words "Bei mir bist du schoen" are not English and that the string of words "Quickly peaches sheep deserve" is not an acceptable sentence. Children the world over learn language with impressive speed and regularity.

Developmental psychologists have painstakingly detailed the steps in this process. In Chapter 2, we discussed the earliest steps: the babblings of infants and the one-word speech of young children. By eighteen to twenty-four months of age, children usually have a vocabulary of some fifty words. Then their language undergoes an explosion; it is not uncommon at this point for children to learn several new words a day and to begin to put words together.

At first, children's sentences consist of two-word pairs. These are more elaborate, less ambiguous, and somewhat less tied to gestures than children's one-word expressions. For example, to call attention to a dog, which was once done by pointing and saying, "Doggy," the child now says, "See doggy." Still, children's two-word utterances are **telegraphic.** Brief and to the point, they leave out any word that is not absolutely essential. If she wants her mother to give her a book, the twenty-month-old might first say, "Give book," then, "Mommy give," and, if that does not work, "Mommy book." The child also uses rising intonation to indicate a question ("Go out?"), and word stress to indicate location ("Play *park*") or asserted information ("*Big* car").

Three-word sentences come next in the development of language. They are still telegraphic, but more nearly complete: "Mommy give book." The child can speak in sentences that have the usual subject-verb-object form of adult sentences. Other words and word endings begin appearing, too (Brown, 1973; Dale, 1976). For most children, the suffix *-ing* comes first ("I walking"); then the prepositions *in* and *on*. The plural *s* comes next; then come some irregular

As children grow, their ability to use language progresses from one-, two-, or three-word sentences to more complex and sophisticated utterances that eventually make it possible to communicate all the subtle nuances of human experience.

past tenses ("It broke," "I ate"). Later, children learn to use the suffix *-ed* for the past tense ("I walked"). But once they have mastered the rule for using *-ed* to express past events, they overapply the rule to irregular verbs that they previously used correctly, saying, for example, "It breaked" or "It broked" or "I eated."

Children also expand their vocabularies with adjectives. At first, they do not always get the antonyms straight. They know that *tall* and *short* both refer to height, *more* and *less* to quantity, *wide* and *narrow* to breadth; but they are likely to use both *less* and *more* to mean "more" or *tall* and *short* to mean "tall" (Donaldson & Balfour, 1968).

After acquiring some adjectives, children begin to use auxiliary verbs ("Adam is going") and to ask questions using *wh-* words (*where, whose, who, why, how, when,* in roughly this order). They begin to put ideas together in sentences. They elaborate on nouns ("Here's the ball I was looking for") and link ideas together ("I want to draw if Jimmy does"). Until they are about five years old, however, children join events in the order in which they occur ("We went to the zoo and had ice cream") and understand sentences better if they follow this order (Clark, 1978; Kavanaugh & Jirkovsky, 1982). By age five, children have acquired most of the syntax of their native language.

How Is Language Learned?

Despite all that has been learned in recent years about the steps children follow in learning language, mystery still surrounds the question of just how they learn it. We know a great deal about what happens, but why and how it happens is still open to debate. Obviously, children pick up the specific content of language from the speech they hear around them; English children learn English, French children learn French. As parents and children share meals, playtime, and conversations, children learn that words refer to objects and actions and what the labels for them are. But how do they learn syntax?

Conditioning and imitation   Our discussion of conditioning in Chapter 7 suggests one possibility: perhaps children learn syntax because of the way their parents reinforce them. In fact, however, observations of parents and children suggest that reinforcement cannot fully explain the learning of syntax. Usually parents do not deliberately instruct their youngsters in the fine points of syntax. Most parents forego correcting the grammar of their young children or reprimanding them for syntactic mistakes. They are more concerned about *what* is said than about its form (Hirsch-Pasek, Treiman & Schneiderman, 1984). When the little boy with chocolate crumbs on his face says, "I not eat cookie," the mother is more likely to respond "Yes, you did eat it" rather than asking the child to say, "I did not eat the cookie." Parents may offer the child a correct version of the incorrect sentence, but they do not reprove the child.

Although adults do not give lessons on grammar, they do greatly modify their speech when talking to their language-learning children. They shorten their sentences and use concrete, basic nouns and active verbs—not pronouns, adjectives, conjunctions, or past tenses. They exaggerate, repeat, enunciate clearly, and stick to the here-and-now, in grammatically correct utterances. This kind of talk, which parallels children's own, has been called **motherese**— although fathers, aunts, uncles, and older siblings also speak it. Parents seem to use motherese to help children understand what is being said. But does it help children acquire language? Apparently not. Children do not learn to speak correctly earlier if their mothers speak down to their level (Chesnic et al., 1983; Nelson et al., 1983). In fact, within the range of language spoken by most mothers to their children, the more complex the mother's language, the earlier and more rapidly their children learn to speak in complex sentences (Clarke-Stewart & Hevey, 1981; Gleitman, Newport & Gleitman, 1984).

If the aim is to help a child learn syntax, expanding the child's utterances is more helpful than speaking motherese. Children learn syntax most rapidly when adults offer simple revisions of their sentences, implicitly correcting their syntax, and continue with the topic they are discussing. For example,

Child: Mommy fix.
Mother: Okay, Mommy will fix the truck.
Child: It braked.
Mother: Yes, it broke.
Child: It broke.
Mother: Let's see if we can fix it.

This recasting obviously involves modeling correct speech forms, and as we noted in Chapter 7, modeling, or imitation, is an important source of learning. Especially if the child is given approval for imitating recast forms, adults' recasting of language cannot help but shape language development.

But if children learned syntax by imitation, why would they overgeneralize rules for past tenses and plurals? Neither conditioning nor imitation seems entirely adequate to explain how children learn language. Children must still analyze for themselves the underlying patterns in the welter of language examples they hear around them.

Nature and nurture   The ease with which children everywhere discover these patterns and learn language has encouraged some to argue that humans are "prewired" or biologically programmed to learn language. Chomsky (1957)

has suggested that human beings possess an innate **language acquisition device**—a **LAD,** for short—that processes speech and allows children to understand the regularities of speech and fundamental relationships among words. The LAD permits youngsters to gather ideas about the rules of language without even being aware of doing so. They then use these ideas to understand and construct their native language.

Evidence to support this hypothesis is hard to come by, however. One suggestive finding is that there is some similarity in the syntax of all languages. Another is the fact that children born deaf and never exposed to language make up gestural systems that have several properties of natural spoken language, including placement of subjects before verbs and agent-action-object sequences, such as "June saw Bob" (Goldin-Meadow & Feldman, 1977).

Even if there is a LAD, it has a limited warranty. One unfortunate child was confined by her father to isolation and abuse in a small room until she was discovered and rescued at age 13½ (Curtiss, 1977). Like the Wild Boy of Aveyron, whom we described in Chapter 2, she had not heard any language, and she could not speak at all when she was discovered. After six years of therapy and language training, she still had not learned to use language forms like *what, which,* and *that;* possessive sentences; or auxiliary verbs. She could not combine ideas into a single sentence. Her speech was the equivalent of a two- or three-year-old's. The Wild Boy was also unable to learn adult language. Such cases suggest that, to acquire complex features of language, it may be that a person must be exposed to speech before a certain age. That is, there appears to be a *critical period* for learning language similar to the critical periods for such developmental dimensions as binocular depth perception, discussed in Chapter 5. This suggestion is supported by research showing that people who learn a second language after the age of thirteen or fourteen are unlikely ever to speak it without an accent (Lenneberg, 1967).

How Important Is Language?

The impressive power of language, and the complexities encountered when one tries to explain it, have helped generate many claims about its importance. Language, some say, is qualitatively different from all other forms of communication, is unique to humans, and sets humans apart from other creatures. Others suggest that language determines how people perceive the world or that, without language, there can be no thought.

Is human language unique?   Animals readily use symbols to communicate. Bees dance in a way that indicates the direction and distance of sources of nectar; the grunts and gestures of chimpanzees communicate various attitudes and emotions. However, no one has yet found a nonhuman species that consistently and naturally orders symbols according to specific rules like the grammar that governs human language. Indeed, as we described in Chapter 2, even when years of training result in a primate with some fundamental language skills, it is by no means clear that those skills constitute language as it appears in humans. Thus, human language does seem to be unique, and humans appear to be uniquely prepared biologically to acquire it. This biological preparedness is reflected in such brain regions as Broca's area and Wernicke's area, discussed in Chapter 2 and illustrated in Figure 3.15.

Does language determine perception?   The language that people speak forms part of their knowledge of the world, and that knowledge, as we noted in Chapter 5, guides perceptions. This relationship raises the question of whether there is an even closer relationship between the two. Do differences among the languages of the world create differences in how people perceive

THOUGHT, LANGUAGE, AND ABNORMAL PSYCHOLOGY

What Is Different About the Thought and Language of Schizophrenics?

People usually take it for granted that most human beings think and speak in the well-organized, logical, and comprehensible ways we have described in this chapter. But consider the following conversation:

Interviewer: Have you been nervous or tense lately?
Patient: No, I got a head of lettuce.
Interviewer: I don't understand.
Patient: Well, it's just a head of lettuce.
Interviewer: Tell me about lettuce. What do you mean?
Patient: Well, . . . lettuce is a transformation of a dead cougar that suffered a relapse on a lion's toe. And he swallowed the lion and something happened. The . . . see, the . . . Gloria and Tommy, they're two heads and they're not whales. But they esaped with herds of vomit, and things like that. (Neale & Oltmanns, 1980, p. 102)

This patient was diagnosed as having schizophrenia, a severe and debilitating mental disorder. Disorders in thought and language are among the most prominent signs of schizophrenia.

Because schizophrenics use language in such odd, idiosyncratic, and often incomprehensible ways, it sounds as if they do not understand the rules of grammar and syntax. Actually, they do (Neale & Oltmanns, 1980). However, they seem not to take their listeners into account when they speak, and they violate the unwritten laws of communication we described earlier. These failures have been demonstrated in numerous experiments. In one, schizophrenic and normal people were asked to look at two sets of colored disks and then describe one of them aloud in a way that would allow someone else to identify the set of disks they were talking about (Kanterowitz & Cohen, 1977). When the sets were very different, both groups did about equally well. But when the sets were very similar, the schizophrenics did far worse. They gave repetitive descriptions of what they saw and did not say anything about how one set of disks differed from the other. In other words, they did a poor job of putting themselves in the listener's place and anticipating what information the listener needed to comprehend the message.

The failure of schizophrenics to take the listener into account is also demonstrated by two specific differences between their language and that of other people: they use fewer conjunctions that help tie sentences together, and they use more ambiguous words (Rochester, Martin & Thurston, 1977). A normal person might say, "My brother and his friend, Jim, packed their bags last night and left for the airport early this morning." A schizophrenic might say, "They packed gone."

Psychologists do not yet know what the sources of these difficulties are. Researchers are exploring the possibility that they reflect an inability to recognize what listeners need to know, or an inability

the world? Benjamin Whorf thought that the answer was yes (Whorf, 1956). He noted, for example, that Eskimos have some twenty names for snow, whereas most Americans have only a few. Whorf proposed that this difference in language would lead to a greater ability to discriminate between varieties of snow—a perceptual ability—and when the discrimination abilities of Americans and Eskimos are compared, there are indeed significant differences. However, these results leave another question unanswered: Are the differences in perception the *result* of differences in language?

One of the most interesting tests of Whorf's ideas was conducted by Eleanor Rosch (1972). She compared the perception of colors by Americans with that by members of the Dani tribe of New Guinea. In the language of the Dani, there are only two color names, one for dark, "cold" colors and one for lighter, "warm" ones. In contrast, English speakers have names for a vast number of different hues. Of these, it is possible to identify eleven *focal* colors; these are prototypes, the particular wavelengths of light that are the best

to control one's own mental processes sufficiently to meet listeners' needs, or deficits in attention or memory that make it difficult to focus on or recall what has been said or not said.

Schizophrenics do appear to be less able than others to filter out irrelevant information or to concentrate on important information (McGhie & Chapman, 1961; Payne, Matussek & George, 1959). For example, when schizophrenics are asked to repeat a series of numbers spoken by an experimenter, their performance is disrupted far more than that of normals if another experimenter is saying a different set of numbers at the same time (Lawson, McGhie & Chapman, 1964). Further, compared with other people, schizophrenics seem to be less able to use cues that might help them focus attention during such tasks (see Figure A). These deficits in the ability to control attention might account for the trouble so many schizophrenics have in conversing logically about one subject at a time.

Difficulties in later stages of information processing, particularly those requiring conscious control, also contribute to the thought and language disorders associated with schizophrenia. For example, we noted in Chapter 8 that the amount of information people can store in short-term memory depends largely on how they organize the information into chunks. Schizophrenics seem to be deficient in organizing chunks, even when they are given help (Bauman, 1971). They also fail to use word meanings to facilitate

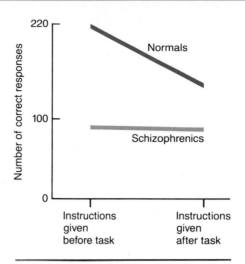

Figure A
Attentional Differences Between Schizophrenics and Normals
When normal people are told beforehand which of two experimenters to listen to, they do better at recalling what that experimenter said, but these instructions have little effect on the performance of schizophrenics.

recall (Koh, Kayton & Berry, 1973). In one study, even after they learned a list filled with concepts, schizophrenics recalled the words in random order rather than in groups of related items (Koh, Kayton & Berry, 1973).

We will see in Chapter 15 that the causes of schizophrenia are still not clear, but the link between thought disorder and mental disorder is.

examples of the eleven major color categories (red, yellow, green, blue, black, grey, white, purple, orange, pink, and brown). Thus, fire-engine red is the focal color for red. Rosch reasoned that, if Whorf's views were correct, then English speakers, who had verbal labels for focal colors, should recognize them better than nonfocal colors. For the Dani, the focal-nonfocal distinction should make no difference. Yet, in spite of the language differences between the groups, Rosch found that both the Dani and the Americans perceived focal colors more efficiently than nonfocal ones (Heider, 1972).

There are correlated differences in language and in perception between cultures. For example, Eskimos perceive and have verbal labels for subtle, but important differences among snow textures. Americans do not. But it appears doubtful that language *causes* the differences in perception, as Whorf claimed. It seems far more likely that, beneath the differences in both language and perception, there is a third variable: frequency of use and the society's need for certain objects. Eskimos, for example, live in a snowy world. Their lives depend on making fine discriminations about the snow—between the snow bridge that is old and the one that will collapse, between the snow field that can be crossed easily and the one that must be avoided. Hence, they learn to discriminate differences that are unimportant to people in warmer climates, and they attach names to those discriminated differences.

Is language ability necessary for thought?   Much of human thought seems to be language-bound; people often use words to express ideas and silently spoken sentences to solve problems. We saw earlier that thought can be carried out without the muscular structures involved in language (Smith et al., 1947), but are the *cognitive structures* of language necessary to allow thought? Hans Furth (1964) looked for an answer to this question by studying the cognitive abilities of deaf children. Most deaf children are taught American sign language (ASL) quite early. But Furth studied children who were not taught any language, because their parents felt that learning ASL might retard their eventual acquisition of vocal speech and lip reading. Therefore, these children were language-deficient. Were they also deficient in thinking ability? Furth carefully tested their ability to solve problems that did not involve language, and he found no cognitive deficits. At the very least, his experiment suggests that there can be thought without language.

Furth himself offered a stronger conclusion. Thought, he said, is unhampered by the loss of language. Many psychologists dispute this view, because language seems to provide an effective organizing tool for guiding people's thinking, as well as a rich vocabulary to help give meaning to concepts (Bruner, 1964). The precise relationship between thought and language may never be fully established, mainly because there is probably no single relationship involved. As we have seen, thinking sometimes requires language, but it can also be based on visual images. Further, the importance of language for thought varies from person to person.

FUTURE DIRECTIONS

As some of the simpler, more observable phenomena of cognition yield up their secrets, the challenge grows to understand the most complex mental phenomena, including thought, decision making, and problem solving. Techniques such as brain wave recording, verbal reports of thought processes, and computer simulations of thought have all been enlisted in this effort. For example, researchers are studying how well-established findings regarding reaction time can be used to build better computers, airplanes, automobiles, and other systems. (This is the field of engineering psychology, which was discussed in Chapter 1.) Verbal narratives, spoken by expert problem solvers, are used to help create computer programs that will solve new problems in the same way the experts do. Evoked potentials help us to understand precisely how the fastest decisions are carried out.

The issue of mental models is very much at the core of modern cognitive psychology. Among the questions still to be answered are: Do we need to talk about mental models at all in order to describe thought? If so, are they verbal or spatial, neither or both, accurate or biased? How do they differ between experts and novices, or among people with differing mental abilities? How do we measure them? Designers of computers and other complex systems would like to know what the user's mental model of the system is, so that the system can be built in a way that is compatible with that model.

Numerous questions about problem solving and decision making are also on the agenda for coming years. How good or bad is human decision making

(Einhorn & Hogarth, 1981)? To what extent do decision-making heuristics save work and produce good results? How often and to what extent do they get people into trouble? Does laboratory research on decision making by mock juries have applications in the real world? Can debiasing procedures be taught to improve decision making outside the laboratory? Several companies have marketed products that are supposed to help people make decisions, but it is extremely difficult to evaluate the effectiveness of these aids. Their true value remains questionable (Wickens, 1984).

The study of artificial intelligence is one of the most rapidly expanding areas in science. It draws on concepts of psychology, engineering, computer science, and many other fields. One of the challenges in this multidisciplinary area is that of getting computers to think, reason, and communicate effectively. Most people remain skeptical that computers will ever be able to match human mental abilities (Dreyfus & Dreyfus, 1986). However, efforts to achieve this goal have already helped scientists learn more about the human mind and, as we have seen, have led to the design of computer-based expert systems that can help solve problems. Psychologists' involvement in future research in this area will lead not only to more sophisticated computers, but also to a fuller understanding of complex mental processes in humans.

Indeed, cognitive psychology is rapidly becoming one of the most exciting areas in psychology. To learn more about the research explosion taking place in the areas of thought, decision making, problem solving, and language, you might take courses in experimental psychology, cognitive psychology (sometimes called *higher processes* or *thinking*), psycholinguistics, or engineering psychology (which is sometimes called *human factors*).

SUMMARY

1. The information-processing approach offers a general model of human cognition. According to this model, between the presentation of a stimulus and the execution of a response, information is received, transformed, and manipulated through a series of stages. The minimum time to process information through these stages is the reaction time. It is affected by the intensity of the stimulus, the ease with which different stimuli can be discriminated, the complexity of the choice of a response, stimulus-response compatibility, expectancy, and the tradeoff between speed and accuracy. Researchers have begun to examine evoked brain potentials as a way of measuring the timing of different mental events.

2. Concepts are basic units of thought. They are categories of objects, events, or ideas with common properties. They may be natural or artificial. Artificial concepts are precisely defined by the presence or absence of certain features. Natural concepts are fuzzy; there is no fixed set of defining properties determining membership in a natural concept, as there is for artificial concepts. The difficulty of learning a particular concept depends on the number of relevant and irrelevant attributes and on the rule that determines membership in the concept.

3. Propositions are larger units of thought. They are assertions that state how two or more concepts are related. Propositions can be true or false. Mental models are essentially large clusters of propositions describing physical devices or processes.

4. Conscious thought involves the manipulation of words, propositions, and images. Mental representations of real geographical environments are often systematically distorted and simplified.

5. Syllogisms are propositions with premises and conclusions that logically follow from the premises. People's belief in the conclusions are only partly based on the logic of the premises. They are also based on whether the conclusions are consistent with their attitudes.

6. Much thinking is best described in terms of heuristics. These mental shortcuts or rules of thumb work most of the time but sometimes produce errors. Three important heuristics are the anchoring heuristic (people are reluctant to adjust their probability estimates far from a starting value); the representativeness heuristic (people categorize events by how representative the events are of classes, without considering how probable or likely these classes are); and the

availability heuristic (people estimate probability by how available an event is in memory).

7. Many of the difficulties that people experience in solving problems arise when dealing with hypotheses. People do not easily entertain multiple hypotheses about what is wrong, and they persevere in applying one hypothesis even when it is obviously unsuccessful. People are reluctant to revise or change hypotheses on the basis of new data, preferring to confirm what they already believe to be true. People also fail to use the absence of symptoms as evidence in solving problems and often focus on the representativeness of a pattern of symptoms rather than on its probability.

8. Limitations in problem solving can be addressed in various ways. Pictures or Venn diagrams help solve syllogistic reasoning problems. Incubation, or putting the problem aside, can help. Problems can sometimes be broken down or decomposed into smaller, more manageable elements. Experts are superior to novices in problem solving because of their knowledge and experience. They can draw on knowledge of similar problems they have solved, and they can visualize several related components of a problem as a single chunk. However, expertise can prevent the expert from seeing problems in new ways. There is no shortcut to obtaining the extensive knowledge that is the main component of expertise.

9. Artificial intelligence's goal is to program computers to perceive, think, and solve problems like humans. Computers may use algorithms but often employ humanlike heuristics that simplify the problem-solving process. Expert systems contain knowledge and solve problems in restricted domains, such as medical diagnosis. The effectiveness of these systems is currently restricted by problems in developing an adequate knowledge base for the computer, by the computer's inability to know what it does not know, and by difficulties in giving computers the ability to draw on knowledge from many domains.

10. Decisions are sometimes difficult to make accurately because there are too many alternatives and too many attributes to consider at one time. Multiattribute utility theory offers a technique to help people cope with this problem. But decision making is also complicated by the fact that the world is unpredictable.

11. People's decision making under uncertainty reflects important biases in how both value and probability are perceived. Equal changes in objective value are not perceived as equal changes in utility. In particular, the utility of a specific gain depends on how much a person had to begin with, and a loss of a given amount is viewed as more of a cost than a gain of the same amount is viewed as a benefit. When facing a choice between gains, people tend to prefer the sure thing; but risk-seeking behavior governs the choice between losses. Risky decisions are also shaped by the fact that people tend to overestimate the probability of very rare events, underestimate very frequent events, and feel overconfident in the accuracy of their forecasts.

12. Research on legal decision making suggests that juries are not as sensitive as they should be to the unreliability of eyewitnesses. Therefore, juries' judgments and decisions are often made with greater confidence than they should be.

13. Language consists of words or word symbols and rules for their combination—a grammar. Spoken words are made up of phonemes, which are combined to make morphemes. Combinations of words must have both syntax (grammar) and semantics (meaning). Behind the word strings, or surface structures, is an underlying representation, or deep structure, that expresses the relationship among the ideas in a sentence. Ambiguous sentences occur when one surface structure could reflect two or more deep structures.

14. When people listen to speech, the perceptual mechanism allows them to perceive gaps between words, even where these gaps are not physically present in the stream of sound. The syntax as well as the semantics helps people to understand spoken messages. In addition, understanding of language is shaped by people's knowledge of the world, the context, and unwritten laws of communication.

15. Children develop grammar according to an orderly pattern. Babbling and one-word speech come first; then telegraphic two-word sentences. Next come three-word sentences as well as grammatical forms in a somewhat predictable order. Once children learn certain regular verb forms and plural endings, they overgeneralize rules, applying them even to nouns with irregular plurals or verbs with irregular endings. Children acquire most of the syntax of their native language by the time they are five years old.

16. Conditioning and imitation both play some role in a child's acquisition of language, but neither can provide a complete explanation of how children acquire syntax. They cannot explain, for example, children's overgeneralization of certain grammatical rules or the fact that parents reinforce children for the meaning of their sentences, not the syntax. Children learn language more rapidly if more complex sentences are spoken to them. It has been suggested that some portion of language acquisition may be genetically determined. It appears that language must be learned during a certain critical period, if normal language is to occur.

17. Humans appear to be the only species that possesses all of the characteristics of language. Although language and perception are closely related, the differences among the world's languages do not create differences in how people perceive the world. Instead, both language and perception are influenced by the frequency of objects, events, and actions in society. Language appears to be important, but not always essential for thought.

KEY TERMS

Definitions of terms appear on the pages shown in parentheses.

affirmation (one-feature) rule (331)
algorithm (335)
anchoring heuristic (335)
artificial concept (328)
artificial intelligence (342)
availability heuristic (336)
average evoked potential (326)
base-rate frequency (336)
concept (328)
conjunctive rule (331)
decomposition (340)
deep structure (353)
disjunctive rule (331)
evoked brain potential (326)
expected utility (347)
expert system (343)
functional fixedness (337)
gambler's fallacy (349)
grammar (351)
heuristic (335)
incubation (340)
information-processing system (323)
language (351)
language acquisition device (LAD) (359)
logic (333)
mental chronometry (324)
mental model (332)
mental set (337)
morpheme (352)
motherese (358)
natural concept (329)
phoneme (351)
premise (333)
proposition (332)
prototype (329)
reaction time (324)
reasoning (333)
representativeness heuristic (335)
semantics (352)
speech spectrograph (354)
surface structure (353)
syllogism (333)
syntax (352)
telegraphic speech (356)
thinking (328)
utility (346)
word (352)

RECOMMENDED READINGS

Andersen, J. (1985). *Cognitive psychology and its implications.* (2nd ed.). San Francisco: W. H. Freeman. A nice overview of the different mental representations involved in thinking and of the processes involved in concept learning. Many general issues in cognitive psychology and information processing are also discussed.

Clark, H. H., & Clark, E. V. (1977). *Psychology and language.* San Diego: Harcourt Brace Jovanovich. An excellent overview of the psychology of language.

Kahneman, D., Slovic, P., & Tversky, A. (1982). *Judgment under uncertainty: Heuristics and biases.* Cambridge, Eng.: Cambridge University Press. An outstanding collection of readings on human decision making and heuristics.

Lachman, R., Lachman, J., & Butterfield, E. (1979). *Cognitive psychology and information processing.* Hillsdale, N.J.: Lawrence Erlbaum. Another good general reference on cognitive psychology, which also covers the concept of information-processing stages and their importance in reaction time.

Mayer, R. (1983). *Thinking, problem solving and cognition.* San Francisco: W. H. Freeman. A very readable discussion of issues in problem solving.

McCorduck, P. (1979). *Machines who think.* San Francisco: W. H. Freeman. This book offers a good representation of many of the important issues in artificial intelligence.

Slobin, D. I. (1985). *Psycholinguistics.* Glenview, Ill.: Scott, Foresman. Another fine overview of the psychology and language area.

Wickens, C. (1984). *Engineering psychology and human performance.* Columbus, Ohio: Merrill. This volume discusses decision making and the stages of information processing, especially in relation to their role in human-machine interactions.

A mong many new programs of President Lyndon B. Johnson's Great Society was Project Head Start, which was to offer early enrichment through special academic preparation classes for preschool children whose home and cultural backgrounds put them at risk for failure at school (Zigler & Valentine, 1979). During the 1970s and 1980s, however, government spending on domestic programs declined in popularity. Critics argued that the expense of Head Start and similar programs was not justified. Such programs, they felt, could not produce improvements in academic performance that were sufficiently large and enduring to substantially affect disadvantaged childrens' chances for ultimate success. The arguments continue.

Psychologists have been at the forefront of research to evaluate programs like Head Start. Their research has revealed that, indeed, the academic effects of such programs are not permanent. However, the benefits—especially in terms of social skills, involvement of parents in children's lives, and the like—are significant. Psychologists' contributions to early enrichment programs are just one aspect of their research on the nature, measurement, and improvement of all kinds of mental abilities. In this chapter, we describe some of this research and its implications.

In Chapter 9, we discussed thought, reasoning, problem solving, decision making, and language. There we approached these mental activities by examining what people have in common. In contrast, this chapter focuses on how people differ in their ability to carry out mental activities. Here we discuss differences in people's **mental ability,** their capacity to perform the higher mental processes of reasoning, understanding, and problem solving. Understanding differences in mental abilities is important for both intellectual and social reasons. Exploring these differences provides another avenue for understanding how the brain works and what mental processes are involved in thinking, problem solving, and other forms of intelligent behavior. Furthermore, if psychologists can describe the mental abilities of people, and if they understand the sources of these differences, then they may be able to prescribe ways of improving those abilities. Finally, knowledge of mental activities may be useful for prediction. By using tests of mental abilities, psychologists may be able to predict how well people will do in college or in various jobs. Thus, such tests may help people select careers or help employers choose people for specific jobs.

Western society places special emphasis on one mental ability: intelligence. Each year, millions of people from infancy through adulthood are tested to measure their intelligence. How children score on these tests can sometimes affect where they go to school and, as result, where they will work, which opportunities will be open to them, and what kind of economic future they will have.

We begin by discussing how psychologists have tried to measure intelligence through IQ tests. This discussion leads us to consider the fundamentals of psychological testing. What characteristics make a test good or bad, and how do IQ tests measure up to these criteria? Next, we consider differences

10

Mental Abilities

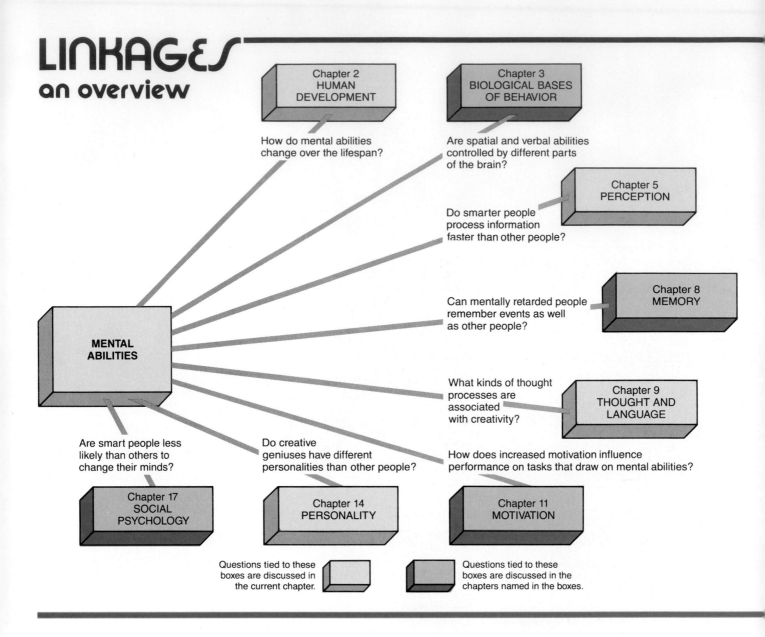

LINKAGES
an overview

Chapter 2
HUMAN DEVELOPMENT

How do mental abilities change over the lifespan?

Chapter 3
BIOLOGICAL BASES OF BEHAVIOR

Are spatial and verbal abilities controlled by different parts of the brain?

Chapter 5
PERCEPTION

Do smarter people process information faster than other people?

Chapter 8
MEMORY

Can mentally retarded people remember events as well as other people?

Chapter 9
THOUGHT AND LANGUAGE

What kinds of thought processes are associated with creativity?

How does increased motivation influence performance on tasks that draw on mental abilities?

MENTAL ABILITIES

Are smart people less likely than others to change their minds?

Do creative geniuses have different personalities than other people?

Chapter 17
SOCIAL PSYCHOLOGY

Chapter 14
PERSONALITY

Chapter 11
MOTIVATION

Questions tied to these boxes are discussed in the current chapter.

Questions tied to these boxes are discussed in the chapters named in the boxes.

in IQ scores among individuals and groups, the possible causes of those differences, and how IQ scores are used. Finally, we look beyond the IQ to consider research on various theories of intelligence and on the relationship between intelligence and other mental abilities.

IQ TESTS

One very broad definition of **intelligence** holds that it is "those attributes that center around reasoning skills, knowledge of one's culture, and the ability to arrive at innovative solutions to problems" (Scarr & Carter-Salzman, 1982). David Wechsler (1975) argued that intelligence is the purposeful and rational ability to deal with the environment—a definition that suggests that we cannot quantify intelligence in an absolute sense, since the ability that serves you well in one environment (for example, escaping from a mountain ridge during a thunderstorm) may be totally different from the ability that is important elsewhere (for example, solving a family crisis at home). E. G. Boring (1923) said that intelligence is whatever an intelligence test measures. In short,

MENTAL ABILITIES AND PSYCHOLOGY

The chapter on thought and language discussed how people think, reason, and decide. But those discussions considered the average person and did not examine how people differ from each other. Why are some people better at reasoning and problem solving than others? How is the creative genius different from others? Does the genius have more attention, better logic, faster reactions, or just more knowledge? How are all of these abilities related to what we call "intelligence"? Although psychologists know a lot about how to measure differences in mental abilities, they are uncertain about what causes them. One possibility is that mental abilities are inherited characteristics, like eye color or height. Another possibility is that the environment in which a child is raised has a strong effect. More stimulating environments may allow the child to learn more and to have greater opportunities to exercise the mental powers of thinking, reasoning, and problem solving. Or, as is so often the case, there may be an interaction between heredity and environment. Those whose genes have provided them with better mental abilities may be more motivated to understand what the environment has to offer.

In answering these and other questions, psychologists have tried to understand what sorts of differences in mental abilities distinguish people, how the differences can be reliably measured, and how much they affect people's success in school and jobs.

psychologists do not agree on how to define intelligence. Pioneers in the study of intelligence focused on the effort to measure it. We will follow their productive lead and begin by examining how intellectual abilities have been measured.

A Brief History

In the late 1800s, Sir Francis Galton tried, unsuccessfully, to develop a test of intellectual ability by measuring people's perceptual and motor abilities, such as how fast they responded to simple stimuli and how sensitive they were to pain. Other researchers soon concluded that these abilities had very little to do with intelligent behavior (Wissler, 1901). Alfred Binet, a French psychologist, took a more successful path; his test provided the model for today's IQ tests.

The Stanford-Binet test In 1904 the French government commissioned Binet to find a way to identify students who might need special instruction. His test included items of varying difficulty, like those in Table 10.1 (p. 370).

TABLE 10.1 _____
Items of the Type Included in the
Stanford-Binet

Age	Task
2	Place geometric shapes into corresponding openings; identify body parts; stack blocks; identify common objects.
4	Name objects from memory; complete analogies (e.g., fire is hot; ice is _____); identify objects of similar shape; answer simple questions (e.g., "Why do we have schools?").
6	Define simple words; explain differences (e.g., between a fish and a horse); identify missing parts of a picture; count out objects.
8	Answer questions about a simple story; identify absurdities (e.g., in statements like "John had to walk on crutches because he hurt his arm"); explain similarities and differences among objects; tell how to handle certain situations (e.g., finding a stray puppy).
10	Define more difficult words; give explanations (e.g., about why people should be quiet in a library); list as many words as possible; repeat 6-digit numbers.
12	Identify more difficult verbal and pictured absurdities; repeat 5-digit numbers in reverse order; define abstract words (e.g., "sorrow"); fill in missing word in a sentence.
14	Solve reasoning problems; identify relationships among points of the compass; find similarities in apparently opposite concepts (e.g., "high" and "low"); predict the number of holes which will appear when folded paper is cut and then opened.
Adult	Supply several missing words for incomplete sentences; repeat 6-digit numbers in reverse order; create a sentence using several unrelated words (e.g., "forest," "businesslike," and "dismayed"); describe similarities between concepts (e.g., "teaching" and "business").

SOURCE: Michael T. Nietzel/Douglas A. Bernstein, _Introduction to Clinical Psychology_, 2/e, © 1987, p. 133. Reprinted by permission of Prentice-Hall, Inc., Englewood Cliffs, New Jersey.

Children of high mental ability would be expected to answer most questions correctly, and those in need of special schooling would be likely to miss them.

Two assumptions guided Binet when he created his set, or _battery_, of questions. First, he assumed that intelligence is involved in many reasoning, thinking, and problem-solving activities. Therefore, instead of looking at performance on perceptual and motor tasks, as Galton had, Binet looked for test items that would highlight differences in children's ability to judge, reason, and solve problems (Binet & Simon, 1905). Included in Binet's original test were such tasks as unwrapping a piece of candy, repeating numbers or sentences from memory, and identifying familiar objects (Frank, 1976). Second, Binet assumed that children's intelligence increases with age. Therefore, if certain children did better on a test than other children their own age, then those children were mentally "older" and thus more intelligent. To select the items for his test, Binet administered potential questions to many children of various ages and then categorized the questions according to the age at which the average child could answer them correctly. For example, a "six-year-old item" was one that a substantial majority of the six-year-olds could answer.

Thus, Binet's test included a series of age-graded tasks. By determining the number of items a child answered correctly at different age levels, the tester identified the child's _mental age_. Children whose mental age equaled their actual, or chronological, age were considered of "regular" intelligence. Those whose mental age was higher than their actual age were known as "advanced." Those with a lower mental than actual age were labeled "retarded" and in need of special education (Reisman, 1976).

About a decade after Binet published his test, Louis Terman at Stanford University developed an English version known as the **Stanford-Binet** (Terman, 1916). It became a model for later mental tests and a standard against which they were judged. Terman added items to measure the intelligence of adults, and he revised the method of scoring. A child's mental age was divided by his or her chronological age, and the quotient was multiplied by 100; the result was called the *intelligence quotient,* or IQ. Thus, a child whose mental age and chronological age were equal would have an IQ of 100, which is considered "average" intelligence. A child who was ten years old but scored at the mental age of a twelve-year-old would have an IQ of $12/10 \times 100 = 120$.

Early testing in America   The method of scoring used on the Stanford-Binet provided a way of ranking all test takers, and it reflected significant differences between Binet and the pioneers of IQ testing in the United States. Binet did not believe his test was measuring a fixed or inherited trait; it was, he thought, simply a useful tool for determining which children should receive special help in school. Terman and others who popularized the test in the United States, however, had very different ideas. They believed that intelligence was a fixed and inherited entity; that different groups were favored with varying amounts of this thing called *intelligence;* and that IQ tests could pinpoint who did and who did not have the right genes to produce a suitable amount of intelligence.

Enthusiasm for testing soon outpaced understanding of what was being tested and what the results meant. Even before Terman developed the Stanford-Binet, psychologist Henry Goddard had made his own translation of Binet's test. In 1912 the U.S. immigration office asked Goddard to identify immigrants who were mentally defective and therefore subject to deportation. Goddard's test included questions that required familiarity not only with writing skills, but also with American culture. Today it is painfully obvious that such tests are not a fair measure of the intelligence of immigrants or anyone else unfamiliar with the English language or American culture. Nevertheless, Goddard concluded from the test results that 83 percent of Jews, 80 percent of Hungarians, 87 percent of Russians, and 79 percent of Italians immigrating to America were "feeble-minded" (Goddard, 1917).

Mental tests were also used to deal with another social problem: how to screen out army recruits of low mental ability and make appropriate job assignments for recruits. When the United States entered World War I, a team of psychologists (including Goddard) was commissioned to develop and administer an intelligence test to all recruits. The team created two versions of their test: the Alpha Test, which required normal English reading skills, and the Beta Test, designed for those with a poor grasp of English. The Beta Test made heavy use of pictures, and the person giving it acted out many of the instructions. Still, the tests favored those familiar with a particular culture. For example, the Alpha Test included tasks such as the multiple-choice question "Five hundred is played with (*rackets, pins, cards, dice*)."

Altogether, 1,726,966 men were tested—an impressive effort. Unfortunately, the fact that these recruits were under stress, in crowded testing rooms where instructions were not always audible, made the conditions of group testing far from ideal. It is thus not surprising that test scores were low compared with those obtained in more relaxed, individualized test settings. Unfortunately, psychologist Robert Yerkes's conclusion, buried in a mass of other data, that 47 percent of the tested population had a mental age of thirteen or lower was widely publicized. In a book based on the army's test statistics (especially on those from the Beta Test), Canadian psychologist C. C. Brigham (1923) concluded that, from 1890 to 1915, the mental age of

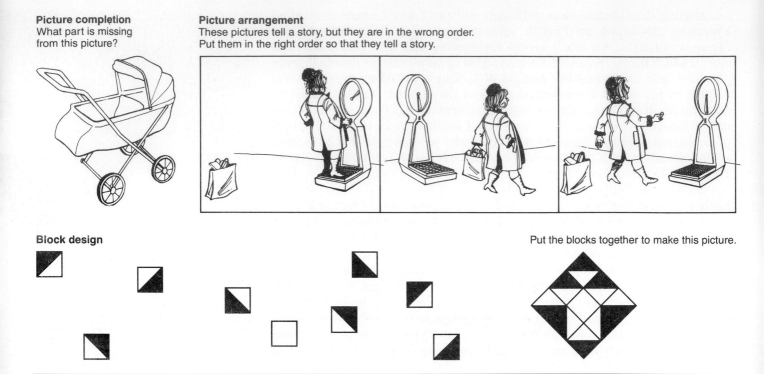

Picture completion
What part is missing from this picture?

Picture arrangement
These pictures tell a story, but they are in the wrong order. Put them in the right order so that they tell a story.

Block design

Put the blocks together to make this picture.

Figure 10.1
Sample Items from the Spatial Abilities Section of the Wechsler Test
(Wechsler Intelligence Scale for Children. Copyright © 1949 by The Psychological Corporation. Reproduced by permission. All rights reserved.)

immigrants to America had declined from 13.8 to 11.4 and that the main source of this decline was the increase in immigration rates from southern and eastern Europe.

Brigham's statistic, along with the results of Goddard's tests, became part of the "scientific" evidence that was used to justify the Immigration Act of 1924, which established differential quotas for immigrants from various nations. Test results were also used by some to argue for segregation of blacks, and in some states, people whose IQ scores earned them the label of "imbecile" could be sterilized against their wishes, or even without their knowledge (Gould, 1983).

The Wechsler scales   In 1930 Brigham repudiated the conclusions he had drawn from the army tests. The methods used to reach conclusions about the intelligence of national groups on the basis of the test scores were wrong, he acknowledged. And the tests themselves, he said, measured not innate intelligence, but familiarity with American language and culture (Gould, 1983).

A new test developed by David Wechsler (1949) was designed to address these concerns. It includes eleven subtests. Six require verbal skills and make up the **verbal scale** of the test. The remaining five tests have little or no verbal content and make up what is called the **performance scale.** They include tasks that require spatial ability and manipulation of materials—for example, assembling blocks, solving mazes, and completing pictures (see Figure 10.1). Wechsler's test allows the tester to develop a profile describing an individual's performance on each of the eleven subtests and to compute a verbal IQ and a performance, or nonverbal, IQ, as well as an overall IQ.

IQ Tests Today

The latest edition of the Stanford-Binet test also uses a subtest format, providing scores on verbal reasoning, quantitative reasoning, abstract/visual reasoning, and short-term memory, along with the composite, or summary, IQ (Thorndike,

Hagan & Sattler, 1986). It is used to test individuals from age two to adult. Different forms of Wechsler's tests have been developed for different age ranges. For example, the *Wechsler Adult Intelligence Scale—Revised (WAIS-R)* is a test for adults; the *Wechsler Intelligence Scale for Children—Revised (WISC-R)* is for children five to fifteen, and the *Wechsler Preschool and Primary Scale of Intelligence (WPPSI)* is for preschoolers. Together, the Stanford-Binet and the Wechsler scales are the most widely used individually administered IQ tests in schools.

In a typical IQ test, the tester presents items from each subtest and gives points for each correct answer. Other tests similar to the Stanford-Binet and Wechsler scales have been designed for groups rather than individuals. Group tests allow more data to be collected in less time but can have drawbacks. As we have already seen, the group tester has less opportunity to learn whether instructions are understood and followed correctly or to discover if motivation is adequate. Furthermore, compared with tests administered individually, those designed for group testing contain a larger proportion of multiple-choice questions and fewer questions that are performance based or open-ended. Thus, group tests generally sample a narrower range of behaviors.

Scoring IQ tests   IQ scores are no longer calculated by dividing mental age by chronological age. When people take an IQ test today, the points they earn for each correct subtest or age-level answer are summed. These raw scores are then compared with the raw scores received by other people. The average raw score obtained by people at each age level is *assigned* the IQ score of 100. Other raw scores are assigned IQ values that reflect how far each score deviates from the age-group average. This procedure is based on the well-documented assumption that IQ, like many other physical and psychological characteristics, follows a normal, or bell-shaped distribution (discussed in the appendix on statistics), in which most people's scores fall in the middle of the IQ range (see Figure 10.2). Thus, your **intelligence quotient**, or **IQ score**, reflects your *relative* standing within a population of your age.

Culture-fair tests   Our review of the history of early testing in the United States suggests an obvious question: Are these tests fair or do they put particular groups at a disadvantage? Some early IQ tests contained vocabulary items that would be unfamiliar to lower-income youths even if they were not foreign-born. For example, consider the question "Which is most similar to a xylophone? (*violin, tuba, drum, marimba, piano*)" No matter how intelligent

Taking an intelligence test. Comparison of verbal and performance scores on the Wechsler scales can provide useful information. For example, a high score on the performance scale and a low verbal score could mean that the child has a language deficiency that prevents the verbal scale from accurately measuring that child's mental abilities.

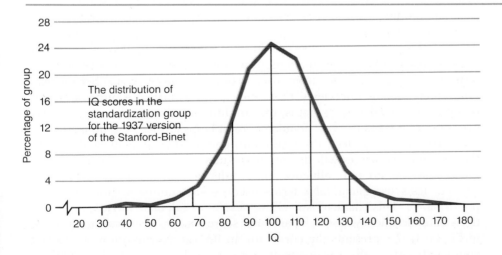

Figure 10.2
The Distribution of IQ Scores in a Population
This distribution is typical of the normal curve described in the statistics appendix. Each raw intelligence test score is given an IQ value that reflects how far it deviates from the average of 100 in a given age group. As a result, half the population ends up with an IQ below 100 and half above 100; about two-thirds of a given age group's IQ scores fall between 85 and 115; about one-sixth fall below 85 and one-sixth above 115.

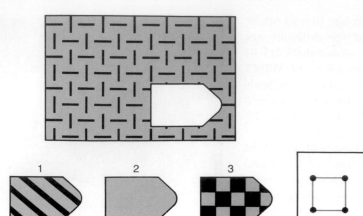

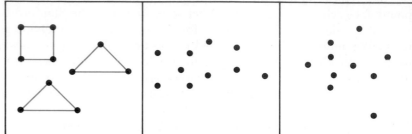

(a) Raven Progressive Matrices Test   (b) Learning Potential Assessment Device

Figure 10.3
Culture-Fair Tests
(a) Items from the Raven Progressive Matrices Test. The task is to complete the patterns by choosing from a group of alternative patches. In the figure, patch 4 will complete the pattern. (b) Items from the Learning Potential Assessment Device (LPAD). In this example, the task is to outline the square and two triangles embedded in patterns of dots, using each dot only once. The LPAD is unusual in that it not only measures children's ability to deal with such problems, but also allows them to try solving them again after receiving some training. Thus, the baseline performance is supplemented by evidence of potential for learning (Feuerstein, 1980).
(Part A: From J. C. Raven, 1948, "The Comparative Assessment of Intellectual Ability," *British Journal of Psychology, 39,* 12–19. Reprinted with permission of the British Psychological Society. Part B: From *The Dynamic Assessment of Retarded Performers* by Reuven Feuerstein. Copyright © 1979 by Scott, Foresman and Company. Reprinted by permission.)

children are, if they have never had a chance to see an orchestra or to have any experience with these instruments, they may easily miss the answer.

To avoid culturally problematic questions, the makers of some tests, such as the Wechsler Adult Intelligence Scale, have tried to assess people on a vocabulary-free performance scale, based on picture perception, spatial skills, and so forth. Others have made more radical efforts to develop tests that are **culture-fair.** The items on these tests have been very carefully chosen to limit the extent to which they depend on ideas and vocabulary that are tied to a specific culture; Figure 10.3 shows two examples. But before assessing these, as well as more traditional IQ tests, we need first to examine some principles of psychological testing and some criteria for evaluating tests.

Some Principles of Psychological Testing

Any **test** is a systematic procedure for observing behavior in a standard situation and describing it with the help of a numerical scale or a category system (Cronbach, 1970). Tests present certain planned stimuli (such as true-false statements) and ask the test taker to respond to them in some specified manner. The test taker's reactions are recorded and scored using a set of rules to obtain a number (or set of numbers or categories) that summarizes the test taker's performance.

Unless you are very unusual, you have taken innumerable tests in your life—IQ tests, school examinations, tests for admission to college. Why are tests so widely used? They have three major advantages over other means of evaluation, such as interviews. First, their administration, scoring, and interpretation are *standardized;* that is, the conditions are as similar as possible for everyone who takes the test. Standardization helps ensure that, no matter who gives and scores the test, the results are comparable. It reduces the chance that extraneous factors will distort the results. Insofar as the biases of those giving the test do not influence the results, a test is said to be *objective.* Second, tests use *quantifiable* terms—scores—to summarize the test taker's performance. This characteristic allows testers to calculate **norms,** or descriptions of the frequency at which particular scores occur. The distribution shown in Figure 10.2 represents the norms for an IQ test. Norms allow scores to be compared statistically. As a result, you can tell, for example, whether a particular score is above or below the average score obtained by hundreds or even thousands of people of the same age or class. Third, tests are *economical* and *efficient*. Once a test has been developed, it can often be administered to many people in less time and for less money than other ways of obtaining information.

Of course, some tests are better than others. Two characteristics are important in determining how good a test is: reliability and validity. Both are expressed in terms of a *correlation*, a measure of the relationship between two variables. (You may want to review the discussion of correlation in Chapter 1.)

Reliability   If you stepped on a scale, checked your weight, stepped off, stepped immediately back on, and found that your weight had decreased by twenty pounds, you would be wise to try a different scale. A good scale, or a good test, must have **reliability;** in other words, the results must be repeatable or stable. If a person receives a very high score on a reasoning test the first time it is given but gets a very low score when the test is given again, the test is probably unreliable. The higher the reliability of a test, the less susceptible its scores are to insignificant or random changes in the test taker or the testing environment. In other words, reliability reflects the extent to which test scores are affected by chance factors, such as the temperature of the room or a person's ability to follow directions.

To estimate reliability, researchers obtain two sets of scores on the same test from the same people and compute the correlation coefficient between the scores. When the correlation is high and positive (usually above +.80 or so), the test is considered reliable. There are several methods for obtaining the scores used to measure reliability. Perhaps the most obvious method is to give the same test to the same people on two different occasions. This method is called *test-retest reliability*. Of course, you cannot expect high test-retest reliability if the trait or ability you are measuring changes between administrations of the test. If a test measures verbal fluency and you learn a lot of words between the first and second time you take the test, then your second score might be considerably higher than the first.

The test-retest method has an obvious problem: some people may benefit more than others from the experience of the first test. Other methods of calculating reliability alleviate this problem. One method uses an *alternate form* of the test on the second testing. The two forms of the test must cover the same material, with items written in the same fashion, reflecting the same level of difficulty. Still another method is to use *split halves*. Just one test is given, but when it is scored, the test is divided into two comparable halves. Of course, if you just divided a test between a first and a second half, the test takers' fatigue or boredom would make the second half different from the first. Instead, a test is usually divided by placing the even-numbered test items into one half and odd-numbered items into the other half. Each half is scored separately, and then the correlation between the two scores is calculated.

Validity   A test may be very reliable and still not be valid. The **validity** of a test is the degree to which it measures what it is supposed to measure (Anastasi, 1976). No test has "high" or "low" validity in an absolute sense; its validity depends on how the test is being used. For example, Galton administered a test that was good at measuring an individual's threshold for pain, but it turned out to be an invalid measure of intelligence.

Validity, like reliability, can be measured with a correlation coefficient, but determining what the test scores should be correlated with may be troublesome. The answer depends on what the test is supposed to measure. There are three basic approaches. One method is to analyze how much the

If a yardstick yields the same reading on two occasions on the same day, it is said to be a reliable measure of height. Tests that yield similar results on repeated occasions are also said to be reliable.

test content covers a representative sample of the domain to be measured; the resulting measure is called *content validity*. If an instructor spends five minutes out of twenty lectures discussing the mating behavior of the tree frog, then focuses half the items of the midterm on this topic, you might want to tactfully question the content validity of the exam. A content-valid test includes items relating to the entire area of interest, not just to a narrow slice of it.

Another way of assessing validity is to measure *construct validity*, the extent to which scores on a test behave in accordance with a theory about the underlying trait or construct of interest. For example, if your theory holds that an intelligent person will be very good at solving problems, people who score high on an intelligence test should also score high on tests of problem-solving ability. If they do not, the test can be said to have low construct validity, at least with regard to one particular theory of intelligence. A third approach is to measure *criterion validity*, which is the extent to which the scores on a test correlate with another direct and independent measure of what the test is supposed to assess. For example, to assess the criterion validity of a test of eye-hand coordination, you might calculate its correlation with a test of skill at video games. This independent measure is called the *criterion*.

When the goal is to predict future behavior, the criterion will be some measure of future performance; criterion-related validity is then called *predictive validity*. For example, one way to measure the validity of the Scholastic Aptitude Test (SAT) is to determine its ability to predict the grade-point average (GPA) of first-year college students. These grade-point averages, then, are the criterion, and the SAT is valid insofar as it is correlated with them. By this measure, the SAT does its job reasonably well. The correlation between the verbal portion of the SAT and first-year grade-point averages is roughly +.38; the correlation for the mathematical portion, +.35 (Linn, 1982).

HIGHLIGHT

The Case of the SAT

Controversies over the SAT test indicate some of the difficulties of constructing a good test and of determining a test's validity. The name of the test—Scholastic Aptitude Test—suggests that it assesses *aptitude*, or the potential for success. The purpose of the test (and its equivalent, the American College Testing program, or ACT) is to predict a student's potential for success in college. Admissions committees of colleges around the country use the test to help them decide whom to accept and whom to reject—a practice that has stimulated considerable debate.

One criticism is that the test may not measure potential, because students can in a sense "cheat" the SAT, raising their scores by taking special courses or by taking the test several times. If these ploys work, then the test is measuring other factors besides academic potential, and those who can afford multiple tests or special courses have a distinct advantage.

But do these extra aids work? It depends. It is unlikely that merely taking the test again will improve a student's score very much, unless some particular event, such as illness, artificially lowered the first score. SAT courses may teach about test taking, such as how to distribute time wisely and when to guess. This information is most likely to alter students' scores only if they are unfamiliar with standardized tests like the SAT. Courses may also provide information on the content covered by the test. This information may indeed help people who have been out of touch with the content—for example, someone who has had no math courses during the previous year (Carroll, 1982; Messick, 1980). Otherwise, cram courses do not seem to offer substantial

The Scholastic Aptitude Test (SAT) and its equivalent, the American College Test (ACT), are designed to yield scores that predict students' potential for success in college. The degree to which they do so is a matter of some debate.

advantages. Samuel Messick and Ann Jungeblut (1981) concluded that SAT-preparation courses can raise SAT scores only by ten to fifteen points, which is rarely enough to substantially alter the chances for admission into a college.

A second criticism is that the SAT is not an aptitude test at all, but an achievement test. **Achievement tests** try to assess knowledge gained in a specific area and indicate a person's current status; examinations in academic courses are an obvious example. When test makers want instead to assess aptitude, they try to minimize the effects of specific knowledge (1) by asking questions about material with which it is assumed everyone is equally unfamiliar, such as harvesting rubber in Burma, or (2) by asking questions that should be equally familiar to people with a given aptitude, such as verbal analogies. Even on these tasks, however, performance depends to some extent on past experience. The verbal portion of the SAT, for example, depends greatly on vocabulary, which in turn depends on previous learning—in other words, on achievement. But this difficulty is not unique to the SAT. In practice, the difference between aptitude and achievement tests is hazy at best.

The fact remains that, whether we call the SAT an aptitude test or an achievement test, it has some predictive validity for academic success. As we have seen, the correlations between SAT scores and first-year grade-point averages are around +.35, indicating that the test is reasonably, but not spectacularly, valid.

One reason why the validity of the SAT is not higher is the criterion measure itself: the GPA. Specifically, certain areas of study have stricter grading standards than others. Suppose a large number of students took both introductory psychology and introductory biology, and their mean grade-point averages were 3.0 in the psychology course and 2.5 in the biology course. We would conclude that the psychology course was half a grade point easier than the biology course. Surveys show that such differences in use of the grading scale do exist (Ory, 1986; Williams, 1985). Furthermore, people with higher SAT scores tend to gravitate toward disciplines with stricter grading standards (Goldman & Widawski, 1976). Thus, the GPA for people in strict courses is depressed to a lower level than it would be if uniform grading standards were applied. The result is a lowering of the validity correlation of the SAT.

Actually, high school grade-point averages are a better predictor of college success than are SAT scores; their correlation with first-year GPA is nearly +.50. The best predictor, however, takes into account both high school GPA and SAT scores (Anastasi, 1982). ■

Evaluating IQ Tests

Reliability and stability of IQ scores How reliable are IQ tests? When split-half reliability is computed, the reliability is quite high, generally around $r = +.90$. But when IQ tests are administered to the same people several years apart, the correlations are lower. For example, correlations between tests taken by people when they were around three years old and when they were teenagers have been found to be only about +.54 (Brody & Brody, 1976). Earlier studies have reported even lower correlations (Honzik, MacFarlane & Allen, 1948). (Note that an r of +.54 would be a respectable predictive validity coefficient, but as noted earlier, standards for reliability are more stringent).

Such findings do not necessarily indicate that IQ tests are unreliable. Instead, they indicate that intelligence probably changes somewhat over the years. After all, as noted in the chapter on human development, childhood is a time when many cognitive skills are developing and changing at a rapid rate, a fact that is reflected to some extent in intelligence test scores (see Figure 10.4). For example, a child may show particular strength in spatial abilities, but weak verbal skills, when tested at age four, then show a dramatic increase in verbal ability when tested a few years later.

What do IQ scores predict? Assessing the validity of the IQ test is more difficult than evaluating its reliability. If one wants to know whether IQ tests measure intelligence, for example, what is the criterion with which the test scores should be correlated?

Figure 10.4
Changes in IQ Scores
The average score on intelligence tests tends to increase in childhood and adolescence, level off in adulthood, and then begin to decline late in life. But the decline is based on a comparison of different people at different ages. When the same people are tested repeatedly over time, the decline is much less dramatic. For many individuals, IQ remains stable; for some, it even increases (Horn & Donaldson, 1980; see this chapter's Linkages box).
(From *Development of Mental Abilities* by N. Bayley in P. H. Mussen, ed., *Carmichael's Manual of Child Psychology,* 3rd ed., Vol. 1, New York: John Wiley and Sons, Inc. © 1970, p. 1176. Reprinted with permission of John Wiley and Sons, Inc.)

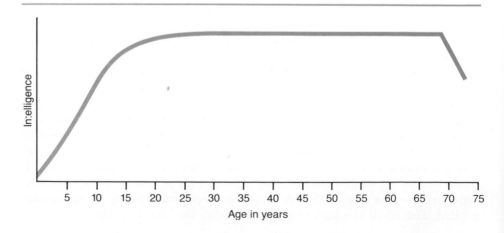

Albert Einstein was unquestionably a genius, but his superior mental abilities were not evident in his early scholastic performance.

One approach to this question assumes that academic success is a criterion that reflects intelligent behavior. IQ tests do a reasonably good job of predicting success in school (the correlation of IQ with high school grades is approximately +.50; Cronbach, 1970), but do they predict anything else? Academic success, after all, may reflect intellectual behavior, but it certainly does not define intelligent behavior. Winston Churchill, for example, was a modest student at best, and there are many other obviously intelligent figures, including Leonardo DaVinci, Thomas Edison, and Albert Einstein, whose early problems in reading, writing, or mathematics would no doubt have resulted in low IQ scores (their problems were related to learning disabilities, which are discussed in Chapter 15). Still, one study that kept track of people for over fifty years found that children with high IQs did tend to grow up to be successful adults (Terman & Oden, 1947). Terman had identified more than a thousand children who had scored very high on intelligence tests; most had IQ scores over 135 when they were ten years old. Only eleven failed to graduate from high school, and more than two-thirds graduated from college. Ninety-seven earned PhDs; ninety-two, law degrees; and fifty-seven, medical degrees. In 1955 their median family income was well above the national average.

Are IQ tests biased?   There are several factors that tend to limit the validity of IQ tests for predicting academic success. First, numerous factors besides intelligence influence academic success: hard work, easy courses, and just plain luck. Hence the criterion itself is not altogether stable. Second, IQ test scores may reflect factors that are not directly related to overall intelligence. For example, motivation can affect test taking in several ways. You may have experienced the phenomenon of being too motivated or anxious and, as a result, "choking" on a test. In undermotivated people, IQ scores may be increased simply by introducing incentives to increase motivation (Johnson et al., 1984). In short, differences in motivation cause the test to measure things unrelated to the abilities it is supposed to assess and therefore lower its validity.

Another possibility is that biased content may lower the predictive validity of IQ tests. As mentioned earlier, tests may be biased against certain groups, because the content requires knowledge that is likely to be gained only by people living in certain kinds of environments, such as white, upper-middle-class homes. Concern over this potentially score-reducing bias has led courts in some states—California, for one—to ban the use of IQ tests in deciding whether black children should be placed in special education classes (Landers, 1986). We noted that new, culture-fair tests have been devised to minimize such content. However, conventional IQ tests predict academic success equally well for various groups, white and nonwhite. And conventional IQ tests are more valid predictors of later scholastic achievement than are these culture-fair tests.

This result does *not* mean that conventional IQ tests measure more fundamental abilities than culture-fair tests do or that conventional IQ tests do a better job of measuring intelligence. It only means that, whatever abilities IQ tests do measure, these overlap more strongly with the abilities reflected in school grades than do the abilities measured by culture-fair tests. This may be because both school grades and IQ scores reflect the degree to which children perform in ways that are valued, taught, and rewarded by the dominant culture in which they live.

INTERPRETING AND USING IQ SCORES

It is one thing to know that IQ tests predict academic success; it is something else to know what to make of particular test scores. What do differences between the test scores of two individuals mean? And what about differences between the average scores of two groups? Can anything be done about the scores?

Heredity and Environment

The history of mental testing has been dominated by questions about the importance of genetics and the environment. As we noted in the chapter on development, both factors influence mental abilities, but psychologists continue to study how much each contributes. To what extent is an individual's score determined by the genetic makeup inherited from his or her parents, and to what extent can intellectual abilities be modified by the environment?

It is unlikely that anyone will ever determine the exact contributions of heredity and environment, for several reasons. First, the effects of heredity and environment *interact*. For example, initial intelligence may create a more enriching environment, because bright children tend to take better advantage of their environment—asking more questions, for example (Scarr & Carter-Salzman, 1982). In addition, in the real world, the influences of heredity and environment are usually *confounded*. Bright parents typically give their children an environment favorable to the development of intelligence, so such children are favored by both heredity and environment. Furthermore, the relative contributions of heredity and environment *vary* from person to person and from culture to culture. If a society treated everyone exactly alike, for example, there would be little room for the environment to influence differences in scores.

Despite these difficulties, exploring the nature of genetic and environmental influences is still useful. Understanding them can improve both understanding of human abilities and decisions about social and educational policies. Studying these influences may, for example, help policy makers determine whether it is worthwhile to spend millions or billions to improve preschool education.

Two primary methods for analyzing the contributions of heredity and environment are correlational studies and environmental intervention.

Correlational studies   To test the influence of genetics on individual differences in IQ scores, psychologists have compared the scores of people who have different degrees of genetic similarity—in particular, identical versus fraternal twins. Because *identical twins* develop from just one fertilized egg, they have exactly the same genetic makeup. In contrast, the genetic makeup of *fraternal twins* is no more similar than that of any other pair of siblings. Therefore, if genetic factors have an important influence on how well people perform on IQ tests, the correlation between the scores of identical twins should be higher than the correlation between the scores of fraternal twins. Indeed, many studies have found that the correlation between measures for identical twins is significantly higher than that for fraternal twins (Nichols, 1978). But the difference between these correlations may reflect something besides the effect of heredity. Identical twins may share more than genetic makeup; they may experience a nearly identical environment. They may be dressed the same, have similar experiences, and be treated in the same way because they are physically identical.

To separate the genetic and environmental effects, psychologists have examined the small population of identical twins who were separated when very young and reared in different environments—perhaps in different orphanages or by different adoptive parents. Twins reared apart are likely to have less similar environments than twins reared together; therefore, if the correlation between the IQs of identical twins reared apart is still high, chances are that genetic similarity is more important than environment in determining their mental ability. There are many studies that support the view that heredity has a strong effect on intelligence. For example, studies of how parents treat identical twins indicate that the similarity of their environment alone cannot account for the twenty-point difference in the correlations found for fraternal versus identical twins (Loehlin & Nichols, 1976; Scarr & Carter-Salzman, 1982). And David Rowe and Robert Plomin (1978) reported that, although the correlation of IQ scores for identical twins reared apart is somewhat less than the figure for identical twins reared together, it is still +.74. This correlation is high enough to provide good evidence for a hereditary influence on IQ scores.

Viewed in another way, correlational studies also provide evidence for the importance of environmental influences. Consider any set of people—a set of identical twins, a set of fraternal twins, a pair of siblings of different ages, or a pair of unrelated children brought into a foster home. No matter whether the degree of genetic similarity in these pairs is high or low, the correlation between their IQ scores will be higher if they share the same home than if they are raised in different environments, as Figure 10.5 (p. 382) shows (Scarr & Carter-Salzman, 1982). Other correlational studies also document the influence of the environment. For example, one study found that higher levels of chaos and noise in the home were associated with lower test scores (Wachs & Gruen, 1982).

Environmental intervention   Correlations tell whether two variables are related, but they do not tell directly whether one variable causes the other. As we discussed in Chapter 1, experimental manipulation is one way to find out whether there is a causal link. Ethics prohibit selective breeding or other experimental manipulations of genetic factors in humans, but manipulations of childrens' environments happen naturally all the time. Adoption, for example, provides an excellent opportunity to examine the effects on mental ability of a change in a child's environment.

By providing a stimulating intellectual environment, parents help children make the most of their inherited intellectual abilities.

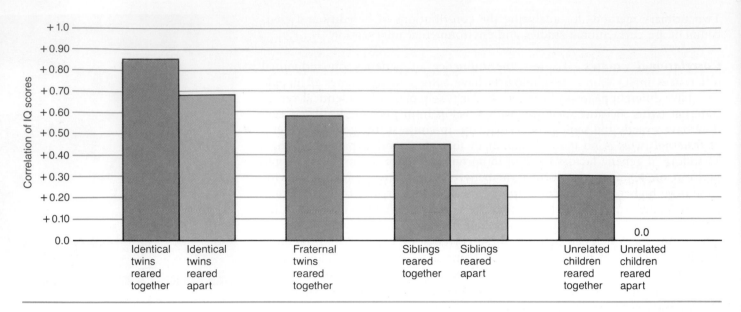

Figure 10.5
Correlation of IQ Scores for People of Varying Hereditary and Environmental Relatedness
In spite of some variation between different studies that have been performed for each type of relatedness, it is clear that the correlation between pairs increases as hereditary or environmental similarity increases.
(From "Familial Studies of Intelligence: A Review," T. Bouchard et al., *Science*, Vol. 212, #4498, pp. 1055–9, 29 May 1981. Copyright 1981 by the American Association for the Advancement of Science.)

The first major study of the effects of adoption was conducted by Harold Skeels (1938). Two infants had been placed in an orphanage because they had been neglected by their "feeble-minded" mothers. Both had been diagnosed as having very low intelligence, both were somewhat unresponsive to outside stimulation, and both were somewhat retarded in many aspects of their development. When they were a little more than a year old, both children were taken from the orphanage and placed in the care of mentally retarded women in an institution. The women ranged in age from eighteen to fifty, but tests indicated that they had an average mental age of seven. The women quickly made the babies the center of attention and gave them considerable care and love. The babies grew increasingly alert and responsive.

Encouraged by these results, Skeels took eleven other babies who had been diagnosed as mentally retarded and placed them in similar care, so that they received affection and attention. After a few years, their IQ scores had risen by an average of twenty-nine points. Over the same period, Skeels also examined a control group of twelve infants who had been diagnosed as relatively bright but who had remained in the orphanage. The IQ of these unfortunate children declined by twenty-six points. The decline testified to the importance of the environment for the development of mental ability and to the harmful effects of an absence of stimulation.

Other investigations, using conditions more controlled than those in Skeels's study, have not always found the large gains in IQ that he reported (Horn, Loehlin & Willerman, 1979; Scarr & Weinberg, 1976; Skodak & Skeels, 1949). Nevertheless, studies have been conducted of children from relatively impoverished backgrounds, adopted into homes that provided more enriching intellectual environments—environments with interesting materials and experiences, as well as a supportive, responsive adult. Such studies have consistently found modest increases in the childrens' IQ scores. They have also found higher levels of cognitive development and better success and adjustment in school for the adopted children compared with those from similar backgrounds who remained with their biological parents (Scarr & Carter-Salzman, 1982; Scarr & Weinberg, 1976). Michel Schiff and his colleagues, for example, compared the IQ scores of pairs of siblings, one of whom had been adopted while the other remained with the biological parent in a poorer environment (Schiff et al., 1978). The adopted siblings' IQ scores were an average of fourteen points higher.

Further evidence for the impact of the environment comes from studies in which investigators have intervened in the lives of youngsters by providing lessons and stimulating experiences that the children otherwise would not have received. As mentioned at the beginning of the chapter, the most prominent of these interventions is Project Head Start, a wide-ranging package of early enrichment programs that focus on two- to five-year-olds from lower-income homes. Some Head Start components involve home visits by teachers who work with both child and parents on concept learning and other cognitive skills. Other activities include group classes in nursery schools. There is also emphasis on health and nutrition. Benefits in this latter area have been clear and strong (Zigler & Seitz, 1982), and substantial improvements in academic and intellectual skills have been found as well.

HIGHLIGHT

Evaluating Enrichment Programs

For practical purposes, parents, educators, and policy makers want more than testimony to the possibility of raising IQ scores. They want to know what environmental factors are important, what types of enrichment programs work best, and whether their benefits last.

As mentioned in Chapter 2 and in the adoption studies described earlier, it is certainly important to provide children with a home in which there is a variety of interesting materials and experiences, along with a warm and attentive adult to help them learn about and explore the world. This is also true in preschool programs outside the home. The most consistently effective preschool programs for poor children have a moderate degree of structure. They have an orderly physical setting and a predictable schedule; educational materials are available; and the teachers' interactions with children are aimed at providing regular opportunities for learning (Zigler & Seitz, 1983).

Do the gains achieved by these programs last? Findings vary somewhat. Data from Project Head Start show that the effect on IQ scores often diminishes after a year or two. One study, for example, found that gains in cognitive development from preschool programs disappeared by the time the children were in high school, if not before (Lazar et al., 1982). But other studies have

Project Head Start is designed to provide children from impoverished backgrounds with the preparation they will need to succeed in grade school. Such early enrichment programs have resulted in IQ gains of from five to fifteen points (Lazar et al., 1982; Zigler & Seitz, 1983).

found that this fadeout does not always occur (Zigler & Seitz, 1982). For example, one study (Seitz, Apfel & Rosenbaum, 1981) found that improvements on tests of mathematical aptitude and general information persisted from the third into the ninth grade, but improvements did not persist on tests of verbal ability. Furthermore, even when IQ advantages fade out, other, more general academic gains may remain. Francis Palmer and Lucille Anderson (1979) found that children who had taken part in enrichment programs were less likely to be held back in school or to need special education programs. Recent studies have also found that children participating in Head Start programs in the 1960s and 1970s were significantly more likely to have completed high school and attended college than children of the same age who were not exposed to Head Start (Jordan et al., 1985).

When fadeout does occur, reduced motivation, not loss of mental ability, may be the cause (Zigler & Seitz, 1982). Children may lose motivation when they are moved from the stimulating environment of a special preschool program into the substandard schools that often serve poor children. In other words, the effects of early enrichment may provide the basis for future academic achievement, but even the best preschool programs cannot protect disadvantaged children from the negative effects of subsequent understimulation. ▪

The interplay of heredity and environment   The effects of heredity and environment on intelligence may be best expressed by the concept of *reaction range*. Genetics seems to define a limit, or potential range, of intelligence, within which the effects of environment can push a child up or down. This range may be quite broad, on the order of twenty to twenty-five IQ points (Zigler & Seitz, 1982).

Generally, genetic makeup seems to exert its influence through the action of many genes, perhaps groups of genes. Some specific genetic defects can severely limit intelligence. **Down's syndrome,** for example, is caused by the presence of an extra chromosome. Children with Down's syndrome typically have IQ scores around 40 to 50, although their scores may be raised up to ten points through careful education (Bayley et al., 1971).

Environmental conditions can also have severe effects, especially when there are abnormal conditions during pregnancy or in the very early years of a child's life. In the chapter on development, we reviewed several of these conditions, such as the mother's excessive use of alcohol or exposure to German measles (rubella) during the early months of pregnancy. Malnutrition may also cause severe problems. Certain nutritional deficits before or at birth may lead to losses in intelligence that cannot be fully restored through later intervention. Severely malnourished children have lower IQ scores than children from the same countries and environments who have received adequate nutrition (Birch & Gussow, 1970).

As we have seen, however, the effects of many environmental deficiencies can be compensated for—to a substantial degree—by later opportunities. This reversibility also means, unfortunately, that the many benefits of early enrichment may fade away, as in the case of some Head Start children, if the environment becomes barren, threatening, or unmotivating.

A genetic restriction on mental ability is a two-edged sword. It can blunt the effects of bad environments and limit the benefits of good ones. Thus, a child's inherited mental ability may be robust enough to limit the damage done by an impoverished home situation, inadequate nutrition, poor day care or schooling, and other environmental features. On the other hand, several adoption studies (Horn, Loehlin & Willerman, 1979; Scarr & Weinberg, 1977) have found that the correlation between the child's IQ and the IQ of the biological parent (the latter reflecting mainly the genetic component) remained at least as high as, if not higher than, the correlation with the new parents' IQ (reflecting the environmental contribution). Thus, even when the environment improves dramatically, the influence of unfortunate genetic factors remains.

Group Differences

Much of the controversy about the causes of differences in IQ scores has concerned, not differences among individuals, but differences in the mean scores of groups. For example, the mean IQ score of black Americans tends to be around fifteen points lower than the mean score of whites. Significant differences in the scores of different socioeconomic groups have also been found. Julia Vane (1972) found that upper-class American communities had mean IQ scores seventeen points higher than those of lower-class communities with the same racial-ethnic makeup. The correlation between family income and children's IQ scores is + .30 (Cleary et al., 1975).

To interpret these differences and analyze the possible reasons for them, we need to be careful to avoid some pitfalls. First, group scores are just that; they do not tell you about individuals. For example, the range of differences in IQ scores among whites (and among blacks) is greater than the average difference between blacks and whites as groups. Large numbers of blacks score well above the mean score of whites, and large numbers of whites score below the mean level of blacks. Second, people tend to think of something inherited as being fixed and of something environmentally determined as being changeable; but such ideas can be misleading. We have seen that a favorable environment may improve a child's performance, even if the inherited influences on that child's IQ are poor. But simply because harmful environmental influences are identified does not mean that the effects can be corrected (Humphreys, 1984).

Socioeconomic differences   There are two possible explanations for the relationship between IQ and socioeconomic status. First, perhaps the father's job, and therefore his salary and status, are determined by characteristics related to his IQ, and perhaps his IQ reflects a genetic component that in turn influences his child's IQ. Second, perhaps the father's job and level of education determine his income, and his job, education, and income in turn affect the child's environment, which may influence the child's IQ score (Cronbach, 1975). Research supports the conclusion that a child's ability is determined jointly by genetic factors and by the effects of the father's occupation and education on the home environment (Mackenzie, 1984).

Motivational differences may also play a role in the IQ-socioeconomic status link. Upper- and middle-income families demonstrate a higher level of motivation to succeed and excel (Atkinson & Raynor, 1974). (We will discuss this motivation in the next chapter.) Perhaps these families instill in their children greater motivation to succeed on IQ tests. As a result, children from middle- and upper-class families perhaps make a greater effort and therefore obtain higher scores (Zigler & Seitz, 1982).

Racial differences   What about the fifteen-point difference between the mean IQ scores of black and white Americans? Some say that the gap is due mostly to hereditary differences between the two groups. In support of this view, Arthur Jensen (1969) noted that heredity makes an important contribution to the differences in IQ scores within groups. Jensen also argued that tests of response times support a genetic explanation for the black-white difference in IQ scores. Black subjects had slower response times in the tests of reaction time that correlate with some IQ scores (Jensen, 1983). It is important to note, however, that the fact that there are hereditary differences among individuals *within* groups does not tell us whether differences *between* groups result from similar genetic causes. For example, height is certainly determined genetically, but it cannot be said that the difference in height between a group of ten-year-olds and a group of fifteen-year-olds is due to hereditary factors alone.

Critics of Jensen's view point to the very large differences between the environments in which the average black and the average white child grow up. To take only the most blatant evidence, consider the fact that, in 1986, 31.3 percent of black families in America lived at or below the poverty level compared to 11.4 percent of white families (U.S. Department of Commerce, 1986). Compared with whites, blacks are also more likely to have parents with poor educational backgrounds, as well as inferior nutrition, health care, and schools. All of these conditions are likely to pull down performance on IQ tests. Evidence for the influence of environmental factors on the average black-white IQ difference comes, too, from adoption studies. In one of these, black children from disadvantaged homes were adopted by white middle- to upper-class families within the first years of their lives (Scarr & Weinberg, 1976). Within a few years, the mean IQ score of these children was 110. Using the scores of nonadopted children from similar backgrounds as a base suggests that adoption raised the children's IQ scores about ten points.

Like the link between IQ and socioeconomic status, racial differences in IQ scores may be due in part to differences in motivation (Zigler & Seitz, 1982). One group of psychologists administered IQ tests to thirty-three black inner-city children and to a control group of middle-class white children (Johnson et al., 1984). Half of the children in each group were given tokens as reinforcement for correct responses. The tokens could be exchanged for toys after the test. The other half of each group received no rewards. The black children who received tokens obtained IQ scores that were a significant thirteen points higher than those of the black students who received no reinforcement. In contrast, the presence or absence of reinforcement had no significant effect on the IQ scores of the white children. The best explanation for the difference, the investigators concluded, was that the motivation of the white children was already high and could not have been substantially improved by further incentives.

In short, there appear to be very important nongenetic factors working to decrease the mean score of black children. It is easy to argue that, given identical environments and educational advantages, the differences in the mean IQ scores of black and white children would be reduced. But it is difficult to conclude for certain that the gap would be *eliminated*. Still, many psychologists have urged that research should now focus, not on the source of the racial differences in mean scores, but on how children should be cared for and educated (Humphreys, 1984; Scarr & Carter-Saltzman, 1982; Zigler & Seitz, 1982). After all, whatever hereditary component might be contributing to children's performance, it may be possible for children to improve greatly, given the right conditions.

IQ Scores in the Classroom

As Alfred Binet had hoped, intelligence tests have been enormously helpful to educators in identifying children who need special educational attention. These tests have also assisted teachers, guidance counselors, and others working with students at all levels of ability. In particular, the encouragement some "slow" students receive to work harder is often based on a very high IQ score, indicating their ability to excel. Along with these benefits come some pitfalls—particularly if the limits of IQ scores are not kept in view. IQ scores are neither a crystal ball into some predestined future nor a measure of some fixed quantity.

Perhaps the most serious potential mismeasurement occurs when people of normal intelligence receive scores below 70—a level that indicates they are mentally retarded. Consider the case of Philip R., a black man now in his forties. When Philip was two, a physician labeled him mentally retarded, and he was sent to a state institution. His Stanford-Binet IQ score of 60 confirmed the doctor's label, and Philip remained in the institution for fifteen years. Because he communicated mainly with grunts and gestures, Philip received no formal training in academic subjects, but he did become highly proficient at daily living skills. At fifteen, Philip began to work with a local shoemaker who was impressed with how rapidly the youngster mastered tasks that were demonstrated for him. Through this man's efforts, Philip began to learn to speak a few words. At seventeen, Philip took an army physical; it revealed that he had a severe hearing loss in both ears. When surgery and dual hearing aids improved his hearing, Philip rapidly began to acquire expressive language. After spending years learning basic academic skills from the shoemaker, Philip entered a public high school at the age of twenty-three. He graduated in three years, went to college, and completed medical school at the age of thirty-three. Today he is a successful orthopedic surgeon (DeStefano, 1986).

Using IQ scores or other labels to categorize people may also have more subtle effects on how they are treated and how they behave. In a controversial study, Robert Rosenthal and Lenore Jacobson (1968) found that labels create *expectancies* that can have dramatic effects. Teachers were told that a test could indicate which grade-school students were about to enter a "blooming" period of rapid academic growth, and they were given the names of students who had supposedly scored high on the test. In fact, the experimenters *randomly* selected the "bloomers." But during the next year, the IQ scores of the bloomers dramatically increased; two-thirds showed an increase of at least twenty points. Only one-quarter of the children in the control group showed the same increase.

Apparently, the teachers' expectancies about the children influenced them in ways that showed up on IQ tests. How can expectancy exert such an influence? To find out, Alan Chaiken and his colleagues (1974) videotaped teacher-child interactions in a classroom in which teachers had been informed (falsely) that certain pupils were particularly bright. They found that the teachers favored the "brighter" students in several ways. They smiled at these students more often than at others, made more eye contact, and generally reacted more positively to their comments. Children receiving this extra social reinforcement are not only getting more intense teaching, but are also more likely to enjoy school, to have their mistakes corrected, and to continue trying to improve.

These results suggest that the "rich get richer": those perceived to be blessed with high mental abilities are given better opportunities to improve those abilities. Is there also a "poor get poorer" effect? Clearly, we would not want to conduct an experiment in which children were falsely labeled dumb. But there is evidence that teachers tend to be less patient, less encouraging, and less likely to try teaching as much material to students whom they do not consider bright (Cooper, 1979; Luce & Hoge, 1978; Trujillo, 1986). Thus, it is not hard to imagine that being tagged with a low IQ score or some other negative label may limit a person's educational opportunities.

Attempts to replicate Rosenthal and Jacobson's findings have not always been successful (Elashoff, 1979). It is probably safest to conclude that

Reinforcement from teachers encourages children to try harder and do better, which leads to more encouragement and further effort. Without such reinforcement, a child's scholastic performance may suffer.

expectancies may influence pupil performance under some circumstances, but not others, and that, even if expectancies do not affect IQ scores, they may influence academic performance (Snow & Yallow, 1982).

Obviously, intelligence tests are far from perfect. Like any enterprise in which one tries to "summarize" people with a label, a test score, or a profile, they carry with them the danger of misuse and error. On the other hand, they can also prevent errors. For example, boredom or lack of motivation at school can make a child appear mentally slow, even retarded. But an IQ test conducted under the right circumstances is likely to reveal the child's normal, perhaps even superior, mental abilities. In such cases, IQ tests can not only highlight the motivational problem, but also prevent the mistake of moving a bright child to a class for the mentally handicapped. In short, despite their limitations, intelligence tests seem to provide a standardized and often helpful way of assessing and comparing some of the important mental abilities of large numbers of people.

INTELLIGENCE AND THE DIVERSITY OF MENTAL ABILITIES

If you are a teacher or administrator who cannot possibly know all your students well and you want one score to tell you something about their potential for academic success, then IQ tests are probably your answer. But, does it make sense to rank children by just one score, in particular by an IQ score? The answer depends not only on what IQ scores measure, but also on what intelligence is and how it is related to other mental abilities.

As we have said, IQ scores do distinguish people in ways that roughly correspond to notions of who is or is not intelligent, and IQ scores do a reasonable job of predicting academic success. But differences in mental abilities extend well beyond the differences measured by IQ tests. Do IQ tests measure all aspects of intelligence? Is there a single trait that can be called *intelligence*? To examine these questions, we look first at three other ways of studying intelligence and then at some differences in cognition that are not measured by IQ tests.

The Psychometric Approach: General and Specific Intelligence

One method of studying intelligence analyzes test scores in order to describe the structure of intelligence. Much of the research using this **psychometric approach** has tried to answer the question: Does intelligence consist of one general factor? The answer has practical implications. For example, if intelligence is truly a single characteristic, a potential employer might assume that someone with a low IQ could not be expected to do any mental task well. On the other hand, if intelligence is composed of a multitude of subdimensions or specific abilities, a poor showing in one area—say, problem solving—might not rule out better performance in memory or comprehension of information.

Spearman's g   In the late 1920s, Charles Spearman, a well-known statistician who helped develop the methods for calculating the correlation coefficient, noted that there was a positive correlation between scores on almost all tests of mental abilities (Spearman, 1927). That is, people who did well on one test tended to do better than average on all of the others. Spearman concluded that these correlations were created by a very general factor of mental ability, which was called **g,** or the **g-factor** of intelligence.

At first, Spearman held that people's scores on a test resulted from the g-factor plus an s-factor, which represented the specific information and skills needed for a particular test. Thus, in Spearman's view, scores on an IQ test depend on just two things: general intelligence and the specific abilities needed for a particular test. As correlations among test scores were examined further, however, researchers found correlations that could not be explained by either g or s. Narrower than g and broader than s, they were called *group factors.* Spearman soon modified his theory to try to accommodate these factors, but he continued to maintain that g represented a controlling mental force (Gould, 1983).

Other views   L. L. Thurstone in particular disagreed with Spearman's theory. In 1938 he published a paper criticizing Spearman's mathematical methods and denying the significance of Spearman's g. Using a statistical technique called **factor analysis,** he analyzed the correlations among IQ tests, and instead of a dominating g factor, he found several independent *primary mental abilities.* He identified these as numerical ability, reasoning, verbal fluency, spatial visualization, perceptual ability, memory, and verbal comprehension. Thurstone said that Spearman's g-factor contributes little to the correlation among scores. It is, he argued, secondary to the primary mental abilities, rather than the controlling force that Spearman had postulated.

Decades later, Raymond B. Cattell (1971) contested Thurstone's analysis, reanalyzed data, and argued that g exists but that there are two kinds of g, which he labeled fluid (gf) and crystallized (gc). **Fluid intelligence** is the basic power of reasoning and problem solving. It produces induction, deduction, reasoning, and understanding of the relationships between different ideas. **Crystallized intelligence,** in contrast, involves specific knowledge gained as a result of applying fluid intelligence. It produces verbal comprehension and skill at manipulating numbers. Since people with greater fluid intelligence are likely to gain more crystallized intelligence, measures of the two sorts of intelligence are positively correlated.

Conclusions   Most psychologists acknowledge the existence of g, but what does it mean? Spearman believed that there was an actual factor that is measured by g. In some of his early work, he proposed that this factor is attention or mental effort. A contrasting position is that g reflects merely a collection or bundle of component abilities. For example, this bundle might include reasoning ability, test-taking skill, reading ability, and so forth (Humphreys, 1984). The small positive correlation among test scores represented by g, in this view, results from the fact that many of these abilities are needed to perform well on tests.

How important is g? Because g is the result of an analysis of the correlations among scores, the answer depends on who is taking the tests. The nature of the correlation coefficient is such that, if the range of abilities reflected by the test scores is large, then there will generally be a positive correlation between most tests, and mathematical analysis will reveal the g factor. But when the range of ability is small, correlations decline; therefore, mathematical analysis will give little evidence of the g factor. To see why correlations decline when the range of scores is reduced, consider the correlation between height and weight. If all ages in the population are included—from infants to adults— this correlation will be rather high, because infants are always much shorter and lighter than adults. But if the range of scores is restricted by studying only adults—a category that includes many short, heavy people and many tall, skinny people—the relationship between height and weight will be weaker (and the correlation smaller).

In other words, the psychometric approach to the study of intelligence has its limitations (Frederiksen, 1986). The data it generates depend in part on which tests are used, which subjects take those tests and under what conditions, what methods of statistical analysis are chosen, and what labels are chosen to describe the factors that emerge. For these and other reasons, some scientists argue that the ultimate answers to questions about the fundamental nature of mental abilities can only be found by turning to evidence other than the test scores used by the psychometric approach.

The Information-Processing Approach

IQ tests, the various analyses of *g,* and Thurstone's analysis of primary mental abilities all focus on the *products* of intelligence—the answers to a test. Another approach looks instead at the *process* of intelligent behavior (Hunt, 1983; Sternberg, 1982). It asks: What mental operations are necessary to answer the questions on an IQ test or to perform other intellectual tasks? What components of this performance depend on past learning, and what components depend on attention, short-term memory, and processing speed? In short, one can examine intelligence by focusing on differences in information processing. This approach relates the basic mental processes discussed in earlier chapters— such as the transfer of information from short- to long-term memory, the measurement of reaction time, and access to long-term memory—to research on intelligence tests. Are there individual differences in these mental processes that correlate with differences in IQ scores or other measures of intelligence?

Components and metacomponents   One possibility is that people with high IQ scores carry out basic mental processes more quickly than people with low scores; as Sir Francis Galton suggested in the nineteenth century, perhaps they have "faster brains." It might make little difference if a "fast brain" allows you, say, to save 200 milliseconds on a simple task like performing an easy arithmetic calculation. But when a task is complex, having a "fast brain" might decrease the chance that information will be lost before it can be used (Carlson, Jensen & Widaman, 1983). Or a "fast brain" might allow you to do a better job mastering material in everyday life and therefore allow you to build up a good knowledge base (Vernon, 1983).

In the 1970s, Earl Hunt explored the possibility that intelligence was correlated with the speed of basic cognitive processes. In one study, for example, Hunt and his colleagues measured the speed with which people could decide whether two letters (for example, *a* and *A*) shared the same name. This test provided a measure of speed of access to long-term memory. They did find a significant correlation between speed on this test and IQ test scores of verbal fluency and comprehension. But the correlation was just +.33. Other correlations between measures of basic cognitive processes and measures of verbal intelligence were also rather modest. This led researchers to conclude that only a small portion of individual differences in performance on tests of reasoning or general comprehension could be tied to differences "in any one type of mechanistic information processing" (Hunt, 1983).

Robert Sternberg also examined the speed of basic mental processes and, like Hunt, found that the correlations with measures of intelligence were not impressive. But Sternberg argued that there are two major aspects of intelligent behavior: components and metacomponents (Sternberg, 1977, 1982). **Components** are the information-processing capacities of perceiving stimuli, holding information in working memory, comparing values, retrieving things from memory, and calculating sums and differences. Of greater importance to intelligence, according to Sternberg, are **metacomponents**—the processes involved in organizing and setting up a problem. For example, metacomponents determine how people decide on the nature of a problem, know what needs to be known before trying to solve it, and adopt a strategy for solving it.

Sternberg's ingenious way of separating the influence of components from that of metacomponents involved asking subjects to complete such analogies as "Hot is to cold as high is to————" by choosing from several alternatives (such as *green, low, dark,* and *bright*). In one series of experiments, he first showed subjects just part of each analogy (such as "Washington is to 1") and asked them to press a button when they understood it. The elapsed time represents component processing—reading the words and storing them in short-term memory. Then subjects saw the rest of the problem ("as Lincoln is to: *2, 5, 10, 20*") and pressed the button when they had the solution (in this case 5; Washington appears on the one-dollar bill, Lincoln appears on the five-dollar bill). By varying the amount of each problem revealed at each step, Sternberg was able to show that component-processing times did not correlate with intelligence test scores, but that the time taken to understand and set up the problem—metacomponent processing—was related to scores on tests of reasoning ability. In our example, metacomponent processing involves determining in advance the possible relationships between *Washington* and *1* (such as order of the presidents' portrait on the currency). People with better reasoning ability spent more time on understanding problems but reached solutions faster and more accurately than those with lower reasoning scores.

The role of attention   In addition to components and metacomponents, psychologists have proposed that there is a third major determinant of cognitive functioning: attention. This idea builds on the results of research by Hunt and others (Hunt, 1980; Hunt & Lansman, 1983; Stankov, 1983). As mentioned in the chapter on perception, attention represents a pool of resources or mental energy that can be applied to a task. When people perform difficult tasks or perform more than one task at a time, they must call on greater amounts of these resources. Does intelligent behavior depend on how well people can mobilize the resources of attention?

In one experiment on this question, Hunt (1980) used the Raven Progressive Matrices Test as a test of complex spatial ability (see Figure 10.3). The difficulty of the problems in the test can be varied. Hunt had people perform the task twice. The first time, he increased the difficulty of the problems until the subject made an error; the person's score on this version of the test provided a measure of intelligence. The second time the person took the test, Hunt kept the level of the problems easy. However, the person had to perform another task at the same time: pressing a switch whenever a particular tone was heard. People could perform this concurrent task well, Hunt reasoned, only if performing the easy spatial-ability task left extra attentional resources. Thus, if intelligence depends on the availability of attentional resources, performance on this concurrent task should relate to performance on the first version of the spatial-ability test. And it did. Hunt reasoned that those with greater intellectual ability also had more attentional resources available. These abundant resources not only allowed better performance of the easy problems but also left sufficient resources for superior performance on the concurrent task.

Conclusions   Does this mean that attention *is* the g factor of intelligence, as Spearman had speculated decades ago? No. Researchers in information processing are not claiming that attention or any other single entity underlies intelligent behavior. They are examining how particular processes are important elements of many intellectual tasks (Sternberg, 1984). There may indeed be other important processes, just as it is possible that the processes they have examined may be unimportant for some intellectual tasks.

Research on information processing holds considerable promise. The development of the Kaufman Assessment Battery for Children (K-ABC; Kaufman & Kaufman, 1983) is one indication that this approach to mental abilities is here to stay. Like other IQ tests, this test assesses factual knowledge and academic skills, but it also contains subscales designed to assess information-processing abilities related to intellectual performance. A sequential processing scale contains tasks (such as imitating a sequence of hand movements) that require the orderly use of one piece of information at a time, while a simultaneous processing scale presents problems (such as identifying a picture from small glimpses visible as it moves past a narrow slit) that can be solved only by integrating several sources of information.

HIGHLIGHT

Understanding and Treating Mental Retardation

The usefulness of both IQ tests and studies of information processing is evident when one considers the problem of mental retardation. IQ tests have long been used to define and diagnose mental retardation. More recently, studies of information processing have provided useful information about how the cognitive skills of mentally retarded people are deficient and how these people can best be helped.

What is mental retardation? The label "mentally retarded" is applied to people whose measured IQ is less than about 70. But people within this very broad category differ greatly in their mental abilities and their ability to function independently in daily life. Table 10.2 shows a classification that divides the range of low IQ scores into categories that reflect these differences.

Often, the most severe cases of retardation are associated with a specific genetic defect. We have described the best-known example: Down's syndrome. Children with Down's syndrome typically have IQ scores around 40 to 50. As we have seen, environmental conditions may also limit intelligence, sometimes permanently. In most cases of mental retardation, however, no environmental

TABLE 10.2
Categories of Mental Retardation

Level of Retardation	IQ Scores	Characteristics
Mild	50–70	A majority of all the mentally retarded. Usually show no physical symptoms of abnormality. Individuals with higher IQs can marry, maintain a family, and work in menial, unskilled jobs. Abstract reasoning is difficult for those with the lower IQs of this category. Capable of some academic learning to a sixth-grade level.
Moderate	35–49	Often lack physical coordination. Can be trained to take care of themselves and to acquire some reading and writing skills. Abilities of a four- to seven-year-old. Capable of living outside an institution with their families.
Severe	20–34	Only a few can benefit from any schooling. Can communicate vocally after extensive training. Most require constant supervision.
Profound	Below 20	Mental age less than three. Very limited communication. Require constant supervision. Can learn to walk, utter a few simple phrases, and feed themselves.

or genetic cause can be found. Most often, these are cases of mild retardation, known as **familial retardation** for two reasons: most people in this group come from families of lower socioeconomic status, and they are more likely than those suffering from a genetic defect to have a relative who is also retarded (Johnson, Ahern & Johnson, 1976). These facts have led psychologists to conclude that familial retardation results from a complex, not well understood interaction between heredity and environment.

Exactly *how* are the mentally retarded deficient in their cognitive skills? Studies of information processing show that there are some significant ways in which the retarded do *not* differ from those with higher IQs. For example, they are just as proficient at recognizing simple stimuli, and their rate of forgetting information from short-term memory is no more rapid (Belmont & Butterfield, 1971). But Joseph Campione, Ann Brown, and Roberta Ferrara (1982) found that mildly retarded children do differ from other people in three important ways.

1. They perform certain mental operations, such as those involved in retrieving information from memory, more slowly.

2. They simply know fewer facts about the world. It is likely that this deficiency has a great deal to do with a third problem.

3. They are not very good at using particular mental *strategies* that may be important in learning and problem solving. For example, they do not spontaneously rehearse material that must be held in short-term memory.

What are the reasons for this deficiency in using strategies? As we saw in the chapter on memory, the differences between normal and retarded children in some ways resemble differences between older and younger children. Both younger children and retarded children show deficiencies in *metamemory*—the knowledge of how their memory works. More generally, retarded children are deficient in **metacognition:** the knowledge of what strategies to apply, when to apply them, and how to deploy them in new situations so that new specific knowledge can be gained and different problems mastered. Yet it is this knowledge that is most critical to intelligent behavior. Thus, deficiencies in metacognition most limit the intellectual performance of the mildly retarded. It may be easy to teach *what* a strategy like rehearsal is, but it is not so easy to teach when and how it should be used. If retarded children are simply taught a strategy, they are not likely to use it again on their own or to transfer the strategy to a different task. Can they be taught to do so?

In one experiment, Ann Brown, Joseph Campione, and Craig Barclay (1979) taught children to use rehearsal strategies to remember pictures that appeared in different windows on a display screen. They also carefully taught the children why rehearsal was valuable and how to monitor their own performance to make sure that they were rehearsing effectively. In this case, the children transferred the use of rehearsal from the window task to a different memory task and still used this strategy up to a year later (Brown, Campione & Barclay, 1979). The researchers concluded that retarded children can be taught to employ a rehearsal strategy on a variety of tasks.

It is too early to judge the success that can be achieved through intervention programs like those suggested by this research. But it is fair to conclude that the intellectual abilities of the retarded, like those of other people, can be raised by carefully tailored programs that focus on specific weaknesses. Designing these programs is complicated by the fact that people are not machines that can simply be programmed; how people learn depends not just on cognitive skills, but also on social and emotional factors.

Consider, for example, the debate about *mainstreaming,* which is the policy of educating handicapped children, including those who are retarded, in

Abnormal conditions during pregnancy—such as a mother's exposure to German measles or excessive amounts of alcohol—can lead to the birth of a mentally retarded child, but, in most cases, the cause of retardation is unknown.

regular classrooms, along with those who are not handicapped. Is mainstreaming good for retarded children? Susan Harter and Edward Zigler (1974) concluded that retarded children who are taught in separate settings, especially in institutions, may demonstrate less curiosity and exploration than others, perhaps as a result of many institutions' sterility. Yet these individuals also showed greater confidence in tackling problems than children who were mainstreamed. Given a choice, the mainstreamed children tended to select very easy or unchallenging tasks that they could be sure of doing well; the segregated children did not. Perhaps the confidence of retarded children who are mainstreamed is damaged by the contrast they see with the brighter pupils around them.

Observations like this suggest that educators should focus less on training the retarded to learn specific cognitive skills and on raising their IQ scores. Instead, educators might emphasize improving motivation to succeed, confidence, emotional well-being, and general social competence (Zigler & Seitz, 1983). ■

The Symbols-Systems Approach

Some retarded people show incredible skills in one narrowly defined area. One such child, though his IQ tested at 50, could accurately state the day of the week for any date between 1880 and 1950 (Scheerer, Rothman & Goldstein, 1945). He could also play melodies on the piano by ear and could sing Italian operatic pieces he had heard, although he had no understanding of what he was doing. Similarly, he could spell (forward or backward) any word spoken to him and memorize long speeches.

Such children, who are retarded in most areas but amazingly proficient at some mental skill, are called **idiots savants.** Their amazing abilities, as well as those of child prodigies, constitute one piece of evidence cited by Howard Gardner (1983) for his theory of *multiple intelligences.* The theory is a descendant of Thurstone's analysis of primary mental abilities, but it represents a quite different approach, called the **symbols-systems approach.** This approach to intelligence focuses, not on the mathematical analysis of paper-and-pencil tests, but on how people learn and use various symbol systems, such as language, mathematics, music, and so on. Do these systems all require the same abilities and processes, the same "intelligence"?

To find an answer, Gardner looked, not just at test scores and information-processing experiments, but also at developmental data, the abilities of idiots savants and child prodigies, biological research, and various cultural factors. If one examines the behavior of children and the biological findings, he argued, one finds evidence that certain abilities are relatively independent. We saw in the chapter on biological psychology, for example, that damage to the left cerebral hemisphere in most people leads to a loss of linguistic ability, with little damage to spatial abilities; this supports the idea that spatial intelligence and verbal intelligence are distinct. If we examine various cultures, we can identify those sets of skills that are genuinely important to human beings. Spatial skills, for example, are valued by the navigator of a small boat sailing at night in the seas of Micronesia, just as they are valued by the architect or circuit board designer in the United States.

The specific intelligences that Gardner proposed are (1) linguistic intelligence; (2) logical-mathematical intelligence; (3) spatial intelligence; (4) musical intelligence; (5) body-kinesthetic intelligence, which is demonstrated by the skills of dancers and athletes; and (6) personal intelligence, which refers to knowledge and understanding of oneself and of one's relations to others. Conventional IQ tests sample only the first three of these intelligences.

According to Howard Gardner, shown here working with a child, there are a small number of intellectual potentials, or "intelligences," that are possessed by all humans and are capable of being involved in symbol systems. Biology provides a raw capacity unique to each of these intelligences; cultures provide a symbolic system that mobilizes that capacity. Each intelligence involves a set of skills that allows people to solve problems and is valued in at least some cultures. Although normally the intelligences interact, they can function with some independence, and individuals may develop certain intelligences further than others.

Evidence for *g,* Gardner argued, results from the fact that most IQ tests rely heavily on just linguistic and logical-mathematical intelligences. And IQ tests predict academic success because schools value these particular intelligences. But conventional IQ tests, he claimed, fail to do justice to the diversity of intelligences.

Like other theories of mental abilities, determination of the validity or usefulness of Gardner's theory must await further research. It does, however, serve to highlight the fact that there are aspects of mental ability not measured by IQ tests and aspects that vary considerably from one domain to another. Indeed, as we discuss in the following sections, some of these aspects seem to be somewhat independent of intelligence.

Creativity

In each area of ability identified by Gardner there are people who are able to produce original solutions or novel compositions—in short, *creative* people. To measure **creativity,** some psychologists have generated tests of **divergent thinking,** which is the ability to think along many alternative paths to generate many different solutions to a problem (Guilford & Hoepfner, 1971). One example is the Consequences Test. It asks questions like "Imagine all of the things that might possibly happen if all national and local laws were suddenly abolished" (Guilford, 1959). Divergent thinking tests are scored by counting the number of *different,* but plausible responses that a person can list for each item or by the extent to which a person's answers are different from those given by most test takers.

Of course, the ability to come up with different answers or different ways of looking at a situation does not guarantee that you will produce anything creative. It is necessary, too, for divergent thinking to be *appropriate* for a situation or problem. Otherwise your ideas might be considered, not creative, but bizarre or nonsensical. More generally, to be productive, a creative person must have an anchor attached to reality, understand society's needs, and learn from the experience and knowledge of others. These are qualities that are associated with intelligence. An inventor who does not possess them might spend years perfecting a belt-driven, gas-powered, energy-efficient, portable pooper-scooper for urban dog owners who already have a perfectly usable hand-operated alternative.

Creativity and IQ Is creativity, then, associated with a high IQ? When Terman followed the lives of children who had very high IQ scores, he found that few, if any, developed into truly creative geniuses—into world-famous inventors, authors, artists, or composers (Terman & Oden, 1959). And comparisons of people's scores on IQ tests and on tests of creativity have found only modest correlations, ranging between +.10 and +.30 (Anastasi, 1971; Barron & Harrington, 1981; Dellas & Gaier, 1970).

Since creativity requires divergent thinking, this result is not really surprising: novel behavior is precisely what the typical IQ test score does *not* measure. It measures **convergent thinking**—the ability to apply the rules of logic and what one knows about the world in order, say, to narrow down the number of possible solutions to a problem. The qualities that might lead a person to score high on an IQ test are not the same as those that lead to creative abilities.

The low correlation between IQ and creativity does not mean that the two are completely unrelated. Research suggests that, for creativity to lead to productive behavior, a person's IQ score must be above the average level of 100 (Barron & Harrington, 1981). Creativity also appears to be related to IQ

Vincent Van Gogh, the brilliant artist who severed his own ear and later committed suicide, exemplifies the alleged relationship between creativity and personality disorder. Despite such stereotypes, creativity is not generally associated with personality disturbances or other mental disorders.

in another way: high levels of creativity may sometimes compensate for lower IQ scores. At least this was the conclusion drawn by Jacob Getzels and Philip Jackson (1962). After giving adolescents various tests of creativity, they divided them into two groups. One group had received very high scores on tests of creativity and a mean IQ score of 127. The second group had a mean IQ score of 150 but showed no particular signs of creative behavior. The interesting finding was that the two groups received nearly identical scores on basic achievement tests. It appeared that the creativity of the first group had compensated for their relatively lower IQs.

Creativity and personality   People sometimes associate the creative mind with bizarre behavior and a strange personality. Of course, there are some well-known creative artists who have suffered from emotional disturbances—Vincent van Gogh, for example. But many mentally disturbed people are not creative, and many creative people are emotionally well balanced. Research indicates that personality disorders are no more likely to occur in the creative than in the noncreative person (Coleman, Butcher & Carson, 1984). There is some evidence, however, that creative people share certain characteristic personality traits. In particular, they tend to be more independent, rely more on intuitive thinking, and have higher self-acceptance and energy (Barron & Harrington, 1981).

Cognitive Style

Suppose you are on the board of directors of a corporation that specializes in complicated systems, such as the rockets used to launch ICBMs or the space shuttle. You hold in your hand a proposal from a company that makes mostly automobile parts. The company wants to buy your corporation. They are offering a very good price, and you are certain of maintaining your seat on the board. Do these facts settle your decision? Not necessarily. You might also consider that the automobile company has no experience handling products

Complex problems require decision-makers to take numerous interacting factors into account and to anticipate the consequences of all the available options. These abilities are part of what is meant by cognitive complexity.

like yours—products that are technically very complex and require many years of research, testing, and production. Would they demand changes in middle management? What effects would a takeover have on employee morale and productivity? On your customers' confidence? Would the automobile company consolidate corporate offices, closing your headquarters and disrupting employment in the community?

Some people are likely to ask questions like these before making any important decision. They demonstrate **cognitive complexity,** a set of abilities related to flexibility of thought, the ability to anticipate future events and to alter a chosen course of action based on unexpected happenings. Most importantly, cognitively complex people can think *multidimensionally*. In other words, they can interpret the consequences of their actions in a variety of ways and appreciate several aspects of a problem.

To measure cognitive complexity, Siegfried Streufert (1986) asked several executives to play a game that simulated business decison making (see Figure 10.6). The subjects managed a fictitious company, making decisions about

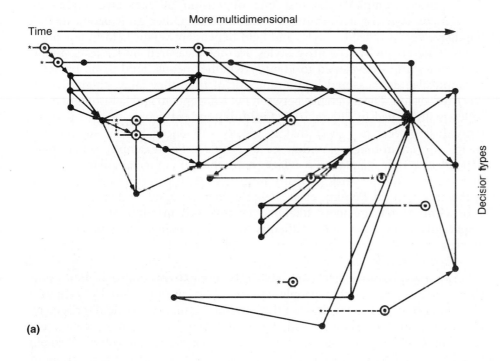

(a)

(b)

Figure 10.6
Cognitive Complexity
Each node or point in both graphs represents a decision point. The different horizontal "streams" reflect decisions regarding one category (for example, profits to the company). The horizontal axis represents the "stream" of information seeking and decision making that occur over time; the vertical axis indicates different aspects of the business environment. The differences between the two subjects are quite pronounced. (a) The many vertical branches in the top profile indicate that information about one class of events was used to help make decisions regarding a completely different class. For example, knowledge of economic factors outside the company might be used to help decide what to do in the face of a potential strike. (b) The bottom profile represents decision making by an executive who demonstrated less cognitive complexity.
(Permission granted by Dr. Siegfried Streufert.)

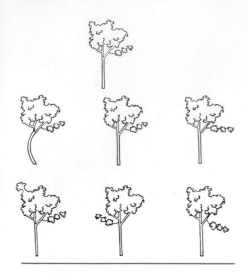

Figure 10.7
Impulsive and Reflective Styles
These are samples of the types of items on the Matching Familiar Figures (MFF) Test, which is used to identify one dimension of cognitive style: reflectivity versus impulsivity (Kagan, 1966; Messer, 1976). On this test, people are asked to select which of the six alternatives is identical to the one at the top. The time to make the first choice is measured, along with the number of errors, until a final decision is reached. Impulsive people often make rapid judgments without fully considering all alternatives. They are fast, but prone to errors. On this test, they tend to have short response times and make many errors. Reflective people, in contrast, ponder alternatives, censor their ideas, and generate slower, but more accurate performance.
(From "Reflection-Impulsivity: The Generality and Dynamics of Conceptual Tempo" by Jerome Kagan, *Journal of Abnormal Psychology, 71,* 17–24, 1966. Copyright © 1966 by the American Psychological Association.)

investments, expansion, marketing, salaries, and so forth. Streufert analyzed the relevance of the subjects' decisions to various aspects of the company and the extent to which new information was used in making decisions. Figure 10.6 shows the resulting profiles of two executives' decision making. Two findings were especially significant.

First, Streufert found that cognitive complexity is *domain-specific.* People who are cognitively complex in dealing with one domain or area, such as business decisions, may not show cognitive complexity in dealing with another area, such as family relations. Thus, executives who can consider all sides of a business issue may react to their son or daughter in rigid, intolerant ways that show no appreciation for the child's point of view. Second, Streufert found that measures of cognitive complexity do not correlate with IQ scores. The significance of this finding is clouded by the fact that the subjects from his studies generally had above-average IQs to begin with. (As noted earlier, correlations involving a narrow range of scores will be smaller than for a wider range of scores.) Like creativity, cognitive complexity does not appear to correlate with IQ for those who have been previously identified as quite intelligent.

Cognitive complexity is just one dimension of **cognitive style**—the manner, or style, of performing cognitive tasks. Other dimensions include impulsive versus reflective styles and field-dependent versus field-independent styles. Like creativity, cognitive styles are not measured by IQ tests. Figure 10.7 shows a test developed to identify whether people tend to be reflective or impulsive, as measured by the amount of time they allow themselves to reach a decision. The difference between field-dependent and field-independent styles is illustrated in Figure 10.8. **Field-dependent** people tend to perceive individual objects in a way that is greatly influenced by the surrounding "field," or environment (Witkin et al., 1962). For example, when field-dependent people are placed in a dark room, the sight of rectangular structures that are tilted off the vertical greatly influences their perception of which way is the true vertical (Witkin et al., 1962). There is good evidence that field-dependent people are more likely to be involved in automobile accidents. Apparently, they have more difficulty than field-independent perceivers in picking out traffic signs from a complex background, and they are slower at identifying hazards (Goodenough, 1976).

Although cognitive styles are labeled by the extremes of each dimension, much as one might label people tall or short, people actually exhibit a continuous range of styles between the extremes. Usually, a particular cognitive style is not in itself good or bad; instead, it may be more or less effective, depending on the circumstances. For example, when one behavior is obviously best in an emergency situation, the impulsive person will probably be more effective. But impulsive behavior may be less adequate when the situation is complex or when making a mistake would be dangerous.

FUTURE DIRECTIONS

The study and testing of intelligence and other mental abilities have very far reaching implications for education; for who is hired, fired, or promoted; and for governmental policies for the socially and economically disadvantaged. Because of this broad reach, these topics inevitably stir heated debates, conflicting opinions, and biases that may have little to do with scientific findings on mental abilities. Yet, despite the complexity of the field, some solid conclusions about intelligence and mental ability are emerging, although even these are not shared by all experts in the field.

First, there seems to be an emerging consensus that there is no *single* definition of intelligence. Instead, different definitions of intelligence must be offered to serve different purposes. There are varying views about how far beyond the academic domain it is appropriate to look for the characteristics of intelligent behavior. Robert Sternberg (1985), for example, has argued for the importance of considering how intelligence is applied to solve everyday problems. And we have seen that Gardner (1983) argues that the concept of intelligence must include all skills and talents that are valued by different societies. But others have cautioned against casting the net of definition too widely, for fear of losing any unifying theme (Humphreys, 1986). Second, most psychologists concur that the brain probably does not "contain" some unified "thing" that we call intelligence. Even the g factor of intelligence is likely to be a collection of subskills and mental abilities, many of which are needed to succeed on any test of intelligence. Third, many psychologists acknowledge that there *is* a positive correlation between several tests of mental ability, a correlation that can be described by one number, labeled g. But they caution against emphasizing g so much that the diverse abilities underlying it are ignored. And, fourth, most psychologists are now in substantial agreement that the mental abilities of a particular individual result from a complex interaction between heredity and environment.

Where is the field moving? What are its future directions? Some insight is provided by a recent book compiled by most of the best researchers in the field (Sternberg & Detterman, 1986). From their thoughts and conclusions, it is apparent that much effort will be given to understanding the cognitive information-processing operations that underlie intelligent behavior, as psychologists strive to understand, not only what these operations are, but also how they underlie more traditional or more global measures of intelligence. For example, psychologists are making progress in identifying what the component skills of g are and are beginning to apply them to the understanding of such areas as mental retardation (Campione, Brown & Ferrara, 1982).

There will be growing concern for evaluating mental abilities not just in the abstract, but in the context of how the individual relates to the surrounding society. This concern is likely to be reflected in studies of the sort of intelligent behavior shown in everyday problem-solving situations, in research on the role of intelligence in the ability to deal successfully with other people, and in continued interest in the heredity-environment issue. Researchers in the field are also more closely examining the development of intelligence—no longer as a single g-factor that increases with age, but as a set of information-processing components or mental operations.

Finally, the focus on mental operations is likely to lead psychologists to consider how these operations are related to the functions carried out by two important systems: the human brain and the computer. Their progress at linking intelligent behavior to neural or chemical mechanisms may be slower than similar attempts to link perception, memory, and mental illness to biological processes. Progress will take time, if only because the gulf between intelligent behavior and the microscopic level at which the brain is studied will be harder to cross until there is a better understanding of the component processes of intelligence. Nevertheless, there will be progress. Similarly, as we discussed in the chapter on thought, the growing interest in artificial intelligence among psychologists and computer scientists will surely lead to revolutionary developments in the design of computers and computer programs capable of ever more "intelligent" information processing. Such work may also help researchers to better understand the mechanics and processes involved in human mental abilities.

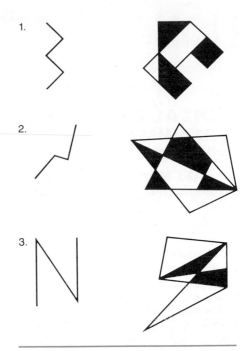

Figure 10.8
Field Dependence and Field Independence
If you have trouble locating the shapes at the left in the more complex pattern on the right, your cognitive style might be characterized as field dependent.
(Adapted from Witkin et al., "Field Dependent and Field Independent Cognitive Styles and Their Educational Implications," *Review of Educational Research*, 1977, 47, 1–04.)

MENTAL ABILITIES AND HUMAN DEVELOPMENT
How Do Mental Abilities Change over the Lifespan?

This chapter has dealt with intelligence and mental abilities—how to define them and measure them, what they mean, and how they vary. But we have not said very much about one important variation in mental abilities: the changes that occur during a person's own lifetime.

One way to describe how mental abilities change with age is to look at changes in IQ scores. Figure 10.4 showed that IQ scores tend to increase in the early years, level off during adulthood, and then decline somewhat in old age. But these data were based on a comparison of different people at different ages. In other words, the data came from a **cross-sectional study,** a study in which data collected simultaneously from people of different ages are compared. Changes associated with age can also be examined through **longitudinal studies,** in which a group of people is repeatedly tested as they grow older. The difference between these two methods can have a significant effect on the results.

Cross-sectional studies contain a major confounding variable: older subjects have not only aged more than younger ones; they were also born in a different year. As a result, they may well have been exposed to very different educational, cultural, nutritional, and medical experiences. These differences, and not just younger age, might account for higher IQ scores among younger people. To some extent, experimenters can address this confound between age and date of birth by careful selection of subjects; for example, by attempting to match the educational levels of the older and younger groups.

Many researchers feel that a better strategy is to use a longitudinal design, but longitudinal studies may be marred by another problem: the availability of subjects. As a group of people the same age (a *cohort*) is tested through the years, fewer members of the group can be tested, because some die or become incapacitated through hospitalization, failing eyesight, and the like. The remaining people are likely to be the healthiest in the cohort and may also have retained better intellectual powers than the dropouts (Botwinick, 1977). If this is the case, the average intelligence score of the sample will be higher as it ages than it would have been had the entire sample remained intact. Hence, longitu-dinal studies may *underestimate* the degree to which mental abilities decline with age. Indeed, longitudinal studies indicate that age has somewhat less effect on intelligence than cross-sectional studies suggest and that the decline tends to appear somewhat later than Figure 10.4 shows (Botwinick, 1977; Schaie & La-bouvie-Vief, 1974; Willis & Baltes, 1980).

In short, cross-sectional studies are likely to overestimate and longitudinal studies to underestimate the effects of age on intellectual ability. But the general picture painted by both types of studies is reasonably consistent: people's IQ scores usually remain fairly constant from early adulthood until about sixty to seventy years of age. Then—excluding cases of senility, Alzheimer's disease, and other organic disorders—some components of intelligence, but not others, begin to fail. The classic pattern is that capacities related to numerical skills, speeded performance, and spatial processing decline and that little or no loss, and possibly even some improvement, occurs in verbal ability and general knowledge (Botwinick, 1977).

In other words, different aspects of mental ability show a different developmental course over the lifespan. *Crystallized intelligence,* which depends on retrieving information and facts about the world from long-term memory, may continue to grow well into old age. *Fluid intelligence,* which involves rapid and

SUMMARY

1. Psychologists do not fully agree on the definition of intelligence, but most psychologists focus on its role in reasoning, problem solving, and dealing with the environment.

2. Binet developed the first test of intelligence in an effort to identify children in need of special instruction. The test offered reasoning and vocabulary questions of varying levels of difficulty and produced a mental-age score. A revision of Binet's test, developed by Terman and known as the Stanford-Binet test, also included items designed to assess adult intelligence and became the standard for modern intelligence tests. In scoring his test, Terman used the intelligence quotient (IQ), which is the ratio of mental age divided by chronological age times 100.

3. Early uses of intelligence tests to assess immigrants arriving from Europe and to screen out World War I army recruits of low mental ability failed to acknowledge that cultural differences and the content of the questions, as well as poor test-taking environments, lead to large biases in test scores. These biases had unfortunate consequences for many of the cultural groups involved and helped lead to the establishment of immigration quotas.

4. The Wechsler test of intelligence offers eleven subtests and generates scores of both verbal and performance intelligence, the latter assessing spatial and manipulative abilities. There are currently different versions of the Wechsler test for preschoolers (WPPSI), children (WISC-R), and adults (WAIS-R).

flexible manipulations of ideas and symbols, remains stable during adulthood and then declines in late life (Hayslip & Sterns, 1979).

Does this decline show up in daily tasks that require intelligent behavior, such as problem solving and decision making? As we described in Chapter 2, the decline in fluid intelligence is evident in somewhat slower processing of new information and the need for more time to solve new and unfamiliar problems. More specifically, among those over sixty-five or seventy, problems in four areas of information processing—all of them important components of fluid intelligence—often seem to impair problem-solving ability.

1. *Short-term memory* There is good evidence that the ability to hold and organize material in short-term memory declines beyond age fifty or sixty, particularly when attention may have to be redirected. This decline is commonly seen when older people try to solve mathematical word problems that require that they attend to stimuli relevant for deciding how to solve the problem while also making the necessary computations (Craik, 1977; Fozard, 1980).

2. *Processing speed* One of the clearest changes associated with age is a general slowing of all mental processes (Salthouse, 1985; Strayer, Wickens & Braune, 1987). For many tasks, this may not create obstacles. But when solving a problem that requires manipulating material that remains in short-term memory for only twenty seconds or so, the ability to process this information quickly is critical to success (Rabbitt, 1977). If you want to multiply two two-digit numbers mentally, for example, you must work rapidly enough to combine the subsums before they decay.

3. *Organization* Older people seem to be less likely to solve problems by adopting specific search strategies, or heuristics (Young, 1966, 1971). For example, a good heuristic for locating a problem in the wiring of a circuit is to perform a test that narrows down the regions where the problem might be. Marguerite Young (1966, 1971) found that the tests carried out by older people tended to be more random and haphazard. As noted in Chapter 2, this may be due in part to the fact that many are out of practice at solving such problems.

4. *Conservatism* Older people tend to be more conservative in problem solving than their younger counterparts. They are less likely, for example, to abandon an old, incorrect hypothesis in favor of a new one (Offenbach, 1974). They also require more information before making a tentative decision or judgment (Rabbitt, 1977). Laboratory studies suggest that older people are also more likely than younger ones to choose conservative, risk-free options over more radical, riskier ones (Botwinick, 1966).

In summary, in old age, as in earlier life, we find a gradual, continual accumulation of knowledge about the world; some systematic changes in the limits of mental processes; and qualitative changes in how those processes are carried out. But our discussion might have suggested an overly grim picture of the limits and changes in mental processes during old age. It is important to emphasize that, for much of people's everyday lives, they depend more on crystallized intelligence, which seems not to decline in old age, than on fluid intelligence. Furthermore, the correlation values for those measures of fluid intelligence that *do* decline indicate that more than three-fourths of the variability in these abilities is not related to age. Thus, many of the elderly will score well above their younger counterparts even on measures of fluid intelligence. Indeed, some investigators have argued that the most appropriate question to ask about the intellectual abilities of the elderly is how they maintain such a high level of intellectual functioning in spite of obvious changes in information-processing capacity (Rabbitt, 1977).

5. Culture-fair tests are those designed to have a minimum dependence on concepts and vocabulary from any one particular culture. These tests have typically not done as well as the Wechsler and the Stanford-Binet tests in predicting scholastic success.

6. Tests have advantages over other techniques of evaluation because they are *standardized*, making scores comparable between people; they are *quantifiable*; and they are *economical* and *efficient*.

7. Tests should be reliable, which means that the results for each person should be stable. Reliability can be measured by the test-retest, the alternate-forms, or the split-halves method. Using each method, reliability is expressed as a correlation coefficient.

8. Test validity determines the extent to which a test measures what it is supposed to measure, in terms of content and constructs. Criterion validity is measured by the correlation between the test score and some criterion measure of performance that the test is supposed to predict.

9. The purpose of the Scholastic Aptitude Test (SAT) is to predict success in college. Special courses designed to improve SAT scores will help some people who are unfamiliar with the testing environment, the general material of the test, or important test-taking strategies. Such courses may be expected to raise test scores by only ten to fifteen SAT points, however. The correlation of SAT scores with college grade-point averages is reduced because students with higher scores tend to take more difficult courses, in which lower grades tend to be given.

10. The validity of IQ tests in predicting high school grades is around $r = +.50$. Studies have found that

children with exceptionally high IQs attained a high degree of success in later life.

11. Heredity and environment interact in their effects on intelligence. This interaction is specified by a *reaction range*. Heredity sets limits on how much environmental factors can raise or lower IQ. The relative influences of heredity and environment are examined by correlational studies and by environmental interventions. In correlational studies comparing the similarity of mental abilities between siblings who have different degrees of genetic similarity, correlations in IQ are highest when both heredity and environment are identical (identical twins from the same home).

12. Environmental interventions have been accomplished either through adoption into warm and stimulating home environments or through early enrichment programs, such as Head Start, that have stressed nutrition, health care, parent involvement, and intellectual stimulation. These interventions sometimes raise IQ, but do not always. Initial large gains in cognitive performance that result from intervention may decline over time, but the programs do produce lasting gains in other aspects of scholastic competence.

13. There are differences in aptitude and IQ scores between different socioeconomic and racial groups. These differences result from both environmental and heredity factors, and the precise amount of each is difficult to establish. Motivational differences and environmental enrichment are major sources of differences between IQ scores of black and white children.

14. Intelligence test scores may interact with schooling opportunities. Studies have shown that children labeled as having low intelligence may be offered fewer, or lower-quality, educational opportunities. On the other hand, intelligence test scores, if used properly, may help to identify those who can benefit from a changed scholastic environment.

15. There are a variety of different kinds of intelligences. The psychometric approach to identifying these intelligences examines the correlations between different tests of intelligence. These correlations suggest that there is some general factor of intelligence called *g*. Other aspects of these correlations have also suggested progressively more specific kinds of subintelligences: fluid intelligence which describes a basic power of reasoning, and crystallized intelligence, which reflects gained knowledge. Other analyses suggest still more specific kinds of intelligence.

16. The information-processing approach to intelligence has focused on the processes by which intelligent behavior is produced. Small positive correlations have been found between IQ scores and measures of the speed of information-processing components. Robert Sternberg has found that the metacomponents, or strategies by which information-processing components are employed, are more closely related to intelligence. Studies have also shown that intelligence is related to the amount of attentional resources available.

17. Mental retardation describes people with an IQ lower than 70. Severe retardation is associated with genetic defects. Milder retardation results from an interaction of heredity and environment. Compared to those of normal intelligence, retarded people process information more slowly, know fewer facts about the world, and are poorer at using information-processing strategies, such as rehearsal. However, strategies can be taught to the mentally retarded. Studies have also demonstrated the benefits of developing social competence in the retarded.

18. Gardner's symbols-systems approach to different intelligences focuses on evidence from tests, child prodigies, information processing, brain function, and cross-cultural values to define separate intelligences related to language, logic-mathematics, spatial awareness, music, body-kinesthesia, and interpersonal relations.

19. Creativity is measured by tests of divergent thinking. But the thinking must be appropriate to be effective. Creativity does not appear to be closely associated with high IQ, but IQ must be above average for creativity to emerge. Creative people are not particularly prone to emotional or personality disorders.

20. Cognitive style refers to a set of characteristics of mental abilities that are not directly related to IQ. Different styles may be helpful or harmful under different circumstances. Cognitive complexity is a style that refers to a person's ability to think multidimensionally and is useful, for example, in business decision making. Cognitive complexity does not necessarily generalize from one domain to another. Impulsivity/reflectivity refers to the amount of time people allow themselves to reach a decision. Field dependence/independence refers to the extent to which objects are perceived independently of their surroundings.

KEY TERMS

Definitions of terms appear on the pages shown in parentheses.

achievement test (377)	crystallized intelligence (389)
cognitive complexity (397)	culture-fair test (374)
cognitive style (398)	divergent thinking (395)
component (390)	Down's syndrome (384)
convergent thinking (395)	factor analysis (389)
creativity (395)	familial retardation (393)
cross-sectional study (400)	field-dependent (398)

fluid intelligence (389)
g (g-factor) (388)
idiots savant (394)
intelligence (368)
intelligence quotient (IQ score) (373)
longitudinal study (400)
mental ability (366)
metacognition (393)
metacomponent (390)

norm (374)
performance scale (372)
psychometric approach (388)
reliability (375)
Stanford-Binet (371)
symbols-systems approach (394)
test (377)
validity (375)
verbal scale (372)

RECOMMENDED READINGS

Gardner, H. (1983). *Frames of mind: The theory of multiple intelligences.* New York: Basic Books. This book offers a refreshing view of the many diverse ways in which intelligence can be defined across different abilities in different cultures.

Gould, S. J. (1981). *Mismeasure of man.* New York: Norton. This book traces many of the historical controversies in the measurement of mental abilities, highlighting some of the abuses in mental testing.

Sternberg, R. J. (Ed.). (1982). *Handbook of human intelligence.* New York: Cambridge University Press. A collection of advanced and detailed chapters by experts in the field of intelligence.

Sternberg, R. J. (1985). *Beyond IQ: A triarchical theory of human intelligence.* New York: Cambridge University Press. This book provides an important overview of Sternberg's efforts to integrate information-processing approaches to intelligence with considerations of the broader relations between intelligence and experience, and between intelligence and the external world.

Sternberg, R. J., and Detterman, D. (1986). *What is intelligence?* Norwood, N.J.: Ablex. This is a collection of chapters by eminent names in the field, each describing in a few readable pages his or her own conceptions of and perspectives on the topic of intelligence.

Willerman, L. (1979). *The psychology of individual differences.* San Francisco: W. H. Freeman. This is a good basic introduction to the assessment of individual differences in mental abilities, and provides an introduction to some of the issues in the area.

Wolman, B. B. (Ed.). (1985). *Handbook of intelligence: Theories, measurements and applications.* New York: John Wiley. Another volume of chapters by experts on intelligence which provides advanced treatments of practically all aspects of the field.

When he was nineteen years old, one of the authors and his mother decided to go to a distant movie theater, in the middle of a blizzard, to see a Japanese horror movie called *Gorgo*. He should have known better, and his mother should *certainly* have known better. It took them twenty minutes to shovel a path to the car and five more to discover that they could not get it out of its snowbound parking space. Undaunted, they trudged back inside to call a cab. Certain that, on such a foul day, the call had to involve a life-threatening emergency, the cab driver was astonished to discover where his apparently demented customers wanted to go, and why. After a drive that took twice as long (and cost twice as much) as it would have without two feet of snow on the ground, the intrepid moviegoers reached their destination, startled the ticket taker, and contentedly munched licorice drops while they watched a film of, at best, dubious virtue in an otherwise empty movie house.

Why did they do this? Why, for that matter, do people help others or ignore them, eat a lot or starve themselves, mow their lawns or let them grow wild, haunt art museums or sleazy bars, go to college or drop out of high school? These questions illustrate that it is not enough to know *how* people behave. We also need to know *why* they do what they do.

Like the question of how people behave and think, the puzzle of why they do so involves concepts and research from many areas of psychology (see Linkages diagram, p. 406). One way to approach this puzzle is to use concepts of motivation. In this chapter, we provide a general overview of those concepts and look at some important examples of motivated behavior.

BASIC CONCEPTS OF MOTIVATION

The word *motivation* comes from *movere,* the Latin word meaning "to move." Psychologists who study motivation focus on internal and external influences that might "move" a person. They ask such questions as: What starts a person acting in a particular way? What determines the direction, strength, and persistence of that action? In short, **motivation** can be defined as the influences that account for the initiation, direction, intensity, and persistence of behavior (Geen, Beatty & Arkin, 1984).

Finding Unity in Diversity and Change

People often talk about motivation in everyday life. An actor or actress seeking the director's guidance about how to play a scene might ask, "What's my motivation?" meaning "Why should I be saying these lines?" A prosecuting attorney must show that the defendant not only had an opportunity to kidnap the neighbors' schnauzer, but also had a motive for doing so. People use motivational concepts to make sense of apparently senseless behavior and to

11

Motivation

LINKAGES
an overview

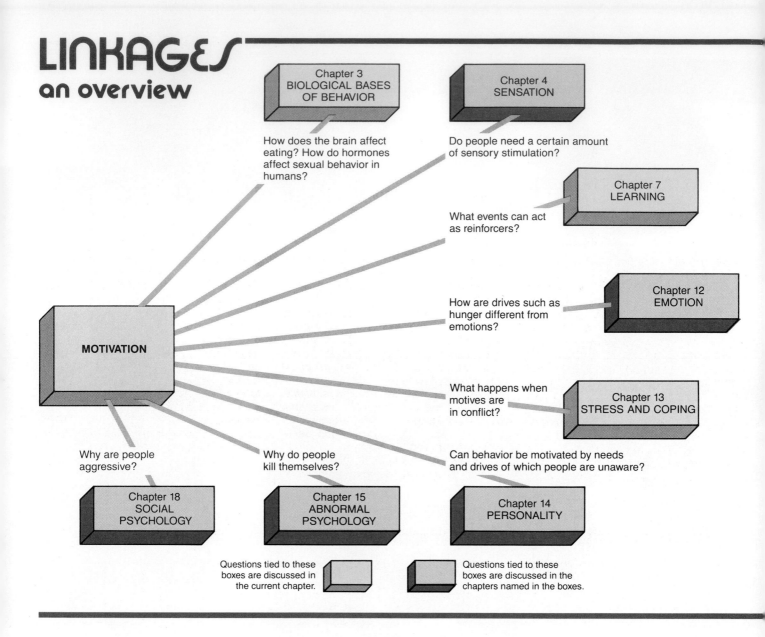

Chapter 3
BIOLOGICAL BASES
OF BEHAVIOR

How does the brain affect
eating? How do hormones
affect sexual behavior in
humans?

Chapter 4
SENSATION

Do people need a certain amount
of sensory stimulation?

Chapter 7
LEARNING

What events can act
as reinforcers?

Chapter 12
EMOTION

How are drives such as
hunger different from
emotions?

MOTIVATION

What happens when
motives are
in conflict?

Chapter 13
STRESS AND COPING

Why are people
aggressive?

Why do people
kill themselves?

Can behavior be motivated by needs
and drives of which people are unaware?

Chapter 18
SOCIAL
PSYCHOLOGY

Chapter 15
ABNORMAL
PSYCHOLOGY

Chapter 14
PERSONALITY

Questions tied to these
boxes are discussed in
the current chapter.

Questions tied to these
boxes are discussed in the
chapters named in the boxes.

---

infer what cannot be seen. In particular, concepts of motivation help psychologists to accomplish what Albert Einstein once said was the whole purpose of science: to discover unity in diversity.

Suppose that a man holds down two jobs, consistently turns down friends' invitations to the movies, wears old clothes, drives an old car, eats food left behind from other people's lunches, refuses to give to charity, and keeps the furnace set at sixty degrees in the dead of winter. Why? Possibly he does so because he likes to work hard, hates movies, fears new clothes and new cars, enjoys other people's cold leftovers, does not care about the poor, and likes cold air. This set of statements certainly covers all of this man's behaviors. But a far simpler way of accounting for those behaviors is to suggest that the man is trying to save as much money as possible. In other words, by suggesting a **motive,** a reason or purpose for behavior, you can find unity beneath the apparent diversity of many behaviors.

In more formal terms, we say that motivation can serve as an **intervening variable,** which is a variable that is not observed directly but that helps to account for relationships between various stimuli and responses. Figure 11.1

MOTIVATION AND PSYCHOLOGY

Explaining behavior is one of psychology's basic research tasks. If human beings were just like computers, earlier chapters would have outlined the basic elements that predict how each person will think and behave in any situation. But people, and even animals, are far more complicated and far less predictable than any computer. One of the most important complications is the fact that people, unlike machines, are motivated to act as they do by a wide variety of complex biological, psychological, and social forces. Psychologists in many specialties study these forces, forging numerous links between these areas and motivation.

The close tie between learning and motivation is one example. Imagine that you want to teach a rat to press the bar in a Skinner box, and you have only a jar of pennies and a bag of corn kernels to use as reinforcers. Which will be the more effective reward? What if your goal were to teach a six-year-old to read? Your choice of reinforcers in each case would depend on your knowledge of what motivates different creatures. In this case, the choice would be easy, but teachers, parents, therapists, employers, and others face far more difficult decisions about how to encourage desired behaviors. For example, if a parent tries to reinforce a boy for doing his homework by offering him the opportunity to play soccer, the opportunity will not be an effective reinforcer if the child thinks soccer is silly or has just spent six hours at it. The effectiveness of a particular reinforcer differs from person to person and can change over time. There is no universal reinforcer. Quite the contrary: changing behavior through learning is best accomplished by matching rewards to each individual's characteristics and situation. In this chapter, we will review some of the other facts and principles about motivation that have emerged from psychological research.

(p. 408) shows one example. In this case, diverse environmental stimuli lead to diverse behavioral responses. All the responses can be organized and understood by viewing them as guided by the single unifying motive of hunger. If a different motive were present, the person's responses to these stimuli would likely be different as well. Suppose a person is in desperate need of money for an addictive drug. Now the vending machine or the bakery window might prompt an effort to break in and steal cash, and the pizza ad might stimulate a robbery of the delivery truck. As an intervening variable, motivation helps us to understand how the same stimulus can bring about diverse responses in different people.

Similarly, motivation provides a way to explain fluctuations in behavior over time. For example, some college students respond little to the stimuli provided by their courses until they are put on academic probation. The same stimulus elicits very different responses at different times. Why? The idea that a person's motivation somehow changes may be useful in accounting for such fluctuations, from changes in eating, drinking, or smoking habits to alterations in the amount of effort put into a marriage, a job, or leisure activities.

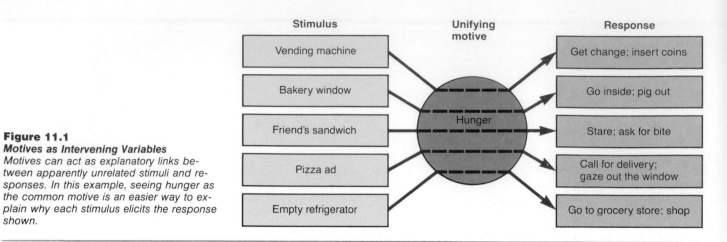

Figure 11.1
Motives as Intervening Variables
Motives can act as explanatory links between apparently unrelated stimuli and responses. In this example, seeing hunger as the common motive is an easier way to explain why each stimulus elicits the response shown.

Sources of Motivation

For centuries, philosophers assumed that reason and free will guide human behavior. But psychologists' research with humans and animals forced them to conclude that not all human behavior is guided by reason, and they began to study other factors that might serve as sources of motivation. These sources fall into four categories.

First, some human behavior, like most animal behavior, is motivated by basic *biological factors,* particularly the need for food, water, temperature regulation, and the like. Second, *cognitive factors* motivate human behavior. These are not always rational. A person who once nearly starved to death might later hoard food, not because there is any real danger of future famine, but because the thought of running out of food creates panic. This example highlights yet a third source of motivation: *emotional factors* (Petri, 1986). Panic, fear, anger, love, and many other emotions can be crucial in behaviors ranging from selfless giving to brutal murder. Fourth, people react to parents, teachers, siblings, friends, television, and other forces. The combined influence of these *social factors* in motivation has a profound effect on virtually every aspect of human behavior.

There is no one theory that provides a complete explanation of why humans behave as they do. Here we review six of the most prominent theories, because each offers a useful perspective on motivation.

Instinct Theory

William McDougall was one of the first psychologists to search for a unifying thread connecting diverse human behaviors. In doing so, he was strongly influenced by Darwin's theories about the role of instincts in motivating animal behavior. An **instinct** is an innate, automatic disposition to respond in a particular way when confronted with a specific stimulus; instincts produce behavior over which an animal has no control. McDougall argued that much of human behavior is also the result of innate forces, and he became one of the earliest proponents of an *instinct theory* of human motivation, which held that fixed, unlearned patterns of responses are often motivated by specific signals. But instinct as a primary theory of human motivation has faded because of three significant problems.

First, theorists began to propose the existence of more and more instincts. McDougall (1908) postulated eighteen human instincts, including self-assertion, reproduction (sex), pugnacity (quarrelsomeness), and gregariousness (socializing). Soon the list of proposed instincts became so long that critics argued that instincts had become meaningless labels that merely describe behavior. Saying that someone gambles because of a gambling instinct, watches television because of a television-watching instinct, and works hard because of a work instinct explains nothing. Second, there is no scientific way to disprove the existence of an instinct. If Mary wears a watch, someone might claim that she does so because of an instinct to wear a watch, to own gold, to know the correct time, or to look attractive. There is no clear-cut way to decide which of these possibilities should be ruled out. Third, many psychologists during the early 1900s pointed out that, far from being rigid and predetermined, much human behavior changes as a function of changing contingencies of reward and punishment. Instinct theory failed to accommodate the role of learning.

Instinct continues to play a role in psychology, however. For example, in later chapters, we will describe the influence wielded by Sigmund Freud's theory of psychoanalysis. He based his theory on the idea that human behavior is motivated primarily by the attempt to satisfy sexual and aggressive instincts. More broadly, the strong, enduring, and widespread tendency for humans to be aggressive, to seek sexual gratification, and to fiercely protect their young continues to suggest that some behaviors may be "wired-in" predispositions that cannot be suppressed or eliminated. Further, as we saw in Chapter 7, people, like animals, may be especially likely or "biologically prepared" to learn certain fears or aversions. However, behavioral predispositions are subject to modification by learning; civilization controls and shapes "wired-in" human tendencies. In short, instincts play a far less significant role in human motivation than McDougall suggested. However, sometimes they intensify or moderate behavior based on other sources of motivation and thus cannot be entirely ignored.

Drive Theory

The shortcomings of instinct theory eventually led to the drive theory of motivation. Like instinct theory, drive theory emphasizes the role of biological factors, but it is based on the concept of homeostasis. **Homeostasis** is the tendency for animals and humans to keep their physiological systems at a steady level, or *equilibrium,* by constantly adjusting themselves in response to change. We described a version of this concept in Chapter 3 when we discussed the feedback loops that allow smooth bodily movements and keep various hormones at desirable levels.

According to **drive theory,** much motivation arises from imbalances in homeostasis. When an imbalance occurs, it creates a **need**—a biological requirement for well-being. This need, in turn, creates a **drive**—a psychological state of arousal that prompts the organism to take action to restore the balance and, in the process, to reduce the drive (Hull, 1943). For example, if you have had no water for some time, the chemical balance of your body fluids is disturbed, creating a biological need for water. The psychological consequence of this need is a drive—thirst—that motivates you to find and drink water. After drinking, the need for water is satisfied, and the drive to drink is reduced. In other words, drives push people to satisfy needs, thus leading to drive reduction and a return to homeostasis (see Figure 11.2, p. 410).

Drive theory incorporates the influence of learning by distinguishing between primary and secondary drives. **Primary drives** are those that arise from basic biological needs, such as the need for food or water. (You may recall from the learning chapter that food, water, and other things that satisfy

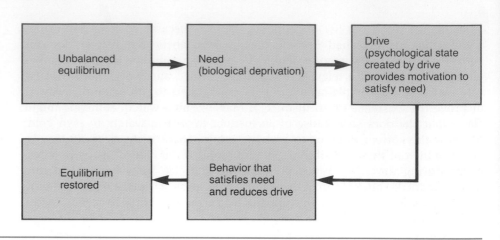

Figure 11.2
Drive Theory and Homeostasis
An analogy is often drawn between internal homeostatic mechanisms, such as body temperature regulation or other states of equilibrium, and a thermostat. If the temperature in a house drops below the desired thermostat setting, the heat comes on and brings the temperature up to some preset level, achieving homeostasis. When the temperature reaches or exceeds the preset point, the furnace shuts off.

Figure 11.3
Curiosity
This monkey learned to perform a complicated task simply in order to look at a moving electric train.
(Photo by Fred Sponholtz.)

primary drives are known as *primary reinforcers.*) Neither basic biological needs nor the primary drives to satisfy them require any learning (Hull, 1951). But, through classical conditioning or other learning mechanisms, people can acquire other drives. These learned drives are known as **secondary drives.** (Here, too, is a link with learning principles; we saw in the learning chapter that neutral stimuli can, through association with primary reinforcers, become learned, or secondary, reinforcers.) Once a secondary drive is learned, it motivates people to act *as if* they have an unmet basic need.

For example, coins, paper money, and checks cannot themselves satisfy any primary drive, but through classical and operant conditioning, modeling, and cognition, people learn that money can buy food, water, housing, and other primary reinforcers. As having money becomes associated with the satisfaction of primary drives, it becomes a learned, or secondary, drive. Having too little money (a situation most people feel they are in most of the time) thus motivates a wide variety of behaviors, from hard work to thievery, designed to obtain more funds. Similarly, people have a primary drive to avoid pain. If, as noted in Chapter 7, they associate dogs or the dentist's office with pain, they may develop a *phobia,* a secondary drive to avoid those stimuli.

Thanks in part to the concept of secondary drives, drive theory was able to account for far more behavior than was instinct theory. Still, drive theory has lost much of its influence, primarily because it does not appear capable of adequately explaining certain aspects of behavior. Particularly puzzling are behaviors in which humans and animals go to great lengths to do things that do not obviously reduce any primary or secondary drive.

Consider curiosity. Animals frequently explore and manipulate what is around them, even though such activities do not lead to drive reduction. When new objects are placed in most animals' environments, they smell them, touch them, and manipulate them in countless ways. Rats will carefully explore every inch of a maze they have never seen, but the time they spend investigating a second maze depends on how similar it is to the first. If it is identical, little additional exploration occurs; but if its appearance, smell, or layout is different, the animal will again cover every nook and cranny (Montgomery, 1953). Monkeys are actually willing to "pay" for the opportunity to satisfy their curiosity (Bolles, 1975), as Figure 11.3 demonstrates. Even rats will exert an extraordinary effort simply to enter a new environment, especially if it is complex and full of novel objects (Berlyne, 1960; Dember, Earl & Paradise, 1957; Myers & Miller, 1954).

People are no less curious. Most find it difficult to resist checking out anything that is new or unusual. They will go to the new mall, read the newspaper, and travel around the world just to see what there is to see. Sometimes this creates problems, as when curious crowds prevent rescue workers from reaching a fire scene.

Other human behaviors are equally difficult to explain through drive reduction. People go out of their way to ride roller coasters, climb mountains, go to horror movies (even in blizzards), and do countless other things that, like curiosity-motivated behaviors, fail to reduce any known drive (Csik-szentmihalyi, 1975; Deci, 1980). Quite the opposite. These behaviors appear to *increase* people's levels of activation, or arousal. The fact that people are sometimes motivated to reduce arousal through drive reduction and sometimes seek to increase it (Smith & Dorfman, 1975) led to theories tying motivation to the regulation of arousal.

Arousal Theory

Most theorists think of **arousal** as a general level of activation reflected in the state of several physiological systems (Geen, Beatty & Arkin, 1984; Pribram & McGuiness, 1975). Thus, your level of arousal at any given moment can be measured by electrical activity in the brain, by heart action, by muscle tension, and by the state of many other organ systems (Petri, 1986). Normally, arousal is lowest during deep, quiet sleep and highest during periods of panic or extreme excitement. Arousal is increased by the presence of such biological drives as hunger or thirst. It is also elevated by very intense stimuli (bright lights or loud noises, for example), by unexpected or novel events, and by caffeine and other stimulant drugs.

Arousal theories of motivation suggest that people are motivated to behave in ways that maintain what is, for them, an *optimal level* of arousal (Fiske & Maddi, 1961; Hebb, 1955). Research suggests that people perform best, and often feel best, when arousal is moderate. The general relationship between efficiency of performance and level of arousal is depicted in Figure 11.4. Overarousal can be particularly detrimental to performance. Reports from the Korean War, for example, indicated that overarousal during combat caused up to 25 percent of U.S. soldiers' being "frozen" and unable to fire

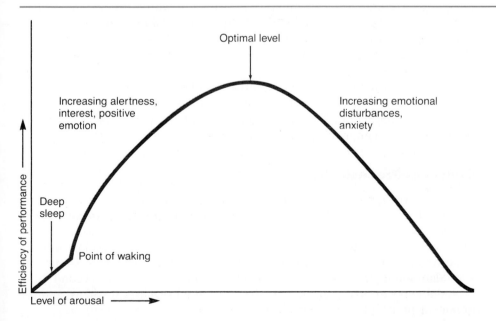

Figure 11.4
The Arousal-Performance Relationship
Note that performance is very poor when arousal is very low or very high and that it is best when arousal is at some intermediate level. When a person is nearly asleep, it is difficult to process information efficiently, or organize verbal or physical responses. As described in the chapters on perception and thought, overexcitement can also interfere with attention, perception, thinking, and the smooth coordination of physical actions. In general, the optimal level of performance comes at a lower level of arousal on difficult or complex tasks and at a higher level of arousal on easy tasks.
(From D. Hebb, "Drives and the CNS," *Psychological Review, 62,* 243–253, 1955. Copyright © 1955 by the American Psychological Association.)

People who characteristically enjoy high levels of arousal tend to be more likely to smoke, drink alcohol, engage in frequent sexual activity, listen to loud music, eat spicy foods, and do things that are novel and risky (Farley, 1986; Zuckerman, 1979). Those with a lower optimal arousal level tend to behave in ways that involve less intense stimulation and risk taking. Most of these differences in optimal arousal have a strong biological basis and help create each individual's personality.

their weapons (Hebb, 1955). The negative effects of overarousal are particularly strong on complex mental tasks. Overarousal may cause students to perform far below their potential on tests. Excessive arousal also plays a role in a variety of psychological and physical disorders discussed in the chapter on stress.

In general, people are motivated to increase their arousal level when it is too low and to decrease it when it is too high. They seek excitement when they are bored and relaxation when they have had too much excitement. After listening to lectures in the morning and studying all afternoon, for example, you might feel the urge to see an exciting movie that evening. However, an evening of quiet relaxation might seem ideal if your day was spent playing baseball, going to a rock concert, and helping a friend move. If you do not agree with this, it may be because you have a very high optimal level of arousal. Indeed, people differ considerably in the amount of arousal at which they are at their personal "peak" (Zuckerman, 1984).

Historically, arousal theory has centered on accounting for people's preferences for various activities and on how their performance on various tasks changes as a function of arousal. However, arousal theory may also hold the key to better understanding the relationship between motivation and emotion. As we will see in Chapter 12, high degrees of arousal are present during emotional episodes, and emotionally aroused people are intensely motivated. The reciprocal influence of motivation and emotion is an issue that theorists in both areas are currently working to understand (Petri, 1986).

Incentive Theory

Instinct, drive, and arousal theories of motivation all have one thing in common: they focus on internal processes that push people to behave in certain ways. Incentive theory, in contrast, emphasizes that environmental stimuli may motivate behavior by pulling people toward them. According to **incentive theory,** behavior is goal-directed; actions are directed toward attaining desirable stimuli, or *positive incentives,* and avoiding unwanted *negative incentives.*

The specific nature of positive and negative incentives varies widely from one person to another. The prospect of free tickets to see a movie about the life of Mozart might motivate an adult to study but would probably have little effect in prompting a retarded child to do so. The value of an incentive can also change over time and situations. For example, food is a more motivating incentive when you are hungry than when you are satiated (Logue, 1986; Revusky, 1967).

Along with arousal theory, incentive theory helps explain why people play chess, ride roller coasters, and engage in other activities that do not involve drive reduction. The mental and physical stimulation associated with these activities is enough to pull people toward them, at least for a while.

Opponent-Process Theory

Both the changing value of incentives and the regulation of arousal are combined in an approach to motivation called **opponent-process theory** (Solomon, 1980; Solomon & Corbit, 1974). This theory is based on two assumptions. First, any reaction to a stimulus is automatically followed by an opposite reaction, called the *opponent process.* For example, being startled by a sudden sound is typically followed by relaxation and relief. Second, after repeated exposure to the same stimulus, the initial reaction weakens, and the opponent process becomes stronger.

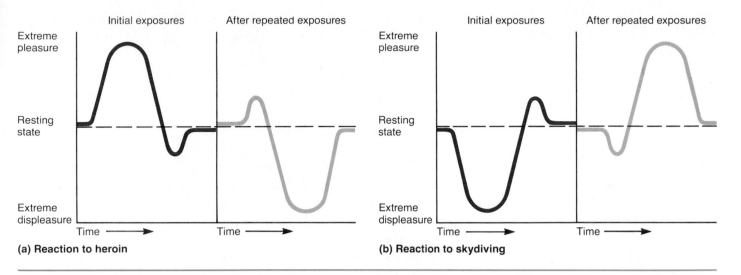

(a) Reaction to heroin

(b) Reaction to skydiving

Figure 11.5
Opponent Processes
Panel A shows how experiences of pleasure and displeasure change over time as a person continues to use heroin. Panel B shows the sequence of skydivers' emotional reactions to their sport. During the first few jumps, most novices are terrified. Once safely on the ground, however, they feel a certain amount of pleasure and relief. After repeated jumps, the initial terror becomes mild anxiety, and the pleasurable reaction becomes an intense euphoria that lasts longer with practice. According to Solomon (1980), people can become so motivated to repeat experiences like this that it becomes a special type of addiction.
(R. L. Solomon & J. D. Corbit, "An Opponent-Process Theory of Motivation. I. Temporal Dynamics of Affect," *Psychological Review, 81,* 119–145, 1974. Copyright © 1974 by the American Psychological Association. Adapted by permission of the publisher and author.)

Opponent-process theory uses both assumptions to account for drug addiction. As Figure 11.5 shows, the first several exposures to heroin produce an intensely pleasurable rush, followed by a reduction in pleasure and a mild, unpleasant feeling of withdrawal associated with a craving for another dose. After continued drug use, however, the initial reaction becomes less intense, and the withdrawal reaction occurs more quickly, becomes more intense, and lasts longer. In fact, as people become addicted, withdrawal becomes so aversive that they are motivated to use the drug again, not so much for what is left of the pleasure, but to avoid the discomfort of *not* using it.

Opponent-process theory is especially useful for understanding changes in affective states and explaining patterns of behavior in which people appear motivated to put themselves in danger through such activities as skydiving.

Maslow's Hierarchy

At any time, many motives might guide your behavior. What determines which ones will? Abraham Maslow (1970) proposed a theory that addresses this question. He suggested that five basic classes of needs or motives influence human behavior. These motives are organized in a hierarchy, as illustrated in Figure 11.6 (p. 414). According to Maslow, motives at the lowest level of the hierarchy must be at least partially satisfied before people can be motivated by higher-level motives.

From the bottom to the top of the hierarchy, the five levels of motives, according to Maslow, are:

1. *Biological, or physiological* These motives include the need for food, water, oxygen, activity, and sleep.

2. *Safety* Being cared for as a child and having a secure source of income and a place to live as an adult are examples of safety needs. Many people spend most of their lives in an attempt to satisfy needs at this level.

3. *Belongingness and love* *Belongingness* is integration into various kinds of social groups, such as clubs and other formal social organizations. By *love* Maslow meant affectionate relationships with others. Some of these relationships may have a sexual component; ideally, all of them are based on mutual respect, admiration, and trust.

4. *Esteem* An honest, fundamental respect for a person as a useful, honorable human being constitutes esteem. Esteem brings feelings of competence and confidence and a sense of achievement and individuality. The

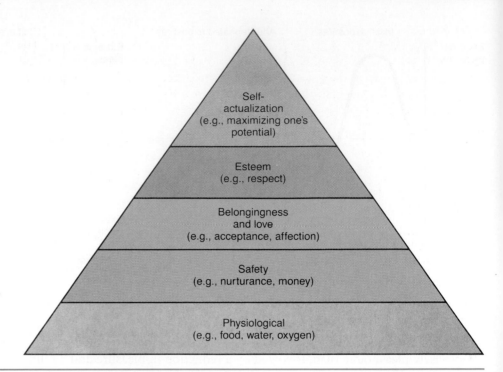

Figure 11.6
Maslow's Hierarchy of Motives
*According to Maslow, motives are orga-
nized in a hierarchy in which motives at
lower levels take precedence over those at
higher levels. Thus, motives at lower levels
must be at least partly satisfied before those
above them can significantly influence an
individual's behavior.*
(Adapted from A. H. Maslow (1943), A theory of
human motivation, *Psychological Review, 50,*
370–396.)

effort to meet esteem needs can take infinitely varied forms. Some people
pursue esteem through their careers; others through their relationships with
family, friends, or the larger community.

5. *Self-actualization*   When people are motivated not so much by unmet
needs as by the desire to become all they are capable of, then they are seeking
self-actualization. This means, for example, exploring and enhancing relationships with others, following leisure-time interests for pure pleasure rather
than for status or esteem, and being concerned with issues and problems
affecting all people, not just oneself. Maslow viewed self-actualizing motives
as the essence of mental health.

Although Maslow saw self-actualization as a motive inherent in all people
that pushes them to the limits of their potential, he admitted that very few
people spend much time or effort doing so. Only the rare individual, such as
Gandhi or Martin Luther King, approaches full self-actualization. Why does
self-actualization apparently motivate so few people? Maslow's hierarchy
suggests one possible reason. Most people are so oriented toward lower-level
motives that they seldom concern themselves with self-actualization. Culturally
reinforced sex roles are another factor inhibiting self-actualization. In American
society, for example, women often feel constrained about expressing a desire
for authority and power; men frequently find it difficult to display tenderness,
fear, dependency, or other feelings stereotyped as unmanly. American society's
emphasis on esteem also inhibits self-actualization. Accordingly, many people
spend their lives motivated by the desire to acquire more things, to show that
they are somehow better than others.

One weakness of Maslow's system is that it is too simplistic. People do
not always act according to his hierarchy; even when lower-level needs are
unmet, some people continue to be motivated by higher levels in the hierarchy.
Examples of the inversion of the traditional motivational hierarchy abound in
the history of political and moral causes. In 1981, for example, Bobby Sand,
Kieran Doherty, and seven other imprisoned men starved themselves to death
to protest continued British rule over Northern Ireland. Nevertheless, Maslow's

classification is useful for organizing discussions of human motivation. Most researchers agree that his system includes the basic human motives. His hierarchy provides an organized description of the basic sources of motivation referred to in other theories. And it appears that, *in general,* motives lower in Maslow's hierarchy do take precedence over those higher in the hierarchy. For example, people deprived of food may become completely dominated by it (Keys et al., 1950). In the following sections, we use Maslow's classification as our framework for discussing in detail some of the motives that are best understood and have generated the most empirical research.

BIOLOGICAL MOTIVES

Generally speaking, biological needs are the most basic and powerful of all motives. When people can routinely satisfy their biological needs, as most Americans can, they may remain unaware of the power of those needs unless a disaster or accident refocuses their attention on getting enough food, water, or air to survive. In this section, we consider three biological motives: hunger, thirst, and sex.

Hunger

Hunger is deceptively simple; people get hungry when they do not eat. But once we try to specify what causes hunger or what determines whether people eat and when they stop eating, even this very basic motive becomes complicated. Here we focus on the biological processes involved in hunger and eating, including the physical changes that make people experience hunger and the factors that start and stop eating.

The role of stomach cues The stomach seems a logical place to look for mechanisms that control hunger and eating. After all, people often get "hunger pangs" in the stomach when they are hungry and complain of having a "full stomach" after eating a large meal. To study the role of the stomach, physiologist Walter Cannon arranged for a subject to swallow a deflated balloon. Then the balloon was inflated and attached by a tube to a machine that measured the pressure that stomach contractions exerted against the balloon. The subject reported strong hunger pangs when the contractions were strong and few pangs when the contractions were weak or absent (Cannon & Washburn, 1912). These results supported the idea that hunger pangs are related to stomach movements, but they did not clarify what caused hunger itself.

When other researchers placed a large amount of dry material with no nutritional value directly into dogs' stomachs, the animals ate very little. Some stopped eating completely, even though nutritious food was easily available (Janowitz & Grossman, 1949, 1951). These experiments suggested that the stomach might control the hunger motive; but hunger, it turns out, is not that simple (Quartermain et al., 1971). For example, people who have had their stomachs removed because of illness still experience hunger pangs when they do not eat and still eat normal amounts of food (Janowitz, 1967). These and other studies suggest that hunger and the regulation of eating must stem from somewhere other than the stomach alone.

The role of taste cues There is another obvious candidate in the search for mechanisms that might control eating: the taste of food. Many experiments have demonstrated that taste does have an important influence on eating. For example, when one group of animals was offered just one type of food, while another group was offered a succession of distinctly different-tasting foods, the group receiving the varied menu ate nearly four times more than the one-food animals. As each new food was introduced, the animals began to eat voraciously, regardless of how much they had already eaten (LeMagnen, 1971; Peck, 1978). Similar experiments with humans lead to essentially the same conclusion (Cabanac, 1971). All things being equal, people consume more food during a multicourse meal than when only one type of food is served. This is due in part to the fact that the taste of a given food becomes less and less enjoyable as more of it is eaten (Woody et al., 1981).

Is taste, then, the controller of hunger and eating? If it were, animals without the ability to taste would not know when to stop eating. But somehow they do (Jordan, 1969; Snowdon, 1969). Similarly, when intravenous feeding prevents people from tasting their nutrients, they eat very little by mouth when allowed to do so and thus maintain a roughly constant body weight (Deutsch, Young & Kalogeris, 1978). In other words, though taste cues have some influence over eating, they do not appear to be the main determinant.

The role of the brain   Other research has shown that the brain is central to both hunger and the regulation of eating. Research on the role of the brain has focused on the hypothalamus, a structure in the forebrain that we described in the chapter on biological psychology. Two regions of the hypothalamus in particular have been studied: the **lateral area** and the **ventromedial nucleus,** which are indicated in Figure 11.7.

When fibers in the lateral area of the hypothalamus are *destroyed,* rats stop eating almost entirely. Most resume eating eventually, but they consume only small amounts of their most preferred foods and maintain a much-reduced weight (Keesey & Powley, 1975). In contrast, if the lateral hypothalamus is electrically *stimulated,* one result is that the rats begin to eat vast quantities, even if they have just consumed enough food to have stopped eating. In short, the lateral area of the hypothalamus seems to act as a "start-eating" center. When stimulated, it causes eating; when it is destroyed, the tendency to start eating is destroyed as well.

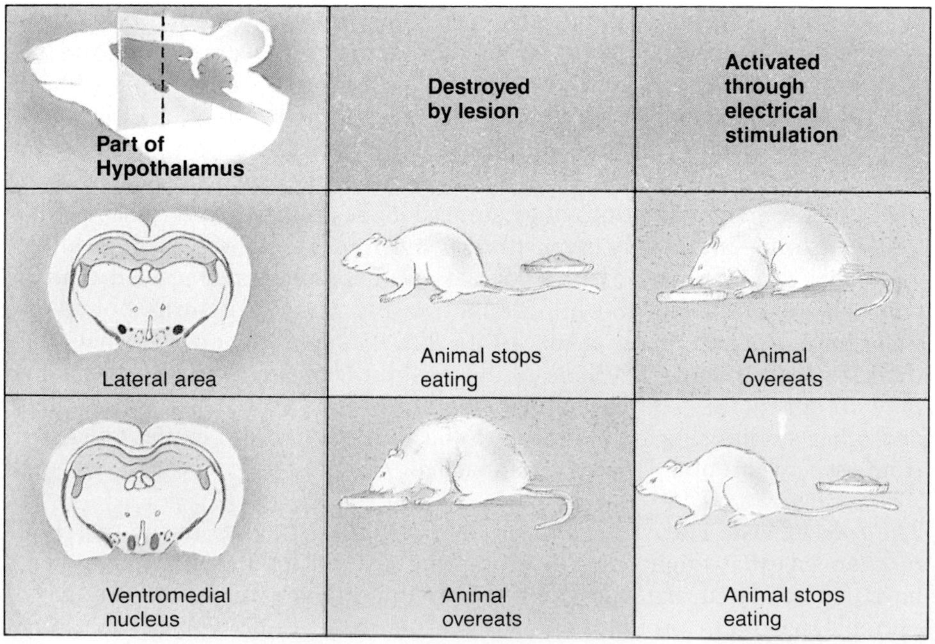

Figure 11.7
The Hypothalamus and Hunger
Studies of the hypothalamus have concentrated on either stimulating or destroying fibers passing through the lateral area and the ventromedial nucleus. Here are some of the results of this research.

The story is the opposite for the ventromedial nucleus. If surgery *destroys* fibers in a rat's ventromedial nucleus, the animal will eat far more than usual, increasing its weight up to threefold. Then the rat begins to eat enough food to maintain itself at the higher weight it has reached (Teitelbaum, 1961). If the ventromedial nucleus is electrically *stimulated,* the rat stops eating. Thus, it appears that the ventromedial nucleus is a "stop-eating" center. Stimulate it and animals stop eating; destroy it and their tendency to stop eating is disrupted. Other motivated behaviors are also affected by the lateral and ventromedial areas, so designating these areas as "hunger" and "satiety" areas is an oversimplification.

Still, some theories of hunger and the regulation of eating rely heavily on studies of the hypothalamus. For example, the **set-point concept** suggests that a homeostatic mechanism in the brain establishes a level, or set point, based on body weight, or some related metabolic signal, much as a thermostat sets temperature (Keesey & Powley, 1975; Nisbett, 1972; Powley & Keesey, 1970). This view suggests that normal animals eat until their set point is reached, then stop until their brain senses a drop in desirable intake, at which time they eat again. Destruction or stimulation of the lateral or ventromedial areas may act to alter the established set point. Thus, when animals with ventromedial damage eat more and maintain themselves at a higher weight, it may be because their set points have been dramatically raised. Similarly, damage to the lateral hypothalamus may lower the set point, causing far less eating and maintenance of a lower weight.

Following surgical destruction of its ventromedial nucleus, this rat ate enough to triple its body weight. Interestingly, such animals become picky eaters, choosing only foods that taste good and ignoring all others (Teitelbaum, 1957).

Signals for hunger   How does the brain "know" when you should eat and when you should stop? It appears to gather its cues by constantly monitoring the contents of the blood. This was established years ago when researchers deprived rats of food for long periods of time and injected some of the deprived rats with the blood of rats that had just eaten. When finally given access to food, the injected rats ate very little, if anything (Davis et al., 1969). Apparently, these hungry animals' brains "read" something in the satiated animals' blood that told them there was little need to eat. Exactly what the brain "reads" in the blood is not fully understood, but the level of glucose (sugar) is part of the story. When the level of blood sugar drops, eating increases dramatically (Friedman & Stricker, 1976; Mogenson, 1976). When large doses of glucose are injected into the blood of a food-deprived animal, it refuses to eat.

The suppression of eating after glucose injections is particularly strong when the injection is given in a vein that provides blood to the liver. Some researchers have suggested that the liver plays an important intermediary role in hunger and eating, by receiving information about the blood and then passing that information on to the brain through nerve connections (Russek, 1971). Even when these connections are severed, however, the brain still manages to regulate eating in relation to blood sugar. Thus, it appears that the brain directly monitors the blood passing through it (Granneman & Friedman, 1980).

Whatever their exact nature, the signals that prompt a person or animal to start eating are probably different from those that cause eating to stop. One possible "stop-eating" signal is cholecystokinin, or CCK. During a meal, CCK is released from the gut and from neurons in the hypothalamus (Schick et al., 1986). When CCK is injected into animals' brains, they not only stop eating but also show other signs of being satiated, such as grooming and sleeping.

Figure 11.8 (p. 418) summarizes the biological processes contributing to hunger and the regulation of eating. Notice, however, that these biological processes do not by themselves explain when animals or people start or stop eating. For example, animals come to associate calorie-rich meals with satiety,

Biological factors　　　　　　　　　　　　　　　Psychological and social factors

| Activity of hypothalamic areas |
| Metabolic rate |
| Number and size of fat cells |
| Characteristic set-point |
| Blood-sugar level |
| CCK |

Hunger and the regulation of eating

| Family customs about eating |
| Conditioned cues for eating |
| Conditioned satiation |
| Learned self–control of eating |
| Stress |

Figure 11.8
Some Important Factors Influencing Hunger and the Regulation of Eating
Notice that these factors are numerous and represent biological, psychological, and social variables. Adding to the complexity of the hunger motive is the fact that these factors can all exert their sometimes opposing influences simultaneously.

and they stop eating sooner after a high-calorie meal than when eating a lower-calorie meal. In other words, satiation and the termination of eating also depend in part on learning, in this case on conditioned satiation. Similarly, eating can be triggered, not by a drop in blood sugar, but by the sight of something appetizing. After stuffing yourself at Thanksgiving dinner, you usually recover your appetite long enough for dessert. In fact, even the biological need to eat can be modified by cognitive, social, and emotional factors. On hearing of a death in the family, for example, a hungry person may not feel like eating. The role of such nonbiological factors in hunger and eating has been of special interest to researchers studying eating disorders.

HIGHLIGHT

Eating Disorders

For reasons that are not always clear, the regulation of food intake sometimes goes awry, resulting in eating disorders. The most common and health-threatening of these are obesity (severe overeating), anorexia nervosa (drastic undereating), and bulimia (overeating followed by self-induced vomiting).

Obesity It has been estimated that about 12 percent of Americans between the ages of fourteen and sixty-one display **obesity,** a condition of severe overweight, often by as much as one hundred pounds (Stewart & Brook, 1983). Obesity threatens the health of millions of Americans, often contributing to diabetes, high blood pressure, and increased risk of heart attack (Wilson, 1984).

In most cases, obesity results when someone consumes more calories than the body can metabolize, or burn up; obese people usually eat more than those of normal weight. Almost like rats with damage to the ventromedial nucleus, they are also finicky eaters; they eat larger-than-average amounts of foods they like and less-than-average amounts of less-preferred foods (Peck, 1978). Obese people are also less willing than those of normal weight to expend effort to obtain food. For example, one study found that obese people will eat more shelled nuts than will people of normal weight, but that obese people will eat *less* than normal people if they must remove the shells themselves (Schachter & Friedman, 1974).

It has long been thought that one reason why obese people eat so much is that they have a higher-than-average sensitivity to environmental cues, including the sight, smell, and taste of food (Rodin, 1973; Schachter, 1971; Schachter & Rodin, 1974). This view suggests that a person of normal weight is less likely than an obese person to notice the goodies in a bakery window. But there is now some question about whether obese people are actually more sensitive to their environments (Rodin, 1980) and, even if they are, whether this sensitivity can fully account for obesity. For example, not all people who eat a lot become obese. Why?

Several physiological characteristics may make certain people prone to obesity. First, some research suggests that certain body types (for example, short limbs and barrel chests) predispose people to obesity (Mayer, 1975). Second, other investigators have found that the tendency to accumulate fat stems from the presence of more and larger fat cells in obese individuals than in normal-weight people, especially if they were overweight in childhood (Hirsch & Knittle, 1970; Knittle et al., 1979). Third, obese people may also have a higher set point for body weight and therefore feel hungry more often than other people (Keesey, 1980; Nisbett, 1972). These higher set points may be the joint result of genetics and early, even prenatal, nutrition that may have created particularly large and numerous fat cells (Foreyt & Kondo, 1984).

Basic differences in the rate at which people metabolize food may also play a role in obesity. The body maintains a set point for weight by changing both food intake and energy output (Keesey & Powley, 1986). If intake is lowered, the metabolic rate also drops, thus conserving energy and curbing weight loss. (This is one reason why it can be so frustrating and ultimately counterproductive to try losing weight through diet plans that focus on drastically reduced food intake.) Increasing physical activity is an important adjunct to gradual and permanent weight loss, because it burns calories without altering the metabolic rate (Donahoe et al., 1984). When obese people reduce to a normal weight, their metabolic rate tends to drop below a normal level. As a result, they begin to gain weight again even if they eat an amount that would maintain a constant weight in a normal person. These facts suggest that long-term overeating can raise set points for weight (Keesey & Powley, 1986; Kolata, 1985).

Among the psychological factors associated with obesity may be a failure to develop conditioned satiety that is strong enough to prevent overeating (Booth, 1980). The physical and psychological stressors discussed in Chapter 13 may also contribute to obesity. Many people tend to eat more when under stress; this reaction may be particularly extreme among those who are obese (Herman & Polivy, 1975; McKenna, 1972).

Anorexia nervosa   Even more perplexing than obesity is **anorexia nervosa,** a very different eating disorder characterized by self-starvation and dramatic weight loss. Some anorexics are obsessed with food and its preparation but eat almost nothing. The self-starvation of anorexics creates serious, often irreversible, physical damage. Between 4 and 30 percent of these people actually starve themselves to death (Eisner et al., 1985; Hsu, 1980). Occurring in females about 95 percent of the time, the incidence of anorexia has increased greatly in the last few decades, affecting as many as 1 percent of American women between the ages of fifteen and thirty (Gilbert & DeBlassie, 1984).

The causes of anorexia are not yet known. It has been speculated that anorexics have an abnormally low set point or some physiological abnormality (Gwirtsman & Germer, 1981), but there is not much evidence for this view (Bemis, 1978). For one thing, no specific abnormalities have been found in the hypothalamus or elsewhere in the brains of anorexics. Further, anorexics often report strong hunger yet still refuse to eat. Psychological factors that might contribute to the problem include America's apparent obsession with thinness and young people's concern with appearing attractive. In other words,

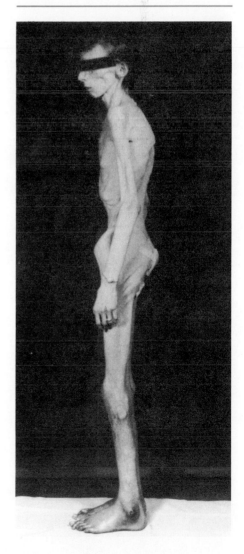

Some anorexics literally starve themselves to death. This woman weighed only forty-seven pounds when she began a treatment program that saved her life.

anorexics appear to develop a fear of being fat, which they take to dangerous extremes (Achenbach, 1982). Many anorexics continue to view themselves as too fat or misshapen even as they are wasting away (Davis, 1986).

Drugs, hospitalization, and psychotherapy are all used to treat anorexia. In about 70 percent of cases, some combination of treatment and the passage of time brings recovery and maintenance of normal weight (Hsu, 1980).

Bulimia   About half of all anorexics display another eating disorder: bulimia (Casper et al., 1980). **Bulimia** involves eating massive quantities of food (say, several boxes of cookies, a loaf of bread, a half gallon of ice cream, and a bucket of fried chicken) and then eliminating the food by self-induced vomiting or strong laxatives (Garfinkel, Moldofsky & Garner, 1980). The frequency of these "binge-purge" episodes ranges from once a week to several times a day (Fairburn, 1981; Pyle, Mitchell & Eckert, 1981). Like anorexics, bulimics are usually female; their eating problems usually begin when they are about fifteen years old; and they are obsessed with being slender. However, bulimia and anorexia are separate disorders. For one thing, most bulimics maintain a reasonably normal weight.

Although some bulimics attempt suicide, most do not suffer life-threatening consequences of their disorder (Fairburn, 1981; Schlesier-Stroop, 1984). There *are* consequences, however, including dehydration, nutritional imbalances, and intestinal damage. Many bulimics also develop raw throats from frequent vomiting and from the objects they insert to induce vomiting. More generally, their preoccupation with eating and with avoiding fatness prevents many bulimics from working productively (Herzog, 1982).

Informed guesses have placed the incidence of bulimia in the United States at about five million people. The exact figure is unknown, because shame and guilt keep some victims from reporting the problem. Unfortunately, little is known about the causes of the disorder or about effective treatment. Because bulimics are now seeking treatment in greater numbers, researchers will undoubtedly begin to learn more about the disorder. ■

Thirst

Every cell in the human body is surrounded by water. In fact, water accounts for 75 percent of total body weight. As water is lost in perspiration, urine, feces, and even breathing, it must be quickly replaced if the body is to function normally. You can live for weeks without food, but you would die after two or three days without water.

Intuitively, it might seem as if thirst and drinking are based on dryness and other cues in the mouth. But even if your mouth is dry, your thirst will be reduced if water is injected directly into your stomach (Montgomery, 1931). Moreover, people who are born without the salivary glands that keep the mouth moist still show normal drinking patterns (Steggerda, 1941). In fact, signals from the mouth have rather little to do with thirst. In thirst, as in hunger, the hypothalamus plays an important role. Surgical damage to the lateral nucleus inhibits drinking as well as eating (Blass & Epstein, 1971; Peck, 1973). Electrical stimulation of anterior parts of the hypothalamus in rats and other animals typically produces dramatic increases in drinking (Andersson & McCann, 1955). The brain receives information about the need for water through two mechanisms. One is sensitivity to events within body cells and the other is extracellular. These mechanisms provide information about the fluids in the body and the balance of salt and water in the cells. Imbalances prompt drinking; when drinking restores the normal volume of fluids and the normal salt-water balance inside and outside the body's cells, the thirst motive disappears.

First, consider the mechanism within cells that regulates thirst. If water deprivation, exercise, or other factors reduce the amount of water in the blood and other fluids outside the cells, these fluids become salty. Water within the cells then begins to seep out, a process that equalizes the salt balance on each side of the cell membrane but leaves the fluid within the cells too salty. This fact is detected by **osmoreceptor cells** in the hypothalamus and leads to feelings of thirst.

The second thirst mechanism depends on **volumetric receptors** in the heart and kidneys; they monitor the volume and pressure of blood and other fluids outside the cells (Carlson, 1980). Water deprivation, bleeding, or inadequate salt intake can produce a drop in the volume of blood or in blood pressure. For example, if fluids outside the cells are not as salty as the fluid within them, water from the blood enters the cells, equalizing the saltiness on each side of the cell membranes but reducing blood volume. When the amount of blood or the pressure against its vessels drops significantly, the volumetric receptors stimulate the kidneys to begin a process that releases a hormone called *angiotensin* into the bloodstream. When it reaches the brain, angiotensin stimulates a feeling of thirst (Ganong, 1984).

Sex

Unlike food and water, sex is not necessary for individual survival. A successful species, however, must have strong motivation for sex; if other motives were always more potent than sex, the species would die out.

For some species, sexual motivation, particularly the appropriate time for mating, appears to be controlled almost entirely by instinct (Crews & Moore, 1986). For example, one species of desert bird is not at all motivated for sexual behavior until the rainy season begins. Then, within ten minutes of the first rainfall, vigorous copulation occurs. In contrast, although the human species has a strong motivation for sex, this motivation is expressed in many ways, at varying times. Biology alone cannot explain human sexual behavior. Indeed, much of human sexual motivation stems from environmental stimuli (particularly from sexually attractive people) that act as incentives for sexual

Though no one has ever died from a lack of sex, it is a strong source of motivation for most people.

behavior. Further, human sexual relations typically occur between two individuals who have an emotional bond. As a result, it is often difficult to disentangle the purely sexual motivation from the motivation for emotional closeness.

In the following sections, we provide a brief description of sexual behavior, some discussion of several sources of human sexual motivation, and an overview of sexual problems. We focus on **heterosexual behavior,** or sexual activity between people of opposite sexes, and on sexual intercourse in married couples, because these are the most common forms of sexual activity in American society. The same basic facts and principles apply to unmarried couples, and the biological mechanisms are the same for homosexuals.

Describing sexual behavior Much of what we know about human sexual behavior has been obtained by surveys. Two of the earliest and most widely known surveys of human sexual behavior were published by Alfred Kinsey and his colleagues (Kinsey, Pomeroy & Martin, 1948; Kinsey et al., 1953). As we noted in Chapter 1, however, surveys do not always provide the most reliable data, especially if they do not contact a representative sample of people. Kinsey's work was immediately criticized because, among other things, his sample was far from random and representative; only white volunteers were included, for example (Hyman & Barmack, 1954; Terman, 1948). Nevertheless, because Kinsey's interviews covered many aspects of respondents' sex lives, desires, and fantasies, they provided a very important glimpse into human sexuality.

Another milestone occurred in 1966, when William Masters and Virginia Johnson published *Human Sexual Response.* They offered the first extensive report of laboratory research on human sexual behavior. Their book contained detailed descriptions of the physical and psychological responses of more than six hundred males and females as they received natural or artificial sexual stimulation. Figure 11.9 shows one result of their research. It depicts the **sexual response cycle,** which is the pattern of arousal during and after sexual activity (Masters & Johnson, 1966).

The areas of the body that produce sexual arousal when stimulated are called *erogenous zones.* Most people think of erogenous zones as the genitals, breasts, lips, thighs, neck, shoulders, and ears. There is great variety in what people find stimulating, however, and for the same person, the same stimulation can be arousing or annoying at different times. Oral-genital stimulation is a common component of sexual foreplay for many people and may even take the place of coitus during some sexual encounters. The frequency of intercourse varies greatly among couples, ranging from several times a week to a few times per month or even less (Hunt, 1974).

The biological basis of sexual motivation In humans, instinctual biological factors are less important in the regulation of sexual behavior than what people learn about how and when to express themselves sexually. Still, biological factors provide the raw material for sexual motivation, and anomalies or dysfunctions in sexual "equipment" can interfere with normal patterns of sexual motivation and behavior.

For sex, as for hunger and thirst, the brain, particularly the hypothalamus, plays a critical role. The hypothalamus controls the activity of the pituitary gland, which is located just under the hypothalamus. The pituitary gland controls the secretion of **luteinizing hormone (LH)** into the bloodstream. And LH, in turn, controls the rate at which the *gonads*—the ovaries in females and the testes in males—secrete masculine or feminine hormones. The sex hormones secreted into the bloodstream in turn act on the hypothalamus, as

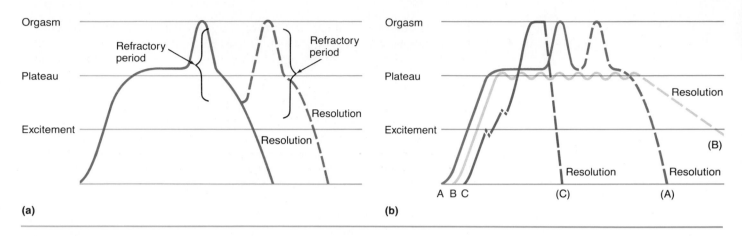

Figure 11.9
The Sexual Response Cycle
(a) Men show one primary pattern of sexual response, whereas (b) women display at least three different patterns from time to time (A, B, and C). The first, or excitement, *phase of the sexual response cycle occurs in response to some kind of sexually stimulating input, either from the environment or from one's own thoughts. If this stimulation continues, it leads to intensification of the excitement in the second, or* plateau, *phase. Sexual tension becomes extreme in this phase. If stimulation continues, the person reaches the third, or* orgasmic *phase, which, though lasting only a few seconds, provides an intensely pleasurable release of physical and psychological tension. The* resolution *phase follows, during which the person returns to a state of relaxation. At this point, men enter a* refractory period, *during which they are temporarily insensitive to sexual stimulation. Women are capable of immediately repeating the cycle if stimulation continues.*
(From *Human Sexual Response* by W. H. Masters and V. E. Johnson, 1966, p. 5. Adapted with permission of Little, Brown and Company.)

Figure 11.10 (p. 424) describes. The masculine hormones are called **androgens**; the principal androgen is **testosterone.** The feminine hormones are **estrogens** and **progestins**; the main ones are **estradiol** and **progesterone.** Actually each of these hormones circulates in the bloodstream of members of *both* sexes, but relatively more androgens circulate in men and relatively more estrogens and progestins circulate in women. Androgens affect sexual motivation in both sexes (Davidson, Kwan & Greenleaf, 1982; Sherwin, Gelfand & Brender 1985).

The sex hormones have both organizational and activational effects on sexuality. The *organizational effects* are those that determine the form of sexual behavior: male or female. These effects occur very early in life and are usually permanent. *Activational effects* occur during adulthood, when hormones temporarily change behavior or reproductive physiology. These changes appear soon after hormone levels increase and disappear soon after hormone levels drop.

Research on the organizational effects of hormones in animals has shown sexual behavior patterns to be established by the actions of androgens during development. For example, if a male animal fetus is exposed to androgens during development, its adult sexual behavior will be that of a normal male. If its testes are removed before the androgens have a chance to act, it will appear to be a female and will behave as one if exposed to the activational effects of estrogen and progesterone. Control of its pituitary gland by the hypothalamus will also follow the feminine pattern described in Figure 11.10. If an ovary is implanted in such a male, it will show cyclical hormonal changes, as in a female.

The activational effects of hormones are most easily seen in animals. But, even in animals, hormones do not rigidly determine behavior; they only change the likelihood that certain behaviors will occur. In humans, the

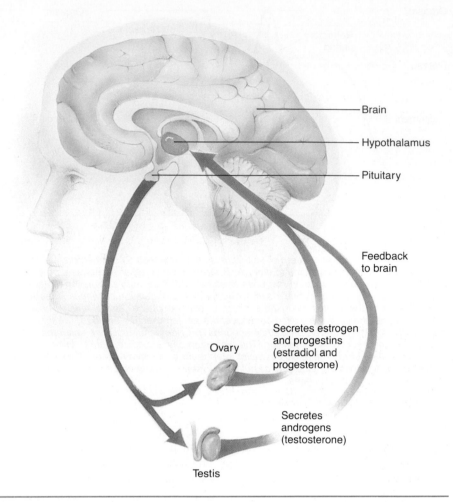

Figure 11.10
The Regulation of Sex Hormones
In males, high levels of testosterone reduce activity in the hypothalamus, which lowers LH secretion, which causes less testosterone to be secreted. This tends to keep the secretion of testosterone reasonably constant. In females, these feedback loops are more complex. High levels of estrogen increase hypothalamic activity, causing more LH to be secreted, which causes more estrogen to be secreted. At some point, the secretion of LH increases very rapidly, and a surge of hormone is released. This increased LH not only prompts the release of more estrogen but also causes the ovary to release an egg, or to ovulate.

activational effects of hormones are even less pronounced. People who have had their gonads removed for medical reasons do show a decline in sexual motivation and behavior, but there is great variability from one person to the next (Sherwin et al., 1985). Similarly, some people have decreased hormone levels as a result of chemical imbalances or surgical removal of the gonads. When they are treated with appropriate hormones, their sexual interest and behavior increase (Sherwin et al., 1985).

Activational effects of hormones are clearly seen in female animals, as cyclical changes in the levels of circulating sex hormones produce dramatic changes in sexual motivation. Women are also influenced by the changes in hormone levels that occur during the menstrual cycle. For example, there is increasing evidence that, on the average, women are more interested in sex and more likely to have intercourse at the middle of the menstrual cycle, when the levels of estrogen and androgen are relatively high.

Social and psychological influences on sexual motivation   Overlaying, and often overwhelming, the biological sources of human sexual motivation are social and psychological influences. These include what people learn about sex, how they come to feel about it, cultural backgrounds, the characteristics of available sex partners, and many other sources of information and stimulation. Some of the influential factors relate to interpersonal attraction in general, a topic we discuss in some detail in Chapter 17.

Attitudes about sex can be very important. People whose early experiences with sex involved abuse or other traumas may display unusually limited or overly expressive sexual behavior. And, as sexuality has become a more acceptable topic in the United States, members of both sexes, but especially women, have come to enjoy sex more and to expect more from it. In a survey in the 1920s, most husbands wanted more frequent sexual contact with their wives, whereas the wives wanted less (Davis, 1929). In a similar survey in the 1970s, only 2 percent of wives said that intercourse was too frequent, and 32 percent thought it was too infrequent (Bell & Bell, 1972). This trend is also evident among unmarried women, especially those involved in a serious relationship (Sherwin & Sherry, 1985).

Increasing experience with a partner can increase sexual motivation, but novelty can be enticing as well. The physical characteristics of a potential sex partner can also increase or decrease sexual interest, arousal, and activity. What makes someone sexually motivating? It depends on what is considered "sexy" in a person's culture and on what he or she has learned to find sexually arousing. Even time and fashion can change how people respond to sexual stimuli. Decades ago plumpness was viewed as sexually stimulating; today, "thin is in."

Fantasizing is another important nonbiological source of sexual arousal and motivation. Just over half of men and women report that they fantasize sometimes or always during intercourse (Sue, 1979). This is not surprising, since so much of sexual arousal is mental, rather than purely physical. Although the most common sexual fantasy involves an imaginary lover, the use of fantasy is generally not related to either sexual or marital problems. It is simply a way of enhancing arousal (Hariton & Singer, 1974).

Sexual orientation   Human sexual motivation is usually oriented toward members of the opposite sex, but it is sometimes **homosexual**—that is, focused on those of one's own sex. Several criteria may be used to define homosexuality. Defined in terms of behavior, homosexuality means engaging

Because of differing definitions of homosexuality, estimates of its prevalence vary widely. Hunt (1974) found that only 7 percent of males had had homosexual experiences during more than three years of their lives, and only 2 to 3 percent of males were predominantly or exclusively homosexual. Female homosexuality is somewhat less prevalent. Hunt's (1974) figures suggest that less than 2 percent of women are predominantly homosexual. Thus, homosexuality is not so widespread that it threatens the species with extinction; nor is it so rare as to be considered an extreme aberration.

in sexual activity with a partner of one's own sex. Defined by sexual attraction, it means being attracted to or aroused by members of the same sex. And defined by sexual identification, homosexuality means a self-acknowleged preference for members of one's own sex. These three components of homosexuality do not necessarily go together, and they do not exclude having sexual activities with the opposite sex. People who engage in activities with partners of both sexes are called **bisexual.**

HIGHLIGHT

Origins of Homosexuality

Animal studies have fostered the idea that some instances of male homosexuality arise from low levels of androgen during prenatal development. Two studies have reported that the pattern of pituitary hormone control in exclusively homosexual males is in some ways similar to that of females (Gladue et al., 1984). Further, studies of identical twins reared apart support the idea that the development of male homosexuality may be partly determined by genetic factors (Eckert et al., 1986; Ellis & Ames, 1987).

Nevertheless, there is little evidence for either a genetic or a hormonal cause in most cases of homosexuality. In neither male nor female homosexuals have levels of sex hormones been found to differ from those in heterosexuals. Furthermore, administering androgens to male homosexuals does not change their sexual orientation (although it may increase their sex drive). Likewise, there is little evidence that the organizational effects of hormones during development affect sexual orientation, at least not when genetic females are exposed to excessively high androgen levels.

If hormones alone do not account for homosexuality, what about family relationships? There is some retrospective evidence that, compared with the fathers of a control group of male heterosexuals, the fathers of male homosexuals were more likely to be rejecting or distant (Saghir & Robins, 1973; Siegelman, 1974). In one study, 39 percent of lesbians, compared with 5 percent of heterosexual women, had lost one or both parents due to death or divorce before the age of ten (Saghir & Robins, 1973). And, whereas 83 percent of heterosexual women reported having a close relationship with their mothers, only 23 percent of lesbian women reported such a relationship.

However, though some male and female homosexuals have had less-than-satisfactory relationships with the same-sex parent, many homosexuals have had very good relationships with both parents. These responses come from retrospective studies, in which recollections can be influenced by current attitudes and stereotypes. But to the extent that retrospective reports can be relied upon to capture without distortion the flavor of early family life, there appear to be no consistent differences between the family backgrounds of homosexuals and of heterosexuals (Bell & Weinberg, 1978).

There is some evidence that certain patterns of behavior in early childhood are associated with adult homosexuality in males. Especially where sex-role stereotypes are heavily emphasized, as in American culture, people who do not fit these stereotypes may be pressured into rejecting the male sex role. In one survey, 67 percent of male homosexuals, as opposed to 3 percent of heterosexual males, considered themselves to be effeminate during preadolescence (Saghir & Robins, 1973). These males reported what researchers call *gender nonconformity,* such as playing more with girls, patterns that got them called "sissies" by their male peers (Adams & Chioto, 1983; Bell, Weinberg & Hammersmith, 1983). Although those responses are retrospective, their validity is strengthened by longitudinal data showing that, of forty-four extremely effeminate boys studied from early childhood to young adulthood,

75 percent became bisexual or homosexual. Only one bisexual was identified in a comparison group of more masculine boys (Green, 1987). Lopsided as these figures are, there are still many homosexual males (25 percent in Green's study) who do not fit this developmental pattern.

In short, homosexuals are very diverse in their personalities and sexual patterns, and they do not share a common developmental pattern or family history. It would appear that a homosexual orientation, preference, or identity stems from the interaction of family, sociosexual, and biological factors, not from any single cause (Money, 1987). ∎

Sexual problems   Whatever one's sexual orientation, problems with sex sometimes arise. Known as **sexual dysfunctions,** these problems can involve sexual motivation, arousal, or orgasmic response.

Some problems with sexual motivation involve a level of desire that is lower than what a person (or his or her partner) feels is satisfactory or appropriate. Most often, low desire is associated with emotional problems, such as depression, or with other factors, such as anxiety. Treatment focuses on these problems rather than on low desire per se.

Problems of arousal respond more directly to therapy. For men, the most common arousal problem is *erectile dysfunction* (once known as *impotence*), which is the inability to gain or maintain an erection sufficient for intercourse. In women, arousal problems usually involve inadequate vaginal lubrication and inhibition of other aspects of the excitement phase of the sexual response cycle. Though such inhibition may not prevent intercourse, it can nevertheless significantly reduce sexual satisfaction.

Erectile dysfunction can arise from fatigue, general stress, or excessive use of alcohol or other drugs. Most men experience the problem at some point in their lives. However, if erectile difficulties occur consistently enough to interfere with sexual functioning and a partner's satisfaction, they are considered a sexual dysfunction. Traditionally, psychological causes such as anxiety were considered the source of 95 percent of cases of severe erectile dysfunction (Kaplan, 1974). But physical problems—including kidney disease, diabetes, and hypertension, as well as prescription drugs used for these and other disorders—may also be responsible. In fact, these organic factors may account for as many as one-third of the cases of erectile impotence (Shrom et al., 1979). Hormonal abnormalities may also be involved. When they are, hormonal therapies are effective (Spark, White & Connolly, 1980).

Infrequent orgasms or lack of orgasms are common problems in women. The number of women who have never had an orgasm has dropped from 17 percent in the Kinsey survey of 1953 to less than 10 percent in later surveys (Bell & Bell, 1972; Hunt, 1974). The percentage of women who have an orgasm "always or most of the time" has held steady at 60 to 70 percent. However, 73 percent of the women in one study reported that orgasm was not necessary to enjoy sex (Butler, 1976).

Some clinical reports indicate that women who have never had an orgasm tend to have had restrictive upbringings and to be religious, with conflicts about their sexuality (Geer et al., 1986). But some surveys find that women who describe themselves as "very religious" are *more* likely to have frequent orgasms. There is a consistent finding that nonorgasmic women are more depressive and more sensitive to criticism by others (Derogatis et al., 1981). Interestingly, partners of nonorgasmic women also tend to be depressive and lack self-confidence (Clement & Pfafflin, 1980). Treatment for women's orgasmic difficulties typically involves helping the client to explore the basis for her sexual inhibition, to relax about sex, and to enjoy sexual feelings as they occur.

The analogous problem in men, retarded ejaculation, is rare in youth and adulthood but can become a problem with advancing years. The more common problem in men is *premature ejaculation,* or ejaculating sooner than they or their partner would like. Men who seek help for this problem usually ejaculate within ten seconds of penetration or even before penetration. In one study of a nonclinical population, such "instant" orgasms were rare, but 36 percent of men reported ejaculating more quickly than desirable (Frank et al., 1978). Although men who experience premature ejaculation may have high levels of physiological arousability, usually there is a learned component to the problem. Characteristically, these men have had early sexual experiences that were "secret" encounters fraught with guilt and anxiety, during which rapid ejaculation was helpful (Masters & Johnson, 1970). Treatment usually entails first helping the client to reduce his concern over the timing of ejaculation and then setting up practice sessions, in which he and his partner work to gradually lengthen the amount and duration of sexual stimulation he can experience without reaching orgasm.

SAFETY MOTIVES

The desire to establish a reasonable degree of safety and predictability is an important motivation. Adults show this motive when they strive for a secure job, a place to live, and money and other material possessions. As Maslow suggested, a child's safety needs are satisfied through a stable environment, typically provided by the parents. As described in the chapter on human development, young children's search for safety may be particularly evident in a close attachment to the mother or other caregiver. Youngsters who are away from their mothers for prolonged periods (for example, during hospitalization) often become terrified and later cling to her, screaming at any hint that she might leave even for a moment. Observations like these suggest that the need to be physically and emotionally supported by a caregiver resembles a physiological drive like hunger or thirst. Yet children who grow up without such support do not die. Why is their motivation for the safety of attachment so strong?

One explanation focuses on the association, through classical conditioning or some other learning mechanism, of safety needs and physiological drives (Gewirtz, 1972; Sears, 1972). In other words, children may become fiercely attached to their mothers because it is the mother who provides the food and water vital to life. Experiments by Harry Harlow, however, suggest that motivation for safety may also have a source independent of this association.

Harlow (1958) separated newborn monkeys from their mothers and then reared the monkeys in cages containing two artificial mothers (see Figure 11.11). One was made of wire, but it had a rubber nipple from which the infant could obtain milk. This "mother" provided food but no physical comfort. The other mother substitute had no food nipple, but it was made of soft, comfortable terrycloth. If safety motivation were based entirely on the association of physical contact with food, the infants would be expected to prefer the wire mother. In fact, they spent most of their time with the terrycloth mother. And when they were frightened by a mechanical robot or an unfamiliar room, the infants immediately ran to their terrycloth mother and clung to her. Harlow concluded that the monkeys were motivated by the need for *contact comfort.* The terrycloth mother provided feelings of softness and cuddling, which were things the infants needed when their safety was in jeopardy.

Young children's search for safety may be particularly evident in a close attachment to the mother or other caregiver. To a lesser degree, teddy bears, "security blankets," and other cuddly objects sometimes become safety symbols as well.

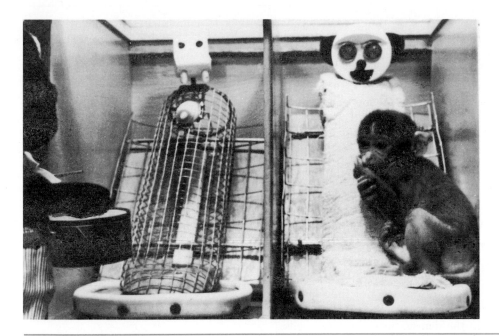

Figure 11.11
Wire and Terrycloth Mothers
Here are the two types of artificial mothers used in Harlow's research. Although baby monkeys received milk from the wire mother, they spent most of their time with the terrycloth version and would cling to it when frightened.
(Harlow Primate Laboratory, University of Wisconsin.)

What happens when safety needs are not met? Harlow raised monkeys isolated from all maternal, social, and other safety-related stimuli from birth. After a year of this isolation, they showed dramatic disturbances (see Figure 11.12). When visited by normally active, playful monkeys, they withdrew to a corner, huddling or rocking back and forth for hours. If one of the normal monkeys approached, those that had been isolated often bit themselves until left alone. These monkeys' problems continued into adulthood. Neither males nor females were able to develop appropriate sexual relationships. Though

Figure 11.12
Monkeys Raised in Isolation
Monkeys reared without any social contact develop a variety of disorders. (a) Many of them spend most of their time huddled in a corner of the cage. (b) One of these animals began to bite itself when a stranger approached.
(Harlow Primate Laboratory, University of Wisconsin.)

Motivation for belongingness sometimes becomes a desire to contact a national or global community, as illustrated by the success of such epic charitable efforts as Hands Across America, Live Aid and USA for Africa.

Figure 11.13
Parenta! Devotion
An early study examined parental devotion in rats by counting the number of electric shocks a female would tolerate in order to (1) have sex after being sexually deprived, (2) eat when very hungry, (3) drink when very thirsty, or (4) reach her distressed baby. It is easy to see that the strongest motivation was engendered by the sounds of a distressed infant.
(Adapted from *Animal Motivation: Experimental Studies on the Albino Rat*, by C. J. Warden, 1931. By permission of Columbia University Press.)

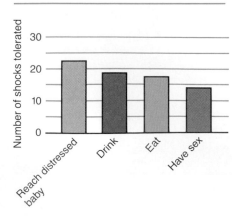

the males sometimes tried to mate with a female, they seldom got further than touching a potential partner. Isolated females quickly ran from any male who made a sexual advance. When some of the females were made pregnant through artificial insemination, their maternal behaviors were woefully inadequate. In most cases, these mothers totally ignored their infants. When the infants began to send distress signals, the mothers physically abused and sometimes even killed them. In short, it seems that when the safety needs of young monkeys are not met because they are socially isolated, the animals are permanently deficient, socially and emotionally.

Are there parallels here to human development? It would certainly be tempting to conclude that there are. In Chapters 1 and 2, for example, we noted evidence that social, emotional, and intellectual deficits are common among children raised in institutions that offer little warmth or other social contacts associated with safety needs (Dennis, 1973; Provence & Lipton, 1962). Some of these children's behavior resembles that of Harlow's monkeys: they may be withdrawn and terrified of others, often failing to respond to any social contact and resistant to physical contact. People do not die when safety needs are unmet, but they may develop social, emotional, and psychological problems. Many theories (discussed in later chapters) relate abnormal behavior to the deprivation of safety needs.

Still, it is important to recognize the limits of the analogy between Harlow's monkeys and human beings. For one thing, there is now considerable evidence that unfortunate early experiences, including unmet safety needs, may be less devastating and less permanent in humans than in lower animals (Clarke & Clarke, 1976; Kagan, 1984; Lerner, 1984). Also, the total isolation suffered by Harlow's monkeys has almost no parallel in human experience. They lost not only comfort and safety but also the opportunity to learn anything about social interaction and behavior.

In summary, it seems that motivation for safety and security may be as strong as physiological drives; it is not just a by-product of the reduction of a primary drive, such as hunger. Further, it appears that failure to satisfy safety motives, although not deadly, can have significant social and emotional consequences.

MOTIVES FOR BELONGINGNESS AND LOVE

Many people whose financial success amply provides for satisfaction of safety needs find themselves endlessly seeking love and a sense of belonging. Humans are notoriously social creatures; they seek to belong—to cliques of friends, to teams, to religious groups, and, perhaps most of all, to one another. The strength of this apparent need to belong is also reflected in the loyalty people display toward social, political, religious, and occupational groups. In this section, we consider two types of behavior—parenting and affiliation—that can satisfy motives for belongingness and love.

Parenting

Parental devotion to the care and protection of their children is one of the world's strongest forces. Infants' signals of discomfort or danger typically elicit an immediate helping response from the mother. Figure 11.13 shows the results of one study that examined the strength of this response in rats (Warden, 1931). Not all creatures, however, exhibit parental devotion. The treatment of offspring varies considerably from one species to another. Many

Parents' motivation to protect their children can be strong enough to overcome concern for personal safety, as when a mother or father dies in the attempt to save a child from danger. Some animals will also jeopardize their own lives in order to protect their young.

types of fish and reptiles, for example, do nothing to care for their numerous young. Most of these newborns soon die, leaving only a minority to preserve the species. Mammals have far fewer babies but provide much more intense care (Brazelton & Tronick, 1983). Typically, the mother feeds the young, keeps them warm, cleans them, protects them, and teaches them skills needed for survival. This period of dependency can last from months in animals like dogs, to years in monkeys, to decades in humans.

What creates a parenting motive so intense that in some species it can overcome a parent's motive to survive? No one knows for sure. Some instinct-oriented theorists believe that nurturing, in humans and animals, involves automatic responses to such signals as smiling or crying. Nurturance in response to distress signals certainly appears to be as automatic as the responses of animals to sign stimuli and releasers. A crying, lost child in a department store instantly attracts a crowd of concerned adults, for example. These theorists might suggest that parenting behaviors involve unlearned responses to sign stimuli generated by the young.

In some animals, parenting behavior is controlled to some extent by biological factors, especially hormones. In several studies, for example, when blood from a mother rat was injected into another rat, male or female, that rat immediately began to build a nest; lick, clean, and protect newborn rats; and even attempt to nurse them (Terkel & Rosenblatt, 1972). In monkeys and other higher animals, parenting behaviors appear to require some learning. These animals normally spend a great deal of time playing with their young, but as illustrated in research by Harlow and others, parenting behaviors do not develop automatically. Monkeys separated from their parents at an early age often fail to care for or play with their own offspring (Harlow, Harlow & Suomi, 1971; Rock, 1978).

Similarly, children who are neglected or abused by their parents may grow up to be neglectful or abusive of their own youngsters. A National Institute of Mental Health study estimated that 1.7 million children are hit or kicked by their parents each year and that as many as 750,000 are beaten severely enough to require medical care (Vander Zanden, 1981). Less than 10 percent of abusing parents manifest symptoms of severe mental disorder, but more than half of them were themselves abused as children (Gil, 1979). Thus, parenting appears to involve an interaction of innate and learned behaviors whose proportions vary from one species to another.

Affiliation

The tendency for people to affiliate with others may come simply from a need to feel part of a community or group or to feel loved. It may also reflect the fact that, as we have seen, people can help other people meet needs for safety. In fact, there are many things that people can do only with others.

For one thing, people provide a source of *social comparison*. For example, there are many situations in which it is difficult to evaluate your own decisions, opinions, abilities, and the like. Suppose you just refused to let a classmate borrow your lecture notes and now you are not sure if you acted appropriately. This is when many people ask others for their opinions. People also routinely consult others before making major decisions, in an effort to avoid errors in judgment. These and other aspects of social comparison are discussed in more detail in Chapter 17.

Other people can also provide support and comfort in times of trouble. As described in the chapter on stress, having a network of friends helps people to cope with the stress of divorce, illness, a death in the family, and other negative events (Fischer & Phillips, 1982; Hirsch, 1980; Stokes, 1983, 1985).

The existence of mutual-support groups for parents of retarded children, spouses or children of alcoholics, unwed mothers, AIDS patients, and people facing all kinds of serious adjustment problems suggests that people in trouble are especially motivated to affiliate with others. Stanley Schachter (1959) found evidence of this tendency in a laboratory experiment. The subjects were two groups of female college students. Those in the high-anxiety group were told that the experiment for which they had volunteered would include some very painful electric shocks. Those in the low-anxiety group were told that they would receive only mild, "tickling" shocks. Members of both groups had to wait several minutes before the experiment began and were given the option of waiting alone or with another volunteer. Those in the high-anxiety group were much more likely to wait with someone else, even though the other person was presumed to be just as worried about the shocks. In fact, there is some evidence that the motive to affiliate when anxious is reduced if the other person is *not* anxious. In a follow-up study, for example, Schachter (1959) gave high-anxiety subjects the choice of waiting alone or with another woman who was there merely to see an academic adviser. Given these options, the women preferred to be alone.

A final benefit of affiliation is the attention and praise people can receive from others. In other words, other people can help satisfy our esteem needs.

MOTIVATION FOR ESTEEM

This sentence was written at 6 A.M. on a beautiful Sunday in June. Why would someone get up that early to work on a weekend? Why do people take their work seriously and do the best job they can, even without special compensation? Most people work at least in part to receive financial compensation, but it would be a mistake to assume that the sole motivation for work is monetary.

The next time you visit someone's home or office, take a look at the mementos displayed there. There may be framed diplomas, certificates of appreciation, photographs of memorable events, stuffed fish or game, photo-

Diplomas and other signs of personal achievement function as badges of self-worth, affirmations that the person who earned them deserves approval or admiration. Displaying these items reflects the strength of people's motivation for esteem.

graphs of children and grandchildren, or cases filled with trophies and ribbons. All of these are badges of worth, affirmations that the person deserves approval or admiration. The fact that so many people proudly display such outward signs of their value serves as a reminder that much human behavior is motivated by the desire for approval, admiration, and other positive evaluations—in short, for *esteem*—from others and from themselves. In this section, we examine two of the most prominent avenues to esteem: achievement in general and a job in particular.

Achievement Motivation

Motivation to achieve is reflected in the degree to which people establish specific goals, care about meeting those goals, and experience feelings of satisfaction doing so. Over the last few decades, a great deal of research in psychology has focused on the characteristics and consequences of **need achievement,** a specific motive first postulated by Henry Murray (1938). An individual's need for achievement is often measured by the Thematic Apperception Test (TAT), a set of ambiguously drawn pictures like Figure 11.14 (Morgan & Murray, 1935).

Characteristics of achievement motivation How do people with strong motivation to achieve differ from other people? To find out, researchers gave children a test designed to measure their need for achievement and then asked them to play a ring-toss game. Children who scored low on the need-for-achievement test tended either to stand so close to the target that they never failed to score or so far away that it was impossible for them to succeed. In contrast, the children who scored high on the need-achievment test chose to stand at an intermediate distance from the target, making the game challenging but not impossible. These children were happy when they succeeded, and they saw the game as even more challenging when they failed (McClelland, 1958).

These and other experiments indicate that individuals with high achievement motivation tend to establish challenging and difficult, but realistic goals. Perhaps most important, they actively pursue success and are willing to take risks in that pursuit. They experience intense satisfaction from success; in fact, one classic definition of high achievement motivation is the capacity to experience pride in success. But, if they feel they have tried their best, individuals with high achievement motivation are not particularly bothered by failure. Those with low achievement motivation also prefer to succeed. For the most part, though, success brings them, not joy, but relief at having avoided failure (Atkinson & Birch, 1978).

In general, people who are very motivated to achieve tend to be preoccupied with their own performance and level of ability. They prefer tasks that have clear-cut outcomes, tasks that leave no question about whether they succeeded or failed. They tend to persist at a task, even after repeated failures. People less motivated to achieve tend to quit trying much sooner (Weiner, 1980). These people also tend to seek help from others. In contrast, people with a high need for achievement struggle with a problem on their own much longer before asking for assistance. In general, they enjoy receiving concrete feedback about their progress. They would rather receive feedback from a harsh but competent critic than from a friendlier but less competent one (McClelland, 1985). Finally, people with high levels of achievement motivation tend to delay immediate gratification and to make careful plans about the future, especially about career goals (Mischel, 1961; Raynor, 1970).

Figure 11.14
Assessment of Need Achievement
This picture is similar to those included in the Thematic Apperception Test, or TAT. The strength of people's achievement motivation is inferred from the stories people tell about what has happened and will happen in TAT pictures. A response like "The young man is hoping that he will be able to make his grandmother proud of him" would reflect clear achievement motivation.
(Reprinted by permission of the publishers from Henry A. Murray, *Thematic Apperception Test,* Cambridge, Mass.: Harvard University Press, copyright © 1943 by the president and fellows of Harvard College, © 1971 by Henry A. Murray.)

People with high achievement motivation tend to set challenging but not unrealistic goals, work hard to attain them, and experience intense satisfaction when they succeed.

Development of achievement motivation   Achievement motivation appears to be largely learned in early childhood. For example, one study found that ten-year-old boys who scored high on tests of achievement motivation had mothers who very strongly encouraged independent thinking and who rewarded their success with hugs and other signs of affection (Winterbottom, 1953). In another study, young boys were given a very difficult task at which they were sure to fail. Fathers whose sons scored low on achievement motivation often became irritated, discouraged their boys from continuing to try, and often interfered or even completed the task themselves (Rosen & D'Andrade, 1959). More recently, David McClelland (1985) described the pattern of parenting that is typically associated with children who score high on achievement motivation tests. The parents of these children tend to (1) encourage the child to attempt difficult tasks, especially new ones; (2) offer praise and other rewards for success; (3) encourage the child to find ways to succeed, instead of complaining about failure; and (4) prompt the child to go on to the next, somewhat more difficult challenge.

The culture also shapes the strength of a person's achievement motivation. The written material used to teach children to read provides one source of cultural influence. Obviously, reading primers do not contain statements like "You're no good if you don't do well in school" or "Success in life doesn't matter." However, the events and themes of simple stories give children subtle messages about what their culture values. Is the hero or heroine someone who worked hard and overcame obstacles to achieve success (thus modeling reinforcement of persistence and hard work) or someone who loafed and then won the lottery (suggesting that rewards come randomly and that commitment to achievement is irrelevant)? Does the description of living "happily ever after" include a nice house and a big car? These are examples of differing *achievement themes* in children's stories.

We do not know whether differences in these messages actually *cause* differences in achievement motivation. However, a study by Richard de Charms and Gerald Moeller (1962) found a strong positive correlation between the number of high-achievement themes in children's reading material and the industrial achievements in these children's countries years later, when they became adults. For example, the number of industrial patents issued was much higher in countries in which children's books contained many high-achievement themes.

HIGHLIGHT

Increasing Achievement Motivation

Achievement motivation can be developed in later years, even among people whose early backgrounds did not encourage it. David McClelland developed a procedure through which individuals can increase their achievement motivation and, with it, their success in life. In one early study, for example, high school and college students with low achievement motivation were helped to develop fantasies about their own success. They imagined setting goals that were difficult but not impossible. Then they imagined themselves concentrating on breaking a complicated problem into smaller, more manageable steps. (You might recall from the chapter on thought and language that this decomposition heuristic can be very useful in problem solving.) They fantasized about working intensely, failing but not being discouraged, continuing to work, and finally feeling elated at success. After the program, these students' grades and general academic performance improved, which suggested that their achievement motivation had been intensified.

As part of a much more difficult project, McClelland went to a village in India. There was very little economic development in the region, and earlier government-supported efforts to develop the economy had had only limited success. McClelland encouraged members of the local business community to have fantasies of high achievement. He taught them to go step by step, to make concrete and elaborate plans for what they needed to do to succeed, and to imagine running large business organizations. He encouraged them to imagine both setbacks and working to overcome them. This program had considerable success (McClelland & Winter, 1969). Many of the participants became successful entrepreneurs. Over the next ten years, they expanded their businesses and started several large industrial concerns that employed thousands of workers (McClelland, 1978). ■

Sex differences in achievement motivation One set of findings about achievement motivation continues to be perplexing. Specifically, the behavior of women with a high level of achievement motivation is much more variable than that of men equally motivated by achievement. In particular, women who are highly motivated to achieve do not always establish challenging goals for themselves when given a choice. And they do not always persist when confronted with failure (Dweck, 1986; Nicholls, 1984). In fact, some of them withdraw from and even avoid academic or business situations in which their achievement could be evaluated. The question of why these sex differences occur is the subject of considerable research and debate. One thing is clear: females are much more likely than males to attribute failure on school-related tasks to a lack of ability, and they tend to begin doing so at a very early age (Dweck & Gillard, 1975). Many continue to see themselves as incompetent even in the face of objective evidence that they do better academically than their male counterparts (Licht & Dweck, 1984).

Girls' readiness to deprecate their own abilities in school may stem in part from classroom experiences. For reasons that are not yet fully understood, elementary school teachers tend to use different styles of criticism for boys and girls. Girls are likely to be told what they did wrong and what they should do instead; in other words, their poor *performance* is highlighted. Boys are also likely to hear this kind of criticism; but in addition, boys are often told that they are not concentrating or are not being careful enough (Dweck et al., 1978). Carol Dweck suggested that the feedback given to girls leads them to think of *themselves* as incompetent, whereas the boys conclude that any failure was due only to lack of effort or some other situational factor. To investigate the effects of criticism by teachers, Dweck and her colleagues (1978) arranged for girls who were very motivated to achieve to receive the type of criticism normally directed toward boys. Under these conditions, the girls' behavior became more like that of boys with high achievement motivation. The girls tended to adopt challenging goals, to try hard, and to persist in the face of failure.

There is little doubt that early parent-child interactions can have a large influence on a child's achievement orientation. It is also clear, however, that this orientation continues to be affected in the early school years and, as McClelland's research demonstrates, even into adulthood.

Jobs and Motivation

Employers are less likely to be interested in a worker's personal need to achieve than in whether their employees are motivated to work hard. One of the most influential theories about motivation on the job was proposed by Frederick Herzberg.

Job satisfaction and dissatisfaction Herzberg suggested that the factors associated with job *satisfaction* are different from those linked to *dissatisfaction* (Herzberg, 1966, 1968). According to Herzberg's theory, dissatisfaction relates primarily to external, or *extrinsic,* aspects of a job, especially inadequate job security, salary and fringe benefits, working conditions, job status, quality of supervision, and relationships with coworkers and supervisors.

However, high pay, high status, good working conditions, and the like do not necessarily bring employee satisfaction. Satisfaction is more closely tied to other, *intrinsic,* aspects of the job, especially those that permit the fulfillment of esteem needs. The important factors in satisfaction include being given individual responsibility, having opportunities for advancement, and doing work that is challenging, allows one to demonstrate unusual degrees of achievement, and fosters personal growth and development. If these conditions are not present, workers may not be satisfied, but they will probably not be dissatisfied either unless the extrinsic factors we described are also lacking.

There is substantial evidence for Herzberg's theory separating satisfaction and dissatisfaction (Petri, 1986). Consider assembly line workers. Their jobs are very repetitive, often boring, and generally unrewarding. Employers have generally attempted to improve these workers' performance by altering extrinsic aspects of jobs—increasing pay, benefits, and job security. Research indicates that this approach can decrease dissatisfaction but does little to increase job satisfaction (Szilagyi & Wallace, 1980).

Designing jobs that motivate Intentionally or not, managers structure jobs in ways that reflect a theory about what motivates people. Employers who see employees as basically lazy, untrustworthy, ambitionless creatures, who have little creative insight about their jobs and prefer to avoid responsibility, tend to design jobs that are very structured, heavily supervised, and allow employees very little flexibility to decide what to do and how to do it. Tightening the same set of nuts on the same part on an endless assembly line exemplifies such jobs. People in jobs structured this way tend not to be satisfied and show a lack of motivation to perform at peak efficiency (Wexley & Yukl, 1984). Edward Deci and Richard Ryan have suggested that these problems arise

Once associated mainly with Japanese firms, job enhancement and a more flexible and humanistic style of job design are now beginning to appear in American companies (Ouchi, 1981; Peters & Waterman, 1983). The hope is to increase both employee productivity and job satisfaction.

largely from the feeling of having little or no control over the work environment (Deci, Connell & Ryan, 1987). This view is consistent with evidence discussed in Chapter 13 that a sense of control over important aspects of life is an important buffer against stress and that lack of control can lead to many kinds of psychological and physical problems.

Employers who view employees as creative, responsible individuals who enjoy a challenge, will show initiative, and are capable of self-direction, are likely to design jobs in which workers are (1) encouraged to participate in decisions about how work should be done; (2) given problems to solve, without being told how to solve them; (3) taught more than one skill; and (4) given lots of individual responsibility. In such organizations, potentially deadening assembly line jobs are enhanced by having workers rotate from one responsibility to another, having employees work in teams to discuss and solve problems, and arranging for teams to produce a finished product from beginning to end, rather than doing something to an incomplete product as it rolls by. Researchers have discovered that the greater sense of control and competence in jobs like these can increase workers' job satisfaction, as well as reduce dissatisfaction (Deci, Connell & Ryan, 1987). Workers in these "enhanced" jobs tend to be more satisfied and productive than their counterparts in more traditionally structured jobs.

The importance of goals   One key component of jobs that are satisfying is that they allow people to set and achieve clear goals (Latham & Yukl, 1975; Steers & Porter, 1979). Reaching these goals, in turn, brings satisfaction of esteem needs. The goals most effective in maintaining work motivation have two distinguishing characteristics.

First, the goals must be personally meaningful. You may have found that you studied harder and received better grades in high school if you, rather than your parents or teachers, set your academic goals. Similarly, when employees are told through a memo from a faceless administrator that their goal should be an increase in production, they are likely to feel put upon and may not be motivated to meet the goal. Second, goals must be specific and concrete. The goal of "doing better" is usually not a very effective motivator. A particular target—such as no customer complaints or a 10 percent increase in sales—makes a far more motivating goal. If the goal is explicitly stated, it is there for all to see, and it is easy to know if it has been reached.

MOTIVATION AND STRESS
What Happens When Motives Are in Conflict?

If people's motivation were always clear and simple, human behavior would be relatively easy to understand. However, the motivation for people's actions is sometimes so obscure and complicated that their behavior appears to make no sense, even to them. The healthy and popular child of wealthy parents commits suicide; the former spouse of an alcoholic marries another alcoholic; a successful executive suddenly abandons a high-pressure job and family commitments for a life of beachcombing with a new lover. Sometimes, actions like these are responses to stress, and stress, in turn, often reflects conflicting motives, such as

the desire to live but to avoid the pain of life, or to have money as well as freedom. Anyone trying to understand human behavior must recognize not only that there are numerous sources of motivation, but also that several motives often operate at the same time, thus provoking stress.

Suppose it's late on a Saturday night and you're bored, so you think about going to a convenience store for a snack. What are your motives? Hunger might play a role in sending you out, as might the prospect of the boredom-fighting stimulation (arousal) you will obtain from a trip to the store. Even sexual motivation might be involved, as you think about the possibility of meeting someone exciting in the frozen pizza aisle. But safety-related motives might make you hesitate. What if you should get mugged? And an esteem motive might prompt you to shrink from being seen without a companion on an evening seemingly filled with couples.

These are just a few of the motives that might be relevant to a trivial decision. When the decision is important, the number and strength of motivational pushes and pulls is likely to be even greater,

creating stress through conflicting behavioral tendencies. Neal Miller (1959) identified four basic types of motivational conflict, each of which may play a role in stress.

1. *Approach-approach conflicts* When a person is motivated to engage in two desirable activities that cannot be pursued simultaneously, an *approach-approach conflict* exists. If you are trying to choose which of two movies to see or must decide between going to a prestigious law school versus accepting a lucrative job, you face an approach-approach conflict. As the importance of the decision increases, so does the difficulty of making it. Still, approach-approach conflicts are usually resolved with relative ease.

2. *Avoidance-avoidance conflicts* An *avoidance-avoidance conflict* arises when a person faces two unattractive situations, and avoidance of one forces exposure to the other. For example, a woman with an unwanted pregnancy may be morally opposed to abortion. In this case, neither having the baby nor terminating the pregnancy is desirable. Like most

The effectiveness of goals in motivating work also depends on how management treats them. They are likely to be very effective if management supports goal setting by employees themselves, offers special rewards for reaching goals, and provides encouragement after failure. In short, jobs that offer personal challenges, independence, and rewards of many kinds provide enough satisfaction of esteem needs for people to feel excitement and pleasure in continuing hard work.

FUTURE DIRECTIONS

Because the concept of motivation centers around the initiation, persistence, and change of behavior, the study of motivation is fully intertwined with most other areas of psychology. For example, we reviewed biological psychology research in discussing hunger and thirst, developmental research in the context of parent-child attachment, social psychology research in examining affiliation and work motivation, and personality research in discussing the need for achievement. Indeed, as suggested in the Linkages diagram, most theorists today prefer not to think of motivation as a separate area of psychological research.

A recent trend in motivational research is to examine long-term life goals, or *personal strivings,* that people try to achieve through their everyday actions (Emmons, 1986). Personal strivings might include developing a coherent philosophy of life, becoming a respected scholar in a given area, contributing

avoidance-avoidance conflicts, this conflict is very difficult to resolve and creates intense emotions.

3. *Approach-avoidance conflicts* When one event or activity has both attractive and unattractive features, an *approach-avoidance conflict* is created. Acting to attain the desirable features requires exposure to the undesirable ones as well; avoiding the negative features means giving up something desirable. Consider, for example, the dilemma of the student who is offered a stolen copy of an important final exam. Cheating will bring guilt and reduced self-esteem, but also a good grade.

Approach-avoidance conflicts are very difficult to resolve (Weiner, 1972). As the person moves toward the situation or thinks about entering it, the negative aspects become more prominent, and the person begins to back away or decides to stay away. This makes the negative aspects of the situation more remote and highlights the positive side. The result is a continuing vacillation between approach and avoidance, creating a great deal of emotional upset.

4. *Multiple approach-avoidance conflicts* Suppose you must choose between two jobs. One offers a high salary with a prestigious organization but requires long working hours and moving to a miserable climate. The other boasts plenty of opportunity for advancement and good fringe benefits, in a better climate, but offers lousy pay and an unpredictable work schedule. This is an example of a *multiple approach-avoidance conflict*, a situation in which a choice must be made between two or more alternatives, each of which has both positive and negative features. Multiple approach-avoidance conflicts are the most difficult to resolve, partly because the features of each option are often difficult to compare. For example, how much is a good climate "worth" in terms of unpredictable working hours? To what extent will the chance for rapid advancement compensate for a low starting salary?

While in the midst of motivational conflicts, most people tend to be tense, irritable, and vulnerable to many other stress-related problems described in Chapter 13. This is especially true when the correct choices are not obvious, when varying motives have approximately equal strength, and when a choice can bring frightening or irrevocable consequences (as in decisions to marry, to divorce, or to approve disconnection of a life-support system). Resolution of such conflicts may be a long time in coming or may be made impulsively and thoughtlessly, just to end the discomfort of uncertainty. Even after the conflict is resolved, signs of stress may continue, in the form of anxiety about the correctness of the decision or guilt over bad choices. Sometimes, these and other consequences of conflicting motives create depression and other serious disorders. Since motivational conflicts are inevitable, it is important to understand their effects and to have some idea of how to resolve them effectively and with a minimum of residual distress. In Chapter 13, on stress, we mention one approach to resolving motivational conflicts, which utilizes a systematic analysis of alternatives reminiscent of the more general problem-solving skills described in the chapter on thought.

to a successful and happy family, or becoming a highly competitive chess player. Although the personal strivings that people adopt can vary widely, the common element is that they must be pursued over long periods of time. Research indicates that personal strivings play an important role in life satisfaction. People who report high levels of life satisfaction tend to be committed to at least one long-term life objective (Klinger, Barta & Maxeiner, 1980). They also perceive themselves as striving to attain that goal on a regular basis, and they see the goal as difficult, but not impossible, to attain (Emmons, 1986).

Low levels of life satisfaction come about for several reasons. One is a preoccupation with avoiding negative results rather than achieving positive ones (Emmons, 1986). For example, rather than striving to become the best criminal lawyer possible, a person might constantly think in terms of not making a mistake, not losing a big case, or not being embarrassed. A related factor is the belief that actually attaining the goal is nearly impossible (Emmons, 1986).

From a motivational perspective, the most important factor leading to low levels of life satisfaction is perceived conflict (Palys & Little, 1983). This can come about in two ways. One is a perceived conflict between strivings themselves. For example, career and family concerns are often perceived to be in conflict. As long as this is the case, there will be almost daily stress. People who perceive their lives as in balance and see their various goals as complementing one another, rather than in conflict, tend to report very high levels of life satisfaction (Emmons, 1986). A second type of conflict is often called *ambivalence*, or conflicting motives within a given situation. For example, a person might feel anger over something that a spouse has done. The person might believe that this anger "should" be expressed because it is personally distressing, but also that it "should not" be expressed because it will only create stress in the family. Many types of ambivalence appear to be due to cultural norms against public displays of emotion and can be traced to early childhood experiences (Tavris, 1984). Researchers have found that inhibiting the expression of such emotions results in a heightened degree of autonomic arousal and can contribute to various types of physical illness (Pennebaker, 1985; Pennebaker & Hoover, 1986).

Thus, whereas motivational research has historically been concerned with short-term motives, researchers are increasingly turning their attention to those that are pursued over the long term. Personality, clinical, social, developmental, and biological psychologists are all contributing to this effort. If you are interested in studying motivation in more detail, you can expect to find motivational issues discussed in courses in all of these areas, as well as in a course usually labeled motivation and emotion.

SUMMARY

1. Motivation can be defined as those processes that account for the initiation, direction, intensity, and persistence of behavior. Motivational concepts are often used to identify the underlying themes in behaviors that appear to be quite different and to explain fluctuations in behavior over time. Motivation often involves interactions among biological, cognitive, emotional, and social determinants of behavior.

2. Psychologists have developed numerous theories of motivation. Some focus on the instinctual or physiological basis of motivated behavior; others emphasize the homeostatic drives to keep biological systems in a balanced state. Arousal theories suggest that people are motivated to maintain an optimal level of arousal. Incentive theory highlights the role of the environmental incentives that pull people toward certain behaviors. Opponent-process theory is based on the fact that any reaction to a stimulus is followed by an opposite reaction, which becomes stronger over time. Maslow's approach organizes motives into a hierarchy ranging from the most basic biological needs, safety needs, belongingness and love needs, and esteem needs to the uniquely human desire for self-actualization.

3. The regulation of hunger is controlled less by cues from the stomach or by the taste of food and more by the brain. The brain monitors glucose levels in the blood and then, through the lateral and ventromedial areas of the hypothalamus, acts to begin and stop eating as necessary.

4. Eating disorders have become serious health problems. Obesity may result from some combination of certain body types, more and larger fat cells, a higher-than-

average set point for food intake, a lower-than-average metabolic rate, and a tendency to cope with stress by eating. Anorexia nervosa is marked by self-starvation, sometimes leading to death. Bulimia is characterized by eating large quantities of food, then purging with laxatives or self-induced vomiting.

5. As in hunger, the brain plays a central role in the regulation of thirst.

6. Sexual motivation is quite strong, even though lack of sex is not life-threatening. In humans, sexual motivation stems from a combination of hormonal and environmental factors. Because social and cultural factors tend to outweigh hormonal determinants in humans, the specifics of their sexual behavior and preferences vary more than in lower animals. Sexual problems can involve sexual motivation, arousal, or orgasmic response.

7. The motive to seek stability and safety is reflected in infants' development of a strong attachment to the primary caretaker, usually the mother. The absence of a strong mother-child bond can have numerous negative consequences.

8. Two types of behavior—parenting and affiliation with others—can satisfy motives for belongingness and love. The parenting motive can overcome a parent's motive to survive. Affiliation with others provides a source of social comparison and support in times of trouble.

9. Achievement motivation is reflected in the capacity to experience pride in success. Individuals with high achievement motivation tend to establish challenging but realistic goals and usually persist in the face of failure.

10. The motivation to work comes from factors that produce job satisfaction and that eliminate dissatisfaction. Workers tend to perform best when they are working toward their own goals and receive recognition for attaining them.

KEY TERMS

Definitions of terms appear on the pages shown in parentheses.

androgen (423)
anorexia nervosa (419)
arousal (411)
arousal theory (411)
bisexual (426)
bulimia (420)
drive (409)
drive theory (409)
estradiol (423)
estrogen (423)
heterosexual behavior (422)
homeostasis (409)
homosexual (425)
incentive theory (412)
instinct (408)
intervening variable (406)
lateral area (416)
luteinizing hormone (LH) (422)

motivation (404)
motive (406)
need (409)
need achievement (433)
obesity (418)
opponent-process theory (412)
osmoreceptor cell (421)
primary drive (409)
progesterone (423)
progestin (423)
secondary drive (410)
set-point concept (417)
sexual dysfunction (427)
sexual response cycle (422)
testosterone (423)
ventromedial nucleus (416)
volumetric receptor (421)

RECOMMENDED READINGS

Geen, R. G., Beatty, W. W., & Arkin, R. M. (1984). *Human motivation: Physiological, behavioral, and social approaches.* Boston: Allyn and Bacon. This book provides a general introduction to human motivation. The material is current and all major approaches are covered.

Logue, A. W. (1986). *The psychology of eating and drinking.* New York: W. H. Freeman. This excellent text covers all aspects of eating and drinking and contains separate chapters on obesity, anorexia and bulimia, and alcohol abuse.

McClelland, D. C. (1985). *Human motivation.* Glenview, Ill.: Scott, Foresman. This introductory text includes a major section on achievement motivation and discusses issues concerning the development, measurement, and effects of achievement motivation.

Petri, H. L. (1986). *Motivation: Theory and research* (2nd ed.). Belmont, Calif.: Wadsworth. This introductory text provides an excellent overview of the field and highlights the relationship between motivation and emotion. The text includes a separate chapter on work motivation.

Pfaff, D. W. (Ed.). (1982). *The physiological mechanisms of motivation.* New York: Springer-Verlag. This book provides a detailed examination of the physiological aspects of motivation. Each chapter covers a different topic and is written by one of the leading experts in the field.

T

he laboratory rat you have been observing is acting strangely. It is hungry and thirsty, but instead of eating the food or drinking the water in its cage, it spends hours pressing a lever. What could take precedence over the rat's basic needs for food and water? You notice a thin wire leading from the top of the animal's head to some equipment and find out that, each time the rat presses the lever, an area deep in its brain receives a small amount of electrical stimulation through the wire. The animal will go to great lengths to continue receiving the stimulation, presumably because it feels so good.

This rat's self-stimulation is but one example of how emotions can motivate behavior. People vigorously pursue safety, belongingness, and esteem because of the happiness, satisfaction, and other positive feelings they expect to experience when they achieve those goals. Some drug addicts will do anything to get the drugs that make them feel good or keep them from feeling bad. The relationship between emotions and motivation works in the other direction as well: emotions can be created by strong motivation. When people cannot satisfy their needs, reach their goals, or resolve their motivational conflicts, for example, they are likely to be disappointed, depressed, angry, or frustrated.

We now consider the emotions that are so inextricably bound up with motivation, as well as with other aspects of human psychology (see Linkages diagram, p. 444). We address four basic questions about emotions.

1. *What is emotion?* Specifically, what do the various experiences called *emotions* share, and how many different emotions are there?
2. *Where is emotion?* That is, what are the origins of emotional experience?
3. *How do people express and recognize emotions?*
4. *What are the functions and effects of emotions?*

WHAT IS EMOTION?

Joy, sorrow, anger, fear, love, hate, mirth, and lust are a few of the 558 emotions in Averill's *Semantic Atlas of Emotional Concepts* (Averill, 1980). What properties do all these experiences share that make them emotions?

A Definition

Emotions are transitory states, characterized by four features. First, emotions are neither overt behaviors nor specific thoughts; they are experiences. As a result, they can sometimes be ambiguous. Very often, emotions seem mixed and contradictory, and you may have trouble assigning specific labels to them. Faced with news of a friend's serious illness, for example, you might find it difficult to determine all of your feelings. Certainly you feel sadness, but it may be mixed with guilty relief that you remain healthy yourself.

442

12

Emotion

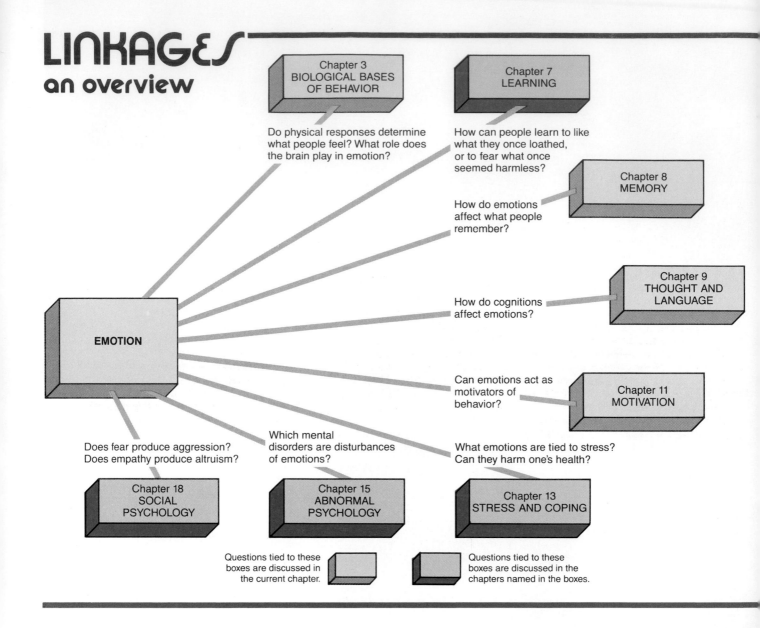

LINKAGES
an overview

Chapter 3
BIOLOGICAL BASES
OF BEHAVIOR

Chapter 7
LEARNING

Do physical responses determine
what people feel? What role does
the brain play in emotion?

How can people learn to like
what they once loathed,
or to fear what once
seemed harmless?

Chapter 8
MEMORY

How do emotions
affect what people
remember?

Chapter 9
THOUGHT AND
LANGUAGE

How do cognitions
affect emotions?

EMOTION

Can emotions act as
motivators of
behavior?

Chapter 11
MOTIVATION

Does fear produce aggression?
Does empathy produce altruism?

Which mental
disorders are disturbances
of emotions?

What emotions are tied to stress?
Can they harm one's health?

Chapter 18
SOCIAL
PSYCHOLOGY

Chapter 15
ABNORMAL
PSYCHOLOGY

Chapter 13
STRESS AND COPING

Questions tied to these
boxes are discussed in
the current chapter.

Questions tied to these
boxes are discussed in the
chapters named in the boxes.

Second, emotions are *passions,* not actions. Eating, for example, is an action, but hunger is a passion; the two represent very different relationships between the self and the experience of consuming food. Actions are initiated by the actor, whereas passions happen to the actor. You are thus expected to be able to control whether you eat but not whether you feel hungry. Hunger happens to you. As passions, emotions also happen to you; they are experienced passively. You cannot decide to experience joy or sorrow; instead, you "fall in love" or are "overcome by grief."

Emotions are more complex than bodily passions like hunger, however, because of a third feature: emotions arise in part from a cognitive appraisal of a situation (Averill, 1980). Seeing a lion elicits totally different emotions depending on whether you think the animal is a tame pet or a wild, hungry beast; your *interpretation* of the situation can alter your emotional reaction to it. This does not mean that emotions are determined consciously. But emotions do depend, not just on situations, but on what you think about those situations, such as how you interpret their potential for threat or pleasure. When the

EMOTION AND PSYCHOLOGY

"Intellect is to emotion as our clothes are to our bodies," observed the British philosopher Alfred North Whitehead; *"we could not very well have civilized life without clothes, but we would be in a poor way if we had only clothes without bodies."* So far, we have said more about the *"clothes"* of the intellect than about emotions. Indeed, for years many psychologists avoided the study of emotional experiences, because emotions are not overt behaviors that can be easily measured. Still, as we saw in the chapter on learning, behaviorists often examine emotional responses, *such as anxiety, in order to develop general laws of learning. And emotions have a way of making their importance felt even when psychologists hope to study some other type of experience or behavior. For example, as described in the memory chapter, Ebbinghaus invented the nonsense syllable in part to eliminate the effect of the feelings associated with words.*

Emotions, in short, are a major category of mental experience, linked with many other aspects of psychology. The strongest tie is between the study of emotions and biological psychology, because the bodily responses that accompany emotions provide the added dimension that distinguishes emotions from other types of mental processes. Whether emotions would be the same without the bodily responses is a question that has been studied for many years and one that we consider in this chapter.

space shuttle *Challenger* exploded, for example, most youngsters did not become upset until the situation had been explained to them.

Finally, emotions are accompanied by bodily responses, such as movements of the face and body. People experiencing surprise, for example, typically show a wide-eyed, open-mouthed expression and may raise their hands to the face. Internal, visceral responses—changes in heart rate, for example—also accompany emotion. But visceral responses are reflexive, occurring as automatically as salivation in response to food. Facial and bodily movements, on the other hand, are partly reflexive and partly learned, as we will see later.

In summary, an **emotion** is (1) an experience that (2) is felt as happening to the self, (3) is generated in part by one's cognitive appraisal of a situation, and (4) is accompanied by both learned and reflexive physical responses. Emotions are therefore experiences that are both triggered by the thinking self and experienced by the self as happening to the self. They reveal the individual as both agent and object, as both I and me, both the controller of thoughts and the victim of passions.

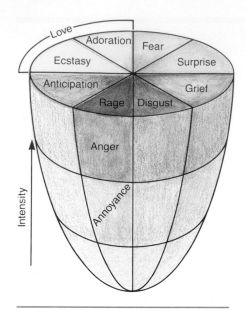

Figure 12.1
Plutchik's Multidimensional Model of Emotions
Studies of how people use words to describe emotions have shown that emotions cluster together in a few dimensions: similarity, intensity, and polarity, or positivity or negativity. Here, similar emotions are pictured adjacent to each other, and opposite emotions are pictured opposite each other on a circle. Adding intensity as a vertical dimension makes the model a three-dimensional solid, with the most intense emotions at its top. Combinations of adjacent primary emotions produce complex emotions (love is a combination of ecstasy and adoration). The shape of the model indicates that, as emotions become less intense (toward the bottom of the solid), they become less distinguishable.
(From R. A. Plutchik, "A Psychoevolutionary Theory of Emotions," *Social Science Information, 21,* 1984. Published by Sage Publications Ltd., London.)

Classification of Emotions

Is fear a shade of panic? Is love a more intense version of infatuation? You can easily distinguish anger from mirth, but jealousy, envy, and many other emotions seem to differ from one another less dramatically, by shades. In fact, as we noted earlier, people often have difficulty deciding exactly what emotion they are experiencing.

Descriptions of emotions can be, as William James once said, as interesting as "descriptions of the shapes of rocks on a New Hampshire farm" (James, 1890/1952, p. 742). But if psychologists could establish that there are a limited number of *primary* emotions, this knowledge might illuminate how emotions are generated. Perhaps the full spectrum of emotional life could then be represented as mixtures of a few basic emotions, which produce emotional shades that vary in intensity, as colors do.

For centuries, philosophers and psychologists have attempted to discern a set of fundamental emotions, but it is difficult to verify the correctness of any one taxonomy of emotion. Robert Plutchik (1980) proposed a classification that resembles the system for color vision described in the chapter on sensation. Emotions, he said, can be characterized by their intensity, similarity, and polarity. There are eight primary emotions, made up of four pairs of opposites (see Figure 12.1). Mixtures of these emotions produce other, secondary emotions. Jaak Panksepp (1982) proposed a different classification, based on an attempt to link primary emotions to particular anatomical systems of the brain (see Figure 12.2). In his view, there are four basic emotions (expectancy, rage, panic, and fear), each linked to the activity of a different part of the hypothalamus. Only time and research will tell whether either of these particular categorizations will further the understanding of emotions.

WHERE IS EMOTION?

Earlier we described the interacting elements of emotion—the feeling of emotions, the cognitions related to them, and the behavioral and visceral responses. Is one element the core of emotion that causes the others? When you are angry, for example, does the experience of anger arise from what you think about a situation or from your physical response to it? Different answers to such questions represent the primary difference among various theories of emotion. But before investigating those theories, we need to look at the visceral responses that are part of emotion and at how those responses are controlled.

Emotions and the Autonomic Nervous System

If you get red in the face when you are angry or embarrassed, it is because the autonomic nervous system has increased the flow of blood to your face. This system, which we described very briefly in the chapter on biological psychology, plays an integral part in the experience and expression of emotion.

Recall that the **autonomic nervous system,** or **ANS,** is the part of the peripheral nervous system that carries information between the brain and all organs of the body except the striated muscles (such as the arm and leg muscles). As Figure 12.3 (p. 448) shows, there are exactly two synapses between the central nervous system (the brain and spinal cord) and each target organ. First, a central nervous system cell connects to an ANS cell out in the body; a collection of ANS cells is a *ganglion.* It then synapses on the target organ. For example, in order to increase heart rate, cells in the spinal cord stimulate an ANS ganglion, which then transmits the message to the heart.

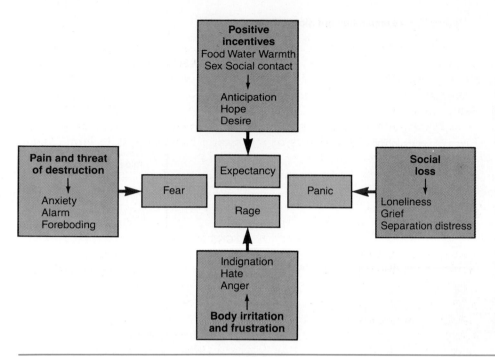

Figure 12.2
Panksepp's Classification of Emotions
Panksepp's scheme, based on challenges that all animals must face, sees emotions as part of the creature's response to a class of environmental stimuli. Four types of environmental stimuli converge on command systems in the brain that trigger sensorimotor patterns particular to each species. The four basic emotions are expectancy, which may be experienced as hope or desire for positive results; rage, which may be felt as anger or hate; panic, which is experienced as loneliness or grief; and fear, which is felt as anxiety or foreboding.
(From "Toward a General Psychological Theory of Emotions" by J. Panksepp, *Behavioral and Brain Sciences*, Vol. 5, 1982. Copyright © 1982 by the Cambridge University Press. Reprinted with permission.)

The ANS as a modulator The autonomic nervous system affects all of the organs—the heart and blood vessels, the digestive system, the reproductive organs, glands such as the adrenal gland, and so on. Each of these organs has ongoing activity independent of the autonomic nervous system, but input from the autonomic system *modulates* this activity, increasing or decreasing it. For example, the heart continues to beat even without input from the autonomic system, but input from the autonomic system may increase or decrease the heartbeat.

By modulating the organs' activity, the autonomic system coordinates their functioning to meet the needs of the whole organism and prepares the body for changes. For example, if a person is aroused to increased activity, more glucose is needed to fuel the muscles. Actions of the autonomic nervous system provide that needed energy by stimulating secretion of glucose-generating hormones and by promoting blood flow to the muscles. Much of the *arousal,* or general physiological activation, discussed in the chapter on motivation involves the autonomic nervous system.

The sympathetic and parasympathetic systems There are two divisions in the autonomic nervous system: the sympathetic nervous system and the parasympathetic nervous system. The **parasympathetic nervous system** typically influences activity related to the protection, nourishment, and growth of the body; digestion is one example. Thus, for example, the parasympathetic system increases movement of the intestinal system, allowing more nutrients to be extracted from what you eat. The **sympathetic nervous system** usually prepares the organism for vigorous activity. This system gets its name from the fact that, when one part of it is stimulated, other parts are stimulated "in sympathy" with it (Gellhorn & Loofbourrow, 1963). Activation of the sympathetic nervous system usually produces increased heart rate and blood pressure, rapid or irregular breathing, dilated pupils, perspiration, dry mouth, increased blood sugar, decreased gastrointestinal motility, piloerection ("goose bumps"), trembling, and other changes. You have probably experienced these reactions after a near-accident. They are sometimes called the **fight-or-flight**

Parasympathetic functions

Sympathetic functions

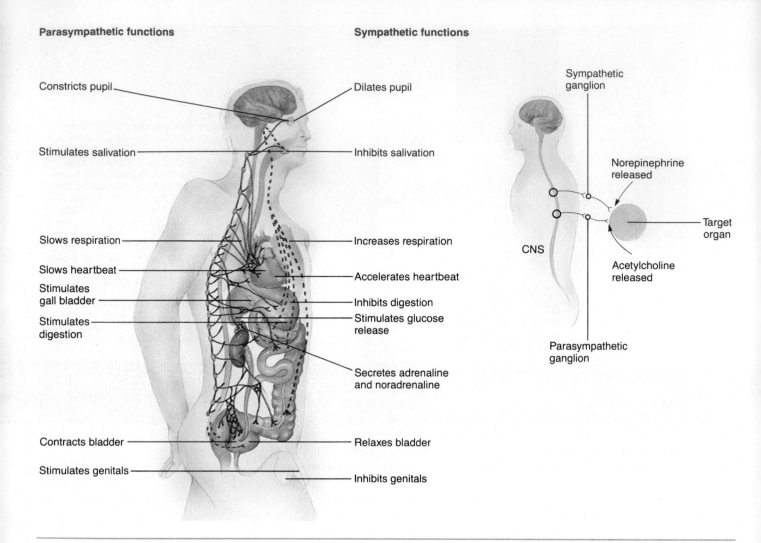

Constricts pupil

Stimulates salivation

Slows respiration

Slows heartbeat

Stimulates gall bladder

Stimulates digestion

Contracts bladder

Stimulates genitals

Dilates pupil

Inhibits salivation

Increases respiration

Accelerates heartbeat

Inhibits digestion

Stimulates glucose release

Secretes adrenaline and noradrenaline

Relaxes bladder

Inhibits genitals

Sympathetic ganglion

Norepinephrine released

Target organ

CNS

Acetylcholine released

Parasympathetic ganglion

Figure 12.3
The Autonomic Nervous System
Emotional responses involve activation of the autonomic nervous system, which includes sympathetic and parasympathetic subsystems. Which bodily responses depicted do you associate with emotional experiences?

syndrome, because they prepare the body to combat or to run from a threatening situation.

In both systems, the neurotransmitter at the ganglia is always acetylcholine (see Figure 12.3). In the *parasympathetic* system, the neurotransmitter at the target organ is also acetylcholine. But in the *sympathetic* system, the neurotransmitter at the target organ is almost always norepinephrine (also known as noradrenaline). Very often, the same organ is innervated by fibers of both the sympathetic and the parasympathetic system, each of which may produce opposite effects. For example, norepinephrine released by the sympathetic nerves on the heart speeds up the heart, whereas acetylcholine released by the parasympathetic nerves slows it down.

One part of the sympathetic nervous system deserves special mention: the **adrenal gland.** There are actually two adrenal glands, one on each side of the body just above the kidney. The inner part of the adrenal gland, called the *adrenal medulla,* acts as a ganglion of the sympathetic system, since it facilitates communication between the brain and various target organs. Like other ganglia, the adrenal medulla receives stimulation from the central nervous system via fibers that use the neurotransmitter acetylcholine. Unlike other ganglia, however, the cells of the adrenal gland do not have axons that travel to a target organ. Instead, its cells simply dump noradrenaline and adrenaline into the bloodstream, thereby activating all target organs of the sympathetic system. The release of adrenaline is responsible for the fight-or-flight syndrome. Another part of the adrenal gland, the *adrenal cortex,* releases hormones, such as cortisol, that are involved in stress reactions. We will discuss the fight-or-flight syndrome and other aspects of the body's response to threat in the chapter on stress.

Emotions are associated with arousal of either branch of the ANS. However, the link between the amount or location of this arousal and the experience of a particular emotion is neither clear nor consistent. To take but one example, one person who is afraid and another who is excited about meeting a blind date may show the same increase in heart rate. A major task still facing researchers is to better understand the relationship between physiological arousal and emotional experience.

The autonomic system and consciousness   The autonomic system and the parts of the brain involved in consciousness are connected, but only indirectly. For example, the autonomic system does not provide immediate feedback to the sensory areas of the cerebral cortex. Thus, you are not immediately aware of the fact that your stomach has secreted gastric juices. The feedback that is available to your consciousness is indirect; you might hear your stomach grumbling.

Similarly, you can influence the activities of the autonomic nervous system only indirectly. You cannot consciously will changes in the activity of the ANS, such as a rise in blood pressure or an erection. But you can decide to do certain things that will, in turn, alter the activities of the ANS. Through the procedure known as *biofeedback,* in which special monitoring equipment "feeds back" information about autonomic activity in the form of a varying tone or meter reading, people can learn to use certain thoughts that will affect heart rate or blood pressure.

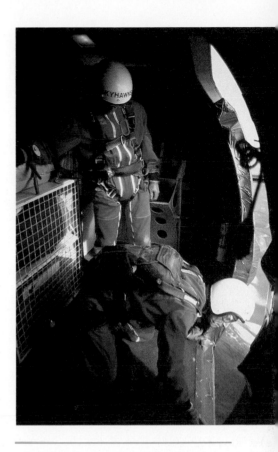

These skydivers are likely to show notable changes in autonomic arousal just before a jump, but it would probably be unclear from their physiological activity alone whether the emotion they experience is fear or excitement.

Detecting Lies Through the Physiology of Emotion

The involuntary nature of the autonomic nervous system provides the basis for using polygraphs as lie detectors. *Polygraphs* are instruments that record several types of physiological activity. For lie detection, polygraphs record physiological responses that are under the control of the autonomic nervous system—usually heart rate, respiration, and skin resistance (which is affected by slight changes in perspiration). There is no specific *lie response;* there are only *emotional responses,* and the use of the polygraph as a lie detector assumes that emotional responses will accompany lies. Most people will in fact have some emotional responses when they attempt to deceive another person. This is due either to guilt or to fear of being found out.

Lie detectors are used by agencies that have a need to determine whether someone is lying. They are used in the interrogation of suspects in criminal investigations, often in order to generate a confession. They are also used by security agencies, such as the CIA, as one aspect of security clearance procedures. And increasingly they are being used by businesses for routine preemployment screening to eliminate such problems as employee theft or drug abuse.

Practitioners of polygraph testing are trained both in reading polygraph responses and in asking questions that will elicit responses establishing guilt or innocence. In attempting to identify the perpetrator of a crime, for example, the investigator will ask questions that are specifically related to the crime. "Did you stab anyone on January 23, 1988?" exemplifies such *relevant* questions.

Responses to relevant questions are then compared to responses to *control* questions; that is, more general inquiries, such as "Have you ever tried to hurt someone?" The assumption underlying this comparison is that an innocent person will display a stronger emotional response to control than to relevant questions (Raskin & Podlesny, 1979). Some researchers claim that a guilty person can learn to "fool" this version of the lie detector test by generating a response to items that an innocent person might be expected to be uneasy about (Lykken, 1979).

Statistics about the polygraph's accuracy in detecting deception are very difficult to obtain, and estimates made by reputable scientists differ widely. For example, David Raskin (Raskin & Podlesny, 1979) estimates that an objectively analyzed polygraph record can be correct in detecting 90 percent of guilty individuals and 89 percent of innocent suspects. On the other hand, David Lykken (1979) cites several studies with much less impressive statistics, in which innocent persons are deemed guilty as often as 50 percent of the time.

In Great Britain, the British Psychological Society studied the evidence on the effectiveness of polygraphic lie detection. Their report (British Psychological Society, 1986) concluded that the factors that determine whether a polygraph will be effective in a given case are still not fully known, but that they include the *belief* on the part of the person tested that the machine is infallible in its ability to detect lies. Thus, effective use of the polygraph may actually require lying to the person being tested. A more serious concern expressed in the British report is that correct identification of liars comes at the expense of false accusation of the innocent (up to 50 percent of the time, as mentioned above). This is especially serious when most people being tested are innocent and only a small number are lying. When there are few liars and many innocent people, even polygraph tests capable of catching 90 percent of liars and exonerating 90 percent of the innocent will falsely accuse a large number of people of lying. Furthermore, even if the test can catch people who are lying when they take the test, the polygraph can neither predict subsequent behavior nor guarantee an applicant's moral character.

Nevertheless, in the United States, the federal government's use of the polygraph more than tripled from the early 1970s into the 1980s, with about 23,000 examinations in 1982 (U.S. Congress, 1983). Most of these tests, except by the CIA and the National Security Agency, were for criminal investigations. However, in 1983 the Justice Department authorized polygraph use for screening personnel applicants in agencies other than the CIA. Twenty-three states allow polygraph testing, and it has been estimated that about a million tests are conducted in the United States each year (Dulewicz, 1984). However, pressures may be building to limit reliance on the polygraph as a lie detector. For example, the American Psychological Association has issued a policy statement acknowledging that the scientific evidence is incomplete and expressing "great reservations about the use of polygraph tests to detect deception" (Abeles, 1985). ∎

Self-Observation:
The James-Lange Theory

Suppose you are walking in the woods and come upon a mean-looking bear. The encounter scares the daylights out of you, and you begin to run for dear life. But do you run because you are afraid, or are you afraid because you run? The example and the question come from the work of William James, one of the first psychologists to propose a formal answer to questions about how autonomic responses are related to the experience of emotion. James argued that you are afraid because you run. Your running and other physiological responses, he said, follow directly from the perception of the bear. Without some form of these responses, you would feel no fear. Presented like this, in its simplest form, James's theory may sound preposterous. It goes against common sense, which says that it makes no sense to run from something unless you are already afraid of it. How did James come to conclude otherwise?

James based his theory in part on a similar view proposed by Carl Lange, a Danish physician; as a result, it is usually called the *James-Lange theory*. James's main method of analysis was to scrutinize his own mental processes. James found that, after stripping away all physiological responses, there was *nothing* left of the experience of an emotion (James, 1890). Figure 12.4 outlines James's view of the source of emotion. First, a perception affects the cerebral cortex, said James, then

> quick as a flash, reflex currents pass down through their pre-ordained channels, alter the condition of muscle, skin, and viscus; and these alterations, perceived, like the original object, in as many portions of the cortex, combine with it in consciousness and transform it from an object-simply-apprehended into an object-emotionally-felt. (James, 1890, p. 759)

In other words, the brain interprets a situation in such a way that physiological responses are called for, but the interpretation is not necessarily conscious. Only when responses occur are they consciously perceived. This subsequent

Experience of Emotion

4. Perception of bodily responses (Heart rate is increasing; I'm running.)

2. Perception (It's a bear!)

1. Sensation (Bear stimulus)

3. Bodily responses (Brain to body: increase heart rate; run.)

Figure 12.4
The James-Lange Theory of Emotion
This theory states that bodily responses are the core of the emotional experience. James argued that the conscious experience of emotion does not occur until the brain receives feedback about physiological responses.

perception of the peripheral responses, according to James, constitutes the experience of emotion.

Thus, the **James-Lange theory** holds that automatic, *peripheral responses*—for example, a palpitating heart, sinking stomach, flushed cheeks, and perspiration—precede the experience of emotion. The conscious aspect of emotion arises later, when the brain observes these responses. Notice that, according to this view, there is no emotion generated solely by activity of the central nervous system. There is no special "brain center" where emotion is experienced. This theory therefore suggests one reason why you may have difficulty knowing your true feelings: you must interpret your feelings from your responses; there is no direct access to feelings from one part of the brain to another.

Evaluating James's theory   James's theory has at least three implications. First, if the perception of peripheral physiological responses constitutes emotion, then each shade of emotion should stem from distinguishable patterns of physiological arousal. For example, fear should be tied to one pattern of bodily responses, and anger should arise from a different pattern. According to James's theory, if the patterns of responses are not different, then you cannot distinguish the two emotions.

Walter Cannon, a distinguished physiologist of the 1920s, disagreed with this and other aspects of James's theory, arguing that separate patterns of arousal do not occur for each emotion. Subsequent research indicated that the pattern of autonomic changes *does* in fact vary with different emotional states. For example, anger and fear both cause heart rate to rise; but anger *increases* blood flow to the hands and feet, whereas fear *reduces* blood flow to the hands and feet (Ekman, Levenson & Friesen, 1983). (Thus, fear produces "cold feet"; anger does not.) Also, when people mentally "relive" different emotional experiences, they show different patterns of autonomic activity (Ekman, Levenson & Friesen, 1983). Whether these results mean that peripheral responses are different enough to be distinguishable as separate emotions is still not clear, however.

A second implication of James's theory is that individuals who are cut off from feedback about physiological changes in the body's periphery should not experience emotions. Cannon argued against James's theory on this point by demonstrating that animals show emotional behavior even after their visceral sensory fibers have been surgically disconnected from the brain. But Cannon's work left an important question unanswered: Do animals *experience* emotions in the same way after surgery? George Hohman (1966) addressed this question by studying people with spinal cord injuries. The amount of peripheral

Figure 12.5
Voluntary Facial Movements Can Evoke Emotional Autonomic Responses
In these experiments, actors were instructed to move certain parts of the face, without being asked to experience an emotion. For example, this man was instructed to (a) "raise your brows and pull them together"; (b) "raise your upper eyelids"; and (c) "also stretch your lips horizontally, back toward your ears." Carrying out these instructions produced heart rate changes characteristic of fear and to some extent the experience of fear.
(Copyright, Paul Ekman, 1983. Photos of actor Tom Harrison, from Ekman, P., Levenson, R. W. and Friesen, W. V. "Autonomic nervous system distinguishes among emotions," *Science*, 1983, 221.)

feedback to their brains depended on the location of the damage: the higher the point of damage, the less feedback these people received from their bodies. Hohman reasoned that, if peripheral feedback is important to the experience of emotion, then the higher on the spinal cord damage occurs, the less intense the experience of emotions should be. The results of Hohman's study matched this prediction. His subjects reported that they still felt emotions, but less intensely, and the level of spinal damage was correlated with the loss of intensity. One person with spinal damage, for example, described anger as "cold anger . . . it doesn't have the heat to it that it used to. It's a mental kind of anger" (Hohman, 1966, p. 151). These results suggest that emotions *may* occur without extensive feedback from peripheral responses, but that feedback contributes greatly to the intensity of emotions.

A third implication of James's theory is that, if people could voluntarily control peripheral responses, then the emotions associated with those responses should follow. A person who can voluntarily produce the physiological responses associated with fear should feel fear, even if there is nothing in the environment to be afraid of. Similarly, if you loathe Brussels sprouts, you could come to love them by somehow bringing on the physiology of happiness while eating them. Recent experiments, directed at a refinement of James's ideas, called the *facial feedback hypothesis*, have lent some limited credence to this part of his theory.

Facial feedback and emotion   According to the **facial feedback hypothesis,** movements of the face provide information about what emotion is being felt (Izard, 1971; Laird, 1984). Thus, if you find yourself frowning, you must be unhappy. The facial movement is involuntary, and the feedback from that movement directs further emotional responses. As a result, if you can control your facial muscles to reproduce the movements associated with specific emotions, you should to some extent experience those emotions.

Paul Ekman and his colleagues (Ekman, Levenson & Friesen, 1983) tested this prediction by instructing professional actors to move specific facial muscles or parts of the face. Ekman found that various facial configurations did produce autonomic responses like those normally accompanying emotion. Furthermore, different facial configurations led to very different patterns of responses (see Figures 12.5 and 12.6).

In another study, with nonactors, more than 90 percent of the subjects reported feeling the emotion associated with the facial expression they had created, even though they did not realize that this specific emotion was being elicited. Interestingly, the effect works for expressions of fear, anger, disgust, and sadness, but not for smiling. Presumably smiling is so often used as a social signal that it is less closely connected to the emotional experience than are the other facial expressions (Ekman, 1985). These effects do support James's theory that emotion requires feedback about peripheral responses, but it may also be that facial expressions are associated with past emotional experiences and that producing these expressions arouses emotions by activating memories (Izard, 1971).

Further, in spite of facial feedback data, it is still not clear whether, as James claimed, *nothing* is left of emotion if information about peripheral responses is eliminated. Are those responses the sole cause of emotion?

Direct Central Experience: The Cannon-Bard Theory

Walter Cannon did more than criticize James's theory; he and Philip Bard suggested an alternative. In their view, you feel fear at the sight of a wild bear without ever taking a step. The responses of the autonomic nervous system, they said, do not help generate emotion (Cannon, 1927).

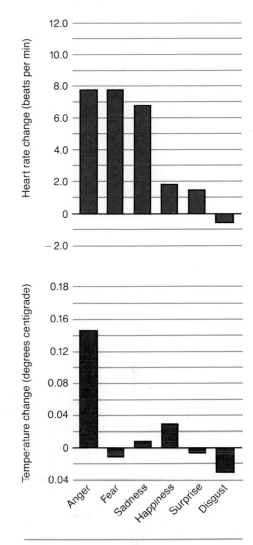

Figure 12.6
Physiology and Facial Movements
Movements of the face characteristic of different emotions produced different patterns of change in (a) heart rate and (b) peripheral blood flow, as indexed by finger temperature (Ekman, Levenson & Friesen, 1983). For example, making an angry face causes heart rate and finger temperature to rise, whereas making a fearful face raises heart rate but lowers finger temperature. (From "Autonomic Nervous System Activity Distinguishes Among Emotions," P. Ekman et al., Science, Vol. 221, #4616, pp. 1208–1210, 16 September 1983. Copyright © 1983 by the American Association for the Advancement of Science.)

Figure 12.7
The Cannon-Bard Theory of Emotion
Cannon argued that emotion is a direct central nervous system experience and that peripheral responses occur independently of the central experience of emotion. The brain "knows" that fear is being experienced even before feedback from the autonomic nervous system reaches the brain.

How, then, does emotion occur? Cannon and Bard proposed that the experience of emotion originates in the thalamus, the structure in the brain that relays information from various sense organs to the cortex (see Figure 3.14). According to the **Cannon-Bard theory** of emotion, the brain interprets an emotional situation through the thalamus. The thalamus sends sensory signals both to the cerebral cortex, where the emotion becomes conscious, and simultaneously to the autonomic nervous system. When you see that bear in the woods, the brain receives sensory information about it, interprets that information as a bear, and *directly* creates the experience of fear while *at the same time* sending messages to the heart, lungs, and legs to initiate a rapid departure. According to the Cannon-Bard theory, then, there is a direct, central experience of emotion, with or without feedback about peripheral responses, as Figure 12.7 shows.

Recent work suggests that the thalamus does not produce the direct central experience of emotion, as Cannon had theorized. But are there other parts of the brain that produce this experience? An updated version of the Cannon-Bard theory suggests that some parts of the brain play the same role for other parts of the brain as the autonomic nervous system does for the rest of the body (Hartman et al., 1986). Fibers from the sympathetic or the parasympathetic branches of the autonomic nervous system do not enter the brain, but the brain appears to contain a kind of "autonomic nervous system" of its own. Just as the autonomic nervous system modulates the activity of organs that can function without input from the ANS, several neurotransmitter systems in the brain appear to modulate the activity of other brain cells. These neurotransmitter systems resemble the autonomic nervous system in another way. Recall that cholinergic fibers (those using acetylcholine for neural communication) activate noradrenergic cells in the sympathetic branch of the autonomic nervous system. Similarly, some of the brain's cholinergic fibers connect to cells in the brain that use noradrenaline. For example, noradrenergic cells in the *locus coeruleus* play this "autonomic" role, releasing noradrenaline and modulating the activity of other brain cells, as well as sending descending signals to the peripheral autonomic nervous system (Olpe, Steinmann & Jones, 1985). These noradrenergic cells appear to be involved in emotions and disturbances of emotions, such as depression.

The involvement of these and other brain cells in directly sensing emotional feeling is exemplified by the rat described at the beginning of the chapter. The brain areas in which stimulation is experienced as pleasurable include the locus coeruleus and other areas associated with the brain's "autonomic nervous system" (Segal & Bloom, 1976; see Figure 12.8).

However, noradrenergic cells are by no means the only ones whose activation is pleasurable enough to reinforce self-stimulation (Wise, 1978). And there are brain cells whose stimulation is so aversive that animals will work hard to avoid that stimulation. Presumably, part of the direct central experience of emotions involves activity in areas of the brain that are either reinforcing or aversive.

The idea that the brain contains its own "autonomic nervous system" unifies the picture of emotional responses. The same cells of the locus coeruleus and elsewhere that project fibers down the spinal cord to activate the traditional

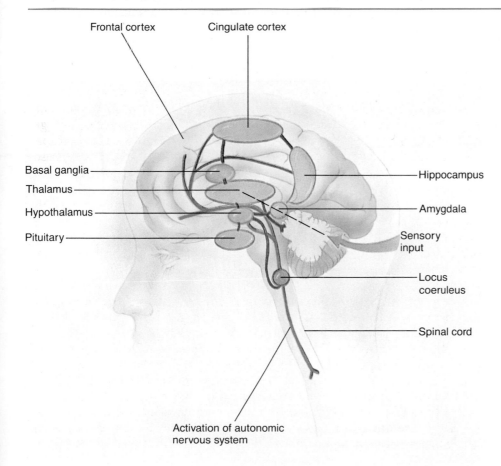

Figure 12.8
Parts of the Brain Involved in the Experience of Emotion
In all theories, sensory information comes into the brain to alert the individual to an emotion-evoking situation. Most sensory information goes through the thalamus, and the cingulate cortex and hippocampus are involved in the interpretation of the sensory input. Output from these areas goes to the amygdala and hypothalamus, which control the autonomic nervous system via brainstem connections. The locus coeruleus is one area of the brainstem that causes both widespread arousal of cortical areas and changes in autonomic activity.

autonomic nervous system also appear to send fibers into the rest of the brain, activating cells in areas such as the hypothalamus and the limbic system. Thus, an emotional situation energizes the entire body, including parts of the brain, creating changes in the central nervous system that are part of the same response that produces a racing heart or other symptoms of emotion in the peripheral autonomic system.

In short, in this updated version of the Cannon-Bard theory, a direct experience of emotion results from the modulation of the activity of brain cells, contributing to a tone or feeling rather than to specific thoughts, just as color adds feeling to a black-and-white picture without changing its form. There is solid evidence that changes in the activity of noradrenaline cells in the central nervous system affect mood, but we still do not know whether the firing of those cells constitutes the primary basis for the experience of emotion.

Attribution of Arousal: The Schachter Theory

The James-Lange and the Cannon-Bard theories of emotion both provide helpful guides to the study of emotion. However, although both recognized that the interpretation of situations or autonomic feedback is important, neither devoted much attention to how interpretation takes place. Modern research on this aspect of emotion was sparked largely by a creative proposition by Stanley Schachter.

Schachter agreed with James that the feeling of emotions arises from perceiving feedback from bodily responses, but he also agreed with Cannon's view that this feedback is not sufficiently varied to generate subtle emotional differences. To reconcile these views, Schachter and Jerome Singer proposed that emotions are produced by both feedback from peripheral responses *and* cognitive appraisal of what caused those responses (Schachter & Singer,

Schachter's theory of emotion predicts that these sports fans would attribute their physiological arousal to the game they are watching and label their emotion "excitement."

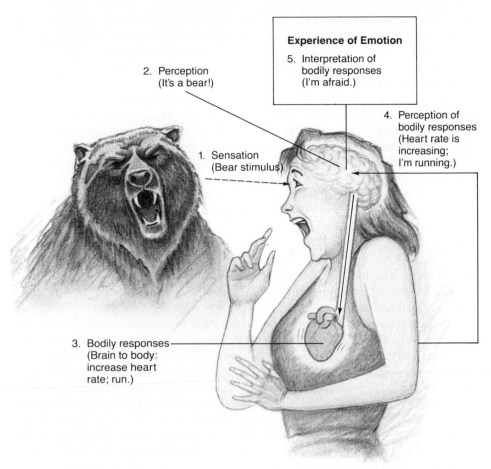

2. Perception
(It's a bear!)

1. Sensation
(Bear stimulus)

3. Bodily responses
(Brain to body:
increase heart
rate; run.)

Experience of Emotion

5. Interpretation of
bodily responses
(I'm afraid.)

4. Perception of
bodily responses
(Heart rate is
increasing;
I'm running.)

Figure 12.9
The Schachter Theory of Emotion
*A modification of the James-Lange theory,
the Schachter theory adds the idea that peripheral feedback must be interpreted in
light of knowledge about what might have
caused autonomic responses.*

1962). Thus, cognitive interpretation comes into play twice: once when you perceive the situation that leads to visceral responses and again when you identify feedback from those responses as a particular emotion.

Figure 12.9 outlines the **Schachter theory.** As in the James-Lange theory, the first step is the perception of a situation, followed by bodily responses. However, whereas James said that the brain perceives the responses as a particular emotion solely on the basis of the feedback, Schachter argued that the brain may interpret a single pattern of feedback in many ways and give it many labels. According to Schachter and Singer (1962), this cognitive act of *labeling* an originally undifferentiated pattern of physiological arousal constitutes the core of emotion. The labeling depends on an **attribution,** which is the process of identifying the cause of some event. People may attribute physiological arousal to different emotions depending on the information that is available about the situation. For example, if you are watching a close football game, you might attribute your racing heart, rapid breathing, and perspiration to excitement; but you might attribute the same physiological reactions to anxiety if you are waiting for an important exam to begin. Thus, the emotion you experience seeing a bear in the woods might be fear, excitement, astonishment, or surprise, depending on how you label your reaction.

Evaluating the Schachter theory   Many experiments have supported Schachter's view that both physiological responses and the cognitive labeling of those responses play a role in emotion. For example, consider the results of research on three hypotheses generated by the Schachter theory.

First, Schachter's theory predicts that, if physiological responses are reduced or eliminated, the experience of emotion should be reduced or eliminated as well. James's theory also led to this prediction, and we have seen that it was supported by Hohman's studies of individuals with spinal cord damage (Hohman, 1966).

Second, if you attribute emotional arousal to a nonemotional cause, then the experience of emotion should be reduced. If you notice your heart pounding before an exam but say to yourself, "Sure my heart's pounding, but I'm not nervous—I just drank five cups of coffee!" you should feel "wired" from caffeine rather than afraid or worried. This prediction has also received some support. In one series of experiments, people were given an injection of a placebo, a substance with no physiological effect (Schachter & Singer, 1962). But the people were told, falsely, that the injection would increase their heart rate and blood pressure and produce trembling and other signs of arousal; then they were placed in situations designed to produce an emotion such as anger. They reported experiencing less intense emotion than did people who had had no injection. Presumably, these misinformed subjects attributed some of their physiological arousal to the injection rather than to their own emotions.

A third prediction from the Schachter theory is that, if arousal is artificially induced—by drugs, for example—people should experience emotion if there is a situation to which they can reasonably attribute the drug-induced arousal. By the same logic, artificially induced physiological responses should *intensify* emotion if they can be attributed to an emotion-producing situation.

To test this prediction, Schachter and Singer (1962) attempted to separate the physiological and cognitive components of an emotional experience. To produce physiological arousal, they injected subjects with adrenaline. Some of the people were told that they were receiving an injection of a new vitamin; the others were given accurate information about the injection and its likely arousing effects. Then the subjects were placed in a situation designed to generate emotion. With them was an actor working for the experimenters, who appeared to be another subject. Some subjects were given a questionnaire containing insulting items about such topics as their mothers' extramarital sexual activity. In these cases, the actor-subject responded angrily to the questionnaire. With other subjects, who did not receive the questionnaire, the actor pretended to feel happy, even euphoric.

The Schachter theory predicts that those who were correctly informed about the injection and its effects would not be influenced much by the social cues in the environment—that is, by the confederate's anger or joy—because they would attribute any arousal to the injection, not to an emotion. In contrast, the theory predicts that people who did not know that the injection could cause arousal would attribute the arousal to emotion. They would therefore not only experience stronger emotions but also look to the environment for clues to what particular emotion they were experiencing. Thus, people who were misinformed about the injection and were with an apparently euphoric actor should attribute their otherwise unexplained arousal to euphoria (a cue provided by the actor) and therefore experience positive emotions. Those in the presence of an angry actor should label their physiological responses as anger, not only because of the actor's behavior, but also because of the questionnaire.

The results matched these predictions (Schachter & Singer, 1962). Thus, key predictions of Schachter's theory were supported, namely that attributing arousal to an emotion intensifies the emotion and that social cues in the environment can guide the labeling of one's own emotional arousal. However, the magnitude of the effects was quite small. Indeed, some investigators have

Several theorists have expanded on Schachter's theory of emotion, suggesting that the emotions people experience depend not just on their labeling of physiological activity but also on their cognitive interpretation of situations (Lazarus & Folkman, 1984). Those viewing an event as a disaster will experience negative emotions, while those thinking of it as an adventure or a challenge may feel more positive.

been unable to replicate Schachter's results (Leventhal & Tomarken, 1986; Marshall & Zimbardo, 1979, Maslach, 1979).

The transfer of excitation   In spite of its problems, the Schachter theory of emotion is still influential and has stimulated interesting research. Some of this research has shown that physiological arousal can be attributed to emotion and can intensify emotional experience *regardless* of the source of arousal (Zillman, 1984). For example, people who have been aroused by physical exercise show greater anger when provoked than people who have been physically less active. The person attributes the exercise-produced arousal to anger, thus intensifying the emotion. Similarly, compared with a person at rest, exercise-aroused people experience stronger feelings of attraction or dislike when they meet an attractive or unattractive member of the opposite sex (White, Fishbein & Rutstein, 1981).

When arousal from one experience carries over to an independent situation, it is called **transferred excitation** (Reisenzein, 1983). The transfer of excitation is especially likely when the pattern of arousal from the nonemotional source is similar to the pattern associated with a particular emotion. Thus, the pounding heart, increased respiration, and facial redness created by exercise are more likely to be mistaken for anger than for contentment.

The fact that people remain physiologically aroused longer than they think they do also helps explain transfer of excitation and its "accidental" intensification of emotion. A person still activated from exercise may feel calm, thus making it easier to attribute any subsequently noticed arousal to anger. If the person still *feels* aroused, however, he or she will accurately attribute the arousal to exercise (Zillman, 1978). For the transfer to occur, there must be a period during which the overt signs of arousal subside but the sympathetic nervous system is still active.

Arousal created by one emotion can also transfer to intensify another. For example, arousal from fear, like arousal from exercise, can enhance sexual feelings. In one study that found this result, the scene was a deep gorge in British Columbia with roaring rapids that could be crossed either by a precarious swinging bridge or by a safe wooden structure across a quiet part of the river. A female experimenter asked men who had just crossed each bridge to fill out a questionnaire based on the Thematic Apperception Test, which includes a measure of sexual imagery. The men who met the woman after crossing the dangerous bridge had much higher sexual imagery scores than the men who had crossed the safe bridge. Furthermore, they were more likely to rate her as attractive (Dutton & Aron, 1974). When the person giving out the questionnaire was a male, however, the bridge crossed had no impact on sexual imagery. The implication is that the excitement from crossing the bridge transferred to the men's interaction with the woman.

However, you might have thought of another possibility: perhaps the men who crossed the dangerous bridge were simply more adventurous in both bridge crossing and sexual encounters. This possibility was tested by repeating the experiment, with one change. This time, the woman approached the men farther down the trail, long after the arousal from crossing the bridge had subsided. In this case, the apparently adventurous men were no more likely than others to rate the woman as attractive or to call her for a date, suggesting that it was indeed transfer of excitation, not just adventurousness, that produced the original difference between groups.

Conclusions   Looking back on the theories of emotion we have discussed, it appears that, on balance, there is a role for both peripheral autonomic responses and the cognitive interpretation of those responses. In addition, there appears to be some direct central experiencing of emotion by the brain, independent of physiological arousal. No theory has completely resolved the issue of which, if any, component of emotion is primary, but all of them have helped psychologists to better understand how these components interact to produce emotional experience.

EXPRESSING AND RECOGNIZING EMOTIONS

Imagine a normal American male sitting down to watch television. You can see his face, but you cannot see what he is watching. He might be involved in complex patterns of thought, perhaps comparing his investments with those of the experts on "Wall Street Week." Equally plausibly, his mind might be reaching the consistency of leftover mashed potatoes while he watches reruns of "Gilligan's Island." There is very little you can observe that indicates the nature of his thought patterns. However, if the television program creates an *emotional* experience, you could make a reasonably accurate guess about what kind of emotion it is by watching his face (Patrick, Craig & Prkachin, 1986; Wagner, MacDonald & Manstead, 1986). Why should an emotional experience cause the muscles of the face to contract in a distinct pattern? So far, we have looked at emotion from the inside, as people experience their own emotions. In this section, we examine how they express and recognize emotions; in other words, how they communicate emotions.

Different species have evolved a variety of ways to communicate emotions. For people, even movement and body positioning can convey a certain amount of emotional information. In conversation between members of the opposite sex, for example, leaning toward and looking directly at one another usually indicate liking, possibly even arousal of sexual interest; leaning back and looking away tend to suggest boredom or hostility. But such cues are often complex and subtle. Contrary to the claims of popular books and articles on body language, there is no fixed set of signals in body movement or posture that always conveys a specific set of emotional messages (Goleman, 1986). Indeed, in humans, *facial* movement and expression play the primary role in communicating emotions.

Facial Movements and Emotions

The human face can generate six to seven thousand different expressions (Izard, 1971). Observers can discriminate very small changes in facial patterns; a twitch of the mouth can carry a lot of information. Are facial expressions of emotion innate, or are they learned? How are they controlled?

Innate and learned expressions People do seem to be programmed to express some emotions in certain ways; to some extent at least, facial expressions of emotions appear to be innate. People of all cultures show similar facial responses to similar emotional stimuli (Ekman, 1984; Ekman & Friesen, 1986). For example, the pattern of facial movements we call a smile is universally related to positive emotions. In all cultures, sadness is accompanied by slackened muscle tone and a "long" face. And in all cultures, people contort their faces in a similar way when presented with something disgusting. Additional evidence suggesting that basic emotional expressions are innate comes from infants. They do not need to be taught to grimace in pain or to smile in pleasure; they show facial movements that are appropriately correlated with their well-being. Even blind infants, who cannot see adults in order to imitate them, show the same emotional expressions as do sighted infants (Goodenough, 1932).

In addition, however, there are many expressions that are neither universal nor innate. People learn how to express certain emotions in particular ways specified by cultural rules. For example, suppose you say, "I just bought a new car," and everyone sticks their tongue out at you. In North America, this

The innate origin of some emotional expressions is supported by the fact that the facial movement pattern we call a smile is related to happiness, pleasure, and other positive emotions in human cultures throughout the world.

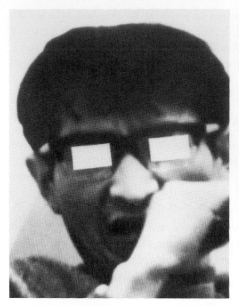

The extent to which control of emotional expression is expected varies from one culture to another. This was illustrated in a study of Japanese and American students who were shown movies that contained distressing scenes. When the subjects viewed the movie with a group of peers, the Japanese students showed little facial expressiveness compared with the American students. But, as pictured here, when they viewed the movie by themselves Japanese and American students showed the same facial expressions (Ekman, Friesen, and Ellsworth, 1972).

Figure 12.10
Control of Voluntary and Emotional Facial Movements
This man has a tumor in the motor cortex that prevents him from voluntarily moving the muscles on the left side of his face to form a smile. (a) The man is trying to smile in response to a command from the examiner. Even though he cannot smile on command, he is perfectly capable of (b) smiling with genuine happiness, because these movements are controlled by the extrapyramidal motor system.
(From *The Neurological Examination,* 4th ed., by R. N. Dejong. New York: Lippincott/Harper & Row, 1979.)

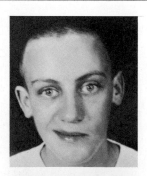
(a)

(b)

probably would mean that these people feel jealous or resentful. In China, such a response would express surprise.

The effects of learning are evident in a child's expanding repertoire of emotional expressions. Although infants begin with an innate set of emotional responses, they soon learn to imitate facial expressions and to use facial expressions to signal an ever-widening range of emotions. As they grow older, these expressions become more precise and somewhat more individualized, so that a particular expression conveys an unmistakable emotional message to anyone who knows that person well.

If a person's expressions become too idiosyncratic, however, no one knows what the expressions mean, and they fail to elicit the desired response from others. Operant shaping, which we described in the chapter on learning, probably helps keep emotional expressions within certain limits. If we could not see other people's facial expressions or observe their overt responses to ours, we might show fewer, or at least less intense, facial signs of emotion. Indeed, as congenitally blind people grow older, their facial expressions tend to become less animated (Izard, 1977).

People even learn to use facial expressions ironically or to hide or miscommunicate their feelings. They can show a smile that communicates contempt or derision rather than friendliness. They may look mock-serious before revealing a happy surprise or smile a greeting that is not particularly joyful. And, of course, even facial expressions that do arise from emotions can be controlled to some extent, as any poker player knows.

The brain and facial expressions   A forced smile and a smile that reflects real happiness not only look somewhat different but are controlled by different neurons in the brain (Rinn, 1984). Voluntary facial movements are controlled by a part of the motor cortex known as the **pyramidal motor system.** Involuntary facial movements accompanying emotions are controlled by the **extrapyramidal motor system,** which is controlled by subcortical areas, such as the basal ganglia (see Figure 12.8). People can partially suppress emotion-driven facial expressions because the cortical, pyramidal system can control the extrapyramidal system.

Neurological damage can disrupt these control systems. For example, the cortical motor system of the man shown in Figure 12.10 has been damaged.

As a result, he can smile reflexively when he is happy, but he cannot *make* himself smile. Damage to the extrapyramidal motor system can produce either the inability to display emotional facial movements, as in the masklike face of patients with Parkinson's disease, or an inability to inhibit emotion-driven facial movements. The woman shown in Figure 12.11, for example, laughs uncontrollably as a result of the neurological disease amyotrophic lateral sclerosis ("Lou Gehrig's disease"). Her laughter is involuntary and not accompanied by any felt emotion of mirth (Poeck, 1969).

Studies of people with different kinds of brain damage have revealed another characteristic of emotional expression. Recall from the chapter on biological psychology that, although the cerebral hemispheres normally operate in an integrated fashion, the hemispheres play somewhat different roles in such functions as language. Similarly, the perception, experience, and expression of emotion are not controlled equally by each half of the brain.

In particular, people who suffer damage to the left hemisphere but have an intact right hemisphere tend to express an unusual amount of negative affect, such as pathological crying. Furthermore, some people with damage to the left hemisphere no longer laugh at jokes, even though they understand their meaning, logic, and punch lines. And compared with normal individuals, depressed people show greater electrical activity of the right frontal cortex (Schaffer, Davidson & Saron, 1983). In contrast, patients with right-hemisphere damage but intact left hemispheres often exhibit pathological laughter (Sackeim et al., 1982). These findings suggest that the right hemisphere is somewhat more involved than the left in the expression of negative emotion, whereas the left is more involved in expressing positive emotion. This asymmetry is found even in infants. In both newborns and ten-month-olds, positive emotional expression is accompanied by greater electrical activity in the left hemisphere; negative emotions are accompanied by greater activity in the right frontal cortex (Davidson, 1984).

Even though the left hemisphere appears more active during the expression of some emotions, the right hemisphere is more involved in the expression of emotion in general. Because the nerves controlling muscles cross over the midline, just as the sensory systems do, the contribution of the right side is observable in the left side of the face (Sackeim, Gur & Saucy, 1978).

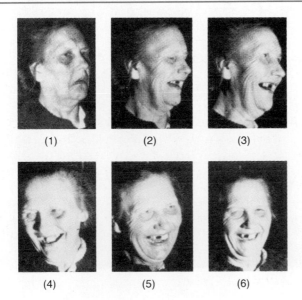

(1)   (2)   (3)

(4)   (5)   (6)

Figure 12.11
Separation of Emotional Experience from Emotional Expression
This woman has a neurological disease (amyotrophic lateral sclerosis) that causes involuntary nonemotional laughing. She reported that the laughter was painful and she was struggling to suppress it.
(From "Pathophysiology of emotional disorders associated with brain damage" by K. Poeck, in P. J. Vinken and G. W. Bruyn (Eds.) *Handbook of Clinical Neurology* Vol. 3, New York: American Elserier, 1969.)

HIGHLIGHT

Laterality and the Suppression of Emotion

The relationship between the cerebral hemispheres may also be important in suppressing the expression of emotions. Specifically, Richard Davidson (1984) offered the suggestion that communication between the hemispheres may be important in the development of this ability.

Some evidence for this idea comes from observations of infants. Anyone with intact hearing will testify that infants do not inhibit emotional expressions, especially negative ones. Infants also have less well developed functional connections between the hemispheres (Rakic & Yaklovlev, 1968). In fact, until about the age of thirteen the corpus callosum (the structure connecting the hemispheres) is not fully myelinated; that is, its axons are not yet covered with the fatty sheath that speeds neural activity (Rakic & Yaklovlev, 1968). Perhaps the developing fibers of the corpus callosum speed interhemispheric cooperation in the inhibition of emotion and contribute to the child's ability to suppress negative emotional displays.

Among adults, individual differences in interhemispheric communication may likewise be partly responsible for differences in the ability to suppress emotional expression. One possibility is that the suppression of negative emotions involves cutting off the communication of emotional information from the right hemisphere (where negative emotions tend to be generated) to verbal areas in the left hemisphere (Galin, 1974). Therefore, among people who characteristically suppress emotions, the autonomic responses to emotion and the ability to report an emotional experience may be disconnected. In fact, when mildly stressful stimuli are presented to people who typically suppress emotion, their autonomic activity increases, even though they report feeling little or no anxiety (Weinberger, Schwartz & Davidson, 1979).

Young children's relative inability to suppress emotions, especially negative ones, may be related to the fact that neural pathways between their cerebral hemispheres are not yet fully developed or functional.

Some preliminary experimental evidence supports the idea that this dissociation of verbal reports from physiological responses is due to reduced interhemispheric communication (Davidson, 1984). An apparatus that presented images either to the right or to the left side of the brain, but not both, showed subjects known to be suppressors or nonsuppressors of emotion brief glimpses of faces exhibiting emotions. The subjects were asked to describe the emotion in each face. (Asking for an oral response ensured that the information passed through the left hemisphere, where language production occurs.) When the faces were presented to the *left* hemisphere, suppressors and nonsuppressors were equal in their ability to recognize and report the emotion shown. However, when the faces were seen only by the *right* hemisphere, suppressors did significantly worse than nonsuppressors. This difference did not occur when the subjects were asked to report just the sex of the face. These results suggest that suppression of emotional expression may involve reduced interhemispheric communication, rather than a failure to experience emotion. ◼

Perceiving Emotions

For perceiving as well as expressing emotion, the right hemisphere is more active than the left. Psychologists discovered this by studying the perception of the face, the primary carrier of human emotional expression. They found, first, that the right hemisphere is better at recognizing faces than the left hemisphere (the left hemisphere is better at recognizing words). That is, the image of a face can be recognized faster when flashed to the right hemisphere. The right hemisphere's advantage is even greater when the face is portraying an emotion, especially a negative emotion, such as sadness (Suberi & McKeever, 1977). Furthermore, the right hemisphere can recognize a particular emotion even if the face is presented too briefly for the subject to recognize the person. In other words, the right hemisphere appears to detect a person's emotion first and his or her identity second.

FUNCTIONS AND EFFECTS OF EMOTION

Earlier, we said that one defining characteristic of emotions is that they happen *to* people; people do not make them happen. Like the heartbeat and the physiological need for food and water, emotions are a basic part of being human. But what purposes do they serve?

The Functions of Emotional Expressions

Charles Darwin provided one influential view of the function of emotions. Because he observed that certain facial expressions seem to be universal, Darwin proposed that these expressions are biologically determined, passed on genetically from one generation to the next. Consistent with his evolutionary theory, Darwin also argued that the facial expressions seen today are those that have been most effective at serving communicative functions. That is, facial expressions survive in a particular form because they tell others something about how a person is feeling and what he or she is about to do. If someone is red in the face and scowling, for example, you will probably assume that he or she is angry, and you will be unlikely to choose that particular moment to ask for a loan.

Darwin's theory about facial expressions is widely, but not universally, accepted (Zajonc, 1985). It has been criticized on two grounds. First, although

People's facial expressions can be eloquent communicators of their emotional state and provide unspoken cues as to how one should behave around them.

it may be beneficial for an animal or person to communicate some emotions, such as anger, in order to avoid open conflict, other emotions are better left concealed. Every gangster and politician knows that it can be conducive to survival to conceal one's true feelings and intentions. Second, Darwin himself suggested that, in order to understand emotional expressions, one should be able to explain why certain movements of the face are related to certain emotions. But Darwin's theory did not indicate why particular muscles are used to express specific emotions.

Another idea about the function of emotions emphasizes, as Darwin did, their role in communication but focuses more specifically on how communicated information is used. For example, infants who cannot yet understand spoken language depend to a large degree on adults' emotional expressions for information (Campos & Barrett, 1984). Joseph Campos has shown how the communicative value of emotional expressions depends on context. One of the most interesting examples is the **social referencing** phenomenon (Campos & Stenberg, 1981). In an uncertain situation, other people provide a *reference,* to reduce uncertainty. People may look to the facial expressions, tone of voice, and bodily gestures of others for guidance about how to proceed. A novice chess player, for instance, might reach out to move the queen, catch sight of a spectator's grimace, and infer that another move would be better. The person providing facial cues in situations like this may or may not have any intention of communicating information. If a situation has no ambiguities, people may not pay attention even if the cues are present.

For infants, the visual-cliff experiments described in the chapter on perception provide an example of an uncertain situation. To reach its mother, an infant in these experiments must cross the visual cliff (see page 198). If there is no apparent dropoff or if the drop is very dramatic, like that of a four-foot cliff, there is no ambiguity, and a one-year-old knows what to do. It crawls across in the first case and stays put in the second case. However, if the apparent dropoff is shallow enough to create uncertainty (say, two feet), then the infant looks to its mother's emotional expressions to relieve uncertainty. In one study, mothers were asked to display either a fearful or a joyful face. When the mothers made a fearful face, no infant crossed the glass floor.

But when they posed a joyful face, fifteen out of nineteen infants crossed (Sorce et al., 1981).

Communication through emotional expression may explain some behaviors that many have considered biologically "wired in." For example, infants' fear of strangers is greatly influenced by the mother's emotional expressions. If a stranger enters the room and the mother abruptly says "Hello" and frowns, an eight-month-old infant will have an increased heart rate and show distress when the stranger approaches. But if the mother says a cheery "Hello," the infant's heart rate actually slows down, and it shows less distress (Sorce et al., 1982). Thus the emotional expression of one person can communicate values and shape the behavior of another person. This type of emotional communication is an important source of knowledge about the world, and it continues to influence people even in adulthood.

An alternative theory of the purpose of emotional expression, proposed more than eighty years ago by Israel Waynbaum and recently revived by Robert Zajonc (pronounced "zi-onze") (1985), suggests that facial expressions of emotions have important physiological functions. Specifically, Waynbaum suggested that, when facial muscles contract, the flow of blood to different regions of the brain is redistributed. For example, he suggested that laughing is beneficial because it constricts some arteries and veins, causing more blood to be shunted to the brain and thus providing more oxygen there. These ideas are speculative, but they are testable hypotheses.

The Effects of Experiencing Emotions

Whatever their purpose, emotions also have a variety of short- and long-term effects on people, especially on their motivation and health.

Motivation and emotions   As we noted earlier, emotions can alter motivation. Most people tend to act in ways that bring about happiness, satisfaction, and other positive emotions and to avoid doing things that cause pain, anxiety, disgust, or sadness. People who consistently behave in ways that result in unpleasant emotional consequences are commonly considered to have some form of mental disorder.

Emotions also arouse the brain and body in preparation for needed action. The importance of this is evident in people whose emotional intensity is very low. Nothing seems to get them excited; they appear to take no real pleasure in anything; and they do not get very upset about anything. If lack of emotion is extreme, they find it difficult or impossible to hold a job or to function normally in other ways. Too much emotional arousal can also cause problems, as we discussed in the chapter on motivation. An overly emotional person becomes unable to concentrate or to coordinate thoughts and actions efficiently. For example, stage fright, which brings sweaty palms, dry mouth, tremors, and other signs of strong arousal of the sympathetic nervous system, can lead to forgotten lines, botched musical numbers, and other performance disasters.

People can learn to reduce their emotional arousal in order to improve their performance. (Some of the methods are described in more detail in the chapter on psychotherapy.) Drugs can also be used. In studies with music students, preventing the peripheral symptoms of sympathetic nervous system arousal with the drug propranolol not only reduced anxiety but also improved performance (Brantigan, Brantigan & Joseph, 1978).

Emotions and health   Norman Cousins popularized another idea about the effects of emotion: the notion that positive emotions may promote or maintain health. Cousins believes that he recovered from an incurable disease because

EMOTION AND MEMORY

How Do Emotions Affect What People Remember?

We noted earlier that emotions happen to us; we do not usually "decide" to have them. However, most people have found that retrieving memories from long-term storage is often accompanied by the happiness, sadness, or other emotions originally associated with the remembered events. Thus, it is possible to recreate emotions by recalling memories, a fact that many actors have recognized and used to advantage. The biological basis of this interaction of memory and emotion may lie in the fact that the emotional, as opposed to the informational, components of memories may have their own storage regions in the brain (Mishkin & Appenzeller, 1987). Psychologists have recently begun to make studies of the numerous ways in which evoking one of these types of components may trigger the other.

Consider, for example, *emotion-dependent memory.* When your current emotion matches the emotion that you felt when you stored a certain memory, then retrieval is better than if your emotional state is different (Bower, 1981; Bower & Cohen, 1982). For example, if you are in a good mood when you learn something, you will have better recall if you are in a good mood when you try to remember it. Emotion-dependent mem-

ory represents a form of state-dependent memory and is another example of the encoding specificity principle discussed in the chapter on memory. Recall that your internal psychological environment is one more cue associated with what you learn, and your emotional state is part of this internal environment. Thus, the existence of emotion-dependent memory supports the view that the chunks that make up memory are organized into networks and that emotions form part of these networks (Bower, 1981).

Emotional state may also facilitate the processing of information that is similar in tone to that state. For example, Gordon Bower and his colleagues found that people who read a story remembered more happy incidents if they were made to feel happy before reading it than if they had been made to feel sad (Bower et al., 1981). Notice that this effect occurs because of a match between a person's emotional state and the content of what is to be learned, whereas emotion-dependent memory reflects a match in a person's emotional state at two different times. Researchers are trying to discover whether this *mood congruency effect* is due to the way information is encoded, the way it is retrieved, or both. Preliminary evidence suggests that both encoding

he treated himself with "laughter therapy," which included watching Marx Brothers movies in the hospital. However, many people recover from incurable diseases even though they remain grumpy.

There is evidence that very desirable rewards (which presumably elicit positive emotions) can inhibit the experience of pain. Decades ago, Ivan Pavlov discovered that pain responses are inhibited in very hungry animals if the pain also serves as a signal for the delivery of food (Pavlov, 1927). More recently, animals allowed to eat, drink, and achieve other important goals showed reduced blood levels of stress-related hormones called corticosteroids (Hennessy & Levine, 1979). Perhaps the reduction was at least in part related to the positive emotions the animals presumably experienced as they reached their goals. How and why positive emotions might reduce pain or the level of stress-related hormones is still unclear. It may be that positive emotions alter the body's responses to all sorts of negative events, including the agents of disease. If so, positive emotions may indeed play as great a role in promoting physical health as they do in promoting mental health.

More solid research is required before psychologists and medical scientists will fully understand the role of positive emotions in health. Much more is known about the role of such negative emotions as anger, depression, worry,

and retrieval factors are involved (Leventhal & Tomarken, 1986).

For both emotion-dependent learning and mood congruency, positive emotions have a stronger effect on memory than do negative ones. Negative emotions tend to interfere with memory processes in general, perhaps because they are so often accompanied by angry or panicky thoughts that distract people's attention from the retrieval process at hand. This interference may obscure emotion-dependent learning in some cases. The impact of emotions on memory is greatest if the material does not have many links with what is already known (Leventhal & Tomarken, 1986). This is partly because, as noted in the memory chapter, retrieval of information from long-term memory is easier when the material is well integrated with existing knowledge. When there is little integration, the emotion associated with the information may be one of the only retrieval cues available.

Very intense emotional experiences exert special effects on the way people remember events. Most people have vivid memories of their wedding day and recall exactly where they were and what they were doing when they learned of a relative's death. Memory for events that are very emotionally arousing tends to be vivid, detailed, and long-lasting. In fact, these memories are called *flashbulb memories,* because they preserve particular experiences in such great detail (Brown & Kulik, 1977; Thompson & Cowan, 1986). Flashbulb memories occur primarily because of the many consequences the event has for one's life. When people get married or are told that a parent has died, they know that their life will change, often dramatically. This knowledge leads them to think about the event and to form an elaborate network of associations with other areas of knowledge, thus making accurate retrieval of the event more likely.

Negative emotions can also have a very different effect on memory, however: people may be motivated *not* to recall certain particularly painful events or to distort them in ways that make them less upsetting (Erdelyi, 1985; Erdelyi & Goldberg, 1979). In fact, some people intentionally dwell on positive memories in order to make themselves feel better (Clark & Isen, 1982). These tendencies may well serve as the basis for some of the defense mechanisms to be discussed in the chapters on stress and personality

and anxiety in creating or intensifying such health problems as headaches, high blood pressure, and heart disease. These negative emotions and their adverse effects on health will be discussed in Chapter 13, on stress.

FUTURE DIRECTIONS

The James-Lange, Cannon-Bard, and Schachter theories clearly state relatively simple relationships between physiological responses, cognitive activity, and the experience of emotion; but psychologists have still not pinpointed exactly how emotional experiences are produced. As PET scans, magnetic resonance imaging, EEG recordings, and other techniques for monitoring brain activity are refined, researchers may be able to observe brain activity more precisely and to relate that activity to subjective reports of emotional experience. Determining the areas of the brain that generate emotions may also clarify how emotions and motivational systems interact.

Several of the recent studies that we discussed have opened new and interesting lines of investigation. For example, observations that some aspects of emotional expression do not vary across cultures and that some of these expressions occur in infants provide evidence that biology plays an important role in determining emotional expressions. Yet social factors are critical in shaping the way emotions are expressed, in communicating values, and in shaping behavior. Future research will be needed to clarify the interactions of social and biological factors in emotional experience and expression.

Current knowledge suggests that future studies will find that thinking and feeling cannot be as neatly separated as psychologists in the past might have wished. Psychologists working in the field of artificial intelligence have even begun to attempt computer simulations of human thinking that include emotions.

In all of these areas, future research is likely to emphasize the adaptive functions of emotions, instead of portraying them as disruptions to smooth functioning. If you wish to study the topic of emotion in more detail, consider taking a course in motivation and emotion. You will also find that most courses in biological psychology deal to some degree with the physiological and anatomical bases of emotion. A course on stress and coping may also offer valuable coverage of the negative effects of emotional overarousal.

SUMMARY

1. An emotion is an experience that is felt as happening to the self, generated in part by one's cognitive appraisal of a situation, and accompanied by both learned and reflexive responses. There is no consensus on how many distinct basic emotions exist.

2. The visceral responses that are part of emotional experiences are produced by the autonomic nervous system. This system modulates the activity of all the body's organs, allowing the body to respond to demands from the environment in a coordinated fashion. The autonomic nervous system has two divisions: the sympathetic and the parasympathetic nervous systems. The parasympathetic system is involved mainly in the protection, nourishment, and growth of the body, whereas the sympathetic system usually prepares the body for vigorous action. The adrenal glands, acting as specialized cells of the sympathetic nervous system, contribute to the fight-or-flight response by releasing adrenaline into the bloodstream. Activity of the autonomic nervous system does not reach consciousness directly but can be detected indirectly, as through biofeedback.

3. The James-Lange theory of emotion holds that visceral and reflexive behavioral responses are the primary source of emotion and that self-observation of these responses is perceived as an emotional experience.

4. The Cannon-Bard theory suggests that visceral responses occur independently of emotional experience and that there is a direct experience of emotion based on activity of the central nervous system. An updated version of this theory suggests that the experience of emotion depends on pathways in the brain, such as those from the locus coeruleus, which constitute a kind of "autonomic nervous system" within the brain. These pathways probably mediate the connections between motivation and emotion.

5. The Schachter theory suggests that peripheral responses are primary sources of emotion but that cognitive interpretations of the eliciting situation are required to label the emotion. Attributing arousal from one situation to stimuli in another situation can intensify the emotion experienced in the second situation.

6. People's facial expressions are the primary source of information about the emotions they are experiencing. Certain facial movements are innate and universally associated with certain emotions, but many other expressions must be learned. As a result, the same emotion may be expressed facially in different ways in different cultures.

7. The right and left cerebral hemispheres play somewhat different roles in emotion. Overall, the right hemisphere seems to play the dominant role in both the expression and the perception of emotion. However, there may be differences in the hemispheres' roles in expressing positive and negative emotions. Suppression of emotions may involve reduced communication between the hemispheres.

8. Darwin suggested that facial expressions of emotion evolved because they communicate an animal's emotional condition to other animals. Especially in ambiguous situations, other people's facial expressions of emotion may also be vital sources of information about what to do or what not to do. The Waynbaum-Zajonc hypothesis suggests that emotional facial movements serve physiological functions because these movements modify the flow of blood to the brain.

9. Emotions can create motivation, and motivation can generate emotions. Researchers have not determined whether positive emotions promote physical health, but it is clear that negative emotions can contribute to physical health problems.

KEY TERMS

Definitions of terms appear on the pages shown in parentheses.

adrenal gland (448)

attribution (457)

autonomic nervous system (446)

Cannon-Bard theory (454)

emotion (445)

extrapyramidal motor system (462)

facial feedback hypothesis (453)

fight-or-flight syndrome (447)

James-Lange theory (452)

parasympathetic nervous system (447)

pyramidal motor system (462)

Schachter theory (457)

social referencing (466)

sympathetic nervous system (447)

transferred excitation (459)

RECOMMENDED READINGS

Izard, C. E., Kagan, J., & Zajonc, R. B. (Eds.). (1984). *Emotions, cognition, and behavior.* Cambridge, Eng.: Cambridge University Press. Contains an interesting variety of papers, some fairly technical, but some general enough for the nonspecialist.

James, W. (1890). *Principles of psychology.* New York: Henry Holt. This classic treatment of emotions is surprisingly readable, relatively short, and well worth reading.

Leventhal, H., & Tomarken, A. J. (1986). Emotion: Today's problems. *Annual Review of Psychology, 37,* 565–610. This review assesses the status of classical theories of emotion and addresses some of the newer directions that research on emotion is taking.

Plutchik, R. (1980). *Emotions in humans and animals: A psychoevolutionary synthesis.* New York: Harper & Row. Plutchik's theory considers the functions of emotions from a variety of viewpoints and does not require a great deal of technical knowledge to appreciate.

N

ot too long ago, dentists were encouraged to deal with fearful, screaming child patients by using the Hand Over Mouth Exercise (HOME). They were told to pin the terrified child in the dental chair, hold a towel over its mouth, and calmly state that there would be no escape until all crying and uncooperative behavior ceased (Levitas, 1974). Needless to say, the technique often made matters worse. Even with adult patients, dentists of an earlier era often said little or nothing about what they were about to do. Fortunately, today's dental students learn that patients will be less upset, even less pained, when they are told what is coming and are given some control over it, such as raising one's hand to request a break. This insight comes from research on stress and stress management.

Of course, stress is not limited to the dental office. You have probably heard that death and taxes are the only two things you can be sure of in life. If there is a third, it must surely be stress. Stress is basic to life, no matter how wealthy, powerful, good looking, or happy you might be, and it is related to many areas of psychology (see Linkages diagram, p. 474). Mild stress can be stimulating, motivating, and sometimes even desirable. But as it becomes more severe, stress can bring on a variety of physical, psychological, and behavioral problems. In this chapter, we consider what stress is, where it comes from, what its effects are, and how people can cope with it.

WHAT IS STRESS?

Stress is the process of adjusting to circumstances that disrupt, or threaten to disrupt, a person's equilibrium (Burchfield, 1979; Lazarus & Folkman, 1984; Selye, 1976). Here are two examples:

Marlene has spent ten hours of a sweltering August day on a crowded bus from Toledo, Ohio, to Muncie, Indiana. The air conditioner is not working, and she discovers that the person next to her has apparently not had a bath since the beginning of the decade. By the time she reaches Muncie, Marlene is hot, dizzy, depressed, tired, and irritable.

Jack is waiting in a roomful of other college seniors to interview for a job with a large accounting firm. His grades are not outstanding, but he hopes to get by on his personality. He feels that his parents and his fiancée expect him to land a high-prestige, high-paying position. He is very nervous. His mouth is dry, his stomach feels tight, his heart is pounding, and perspiration has already begun to soak through his new suit.

These sketches emphasize that stress always involves a relationship between people and their environments—more specifically, between stressors and stress reactions. **Stressors** are events and situations (such as uncomfortable bus rides) to which people must adjust. **Stress reactions** are the physical, psychological, and behavioral responses (such as nausea, nervousness, and tiredness) people display in the face of stressors.

To a considerable degree, the impact of stressors and how people react to them depend on the circumstances in which the stressors occur and on each person's physical and psychological characteristics. This is why stress is

13

Stress and Coping

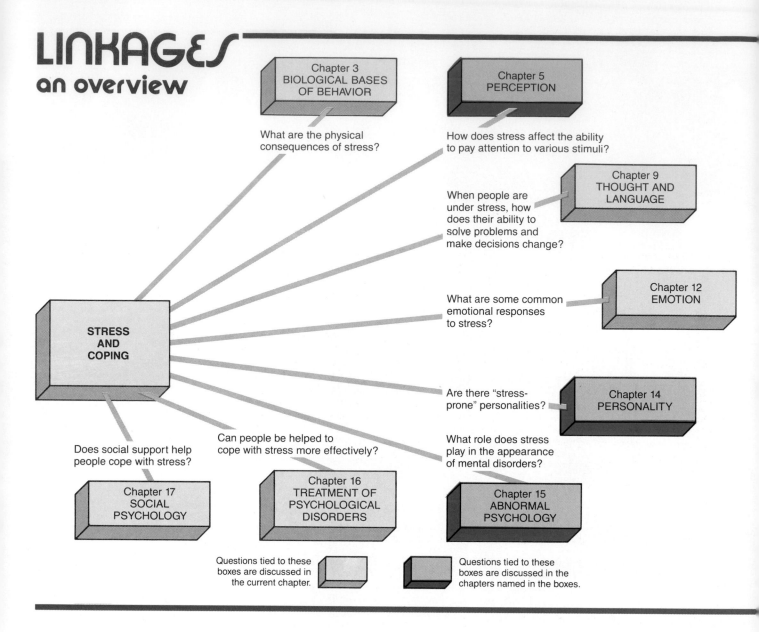

LINKAGES
an overview

Chapter 3
BIOLOGICAL BASES
OF BEHAVIOR

What are the physical
consequences of stress?

Chapter 5
PERCEPTION

How does stress affect the ability
to pay attention to various stimuli?

Chapter 9
THOUGHT AND
LANGUAGE

When people are
under stress, how
does their ability to
solve problems and
make decisions change?

STRESS
AND
COPING

Chapter 12
EMOTION

What are some common
emotional responses
to stress?

Are there "stress-
prone" personalities?

Chapter 14
PERSONALITY

Does social support help
people cope with stress?

Can people be helped to
cope with stress more effectively?

What role does stress
play in the appearance
of mental disorders?

Chapter 17
SOCIAL
PSYCHOLOGY

Chapter 16
TREATMENT OF
PSYCHOLOGICAL
DISORDERS

Chapter 15
ABNORMAL
PSYCHOLOGY

Questions tied to these
boxes are discussed in
the current chapter.

Questions tied to these
boxes are discussed in the
chapters named in the boxes.

defined, not as a specific occurrence, but as a process. Figure 13.1 shows that understanding the stress process requires attention to environmental stressors, to the mediating factors that make people more or less sensitive to stressors, and to the nature of different stress responses. We will consider stressors and stress responses first, and then we examine some of the factors that influence the relationship between them.

STRESSORS

Many stressors involve *physical demands;* infections and extreme temperatures are examples. In humans, however, many of the most significant stressors are *psychological.* The person who must give a speech to impress a professor or potential employer is facing stressors that can be just as demanding as a day of hard physical labor. Many, perhaps most, human stressors include both physical and psychological components. Athletes, for example, are challenged by the demands of physical exertion, as well as by the pressure of competition. In this section, we focus on psychological stressors.

STRESS AND PSYCHOLOGY

Constant interaction with an ever-changing world is the basis for stress. Why are some people able to withstand the stress of life, whereas others in similar circumstances burn out psychologically and wear out physically? What rules govern the impact of stressors on individual people? These are some of the questions psychologists are trying to answer. And some of the answers are surprising. For example, one study found that health problems, missed workdays, and other occupational difficulties among university administrators were less related to the number or intensity of job stressors (such as deadlines or conflicts) than to how well the job situations allowed the administrators to use their most preferred way of interacting with others and display other aspects of their leadership style (Chemers et al., 1985).

Results like these have helped researchers to recognize that understanding stress requires that they link the study of stress to concepts and evidence from numerous other areas of psychology. Cognitive psychology, for example, assumes an important role in stress research, because the way people think about stressors can significantly alter the stressors' impact. Similarly, one cannot understand human stress without taking social psychology into account. The presence or absence of social support from friends or family can sometimes determine whether people keep trying to cope with stressful circumstances or succumb to drugs or suicide. These and other links appear throughout this chapter.

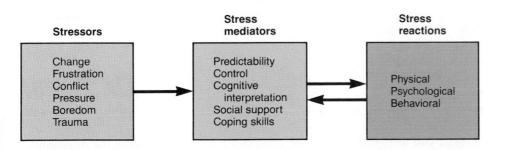

Stressors	Stress mediators	Stress reactions
Change Frustration Conflict Pressure Boredom Trauma	Predictability Control Cognitive interpretation Social support Coping skills	Physical Psychological Behavioral

Figure 13.1
The Process of Stress
Stressful events, a person's reactions to those events, and interactions between the person and the situation are all important components of stress. The interactions are stress mediators; they moderate or intensify the impact of a stressful situation. For example, just one or two minor stressors might create extreme stress reactions if they are not controllable and are the latest of dozens of hassles in the life of a stress-prone individual with few coping skills. The same circumstances might not have much effect if that individual is more skilled or has more support from family or friends. Note the two-way relationship between stress mediators and stress responses. Coping well with a stressor on one occasion, for example, can make it easier to cope well the next time.

Long periods of potentially boring quiet unpredictably punctuated by episodes of intense pressure are among the factors that can create significant stress for firefighters and emergency medical personnel.

Some Major Psychological Stressors

Even very desirable events can be stressors if they require that one adapt to them. For example, the increased salary, responsibility, and status associated with a promotion may be very desirable; but the upgrade also creates new circumstances and pressures that require physical and psychological adjustments. Similarly, it is not uncommon for people to report feeling exhausted after a vacation and somewhat depressed after the excitement of a joyous event such as a wedding or birth. Still, unpleasant events and situations—those involving frustration, pressure, boredom, trauma, conflict, or change—are more likely to be associated with stress (Mueller, Edwards & Yarvis, 1977; Suls & Mullen, 1981).

Frustrating situations contain some obstacle that stands between a person and his or her goals. Waiting in a long line at the bank or being unable to find a phone to make an important call are simple examples of frustrating situations. More substantial illustrations include being unable to earn a decent living because of adverse economic conditions or job discrimination or failing in repeated attempts to find a love relationship.

Pressure situations require a person to do too much in too short a time. If you are trying to fix Thanksgiving dinner for twenty people on a day's notice, or if you are struggling to finish the last two questions on an essay test in ten minutes, you are under pressure. Even more problematic are situations in which pressure is constant or long-lasting, as it sometimes is for air traffic controllers, physicians, nurses, police officers, and others. These people must make many difficult decisions, sometimes involving life and death, under heavy time pressure. People under such pressure day after day sometimes begin to perform poorly and develop physical illness, alcoholism, anxiety, and many of the other stress-related problems described later in this chapter.

Boredom, or understimulation, is the opposite of pressure, but it, too, can be a stressor, especially if it continues for a long time. The agony of solitary confinement in prison or the tedium of a remote military post are probably the most extreme examples, but there are many others. If you have ever spent several hours doing an easy, but repetitive task, such as stuffing hundreds of envelopes, you can understand the stress experienced by factory workers who must do the same task over and over again every day.

Trauma, a shocking physical or emotional experience, can create what is perhaps the ultimate stress situation. Such catastrophes as rape, assault, military combat, fire, tornadoes, plane crashes, torture, or bomb blasts are only a few examples. Fortunately, few people ever have to endure such traumatic events, but more common disasters, such as a divorce or the sudden death of someone close, can be equally devastating.

Conflict is almost always stressful. The most obvious examples are the all-too-common disputes in which friends, family members, coworkers, or total strangers fight with, insult, or otherwise get nasty with each other. If you can recall the last time one of these interpersonal conflicts occurred in your life (even if you were just a spectator), you can probably also recall the discomfort you felt. Internal motivational conflicts can be equally, if not more, distressing than those with other people. Imagine, for example, the stress that might result when a woman stays with a man she does not love, only because she fears he will commit suicide if she leaves. Other examples were described in Chapter 11 as approach-approach, approach-avoidance, avoidance-avoidance, and mutiple approach-avoidance conflicts.

Change, whether positive or negative, can be a major stressor. Divorce, illness in the family, unemployment, and moving to a new city are just a few examples of situations that create social, psychological, financial, and physical changes to which people must adjust. Thomas Holmes and Richard Rahe included a wide range of change-related stressors in the forty-three items of their Social Readjustment Rating Scale (SRRS), developed in 1967. They asked a large number of people to rate these stressors in terms of *life change units* (*LCUs*), the amount of change and demand for adjustment they introduce into a person's life. The items on the SRRS and their LCU ratings are presented in Table 13.1. Getting married (the anchor point against which raters were told to compare all other stressors) was considered to be slightly more stressful than losing one's job.

TABLE 13.1

The Social Readjustment Rating Scale

Note that each event in the scale has a life change unit (LCU) value associated with it. People with a higher total of LCUs may experience more stress-related problems, but stress mediators, such as social support and coping skills, are also important factors.

Rank	Event	LCU Value
1	Death of spouse	100
2	Divorce	73
3	Marital separation	65
4	Jail term	63
5	Death of close family member	63
6	Personal injury or illness	53
7	Marriage	50
8	Fired at work	47
9	Marital reconciliation	45
10	Retirement	45
11	Change in health of family member	44
12	Pregnancy	40
13	Sex difficulties	39
14	Gain of new family member	39
15	Business readjustment	39
16	Change in financial state	38
17	Death of close friend	37
18	Change to different line of work	36
19	Change in number of arguments with spouse	35
20	Mortgage over $10,000	31
21	Foreclosure of mortgage or loan	30
22	Change in responsibilities at work	29
23	Son or daughter leaving home	29
24	Trouble with in-laws	29
25	Outstanding personal achievement	28
26	Wife begins or stops work	26
27	Begin or end school	26
28	Change in living conditions	25
29	Revision of personal habits	24
30	Trouble with boss	23
31	Change in work hours or conditions	20
32	Change in residence	20
33	Change in schools	20
34	Change in recreation	19
35	Change in church activities	19
36	Change in social activities	18
37	Mortgage or loan less than $10,000	17
38	Change in sleeping habits	16
39	Change in number of family get-togethers	15
40	Change in eating habits	15
41	Vacation	13
42	Christmas	12
43	Minor violations of the law	11

SOURCE: T. H. Holmes and R. H. Rahe, "The Social Readjustment Scale," *Journal of Psychosomatic Research*, Vol. 11, 1967. Reprinted by permission of Pergamon Press and T. H. Holmes.

Stress problems may stem not only from such major life events as divorce but also from daily hassles like crowded urban commuting or neighborhood noise.

Measuring Stressors

If you want to use the SRRS to measure the stressors in your own life, add the LCUs associated with each item you have experienced within the past year. If your score strikes you as being high, don't be surprised. College students routinely face numerous stressors having to do with everything from coursework to social life.

Tests like the SRRS provide a general impression of the stressors in a person's life. In fact, a great deal of research with such tests has suggested that the more stressors a person experiences (especially negative ones), the more likely it is that physical illness, mental disorder, or other problematic stress responses will follow. This conclusion is based in large measure on the fact that most patients who suffer from certain physical illnesses or mental disorders report having experienced one or more major stressors just before their disorders appeared (Barrett, 1979; Rahe et al., 1974). Does this mean that you can predict the stress problems in a person's life just by using the SRRS? No. Many people with high scores on the SRRS do not develop serious problems. And low scores do not guarantee a life free of the dangers of stress. Why?

One reason is that mediating factors, such as those listed in Figure 13.1, play an important role in determining the impact stressors will have on each individual. For example, it is difficult to predict who will develop stress-related problems by looking only at major life changes and not at such "daily hassles" as living in a noisy or overcrowded neighborhood, working at an unsatisfying job, or contending with urban commuting (Cohen, 1980; Kahn & French, 1970; Lazarus & Cohen, 1977). If you have ever had a day when everything seemed to go wrong—you overslept, could not get the car started, got to class late, and found that your pen was out of ink—you can understand the contribution of daily hassles to a person's total stress load.

One group of researchers (Kanner et al., 1981) developed special questionnaires to assess both major and minor hassles, as well as the uplifts people experience on a daily basis (see Table 13.2). Research with these scales has suggested that the accuracy of predictions about the severity of a person's

TABLE 13.2

Daily Hassles and Uplifts
Here are some items from the Daily Hassles and Uplifts Scales. The respondent is asked to identify which of these items he or she has experienced in the past month and to rate on a three-point scale the severity of the hassles and the intensity of the uplifts.

Hassles	Uplifts
Misplacing or losing things	Saving money
Troublesome neighbors	Being rested
Someone owes you money	Feeling healthy
Too many responsibilities	Completing a task
Planning meals	Meeting your responsibilities
Care for pet	Eating out
Too many interruptions	Relaxing
Unexpected company	Getting a present
Not enough money	Traveling
Silly mistakes	Resolving conflicts
Rising prices	Paying off debts
Job dissatisfaction	Getting love

SOURCE: A. D. Kanner, J. C. Coyne, C. Schaefer, and R. S. Lazarus, "Comparison of Two Modes of Stress Measurement: Daily Hassles and Uplifts versus Major Life Events," *Journal of Behavioral Medicine,* Vol. 4, 1981. Reprinted by permission of Plenum Publishing Corporation and the authors.

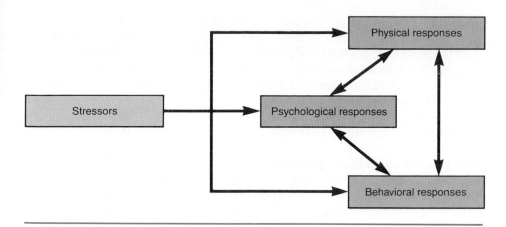

Figure 13.2
Stress Responses
The three main kinds of stress responses can occur in reaction to outside stressors or to one another. For example, suppose your instructor suddenly announces that a major paper will be due in two weeks (an environmental stressor). If your psychological response involves becoming worried about the assignment, that worry might act as an internal stress stimulus, perhaps causing such behavioral stress responses as insomnia, which in turn creates physical stress due to lack of sleep. The psychological response to the loss of sleep might include an inability to concentrate, thus slowing down work on the paper (a behavioral effect) and prompting increased worry. To some extent, stress can come from within ourselves, not just from the outside world.

stress responses may be improved when based on hassles rather than on major stressors alone (DeLongis et al., 1982; Eckenrode, 1984; Monroe, 1983).

STRESS RESPONSES

Stress reactions can be physical, psychological, or behavioral. For the sake of clarity, we will discuss each type of response separately, but all three types of stress reactions can, and often do, occur together, especially as stressors become more intense. For example, Marlene's responses to the stress of her bus ride were physical (dizziness), psychological (depression), and behavioral (irritability).

Furthermore, because the mind and body are so closely related, a stress response in one dimension can act as a stimulus setting off a stress response in another dimension (see Figure 13.2). For example, a physical stress reaction, such as mild chest pains following a family crisis, may lead to such psychological and behavioral stress responses as worrying about a heart attack and reluctance to have sex. We will come back to these ideas when we discuss research on how stress can cause illness and how illness can create stress.

Physical Stress Responses

Anyone who has experienced a near-accident or some other sudden and very frightening event knows that the physical responses to stress include rapid breathing, increased heartbeat, sweating, and a little later, general shakiness, especially in the muscles of the arms and legs. These reactions are all part of the fight-or-flight syndrome. As we saw in the chapter on emotion, this syndrome, created by the sympathetic branch of the autonomic nervous system, prepares the body to face or to flee an immediate threat. When the danger is past, these responses subside.

However, pioneering research by Hans Selye (pronounced "sell-yay") showed that, when stressors are longer-lasting, fight-or-flight responses are only the beginning of a longer sequence of bodily reactions. Careful observation of animals and humans exposed to infections, radiation, temperature extremes, and other extended stressors led Selye to suggest that this longer sequence of physical responses occurs in a consistent and very general pattern, or *syndrome,* which is triggered by the effort to adapt to any stressor. He called this sequence the **general adaptation syndrome,** or **GAS** (Selye, 1956, 1976).

The general adaptation syndrome   There are three stages in the GAS, as Figure 13.3 shows. The first stage is the **alarm reaction,** which involves some version of the fight-or-flight syndrome. In the face of mild stressors, such as a hot room, the reaction may simply involve changes in heart rate, respiration, and perspiration that help the body regulate its temperature. More severe stressors prompt more dramatic alarm reactions, rapidly mobilizing the body's adaptive energy, much as a burglar alarm alerts the police and mobilizes them to take action (Selye, 1956).

If the stressor persists, the stage of **resistance** begins. Here, signs of the initial alarm reaction diminish, but the body settles in to resist the stressor on a long-term basis. The drain on adaptive energy is slower during the resistance stage than it was during the alarm reaction; in fact, there may be few outward signs that anything is wrong. But the body is working very hard, just as if it were in a tug-of-war, pulling steadily against an opponent of equal strength. Organs such as the adrenal glands, the thymus, the liver, and the kidneys release several substances that increase blood pressure, fight inflammation, enhance muscle tension, increase blood sugar, and promote all the physical changes needed to cope with stressors (see Figure 13.4). Among these substances are *catecholamines* (especially adrenaline and noradrenaline) and *corticosteroids,* such as cortisol; the overall effect is to generate emergency energy. The more stressors there are (especially if new ones appear before recovery from the last one can take place) and the longer they last, the longer people need to expend resources in an effort to resist them.

This continued campaign of biochemical resistance is costly. It slowly but surely uses up more and more of the body's reserves of adaptive energy until, just as a slowly leaking tire eventually goes flat, the capacity to resist is gone. The body enters the third GAS stage, known as **exhaustion.** In extreme cases, such as prolonged exposure to freezing temperatures, the result is death. More commonly, however, the exhaustion stage is associated with signs of physical wear and tear, especially in organ systems that were weak in the first place or heavily involved in the resistance process. For example, if the catecholamines and corticosteroids, which help fight stressors during the resistance stage,

Figure 13.3
The General Adaptation Syndrome
Hans Selye's research suggested that physical reactions to stress occur in three phases: the alarm reaction, the stage of resistance, and the stage of exhaustion. During the alarm reaction, the body's resistance temporarily drops below its normal, ongoing level as it absorbs the initial impact of the stressor. However, the resistance soon increases dramatically, leveling off in the resistance stage, but ultimately declining if the exhaustion stage is reached. The GAS has been very influential in stress research, but more recent approaches suggest that this sequence of events is not always as consistent and predictable as Selye suggested.
(Adaptation of Figure 3, p. 39, from *Stress Without Distress* by Hans Selye. J. B. Lippincott. Copyright © 1974 by Hans Selye, M.D. Reprinted by permission of Harper and Row, Publishers, Inc.)

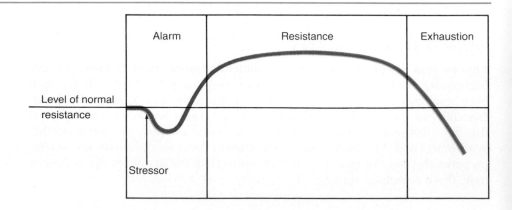

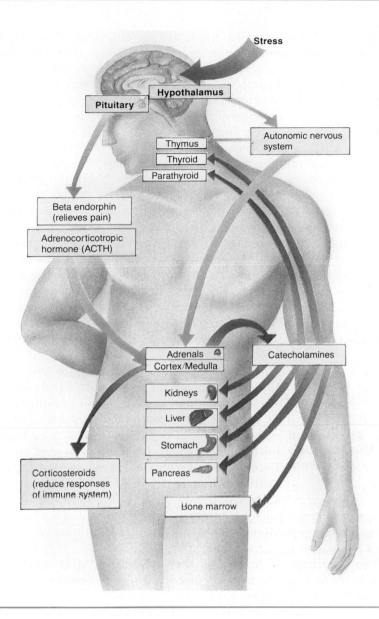

Figure 13.4
Organ Systems Involved in the GAS
Stressors produce a wide variety of physiological responses that begin in the brain and spread to many organs throughout the body. For example, catecholamines from the medulla of the adrenal glands cause the kidneys to raise blood pressure. The pituitary gland triggers release of endogenous opiates, the body's natural painkillers. It also stimulates release of corticosteroids, which help resist stress but, as we describe later, also tend to suppress the immune system, making the body more vulnerable to infection.
(Copyright © 1983 by The New York Times Company. Reprinted by permission.)

remain at high levels for an extended time, they can promote illnesses ranging from heart disease, high blood pressure, and arthritis to colds and flu (Ross & Glomset, 1976). Selye called illnesses that are caused or promoted by stressors **diseases of adaptation.**

Beyond Selye's model   Selye's model has been very influential, but it has also been criticized. At least in the case of humans, Selye overemphasized the role of fixed biological processes in determining stress responses, and he underestimated the role of such psychological factors as emotional state or the way a person thinks about stressors (Lazarus & Folkman, 1984; Mason, 1971). Research has shown, for example, that the alarm reaction of the GAS may not be as general and automatic as Selye described it and that specific responses later in the GAS are quite individualized. In terms of our earlier analogy, the burglar alarm might sound somewhat different depending on which door or window is invaded (the alarm reaction), and what the police do after they arrive (the resistance stage) depends on their interpretation of the situation.

Criticisms of Selye's model led to the development of several broader approaches to understanding stress responses. Although they differ somewhat in detail, these *psychobiological models* emphasize the importance of psychological as well as biological variables in regulating and producing stress responses (Mason, 1975; Schwartz, 1982). For example, one study of autopsy data found that those terminally ill patients who had been conscious until they died showed some classic signs of stress (such as enlarged adrenal glands), whereas those who had remained in a coma until death did not (Symington et al., 1955). According to psychobiological models, this variation in stress responses reflects the influence of psychological variables on physical stress reactions. That is, although the physical stressors were similar in both groups, patients who could think about and become emotional about their impending death displayed more severe stress responses.

According to psychobiological models, psychological variables, such as how a person thinks about a stressor, shape the impact of that stressor. For example, they suggest that a given stressor will have a more negative impact if the person thinks about it as an uncontrollable threat rather than as a controllable challenge (Lazarus & Launier, 1978). Furthermore, threat, conflict, frustration, pressure, boredom, and other psychological stressors can stimulate some of the same responses as physical danger (Frankenhaeuser et al., 1971).

HIGHLIGHT

Stress and the Immune System

We mentioned earlier that physical and psychological stressors promote the excessive or prolonged secretion of catecholamines and corticosteroids. These effects may in turn lead to illness because they hamper the functioning of the body's immune system (Jemmott & Locke, 1984; Tecoma & Huey, 1985). The **immune system** is the first line of defense against invading substances and microorganisms. Among the cells that form the armies of the immune system are *T-cells,* which attack virally infected cells; *B-cells,* which form antibodies against foreign substances; and *natural killer cells,* which kill invaders like tumor cells and virally infected cells.

When corticosteroid hormones, such as cortisol, are released from the adrenal cortex in response to stress, they tend to suppress the responsiveness of the immune system, thus leaving the body more vulnerable to infection (see Figure 13.4). Adrenaline secreted from the adrenal medulla under stress also influences immune cells, as do endogenous opiates, which, as we described in Chapter 3, ease pain. Immune cells of the thymus gland are also directly activated by the autonomic nervous system. The role played by these and other physiological stress responses in reducing the body's ability to fight disease was demonstrated more than a century ago. On March 19, 1878, at a seminar before the Académie de Médécine de Paris, Louis Pasteur showed his distinguished audience three chickens. One healthy bird, the control chicken, had been raised normally. A second bird had been intentionally infected with bacteria but given no other treatment; it was also healthy. The third chicken Pasteur presented was dead. It had been infected with the same bacteria as the second bird, but it had also been physically stressed by being exposed to cold temperatures (Kelley, 1985); as a result, the bacteria killed it.

Since Pasteur's time, much has been learned about how stressors affect the immune system. The effects are not straightforward. For example, the stress of crowded living conditions increases chickens' susceptibility to some diseases but reduces their susceptibility to others (Gross & Colmano, 1969). Still, two characteristics of physical stress reactions in general also apply to the effect of stressors on the immune system.

First, both psychological and physical stressors can influence the immune system. For example, husbands of women who died of breast cancer have shown diminished immune function for several months during bereavement (Schleifer et al., 1983). And among students the activity of natural killer cells was significantly lower during the week of finals than one month before or one month after exams (Kiecolt-Glaser et al., 1984). Second, psychological variables help regulate the impact of a stressor. More specifically, the effect of a stressor on the immune system depends on how the organism *copes* with it. For example, in several studies, rats were given mild but distressing shock to the toes, which they either could or could not escape by pressing a bar in the cage. Even though animals in both conditions experienced the same amount of shock, those unable to cope with it through bar pressing showed impaired functioning of the immune system (Laudenslager et al., 1983).

Psychoneuroimmunology is the field that examines the interaction of psychological and physiological processes that affect the body's ability to defend itself against disease. Research in this new area promises to reveal vital links in the complex chain of mental and physical events that determine whether people become ill or stay healthy. ◾

Psychological Stress Responses

When people describe stress, they are more likely to say, "I got confused and felt angry and frustrated!" than "My heart rate increased and my blood pressure went up." In other words, when people describe stress, they are likely to mention changes in how they think or feel. These *psychological changes*, changes in emotion and cognition, make up the second major category of stress responses.

Emotional stress responses   As we discussed in the chapter on emotion, there has been considerable debate among psychologists about the timing and importance of physical arousal, behavioral responses, and the experience of emotion in the face of stressors. It is safe to say that physical responses to life's stressors are usually accompanied by emotional responses. If someone

Emotional stress responses can be quite severe, but they normally subside with time. However, people facing numerous stressful events in quick succession may experience negative emotional reactions for months or even years.

puts a gun to your head and demands your money, you will no doubt experience the GAS alarm reaction, but you will also feel some strong emotion, probably anxiety or fear, maybe anger. Among the most common emotional stress reactions are anxiety, anger, and depression. In fact, it is hard to imagine feeling these emotions in the absence of a stressor. When was the last time you felt anxiety? Perhaps it was before a major exam or while waiting for an important interview. Anger or depression often occurs during or after some conflict, failure, disappointment, or loss.

Emotional stress responses usually occur in relation to clearly identifiable situations, such as lack of job security, a spouse's unfaithfulness, or the constant pressure of daily hassles. And, in most cases, emotional stress reactions subside soon after the stressors are gone. Anxiety is usually immediately replaced by relief, even euphoria, as soon as a dreaded exam or interview is over.

If stressors continue for a long time or come in a tight sequence, emotional stress reactions may also continue, and the consequences can be serious. When people do not have a chance to recover their emotional equilibrium, they commonly report feeling tense or anxious more and more of the time. Eventually, if stressors continue, people describe themselves as a "nervous wreck." Increasingly intense feelings of fatigue, depression, and helplessness may also appear, as the long battle against stressors continues.

Sometimes, constant emotional arousal becomes so routine that the person can no longer pinpoint why it is there. The result may be a clinical pattern called **generalized anxiety disorder** (or **free-floating anxiety**), in which the person is at a loss to explain his or her constant feelings of tension and anxiety. In other cases, the person may keep obvious emotional stress responses more or less under control most of the time, but then suffer occasional, sudden, and intense attacks of anxiety or panic for no apparent reason. We discuss stress-related emotional disorders and ways to treat them in Chapters 15 and 16.

Cognitive stress responses   Cognitive stress responses typically appear as reductions in the ability to concentrate, to think clearly, or to remember things accurately. As we will see in this chapter's Linkages box, these problems usually occur as stressors elevate a person's arousal above the moderate level that tends to be optimal for maximum performance, especially on problem solving and other tasks requiring complex mental operations.

One of the most common cognitive stress responses is **catastrophizing,** or dwelling on and overemphasizing the consequences of negative events (Sarason et al., 1986). For example, Irwin Sarason (1978, 1984) found that, during examinations, test-anxious college students are likely to say to themselves, "I'm falling behind," "Everyone else is doing better than I am," or "If I don't do well on this test, I won't get an A and I'll never get into medical school and I'll be a failure." Such cognitive stress reactions can be especially severe for those of moderate ability or those who are most uncertain about how well they will do (Defares, Grossman & de Swart, 1983; Spielberger, 1979). Catastrophizing can not only interfere with the smooth cognitive functioning necessary for coherent speech but can actually intensify emotional and physiological arousal, which in turn adds to the total stress response and further hampers performance (Geen, 1985; Sarason, 1984). Students who have studied adequately and feel they are prepared but who cannot think clearly during examinations typically refer to these cognitive problems as "choking" or "blocking." They illustrate how cognitive reactions to stressors can themselves create additional stress responses, so that having thoughts about failure may help bring about failure.

Other cognitive reactions to stress act to minimize the impact of stressors,

Defense Mechanism	Example
Denial	A man is severely overworked. He is not getting enough sleep, is eating poorly, and is beginning to show signs of physical and mental exhaustion. Nevertheless, he responds to expressions of concern from his wife and coworkers with "Everything is fine. I'm too strong to be bothered by a little hard work."
Repression	A working mother who is the sole support of her four children has begun to experience episodes of rapid heartbeat and dizziness, especially on hectic days when job responsibilities conflict with child care requirements. At her annual physical examination, she forgets to mention these symptoms to her physician.
Intellectualization	A college student who has fallen hopelessly behind in his classwork spends most of his time discussing with professors, friends, and anyone else who will listen the philosophical meaninglessness of grades and achievement.
Displacement	A business executive, who is under constant stress brought on by fierce competition from other companies, routinely blames her stomach ulcer and irritability on "aggravation" caused by the incompetence of her employees.
Projection	A professor claims that the stress reactions displayed by several colleagues have created such a tense atmosphere that it is impossible to get any work done in the department.

TABLE 13.3

Psychological Defenses Against Stress

These and other defense mechanisms are sometimes helpful in dealing temporarily with stressors, but over-reliance on them as avoidance tactics usually leads to trouble in the long run, mainly because they do nothing to eliminate sources of stress.

at least temporarily. For example, some people automatically (and perhaps unknowingly) respond to stressors with denial, repression, intellectualization, displacement, projection, and other cognitive strategies that Freud called defense mechanisms. **Defense mechanisms** are psychological responses that help protect a person from anxiety and the other negative emotions accompanying stress. Table 13.3 contains several illustrations.

Defense mechanisms may cushion the emotional impact of stress, but they do little or nothing to eliminate the source of stress. For example, denying to yourself that a recent bad grade bothers you may make you feel better, but it will not improve your study habits. If you are facing a natural disaster or some other stressor you can do little about, defense mechanisms may work well. They can also be valuable to get through short-lived crises. However, serious problems can result if you rely on defense mechanisms all the time and if they prevent you from recognizing and acting against stressors that can be changed (Moos & Schaefer, 1984). For example, people may suffer needlessly if defense mechanisms prevent them from seeking help in response to early signs of illness.

In short, physical and emotional stress reactions provide signals that something is wrong, but cognitive reactions can jam those signals, stopping a person from developing strategies to cope with or eliminate sources of stress. Fortunately, many people routinely display rational and constructive cognitive reactions. While one unemployed person might think that all is lost or deny that there is a problem, another might calmly review alternative ways to obtain a new job.

Behavioral Stress Responses

Clues about the physical and emotional stress reactions of other people come from *behavioral stress responses;* that is, from changes in how people look, act, or talk. For example, as we noted in the chapter on emotion, emotional

BLOOM COUNTY   **by Berke Breathed**

Moderate arousal can facilitate performance, but overarousal can interfere with it.

Figure 13.5
One Behavioral Response to Stress
Deterioration of handwriting is one of many behavioral signs of stress. On the top is a sample of President Richard Nixon's signature when all was well. On the bottom, you can see what happened to his handwriting during the stress of the Watergate investigations that ultimately forced him from office.

responses usually show up in facial expressions, which most of us can "read" in other people. Perspiration, a shaky voice, tremors or spasms in facial or other muscles, and the jumpiness that suggests general tension provide other indicators of physiological stress responses. Posture can also convey information about stress, a fact used by skilled interviewers. In one experiment, unsuspecting people were subjected to sudden and rather nasty verbal attacks by a previously friendly interviewer (Ekman, 1964). Later, students looking at photographs that showed only silhouettes of the conversing pair were able to judge when the subjects were under stress.

Many behavioral stress responses reflect the effects of stress-related physiological and emotional arousal. As we described in the chapter on motivation, moderate arousal can help people do their best; actors and athletes usually turn in peak performances when they feel "up" and even slightly nervous before a performance or a game. However, if the stress process pushes arousal beyond some optimal point, physical coordination, behavioral skills, and other aspects of behavior may be disrupted (Baumeister, 1984). Figure 13.5 shows one example of disruption of behavior by stressors. Another was provided in a study which, for ethical reasons, could not be conducted today. Soldiers were given two-way radios and left alone at remote locations during what they thought were war games (Berkun, 1964). Told to report on any aircraft they saw, each recruit heard radio reports that artillery shells were being mistakenly fired into supposedly safe areas. After a five-pound charge of TNT buried 150 yards from the subject's post was exploded, the soldier was told that his radio was no longer transmitting and that he should use recently learned procedures to switch to an emergency transmission circuit. The speed and skill with which he completed this task were 33 percent lower than for soldiers who performed the same job under low-stress conditions.

Even more obvious behavioral stress responses appear as people attempt to escape or avoid stressors. Some people quit their jobs, drop out of school, run away from home, or pursue extramarital affairs in order to escape or avoid stressors. Unfortunately, as we discussed in the learning chapter, escape and avoidance deprive people of the opportunity to learn new, more adaptive ways of coping with a stressful environment.

Perhaps the most dramatic and tragic form of escape from stress is suicide. In 1929 a number of people literally jumped out of office windows when the stock market crash wiped out their financial holdings. Today, ten thousand college students attempt suicide every year, in part because of difficulty in coping with stressors such as academic requirements, social pressures, financial problems, detachment from family support, and relationship problems.

Other behavioral responses to stressors may bring different brands of tragedy. As shown in Figure 13.6, one of the more common examples is an increase in aggression, especially directed toward one's own family. Aggressiveness is particularly likely in those who try to blunt the impact of stressors with alcohol or drugs. If this pattern evolves into alcohol or drug abuse, the person may not only become dependent on the substance, but also find that using it *produces,* rather than relieves, anxiety and depression (Nathan et al., 1970).

Facial expressions and other behavioral responses commonly reflect less obvious emotional and physiological reactions to stressful events.

HIGHLIGHT

Posttraumatic Stress Disorder and Burnout

Many of the physical, psychological, and behavioral stress responses we have discussed sometimes appear together in patterns known as burnout and posttraumatic stress disorder.

Burnout is a gradually intensifying pattern of physical, psychological, and behavioral dysfunction in response to a continuous flow of stressors (Farber, 1983; Paine, 1982; Riggar, 1985). Burnout typically begins with normal reactions to the conflict, frustration, and pressure of one's job (especially such high-stress jobs as police work or air traffic control), but they eventually become so severe as to impair functioning at work. The stress reactions can become so general that the person may appear to have developed a new personality, on and off the job. Previously reliable workers or once-attentive spouses may become indifferent, disengaged, impulsive, or accident prone. They may miss work frequently, oversleep, perform their jobs poorly, and become irritable, suspicious, withdrawn, depressed, and unwilling to talk about stress or anything else. Because their problem develops gradually, people who suffer from burnout frequently fail to seek assistance. Attempts by family and friends to help may be met with aggressiveness, especially if alcohol or drugs are involved (see Figure 13.6). College students sometimes display stress reactions similar to burnout, from the pressure of heavy course loads, part-time jobs, constant deadlines, and a competitive atmosphere. Coping with these stressors is a major challenge; later in this chapter, we describe some methods for doing so.

A different pattern of severe stress reactions is illustrated by the case of Mary, a thirty-three-year-old nurse who was raped at knifepoint by an intruder in her apartment (Spitzer et al., 1983). In the weeks following the attack, she became afraid of being alone and was preoccupied with the attack and with thoughts that it could happen again. She had additional locks installed on doors and windows, but had such difficulty concentrating that she could not immediately return to work. She was repelled by the thought of sex and stated that she did not want to have sex for a long time.

Mary suffered from **posttraumatic stress disorder,** a pattern of adverse and disruptive reactions following a traumatic event. Among the characteristic reactions are anxiety, irritability, jumpiness, inability to concentrate or work productively, sexual dysfunction, a lack of feeling (known as *emotional numbness*), and difficulty in getting along with others. The most common feature of posttraumatic stress disorder is reexperiencing the original trauma through nightmares or vivid memories. In rare cases, very disturbing waking recollections, known as *flashbacks,* occur, in which the person behaves for minutes, hours, or days as if the trauma is occurring again. People who survive events in which others perished or those who feel somehow to blame for others' deaths may also experience severe guilt or depression; some of the engineers who tried unsuccessfully to halt the ill-fated launch of the space shuttle Challenger apparently suffered such reactions.

These problems may occur immediately, or they may be delayed; they may be temporary or continuing. The most severe and long-lasting difficulties

Figure 13.6
Stress and Violence
Many researchers have found that unemployment, inadequate pay, job dissatisfaction, and other economically related stressors are associated with increases in the rate and severity of domestic violence (Ponzetti, Cate & Koval, 1982). The graph illustrates this relationship in a sample of thirty-eight women whose husbands had subjected them to either mild or severe physical abuse. The proportion of incidents in which physical injury occurred is clearly much higher in homes where husbands were unemployed.
(Prescott & Letko, 1977)

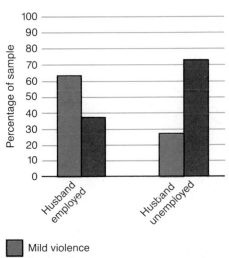

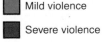
■ Mild violence
■ Severe violence

Burnout on the job is especially likely when people face unrelenting pressure brought on by a heavy workload and the need to make split-second, life-and-death decisions. Air traffic control typifies such occupations, but burnout is also a problem in law enforcement, medicine, nursing, and many other fields.

usually appear as the result of experiences in military combat and concentration camps. Indeed, posttraumatic stress disorder has become familiar to many people because of the publicity given to American veterans' difficulties after they returned from the war in Vietnam (Stretch, 1985). Some individuals who display posttraumatic stress disorders require professional help; others seem to recover without it. For most, improvement takes time; for nearly all, the support of family and friends is vital to recovery. ◼

Interactions Between People and Stressors

As we have seen, just counting and rating the stressors in a person's life cannot always predict how much difficulty that person will experience. One individual can survive, even thrive, under the same circumstances that lead another to break down, give up, and burn out. What determines how much and what kind of impact stressors will have? Research suggests that the answer lies in the *interaction* of particular stressors and particular people. In the sections that follow, we review some of the characteristics of people and stressors that appear to moderate or intensify stress responses.

Predictability   Researchers have found that predictable stressors have less impact than those that are unpredictable (Cohen, 1980). This is especially true when the stressors are intense and occur for relatively short periods of time (Abbott, Schoen & Badia, 1984). For example, rats given a reliable warning signal every time they are to receive a shock show less severe physiological responses, fewer stomach ulcers, and more normal eating and drinking habits than animals receiving no warnings (Weiss, 1970). Humans also seem to be less stressed by shocks they know are coming (Badia, Suter & Lewis, 1967). For example, people often seem to suffer more stress-related problems when a death in the family is unforeseen. In one study, men and women whose spouses had died suddenly displayed more immediate disbelief, anxiety, and depression than those who had weeks or months to prepare themselves for the loss (Parkes & Brown, 1972).

This is not to say that predictability provides total protection against stressors. Laboratory research with animals has shown that predictable stressors, even if relatively mild, can be more damaging than unpredictable ones if they occur over long periods of time (Abbott, Schoen & Badia, 1984).

Control Numerous studies indicate that stressors usually have less impact if people can exert some control over them. In one experiment, subjects given the option of turning off loud bursts of aversive noise reported less discomfort and showed less physiological reaction to the stressor than those who could not control it (Corah & Boffa, 1970).

Simply believing that a stressor is controllable, whether it is or not, can reduce its impact (Cohen, 1980). For example, in one study some subjects were told that the duration of the shock they were to receive could be reduced from six seconds to three seconds if they responded quickly enough to a warning light (Geer, Davison & Gatchel, 1970). Other subjects were given no such instructions. In fact, everyone received three-second shocks regardless of what they did, but those who thought they had control showed milder physiological responses than the others.

People who do not think they have control over stressors often develop feelings of helplessness and hopelessness; these emotions may promote depression or other mental disorders. These people may also be more vulnerable to disease. In one study on women undergoing tests for cervical cancer, researchers were able to correctly predict 74 percent of the malignancies just by knowing which subjects tended to react helplessly to recent stressors (Schmale & Iker, 1966).

How stressors are interpreted The effects of perceived control on stress responsiveness are just part of a more general relationship between cognition—how people think about stressors—and the impact of stressors. In the chapter on perception, we pointed out that perceptions of the world are determined not only by the many things that are "out there," but also by which of them people attend to and how they interpret them. You might see a bright light as "glaring" or "glowing," and a broad smile as "warm" or "phony." Similarly, in Chapter 12, we saw that emotional reactions to stressors and other events can depend on whether people think of them as dangerous or merely interesting. Thus, a given stressor, be it a hot elevator or a deskful of work, usually has more impact on those who perceive it as threatening or potentially harmful than on those who view it as stimulating or challenging. Some theorists, such as Richard Lazarus (1966, 1976), go so far as to argue that, unless a person interprets something as stressful, there will be no stress response.

Of course, the influence of cognitive responses weakens somewhat as stressors become more extreme; a bomb going off next to you will probably not be any less stressful if you think of it as fireworks. Still, even the impact of natural disasters and other major stressors may be less severe for those who think of them as challenges to be overcome rather than as the end of the world.

In a classic demonstration of how thinking can influence stress responses, Lazarus and his colleagues showed three groups of students a film containing graphic scenes of bloody industrial accidents (Lazarus et al., 1965). As you can see in Figure 13.7 (p. 490), the film caused significantly less physiological arousal among the intellectualizers than among those in the unprepared group. The reactions of those in the denial group were less extreme than those in the unprepared subjects, but stronger than in the intellectualizers.

Thus, in Lazarus's study, the intensity of students' physiological arousal during the film depended on how they had been instructed to interpret it. Other data show that noise-related distress among people living near airports

Stress responses do not always cease when the stressors that created them are gone. A pattern of lingering problems known as posttraumatic stress disorder is especially likely following such catastrophic events as combat or rape.

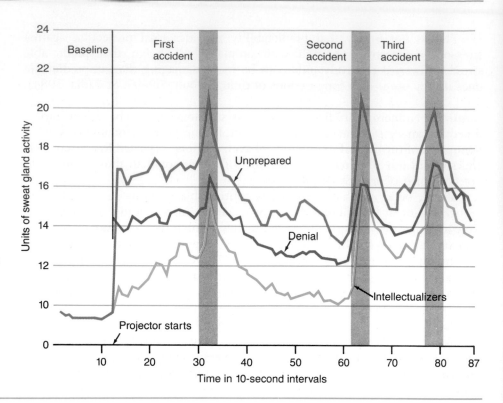

Figure 13.7
Cognition and Stress
When subjects were given different instructions about what to think about during a stressful film that showed industrial accidents, there were clear differences in physiological arousal during the film, as measured by sweat gland activity. Those who were instructed to remain detached from the bloody scenes (the intellectualizers) or to think of them as unreal (the denial group) were less upset than those in an unprepared control group. These results provide one of many demonstrations of the effect of how people think about stressors on their responses to those stressors.
(Adapted from Lazarus, Opton, Nornikos, and Rankin, *Journal of Personality* 33:4. Copyright 1965 Duke University Press.)

appears to have more to do with how they evaluate the airport (for example, as a nuisance or as a source of employment) than with how much noise they must endure (Tracor, 1971). Even such major stressors as divorce can be altered by a person's view of them. One member of a divorcing couple might be devastated by feelings of failure and shame, whereas the other might be invigorated by the prospect of beginning a new life.

The reasons why some people tend to think about stressors in constructive, organized ways, whereas others catastrophize or try to deny their existence are not entirely clear. Some personality theorists suggest that people learn how to think about stressors by watching and listening to others; they imitate cognitive styles, especially if they find that it helps them through stressful times. It may be that people have generalized cognitive coping styles. For example, Don Byrne (1964) suggested that some individuals tend to be *repressors,* who deny and cognitively avoid all stressors. Others, according to Byrne, are *sensitizers;* they seek out information about stressors and try to cope more actively with them.

It may also be that people who have an **internal locus of control**—that is, who think of themselves as generally capable of controlling what happens to them—have a greater sense of personal control over stressors, thus making those stressors appear less threatening (Anderson, 1977). This may explain why "internals" often appear to be better than "externals" (those who see events as less controllable) at managing everyday stressors (Tanck & Robbins, 1979). Indeed, a sense of personal control over life's events is characteristic of people who have stress-resistant, or *hardy,* personalities (Kobasa, Maddi & Kahn, 1982). The relationship between personality characteristics and stress responsiveness is discussed further in Chapter 14.

Social support   If you have ever appreciated the comforting presence of a good friend during troubled times or had to endure a bad experience on your own, you can probably vouch for the importance of social support in tempering the impact of stressful life events.

Psychologists refer to the friends and social contacts on whom one can depend for help and support as one's **social support network** (Gottlieb, 1981). Members of this network provide support in many forms, including companionship, help with daily hassles, and financial assistance (Rook, 1987). Perhaps most important, they offer reassurance that one is cared about and valued and that everything will eventually be all right again (Cohen & Wills, 1985; Sarason & Sarason, 1985; Schaefer, Coyne & Lazarus, 1982).

The stress-reducing effects of social support have been documented in a wide range of research on mental and physical problems (Broadhead et al., 1983; Heller & Swindle, 1982; Leavy, 1983; Thoits, 1986). For example, socially isolated students suffered more emotional distress during the first year of graduate school than classmates who were part of a supportive social network (Goplerud, 1980). Andrew Billings and Rudolph Moos (1984, 1985) found that depression over major life stresses (divorce, unemployment, illness, or family conflict) was less severe among people who had more supportive social networks. This relationship between support and depression was especially strong for women.

Interestingly, having too much support can be as bad as not having enough. When friends and family overprotect a person under stress, he or she may put less energy into coping efforts. Overly concerned and protective family support has been associated, for example, with increased disability and a tendency not to return to work after an accident or illness (Garrity, 1973; Hyman, 1971; Lewis, 1966).

Coping skills   Just as a football player in a sturdy helmet and protective pads is far less likely to be hurt in a game than someone wearing a T-shirt and cutoffs, people who are better equipped to cope with stress usually suffer fewer ill effects. Coping skills may take the form of thinking about stressors as challenges rather than threats. They may also include overt behavior, such as efficiently budgeting time, carefully planning strategies for handling problems, learning how to relax, or getting enough rest, exercise, and proper nutrition. We will discuss these and other stress-coping skills shortly.

It is also important to know how and when to use one's coping skills, a dimension on which people differ. Some research suggests, for example, that people with optimistic expectations about handling stress tend to deal with disappointments, such as being turned down for a date or a job, by formulating a new plan to reach their goal. Instead of utilizing their coping skills at this point, people with a more pessimistic view tend to focus on negative emotions and give up (Scheier, Weintraub & Carver, 1986). Similarly, individuals with an internal locus of control have often been found to be better able than externals to utilize their coping skills. They may also be better at selecting the right strategy for coping with each type of stressor. In one study, student nurses who were internals reported taking direct action to alter changeable stressors, while tending to accept or just not think about those that they saw as unchangeable. Externals, on the other hand, took less direct action and engaged in more inefficient, often wishful, thinking and denial—regardless of whether the stressors were changeable (Parkes, 1984).

Our review of factors that can alter the impact of stressors should make it obvious that what is stressful for a given individual is not determined simply by predispositions, by cognitive style, or by events and situations. What seems most important are person-situation interactions, the mixture of each individual's resources and the specific characteristics of the situations he or she encounters.

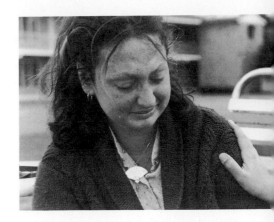

Social support can be an important factor in helping people to cope with all kinds of stressors. For example, people usually adjust better to a divorce (and do a better job of child care) if they have supportive friends and family around them (Colletta, 1979; Raschke, 1977).

Stress and Illness

Earlier, we discussed research on the relationship between stress and immune system functioning. These investigations are part of a larger scientific effort, which for decades has been aimed at understanding the link between stress and illness. During the 1940s and 1950s, for example, an enormous amount of research focused on the role of psychological factors in the appearance of Selye's diseases of adaptation. Particular attention was directed at bronchial asthma, high blood pressure, migraine headaches, skin problems (such as dermatitis), stomach ulcers, arthritis, and other disorders associated with overarousal of the autonomic nervous system. Official classifications of mental disorders began to include special sections on *psychosomatic* or *psychophysiological* disorders; that is, physical problems that can clearly be brought on by psychological factors, such as frustration or conflict.

Research now suggests that physical and psychological stressors and stress responses can set the stage for, worsen, or even directly cause almost any kind of physical illness, not just those that had been considered psychosomatic. One example is Alzheimer's disease, which, as described in Chapter 3, causes severe memory loss. There is some evidence that the degeneration of the brain in Alzheimer's disease is worsened when cortisol is released from the adrenal glands during stress (Landfield et al., 1981; Sapolsky, Krey & McEwen, 1985).

Stress responses have also been linked to coronary heart disease. The discovery of this relationship began years ago, when two cardiologists, Meyer Freidman and Ray Rosenman (1959, 1974) noticed that the front edges of their waiting room chairs were being worn out especially fast. It was as if patients with heart disease were always on the edge of their seats. Interviews with these patients revealed that, indeed, many of them tended to display a pattern of behavior that Friedman and Rosenman ultimately called *Type A*. People who display the **Type A** pattern tend to be nonstop workers, intensely competitive, aggressive, and impatient. They constantly attempt to do more and more in less and less time. They display an especially strong need to control events around them and tend to become very upset if they cannot, or feel they cannot, do so (Glass, 1977).

Apparently, it was no accident that a disproportionate number of Type A's appeared in a cardiology office. Several studies have found that people who display the Type A pattern are more than twice as likely to suffer heart disease as their **Type B** peers, who are more relaxed and easygoing (Matthews, 1982; Rosenman et al., 1975; Suinn, 1982). The precise mechanism underlying this relationship is not clear, but it may be that the more or less constant emotional stress responses of Type A's are accompanied by surges of chemicals (such as catecholamines) into the bloodstream, which lead to increased fatty deposits in the arteries and, in turn, to heart disease.

It is also unclear whether all Type A's are at equal risk; some research shows, for example, that the link between Type A behavior and heart disease is not always as strong or consistent as was originally thought (Houston & Snyder, 1987; Matthews & Haynes, 1986; Shekelle et al., 1985). Indeed, some researchers suggest that it is not the Type A pattern as a whole, but only certain of its elements, particularly hostility, anger, cynicism, and selfishness, that predict heart problems (Barefoot, Dahlstrom & Williams, 1983; Matthews et al., 1977; Scherwitz, Graham & Ornish, 1985; Williams et al., 1980).

These particularly stress-enhancing components of the Type A pattern may also increase the risk of many other kinds of illness (Lazarus & Folkman, 1984). This is consistent with the notion that, when the body reaches the exhaustion phase of the GAS, its immune system may have been weakened, thus making it more vulnerable to colds, mononucleosis, and many other infections (Jemmott & Locke, 1984). There is even some evidence that stress-

Type A individuals are far more interested in their achievements in the world of work than in social relationships. They often display selfishness, a strong fear of failure, and considerable hostility toward those whom they feel stand in the way of their success (Ditto, 1982; Gastorf & Teevan, 1980; Rhodewalt, 1984). The Type A pattern has been detected in people as young as eleven (Matthews & Siegel, 1983).

related suppression of the immune system may create vulnerability to certain forms of cancer (Cooper, 1985; Jacobs & Charles, 1980; Justice, 1985).

Just as the Type A pattern tends to increase the risk for stress-related illness, other evidence suggests that the stress-mediating factors we discussed earlier appear to reduce that risk. Research in this area has focused largely on the benefits of social support (Chen & Cobb, 1960; Cohen & Hoberman, 1983; Cohen & Wills, 1985). For example, Susan Gore (1978) studied the physiological stress responses of men who had recently lost their jobs in a factory closing. She found that problems were significantly milder among those who received higher levels of emotional support from friends and family. Social support may also help speed the healing process. Richard Lucas (1975) found faster recovery from surgery among patients who received extra attention and reassurance from the medical staff. Indeed, there is general evidence that people with better social support networks live longer than those with less support (Berkman & Syme, 1979).

James Pennebaker (1985) has suggested that social support helps prevent illness mainly because it can provide the person under stress with an opportunity to express pent-up thoughts and emotions. Keeping important things to oneself, says Pennebaker, is itself a form of stress. In the laboratory, for example, subjects who were asked to try to deceive an experimenter revealed the effort required to inhibit self-expression in the form of physiological arousal (Pennebaker & Chew, 1985; Waid & Orne, 1981). (We saw in the emotion chapter that lie detection devices are essentially designed to measure such arousal.) Further, the spouses of suicide or accidental death victims who do not or cannot confide in others about their feelings are most likely to develop physical illnesses during the year following the death (Pennebaker & O'Heeron, 1984). Confiding in people may not only reduce harmful physiological arousal, but also allow a person to make sense of stressors and to recognize that others have experienced (and survived) similar events (Silver & Wortman, 1980; Wortman & Dunkel-Schetter, 1979).

HIGHLIGHT

Behavioral Medicine

During the 1970s, evidence began to accumulate indicating that psychological stress is but one of several factors that can increase the risk of illness. Survey studies showed, for example, that certain diseases are more prevalent among people who behave in certain ways. Smoking cigarettes, eating a high cholesterol or high salt diet, and getting too little exercise were identified as particularly important risk factors for heart disease, stroke, cancer, emphysema, and many other serious illnesses. In one decade-long study in Alameda County, California, the death rate for men who did not smoke, drank alcohol in moderation, regularly slept seven or eight hours a night, ate breakfast, kept their weight within normal limits, and got regular exercise was almost four times lower than for those who followed three or fewer of these practices (Wiley & Camacho, 1980).

The 1970s were also a time of increased recognition that people's knowledge of illness and their reaction to illness can have a lot to do with its impact on them. Those who pay attention to their bodies (for example, through regular checkups), seek medical attention if symptoms appear, and carefully follow instructions about taking medication tend to be more likely to remain healthy or at least to have serious illnesses detected and treated early enough to make cure and rehabilitation possible.

In short, it became obvious that the way people think and behave has an enormous effect on health and illness. Accordingly, physicians, psychologists, dentists, nurses, social workers, and other health-related professionals began working together to find ways to use behavioral science to aid in the prevention, detection, and treatment of physical disease (Schwartz & Weiss, 1978). This broad-based movement focused on how behavior and illness are linked has become known as **behavioral medicine.** It includes, for example, smoking-cessation clinics, weight-control programs, public education campaigns about high blood pressure, and similar prevention efforts. It also includes efforts to teach patients to think pleasant thoughts and to use regulated breathing to ease the discomfort of painful tests; to prepare themselves mentally for the stress of surgery; and to reduce the frequency of headaches through biofeedback or other special training.

Behavioral medicine is a rapidly growing field that offers many career opportunities, especially for people trained in psychology. In fact, a subfield within behavioral medicine, known as *health psychology*, focuses on the use of psychological theory and research to help people maintain good health and cope with illness (Gatchel & Baum, 1983). In the following section on coping with stress, we give further examples of research and treatment programs related to behavioral medicine and health psychology. ◖

COPING WITH STRESS

Just as people with extra money in the bank can weather a financial crisis, those with stress-coping skills may escape even the harmful effects of intense stress. Like family money, the ability to handle stress appears to come naturally to some people, but coping can also be learned. In this section, we review the basic components of an effective stress-coping plan, some specific coping methods, and some examples of programs designed to help people with particularly severe stressors.

A Plan for Coping

The first step in learning to cope with stress is to make a systematic assessment of the problem. This assessment involves (1) identifying the sources of stress, which means carefully listing events and situations that contain conflict, change, frustration, pressure, and other stress factors; and (2) noting the effects of stress. To assess the stressors, you might use the Social Readjustment Rating Scale or the Daily Hassles Scale (see Tables 13.1 and 13.2), but people usually create more specific and personalized lists (for example, "My sister keeps leaving her wet socks on my bed to dry"). Assessing the effects of stress requires an objective survey of physiological, psychological, and behavioral responses such as headaches, lack of concentration, feelings of tension, or heavy drinking. This survey helps establish the degree to which stress is disrupting your life.

Once you have pinpointed the sources and effects of stress, it is important to select an appropriate goal. Should you try to eliminate stressors or to alter your response to them? Sometimes it makes sense to do the former, such as changing your academic major if your current one has become a source of severe stress since you lost interest in it. Often, however, such changes are either impossible or unwise. For example, if test taking or daily commuting are major stressors, you could eliminate them simply by refusing to take exams or go to work, but doing so would not do much for your academic or employment record. An alternative is to reduce the tension and anxiety related to these situations, perhaps by moving nearer the workplace, improving your test-taking skills, or learning to be more relaxed.

The most effective coping plans aim at removing the stressors that can be changed and reducing stress responses to those that remain (Silver & Wortman,

Stage	Task
1. Assessment	Identify the sources and effects of stress.
2. Goal setting	List the stressors and stress responses to be addressed. Designate which stressors are and are not changeable.
3. Planning	List the specific steps to be taken to cope with stress.
4. Action	Implement stress-coping plans.
5. Evaluation	Determine the changes in stressors and stress responses that have occurred as a result of stress-coping methods.
6. Adjustment	Alter coping methods to improve results, if necessary.

TABLE 13.4
Stages in Coping with Stress
Most successful stress-coping programs progress systematically through several logical stages.

1980). In fact, stress-related problems may be especially prevalent among people who either exhaust themselves trying to change stressors that cannot be changed or who pass up opportunities to alter those that can be altered (Folkman, 1984). This was well illustrated in a study of people who lived near the Three Mile Island nuclear reactor when the accident occurred there. Those who acted as if they could somehow alter the consequences of the accident reported more psychological stress symptoms than those who focused on learning to accept their situation (Collins, Baum & Singer, 1983).

Systematic stress assessment, goal setting, and plans for coping all set the stage for the implementation and evaluation of a stress-management program. The entire sequence is laid out in Table 13.4.

Methods of Coping

People use a variety of methods to cope with stressors, as Table 13.5 illustrates. Like stress responses, strategies for coping with stress can be cognitive, behavioral, or physiological.

Cognitive coping strategies   As we saw earlier, the way people think about stressors can have a great deal to do with the intensity of the stress process. Cognitive methods involve changing how people interpret stressors and thus changing to some extent how they respond to stressors.

Method	Description
Distraction	Diverts attention away from the problem by thinking about other things or engaging in some activity.
Situation redefinition	Tries to see the problem in a different light, which makes it seem more bearable.
Direct action	Thinks about solutions to the problem, gathers information about it, or actually tries to do something to try to solve it.
Catharsis	Expresses emotions in response to the problem to reduce tension, anxiety, or frustration.
Acceptance	Accepts that the problem had occurred, but that nothing can be done about it.
Seeking social support	Seeks or finds emotional support from loved ones, friends, or professionals.
Relaxation	Does something with the implicit intention of relaxing.
Religion	Seeks or finds spiritual comfort and support.

SOURCE: Stone, A. A., & Neale, J. M. (1984). New measure of daily coping: Development and preliminary results. *Journal of Personality and Social Psychology, 46*, 892–906.

TABLE 13.5
Categories of Coping Methods
People use a variety of methods to cope with stressors.

Cognitive coping strategies help people think more calmly, rationally, and constructively in the face of stress. For example, suppose you are a counselor working with Chris, a student whose heavy courseload, conflicts with parents, and numerous daily hassles have engendered anxiety, confusion, discouragement, a lack of motivation to study, and a tendency to escape by drinking. Not surprisingly, his grades are beginning to suffer. Your initial assessment might reveal that the main sources of Chris's stress are the increase in work pressure from high school to college and frightening thoughts about that pressure. To cope with this source of stress, Chris must start substituting other thoughts for those now paralyzing him. This substitution process is often called **cognitive restructuring** (Lazarus, 1971; Meichenbaum, 1977). It can be done by writing down and actively practicing constructive new thoughts such as "All I can do is the best I can."

Successful cognitive coping does not eliminate stressors, but it can make them less threatening and disruptive. Chris will still feel the pressure of college and will still want to succeed, but the prospect of failure will seem less horrible and the need for perfection less pressing. Coping by "talking to yourself" also allows a person to focus on constructive work rather than on fruitless worry and may generate a more hopeful emotional state.

Behavioral coping strategies   Even after Chris learns to think more calmly about deadlines and other stressors, he may have too many stressors occurring too close together and no plan for dealing with them. This is where behavioral coping methods come in. If you rearrange your world in ways that minimize the impact of stressors, you are using *behavioral coping strategies.*

Time management is one form of behavioral coping. For example, you might suggest that Chris keep track of his time for a week. How much time is he devoting to study, work, meals, sleep, worrying, and relaxation? Using this information, Chris can draw up a *time-management plan,* a schedule that specifies periods for each of these categories of activity (except perhaps worrying), as Table 13.6 illustrates.

TABLE 13.6

Time Management Planning
The goal is to lessen stress by using time more efficiently. The complete plan would include schedules for each day of the week, with adjustments for special occasions and exam periods.

A Typical Day		Plan for a Day	
Time	**Activity**	**Time**	**Activity**
8:00 A.M.	Sleep	6:30–7:15 A.M.	Exercise
8:30 A.M.	Continue sleeping	7:15 A.M.	Shower; dress
9:00 A.M.	Shower; dress	8:00–8:45 A.M.	Breakfast; read paper; review class notes
9:50 A.M.	Leave for second class of the day	9:00 A.M.—Noon	Classes
10:00 A.M.–Noon	Classes	Noon–1:00 P.M.	Lunch; talk with friends
Noon–1:55 P.M.	Lunch; talk with friends	1:00–2:00 P.M.	Do assigned readings
2:00–4:00 P.M.	Classes	2:00–4:00 P.M.	Classes
4:00–6:00 P.M.	Library job	4:00–6:00 P.M.	Library job
6:00–7:30 P.M.	Dinner; talk with friends	6:00–7:00 P.M.	Dinner; talk with friends
7:30–9:00 P.M.	Study	7:00–11:00 P.M.	Study
9:00–Midnight	Drink with friends at campus bar	11:00 P.M.–Midnight	Watch TV with friends

Such a plan demonstrates that time is limited and might have been wasted in the past. It can help Chris see all the things that need to be done and how much time is available for each activity. If Chris really has too little time, something may have to go. If not, he may decide to follow a more efficient and disciplined schedule or perhaps enroll in a course that would teach him to study more efficiently. Time management can also help control catastrophizing by assuring Chris that there is enough time for everything and a plan for handling it all.

Some of the general-purpose problem-solving strategies we discussed in Chapter 9 can also be useful behavioral coping methods. Suppose you have a full course load, a part-time job, and a busy social life. You are sometimes tired but manage to handle everything reasonably well. Now a professor offers you an unpaid research job that will increase your stress, possibly beyond your ability to cope with it. Should you accept the job? As mentioned in the motivation chapter, conflicts—especially approach-avoidance conflicts like this one—prompt some people to make almost any decision impulsively, just to have it over with. But there is a better way of coping with the stress of the conflict. By listing and examining the pros and cons and the potential costs and benefits of each course of action, you can analyze the problem carefully and rationally, then reach a decision based on that analysis (review Figure 9.12 for an example).

In short, behavioral methods of coping with stress involve paying attention to the total load of stressors and acting to keep it within manageable limits. Behavioral and cognitive skills often interact closely. Thinking calmly makes it easier to develop and use sensible plans for behavioral coping; when behavioral coping eliminates or minimizes stressors, people find it easier to think and feel better about themselves.

Physiological coping strategies
People also cope with stress by directly altering the physical responses that occur before, during, or after stress. The most common example of *physiological coping strategies* is the use of drugs.

But chemical coping methods provide only temporary relief. That may be fine in some cases, as when prescribed sedation helps parents endure the immediate but temporary shock that follows the death of a child. But using short-term methods to deal with long-term stressors such as unemployment or marital discord can lead to continued use of drugs and thus to addiction, physical illness, debt, and other problems. Moreover, when people come to depend on drugs to help them face stress, they often attribute any success they have to the drug, not to their own skill. This loss of perceived control over stressors may make those stressors even more threatening and disruptive. Finally, the same drug effects that blunt stress responses may also interfere with the ability to plan and to apply cognitive and behavioral coping strategies.

These are some of the reasons why many stress-management programs emphasize reduction of physical stress reactions through nonchemical means, including progressive relaxation training, biofeedback, and meditation (described in Chapter 6), among others. These procedures lead to a pleasant state of reduced physiological arousal (Carrington, 1984; Tarler-Benlolo, 1978), and people can learn to use them at will, either to help combat stressors as they occur or to calm down afterward. We will describe just two examples.

In **biofeedback training,** special equipment records the state of stress-related physiological activity, such as heart rate, blood pressure, and muscle tension. The equipment continuously feeds this information back to a person in the form of a changing tone or meter reading. With practice, many people can develop mental strategies that control these physiological processes and can use the same strategies to control stress responses in everyday situations (Budzynski & Stoyva, 1984).

Exercise provides an important physiological strategy for coping with stress. It improves physical fitness and reduces the threat of coronary heart disease and other stress-related illnesses. There is also some evidence that physical exercise can reduce feelings of anxiety and depression for periods ranging from thirty minutes to several hours (Sime, 1984).

Progressive relaxation training is one of the most popular physiological methods for coping with stress. Edmund Jacobson developed progressive relaxation techniques during the 1930s as a way of reducing tension in muscles that are under voluntary control, thus leading to reductions in heart rate and blood pressure and creating mental and emotional calmness (Jacobson, 1938; Paul, 1969). Today, progressive relaxation training is learned by tensing a group of muscles (such as the hand and lower arm) for a few seconds, then releasing that tension and focusing attention on the resulting feelings of relaxation. This procedure is repeated at least once for each of sixteen muscle groups throughout the body (Bernstein & Borkovec, 1973). The basic procedures are first learned and practiced while reclining comfortably in a quiet, dimly lit room. Once a person has developed some skill at relaxation, he or she can use it to calm down anywhere and anytime, often without having to lie down (Wolpe, 1982).

Together, cognitive, behavioral, and physiological coping strategies can help reduce or eliminate stressors, as well as minimize the intensity of stress responses. Once people know how to plan and carry out this three-pronged attack, they usually feel more in control and less threatened about confronting stressors.

Some Stress-Coping Programs

Sometimes stressors and stress reactions are too intense, surprising, or otherwise overwhelming for people to handle them alone or even with the help of their normal social support network. To provide extra assistance, psychologists and others involved in mental health care offer special, usually short-term, stress-coping programs. Most of these programs give information, support, and training in coping skills. When people develop these skills and take them along when they leave the program, they are more likely to be able to handle the next set of stressors on their own. Here we take a brief look at a few stress-management programs, in order to see how cognitive, behavioral, and physiological strategies are taught by professionals and to assess the effectiveness of these formal interventions.

Changing Type A behavior   We saw earlier that people who display a Type A behavior pattern are hard-driving, competitive, hostile, and impatient and that they perceive stressors as threats (Glass, 1977). Compared with their more relaxed Type B peers, they show especially strong physical reactions to stressors and appear particularly vulnerable to coronary heart disease. Researchers in behavioral medicine have developed programs to reduce the health risks faced by Type A individuals by altering their frantic lifestyles and the intensity of their stress reactions (Roskies, 1980).

In one experiment, healthy male Type A executives participated in eight ninety-minute group sessions that provided training in stress reduction (Levenkron et al., 1983). First, the staff sought to show the executives that their Type A behavior was not only potentially dangerous, but often inefficient. Next, the staff reviewed ways of anticipating and planning to avoid or cope with stressful situations ranging from slow-moving traffic to short deadlines. They gave instructions on how to limit work to a reasonable amount, set realistic deadlines, work more slowly and carefully, bring less work home at night, and in general, take life easier. The executives also developed cognitive coping skills by practicing thoughts that justified and encouraged working at a more normal pace. Finally, the men learned relaxation skills and practiced using them while imagining themselves in stressful situations. After the executives took part in this multifaceted program, their scores on a written test that measured Type A characteristics dropped significantly. Also, changes

Figure 13.8
Results of a Stress-Management Program
Stress responsiveness among participants in a comprehensive stress-management program were compared with that for people who merely discussed the problems created by Type A behavior (group support condition) or were simply told by a doctor to slow down (brief information condition). One of the outcome measures involved giving subjects a stressful mental arithmetic task and observing the consequent change in the level of free fatty acids in their blood—a physical stress response. Note that, before treatment, all three groups responded to stress with an increase in free fatty acids, but after treatment, subjects in the comprehensive treatment group actually showed negative change scores, indicating that their fatty acid levels dropped rather than increased under stress. These subjects' scores on written measures of Type A behaviors were lower as well, but not enough to call them Type B's.
(From J. D. Levenkron et al., "Modifying the Type A Coronary Prone Behavior Pattern." *Journal of Consulting and Clinical Psychology*, Vol. 51, #2, pp. 192–204. Copyright 1983 by the American Psychological Association. Adapted by permission of the publisher and the author.)

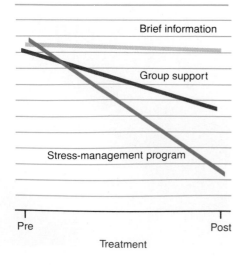

Brief information

Group support

Stress-management program

Pre   Post

Treatment

in levels of free fatty acids in their blood were measured during a stressful task. As Figure 13.8 shows, participants' stress responses on this test were greatly reduced after treatment.

These results must be interpreted with caution, however, because the subjects' blood cholesterol levels actually increased slightly, indicating that their risk for coronary heart disease may not have been significantly altered. Reduced risk was found, however, in a similar study of men who had already survived a heart attack (Friedman et al., 1984). More research is needed before the value of stress-management programs for Type A behavior can be firmly established. The benefits of future programs may be enhanced by aiming treatment more specifically at reducing hostility and other elements of the Type A pattern that research shows to be particularly dangerous.

Facing illness and surgery   Illness and surgery bring pain, lack of control, and other stressors. People who are the least prepared to deal with such stressors often become especially angry, anxious, and depressed (Cohen & Lazarus, 1979). They also tend to experience more pain, need more medication, recover more slowly, and at least among heart attack patients, have a lower survival rate (Garrity, 1975; Melamed & Siegel, 1980). To combat these problems, many hospitals offer programs to help patients cope with the stress and pain of surgery or with such chronic illnesses as cancer, heart disease, and asthma (MacDonald & Kuiper, 1983).

In one experiment designed to evaluate such programs, adult surgical patients were given relaxation training, information about surgical procedures and postoperative pain, or both (Wilson, 1981). Compared with a control group that received no special preparation, patients who received both treatments had less pain and pain medication, felt better emotionally, began walking sooner, and went home earlier. Studies like this suggest that simply telling patients what to expect might not be enough to significantly reduce the impact of surgery-related stressors. Patients should also be helped to develop behavioral coping strategies to use before and after surgery (MacDonald & Kuiper, 1983).

Dealing with trauma   As we noted earlier, stress reactions to traumas, such as rape, natural disaster, or military combat, may be temporary or chronic, immediate or delayed. Hospitals, government agencies, and community groups have created programs designed to help traumatized people cope with their experience and minimize the severity of their stress reactions.

Efforts to help the victims of rape are one example. In many cities and towns, rape victims now have access to stress-coping programs run by hospitals, mental health clinics, or women's advocacy and support groups. These programs make it easier for the victim to report a rape (there may be a special hotline number). They often dispatch female counselors to provide information, advice, and support while the victim is being examined at a hospital or questioned by police. Perhaps most important, staff members offer individual or group counseling sessions in which victims can express and start coping with the anger, humiliation, fear, guilt, and other emotional stress responses stemming from the attack, which they might not be able to talk about with family or friends. These sessions also provide a good place to discuss cognitive and behavioral strategies for coping with such problems as fear of being alone, aversion to sexual activity, or conflict with husbands or boyfriends (Peters, 1977). The staff also guides the most seriously disturbed individuals to seek more formal psychotherapeutic help.

Coping with major changes: Widowhood and divorce   The breakup of a marriage and the death of a spouse are among the most intense stressors a

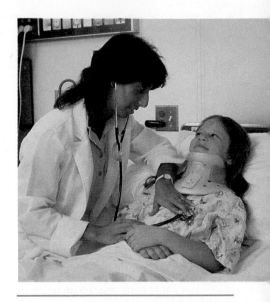

Most presurgery programs for managing stress attempt to reduce patients' uncertainty by telling them exactly what procedures will take place when and what sensations, including pain, are likely to occur. They also provide training in cognitive coping strategies and relaxation. And they offer social support in the form of reassurance and encouragement.

STRESS AND THOUGHT

When People Are Under Stress, How Does Their Ability to Solve Problems and Make Decisions Change?

The physiological arousal associated with stress can affect performance on all kinds of tasks. If arousal is moderate, it may improve a person's ability to perform a task, but overarousal or underarousal may interfere with the efficient processing of information, and performance may suffer (see Figure 11.4 in the chapter on motivation). This relationship between arousal and performance has special implications for people's ability to think clearly about complex material when confronted with stressors.

For one thing, the presence of environmental stressors tends to narrow the range of attention, which may in turn worsen many of the problems in problem solving that we discussed in Chapter 9. For example, stress-narrowed attention can accentuate the general tendency to cling to mental sets, which are established, though possibly inefficient, approaches to problems. The consequent inability to scan a wide range of creative solutions may add to the time needed to solve problems (Berkun, 1964; Easterbrook, 1959). More specifically, stress can intensify functional fixedness, which is the tendency to use objects for only one purpose. People in hotel fires, for example, sometimes die trapped in their rooms because it did not occur to them to use the telephone or a piece of furniture to break a window.

The disruption of thinking ability by stress may also come from a splitting of attention. A person who is trying to perform a complex mental task under time pressure or other stressors tends to be distracted by catastrophizing thoughts, worry about how much time is left, or concern over physical and emotional discomfort (Baumeister, 1984). It is difficult to do well on demanding mental tasks when attention is split in this way. For example, in one study conducted by the army, soldiers who thought their transport plane was in danger of crashing were less able to recall previously learned crash-landing procedures than soldiers who were asked to remember the same information during a normal flight. Far more familiar examples happen every day, as participants on "Wheel of Fortune" and other television game shows try to solve puzzles, recall information, and perform other tasks requiring thought and memory under time pressure and the eyes of millions of viewers. In these very

person can face. We mentioned earlier that such changes can be especially disruptive when they occur unexpectedly and the person feels unable to control what is happening. Special stress-management programs are available all over the country to help individuals deal with these stressors.

For example, Carol Barrett (1978) offered widows in the Los Angeles area one of three experiences: a confidant group, which emphasized the development of social support through close personal friendships; a consciousness-raising group, which focused on discussing the social role of widows; and a self-help group, which discussed ways of dealing with loneliness, grief, financial difficulties, legal matters, social interaction with men, and other problems that widows typically face. Each group met for two hours a week for seven weeks. Measures of personality, attitudes, and behaviors were taken before and as long as fourteen weeks after the program. Compared with an untreated group, the women in all three groups tended to feel more in control of their lives and more optimistic about their health.

Valuable as stress-management programs can be, however, they are not cures for stress. Long-term success in the form of reduced stress responsiveness and improved coping skills usually comes only to those who not only learn, but also work on their own to practice and improve on what formal programs have to offer.

FUTURE DIRECTIONS

Early conceptions of stress characterized stressors as fixed forces acting on people who display relatively automatic stress responses, much as a shelf might sag under the weight of heavy books. As we have seen, this perspective has been superseded and expanded by psychobiological models and other more complex approaches. These newer approaches view stress, not just in

stressful circumstances, contestants sometimes miss questions that seem ridiculously easy to viewers watching calmly at home.

The *confirmation bias*—the tendency to ignore information that does not fit one's initial approach to a problem—can also be intensified by stress. This was nicely illustrated in *The Poseidon Adventure,* a film about passengers aboard a capsized luxury liner. All those who, under the stress of the moment, adhered to the hypothesis that the best escape route would be downward and out, the way they had entered, died. Only those few who climbed upward toward the bottom of the ship were saved by rescuers who had cut through the ship's hull.

Decision making may also suffer when people face stressors. People who normally examine and think about all aspects of a situation before making a decision may, under stress, act impulsively and sometimes foolishly (Keinan, 1987). Couples whose dating relationships have been full of conflict and argument may suddenly decide to break up and then, just as suddenly, get married. High-pressure salespeople try to take advantage of people's tendency to act impulsively when under stress. They may create artificially time-limited offers or tell customers that others are waiting to buy an item.

These and other examples of the disruptive impact of stressors on cognitive functioning highlight the importance of taking their effects into account when assessing performance. Sometimes this means placing less faith in the validity of a low score on an intelligence test if the test was taken under unusually stressful circumstances. Similarly, the best candidate for a particular job may not make the best presentation under the stress of an interview. Skilled managers and recruiters view interviews in the light of academic transcripts, letters of recommendation, and other sources of information that reflect how a person can perform under less intense stress. Oc-

casionally, however, interviews or other assessments are conducted under conditions designed to be as stressful as possible, in order to get some idea of how a person is likely to perform under stress. This is especially important when trying to identify those most likely to perform well in the astronaut corps, a big-city police force, or other dangerous work.

Research on the link between stress and thinking has also indicated the need to try to limit the stress placed on people in jobs that require complex mental activity. As a result, pilots are not permitted to fly more than a certain number of hours per day, and air traffic controllers are encouraged to take breaks every two hours. Measures like these are designed to reduce the possible lapses in attention, judgment, or decision making that could cause a tragedy.

terms of stressors and stress responses, but as an interactional process in which stressors and a person's thoughts, emotions, and coping efforts all play important roles. The prominence of interactional models of stress (Fleming, Baum & Singer, 1984; Gatchel & Baum, 1983; Hamberger & Lohr, 1984) reflect a more general tendency toward thinking about human behavior and behavior problems as determined by both person-specific and situational variables. This trend is also evident in the chapters on personality and abnormal psychology.

Contemporary research has broadened to include the context in which stressors occur. What makes a stressor stressful? Is there anything inherently damaging in certain events or situations, or does their impact come from the broader circumstances in which those events and situations occur? At one time, for example, it was thought that change alone was the key to the creation of stressors, but this view now seems too narrow. In future years, researchers will be exploring the role of such factors as how predictable and controllable stressors are. Indeed, some psychologists are now suggesting that control is a particularly important dimension and that the feeling of control may be central not only to minimizing the effects of stressors, but to mental health in general (Rodin, 1986).

Viewing stress as a dynamic process has widened the scope of research in the field in other ways as well. For one thing, it has increased the attention devoted to understanding how individual differences, such as physical predispositions and cognitive styles, influence responses to stressors. For example, it may be that lack of control over stressors amplifies stress responses in an especially dangerous way among Type A's or others with an especially strong need for control. Special tests have been designed to measure need for control and to relate that need to stress responsiveness (Burger, 1985). Similarly, it may be that the benefits of social support are greatest for people with an internal locus of control (Lefcourt, Martin & Saleh, 1984).

The process of coping has become at least as prominent in stress research as stressors and stress responses. Research now suggests, for example, that people whose defense mechanisms prompt them to cope with stress by denying, minimizing, or otherwise avoiding confrontation of stressors are at greater risk for stress-related illness and psychological distress than those whose coping is more active and direct (Holahan & Moos, 1987). Research on the relationship between coping styles and stress outcomes has increased and is likely to receive even more attention in coming years (Menaghen, 1983). Also of interest are questions about how coping skills develop and the degree to which they can be strengthened through modeling, formal training, and other means.

Because researchers today are trying to understand the entire stress process as it occurs in the lives of individual human beings, they face a huge undertaking, one that involves virtually every aspect of psychology. Current concepts of stress have also helped to build bridges between psychology and other disciplines, from physiology to sociology. The field of psychoneuroimmunology is a case in point. Research that views stress from a broad, interdisciplinary perspective is likely to have potentially sweeping implications for enhancing well-being, improving health, and prolonging life. It has already stimulated research on ways to protect elderly people's weakened immune systems from the stress of feeling out of control over their environment. In one nursing home, this source of stress was reduced by giving residents a greater sense of control over such simple things as what they ate, how their rooms were arranged, and whether their personal telephones were turned on or off. Over an eighteen-month period, the death rate among these residents was 50 percent lower than for a group whose decision-making power was unchanged (Rodin, 1986).

In short, stress and stress management are likely to be exciting fields as time goes on. For a more detailed look at their development, consider taking courses in such areas as health psychology, behavioral medicine, stress and coping, or other stress-related topics. Most courses in abnormal psychology and some in personality also spend time on the relationships between stress, mental disorder, and individual characteristics.

SUMMARY

1. The term *stress* refers in part to stressors, which are events and situations that place physical or psychological demands on people. The term is also used to refer to reactions to stressors. Most generally, however, stress is viewed as an ongoing, interactive process that takes place as people adjust physically and psychologically to their environment.

2. Stressors may be physical or psychological. Major psychological stressors include frustration, pressure, boredom, trauma, conflict, and change. Stressors can be measured by tests like the SRRS and the Daily Hassles Scale.

3. Reactions to stressors include physical, psychological, and behavioral responses. These stress responses can occur alone or in combination, and the appearance of one can often stimulate the others.

4. Physical stress responses include short-term changes in heart rate, respiration, muscle tension, and other processes associated with the fight-or-flight syndrome. These responses subside when the stressor does. Longer-lasting stressors bring on a more elaborate physical response pattern known as the general adaptation syndrome, which helps people resist stress but which, if present too long, can also lead to a variety of physical illnesses. One of the more recently discovered physiological responses to stress is the suppression of the immune system.

5. Psychological stress responses include emotional and cognitive reactions. Anxiety, anger, and depression are among the most common emotional stress reactions. Cognitive stress reactions include disruptions in the ability to think clearly, remember accurately,

and solve problems efficiently. They can also include catastrophizing about stressors, which increases their impact, and utilizing various defense mechanisms in an effort to minimize their impact. Severe psychological stress responses may ultimately create some form of mental disorder.

6. Behavioral stress responses include specific changes in posture, coordination, and other actions, including facial expressions, tremors, or jumpiness, which reflect physical tension or emotional stress reactions. More global behavioral stress responses include everything from irritability and excessive escapism to suicide attempts and drug abuse. Certain patterns of behavioral response to severe, long-lasting stressors or to trauma have been identified as burnout and posttraumatic stress disorder, respectively.

7. The key to understanding stress appears to lie in understanding how specific stressors interact with particular people. Stressors are likely to have greater impact if they occur without warning, are uncontrollable, or involve a continuous parade of daily problems. The people most likely to react strongly to a stressor are those who perceive stressors as frightening, uncontrollable threats or who have the least social support or stress-coping skills.

8. Psychological as well as physical stressors can create illness. This is especially true for people who live high-pressure, competitive, Type A lifestyles. Recognition of the stress-illness link, as well as the association between risk factors such as smoking, prompted the development of behavioral medicine. Researchers in this field seek to understand how psychological factors are related to physical disease and to use behavioral sciences, such as psychology, to help people behave in ways that will prevent or minimize disease.

9. In order to cope with stress, a person must first clearly recognize stressors and develop a systematic plan for dealing with them through cognitive, behavioral, or physiological coping skills. Important skills include learning to think rationally about stressors, acting to minimize the number or intensity of stressors, and developing relaxation or other techniques for reducing the intensity of physical stress reactions.

10. Formal stress-management programs have been developed to help people who are most vulnerable to stress-related illnesses or who face such major stressors as heart attack, cancer, surgery, military combat, or rape. Training in the development of psychological, behavioral, and physiological coping skills is a basic part of such programs.

KEY TERMS

Definitions of terms appear on the pages shown in parentheses.

alarm reaction (480)
behavioral medicine (494)
biofeedback training (497)
burnout (487)
catastrophizing (484)
cognitive restructuring (496)
defense mechanism (485)
diseases of adaptation (481)
exhaustion (480)
free-floating anxiety (484)
general adaptation syndrome (GAS) (480)
generalized anxiety disorder (484)
immune system (482)

internal locus of control (490)
posttraumatic stress disorder (487)
progressive relaxation training (498)
psychoneuroimmunology (483)
resistance (480)
social support network (491)
stress (472)
stressor (472)
stress reaction (472)
Type A (492)
Type B (492)

RECOMMENDED READINGS

Beech, H. R., Burns, L. E., & Sheffield, B. F. (1982). *A behavioural approach to the management of stress.* New York: Wiley. A concise guide to stress-management techniques, from assessment of sources of stress through implementation of a full-scale stress-reduction plan.

Davis, M., Eshelman, E. R., & McKay, M. (1982). *The relaxation and stress reduction workbook.* Oakland, Calif.: New Harbinger Publications. A workbook containing clear and basic descriptions of progressive relaxation, meditation, self-hypnosis, and other antistress methods.

Farmer, R. E., Monahan, L. H., & Hekeler, R. W. (1984). *Stress management for human services.* Beverly Hills, Calif.: Springer. This is a "how-to" manual, mainly for people already working in high-stress human services jobs. Even if you are not working in such a job, you may find it instructive to consider the program of self-help suggested in this slim volume.

Lazarus, R. S., & Folkman, S. (1984). *Stress, appraisal, and coping.* New York: Springer. An excellent treatment of the history of the stress concept and researchers' various approaches to it. This volume also contains a full statement of Lazarus's views on the importance of cognitive interpretation of stressors.

Selye, H. (1976). *The stress of life.* New York: McGraw-Hill. This is the classic volume that describes Selye's research on and theories about stress and its effects.

Spielberger, C. (1979). *Understanding stress and anxiety.* New York: Harper & Row. A fine, basic introduction to the concept of stress and to the wide range of anxiety-related disorders it can engender.

D

uring World War II, the U.S. government needed spies, assassins, saboteurs, and other specialists, for secret operations behind enemy lines. Candidates for these jobs were taken to special camps, where they were subjected to physical and psychological tests. In one of these tests, a candidate was given just a few minutes to instruct and supervise two enlisted men—"Buster" and "Kippy"—in the construction of a five-foot, cube-shaped wooden frame. What the candidate did not know was that the men were psychologists whose job was to frustrate and enrage him. Buster and Kippy were so good at acting lazy, stupid, and hostile that the cube was never built in the allotted time.

Did the government think that its spies would someday need to build giant Tinker Toy cubes in Nazi Germany? No, but the government did need to assess the likelihood that a person could act under extremely dangerous and stressful working conditions. The construction test was supposed to measure candidates' skill, ingenuity, endurance, and resistance to stress. The testers assumed that, if a candidate did well on the test, then these characteristics were part of his personality and would come to the fore when needed.

These assumptions reflect just one of several ways of looking at personality. In everyday conversation, you might use the word *personality* to mean "charm" ("Abercrombie has a lot of personality"), to refer to a person's most prominent characteristic ("She has a trusting personality"), or as a general cause of behavior ("He wouldn't have so many problems if he didn't have such a rotten personality"). Psychologists' definitions of personality are just as varied. Some describe it as a collection of character traits. Others believe it to be something inside the person that guides behavior. Still others hold that one's personality *is* one's behavior, no more and no less. To make a long story short, there never has been a universally agreed-upon definition of personality. We define **personality** as the pattern of psychological and behavioral characteristics by which each person can be compared and contrasted with other people. It is this unique pattern of characteristics that emerges from the blending of inherited and acquired tendencies to make each person an identifiable individual.

When they study personality, researchers look at the consistencies or inconsistencies that people display within themselves and the similarities and differences among people. We will see that personality research uses many of the concepts introduced in previous chapters. Indeed, personality has been said to lie at the crossroads of all psychological research (Mischel, 1981) (see Linkages diagram, p. 506). In this chapter, we consider several approaches to the topic and some of the ways in which personality theory and research are being applied.

STUDYING PERSONALITY

Why does a person who is usually quiet and friendly sometimes get nasty and mean? What makes one person consistently confident and optimistic, whereas

14

Personality

LINKAGES
an overview

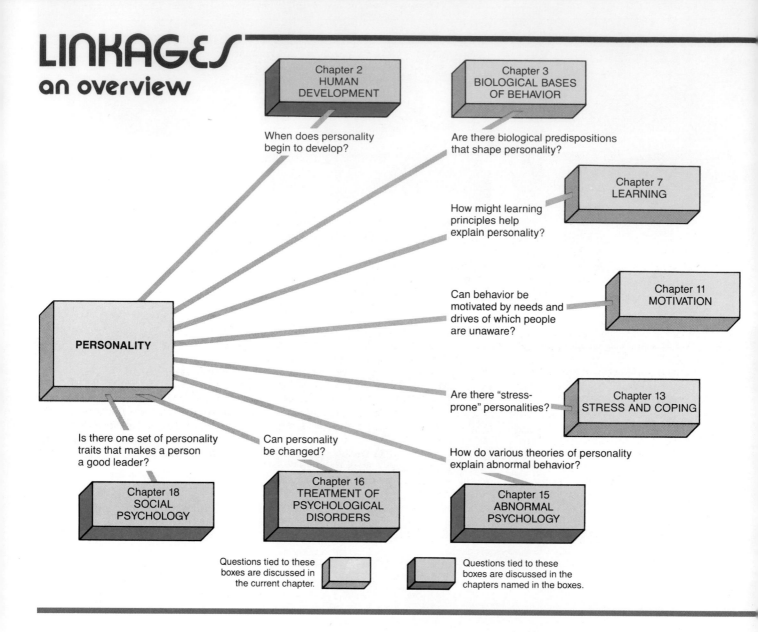

Chapter 2
HUMAN DEVELOPMENT

When does personality begin to develop?

Chapter 3
BIOLOGICAL BASES OF BEHAVIOR

Are there biological predispositions that shape personality?

Chapter 7
LEARNING

How might learning principles help explain personality?

Chapter 11
MOTIVATION

Can behavior be motivated by needs and drives of which people are unaware?

PERSONALITY

Are there "stress-prone" personalities?

Chapter 13
STRESS AND COPING

Is there one set of personality traits that makes a person a good leader?

Can personality be changed?

How do various theories of personality explain abnormal behavior?

Chapter 18
SOCIAL PSYCHOLOGY

Chapter 16
TREATMENT OF PSYCHOLOGICAL DISORDERS

Chapter 15
ABNORMAL PSYCHOLOGY

Questions tied to these boxes are discussed in the current chapter.

Questions tied to these boxes are discussed in the chapters named in the boxes.

another is usually fearful and negative? How much behavior is controlled by people's characteristics and how much by the situations they are in? These are among the unanswered questions in the field of personality. To address these questions, psychologists must have some way of assessing personality and some concepts to guide that assessment.

Methods of Assessing Personality

Suppose you were one of the psychologists choosing people for undercover work during World War II. How would you go about judging whether a person was a good candidate? All of the methods typically used to measure, or assess, personality employ some combination of three basic tools: *observations, interviews,* and *tests.*

Observation of people's behavior (always done with appropriate permission) can highlight their styles of social interaction. For example, observation may involve visiting a home to observe a family's interactions during meals, watching schoolchildren in a playground, or asking people to monitor themselves by keeping track of, say, every hostile remark made during the

PERSONALITY AND PSYCHOLOGY

Like snowflakes, no two people are entirely the same. Even identical twins, who share exactly the same genetic characteristics, develop their own personal styles. The unique pattern of psychological and behavioral characteristics that emerges from the blending of inherited and acquired tendencies to make each person an identifiable individual is known as personality. It has great importance in psychology.

Indeed, one might think of personality as the coalescence in a particular individual of all the psychological, behavioral, and biological processes discussed in other chapters. Personality researchers focus their attention on how this coalescence takes place, on the resulting range of personalities, on the course of personality development over the lifespan, and on how personality influences (and is influenced by) the environment. One result of this work has been the construction of several theories that have proven helpful in measuring personality characteristics, explaining normal and abnormal personality development, and creating therapies aimed at personality change.

Whatever aspect of personality they choose to address, researchers almost always find themselves working with variables and data from other areas of psychology. For example, the differences in optimum level of arousal and arousal seeking that we discussed in the chapter on motivation have been tied to differences in introversion-extraversion—the degree to which a person is socially outgoing and adventurous (extraverted) or shy and withdrawn (introverted). Introverts may have a lower optimum level of arousal than extraverts or may be so sensitive to stimulation that they restrict their exposure to it in order to avoid the discomfort of overarousal. On the other hand, extraverts may have a high optimum level of arousal or an insensitivity to stimulation, so that they require greater-than-average stimulation to reach an optimum level. Because variations in optimum arousal level or sensitivity to stimulation may be biologically based, perhaps even inherited, the study of this personality dimension reaches not only into motivation but also into biological psychology. There are many other links like these; indeed, it is difficult to imagine any aspect of human psychology that does not overlap in some way with personality.

Interviews provide a way of gathering information about personality in which the interviewer can adjust the pattern of inquiry to focus on the details of particularly significant aspects of behavior or thought.

day. Of all the methods of assessing personality, however, interviews and tests are by far the most popular. Interviews provide a relatively natural way to gather information about personality from the person's own point of view. Personality tests, like the mental abilities tests discussed in Chapter 10, offer a more standardized and economical way of gathering information; they are usually classified as either *objective* or *projective.*

Objective tests   A typical **objective test** is a paper-and-pencil form containing clear, specific questions (such as "Have you ever worried about your family without good reason?"), statements ("I think about sex more than most people"), or concepts ("Myself"), to which the respondent is asked to give yes-no, true-false, or multiple-choice answers or ratings. These personality tests can be scored objectively, much like the multiple-choice tests so common in the classroom. And, just as in the classroom, results from many people can be compared mathematically. For example, before interpreting the meaning of your apparently high score on an objective test of anxiety, a psychologist would first compare the score with *norms,* or average scores obtained from others of your age and sex. Only if you were well above these averages might you be considered unusually anxious.

Projective tests   Personality tests made up of relatively unstructured stimuli, such as inkblots, which can be perceived and responded to in many ways, are known as **projective tests.** Indeed, the whole idea behind projective tests is to provide stimuli that are so unstructured and allow such a wide range of interpretations that particular responses will be a reflection (or *projection*) of the individual's needs, fantasies, conflicts, thought patterns, and other aspects of personality. Some projective tests ask people to say what they associate with the shape of an inkblot (see Figure 14.1) or with a particular word. In others, the person is shown a drawing like those in the Thematic Apperception Test (described in the motivation chapter) and is asked to construct a story about what is going on in the picture. Still others ask respondents to make their own drawings of such items as a house, a person, or a tree; they may also ask people to fill in the missing parts of incomplete pictures or sentences.

Compared to the true-false answers or ratings generated by objective tests, the stories, drawings, associations, and other responses to projective tests are difficult to translate into clear numerical scores. Experts in the use of certain tests have summarized their experience and research, thus providing guidelines for interpreting projective test answers. Still, for the most part, statements about what these patterns say about any given individual's personality vary from one tester to the next. This looseness and subjectivity in scoring projective tests has been widely criticized. Indeed, research showing relatively low validity coefficients for projective tests has tended to make them less scientifically acceptable than objective varieties. Yet even objective tests are not totally objective, because the test taker must interpret what an item means before responding to it. This point was beautifully summarized by the psychologist who said, "When a subject is asked to guess what the examiner is thinking, we call it an objective test; when the examiner tries to guess what the subject is thinking, we call it a projective device" (Kelly, 1958, p. 332).

Using personality tests   Whether personality tests are objective or projective, their usefulness must be evaluated by the same criteria applied to tests of mental abilities. As we discussed in the chapter on mental abilities, tests must meet certain standards of reliability and validity. Yet, even when a test is reliable and valid, the information it gathers may not be worth the disadvantages of testing. One concern is that tests must be administered by qualified people,

Figure 14.1
A Projective Test
Here is an inkblot similar to those included in the Rorschach test, which contains a set of ten patterns, some in color, others in black and white. The subject is asked to tell what the blot might be and then to explain why. What do you see? Most scoring methods pay attention to (1) what part of the blot the person responds to; (2) what particular features (such as small details or color) appear to determine each response; (3) the content of responses (for example, animals, knives, blood, maps, body parts); and (4) the popularity or commonness of the subject's responses compared to those of others who have taken the test. As is true of most projective tests, scoring of Rorschach responses and interpretation of what they say about personality depends to a considerable extent on the tester, but several researchers have developed systems designed to provide some guidance and make the process more objective (Exner, 1974).
(© Andrew Brilliant/Carol Palmer.)

scored, interpreted, and used properly. Otherwise, for example, qualified applicants might unfairly lose out on a job, or inappropriate people might be hired.

There are also questions of who should have access to personality test results and how those results should be presented. In most situations, people have a legal right to review their own test results, but this does not mean that they will understand those results. A qualified person should be available to explain how the results and conclusions were reached and to put them into perspective. Without this guidance, individuals could easily misunderstand and become upset or depressed about what they might see as serious flaws in their personality. Many people also worry about having personality test information kept in their school or work records because of uncertainty over who might be allowed to review them and whether the information might create a negative bias. These and other concerns have led the American Psychological Association to establish a set of ethical standards regarding the development, publicity, and use of personality and all other types of psychological tests (American Psychological Association, 1974, 1981).

Systematic Approaches to Personality

Researchers in personality can approach their task from many different points of view, depending on their basic assumptions about people. For example, suppose your background is in anatomy (the study of physical structure) and you notice how bumpy the human skull is and how lumpy the brain is underneath it. It might occur to you that those lumps and bumps might mean something. Maybe a bump reflects a better-developed part of the brain and thus a stronger tendency to think or behave in some particular way. With these basic assumptions as a guiding theory, you could study personality by investigating which part of the brain controls which behavior, emotion, or attitude. This might allow you to describe people's personalities and even to make predictions about their behavior on the basis of skull examinations. The degree to which your descriptions and predictions actually correspond to a person's actions would provide a test of the validity of your theory and techniques. If the results were positive, you might be encouraged to try using your "lump-and-bump" method to detect criminals applying for jobs as bank guards or to match people in a dating service.

As it happens, a theory similar to this one was actually proposed by the eighteenth-century anatomist Franz Gall. He believed that each of thirty-five faculties (such as sense of humor or hostility) was localized in a specific part of the brain. He called his theory of personality *phrenology*. When phrenology was subjected to scientific evaluation by other researchers, it proved inadequate. But it illustrates that all approaches to personality, even unsuccessful ones, contain certain basic components:

1. A set of assumptions that forms a personality theory (in this case, phrenology).
2. Theory-guided decisions about where to look for evidence about personality. (Gall chose the brain.)
3. Ways of measuring or assessing personality. (Gall used physical examination of the skull.)
4. A set of special research methods designed to evaluate the personality theory. (Gall tried to relate bumps to behavior.)

Most approaches to personality also contain a fifth basic component: methods for helping people change, usually known as *psychotherapy*.

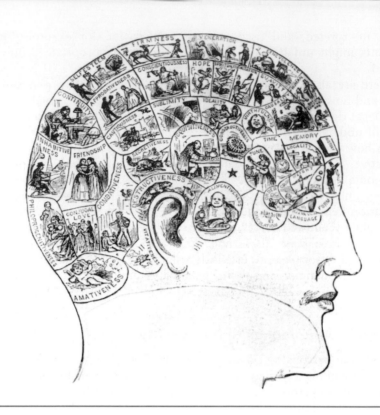

Franz Gall, founder of phrenology, mapped out what he believed to be the physical location of each mental faculty and then used this map to translate skull examinations into personality sketches.

The four most prominent approaches to personality today include the psychodynamic approach, the dispositional approach, the behavioral approach, and the phenomenological approach.

THE PSYCHODYNAMIC APPROACH

Some people think of personality as a quality that is clearly reflected in behavior. A person with an "obnoxious personality," for example, shows it by acting obnoxiously. But is that all there is to personality? Not according to Sigmund Freud, who likened personality to an iceberg, with the tip visible but the bulk underwater. He created the **psychodynamic approach** to personality, which emphasizes the interplay of unconscious mental processes in determining human thought, feelings, and behavior.

The development of Freud's psychodynamic approach began during the 1890s, when, as a physician, he specialized in the treatment of "neurotic" disorders, including such problems as blindness, deafness, or paralysis for which there was no physical cause. His patients did not appear to be faking, but their puzzling symptoms could often be made to disappear under hypnosis. Freud's experience with these cases eventually led him to believe in *psychic determinism,* the idea that psychological factors play a major role in determining behavior and shaping personality. He proposed, further, that people may not know why they feel, think, or act the way they do, because these activities are partly controlled by the unconscious part of the personality—the part of which people are not normally aware. Most of what is in the unconscious, he said, is frightening or socially taboo, and people keep this material out of awareness by using various psychological defenses.

These defenses make the unconscious difficult to explore, but Freud developed methods for doing so. For example, he asked patients to use **free association,** or saying whatever comes to mind. He believed that the pattern

Sigmund Freud (1856–1939) worked on revising and applying his psychodynamic theory of personality right up until his death. Here, late in life, he works in his study accompanied by his dog, Jo-Fi.

of association can disclose thoughts, feelings, and impulses that are normally unconscious (for instance, "I saw a dead rat in the street this morning. . . . Boy, it's been a long time since I've talked to my Dad"). Hidden aspects of personality can also be inferred from apparently accidental behaviors, such as being late for an interview or making a "Freudian slip" of the tongue ("What thighs. . . . I mean, what size do you wear?"). The nature and content of a person's dreams also provide data for personality assessment. These methods became part of Freud's theory of personality, his approach to research, and his therapy techniques, which are collectively known as **psychoanalysis.** We will discuss psychoanalytic treatment in more detail in Chapter 16.

Freud's psychodynamic theory of personality began with the assumption that people are born with basic instincts or needs—not only for food, water, and air, but also for sex and aggression. The needs for love, knowledge, security, and the like are based, he said, on these more fundamental desires. Each person is faced with the task of figuring out how to meet his or her needs in a world that often frustrates one's efforts. According to Freud, personality develops out of each person's struggle with this task and is reflected in how he or she goes about satisfying a wide range of needs.

The Structure of Personality

Figure 14.2 illustrates Freud's view of the structure of personality. He described personality as having three major components: the id, the ego, and the superego.

The **id** is a reservoir of unconscious energy, sometimes called psychic energy or **libido,** which includes the basic instincts, desires, and impulses with which all people are born. Prominent among these are *Eros,* which is the instinct for pleasure and sex, and *Thanatos,* a death instinct, which can motivate aggression or destructiveness toward oneself or others. The id seeks immediate satisfaction, regardless of society's rules or the rights or feelings of

Figure 14.2
Freud's Conception of the Personality Structure
This theoretical organization consists of the primitive, impulsive id; the stern, demanding superego (which includes the conscience); and the reality-oriented ego, which must work out compromises between internal demands and the limitations of the external world. Notice that parts of the personality are conscious, parts unconscious. Further, Freud recognized that between these levels is the preconscious, *a region discussed in the consciousness chapter as the location of memories and other material not usually in awareness, but which can with little or no effort be brought into consciousness.*
(As adapted from Robert M. Liebert and Michael D. Spiegler: *Personality: Strategies and Issues,* Chicago, Ill.: The Dorsey Press. © 1987, p. 95.)

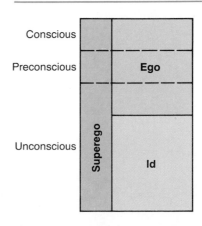

others. In other words, the id operates according to the **pleasure principle,** which guides people toward whatever feels good. Throwing a temper tantrum at your noisy neighbor's front door would reflect an id impulse.

As children grow, however, they learn that doing whatever they want is not always acceptable. Drawing with Mom's lipstick on the living room wall might be fun, but it might also lead to a spanking. As parents, teachers, and others place more and more restrictions on the direct expression of id impulses, a second part of the personality—the **ego** (or "self")—evolves from the id to create ways to get what one wants in a world full of rules. Because the ego makes compromises between the unreasoning demands of the id and the demands of the real world, it is said to operate on the **reality principle.** Suggesting to your neighbor certain "quiet times" is an example of ego activity. The ego has been called the "executive" of the personality, because it tries to get needs met while protecting people from the physical and emotional harm that might result if they became aware of, let alone acted out, their id impulses.

The more experience people have with the rules and morals of society, the more they tend to adopt them. As a result, children learn that certain behaviors are "wrong" and will even scold themselves for doing "bad" things. **Introjection** is the term Freud used for this process of *internalizing* parental and societal values into the personality. Introjected values, our "shoulds" and "should nots," form the third component of personality: the **superego.** "Should nots," the things people know are wrong, make up the part of superego known as the *conscience.* Pressure to conform to "shoulds," the ideal behaviors that people know are right, comes from a second part of superego, known as the *ego ideal.* You might think of the superego as operating on the *morality principle,* since violating either category of its rules results in guilt.

Unfortunately, basic needs (id), reason (ego), morality (superego), and the demands of the environment are often at odds. This creates inner turmoil known as *intrapsychic* or *psychodynamic conflict* (see Table 14.1), which the ego must try to resolve. Freud believed that the number, nature, and outcome of intrapsychic conflicts shape each individual's personality and determine many aspects of behavior. For example, he saw neurotic anxiety as a signal that unconscious impulses are threatening to overwhelm the ego's defenses and reach consciousness. (This differs from *realistic* anxiety, which results when you face a snarling dog or other physical danger.) Normal, adaptive behavior is associated with having relatively few conflicts or with resolving them effectively. Having numerous, severe, or poorly handled conflicts can result in anything from unusual or unique personality characteristics to the major mental disorders discussed in Chapter 15.

Ego Defense Mechanisms

One of the ego's most important functions is to defend against anxiety and guilt. Often it does so by organizing realistic actions, as when a person decides to seek help because of impulses to abuse a child. However, the ego may also deal with anxiety or guilt by resorting to **defense mechanisms,** the unconscious psychological and behavioral tactics that help protect a person from unpleasant emotions. Everyone uses defense mechanisms at one time or another, but overreliance on them can lead to problems.

To illustrate, suppose you find yourself strongly attracted to your best friend's lover but find it impossible to admit it, even to yourself. Your most primitive unconscious impulse might be to kill your friend or abduct the lover, but becoming aware of this impulse would bring a flood of anxiety and guilt. To prevent this, your ego might employ repression. Unlike suppression, in which one consciously denies certain feelings, **repression** unconsciously forces unacceptable impulses out of awareness, leaving you unaware that you

Conflict	Example
Id vs. ego	Choosing between a small immediate reward and a larger reward that requires some period of waiting (i.e., delay of gratification)
Id vs. superego	Deciding whether to return the difference when you are overpaid or undercharged
Ego vs. superego	Choosing between acting in a realistic way (e.g., telling a "white lie") and adhering to a potentially costly or unrealistic standard (e.g., always telling the truth)
Id and ego vs. superego	Deciding whether to retaliate against the attack of a weak opponent or to "turn the other cheek"
Id and superego vs. ego	Deciding whether to act in a realistic way that conflicts both with your desires and your moral convictions (e.g., the decision faced by devout Roman Catholics as to the use of contraceptive devices)
Ego and superego vs. id	Choosing whether to "act on the impulse" to steal something you want and cannot afford—the ego would presumably be increasingly involved in such a conflict as the probability of being apprehended increases

SOURCE: R. M. Liebert and M. D. Spiegler, *Personality: Strategies and Issues,* 1987. Reprinted by permission of Dorsey Press.

TABLE 14.1
Examples of Intrapsychic Conflicts
According to Freud, some of these conflicts may be wholly or partially conscious, but most of them tend to be unconscious.

had the taboo desires in the first place. Keeping such strong feelings under wraps involves a distortion of reality that takes tremendous effort, like trying to hold an inflated beach ball under water.

Other ego defense mechanisms may help keep repressed material from surfacing or disguise it when it does. (We describe a few of these in the chapter on stress; see Table 13.3.) For example, through **projection,** people see their own unacceptable desires in others. Projection might operate in our illustration to make you fearful that others are out to steal your possessions (just as you want to "steal" from your friend). **Reaction formation** is a defense in which one's behavior runs exactly opposite to one's true feelings. Thus, you might develop a sudden, intense dislike for your friend's lover. In **displacement,** unacceptable impulses are diverted toward alternative targets. This could cause you to express hostility toward people who remind you of your friend or to fall temporarily in love with everyone you date.

Intellectualization helps a person to minimize anxiety by viewing threatening issues in cold, abstract terms. Thus, you might engage in endless talk about such conflict-related topics as platonic love, loyalty, or trust. **Rationalization** attempts to "explain away" unacceptable behavior. So, if you blurt out at a party how you really feel, you might later blame it on drunkenness. **Denial,** the most primitive defense, distorts reality by leading one to act, feel, and think as if the impulses are not there. In our example, denial would lead you to acknowledge no romantic interest in the person you love. Finally, there is **sublimation,** the conversion of repressed yearnings into socially approved action. This might prompt you to throw yourself into hard physical labor or creative intellectual or artistic activity.

Stages in Personality Development

Freud believed that internal and external conflicts focus on different issues and problems as people grow, which led him to propose that personality develops during childhood in several stages, which we outlined in Chapter 2.

These are called **psychosexual stages;** each one relates to the part of the body that is the main area of pleasure at that stage. Freud said that failure to resolve problems and conflicts at any given stage can leave a person *fixated;* that is, overly attached to or unconsciously preoccupied with the pleasure area associated with that stage.

The oral stage   A child's first year or so is called the **oral stage,** because the mouth is the center of pleasure then. The infant uses its mouth not only to eat but also to explore its world, mouthing everything from plastic toys to its own hands and feet. Personality problems occur mainly when oral needs are either not met or overindulged. Thus, early weaning or greatly delayed weaning may leave a child longing for or overly attached to the bottle, the breast, and other forms of oral satisfaction.

In the adult personality, fixation at the oral stage might result in such "oral" characteristics as talking too much, overeating, smoking, alcoholism, or even using "biting" sarcasm. Excessive dependence on others (like an infant on its mother) is another possible sign of oral fixation. Especially under stress, an adult fixated at the oral stage may tend to exaggerate these characteristics as he or she regresses toward behaviors once used as an infant.

The anal stage   The second psychosexual stage usually occurs during the second year, when the demand for toilet training conflicts with the child's instinctual pleasure in having bowel movements at will. Because the focus of pleasure and conflict shifts from the mouth to the anus during this period, Freud called it the **anal stage.** If toilet training is too harsh and demanding or is begun too early or too late, conflicts may result.

Followers of Freud's psychodynamic theory argue that unresolved conflicts from the anal stage can create an "anal personality." The adult fixated at the anal stage might symbolically withhold feces by being controlling, stingy, highly organized, stubborn, and perhaps excessively concerned with cleanliness, orderliness, or details. At the other extreme are those who symbolically expel feces by being sloppy, disorganized, or impulsive.

The phallic stage   By the age of three or so, and for about two years thereafter, the focus of pleasure shifts to the genital area. Emphasizing the psychosexual development of boys, Freud called this period the **phallic stage.** Freud said that, during the phallic stage, a boy's id impulses involve sexual desire for the mother and a desire to eliminate, even kill, the father, with whom the boy must compete for the mother's affection. He called this constellation of impulses the **Oedipus complex,** because it parallels the plot of the Greek tragedy *Oedipus Rex,* in which Oedipus unknowingly kills his father and marries his mother. The boy's hostile fantasies and impulses about his father create a fear of retaliation called *castration anxiety.* The fear becomes so strong that the ego represses the incestuous desires. Then the boy seeks to become like, or identify with, his father and in the process begins to learn male sex-role behaviors, which will later help him form a sexual relationship with a woman other than his mother.

Resolution of these conflicts is more complicated for the female child. According to Freud, she begins with a strong attachment to her mother but, as she realizes that boys have penises and girls do not, she begins to hate her mother, perhaps blaming her for the lack and considering her inferior. She allegedly experiences *penis envy* and transfers her love to her father, who has the sex organ she wants. But the girl must still avoid her mother's disapproval; she does so by identifying with her mother, adopting female sex-role behaviors, and subsequently choosing a male mate other than her father.

According to Freud, successful resolution of young boys' Oedipal conflicts results in identification with the father and adoption of behaviors traditionally associated with the male sex role.

Freud believed that the prevalence of interpersonal problems indicates that most people are to some degree fixated at the phallic stage. The person who displays extreme fear, aggression, or other difficulties in dealing with a boss, teacher, or other authority figure may be demonstrating unresolved conflicts with his or her same-sex parent. Uncertainty about one's sexual identity as a male or female, problems in maintaining a stable love relationship, and the appearance of disordered or socially disapproved sexual behavior may also stem from poorly resolved conflicts of the phallic stage.

The latency period and the genital stage   As the phallic stage draws to a close, its conflicts, resolved or not, are repressed or otherwise kept out of consciousness by the ego. An interval of peace known as the **latency period** ensues, during which sexual impulses lie dormant and the child focuses on education and other matters. When he or she begins to mature physically during adolescence, sexual impulses begin to reappear at the conscious level. The genitals again become the focus of pleasure, and the young person begins to seek relationships through which sexual impulses can be gratified. Thus begins what Freud called the **genital stage,** a period that spans the rest of life. The quality of relationships and the degree of fulfillment and contentment that one experiences during this long stage are, according to Freud, tied directly to the success one had at resolving conflicts during the earlier stages.

Variations on Freudian Personality Theories

Freud's ideas, especially the Oedipal theory, created controversy from the moment he presented them. Perhaps the most important reactions came from the psychologists and psychiatrists who were impressed, but not completely satisfied, with Freud's approach. Several of them developed personality theories of their own, in which they retained Freud's emphasis on psychodynamics but downplayed his preoccupation with instincts, the unconscious, and infantile conflicts.

Carl Jung's analytic psychology   Carl Jung (pronounced "yoong") believed that the psychic energy Freud called libido was not based just on sexual and aggressive instincts (1916). He saw it as a more general life force containing within itself an innate drive not only for instinct gratification, but also for the productive blending of basic drives with real-world demands. Jung called this tendency toward growth-oriented resolution of conflicts the *transcendent function.*

Jung also believed that everyone has not only a personal unconscious (containing individually repressed or controlled memories and impulses), but also a **collective unconscious,** a kind of memory bank in which are stored all the images and ideas the human race has accumulated since its evolution from lower forms of life. Some of these images are called **archetypes,** because they consist of classic images or concepts. The idea of *mother,* for instance, has become an archetype; everyone is born with a kind of predisposition to see and react to certain people as mother figures. More ominous is the *shadow* archetype (similar to Freud's notion of id); it contains the most basic instincts from our prehuman centuries. Jung saw the shadow as responsible for such notions as sin and the devil.

Instead of identifying specific stages in personality development, Jung suggested that people come to display differing degrees of introversion (a tendency to focus on one's inner world) or extraversion (a tendency to focus on the social world) and differing tendencies to rely on specific psychological functions, such as thinking versus feeling. The combination of these tendencies, said Jung (1933), creates personalities that display distinctive and predictable patterns of behavior.

Alfred Adler's individual psychology Alfred Adler's (1927) individual psychology emphasized the role of inborn social urges in forming personality. Adler began with the assumption that each person is born in a helpless, totally dependent state, which creates unpleasant feelings of inferiority. These negative feelings, combined with an innate desire to become a full-fledged member of the social world, provides the impetus for the development of personality, according to Adler. He referred to this process as *striving for superiority,* by which he meant a drive for fulfillment as a person, not just a desire to do better than others. If feelings of inferiority are very intense, they can motivate the person to compensate, even overcompensate, for that perceived inferiority. This is sometimes called an *inferiority complex,* in which the individual's personality revolves around trying to make up for some deficit.

According to Adler, the ways in which each person goes about trying to reach personal and social fulfillment constitutes personality or, as he called it, **style of life.** Adler suggested that the style of life is guided by conscious ideas, goals, and beliefs (not by the unconscious, as Freud had said), and that these ideas come about through experience. For example, a child who is pampered and protected may come to believe that he or she is "special" and exempt from society's rules. This *guiding fiction* that "I'm special" is likely to lead to a selfish style of life, in which personal fulfillment comes at the expense of others. In contrast, "There is good in everyone" and "Tomorrow will be better than today" are examples of guiding fictions that, whether true or not, are likely to create positive, upbeat lifestyles.

Ego psychology and the neo-Freudians The importance of social factors in personality is also highlighted in a number of other psychodynamic theories, including that of Freud's daughter, Anna. These theories have retained many of Freud's ideas but have deemphasized the roles of instincts and the unconscious. For example, **ego psychologists** see the ego not just as a mediator in conflicts among id, superego, and environment, but as a creative, adaptive force in its own right (A. Freud, 1946). It is responsible for language development, perception, attention, planning, learning, and many other psychological functions (Hartmann, 1939).

Neo-Freudian theorists, such as Erich Fromm (1941), Karen Horney (pronounced "horn-eye"; 1937), and Harry Stack Sullivan (1953) followed Adler's lead by focusing on how other people help shape an individual's personality. They argued that, once biological needs are met, the attempt to meet *social needs* (to feel protected, secure, and accepted, for example) is most influential in forming personality. When these social needs are unmet, people feel great discomfort and are strongly motivated to correct the problem by somehow getting others to give them what they need socially. The strategies people use to do this, such as taking advantage of other people or becoming extremely dependent on them, become the personality (note the similarity to Adler's style of life concept). Sullivan went so far as to say that the concept of personality is just an illusion, a name for each person's pattern of interpersonal behaviors. This trend within the psychodynamic approach toward emphasizing social factors in personality development is also reflected in the work of Erik H. Erikson (1963, 1968). Erikson proposed eight **psychosocial stages,** suggesting that the most important developments occur in relation to social crises rather than to sexuality. We discussed these stages in the chapter on human development (see Table 2.3).

Another example of the expanded role of social needs and relationships in modern psychodynamic approaches is the work of *object relations* theorists, such as Melanie Klein (1975), Otto Kernberg (1976), and Heinz Kohut (1984). **Object relations** theories focus on the importance for personality development of the very early relationships between infants and their love objects, usually the mother and other primary caregivers. Especially critical is how the primary caregivers provide support, protection, acceptance, and recognition and otherwise meet the infant's physical and psychological needs (Blatt & Lerner, 1983). The nature of these object relations has a significant impact on personality development, including secure early attachment to the mother or other caregiver, gradual separation from the object of attachment, and finally the ability to relate to others as an independent individual. Distorted object relations can create problems that interfere with personality development and lead to inadequate self-esteem, difficulties in trusting or making commitments to others, or more serious mental disorders.

In addition to revising and adding theoretical concepts, psychodynamic theorists after Freud suggested new personality assessment methods. The most familiar of these are projective personality tests. For example, Carl Jung developed a test designed to detect unconscious personality themes in the associations people make to particular words. For example, dark–heart, baby–dead, and hot–blood would suggest more aggressive unconscious impulses than, say, dark–light, baby–bottle, and hot–cold. Psychodynamic theory also forms the basis for other projective tests, including the Rorschach test.

Some Practical Applications

Probably the most common application of psychodynamic personality concepts is in **psychotherapy,** which is the attempt to alleviate various forms of mental disorder through psychological means. Psychodynamic forms of therapy are based on the idea that, if troubled patients can be made conscious of previously unconscious aspects of their personality, they will be better able to understand themselves and to resolve old conflicts. Psychodynamic therapies are discussed in detail in Chapter 16.

To guide their judgments about mental disorder, psychologists and psychiatrists frequently use psychodynamic interviews and projective tests. This process is called *psychodiagnosis.* Figure 14.3 shows how the interpretation of drawings made by a teenage burglary suspect suggest unconscious material. Psychodynamic assessments of personality are also used by those who want to know about a person's unconscious impulses before deciding whether that person might harm other people, attempt suicide, or have trouble living outside a mental institution.

The psychodynamic approach has also stimulated research on how the mind can influence the health of the body. As described in the chapter on stress, the mind and the body can affect each other in many ways. Especially important from the psychodynamic perspective is the ability of anxiety or conflict to bring about physical disorders, such as headaches or high blood pressure. For example, some researchers have found that an inability to describe one's feelings (presumably because of repression) is associated with certain physical disorders, including cancer (Dattore, Shontz & Coyne, 1980; Nemiah, 1975).

Because early childhood experiences are seen as so important to the development of personality and to the appearance of mental disorder, many psychodynamic theorists have also provided tips on child rearing. They have offered books, articles, and courses that advise parents on how to handle such

Figure 14.3
Interpretations Based on a Draw-a-Person Test
These drawings are by an eighteen-year-old male who had been caught stealing a television set. Using a psychodynamic personality approach, a psychologist interpreted the muscular figure as the young man's attempt to boast of masculine prowess, but also saw the muscles as overinflated into a "puffy softness," suggesting feelings of inadequacy. The drawing of the babylike figure was seen to reveal feelings of vulnerability, dependency, and a desire for affection. Appealing as these interpretations may be, the use of projective tests in personality assessment is not generally supported by research. In most cases, projective test results have generally low predictive validity or add little information beyond what the psychologist might have inferred from the case history or other more directly available information.
(Emanuel F. Hammer, Ph.D., "Projective Drawings," in Rabin, ed., *Projective Techniques in Personality Assessment,* pp. 375–376. Copyright © 1968 by Springer Publishing Company, Inc., New York. Used by permission.)

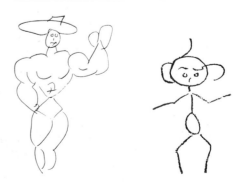

potentially conflict-producing processes as weaning, toilet training, and discipline (Fraiberg, 1959). Object relations theories have also focused special attention on the first days and weeks of life, a time when a strong bond should begin to form between an infant and its parents. Babies who are deprived of this important bonding experience, because they have been abandoned, orphaned, or isolated from their parents by premature birth or physical illness, appear especially prone to develop psychological problems. As noted in Chapter 2, hospitals seek to minimize these problems by allowing increased early contact between babies and parents.

Criticisms of the Psychodynamic Approach

Freud's writings have been extraordinarily influential, but critics of the psychodynamic approach point out that Freud based his theory on observations of a very unrepresentative sample of humankind: a relatively small number of upper-class Viennese patients (mostly women), who not only had mental problems but were raised in a society that considered discussion of sex to be uncivilized. Moreover, Freud's focus on male psychosexual development and his apparent bias toward male anatomy as something to be envied by women has earned him a sexist label and has caused male as well as female feminists to reject his ideas. Some observers have also pointed out that conflicts involving sex and one's parents may relate, not to a desire to have sexual relations with them, but to memories of sexual abuse. In fact, as the reality of child sexual abuse has become clearer, Freud has been faulted for refusing to believe his patient's tales of abuse by parents and other adults and for attributing them to fantasies and wish fulfillment (Masson, 1983).

Questions have also been raised about the existence and operation of such basic psychodynamic concepts as id, ego, unconscious conflicts, defense mechanisms, and archetypes. These constructs are generally considered too vague to measure scientifically. For example, suppose a psychologist suspects that a man harbors strong, unconscious aggressive impulses. The suspicion would be confirmed if the man is often angry and hostile. But if he is unusually even-tempered, this calm could be seen as a defense against aggressive impulses. Occasional angry outbursts might be viewed as wavering ego control. In short, there is almost nothing the man can do that could not be interpreted as reflecting unconscious aggression. Projective instruments are supposed to detect hidden anger, but the value of such tests for accurately predicting behavior has not been strongly supported by psychological research (Geller & Atkins, 1978).

Finally, Freud's view of human beings as creatures driven mainly by instinct and the unconscious has been criticized. Much human behavior goes beyond instinct gratification. The conscious drive to attain lofty personal, social, and spiritual goals is also an important determinant of behavior, as is learning from others. Ego psychologists and others who altered some of Freud's original concepts have helped to divert some of this criticism. Indeed, though it is much less popular than it once was (Garfield & Kurtz, 1976; Smith, 1982), the psychodynamic approach is far from extinct. Many therapists depend heavily on it, and researchers continue to evaluate it (Silverman, 1976). Still, the goal of measuring personality more precisely and the belief that psychodynamic theories underestimate the importance of learning principles or conscious intent have increased the popularity of several alternative approaches. We shall now consider some of these approaches, beginning with the dispositional approach.

THE DISPOSITIONAL APPROACH

If you were to ask a friend to describe the personality of someone you both know, he or she could probably do it without too much trouble. The personality sketch would probably be organized into a small number of descriptive categories. For example:

> She is a truly *caring* person, a real *extrovert*. She is *generous* with her time and she *works very hard* at everything she does. Yet, I think she also *lacks confidence*. She is *submissive* to other people's demands because she *needs to be accepted* by them.

In other words, most people describe others, not in psychodynamic terms, but by referring to the type of people they are ("extrovert"), to their most notable traits ("caring"; "lacks confidence"), or to their needs ("needs to be accepted"). Together, these statements describe a person's *dispositions,* the ways he or she generally thinks and behaves. This dispositional approach to personality is without a doubt the oldest and most common of the approaches we will consider.

The **dispositional approach** makes three basic assumptions.

1. Each person has stable, long-lasting dispositions to display certain behaviors, attitudes, and emotions. Thus, a basically gentle person tends to stay that way day after day, year after year.

2. These dispositions are general, in that they appear in diverse situations. A person who is fiercely competitive at work will probably also be that way on the tennis court or at a party.

3. Each person has a different set of dispositions, or at least a set of dispositions of varying strengths, which assume a unique pattern. This creates an endless variety of human personalities.

People's tendencies to think and act in characteristically different ways make up part of what is meant by their disposition.

Figure 14.4
Types of Personality
What can you say about people's personalities by looking at them? Remarkably little, even though, as we mentioned in Chapter 9, people tend to use representativeness heuristics to place others in personality types based on appearance. Thus, it is tempting to decide that a small, tidy-looking person is more reliable or trustworthy than a big, slovenly one. Every year, well-dressed con artists exploit the trust engendered by mistaken type theories.

Personality Types

When you hear someone say, "He's not my type," or "I'm not that type of person," you are hearing the echoes of an age-old dream: to be able to classify people into a few basic kinds of personalities. The attempt to establish *types* of people goes back at least as far as Hippocrates, the ancient Greek physician who suggested that a certain temperament or behavior pattern is associated with each of four bodily fluids, or *humors:* blood, phlegm, black bile, and yellow bile. Personality type, said Hippocrates, depends on how much of each humor one has. The terms for these personality types—sanguine, phlegmatic, melancholic, and choleric—still survive.

The idea of typing people's personalities based on biological factors also appears in theories that relate the appearance people inherit to the personality they develop (Williams, 1967). This notion has great appeal. For example, look at Figure 14.4. Which of these men do you think is a photographer? an executive? a convicted rapist? a successful con artist? Most likely, you decided on the basis of some kind of personal system, which told you that certain types of people have a certain "look" (check the bottom of the next page to see how well you did). Many people use a personal typing system to make assumptions about people on a first meeting (Warner & Sugarman, 1986); in Chapter 17, we will see how this can influence attraction.

The formal study of the relationship between personality and the face or body is called *physiognomy* and goes back to Gall's phrenology. Modern physiognomy was promoted in the 1940s by William Sheldon, an American physician and psychologist. However, research has not supported the validity of compressing the full range of human personality into a few types based on facial or bodily characteristics.

Personality Traits

In a sense, personality *types* are really labels for groups of personality *traits*. Many researchers have focused on traits as the building blocks of personality. They start with the assumption that each personality can be described in terms of how strong it is on various traits, such as hostility, dependency, sociability, and the like (see Figure 14.5). Thus, from the trait perspective, personality is like a fabric of many different-colored threads, some bright, some dull, some thick, some thin, which are never woven together in exactly the same way twice.

Allport's trait theory   Gordon Allport, one of the founders of trait research, spent thirty years studying the way traits combine to form the normal personality. He found at least eighteen thousand traits. He also found that many of the labels for these traits refer to the same thing ("hostile," "nasty," and "mean" all convey a similar meaning), so that, when people are asked to give a personality sketch, they are usually able to do the job using only about seven trait labels. Of course, those seven labels might be very different for each person being described, but Allport believed that such a set of labels represents a person's *central traits,* which organize and control his or her behavior across many different situations. In addition, Allport found what he called *secondary traits.* These are more specific to certain situations and control far less behavior. "Hates salad bars" would be an example of a secondary trait. In a few people, Allport found *cardinal traits*—dispositions that are so general and pervasive that they govern virtually everything a person does. People who have cardinal traits often become famous: Albert Schweitzer and Mother Theresa, for example, illustrate the cardinal trait of humanitarianism.

The factor-analytic methods of Eysenck   Suppose that everyone has one hundred common traits, each of which appears in some strength in the personality. If you want to compare the personalities of even two people (say, to match them up in a dating service), you would have to measure all hundred traits. It would be far more convenient to know whether some of those hundred traits are related to, or correlated with, others, so that if someone is strong on, say, optimism, that person is also going to be strong on happiness, friendliness, and hopefulness. If you knew these correlations, you could compare personalities more efficiently by measuring just a few specific traits.

It would be even better if, after identifying these "trait clusters," you could determine *why* they appear together. Perhaps each cluster belongs to a more basic dimension of personality. If so, personality could be fully described by finding out where a person lies on just these basic dimensions. Several personality researchers have done just that. Using complex mathematical methods known as **factor analysis,** they identified groups of traits that are correlated with each other, but uncorrelated with other groups. They then gave each group a label describing the basic personality dimension that underlies it.

Factor analytic research by British psychologist Hans Eysenck (pronounced "eye-sink") has identified three basic personality factors—*psychoticism, introversion-extraversion,* and *emotionality-stability*—which he believes can describe and explain both normal and abnormal aspects of personality (Eysenck, 1970, 1981). People high on psychoticism show such traits as cruelty, hostility, coldness, oddness, and rejection of social customs (Eysenck, 1975).

Eysenck's extravert is sociable and outgoing, someone who enjoys parties and other social activities but is also an impulsive risk taker, who loves excitement, change, and being "where the action is." The person strong on introversion tends to be quiet, thoughtful, and reserved, enjoying study and other solitary pursuits and avoiding excitement or social closeness.

On Eysenck's other major personality dimension, emotionality-stability, there are at one extreme such traits as moodiness, restlessness, worry, anxiety, and a general tendency toward the open display of emotion. People at the other end of the scale are calm, even-tempered, carefree, relaxed, and emotionally stable. Most people fall somewhere between the extremes on both

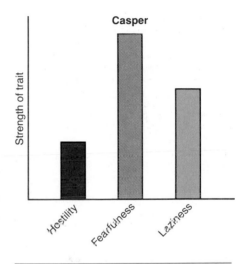

Figure 14.5
Two Personality Profiles
Personality traits can have different strengths in different people. Here, even though Spike and Casper can be said to have the same traits, their behavior when insulted, for example, is likely to be quite different. Spike might return the insult in even harsher terms, whereas Casper would probably feel some anger but fail to express it for fear of retaliation.

The men shown in Figure 14.4 are as follows (left to right): a photographer; Richard Speck, a convicted rapist and murderer; an executive; and Billy Sol Estes, a con artist. Photos (left to right) by Carol Palmer, UPI/Bettmann Newsphotos, Steven Gyurina, and Wide World Photos.

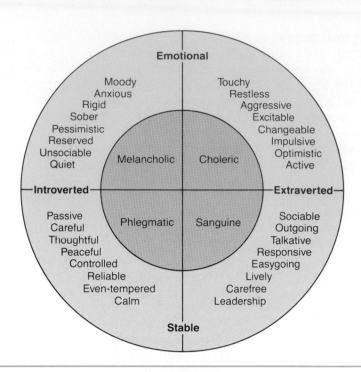

Figure 14.6
Eysenck's Major Personality Dimensions
Combining varying degrees of emotionality-stability and introversion-extraversion suggests characteristic combinations of traits. Thus, for example, an introverted but stable person is likely to be controlled and reliable, whereas the combination of introversion and emotionality tends to be associated with rigidity and anxiety. This figure also illustrates the rather amazing fact that the traits appearing in the four quadrants created by crossing Eysenck's two personality dimensions correspond roughly to Hippocrates' four temperaments!
(Eysenck, H. J., Rachman, S.: "The Causes and Cures of Neurosis: An Introduction to Modern Behavior Therapy Based on Learning Theory and the Principle of Conditioning." 1965. EDITS.)

of these latter dimensions. Figure 14.6 illustrates some of the characteristics of people who display various combinations of scores on each.

Eysenck found that people who display certain kinds of behavior disorders also show characteristic scores on the last two of his basic personality dimensions, as measured by a test called the Eysenck Personality Inventory. He has suggested that a person's position on these dimensions is determined largely by biological variables. He says, for example, that if you inherit a highly sensitive, "overaroused" nervous system, you are likely to be strongly affected by environmental rewards and punishments and thus to develop conditioned responses very easily. This high conditionability will result in someone who learns and follows rules and avoids too much stimulation; in other words, an introvert. Someone with an "underaroused" nervous system, on the other hand, will not be as sensitive to rewards and punishments and thus will not easily learn to play by the rules. Further, underarousal will prompt such a person constantly to seek arousal through excitement and change, thus creating an extroverted behavior pattern.

Personality as Reflecting Needs

A final dispositional approach to personality begins with the assumption that people have unique mixtures of needs, some inborn, some learned, which motivate them to think and behave as they do. The most prominent representative of this approach is Henry A. Murray, a physician and psychologist whose personality research began in the 1930s. Much as trait theorists look for basic trait dimensions, Murray attempted to identify basic human needs. Murray's list of needs included twelve primary, or biological, needs, such as food, water, and air, and twenty-seven secondary, or psychological, needs, such as recognition, dominance, and, as noted in the motivation chapter, achievement (Murray, 1938, 1962).

Reflecting Freud's influence, Murray argued that personality develops as people find ways to meet their needs while adjusting to the circumstances in which they live. Murray also believed that some needs are unconscious and can only be measured through projective methods, such as the Thematic

Apperception Test (TAT). This widely used instrument, described in the motivation chapter as a measure of the need for achievement, is also used in more general personality assessment. Thus, if a person's stories about TAT pictures all contain a central character who feels abandoned and unloved, this might indicate a strong need for security and acceptance.

HIGHLIGHT

Is Personality Inherited?

Dispositional theories have helped focus attention on the possibility that personality might be determined in part by biological factors. Especially influential is the suggestion that psychological characteristics may be inherited (Goldsmith, 1983; Williams, 1967).

For example, newborns differ markedly in irritability, tendency to cry, and duration of interest in a new stimulus, suggesting that these differences are inherited (Korner, 1971). Several studies have also found small but significant correlations between children's personality test scores and those of their parents and siblings (Dixon & Johnson, 1980; Loehlin, Horn & Willerman, 1981; Scarr et al., 1981). Is this because they all share the same environment? Apparently not, because even adopted children's personalities tend to resemble those of their real parents and siblings more than those of their new families (Loehlin, Willerman & Horn, 1985; Scarr et al., 1981). Further, identical twins (who share exactly the same genes) appear more similar than nonidentical twins (who have different genes) on some personality tests (Gottesman, 1963; Henderson, 1982; Loehlin & Nichols, 1976). They are also more alike than nonidentical twins on such basic

Separated at birth, the Mallifert twins meet accidentally.

The effects of heredity on personality are most dramatically illustrated in identical twins who grow up in different environments yet show all sorts of similarities. For example, one study described a pair of male twins who had been separated at five weeks of age and did not meet until thirty-nine years later. Both men drove Chevrolets, had a white bench around a tree in their yards, chain-smoked the same brand of cigarettes, had divorced a woman named Linda, and were remarried to a woman named Betty. Both had sons named James Allan, had dogs named Toy, enjoyed similar hobbies, and had served as sheriff's deputies (Tellegen et al., 1987).

The bodies people inherit help to shape their personalities by affecting what they can do and how others treat them.

behavioral characteristics as general activity level, sociability, anxiety, emotionality, and helpfulness (Buss, Plomin & Willerman, 1973; Plomin, 1981; Plomin & Rowe, 1979; Rushton, Russell & Wells, 1984). Other characteristics, such as aggression and distractibility, do not show as strong a genetic component (Plomin & Foch, 1980).

Similarities in traits and behavior patterns do not mean, however, that there are actually specific genes for each aspect of personality. Probably the best way to summarize research on the issue of the heritability of personality is to say that, in addition to physical appearance, people inherit general predispositions toward certain levels of activity, forcefulness, emotionality, or sensation seeking, as well as toward left- or right-brain dominance, intelligence, optimum arousal level, and cognitive style (Tellegen et al., 1987; Eysenck, 1981). These predispositions and physical features then interact with the environment to produce the specifics of personality.

Thus, children who inherit a frail, slender body may be especially likely targets for aggression by other children. This common set of social experiences might help create a tendency to avoid social interaction and thus encourage the development of an introverted personality, characterized by self-consciousness and a preference for privacy. On the other hand, strong, well-built children are more likely to be encouraged to take part in athletic and social pursuits, which help them to develop self-confidence and boldness. If the slender child has also inherited a predisposition toward social shyness or introversion, and if the muscular child has a genetic tendency toward sociability and vigorous activity, the development of their personalities in very different directions would be even more pronounced (Kagan, Reznick & Snidman, 1987). Thus, it appears that, rather than inheriting personality, people inherit the raw materials out of which it is shaped by the world. ■

Some Practical Applications

Personality assessment based on the dispositional approach has been used in a number of ways to make statements and predictions about people. Interviews and projective tests are often combined with dispositional measures, such as the *Minnesota Multiphasic Personality Inventory (MMPI)*, to determine what type of mental disorder a person has, to predict a person's potential for violent behavior or suicide, and even to judge sanity for legal purposes. The test's authors, Starke Hathaway and J. C. McKinley, began with a vast pool of true-false items but retained only those that tended to be answered differently by people with different kinds of mental disorders. All the items that tended to be answered the same way by particular groups of patients were gathered together into *clinical scales*. As illustrated in Figure 14.7, this allows each person's responses to be plotted in a profile showing the relative strength of the personality dimensions associated with each scale. This profile is then compared to the profiles of people known to have various kinds of behavioral tendencies or behavior disorders, in order to make statements and predictions.

The dispositional approach has also been used to select people who, on the basis of their personality profile, appear especially well suited to certain jobs. Today, many businesses and industries require potential employees to take one or more personality tests before being hired. Unfortunately, although personality tests may be capable of identifying mental disorder in job applicants (Butcher, 1979), they have not generally done very well at predicting exactly which individuals will be best at a particular job (Hunter & Hunter, 1984). Moreover, some of the questions asked on personality tests strike many people as an invasion of privacy and irrelevant to their ability to do a job. Antitest protests and even lawsuits against testing have become frequent in recent

MMPI scale

1. Hypochondriasis
(concern with bodily functions and symptoms)
2. Depression
(pessimism, hopelessness, slowed thinking)
3. Hysteria
(use of physical or mental symptoms to avoid problems)
4. Psychopathic deviancy
(disregard for social customs; emotional shallowness)
5. Masculinity/femininity
(interests associated with a particular sex)
6. Paranoia
(delusions, suspiciousness)
7. Psychasthenia
(worry, guilt, anxiety)
8. Schizophrenia
(bizarre thoughts and perceptions)
9. Hypomania
(overactivity, excitement, impulsiveness)
10. Social introversion
(shy, insecure)

Scale score

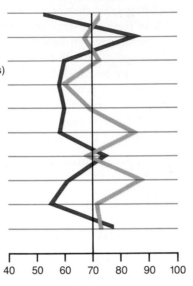

40   50   60   70   80   90   100

Figure 14.7
Profiles of MMPI Test Scores
Plotting a person's score on each of the MMPI's subscales creates a profile that summarizes the overall pattern of results. A score of 70 or more on any scale means that that personality characteristic is more extreme than in at least 95 percent of the normal population. Here, the red line represents the profile of a person who tends to be anxious, depressed, and introverted; the brown line suggests a seriously disturbed personality with tendencies toward paranoia and bizarre thinking.

years. In one case, would-be firefighters sued to stop the use of the MMPI as part of the hiring evaluation process in the Jersey City, New Jersey, fire department. Their suit was unsuccessful, but in other cases, such as in the hiring of federal employees, personality testing has been banned.

A special kind of personnel selection is done when dispositional concepts are applied in the courtroom to assist attorneys in the jury selection process. Actually, juries are "deselected," as lawyers reject individuals they feel might not be sympathetic to their case. Psychologists sometimes help by looking for clues to prospective jurors' personality traits in their physical appearance, dress, or overt behavior. For example, a sweet-looking elderly woman who wears a print dress, lace shawl, and bright orange combat boots would probably be judged eccentric or unconventional, traits that might cause her to stick to a not-guilty vote even if evidence of guilt was very strong (Suggs & Sales, 1978, 1979).

Does this use of the dispositional approach work? Yes and no. In several famous trials, such as that of Joan Little, a black prisoner who killed the male jailer she said tried to rape her, juries selected with the help of defense psychologists have voted for acquittal. But research indicates that jurors who vote to acquit do not differ significantly in personality from those voting to convict and that the verdicts of mock juries selected with psychological guidance were no more predictable than those selected as usual (Horowitz, 1980; Saks, 1976). And how do we know that a "scientifically selected" jury would not have reached the same verdict on the basis of trial evidence alone? This new use of the dispositional approach will remain controversial unless it is better supported in future research.

Criticisms of the Dispositional Approach

Dispositional approaches to personality have been criticized on a number of counts. For one thing, it has been argued that dispositional theories are better at describing people than at understanding them. You might say, for example, that Sally is nasty to others because she has a strong hostility trait, but doing so can lead you to a logical dead end. (Why is Sally nasty? Because of her hostility trait. How do you know she has that trait? Look how nasty she is!)

To avoid this sort of circular reasoning, it is important to go beyond merely inventing trait names to describe behavior. Some dispositional researchers, such as Eysenck, have tried to solve the problem by isolating just a few trait dimensions, which can be used to predict how people will behave across a wide range of situations. Indeed, it has been suggested that this is where trait theory may be most useful (Epstein & O'Brien, 1985).

A second problem with dispositional descriptions of personality is that, though they sound reasonable, even impressive, they may not say much about a person that is truly unique. To illustrate, consider how you might react to the following trait-oriented personality sketch:

> You have a strong need for other people to like and admire you. You have a tendency to be critical of yourself. You have a great deal of unused capacity, which you have not turned to your advantage. . . . Disciplined and controlled on the outside, you tend to be worrisome and insecure inside. . . . At times you are extraverted, affable, and sociable; at other times, you are introverted, wary, and reserved. . . .

Does this sound familiar? Does it describe anyone you know? Don't be surprised if it sounds like you. When psychology professors gave a longer version of this sketch to college students who had just taken a personality test, nearly all of them said it was a "good" or even "excellent" description of their own personality (Ulrich, Stachnik & Stainton, 1963). At their worst, dispositional personality variables may be general enough to apply to most people.

The fact that dispositional theories of personality rely so heavily on personality tests has also been a target of criticism, because research has shown these tests to have numerous weaknesses. They tend to have low reliability, often giving different results depending on whether the test respondent was, say, tired, in a good mood, or depressed. The testing situation itself may also affect responses. For example, hospitalized mental patients have been shown to fake personality test responses toward normal or abnormal extremes, depending on whether they wished to leave or to stay in the hospital (Braginsky, Grosse & Ring, 1966). Results like these are especially troubling, because dispositional theorists view personality as a set of relatively stable features.

The validity of personality tests, especially the degree to which they can lead to accurate statements or predictions about people, has also been questioned. For example, scores on the MMPI have not been very good predictors of a person's potential for suicide (Clopton, Pallis & Birtchnell, 1979) or violence (Mulvey & Lidz, 1984); in general, the correlations between personality test scores and future behavior is often only around +.30 (Mischel, 1965, 1968; Nietzel & Bernstein, 1987; Nisbett, 1980).

Defenders of the dispositional approach (Hogan, DeSoto & Solano, 1977) argue that, though prediction of individual behavior is always difficult, some personality tests do quite well. For example, scores on the California Personality Inventory have been shown to correlate +.73 with juvenile delinquency (Gough, 1965) and to correctly separate marijuana users from nonusers over 80 percent of the time (Hogan et al., 1970). Further, they point out, tests like the MMPI are constantly being studied and revised in an attempt to improve their reliability and validity (Holden, 1986).

It appears, then, that some tests of some aspects of personality can be accurate predictors of some of the people, some of the time. But we must be careful not to expect too much of them. A person's responses to such tests are determined not by personality alone, but also by the circumstances under which the test was taken. The notion of personality as the product of person-situation interactions is an important one, to be discussed in the next section.

THE BEHAVIORAL APPROACH

In the psychodynamic and dispositional approaches discussed so far, outward behavior is viewed as a *sign* of inner personality. The **behavioral approach** contrasts sharply with this notion by viewing personality and behavior as basically the same thing. *Personality* becomes, for behavioral theorists, a label for the sum total of a person's behavior patterns, of which any specific behavior is merely a sample. The basic assumption made by behavioral theories is that human behavior is determined mainly by what a person has learned in life, especially by what one has learned from interacting with other people. Behavioral theorists suggest that the consistency of people's learning histories, not an inner personality structure, produces characteristic patterns of behavior. Successfully cheating on one test, for example, may encourage a person to do the same on other tests. Continued reinforcement and stimulus generalization may lead to a generally dishonest behavioral style, including cheating on job assignments or a spouse.

But what about the obvious inconsistencies in human behavior? People who are sociable in groups are sometimes shy and awkward on a date; big, friendly men can become wildly aggressive on a football field; a meek office worker might be found guilty of a string of grisly murders. Unlike psychodynamic and dispositional theories—which suggest that different behaviors can reflect the same underlying trait, need, conflict, or defense—the behavioral view offers the concept of **situational specificity.** In other words, in different situations, people are capable of many different behaviors, not all of which are necessarily compatible or consistent. Yet all are genuine parts of a person's being, part of the endless interaction between learned (and inherited) behavioral tendencies and the situations of life.

The behavioral approach was not the first to recognize the importance of person-situation interactions in determining behavior; recall, for example, Freud's notion of the ego mediating between the id and environmental demands. But behavioral theorists have paid the most systematic attention to *situational* rather than *person* variables in personality, beginning with the *radical behaviorism* of John B. Watson. Building on the classical conditioning research of Ivan Pavlov and others, Watson (1924) claimed that all human behavior, from mental disorder to scientific skill, is determined by the learning situations a child faces, not by anything present at birth.

Today, most behavioral theorists recognize that Watson's view was too extreme, but there is still a clear environmental flavor to their approach. There is also a strong commitment to studying personality by focusing on objectively measurable behaviors. Finally, there is a conviction that all behavior, normal and abnormal, develops through common learning processes; even people with "disturbed" personalities are thought to have *learned* to behave in problematic ways.

B. F. Skinner and the Functional Analysis of Behavior

Harvard psychologist B. F. Skinner developed a behavioral approach that analyzes how *observable* behavior is learned in relation to *observable* environmental events. He referred to the interactions between behavior and the environment as *functional relationships,* and he sought to understand these relationships by employing what he called the **functional analysis of behavior.**

Suppose a schoolboy causes trouble by hitting other children. Skinner would argue that it is pointless to speculate about the motivation or personality traits that might underlie such behavior. He would seek to understand the

A behavioral approach to personality might suggest that aggressive behavior is maintained by the attention or other rewards it brings, not by an underlying trait of aggressiveness.

behavior (and thus the child) by analyzing exactly what responses are occurring and under what conditions. Careful observation may reveal that the aggression is not very violent and occurs mainly when a particular teacher is present to break up the fight. Perhaps the boy's aggression is being rewarded by the extra attention he gets from that teacher. This could be confirmed experimentally by assigning the child to another teacher and observing the effect on his aggressive behavior. Notice that functional analysis does not describe the boy's personality but summarizes what he finds rewarding (social attention), what behaviors he is capable of (punching others), and what skills he lacks (for example, asking for attention in appropriate ways).

Notice also that Skinner's approach emphasizes the role of *operant conditioning,* a set of procedures, described in Chapter 7, through which behavior is shaped by its environmental consequences. From Skinner's perspective, a "dependent" person is one who has been rewarded for dependence, just as a "hostile" person has been reinforced for aggression. The same logic is also applied to understanding how some behavior disorders develop. Consider the mental patient who stares into space, refusing to speak. These behaviors might have begun in milder form, perhaps as responses to stress, but through inadvertent reinforcement by others, they became worse (Ayllon & Azrin, 1968; Ullmann & Krasner, 1975).

Cognitive-Behavioral Theories

The views of Watson and Skinner focus primarily on how the *external* environment determines personality through classical and operant conditioning. They say little or nothing about the role of the *internal* environment—what people *think* about themselves and about the things that happen to them. Yet, as discussed in the chapters on perception, thought, and stress, what people think and expect can have a great deal to do with how the outside world affects them. The importance of these cognitive variables has been emphasized, along with classical and operant conditioning, in the *cognitive-behavioral theories* of Julian Rotter, Albert Bandura, and Walter Mischel.

Rotter's expectancy theory   Rotter (1954) argued that past learning creates cognitive expectancies and that these expectancies guide behavior. Specifically, he suggested that any given behavior is determined by (1) what the person expects to happen following the behavior and (2) the value the person places on the outcome. For example, people commonly spend a lot of money on rock concert tickets because (1) past learning leads them to expect that doing so will get them into the concert and (2) they place a high value on being there.

Rotter hypothesized that people learn very general ways of thinking about the world, especially about how life's rewards and punishments are controlled. He developed a personality test, called the *Internal-External Locus of Control Scale,* or *I-E,* which measures the degree to which people expect events to be controlled by their own internal efforts (*internals*) or by external forces over which they have no influence (*externals*).

A great deal of research has examined how internals and externals differ. One study found that internals do better at work in which they can set their own pace, whereas externals work better when a machine controls the pace (Eskew & Riche, 1982; see also Phares, 1973). Others have found that internals are more health conscious and more likely to seek medical treatment when they need it (Strickland, 1978). An internal locus of control is also an aspect of the stress-resistant, or *hardy,* personality disposition mentioned in this chapter's Linkages box; internals generally suffer less stress-related illness and seem to handle stress especially well.

Albert Bandura and observational learning   Albert Bandura has emphasized the role of cognition in *observational learning,* or learning by watching others. As we discussed in the chapter on learning, cognitive processes allow people to observe or hear about the behavior of others and then to imitate these models or not (Bandura, 1977). For example, preschool children in one experiment observed films in which models either sat quietly beside or viciously attacked an inflatable Bobo doll (Bandura, Ross & Ross, 1963). When the children were later left in a room with the same doll, those who had seen the aggressive models were not only most aggressive, but often exactly matched the forms of attack they had seen.

Through observational learning, said Bandura, people can (1) learn new behaviors, such as how to tie shoes; (2) inhibit responses, as when you do not try to open a door that someone else has found locked; (3) disinhibit responses, as when you start complaining about bad restaurant service after hearing someone else do so; and (4) facilitate or prompt responses, as when a crowd of curious pedestrians gathers when one or two pranksters stare and point at the top of a building. Bandura (1978) has also focused on the ways in which people's overt behaviors, cognitions, and the environment constantly influence one another, in what he called **reciprocal determinism.** Figure 14.8 illustrates this idea.

Bandura has also placed special emphasis on the role of learned expectations for success or, as he calls it, **self-efficacy.** Going to a party with the firm belief that you have the skills necessary to be a social success may be enough in itself to create that success and even to blunt the impact of minor failures.

Mischel's person-situation theory   Walter Mischel (1973, 1981) extended many of Bandura's ideas by noting that person-situation interactions involve not only situation variables, but also *person variables.* The most important learned person variables, according to Mischel, are (1) competencies (the thoughts and actions the person can perform); (2) perceptions (how the person perceives the environment); (3) expectations (what the person generally expects to follow from various behaviors); (4) subjective values (the person's ideals and goals); and (5) self-regulation and plans (the harshness of the person's standards for self-reward and plans for reaching goals).

Mischel sees these learned person variables as being primarily responsible for differences in the way each individual handles each new situation. When person variables dominate situational ones, the person behaves as he or she normally does. For example, someone who expects that bad things do not happen to him or her would probably remain calm during a crisis, such as being stuck in an elevator. This calmness would be disrupted, however, if situational variables became more dominant (as when the elevator cable is in danger of snapping). Mischel's formulation thus highlights the more general cognitive-behavioral view that personality is a process, a continuously changing outcome of the interplay of a conscious, rational person and the world in which he or she lives.

Behavioral personality assessment   From the behavioral perspective, personality data can be gathered in interviews aimed at eliciting a person's report of what he or she does or thinks about at parties, at work, in sexual interactions, and in other situations. In addition, observations might be set up in which the person is asked to role-play social situations. For example, you might be asked to act out what you would do if the person in front of you in a theater line suddenly invited six friends to cut in. With this procedure, a researcher might obtain not only a "live" sample of overt social behavior, but also measurements of heart rate and other physical reactions. A person might even be asked to observe his or her own social behavior through a procedure called

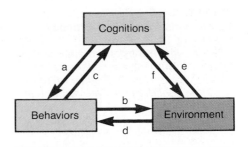

Figure 14.8
The Concept of Reciprocal Determinism
Bandura suggests that the way we think, how we behave, and the nature of our environment are all determined by one another. Thus, for example, hostile thinking can lead to hostile behavior (line a), which in turn can intensify hostile thoughts (line c). At the same time, all that hostility is likely to offend others and create an environment of anger (line b), which calls forth even more negative thoughts and actions (lines d and e). These negative thoughts then alter perceptions, making the environment more threatening (line f).

TABLE 14.2

Some Items from a Self-Efficacy Scale

Respondents are asked to state which of the following situations they could handle and to rate on a scale of 10 to 100 how confident they are about their judgments.

1. Attend a social gathering at which there is no one you know.
2. At a social gathering, approach a group of strangers, introduce yourself, and join in the conversation.
3. Complain about poor service to an unsympathetic sales or repair person.
4. In a public place, ask a stranger not to do something that annoys you, such as cutting in line, talking in a movie, or smoking in a no-smoking area.
5. Ask neighbors to correct a problem for which they are responsible, such as making noise at night, or not controlling children or pets.

SOURCE: From *Introduction to Personality*, 3/e, by Walter Mischel. Copyright © 1971 by Holt, Rinehart & Winston. Copyright © 1976 by Holt, Rinehart & Winston. Copyright © 1981 by CBS College Publishing. Reprinted by permission of Holt, Rinehart & Winston, Inc.

self-monitoring. He or she would keep a written record of thoughts, feelings, and performance in each social situation for a week or more. Finally, written tests, such as the self-efficacy scale in Table 14.2, might ask for the person's predictions of social success.

Some Practical Applications

There are many uses of the behavioral approach. We will cover only three of them: predicting behavior, training in social skills, and training in child rearing.

We mentioned earlier that attempts to predict human behavior using psychodynamic and dispositional approaches have often been unsuccessful. For example, predictions of violence on the basis of standard personality tests have repeatedly been shown to be accurate only about 33 to 40 percent of the time (Megargee, 1976; Monahan, 1981; Werner, Rose & Yesavage, 1983). Behavioral theorists suggest that the best predictor of future behavior is *past* behavior under similar circumstances. People who have already committed crimes, especially violent crimes, are the ones most likely to do so again (Litwack, 1985; Wolfgang, 1978). Situational factors, such as having a family or peer group that encourages crime, being unemployed, having easy access to victims, being intoxicated, or possessing a weapon, are all likely to help determine whether or not a person will commit a crime and how violent that crime will be (Monahan, 1981). Prediction of suicide attempts is also improved by looking at behavioral, situational, and demographic variables instead of, or in addition to, personality traits.

Behavioral theorists have also been active in helping people to alter their personalities through new learning experiences. Consider unpopular school-children, for example. They are far more likely than their more popular peers to experience academic, social, and psychological problems. Observational assessments have shown that their unpopularity stems from a lack of skill at cooperative play or at joining a group without disrupting it. They also tend to display such inappropriate social behaviors as hitting or shouting at other children (Putallaz & Gottman, 1983). Learning-oriented psychologists have set up social-skills training programs, which literally teach unpopular children how to behave in more acceptable and socially rewarded ways (Bierman et al., 1987; Ladd & Mize, 1983; Oden & Asher, 1977). Similar programs for adults are discussed in Chapter 16.

Behavioral principles have also been incorporated in a number of useful child-rearing books, which offer parents of unruly children a wide range of methods designed to alleviate and even prevent child behavior problems

(Becker, 1971; Patterson, 1976; Smith & Smith, 1976). For the most part, these methods involve applying the principles of modeling and operant reinforcement to the creation of a stable, consistent home environment. The goals are to have parents (1) show and tell a child how to behave appropriately, (2) provide consistent rewards for good behavior, and (3) either ignore or mildly reprimand misbehavior. A simple example of such a program is illustrated in Figure 14.9.

Criticisms of the Behavioral Approach

To many, the behavioral approach, with its emphasis on conscious, objectively measured behaviors and its careful analysis of person-situation interactions, provides an attractive and scientific way of thinking about, assessing, and changing personality. It has achieved wide popularity in recent years but has not escaped its share of criticism.

Behavioral assessment has been one target. It has been suggested, for example, that the information people give in response to behavioral interviews and tests can be just as unreliable or invalid as that collected through dispositional and psychodynamic assessment. In fact, most behavioral tests have not been as carefully designed, constructed, or evaluated as those of the dispositional approach (Cone, 1977). Even supposedly objective observational measures of personality have been shown to be vulnerable to distortion. A young man's conversational skill during a role-played interaction with a female research assistant may or may not accurately reflect his true capabilities in real-life social situations. Further, critics point out that, even though behavioral assessment may be fine for measuring some overt behaviors, it may not be able to measure more subtle cognitive variables.

Critics also object to the behavioral approach's oversimplified reduction of human personality to a by-product of lawful, systematic, or mechanical forces. They see this approach as doomed to failure because people are more than the sum of what they have learned, or even of what they have learned and inherited. Human personality, the criticism goes, is not learned and changed in the same way as overt behavior. Even the broader cognitive-behavioral theories of Rotter, Bandura, and Mischel have failed to satisfy critics who see the behavioral approach as focusing so narrowly on individual behavior that it ignores the individual. The individual personality, they argue, cannot be understood without focusing more on nonbehavioral factors, such as perceptions, values, beliefs, expectancies, and intentions. These factors are the focus of the phenomenological personality theories discussed next.

THE PHENOMENOLOGICAL APPROACH

Phenomenological approaches to personality begin with the assumption that each personality is created out of each person's unique way of perceiving and interpreting the world. Proponents of this view believe that one's personal perception of reality—not instincts, traits, or rewards—shape and control behavior from moment to moment. Other approaches have also recognized this active aspect of personality. Ego analysts, for example, focused on the role of ego in planning and directing one's efforts toward growth, and cognitive-behavioral theorists' "person variables" include the active, aware, and planful nature of the human being. Still, the phenomenological approach has emphasized this aspect of personality more than others have.

To illustrate, suppose you and a friend meet someone new at a party. When comparing notes later, you discover a major discrepancy in your

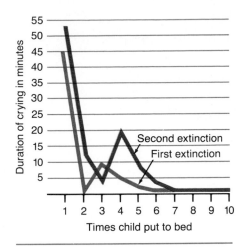

Figure 14.9
A Behavioral Program to Control Crying
A child whose excessive bedtime crying had been inadvertently rewarded by parental attention was lovingly tucked in each night. Then all crying and other requests for attention were ignored. Based on the principle of extinction, this procedure not only reduced crying, but created a more pleasant bedtime. The purple line shows the duration of crying on successive nights when the parents first used the extinction program. The reddish line shows the results of a second extinction program that became necessary after the child's aunt rewarded his crying when the parents were away.
(From C. D. Williams, 1959, "The Elimination of Tantrum Behavior by Extinction Procedures," *Journal of Abnormal and Social Psychology, 59,* p. 269. Copyright 1959 by the American Psychological Association. Adapted by permission of publisher and author.)

reactions. You thought the new person was entertaining and humorous and showed a genuine interest in others. Your friend saw the same person as a shallow and insincere individual, who was hiding a lack of anything to say behind a humorous style and was merely pretending to be interested. How can two people draw such opposite conclusions from the same conversation? According to the phenomenological view, it was not the same conversation. Just as each person sees something different in an inkblot or a sunset, each of you perceived a different reality, a different conversation, and a different person, toward whom each of you then behaved differently.

From this perspective, the specific ways in which each person perceives and interprets the world make up personality. Humans are not merely passive carriers of traits, arenas for the resolution of intrapsychic conflict, or behavioral clay that is molded by learning. In fact, the phenomenological approach deemphasizes the instincts and learning processes that humans and lower animals seem to have in common. Instead, it focuses on those special mental qualities that set humans apart: consciousness, self-awareness, creativity, the capacity for making plans and decisions, and responsibility for those decisions. For this reason, the phenomenological approach is sometimes also called the *humanistic* view of personality.

Among the other important assumptions of this view is the belief that the primary human motivator is an innate drive toward growth, which, if unobstructed, prompts people to fulfill their unique and natural potential. Like the planted seed that naturally becomes a flower, humans are seen as naturally inclined toward goodness, creativity, love, joy, and other higher goals. The phenomenological view also implies that no one can truly understand another person's behavior or personality without somehow perceiving the world through that person's eyes. Phenomenologists therefore assume that all behavior, even that which appears strange or puzzling, is sensible or meaningful to the person displaying it.

The phenomenological perspective has evolved from several sources. It stems partly from the reaction against Freud by Adler and Jung, both of whom emphasized positive as well as negative aspects of human nature. It also comes from philosophy. (In the language of philosophy, the mental experiencing of the environment is called a *phenomenon,* and the study of how each person experiences reality is *phenomenology.*) The idea that people perceive, not reality, but their own personal interpretation of reality comes partly from existential philosophers, such as Kierkegaard, Sartre, and Camus, and partly from the work of the Gestalt psychologists. (As we saw in Chapter 5, the Gestalt psychologists emphasized that people are active participants in the process of perception.) In the sections that follow, we consider some specific phenomenological theories of personality.

The Personal Construct Theory of George Kelly

George Kelly (1955) was an experimental psychologist-turned-therapist, who suggested that people's view of reality is guided by a set of learned expectations. Expectations, said Kelly, form **personal constructs,** or generalized ways of anticipating the world. A person may not be aware of all of them, but according to Kelly, the nature of each person's unique set of constructs determines personality and guides behavior. For example, if you have one simple, general construct about people, such as "All people are either good or bad," your outlook will be far different from that of someone with a more complex construct, such as "Some people can be good and bad, depending on the circumstances."

When the world goes as personal constructs lead one to expect, a person feels comfortable, and his or her constructs are strengthened, or *validated*. If not, one's ability to accurately anticipate the world is diminished, and the result is discomfort or anxiety. Kelly saw personality development stemming from people's search for a set of constructs that allows them to accurately predict and understand themselves and others.

The Self Theory of Carl Rogers

In contrast to Kelly's views, which received relatively little popular acclaim and were obviously flavored by learning principles, the prolific writings of Carl Rogers (1942, 1951, 1961, 1970, 1980) more clearly differentiated the phenomenological approach from all others and in the process made Rogers's name almost synonymous with that approach. Like phenomenological philosophers and psychologists before him, Rogers assumed that each person responds as an organized whole to reality as he or she perceives it. He particularly emphasized **self-actualization,** which he considered an innate tendency toward growth, which motivates all human behavior. To Rogers, personality was the expression of each individual's self-actualizing tendency as it unfolds in that individual's uniquely perceived reality. If unimpeded, this process results in the full realization of the person's highest potential. If the process is thwarted, however, that potential may be distorted as various problems appear.

The concept of self   Central to Rogers's theory is the *self,* that part of experience that a person comes to identify early in life as "I" or "me." Rogers suggested that people constantly evaluate all experiences, including the self, as positive or negative, depending on whether they enhance or impede self-actualization. People have a natural tendency to seek positive experiences and avoid negative ones, simply on the basis of genuine organismic reaction to them. A child would probably say, "I like ice cream," because it tastes good, or "I hate cough syrup," because it tastes bad. The child is clearly aware of these self-experiences and is quite relaxed about saying, "I like what feels good." In Rogers's terms, the child's organismic experience and self-experience are consistent, or *congruent.*

Very early in life, however, children learn to need others' approval or, as Rogers called it, their *positive regard.* As a result, the evaluations provided by parents, teachers, and others begin to enter into children's evaluations. When others' evaluations agree with one's own (as when the pure organismic pleasure of finger-painting is enhanced by a parent's approval), a person not only feels the other's positive regard but also evaluates the self as "good" for having earned that approval. The result is a clearly identified and positively evaluated experience of the self ("I like to paint") that one gladly acknowledges. This self-experience becomes part of the **self-concept,** the way one thinks of oneself. Unfortunately, things do not always go so smoothly. If a basically pleasurable self-experience is evaluated negatively by others, one must either do without their positive regard or reevaluate the experience. Rogers argued that, since having positive regard from others allows a person to have positive self-regard, people often choose to suppress their genuine feelings in order to get approval. Thus, a little boy who is chided by his parents for enjoying dolls might adopt a distorted self-experience ("I don't like dolls" or "Feeling good is bad").

Thus, personality is shaped partly by the self-actualizing tendency and partly by others' evaluations. In this way, people come to like what they are "supposed" to and to behave as they are "supposed" to. To a certain extent,

Carl Rogers believed that the need for positive regard can become so powerful as to distort people's personalities, especially if they seek to please others by acting at variance with their true feelings.

this process is adaptive, allowing people to get along in society. But often it requires that they stifle the self-actualizing tendency and distort experience. Rogers argued that psychological discomfort, anxiety, or mental disorder can result when the feelings people let themselves experience or express are inconsistent, or *incongruent,* with their true feelings.

Conditions of worth   Incongruence is especially likely when parents and teachers lead a child to believe that his or her worth as a person depends on displaying the "right" attitudes, behaviors, and values. These **conditions of worth** are created whenever *people* are evaluated instead of their behavior. For example, parents who find their children smearing Jell-O on the kitchen floor are unlikely to say, "I love you, but I do not approve of this particular behavior." They are more likely to angrily shout, "Bad Boy!" or "Bad Girl!" thus suggesting that the child can only be loved and considered worthwhile by being well behaved. As a result, the child's self-experience is not "I like smearing Jello-O, but Mom and Dad don't approve," but "Playing with Jell-O is bad, and I am bad if I like it, so I don't like it," or "I like it, so I must be bad." The child may then display especially neat and tidy behaviors, which, though not a part of the real self, are part of the ideal self dictated by the parents. Or the child may become quite naughty, in line with the new belief that he or she is "bad."

Methods of assessment   To learn about personality, Rogers relied heavily on interviews. Rogerian interviews are unstructured, allowing the interviewee to decide what he or she wants to talk about. The assumption is that, given sufficient freedom and encouragement, the person will eventually and spontaneously reveal whatever is important about his or her personality. Rogers also used a technique called the *Q-sort.* The person is given a large number of cards containing statements like "I am generally happy" or "I am overly suspicious." The task is to sort the statements into, say, ten categories ranging from "very uncharacteristic of me" to "very characteristic of me." This sorting is done twice, first on the basis of the person's *real self,* then on the basis of how he or she would like to be (*ideal self*). If the two sortings are very dissimilar, the person seems to be saying that his or her real and ideal self-concepts are not very close; there is little congruence. Repeated Q-sorts are often used during therapy to chart changes in self-concept and reductions in incongruence.

Maslow's Humanistic Psychology

Like Rogers, Abraham Maslow (1954, 1962, 1971) believed there is a basic human tendency toward growth and self-actualization and saw personality as the expression of that tendency. Maslow saw self-actualization not only as a human capacity, but as a human need. It is not the strongest need; as we discussed in the chapter on motivation, Maslow described it as the highest in a *hierarchy of needs.*

To Maslow, personality reflects people's perceptual orientation and the level of needs on which they focus their attention and energy. He believed that people are less likely to achieve their full potential if they are distracted from self-actualization by preoccupation with other needs. Maslow noted that most people, even those whose basic needs are met, tend to be preoccupied with meeting perceived needs for the material things they do not have. This **deficiency orientation** can lead to perceptions that life is a meaningless exercise in disappointment and boredom. People holding these perceptions are likely to behave in problematic, even disordered, ways. For example, in an attempt to satisfy the need for love and belongingness, many people focus more on what love can give them (security) than on what they can give to another. According to Maslow, this deficiency orientation may lead a person to be possessive and jealous of the partner or to make the partner the target of hostile "put-downs" designed to make the person feel superior and powerful. The person will never truly experience love and security; he or she will always focus on what is missing.

Among a very few notably self-actualized people, such as Albert Einstein and Eleanor Roosevelt, Maslow found what he called a **growth orientation,** a focus not on what is missing, but on drawing satisfaction from what there is. Those who break away from a deficiency orientation not only escape dismal feelings, but make it possible to have what Maslow called *peak experiences,* in which one feels great joy, even ecstasy, in the mere fact of being alive, being human, and knowing that one is utilizing one's fullest potential.

Some Practical Applications

Probably the best-known applications of the phenomenological approach to personality are methods of psychotherapy, especially the client-centered therapy of Carl Rogers and the Gestalt therapy of Fritz Perls. We discuss these methods in Chapter 16. The phenomenological approach also helped inspire a variety of short-term group experiences, variously labeled as sensitivity training, encounter groups, and personal growth groups. These experiences are designed to help "normal" people become more aware of themselves and the way they relate to others, to recognize and begin breaking down the false fronts or barriers they use to protect their self-esteem, and to interact more genuinely with others.

The concepts of the phenomenological approach also have applications to education. In most American schools, students are treated as passive recipients of facts, which are fed to them on a fixed schedule, without regard for individual needs, readiness, or interest. This system, said Rogers, may

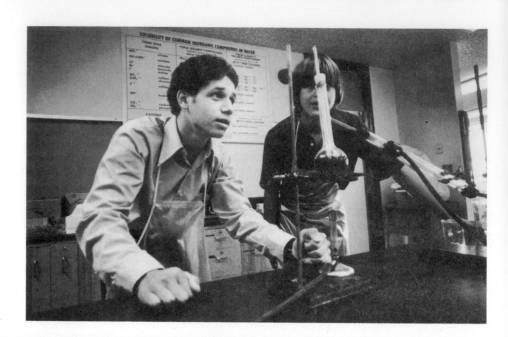

A phenomenological approach to education emphasizes the importance of allowing students to progress at their own pace and to become active participants in learning rather than passive recipients of information.

discourage and stifle the growth potential of many students. Students may be most likely to learn and to enjoy learning if they are allowed to choose what and how to study and to learn by doing rather than merely by listening. Indeed, Rogers wanted to replace the term *teacher* with *facilitator*, to emphasize the idea that one should not so much *teach* things to students as create an atmosphere in which they want to learn.

For parents, the phenomenological approach has generated programs designed to help them avoid creating conditions of worth while maximizing their childrens' potential. Most popular of these is a course called *Parent Effectiveness Training*, or *PET* (Gordon, 1970). Based on Rogers's self theory, the course helps parents learn to see their child as a human being with legitimate needs, feelings, and worth, not as a creature to be shaped, dominated, and controlled. The focus is on improving communication between parent and child and on resolving conflicts in a fashion that does not always create a winner and a loser. PET also helps parents to evaluate a child's behavior independently of his or her self. They are urged to make statements like "I don't want you to do that" or "I feel proud when you act that way," instead of giving judgments, such as "You are a good girl" or "You are a bad boy."

Criticisms of the Phenomenological Approach

The phenomenological approach to personality has attracted many loyal adherents among psychologists and the general public, largely because it coincides with how many people view themselves. Yet the phenomenological view has also been called naive, romantic, and unrealistic. Are we all as inherently good and "growthful" as humanists suggest? The violence, aggression, and cruelty of which only humans appear capable calls this notion into question.

Phenomenologists have also been criticized for their emphasis on subjective experience as the main determinant of behavior. Depending on their own favorite approach, various observers have chided phenomenologists for deemphasizing such factors as inherited characteristics, biological processes, learning, situational influences, and unconscious motivation. They also argue that, given the complexity of human motivation, the idea that everyone is driven primarily by an innate growth potential is an oversimplification. The same has been said of the phenomenological assumption that all human problems stem from blocked self-actualization. This assumption leads, say skeptics, to overly general forms of therapy in which everyone is treated in basically the same way. The reliability and validity of phenomenological personality assessment methods have also been questioned. Does a person's Q-sort really represent his or her self-perceptions, or was it distorted by a desire to appear self-confident or "normal"?

Critics argue that, like the dispositional approach, phenomenological theories are better at describing personality than at explaining it. Saying that people behave as they do because of their perceptions, constructs, or actualizing tendencies provides a temporarily satisfying way of thinking about personality, but it does not deal with some important underlying questions. Where does the actualizing tendency come from? How do perceptions and constructs develop? General notions that personality simply unfolds are seen as incomplete and unsatisfying by those interested in understanding personality development in detail.

Finally, many phenomenological concepts, like many psychodynamic variables, are seen as too vague and therefore as unscientific. Indeed, although phenomenologists like Kelly and Rogers devoted years to systematic research on their concepts, many others actively avoid the scientific approach. They believe that people can understand themselves only through personal experience, not through experiments. This point of view has made the phenomenological approach unacceptable to those who favor careful, controlled experimental research as a means of learning about personality.

FUTURE DIRECTIONS

We have seen that there are many approaches to the concept of personality. Table 14.3 contains a comparison of the basic features of each, so that you can more easily compare and contrast the consequences of their assumptions for personality assessment and research. In spite of differences among the approaches, there are also some important similarities.

	Psychody-namic	Dispositional	Behavioral	Phenomeno-logical
Basic assumptions about behavior	Determined by intra-psychic conflicts	Determined by types, traits, or needs	Determined by learning and specific situations	Determined by perception of reality
Assessment methods	Interviews; projective tests	Personality tests	Interviews; self-report tests; observations	Interviews and tests
Typical research methods	Case reports; group studies showing operation of unconscious processes	Analysis of tests for basic personality dimensions	Analysis of person-situation interactions	Studies on relationship between perceptions and behavior

TABLE 14.3

A Comparison of Major Approaches to Personality
Notice that each approach is associated with a set of assumptions that allows those adopting the approach to deal with personality assessment and research in a way that follows logically from those assumptions.

PERSONALITY AND STRESS

Are There "Stress-Prone" Personalities?

We noted in the chapter on stress that some people tend to overreact to stress. Often they add their own catastrophizing thoughts to externally generated arousal, and they usually experience psychological and physical problems ranging from nervous tension to heart disease. Some people handle stress better, suffering occasional symptoms but coping well overall. Others actually seem to thrive on stress. Personality research has helped shed light on what makes the difference.

For example, Aaron Beck (1984) described two personality patterns that his research linked with sensitivity and overreaction to stress. The first, called the *socially dependent type,* is characterized by a preference for and dependence on interactions in which other people provide approval, acceptance, support, understanding, and the like. These individuals, says Beck, thrive on such rewards, are greatly influenced by them, and become very upset if they are not forthcoming. Any behavior by others that is perceived as rejection, exclusion, abandonment, or disapproval is likely to be a significant stressor for those displaying characteristics of the socially dependent personality.

Beck's second stress-prone personality is called *autonomous;* it is characterized by a strong desire to be independent, a tendency to take immediate action to solve problems, and an abhorrence of people or circumstances that

might limit or restrict freedom. According to Beck, autonomous people tend to think of rules, other people's needs, and many other aspects of social life as threats to their independence or their efforts at solitary achievement. As a result, they are particularly sensitive to interruptions and to anything they interpret as intrusions or coercion by others. They may fly off the handle if someone suggests they take a break from work, for example. Even physical restraints can be major stressors for some of these individuals, as illustrated by a war hero who suffered a severe anxiety attack while crawling through a narrow cylinder at an amusement park (Beck, 1984).

Beck's autonomous personality is similar in many ways to the *Type A* personality described in the chapter on stress. Recall that the primary characteristics of the Type A personality include competitiveness, a hard-driving approach to life, concern about wasting time, im-

For example, all approaches recognize the importance of childhood as a time when personality begins to form. They also recognize that much of personality develops through experience. Further, they all focus on the fundamental struggle each person faces in adapting to the world, even though that adaptation may be described in terms of dealing with intrapsychic conflicts, developing traits, learning behavioral responses, meeting various needs, or growing toward self-actualization. Finally, the fact that thoughts can affect (and be affected by) one's behaviors and emotions has required all approaches to deal with cognitive processes in personality.

Progress toward a fuller understanding of human personality seems most likely to come from an intelligent integration of the wisdom and research of more than one point of view. The trend toward this way of thinking is reflected in articles and books whose theme is the integration of apparently diverse approaches to personality (Krasner, 1978; Wachtel, 1977; Wandersman, Poppen & Ricks, 1976). This trend is also reflected in the fact that modern personality researchers have become more eclectic and less concerned with trying to establish one approach as the best. They are engaged instead in research on more specific variables and relationships.

One major area of personality research is the exploration of individual differences. This research provides not only scientific descriptions of human behavior, but also a basis for relating these individual difference variables to how people handle stress and other life situations. The contents of any issue of the *Journal of Personality and Social Psychology* illustrate this individual differences orientation. In one study, subjects were asked to rate the frequency with which they had various types of sexual fantasies (Arndt, Foehl & Good, 1985). These ratings were then related to reported sexual behavior and to scores on a personality test that measured such traits as emotional stability and sociability. Males and females not only had different types of sexual

patience, hostility, and a view of life as very threatening. Type As display these characteristics on laboratory tasks, in friendly sports competitions, and at work (Glass, 1977). These people are more likely than others to suffer ill effects from stress, including heart attacks or high blood pressure (Harrell, 1980; Rosenman et al., 1975).

Fortunately, there may also be stress-resistant, or *hardy,* personalities. The hardy personality pattern was first described by researchers working on the Chicago Stress Project, a study of stress among business executives (Kobasa, 1979). The project identified and gave personality tests to two groups of executives. Both groups worked in very stressful situations, but one group showed many symptoms of illness and the other group showed few. The scores of the low-illness, or hardy, group revealed a personality pattern characterized by what Suzanne Kobasa (1979) called commit-

ment, control, and challenge. Commitment was reflected in a strong involvement in personal values and goals; hardy individuals believed in what they were doing rather than merely "going through the motions." Control involved a firm belief in one's ability to control and take direct action to deal with problems; this is similar to Rotter's concept of an internal locus of control. These executives preferred actively confronting, rather than shrinking from, the world around them. Though they may sound like Beck's autonomous personality, there was a major difference. Hardy individuals perceived even stressful events as challenging opportunities for personal development rather than as threats to their esteem, security, independence, or freedom.

Later research with executives, as well as with attorneys, students, and other nonexecutives, has found that those displaying the characteristics of the hardy personality appear less likely to become

physically sick as the result of stress (Holahan & Moos, 1985; Kobasa, Maddi & Kahn, 1982). This is especially true if other stress-moderating factors, such as a strong physical constitution or abundant social support, are present (Ganellen & Blaney, 1984; Kobasa & Puccetti, 1983; Kobasa, Maddi & Courington, 1981).

Research on stress-prone and stress-hardy characteristics not only has helped establish the link between personality and the probability of stress-related illness but also, as noted in the stress chapter, has prompted the development of programs for helping stress-prone individuals moderate their health risks by altering potentially dangerous patterns of behavior and thinking.

fantasies (for instance, romantic versus forceful), but showed different relationships between fantasy, test scores, and sexual behavior. In another experiment (Pekala, Wenger & Levine, 1985), subjects completed a questionnaire about their ability to become absorbed in various tasks. They then participated in a series of short sessions of reading, relaxation, meditation, and sitting quietly, all of which might alter their state of consciousness somewhat. Results showed that higher "absorption" scores were associated with increased ability to become involved in consciousness-altering activities. Future research will continue to explore individual differences in an ever-growing number of variables, including how different people perceive and process information about their environment, what attributions they make about other people's behavior and personality, and how their emotions and thoughts interact to influence their attitudes and behavior.

Another aspect of modern personality research focuses on how individual differences interact with the situations in which people find themselves. For many years, the debate over this issue centered on whether behavior is determined by personality traits or by environmental situations (Bem & Allen, 1974; Mischel, 1968). More recently, however, advocates of both points of view have acknowledged that the argument will probably never be settled (Funder, 1983; Mischel & Peake, 1983). Each side has recognized the necessity of dealing with both person and situation variables, because (1) people are often consistent from one day or year to the next and across many situations (Conley, 1984), and (2) they can be quite inconsistent as well, behaving very differently toward different people and from one situation to the next.

Research is now focusing, not on whether people show consistency in thought and behavior, but on how consistency develops over the course of a lifetime, how much of it is real, how much lies in the perceptions of those who observe it, and how much is determined by the situation. Similarly, research on people's inconsistency is beginning to look beyond the influence of obviously different situations to explore such questions as how situations exert their influence and the degree to which the person's view of a situation changes its meaning and therefore its impact (Mischel, 1984).

If you want to learn more about personality or to follow the progress of research in the area, consider taking a basic course in personality psychology, perhaps also a laboratory in personality research methods.

SUMMARY

1. Personality is a commonly used term with no universally accepted definition. It refers generally to the pattern of psychological and behavioral characteristics that distinguishes each person from everyone else.

2. The assessment of personality is usually accomplished through some combination of observations, interviews, and tests. Tests can be classified as either objective or projective.

3. Personality can be approached from many perspectives. The four main approaches to personality are the psychodynamic, the dispositional, the behavioral, and the phenomenological. Each contains its own basic assumptions and methods of measuring personality.

4. The psychodynamic approach was founded by Freud and assumes that personality is formed out of conflicts between basic needs and the demands of the real world. Most of these conflicts occur at an unconscious level, but their effects can be seen in everyday behavior. Freud believed that personality has three components—the id, the ego, and the superego—which are often in unconscious conflict. Various ego defense mechanisms serve to keep these conflicts from becoming conscious. The focus of conflicts changes as the personality develops from the oral stage of infancy through the anal stage, the phallic stage, the latency period, and the genital stage.

5. Numerous psychodynamic theories have been based on Freud's original formulations. These variations on his approach tend to downplay the role of instincts and the unconscious, emphasizing instead the importance of conscious processes, ego functions, and the influence of social and cultural factors on behavior and thought.

6. The psychodynamic approach is found in many forms of psychotherapy, as well as in attempts to understand certain forms of physical illness and in efforts at preventing psychological problems that have their origins in early childhood.

7. Critics fault the psychodynamic approach—especially Freud's—for its lack of a scientific base, for the vagueness of its concepts, and for its view of humans as driven by instincts.

8. The dispositional approach assumes that personality is made up of a set of stable internal characteristics that guide behavior. These characteristics have been described as personality types, but more often as each person's unique combination of traits, factors, or needs. Personality may have a genetic origin in the sense that inherited tendencies become the raw materials out of which environmental experience molds each unique personality.

9. Dispositional personality tests are commonly used in personnel selection to identify people whose personalities best suit them for certain kinds of employment. Unfortunately, this use of dispositional tests does not usually work as well as employers might wish. Dispositional theories are also more generally criticized because they seem better at describing personality than at explaining it.

10. The behavioral approach assumes that personality is just a label that summarizes the unique patterns of learned behaviors that people display in various situations. Some behavioral theorists think of personality only as overt behavior, but others, such as Rotter, Bandura, and Mischel, include learned patterns of thinking as well. Especially important in this cognitive-behavioral approach is the emphasis on behavior as the outcome of person-situation interactions. Behavioral approaches form the basis for many newer forms of psychotherapy. They also help people learn the social and cognitive skills they need to improve their personality and provide suggestions for systematic child-rearing practices. Still, critics of the behavioral approach see it as cold, mechanistic, and not capable of capturing, let alone changing the essence of, what most psychologists mean by personality: beliefs, intentions, and values.

11. The phenomenological, or humanistic, approach is best represented in the theories of Carl Rogers and Abraham Maslow. It is based on the assumption that personality is determined by the unique ways in which

each individual views the world. These perceptions form a personal version of reality and guide behavior as people strive to reach their fullest human potential. The phenomenological approach is evident in humanistic approaches to child rearing and education and in the many personal growth experiences offered to the public. Though the approach has a large following, it has been faulted for being too vague and unscientific.

KEY TERMS

Definitions of terms appear on the pages shown in parentheses.

anal stage (514)
archetype (515)
behavioral approach (527)
collective unconscious (515)
condition of worth (534)
defense mechanism (512)
deficiency orientation (535)
denial (513)
displacement (513)
dispositional approach (519)
ego (512)
ego psychologist (516)
factor analysis (521)
free association (510)
functional analysis of
    behavior (527)

genital stage (515)
growth orientation (535)
id (511)
intellectualization (513)
introjection (512)
latency period (515)
libido (511)
objective test (508)
object relations (517)
Oedipus complex (514)
oral stage (514)
personal construct (532)
personality (504)
phallic stage (514)
phenomenological approach
    (531)

pleasure principle (512)
projection (513)
projective test (508)
psychoanalysis (511)
psychodynamic approach
    (510)
psychosexual stage (516)
psychosocial stage (514)
psychotherapy (517)
rationalization (513)
reaction formation (513)

reality principle (512)
reciprocal determinism (529)
repression (512)
self-actualization (533)
self-concept (533)
self-efficacy (529)
situational specificity (527)
style of life (516)
sublimation (513)
superego (512)

RECOMMENDED READINGS

Hall, C. S., & Lindzey, G. (1970). *Theories of personality* (2nd ed.). New York: Wiley. A classic treatment of a wide range of personality theories, representing all the approaches described in this chapter.

Hogan, R. (1986). What every student should know about personality. In V. P. Makosky (Ed.), *The G. Stanley Hall lecture series:* Vol. 6. Washington: American Psychological Association. A brief and readable summary of the history of the personality construct and of the issues with which researchers in personality psychology concern themselves.

Liebert, R. M., & Spiegler, M. D. (1987). *Personality: Strategies and issues* (5th ed.). Homewood, Ill.: Dorsey Press. A good, balanced textbook on all major approaches to personality.

*B*ob D, a twenty-two-year-old carpenter, was referred to the psychiatric department of a community hospital. Three months earlier, Bob's father had died after a long illness. The day of his father's funeral, Bob had experienced an episode of dizziness, sweating, and a strange feeling that things around him did not look quite real. This feeling waxed and waned for an hour or so and then disappeared. Over the ensuing months, similar episodes became longer and more frequent, until he was never free of uncomfortable physical sensations. During an initial interview, Bob seemed tense, worried, and frightened. He sat on the edge of his chair, tapping his foot and fidgeting with a pencil. Several times during the previous two weeks, he had been unable to go to work because he was "too nervous." Recently he felt easily distracted by roadside stimuli while driving and experienced a frightening sensation that trees he passed were falling onto his car. He tied the onset of his difficulties to the funeral, but he could not understand why.[1]

Marlene T, a thirty-one-year-old divorced mother, was admitted to a general hospital after attempting suicide. She had previously experienced noticeable mood changes; then, soon after the birth of her child, these mood swings became greatly exaggerated. She began having periods of considerable activity, during which she was very outgoing and sociable, and periods when she was very irritable and depressed. Then, after an argument with her mother, Marlene took an overdose of sleeping pills. (Adapted from Zax & Stricker, 1963, pp. 198–199)

When Philip L was twenty-one, he met and married a waitress twelve years his senior. He did so, he said, not because of loving feelings for her, but because of the "practical" advantages, such as her income. Throughout the seven-year marriage, Philip managed to get a variety of jobs as an unskilled worker but could hold none of them. Usually he would get into a conflict with bosses or fellow workers and then quit or be fired. As a result, his wife was forced to work particularly long hours; on occasion, the couple was forced to live on welfare. When he appeared at a mental health clinic, Philip admitted that he came only to please a welfare worker. He did acknowledge that he had a poor attitude toward life and could not stick to activities. In general he complained of a lack of will power. He also pointed out that he did not have very strong feelings about other people. He recognized that he was different from others in this respect, but this did not bother him much. (Adapted from Zax & Stricker, 1963, pp. 189–190)

Obviously, these people have problems. In fact, the professionals who interviewed them ultimately diagnosed them as displaying some form of mental disorder, or *psychopathology*. **Psychopathology** is a social as well as a personal matter; it involves patterns of thinking and behaving that are maladaptive, disruptive, or uncomfortable either for the person affected or for those with whom he or she comes in contact. Psychopathology has fascinated and frightened human beings for centuries. It has also attracted the attention of psychologists in many specialty areas (see Linkages diagram, p. 544), not only because it encompasses puzzling behavior, but also because its appearance

[1] R. L. Spitzer et al., *Psychopathology: A Casebook,* 1983, pages 11–12. Reprinted by permission of McGraw-Hill.

15

Abnormal Psychology

LINKAGES
an overview

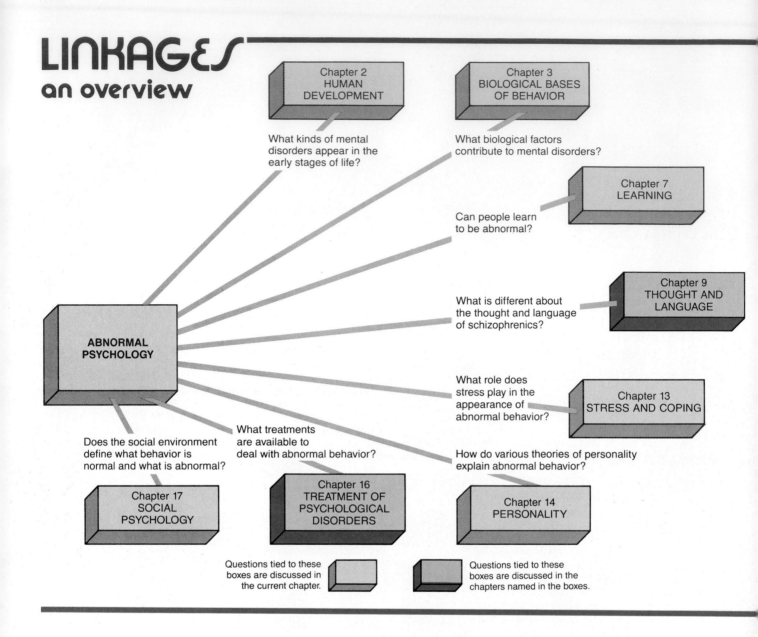

Chapter 2
HUMAN DEVELOPMENT

What kinds of mental disorders appear in the early stages of life?

Chapter 3
BIOLOGICAL BASES OF BEHAVIOR

What biological factors contribute to mental disorders?

Chapter 7
LEARNING

Can people learn to be abnormal?

Chapter 9
THOUGHT AND LANGUAGE

What is different about the thought and language of schizophrenics?

ABNORMAL PSYCHOLOGY

What role does stress play in the appearance of abnormal behavior?

Chapter 13
STRESS AND COPING

Does the social environment define what behavior is normal and what is abnormal?

What treatments are available to deal with abnormal behavior?

How do various theories of personality explain abnormal behavior?

Chapter 17
SOCIAL PSYCHOLOGY

Chapter 16
TREATMENT OF PSYCHOLOGICAL DISORDERS

Chapter 14
PERSONALITY

Questions tied to these boxes are discussed in the current chapter.

Questions tied to these boxes are discussed in the chapters named in the boxes.

is so hard to predict. For example, sometime in their lives, most people encounter episodes of tragedy or trauma—a death, the loss of a job, a financial disaster—but somehow they adjust and go on. But for some people, a single crisis can be psychologically shattering, bringing about behavior problems and lifelong maladjustment. And some individuals suffer mental problems for no apparent reason.

Large-scale surveys have found that, in any six-month period, nearly 20 percent of the American population shows some form of mild to severe mental disorder and that nearly one-third have experienced some disorder sometime in their lives (Meyers et al., 1984; Robins et al., 1984; see Figure 15.1, p. 546). What determines who will "break down" and who will not? Is it a matter of will power, genetics, learned skills, or sheer luck? We will consider these questions throughout this chapter, as we describe the characteristics of several major categories of psychopathology and some of their possible causes.

ABNORMAL PSYCHOLOGY AND PSYCHOLOGY

In the chapter on development and elsewhere, we have provided a general picture of the way thought, perception, motivation, emotion, language, and personality normally develop over the lifespan. Unfortunately, development along these dimensions is often disrupted or distorted, resulting in numerous problems, some of which may take the form of mental or behavioral disorders. These disorders define the realm of abnormal psychology, the topic of this chapter.

Psychologists working to describe or explain abnormality rely heavily on concepts and data from other areas of the discipline. The theories of personality described in the previous chapter have been of enormous value in focusing research on certain likely causes of these disorders, including psychodynamic conflicts, maladaptive learning experiences, and blockages in the expression of a person's potential. Genetic and biochemical problems, including brain disorders, are also important causal factors. Currently, there is great interest in using information-processing tasks to try to understand more precisely the mental capacities and information-processing problems of people who display disturbances in the ability to think and communicate with others. Similarly, psychologists have looked to the learning principles discussed in Chapter 7, especially classical, operant, and vicarious conditioning, to help them understand the circumstances under which intense fears develop. In the course of this chapter, we will see many other linkages as well.

NORMALITY AND ABNORMALITY

Who decides what is maladaptive or abnormal? When is treatment required? In large measure, the society or culture shapes the answers to such questions. If you live in a tolerant society and do not upset other people too much, you can behave in some rather unusual ways and still not be officially diagnosed or treated for psychopathology. For example, our collection of recent news clippings contains stories about (1) a man in Long Beach, California, who moved out of his apartment, leaving behind sixty thousand pounds of rocks, chunks of concrete, and slabs of cement neatly boxed and stacked in every room; and (2) a Richmond, California, woman whose unexplained habit of opening all her faucets (some connected to garden hoses hanging from trees) regularly consumed over twenty thousand gallons of water a day until a judge ordered a flow restrictor placed on her meter. In a less tolerant country, these

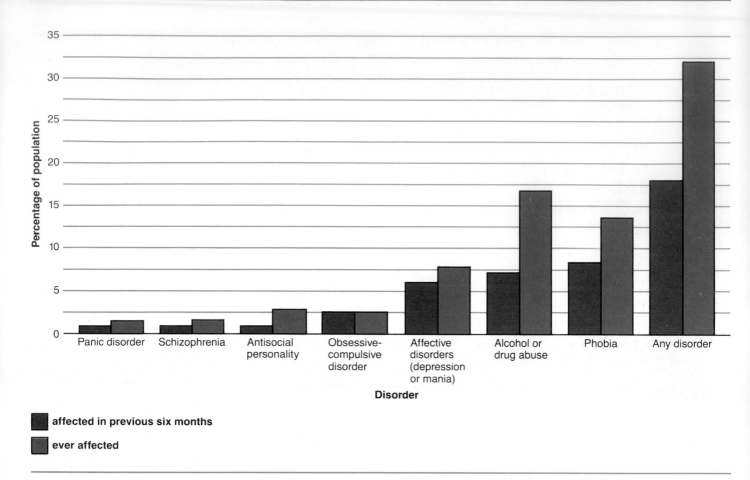

Figure 15.1
Mental Disorders in the American Population
A three-city survey of 9,543 people revealed that almost 1 in 5 displayed some form of mental disorder, either within the previous six months (Meyers et al., 1984) or at some time (Robins et al., 1984). Shown here are the estimated percentages of the population who exhibited various disorders described later in this chapter. Note that the total percentage for all disorders is smaller than the total of the individual percentages, because some people had more than one disorder.

individuals might be taken into custody and subjected to treatment or imprisonment.

We begin our exploration of psychopathology by considering some of the factors that determine what is considered normal and abnormal today and by reviewing some of the changes that have taken place over the years. In the process, we will see that the concept of psychopathology and what to do about it changes constantly, that even today's answers are just steps toward knowledge in an area where much is still unknown or poorly understood.

What Is Abnormality?

Certainly, most people would call it abnormal to think small children should be killed because they are beings from another planet. And just as certainly, very few people would use the "abnormal" label on someone who prefers to wear long-sleeved shirts in the summer. It is the vast range of behaviors between these extremes that causes debate over just what is normal and what is not.

The statistical approach   One apparently simple way of deciding whether behavior is abnormal is to ask how common it is. For example, most people probably wash their hands three or four times a day. We could label as "normal" anyone whose handwashing frequency falls close to the average; everyone else could be said to show abnormal handwashing behavior. From this strictly statistical point of view, normality describes the behavior of the greatest number of people, or what the average person does. Thus, as we noted in Chapter 10, those who score significantly below the average range on IQ tests are often given labels such as "mentally retarded." This certainly provides a clear criterion for abnormality, but are we also willing to call a person abnormal if he or she has an unusually high IQ? A problem with the statistical approach is that it does not take into account the fact that some kinds of deviant behaviors, such as the ability to speak twelve languages, are valuable and desirable. Another problem with the statistical view is that it equates normality with *conformity*. Nonconformists, however, are often a society's most creative thinkers. If everyone behaved just like everyone else, for instance, the research that led to computers, miracle drugs, and space travel might never have been done.

The valuative approach An obvious alternative to a statistical view of abnormality is to use *valuative* criteria: behavior is abnormal if a person acts in ways that are not valued, no matter how many other people also behave that way. This gets around the problem of calling geniuses and certain valued nonconformists "abnormal." Common valuative criteria for normality include *intelligibility* (does behavior make sense?); *consistency* (does one appear to be the same person from day to day?); *control* (is behavior guided by one's intentions?); and *morality* (does behavior conform to prevailing legal and moral standards?).

The valuative approach is inherent in our legal system and social and moral codes, but it is not without problems. Chief among these is the question of who determines official values, the criteria for normality. If law or custom says that a behavior, such as oral sex, is wrong and therefore abnormal, but many or even most people do it anyway, is that behavior really abnormal? If the answer is yes, very few people could be considered normal because there are so many ways of being abnormal and because most people probably display at least one of them.

A practical approach In everyday life, both mental health professionals and the public use a combination of the statistical and valuative views. In this *practical* approach, judgments about abnormality and about who should receive treatment are tempered by consideration of (1) the *content* of behavior (what a person does), and (2) the *context* of behavior (where and when the person does it).

With regard to content, behavior is likely to be judged abnormal by society if it (1) causes discomfort, (2) appears bizarre or weird, and (3) is inefficient or dysfunctional (Buss, 1966; Davison & Neale, 1986; Rosenhan & Seligman, 1984). People will tolerate a considerable amount of discomfort and even bizarreness in themselves and others if the behavior is not so frequent or disruptive that it interferes with the demands of everyday life. This is the vitally important dysfunction criterion. From the practical viewpoint, behavior is unlikely to be formally considered abnormal if the person displaying it can get along from day to day and in the process not cause others too much trouble. For example, a successful businessman was found to have lined all his clothes with newspaper to protect himself against harmful radiation from alien spacecraft. Everyone at the office thought this was bizarre, but because he was able to do his job efficiently enough to be useful to his company, his behavior did not lead to a formal diagnosis or to treatment of any kind.

The second criterion used in the practical approach is *context*—where and when behavior occurs. How would you feel if you were asked to enter an elevator and stare directly at another passenger during the ride? Or to tell sexually oriented jokes during a funeral? If you would hesitate, it is prob-

If our society adhered strictly to a statistical view of abnormality, Christo, an artist fascinated with wrapping buildings, and even islands, with plastic or canvas might be considered abnormal. Similarly, many writers, scientists, political activists, religious leaders, and anyone else with unusual ideas could all too easily be labeled abnormal and perhaps be "put away" (as they often have been in the Soviet Union).

ably because you recognize that these actions would be inappropriate to the situation. Behavior may be labeled abnormal if a person uses poor judgment about where he or she displays it. At the same time, the practical approach to abnormality says that people can perform all sorts of bizarre activities as long as they do not create discomfort and as long as they confine these activities to private places or to situations where everyone present approves.

The question of just what behaviors are approved in what situations is largely determined by the culture or subculture. What is normal in one culture could be abnormal in another. For example, in one Pacific island society, social life is governed by hostility and suspicion. Gifts of food are assumed to be poisoned, and a poor crop is attributed to theft, by magic, of nutrients from the soil. Anyone who is friendly is considered crazy (MacAndrew & Edgerton, 1970). Even in a culture like ours, there are significant differences among subcultural groups as to what is considered normal and abnormal. A street gang member who decides to devote more time to studying, household chores, or other behaviors considered normal by the dominant culture is likely to be considered abnormal by other gang members and subjected to punishment, or even banishment.

In summary, it is difficult to identify behaviors that are universally considered deviant or abnormal. The practical approach defines as *abnormal* statistically frequent or infrequent behavior that makes the person uncomfortable or that disrupts the lives or offends the social or cultural values of others.

Changing Beliefs About Abnormality

Mental disorder has been viewed at one time or another as the work of gods or demons, as physical disease, as the result of mental conflicts, as learned maladaptive habits, and as the product of the way one looks at the world.

Ancient concepts   The earliest explanations for behavior disorders followed the *demonological model* of abnormality, which attributed abnormal behavior to the supernatural powers of devils or gods. This view was dominant until about the fourth century B.C. It was then that the Greek physician Hippocrates suggested a **medical model** of abnormality, in which behavior disorders, such as epilepsy and depression, were seen, not as godly punishments, but as physical diseases whose causes were natural and related mainly to the brain. Later Greek and Roman physicians expanded on or revised Hippocrates' views, giving birth to the notion of mental illness, or psychopathology.

The Middle Ages   During the Middle Ages (from about the fifth to about the fifteenth century A.D.), supernatural explanations of behavior disorders returned to prominence. A great deal of deviant behavior was tolerated and even encouraged if it was attributed to devotion to God. Thus, whipping oneself for one's sins or participating in the "dancing manias" that often afflicted whole towns was generally viewed as godly (Kroll, 1973). By the fourteenth and fifteenth centuries, however, the church became very concerned about the influence of groups of nonbelievers, or heretics, and dealt with them harshly. Heretics were burned at the stake, and it ultimately became common knowledge that heresy and other unusual behavior was brought on by the devil and his witches.

As the Middle Ages drew to a close, specialized hospitals, or *asylums,* for the insane began to appear throughout Europe. After the Middle Ages, medical doctors again took over responsibility for those considered mentally ill.

Hogarth's eighteenth-century portrayal of "Bedlam," the colloquial name for London's St. Mary's of Bethlehem hospital. Most early mental hospitals were little more than prisons where the public could buy tickets to gawk at the patients, much as people go to the zoo today.

Although doctors generally agreed that behavior disorders were due to physical causes, there was little agreement about what those causes were, and even less certainty about treatment methods.

Biological and psychodynamic models   The assumption that hospitals are the proper place for those who display abnormality was given added support during the 1850s, when medical research began to discover organic causes for some disorders. Confidence grew among physicians that it was only a matter of time before a physical cause would be found for all mental disorders. Consequently, by 1850 almost every state in the United States had many state-run mental hospitals, each capable of housing thousands of patients. These hospitals kept patients under far better conditions than their counterparts in earlier times had, but the search for organic causes proved difficult. Even today, the medical model (also known as the **biological model**) has yet to fully explain most behavior disorders.

Late in the 1800s, Sigmund Freud began to develop a reconceptualization of the medical model. He created the *psychodynamic approach,* described in the chapter on personality. In Freud's view, abnormal behavior results from unresolved, mostly unconscious conflicts between instinctual desires and the demands of the environment and society. The more basic, severe, or numerous the conflicts, the more severe the behavior disorder. The causes of behavior disorders are seen as psychological, not physical, and often stem from early childhood. But the medical and psychodynamic models of psychopathology are closely connected. In the psychodynamic model, behavior disorder is like physical illness, in that there are problematic symptoms stemming from an underlying cause, which can be diagnosed, treated, and cured. Both the medical and psychodynamic models have been supported mainly by psychiatrists and other medical doctors. The popularity of the terms *psychopathology* and *mental illness* and the frequency of such casual comments as "She's really sick" or "He should have his head examined" reflect the way biological and psychodynamic models have dominated contemporary thinking about abnormal behavior.

Biological and psychodynamic models have generated many useful hypotheses about the causes and treatment of abnormal behavior. But critics point out that all abnormal behavior may not have physical causes and that the unconscious problems alleged to create disorder are not useful explanations because they are too difficult to measure objectively. Further, thinking of abnormal behavior as physical or mental illness casts the deviant person in the role of a patient who may be labeled abnormal along with his or her behavior. This labeling can lead to reduced expectations for improvement and to other significant problems, as we will see later. Concern about these and other issues prompted the development of two alternative ways of looking at abnormal behavior: the behavioral model and the phenomenological model.

The behavioral model   The *behavioral model* emphasizes the view that most normal behavior is learned, usually in social situations. Behavioral theorists (Bandura, 1971; Mischel, 1978; Skinner, 1953; Ullmann & Krasner, 1975) bring the same point of view to the problem of behavior disorder, which they see as caused by unfortunate learning experiences and the influence of situations in the present, rather than by biological imbalance or unconscious conflicts from the distant past. In fact, they argue that people learn many maladaptive, abnormal behaviors in the same basic ways that they learn adaptive, normal behaviors. Just as you learned to enjoy your favorite food by discovering the rewards of its taste, a person who is terrified of crossing bridges probably learned this fear through past negative experiences on a bridge. Although physical or biochemical problems (such as paralysis or mental retardation) may set certain limits on a person's behavior, the degree to which that person displays abnormal behavior depends mainly on how he or she learns to behave within those limits.

Looking at abnormality as learned, maladaptive behavior allows one to call behavior abnormal without calling the person abnormal, thus focusing attention on the person's strengths as well as problems. Also, society's deviants need not be seen as sick people, but as individuals who have learned specific maladaptive ways of thinking and behaving and who need help in learning more adaptive thoughts and actions. They are usually referred to as *clients,* not patients, and the preferred term for describing their problems is *behavior disorders,* rather than *mental illness.*

The phenomenological model   The other major alternative to medical/ biological and psychodynamic models is the *phenomenological model.* As noted in the personality chapter, this model sees human behavior as guided by the way each person perceives the world. If all goes well, each person naturally develops his or her unique potential. But if something gets in the way of self-actualization, psychological growth stops, and behavior disorder appears as a signal of the problem. The "something" that obstructs growth usually is a failure to be in touch with and express one's own true feelings, some of which may be unacceptable to oneself or to others. When this happens, the person begins to distort his or her perceptions of reality. The greater the perceptual distortion and the less emotional contact one has with one's feelings, the more serious the behavior disorder. Like behavioral theorists, phenomenologists do not talk of "sick patients," but of disturbed clients. Further, abnormal behavior, no matter how unusual or seemingly irrational, is presumed to be a reasonable reaction to the world the client perceives.

Approach	Possible Causes	Possible Treatment
Medical/ biological	Organic disorder; perhaps overly reactive nervous system or biochemical imbalance, making Mr. A vulnerable to stress	Drugs
Psychodynamic	Unconscious conflicts, perhaps related to unacceptable impulses toward older daughter	Talking therapy, aimed at gaining insight into and resolving conflicts
Behavioral	Learned response to stress brought on by family and job responsibilities; symptoms rewarded by relief from duties	Development of stress-coping techniques
Phenomenological	Failure to recognize true feelings about family and job; perhaps feelings of wanting to be free are incongruent with his self-image and result in symptoms	Therapy experiences designed to put Mr. A in closer touch with his real feelings so that he can make some thoughtful decisions

TABLE 15.1

Four Ways of Viewing Psychopathology
Mr. A is a forty-two-year-old man who lives with his wife and two teenage daughters in a large city on the West Coast. For over a year, he has been experiencing attacks of dizziness, accelerated heartbeat, and most recently, fainting. These attacks come only when he is away from home or when his older daughter is there. The problem has become so severe that Mr. A has had to take a leave of absence from his job. Here is a summary of how the four main approaches to psychopathology might view Mr. A's problems.

An integrated view: The diathesis-stress model Today, the medical/biological, psychodynamic, behavioral, and phenomenological approaches represent the main views of psychopathology. All of them are valid and useful to some degree, at least in the sense that they all provide a logical explanation for many behavior disorders and have generated potentially helpful methods of treating those disorders. Table 15.1 illustrates this point.

It is up to researchers in abnormal psychology to present evidence that one model is better than another in understanding a particular disorder. Since no single model can fully account for all forms of abnormality, physical factors (such as chemical imbalances), as well as psychological and environmental factors (such as learning and conflicts), are included in more general formulations, such as the **diathesis-stress model** of psychopathology.

This integrative alternative recognizes that each person inherits certain physical predispositions that leave him or her vulnerable to problems, which may or may not appear, depending on other factors. This predisposition is called a **diathesis** (pronounced "die-a'-thesis"). Whether a predisposition actually leads to problematic behavior depends on what kinds of situations —especially conflicts, frustrations, pressure, and other kinds of stressors—a person confronts. Thus, a person may inherit a tendency toward sadness and depression, but this tendency may appear only in stressful situations, such as a financial crisis. If no such situations occur, depression may not occur either. Similarly, as noted in Chapter 13, people who must deal with particular stressors may or may not show signs of psychopathology, depending on their ability to cope with those stressors.

Classification of Abnormal Behavior

In spite of variations in what is called abnormal, there does seem to be a core of behavior patterns that at least roughly defines abnormality. It has long been the goal of those who study abnormal behavior to establish some way of classifying these patterns in order to understand and deal with them. In the traditional medical model, the process of deciding what to call each pattern of disorder is called *psychodiagnosis*. Proponents of the behavioral and phenomenological models favor the term *assessment*.

In 1917 the American Psychiatric Association began publishing an early version of what has become the "official" diagnostic classification system, the *Diagnostic and Statistical Manual of Mental Disorders* (DSM). In each of its editions, the DSM has been expanded to include more categories. The revised third edition, DSM-III-R, was published in 1987 and contains over two hundred specific diagnostic labels.

DSM-III-R is basically a list of abnormal behavior patterns, but unlike the earlier DSM-I and DSM-II, it does not attempt to state the causes of all disorders (or directly endorse any particular theoretical model). Instead, DSM-III-R describes each form of disorder and provides criteria outlining what conditions must be present before making each diagnosis. The system allows for not just one diagnosis, but a series of evaluations on five dimensions, or *axes*, which, taken together, are designed to provide a picture of the person's problems, as well as some information about the context in which they have occurred. On Axis I there are sixteen major mental disorders (see Table 15.2). On Axis II there are two additional types of disorder: developmental problems and personality disorders. These have been placed on a separate axis to help ensure that they are not overlooked when an Axis I problem attracts the most

TABLE 15.2

The Diagnostic and Statistical Manual (DSM) of the American Psychiatric Association
On Axis I of the revised third edition (DSM-III-R) are listed the major categories of mental disorder. Axis II contains personality disorders and problems in various areas of development.

Axis I (Major Mental Disorders)

1. *Disorders usually first evident in infancy, childhood, or adolescence.* Problems such as hyperactivity, childhood fears, abnormal aggressiveness or other notable misconduct, failure to identify with one's own gender, frequent bedwetting or soiling, and other problems in normal social and behavioral development. Problems associated with eating too little (anorexia) or binge eating followed by self-induced vomiting (bulimia). These disorders are discussed in Chapter 11.

2. *Organic mental disorders* Problems caused by physical deterioration of the brain due to aging, disease, drugs or other chemicals, or other possibly unknown causes. These problems can appear as an inability to "think straight" (delirium) or as loss of memory and other intellectual functions (dementia).

3. *Psychoactive substance-use disorders* Psychological, behavioral, and physical problems caused by dependence on a variety of chemical substances, including alcohol, heroin, cocaine, amphetamines, hallucinogens, PCP, marijuana, and tobacco.

4. *Schizophrenia* Severe conditions characterized by abnormalities in thinking, perception, emotion, movement, and motivation that greatly interfere with daily functioning.

5. *Delusional (paranoid) disorders* Problems involving false beliefs (delusions) about such things as being loved by some high-status person, having inflated worth or power, or being persecuted, spied on, cheated on, followed, harassed, or kept from reaching important goals.

6. *Other psychotic disorders.* Serious mental problems that are similar to, but not as intense as schizophrenic or delusional (paranoid) disorders.

7. *Mood disorders* (also called *affective disorders*) Severe disturbances of mood, especially depression, overexcitement (mania), or alternating episodes of each extreme (as in bipolar disorder).

8. *Anxiety disorders* Specific fears (phobias), panic attacks, generalized feelings of dread, rituals of thought and action (obsessive-compulsive behavior) aimed at controlling anxiety, and problems caused by traumatic events, such as rape or military combat (see Chapter 13 for more on posttraumatic stress disorder).

attention. Any physical conditions or disorders that might be important in understanding a person's problems are listed on Axis III. On Axis IV the diagnostician rates (from 1 to 6) the amount of stress the person has been under in the past year. Finally, ratings (from 90 down to 1) of the person's psychological, social, and occupational functioning, currently and during the past year, appears on Axis V. Here is a sample DSM-III-R diagnosis.

Axis I   Major depression, single episode; alcohol dependence.

Axis II   Dependent personality disorder.

Axis III   Alcoholic cirrhosis of the liver.

Axis IV   Stressors: death of child. Severity: 6—catastrophic.

Axis V   Global assessment of functioning: currently, 50; highest in past year, 65.

A final notable feature of DSM-III-R is the absence of the time-honored major categories known in DSM-I and DSM-II as neurosis and psychosis. **Neurosis** referred to conditions in which a person is uncomfortable (usually anxious) but can still function. **Psychosis** included conditions involving loss of contact with reality or an inability to function day to day. Problems like these have not disappeared; they appear throughout Axis I in various specific disorders.

9. *Somatoform disorders*   Physical symptoms, such as paralysis and blindness, that are found to have no physical cause. Also, unusual preoccupation with physical health or with nonexistent or elusive physical problems (hypochondriasis).

10. *Dissociative disorders*   Psychologically caused problems of consciousness and self-identification, including loss of memory (amnesia) or the development of more than one identity (multiple personality).

11. *Sexual disorders*   Problems related to (a) finding unusual objects or situations (like baby carriages or exposing oneself) sexually arousing or (b) unsatisfactory sexual activity (sexual dysfunction). See Chapter 11 for more about problems in category b.

12. *Sleep disorders*   Severe problems involving the sleep-wake cycle, especially an inability to sleep well at night or to stay awake during the day.

13. *Factitious disorders*   False mental disorders, which are intentionally produced to satisfy some economic, psychological, or other need.

14. *Impulse control disorders*   Compulsive gambling, stealing, or fire setting.

15. *Adjustment disorders*   Failure to adjust to or deal well with such stressors as divorce, financial problems, family discord, or other unhappy life events.

16. *Psychological factors affecting physical condition*   True physical problems, such as headaches, high blood pressure, or ulcers that are caused or made worse by such psychological factors as anxiety (see Chapter 13, on stress).

Axis II (Developmental and Personality Disorders)

1. *Specific developmental disorders*   Mental retardation and autism (severe impairment in social and behavioral development), as well as other problems in the development of skill in reading, speaking, mathematics, or English.

2. *Personality disorders*   Individuals who may or may not receive an Axis I diagnosis but who show lifelong behavior patterns that are unsatisfactory to them or that disturb other people. The problematic features of their personality may involve unusual suspiciousness, unusual ways of thinking, self-centeredness, shyness, overdependency, excessive concern with neatness and detail, or overemotionality.

HIGHLIGHT

The Value of Psycho-diagnosis

When an observer makes an official diagnosis that affects another person's life, the consequences of an ill-informed decision can be enormous. One especially tragic example came to light in 1983, when it was discovered that David Tom, a Chinese immigrant who had been kept in mental institutions for over thirty years, suffered mainly from an inability to speak English. While Mr. Tom was in a hospital for treatment of tuberculosis, the diagnostician who examined him failed to realize that Mr. Tom spoke an unusual Chinese dialect and labeled him psychotic. When the error was finally discovered, Tom was released, but his physical and mental condition had deteriorated so much during his hospital stay that he would spend the rest of his life in a group home for former mental patients.

This incident illustrates some of the dangers of the diagnostic enterprise: (1) that diagnostic labels reflect an incomplete understanding of a person; (2) that the labels given often depend too much on the personal opinion of a single diagnostician; and (3) that, after all is said and done, labels do not always tell very much about a person.

The first of these problems can be lessened by spending more time on each case, giving (instead of DSM-III-R labels) a longer, more descriptive summary of the person's background, present problems, and potential strengths. In practice, however, this may not be possible. Furthermore, many professionals want a shorthand way of summarizing a person's problems. How good are those summary labels? One major concern has been about their *inter-rater reliability,* the degree to which different diagnosticians give the same label to the same person. Early studies of the reliability of psychodiagnosis (using pre-DSM-III systems) were notoriously disappointing. Frequently, diagnosticians could not agree more than 50 percent of the time on the major category in which a person belonged (for example, neurosis versus psychosis). Agreement about specific subcategories was even worse (Ash, 1949; Schmidt & Fonda, 1956).

Since most disagreements still seem to stem from confusion over what a person must do to receive a particular label (Ward et al., 1962), it is not surprising that the inclusion in DSM-III and DSM-III-R of specific criteria for giving each diagnosis has helped. More recent studies indicate interjudge agreement as high as 83 percent on such categories as schizophrenia and mood disorder, and agreement for all Axis I categories in the high 70s (Matarazzo, 1983; Spitzer, Forman & Nee, 1979). Though these figures represent great improvements, remember that they reflect the results of special experimental trials. High reliability figures are likely to be duplicated in everyday clinical practice only if diagnosticians adhere to DSM-III-R criteria. That they may not is suggested by a study at a New York psychiatric hospital, where very different diagnoses were given to the same patients by different clinicians in as many as 75 percent of 131 randomly chosen cases (Lipton & Simon, 1985). Further, there is evidence that diagnosticians in different places may use different standards (see Table 15.3).

A second important question about psychodiagnosis concerns how *valid* it is; that is, what do labels actually tell about the person? Again, early research found little evidence for validity. A classic study showed that a person labeled "neurotic" commonly had some of the same symptoms as someone labeled "schizophrenic" or "manic depressive" (Zigler & Phillips, 1961).

Today, the validity of DSM-III diagnoses is still debated. One thing seems certain: no shorthand label can be valid enough to specify exactly what each person's problems are or exactly how that person will behave in the future.

	Percentage Given at		
Label	North Carolina	London	Glasgow
Schizophrenia	18	20	13
Manic depression	9	18	18
Neurosis	29	15	10
Personality disorder	18	22	38

SOURCE: M. G. Sandifer et al., "Psychiatric diagnosis: A comparative study in North Carolina, London, and Glasgow," *British Journal of Psychiatry*, 1968, *114,* 1–9. Reprinted by permission.

TABLE 15.3

Effect of Geography on Diagnosis
These data show the diagnoses given by a group of diagnosticians in three countries who saw films of the same thirty people being interviewed in an American hospital. Even more dramatic effects have been found in other studies (Chapman & Chapman, 1973; Cooper et al., 1972; Kendall, 1975). Differences in training, diagnostic traditions, and even personal bias appear to account for these data (Lee & Temerlin, 1970; Temerlin, 1968).

Indeed, all that can be reasonably expected may be a system that allows informative, general descriptions of the types of problems displayed by people in different major categories. Still, it is worth noting that current research on the validity of diagnostic categories goes beyond trying to predict how people will behave. Researchers are also attempting to determine whether everyone in a particular diagnostic group shares patterns of family history, genetic and biochemical factors, responses to specific treatments, and other characteristics (Pope & Lipinsky, 1978). We will see evidence of this approach as we discuss various specific disorders. ∎

Although DSM-III-R is by no means a perfect system of classification, it does represent the state of the art in psychodiagnosis. The future will no doubt see further changes and improvements; DSM-IV is due to be published in about 1993. For now, however, DSM-III-R provides a convenient framework for our description of abnormality. We will not have the space to cover all DSM-III-R categories, so we will focus on several of the major disorders on Axis I. In each instance, we will provide a general description, some clinical examples, and a brief discussion of possible causes of the disorder.

As you read, try not to catch "medical student's disease." Just as medical students often think they have the symptoms of every illness they read about, psychology students frequently worry that their behavior (or that of a family member or friend) signals some type of mental disorder. This is usually not the case; it is just that everyone has some problems, some of the time. It might be a good idea to review the criteria of the practical approach to abnormality and consider how frequently a problem occurs before deciding whether you or someone you know needs psychological help.

ANXIETY DISORDERS

If you have ever been tense before an exam, a date, or a visit to the dentist, you know what anxiety feels like. Increased heart rate, sweating, rapid breathing, a dry mouth, and a sense of apprehension are common components of anxiety. Brief episodes of moderate anxiety are a normal part of life. For some people, though, anxiety is so intense, longstanding, or disruptive as to be called an **anxiety disorder.** We will consider four types of anxiety disorders: phobia, generalized anxiety disorder, panic disorder, and obsessive-compulsive disorder.

Luposlipaphobia: The fear of being pursued by timber wolves around a kitchen table while wearing socks on a newly waxed floor.

The fact that phobias can be very specific and unusual has provided grist for the humor mill, but the discomfort caused by severe phobias is no laughing matter.

Phobia

Anxiety disorders called **phobias** involve a strong, irrational fear of an object or situation that should not cause such a reaction. The phobic individual usually realizes that the fear makes no sense but cannot keep it from interfering with daily life. There are literally thousands of phobias, most of which have been given Greek names; examples include acrophobia (fear of heights), ailurophobia (fear of cats), and xenophobia (fear of strangers). In DSM-III-R, phobias are divided into simple and social subtypes.

Simple phobias involve fear of physical things, such as heights, darkness, animals, and air travel. Here is a case from one of the authors' files.

> Mr. L was a fifty-one-year-old office worker who became terrified whenever he had to drive over a bridge. For years, he avoided bridges by taking roundabout ways to and from work, and he refused to be a passenger in anyone else's car, lest they use a bridge. This very inconvenient adjustment was shattered when Mr. L was transferred to a position requiring frequent automobile trips, many of which crossed bridges. He refused the transfer and was fired.

Social phobias usually center on the prospect of being negatively evaluated by others or publicly embarrassed by doing something impulsive, outrageous, or humiliating. These fears can create extreme discomfort in social situations and motivate all sorts of logical and illogical excuses to escape or avoid them. Fear of public speaking, "stage fright," and even fears of eating or writing in front of others are illustrations of this problem.

Generalized Anxiety Disorder

The condition called **generalized anxiety disorder** involves relatively mild, but long-lasting anxiety that is not focused on any particular object or situation. For weeks at a time, the person feels anxious and worried, sure that some, usually unspecified, disaster is going to happen. The person becomes so jumpy and irritable that sound sleep is impossible. Fatigue, inability to concentrate, and physiological signs of anxiety are also common. Because the problem occurs in virtually all situations and because the person cannot pinpoint its source, this condition is sometimes called *free-floating anxiety*. The Bob D. case at the beginning of this chapter is a good example.

Panic Disorder

For some people, anxiety takes the form of **panic disorder,** consisting of terrifying *panic attacks* that come without warning or obvious cause. These attacks are marked by heart palpitations, pressure or pain in the chest, dizziness or unsteadiness, sweating, and faintness. They may be accompanied by feeling detached from one's body or feeling that people and events are not real (Barlow et al., 1985). The person may think he or she is about to die or "go crazy." After a few minutes, the attack subsides. The person may worry constantly about having one of these unpredictable attacks and eventually curtail business or social activities to avoid possible embarrassment. This may ultimately lead to a very severe phobia called agoraphobia.

Agoraphobia is a strong fear of being alone or away from the security of home. Any attempt to go out alone leads to increasing anxiety, nausea, dizziness, or fainting. Crowded public places like theaters or shopping malls are especially upsetting because the person fears becoming helpless and incapacitated by some unspecified disaster. In severe cases, being alone at all, even at home, brings terror. Like other phobias, agoraphobia is more often seen in women, many of whom are totally housebound by the time they seek help. Although agoraphobia occurs in less than 0.5 percent of the population, it is the phobia that most often brings people into treatment, mainly because of its disruptive effects on everyday life (Chambliss & Goldstein, 1980).

Obsessive-Compulsive Disorder

Anxiety is also at the root of **obsessive-compulsive disorder,** in which a person becomes obsessed with certain thoughts or images or feels a compulsion to do certain things. If the person tries to interrupt obsessive thinking or compulsions, severe agitation and anxiety usually result. This pattern is very different from the occasional experience of rechecking to see that a door is locked. In obsessive-compulsive disorder, the thoughts and compulsions are constant, unwelcome intrusions that can severely impair daily activities. Typical obsessive thoughts revolve around the possibility of harming someone or being infected. Compulsive behaviors often take the form of repetitive rituals, such as counting or touching things, or arranging objects "just so." Here is an example of a rather severe case.

> Marcia's symptoms began at a family Christmas party when she began to doubt whether she had correctly made the dessert. This doubt was accompanied by the fear that she might have harmed her children and guests, which soon spread to other areas. Marcia became unable to give her children vitamins for fear of making a mistake and injuring them, and she could not cook for fear that she would poison someone. She gave up driving the car, plagued by the thought that she might kill someone. She repeatedly checked locks, faucets, the fireplace, and her husband's tools as possible sources of danger. She began to bathe as often as six times a day, particularly if she happened to brush against something, such as the garage door, that she saw as carrying germs. Her hands became swollen from repeated washings. (Based on Zax & Stricker, 1963, p. 171)

Causes of Anxiety Disorders

As with all the forms of psychopathology we will consider, the exact cause of anxiety disorders is a matter of some debate. All theoretical approaches offer explanations, but research suggests that the biological and behavioral models are particularly important.

The biological model suggests that the development of anxiety disorders may be based on a predisposition to react with anxiety to a wide range of situations. The predisposition may be based on having too little of a particular neurotransmitter. Such a deficiency, possibly inherited, might create an autonomic nervous system that is oversensitive to stress. The possibility of inherited autonomic oversensitivity is supported by research showing that identical twins share anxiety disorders more often than other twins (Eysenck, 1975). Another biological hypothesis is that panic attacks may result from an overreaction to lactic acid, a substance produced naturally when the body is under stress (Fishman & Sheehan, 1985). This overreaction is visible not only in the panic symptoms produced in lactic acid-sensitive volunteers, but also in the pattern of blood flow through their brains (Reiman et al., 1984; see Figure 15.2, p. 558). Additional biological predispositions are likely to be discovered in the future. However, most researchers seem to agree that these predispositions are less critical than environmental stress in bringing about most anxiety disorders.

The behavioral model emphasizes learning. Obsessive-compulsive behaviors are seen as learned habits that allow a person to escape or avoid anxiety-

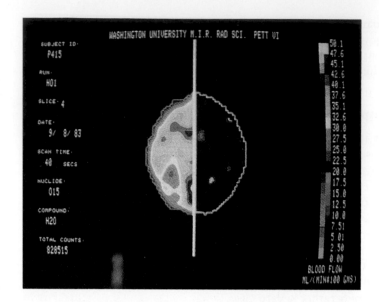

Figure 15.2
Anxiety and the Brain
This PET scan of a patient susceptible to panic attacks shows that blood flow in the right side of the parahippocampal gyrus (an area involved in emotion) is unusually high compared to that in the left. People not especially sensitive to lactate showed equal amounts of blood flow on both sides.
(Reprinted from *Psychology Today Magazine.* Copyright © 1985 American Psychological Association.)

provoking situations, such as studying or discussing personal feelings. Phobias are explained in part on the basis of unpleasant personal experiences; fear of dogs may result from an attack by a dog. Seeing or hearing about other people's bad experiences can produce the same result; most people who fear flying have never been in a plane crash. Once the fear is learned, avoidance of the feared object prevents the person from finding out that there is no need to be afraid. This vicious cycle explains why many fears do not simply disappear.

HIGHLIGHT

Phobias and Preparedness

Some phobias are common, and others are rare. Why? And why, if you are frightened by a snarling, chained dog, do you not develop a fear of chains as well as of dogs? The answer may be that people are physiologically prepared to learn certain fears, especially those that are self-protective, such as fear of heights or of snakes (Seligman, 1971). Some laboratory evidence supports this notion. A group of Swedish psychologists attempted to teach people to fear certain stimuli by associating the stimuli with electric shocks (Ohman, Erixon & Lofberg, 1975). The subjects developed about equal conditioned anxiety reactions to slides of houses, human faces, and snakes. But later, when they were tested without shock, the reaction to snakes remained long after the houses and faces had failed to elicit a fear response.

Thus, it may be that rare phobias are learned on the basis of specific negative experiences; fear of, say, flashbulbs may stem from previous startle reactions to them. Other, more common fears may appear because people are biologically prepared to react negatively to certain things. We encountered this notion of preparedness earlier, in the chapter on learning. We saw there that people and animals quickly learn to avoid a certain food after its taste has been associated with nausea, but they may never develop an aversion to bright lights or unusual sounds that are paired with nausea just as many times. In other words, certain stimuli and certain responses appear to be especially easy to link.

It has been suggested that preparedness stems from thousands of years of experience with poison, fire, heights, snakes, insects, and other objects and situations that were dangerous to our prehistoric ancestors. Those who quickly learned to avoid these things were more likely to survive than those who did not (De Silva, Rachman & Seligman, 1977). Some research suggests that the preparedness effect may not be as strong as originally thought (Cook, Hodes & Lang, 1986; McNally, 1987; Zafiropoulou & McPherson, 1986), but it nonetheless remains an important phenomenon. ■

SOMATOFORM DISORDERS

Sometimes people show the symptoms of some physical (somatic) disorder, even though there is no physical cause. These are psychological problems that take the form of a somatic problem; thus, they are called **somatoform disorders.** The classic example is **conversion disorder,** a condition in which a person appears to be, but actually is not, blind, deaf, paralyzed, insensitive to pain in various parts of the body, or even pregnant. In Freud's day, this disorder was called *hysteria*. Conversion disorders are rare, accounting for only about 2 percent of psychiatric diagnoses (Stephens & Kamp, 1962). Although they can occur at any point in life, they usually appear in adolescence or early adulthood. Conversion disorders are different from true physical disabilities in several ways. First, they often help to reduce stress. An opera singer, for example, may develop laryngitis or go deaf just before a performance and thus avoid facing the audience. Second, the person may show remarkably little concern about what is apparently a rather serious problem. Finally, the symptoms may be organically impossible, as Figure 15.3 illustrates.

Can people displaying conversion disorder see and hear, even though they act as though they cannot? Experiments show that they can (Grosz & Zimmerman, 1970), but does this mean that the person is lying about the

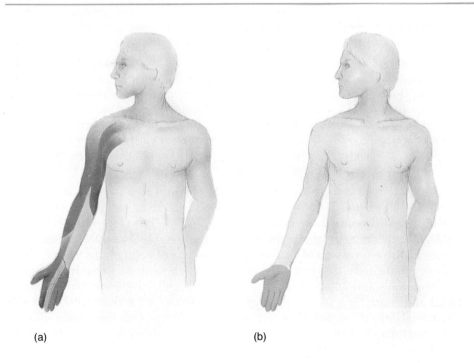

(a)   (b)

Figure 15.3
Glove Anesthesia
In this conversion disorder, the person's insensitivity stops abruptly at the wrist (b). But if the nerves shown here (a) were actually impaired, part of the arm would also lose sensitivity. Other neurologically impossible symptoms seen in conversion disorder include sleepwalking at night on legs that are "paralyzed" during the day.

problem? Possibly not. Research on attention and consciousness suggests that people can be influenced by information even though they may not be aware of it (Bargh, 1982; Nisbett & Wilson, 1977; Zajonc, 1980).

Another form of somatoform disorder is known as *hypochondriasis,* a strong fear of heart disease, cancer, or illness in general, which is usually accompanied by reports of many vague symptoms. People in this category are known as hypochondriacs. *Somatoform pain disorder* is characterized by severe, often constant pain, commonly in the neck, chest, or back, for which even elaborate tests can find no physical cause. The pain may become especially intense when the person faces stress, and it may prevent the person from engaging in certain activities (especially disliked activities).

Traditional explanations of somatoform disorders focus on conversion disorder. Freud believed that conversion disorder results when anxiety related to unconscious conflict is converted into physical symptoms. (This belief is, in fact, the source of the term *conversion disorder.*) In explaining somatoform disorders, behavioral as well as psychodynamic theorists point to the fact that somatoform disorders can produce benefits by relieving sufferers of unpleasant responsibilities. Genetic factors do not seem important in somatoform disorders.

DISSOCIATIVE DISORDERS

Dissociative disorders involve a sudden and usually temporary disruption in a person's memory, consciousness, or identity. In some cases, a person suddenly suffers a memory loss. This loss may include the person's name, home address, occupation, and all other identifying information. These are rare conditions, but tend to attract intense publicity when they occur.

The most famous and least commonly seen dissociative disorder is **multiple personality,** a condition in which a person reports having more than one identity, each of which speaks, acts, and writes in a very different way. Each personality seems to have its own memories, wishes, and (often conflicting) impulses. Some personalities may be aware of the existence of the others; some may not. Shifts among personalities are sudden, dramatic, and often stress related. Though commonly confused with schizophrenia (a more incapacitating disruption of thought and emotion), "split" or multiple personality is a very different disorder. Here is a famous case.

> "Eve White" was a shy, reserved housewife and mother who began complaining of headaches and blackouts. It soon became obvious that, during these blackouts, she became "Eve Black," a hard-drinking, promiscuous woman, who frequented the bar scene and was not very kind to her daughter. Since "Eve White" had no apparent knowledge of "Eve Black," she denied her husband's accusations of unfaithfulness and child neglect. Ultimately she was divorced. During psychiatric treatment, a third, far more balanced personality, known as "Jane," emerged and appeared to take over. (Sizemore & Pittillo, 1970)

Psychodynamic theorists see massive repression of unwanted impulses or memories as responsible for dissociative disorders. In multiple personality, this repression creates a "new person," who acts out taboo impulses. Phenomenological theorists might argue that an individual's multiple personalities represent the expression of dramatically conflicting perceptions of the world. Behavioral theorists suggest that everyone is capable of behaving in many different ways and learns to behave differently under different circumstances (loud and boisterous in a bar; quiet and respectful in a church). Under rare circumstances, these behavior patterns may become so discrepant that an individual may feel like and be seen by others as a different person from time to time (an extreme form of "not being oneself").

The apparently happy ending to the story of "Eve White's" multiple personality was marred in later years when the real patient in the case, Chris Sizemore, came forward to report on nineteen more personalities that had appeared during the twenty years since her therapy. Here, she shows paintings she completed while displaying some of these personalities. She apparently now maintains just one personality (Sizemore & Pittillo, 1970).

Some people displaying major depression sit quietly, weeping or staring off into space for hours; others cannot sit still and pace about, wringing their hands, pulling at their hair or clothing, perhaps wailing or shouting about their worthlessness.

MOOD DISORDERS

Everyone's emotional feelings, or *affect,* tend to rise and fall from time to time. But when people experience extremes of mood—wild elation or deep depression—for long periods, when they shift from one mood extreme to another, and especially when their moods are not consistent with the happy or sad events around them, they are said to show a **mood disorder** (also known as **affective disorder**). We will examine two main types.

Depressive Disorders

Depression plays a central role in many mood disorders and can range from occasional "down" periods to episodes severe enough to require hospitalization. A person suffering **major depression** feels sad and hopeless for weeks or months, often losing interest in all activities and taking pleasure in nothing. Feelings of inadequacy, worthlessness, or guilt are common. Everything, from conversation to bathing, is an unbearable, exhausting effort. Weight loss and lack of sleep or, in some cases, overeating and excessive sleep are frequent accompaniments, as are problems in concentrating, making decisions, and thinking clearly. In extreme cases, the person may express false beliefs, or **delusions,** worrying, for example, that the CIA is coming to mete out punishment for past sins. Major depression may come on suddenly or gradually. It may consist of a single episode or, more commonly, an irregular, sometimes lifelong pattern of depressive periods. Here is one example of a case of major depression.

> Mr. J was a fifty-one-year-old industrial engineer. . . . Since the death of his wife five years earlier, he had been suffering from continuing episodes of depression marked by extreme social withdrawal and occasional thoughts of suicide. . . . He lost all capacity for joy; . . . his gait was typically slow and labored, his voice usually tearful, his posture stooped. . . . His work record deteriorated markedly. . . . He was referred by his physician for psychotherapy after he had spent a week closeted in his home. (From Davison & Neale, 1982, p. 231)

Most cases of depression do not become this severe. A far more common pattern is **dysthymia,** in which the person shows the sad mood, lack of interest, and loss of pleasure associated with major depression, but to a lesser degree and for a shorter time. Mental and behavioral disruption may also be less severe.

Usually people exhibiting dysthymic disorder do not require hospitalization. Like major depression, however, dysthymic disorder may plague a person for years, either as a constant condition or in episodes lasting days or weeks. Some of these episodes may be very intense and can lead to suicide attempts.

For reasons that are not fully understood, about twice as many women as men appear to suffer from depression. Since depressive episodes often begin in response to stress, it should not be surprising that most college students, especially freshmen, experience some degree of severe depression from time to time (Bosse et al., 1975).

HIGHLIGHT

Suicide and Depression

At least 200,000 suicide attempts take place every year in the United States and Canada; about 26,000 succeed (Wekstein, 1979). These tragic events affect all socioeconomic groups, both sexes, every racial and cultural group, and any age group, from nine to ninety. Not all of these people are depressed, and not all depressed people attempt suicide, but the two problems are closely linked. Although the risk of suicide is about 1 percent during the year following a single depressive episode, it reaches about 15 percent during the lifetime of those who experience repeated episodes (Klerman, 1982). For this reason, people who suffer major depression or intense episodes of dysthymic disorder are often hospitalized as a preventive measure.

Virtually all of the factors related to depression are also associated with suicide. These include interpersonal crises, such as divorce; financial failure; sudden death in the family; intense feelings of frustration, anger, or self-hatred; and an absence of long-term or meaningful life goals (Farberow, Shneidman & Leonard, 1963; Paykel, Prusoff & Myers, 1975; Slater & Depue, 1981; Weissman, Fox & Klerman, 1973; Wekstein, 1979). Constant stress often leads to depression, so it is not surprising that those leading stress-filled lives show significantly higher suicide rates than the general population. Among students, the suicide rate increases dramatically at the beginning of each school year and at the end of each term (Klagsbrun, 1976). It also rises following the breakup of an engagement or other romantic relationship (Hendlin, 1975; Miller, 1975). About ten thousand college students try to kill themselves each year and about one thousand succeed. This rate is much higher than for the eighteen- to twenty-four-year-old noncollege population, but it is much lower than for the elderly, who often find themselves sick and alone (Blazer, Bacher & Manton, 1986).

Suicide attempts often reflect uncertainty about wanting to die. Only about 5 percent of all attempters appear truly intent on dying; they give little or no warning to others, and they choose such quick and lethal methods as shooting or hanging (Farberow & Litman, 1970). Most attempters (about 65 percent) do not actually want to die but use the suicide attempt to communicate a desperate "cry for help." Usually these individuals select relatively slow methods (nonlethal drug overdoses or minor wrist cuts, for example) and choose times and places that virtually guarantee that someone will arrive to save them. The remaining 30 percent are ambivalent; they face serious problems in life but still harbor hope that things will improve. They usually

"I TRIED TO COMMIT SUICIDE AND I KNOW HOW HELPLESS YOU CAN FEEL. SAMARITEENS CAN HELP. CALL AND TALK AND THEY'LL LISTEN. IT'S KIDS YOUR OWN AGE AND IT'S TOTALLY CONFIDENTIAL."

SAMARITEENS · 247-8050

HELP FOR TEENS CONSIDERING SUICIDE.

The suicide rate is increasing fastest among those who are fifteen to twenty-four years old. This includes not only college students but a growing number of troubled adolescents (Wells & Stuart, 1981). Familiarity with guidelines about who is most likely to make good on suicide threats is vital to those who staff suicide prevention hotlines.

use lethal, but slow methods (such as a drug overdose) and let fate decide whether or not they will survive.

One myth about suicide is that people who talk about it will never try it. On the contrary, those who say they are thinking of suicide are much more likely to try suicide than the general population. In fact, according to Edwin Shneidman (1987) 80 percent of suicides are preceded by some kind of warning, whether direct ("I think I'm going to kill myself") or vague ("Sometimes I wonder if life is worth living"). However, not everyone who threatens suicide follows through. Knowing who will and who will not attempt suicide is difficult, but here are some useful guidelines (Shneidman, 1973, 1985, 1987):

1. People who attempt suicide tend to be those in psychological pain, often stemming from frustration over an inability to meet needs on Maslow's hierarchy, ranging from basic physical necessities to security, love, and esteem (see Chapter 11).

2. Suicide attempts are often associated with a tendency to seek instant escape from difficult problems. This behavioral style may in turn stem from what George Kelly (Chapter 14) called personal constructs that limit one's perceptions of the world to black-and-white, either-or terms, with few options. Suicidal people see no option to pain but death.

3. Three times as many women attempt suicide as men, but three times as many men succeed.

4. Males who are forty-five to sixty years old, divorced, living alone, and with few family and friends are especially likely to attempt suicide.

5. Previous suicide attempts suggest that future attempts are more likely.

6. Suicide attempts among people prone to depression tend to occur either just after their energy returns following a bout of deep depression or while they are still depressed, but in a desperate, overactive state.

7. Suicide is more likely when the person has not only talked about dying but developed a plan and given away possessions. ∎

Bipolar Disorder

Bipolar disorder refers to the alternating appearance of two emotional poles, or extremes. We have already described one emotional pole: depression. The other is **mania,** which is an elated, very active emotional state. In bipolar disorder, mania usually alternates from day to day or even hour to hour with deep depression. This pattern has also been called *manic depression.* Compared with major depression, bipolar disorder is rare; it occurs in only about one person out of a hundred.

People in a manic state tend to be totally optimistic, boundlessly energetic, certain of having extraordinary powers and abilities, and bursting with all sorts of great, though nonsensical ideas. They may also become very irritated with anyone who tries to reason with them or "slow them down." Manic speech is rapid and jumps unpredictably from one topic to the next. During manic episodes, which may last from a few days to many weeks, the person may make impulsive and very unwise decisions. One man suddenly quit his job and spent all his savings on tropical fish equipment, which, he said, could be modified so the fish would never die.

Causes of Mood Disorders

Psychological theories Traditional psychodynamic theory suggests that depression is most likely to appear in people with especially strong dependency needs, needs that greatly exaggerate grief over, say, rejection or the death of a loved one. Further, because the lost loved one has become part of such a person's identity, the target of conscious or unconscious feelings of anger and resentment over being abandoned becomes the self. Thus, the feelings of worthlessness, guilt, and self-blame that are so common in depression are emotions that were meant for others but have been turned inward.

Other psychological theories about mood disorders are currently more influential. For example, the behavioral model also recognizes that people become depressed when they lose important rewards or reinforcements. Unemployment or the loss of a relationship brings not only natural feelings of depression, but also a consequent reduction in pleasant activities. This may lead in turn to more depression and to extra attention and sympathy from others, which can therefore maintain the problem by reinforcing it (Lewinsohn, 1974).

Reinforcement appears to be only part of the story, though; how people think about their world also seems important (Sweeney, Shaeffer & Golin, 1982). The cognitive-behavioral view (Beck, 1967, 1970) suggests that depressed people develop mental habits of (1) blaming themselves when things go wrong; (2) focusing on and exaggerating the dark side of events; and (3) jumping to overly generalized pessimistic conclusions. These cognitive habits constitute logical errors, which lead to very depressing thoughts and other signs of depression. Another cognitive-behavioral theory of depression is based on *learned helplessness*. You might recall our description of this phenomenon in the chapter on learning. When animals have no control over shock or other aversive events, they begin to appear depressed and become inactive.

Interestingly, people who learn this temporary helplessness in the laboratory deal with laboratory tasks in ways similar to truly depressed individuals (Hiroto & Seligman, 1975; Klein & Seligman, 1976). Thus, lack of control over one's life, especially over its rewards and stressors, may be an important factor in depression. The extent to which women have less control in their lives may help explain why more women than men become depressed (Radloff, 1975). But many people have limited control; why are they not depressed? Some researchers suggest that severe, long-lasting depression is far more likely in people who attribute their lack of control to some permanent, generalized lack of personal competence rather than to "the way things are" (Abramson, Seligman & Teasdale, 1978; Miller & Norman, 1979). Research on this and other promising cognitive-behavioral theories is continuing (Alloy & Ahrens, 1987; Metalsky, Halberstadt & Abramson, 1987).

Physiological theories   Cognitive-behavioral and physiological theories of mood disorders are linked by findings that, when animals become "helpless," they show changes in the neurotransmitters norepinephrine and serotonin. We mentioned, in the chapter on the biological bases of behavior, that these neurotransmitters are important in the regulation of moods. Abnormalities in the amount of norepinephrine, serotonin, or chemicals related to them have consistently been found in depressed people, and drugs that relieve depression modify the operation of synapses that use these neurotransmitters. Further, mania may be related to an excess of norepinephrine (Bunney, Goodwin & Murphy, 1972). The exact nature of the malfunction of these neurotransmitter systems is not yet known. The *dysregulation hypothesis* suggests that the adjustments in neurotransmitter levels that normally accompany variations in people's activity somehow go awry in depressed individuals (Siever & Davis, 1985).

People who suffer from major depression also differ from other people on a variety of biological variables. These biological markers of depression may suggest possible causes of depression or confirm a clinical diagnosis. For example, the control of the stress-related hormone cortisol is abnormal in about 70 percent of people diagnosed as major depressives (Carroll et al., 1981). A synthetic hormone that normally suppresses the secretion of cortisol does not work in depressed people. This suggests that depression involves, not just a maladaptive way of thinking about stressful events, but an abnormality in the biological systems that help people cope with stress.

The frequently cyclical nature of mood disorders also suggests an abnormality in basic biological rhythms. For example, a person with bipolar disorder might become depressed every six months, regardless of whether life is going well or not. Depressed people also tend to have trouble sleeping; in most cases, they wake up abnormally early. Thus, depression may be a consequence of improper coordination among various biological cycles (Wehr et al., 1983). Depressed people may feel the way they do, because according to their biological clocks, they are trying to function in the middle of the night. Animal studies have found that antidepressant drugs can shift these biological rhythms. And, in some human cases, depression has been relieved by "resetting" the biological rhythms through sleep deprivation or by changing the times of sleeping and awakening.

Whatever their primary physiological basis, there is strong evidence that mood disorders, especially bipolar disorder, may be inherited. One review of research with twins found that, if one member of a pair of identical twins developed bipolar disorder, 72 percent of the other members showed the same disorder. This happened in only 14 percent of nonidentical pairs (Allen, 1976). Other studies have found similar results (Egeland et al., 1987; Nurnberger & Gershon, 1984; Winder et al., 1986). The children of parents who show major depression are more likely to develop depression themselves, but because there may be several types of depression, each possibly caused by different factors, the evidence for its inheritability is not as strong as for bipolar disorder. The number and complexity of causal factors in mood disorders makes a diathesis-stress model—which recognizes the interaction of predispositions and life stresses—an especially appropriate guide for future research.

SCHIZOPHRENIA

The following letter arrived in the mail recently:

> Dear Sir:
>   I want to buy a good book of Psychology without any bad topics of the mind such as suicide. Unfortunately, I recently purchased a William James Psychology Book. But I found something in it bad and the man was related to a very bad group of people in London. Therefore, I terrestrialize of want to possess one that teaches of all the good things of the mind. After all and before good is what victorizes and is preeminated and is naturally given and willed before any bad. So will you please teach me of the best author of Psychology to buy so I am not betrayed as I was before. Please correspond to very truly yours.

The author of this letter would probably be diagnosed as schizophrenic. **Schizophrenia** is a pattern of severely disturbed thinking, emotion, perception, and behavior that constitutes one of the most serious and disabling of all mental disorders. It occurs in only about 1 percent of the population, in about equal numbers of men and women, and tends to appear in adolescence or early adulthood. Those labeled schizophrenic usually require hospitalization, sometimes for weeks or months, sometimes for many years. At any given time, this diagnostic group occupies about half the beds in mental hospitals and constitutes a large proportion of outpatients. In addition, about three or four million of these individuals are permanently unemployed and often unemployable.

Symptoms of Schizophrenia

Although the economic costs of schizophrenia run into billions of dollars (Gunderson & Mosher, 1975), the cost in human suffering is even greater because of the wide range of dysfunctions associated with the disorder. These include disorders in thinking, perception, attention, emotion, motor behavior, personal identity, motivation, and day-to-day functioning.

Disorders of thought   As illustrated in the Linkages box in Chapter 9, schizophrenics typically display disorders in both how they think (thought form) and what they think (thought content). The *form* of their thought is often incoherent. *Neologisms* ("new words" that have meaning only to the person speaking them) are common; *terrestrialize* is one of several examples in the letter at the beginning of this section. That letter also illustrates *loose associations,* the tendency for one thought to be logically unconnected or only superficially connected to the next. Sometimes the associations are based on double meanings or on the way words sound ("clang" associations). For example, "My true family name is Abel or A Bell. We descended from the

Disordered thoughts and perceptions are often reflected in the artistic creations of schizophrenics. Here is one example from the collection of Hans Prinzhorn, a German psychiatrist who studied such paintings early in this century.

clan of Abel, who originated the bell of rights, which we now call the bill of rights." In the most severe cases, thought becomes just a jumble of words known as *word salad*. For example,

> Upon the advisability of held keeping, environment of the seabeach gathering, to the forest stream, reinstatement to be placed, poling the paddleboat, of the swamp morass, to the forest compensation of the dunce. (Lehman, 1967, p. 627)

It is this apparent loosening or breaking of associative bonds among thoughts that prompted nineteenth-century psychiatrist Eugen Bleuler to coin the word *schizophrenia,* or "split mind" (see Neale, Oltmanns & Winters, 1983). Thus, contrary to popular belief, *schizophrenia* does not mean "split personality."

The *content* of schizophrenic thinking is equally disturbed, often including a bewildering variety of delusions. Delusions of persecution are among the most common. The person may think that the FBI or the Russian KGB is trying to harm him or her and may interpret everything from radio programs to people's gestures as part of the plot. Delusions that everything in the world is somehow related to oneself are called *ideas of reference*. Delusions of grandeur may also be present, as may several others. Examples include *thought broadcasting,* in which the person believes that his or her thoughts are being heard by others; *thought blocking* or *withdrawal,* which is the belief that someone is either preventing thoughts or "stealing" them as they appear; and *thought insertion,* which is the belief that other people's thoughts are appearing in one's mind. Some schizophrenics believe that, like a puppet, their behavior is being controlled by others.

Disorders of perception and attention   People labeled schizophrenic often report that they cannot focus their attention. They may also feel overwhelmed as they try to attend to everything at once. Various perceptual disorders may also appear. The person may feel detached from the real world; other people may appear to be flat, black-and-white cutouts. The body may feel like a machine, or parts of it may feel as if they are dead or rotting. About 75 percent of those diagnosed as schizophrenic report **hallucinations,** or false perceptions, usually of voices (Sartorius, Shapiro & Jablensky, 1974). Sometimes these voices talk directly to the person, urging the person to do or not to do things, commenting on or narrating the person's actions. Several voices may even be heard arguing about the person's strengths and weaknesses.

Disorders of emotion and movement   Unlike people suffering from mood disorders, people diagnosed as schizophrenic usually do not experience extreme emotions. In fact, they may experience a "flat" affect, showing little or no emotion even in the face of happy or sad events. Those who do display emotion often do so inappropriately, laughing while telling a sad story, crying for no apparent reason, or flying into a rage in response to a simple question. This lack of a coherent relationship between thoughts and feelings represents another way in which schizophrenia involves a kind of "split mind."

Some schizophrenics appear very agitated, ceaselessly moving their limbs, making facial grimaces, or pacing the floor in highly ritualistic sequences. Others become so withdrawn that they move very little.

Other schizophrenic symptoms   Lack of motivation and social skills, deteriorating personal hygiene, and an inability to function from day to day are other common characteristics of schizophrenia. The classic picture of the long-term, chronic schizophrenic includes lack of interest in anything, total preoccupation with an inner world (a condition known as *autism*), and loss of a sense of self. But not all persons labeled "schizophrenic" end up this way.

Types of Schizophrenia

DSM-III-R includes three main subtypes of schizophrenia, each with a particular syndrome of problems. These subtypes are known as *disorganized, catatonic,* and *paranoid schizophrenia.*

Disorganized schizophrenia   The main features of the **disorganized** subtype include a variety of jumbled and unrelated delusions and hallucinations. There may be incoherent speech and a consequent inability to communicate effectively. Strange facial grimaces and meaningless ritual movements are common. Affect is flat, though there may be inappropriate laughter or giggling. Personal hygiene is neglected, and the person may lose bowel and bladder control. Although many people think of this pattern when they think of schizophrenia, the disorganized type is rare, accounting for only about 5 percent of schizophrenia diagnoses.

Catatonic schizophrenia   The most significant characteristic of **catatonic schizophrenia** is movement disorder, in which the individual alternates between total immobility or stupor (sometimes holding bizarre, uncomfortable poses for long periods) and wild excitement. About 8 percent of schizophrenics fall into this subtype.

Paranoid schizophrenia   About half of all schizophrenics appear in the **paranoid** subtype. Its most prominent features are delusions of persecution or grandeur accompanied by anxiety, anger, superiority, argumentativeness, or jealousy. Sometimes these feelings lead to violence. Compared with the other subtypes, paranoid schizophrenia tends to appear later in life, typically

Especially during stupor, people who display catatonic schizophrenia may not speak, ignore all attempts at communication, and either become rigid or show a "waxy flexibility" that allows them to be "posed" in virtually any posture.

after the age of twenty-five or thirty, and there is much less impairment of affect and perception. In most cases, the person is able to complete an education, hold a job, and even have a family before problems become severe.

The Search for Causes

There is probably more research on the causes of schizophrenia than on any other form of behavior disorder. Though scientists are still far from their goal, one thing is certain: no single theory can adequately account for all forms of schizophrenia.

Biological factors   Schizophrenia may be due in part to problems in the brain, which, along with other causal factors, may be inherited (Faraone & Tsuang, 1985; Rosenthal, 1977). Schizophrenia certainly does seem to run in families. The children and siblings of people diagnosed as schizophrenic are, overall, about ten times more likely than other people to develop schizophrenia. Identical twins share schizophrenia more often than nonidentical twins, and children of schizophrenics who are adopted by normal parents still tend to display schizophrenia more often than the general population (Allen, Cohen & Pollin, 1972; Gottesman & Shields, 1972, 1976; Heston, 1966; Kety et al., 1975). Still, most people with schizophrenic relatives are not schizophrenic. What may be inherited is a *predisposition* toward schizophrenia (Meehl, 1962).

Part of this predisposition may have to do with biochemistry. A great deal of current research is focused on the possibility that the brain's neurotransmitters, especially dopamine, play a role in causing or at least intensifying schizophrenic thought and behavior. The dopamine hypothesis came about in part because drugs that are used to treat schizophrenia blunt the action of dopamine in the brain. In fact, there is a high positive correlation between the clinical effectiveness of these drugs and their ability to block dopamine receptors (Seeman & Lee, 1975). Some treated patients even show signs of Parkinsonism, a nervous disorder related to the presence of too little dopamine. Furthermore (as described in Chapter 6), both schizophrenialike symptoms and the stimulation of dopamine systems in the brain have been tied to heavy amphetamine use (Snyder, 1978). Indeed, giving schizophrenics amphetamines makes their problems worse (Angrist, Lee & Gershon, 1974). It has thus been suggested that excess dopamine or oversensitivity to dopamine may be responsible either for some forms of schizophrenia or for the intensity of their symptoms (Davis, 1978; Meltzer & Stahl, 1976).

Data from autopsies, X rays, and computer-assisted tomography (CT scans) have spawned biological theories that suggest a relationship between schizophrenia and other brain abnormalities. These abnormalities may involve a shrinking or deterioration of cells in the cerebral cortex or cerebellum; enlargement of the ventricles (fluid-filled cavities deep in the brain); disorganization of cells in the hippocampus (an area involved with the expression of emotion), as Figure 15.4 (p. 570) shows; or other physical anomalies (Andreasen et al., 1982; Colon, 1972; Golden et al., 1981; Luchins, Pollin & Wyatt, 1980). Of course, not all schizophrenics display these problems—and some normal people do. But the relevance of brain disorders for schizophrenia is supported by evidence that the specific nature of the brain abnormality may be related to the person's symptoms. Some researchers have found that, among people labeled schizophrenic, those with abnormal brain structures tend to show passive or "negative" symptoms, such as reduced affect, apathy, and withdrawal; those with more normal-looking brains tend to show more active or "positive" symptoms, including hallucinations and delusions (Crow, 1980).

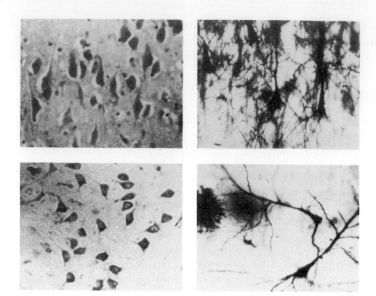

Figure 15.4
Brain Abnormalities and Schizophrenia
*Orderly pyramidal cells in the hippocampus
of a normal brain (top) are contrasted in
these microscope photographs with the disorganized cells from the brain of a person
diagnosed as schizophrenic. Such anomalies have been implicated in the appearance
of certain schizophrenic symptoms.*
(Kovelman and Scheibel)

Other research has suggested that schizophrenia may also be associated with reduced blood flow in certain parts of the brain, especially the frontal lobes (Buchsbaum et al., 1982). Reduced blood flow is usually a consequence of reduced neural activity in the region. Evidence suggesting abnormalities in *brain lateralization,* the pattern of dominance of one cerebral hemisphere over the other, has also been reported, especially in the way the hemispheres communicate with one another and in the activity of the left hemisphere (Newlin, Carpenter & Golden, 1981). Firm conclusions about the meaning of all of these correlations await further research (Seidman, 1983).

Psychological factors   Several psychological and social factors have been proposed as completing part of the causal puzzle in schizophrenia. Psycho-dynamic theorists suggest that schizophrenic symptoms may be generated by anxiety that stems from the threat of expressing or becoming aware of unacceptable unconscious impulses. The person labeled schizophrenic re-sponds to this anxiety by going symbolically backward to an easier time or inward to a less threatening private world. Lack of strong research support for this view has focused more attention on other psychological theories.

For example, behavioral theories suggest that the problematic thoughts and behaviors of people labeled as schizophrenic reflect their learned, though maladaptive, way of trying to cope with anxiety (Mednick, 1958, 1970). Problems may also stem from patterns of reinforcement and punishment early in life: unfortunate learning experiences may have extinguished the normal process of attention and behavioral development and at the same time inadvertently rewarded maladaptive behaviors and thoughts (Ullmann & Krasner, 1975). Though far from conclusive, evidence in favor of this view comes from many studies that show that some schizophrenic behaviors can be reduced or eliminated by ignoring them, while systematically rewarding more adaptive alternatives (Paul & Lentz, 1977). Such "token economy" programs are described in the chapter on therapy.

Since the experiences that are thought to lead to schizophrenia seem to occur in childhood, some researchers have looked for the psychological origins of the disorder in the structure of and interactions in the families of schizophrenics. These theories have focused especially on the potentially damaging effects of conflict, coldness, and poor communication in the family, but research has so far failed to clarify just which family conditions might cause schizophrenia and how. For example, in a wildly disturbed family, only one child out of several may be affected. And the same conditions associated with schizophrenia in one person's family background may be associated with other, less severe disorders or no disorder at all in someone else's history (Davison & Neale, 1986). This brings us back to the diathesis-stress approach, which presently seems best able to handle all the perspectives on the problem.

Paul Meehl (1962) proposed that schizophrenics inherit a neurological or biochemical *predisposition* for schizophrenia. Under normal stress, such individuals may show only unusual personality characteristics, such as shyness or odd dress. But under severe stress, these people (and only these people) will become schizophrenic. This "all-or-nothing" notion of an inherited diathesis was subsequently expanded into the **vulnerability model** of schizophrenia (Zubin & Spring, 1977). This model suggests that (1) different people have differing degrees of vulnerability to schizophrenia; (2) this vulnerability may not be entirely inherited; and (3) it may involve psychological components, such as a history of poor parenting, as well as biological components, such as a highly reactive autonomic nervous system. According to this vulnerability model, many different blendings of vulnerability and stress can lead to schizophrenia, as Figure 15.5 illustrates.

Can knowledge of the particular blend in an individual allow for an accurate prediction of his or her becoming schizophrenic? This is just one of the research questions whose answers will ultimately strengthen the vulnerability model or lead in other directions.

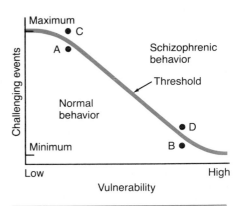

Figure 15.5
The Vulnerability Model of Schizophrenia
In this model, a person can cross the threshold into schizophrenia by having a very strong predisposition for it and very little stress (point D); by having only a weak predisposition, but a great deal of stress (point C); or any other sufficiently potent combination.
(From J. Zubin and B. Spring, 1977. "A New View of Schizophrenia," *Journal of Abnormal Psychology,* 86, pp. 103–126. Copyright 1977 by the American Psychological Association. Adapted by permission of the publisher and author.)

PSYCHOACTIVE SUBSTANCE-USE DISORDERS

When people use psychoactive drugs for months or years in ways that harm themselves or others, they are said to show a **psychoactive substance-use disorder.** The substances most often involved include alcohol and other depressants, such as barbiturates and quaaludes; opiates, such as heroin; stimulants, such as cocaine or amphetamines; and psychedelics, such as cannabis. We described these drugs and their impact on consciousness in Chapter 6; here we are interested in their broader effects and what causes people to use them.

As noted in Chapter 6, one effect of the use of some substances, including alcohol, heroin, and amphetamines, is **addiction,** or a physical need for the substance. In DSM-III-R, addiction is called *dependence.* Usually, addiction is evident when the person begins to need more and more of a substance to achieve the desired state; this is called *building a tolerance.* If an addicted person stops using the substance, he or she experiences painful, often terrifying, *withdrawal symptoms,* as the body tries to readjust to a substance-free state. Even when use of a drug does not create physical addiction, some users may overuse, or *abuse,* it because it gives them self-confidence, enjoyment, or relief from tension. Thus, people can become *psychologically* dependent on psychoactive substances, but not addicted to them.

Psychoactive substance abuse or dependence causes many serious problems. The physical consequences are associated either with the intoxicating (poisoning) effects of the substance or with the dangerous effects of withdrawal. For example, prolonged overuse of alcohol can result in life-threatening liver damage, vitamin deficiencies that can lead to an irreversible brain disorder called *Korsakoff's psychosis,* and a host of other physical ailments. Similarly, the process of withdrawal from barbiturates can be so physically stressful as to end in death.

The psychological, social, and occupational problems attributable to psychoactive substance abuse or dependency are hardly less severe. The person may become so preoccupied with getting and using the substance that family relationships and job obligations are neglected or ignored. Family violence is common around those who become physically or psychologically dependent on drugs. So is unemployment, which, combined with the high cost of illegal drugs, frequently leads to criminal acts aimed at supporting the habit. The yearly cost to society is over $100 billion. Consider just a few of the most serious problems that come under the heading of psychoactive substance-use disorders.

Alcoholism

Over 100 million Americans drink alcohol on a regular basis, usually without serious consequences. But about 12 million have developed **alcoholism,** a pattern of continuous or intermittent drinking that may lead to addiction and almost always causes severe social, physical, and other problems. Alcoholism or alcohol abuse have been implicated in half of all the traffic fatalities, homicides, and suicides that occur each year and also figure prominently in rape and child abuse (Mayer, 1983; Alcohol and Health Report, 1984).

Alcoholism usually begins with social drinking, which gradually changes over a period of years into a very different and far more problematic pattern, as Table 15.4 describes. In most cases, alcoholism tends to stabilize into one of three patterns identified by Elvin Jellinek (1960): (1) regular daily drinking of large amounts of alcohol; (2) regular heavy drinking on weekends only; or (3) binges of heavy drinking for weeks or months at a time, separated by long periods of sobriety. Addicted alcoholics continue to drink because they physically need alcohol. Not drinking can be painful, sometimes causing frightening hallucinations known as *delirium tremens,* or *DTs.*

Causes of alcoholism   Tragically, the roots of alcoholism are still largely unknown. Psychoanalytic theories suggest that alcoholism represents unfulfilled oral needs (a desire to literally return to the bottle). These theories have enjoyed relatively little research support and are less influential than other approaches.

One of these approaches is a behavioral theory suggesting that people learn to use alcohol because it helps them cope with stressors and reduce

TABLE 15.4

Social Drinking Versus Alcoholism
Social drinking patterns differ markedly from those of alcoholics, yet social drinking can easily evolve into alcoholism.

Social Drinkers	Alcoholics
Usually drink in moderation and can control the amount they consume	Drink increasing quantities, often reaching an amazing capacity to drink more than other people. Sometimes drink until blacking out. May not remember events that occur while drinking
Usually drink to enhance the pleasure of social situations	Drink for the chemical effect, often to relieve tension or face problems; often drink alone, including in the morning to reduce hangover or to face the day
Do not usually think about or talk about drinking in nondrinking situations	Become preoccupied with getting their next drink, often sneaking drinks during working hours or at home
Do not experience physical, social, or occupational problems caused by their drinking	Suffer physical disorders, damaged social relationships, and impaired capacity to work because of drinking

Contrary to popular belief, only a small proportion of alcoholics are "skid row bums"; the rest are found throughout the population, including an increasing proportion of women and teenagers (Becker & Kronus, 1977).

emotional stress reactions. Use becomes abuse, often addiction, if drinking is a person's main coping strategy. The stress-reduction theory of alcoholism has been supported by studies showing that alcohol can reduce animals' learned fear of a particular location and that animals in a stressful conflict situation will choose to drink alcohol if it is available (Conger, 1951; Freed, 1971). The stress-reducing effects of alcohol have also been demonstrated in humans (Sher & Levenson, 1982).

The importance of learning is suggested by evidence that alcoholism is more common in ethnic and cultural groups (such as the Irish and English) where frequent drinking tends to be socially reinforced than in groups like Jews, Italians, and Chinese, where all but moderate drinking tends to be discouraged (Frankel & Whitehead, 1981). Learning would also help explain why alcoholism is higher among people working as bartenders, cocktail servers, and other jobs where alcohol is available and drinking is socially reinforced, even expected (Fillmore & Caetano, 1980).

But alcoholism also appears to run in families, especially among males. The sons of alcoholics are more likely than others to become alcoholics themselves; if the sons are identical twins, both are at increased risk for alcoholism, even when they are raised apart (Goodwin, Crane & Guze, 1973). Data like these suggest that alcoholism may be due in part to an inherited predisposition of some kind, perhaps a greater ability to tolerate alcohol's short-term physical effects (Goodwin, 1979; Schuckit, 1983). It is easy to see how a diathesis of this kind could interact with cultural traditions and other learning factors to create alcoholism, especially in those who have stressful lives. Still, the fact that many alcoholics do not fit this neat picture makes it painfully obvious that there is much that remains to be learned about the causes of alcoholism.

Heroin and Cocaine Dependence

Heroin is a highly addictive illegal drug that produces a pleasurable reaction, or "rush." Like alcoholics, heroin addicts suffer a variety of health problems, as a result of the drug itself and the poor eating habits it engenders. Further, the danger of death from an overdose, contaminated drugs, or AIDS (acquired immune deficiency syndrome; contracted through blood in shared needles) is always present.

Cocaine is a stimulant whose pleasurable effects include a feeling of self-confidence, well-being, and optimism. Continued use or overdoses of cocaine can cause serious problems ranging from nausea and hyperactivity to paranoid thinking, sudden depressive "crashes," and even death. An estimated one million Americans have become dependent on cocaine. Because it is a "luxury drug" (selling for over $2,000 per ounce), cocaine has become particularly popular among middle- to upper-income groups.

Addiction to drugs like heroin is largely a biological process. The causes of initial abuse are even less well established than the reasons for alcohol abuse, but the problem does not seem to be inherited. Psychological factors, such as the need to reduce stress, emulation of drug-using peers, thrill seeking, and social maladjustment, have all been suggested. The desire to gain social status appears to be partially responsible for the fact that the use and abuse of cocaine have increased in recent years. Research has not yet established why drugs become a problem for some people and not for others.

SEXUAL DISORDERS

As noted in Table 15.2, **sexual disorders** include *sexual dysfunction,* in which one's sexual activity is unsatisfactory for some reason, and **paraphilias,** in which a person's sexual interest is directed toward stimuli that are culturally or legally defined as inappropriate. The most common sexual dysfunctions, including difficulty in becoming aroused or reaching orgasm and (in males) reaching orgasm too quickly, are covered in Chapter 11 on motivation. Accordingly, our discussion here focuses on paraphilias.

People displaying paraphilias have recurrent sexual fantasies and strong sexual urges that involve nonhuman objects (such as women's shoes or purses), children or other nonconsenting partners, and the infliction of suffering or humiliation on oneself or one's sexual partner. These people are usually males. Whether or not they act on their urges, they are usually very distressed by them and the fantasies related to them. In many cases, the person is unable to become sexually aroused or to reach orgasm without these stimuli or without having fantasies about them. The most common paraphilias are listed in Table 15.5.

Though relatively rare, paraphilias are of great concern, not because people find particular stimuli to be sexually arousing, but because, by acting on their sexual urges, these people coerce or abuse others (especially children), invade other people's privacy, or display their sexuality in public places. From a practical perspective, individuals who comfortably engage in paraphilia-driven sexual activities in private or with consenting partners might not be considered abnormal. However, a valuative perspective would consider paraphilias abnormal no matter how or where they appear.

PERSONALITY DISORDERS

People labeled as having personality disorders are more disturbing than disturbed. **Personality disorders** are, to put it simply, long-standing ways of behaving that are not so much severe mental disorders as styles of life, which, from childhood or adolescence, create problems, usually for others (Millon, 1981). We will consider two examples.

This collection of stolen shoes was recovered from a man in Seattle, Washington, whose paraphilia involved using them in his solitary sexual activities.

Pedophilia	Adult sexual gratification through sexual contact with children under the age of thirteen.
Exhibitionism	Achieving sexual arousal through exposing one's genitals to unsuspecting strangers in public.
Sexual sadism	Gaining sexual pleasure from inflicting real or simulated physical pain or psychological distress on another person. Beatings, bondage, and humiliation are often involved.
Sexual masochism	Gaining sexual pleasure from being the victim of the physical or psychological abuse described in sexual sadism.
Voyeurism	Achieving sexual arousal and orgasm by watching unsuspecting persons who are naked, undressing, or engaging in sexual activity. The voyeur often tries to look in the windows of private homes.
Fetishism	Using inanimate objects such as women's shoes, purses, and undergarments to achieve sexual arousal and gratification. The person may wear the items or merely use them as aids in masturbation.
Frotteurism	Achieving sexual arousal and orgasm from touching or rubbing against unsuspecting people in elevators, buses, or other (usually crowded) public places.

TABLE 15.5

Some Typical Paraphilias
According to DSM-III-R, in order to be diagnosed as a paraphilia, a person's distressing sexual fantasies or inappropriate sexual acts must have taken place repeatedly for a period of at least six months.

Narcissistic Personality Disorder

The main characteristic of **narcissistic personality disorder** is an exaggerated sense of self-importance. People who earn this label act as though they are very special, even unique, and deserving of extraordinary privileges and consideration. They are often flamboyant, constantly need to be the center of attention, and tend to wildly overestimate their abilities and achievements. These individuals commonly want to be seen with the "right people," but actually have few, if any, real friends. They are filled with self-doubt, as evidenced by an extreme sensitivity to criticism or emotional hurt.

Antisocial Personality Disorder

From the perspective of public safety and security, the most serious personality disorder is the **antisocial personality.** The main problem here is a long-term, persistent pattern of impulsive, selfish, unscrupulous, even criminal, behavior. In the nineteenth century, the pattern was called *moral insanity*, because such a person appears to have no morals or common decency; more recently, people in this category have been called *psychopaths* or *sociopaths*. Males displaying antisocial personality outnumber females three to one.

At their least troublesome, these people are an inconvenience. They borrow money and fail to return it, they lie, and they "con" others into doing things for them. In fact, they are expert at taking advantage of the decency and trust of others, in order to reach selfish goals. A hallmark of those displaying antisocial personalities is a lack of remorse or guilt, whether they have wrecked a borrowed car, ruined a family's finances, or killed an innocent person. The following list, based on Hervey Cleckley's (1976) summary of classic antisocial personality characteristics, captures the essence of the disorder: (1) considerable superficial charm; (2) average or above average intelligence; (3) absence of anxiety; (4) considerable poise, calmness, and verbal skill (a "good talker"); (5) unreliability and no sense of responsibility; (6) untruthfulness and insincerity; (7) lack of guilt or shame; (8) complete self-centeredness; (9) absence of any real or deep feelings, including love; and (10) an impulsive, disorganized, and ultimately self-defeating lifestyle that does not change in spite of repeated punishment. Philip L, whose story appears at the beginning of this chapter, is a case in point. Philip's behavior stopped short of crime, but many psychopaths are not so restrained. The senseless crime sprees documented in Truman Capote's *In Cold Blood* and Norman Mailer's *The Executioner's Song* represent the antisocial personality at its worst. There are presently no successful methods for permanently altering the behavior of people with antisocial personalities. Those who commit crimes often end up in prison. Whether incarcerated or not, however, they seem to become less active and dangerous as they reach middle age.

What causes antisocial personality? There are numerous theories. Research on biological factors has found these people to be less sensitive than normals to electric shock and other punishments and to display an unusually low level of emotional arousal (Eysenck, 1960; Fenz, 1971; Newman & Kosson, 1986). These findings, along with the appearance of abnormal brain wave patterns in some cases, have been used to account for the irresponsibility, impulsiveness, thrill seeking, and lack of anxiety and guilt associated with the disorder (Hare, 1970). From psychological and social perspectives, broken homes, rejection by parents, lack of good parental models, conflict-filled childhoods, and living in poverty have all been suggested as contributing to the problem. But all of these biological and psychosocial factors also appear in the backgrounds of people who do not develop antisocial personalities, so the causal picture is still cloudy.

ORGANIC MENTAL DISORDERS

The causes of most of the abnormal behavior discussed so far are, as we have noted, unknown, poorly understood, or debatable. However, there are other forms of abnormality that have a clearly biological basis. These are the **organic mental disorders;** they include such symptoms as delirium and dementia.

Delirium is a clouded state of consciousness. The delirious person has trouble "thinking straight," may be unable to focus on a conversation or other environmental events, and may appear confused. The normal sleep-waking cycle may be disturbed, such that the individual may fall asleep in the middle of a sentence or stay up all night muttering incoherently. Delusions and hallucinations sometimes occur. Depending on the cause of the problem, delirium may come and go in episodes or become a permanent condition.

Dementia is mainly a loss of intellectual functions; it may occur alone or in combination with delirium. The most common symptoms involve loss of memory-related functions. In mild cases, this involves such minor errors as leaving the television on or the water running. In severe cases, such as Alzheimer's disease, the person may eventually become unable to recognize family members or give his or her own name, address, or occupation. The learning of new information may be as difficult as recalling old facts. Judgment and impulse control may also be affected; a perfectly respectable person may suddenly begin propositioning strangers or committing petty crimes. Personal hygiene and appearance may be neglected, and new or exaggerated personality traits, such as withdrawal, irritability, or paranoia, may become prominent. Like delirium, dementia can have a variable course, occurring in episodes of varying length or becoming progressively worse until it is ever-present.

Most often, delirium and dementia are associated with the elderly, but these symptoms can appear at any age. They are brought on mainly by (1) physical deterioration of the brain due to aging or disease, or (2) intoxication by or withdrawal from alcohol or the other drugs and toxins mentioned in our discussion of psychoactive substance-use disorders.

MENTAL ILLNESS IN SOCIETY

As promised, we have reviewed some of the main forms of abnormal behavior. Before concluding, it is important to put abnormal psychology into perspective by considering two important social issues.

Does Mental Illness Exist?

In the case of organic mental disorders, the concept of mental illness seems perfectly appropriate. But what about the majority of behavior disorders, for which no clear physical basis has been found? Should those who display such disorders be called "sick"? Traditionalists in psychiatry and psychology say yes, either because a physical cause is suspected or because these disorders are like physical illness. But critics say no. Prominent among these is psychiatrist Thomas Szasz (pronounced "zaws"), who believes that the concept of mental illness is not only inappropriate but harmful. Szasz prefers to think of the disorders listed in the DSM as "problems in living." He first spelled out his objections in an influential 1960 article called "The Myth of Mental Illness." Here is a summary of the arguments against the concept of mental illness presented by Szasz and like-minded critics (Bandura, 1969; Rogers, 1961; Ullmann & Krasner, 1969).

1. Calling a person "sick" when he or she has problems in living puts that person in the inferior, passive role of being a patient, a role in which the person may no longer be treated as a responsible adult.

2. When the concept of mental illness is applied, a kind of psychiatric tyranny may result, in which people who displease those in authority can

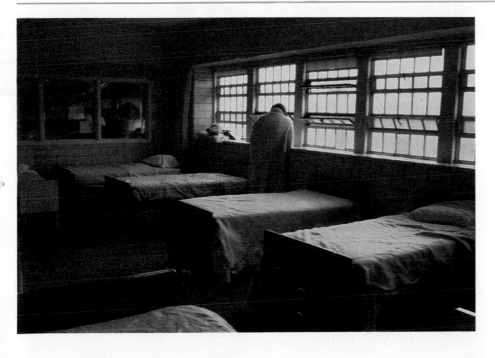

Thomas Szasz and others blame the concept of mental illness for encouraging the use of drugs and hospitalization to try solving problems in living that may have nothing to do with physical illness. This approach, they say, can result in an atmosphere of hopelessness while patients wait passively for a "cure."

ABNORMAL PSYCHOLOGY AND HUMAN DEVELOPMENT
What Kinds of Mental Disorders Appear in the Early Stages of Life?

As we saw in Chapter 2, childhood is a period that, in our culture, is associated with special privileges and a relative lack of responsibility, but it is also a period of rapid physical, cognitive, emotional, and social changes. These changes and the stress associated with them can create or enhance disorders in children. Stress can do the same in adults, especially among those who are biologically predisposed toward disorder or who must deal with particularly demanding circumstances. But childhood disorders are not just miniature versions of adult psychopathology. Indeed, the facts that children's mental, physical, and behavioral development is still incomplete and that their capacity to cope with stress is not at full strength means that they may be vulnerable to several special types of disorders, of which we will be able to discuss only a few. As shown in Table 15.2, DSM-III-R lists these disorders in two places: on Axis I, as disorders usually first seen in infancy or childhood, and as developmental disorders on Axis II. One of the latter, mental retardation, was described in the chapter on mental abilities.

Another very severe and puzzling developmental disorder, known as *infantile autism,* is usually identified within the first thirty months of life. The autistic baby shows no sign of attachment to the mother, the father, or anyone else. There is none of the smiling, laughing, and eye contact with parents that characterize normal infants. Nor will autistic infants tolerate being held and cuddled; they prefer to remain in a world of their own. As years go by, they ignore others and instead engage in repetitive rocking or endless play with ashtrays, keys, or other inanimate objects. Language development is seriously disrupted in these children; half never learn to speak at all. Those who do speak show such abnormalities as *echolalia,* the mere repetition of what they hear. Autism is rare, occurring in fewer than five children per ten thousand births, but with rare exceptions (Lovaas, 1987), it leads to a life of marginal adjustment, often within an institution.

The causes of autism remain largely unknown. Parents' emotional coldness (Bettelheim, 1967) or lack of attention (Ferster, 1961) were once thought to be prime ingredients, but these characteristics are not always present (Cox et al., 1975). Possible biological roots of autism include oversensitivity to stimulation (Zentall & Zentall, 1983) or abnormally high levels of natural opiates (similar to the endorphins discussed in Chapter 4), which may make autistic children less needful of comfort and other social interaction (Herman et al., 1986). Other research suggests that autistic children may have problems with cell communication in the brain's language areas (Minshew, Payton & Sclabassi, 1986).

Many of the other childhood disorders listed in DSM-III-R involve too little or too much control over behavior (Davison & Neale, 1986). Lack of control in many grade school and high school students, especially boys, shows up in *conduct disorders* characterized by aggression, disobedience, destructiveness, and other obnoxious behaviors. Often these behaviors involve criminal activity. There

be called sick and then either discredited or conveniently deposited in mental hospitals.

3. The patient role inhibits people from trying to improve, because they are expected simply to follow a doctor's orders and wait for a cure.

4. Calling a disorder a "mental illness" implies that only medical doctors are qualified to deal with it. But experience has shown that psychologists and other professional and nonprofessional helpers can play a beneficial role in treating behavior disorders.

5. A person who is called mentally ill bears a social stigma. Others may fear or avoid social contact, hesitate to offer a job, and in general fail to provide the support the person needs to function adequately.

may be a genetic predisposition for conduct disorders (Eysenck, 1975), but it is also clear that something goes seriously wrong with these children's moral development (Herbert, 1982).

Another form of undercontrol is evident in *attention deficit disorder (ADD)*. This label is given to children who show an inability to concentrate on a task or activity as well as other children their age. Many of these children are also labeled *hyperactive,* because they appear far less able than their agemates to sit still or otherwise control their physical activity. Their immaturity and astonishing ability to annoy and exhaust those around them creates numerous problems, especially at school. As many as 9 percent of elementary school boys and 3 percent of girls may be hyperactive (Miller, Palkes & Stewart, 1973). The problem often moderates or disappears by young adulthood, but some formerly hyperactive males continue to show problems in social adjustment (Wallander & Hubert, 1985). Genetic predisposition, the occurrence of brain damage or poisoning, and overly harsh parenting have all been proposed as possible causes of hyperactivity, but the jury is still out on just what role each of these factors may play

At the other extreme are children whose problems involve overcontrol, especially anxiety and social withdrawal. In *separation anxiety disorder,* for example, the child worries incessantly that either some harm may come to a parent (usually the mother) or that he or she will be lost, kidnapped, or injured. As a result, the child clings desperately to the parent and becomes emotionally upset or physically ill at the prospect of even temporary separation. This anxiety may prevent the child from sleeping alone, going to school, or developing normal friendships and play patterns. Though most childhood anxieties tend to disappear with the onset of adolescence, others, especially those involving physical injury or danger, may develop at about that time (Bauer, 1976). One out of every two hundred adolescent females (and about one of every four thousand males) may also develop a fear of becoming overweight that may lead to anorexia nervosa or bulimia; these eating disorders were described in the chapter on motivation (Crisp, Palmer & Klucy, 1976).

Disorders of childhood and adolescence differ from adult disorders not only because of their characteristic patterns of maladaptive behavior, but also because their early onset renders them especially capable of disrupting subsequent development. To take but one example, children whose speech problems or fear of school causes shyness or spotty attendance may not only fall behind academically but also fail to form the relationships with peers that promote normal social development. Some of these children may never recover from or compensate for this deficit and thus live a life filled with conflict and isolation. For some, the long-term result may be the appearance of more serious adult forms of mental disorder.

6. It is too easy to give up trying to help people if they are afflicted with a "mental illness" that has a poor prognosis. More aggressive and systematic treatment may occur if one believes that improvement is possible.

These objections have stimulated a great deal of debate. One result is that, during the last twenty-five years, there has been a shift toward a broad view that recognizes the value of nonmedical concepts of abnormal behavior. The controversy has also highlighted other implications of calling people mentally ill. If they are indeed "sick" mentally, can we trust them to vote or make choices about their own treatment? And are they really responsible for their own behavior? These important questions have legal as well as personal implications.

Behavior Disorder and Criminal Responsibility

If a person is "mentally ill," should he or she be prosecuted or punished for criminal behavior? Consider the following case:

> Cheryl was barely twenty when she married Glen, a graduate student in biology. They moved into a large apartment complex near the university and within three years had two sons. Cheryl's friends had always been impressed by the attention and affection she showered on her boys; she seemed to be the ideal mother. She and Glen had serious marital problems, however, and she felt trapped and unhappy. One day Glen came home to find that Cheryl had stabbed both children to death. At her murder trial, she was found not guilty by reason of insanity and was placed in a state mental institution.

In most states the law says that mental illness can protect a person from prosecution or punishment for a crime. First of all, one cannot be prosecuted unless one is both physically and mentally present. If a defendant is found to be too mentally disturbed to understand the charges or to assist in the preparation of a defense, he or she can be declared incompetent to stand trial. In some cases, such as Cheryl's, the defendant is initially declared incompetent but, after some time in a mental institution, recovers sufficiently to stand trial. In other cases, the court may decide that the defendant might never be competent to go to trial, and he or she is usually committed, in civil court, to a mental institution. This is happening less frequently, however, because competency rules are being relaxed somewhat. For example, a person for whom drugs can produce temporary mental competence may often go to trial instead of being sent for years, untried, to a hospital.

Second, once in court, a person can be found not guilty by reason of insanity if, at the time of the crime, mental illness prevented him or her from (1) understanding that the act was wrong or (2) resisting the impulse to do wrong. These criteria are based on several important court decisions. The concept of irresistible impulse was first used successfully as a defense against a murder charge in Ohio in 1834. In England in 1843, a man named Daniel M'Naghten, on hearing "instructions from God," tried to kill Prime Minister Robert Peel. He was found not guilty by reason of insanity and put in a mental institution for life. The principle behind this decision was that M'Naghten's mental condition made him unable to understand what he was doing or know that it was wrong. This test of knowing right from wrong became known as the *M'Naghten rule.*

The laws of most states now follow rules governing the insanity plea that were set forth by the American Law Institute (ALI) in 1962. The most important of these rules states that "a person is not responsible for criminal conduct if at the time of such conduct as a result of mental disease or defect he lacks substantial capacity either to appreciate the criminality (wrongfulness) of his conduct or to conform his conduct to the requirements of law" (American Law Institute, 1962, p. 66). This was Cheryl's defense, and the court agreed. In such cases, if the defendant is still considered insane, he or she is required to receive treatment, usually through commitment to a hospital, until cured or no longer dangerous. But if by the time of the trial the person is judged free of mental illness, he or she can be released—a rare event.

The ALI guidelines were designed to protect the mentally ill, especially from being punished as criminals. But that, according to Szasz and other critics, is precisely the problem. From their point of view, there is no such thing as mental illness, so people should not be allowed to escape responsibility for their crimes. Whether one entirely agrees with Szasz or not, there are other significant problems with the insanity defense. The most important of these is that psychological and psychiatric experts called by both defense and prosecution often give conflicting testimony about the defendant's sanity at the time of the crime. (In Cheryl's case, one expert said she was sane, and the other concluded she was insane.) The jury is left in the almost impossible position, as nonexperts, of deciding which expert to believe. A second major problem is that, even if a person is found not guilty by reason of insanity, he or she may end up spending more time in a mental hospital awaiting cure than if he or she had entered a guilty plea. In some cases, this result may be fortunate; in others, a miscarriage of justice.

What can be done about these problems? Some have suggested abolishing the insanity defense, but that appears unlikely. In many states, a new verdict, *guilty but mentally ill,* can be rendered. This verdict allows the jury simply to say whether the person committed a crime and leaves to the judge, with expert help, the task of choosing whether to imprison or commit the defendant. Unfortunately, this may merely put the judge instead of the jury in a confused position. Finally, some states have changed their insanity laws to require the *defendant* to prove that he or she was insane at the time of the crime, rather than requiring the prosecution to prove that the defendant was sane. In short, no generally satisfactory solution has yet been found; the wisdom or folly of the insanity defense continues to be argued case by case.

FUTURE DIRECTIONS

It should be clear by now that there have been many different ideas over the years about what constitutes abnormality and that even today the criteria for calling someone "crazy" differ greatly from one culture or subculture to the next. During the last twenty-five years, mental health professionals have become increasingly sensitive to the relative nature of abnormality and to the value of a practical approach. Future editions of the DSM, for example, are likely to continue the current trend toward basing diagnoses on both what a person does and where and when it is done.

Another trend in the categorization and labeling of abnormality is the development of more specific diagnostic criteria. This trend is already evident in the evolution of the DSM. Each edition specifies more clearly than the one before the rules to be followed in placing people in various categories. This has made it easier for different diagnosticians to agree than it was in years past, and as the rules become clearer, reliability is likely to increase even further. Yet, concerns remain over the validity of DSM diagnoses, especially for predicting behavior. Indeed, while the American Psychiatric Association prepares DSM-IV, the American Psychological Association is considering developing its own manual whose focus may be less on diagnosis and more on setting forth research-based guidelines for choosing the most effective therapy for various disorders (Landers, 1986, 1987).

While the diagnostic debate goes on, researchers will continue to devote attention to isolating some of the factors associated with, and possibly responsible for, various reliably identified disorders. Much of that research reflects increasing interest and attention to biological explanations. For example, recent research suggests that anxiety disorders may be related to an overabundance of a newly discovered brain peptide molecule known as DBI (diazepam-binding inhibitor), which appears in areas of the brain involved with emotion and which acts to heighten anxiety responses (Marx, 1985). Studies also indicate that, in certain people, the nervous system seems especially capable of blocking incoming sensations, especially during stress-related emotional arousal. This blocking capability might be partially responsible for the appearance of conversion or other dissociative disorders.

In one sense, studies like these reflect some of the medical/biological models that have been prominent for centuries, but there is a difference. Future research will not be as oriented toward finding single causes for particular disorders. Some of the same descriptive research that has led to better interjudge agreement on diagnosis has also led to a growing awareness that every category of mental disorder not only contains a number of subtypes and variants, but also may have its own set of causal factors. This trend is already exemplified by the research mentioned earlier suggesting that different biological factors may be associated with different subtypes of schizophrenia. It is also illustrated by the popularity of the diathesis-stress approach. This perspective, rather than trying to establish the cause of a disorder, leaves room for a variety of interacting biological, psychological, environmental, and social factors, which, depending on their particular combination, may or may not produce abnormality.

Partly because of the diathesis-stress model and other integrative formulations, proponents of differing theoretical orientations within abnormal psychology will tend to become more open and less stridently dogmatic in their writings than was once the case. Because it now seems clear that no single perspective is capable of explaining mental disorders, we expect that the future will see increasing cooperation among researchers from many perspectives.

We have offered only a glimpse of the problems, issues, and theories that characterize the study of abnormal psychology. For more detailed coverage, consult the list of recommended readings at the end of this chapter or, better yet, enroll in a course in abnormal psychology.

SUMMARY

1. Mental disorder, or psychopathology, involves patterns of thinking and behaving that are maladaptive, disruptive, or uncomfortable either for the person affected or for others.

2. Exactly what is considered abnormal can be defined statistically, in comparison to what most people do, or valuatively, in relation to what is most highly valued by society. Each view has its problems. A practical approach looks both at what people do (the content of behavior) and where they do it (the context of behavior) and labels as abnormal those behaviors that prevent people from functioning on a day-to-day basis or that interfere substantially with the lives of others.

3. Abnormal behavior has been attributed, at one time or another, to the action of gods or the devil (the demonological model), to physical disease (the medical/biological model), to internal mental conflicts (the psychodynamic model), to learned maladaptive behavior (the behavioral model), and to a person's way of looking at the world (the phenomenological

model). Because no one explanatory model of abnormal behavior is fully satisfactory, aspects of several of them have been combined in diathesis-stress theories. These approaches highlight the interaction between inherited predispositions for disorder and the stresses of life.

4. The dominant system for classifying abnormal behavior is contained in the *Diagnostic and Statistical Manual* (DSM) of the American Psychiatric Association. This multidimensional system includes sixteen major types of mental disorder, as well as a variety of less severe behavior problems. Even though it represents an improvement over previous diagnostic systems, many psychologists are dissatisfied with the reliability and the validity of the DSM.

5. Anxiety disorders include such problems as phobia, generalized anxiety disorder, panic disorder, and obsessive-compulsive disorder.

6. Somatoform disorders include conversion disorder, or physical problems, such as paralysis, blindness, or

deafness, that have no apparent physical cause. Another example is hypochondriasis.

7. Dissociative disorders involve such rare conditions as amnesia and multiple personality, in which a person develops two or more separate identities.

8. Mood, or affective, disorders are all too common and involve extremes of mood, such as depression or mania. Suicide is often related to these disorders, especially to depression. Mood disorders have been attributed to loss of significant sources of reward, to pessimistic patterns of thinking, to disruptions in the level of certain neurotransmitters in the brain, and to irregularities in daily biological rhythms. Some of these problems may be inherited.

9. Schizophrenia is perhaps the most severe and puzzling disorder of all. Its symptoms include problems in thinking, perception, attention, emotion, movement, motivation, and daily functioning. The exact causes of schizophrenia are still unknown, but genetic factors, neurotransmitter problems, brain abnormalities, conflict-filled childhoods, and unfortunate learning experiences have all been implicated.

10. Psychoactive substance-use disorders, such as alcoholism and drug abuse, are very common. They affect millions of people and create disastrous personal and social problems.

11. Sexual disorders include sexual dysfunction and paraphilias, or attraction to inappropriate stimuli.

12. Personality disorders are long-term patterns of behavior, which, though not as severe as other mental disorders and not always associated with personal discomfort, are nevertheless disturbing to others. Included are personalities with such problematic traits as self-centeredness (narcissistic personality) or a reckless disregard for the rights of others (antisocial personality).

13. Organic mental disorders, such as delirium and dementia, are those for which there is a clearly biological basis.

14. The concept of mental illness has raised several controversial social issues. Among these are the question of whether mental illness actually exists and whether insanity can be used as a defense in cases of criminal behavior. Some believe that abnormal behavior is indeed an illness, whereas others argue that *mental illness* is just a term for people's problems in living and that using that term deprives these people of their rights.

KEY TERMS

Definitions of terms appear on the pages shown in parentheses.

addiction (571)
agoraphobia (556)
alcoholism (572)
antisocial personality (575)
anxiety disorder (555)
bipolar disorder (564)
catatonic schizophrenia (568)
conversion disorder (559)
delirium (576)
delusion (561)
dementia (576)
diathesis (551)
diathesis-stress model (551)
disorganized schizophrenia (568)
dissociative disorder (560)
dysthymia (562)
generalized anxiety disorder (556)
hallucinations (568)
major depression (561)
mania (564)
medical model (biological model) (548, 549)

mood disorder (affective disorder) (561)
multiple personality (560)
narcissistic personality disorder (575)
neurosis (553)
obsessive-compulsive disorder (557)
organic mental disorder (576)
panic disorder (556)
paranoid schizophrenia (568)
paraphilia (574)
personality disorder (574)
phobia (556)
psychoactive substance-use disorder (571)
psychopathology (542)
psychosis (553)
schizophrenia (566)
sexual disorder (574)
simple phobia (556)
social phobia (556)
somatoform disorder (559)
vulnerability model (571)

RECOMMENDED READINGS

Davison, G. C., & Neale, J. M. (1986). *Abnormal psychology* (4th ed.). New York: Wiley. An excellent textbook, which provides a balanced and detailed overview of all aspects of abnormal behavior.

Meyer, R. G., & Osborne, Y. V. (1982). *Case studies in abnormal behavior.* Boston: Allyn & Bacon. A fascinating collection of cases covering a wide range of abnormal behaviors.

Schwitzgebel, R. L., & Schwitzgebel, R. K. (1980). *Law and psychological practice.* New York: Wiley. A good introduction to legal issues relating to abnormal psychology.

Spitzer, R. L., Skodol, A. E., Gibbon, M., & Williams, J. B. W. (1983). *Psychopathology: A casebook.* New York: McGraw-Hill. Another excellent collection of case studies of behavior disorder.

Vonnegut, M. (1976). *The eden express.* New York: Bantam Books. The firsthand account of Mark Vonnegut's encounter with severe mental disorder.

Zilboorg, G., & Henry, G. W. (1941). *A history of medical psychology.* New York: Norton. A classic text that provides a detailed picture of the history of mental disorder through the ages.

*U*ntil recently, twenty-nine-year-old Lou S. had never had a serious problem in his life, and as far as he knew, neither had anyone in his family. Within five years after graduating from college, Lou had landed a good job, married, and received two major promotions. Being so far along in his pursuit of the American dream, he hadn't a clue about why he began to feel so depressed or what to do about it. He had long ago adopted his parents' view that anyone with psychological problems was just weak and that solving those problems was a private matter, to be handled without help. Hoping the depression would lift on its own, Lou refused to talk about his feelings, even to his wife, who encouraged him to do so. Instead, he accused her of nagging and consoled himself with alcohol and the company of other women. Unfortunately, drinking and infidelity only made Lou feel worse about himself. Then, while driving drunk on one of his nights out, Lou crashed into a bridge abutment. The coroner's jury ruled his death an accident, but his wife still wonders if it was suicide. The tragedy in this case lies not only in the misery and the loss of life, but also in the fact that they might have been prevented. Lou's prejudice against discussing or asking for help forced him to fall back on his own coping skills, which turned out to be inadequate.

About one out of every ten people in this country is treated for some form of psychological disorder at some time in his or her life (Klerman, 1983). The image of treatment that probably comes most readily to mind is of someone lying on a couch describing dreams to a bearded, pipe-smoking therapist with a Viennese accent. To be sure, some treatment is done this way, but the image fails to capture the full range of treatments currently used. Table 16.1 (p. 588) summarizes the varied settings in which treatment is commonly offered. The specific methods number over a hundred (Corsini, 1981; Herink, 1980). But almost all of them are based on the psychodynamic, behavioral, phenomenological, and biological approaches to personality and behavior disorder described in Chapters 14 and 15.

In this chapter, we review treatment methods for the alleviation and prevention of a wide range of psychological disorders. We also consider research on these methods' effectiveness. We discuss the psychodynamic, phenomenological, and behavioral approaches first. These rely mainly on **psychotherapy,** the treatment of psychological disorders through psychological methods, such as analyzing problems, talking about possible solutions, and encouraging more adaptive ways of thinking and acting. Later, we consider the biological approach, which depends mainly on drugs and other physical treatments. Although we discuss each of these approaches in a separate section, keep in mind that those who offer help for psychological problems do not always adhere to only one set of treatment methods. In fact, current surveys show that the majority of mental health professionals see themselves as **eclectic,** perhaps leaning toward one approach, but also borrowing methods from other approaches as appropriate.

16

Treatment of Psychological Disorders

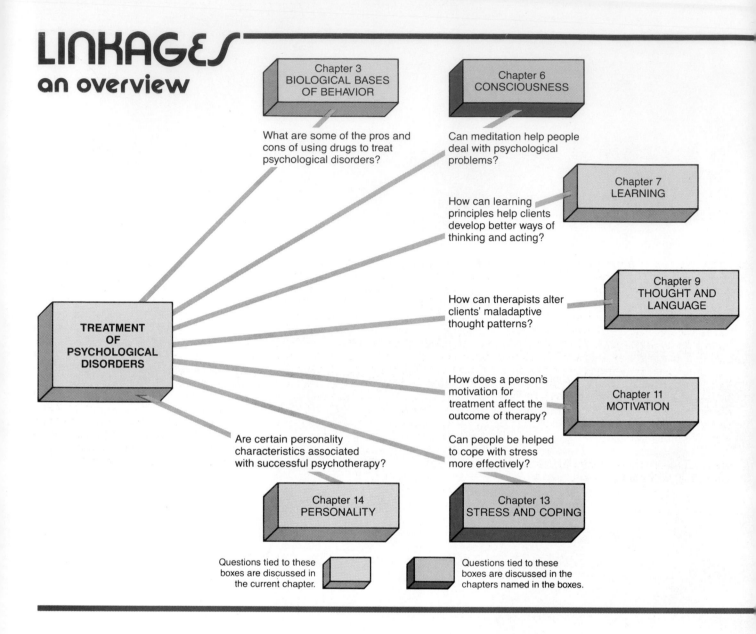

LINKAGES
an overview

Chapter 3
BIOLOGICAL BASES OF BEHAVIOR

What are some of the pros and cons of using drugs to treat psychological disorders?

Chapter 6
CONSCIOUSNESS

Can meditation help people deal with psychological problems?

Chapter 7
LEARNING

How can learning principles help clients develop better ways of thinking and acting?

TREATMENT OF PSYCHOLOGICAL DISORDERS

Chapter 9
THOUGHT AND LANGUAGE

How can therapists alter clients' maladaptive thought patterns?

How does a person's motivation for treatment affect the outcome of therapy?

Chapter 11
MOTIVATION

Are certain personality characteristics associated with successful psychotherapy?

Can people be helped to cope with stress more effectively?

Chapter 14
PERSONALITY

Chapter 13
STRESS AND COPING

Questions tied to these boxes are discussed in the current chapter.

Questions tied to these boxes are discussed in the chapters named in the boxes.

GOALS, METHODS, AND FEATURES OF TREATMENT

The most general goal in treating psychological disorders is to help troubled people change their thinking and behavior so that they will be happier and more productive. In working with individuals, therapists translate this overall goal into more specific ones, such as (1) helping the client better understand his or her problems, (2) reducing emotional discomfort, (3) encouraging the free expression of feelings, (4) providing new ideas or information about how to solve problems, and (5) helping the client try new ways of thinking and behaving outside the therapy situation. Psychological treatments work toward these goals in three main ways.

First of all, therapists provide psychological support. To some extent, this means offering a sympathetic ear and level-headed advice in a crisis. Support also may involve helping a person to recognize and use his or her strengths and skills. A second method in therapy is to eliminate troublesome behaviors and develop new and better ones. The problems may be relatively mild, such

TREATMENT OF PSYCHOLOGICAL DISORDERS AND PSYCHOLOGY

In the previous chapter, we reviewed the many forms of mental disorder that have plagued human beings through the centuries. Until about a hundred years ago, people experiencing these disorders had to depend for relief on what we now recognize as inadequate treatment. Today, as the result of research in psychology, psychiatry, and other mental health professions, there is a wide range of treatment methods with proven value for reducing or eliminating psychological problems. In this chapter, we consider some of these methods.

Much of the basis for psychological treatment lies in the various theories of personality reviewed in Chapter 14. By spelling out proposed explanations for what can go wrong in the development of personality, those theories provided important general guidelines for treatment. For example, we will see in this chapter that the emphasis on learning in behavioral theories of personality resulted in the development of methods that literally teach disturbed people how to think and act in more adaptive ways. Phenomenological theories, in contrast, have promoted treatment aimed at creating conditions in which troubled people can become aware of distorted perceptions that drive distorted thinking and behavior and begin to change those perceptions.

Modern methods of treatment also owe much to research in biological psychology, especially to research on the role of neurotransmitters in the brain. Recognition of the importance of biological processes has led to the development of drugs whose effects on neurotransmitters temporarily alleviate some symptoms of psychological disturbance.

The effectiveness of these and other treatments depends partly on the method itself and partly on clients' motivation and on their expectations about the method's value. These variables highlight the relationship between methods of treatment and the principles of perception, thinking, and motivation discussed in Chapters 5, 9, and 11.

as an awkward conversational style, but more often, difficulties involve the problematic thoughts and actions associated with many of the behavior disorders described in Chapter 15. Finally, therapists attempt to promote insight and self-exploration. This includes a wide-ranging effort to better understand motivations, emotions, perceptions, conflicts, values, goals, and problems. It requires clients to look beyond what is obvious and specific about themselves (such as being afraid of flying or having frequent arguments) and to consider what such problems might suggest about more subtle, general, and previously unrecognized aspects of personality, such as a preoccupation with danger or competitiveness.

The degree to which each of these general methods is used in a particular case depends on several factors, including the problems, preferences, and financial circumstances of the person to be helped; the time available for treatment; and the therapist's theoretical leanings and methodological preferences.

Regardless of differences in specific theories, goals, and procedures, treatment of psychological disorder boils down to one person trying to help

TABLE 16.1 _____
Some Common Treatment Settings
Treatment of psychological problems can take place almost anywhere, but typically in a few general settings. Some of these are supported by public funds, and others are private, profit-making organizations.

Setting	Description
Hospitals	These include state and county mental hospitals, VA hospitals, private mental hospitals, and psychiatric wards in general hospitals of all kinds. Individual or group psychotherapy is usually offered to patients who are full-time residents. It may also be offered to clients who live in the community but spend their daytime hours at the hospital.
Clinics	Included here are privately owned facilities, as well as city, county, or community mental health centers where individual, group, or family therapy sessions are conducted with clients who live full time in the community. Some clinics offer more extensive services similar to those of hospitals.
Halfway houses	These are usually neighborhood houses where former hospital residents and other clients can live temporarily while receiving therapy, supervision, and support. Most of these people either have or are training for a job and are getting ready to move to their own home full time.
Private therapy offices	This is the most traditional and the fastest-growing treatment setting. Here, psychiatrists, psychologists, social workers, and other mental health professionals provide psychotherapy as part of their private practice.
Other settings	Psychotherapy occurs in many settings not mentioned above. They are too numerous to list here, but examples include prisons, orphanages, military bases, alcoholism treatment centers, and clients' homes.

another. Thus, all methods of treatment share certain basic features, not only with one another, but also with efforts to treat the physically ill (Frank, 1973, 1978). These common features include

1. A person who is suffering and seeks relief from a problem. This is the *client,* or patient.

2. A person who, by virtue of training or experience, is socially accepted as capable of helping the client. This is the *therapist,* or healer.

3. A *theory* or rationale that is used to explain the client's problems. In medicine, the theory involves germs, infections, and other biological processes. In some cultures, the theory may involve curses or possession by evil spirits. In psychology the theory may involve psychodynamics, learning principles, or other mental factors.

4. A set of *procedures* for dealing with the client's problems. These procedures usually grow directly out of the theory used and may presume causes ranging from magic spells to infections and everything in between (Frank, 1973). Thus, the witch doctor or exorcist combats the supernatural with special ceremonies and prayers, whereas the medical doctor treats infections with antibiotics. Later we review a number of procedures used by mental health professionals.

5. A special social *relationship* between client and therapist, which helps ease the client's problems. An atmosphere is created in which the client feels optimistic about solving his or her problems, expects that the therapist's methods will help, and is motivated to work toward solutions. These characteristics mark all forms of healing to some extent. In medicine, improvement in a patient's physical or mental condition is usually due mainly to drugs or surgery, but the effects of treatment also depend in

part on the patient's expectations of and confidence in the treatment. In magical/religious healing, on the other hand, specific procedures are far less important than the positive relationship and expectations they create. At this end of the healing spectrum, treatment would probably have no effect without these social factors. Somewhere between these extremes lie psychological methods of treatment. In addition to offering a set of helpful procedures, most psychotherapists try to build a positive relationship because it may enhance the chances of successful treatment. As we will see, some therapists emphasize relationship factors much more than others.

HIGHLIGHT

Rules and Rights in the Therapeutic Relationship

Treatment of psychological disorders can be an intense emotional activity, conducted within a therapy relationship that can profoundly affect the client's life. Professional ethics and common sense require the therapist to assure that this relationship is not harmed or distorted in any way. For example, the Ethical Standards of the American Psychological Association forbid a sexual relationship between therapist and client (APA, 1981). These standards, as well as the ethics of other mental health professions, also require therapists to keep strictly confidential everything a client says in therapy. Confidentiality is one of the most important features of a successful therapeutic relationship, because it allows the client to freely disclose unpleasant or embarrassing feelings or events. Not many clients would reveal that they were sexually attracted to small animals or that they were having an extramarital affair if they thought the therapist would mention these facts at a cocktail party. Professionals may consult with one another about a client, but each is bound by the requirement not to reveal information to outsiders (including members of the client's family) without the client's consent.

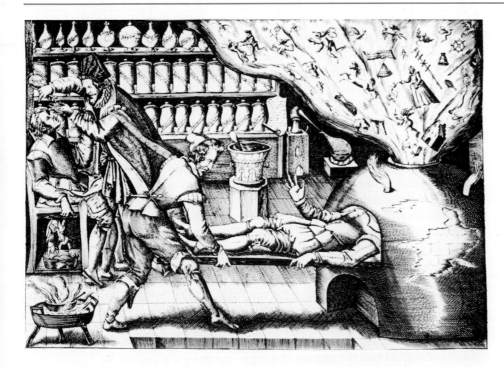

The methods used to treat abnormality are related to the presumed cause of the problems. In the days when gods or demons were blamed for behavior disorder, magical-religious practitioners tried to enlist divine assistance or make the victim's body an uncomfortable place for an evil spirit. Here, an afflicted person's head is placed in an oven, resulting in the the departure of numerous evil spirits.

Professional rules about confidentiality are backed up in most states by laws that recognize information revealed in therapy—like information given to a priest, a lawyer, or a physician—as a privileged communication. This means that a therapist can refuse, even in court, to answer questions about a client or to provide personal notes or tape recordings from therapy sessions. However, there are some special circumstances under which a therapist must violate confidentiality. Among these are cases in which (1) the client is so severely disturbed or suicidal that hospitalization is needed; (2) the client uses his or her mental condition and history of therapy as part of a defense against criminal charges; (3) the therapist must defend against the client's charge of malpractice; and (4) the therapist believes the client may commit a crime, especially a violent crime against others.

This last condition poses a dilemma. Suppose a client says, "Someday I'm going to kill that brother of mine!" Should the therapist consider this a serious threat and warn the brother? In most cases, the danger is not real, but there have been tragic exceptions. The most famous of these occurred in 1969 at the University of California at Berkeley. A graduate student receiving therapy at the student health center revealed his intention to kill Tatiana Tarasoff, a young woman whom he had dated the previous year, but who had since rejected him. The therapist took the threat very seriously, but after he consulted with his supervisor and the campus police, it was decided there was no real danger, so neither Tatiana nor her parents were warned. After terminating therapy, the client killed Ms. Tarasoff. Her parents then sued the university, the campus police, and the therapist. The parents won their case, thus setting an important precedent and making therapists everywhere acutely aware of their legal responsibility to provide a warning whenever a client makes a serious threat to harm a particular person. As noted in Chapter 14, however, accurately predicting violent behavior in specific individuals is difficult, if not impossible. Thus, the responsibility to warn creates difficult decisions for the therapist about when to break confidentiality.

Other rights afforded to people receiving treatment for psychological disorders protect them from being casually committed to a mental hospital. In 1973 a federal court decision provided that a person threatened with commitment can expect the right to written notice; an opportunity to prepare a defense with the help of an attorney; a court hearing, with a jury if desired; and the right to take the Fifth Amendment to avoid self-incrimination. By 1980 other decisions, including one by the Supreme Court, required that, before a person can be forcibly committed, the state must provide "clear and convincing" evidence that he or she is not only mentally ill, but poses an "imminent danger" to self or others. Most states now require a periodic review of every committed person to determine whether he or she should be released. Commitment can no longer become an automatic life sentence. Further, the person now also has the right to receive *treatment* while hospitalized, not just confinement. Finally, people also have the right to refuse certain forms of treatment and to be subjected to as little restriction of their freedom as possible. If these conditions are not being met, the patient must be released.

Rules regarding hospitalized mental patients help protect them from abuse, neglect, and exploitation, but they create some difficulties as well. Staff members at mental health facilities might worry that they could be sued by patients whom they keep unnecessarily confined, but they might also create problems by being too liberal in release decisions. Noncriminal former mental patients are actually less dangerous than the general noncriminal population (Monahan, 1981), but on rare, though well-publicized occasions, tragic release mistakes do occur, and those responsible may be sued by anyone harmed by a former patient. Thus the dilemma: to find a way to balance the legal rights of the individual patient against the legal rights of the public. ■

PSYCHODYNAMIC PSYCHOTHERAPY

The beginning of psychotherapy came with Sigmund Freud's development of psychoanalysis. As we saw in the chapter on personality, this revolutionary theory established the psychodynamic approach to personality. Central to this approach is the assumption that personality and behavior reflect the ego's efforts to referee unconscious mental conflicts in dealing with the pressures of the real world. The key to helping troubled individuals, Freud thought, lay in helping them better understand the unconscious conflicts that he believed lay at the root of their problems. Freud's psychoanalysis offered a set of psychological procedures for achieving this understanding. His one-to-one method of studying and treating people, his systematic search for relationships between an individual's life history and current problems, his emphasis on thoughts and emotions in treatment, and his focus on the client-therapist relationship reappear in most forms of psychotherapy, regardless of their theoretical approach.

The Beginnings of Psychoanalysis

Psychoanalysis developed mainly out of Freud's medical practice, which began in the late 1880s. He was fascinated and puzzled by patients who suffered from hysterical ailments—blindness, paralysis, or other symptoms that have no physical cause. Freud initially used hypnotic suggestions to cure these patients, but found it only partially and temporarily successful. Later, he and a colleague named Joseph Breuer began asking hypnotized patients to try recalling events that might have caused their symptoms. Breuer and Freud (1896) reported a number of successes with this "talking cure." Eventually, Freud stopped using hypnosis and merely had the patient relax on a couch and report the memories that came to mind.

Freud was struck by how many of his patients' symptoms seemed to be traceable to childhood memories of sexual abuse, usually by a parent or close relative. Either child abuse was rampant in Vienna at the time, or his patients' reports were inaccurate. Freud suggested that hysterical symptoms can be based on unconscious wishes and fantasies, not just on memories of actual events. Thus, a person's memory of childhood seduction by a parent might reflect a childhood fantasy or wish about such an encounter. This reasoning not only led to such concepts as infantile sexuality and the Oedipus complex, but also shifted the focus of psychoanalytic therapy from recovering lost memories to exploring unconscious wishes and conflicts. (Today, revelations about the high frequency of child sexual abuse have caused many to wonder how much of what Freud's patients reported was fantasy and how much was reality; Masson, 1984.)

The Goals of Psychoanalysis

Psychoanalysis is a method of treatment that seeks to help clients (1) gain insight by recognizing, understanding, and dealing with unconscious thoughts and emotions that cause their problems and (2) trace, or *work through,* the many ways in which those unconscious causes affect everyday behavior and social relationships. For example, psychoanalysis may help the client recognize hidden, unexpressed feelings of anger toward a parent. This intellectual insight would be followed by further work designed to let the client emotionally experience and release the pent-up anger. The working through would then help the client become aware of how the unconscious conflict and the defenses around it have been creating problems. Thus, the client's hostility toward the boss, an older coworker, or any other "parent

Change takes place very gradually in psychoanalysis, because clients are not only unconscious of the reasons for their problems but have built strong defenses against becoming aware of them. Accordingly, most psychoanalytic methods are aimed at getting around the client's defenses, exploring the unconscious, and helping the client make sense of what emerges.

figure" might be a symbolic, unconscious reenactment of childhood conflicts with a parent.

Psychoanalytic Methods of Treatment

Complete psychoanalytic treatment may require as many as three to five sessions per week for from two to fifteen years. The therapist blends several methods during treatment.

Free association   The method called **free association** requires the client to relax, usually while lying on a couch, and report everything that comes to mind as soon as it occurs, no matter how trivial, apparently senseless, or embarrassing it may seem. The idea is that, within the constant stream of thoughts, feelings, memories, and images that all people experience, there are clues to the unconscious. These clues can be read if the client relaxes defenses and does not disrupt the flow.

Clues to the unconscious often appear more in the way thoughts are linked than in the thoughts themselves. Consider this example from the free association of a middle-aged male.

> My Dad called long distance last night. He seemed upset. . . . (Long silence) I almost fell asleep there for a minute. I used to do that a lot in college. Once I woke up and saw the professor standing over me, shaking me, and the whole class was laughing.

Notice that the client's talking about his father led to a long silence. When clients stop talking or claim that their minds are blank, the psychoanalyst may suspect that unconscious defense mechanisms are keeping threatening material out of consciousness. The fact that the silence in this case was followed by a memory about punishment by a threatening authority figure (a symbolic father) might further support the idea that the client is struggling with unresolved unconscious conflicts about his father.

The interpretation of dreams   It has been assumed for centuries that dreams have meaning. Psychoanalysts believe that dreams express wishes, impulses, and fantasies that the dreamer's defenses keep unconscious during waking hours. Even in dreams, however, defenses usually disguise threatening material so that the dream does not frighten (and awaken) the dreamer. The analyst's task is to help the client search for the unconscious material contained in individual dreams and in the pattern of dreams over time.

The client's description of a dream provides its **manifest content.** Manifest content often contains unimportant features and events from the client's day or reflects temporary needs. The **latent content** of a dream is its unconscious meaning, which lies in the dream's symbolism. For example, "I was sitting in a restaurant, having a conversation with a plate of lasagna, when the president of the United States walked in and started a fistfight with my waiter" is the manifest content of the dream. Perhaps the dreamer just saw the president on television or was hungry at bedtime. But analysis may also reveal latent content. Perhaps, for example, the plate of lasagna represents an Italian friend, and the bout between president and waiter symbolizes the dreamer's conflict about wanting to be wealthy and powerful (the president) but also wanting to be of service to ("wait on") others. To uncover this content, the analyst may ask the client to free associate to parts of the dream or may suggest an interpretation.

The results of dream analysis differ for each client. There are few, if any, universal dream symbols: giants do not always represent an angry father, water does not always represent birth, and long objects do not always represent penises.

The analysis of everyday behavior In *The Psychopathology of Everyday Life* (1914), Freud stated his belief that human actions are never random; they are determined by a combination of conscious intentions and unconscious influences. He reasoned, therefore, that behavior people consider unintentional may hold important messages from the unconscious. In one case, for example, a young male client who was interested in body building referred to that pursuit as "physible culture" (instead of "physical culture"). This *Freudian slip* had no obvious meaning for the client, but when he was asked to free associate to the word *physible,* he thought of *visible* and went on to reveal a previously unconscious wish to exhibit his nude body and to see others naked (Brenner, 1974).

Lapses of memory may also be related to unconscious defenses or impulses. Forgetting the content of a dream or the time of a therapy appointment might reflect a client's unconscious resistance to treatment.[1] Even accidents can be interpreted as meaningful. The waiter who spills hot soup on an elderly male customer might be seen as acting out unconscious aggressive impulses against a father figure.

Giving interpretations Helping clients see what free associations, dreams, and everyday behavior might mean is perhaps the most important contribution the psychoanalyst makes to a client's self-understanding. By asking questions, making comments, and suggesting various interpretations, the therapist gradually leads the client to confront and become fully aware of all aspects of his or her personality, including defenses and the unconscious material behind them. Here is an example of an analytic interpretation relating to a client's resistance to treatment.

Client: I'm sorry to be late, but my brother-in-law called just as I was leaving. He told me my sister is sick again and asked if I had any extra cash to help with her medical bills. I said I did, but I don't know how I can help them and keep coming to see you. Sometimes, everything falls on me at once.

Therapist: You know, last session, we began to see that you have some very negative feelings toward your parents. That was difficult for you to accept. Today, you start off by saying that, through no fault of your own, you may not be able to continue therapy. Could it be that, whenever you are threatened by what you are learning about yourself here, you use something beyond your control to divert our attention. I wonder, because you told me you used to get out of trouble this way as a child. When your parents got angry with you, you always blamed your mistakes on someone else who kept you from doing what you should. What do you think?

Analysis of the transference Psychoanalysts believe that, if they reveal nothing about themselves, clients will begin to *transfer* to the therapist many of the feelings, attitudes, reactions, and conflicts experienced in childhood toward parents, siblings, and other significant people. A "new edition" of the client's problems may appear in this transference. The **transference** may take many forms, including "falling in love" with the therapist, becoming very dependent, or being hostile. By analyzing the transference, the therapist may be able to help the client understand and resolve important problems from the past as illustrated in the present in the client-therapist relationship. This is one reason why therapists focus attention on what goes on during treatment sessions as well as between them.

---

[1] It has been jokingly argued that you cannot win in psychoanalysis, because you are dependent if you show up early, resistant if you miss a meeting or show up late, and compulsive if you are right on time.

Variations on Psychoanalysis

Classical Freudian psychoanalysis is not as popular as it once was, partly because Freud's instinct-based personality theory has fallen into disfavor and partly because psychoanalysis can be so expensive and time consuming. Further, clients in analysis must be able to think and communicate clearly, often about abstract concepts. Thus, most children, as well as adults who lack verbal skills or display very severe disorders, are not candidates for classical psychoanalysis. These limitations of Freud's methods prompted psychodynamic therapists—many of whom were the post-Freudian psychodynamic personality theorists mentioned in Chapter 14—to create variations on psychoanalytic treatment.

Some of these variations focus less on the id, the unconscious, and the past than did Freud; they give more attention to the problems present today and how the power of the client's ego can be harnessed to solve them. Examples of these variations include *ego analysis* (Hartmann, 1958; Klein, 1960), *interpersonal therapy* (Sullivan, 1954), *individual analysis* (Adler, 1963), and *object relations therapy* (Kohut, 1983). In these therapies, clients are helped to gain insight, not into Oedipal conflicts, but into how their deep-seated feelings of anxiety, insecurity, or inferiority create disordered thoughts and problems in relating to others. The therapist is also likely to be somewhat more active than the traditional analyst in providing encouragement and guidance.

Other variations on psychoanalysis retain more of Freud's ideas but alter the format of treatment so that it is less intense, less expensive, and applicable to a broader range of clients. For example, in *psychoanalytically oriented psychotherapy* (Alexander, 1963) or *time-limited dynamic psychotherapy*, basic psychoanalytic methods are used, but more flexibly (Davanloo, 1978; Sifneos, 1979; Strupp et al., 1982). The goal may range from psychological support to basic personality change, and therapy may be completed in thirty sessions or fewer, most of which do not take place every day. Instead of lying on a couch, the client may sit facing the therapist and spend more time in conversation

Some analytically oriented therapists work with children, using fantasy play with toys or puppets, rather than traditional free association, to explore unconscious conflicts and problems.

than in free association. The therapist is often more active than in classical psychoanalysis in directing the client's attention to evidence of particular conflicts. In some forms of psychodynamic treatment, clients may be seen in small groups rather than individually.

HIGHLIGHT

Group and Family Therapies

During World War II, the need to serve an overwhelming caseload prompted therapists to try offering psychodynamic treatment to groups of clients. As the other treatment methods described in this chapter developed in later years, they, too, came to be offered to groups as well as to individuals. Most forms of group treatment involve five to ten clients who meet with their therapist at least once a week for about two hours. All group members agree to hold confidential everything that occurs in treatment.

Group therapy offers several features not found in individual treatment (Yalom, 1985). First, group therapy allows the therapist to observe clients interacting with one another in a real social situation. Second, clients often feel relieved and less alone as they listen to the others and recognize that many people struggle with difficulties similar to or even more severe than their own. This recognition tends to raise each client's hope and expectations for improvement, a factor important in all forms of treatment. Third, group members can bolster each other's self-confidence and self-acceptance as they come to trust and value one another and develop group cohesiveness. Fourth, clients learn from one another. They not only share ideas for solving problems, but also give one another direct, honest feedback about how each member "comes across." In a sense, the group format allows each member to be both a client and a therapist. Finally, the group experience may make clients less guarded, more willing to share their feelings, and more sensitive to other people's needs, motives, and messages.

The psychodynamic theory that many psychological disorders are rooted in family conflicts gave rise to yet another form of treatment: **family therapy.** As its name implies, family therapy involves two or more individuals from the same family, one of whose problems make him or her the initially identified client. As in group therapy, the family format gives the therapist an excellent view of the way the client interacts with others. It also provides a forum for discussing issues important to the family's life. However, family therapy is more than group therapy with people who happen to be related. It is based on the idea that the family is the "client" and that everyone in the family must take part in resolving family conflicts.

The earliest family therapy groups were formed about thirty years ago in the hope of helping schizophrenic adults, but the format has now become popular in the treatment of many other adult and childhood disorders (Gurman & Kniskern, 1978). Whatever the original problem, family therapy usually begins by encouraging the entire family to work on it. Because they are often in a crisis and highly motivated to help the most troubled person, family members usually accept this task readily (Haley, 1970). Very soon, however, attention spreads from the identified client to the entire family, because most family therapists see that client as a part of a total "family system," in which his or her disorder is believed to reflect the conflicts, communication problems, and other difficulties in the family as a whole (Goldenberg & Goldenberg, 1980; Haley, 1971; Minuchin, Rosman & Baker, 1978).

Indeed, the goal of family therapy is not just to alleviate the identified client's problems, but to create harmony and balance within the family by helping each family member better understand the family's characteristic interaction patterns and the problems these patterns create. To take a simple example, suppose the father acts like a bully and, though he manages to control and intimidate his wife and children, they get back at him by accidentally damaging his possessions, creating minor repair jobs around the house, or sabotaging his free time in other subtle ways. The therapist would try to make everyone aware of his or her role in creating and maintaining these problems and help them make constructive changes. Like the group therapist, the family therapist may use psychodynamic, phenomenological, or behavioral methods or some combination of them. ■

Some Comments on Psychodynamic Therapy

Modern variants on psychoanalysis, with their deemphasis on instincts and their focus on the client's potential for insight and self-directed problem-solving, tend to attract more adherents than classical psychoanalysis. In fact, they have helped psychodynamic concepts retain their influence, even though the original psychoanalytic methods have lost much of their popularity.

Critics of psychodynamic therapies continue to point out, however, that ego strength, defense mechanisms, and other concepts underlying these treatments are so vague and difficult to measure that scientific evaluation of change in these variables due to treatment is all but impossible. Indeed, though proponents of psychoanalysis and other dynamic treatments are confident of the value of their techniques, there is not enough high-quality research evidence supporting this view to make it entirely convincing.

PHENOMENOLOGICAL PSYCHOTHERAPY

Until the 1940s, almost everyone doing psychotherapy used some form of psychoanalysis. Then an alternative came from therapists who had been trained in the psychoanalytic tradition but later adopted the phenomenological approach. As we discussed in the chapters on personality and abnormal psychology, phenomenologists view humans as basically good creatures who are capable of consciously controlling their actions and taking responsibility for their decisions. They believe that human behavior is motivated by an innate drive toward growth and is guided from moment to moment by the way people perceive and interpret the world. Disordered behavior reflects a blockage of natural growth, brought on by distorted perceptions or lack of awareness about feelings. When these ideas were applied to psychotherapy, new treatments evolved, each of which operates on the following basic assumptions:

1. Treatment is a human encounter between equals, not a cure given by an expert. It is a way to help clients restart their natural growth and to feel and behave as they really are, not as someone has told them they should be.

2. Clients will improve on their own if the therapist creates the right conditions. The ideal conditions promote clients' awareness, acceptance, and expression of their feelings and perceptions, especially those they have kept hidden and which have blocked their growth. Thus, as in psychodynamic approaches, therapy promotes insight. But in phenomenological therapy, it is insight into current feelings and perceptions, not into unconscious childhood conflicts.

3. The best way to create these ideal conditions is to establish a relationship in which the client feels totally accepted and supported. The client's

experience of this relationship, not any specific techniques, brings beneficial changes.

4. Clients are seen as capable of and fully responsible for choosing how they will think and behave.

There are many forms of phenomenological treatment. We will consider just two, those of Carl Rogers and Frederick S. Perls.

Person-Centered Therapy

Carl Rogers was trained in psychodynamic treatment during the 1930s, but he soon began to question its value. He especially disliked being a detached, expert observer who "figured out" the client. He became convinced that a less formal approach would be more effective for the client and more comfortable for the therapist. Rogers began using what he called *nondirective therapy,* which depended on the client's own drive toward growth or self-actualization. Rogers allowed his clients to decide what to talk about and when, without direction, judgment, or interpretation from the therapist. The approach is now called **client-centered,** or **person-centered, therapy,** to emphasize the client's role. The foundation of Rogers's treatment is the creation of a relationship characterized by three important and interrelated attitudes: unconditional positive regard, empathy, and congruence.

Unconditional positive regard   The therapist must show that he or she genuinely cares about and accepts the client as a person and trusts the client's ability to change. This not only requires a willingness to listen to the client, without interrupting, but also an acceptance of what is said, without judgment or evaluation, no matter how "bad" or "weird" it may seem. The therapist need not approve of everything the client says, but the therapist must accept it as a real part of a valued person. The therapist must also trust clients to solve their own problems; therefore, the therapist does not give advice. Advice, said Rogers, carries the subtle message that clients are incompetent or inadequate, making them less confident and more dependent on help.

Carl Rogers's client-centered, or person-centered, therapy was founded on phenomenological principles and can be offered individually or in groups.

Empathy   Many forms of therapy reflect what Rogers called an *external frame of reference*, looking at the client from the outside. **Empathy** requires an internal perspective, a focus on what the client might be thinking and feeling. The client-centered therapist is supposed to act, not as an outsider who wants to pin a diagnostic label on the client, but as someone who wants to appreciate how the world looks from the client's point of view. Empathy cannot be communicated just by saying, "I understand" or "I know just how you feel." Client-centered therapists convey empathy by showing that they are actively listening to the client. Like other skillful interviewers, they make eye contact with the client, nod in recognition as the client speaks, and give other signs of careful attention. As illustrated in the following example, they also use a tactic called **reflection:**

Client: This has been such a bad day. I've felt ready to cry any minute and I'm not even sure what's wrong!

Therapist: You really do feel so bad. The tears just seem to well up inside, and it must be a little scary to not even know why you feel this way.

Notice that, by restating or paraphrasing what the client has said, the therapist has reflected back not only the obvious feelings of sadness, but also the subtle fear in the client's voice. Reflection shows that the therapist is actively listening and also helps make the client aware of the thoughts and feelings he or she is experiencing. Indeed, most clients respond to empathic reflection by elaborating on their feelings. In our example, the client went on to say, "It *is* scary, because I don't like to feel in the dark about myself. I have always prided myself on being in control."

By simply communicating the desire to listen and understand, the therapist is likely to bring important material out in the open without asking disruptive questions. In therapy, an empathic listener makes clients feel valued and worthy and thus more likely to be confident and motivated to try solving their problems. Even in everyday situations, the people who are thought of as easy to talk to tend to be "good listeners" and often reflect back some of what they hear.

Congruence   Sometimes called *genuineness,* **congruence** refers to a consistency between the way the therapist feels and the way he or she acts toward the client. This means that the therapist's unconditional positive regard and empathy are real, not manufactured. Experiencing the therapist's congruence allows the client to see, possibly for the first time, that openness and honesty can be the foundation of a human relationship. Ideally, this helps the client to try being more congruent in other relationships as well.

Here is an excerpt from client-centered therapy with a depressed young woman. It illustrates the three therapeutic attitudes we have discussed.

Client: . . . I cannot be the kind of person I want to be. I guess maybe I haven't the guts or the strength to kill myself and if someone else would relieve me of the responsibility or I would be in an accident I, I—just don't want to live.

Therapist: At the present time things look so black that you can't see much point in living. [Note the use of empathic reflection and the absence of any criticism.]

Client: Yes I wish I'd never started this therapy. I was happy when I was living in my dream world. There I could be the kind of person I wanted to be. But now there is such a wide, wide gap between my ideal and what I am. . . . [Notice how the client responds to reflection with more information.]

Therapist: It's really a tough struggle digging into this like you are and at times the shelter of your dream world looks more attractive and comfortable. [Reflection]

Client: My dream world or suicide. . . . So I don't see why I should waste your time—coming in twice a week—I'm not worth it—What do you think?

Therapist: It's up to you. . . . It isn't wasting my time. I'd be glad to see you whenever you come but it's how you feel about it. . . . [Note the congruence in stating an honest desire to see the client and the unconditional positive regard in trusting her capacity and responsibility for choice.]

Client: You're not going to suggest that I come in oftener? You're not alarmed and think I ought to come in everyday until I get out of this?

Therapist: I believe you are able to make your own decision. I'll see you whenever you want to come. [Positive regard]

Client: (Note of awe in her voice) I don't believe you are alarmed about—I see—I may be afraid of myself but you aren't afraid for me. [She experiences the therapist's confidence in her.]

Therapist: You say you may be afraid of yourself and are wondering why I don't seem to be afraid for you? [Reflection]

Client: You have more confidence in me than I have. I'll see you next week maybe. (Rogers, 1951, p. 49)

The client was right. At that point, the therapist did have more confidence in her than she had in herself (she did not kill herself, by the way). However, as client-centered therapy progresses, Rogers believed that clients become not only more self-confident, but also more aware of their real feelings, more accepting of themselves, more comfortable and genuine with other people, more reliant on self-evaluation than on the judgments of others, and more effective and relaxed.

Gestalt Therapy

Another form of phenomenological treatment was developed by Frederick S. (Fritz) Perls, a European psychoanalyst who was also trained in Gestalt psychology. We note in the chapter on perception that the term *Gestalt* ("organized whole") refers to perceptual principles through which people actively organize environmental stimuli into meaningful patterns. Similarly, Perls emphasized that the reality each person experiences depends on how he or she perceives the world (Perls, 1969, 1970; Perls, Hefferline & Goodman, 1951). He believed that psychological growth continues naturally, as long as people remain clearly aware of and act on their true feelings, not on other people's expectations. If people are aware of some aspects of themselves but unaware or defensive about other aspects, their perceptions and behavior are not unified. Growth stops, and symptoms appear.

Like client-centered therapy, **Gestalt therapy** seeks to create conditions in which clients can become more unified, self-aware, and self-accepting; then they should be ready to begin growing again in their own unique, consciously guided directions. Gestalt therapy is very often done in groups led by therapists who are far more active than Rogerians. Gestalt therapists use somewhat more dramatic and direct methods as they prod clients to become aware of real feelings and impulses, which they have denied or disowned, and to discard foreign feelings, ideas, and values.

Perls believed that, when people talk about the past or the future, they are avoiding the present, escaping reality. Therefore, Gestalt therapists try to keep clients' attention focused on what they think and feel "here and now." They do this, not by reflecting (as a Rogerian might) the client's desire to avoid dealing with the present, but by clearly pointing out the client's avoidance and insisting that it be stopped. Gestalt therapists pay particular attention to clients' "body language," especially when it conflicts with what they are saying. Here is a brief illustration.

Client: I wish I wasn't so nervous with people.

Therapist: Who are you nervous with?

Gestalt therapists pay particular attention to clients' "body language," especially when it conflicts with what they are saying aloud. For example, if this client had just said she is enthusiastic about treatment, the therapist might wonder.

Client: With everyone.
Therapist: With me, here, now?
Client: Yes, very.
Therapist: That's funny, because you don't look nervous to me.
Client: (Suddenly clasping his hands) Well, I am!
Therapist: What are you doing with your hands?
Client: Nothing, it's just a gesture.
Therapist: Do the gesture again (Client reclasps his hands) and again, harder (client clasps harder). . . . [Exaggerating the gesture helps the client be more aware of the feelings it conveys.] How does that feel?
Client: It feels kind of tight, constricted.
Therapist: Can you play that tightness? What would it say to you?
Client: OK, ah, I'm tight. I'm holding everything together. I'm keeping the lid on so you won't let too much out. [Now the client becomes aware that he fears self-disclosure and wants to keep the therapist at a distance.]

Gestalt therapists may also ask clients to engage in a kind of one-person drama involving imaginary dialogues, not only with people (living or dead), but even with inanimate objects or parts of their own personalities. Like a shy person who can only be relaxed and outgoing while in a Halloween costume, clients often find these dialogues helpful in allowing them to get in touch with and express feelings. Similarly, instead of free associating to a dream, clients are asked to play its various parts.

Some Comments on Phenomenological Therapy

Phenomenological therapies have considerable appeal, largely because of their optimistic, upbeat approach. They do not dwell on a client's problems, but on psychological growth and how to unleash each person's unique strengths and potential. Even so, problems with phenomenological theories, mentioned in the chapter on personality, have implications for phenomenological treatments as well. For example, critics fault the approach for providing idealistic goals, but few specific procedures; many therapists see the idea of adopting certain attitudes or of facilitating growth as too vague. Some problems may be so complex or severe that only a temporary feeling of well-being will occur unless the therapist provides some concrete advice or specific treatments. Finally, with the notable exception of Rogers, most phenomenological therapists have been oriented more toward offering treatment than toward conducting scientific evaluations of its effectiveness.

BEHAVIOR THERAPY

The psychodynamic and phenomenological approaches assume that clients must gain insight into underlying problems, after which the symptoms those problems created will disappear more or less on their own. Behavior therapists emphasize a very different kind of insight. They try to help clients see their problems as learned behaviors that can be changed for the better without first searching for hidden meanings or causes.

This approach is the logical outcome of the assumptions of the behavioral view. As we discussed in the chapters on personality and abnormal behavior, the behavioral approach views learning as the basis of normal personality and of most behavior disorders. According to this approach, disordered behavior and thinking are seen, not as symptoms of more basic and general problems, but as samples of the maladaptive thoughts and actions that the client has learned to display in given situations.

If previous learning experiences can produce problems in the way people behave and think, it is logical to suppose that these problems might be solved by creating new learning experiences. Accordingly, **behavior therapy** (sometimes called **behavior modification**) uses the principles of learning discussed in Chapter 7 to change behavior by helping, often literally teaching, clients to act as well as to think differently. And even though the learning that led to the problems may have begun in childhood, behavior therapists focus on solving today's problems, rather than attempting to explore the distant past for signs of unresolved conflicts. For example, a man whose work suffers because of severe and frequent conflicts with coworkers might be encouraged to examine how he presents ideas, gives and takes criticism, offers rewards, and handles other work-related tasks. He might also be taught to recognize that the problems he reports are the logical result of how he has learned to act in and think about work situations.

Basic Features of Behavior Therapy

Behavior therapists begin by helping the client to set very specific goals, which usually involve (1) eliminating undesirable behaviors and thoughts and (2) developing the new behaviors and ways of thinking that the client needs to be happier and more productive. Some of the most notable features of behavior therapy include

1. Development of a good therapist-client relationship. As in other forms of therapy, this relationship makes it easier for the client to speak freely and to cooperate with treatment procedures.

2. Careful listing of the behaviors and thoughts to be changed. This behavioral assessment and the establishment of specific goals take the place of the psychodiagnosis used in some other approaches. Thus, instead of treating "depression" or "alcoholism" or "schizophrenia," behavior therapists work to change the thoughts, behaviors, and emotional reactions that cause people to be given such labels.

3. A therapist who acts as a kind of teacher/assistant, who may provide special learning-based treatments, give "homework" assignments, and help the client make very specific plans for dealing with problems.

4. Continuous evaluation of the effects of therapy. The therapist and client may decide at any time to alter any procedures that are not working.

Methods of Behavior Therapy

Behavioral approaches to psychotherapy began when a few researchers tried using classical conditioning and other learning principles to explain and change disordered human behavior (Kazdin, 1978). One of the most famous examples is the 1920 report by John B. Watson and his graduate assistant, Rosalie Rayner, in which, as we described in the chapter on development, nine-month-old "Little Albert" developed a phobia toward a white rat through learning. Mary Cover Jones, another of Watson's students, showed that learning principles could also be used to *eliminate* children's fears (Jones, 1924).

In the 1950s, as dissatisfaction with traditional psychodynamic methods grew, behavior therapies based on this early work began to attract serious attention. During the 1960s, behavior therapists showed that troublesome thoughts, as well as troublesome actions, could be altered through learning-oriented methods. By 1970 behavior therapy had become firmly established as one of the most popular approaches to treatment. In the next several sections, we describe some of the more important methods used in behavior therapy today.

Systematic desensitization   This widely known and commonly used treatment is designed to help clients deal with phobias and other irrational forms
of anxiety. Joseph Wolpe (1958) based desensitization methods on classical
conditioning techniques. His most important general principle was that, if a
fearful person can be kept calm while being exposed to gradually more intense
versions of something he or she fears, the learned association between anxiety
and the feared object will be weakened, and the fear will disappear. To make
this happen, Wolpe first arranged for clients to do something incompatible
with being afraid. Since it is hard to be tense and deeply relaxed at the same
time, Wolpe used a technique called *progressive relaxation training* (see Chapter
13) to prevent anxiety during desensitization. The next step is to have the
client relax while imagining an item from an *anxiety hierarchy,* a sequence of
increasingly fear-provoking situations; Table 16.2 presents an example. The
client works through the hierarchy gradually, imagining a more difficult scene
only after being able to tolerate the previous one without feeling any distress.

   Wolpe found that, once clients can calmly imagine being in feared
situations, they are better able to deal with those situations when they actually
occur. Desensitization may be especially effective if the client can work on a
hierarchy *in vivo,* or in real life. In one case of *in vivo* desensitization, a man
who feared closed, dark places was helped to tolerate increasing confinement
until he was comfortable even while completely inside a zipped-up sleeping
bag (Speltz & Bernstein, 1979).

Modeling   Therapists often teach clients desirable behaviors by demonstrating, or **modeling,** those behaviors. For example, *in vivo* desensitization can
be made especially effective by having the therapist show the client how to
behave more calmly in feared situations. In one case, a therapist showed
Louise, a twenty-four-year-old student with a severe spider phobia, how to
kill spiders with a fly swatter and had her practice this skill at home with a

TABLE 16.2 _____
Sample Desensitization Hierarchy
*Desensitization hierarchies present
increasingly fear provoking stimuli
while the client uses relaxation
techniques to remain calm.*

Here are the first fifteen scenes from a hierarchy used with a client who feared
flying.

1. You are reading the paper and notice an ad for an airline.
2. You are watching a television program that shows a group of people
    boarding a plane.
3. Your boss tells you that you need to make a business trip by air.
4. It is two weeks before your trip, and you ask your secretary to make airline
    reservations.
5. You are in your bedroom, packing a suitcase for your trip.
6. You are in the shower on the morning of your trip.
7. You are in a taxi on the way to the airport.
8. You are checking in for your flight and the agent says "Would you like
    smoking or nonsmoking?"
9. You are in the waiting lounge and hear an announcement that your flight is
    now ready for boarding.
10. You are in line, just about to board the airplane.
11. You are in your seat and hear the plane's engines start.
12. The plane begins to move as you hear the flight attendant say, "Be sure
    your seatbelts are securely fastened."
13. You look at the runway as the plane waits to take off.
14. You look out the window as the plane begins to roll down the runway.
15. You look out the window as the plane leaves the ground.

set of rubber spiders (MacDonald & Bernstein, 1974). This careful combination of live modeling with gradual practice, called *participant modeling,* is one of the most powerful fear treatments currently available (see Figure 16.1).

Assertiveness and social skills training   Modeling is also a major part of **assertiveness and social skills training,** a set of methods for teaching clients who are anxious or unproductive in social situations how to interact with others more comfortably and effectively. In assertiveness training, the therapist helps clients learn and practice being more direct and expressive in social situations. (*Assertiveness* does not mean aggressiveness; rather, it means clearly and directly expressing both positive and negative feelings and standing up for one's rights while respecting the rights of others; Lange & Jakubowski, 1976.) Assertiveness training is usually done in groups and involves a great deal of modeling and role-playing of how to handle specific social problems. For example, a client who feels afraid or silly about asking for a raise might perfect the skills needed by repeatedly role-playing the situation with the therapist or other group members of a therapy group.

Behavior therapists also offer help in the development of whatever other behaviors a client may lack. This social skill training might include anything from helping college students to make conversation more easily on a date to rebuilding mental patients' ability to interact normally with people outside the hospital (Curran & Monti, 1982).

Positive reinforcement   Behavior therapists systematically use reinforcement to alter problematic behaviors ranging from nailbiting, childhood tantrums, and rowdy classroom behavior to juvenile delinquency, schizophrenia, and self-starvation. They follow the operant conditioning principles discussed in Chapter 7 to set up special contingencies, or relationships, between the client's behavior and its consequences. Here is one example.

> Ann, a four-year-old preschooler, interacted well with teachers and other adults, but she was shy, silent, and withdrawn around other children (Allen et al., 1964). The psychologist working with the school noticed that Ann's teachers had been inadvertently rewarding her withdrawn behavior with lots of attention and coaxing. Thus, a program was set up in which the teachers were asked to give praise and attention only when Ann was at least standing or playing near another child. Later, they shaped Ann's behavior further by rewarding only genuine interaction with other children. Isolated play was always ignored. Ann soon began to spend most of her time with other children, instead of with adults, and continued to do so.

To improve the behavior of severely disturbed or mentally retarded clients in institutions, behavior therapists sometimes establish a **token economy,** in which desirable behaviors are rewarded with tokens: poker chips, points, or other devices that can later be exchanged for snacks, field trips, access to television, or other rewards and privileges (Ayllon & Azrin, 1968; Kazdin & Bootzin, 1972). The staff, in cooperation with the client when possible, develops a list of desirable target behaviors, depending on the nature of each client's problems. These targets might include speaking clearly, doing school-work, playing cooperatively, or straightening up a bedroom. Next, a payment schedule is arranged, in which the client receives a certain number of tokens immediately after displaying a certain amount of each target behavior.

Token economies can be very effective in altering behavior. For example, among mental patients who once did little more than sit and stare into space, token systems have dramatically improved personal grooming, social interaction, mealtime etiquette, and attendance at individual therapy sessions, while greatly reducing bizarre behaviors (Ayllon & Azrin, 1968). More importantly,

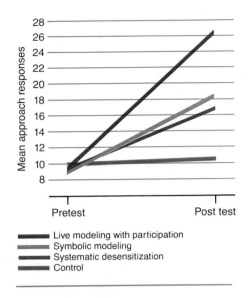

Live modeling with participation
Symbolic modeling
Systematic desensitization
Control

Figure 16.1
Participant Modeling
One study compared the effects of systematic desensitization, participant modeling, symbolic modeling (watching filmed models), and no treatment (control) in the treatment of snake phobia. As the graph illustrates, all three behavioral methods produced more interaction with snakes than no treatment, but participant modeling was clearly the best; 92 percent of the subjects in that group were virtually free of any fear. (From Bandura, Blanchard, Ritter: *Journal of Personality and Social Psychology,* 1969, 13, 173–199. Copyright 1969 by the American Psychological Association. Adapted by permission of publisher and authors.)

token systems have helped prepare even the most severely disturbed patients to live outside the mental hospital. In one major study (Paul & Lentz, 1977), token economy patients were significantly more likely to adjust to community living than those whose hospital treatment had included equal amounts of attention and care, but no contingent reinforcers for specific behaviors. Token systems have also helped mentally retarded children and adults develop self-care, social, and vocational skills (Thompson & Grabowski, 1972), and they have reduced criminal behavior in predelinquent children (Fixen et al., 1976; Kirigin et al., 1982).

Tokens are meant to supplement, not replace, other, more natural forms of reward. The staff also reinforces appropriate client behaviors with praise, encouragement, and attention. Eventually, as improved behavior comes to be supported by these social reinforcers (and the sense of pride and accomplishment they engender), clients can be gradually "weaned" from the token economy and, ideally, reenter the world outside. In fact, token economies are designed to shape and maintain patterns of behavior that will generalize beyond the hospital and thus help clients overcome problems in day-to-day functioning.

Methods based on extinction   Just as they can strengthen desirable behaviors, operant methods can also weaken undesirable behaviors. Sometimes this is done through *extinction,* the process of removing the reinforcers that normally follow a particular response. If you have ever given up calling someone whose line is busy, you know how extinction works; when a behavior does not "pay off," people usually stop it. Though extinction changes behavior rather slowly, it has been a very popular way of treating children and retarded or seriously disturbed adults, because it provides a gentle way to eliminate undesirable behaviors.

Extinction has been used to weaken phobic behavior through a procedure called **flooding,** which keeps people in a feared but harmless situation. The idea is that, once deprived of his or her normally rewarding escape pattern, the client has no reason for continued anxiety. For example, one person who feared riding on escalators was accompanied by her therapist on a continuous twenty-seven-minute ride up and down the escalators of a department store. The client was at first very frightened but later calmed down and had no further trouble (Nisbett, 1973). Most behavior therapists prefer less unpleasant approaches to fear reduction, but extinction methods, especially flooding, are sometimes useful when other techniques fail (Spiegler, 1983).

Aversive conditioning   Many unwanted behaviors, such as alcohol abuse, may be so habitual and temporarily rewarding that they must somehow be made less attractive if the client is to have any chance of learning constructive alternatives. The methods for doing this are known as **aversive conditioning** and act like desensitization in reverse; they employ classical conditioning principles to create rather than relieve a negative response to some stimulus. Just as you might have accidentally learned to stay away from a food that once made you sick, aversive conditioning purposely associates some physical or psychological discomfort with behaviors, thoughts, or situations the client wishes to avoid. For example, alcoholics may be allowed to drink after taking a nausea-producing drug (Cannon & Baker, 1981). This associates the taste and smell of alcohol with nausea rather than with the usual pleasurable feelings. In some stop-smoking programs, smokers consume cigarettes at a very rapid pace so that they will associate smoking with nausea and dizziness (Lichtenstein & Penner, 1977).

Because aversive conditioning is unpleasant and uncomfortable for the client, and because its effects are often only temporary, many therapists avoid

If undesirable behavior is too hard to ignore or is being rewarded by onlookers (as when a child gets laughs by rapping on a classmate's head), the client may be quietly escorted away from the source of reward and placed in a boring waiting room for a few minutes. This "time out" from positive reinforcement interrupts the reward process and gives the client another chance to behave more appropriately after rejoining the group.

this method or use it only long enough to allow the client to learn new behaviors. For example, Michael Serber (1972) showed that the treatment of men who exposed their genitals in public was far more successful when aversive conditioning was combined with training in more appropriate ways to meet women than when used alone.

Punishment   Sometimes the only way to eliminate a dangerous or disruptive behavior is to punish it with an unpleasant but not harmful stimulus (such as a shouted "No!" or a mild electric shock). Unlike aversive conditioning, in which the unpleasant stimulus occurs along with the behavior to be eliminated, punishment is presented after the undesirable response takes place.

The careful use of therapeutic punishment is well illustrated in the case of a brain-damaged and hyperactive six-year-old girl who repeatedly endangered herself by climbing high on furniture, doorframes, trees, and even the side of her house. Her body bore numerous scars from several serious falls. A program of reinforcement for nonclimbing did not work, because when she was not climbing, she merely sat and rocked. Extinction procedures were also ineffective in eliminating this life-threatening behavior pattern. Finally, the child's parents were trained to administer mild electric shock with a hand-held wand while shouting "No!" whenever she was found climbing. This procedure was successful, and by eliminating climbing, it created opportunities for the parents to reward other behaviors (Risley, 1968).

Cognitive Behavior Therapy

Psychodynamic and phenomenological therapists have long recognized that thought patterns may lead to depression, anger, or anxiety, even when there are no obvious reasons to feel those emotions. These problems have also been attacked by behavior therapists through methods known collectively as cognitive behavior therapy. In simplest terms, **cognitive behavior therapy** helps clients change the way they think as well as the way they behave. Thus, instead of practicing new behaviors in assertiveness training, for example, some clients need to identify the habitual thoughts that get in the way of self-expression. Similarly, some clients need help in focusing on the things they have learned to think and say to themselves that may be causing depression, anxiety, or other problems. Once these cognitive obstacles are brought to light, the therapist encourages the client to try new ways of thinking that will make it easier to behave more assertively or feel happier or more relaxed.

Some of the methods known as cognitive behavior therapy were developed by behavior therapists themselves; others have been borrowed from therapists who focus almost entirely on cognitive processes in treatment, but whose techniques are closely allied with the behavioral approach. One of these borrowed methods is **rational-emotive therapy (RET).** Developed by Albert Ellis (1962, 1973; Ellis & Bernard, 1985), RET is based on the rather phenomenological notion that anxiety, guilt, depression, and other psychological problems are not caused by frightening or upsetting events, but by how people think about those events. Ellis says, for example, that you do not get upset because you fail a test, but because you believe failure to be a disaster that indicates you are no good. RET is aimed first at identifying self-defeating, problem-causing thoughts that clients have learned. Among the most common of these thoughts are as follows:

1. It is essential that one be loved or approved by everyone.

2. One must be perfectly competent, adequate, and achieving to consider oneself worthwhile.

3. It is a terrible catastrophe when things are not as one wants them to be.

4. Unhappiness is caused by outside forces over which the individual has no control.

5. There is always a right or a perfect solution to every problem, and it must be found or the results will be catastrophic.

After the client learns to recognize thoughts like these and see how they cause problems, the therapist uses modeling, encouragement, and logic to help the client replace these maladaptive thought patterns with more realistic and beneficial ones. Here is part of an RET session with a thirty-nine-year-old woman who suffered from panic attacks. She has just said it was "terrible" that she had an attack and passed out in a restaurant.

Therapist: . . . Tell me how it is terrible.
Client: Well . . . people should be able to handle themselves!
T: Guess what, Helen . . . you just musturbated.
C: (Looks shocked, then laughs) What do you mean?
T: You said people should do such and such . . . like, people must do such and such . . . that's where the term musturbation comes from. The thing is this: As children we are taught we should do this, or we must do that, or we shouldn't do this. . . . The reality is that the "shoulds" and "musts" are the rules that other people hand down to us, and we grow up accepting them as if they are the absolute truth, which they most assuredly aren't.
C: You mean it is perfectly okay to, you know, pass out in a restaurant?
T: Sure!
C: But . . . now I'm confused . . . I know I wouldn't like it to happen.
T: I can certainly understand that. It would be unpleasant, awkward, inconvenient. But it is illogical to think that it would be terrible, or . . . that it somehow bears on your worth as a person. Thinking this way is also very self-defeating.
C: What do you mean?
T: Well, suppose one of your friends calls you up and invites you back to that restaurant. If you start telling yourself, "I might panic and pass out and people might make fun of me and that would be terrible," you are going to make yourself uptight. And you might find you are dreading going to the restaurant, and you probably won't enjoy the meal very much.
C: Well, that is what usually happens.
T: But it doesn't have to be that way. . . . The way you feel, your reaction, . . . depends on what you choose to believe or think, or say to yourself. . . .
C: Well, what should I think, Doctor?
T: That was a musturbation! Can you state that in a more rational way?
C: (Laughs) Hmmm . . . let's see. What would be a . . . healthy . . . thing to think?
T: Let's role-play it. (Rimm & Masters, 1979)

Many techniques related to RET are used by cognitive behavior therapists to help clients learn to think in new, more adaptive ways. Generally known as **cognitive restructuring** (Lazarus, 1971), these methods can help clients learn calming thoughts that they can use in stressful or anxiety-provoking situations, such as giving speeches, taking tests, or having unpleasant conversations. These thoughts might take the form of "OK, stay calm, you can handle this if you just focus on the task and don't worry about being perfect" (Meichenbaum, 1977). These methods are sometimes expanded into **stress inoculation training,** in which the therapist asks the client to imagine being in some stressful situation so that he or she can practice using new cognitive skills under controlled conditions (Meichenbaum, 1985).

Especially when dealing with depressed clients, behavior therapists often use Aaron Beck's *cognitive therapy.* It helps the client see that depression occurs in part because of extremes of thought in which he or she exaggerates the importance and frequency of negative events ("Nothing ever goes right!") and minimizes the value of personal accomplishments ("Anyone could do that!"). In addition, clients are given homework that helps them keep track of and focus on positive events and personal skills (Beck et al., 1979).

TABLE 16.3
**A Comparative Overview of
Psychological Treatments**
*The three main approaches to
psychotherapy differ on a number of
dimensions.*

Dimension	Psychoanalytic	Phenomeno-logical	Behavioral
Nature of the human being	Driven by sexual and aggressive instincts that create problems	Has free will, choice, and the capacity for self-determination and self-actualization	A product of social learning and conditioning; behaves on basis of past experience
Therapist's role	Neutral; helps client explore meaning of free associations and other material from the unconscious	Facilitator of client's growth potential	Teacher/trainer who helps client replace undesirable thoughts and behaviors with better ones; active, action-oriented
Time frame	Emphasis on uncovering unresolved, unconscious conflicts from the distant past	Here and now; uses data of immediate experience	Current behavior and thoughts; may not need to know original cause in order to create changes
Goals	Psychosexual maturity through insight; strengthening of ego functions	Expanded awareness, fulfillment of potential; self-acceptance	Changes in thinking and behaving in particular classes of situations; better self-management
Attitude toward assessment	Prefers interviews and projective tests aimed at giving clues to unconscious conflicts and personality dynamics	Avoids tests; tries to see world through client's eyes	Behavioral assessment aimed at identifying thoughts and behaviors to be changed; observation, self-reports and self-monitoring favored

Methods of cognitive behavior therapy are also useful as part of behavioral treatments of overeating, drug abuse, cigarette smoking, troublesome sexual practices, and other problems of self-control (Foreyt & Kondo, 1984). Their primary value in these programs lies in helping clients learn to say things to themselves that promote desirable behavior and prevent a relapse into undesirable behavior (Marlatt & Gordon, 1985).

Some Comments on Behavior Therapy

Table 16.3 summarizes key features of behavior therapy and compares it with other approaches to treatment. There is little doubt that behavior therapy methods have been very successful in altering a wide range of problematic behaviors and thoughts (Kazdin, 1984). The treatment of phobia and other anxiety disorders through desensitization and related techniques has been particularly successful, as has the use of reward systems to build new behaviors in adults and children. Furthermore, although not all behavior therapists have adopted them, cognitive-behavioral techniques have proved helpful in dealing with clients' thoughts as systematically as other behavioral techniques deal with more overt behaviors (Dush, Hirt & Schroeder, 1983; Miller & Berman, 1983; Schwartz, 1982).

Yet controversy surrounds behavior therapy. Some critics view it as too mechanical and, in spite of the growth of cognitive-behavioral methods, too focused on overt behavior, which, they say, is only the symptom of deeper problems. Critics also worry that treating symptoms without dealing with the underlying problems will lead to treatment failure or, through a process called *symptom substitution,* the appearance of a new symptom. Particular behavioral methods have also come under fire. For example, though short-term, carefully controlled punishment can be of significant benefit, especially when all else fails, or when the client's behavior problems are life-threatening, some feel that punishment is dehumanizing and should not be used. There is equal or greater concern over aversive conditioning. In addition, assertiveness training, social skills training, and cognitive-behavioral methods, such as RET, are viewed by skeptics as merely persuading clients to adopt the therapist's style of thinking and behaving. Finally, critics note that not all forms of behavior disorder can be effectively addressed through learning-based methods alone.

With respect to the symptom-substitution issue, behaviorists argue that overt behavior and maladaptive thoughts *are* the problems of greatest concern and that only if the therapist fails to detect an important aspect of these problems will treatment fail or create a new problem. As to the allegedly mechanical nature of behavior therapy, it is only fair to say that behavior therapists display just as much humanistic concern for their clients as other therapists. Indeed, the success of behavior therapies, combined with the ease with which they can be applied to an ever-widening array of personal and social problems makes this approach one of the most promising.

EVALUATING PSYCHOTHERAPY

Does psychotherapy work? If so, which approach works best? In one sense, psychotherapy must help clients, since countless case reports and personal accounts published by therapists and their clients attest to significant and often dramatic changes during and after psychotherapy. But believing that therapy helps and demonstrating it scientifically are two very different things.

The Effects of Psychotherapy

In 1952 British psychologist Hans Eysenck compared the effects of traditional psychodynamic therapy to those of routine medical care or no treatment in thousands of neurotic clients. To the surprise and dismay of many, Eysenck (1952) concluded that having this type of therapy did not increase clients' chances of improvement; in fact, he claimed that more untreated than treated clients recovered (72 percent versus about 66 percent). In the years that followed, Eysenck supported his conclusions with additional evidence (Eysenck, 1961, 1966), whereas critics looked at the same data and argued that he was wrong (DeCharms, Levy & Wertheimer, 1954; Luborsky, 1954, 1972). They accused Eysenck of excluding from his analyses several studies that supported the value of psychotherapy. They also pointed out that untreated clients may have been less disturbed in the first place than those in treatment; that untreated clients may have received informal treatment from their doctors; and that the physicians who judged untreated clients' progress might have used different, or more lenient, criteria than the psychotherapists who rated their own clients. The fact that there could be so much arguing about how to interpret Eysenck's data indicated that better methods for evaluating psychotherapy had to be developed. Additional studies of outcomes began to appear and became more sophisticated in design.

Unfortunately, the quality of studies of therapy outcomes is still quite variable. Furthermore, it is difficult to define precisely what is meant by success in treatment. Since some therapists look for changes in unconscious conflicts or ego strength, while others focus on alterations in overt behavior or self-reports of happiness, different observers might make different judgments about whether a given client's treatment was successful. These points must be kept in mind when considering surveys of research on the overall effectiveness of psychotherapy.

These surveys have reached conclusions that are somewhat more optimistic than Eysenck's. For example, Julian Meltzoff and Melvin Kornreich (1970) found that about 80 percent of the 101 studies they reviewed showed positive outcomes following therapy. Allen Bergin (1971) concluded that therapy was superior to no treatment in 22 of the 52 studies he surveyed. A later review (Bergin & Lambert, 1978) found about the same thing. Psychotherapy clients did better than no-treatment controls in 20 of 33 studies reviewed by Lester Luborsky, Barton Singer, and Lise Luborsky (1975); in the other 13 studies, there was a tie. Using special mathematical techniques called *meta-analysis* ("the analysis of analyses"), Mary Lee Smith, Gene Glass, and Thomas Miller (1980) compared the effects of therapy, no treatment, and other control conditions reported in 475 outcome studies. Their main conclusion was that the average therapy client is better off after treatment than 80 percent of those who do not get treatment. Other meta-analyses have supported that conclusion (Landman & Dawes, 1982; Shapiro & Shapiro, 1983).

Together, these reviews suggest that, when the results of all forms of psychological treatment are looked at together, they support the statement that psychotherapy can be effective (Lambert, Shapiro & Bergin, 1986). This is certainly encouraging, for both clients and therapists. But critics of meta-analysis and of other methods of surveying therapy outcomes argue that even sophisticated combination of results from a mish-mash of good and mediocre studies, on the treatment of many different problems by many different methods, may be misleading. Furthermore, these studies cannot answer more important questions about psychotherapy, such as which treatments are best for certain problems (Kazdin, 1985; Paul, 1986; Rachman & Wilson, 1980; Searles, 1985; Strube, Gardner & Hartmann, 1985; Wilson, 1985; Wilson & Rachman, 1983).

Is one therapy approach better than others overall, or for certain problems? Most of the reviews we mentioned found no significant differences in the overall effectiveness of the three main approaches to therapy. Critics argue that these reviews and meta-analyses are not sensitive enough to pick up between-method differences, but even studies that have carefully compared psychodynamic, behavioral, and phenomenological treatments in the same experiment have failed to show one approach to be notably superior to another, though all are superior to no treatment (Cross, Sheehan & Kahn, 1982; Olson et al., 1981; Sloane et al., 1975). When differences in treatment effectiveness do show up, they often tend to favor behavioral methods, especially in the treatment of anxiety (Andrews & Harvey, 1981; Bergin & Lambert, 1978; Giles, 1983; Kazdin & Wilson, 1978; Lichtenstein, 1980; Luborsky, Singer & Luborsky, 1975; Rachman, 1973; Rachman & Wilson, 1980; Searles, 1985). Favorable data on behavior therapy and the basic appeal of phenomenological therapy have made both methods increasingly popular, while the once-dominant psychodynamic therapies have declined somewhat (Garfield & Kurtz, 1976; Prochaska & Norcross, 1982; Smith, 1982).

Recreational therapy with a group of emotionally disturbed children. Working as part of a team headed by a psychiatrist, psychologist, or social worker, recreational therapists, psychiatric nurses, and occupational therapists often provide treatment services, especially in hospitals.

In summary, it appears that (1) psychotherapy works; (2) no single approach has proved unquestionably superior overall; and (3) much more research is needed to determine the combination of therapist, client, and treatment that will most effectively solve each of the many psychological problems that require attention in our society.

Differences Among Therapists

Several professional groups are socially accepted as agents of treatment for psychological disorders. Psychiatrists and psychologists are the most prominent examples. **Psychiatrists** are medical doctors who complete special training in the treatment of mental disorder. **Psychologists** who do psychotherapy have completed a graduate program in clinical or counseling psychology, often followed by additional specialty training. According to the American Psychological Association and the laws of most states, only those who hold a doctoral degree are officially recognized as clinical or counseling psychologists. However, psychotherapy services are often provided by individuals who have completed only a master's degree. (Unlike psychiatrists, psychologists are not permitted to prescribe drugs.) Psychotherapy is also offered by *psychiatric social workers,* who typically hold a master's degree from a school of social work. They usually provide psychotherapy services in a hospital or clinic, though many also enter private practice. *Psychiatric nurses, occupational therapists,* and *recreational therapists* also provide therapy, especially in hospitals where they work as part of a team, usually headed by a psychiatrist or a psychologist.

Interestingly, most people do not actually turn to any of these "official" agents for help—at least not at first (Cowen, 1982; Gurin, Veroff & Feld, 1960). They may go instead to a member of their family; to the clergy; to their physician, teacher, or lawyer; to their friends; to self-help groups (such as Alcoholics Anonymous); and even to their barber, beautician, or bartender. These helpers cannot offer formal treatment, but they are in a position to aid a very large number of distressed people (Lichtenstein, 1980). Recognition of this fact has led to the development of special programs designed to train some of these "invisible therapists" to do an even better job, especially the clergy, who commonly enter formal study to enhance their counseling skills.

No professional group holds a monopoly on competence, but certain people seem to make particularly effective therapists. Usually these are individuals who are especially good at forming productive relationships with people. Some may have had relatively little formal training (Berman & Norton, 1985). In therapy, this interpersonal skill appears as the ability to listen to clients with interest, understanding, and sensitivity; make clients feel accepted; and be supportive while still requiring clients to assume responsibility for solving their problems. These characteristics have been summarized in the acronym SAUNA (Allen, 1977): Sensitive, Active, Unflappable, Nonpunitive, and Amoral (that is, not likely to impose personal moral values on clients).

Although it certainly makes sense that SAUNAs would have more success than people who are nasty or judgmental, the therapist's skill at selecting and using particular methods also has much to do with how effective therapy will be (Lambert, DeJulio & Stein, 1978). The match between client and therapist is also crucial; even a good therapist, using well-established methods, may fail to help certain clients. Thus, the "best" therapists appear to be those whose relationship skills and treatment methods give them the best chance of helping the widest range of clients.

BIOLOGICAL TREATMENTS

Hippocrates, the ancient Greek physician, was among the first to propose that psychological problems have physical causes. He prescribed rest, special diets, laxatives, and abstinence from alcohol or sex as treatments for psychological disorders. In the mental hospitals of Europe and America during the sixteenth through eighteenth centuries, treatment consisted mainly of physical restraints, along with laxative purges, bleeding of "excess" blood, and induced vomiting. Cold baths, heat treatments, hunger, and other physical discomforts were also used to try shocking patients back to normality. In the 1800s, the shock became electrical and was delivered to patients' hands.

The crib, a device used in the nineteenth century to restrain unmanageable mental patients, was gentle compared to some of the treatment methods advocated by Benjamin Rush, an influential American psychiatrist of the late 1700s. He not only endorsed bleedings but advocated curing patients by frightening or disorienting them. This included placing patients in a coffinlike box which was then briefly immersed in water.

Electroconvulsive Therapy (ECT)

In the 1930s, electric shock began to be used in another way. A Hungarian physician had suggested that, since schizophrenia and epilepsy rarely occurred in the same person, the conditions were incompatible and that epilepticlike seizures might therefore combat schizophrenia. He began inducing convulsions in schizophrenics by using a drug. Later, two Italian physicians named Ugo Cerletti and Lucio Bini created convulsions more easily by applying an electric current to schizophrenics' brains. This **electroconvulsive therapy (ECT)** had an effect on schizophrenic symptoms, but it also seemed to relieve the depression that some patients had been experiencing. During the next twenty years or so, ECT became a routine treatment for schizophrenia, depression, and, sometimes, mania.

The standard ECT procedure involved placing electrodes on either side of the patient's forehead and sending 70 to 150 volts of electricity directly through the brain for up to one and one-half seconds. The patient immediately lost consciousness and for a minute or so had a series of convulsions, causing muscle contractions violent enough to dislocate or fracture bones. On awakening after a few minutes, the patient typically remembered nothing about the events just preceding the shock and remained confused for varying periods of time. Although many patients improved following ECT, the benefits were sometimes outweighed by negative side effects, including memory loss, speech disorders, and even some deaths (Breggin, 1979). These problems arose in part because the treatment methods were relatively crude, but also because patients often received dozens, even hundreds, of such treatments.

Several changes have been made in recent years to make ECT safer. First, patients are now given an anesthetic to make them unconscious before the shock is delivered and a muscle relaxant to prevent bone fractures during the convulsions. Second, the duration of shock is now on the order of half a second, and treatment ranges from six to about twelve shocks, given about once every two days. Third, instead of passing current through both cerebral hemispheres (bilateral ECT), some doctors now place both electrodes on the nondominant side of the patient's head. This results in fewer undesirable side effects, but it is not clear whether this method is as effective as the bilateral version (Abrams et al., 1983; Daniel & Crovitz, 1983; Weiner, 1984; Scovern & Kilmann, 1980).

Proponents point out that the risks associated with modern ECT are very slight and that the treatment helps overcome or reduce severe depression and the risk of suicide associated with it (Fink, 1979; Frankel, 1984). Evidence for these benefits has appeared in numerous studies (Scovern & Kilmann, 1980). Nevertheless, critics argue that, too often, ECT's effects are temporary and that it creates memory loss and other problems, which, though rare, can be severe (Breggin, 1979). Furthermore, no one knows for sure how ECT works, other than the fact that the convulsions, not the shock itself, are important. One possibility is that the convulsions somehow increase the amount of the neurotransmitter norepinephrine available at brain synapses (Fink, 1979). Another view is that the neurotransmitters that help the brain recover from the convulsion also reduce activity in areas of the brain associated with depression, thus relieving it (Sackeim, 1985). These are promising leads, but the answer is still in doubt.

ECT continues to be one of the most controversial of biological treatment methods. It is administered to about 100,000 people each year in the United States, far fewer than in past decades. While there have been attempts to outlaw ECT in several states and at least one city (Berkeley, California), committees from both the American Psychiatric Association and the National

Institutes of Health have endorsed the careful use of ECT, especially when other treatments are ineffective (APA, 1978; Holden, 1985). It is now given mainly to those whose depression is profound and fails to respond to antidepressant drugs.

Psychosurgery

In ancient times, the desire to help severely troubled people apparently led to a form of surgery called *trephining,* in which a hole was made in the skull to allow evil spirits to escape. The same good intentions led to **prefrontal lobotomy,** a procedure in which small holes were drilled in the skull and a sharp instrument was inserted and moved from side to side (Freeman & Watts, 1942). The theory was that, in disturbed patients, emotional reactions became exaggerated by processes taking place in the frontal lobes and that the lobotomy disrupted these processes.

Lobotomy is a form of **psychosurgery,** a set of procedures in which various regions of the brain are destroyed in an effort to alleviate psychological disorders. Initial reports of dramatic improvements following these procedures made psychosurgery almost routine during the 1940s and 1950s in the treatment of schizophrenia, depression, anxiety, aggressiveness, obsessive-compulsive disorder, and many other problems involving strong emotional responses (Donnelly, 1978; Valenstein, 1980). Unfortunately, brain surgery is risky and sometimes fatal, and its side effects and complications may be irreversible. Though some patients who had required hospitalization before surgery were able to go home, the treatment was often too "successful." It produced uncharacteristic listlessness and a lack of any emotion. In other cases, patients became more emotional than before. These and other problems prompted the Soviet Union to ban psychosurgery in 1951. Though still legal in the United States, these seldom-performed operations are done only as a last resort, when all less radical treatments have failed. Even then, modern psychosurgery involves destruction of only a tiny amount of brain tissue.

Drugs

The use of ECT and psychosurgery has declined not only because of their side effects, complications, and general distastefulness, but also because biological treatments have come to rely heavily on tranquilizing, antidepressant, and antipsychotic drugs. These drugs began to appear in the 1950s. Today they are used to combat such troubling symptoms as anxiety, depression, mania, and hallucinations or to correct biological imbalances believed to be at the root of some forms of mental disorder (see Chapter 15). Most of the drugs used in the treatment of psychological disorders are listed in Table 6.1, in the chapter on consciousness. They include antipsychotics, antidepressants, lithium, and tranquilizers (also known as antianxiety drugs).

Antipsychotics   In the 1940s, it was discovered that *reserpine,* a drug derived from the root of the snakeroot plant, seemed to act as an **antipsychotic** drug, alleviating mania, schizophrenia, and other severe forms of psychological disorder. Unfortunately, it also caused such side effects as depression and lowered blood pressure. In the early 1950s, a synthetic antipsychotic drug was created. Known as chlorpromazine (and sold as Thorazine), it was the first of a group of *phenothiazines,* whose effects on schizophrenic symptoms were equal to reserpine's but did not cause as many undesirable side effects. Their primary effect is to block the action of dopamine, a neurotransmitter that, as noted in Chapter 15, is thought to be involved in schizophrenia.

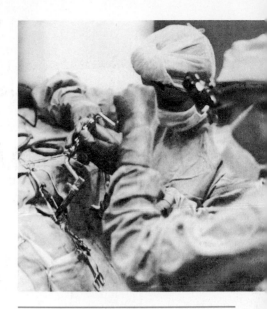

During a prefrontal lobotomy, surgeons used a drill to open the skull. In some places in the United States during the early 1950s, as many as fifty such operations were performed each day (Freeman, 1959).

The phenothiazines created nothing less than a revolution in the treatment of severe psychopathology. Their effectiveness in reducing delusions, hallucinations, and other disturbed behavior allowed mental hospitals to release thousands of patients and to deal with the rest without the padded cells, straitjackets, and other restraints that had been a standard feature of institutional treatment for centuries.

Antidepressants   Shortly after antipsychotic drugs began to appear, they were joined by medications designed to relieve depression. The most common of these **antidepressants** are *monoamine oxydase* (or *MAO*) *inhibitors* and *tricyclics*. Of the two, the tricyclics are used more frequently because they seem to work somewhat better, with fewer side effects. In many cases, the effects of these drugs are quite dramatic, producing a gradual lifting of depression and allowing the person to return to a normal life, often with the help of continued medication, sometimes without it. Antidepressants appear to work by increasing the amount of serotonin or norepinephrine available at brain synapses. Although this idea is consistent with the neurotransmitter theory of depression mentioned in Chapter 15, it remains unclear why the drugs' rapid effect on neurotransmitter levels is often not translated into improved mood for several weeks.

Lithium   Around 1970 the mineral salt **lithium** was found to be helpful not only in relieving depression, but also in reducing and even preventing both depression and the mania associated with bipolar disorder (Berger, 1978; Coppen, Metcalf & Wood, 1982). Lithium appears to control mania by reducing the norepinephrine available at brain synapses (the opposite of how some antidepressants work); why this also lifts depression is a mystery. The drug must be given carefully because an overdose can be harmful, even fatal. Many physicians prefer to try less toxic drugs, such as chlorpromazine or other antipsychotics, in dealing with mania.

Tranquilizers (antianxiety drugs)   In the first half of this century, barbiturates and other potentially dangerous central nervous system depressants were the only drugs available for the treatment of anxiety, or "nervous tension." This changed in the 1950s, with the introduction of **tranquilizers,** such as meprobamate (sold as Miltown or Equanil), chlordiazepoxide (Librium), and diazepam (Valium). The millions of prescriptions written for tranquilizers each year make them the most widely used of all legal drugs. They are administered to people in all walks of life, the vast majority of whom are not hospitalized, but whose anxiety or tension interferes with their lives in some way. Because tranquilizers are so good at producing calmness, even under stress, many people come to depend on them just to get through the day. Yet, for some users, especially those on meprobamate, this calming effect is accompanied by a lack of energy. If the drugs are overused for long periods, psychological dependence on them can become addiction (Levenson, 1981).

HIGHLIGHT

Some Pros and Cons of Drug Treatment

In spite of the widespread success of the "drug revolution" in the treatment of psychological disorders, enthusiasm about drugs has not been universal. Critics point out three major limitations.

First, even if the origin of a disorder is physical, drugs generally cover up or suppress the problem; they do not permanently cure it. For example, though antianxiety drugs do not remove or teach people to cope with the sources of their anxiety, harried physicians may be tempted to prescribe drugs instead of attempting to deal with the person's problems. Second, even clearly beneficial therapeutic drugs may be abused, resulting in addiction or psychological dependence. Third, side effects present a problem. Some are merely annoying, such as the thirst and dry mouth produced by some antidepressants. Others are far more serious. This issue is complicated by the fact that the long-term effects of drugs are not necessarily the same as the initial effects. Neurotransmitter systems tend to adjust to drugs over a long period of time, and the final outcome of such compensatory changes may not be what was expected. Some delayed side effects appear only when it is too late to reverse them.

For example, antipsychotic drugs block dopamine receptors. The early side effects therefore include motor rigidity similar to Parkinson's symptoms (which results from too little dopamine in the striatum). However, as noted in Chapter 3, over a period of years, the dopamine receptors in movement systems compensate for the blockade by becoming more sensitive to dopamine. The movement disorder that results is *tardive dyskinesia,* which creates symptoms that are the opposite of Parkinson's disease and opposite to the initial side effects of the drug. Uncontrollable movements of the face and tongue are especially prominent, and sometimes the person's arms or legs will flail unpredictably. Tardive dyskinesia can be worse than the psychotic symptoms that prompted the drug treatment. One recourse is to increase the dose of the dopamine-blocking antipsychotic (to block the movements), but that only makes the problem worse in the long run. Tardive dyskinesia is the most severe constraint on the usefulness of antipsychotics.

Obviously, drug treatments have their limitations, and there are even greater limitations on knowledge about them. Still, the good done by antipsychotic and other drugs cannot be denied. In addition, even the problems caused by drugs have stimulated research aimed at developing better, less problematic medications. This continuing research may have "side effects" of its own, leading to knowledge about the origin and nature of some psychological disorders. For example, scientists are working to find drugs that will relieve schizophrenia without affecting movement systems. To do so, they will probably have to locate synapses that are defective in cases of schizophrenia, but that have a different receptor type than the synapses at which dopamine affects movement. Finding and differentiating these neural circuits could not only produce a drug that affects one receptor type without affecting the other, but also provide new information about the biological basis of schizophrenia (White & Wang, 1986).

Research on improving antianxiety drugs also promises to reveal important information about the chemical aspects of anxiety. Because these drugs bind to certain receptor sites in the brain, it may be that these sites and the neural circuits to which they connect are fundamental to the experience of anxiety. Indeed, the presence of these receptor sites suggests that there are naturally occurring substances in the body that trigger anxiety. As mentioned in Chapter 3, for example, the neurotransmitter GABA may be involved, since disruptions in GABA-regulated systems may create anxiety. Perhaps there are naturally occurring anxiety suppressors as well, and if so, perhaps they can be isolated or imitated for use in treating anxiety. ▪

COMMUNITY PSYCHOLOGY: FROM TREATMENT TO PREVENTION

Even if we knew exactly what treatment method to use for every human problem, there would not be enough mental health professionals available to provide help for everyone who needed it (Albee, 1968). Recognition of this fact has fostered the rise of **community psychology,** a movement whose goal is to minimize or prevent psychological disorders, not just treat them. These efforts began with community mental health programs designed to make traditional treatment methods more accessible to the poor and others who are unserved or underserved by mental health professionals. Later, community psychology broadened its perspective to include efforts at preventing psychological disorders by altering the conditions that can cause or aggravate them.

Community Mental Health Centers

For the first half of this century, the most seriously disturbed members of society were given routine custodial care, along with electroshock and other medically oriented treatments in large state mental hospitals. Unfortunately, extended hospitalization of this kind tends to cut clients off from their families and the larger community, demoralizing them and often making their condition worse (Ullmann & Krasner, 1975). Providing treatment outside a hospital, usually in the client's home community, was ultimately recognized as a more effective approach, and one that costs state government less (Kiesler, 1982). This awareness, in combination with newly developed antipsychotic drugs that made physical restraints less necessary, fostered a trend in the late 1950s toward treating mental patients in their home communities. During the next thirty years, the patient population in mental hospitals continued to plummet. This process of *deinstitutionalization* placed a heavy burden on already overloaded mental health professionals in local communities.

The *community mental health movement* arose in the 1960s as an attempt by the administrations of Presidents John F. Kennedy and Lyndon B. Johnson to address the need for more abundant and accessible treatment, not only for former mental hospital patients, but for other clients as well. To make it possible for people to obtain low-cost mental health services without entering a hospital, plans were made for a nationwide network of community mental health centers (CMHCs). These centers were designed to provide outpatient therapy, short-term inpatient care, and daytime programs for former hospital patients and others who need supervision but can live at home. Some CMHC staff members were to be psychologists and other mental health professionals, but leaders of the community mental health movement demonstrated that a degree is not always necessary to help people with problems (Berman & Norton, 1985; Cowen, 1982; Durlak, 1979). Accordingly, college students, housewives, and many other community residents were trained to work under professional supervision as mental health workers (Berman & Norton, 1985; Hattie, Sharply & Rogers, 1984).

Prevention

As noted earlier, the community mental health movement is only one component of a larger trend toward community psychology, which focuses primarily on the goal of preventing psychological problems before they require treatment (Albee, 1985). Many of these problems, especially those leading to child abuse, marital strife, failure in school, alcoholism, drug abuse, and suicide, occur in generation after generation. Community psychologists point out that trying to deal with such problems after they appear is like trying to rescue one person after another from a rushing river. Eventually, you must go upstream and do something about whatever is causing all those people to fall in the river (Rappaport, 1977).

Some work by community psychologists involves *primary prevention;* it seeks to head off problems before they start (Caplan, 1964). For example, it is generally agreed that unemployment, poverty, and overcrowded, substandard housing can create stress on the people who live under these conditions. And,

Many community mental health centers include among their services mental health education as well as twenty-four-hour walk-in facilities or "hotlines" for people who are suicidal or in crises related to rape or domestic violence.

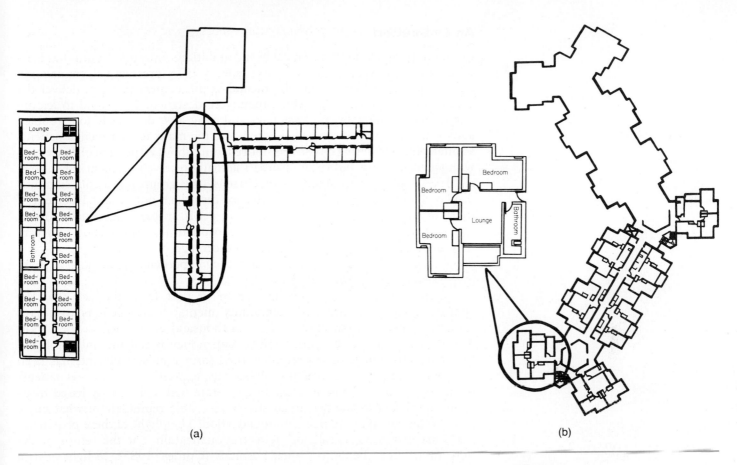

(a)

(b)

Figure 16.2
Community Consultation
Psychologists have shown that the way living space is constructed can affect the stress people experience. One study of college dormitories found that students living in (a) *"hallway" dorms had a greater sense of crowding and discomfort than those who lived in* (b) *suites, even though the same number of people lived in each arrangement (Baum & Valins, 1973). Community psychologists use findings like these to try to prevent excess stress; they remind architects of the importance of privacy for residents of dorms, apartment buildings, and offices. This specific focus on the effects of different physical environments on human behavior is sometimes called* environmental psychology. *(From A. Baum and S. Valins, 1977.* Architecture and Social Behavior: Psychological Studies of Social Density. *Hillsdale, N.J.: Copyright 1977 by Lawrence Erlbaum Associates. Adapted with permission of the publisher.)*

as we noted in the chapters on stress and abnormal psychology, stress appears related to a variety of psychological disorders. Do something about these problems, either directly or by influencing lawmakers, say community psychologists, and you will have reduced more stress and prevented more psychological problems than a battalion of psychotherapists could. To promote primary prevention, some community psychologists have become social and political activists. They may support certain candidates for office or organize neighborhood residents to push for changes in their community. Most often, community psychologists act as consultants, working with schools, groups of newly divorced or retired people, and many other community organizations to suggest ways of preventing psychological problems by easing transitions from one phase of life to another (Felner et al., 1985; see Figure 16.2).

Less ambitious, but perhaps even more significant, are community psychologists' efforts at *secondary prevention,* in which the goal is to detect psychological problems in their earliest stages and keep them from becoming worse. Examples include suicide prevention and the other crisis intervention services, as well as programs like Project Head Start, which identify and offer special help to preschoolers whose disadvantaged backgrounds make them less likely to do well academically. Other programs have trained teachers to identify early signs of behavior problems or abuse.

Community psychology blends into community mental health in third-level, or *tertiary, prevention.* Here, psychological disorders are treated after they appear, with an emphasis on minimizing their long-term effects and keeping them from recurring. The most prominent examples of tertiary prevention are programs designed to allow emotionally disturbed or mentally retarded individuals to live in the community and develop the skills they need for semi-independent living.

An Evaluation

Community psychology is a laudable and ambitious enterprise, but it has been criticized on several counts. For example, a 1978 presidential commission report concluded that community mental health centers may not deliver the broad range of services for which they were designed. They tend to feature one-to-one therapy by professionals and may not do much for troubled adolescents, severely disturbed children, and the many former mental patients so often seen wandering city streets. Indeed, only about 20 percent of Americans with significant psychological disorders actually receive treatment (Shapiro et al., 1984). Worse yet, among poor citizens (the group repeatedly found to display the most serious forms of behavior disorder), only about 1 percent of those in need of help get it, or even try to get it. In particular, many former mental patients are not getting the posthospitalization protection and care they need. In contrast, a much higher percentage of middle- or upper-class people seek and receive treatment when they experience psychological problems (Heller & Monahan, 1977).

These service-delivery problems stem in part from the fact that the approximately eight hundred community mental health centers that have actually opened fell far short of the two thousand envisioned in the 1960s. And they continue to be underfunded. But money is not the only problem. Outpatient treatment of severely disturbed former mental patients has been opposed by some mental health professionals, as well as by homeless patients themselves, many of whom refuse to cooperate with community-based treatment, preferring to wander urban streets as visible reminders of what many claim to be the failure of deinstitutionalization. The plight of these people has led some observers to call for "reinstitutionalization," or the return of the most disordered clients to mental hospitals (Cordes, 1985). In light of data showing the negative effects of hospitalization (Kiesler, 1982), this could be an unfortunate step.

There is also disappointment that the primary prevention efforts made so far have failed to reduce the prevalence of mental disorder (Cowen, 1983).

The presence of thousands of homeless mentally disturbed people on the streets of our cities has fueled criticism that community mental health programs have failed to provide necessary treatment and other services to released mental patients and others in need of long-term care.

Some observers attribute this to the fact that we do not yet understand the causes of mental disorder well enough to know what social changes can prevent them. In spite of criticisms like these, the goal of reaching out to ever-widening circles of those in need and the ideal of prevention are sure to remain with us. As research increases understanding of the causes and cures of psychological disorder, community psychology will become even more valuable.

FUTURE DIRECTIONS

The treatment of psychological disorders is a valuable undertaking that relieves the suffering of thousands of clients each year. Yet the goal is always to do better. Nonstop research makes the treatment field one of the most exciting in psychology. One of the most important and controversial issues in this field is how to choose treatment methods that will be most effective for each client's problems. Should each therapist continue using his or her favorite methods, regardless of what research might say, or should there be a research-based formula for matching treatments to problems? To help therapists decide, the American Psychiatric Association has scheduled for 1988 publication a manual for the selection of treatment. Unlike DSM-III-R, which contains specific criteria for choosing diagnoses of mental disorder, the treatment manual will contain more general recommendations for treatment selection, along with extensive reviews of clinical experience and research on the effects of certain psychological and drug treatments on various disorders. The American Psychological Association is also considering developing a treatment selection manual of its own (Landers, 1986, 1987).

Among the notable features likely to characterize treatment methods in the future is a continued emphasis on altering problematic thoughts, as well as problematic behavior. This focus reflects the cognitive revolution that has influenced research in many areas of psychology. It is most notable in behavioral approaches (where changes in overt behavior were once nearly the exclusive goal), but it runs through the entire range of treatments. To take but one example, research in cognitive psychology has led to greater awareness of the importance of attributional and memory processes in the regulation of behavior. The person who fails at some task and attributes this outcome to his or her general and permanent incompetence is far more likely to become depressed than the individual who perceives the failure as either bad luck or a temporary lack of concentration (Peterson & Seligman, 1984; Raps et al., 1982). Further, depressives may be more likely to recall negative than positive events (Teasdale, 1983). This is a major reason why cognitively oriented psychotherapy for depression focuses on helping clients develop more optimistic ways of thinking, which make self-blame less extreme and focus more on positive events.

Changes in the way that *therapists* think have led to the rise of eclecticism, an orientation in which methods from several approaches, including the biological, are used together in innovative combinations. This integrative approach has been suggested for many years (Thorne, 1950), but it has recently become so popular that most mental health practitioners today no longer identify with just one approach. This broadening of view has been prompted in part by evidence that all the major treatment approaches can be beneficial, but that no single approach is universally successful, and also by recognition of the common features that help make any treatment effective. Thus, the eclectic therapist works to create a good relationship and employs whatever combination of methods appears likely to help a given client with a given problem (Arkowitz & Messer, 1984; Garfield, 1981; Goldfried, 1982;

LINKAGES
an example

TREATMENT OF PSYCHOLOGICAL DISORDERS AND PERSONALITY
Are Certain Personality Characteristics Associated with Successful Psychotherapy?

Table A summarizes three categories of people who receive treatment for psychological disorders. We mentioned earlier that, on the average, treated clients are more likely than untreated people to improve, but a look at individual results shows that some people do far better in therapy than others. What makes the difference?

For the most part, the success of therapy depends mainly on factors such as the severity of the client's problems, the type and length of treatment, the therapist's skill, the circumstances of the client's life, and the client's motivation for change (Bandura, 1969; Garfield, 1986; Howard et al., 1986). For example, it is generally the case that individuals whose problems are of recent origin and not serious enough to prevent them from functioning reasonably well on a day-to-day basis are more likely to improve in therapy than those who display more severe, long-term disorders, such as schizophrenia. Similarly, clients who want to solve their problems and volunteer for therapy tend to do better than those who are forced into treatment or are unwilling to try very hard.

Beyond these differences, do those who improve in treatment exhibit a specific set of personality characteristics? Yes and no. To the extent that personality characteristics relate to the nature and severity of a client's problems, they may predict success in therapy. For example, scores on the MMPI, a personality test described in Chapter 14, are sometimes related to the success of subsequent treatment (Prager & Garfield, 1972). Similarly, clients who see themselves as being in control of what happens to them and who are confident of their ability to overcome their problems—that is, people who score as internal on the Rotter internal-external control scale or who score high on self-efficacy tests (see Chapter 14)—often tend to do better in treatment (Ollendick, Elliott & Matson, 1980; Weisz, 1986). But evidence for a relationship between personality and the outcome of therapy tends to be inconsistent (Stone et al., 1961). Few, if any, specific dimensions of personality reliably predict the outcome of treatment (Garfield, 1986).

Despite this conclusion, personality may indirectly influence the outcome of (continued on page 622)

Kendall, 1982; Lazarus, 1981; Marmor & Woods, 1980; Wachtel, 1982; Wandersman, Poppen & Ricks, 1976). The trend toward integration extends to the ways in which psychological and biological treatments are combined. For example, tranquilizers, antidepressants, and other drugs once used primarily in the biological treatment of inpatients or as an accompaniment to psychodynamic therapy are now sometimes used in support of behavioral and other methods. They may be used in especially difficult cases of agoraphobia, obesity, obsessive-compulsive disorder, panic attacks, and other problems (Craighead, 1984; Hersen et al., 1984; Latimer, 1983; Stern, 1983; Zitrin, 1983).

Research on combined treatment approaches is important not only because it is likely to discover the optimal blending of methods for treating particular problems, but also because studying a wider range of treatment methods makes it easier to address what Paul (1969) once called the "ultimate question" in outcome research: What treatment, by whom, is most effective for this individual with that specific problem, under which set of circumstances? Answering this monumental question and determining how various treatments produce their effects will occupy researchers for many years to come (Stiles, Shapiro & Elliott, 1986).

Several courses can help you learn more about the treatment of psychological disorders. In particular, we suggest that you take courses in psychotherapy, behavior modification, psychopharmacology, and community psychology.

Category	Description
Inpatients Those treated in a hospital or other residential institution	Some display the more serious and incapacitating long-term problems described in the chapter on abnormal psychology. Around half a million of these chronic cases are hospitalized at any given time. Typically, they are older adult males from lower social class backgrounds.
Outpatients Those who receive psychotherapy while living in the community	This group is the largest and most diverse. It includes people who seek help for a wide range of problems, from nail biting to depression, most of which are less severe than those of inpatients. These individuals are usually younger than the average inpatient, more often female than male, and typically come from the middle or upper class. Recently, however, this group has included a growing number of people with more serious disorders.
Those who seek personal growth	These people may or may not have significant psychological problems. They are primarily interested in becoming more aware of themselves, forming more open and genuine relationships, and generally becoming more self-actualized. They are usually young to middle-aged adults who have intellectual curiosity, financial resources, and leisure time.

TABLE A

A Classification of Clients Who Receive Psychotherapy
The three main categories of therapy clients are defined mainly by their problems, their goals, and their resources.

SUMMARY

1. Treatment of psychological disorders is usually based on either psychodynamic, phenomenological, behavioral, or biological theories of personality and behavior disorder. Most therapists, however, combine features of two or more of these approaches, in an eclectic approach.

2. The specific goals of treatment may include (a) providing psychological support, (b) working on changes in certain behaviors, and (c) promoting insight and self-exploration.

3. All forms of treatment include certain general features, including (a) a client; (b) a therapist; (c) an underlying theory of behavior disorder; (d) a set of treatment procedures, which the underlying theory says should help; and (e) a special relationship between the client and therapist, which may make it easier for improvement to occur.

4. Clients in therapy have the right to expect that material discussed in treatment will be held in confidence by the therapist. Clients also have rights governing how and whether they can be placed in a mental hospital and specifying treatment conditions there.

5. Psychodynamic psychotherapy began with Freud's psychoanalysis and is oriented toward helping clients gain insight into unconscious conflicts and impulses and then explore how those factors have created disorders.

6. Exploration of the unconscious is aided by the use of free association, dream interpretation, analysis of slips of the tongue and other everyday behaviors, and analysis of certain features of the therapy relationship, such as transference. The therapist often gives interpretations of what the client says and does, in order to help examine unconscious meanings.

7. Some variations on psychoanalysis focus less on the id, the unconscious, and the past and more on helping clients to harness the ego to solve problems in the present. Others, such as psychoanalytically oriented psychotherapy, retain most of Freud's principles but offer a more flexible treatment format.

(Linkages, *continued*)

therapy, perhaps by making particular people more or less likely to respond to particular methods. Consider, for example, a study comparing the effectiveness of two forms of group therapy with college students. One group received ten non-directive sessions, which, consistent with Rogers's client-centered methods, placed responsibility for treatment on the clients. Other groups received ten sessions in which the therapist took much greater control and responsibility (Abramovitz et al., 1974). On the average, clients receiving the two forms of treatment improved to about the same degree. But the improvement of individuals depended to a considerable extent on the *match* between the kind of treatment they received and their locus-of-control score. Specifically, internal students (those expecting to be in control of change) did better in nondirective rather than directive treatment, whereas externals (who tend to look outside themselves for a source of change) tended to do better in the directive rather than the nondirective treatment.

It makes intuitive sense that the out-come of therapy improves when the client's personality meshes with the methods of treatment, but this relationship does not always hold (Weisz, 1986). Further, this kind of therapeutic matchmaking may be more important in some forms of treatment than others. For example, clients' personality characteristics tend to be less strongly related to the outcome of behavioral therapies than to other forms of treatment (Sloane et al., 1975). Proponents of behavior therapy suggest that this is because their methods are powerful enough to overcome the influence of personality variables.

In summary, the nature and strength of the relationship between personality and treatment success remain a puzzle, and the relationship may be a mirage. Researchers do agree, however, that more general attributes of the client usually predict success in various forms of psychotherapy. These attributes have been described as YAVIS (young, attractive, verbal, intelligent, and successful) (Schofield, 1964). YAVIS clients' success in therapy probably relates to the fact that they (1) tend not to be severely disturbed and (2) tend to have the mental capability, motivation, openness, expectation for change, and spare time to work effectively on their problems. Not surprisingly, these volunteers make up the bulk of most psychotherapists' caseloads.

Is there no hope for change among those who do not share YAVIS characteristics? Must all those who have been uncharitably labeled HOUNDs (homely, old, unattractive, nonverbal, and dull) go without help or be relegated to hospitals where they receive only drugs or electroconvulsive shock, along with recreational activities and some job training? Not necessarily. Using videotapes and other instructional devices, researchers have developed methods for helping previously "inappropriate" clients develop the motivation and skills to benefit from psychotherapy (Heitler, 1976; Levine, Stoltz & Lacks, 1983; Mayerson, 1984; Orne & Wender, 1968; Strupp & Bloxom, 1973; Terestman, Miller & Weber, 1974). Others have tried to translate the concepts and procedures of psychotherapy into terms and methods that do not require great sophistication; this attempt has been especially successful for the behavioral approach (Kanfer & Goldstein, 1986).

---

8. Group and family therapies were originally offered by psychodynamic therapists, but today therapists of all theoretical persuasions employ these special approaches to treatment.

9. Phenomenological psychotherapy helps clients to become more aware of discrepancies between their feelings and their behavior. These discrepancies are seen to be at the root of behavior disorder but will be resolved by the client once they are brought to light in the context of a good therapy relationship.

10. Carl Rogers's client-centered therapy is the most prominent phenomenological method. Rogerian therapists help mainly by adopting attitudes toward the client that express unconditional positive regard, empathy, and congruence. This creates a tolerant, accepting, and nonjudgmental atmosphere, in which it is easier for the client to be open and honest with the therapist, with himself or herself, and with others.

11. Therapists employing the Gestalt therapy of Fritz Perls seek phenomenological treatment goals in a more active way, often confronting and challenging clients with evidence of their defensiveness, game playing, and other efforts to escape self-exploration.

12. Behavior therapy applies laboratory-based principles of learning to eliminating a wide array of undesirable patterns of thought and behavior and to strengthen more desirable alternatives. Behavioral treatments include systematic desensitization, modeling, assertiveness and social skills training, positive reinforcement, extinction, aversive conditioning, and punishment.

13. Many behavior therapists also employ cognitive-behavioral methods, including rational-emotive therapy, to help clients alter the way they think, as well as how they behave.

14. The effectiveness of psychotherapy has been hotly debated over the last forty years. Part of the problem is that there is little agreement on how to measure improvement following therapy and how best to design experiments that can assure that the improvement was due to the treatment and not to some other factor. Most current observers conclude that clients who receive psychotherapy are better off than most clients who receive no treatment, but that no single treatment approach is uniformly better than another. Others argue that asking whether psychotherapy "works"

is not as important as determining which therapy works best for which clients with which problems.

15. Treatment may be offered by mental health professionals (psychiatrists, psychologists, and social workers) or by those with less advanced training, even nonprofessionals. The best therapists are not necessarily identified by their professional degree, but by the degree to which they utilize their methods and their interpersonal style to benefit the widest range of clients.

16. Biological treatment approaches once focused on electroconvulsive shock and psychosurgery but now depend heavily on tranquilizing, antidepressant, and antipsychotic drugs.

17. Concern about the effectiveness of psychotherapy and realization that there will never be enough therapists to treat all who need help has prompted the development of community mental health facilities. They provide the usual forms of treatment but also reach out, with professional and nonprofessional staff, to offer services to those who might not ordinarily ask for them. These services include crisis intervention, suicide prevention, community education, and day treatment for former mental patients. Community psychology attempts to prevent rather than treat behavior disorders.

18. Success in psychotherapy has not been linked to a particular pattern of personality characteristics, but clients who are younger, smarter, less disturbed, and more open to therapy seem to do better.

KEY TERMS

Definitions of terms appear on the pages shown in parentheses.

antidepressant (614)
antipsychotic (613)
assertiveness and social skills training (603)
aversive conditioning (604)
behavior therapy (behavior modification) (601)
client-centered (person-centered) therapy (597)
cognitive behavior therapy (605)
cognitive restructuring (606)
community psychology (615)
congruence (598)
eclectic (584)
electroconvulsive therapy (ECT) (612)
empathy (598)
environmental psychology (617)
family therapy (595)
flooding (604)
free association (592)
Gestalt therapy (599)
group therapy (595)
latent content (592)
lithium (614)
manifest content (592)
modeling (602)
prefrontal lobotomy (613)
psychiatrist (610)
psychoanalysis (591)
psychologist (610)
psychosurgery (613)
psychotherapy (584)
rational-emotive therapy (RET) (605)
reflection (598)
stress inoculation training (606)
token economy (603)
tranquilizer (614)
transference (593)

RECOMMENDED READINGS

Corsini, R. J. (1984). *Current psychotherapies* (3rd ed.). Itasca, Ill.: Peacock. An excellent overview of many forms of psychotherapy, along with a helpful index that allows the reader to compare and contrast the features of all the treatment approaches.

Fancher, R. E. (1973). *Psychoanalytic psychology: The development of Freud's thought.* New York: Norton. A very readable presentation, which describes Freud's background and experience and clearly shows how he came to formulate psychoanalytic theory and therapy.

Kanfer, F. H., & Goldstein, A. P. (Eds.). (1986). *Helping people change* (3rd ed.). New York: Pergamon Press. An excellent overview of the full range of behavior therapy techniques.

Kazdin, A. E. (1978). *History of behavior modification: Experimental foundations of contemporary research.* Baltimore: University Park Press. A fine, detailed overview of the background of behavioral approaches to treatment.

Perls, F. S. (1969). *Gestalt therapy verbatim.* Lafayette, Calif.: Real People Press. This book offers transcripts of treatment sessions that illustrate Gestalt principles and methods.

Rappaport, J. (1977). *Community psychology: Values, research and action.* New York: Holt, Rinehart & Winston. A definitive text on the history, goals, methods, and results of the community psychology movement.

*I*n Australia, an aboriginal tribe casts a spell of death on those who break the group's rules. From then on, no one mentions the offender, and nothing he or she says or does attracts the slightest attention. Reports indicate that, after being treated this way for a short time, the rejected person often dies, sometimes by suicide.

Experimenters skeptical about such reports created similar conditions on a military base. At first, the volunteer selected for social isolation made intense efforts to elicit some response from other soldiers. When nothing he did resulted in attention, the man became withdrawn and apathetic; he stopped talking and, later, stopped eating. He looked vaguely off into the distance and became oblivious to his surroundings. He began walking around aimlessly, tripping over objects in his path. At this point, the alarmed researchers stopped the experiment.

Prisoners kept in solitary confinement and others deprived of human interaction for long periods often show similar behavior. And social isolation very early in life can have particularly severe consequences, as we saw in Chapter 2 in the case of the Wild Boy of Aveyron and in Harlow's experiments with monkeys raised without mothers or peers (Chapter 11, on motivation). People are social beings. They are born into a world of other people and need other people throughout life. To understand human behavior fully, we must take the social world into account.

The effects of the social world on the behavior and mental processes of individuals, pairs, and groups are the focus of **social psychology,** a subspecialty with important links to many other areas of psychology (see Linkages diagram, p. 626). In this chapter, we examine what social psychologists have learned about the social world's influence on the way people perceive, think, feel, and react. In the next chapter, we will focus on some important patterns of group and interpersonal behavior, such as conformity, aggression, and cooperation. Together, these two chapters explore the complex puzzle of how people influence one another and discuss some of the research that psychologists have conducted to put together some of the pieces of that puzzle.

SOME BASIC SOURCES OF SOCIAL INFLUENCE

People sometimes influence one another's behavior actively, as when a car dealer tries to convince television viewers to buy the latest model. Other social influences are more subtle and passive. The mere presence of others, in person or in memory, can affect how well people perform and can shape what they think of themselves, their motivation to act, and the unspoken rules that govern them.

Social Comparison

People spend a good amount of their time thinking about themselves, trying to evaluate their own perceptions, opinions, abilities, and so on. Decades ago,

17

The
Individual in
the Social
World

LINKAGES
an overview

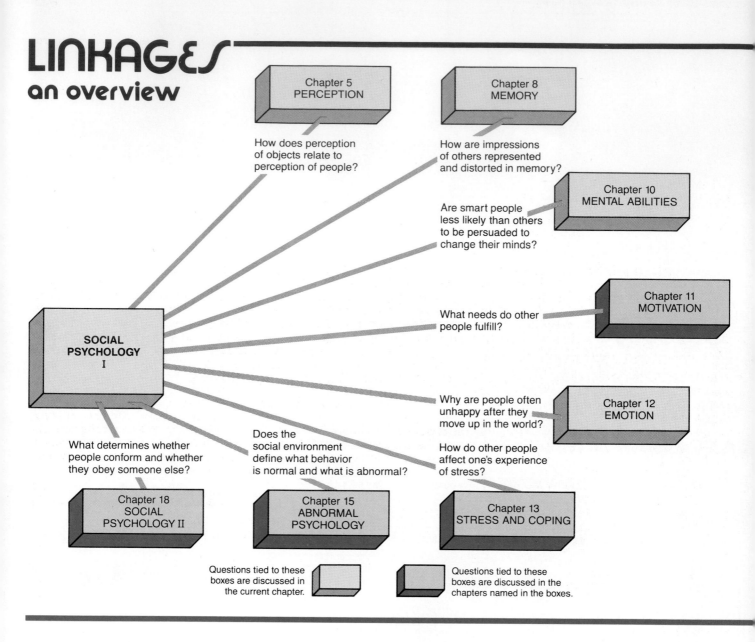

Chapter 5
PERCEPTION

How does perception of objects relate to perception of people?

Chapter 8
MEMORY

How are impressions of others represented and distorted in memory?

Chapter 10
MENTAL ABILITIES

Are smart people less likely than others to be persuaded to change their minds?

Chapter 11
MOTIVATION

What needs do other people fulfill?

SOCIAL PSYCHOLOGY I

Chapter 12
EMOTION

Why are people often unhappy after they move up in the world?

What determines whether people conform and whether they obey someone else?

Does the social environment define what behavior is normal and what is abnormal?

How do other people affect one's experience of stress?

Chapter 18
SOCIAL PSYCHOLOGY II

Chapter 15
ABNORMAL PSYCHOLOGY

Chapter 13
STRESS AND COPING

Questions tied to these boxes are discussed in the current chapter.

Questions tied to these boxes are discussed in the chapters named in the boxes.

Leon Festinger (1954), one of the most influential theoreticians in social psychology, noted that this self-evaluation involves two qualitatively distinct types of questions. One type can be answered by using objective physical criteria of height, weight, and so on. You can answer such questions by taking a simple, objective, physical measurement. But for other types of questions—about physical attractiveness or athletic prowess, for example—there are no objective criteria. In these cases, according to Festinger's theory of **social comparison,** people use other people as a basis of comparison. When you wonder how intelligent, insightful, or funny you are, you use *social* rather than objective criteria.

Reference groups Whom do people use as a basis for comparison? Festinger said that people look to people who are similar to themselves. If you are curious about how good a golfer you are, you are likely to compare your performance, not with that of Jack Nicklaus and other world-class competitors, but with the performance of golfers of your own age and sex (Jones, 1985; Suls & Miller, 1977). The categories of people to which people see themselves

THE SOCIAL WORLD AND PSYCHOLOGY

In Chapter 16, we saw that the relationship between therapist and client can enhance or impair the effectiveness of treatment. The importance of the client-therapist relationship is just one example of the role played in human affairs by social factors. Those factors are the special concern of social psychology, the subfield concerned with how the social world affects the thoughts and behavior of the individual and with how individuals behave toward one another.

A good example of the power of social influences occurred in 1984 when Geraldine Ferraro, the first woman to be nominated by a major political party for the vice presidency of the United States,

debated Vice President George Bush on national television. Who won? The overwhelming majority of Mondale-Ferraro supporters thought that Ferraro was the winner; most supporters of the Reagan-Bush ticket thought that Bush had won. Even though these two groups heard the same debate, their perceptions and their memories of what occurred clearly differed, depending on their attitudes. These attitudes were themselves the product of social influence; they were learned and shaped by what each viewer had read, heard, and come to believe about these candidates and what their attitudes were about men and women.

In this chapter, we focus on this first

aspect of social psychology: the ways in which the social world can influence an individual's attitudes, perceptions, and thoughts and how these influences can affect behavior. As the diagram shows, we have already considered some of these influences in previous chapters. In the next chapter, we will focus on another component of social psychology; namely, some of the characteristic ways in which people think and behave toward each other in groups and other social situations. Together, these two chapters explore the complex puzzle of how people influence and are influenced by one another.

as belonging and to which they habitually compare themselves, are called **reference groups.** In our golfing example, the reference group included people of a certain age and gender.

Relative deprivation   People use different reference groups over the course of their lives. Since their *relative* standing on any dimension may change, relative deprivation may result (Crosby, 1976). Consider the plight of people from a lower-class background who work their way up to a middle-class life. Along with new jobs and more responsibilities comes a higher income, but also new reference groups. As they begin to move up in a business organization, they begin to associate with others with an even higher standard of living. By using these people as a basis for comparison, they begin to experience **relative deprivation**—the sense that, compared with others in the reference group, they are not doing well.

Relative deprivation is part of the reason that moving from the lower to the middle or from the middle to the upper class is often an uncomfortable and frustrating experience (Crosby & Gonzalez-Intal, 1982). Similarly, when

The mere fact that other people are present can alter a person's performance on a variety of tasks. We shall see later that this source of social influence sometimes improves and sometimes disrupts performance.

teenagers move from the relatively high status of being a senior among high school students to the relatively low status of being a freshman in college, the sudden change in reference group and relative standing often creates disorientation, self-doubt, anxiety, and other, usually temporary, problems.

Generally, people do not compare themselves to others who are not in their immediate reference group. Leonard Berkowitz (1980) called this fact the "out of sight, out of mind" phenomenon. One example is provided by an interview of more than twenty thousand people from thirteen countries—industrialized and nonindustrialized, rich and poor (Cantril, 1965). Overall, people who lived in countries with a high standard of living were no happier than those who lived in poor nations. However, those with relatively high status within their own country, regardless of its worldwide standing, were much more satisfied with their life than were those with lower status in that same country. Apparently, people in other nations were "out of sight, out of mind," and the greater well-being of foreigners did not affect people's satisfaction with their own life. But people did seem to use other people within their own nation as a reference group, and their happiness appeared to be based on social comparisons with this group.

Chronic use of extreme reference groups—such as the very rich or very famous—can create depression and anxiety for the average person. One successful middle-aged person we know became upset when someone jokingly pointed out that, by the time Mozart was his age, he had been dead for ten years. The cognitive-behavioral therapy approaches described in the chapter on treatment often help highly self-critical clients toward more positive self-evaluations by encouraging the use of more realistic reference groups.

Social Facilitation and Social Interference

The social world can affect not only what people think about themselves, but also how well or poorly they perform. The term **social facilitation** describes circumstances in which the mere presence of other people improves performance. This phenomenon was the topic of the first experiment in social psychology, conducted by Norman Triplett (1897).

Performance and arousal   Triplett noticed that bicyclists tended to race faster when a competitor was near than when all competitors were out of sight. Did just seeing each other remind the riders of the need to go faster to win? To test this possibility, Triplett arranged for bicyclists to complete a twenty-five-mile course under one of three conditions: (1) riding alone and racing against the clock; (2) riding with another cyclist, but not competing against him; or (3) competing directly with another rider. The cyclists went much faster when another rider was present than when they were simply racing against the clock, whether or not they were competing against the other person. Something about the *presence* of the other person, rather than competition, produced the increased speeds observed during races. Similarly, Triplett later found that, when children were asked to perform certain tasks as rapidly as possible (such as jumping up and down or turning a fishing reel), they did so faster when other children doing the same task were present than when they were alone.

Other psychologists subsequently conducted numerous experiments to describe how the presence of other people affects performance. Like Triplett, many found that the presence of other people improves performance, both when the other people were performing the same task simultaneously and when the other people simply observed (Chen, 1937; Dashiell, 1930; Travis, 1925). However, in other experiments, the presence of other people *impaired* performance (Gates & Allee, 1933; Husband, 1940; Pessin, 1933).

Decades later, Robert Zajonc reviewed this research and suggested that these opposite results only seemed to be contradictory. They could all be explained, he argued, by one process. The presence of other people, said Zajonc, increases a person's general level of arousal or motivation (Zajonc, 1965).

This idea is consistent with the everyday experience that having other people watch you do something can make you nervous and error-prone. But how does it help to explain social facilitation? First, increased arousal increases the tendency to perform those behaviors that are *most dominant,* the ones a person knows best. Second, this tendency may either help or hinder performance in a situation. When a person is performing a familiar or easy task, such as riding a bike or tying a shoe, the best-learned responses are likely to be helpful ones. In such cases, increased arousal due to the presence of others should allow the person to ride a bike or tie a shoe even faster than normal. However, when a task is unfamiliar, complex, or difficult, the best-learned responses may be detrimental. Thus, if you try to perform a recently learned dance in the arousal-producing presence of others, old dance movements may appear, making your performance look awkward.

In other words, according to Zajonc, other people's presence can help or hinder performance depending on whether the most likely behavior in the situation is beneficial or harmful to that performance. Notice that this model is consistent with the effects of arousal that we described in the chapters on motivation and stress: increased arousal impairs performance on complex and difficult tasks more than on easy tasks.

Sources of arousal   What is there about the presence of others that leads to arousal? One possibility is that people recognize that others will evaluate their performance; therefore, they feel apprehensive. This apprehension about evaluation increases the level of arousal (whether the observers are actually judgmental or not), thus strengthening well-learned responses and weakening less dominant ones. Several experiments have found that, indeed, apprehension about being evaluated profoundly increases a person's general level of arousal or motivation, as measured by galvanic skin response and respiration (Chapman, 1974; Geen, 1977; Gore & Taylor, 1973; Sasfy & Okun, 1974).

Athletes usually perform better when competing directly against other athletes. This enhancement of performance when in the presence of others is an example of social facilitation.

Another way in which the presence of others may create arousal is by intensifying self-evaluation. Evidence in support of this notion comes from a comparison of the performance of home and visiting teams during championship games (Baumeister & Steinhilber, 1984). Traditional wisdom has it that home teams have the advantage. In fact, in baseball since 1924, the home team has won 60 percent of the first and second games in the World Series, but only 38 percent of the seventh and deciding games. Moreover, the home team committed twice as many fielding errors in the final game as in the first two. Very similar patterns occurred in professional basketball championships: home teams tended to win games early in a championship series, but visitors more often won the final games. And although visiting teams shot free throws equally well from the first through the last games, the home teams' free throw percentages dropped dramatically. Why? Roy Baumeister and Andrew Steinhilber (1984) reasoned that those playing to a home crowd focus more attention on themselves and on how well they are doing as the prospect of a championship draws nearer. This in turn distracts the home athletes and interferes with their performance.

Social Norms

Probably the most pervasive yet subtle way in which the social world influences people is through norms. **Norms** are learned, socially based rules that prescribe what people should or should not do in various situations. They are transmitted by parents, teachers, clergy, peers, and other agents of culture. Even when they cannot be verbalized explicitly (they are seldom written as laws), norms are so powerful that people often follow them automatically. A good example of an unspoken social norm, in this culture at least, is the fact that it is socially inappropriate to sit right next to the only other passenger on a bus. By telling people what is expected of them and others, norms make social situations more comfortable and less ambiguous. At a movie, for example, norms tell you that you should get in line to buy a ticket rather than push people out of the way; they also give you the expectation that others will do the same.

The reciprocity norm   *Reciprocity*—the tendency to respond to others as they have acted toward you—is a very powerful social norm (Cialdini, 1984). When an investigator sent Christmas cards to strangers, most responded with a card of their own; some even scribbled a personal note of good cheer (Kunz & Woolcott, 1976). During the 1970s, members of the Hare Krishna Society increased the society's revenues by millions by trying a new strategy based on the reciprocity norm. Instead of simply asking people in public places for a donation, they first gave people a small gift, such as a flower. Then they asked for money but told people they could keep the flower whether or not they made a donation (Cialdini, 1984).

The reciprocity norm also operates when people make concessions to one another (Cialdini et al., 1975). Sometimes people gain an advantage by anticipating the effects of this norm. For example, when television script writers are afraid that a particular line will be cut by the censors, they may insert one or two extra (often sexually related) words in the line, words that they expect will be objectionable. When the censors object to the line, the writers agree to delete the objectionable words. Then the censor reciprocates by accepting the rest of the line, as the writers intended it in the first place. There are countless other applications of the reciprocity norm, especially in union-management contract negotiations, in treaty talks between nations, and even in the agreements that couples reach in resolving conflicts.

Hare Krishnas and other fund raisers often give people a flower or other small gift before asking them for money. The donors' money is given not because of the gift's value—the gift is often discarded almost immediately—but apparently because of the reciprocity norm that says one good act deserves another.

Differing norms   Norms are neither universal nor unchanging. For example, social roles and status determine in part which norms influence particular people in particular situations. Imagine yourself in a professor's office. The professor may very well lean back and put his or her feet up on the desk. However, should you put your feet on the professor's desk, you would be breaking a norm.

Norms also differ widely from culture to culture. In some cultures, people crowd around a ticket counter or theater entrance rather than forming a line. In some Near Eastern cultures, people put their faces only inches away from the person with whom they are conversing, displaying a norm that would violate the more moderate distance Westerners usually observe. Norms can also vary within a culture. On some college campuses, hooting and hollering, not silence, is the norm during a movie. And in certain subcultures, youngsters are revered by peers for skill and daring at committing crimes.

When people enter a new subculture, they may adopt the norms of that subculture, especially if its members become an important reference group. One of the few investigations of the influence of a new reference group on people's social norms took place over nearly thirty years. The study, by Theodore Newcomb, began at Bennington College in the 1930s. Because it enrolled only 250 students and was physically isolated from its host town, Bennington created a close, insulated faculty-student community. Most of the faculty were young and constituted a reference group that tended to be liberal politically. The students, all of whom were female, came mostly from wealthy families, a reference group with conservative political beliefs.

Newcomb (1943) surveyed the political beliefs of an entire entering class, throughout their years at Bennington and afterward. He found that the students arrived with quite conservative political beliefs very much in line with the norms established by their parents. The longer they remained at Bennington, however, the more liberal the students became (see Figure 17.1). This change in the students' political orientation suggests that the norms of the faculty became increasingly influential. The change tended to be greatest among students who immersed themselves in the new subculture by spending most weekends on campus and becoming deeply involved in college life. During the twenty-five years immediately after graduation, the women who had become more liberal at Bennington remained so; those who had retained their conservative beliefs during their years at Bennington tended to remain conservative (Newcomb, 1962; Newcomb et al., 1967).

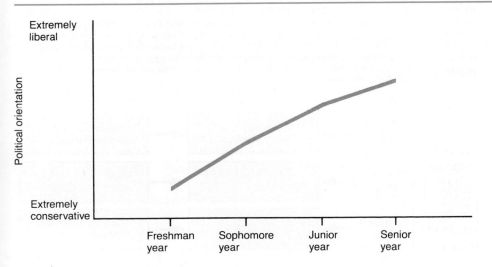

Figure 17.1
The Effect of Norms
This graph shows one class's change in political beliefs over four years at Bennington College. Notice the gradual shift that occurred, apparently as a result of exposure to a new and different reference group.
(From *Personality and Social Change* by Theodore M. Newcomb. Copyright © 1957 by Holt, Rinehart and Winston, Inc. Reprinted by permission of Holt, Rinehart and Winston, Inc.)

The term *subculture* might suggest that it takes hundreds or thousands of people to establish a reference group norm, but this is not the case. We will see in the next chapter that very small groups of people—or even one influential person—can create miniature subcultures with norms powerful enough to produce conformity, compliance, and obedience in their members. For now, we turn to how the social world affects a different aspect of the individual.

ATTITUDES, PERSUASION, AND ATTITUDE CHANGE

The changes in political beliefs charted by the Bennington study represent one example of a much broader phenomenon: changes in attitudes. In this section, we examine both what attitudes are and how they change.

The Nature of Attitudes

An **attitude** is a predisposition toward a particular cognitive, emotional, or behavioral reaction to an object. The object can be almost anything—from inanimate objects, such as nuclear power plants, to individuals or groups, to actions, such as having an abortion. As suggested by its definition, an attitude has three components (see Figure 17.2). The *cognitive* component is a set of beliefs, such as the notion that whales are about to become extinct. The emotional, or *affective,* component consists of an evaluation: a like or dislike of the object of the attitude. Finally, the *behavioral* component of an attitude involves a way of acting toward the attitude object. For example, if your attitude toward whales includes the belief that they are on the verge of extinction and the feeling that this state of affairs is very sad, you might donate to the Save the Whales fund.

If these three components were always in harmony, so that emotions and actions always reflected what people believed, we could measure all aspects of an attitude by measuring any one component. We could even predict how people would act toward an object by noting the beliefs and feelings they expressed. In fact, however, predicting a specific behavior on the basis of a

Figure 17.2
Three Components of an Attitude
The three components of an attitude can be measured separately and through different assessment channels. For example, the cognitive component of people's attitudes is typically assessed through surveys, interviews, and other self-report methods. The affective component might be monitored by physiological recordings taken while a person watches a film about something relevant to the attitude. Measurement of the behavioral component could entail observing what the person does in relation to the attitude object.
(Adapted with permission from Kahn, Arnold S., *Social Psychology,* © 1984 Wm. C. Brown Publishers, Dubuque, Iowa. All Rights Reserved.)

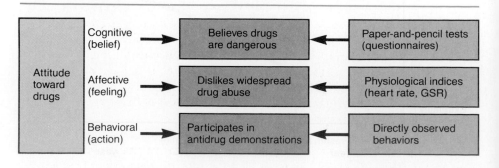

person's attitude is difficult. To take but one example, a recent survey revealed that more than half of American motorists believed that a speed limit of 55 saved lives and should be retained, but that most motorists regularly drove faster than 55 (Associated Press Media General Poll, 1986).

Discrepancies among the components of an attitude can appear for many reasons. First, there are always competing motives and competing attitudes. For example, you might think about donating to the Save the Whales fund but then realize that your father's birthday is coming up. As a result, you might end up spending the money on a gift, even though the cognitive and affective components of your attitude toward whales remain positive. Second, an attitude can be expressed in many ways. One person might donate money, another might display a bumper sticker, another might fire off letters to members of Congress, and still others might picket whaling companies. It is often difficult to predict what action a person will take. Third, social pressure in the form of reference group norms may influence a person to suppress the behavioral aspects of an attitude while retaining the other components. Thus, someone who believes that the rights of homosexuals should be protected might not campaign for this cause because doing so would bring disapproval from valued friends or family members who hold strong antihomosexual attitudes.

Although attitudes tend to be relatively stable, they can and do change. Sometimes, as illustrated in the Bennington study, they change because of shifting reference groups. Sometimes they change in response to altered reinforcement contingencies. For example, the negative attitude of an unemployed American auto worker toward Japanese cars might change if he or she begins working at a new auto plant built by a Japanese company. In the following sections, we examine two other reasons for changes in attitudes: persuasive communications from other people and the nature of a person's own behavior.

Persuasive Communications

Attitudes often change because other people intentionally try to change them through persuasive communication. Whether the attempt succeeds depends on several factors, including (1) characteristics of the communicator, (2) the nature of the message, and (3) the characteristics of the audience (Hovland, Jarnis & Kelley, 1953; Petty & Cacioppo, 1984).

Characteristics of the communicator   Various characteristics of the communicator influence whether a message will change the audience's attitude. The most important is the perceived credibility of the communicator. *Credible* sources, those considered knowledgeable and trustworthy, are more effective at changing attitudes than are low-credibility sources (Cooper & Croyle, 1984).

Another very important characteristic of persuasive communicators is *sincerity*. Listeners are more likely to be persuaded by a sincere, apparently honest speaker than by an obviously dishonest, self-serving individual. For this reason, people's attitudes are more likely to be influenced by a message that is accidentally overheard (and thus is presumably sincere) than by a presentation obviously intended to persuade (which might be insincere) (Walster & Festinger, 1962). To exploit this fact, advertisers often use such devices as testimonials from apparently unpaid consumers, who are supposedly unaware of being photographed.

Finally, as the *similarity* between the communicator and the audience increases, the communicator tends to be more effective in changing attitudes (Berscheid, 1966; Cialdini, Petty & Cacioppo, 1981; Simons, Berkowitz &

Politicians who don mining gear, wear flannel shirts to union meetings, or eat barbecue lunches with ranchers are trying to be as similar as possible to their audiences, so that they will be more likeable and thus more persuasive in vote-getting.

Moyer, 1970). There appear to be two reasons for this effect. First, people perceive communicators who are similar to themselves to be more trustworthy than those who are less similar. Second, all else being equal, people tend to like others who are similar to themselves.

Nature of the message Whether it is best to present one or two sides of an issue depends on the prior attitudes of the audience (Cialdini et al., 1981). Imagine that your school is considering a 50 percent increase in tuition. Most of the administrators favor the proposal, but most of the students are against it. Anyone wishing to promote votes against the proposal should use one message when speaking to a student audience and another when talking to administrators.

In the case of students, an already sympathetic audience, the most effective communication would contain only arguments against the tuition increase. This one-sided communication would bolster the audience's prior beliefs and reinforce its members' tendency to vote against the proposal. Any contrary arguments, such as the need to meet the university's increasing operating costs, can only sow the seeds of doubt, even if they are immediately refuted. However, in talking to an audience that opposes the speaker's point of view, it is usually better to present both sides of the issue. In this way, the communicator shows respect for the audience's attitudes, recognizes the validity of those attitudes, but also provides counterarguments aimed at attitude change. In short, a one-sided message is more effective when the audience is predisposed to the speaker's point of view; a two-sided message is more effective when the attitude of the audience is contrary to that of the speaker (McGuire, 1985; Petty & Cacioppo, 1981).

The amount of attitude change is greatest when a persuasive message states explicit conclusions; for example, "It is therefore obvious that increasing tuition 50 percent would be detrimental to the university." This principle applies with people of all intelligence levels (McGuire, 1969). Having decided to state conclusions, the communicator must determine how mild or extreme those conclusions should be in order to change attitudes most effectively. For example, suppose that administrators favor a 50 percent increase in tuition and the communicator favors no increase. Would it be more effective for the speaker to argue for a 40 percent increase, a 20 percent increase, or no increase?

An answer is suggested by a study in which students first rated several poems and then heard a message purportedly stating the "real" quality of the poems. Some students heard a message that supposedly came from a high-credibility source (a famous poet); others, from a low-credibility source (an uninformed undergraduate from an obscure school). When the students rated the poems again, their attitudes tended to change in the direction suggested by the message they had heard, and the amount of change was always greater for the high-credibility message (see Figure 17.3). However, the amount of change depended on both the credibility of the speaker and the amount of discrepancy between the speaker's message and the students' original ratings. For the high-credibility speaker, the greater the discrepancy between the message and the students' ratings, the larger the attitude change. But for the low-credibility speaker, the most attitude change occurred when the discrepancy between the message and the students' original ratings was moderate (Aronson, Turner & Carlsmith, 1963).

Sometimes communicators try to change attitudes by instilling fear in the audience. A health organization, for example, may suggest that, if you do not eat a healthy diet, you are likely to die prematurely. Can **fear appeals** change attitudes? One of the first experiments to examine their influence was concerned with attitudes toward smoking. Subjects in a low-fear group watched a movie in which the dangers of smoking were demonstrated with a smoking machine and charts describing the relationship between cigarette sales and lung cancer. Subjects in a high-fear condition received the same information, but in addition, they saw an operation for the removal of a smoker's cancer-blackened lung. Compared with those in the low-fear condition, subjects in the high-fear condition were more upset, felt more likely to get lung cancer themselves, and were more eager to quit smoking (Leventhal, Watts & Pagano, 1967).

Fear appeals have limitations, however. For example, more often than not, when fear has provoked efforts to quit smoking, people eventually start smoking again (Glasgow & Bernstein, 1981). Even when fear produces lasting effects on the *cognitive* component of an attitude, the effects on behavior often fade after several weeks or months. Further, fear appeals are most effective when they are not *too* frightening and when they are accompanied by information about what the audience can do to avoid the fearful consequences. If nothing but extremely frightening information is presented, many people tend to block out the message (Leventhal, 1970).

Characteristics of the audience   Whoever is communicating, and whatever the message, some people in the audience change their attitudes, and others do not (Cialdini et al., 1981; Janis & Field, 1956; McGuire, 1968; Petty & Cacioppo, 1981). What general characteristics are important in determining who changes and who does not?

One candidate is general intelligence. Perhaps intelligent people, because they can better comprehend arguments, change their attitudes more easily than less intelligent people. Or perhaps intelligent people are better able to detect logical flaws in the arguments presented, are more likely to think of counterarguments, and are therefore *less* likely to be persuaded to change their attitudes. In fact, research shows that both of these processes occur. Very intelligent people comprehend persuasive arguments better than less intelligent people, but they are also better able to refute them. As a result, there is no overall relationship between intelligence and susceptibility to persuasion (McGuire, 1968, 1985).

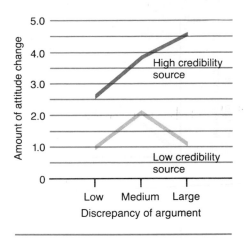

Figure 17.3
Communicator Credibility and Persuasion
In general, highly credible sources of information produce more attitude change as the discrepancy between the speaker's arguments and the audience's attitudes becomes greater. Low-credibility sources are most effective when arguing for more moderate amounts of attitude change.
(From E. Aronson, J. A. Turner, and J. M. Carlsmith: "Communicator Credibility and Communicator Discrepancy as a Determinant of Opinion Change," *Journal of Abnormal and Social Psychology,* 67, 31–36. Copyright 1963 by the American Psychological Association. Adapted by permission of the publisher and authors.)

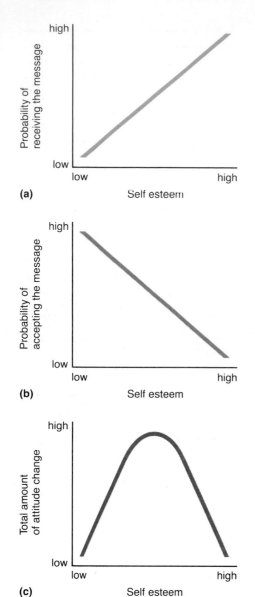

low ─ high
Self esteem

(a)

low ─ high
Self esteem

(b)

low ─ high
Self esteem

(c)

Figure 17.4
Self-Esteem and Attitude Change
*These panels show that people with high
self-esteem pay attention to and understand
a persuasive message but are usually so
confident in their own beliefs that they reject
it. Those with low self-esteem would be
likely to accept the arguments presented,
but because they seldom notice or understand the message, they do not usually
change their attitudes. People with moderate levels of self-esteem tend to show the
greatest susceptibility to a persuasive message, because they not only notice and understand it, but also tend to be uncertain of
the correctness of their own beliefs.*
(From W. J. McGuire, 1968, "Personality and
Susceptibility to Social Influence" in E. F.
Borgatta and W. W. Lambert: *Handbook of Personality Theory and Research*.)

Susceptibility to persuasion does seem related to self-esteem, however. William McGuire (1969) suggested that individuals with low self-esteem are not confident about the correctness of their own attitudes and thus often change those attitudes in response to persuasive messages. However, people with low self-esteem also tend to be inattentive and have little interest in the events that surround them. As a result, although individuals with low self-esteem are prone to accept the arguments of others, they seldom bother to pay attention to or think about those arguments (see Figure 17.4a and b). Individuals high in self-esteem do pay attention to what others think, but they are so self-confident that they are seldom swayed. Consequently, both groups show very little attitude change (see Figure 17.4c). In contrast, those with moderate levels of self-esteem pay a fair amount of attention to what others say; they are also sufficiently unsure of their own attitudes to be persuaded. Thus, these individuals tend to change their attitudes the most (Gergen & Baver, 1967; Nisbett & Gordon, 1967; Zellner, 1970).

HIGHLIGHT

**Pushing Too
Hard May Be
Worse Than Not
Pushing
at All**

What if the combination of communicator, message, and audience does not favor attitude change? One obvious possibility is that some listeners' attitudes will not change, but an even less desirable outcome may occur. Consider an experiment in which students heard arguments in favor of equal treatment for the Communist party of the United States (Worchel & Brehm, 1970). One group was given an extreme message, in which the speaker said that "You cannot believe otherwise" and "You have no choice but to believe this." Of the students in this group, 50 percent accepted the arguments and changed their attitudes in the direction proposed, but 40 percent changed their attitudes in the direction opposite to that argued for. A control group received exactly the same message, but without the two extreme statements. In this case, about 70 percent of the audience changed their attitudes in the direction suggested by the speaker's arguments, but only 15 percent shifted in the opposite direction.

Such attitude reversal is an important and pervasive form of interpersonal influence. When people are told that they may not do something, they tend to become even more motivated to do it. When people are told that they may not have a particular object, they often go to extraordinary lengths to obtain it (Brehm, 1972). In one experiment, for example, children were allowed to choose as a reward any brand of candy bar on display, but the experimenter told some of the youngsters that they should *not* pick brand X (Hammock & Brehm, 1966). The result? Children who were told what not to do chose brand X much more often than those who were given a free choice.

One explanation of this reaction to arbitrary decisions is that most people value their freedom, and when they perceive freedom to be restricted or eliminated, psychological reactance occurs (Brehm, 1966). **Reactance** is a state of psychological arousal that motivates people to restore a lost sense of freedom by resisting, opposing, or contradicting whatever they feel caused the loss.

Perhaps the strongest type of prohibition is a law. Do people who generally respect the law experience psychological reactance to a law they perceive as overly restrictive of their freedom? Evidence suggests that, at least in some circumstances, they do. For example, when alcoholic beverages were declared illegal during the Prohibition era of the 1920s, Americans' desire for beer, wine, and liquor remained strong and may even have intensified.

More recently, on January 1, 1972, the sale, possession, and use of all detergents containing phosphates were banned in Miami, Florida, because the

Even when it is not legally required, many local, state, and federal government agencies hold public hearings at which citizens may comment on proposed new regulations, ordinances, utility rate changes, and the like. These hearings not only support democracy but help to reduce public protests and other forms of psychological reactance.

city's very shallow underground water supply was being contaminated by these chemicals. The law was for the public good, but like most laws, it restricted each individual's freedom of choice. Surveys taken shortly after the law went into effect showed that, compared to pre-ban surveys, Miami residents felt that phosphate detergents were more effective, had greater cleaning power, made clothes fresher, removed stains better, and were gentler. In contrast, residents of Tampa, Florida, where no law had been enacted, showed no change in their attitudes toward phosphate detergents (Mazis, 1975).

Psychological reactance offers a clear lesson for those who wish to make changes that run counter to other people's attitudes and behavior. Acceptance of and cooperation with dictated changes, such as those brought by desegregation laws, may eventually come, but they may take longer than when the changes are first proposed and then discussed by those affected. For example, many companies that once merely informed their employees of changes in production methods, work rules, or personnel policies now *propose* changes and allow employees to comment on them. These efforts do not eliminate employee strikes, but they to some extent reduce reactance. ◥

Behavioral Influences on Attitudes

Although we most often think of attitudes as influencing behavior, people's behavior can also influence their attitudes.

Cognitive dissonance theory   One important explanation of the relationship between behavior and attitudes was provided by Leon Festinger's (1957) theory of **cognitive dissonance.** It holds that people prefer that their many cognitions about themselves and the rest of the world be consistent with one another. When their cognitions are inconsistent, or *dissonant*, people feel uneasy and are motivated to make them more consistent.

Consider again the auto worker who holds very negative attitudes about Japanese cars but then gets a job building them. This person would be expected to experience dissonance between two thoughts: (1) "I don't like Japanese cars" and (2) "I help build Japanese cars." If this worker can justify his job choice, perhaps by pointing to the high pay or the lack of alternative

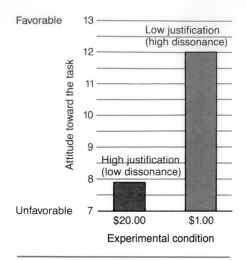

Figure 17.5
Cognitive Dissonance and Attitude Change
People were paid by an experimenter to say that a boring task was enjoyable. According to cognitive dissonance theory, those paid twenty dollars had clear justification for lying and should have experienced little dissonance between what they said and what they felt about the task; indeed, their attitude toward the task did not change very much. However, subjects with little justification to lie (one dollar) should have reduced the dissonance by displaying a more positive attitude toward the task, which they did.
(From L. Festinger and J. M. Carlsmith, "Cognitive Consequences of Forced Compliance," *Journal of Abnormal and Social Psychology, 58,* 203–210. Copyright 1959 by the American Psychological Association. Adapted by permission of the author and publisher.)

employment, there would be little or no dissonance between these apparently discrepant cognitions. If no reasonable justification is available, however, dissonance would probably result, and the worker could only reduce its psychological discomfort by altering one cognition or the other; that is, by either quitting his job or changing his anti-Japanese attitude.

A number of experiments have shown that people usually reduce cognitive dissonance by changing their attitudes. One of the earliest experiments to test cognitive dissonance theory was conducted by Festinger and Merrill Carlsmith (1959). First they asked people to perform a very dull task that involved turning a series of pegs on a board. Later some of these subjects were asked to persuade a waiting subject that the task was "exciting and fun." Some people in this group were told that they would be paid one dollar to tell this lie; the rest were told that they would be paid twenty dollars. The attitudes of these people toward the dull task were measured after they had talked to the waiting subject.

Festinger and Carlsmith (1959) argued that, unless there is adequate financial justification for doing so, telling another person that a boring task is enjoyable will produce dissonance (between the thoughts that "I think the task is boring" and "I am saying it is fun"). One way to reduce this dissonance would be to adopt a more favorable attitude toward the task. Then the cognitions would be more consistent: "I think the task is fun" and "I am saying it is fun." As shown in Figure 17.5, this is exactly what happened. Again, with adequate justification for one's behavior, dissonance can be reduced without attitude change, simply by thinking about the justification. Without adequate justification for one's behavior, the most likely way to reduce dissonance is to change one's attitude to provide that justification.

In another demonstration of the relationships among justification, dissonance, and attitude change, subjects were asked to eat fried grasshoppers (Zimbardo et al., 1965). In some cases, the experimenter made this request in a very friendly and apologetic way, explaining that the grasshoppers had been shipped prematurely and had to be consumed before they spoiled. In other cases, the experimenter acted rude and unfriendly, complaining that the subjects were late and were wasting his time. According to cognitive dissonance theory, those who were asked to eat grasshoppers by the friendly experimenter could easily justify their actions: "I don't like the idea of eating grasshoppers," but "I'm eating them to please this nice person." Like the subjects who were paid twenty dollars to lie, these subjects did not change their attitude toward grasshoppers, reporting them to be very distasteful. However, subjects approached by a rude experimenter could only reduce the dissonance brought on by their agreement to eat something distasteful by changing their attitude toward it. As expected by dissonance theory, these subjects reported that the grasshoppers tasted good.

Self-perception theory Cognitive dissonance theory assumes that attitude change results from a state of psychological tension, but it is extremely difficult to measure this tension or even to confirm its existence. Daryl Bem (1967) suggested an alternative theory, which can help explain the pattern of attitude change we have just examined without presupposing a state of internal tension. According to Bem's **self-perception theory,** situations often arise in which people are not quite sure about their attitudes. When this happens, Bem says, people look back to their behavior in the situation, consider it in light of the circumstances, and then *infer* what their attitude about it must have been. That is, you say, "If I did that under those circumstances, my attitude about it must be this." This process requires no tension to drive it.

Consider again the grasshopper experiment. According to Bem, the subjects' attitudes were determined, not by dissonance reduction, but by their inferences about their actions. Subjects in the nice-experimenter condition may have thought, "Well, if I ate grasshoppers, I must have done it because the experimenter was so nice about it, but they really tasted terrible." This kind of thinking would leave these subjects' relatively negative attitude toward the grasshoppers intact. Subjects in the other condition may have thought, "I ate the grasshoppers, but that experimenter was such a jerk that I never would have done it if they hadn't tasted good."

Obviously, self-perception theory and cognitive dissonance theory often make the same predictions about attitudes and attitude change. Indeed, both may be correct to some extent. There is some evidence that physiological arousal does accompany dissonance-inducing situations (Croyle & Cooper, 1983), but there is no evidence that such arousal is *necessary* to produce attitude change. Researchers are trying to discover the precise conditions under which each of these theories is most applicable to the understanding of attitudes and behavior.

The social world not only influences people's attitudes and behavior, but as shown in the following sections, it also helps shape the way they perceive and think about events and other people.

SOCIAL PERCEPTION

There is a story, perhaps apocryphal, about the president of a company who was having a lunch interview with a person being considered for an executive position. When the candidate salted his food without first tasting it, the president immediately decided not to hire him. The explanation was that "we would never hire a person who acted before collecting all of the relevant information." This process of **social perception**—the way people perceive others (and themselves)—is very significant. It can influence whether one sees a person as hostile or friendly, repugnant, likable, or possibly lovable. It also helps to determine the inferences that one makes about why people behave as they do.

"*You are fair, compassionate, and intelligent, but you are perceived as biased, callous, and dumb.*"

First Impressions

Common sense tells us that first impressions of other people are very important, and research confirms their significance (Dreben, Fiske & Hastie, 1979; Riskey, 1979). First impressions are easily formed, difficult to change, and typically have a long-lasting influence on how one person reacts to another. Why? How do people form impressions of people?

Schemas   The perception of people, like the perception of objects, involves the use of preexisting mental representations and the integration of individual bits of information into organized wholes, or schemas (Wyer & Srull, 1986). A **schema** is a coherent, organized set of beliefs and expectations (Brewer & Nakamura, 1984; Rumelhart, 1984; Taylor & Crocker, 1981). Your schema about grandmothers, for example, probably leads you to expect them to be elderly, sweet, gentle, kind, and conservative dressers. When you are introduced to a grandmother, you are likely to perceive the characteristics that are part of your schema of grandmothers, even if the particular woman in question does not actually display them. It may take a very unusual grandmother (perhaps one who is forty-five years old, wears tight jeans, and rides a motorcycle) to focus your perceptions on her actual attributes (Fiske & Pavelchak, 1986). Schemas allow you to skip the task of perceiving each element of a stimulus separately, to look instead at meaningful configurations, and to fill in missing information on the basis of knowledge stored in long-term memory. (See Figure 5.12 for another example.)

To demonstrate the role of schemas in social perception, consider this. The personality trait of casualness is generally considered to be favorable, as is the occupational role of surgeon. But if you put them together to form the cluster "casual surgeon," you are likely to have an unfavorable reaction, because the trait of casualness, even though it is itself positive, does not fit into your schema of surgeons (Higgins & Rholes, 1976). If people processed each new piece of social information independently, combining two positive attributes, such as "casual" and "surgeon," would not be perceived as negative. Research suggests that the negative reaction comes because, just as in the case of object perception, people look for general configurations of information.

Forming impressions   Schemas help create the tendency for people to infer a great deal about a person automatically, on the basis of very limited information (Srull & Wyer, 1986). This tendency is one reason why first impressions are formed very quickly and easily. Suppose you attend a party where you are introduced to a woman who appears to be in her mid-thirties and is wearing a long black dress with a pearl necklace. You are told that she has just finished writing her third novel. After five minutes of conversation, you might well infer that she is articulate, intelligent, educated, wealthy, witty, and much more interesting than anyone you have met during the past ten years. It is typical for people to take a few isolated bits of verbal and nonverbal behavior and infer from them all sorts of things about a person's life and personality. Some of them may be true, others not.

Two general tendencies influence whether a first impression is positive or negative. First, all else being equal, people tend to give others the benefit of the doubt and form positive rather than negative impressions of them (Matlin & Stang, 1978; Newcomb, 1968). In the absence of contradictory information, people assume that others are more or less similar to themselves (Sears, 1976; Srull & Gaelick, 1983). Since most people tend to have a positive evaluation of themselves, they are predisposed toward liking other people as well.

The second principle is that negative information tends to carry more weight than positive information (Feldman, 1966; Hamilton & Zanna, 1972).

The reason for this is that people may act positively for any number of reasons: because they are nice, because they like us, because they are polite, or because they want to sell us insurance. But it is assumed that negative acts come about only because the person is unfriendly or has some other undesirable characteristic. As a result, people are particularly attentive to negative acts and tend to give them very heavy weight in forming impressions.

Lasting impressions   In addition to being formed easily, first impressions are generally very difficult to change and therefore tend to have a long-lasting influence (O'Sullivan & Durso, 1984; Schneider, Hastorf & Ellsworth, 1979). The major reason they are difficult to counteract is that, as we saw in the chapter on thought, people tend to form impressions with a high degree of confidence. People tend to feel certain that they are correct and that they understand another person, even when they have little objective information about that person (Taylor & Fiske, 1978).

Furthermore, people tend to interpret new information and events so that they will be consistent with an original impression. If you immediately like someone and he or she compliments you, you are likely to interpret the compliment as sincere praise. But if the compliment comes from someone you dislike, you will probably interpret it as insincere ingratiation and begin looking for some ulterior motive. Similarly, self-assured behavior is interpreted as confidence among those one likes, but arrogance or conceit among those one dislikes. In short, the meaning given to new social information is shaped by what is already known about a person (Hamilton & Zanna, 1974).

Self-fulfilling prophecies   A final aspect of impression formation concerns how people behave toward others. People often act in ways that elicit from another person behavior that is consistent with their overall impression of that person (Snyder, 1981; Snyder & Gangestad, 1981). Suppose you hear a man say something at a party that gives the impression of boastfulness. This initial impression may prompt you to ask the man more about his accomplishments and, as he lists them, you become convinced that he is boastful indeed. Thus, an initial impression can constitute a **self-fulfilling prophecy** (Merton, 1948), in which the impression elicits behavior that confirms the impression (Jones, 1976).

The operation of self-fulfilling prophecies has been demonstrated in a number of experiments. In one study, men and women were asked to participate in a "get acquainted" conversation over an intercom system. But before these conversations took place, the men were shown photographs and told falsely that they were pictures of their partners. Some of the men were shown photographs that depicted their female partner as quite attractive. Other men saw pictures that led them to believe their partner was somewhat unattractive. In fact, none of the photographs bore any relationship to the women's actual attractiveness. Independent judges listening to the ensuing conversations (but seeing neither participant) rated the women's behavior and personality. The women whom the men thought were attractive were judged as more articulate, lively, interesting, exciting, and fun to be with. Apparently, when the men thought their partners were physically attractive, they were more friendly and engaging themselves, and this behavior elicited more positive reactions from the women. In contrast, men who thought their partners were unattractive behaved in a way that drew comparatively dull responses (Snyder, Tanke & Berscheid, 1977).

Self-fulfilling prophecies are an important part of why first impressions and overall impressions can have such a long-term impact (Swann, 1984). For example, if the staff in a mental institution believes and acts as if patients diagnosed as schizophrenic are unable to bathe themselves, eat properly, or

As discussed in the chapter on mental abilities, a teacher's first impressions of a student's intelligence can create self-fulfilling prophesies. Teachers may inadvertently or consciously deprive children who impressed them as "dull" of some of the learning opportunities enjoyed by those who appeared "bright." This differential treatment may result in lowered academic performance, thus fulfilling the initial expectation.

take responsibility for attending occupational training and other activities, those patients may become less and less likely to make efforts at self-care and improvement.

Self-fulfilling prophesies also help drive social judgments about even larger groups of people. When people assume that members of a certain minority group, for example, are pushy or aggressive, they may avoid them or act defensively around them. This behavior may prompt members of the minority group to insist on being heard or perhaps to become frustrated and angry. These reactions fulfill the prophecy and perpetuate the original impressions that created it. In the next section, we take a closer look at this process of group stereotyping.

Group Stereotypes and Prejudice

Stereotypes are impressions or schemas of entire groups of people. They are more powerful and potentially more dangerous than individual impressions, because they involve the false assumption that all members of the group share the same characteristics (Fiske & Taylor, 1984). The inferred characteristics that make up the stereotype may be positive or negative, but they are usually negative. The most prevalent and powerful stereotypes focus on observable personal attributes, particularly race, sex, and age.

Stereotyping often, if not always, leads to **prejudice,** a positive or negative attitude toward an entire group of people. *Prejudice* means literally "to prejudge." As an attitude, prejudice has cognitive, affective, and behavioral components. Indeed, stereotyped thinking is the cognitive component of prejudicial attitudes. The hatred, admiration, anger, and other feelings people have about stereotyped groups constitute the affective component. The behavioral component of prejudice often results in **discrimination,** which is differential treatment of various groups.

Stereotyping and prejudice can occur for different reasons, and they can serve very different functions for different individuals. We will describe three major theories of prejudice. Each theory has received empirical support. It therefore seems likely that each of them describes one of several separate processes that together underlie and produce prejudice (Stephan, 1985).

Motivational theories   One of the first attempts to understand prejudice and stereotyping concentrated on the personality structure of the individual. Specifically, the study found that the appearance of prejudice is most likely among people whose parents used punishment or harsh words to instill in them the belief that they must defer to and obey all those with a higher status than themselves (Adorno et al., 1950). According to T. W. Adorno and his colleagues, this upbringing encourages the development of a cluster of traits that they called the **authoritarian personality.** People with an authoritarian personality view the world as a strict social hierarchy. They feel they have the right to demand deference and cooperation from all those who have lower status. In order to know whom to obey and from whom to demand obedience, authoritarian people are motivated to identify other people's status in relation to themselves. This sets the stage for the development of negative stereotypes of those perceived as occupying a lower status, and for prejudice and discrimination against them.

One interesting piece of evidence supporting the concept of the authoritarian personality is that people who are prejudiced against one group also tend to be prejudiced against other groups (Ehrlich, 1973). This suggests that stereotypes and prejudices may serve some psychological need to derogate others. Theorists taking a psychodynamic perspective have suggested that, in downgrading and discriminating against lower-status groups, authoritarian personalities are using a defense mechanism: they are displacing the hostility they may have felt toward their punitive parents onto other, "inferior" people.

Learning theories   A second approach to stereotyping and prejudice emphasizes learning principles. It holds that children often learn stereotypes, prejudice, and discriminatory behaviors from their parents, their peers, and others (Karlins, Coffman & Walter, 1969). These influences are often reinforced by movies and television. One piece of supporting evidence is that people are often prejudiced against groups with whom they have never had any contact. There are people, for example, who have strong prejudices against blacks, Jews, Hispanics, or native Americans, even though they have never interacted with even one member of the group in question.

Learning theories of prejudice have led to the **contact hypothesis,** which states that stereotypes and prejudices about a group should be reduced as contact with that group increases. Specifically, friendly contact, as equals, with members of the group should provide evidence that many aspects of the stereotype are not true, or at least not true of all members, thus breaking down the stereotype, the prejudice, and the discrimination. There is some evidence to support the contact hypothesis. For example, David Hamilton and George Bishop (1976) studied white suburbanites immediately after their neighborhoods had become racially integrated and again a year later. These whites showed much more positive attitudes toward blacks by the end of the year. Contact can also increase prejudice under certain circumstances, however, such as when the contact involves a fistfight or some other negative interaction or when the status of the two parties is unequal. For example, neither the contact between slaves and slave owners in the American South nor that between whites and blacks in South Africa reduced racial prejudice.

Cognitive theories   A third approach to stereotyping and prejudice emphasizes the role of cognitive processes. It holds that stereotypes are inevitable

There are numerous stereotypes about the interests, abilities, and "proper" occupations of males and females. However, as members of both sexes begin to competently perform jobs once associated with only one sex, some of these gender stereotypes have become less influential.

Contact between members of different racial groups can reduce their prejudice toward one another. In one study of summer campers, children who had the most contact with members of another race showed much less prejudice at the end of the camp than did those with less contact (Eaton & Clore, 1975).

responses to an extraordinarily complex social world. There are so many people, so many situations in which one meets them, and so many possible behaviors that they might perform, that one cannot possibly attend to and remember them all. The most effective way to deal with this complexity is to group people into social categories. Just as people form categories for chairs, boats, shoes, and so on rather than remembering every detail about every single object they have ever encountered, people form categories of people. They create categories and mental lists of associated, often accurate, characteristics for teachers, athletes, strangers, politicians, criminals, and so on. These categories represent stereotypes.

How do people categorize other people? As noted earlier, people often focus on characteristics such as age, sex, race, occupation, and other detectable distinctions. They use these characteristics as the basis for creating ingroups and outgroups. An **ingroup** is any category of which people see themselves as a member. If you are black, blacks probably form your ingroup; if you are a black student, black students may form an even more specific ingroup. An **outgroup** is any group of which people do not see themselves as a member. People tend to see ingroup members as more physically attractive than outgroup members and assume that ingroup members have more desirable personality characteristics and engage in more socially accepted forms of behavior (Doise et al., 1972; Taylor & Jaggi, 1974). As might be expected, people tend to give ingroup members preferential treatment (Allen & Wilder, 1975).

In addition to simplifying and giving structure and organization to the world, social categories increase people's ability to anticipate and predict what will occur, as well as help them remember what has already occurred. They help you decide, for example, to ask a doctor rather than a librarian about that pain you have been noticing. But, when social categories are used to define prejudices, they can lead to harm and mistakes.

Attribution Theory

One type of prejudicial mistake appears in the assignment of credit or blame. For example, ingroup as opposed to outgroup members tend to be seen as more responsible for their successes and less responsible for their failures

(Deaux, 1976). Psychologists' interest in how prejudice creates this particular pattern of judgments is part of a larger research effort to understand **attribution,** the process of explaining the causes of people's behavior, including one's own.

Most people tend to attribute other people's behavior in a given situation either mainly to internal or mainly to external causes. *Internal* causes are those that reflect stable characteristics of the person. *External* causes are those that arise, not from the person, but from the situation. For example, suppose you and your friend agreed to meet for dinner at a particular restaurant at 6:00 P.M. It is now 6:45, and your friend has still not arrived. If you attribute this behavior primarily to internal causes, you might decide your friend is late because he or she is disorganized, lazy, inconsiderate, or forgetful. If you consider mainly external causes, you probably attribute the lateness to a flat tire, heavy traffic, an accident, sudden illness, or other characteristics of the situation.

Criteria for attributions   When people decide whether to attribute behavior to internal or to external causes, they use three main criteria: consensus, consistency, and distinctiveness (Kelley, 1973). For example, you could use these three criteria to explain why your father intensely dislikes your friend Ralph.

1. *Consensus* is the degree to which other people's behavior is similar to that of the person in question. If everyone you know thinks Ralph is a twit, your father's behavior has a high degree of consensus, and you would attribute his reaction to something external to him, something in the situation, probably something about Ralph. But if everyone else thinks Ralph is the sweetest guy on the planet, your dad's negative response would have low consensus, and you would probably attribute it to something about him, such as his being an old grouch.

2. *Consistency* is the degree to which the behavior occurs repeatedly in a particular situation. If Dad sometimes warmly invites Ralph to dinner and sometimes throws him out of the house, the consistency of his behavior is low. This suggests that your father's behavior is attributable to something about the external situation—probably something that Ralph sometimes does. If the hostile behavior occurs every time Ralph is around, it has high consistency. But is your father's consistent behavior attributable to a stable internal cause (his consistent grouchiness) or to a stable external cause (a consistently jerky friend)? This is difficult to determine without reference to distinctiveness information.

3. *Distinctiveness* is the predictability of behavior in various situations. If your dad is nasty to all your friends, no matter how they behave, his behavior has little distinctiveness. Low distinctiveness would suggest that Dad's reactions are attributable to his own internal characteristics. But if he gets on famously with everyone you know except Ralph, your attribution about the cause of his behavior is likely to shift toward Ralph as a cause that resides outside your father's personality.

Figure 17.6 (p. 646) shows how the pattern created by information about consensus, consistency, and distinctiveness determines whether behavior is attributed to internal or external causes. An internal attribution is most likely when there is low consensus, high consistency, and low distinctiveness. Thus, if you observe a coworker insulting customers (low consensus; most employees are polite to customers) every day (high consistency) no matter what the customer does (low distinctiveness), you would probably attribute this behavior to his or her negative personality characteristics, rather than to the weather, the customers, the time of day, or some other external cause. On the other hand, if you saw the same person on just one particular day (low consistency) being rude (low consensus) to one particular customer (high distinctiveness), you would be more likely to attribute the incident to the coworker's health

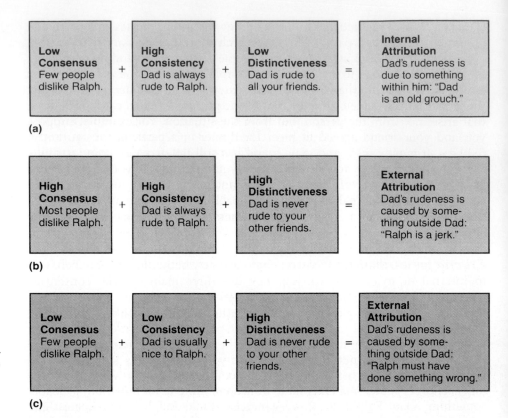

Figure 17.6
Causal Attributions
Here are the most common patterns of consensus, consistency, and distinctiveness information that lead people to make internal or external attributions about the causes of other people's behavior.

(a headache, perhaps), to stress, to the customer's behavior, or to another external factor. External attributions are often made in response to other information patterns as well, as Figure 17.6 illustrates.

Attributional biases   The results of many experiments have supported the principles outlined in Figure 17.6 (Karaz & Perlman, 1975; Kelley & Michela, 1980; McArthur, 1972; Ruble & Feldman, 1976). They suggest that people are often quite logical about how they make attributions about other people's behavior. However, prejudice and other psychological shortcuts sometimes create **attributional biases,** tendencies to distort one's view of behavior. Here are several prominent examples.

The **egocentric bias** is the tendency to assume that others act and believe just as you do. For example, people who choose to sign a petition tend to overestimate the number of others who have done or will do the same. Those who refuse to sign tend to underestimate the number of people who will sign (Ross, Greene & House, 1977). Prejudiced individuals often feel comfortable expressing their bigoted attitudes in public on the assumption that everyone else present will agree.

The **ego-defensive bias** is the tendency to take credit for success (attributing it to one's personal characteristics or efforts) but to blame external causes for failure. In one study, people were asked to explain three of their positive behaviors and three of their negative behaviors. In doing so, they consistently attributed their positive acts to such personal characteristics as generosity and the negative acts to such situational factors as lack of time (Taylor & Koivumaki, 1976).

Another attributional bias is tied to what has been called *belief in a just world.* In other words, many people tend to believe that the world is a just place, where good things happen to good people and bad things happen to bad people (Lerner, 1965). For example, Birnbaum (1973) asked subjects to read one of two stories in which a woman is raped. The stories were identical except for the fact that, in one version, the woman was a nun, and in the other, she was a prostitute. Even though the woman's behavior was exactly the same in both cases, the readers attributed much more responsibility for the rape to the prostitute-victim than to the nun-victim. In other words, they assumed that if a bad thing happened to a nun, it could not be her fault, whereas bad things happen to prostitutes because they bring it on themselves. When the characteristics of the victim are not as clear-cut, people may tend to blame crime victims (especially rape victims), partly because doing so helps maintain the image of a just world.

Attributions are also strongly influenced by the *availability heuristic,* which we described in the chapter on thought. It is the tendency to judge the frequency of an event by how easily an example of the event comes to mind. This bias can lead husbands and wives to attribute the completion of household chores more to their own efforts rather than to their partner's, because it is their own work around the house that they remember best (Ross & Sicoly, 1979).

The final form of attributional bias is known as the **fundamental attribution error:** people tend to be more aware of the influence of situational factors on their own behavior than on the behavior of others. Thus, people tend to be biased toward attributing their own behavior to external situational factors (especially when the behavior is unsuccessful or inappropriate) and toward attributing other people's behavior to internal characteristics (Jones, 1976; Ross, 1977). In other words, if you give the wrong answer to a professor's question in class, you are likely to attribute the mistake to lack of study time, distraction by money problems, or some other external cause. If the person across the room makes the same mistake, you might tend to think he or she is not very bright.

HIGHLIGHT

The Logic and Illogic of the Fundamental Attribution Error

Why do people so often make the fundamental attribution error? For one thing, the kinds and amounts of social information available are usually very different when considering your own and others' behavior. When *you* are acting in a situation—giving a speech, perhaps— the stimuli that are most salient to you are likely to be external and situational, such as the temperature of the room and the size and attitude of the audience. Further, you have access to a great deal of additional information about external factors, such as how much time you had to prepare your talk, the upsetting conversation you had this morning, the speech course you took last term, and the like. Whatever the outcome of your efforts in this situation, it can easily be attributed to one or all of these external causes. When observing the behavior of others, however, the most salient stimulus in the situation is the person. Since you do not know what happened to this person last night, this morning, or last term, it is very likely that you will attribute whatever he or she does to stable, internal characteristics.

The fundamental attribution error is extraordinarily powerful. In one study, students listened to someone give a canned speech either favoring or opposing racial segregation. The audience knew that situational factors were very important in determining the speaker's behavior, because they knew the speech was part of an experiment and that the speaker had been told which side of the issue to support. Nevertheless, even when the speaker unenthusiastically droned out the speech word for word from a printed text, the audience still tended to make internal attributions, judging the speaker's statements to be caused by racial attitudes (Jones & Harris, 1967; Schneider

& Miller, 1975). Attributional errors of this kind are less likely to occur if you know the other person very well, because familiarity allows you to more easily take the other person's point of view and to be aware of external causes that may be affecting his or her behavior.

The fundamental attribution error can lead to a number of problems. One unfortunate result is the tendency for some people to attribute other people's successes to their personal qualities while attributing their own successes to luck or other situational factors. This can undermine self-confidence and lead to the false assumption that everyone else is smart and confident, whereas you are full of faults and weaknesses. (Incidentally, while you are doing this, other people are often doing the same, perceiving you as a paragon of excellence and considering themselves to be shallow, lucky, undeserving recipients of the success that should rightfully belong to others.) As we saw in the abnormal psychology chapter, other attributional patterns, especially those in which people not only attribute their successes to situational factors but attribute their failures to personal shortcomings, can produce feelings of depression.

The fundamental attribution error can also help create or intensify prejudice. Suppose you observe a member of an outgroup with which you have little or no familiarity angrily contesting the amount he or she is being charged for auto repairs. Unacquainted with the person and his or her life situation, it would be easy to assume that here is an example of this outgroup's well-known trait of aggressiveness. In fact, it might simply be the result of a normally level-headed customer's frustration at an obnoxious mechanic who is trying to collect an excessive fee for unsatisfactory work. ◀

Obviously, attributions, as well as other aspects of social perception, can have far-reaching consequences. As shown in the next section, these consequences include the degree to which people come to like or dislike other people.

ATTRACTION

Why do people like other people? For attraction, as for the attribution of causes, both situational factors and a person's characteristics play a role in determining which people will be attracted to each other.

Some Situational Determinants

Among the situational factors influencing attraction to other people are their physical closeness and familiarity, as well as the circumstances associated with them.

Propinquity and familiarity   When thinking about why one person is attracted to another, it is easy to overlook the obvious. One of the most important determinants of attraction is simple physical proximity, or *propinquity*. For example, when friendship patterns in a city housing project were studied, many more friendships were found among people living on the same floor than among those on different floors (Nahemow & Lawton, 1975). Propinquity is apparently tied to attraction, because with proximity comes contact, and people often tend to like people with whom they have a lot of contact. Most of the people named by police cadets as their closest friends at the academy were cadets with whom they had had the most contact: specifically, those who sat nearby in class (Segal, 1974).

In general, the more often we make contact with someone, the more we tend to like that person. This is one reason why next-door neighbors are much more likely to become friends as people who live further from one another (Nahemow & Lawton, 1975).

The circumstances of contact People who meet a stranger under comfortable physical conditions are much more likely to be attracted to that person than if the meeting takes place while enduring heat or other discomfort (Griffitt & Veitch, 1971). And, in a manner similar to the secondary reinforcement described in the chapter on learning, if people receive some reward in the presence of a particular stranger, they tend to like that stranger better (Byrne & Clore, 1970; Lott & Lott, 1972, 1974).

Attraction based on association with rewards occurs even if the other person is not responsible for providing the reward. In one study, an experimenter evaluated the creativity of a subject while another person watched. Compared with those who received a negative evaluation, subjects receiving a positive evaluation tended to like both the experimenter and the observer more, even though the observer did not provide the reinforcement (Griffitt & Guay, 1969). Thus, it appears that secondary reinforcement is an important determinant of attraction, at least among people who are initially strangers.

Some Person-Related Determinants

As we said in the discussion of attitude change, people are more likely to like people whom they perceive as similar to themselves. The similarity can occur along many dimensions but is particularly influential when it involves similarity in attitudes and physical attractiveness.

Similarity in attitudes As Figure 17.7 illustrates, there is a strong and direct relationship between the proportion of attitudes shared by two people and how much one likes the other. This is true of children (Byrne & Griffitt, 1966), college students (Newcomb, 1961), adult workers (Krauss, 1966), and senior citizens (Griffitt, Nelson & Littlepage, 1972).

Among the attitude similarities most predictive of liking are those having to do with people in the same social network. For example, imagine that John likes Terry. Now imagine that John meets Tim. John will be more attracted to Tim if Tim also likes Terry (a *balanced* pattern of attitudes; see Figure 17.8a, p. 650) than if he does not (an *imbalanced* pattern; Figure 17.8c). People greatly prefer balanced attitude patterns over imbalanced ones (Price, Harburg & Newcomb, 1966).

Figure 17.7
Interpersonal Attraction and Attitudes
This graph shows the results of a study in which people first learned about the attitudes of another person. Their liking of this person was strongly influenced by the proportion of attitudes the person expressed that were similar to their own.
(From D. Byrne and D. Nelson, "Attraction as a Linear Function of Proportion of Positive Reinforcements," *Journal of Personality and Social Psychology, 1,* 659–663. Copyright 1965 by the American Psycho-logical Association. Adapted by permission of the publisher and authors.)

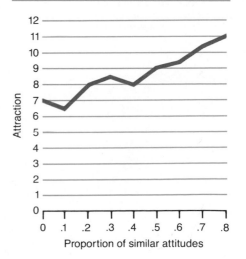

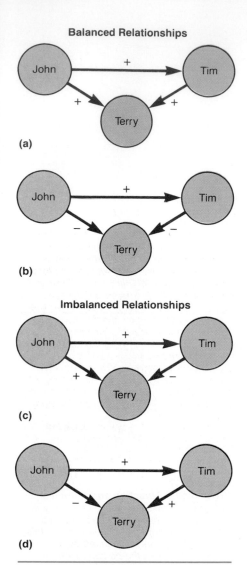

Figure 17.8
Balanced and Imbalanced Relationships
These are the most common balanced and imbalanced patterns of relationships among three people. The plus and minus signs refer to liking and disliking, respectively. Balanced relationships are comfortable and harmonious; imbalanced ones are often full of conflict and friction.

Now imagine a new scenario, in which John dislikes Terry. Under these conditions, John will be more attracted to Tim if Tim also dislikes Terry than if Tim likes Terry. The first set of attitudes would be balanced (Figure 17.8b), and the second set would be imbalanced (Figure 17.8d). Research also indicates that, all else being equal, "the enemy of my enemy is my friend" (Aronson & Cope, 1968).

Physical attractiveness   There is no doubt that physical attractiveness is an important factor in attraction, particularly in determining whether friendships are initiated (Maruyama & Miller, 1975). Even for members of the same sex, physical attractiveness is a key to popularity. This relationship begins to be seen in grade school (Cavior & Dokecki, 1969), and it continues among both male and female college students (Byrne, London & Reeves, 1968).

In one of the first experiments of the role of physical attractiveness on liking, college students completed a personality inventory and were told that they would be matched with a date by computer; in fact, the pairings were done randomly. The couples then attended a large social event. As each couple arrived, judges working for the experimenter rated the physical attractiveness of each person. After the party had been going on for several hours, all the students were asked to complete a questionnaire. The results showed that the more physically attractive the dates, the more they were liked and the more their partners wanted to meet them again in the future. For both males and females, the most attractive people were considered the most desirable dates. Furthermore, intelligence and various personality characteristics were relatively unimportant (Walster et al., 1966). In another study, people were asked whether they were willing to go on a date with someone they had met only briefly. Under these conditions, both men's and women's choices suggested that they tended to be attracted to people whose physical attractiveness was *roughly the same* as their own (Berscheid et al., 1971).

Subsequent dating studies have found more or less the same pattern (Curran & Lippold, 1975), thus lending support to the **matching hypothesis,** which states that a person is most likely to be attracted to others who are similar in physical attractiveness than to those who are notably more attractive or notably less attractive (Berscheid & Walster, 1978). The matching hypothesis has also been supported in studies of married couples, which show that husband and wife are usually about equally attractive physically (Murstein, 1972). In general, then, the factors that shape attraction to another person may also influence the development and maintenance of more intimate relationships.

Developing Intimate Relationships

Even when members of a couple are relatively well matched on appearance, they often find that the physical attractiveness that was so important in bringing them together becomes somewhat less important as the relationship continues and becomes more intimate. As the relationship grows and endures, the two people compensate for any discrepancy between them in physical attractiveness by focusing on deeper, more psychological attributes that keep the pair together (Berscheid et al., 1973). In most cases, this evolution occurs as the pair slowly progresses from *passionate love,* which is characterized by both strong physical attraction and intense emotional attachment (Lee, 1973; Walster & Walster, 1978), toward *compassionate love,* in which each person becomes primarily concerned with the welfare of the other (Hendrick & Hendrick, 1986).

What additional factors motivate people to maintain long-term intimate relationships? (*Intimate,* by the way, may refer not to sexual contact but to

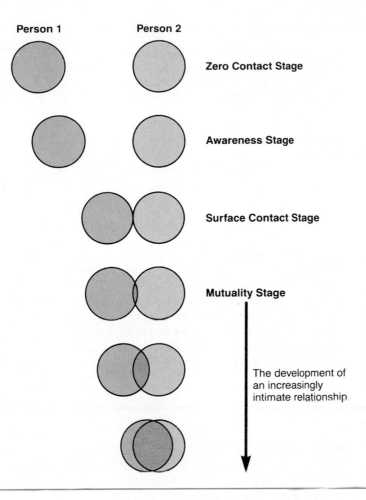

Person 1   Person 2

Zero Contact Stage

Awareness Stage

Surface Contact Stage

Mutuality Stage

The development of
an increasingly
intimate relationship

Figure 17.9
*The Development of Intimate
Relationships*
*During the zero contact stage, two people
have no relationship at all. During the
awareness stage, at least one person becomes aware of the other and begins forming an impression of that person. The entire
impression-formation process discussed
earlier becomes relevant at this stage. The
surface contact stage is the first point at
which two people begin interacting with one
another directly. Since the two people have
been "strangers" up until this point, initial
conversations are typically very superficial.
The mutuality stage involves the sharing of
more and more intimate information and the
development of an increasingly strong psychological bond.*
(Copyright © George Levinger and J. Diedrick
Snoek, 1972. *Attraction in Relationship:
A New Look at Interpersonal Attraction.*
Morristown, N.J.: General Learning Press,
1972.)

psychological closeness. Thus, the principles outlined in this section apply to
the development of intimate friendships in same- and cross-sex pairs, as well
as to marriages and other long-term sexual relationships.) Figure 17.9 outlines
some general steps in the development of intimate relationships (Levinger,
1974; Levinger & Snoek, 1972). Intimacy begins to develop when the
relationship shows *mutuality;* that is, when people share information with one
another, not only about superficial facts, but also about beliefs, preferences,
goals, philosophies, and so on. Mutual relationships begin with a small amount
of intimacy and then may progress to a deeper and deeper level of intimacy.
Eventually, each person begins to care about and identify with the other
person and accepts at least some responsibility for what happens to that
person.

Self-disclosure   One of the major factors in the development of intimate
relationships is *self-disclosure,* the revelation of a person's private world,
background, fears, hopes, beliefs, weaknesses, and the like. There are two
independent dimensions to self-disclosure: breadth and depth (Altman &
Taylor, 1973). *Breadth* refers to the number of topics touched by self-disclosure.
Depth refers to the intimacy level; that is, to how much private information a
person reveals about any given topic. In the early stages of most relationships,
one person offers self-disclosure at a relatively low level on each dimension.
If the other person accepts initial self-disclosures and reciprocates with his or
her own self-disclosures, future disclosures by both parties gradually become
deeper and broader over time. Ideally, when each person's self-disclosure is
received by the other with acceptance, understanding, and caring (responses

PERCEPTION AND SOCIAL PSYCHOLOGY
How Does Perception of Objects Relate to Perception of People?

As suggested earlier, the perception of people follows many of the same laws as the perception of objects, including the Gestalt principles discussed in Chapter 5. Research on how people perceive objects can provide additional insight into social perception, especially into the lasting influence of first impressions. Consider Figure A. As suggested by Gestalt principles, most people would not say that it is composed of eight separate straight lines; they are more likely to describe it as "a square with a notch in one side" (Woodworth & Schlosberg, 1954). They try to impose some meaning on it based on what they know about the world; in other words, they use the schemas they already have to perceive new information. Robert Woodworth suggested that this tendency is based on a **schema-plus-correction process** (the schema is "a square"; the correction is the notch).

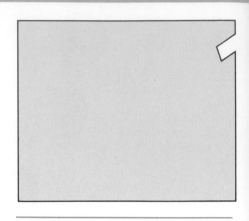

Figure A
A Schema-Plus-Correction
People who see an object like this tend to use preexisting knowledge and perceive it as a schema (in this case, a square) with a correction or modification of some kind (here, a notch). However, they will probably later remember only seeing a square because, over time, people tend to forget corrections and remember only schemas.

Though passion need never die, the basis for most long-term intimate relationships tends to shift over the years from passionate love to compassionate love, characterized by mutual self-disclosure, shared interests, and reciprocal caring.

similar to Rogers's unconditional positive regard, discussed in the chapter on treatment), they begin to develop trust in one another. This trust, in turn, makes the relationship more intimate, leads to further cycles of self-disclosure, greater trust, and deepening intimacy.

Indeed, the most important determinants of the development of intimacy are how each person responds to the other's self-disclosures and whether they also self-disclose (Chaiken & Derlega, 1974; Cozby, 1973). Rejected, neglected, or otherwise unreinforced self-disclosures tend to work against the development of intimacy. On the whole, females tend to value and react to self-disclosure more positively than males. Among female friends, for example, self-disclosure reliably leads to increased liking (Berscheid, 1985). This tends to be less true among males, many of whom find self-disclosure difficult and react to the self-disclosure of others with befuddlement or embarrassment. However, males are by no means incapable of self-disclosure.

Long-term intimate relationships What are the most important factors in maintaining a long-term relationship such as marriage? Psychologists are just beginning to find out. For one thing, both men and women tend to report the highest levels of marital satisfaction when the typical level of self-disclosure in the relationship is high (Levinger & Senn, 1967). Indeed, the mutual sharing of interests and ideas was found to be more important than sex in one study (Sternberg & Grajek, 1984).

Other insights into what makes a successful marriage come from examining the characteristics of couples who stay together happily compared with those who stay together unhappily. Research by Robert Sternberg and Michael Barnes (1985) indicates that the happiness and satisfaction of a couple in a romantic relationship depends not on how strongly they love each other, but on how equally they love each other. People in their study did not rate the sex appeal of their partner as an important factor in their relationship. However, good sex and marital happiness do tend to go together. Of men and

Analogous processes occur in social perception. People have better memory for the impression they form of a person than of any correction that is later added (Graesser & Nakamura, 1982). Imagine that you form a positive impression of someone and then discover that the person has engaged in several unacceptable acts. You will probably think less of the person. Over a period of time, however, you will tend to forget the unfavorable corrections to your schema or impression and remember the positive things the person has done (Graesser et al., 1980). On the other hand, if you dislike someone, you will tend to forget the positive things the person has done and come to like the person even less (Srull & Wyer, 1980, 1983). As a consequence, evaluations of people tend to become polarized over time. This phenomenon has been clearly demonstrated in people's feelings about former President Richard Nixon. Many of those who supported Nixon while he was in office reacted negatively to his Watergate-related behavior but now remember him fondly for his foreign policy achievements. Those who opposed his presidency may once have given him credit for some significant achievements but now despise him, as they recall only his unlawful acts.

women who characterize their marriage as "very close," over 70 percent rate their sex life as "very pleasurable." Only 10 percent of those who feel their marriage is "not too close" still rate their sex life as "very pleasurable" (Hunt, 1974). Unfortunately, correlational studies like these cannot determine whether good sex promotes good relationships or whether good relationships promote good sex.

Besides sex and love, the way in which a couple handles anger is very important to the development of a happy marriage. Anger is a part of both happy and unhappy marriages, but what couples do in response to anger differs. In particular, John Gottman (1979) found that, in both happy and unhappy marriages, men tend to respond to anger from their spouse with anger of their own. In unhappy marriages, however, both the men and the women tend to fall into a cycle in which they merely trade increasingly angry and hurtful remarks until communication about the original problem, or any other problem, breaks down. In happy marriages, the cycle of angry reactions is ultimately broken, usually by the wife, allowing the couple to identify and deal with the problem or conflict at hand during moments of calm. Attempts to understand these and other components of long-term romantic relationships are relatively new, but these relationships are likely to be the subject of much research in the years ahead.

Intimate relationships are but one example of the many consistent patterns of behavior people show toward one another in the social world. In the next chapter, we will consider a number of other examples, including conformity, obedience, aggression, helping, competition, and the like.

FUTURE DIRECTIONS

A tremendous amount has been learned about social behavior, most of it through laboratory experiments. These experiments often provide the best vehicle available for testing specific theories (Aronson, Brewer & Carlsmith, 1985). However, they have a cost. Their settings are artificial, the subjects tend to be college students, and the investigations generally are conducted within a very limited span of time (Sears, 1986).

In the future, we expect that an increasing number of studies in social psychology will study people in naturally occurring situations, and that these studies will last longer. By studying people for longer periods, psychologists will be better able to address the issue of *reciprocal causality*. To illustrate, consider our discussion of attraction. Most theories of attraction postulate a *flow of causality* in only one direction: all else being equal, physical attractiveness leads to more liking, and attitude similarity leads to increased attraction. Is it not possible, however, that once you like someone, your perceptions of their physical attractiveness change? Similarly, once you develop a close interpersonal bond with someone, is it possible that your attitudes on various issues might change to make you more similar or that your perceptions of the other person's attitudes make them appear more similar to your own?

Some trends toward studying reciprocal causality are already apparent in research on such social phenomena as the self-fulfilling prophecy. In one study, subjects were led to believe that another person liked them or disliked them (Curtis & Miller, 1986). These beliefs influenced both their perceptions of the other person and their overt behavior. When subjects thought the other person liked them, they saw that other person as warmer, more friendly, a better listener, and more trustworthy. When interacting with a person seen as liking them, the subjects disclosed more personal information, asked more questions, and otherwise acted more friendly than if the person was said not to like them. One can anticipate that psychologists will devote considerable effort to developing theories that can account for reciprocal causality in the complex relationships between behavior and its social context.

SUMMARY

1. People often use others to evaluate their own characteristics, through social comparison. The people with whom one identifies and whom one habitually uses for comparison are reference groups. Feelings of relative deprivation can occur when a person's relative standing on some dimension decreases as a function of adopting a new reference group.

2. The presence of other people can, through social facilitation, improve one's performance at some task or impair it, through social interference. Both effects appear traceable to increased arousal, which improves performance on easy or well-learned tasks and hampers performance on complex or unfamiliar ones.

3. Norms are learned, socially based rules that prescribe what people should or should not do in various situations. They exert a powerful influence on human behavior.

4. An attitude is a predisposition toward a particular cognitive, emotional, or behavioral reaction to an object, person, or action. Attitudes have cognitive, affective, and behavioral components.

5. Changes in attitudes are often the result of persuasive communications. Attitude change is most likely when the communicator is perceived as credible, sincere, and similar to oneself. Various characteristics of the message are also important in determining whether attitude change will occur. For example, presenting only one side of an issue is usually more effective if the audience is predisposed to the speaker's point of view; presenting both sides is usually best if the audience is antagonistic to the speaker's point of view. Overall, there is no relationship between the audience's intelligence and susceptibility to persuasion. However, people with moderate levels of self-esteem are more likely to change their attitudes than those with either high or low levels of self-esteem.

6. When people perceive their freedom to be restricted or eliminated, a state of psychological reactance occurs, in which the person is less likely than before to do what others might wish.

7. Research on cognitive dissonance indicates that, because people usually prefer to have their behaviors

and attitudes consistent with one another, they often adjust their behaviors and attitudes to eliminate any inconsistencies, or dissonance. Self-perception theory also helps explain attitude change, suggesting that, when people are uncertain, they adjust their attitudes to match their perceptions of the reasons for their behavior.

8. The impression people form of another person or group often takes the form of a schema—a coherent, organized set of beliefs. First impressions are easily formed, difficult to change, and typically have a long-lasting influence on how one person reacts to another. Negative infomation tends to carry more weight than positive information in forming an impression of another person. Self-fulfilling prophecies occur when one acts in a way that elicits behavior from others that is consistent with one's prior impression of them.

9. Schemas about entire groups are called stereotypes. One by-product of stereotyping is prejudice, which is a positive or negative attitude toward the group. Discrimination refers to differential treatment that may be accorded to various groups. There are several theories about the development of stereotyping and prejudice. Motivational theories emphasize the personality structure of the individual. Learning theories emphasize the information that children obtain about various groups from parents, peers, and the media. Cognitive theories emphasize categorization processes

10. Attribution theory suggests that people use several sources of social information to decide whether their own and other people's behavior are due to internal or external causes. Sometimes people use this information logically; at other times, people may be biased, as when they attribute other people's mistakes to those individuals' internal personality characteristics, while attributing their own errors to situational factors or other external circumstances.

11. Many determinants of one person's attraction to another have been identified. All else being equal, people tend to like others (a) with whom they have the most contact, (b) who are present when reinforcement occurs, (c) who share similar attitudes, and (d) who are physically attractive.

12. Intimate relationships usually begin between people of about equal physical attractiveness and develop slowly as each partner discloses more and more personal information. Self-disclosure has two components: breadth and depth. One of the most important keys to the maintenance of such long-term relationships as marriage is how a couple learns to handle anger.

KEY TERMS

Definitions of terms appear on the pages shown in parentheses.

attitude (632)
attribution (645)
attributional bias (646)
authoritarian personality (643)
cognitive dissonance (637)
contact hypothesis (643)
discrimination (642)
egocentric bias (646)
ego-defensive bias (646)
fear appeal (635)
fundamental attribution error (647)
ingroup (644)
matching hypothesis (650)
norm (630)

outgroup (644)
prejudice (642)
reactance (636)
reference group (627)
relative deprivation (627)
schema (640)
schema-plus-correction process (652)
self-fulfilling prophecy (641)
self-perception theory (638)
social comparison (626)
social facilitation (628)
social perception (639)
social psychology (624)
stereotype (642)

RECOMMENDED READINGS

Cialdini, R. B. (1984). *Influence: The new psychology of persuasion.* New York: Quill. An excellent and very well-written analysis of social influence processes. In addition to summarizing experimental investigations, the author provides numerous examples of how social influence operates in everyday life.

Fiske, S. T., and Taylor, S. E. (1984). *Social cognition.* Reading, Mass.: Addison-Wesley. A comprehensive treatment of the role that cognitive processes play in social psychology. The book is highlighted by a very thorough discussion of attribution theory.

Hamilton, D. L. (Ed.). (1981). *Cognitive processes in stereotyping and intergroup behavior.* Hillsdale, N.J.: Erlbaum. A contemporary treatment of prejudice and group stereotyping is provided. Each chapter is written by an expert in the field.

Petty, R. E., and Cacioppo, J. T. (1981). *Attitudes and persuasion: Classic and contemporary approaches.* Dubuque, Iowa: William C. Brown. This is the best introduction to attitudes that currently exists. Virtually all theories of attitude formation and attitude change are included, and the evidence bearing on each is summarized in a clear and concise fashion.

Schneider, D. J., Hastorf, A. H., and Ellsworth, P. C. (1979). *Person perception* (2nd ed.). Reading, Mass.: Addison-Wesley. An excellent introduction to the way we think about ourselves and others. Most of the classic studies in the field are discussed.

I n many a western movie, a few ruthless criminals terrorize an entire town, until a hero rides in off the prairie to send them to Boot Hill. The odd thing about this classic plot is that the decent citizens, all of whom have weapons, always outnumber the outlaws by a hundred to one. They could easily form an army and wipe out the bad guys, but they never do. Why not? The same question can be asked about similar puzzles in the real world of social behavior. For example, compared to the population of most big cities, the number of people involved in organized crime is quite small. Yet this tiny group extorts money and commits many other crimes, secure in the knowledge that their fearful victims will not testify against them. Why? Tyranny over the many by the few is possible, in part, because most individuals in a group act in ways that benefit them in the short run, even when they know that the collective result of those actions will be long-term harm to the group. Tolerating criminals may be the safest thing to do individually, even though it perpetuates the crime problem for everyone.

There are many other examples of how the social world's influence on the individual can create problems for the group. For example, when school districts ask for higher taxes, individuals often vote against them, preferring to minimize their own immediate tax bill, even though this may endanger the long-term quality of education for everyone's children. Such events are examples of **social dilemmas,** situations in which the short-term decisions of individuals become irrational in combination and create long-term, clearly predictable damage for a group.

Social dilemmas illustrate just one of the ways in which the social world—through the influences on the individual that we discussed in the previous chapter—can make for puzzling, dramatic, and sometimes illogical human behavior in groups and other interpersonal situations. In this chapter, we consider some of these phenomena, beginning with people's tendency to behave as others suggest or demand.

CONFORMITY AND COMPLIANCE

Suppose you are with three friends. One says that Franklin Roosevelt was the greatest president in the history of the United States. You think it was Abraham Lincoln, but before you can say anything, another friend agrees that it was Roosevelt, and then the other one does as well. What would you do? Disagree with all three? Maintain your opinion but keep quiet? Change your mind?

This is a very common situation, because the individuals in almost any group—a family, a team, a government body, or a military unit—are likely to harbor differing attitudes and preferences. When people change their behavior or beliefs to match those of other members of a group, they are said to **conform.** It is generally agreed that conformity occurs as a result of real or imagined, though *unspoken,* group pressure (Kiesler & Kiesler, 1969). In Chapter 17, we saw how such pressure caused conformity in the attitudes of many Bennington College students. It can also alter overt behavior. For example, when everyone around you stands up to applaud a performance you

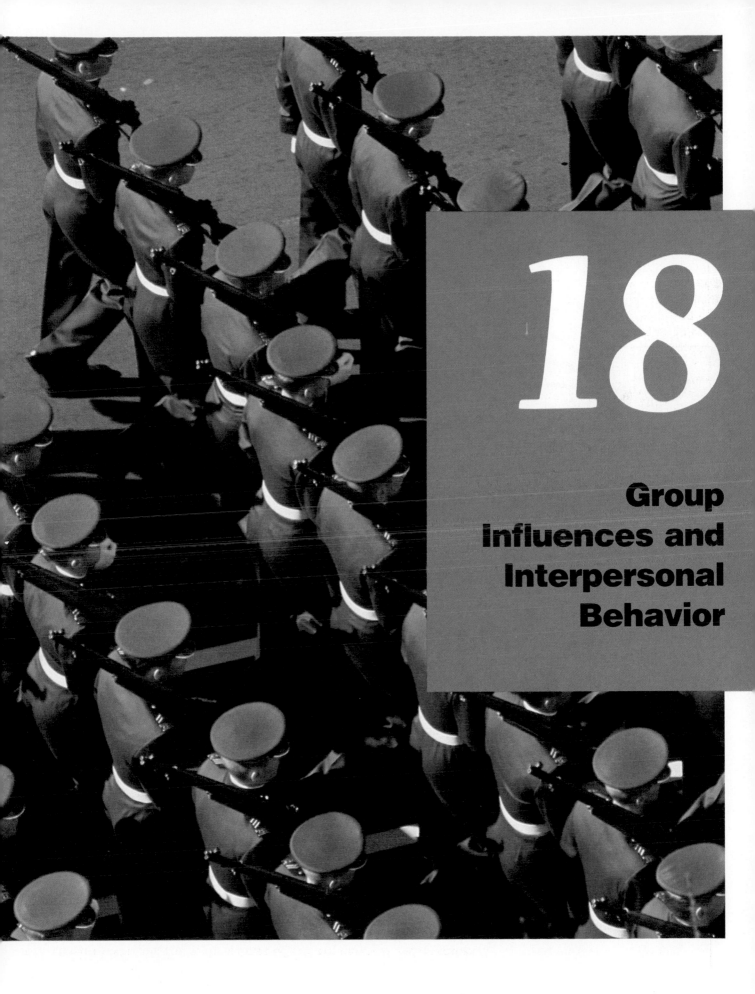

18

Group
Influences and
Interpersonal
Behavior

LINKAGES
an overview

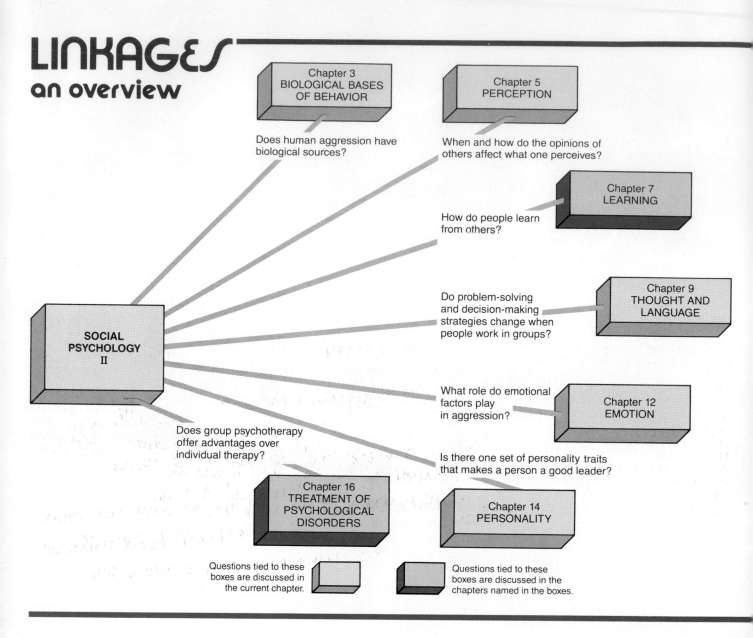

Chapter 3
BIOLOGICAL BASES
OF BEHAVIOR

Does human aggression have
biological sources?

Chapter 5
PERCEPTION

When and how do the opinions of
others affect what one perceives?

Chapter 7
LEARNING

How do people learn
from others?

Chapter 9
THOUGHT AND
LANGUAGE

Do problem-solving
and decision-making
strategies change when
people work in groups?

**SOCIAL
PSYCHOLOGY
II**

What role do emotional
factors play
in aggression?

Chapter 12
EMOTION

Is there one set of personality traits
that makes a person a good leader?

Does group psychotherapy
offer advantages over
individual therapy?

Chapter 16
TREATMENT OF
PSYCHOLOGICAL
DISORDERS

Chapter 14
PERSONALITY

Questions tied to these
boxes are discussed in
the current chapter.

Questions tied to these
boxes are discussed in the
chapters named in the boxes.

---

thought was mediocre, you may conform by standing as well. No one tells you to do this; the group's behavior simply creates a silent but influential pressure to follow suit. **Compliance,** in contrast, occurs when people adjust their behavior to match that of a group because of directly expressed social influence. If the last holdout for acquittal on a jury finally succumbs to the other jurors' browbeating, he or she has complied with overt social pressure.

The Role of Norms

Conformity and compliance are usually generated by a group's spoken or unspoken norms. As we discussed in the previous chapter, *norms* establish rules for behavior in given situations.

Muzafer Sherif (1937) managed to chart the formation of a group norm by taking advantage of a perceptual illusion called the *autokinetic phenomenon.* If a person is placed in a completely dark room and shown a small, stationary

GROUP INFLUENCES AND PSYCHOLOGY

In the previous chapter, we began our discussion of social psychology by focusing on how an individual's behavior and mental processes are influenced by the social world. That chapter made it clear that it is impossible to study the individual in the social world without considering the presence and behavior of other people—the stimuli that, by definition, comprise the social world. For example, it is other people who often help form and change one's attitudes, and it is other people to whom people are attracted or not. Thus, to complete our coverage of social psychology, we devote this chapter to a discussion of the principles that govern how people influence one another. In the process, we will consider a number of fascinating and important social phenomena, including conformity to group norms, obedi-

ence to authority, and aggression against others. As always, there are numerous links between the study of these interpersonal behaviors and other psychological subspecialties.

For example, in studying rape, one of the most troubling and pernicious forms of behavior that can occur between two people, social psychologists often find that their research takes them into the psychological subspecialties of motivation, emotion, thought, biological psychology, personality, and abnormal behavior. Why do rapists often feel they have no personal responsibility for their crime? Many factors appear to contribute. One is an underlying motive to demean women. Learning also appears to play a role. Some men have learned, possibly from their fathers or other adults, that violence, particularly against women,

is an acceptable form of behavior. Cognitive factors also contribute. For example, men who believe that males must be dominant in all of their interactions with women often become sexually aroused at the thought of rape. There also appear to be important personality differences, in that some men have low self-esteem and at the same time equate sexual activity with self-worth. Psychopathic and antisocial tendencies are also associated with rape.

In short, when people interact, all the mental and behavioral processes we have studied in the individual interact as well. One cannot study the interpersonal aspects of social psychology without also touching on almost every other aspect of psychology

point of light, the light will appear to move (*autokinetic* means "self-movement"). Some people tend to see a great deal of movement, whereas others report only a little, but each person's estimates of apparent movement tend to stay within a small, characteristic range, such as from one to two inches or from five to six inches. Sherif put several individuals into the same dark room, switched on a point of light, and asked each person to report aloud how far the light had moved on repeated exposures. Eventually, the subjects' estimates tended to fall within a common *group* range. Even more important, when the individuals in the group were later tested alone, they continued to respond according to this group norm.

Notice that, in Sherif's experiment, the subjects had no way of knowing whether, how far, and in what direction the pinpoint of light moved, because the movement was an illusion. To test whether this ambiguity by itself explained the subjects' conformity, Solomon Asch (1956) asked subjects questions about which they could be sure of the answers. These people were

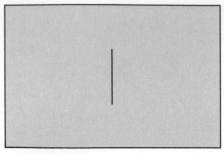

(a) Standard Line

(b) Test Lines

Figure 18.1
Types of Stimulus Lines Used in Experiments by Asch
Such experiments demonstrate that people often conform to the views of others in a group.
(From "Opinions and Social Pressure" by Solomon E. Asch. Illustration on p. 32 by Sara Love. Copyright © 1955 by Scientific American, Inc. All Rights Reserved.)

shown a standard line like the one in Figure 18.1a; then they saw a display like that in Figure 18.1b. Their task was to pick out the line in the display that was the same length as the line they had been shown first.

Each subject performed the task as part of a small group, but in reality all of the other participants were confederates of the experimenter. There were two conditions. In the control condition, the subject had to respond before any of the other participants. In the experimental condition, the subject did not respond until after the confederates did. These confederates chose the obviously correct response on six trials, but they all gave the same, obviously incorrect response on the other twelve trials. Thus, on twelve trials, each subject was confronted with a "social reality"—created by the group norm—which conflicted with the physical reality created by what the person could clearly see. Only 5 percent of the subjects in the control condition ever made a mistake on this easy perceptual task. However, among subjects who heard the confederates' responses before giving their own, about 70 percent made at least one "error" by conforming to the group norm.

Why Do People Conform?

Why did the people in Asch's experiment give so many incorrect responses when they were capable of near-perfect performance? One possibility is that these people did not really change their minds; instead, perhaps they gave an answer they did not believe simply because it was the socially desirable thing to do. This sort of expression of what one does not actually believe is called *public conformity.* Another possibility, of course, is that the subjects used the confederates' responses as legitimate evidence about reality. In other words, they might actually have been convinced that their own perceptions were wrong. Actually changing one's mind in this way is called *private acceptance.*

To better understand this distinction, researchers have asked whether people conform even when they give their responses in private and with complete anonymity. Morton Deutsch and Harold Gerard (1955) reasoned that, if conformity disappeared under these circumstances, Asch's findings must reflect public compliance, not private acceptance. In fact, Deutsch and Gerard found that both public conformity and private acceptance occur in the type of situation studied by Asch. Conformity decreases when people can respond anonymously instead of publicly, but it is not eliminated. This suggests that people will sometimes publicly produce responses that they do not believe, but that the responses of others also influence their own private beliefs (Moscovici, 1980, 1985).

Why do group norms wield such weighty influence? Part of the reason is that norms convey information; they outline what is right or wrong in particular situations, as well as what is expected. In addition, norms guide the dispensation of social reinforcement and punishment (Ross, Bierbrauer & Hoffman, 1976). From childhood on, people learn that conforming to or complying with norms (especially those in family, school, and religious groups) is good and earns material rewards and social esteem. (These positive outcomes presumably help compensate for not always saying or doing exactly what one pleases.) Failure to follow group norms typically brings punishments ranging from spankings for minor violations to imprisonment for nonconformity with norms that have been translated into laws.

Even though conformity has negative connotations for some people, especially those who value independence highly, it does bring certain benefits, particularly for the long-term functioning and cohesiveness of groups. Consider what life would be like if there were no conformity to group norms—if, for example, no one paid attention to norms about taking turns when speaking,

balance between individuality v. conformity

Reverend Sun Myung Moon performs a mass wedding for some of his followers. Cults such as the "Moonies" provide but one example of how groups can exert strong influences over their members' thoughts and behaviors. Conformity to unspoken influences and compliance with explicit rules and requests are basic features of human behavior in many other kinds of groups as well.

knocking before opening a closed door, or respecting people's rights to their own property. At best, life would be chaotic and unpredictable; at worst, the fabric of society would begin to disintegrate. At the same time, if everyone conformed all the time and in exactly the same way, the world might be a rather boring place, bereft of the variety, eccentricity, and even strangeness that makes human beings so fascinating. Thus, members of human social groups constantly search for the delicate balance that will assure group survival without squelching individuality.

When Do People Conform?

Clearly, people do not always conform to group influence. In the Asch studies, for example, nearly 30 percent of the subjects did not go along with the confederates' obviously erroneous judgments. Countless experiments have probed the question of what combinations of people and circumstances do and do not lead to conformity.

Ambiguity of the situation   Ambiguity is very important in determining how much conformity will occur; as physical reality becomes less clear, conformity to a group norm becomes more likely. You can demonstrate this relationship yourself on any street corner. Create an ambiguous situation by forming a group of six or eight people looking up at the top of a building or high in the sky. When curious people ask what is going on, be sure everyone excitedly reports seeing something vague but interesting—perhaps a tiny, shiny object or a faint, mysterious light (the hint of a flying saucer sighting is always helpful in such exercises). In a situation like this, in which the alleged stimulus is fleeting or difficult to see, people are likely to perceive the behavior of your group as providing valid information about the world. If you are especially successful, conforming newcomers will begin persuading other passersby that there is something fascinating to be seen.

The importance of stimulus ambiguity has been repeatedly demonstrated in the laboratory. For example, when Asch (1956) varied his line-comparison task so that it became more difficult to be sure of the correct answer, conformity increased substantially. Other researchers have found that, as the physical reality of a situation becomes less clear, people rely more and more on others' opinions (Shaw, Rothschild & Strickland, 1957).

Unanimity and size of the majority   If ambiguity contributes so much to conformity, why did so many of Asch's subjects conform to a group judgment that was very clearly wrong? The answer has to do with the unanimity of the group's judgment and the number of people expressing it.

Specifically, people experience great pressure to conform as long as the majority is unanimous, but conformity is greatly diminished if even one other person in the group disagrees with the majority view. For example, when Asch (1951) arranged for just one confederate to disagree with the others, the incidence of subjects' conformity was reduced to less than 10 percent. Once unanimity is broken, it becomes much easier to disagree with the majority, even if the other nonconformist does not agree with the person's own view.

Conformity also depends on the size of the group. Asch (1955) examined this relationship by varying the number of confederates in the group from one to fifteen. Figure 18.2 shows the results. Conformity grew as the number of people in the group increased, but most of the increase in conformity occurred as the size of the majority went from one to three or four members.

However, other experiments had different results. Under certain circumstances, conformity may indeed continue to increase significantly as the size of the majority becomes larger than three or four (Gerard, Wilhelmy & Conolley, 1968; Milgram, Bickman & Berkowitz, 1969). The key to the relationship between group size and conformity seems to be how people perceive the majority's opinions (Wilder, 1977). In other words, the majority may have an actual size and a psychological size. The *psychological size* equals the number of members whose assessments are perceived as independent, or as reflecting each individual's carefully considered judgment.

For example, if everyone in a large group gives the same spoken answer to a question, one after the other, you might consider only the first three or four responses to be independent assessments. After that, you might perceive the other people to be giving answers just to be compatible. Those additional assessments may have little effect on you; only the first few assessments, which you perceived as independent, determine the psychological size of the

Figure 18.2
Conformity and Group Size
Asch found that the tendency to conform to a group's judgment increases dramatically as the number of other people in the group increases from about one to about three or four. However, aside from minor variations, further increases in the size of the group do little, if anything, to further increase conformity.
(From "Opinions and Social Pressure" by Solomon E. Asch. Illustration on p. 32 by Sara Love. Copyright © 1955 by Scientific American, Inc. All Rights Reserved.)

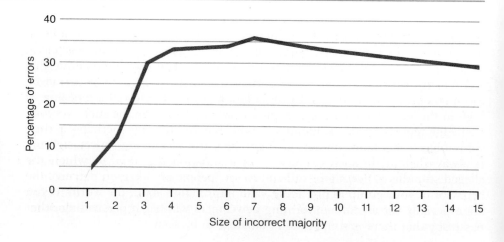

majority. So, if subjects in Asch's original experiment believed that only the first three or four group members were giving independent responses, the psychological size of the majority would remain at three or four, regardless of how many people were actually present. Conformity therefore would not increase with the size of the majority. But when people's responses are perceived to be independent, conformity increases steadily as the number of group members rises (Wilder, 1977).

Personal characteristics   In general, people with high status in a group are less likely to conform than those with relatively low status. One study of this relationship involved groups of fraternity brothers. The men in each group were to look at several displays and indicate which one contained the most dots (Feshbach, 1967). The group scoring the highest number of correct responses could win a large amount of money for its fraternity. Each group included two of the most popular and respected members of the fraternity and two relatively unpopular members. When high-status members made an incorrect judgment about a display, the low-status members were very reluctant to disagree, even when conformity to these erroneous judgments meant the possible loss of money. Compared with low-status members, those with high status disagreed twice as often when they thought the low-status men had made incorrect judgments.

Attraction also influences conformity. People are more likely to conform when they like the various members of the group than when there is little or no attraction (Berkowitz, 1954). The effect of attraction on conformity may occur because people tend to trust the judgment of those they like more than the judgment of those they dislike. It may also occur because people desire the approval of those to whom they are attracted. Conformity based on the desire for approval from attractive group members appears to be particularly likely among those with low self-esteem (Rosenberg, 1961; Stang, 1972). As we mentioned in Chapter 17, people tend to like those whom they perceive as similar to themselves. Thus, people who do not think much of themselves tend to conform in the hope that conformity will make them more similar to, and therefore more liked by, those around them.

Another personal characteristic that may shape conformity is the degree to which people are concerned with being liked or with being correct. People who are preoccupied with being liked are very likely to conform in any group situation, but this is particularly true when they are also very attracted to the other people in the group (McDavid, 1959). In contrast, people who are preoccupied with being right are less likely to conform, no matter how much or how little they are attracted to others in the group (Insko et al., 1985).

Getting X by Asking for Y

Clearly, the experiments we have described involved conformity. The subjects experienced psychological pressure to conform to the views or actions of others, despite the fact that they were not specifically requested to do so. In contrast, the related phenomenon of *compliance* involves changing what one says or does because of a direct request. How is compliance brought about? Many people believe that the direct approach is always best: if you want something, ask for it. But experts on the subject—including salespeople, political strategists, social psychologists, and even certain television evangelists—have learned that often the best way to get something is to ask for something else. This strategy usually takes one of three forms: the foot-in-the-door technique, the door-in-the-face procedure, or the low-ball approach.

The *foot-in-the-door technique* consists of beginning with small requests and working up to larger ones. Psychologists named this approach as the result of a field experiment. The subjects, homeowners in a wealthy California neighborhood, were approached in one of two ways. In some cases, the experimenter claimed to represent a group concerned with reducing traffic accidents in the community and asked the homeowners if a large and unattractive "Drive Carefully" sign could be placed on their front lawn. Approximately 17 percent of the people approached this way complied with the request. In the foot-in-the-door condition, homeowners were first asked only to sign a petition urging their legislators to work toward decreasing the number of accidents in the community. Several weeks later, a different experimenter returned and asked these same people to place the "Drive Carefully" sign on their lawn. In this case, 55 percent of the people complied (Freedman & Fraser, 1966).

Subsequent research has confirmed the compliance-inducing effect of preceding a large request with a much smaller one (Beaman et al., 1983). Why should this be so? First, people are usually far more likely to comply with a request whose cost in time, money, effort, or inconvenience is low rather than high. Second, consistent with the cognitive dissonance and self-perception theories discussed in Chapter 17, complying with a small request makes people think of themselves as supporting and being committed to the source of the request. Thus, signing the traffic safety petition constituted an explicit statement about concern for safe driving. When faced with the higher-cost request (the sign), the subjects were likely to recall their previous action and the perception of their strong commitment to the safety issue. The likelihood of putting up the sign was increased because compliance with this request was consistent with these people's self-perception and past actions (Schwarzwald, Bizman & Raz, 1983).

People take advantage of the foot-in-the-door technique all the time. For example, some companies first ask prospective customers to respond to a mail survey about their product and then ask to visit to explain how it works (with no obligation, of course). Only then is the customer asked to buy the product. In some cases, the initial request requires only that the prospective customer accept a free gift. Agreeing to fill out the forms necessary to receive the gift constitutes the first, low level of compliance, to be followed, the company hopes, by compliance with a later request to buy something. Free gifts not only constitute a foot in the door, but are likely to invoke the reciprocity norm discussed in Chapter 17: many people feel that, once they accept something, they are obligated to reciprocate by buying something.

The opposite approach, known as the *door-in-the-face procedure,* can also be very effective in obtaining compliance. This strategy begins with a very large request that is likely to be denied. Then the person making the original request concedes that it was rather extreme and substitutes a lesser alternative, which is what the requester wanted in the first place. Because it now seems so modest in contrast with the first request, it is more likely to be granted. This is another example of the reciprocity norm in operation.

The door-in-the-face procedure has been found very effective in many situations (Cann, Sherman & Elkes, 1975). It is the heart and soul, for instance, of most bargaining situations. In labor negotiations, for example, both the company and the union usually begin by proposing wage and benefits packages that are obviously unacceptable to the other side. But neither side expects the initial proposal to be accepted; it is only the first and most extreme request, compared to which later proposals will appear to be a compromise.

A third technique for "getting X by asking for Y" is called the *low-ball approach* (Cialdini et al., 1978). The first step is to obtain a verbal commitment from someone to do something. The second step is to show that only a higher-cost version of the initial request will do any good. Finally, that higher-cost request is made. For example, a student we know got a ride to campus every day in time for an 8:00 A.M. class from a friend whose first class was not until 10:00. She did it by first asking him if she could hitch a ride every day. Only after he had said yes did she tell him that she needed to be picked up by 7:30. Apparently the low-ball approach works because, once the initial request is granted, the person feels committed to help even if a later version of the request is a little larger (Burger & Petty, 1981).

The low-ball approach is often used in *bait-and-switch* sales schemes. For example, after a customer agrees to buy a microwave oven at a special sale price, the salesperson may come back from the storeroom to say that there are none of those models left, but that they do have another version that is even better, at a "slightly" higher price. Experts at this tactic use it so skillfully that customers may end up spending two or three times what they had planned. The power and prevalence of low-balling and other questionable sales methods have prompted many states to pass legislation that allows customers to cancel a sales agreement within some specified cooling-off period. ◼

OBEDIENCE

We have seen that compliance involves going along with a request. **Obedience** is a form of compliance in which people comply with a *demand*, rather than with a request, because they think they must or should do so. In short obedience can be thought of as *submissive compliance*.

Hermann Goering (taking notes), Rudolph Hess, Joachim von Ribbentrop, and other members of Adolph Hitler's inner circle listen to testimony during their post–World War II trial for war crimes. The Nazis stimulated interest in the study of obedience because, though they had directly or indirectly participated in the execution of more than six million Jews and members of other minority groups, many of them later denied any responsibility for their actions. They were simply doing their job, they said, merely following orders. Horrified by such behavior, other people wondered how could they have done it. Were they somehow different from other people? Would "normal" people obey such inhumane orders?

Obedience in the Laboratory

Stanley Milgram realized that psychologists knew very little about obedience and developed a laboratory procedure to study it. Through an ad in local newspapers, he recruited forty male volunteers between the ages of twenty and fifty for his first experiment. Among the subjects were professionals, white-collar businessmen, and unskilled workers (Milgram, 1963).

Imagine you are one of the people who answered the ad. When you arrive for the experiment, you meet a fifty-year-old gentleman who has also volunteered and has been scheduled for the same session. The experimenter explains that the purpose of the experiment is to examine the effects of punishment on learning. One of you—the "learner"—will try to learn a list of words; the other—the "teacher"—will help the learner remember the words by administering electric shock whenever he makes a mistake. Then the experimenter turns to you and asks you to draw one of two cards out of a hat. The one you draw says "TEACHER." You think to yourself that this must be your lucky day.

Now the learner is taken into another room and strapped into a chair, as shown in Figure 18.3. Electrodes are attached to his arms. You are shown a shock generator with thirty switches. The experimenter explains that the switch on the far left administers a very mild, 15-volt shock and that each succeeding switch increases the shock by 15 volts; the one on the far right delivers 450 volts. You also notice several labels on the shock generator. The far left section is labeled "Slight Shock." Looking across the panel, you see "Moderate Shock," "Strong Shock," and, at the far right, "Danger—Severe Shock." The last two switches are ominously labeled "XXX." The experimenter explains that you, the teacher, will begin by reading a list of word pairs to the learner. Then you will go through the list again, presenting just one word of each pair; the learner should indicate which word went with it. After the first mistake, you are to throw the switch to deliver 15 volts of shock; after the second, 30 volts; and so on. Each time the learner makes a mistake, you are to increase the shock by 15 volts.

Figure 18.3
Studying Obedience in the Laboratory
In this photograph from Milgram's original experiment, a man is being strapped into a chair with electrodes on his arm. Although subjects in the experiment do not know it, the man is actually a confederate of the experimenter and receives no shock.
(Copyright 1965 by Stanley Milgram. From the film *Obedience*, distributed by the New York University Film Division and the Pennsylvania State University, P.C.R. Courtesy of Alexandra Milgram.)

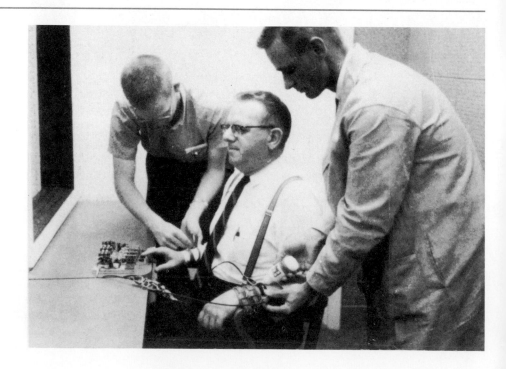

After the learner makes a mistake, you throw the switch to deliver a 15-volt shock. When he makes another mistake, you flip the switch to deliver 30 volts, and so on. But after the switch is thrown for 75 volts, you hear a loud moan. At 90 volts, the learner cries out in pain. At 150 volts, he screams and asks to be let out of the experiment. You look to the experimenter, who says, "Proceed with the next question." You do. After 180 volts, the learner screams that he cannot stand the pain any longer and starts banging on the wall. The experimenter looks at you and says, "You have no other choice; you must go on." After a few more questions, the learner fails to respond to your questions. The experimenter tells you to treat silence as an error and to continue with the procedure. The learner never again responds.

In fact, no shock was delivered in Milgram's experiments. The "learner" was always a confederate of the experimenter, and the moans and other signs of pain were an act. But you do not know that. What would you do in this situation? Would you continue after the learner began to scream in pain? Would you keep going even when he begged to be let out of the experiment and then fell silent? Would you administer 450 volts of potentially deadly shock to a perfect stranger who has done you no harm, just because an experimenter demands that you do?

Figure 18.4 shows what the subjects in Milgram's experiment did. Not one subject stopped before 300 volts. Of the forty subjects in the experiment, twenty-six (or 65 percent) went all the way to the 450-volt level. The decision to continue was a difficult and stressful one for the subjects. Many protested repeatedly; but each time the experimenter told them to continue, they did so. Here is a partial transcript of what one subject said; his reactions were typical.

[After throwing the 180-volt switch]: He can't stand it. I'm not going to kill that man in there. Do you hear him hollering? He's hollering. He can't stand it. What if something happens to him? I'm not going to get that man sick in there. He's hollering in there. Do you know what I mean? I mean, I refuse to take responsibility. He's getting hurt in there. He's in there hollering. Too many left

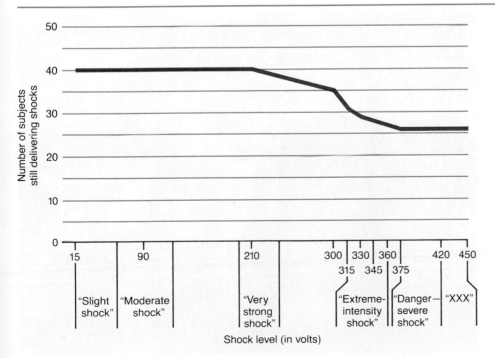

Figure 18.4
Results of Milgram's Obedience Experiment
Note that 65 percent of the people tested gave the maximum amount of shock available. When Milgram asked a group of undergraduates how the people in the experiment would respond, they estimated that fewer than 2 percent of the people would go all the way to 450 volts. He then asked a group of practicing psychiatrists, and they gave very similar predictions.
(Courtesy of Alexandra Milgram. From S. Milgram, "Behavioral Study of Obedience," *Journal of Abnormal and Social Psychology, 67,* 371–378. Copyright 1963 by the American Psychological Association. Adapted by permission of the publisher and author.)

here. Geez, if he gets them wrong. There are too many of them left. I mean, who is going to take responsibility if anything happens to that gentleman?

[After the experimenter accepts responsibility]: All right . . .

[After administering 240 volts]: Oh no, you mean I've got to keep going up with the scale. No sir, I'm not going to kill that man. I'm not going to give him 450 volts.

[After the experimenter says, "The experiment requires that you go on."]: I know it does, but that man is hollering in there sir. (Milgram, 1974)

This subject administered shock up to 450 volts.

Factors Affecting Obedience

Milgram had not expected so many subjects to deliver such apparently intense shocks. Was there something about his procedure that produced such high levels of obedience? To find out, Milgram and other researchers varied his original procedure in numerous ways. The overall level of obedience to an authority figure was nearly always quite high, but the degree of obedience was affected by several characteristics of the situation and procedure.

Prestige   One possibility explored by Milgram was that the status and legitimacy of the experimenter helped produce high levels of obedience in his original experiment. After all, that study was conducted at Yale University, and the newspaper ad had stated that the experimenter was a professor at Yale. A Yale professor was probably a powerful authority figure for most subjects, and they may have thought it socially inappropriate to question research that was sponsored by such a respected institution.

To test the effects of status and prestige, Milgram rented a deserted office building in Bridgeport, Connecticut. He then placed an ad in the local newspaper that made no mention of Yale and instead said the research was sponsored by a private firm. In all other ways, the experimental procedure was identical to the original. Again, the results were surprising. Under these

Milgram's research suggested that the close proximity of an authority figure enhances obedience to authority. This principle is clearly employed in military organizations, where no member is ever far away from a source of authority in the form of a person of higher rank.

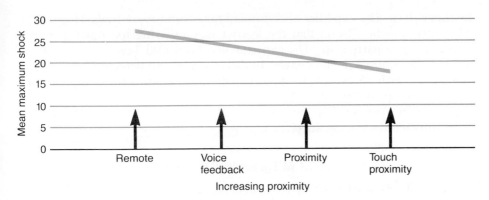

Figure 18.5
Obedience as a Function of Proximity to the Victim
The remote condition was one in which the subject and learner were in different rooms and the subject could neither see nor hear the learner. In the voice feedback condition, the subject could hear the learner but not see him. In the proximity condition, subject and learner were in the same room, so that the learner could be seen and heard. In the touch proximity condition, the subject had to press the learner's hand onto a metal dish in order to administer the shock.
(Stanley Milgram, "Some Conditions of Obedience and Disobedience to Authority." *Human Relations*, Vol. 18, No. 1, 1965, p. 63. Copyright © 1972 by Stanley Milgram. Reprinted by permission of Alexandra Milgram, literary executor.)

Note: The more feedback the subject received from the victim, the less shock he administered to him.

less prestigious circumstances, the level of obedience dropped, but less than Milgram expected; 48 percent of the subjects continued to the maximum level of shock, compared with 65 percent in the original study. Milgram concluded that people were willing to do great harm to another even if the authority figure was not "particularly reputable or distinguished."

Proximity   In another variation on his original design, Milgram altered the contact between the subject and the experimenter. When the experimenter gave instructions over the phone or by tape recording, only 20 percent of the subjects administered the maximum shock level (Milgram, 1965). Other researchers found that when the authority figure gave the instructions by phone, many subjects lied about their behavior, saying that they were continuing to administer higher levels of shock when they were not (Rada & Rogers, 1973). However, obedience remained quite high if the authority figure gave the instructions in person and then left the room (Rada & Rogers, 1973). In other words, it appears that the experimenter's ability to obtain obedience depended on some personal contact, but that once the experimenter had become established as an authority in the subject's mind, the contact did not need to be maintained. As proximity to the authority figure declined, however, obedience tended to drop as well.

Milgram (1965) also tested the effect of proximity between subject and victim. Figure 18.5 shows the results he obtained: as proximity to the victim increased, the level of obedience decreased substantially (Milgram, 1965). These results are consistent with the belief that it is easier for soldiers to follow orders to kill other people by high-altitude bombing than by, say, stabbing.

Presence of others who disobey   Our examination of conformity may lead you to wonder (as Milgram did) how the presence of other people might affect obedience to the authority figure. Milgram (1965) created a situation in which there were three teachers. Teacher 1 (who was a confederate of the experimenter) read the words to the learner. Teacher 2 (who was also a confederate) indicated whether the learner had made a correct or incorrect response. Then it was up to Teacher 3 (the actual subject) to deliver the shock when a mistake was made. At 150 volts, the learner began to complain bitterly that the shock was too painful. At this point, Teacher 1 (a confederate) refused to participate any longer and left the room. The experimenter asked him to come back, but he refused. The experimenter then instructed Teachers 2 and 3 to continue by themselves. The experiment continued for several more trials. However, at 210 volts, Teacher 2 said that the learner was suffering too much pain and also refused to participate. The experimenter then told Teacher 3 (the actual subject) to continue the procedure. In this case, only 10 percent of the subjects (compared with 65 percent in the original study) continued to deliver shock all the way up to 450 volts. Thus, in line with the conformity research we discussed, it appears that the presence of others who disobey is the most powerful factor reducing subjects' obedience.

The Ethics and Value of Milgram's Studies

Although the "learners" in Milgram's experiment suffered no pain, the subjects did. Milgram himself (1963) observed subjects "sweat, stutter, tremble, groan, bite their lips, and dig their fingernails into their flesh. Full-blown uncontrollable seizures were observed for three subjects" (p. 375). Furthermore, Milgram's subjects learned something about themselves that they really did not want to know: that they could be persuaded to inflict severe harm, possibly even death, on an innocent person.

Some observers argue that it was unethical for Milgram to have inflicted such burdens on his subjects. Milgram offered several arguments in his defense. First, although people did experience great stress during the experiment, each subject was told everything about the procedure at the end of the experiment. Each was told that most people went all the way to the 450-volt level and that the learner did not experience any shock at all. Then the "learner" was brought into the room and interacted with the subject in a friendly fashion. Milgram claimed that this debriefing helped the subjects understand that their behavior in the experiment was normal.

Second, when Milgram later sent his subjects a questionnaire, 84 percent indicated they were glad that they had participated in the study. They felt that they had learned something very important about themselves and that the experience had been worthwhile. Less than 2 percent said that they regretted participating. Thus, Milgram argued, the experience was actually a positive one.

Milgram also noted that he expected nearly all of the subjects to stop at some point, certainly before they reached the "danger" level. He claimed that "if everyone had broken off at slight shock or moderate shock, this would be a very reassuring finding and who would protest?" (Milgram, 1977, p. 98). His critics, argued Milgram, were responding not to the procedure, but to the results that were obtained.

Ethical questions are difficult ones. The dialogue between Milgram and his critics has helped push investigators to consider the ethical implications of their research. As we noted in the highlight on ethics in Chapter 1, psychologists are now much more sensitive to ethical issues in research, and it is unlikely that Milgram's study would be approved by today's committees charged with the protection of human subjects.

Milgram's procedures and his results were dramatic, but do they mean that most people are putty in the hands of authority figures? Under the right circumstances, would people all blindly follow inhumane orders from their leaders, as the Nazis did? Some people interpret Milgram's data in just that fashion, and although it may not be a pleasant prospect to contemplate, they may be right. For example, it appears that some American soldiers in Vietnam, like the soldiers of every army in history, followed orders that resulted in inhumane acts against civilians as well as against enemy soldiers. Although many people routinely question and overtly oppose authority figures whenever they feel it is important to do so, most people do what authorities tell them to do, even when they have doubts.

However, drawing broad conclusions about human behavior on the basis of Milgram's results may be a mistake. Reconsider, as Martin Orne did, Milgram's procedures from the subjects' perspective (Orne & Holland, 1968). You are asked to participate in a psychology experiment on the effects of punishment on learning. Exploring this issue is certainly not so cosmically significant that it justifies placing people in mortal danger. So why would the experimenter respond to the learner's suffering by calmly demanding that the experiment continue? And why does the experimenter need you anyway? Why does the experimenter not present the word lists and throw the switches himself?

Orne suggested that such questions caused many of Milgram's subjects to conclude that (1) the experimenter would not actually endanger the life of another human being, and (2) no shock was being administered. If these conclusions led subjects to see that their behavior, not the learner's, was under study, their actions during the experiment may have been governed by the "experimental subject role," a role that dictates full cooperation and an absence of overt skepticism.

Unfortunately, the extent to which people will obey the demands of others, especially when those demands dictate inhumane or other unacceptable behavior, is still not fully understood. If Orne is right, Milgram's ingenious research may have generated overly pessimistic conclusions about human beings. However, continuing news accounts of cruelty by people obeying the authority of military, terrorist, or cult leaders make it impossible to entirely dismiss Milgram's findings. The truth about the extent of human obedience and the circumstances under which it will be displayed remains to be discovered, but it may be less flattering than one might wish. We say this partly because much inhumanity occurs even without pressure for obedience. For example, a good deal of people's aggressiveness toward other people appears to come from within. In the next section, we consider human aggressiveness and some of the circumstances that influence its expression.

AGGRESSION

Carl Panzram proclaimed with perverse pride that virtually his entire life was spent trying to figure out ways to make people suffer (Gaddis & Long, 1970). In the late 1920s, Panzram decided he would build a bomb designed to explode on contact and place it on a train track in the middle of a long tunnel. After the explosion, and before the passengers could escape from the train, he planned to pump poisonous gas into the tunnel and, wearing a gas mask, go in and rob all of the bodies. He estimated that, on a popular route, he could kill nearly four hundred people and collect up to $100,000. Fortunately, Panzram's technical expertise was not sufficient to carry out his plans in full, but he did manage to kill twenty-five people before being caught, tried, and executed (Harrison, 1976). Mr. Panzram was, to say the least, a very aggressive person.

Aggression can be defined as an act that is intended to harm another person (Baron, 1977). Though most people do not display anywhere near the amount, intensity, or duration of aggressiveness shown by Carl Panzram, examples of human aggression abound in everything from playground fights to international terrorism. Under certain circumstances, even the most peaceable person can sometimes lash out aggressively in anger. The questions of

Playing football provides a socially acceptable channel through which people can express aggression and experience catharsis. According to psychoanalytic theory, catharsis can also occur vicariously, as when we watch other people display aggression in contact sports, violent films, and the like.

why human aggression is so prevalent and what circumstances increase and decrease its display have been given considerable attention by psychologists.

Approaches to Aggression

Some theorists believe that aggression is so prevalent because it is an inherent part of human nature. Psychoanalysts and ethologists have proposed the most articulate versions of this view.

The psychoanalytic approach   According to psychoanalysts like Freud, aggression is an instinctive biological urge. It gradually accumulates and at some point must be released. Sometimes it is released in the form of physical or verbal abuse against another. Sometimes the aggressive impulse is turned inward and produces self-punitive actions, even suicide. Sometimes it can be released through socially acceptable activities, such as playing football. It may even be channeled into symbolic forms, such as "beating" an opponent at chess or "destroying" the enemy in a video arcade game. The best we can hope for, according to psychoanalysts, is that aggressive impulses will be channeled into socially acceptable forms. The psychoanalytic approach implies that these and other socially acceptable behaviors can provide direct or symbolic substitutes for overt aggression, thus producing **catharsis,** or the release of pent-up impulses.

Psychoanalysts credit catharsis with temporarily satisfying people's need to be aggressive, but unfortunately, there is very little empirical evidence that it actually does so. In fact, performing violent acts may increase, rather than decrease, the tendency to be aggressive. Some research shows that such activities as hitting a toy doll or engaging in athletic contests lead to more aggression (Bandura, 1973; Berkowitz, 1973). Other researchers have found that watching others engage in aggression on television does not decrease aggression (Gerbner, 1981). In fact, both young children (Peterson & Zill, 1981) and adults (Drabman & Thomas, 1974; Gorney, 1976) who are exposed to televised violence are more likely to see aggression as an acceptable form of behavior. And there is evidence that a nation's homicide rate increases, rather than decreases, during the years immediately after a war when aggressive impulses have presumably been directly or vicariously vented by many people (Archer & Gartner, 1976). Thus, it does not seem that aggressive impulses can simply be "drained off" into substitute activities.

Similarly, empirical evidence for the psychoanalytic view that humans possess an aggressive instinct that presses for expression is scant. True, many people display aggressive behavior, but this behavior can be the product of learning rather than the expression of the inborn, unlearned pattern of behavior defined in Chapter 11 as an instinct. The aggressive instinct is also called into question by the existence of societies, such as the Arapesh of New Guinea, in which aggression is rare and in which peaceful coexistence and cooperation among individuals are the norm (Mead, 1963).

The ethological approach   Ethological theory presents a slightly more complicated approach to aggression. (Recall from Chapter 7 that *ethologists* study the behavior of animals in their natural habitat.) Many ethologists suggest that all animals, including human beings, have an aggressive instinct (Lorenz, 1981). But, unlike Freud, they suggest that, for aggressive behavior to occur, the internal instinct must be accompanied by an environmental stimulus, called a **releaser,** which sets off a stereotyped pattern of behavior—in this case, aggression.

The inherited nature of aggressive impulses is certainly apparent in the animal world, where aggressive behaviors tend to be ritualized, stereotyped, and triggered by specific stimuli. Further, exactly the same behaviors appear in animals that have been raised in isolation, where they could not have learned them from other animals (Flynn et al., 1970). In one study on the role of genetics in aggression, the most aggressive members of a large group of mice were interbred. Then the most aggressive of their offspring were also interbred. After this procedure had been followed for twenty-five generations, the resulting animals were so vicious that they would immediately attack any mouse put in their cage. On the other hand, continuous inbreeding of the least aggressive members of the original group resulted in animals that were so nonaggressive that they would refuse to fight even when attacked (Laperspetz, 1979). Applying ethological theory to human behavior leads to the suggestion that genetic factors may create individual predispositions toward or against aggressiveness and that, whenever aggressive impulses build up sufficiently *and* a releaser is present in the environment, an aggressive response will be triggered (Lorenz, 1966, 1981).

Two major criticisms have been directed at the ethological theory of aggression (Larsen, 1976). First, virtually all of the empirical research has been based on lower animals, where instincts of all kinds clearly play a larger role in behavior than they do in humans. For this reason, many psychologists doubt whether the results of animal research should be extrapolated to aggression in human beings. Second, the ethological theory does not account for the many specific forms that human aggression can take. People aggress with fists, guns, bombs, chemicals, knives, cars, insults, and any number of other weapons. Thus, even if an aggressive instinct or other biological factors set the stage for aggression, the specific form it takes is often determined by learning mechanisms.

The role of learning in aggression   Cognitive-behavioral theorists suggest that most, and perhaps all, human aggression can be explained in terms of learning principles (Bandura, 1977; Zillmann, 1978). Their research has documented, for example, that (1) many aggressive responses are learned by watching others, and (2) the performance of aggressive acts depends greatly on the pattern of rewards and punishments a person has received.

The most obvious illustration of the role of observational learning in aggression is copy-cat crime, in which one person's well-publicized act of aggression (such as poisoning food or medicine in stores) is duplicated within a few days by individuals in other cities. As we saw in Bandura's "Bobo doll" experiments and in studies on the effects of televised violence (both described in the chapter on learning), children learn and subsequently perform many novel aggressive responses that they see modeled by others (Bandura, Ross & Ross, 1963). Further, the amount of violent content watched on television by eight-year-olds predicts aggressiveness in these children even ten years later (Eron, 1980). Laboratory studies have also shown that aggression increases when people view violent content on television (Singer & Singer, 1981). Thanks to individual differences in temperament, parental influences, and other factors, not everyone who sees aggression inevitably becomes aggressive, but observational learning does play a significant, if not primary, role in the development and display of aggressive behavior.

The role of learning in aggression is further supported by research indicating that people become increasingly aggressive when they are positively reinforced

Learning to express aggression is especially easy for children living in war zones, where loaded weapons may serve as "toys" and where deadly aggressive acts are modeled almost daily.

for aggressiveness. Figure 18.6 illustrates one example. Other research has indicated that people will become less aggressive if they are punished for their aggressive acts (Donnerstein & Donnerstein, 1976; Wilson & Rogers, 1975).

From the learning-theory perspective, then, it would appear that, even if impulses toward aggression come partly from unlearned, biological sources, those people who observe, practice, and receive rewards for aggression may be more likely to behave aggressively when the combination of impulse and opportunity occurs. What does this mean for the prevention of aggression? Some researchers believe that portrayals of violence on television and in other media should be restricted, because these portrayals provide models and vicarious reinforcement for aggressive behavior. Another strategy is to discourage and interfere with aggressive play (Brown & Elliott, 1965). For example, parents can express displeasure at children's aggression and not allow them to have the toy guns, knives, and other playtime tools with which to practice and perfect aggressive acts. Finally, learning theory suggests that it is important to teach children by example that conflicts can be dealt with through dialogue and compromise, rather than through aggression.

These strategies are reasonable, but there is reason to expect their effects to be limited. First, because there is so much aggression in the world, it is difficult, if not impossible, to insulate children from seeing some of it modeled somewhere, especially by their friends. Even children who have no aggressive toys play with imaginary ones in fantasy games. Second, telling children that they may not see television shows and movies containing aggressive themes and that they may not have violent toys or engage in aggressive play might create psychological reactance, which, as noted in the previous chapter, can make prohibited activity all the more desirable. Still, learning theory does provide valuable insights into aggression and offers practical suggestions for combating it.

Emotional Factors in Aggression

In general, aggression is most likely in situations where there is physiological arousal associated with some strong emotion, such as anger. People tend to lash out at those who make them angry or, if they use the defense mechanism of displacement, at their children, the dog, or other safe targets. Perhaps the prototypical example is when a person becomes angry and behaves aggressively in response to a verbal attack. This phenomenon helps explain why heated domestic arguments so often end in violent aggression, either against a relative or against outsiders who try to intervene (Geller, 1974). However, aggression can also be made more likely by other forms of emotional arousal. One of the most common of these is frustration, a condition that occurs when obstacles block the fulfillment of goals.

Frustration and aggression   Suppose that a friend interrupts your studying for an exam by coming over unannounced to borrow a book. If things have been going well that day and you are feeling happy and confident about the exam, your response is likely to be friendly and accommodating. But what if you are feeling frustrated? What if you are behind in your preparations, and your friend's visit represents the fifth interruption in the last hour? Under these emotional circumstances, you may react aggressively, perhaps berating your startled visitor for not calling ahead.

Your aggressiveness in this situation conforms to what would be predicted by the **frustration-aggression hypothesis,** a formulation outlined in a book called, naturally enough, *Frustration and Aggression* (Dollard et al., 1939). In

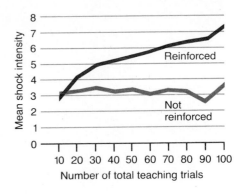

Figure 18.6
Reinforcement and Aggression
In this experiment, people were asked to teach a person new material. They had the opportunity to administer electric shock as punishment for any errors that occurred. Some subjects were reinforced by the experimenter with praise when they delivered the shock. Other subjects were given no reinforcement for delivering shock. People who were reinforced for giving shock clearly became more aggressive over the course of the experiment.
(From R. G. Green and D. Stonner, "Effects of Aggressiveness Habit Strength on Behavior in the Presence of Aggression-Related Stimuli," *Journal of Personality and Social Psychology, 17,* 149–153. Copyright 1971 by the American Psychological Association. Adapted by permission of the publisher.)

it, the authors proposed that "the occurrence of aggressive behavior always presupposes the existence of frustration and contrawise . . . the existence of frustration always leads to some form of aggression" (p. 1). This hypothesis generated hundreds of experiments, many of which indicated that the hypothesis was too simple and too general. Frustration does not always produce aggression (Gentry, 1970). Sometimes it produces depression and withdrawal (Seligman, 1975). And not all aggression is preceded by frustration. For example, in many of the experiments we have described, there were no elements of frustration, but subjects still displayed many aggressive responses.

After many years of research, Leonard Berkowitz (1981) proposed a revised version of the frustration-aggression hypothesis. He suggested that frustration produces a *readiness* to respond aggressively, but that aggression will occur only if there are cues in the environment that invite or are associated with an aggressive response. Neither frustration alone nor environmental cues alone are sufficient to set off or elicit aggression. When combined, however, they do lead to aggression. In general, support for Berkowitz's revision of the frustration-aggression hypothesis has been quite strong (Geen & Donnerstein, 1983; Zillmann, 1978).

Generalized arousal   Imagine you have just jogged two miles. You are hot, sweaty, and out of breath, but you are not angry. Still, the physiological arousal caused by jogging increases the probability that you will become aggressive if, say, a passerby shouts an insult (Zillmann, 1978, 1983). Why? As we describe in the chapter on emotion, through *transfer of excitation,* the physiological arousal caused by jogging may intensify your reaction to an insult (Zillmann, 1978).

However, generalized arousal alone does not lead to aggression. It is most likely to produce aggression when the situation contains some reason, opportunity, or target for aggression (Donnerstein & Wilson, 1976). In one study, for example, people engaged in two minutes of vigorous exercise. Then they had the opportunity to deliver electric shock to another person. The exercise affected the level of shock delivered only if the subjects were first insulted (Zillmann, Katcher & Milavsky, 1972). Apparently the arousal resulting from the exercise made aggression more likely in the first place; the insult "released" it. These findings are in keeping with the notion suggested by learning theorists (and by Berkowitz's revision of the frustration-aggression hypothesis) that aggression occurs, not merely as a function of internal impulses *or* particular situations, but as a result of the interaction of individual characteristics and environmental circumstances.

HIGHLIGHT

Sexual Arousal and Aggression

In both men and women, sexual stimulation produces strong, generalized physiological arousal, especially in the sympathetic nervous system. Heart rate increases, adrenaline is released, breathing changes, and there is an experience of excitement. Can arousal from sexual stimulation, like the other forms of arousal we have considered, also lead to displays of aggression?

The answer appears to be yes, at least under certain circumstances. In a typical study of this type of transfer of excitation, subjects were told that another subject in a separate room (actually a confederate of the experimenter) was performing a learning task and that they were to administer an electric shock every time that person made a mistake. The subjects could vary the intensity of the apparent shock but were told that the intensity would not

Though most forms of pornography do not create aggression in their viewers, research suggests that males may become more aggressive and less sympathetic toward women after seeing aggressive pornography, which portrays rape or other forms of violence against female victims.

affect the speed of learning. Therefore, the intensity (and presumed pain) that they chose to administer was taken as an index of aggressive behavior. Before they administered the shocks, some of the subjects saw a short movie depicting sexually explicit material. Others viewed a film with aggressive, but nonsexual content. A third group was shown travelogues and other monumentally nonarousing films. Then all of them were purposely annoyed by the person they were supposed to shock. The degree of arousal displayed during the films was assessed by measuring changes in blood pressure and heart rate. Aggression was measured by the intensity of shock the subjects administered to the person who annoyed them. The degree of arousal was directly related to aggressive behavior; subjects were most aroused by the sexual film and also gave the strongest shocks after watching it (Zillmann, 1971).

Some people conclude from results like these that sexual arousal inevitably leads to aggression. In 1986, for example, the U.S. attorney general's commission on pornography reported that there is a causal link between erotic material and sexually related crimes. The commission's report created instant controversy, because it appeared to ignore the results of numerous scientific studies showing that the relationship between sexual arousal and aggression is neither consistent nor simple (Donnerstein & Linz, 1986). These studies reveal, for example, that there is no evidence for an overall relationship between any type of antisocial behavior and mere exposure to pornographic literature (Donnerstein, 1983). Researchers have also examined whether watching run-of-the-mill erotic films increases aggression and found that, in general, it does not (Donnerstein, 1980).

However, one particular type of pornography may have different, and much less benign, effects. This material, called *aggressive pornography,* depicts scenes of violence against women (Malamuth & Donnerstein, 1982) and has become increasingly popular in recent years (Malamuth & Spinner, 1980; Yaffe & Nelson, 1982). Many experiments have investigated the effects of aggressive pornography (Malamuth & Donnerstein, 1982, 1984; Yaffe & Nelson, 1982). Although the results remain tentative, the following conclusions seem warranted (Donnerstein, 1984):

1. Aggressive pornography appears to have a strong influence on men's attitudes toward rape. For example, after viewing a rape scene portraying the *rape myth*—in which the victim of sexual violence appears to be aroused by

the aggression (Malamuth, Heim & Feshback, 1980)—males tend to become less sympathetic toward the rape victim and more generally accepting of aggressive acts toward women.

2. In laboratory experiments, males often administer increased levels of shock to females after viewing aggressive pornographic films. However, there is no increase in aggression against other males. This indicates that there is no generalized increase in aggression—only an increase in aggressive responses that are specifically directed toward females.

3. There does appear to be a link between watching aggressive pornography and sexual arousal in some rapists, though not in most men. However, even normal men respond with sexual excitement to aggressive pornography if they are relatively callous toward women and if the film depicts the rape myth. Indeed, there is evidence that repeated exposure to films portraying that myth increases the callousness of men toward women. Aggressive pornography is noted for this portrayal.

Thus, most of the scientific evidence suggests that it is important to distinguish between pornography in general and aggressive pornography in particular. This second form of erotica may indeed be dangerous.

In short, there appears to be no biological mandate for the association of sexual arousal and aggression; for most people, the two remain quite separate. There is also evidence that the association of sex and violence is learned and can sometimes be changed. For example, in one study sexually aggressive males underwent therapy in which they masturbated while viewing films of nonviolent, mutually enjoyable intercourse; they became sexually responsive to such scenes and less sexually responsive to depictions of violence (Abel, Blanchard & Becker, 1976). ■

Environmental Influences on Aggression

We have seen that aggression is influenced by a complex interaction of biological predispositions, learning, emotional arousal, and environmental stimuli. These stimuli are often provided by other people's actions or the availability of a weapon, but general environmental conditions, such as the weather, can also be important in promoting aggression. As Figure 18.7 indicates, for example, the probability of street riots increases as outdoor temperature rises (Carlsmith & Anderson, 1979). And the pattern of rapes and murders occurring over two years in Houston, Texas, indicated that these aggressive crimes are most likely to occur on very hot days (Anderson & Anderson, 1984). High temperatures are a source of stress, and as we saw in Chapter 13, stress often leads people to be more aggressive.

Air pollution and noise are also sources of stress, and they, too, can influence whether a person displays aggression. People tend to become more aggressive when breathing air that contains ethyl mercapton, a mildly un-pleasant-smelling pollutant common in urban areas (Rotton et al., 1979). In addition, a study conducted in Dayton, Ohio, found that the frequency of aggressive family disturbances increased along with the ozone level in the air. Indoors, nonsmokers who inhale the smoke created by cigarettes commonly experience increases in irritability and anxiety (Jones, 1978) and, in laboratory studies, are more likely to become aggressive when breathing smoke-filled rather than clean air (Zillmann, Baron & Tamborini, 1981). Noise—usually defined as any unwanted sound (Kryter, 1970)—tends to make people irritable and more likely to display aggression, especially if the noise is unpredictable and irregular (Ward, 1974). Thus, laws that limit smoking in public places, that control air pollution outdoors, and that limit airport or other urban noise may help make the environment not only healthier, but also less violent.

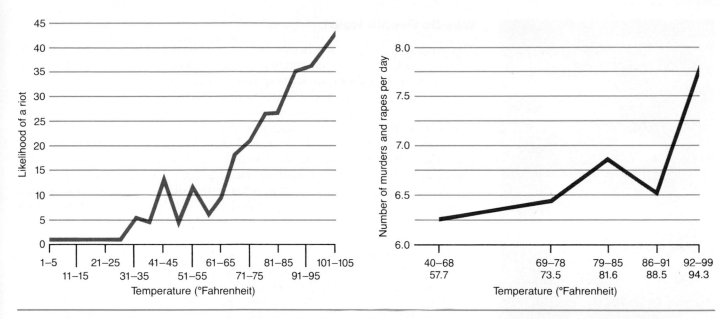

Figure 18.7
Effects of Temperature on Aggression
Outdoor temperature is related to the incidence of aggressive behaviors. For example, studies of police and weather reports suggest that both street riots and violent crimes are more likely to occur as temperatures climb.
(Left graph: From J. M. Carlsmith and C. A. Anderson, "Ambient Temperature and the Occurrence of Collective Violence: A New Analysis," *Journal of Personality and Social Psychology, 37,* 337–344 Copyright 1979 by the American Psychological Association. Adapted with permission of publisher and authors. Right graph: From C. A. Anderson and D. C. Anderson, "Ambient Temperature and Violent Crime: Test of the Linear and Curvilinear Hypothesis," *Journal of Personality and Social Psychology, 46,* 91–97. Copyright 1984 by the American Psychological Association. Adapted with permission of the publisher and authors.)

Living arrangements also influence aggressiveness. Compared with the tenants in high-rise apartment buildings, those in buildings with fewer floors are less likely to behave aggressively (Fisher, Bell & Baum, 1984). This difference appears to be due in part to how people feel when they are crowded. Crowding tends to create physiological arousal and to make people tense, uncomfortable, and more likely to report negative feelings (Epstein, Woolfolk & Lehrer, 1981). This arousal and tension can influence people to like each other less and to be more aggressive. One study of juvenile delinquents found that the number of behavior problems (including aggressiveness) they displayed was directly related to how crowded their living conditions had become (Ray et al., 1982).

We have seen that aggression is a prevalent and durable aspect of human social interaction. Now it is time to consider another frequent, but more uplifting social phenomenon; namely, people's altruism and helping behavior.

ALTRUISM AND HELPING BEHAVIOR

On a winter day a few years ago, an airliner crashed into the ice-filled Potomac River in Washington, D.C. Many of the survivors were thrown, injured or unconscious, into the water and were in danger of drowning or freezing to death. A bystander named Lenny Skutnik dove into the river and helped several people to shore before exhaustion and the frigid temperatures nearly killed him. This man did not act as he did for money or for any other material benefit, but simply to help other human beings in need.

Though the circumstances are rarely this dramatic, it is very common for people to help one another, doing everything from picking up dropped packages to donating kidneys. **Helping behavior** is defined as any act that is intended to benefit another person. **Altruism,** which is closely related, is a desire to help another person, rather than to benefit oneself (Batson & Coke, 1981). In the following sections, we will examine some of the reasons for altruism and helping, as well as some of the conditions in which people are most likely to help others.

The more empathic children are, the more inclined they are to be helpful (Zahn-Waxler, Friedman & Cummings, 1983). Even before their second birthday, empathic children begin to offer help to those who are hurt or crying by snuggling, patting, hugging, or offering food or even their own teddy bears.

Why Do People Help?

The tendency to help others begins quite early. Many children become sensitive to other people's emotional states at a very young age. This soon translates into *empathy,* the ability to actually feel some of the other person's sadness, happiness, or other emotion (Zahn-Waxler & Radke-Yarrow, 1979).

As they grow older, children's efforts at helping become more elaborate (Zahn-Waxler, Iannotti & Chapman, 1982). Their helping behaviors often follow the examples set by those around them and are usually supported and encouraged by the norms communicated through the child's reference groups, especially the family. In our culture, these norms result in praise and other rewards for helpfulness and scoldings for selfishness. Eventually, just as they internalize, or adopt, other social norms, most children come to believe that it is good to be helpful. They form the belief that being helpful is a good thing and that they are good when they are helpful. As noted in the chapter on development, when these norms are communicated by parents through an authoritative rather than an authoritarian socialization style, children are especially likely to internalize and follow them.

If helping norms are internalized, people learn to reward themselves through self-congratulation after acts of good will—saying to themselves something like "I'm a good person for having done that." Numerous studies suggest that, for the most part, people are altruistic and helpful, because in addition to having empathy, they have developed this capacity to mentally reward themselves after acts of good will (Bryan & Walbek, 1970). For example, people who helped Jews escape from the Nazis (London, 1970) and people who have donated kidneys (Fellner & Marshall, 1970) typically express strong feelings of pride and self-satisfaction, as do those who perform volunteer work and good deeds of all kinds.

And then there are people who rarely offer help at all. People who are very concerned about personal discomfort or about failing are less likely than others to display altruism. Even among children, those who are less competent, adjusted, active, or assertive are less likely to act helpful or generous (Barrett & Radke-Yarrow, 1977; Mussen & Eisenberg-Berg, 1977). Thus, an individual's tendency to help others appears related to numerous characteristics. Altruism is most likely among people who are generally (or at least at the moment) not so preoccupied with their own needs that they cannot respond to the needs of others (Hoffman, 1982).

HIGHLIGHT

Sociobiology

Because the development of helping behavior and altruism is so widespread and begins so early in life, some observers see it as inborn. On the face of it, this assertion appears to make little evolutionary sense, since the doctrine of the survival of the fittest suggests that it is the fittest individual, not the most altruistic, that survives. In fact, one might expect that natural selection would be biased against, rather than toward, individuals who help others at the risk of their own welfare. Yet people, like other animal species, do help each other, often at great personal risk. Some even die protecting their family or their home territory. Why?

Some years ago a radical version of the concept of genetic inheritance was put forward by Edward O. Wilson (1975), in his book *Sociobiology.* His claim, and that of the **sociobiologists** who followed in his footsteps, was that altruism, cooperation, aggression, and other human and animal social behaviors that increase the chances of species survival are genetically encoded and passed from generation to generation. Thus, the sociobiologists said, altruistic behavior is inherited because it protects, not the individual, but the individual's genes, which are shared to varying degrees with other members of the species and to a great extent with close family members. Thus, by helping or even dying for a cousin, a sibling, or, most of all, one's own child, the person increases the likelihood that at least some of his or her own genetic characteristics will be passed on to the next generation through the beneficiary's reproduction.

Some psychologists have found the sociobiological perspective useful for understanding why people cooperate with and help one another, for explaining why parents become attached to their infants and invest so much time and energy in caring for them, and for explaining why grandparents help with child care. Nevertheless, the sociobiological approach is often faulted as a misguided view based on abstract theorizing, naive speculation, and unjustified extrapolation from animal studies rather than on solid human evidence (Kitcher, 1985). For example, sociobiologists appear to underestimate the contributions of culture, or nurture, to human social behavior and the fact that human variability cannot be fully accounted for by any genetic theory. Thus, sociobiology may predict the behavior of a species or a group, but it does not appear to be very good at predicting the behavior of specific individuals.

Indeed, the question of how much heredity constrains variation in human social behavior is not answered by sociobiology. The work of developmental psychologists who test sociobiological explanations empirically will be of great value in learning more about the question. It is reasonable to expect that altruism and helping develop in an individual, as many other human behaviors do, through both inborn tendencies and environmental influences; that is, through both nature and nurture. ■

When Are People Most Likely to Help?

The interaction of nature and nurture creates personal characteristics that allow some predictions about who will help and who will not, but a person who helps in one situation will not necessarily help in another (Gergen, Gergen & Meter, 1972). The decision about whether to help others depends on many factors, including the difference between the costs of helping and the anticipated psychological rewards (Lynch & Cohen, 1978).

In short, whether helping and altruism are displayed appears to depend on an interaction between the people involved and the situation in which they find themselves. Deeply rooted and well learned as they are, human altruism and helping behavior are neither automatic nor invariable. This fact was dramatically demonstrated in New York City in 1964, when a woman named Kitty Genovese was repeatedly attacked and ultimately killed by a man with a knife, in full view and hearing of dozens of her neighbors. The tragic episode took more than thirty minutes to unfold, but no one tried to help the screaming victim, and no one called the police until it was too late.

Public dismay and disbelief followed. Psychologists thought it unlikely that everyone in the neighborhood was callous and wondered whether something about the situation that night had deterred people from helping. Numerous studies of helping behavior followed; many of them led to important insights about the characteristics of social situations that promote or inhibit helping. Among the most important of these characteristics are the clarity of the need for help, the attractiveness of the person in need, the familiarity of the situation, and the number of people available to help.

Is the need recognized? The clarity of someone's need for help has a major impact on whether others provide help (Clark & Word, 1974). In one study, undergraduate students waiting alone in a campus building observed what

One of the most fundamental reasons people give for helping others is that it makes them feel good; they experience satisfaction from giving aid or otherwise acting to benefit others rather than themselves.

appeared to be an accident involving a window washer. The man screamed as he and his ladder fell to the ground; then he began to clutch his ankle and groan in pain. All of the students looked out of the window to see what had happened, but only 29 percent of them did anything to help. Other students experienced the same situation, with one important difference: the man said he was hurt and needed help. In this case, more than 80 percent of the subjects came to his aid (Yakimovich & Saltz, 1971). Apparently, this one additional cue eliminated any ambiguity in the situation and led the vast majority of people to offer their help. In a similar experiment, 100 percent of the observers responded to a direct request for help (Clark & Word, 1972).

The attractiveness of the person in need   People are much more likely to provide help to those they find attractive or likable than to others. One study found, for example, that people with a large birthmark are less likely to receive help than those without such a mark (Piliavin, Piliavin & Rodin, 1975). Stranded motorists are more likely to receive help if they are dressed neatly than if their clothes are dirty and their hair is messy (Graf & Riddell, 1972; Morgan, 1973). Males are also more likely to help female rather than male motorists with car trouble (West, Whitney & Schnedler, 1975), and they are more likely to assist physically attractive than unattractive females (West & Brown, 1975).

Familiarity with the surroundings   The probability that people will offer help also increases if they are in a familiar situation. This relationship was demonstrated in an experiment on people's willingness to help in an apparent emergency that took place either in a New York City subway station (where most of the observers were commuters who had been there many times before) or in New York's LaGuardia Airport (where many of the travelers had never been before). A man with a bandaged leg and crutches hobbled along until he came upon a person sitting alone. Then he tripped, fell to the ground, and grasped his knee as if in pain (Latané & Darley, 1970). Over twice as many people helped in the subway station than in the airport. Further, habitual subway users were much more likely to help than those who used the subway infrequently.

The presence of others   The tendency to help is strongly influenced by the number of other people present. Somewhat surprisingly, however, the presence of others is not a social facilitator, but a powerful social *inhibitor* of helping behavior. This was true in the Genovese case and has been demonstrated time and time again in everyday life, when a group of people watches but does nothing to stop a rape or a mugging.

The same phenomenon has been found in controlled experiments. For example, students in one study were told that they would be taking part in a discussion, but that, to encourage truthfulness and guarantee anonymity, they would be left alone and would speak with the others through an intercom system (Latané & Darley, 1968). They introduced themselves and began speaking in turn. Very soon, one participant began breathing heavily, gasped for air, and was apparently having an epileptic seizure. The experimenter arranged the situation so that some students thought they were the only person who knew what was happening; some thought they were one of two people who knew what was happening; and some thought they were one of four people who knew what was happening. When students thought they were alone, nearly everyone did something to help. But the number who helped decreased significantly when they thought even one other person knew about the apparent emergency. And when they thought four others were present, the percentage who helped became quite small. Moreover, even when people did respond, it took them longer to do so when they were in a group than when they were alone.

Clearly, the presence of others inhibited helping behavior in this situation. One explanation for this inhibiting effect is that each person thinks that someone else will help the victim. The tendency to deny any personal responsibility for responding when others are present is known as **diffusion of responsibility** (Mynatt & Sherman, 1975).

The degree to which other people's presence will inhibit helping may also depend on who those other people are. When they are strangers, perhaps poor communication inhibits helping. People have difficulty speaking to strangers, particularly in an emergency situation, and without speaking, it is difficult to know what the others intend to do. People should be less embarrassed with friends and more willing to discuss the problem and what to do about it.

In one experiment designed to test this idea, a female experimenter led the subject to a room where he or she was to wait either alone, with a friend, with a stranger, or with a stranger who was a confederate of the experimenter (Latané & Rodin, 1969). The experimenter then stepped behind a curtain into an office. For nearly five minutes, she could be heard doing normal chores—opening and closing the drawers of her desk, shuffling papers, and so on. Then she could be heard climbing up on a chair. Soon there was a loud crash, and she screamed, "Oh, my God. . . . My foot, I . . . I can't move it. Oh, my ankle. . . . I can't get this . . . thing off me." Then the subject heard her groan and cry.

Would the subject go behind the curtain to help? Once again, as you can see in Figure 18.8, people were most likely to help if they were alone. When one other person was present, subjects were more likely both to communicate with one another and to offer help if they were friends than if they were strangers. When the stranger was the experimenter's confederate (who had been instructed not to help the woman in distress), virtually no subject offered to help. Other studies have confirmed that bystanders' tendency to help increases when they are coworkers, club members, or know each other in some other way (Rutkowski, Gruder & Romer, 1983).

The tendency to interpret emergency situations as emergencies and to take responsibility for doing something about them appears to be strengthened by an understanding of the social psychology of helping. For example, when confronted with a contrived emergency under circumstances unlikely to promote helping, students who had recently learned about diffusion of responsibility offered help nearly twice as often as those who had not received that information (Beaman et al., 1978).

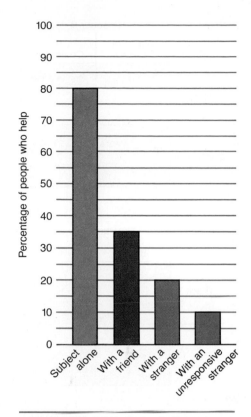

Figure 18.8
Helping in the Presence of Friends or Strangers
People are more likely to help when they are alone than in a group. However, diffusion of responsibility is lessened when the members of the group know each other.
(From B. Latané and J. Rodin, "A Lady in Distress: Inhibiting Effects of Friends and Strangers on Bystander Intervention," *Journal of Experimental Social Psychology, 5,* 189–202. Copyright 1969 by Academic Press. Adapted by permission of the publisher.)

COOPERATION AND COMPETITION

People often cooperate in order to accomplish their goals. For example, several students can drive across the country in three days by changing drivers every few hours; the trip could not be made so speedily by any one of them alone. But people also compete with others for limited resources. For example, on arrival at their destination, these same students might all interview with a company that has only one job opening.

Cooperation is any type of behavior in which several people work together to attain a goal. **Competition** exists whenever individuals try to attain a goal

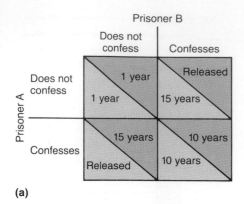

(a)

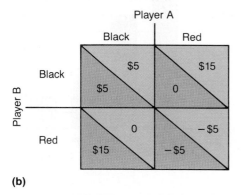

(b)

Figure 18.9
The Prisoner's Dilemma
In many cases, mutual cooperation is beneficial to two parties and mutual competition is harmful to both, but one can exploit the cooperativeness of the other. The prisoner's dilemma provides a model for such situations. These diagrams show the potential payoffs in that situation and in the prisoner's dilemma game described in the text. Each player's payoff is a function of how both people respond.

for themselves while denying that goal to others. Of course, many activities fall somewhere between cooperation and competition or combine elements of both. For example, in team sports, people cooperate with their teammates but compete with members of the opposing team.

The Prisoner's Dilemma

When do people choose to cooperate, and when do they choose to compete? Suppose two people are separated immediately after being arrested for a serious crime. The district attorney believes they are guilty but does not have the evidence to convict them. Each prisoner can either confess or not. The district attorney tells the prisoners that if they both refuse to confess, they will each be convicted of a minor offense and will be jailed for one year. If they both confess, they will be convicted, and the district attorney will recommend a ten-year sentence. However, if one prisoner remains silent and one confesses, the district attorney will allow the confessing prisoner to turn state's evidence and go free, while the other will serve the maximum fifteen-year sentence.

Each prisoner faces a dilemma. Figure 18.9a outlines the possible outcomes in a *payoff matrix.* Obviously, the strategy that will guarantee the best *mutual* outcome—short sentences for both prisoners—is cooperation; both should remain silent. But the prisoner who remains silent runs the risk of receiving a very long sentence if the other prisoner confesses, and the prisoner who talks has the chance of gaining individually if the other prisoner does not talk. Thus, each prisoner has an incentive to compete for freedom by confessing. But if they *both* compete and confess, each will go to jail for longer than if nothing was said.

By setting up analogous situations in the laboratory, psychologists create what is called a **prisoner's dilemma game** (Luce & Raiffa, 1957). In a typical example, two people sit before separate control panels. Each subject has a red button and a black button, one of which is to be pushed on each of many trials. If, on a given trial, both subjects press their black buttons, each wins five dollars. If both press the red button, each loses five dollars. However, if player A presses the red button and player B presses the black button, A will win fifteen dollars and B will win nothing. Thus, pressing the black button is a cooperative response; pressing the red button, a competitive response. Figure 18.9b shows the payoff matrix for this situation. Over the course of the experiment, the combined winnings of the players are greatest if each presses the black button; that is, if they cooperate. But by pressing the black button, one player becomes open to exploitation by the other. To put it another way, each player stands to benefit the most individually by pressing the red button occasionally.

What happens when people play the game? Overall, there is a strong tendency for people to exploit each other (Christie, Gergen & Marlowe, 1970; Rapoport, 1974). Regardless of how many others are being exploited, people tend to respond competitively rather than cooperatively (Komorita, Sweeney & Kravitz, 1980) and find it difficult to resist the competitive choice on any given trial. This choice wins them more money on that trial, but in the long run they gain less than they would have gained through cooperation. People's responses in these laboratory games appear related to their more general behavior outside the laboratory. For example, Daryl Bem and Charles Lord (1979) found that roommates' ratings of subjects' cooperativeness and competitiveness accurately predicted the subjects' performance in the game.

The prisoner's dilemma game parallels numerous real-life dilemmas. When competing companies decide on their advertising budgets or when competing nations plan their military budgets, each side would save enormous sums by cutting their budgets in half. But neither side is certain that the other would in fact cooperate. Fearing that the other side would instead spend enough to pull ahead, they continue to compete.

Factors Affecting Cooperation and Competition

If playing the prisoner's dilemma game competitively leads to smaller rewards in the long run, then why do people persist in being competitive? There seem to be two reasons (Komorita, 1984). First, winning more than an opponent seems to be rewarding in itself. That is, many people feel it is important to outscore an opponent, even if the result is that they win less money overall. Second, and more important, once several competitive responses are made, the competition seems to feed on itself. Each person becomes distrustful of the other, and cooperation becomes increasingly difficult. The more competitive one person acts, the more competitive the other becomes (Hamner, 1974). This self-perpetuating tendency is easily seen in the nuclear arms race between the United States and the Soviet Union. However, the strong tendency to act competitively can be overcome, and even replaced by cooperation, if communication between competing parties is improved, a fact that has been demonstrated in several ways by the prisoner's dilemma game.

Direct communication   Experimenters usually do not permit communication between the players in the prisoner's dilemma game. This constraint seems to interfere with players' ability to develop a cooperative strategy (Nemeth, 1972). In one study, for example, the more visual and auditory communication was possible, the more cooperation occurred (Wichman, 1970). In another study, cooperation increased when one player communicated an intent to cooperate and then immediately followed it up with a cooperative response (Brickman, Becker & Castle, 1979).

Unfortunately, not all communication increases cooperation, just as not all contact reduces prejudice. If the communication takes the form of a threat, people apparently interpret the threat itself as a competitive response and are likely to respond competitively (Smith & Anderson, 1975). Furthermore, the communication must be relevant. In one study, cooperation increased only when people spoke openly about the game and how they would be rewarded for various responses (Dawes, McTavish & Shaklee, 1977).

Communicating a strategy   People can also communicate implicitly, through the strategy they use. We have already noted that being competitive makes the other person less cooperative. It is possible to break this circle by adopting the *reformed sinner strategy*. This happens when one person initially responds very competitively but then shifts to a cooperative strategy. Typically, the other person responds to competitive responses with competitive responses. But once cooperative responses begin, the other person usually reciprocates by cooperating (Deutsch, 1975).

Now imagine that a player consistently acts in a cooperative fashion no matter how the other person responds. This consistent cooperation has a powerful effect (Gruder & Duslak, 1973; Rubin & Brown, 1975). When one person cooperates consistently, it can only be for the maximum gain of both parties. The other person usually adopts the same strategy and begins cooperating as well. Consistent cooperation usually works well, but it is most effective in the very early stages of the game, before any competitiveness has surfaced (Pilisuk & Skolnick, 1968). Sometimes, however, people view consistent cooperativeness as an invitation to exploit (Hamner & Yukl, 1977). For example, when one player is very competitive or has reason to doubt the cooperative player's motives, that player's cooperative strategy may lead to exploitation (Kelley & Stahelski, 1970).

Of all the strategies that can be used, the most simple also appears to be the most effective for producing long-term cooperation. This is to use basic learning principles and play *tit-for-tat,* rewarding cooperative responses with cooperation and punishing exploitation by generating exploitative strategies of one's own. Research indicates that cooperating after a cooperative response and competing after a competitive response produces a high degree of cooperation over time (Kuhlman & Marshello, 1975; Rapoport, 1973). Apparently, the players learn that the only way to come out ahead is to cooperate.

GROUP DECISION MAKING AND GROUP PERFORMANCE

How much should the city's teachers be paid next year? Is the defendant guilty or innocent? What was the cause of yesterday's plane crash? Many questions and problems like these are usually dealt with, not by one person, but by a group of two or more people. In order for groups to make decisions, solve problems, or perform other tasks, they must cooperate. But often there are competing factions in a group, some favoring one solution, others preferring a different approach. How does it all get resolved? How do groups reach their goals?

Decision Making in Groups

In Chapter 9, we described the rational processes, mental sets, and biases that influence an individual's efforts to make decisions. Those processes continue to operate when an individual becomes part of a group, but their influence on the decision is muted somewhat, since the group's interaction also shapes the outcome. Two of the most important factors affecting a group's decisions are (1) the prior opinions of its members, and (2) the order in which various options are considered.

Individual opinions   Each individual in a group has prior beliefs and attitudes. In principle, each person in the group should listen to the others, and the group should evaluate each argument on its merits and try to reach a consensus. In fact, people making decisions in a group often show a strong tendency to stick with their original beliefs. They are seldom persuaded to change their mind, especially when they are not alone in their views. As a result, group discussion often fails to resolve group differences. In most situations, a group's decision simply reflects what individual members already thought (Davis, 1980). In one study, for example, subjects served as members of a mock jury in a rape case. Those who were favorable to the prosecution before the trial began tended to vote for conviction, whereas those who were favorable to the defense before the trial began tended to vote for acquittal (Davis et al., 1978). Moreover, people tended to maintain their beliefs after a thirty-minute group discussion.

The order of discussion   Even though discussions rarely change people's opinions, they do shape a group's decision (Hastie, Penrod & Pennington, 1983). The discussions typically follow a consistent pattern (Hoffman, 1979). At first, various options are proposed and the arguments pro and con are

Group discussions are vital to solving problems and making decisions in the social world, but the give and take of such discussions usually do more to create workable outcomes than to substantially alter individual opinions.

considered. This continues until one option generates a minimally positive response—in other words, the discussion continues until the group perceives that no member has strong objections to one option. At that point, the quality of the discussion changes dramatically (Hoffman, 1979). Rather than seriously considering subsequent options, the group immediately criticizes anything else that is proposed and begins arguing more and more strongly for the minimally acceptable solution. Thus, the first minimally acceptable solution that is offered is likely to survive as the group's decision (Hoffman & Maier, 1979).

One important implication of this process is that the order in which options are considered, rather than the quality of the options, can determine whether or not they will be adopted. Suppose that a group of friends is trying to decide which videocassette movie to rent. Fred and Ginger propose *Footlight Parade,* an old musical, but no one else wants to see a black-and-white film. Jason's nomination of *Friday the Thirteenth, Part 62* is opposed by everyone with a weak stomach. Then Julie mentions *The Sound of Music,* a show that everyone is at least willing to see, even if they are not enthusiastic about it. This is the movie the group is likely to rent, even if someone subsequently mentions a better one, because any ideas that come up after the minimally acceptable option is on the table are likely to meet harsh criticism (Hoffman, Friend & Bond, 1979). The reasons why group members seem to focus prematurely on one solution and close their minds to subsequent alternatives are not entirely clear.

Group polarization   At one time, research suggested that groups almost always make decisions that are riskier or more radical than the average recommendation of the group members. However, evidence now indicates that group decisions are often either riskier *or* more conservative than the average group member might have made individually (Myers, 1975; Myers & Lamm, 1976; Zaleska, 1978). To illustrate, a committee charged with deciding on the appropriate punishment for a student might arrive at a more severe penalty than most members, operating alone, would have chosen. On the other hand, when groups bet on horses, they are more conservative than individuals (Knox & Safford, 1976). This tendency for groups to make decisions that represent a shift toward one extreme or the other is called **group polarization.**

Two mechanisms apparently underlie group polarization. First, most arguments presented during the group discussion will favor the view of the majority, and most criticisms will be directed at the minority view. As a result, the new arguments each member hears are likely to favor what the majority believes. Thus, it will seem rational to those favoring the majority view— whether that view is risky or conservative—to adopt an even stronger version of it (Burnstein & Vinokur, 1977; Burnstein, Vinokur & Trope, 1973).

Second, the social comparison phenomenon described in Chapter 17 may contribute to polarization. Recall that people tend to perceive themselves in relation to those around them, especially to those in their reference groups. Thus, as a group begins to agree that a particular decision is desirable, a group norm is established, and members may try to establish themselves as being the most committed to that norm. (Indeed, various individuals may all claim to have proposed the accepted proposal or policy.) As the competition for most-committed group member continues, each individual may begin to advocate a more and more extreme position, and the group becomes polarized (Myers & Lamm, 1976; Sanders & Baron, 1977).

Especially in small, close-knit groups, extreme decisions and policies reflect not only polarization, but also a more general decision-making process called **groupthink,** a pattern of thinking that, over time, renders group members unable to realistically evaluate the wisdom of various options and decisions (Janis, 1972, 1983). Tape recordings suggest that groupthink held sway in the White House during the early 1970s with President Nixon and his inner circle of advisers. As members of this small group became more and more certain that the press and the "liberals" were to blame for many of the

President Nixon says goodbye after resigning his office. Many of the illegal or unwise tactics that forced the resignation appeared to be the result of groupthink, *a distorted decision-making process to which Nixon and his closest advisors fell victim.*

president's problems in carrying out his policies, they not only decided to authorize illegal acts designed to suppress the influence of their opponents, but came to think that violation of the U.S. Constitution was acceptable in pursuit of their political goals. And later, when these misguided decisions began to come to light, the group compounded the error by trying to cover up and deny the whole affair.

Group Leadership

Whether the goal is to make a decision, set a policy, or solve a problem, groups usually engage in discussion or debate. This process is usually facilitated by a *leader*—a person who organizes, summarizes, and moderates the discussion. A good leader can greatly aid a group in pursuing its tasks, and a poor one can impede a group's functioning. What makes a good leader?

Marvin Shaw (1981) reviewed the past thirty years' research on the personality of leaders and suggested that only three generalizations can be made. First, leaders tend to score very high on whatever skills are crucial to the group. Often they are intelligent, creative, and have good verbal skills. Second, leaders tend to have good social skills. For example, they may have the ability to make others feel important, listened to, and cared for; they certainly can make others like them. Finally, leaders tend to be ambitious. They show initiative and self-confidence, and they enjoy being in a position of leadership. Shaw also discovered, however, that having these traits is not sufficient to ensure that a person will lead well. People who are effective leaders in one situation may not be effective in another (Hollander, 1985). It appears that there is no one single type of good leader. Instead, good leadership apparently depends not just on a person's traits, but also on the situation and on the person's style of handling it.

Psychologists have developed models that attempt to specify the conditions under which different styles of leadership will be most effective (Chemers, 1983). Two main styles have been identified. The first style is **task-oriented** (Shaw, 1981). These leaders provide very close supervision, lead by giving directives, and generally discourage group discussion. Their style may not endear them to group members. Other leaders tend to adopt a **socioemotional** style. They provide loose supervision, ask for group members' ideas, and are generally concerned with subordinates' feelings (Shaw, 1981). They are usually well liked by the group, even when they must reprimand someone (Boyatzis, 1982; Weissenberg & Kavanagh, 1972).

Task-oriented leaders are most effective when the group is working under time pressure. They are also most effective when the task is unstructured and when it is unclear what needs to be done first and how the duties should be divided. People stranded in an elevator in a burning building, for example, need a task-oriented leader. On the other hand, socioemotional leaders are most effective when the task is structured and there are no severe time limitations (Gibb, 1969; Gustafson & Thomas, 1970). These people would be particularly effective, for example, in managing an office in which the workers know their jobs well.

It appears, then, that the "best" leaders are those whose style matches the circumstances and demands of the group's task. Management training programs have been designed to help leaders in business, industry, and government become more aware of leader-situation interactions (Yukl, 1981). High-level executives are trained to select lower-level leaders whose style matches the situation in which they will be operating (Leary et al., 1986). Research suggests that these training programs can help leaders perform more efficiently (Hollander, 1985).

BIOLOGICAL PSYCHOLOGY AND AGGRESSION

Does Human Aggression Have Biological Sources?

In Chapter 3, we discussed some biological bases of behavior, with a special emphasis on the ways in which the nervous and endocrine systems influence the way people feel, think, and act. Indeed, throughout this book we have seen examples of this influence, in the relationship between physiological arousal and emotion, in the role of neurotransmitters in mental disorders, and in the effects of drugs on consciousness, to name just a few. We close by considering what may be one of the most important links between biological variables and behavior: the one tying such biological roots as genetics, brain systems, and hormones to aggression, a social phenomenon that, in the nuclear age, must be better understood and controlled if the human species is to survive.

Aggression and the Brain Charles Whitman, a former altar boy and Eagle Scout, was a student at the University of Texas when he began experiencing episodes of intense anxiety. He had recently been in several fights, assaulted his wife, and, in conversations with several psychiatrists, revealed periodic impulses toward very violent behavior. Shortly thereafter, he murdered his wife and his mother, then took a high-powered rifle with a telescopic sight to the top of a campus observation tower and for two hours shot at everyone he saw. He killed fourteen people and wounded two dozen more before the police killed him. An autopsy on Whitman revealed a tumor the size of a walnut in the area of the forebrain called the amygdala (see Figure 12.8). It is by no means true that all mass murderers have such tumors, but there is evidence that some people who exhibit sudden and extreme forms of aggression are suffering from some type of brain disorder (Mark & Ervin, 1970).

Damage to or electrical stimulation of numerous brain areas can have varying effects on aggression, depending on the precise location and the species involved (Albert & Walsh, 1984). For example, *defensive aggression*—that is, heightened aggressive responsiveness to stimuli that are not ordinarily threatening—is seen following lesions of the septum, the hypothalamus, and other related areas in mice, rats, cats, dogs, and humans. The same lesions produce defensiveness without aggression in gerbils, hamsters, and rabbits.

Stimulating various parts of the hypothalamus in cats produces two different types of aggression (Flynn et al., 1970).

FUTURE DIRECTIONS

We have seen that social interaction is multifaceted. You influence others, and they influence you. People help you and hurt you, cooperate with you and compete against you. Research in social psychology, both in the laboratory and in the field, has helped to illuminate each of these processes and will continue to do so.

One recent trend in social psychology involves placing greater emphasis on the environmental context in which social interaction occurs. This trend was exemplified in our discussion of how certain environmental conditions can increase the likelihood of aggression. Researchers have also described the beneficial effects of certain environments. For example, students living in suite-based dorms often do better in school and are happier than those living in hallway dorms (Baum & Valins, 1977; Figure 16.2 depicted these living arrangements). This difference may reflect the fact that, compared with those in hallway dorms, students living in suite-based dorms have more control over when they interact with others (Baum & Valins, 1977). Both subjective feelings of satisfaction and performance on various tasks increase when people feel they have control (Moos, 1980; Moos & Lemke, 1980; Stokols & Novaco,

The first is an intense rage, in which the cats arch their backs, hiss violently, and attack anything that moves. Another, more ritualistic pattern involves great excitement, but a slower and more gradual attack approach reminiscent of normal feline predatory behavior. When surgical lesions are made in the same hypothalamic regions in cats, aggressive behaviors often cease altogether. Extensive damage to the amygdala (and to nearby cortical tissue) can result in increased aggressiveness in cats. Predatory aggression has also been produced through amygdala lesions in rats. However, most animal studies of amygdala lesions have generally found them to decrease aggression, especially defensive aggression. Indeed, small lesions in the human amygdala have been used to reduce aggression in people suffering from hyperaggressiveness brought on by epilepsy.

There is also suggestive evidence, exemplified in the Whitman case, that human aggression is related to the condition of cortical tissue. For example, a woman who had been thrown from a horse began to display extremely violent and very uncharacteristic episodes of aggression. It was discovered that she had suffered a skull fracture that was putting pressure on part of her temporal lobe. After surgery to relieve the pressure and remove damaged tissue, including some from the amygdala, the aggressive episodes ceased. As mentioned in the chapter on psychotherapy, reports of reductions in aggression following the removal of animal and human brain tissue led to the once-routine use of *psychosurgery* for the treatment of aggressiveness, extreme emotions, and other psychological problems.

Hormonal Factors In both lower animals and humans, males tend to be more aggressive than females (Maccoby & Jacklin, 1974). This gender difference suggests that aggression may be related to differences in the amount of the masculine hormone *testosterone* present in each sex. For example, experiments have shown that aggressive behavior increases or decreases dramatically with the amount of testosterone in an animal's body (Moyer, 1983). However, testosterone appears to have its greatest and most durable influence not through day-to-day effects, but through its impact on early brain development. For example, testosterone was once given to pregnant women as a means of preventing miscarriage. Later research suggested that artificial elevation in testosterone at this early stage of a baby's development is associated with higher levels of aggression in adulthood (Reinisch, 1981). About ten million American fetuses were affected before the practice was halted. In Norway, the testosterone levels of 224 adult males were dramatically lowered by castration following their conviction for aggressive sex crimes. This removal of testosterone did lower their sex drive and greatly reduced sexually related aggressiveness. But, presumably because of more general brain developments, these men still behaved aggressively in situations unrelated to sex (Bremer, 1959).

Hormones that act as the neurotransmitters discussed in Chapter 3 may also play a role in aggression. In animals, for example, aggressive behavior tends to be associated with high levels of adrenaline and noradrenaline and low levels of serotonin. On the other hand, when the level of adrenergic transmitters is low and serotonin is high, behavior tends to be far less aggressive (Whalen & Simon, 1984).

1980). But a sense of control also requires that people have some privacy, that there not be too much noise, and so on. This brand of social psychological research has become known as **environmental psychology;** or the study of the effects of the general physical environment on behavior and mental processes (Proshansky, 1976). Researchers in this field are outlining how the physical environment affects stress, health, competitiveness, cooperation, aggressiveness, and productivity.

One result of this research is that psychologists are working with architects to develop more psychologically comfortable environmental settings. Psychologists have also become active in discussing the implications of environmental psychology for social policy (Craik, 1986; Stokols, 1983). For example, if the physical layout of prisons, mental hospitals, and other institutions affects the aggressiveness or cooperation of their residents, then a psychologically comfortable facility—although it may cost more to build—may both speed rehabilitation and reduce the time and money needed to contend with aggressiveness, uncooperativeness, and damage stemming from violence (Wener et al., 1987). We expect that psychologists will play an increasingly active role in debates about these facilities and their design. This role is consistent with the approach of community psychology, which, as we discussed in

Chapter 16, emphasizes efforts to prevent or minimize human problems, and represents yet another way in which psychological research is being applied to the promotion of human welfare.

You can explore the topics covered in this chapter and the previous one in greater depth by taking courses in social psychology, environmental psychology, community psychology, attitudes and behavior, group dynamics, and other offerings that relate to behavior in its social context.

SUMMARY

1. Social dilemmas occur when people must choose between alternatives that create personal, short-term benefits and those that create longer-term benefits for the group as a whole.

2. Conformity is a change in behavior or beliefs to bring them in line with the norms established by other members of a group. Conformity results in statements or behavior that may or may not reflect a true change in a person's private beliefs. Conformity is greatest when the ambiguity of the situation is high, when the other members of the group are unanimous in their view, and when the group is attractive. Conformity is also greater among those of low status than high status.

3. Compliance occurs when people change their behavior because of a direct request. The foot-in-the-door technique, the door-in-the-face procedure, and the low-ball approach are all effective mechanisms for getting people to change their behavior.

4. Obedience is a change in behavior that results from a specific demand. Stanley Milgram's research indicated that levels of obedience are high even when obedience apparently results in pain and suffering for another person. Although people often obey an authority figure who gives a command, laboratory studies of obedience make it clear that they experience considerable turmoil when inflicting pain on another person. Obedience declines as the authority figure's status declines, as the authority figure becomes more distant, as proximity to the victim increases, and when others are seen disobeying the authority figure. The degree to which apparently blind obedience in the laboratory reflects unflattering basic human characteristics is still unclear.

5. Aggression is any act that is intended to harm another person. Both psychoanalysts and ethologists have suggested that biological factors create a readiness to aggress against another person. However, learning principles play a vital role in human aggression, because many aggressive responses are learned by watching others. The performance of aggressive acts is also affected by the pattern of rewards and punishments a person receives.

6. A variety of emotional factors play a role in aggression. Frustration can lead to aggression, particularly if cues that invite or promote aggression are present in the environment. Arousal from sources completely unrelated to aggression, such as exercise, can also make aggressive responses more likely. This is particularly true when aggression is already a dominant response in that situation. There is no evidence that sexual arousal, in and of itself, produces aggression. However, exposure to aggressive pornography results in men becoming more accepting of aggressive acts toward women. Environmental factors, such as high temperature, air pollution, and noise, also appear to increase the likelihood of aggressive behavior, especially when people are already angry.

7. Although helping another person often entails some sacrifice, there are psychological rewards for helping. The tendency to help others often begins in very early childhood. This observation has led some to propose that helping and altruism have value for the preservation of the species. People are most likely to help others when the need for help is clear, when the person in need is attractive, when the helpers are familiar with the surroundings, and when there are no other people present.

8. People have a strong tendency to compete with one another. This is true even when they receive fewer rewards for competing than for cooperating. Communication between competing parties generally leads to an increase in cooperation, especially if the communication is nonthreatening and relevant to the situation. One of the most effective strategies for producing long-term cooperation is playing tit-for-tat; that is, rewarding cooperative responses with cooperation and punishing exploitation by generating exploitative strategies of one's own.

9. People in groups have a strong tendency to stick with their original beliefs; they are seldom persuaded by

group discussion to change their mind. Nevertheless, group decisions are often affected by the order in which various options are considered. In particular, there is a bias to adopt the first option that generates a minimally positive response from the group. Decisions made by groups are typically more extreme, or polarized, than the ones that individuals would make.

10. There is no single personality type or behavioral style that always results in good leadership. Task-oriented leaders are most effective when the task is unstructured and the group is working under time pressure. Socioemotional leaders are most effective when the task is structured and there are no severe time limitations.

KEY TERMS

Definitions of terms appear on the pages shown in parentheses.

aggression (671)	group polarization (688)
altruism (679)	groupthink (688)
catharsis (672)	helping behavior (679)
competition (683)	obedience (665)
compliance (658)	prisoner's dilemma game
conformity (656)	(684)
cooperation (683)	releaser (673)
diffusion of responsibility	social dilemma (656)
(683)	sociobiologist (680)
environmental psychology	socioemotional leadership
(691)	(689)
frustration aggression	task-oriented leadership
hypothesis (675)	(689)

RECOMMENDED READINGS

Fisher, J. D., Bell, P. A., & Baum, A. (1984). *Environmental psychology* (2nd ed.). New York: Holt, Rinehart and Winston. An excellent text that reviews our current understanding of how the environment influences behavior. Issues such as weather, air pollution, and architectural design are discussed in depth.

Geen, R., & Donnerstein, E. (Eds.). (1983). *Aggression: Theoretical and empirical reviews*. New York: Academic Press. A comprehensive treatment of human aggression. The roles of learning, cognition, emotion, and sexual arousal are highlighted. Various theories are summarized and the evidence relevant to each is reviewed.

Paulus, P. B. (Ed.). (1983). *Basic group processes*. New York: Springer-Verlag. A nice summary of research on leadership, cooperation and competition, bargaining, and group decision making is provided.

Rushton, J., & Sorrentino, R. (Eds.). (1981). *Altruism and helping behavior*. Hillsdale, N.J.: Erlbaum. Experts in the development and instigation of helping behavior review theory and research. There is also a section on how characteristics of the individual influence when helping is most likely to occur.

Yukl, G. (1981). *Leadership in organizations*. Englewood Cliffs, N.J.: Prentice-Hall. The characteristics of effective leaders in business and other organizations are analyzed. The author provides numerous examples of how the principles discovered in laboratory experiments operate in more complex settings.

Statistics in Psychological Research

Whether psychologists conduct experiments, field studies, case studies, naturalistic observations, or surveys, their investigations usually generate a large amount of **data:** numbers that represent their findings and provide the basis for their conclusions. In Chapter 1, we described how psychologists obtain their findings, and we discussed several factors vital to research design if that research is to yield meaningful data. No matter how well a study is designed, however, understanding and interpreting the results also depends on the adequacy of the researcher's *statistical analyses;* that is, on the methods used for summarizing and analyzing the data. In this appendix, we consider various *descriptive statistics* that psychologists use to describe and present their data. Then we discuss *inferential statistics,* the mathematical procedures used to draw conclusions from data and make inferences about what they mean.

DESCRIBING DATA

To illustrate our discussion, consider a hypothetical experiment on the effects of incentives on performance. The experimenter presents a simple list of mathematics problems to two groups of subjects. Each group must solve the problems within a fixed time, but for each correct answer, the low-incentive group is paid ten cents, while the high-incentive group gets one dollar. The hypothesis to be tested is the **null hypothesis,** the assertion that the independent variable manipulated by the experimenter will have no effect on the dependent variable measured by the experimenter. In this case, the null hypothesis holds that the size of the incentive (the independent variable) will not affect performance on the mathematics task (the dependent variable).

Assume that the experimenter has obtained a random sample of subjects, assigned them randomly to the two groups, and done everything possible to avoid the confounds and other research problems discussed in Chapter 1. The experiment has been run, and the psychologist now has the data: a list of the number of correct answers reported by each subject in each group. Now comes the first task of statistical analysis: describing the data in a way that makes them easy to understand.

The Frequency Histogram

The simplest way to describe the data is to draw up something like Table A.1, in which all the numbers are simply listed. After examining the table, you might discern that the high-incentive group seems to have done better than the low-incentive group, but the difference is not immediately obvious. It might be even harder to see if there were more subjects and if the scores included three-digit numbers. A picture is worth a thousand words, so a more satisfactory way of presenting the same data is in a picturelike graphic known as a **frequency histogram** (see Figure A.1, p. 696).

TABLE A.1

A Simple Data Set
Here are the test scores obtained by thirteen subjects performing under low-incentive conditions and thirteen subjects performing under high-incentive conditions.

Low Incentive	High Incentive
4	6
6	4
2	10
7	10
6	7
8	10
3	6
5	7
2	5
3	9
5	9
9	3
5	8

695

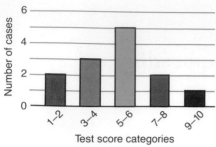

(a) Low Incentive

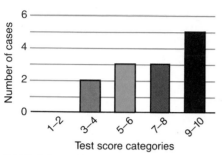

(b) High Incentive

Figure A.1
Frequency Histograms
The height of each bar of a histogram represents the number of scores falling within each range of score values. The pattern formed by these bars gives a visual image of how research results are distributed.

Construction of a histogram is simple. First, divide the scale for measuring the dependent variable (in this case, the number of correct solutions) into a number of categories, or "bins." The bins in our example are 1–2, 3–4, 5–6, 7–8, and 9–10. Next, sort the raw data into the appropriate bin. (For example, the score of a subject who had 5 correct answers would go into the 5–6 bin, a score of 8 would go into the 7–8 bin, and so on.) Finally, for each bin, count the number of scores in that bin and draw a bar up to the height of that number on the vertical axis of a graph. The set of bars makes up the frequency histogram.

Because we are interested in comparing the scores of two groups, there are separate histograms in Figure A.1: one for the high-incentive group and one for the low-incentive group. Now the difference between groups that was difficult to see in Table A.1 becomes clearly visible: more people in the high-incentive group obtained high scores than in the low-incentive group.

Histograms and other pictures of data are useful for visualizing and better understanding the "shape" of research data, but in order to analyze data statistically, the data making up these graphic presentations must be handled in other ways. For example, before we can tell whether two histograms are different statistically or just visually, the data they represent must be described in more precise mathematical terms.

Descriptive Statistics

The numbers that summarize a pool of data are called **descriptive statistics.** The four basic categories of descriptive statistics (1) measure the number of observations made; (2) summarize the typical value of a set of data; (3) summarize the spread, or variability, in a set of data; and (4) express the correlation between two sets of data.

N   The easiest statistic to compute, abbreviated as *N,* simply describes the number of observations that make up the data set. In Table A.1, for example, $N = 13$ for each group, or 26 for the entire data set. Simple as it is, *N* plays a very important role in more sophisticated statistical analyses.

Measures of central tendency   It is apparent in the histograms in Figure A.1 that there is a difference in the pattern of scores between the two groups. But how much of a difference? What is the typical value, the **central tendency,** that represents each group's performance? There are three measures that capture this typical value: the mode, the median, and the mean.

The **mode** is the value or score that occurs most frequently in the data. It is computed most easily by ordering the scores from lowest to highest, as has been done in Table A.2. The mode is 5 in the low-incentive group and 10 in the high-incentive group. Notice that these modes do indicate that the two groups are very different and that the mode of 5 does capture the flavor of the low-incentive group (it falls about in the middle). But, in the case of the high-incentive group, the mode (10) is actually an extreme score; it does not provide a value representative of the group as a whole. Thus, the mode can act like a microphone for a small but vocal minority, which, though speaking most frequently, does not represent the views of the majority.

Unlike the mode, the median takes all of the scores into account. The **median** is the halfway point in a set of data: half the scores fall above the median, half fall below it. To compute the median, arrange the scores from lowest to highest (as in Table A.2) and count the scores from lowest to highest until the halfway point is reached; that point is the median. If there is an even number of observations, so that the middle lies between two numbers, the

Low Incentive		High Incentive
2		3
2		4
3		5
3		6
4		6
5		7
Mode → ⑤	← Median →	⑦
5		8
6		9
6		9
7		10 ⎤ ← Mode
8		10
9		10 ⎦
Mean = 65/13 = 5		Mean = 94/13 = 7.23

TABLE A.2

Measures of Central Tendency
Reordering the data in Table A.1 makes it easy to calculate the mean, median, and mode of the scores of subjects in the high- and low-incentive groups.

median is the value halfway between those two numbers. Thus, if the midpoint is between 17 and 18, the median is 17.5. There are 13 scores in Table A.2; so the median is the seventh score, which is 5 for the low-incentive group and 7 for the high-incentive group.

The third measure of central tendency is the **mean,** which is the *arithmetic average.* When people talk about the "average" in everyday conversation, they are usually referring to the mean. To compute the mean, add the values of all the scores and divide by N (the total number of scores). For the scores in Table A.2, the mean for the low-incentive group is 65/13 = 5, and for the high-incentive group, the mean is 94/13 = 7.23.

Like the median (and unlike the mode), the mean reflects all the data to some degree, not just the most frequent data. Notice, however, that the mean reflects the *actual value* of all the scores, whereas the median gives each score equal weight, whatever its size. This difference can have a huge effect on how well the two statistics reflect the values of a particular set of data. Suppose, for example, that you collected data on the incomes of all fifty families in one small town and that the mean and the median incomes were the same: $20,000. A week later, a person moves to town with an annual income of $1 million. When you reanalyze the income data, the median will hardly change at all, because the millionaire just counts as one score added at the top of the list. However, when you compute the new mean, the actual *amount* of the millionaire's income is added to everyone else's income and divided by the old $N + 1$; as a result, the mean might double in value to $40,000. Because the mean is more representative than the median of the value of all the data, it is often preferred as a measure of central tendency. But sometimes, as in this example, the median may be better because it is less sensitive to extreme scores.

Measures of variability   The **variability,** or spread, or dispersion of a set of data is often just as important as its central tendency. In the histograms in Figure A.1, for example, you can see that there is considerable variability in the low-incentive group; all five bins have at least one score in them. There is less variability in the high-incentive group; only four bins are represented. This variability can be quantified by measures known as the range and the standard deviation.

The **range** is simply the difference between the highest and the lowest value in the data set. For the data in Table A.2, the range for the low-incentive group is $9 - 2 = 7$; for the high-incentive group, the range is $10 - 3 = 7$. Like the median, the range does not reflect the values of all scores.

In contrast, the **standard deviation,** or **SD,** measures the average difference between each score and the mean of the data set. To see how the standard deviation is calculated, consider the data in Table A.3. The first step is to compute the mean of the set, in this case $20/5 = 4$. Second, calculate the difference, or *deviation (D),* of each score from the mean by subtracting the mean from each score, as in column 2 of Table A.3. Third, find the average of these deviations. However, if you calculated the average by finding the arithmetic mean, you would sum the deviations and find that the negative deviations exactly balance the positive ones, resulting in a mean difference of 0. Obviously there is more than zero variation around the mean in the data set. So, instead of employing the arithmetic mean, we compute the standard deviation by first squaring the deviations (which removes any negative values), summing these squared deviations, dividing by N, and then taking the square root of the result. These simple steps are outlined in more detail in Table A.3.

The standard deviation is a particularly important characteristic of any data set. For example, suppose you are a substitute teacher who comes to a new school hoping for an easy day's work. You are offered the choice of teaching one of two classes. In each, the students' mean IQ is 100. At first glance, there would appear to be no major difference between the classes' IQ scores. But it turns out that one class has an SD of 16; the SD of the other is 32. Since a higher standard deviation means more variability, the class with the SD of 32 is likely to be more difficult to teach because its students vary more in ability.

The normal distribution Now that we have described histograms and some descriptive statistics, we will reexamine how these methods of representing research data relate to some of the concepts discussed elsewhere in the book.

In most subareas in psychology, when researchers collect many measurements and plot their data in histograms, the pattern that results often resembles that shown for the low-incentive group in Figure A.1. That is, the majority of scores tend to fall in the middle of the distribution, with fewer and fewer occurring as one moves toward the extremes. As more and more data are collected, and as smaller and smaller bins are used (perhaps containing only one value each), the histograms tend to smooth out, until they resemble the bell-shaped curve known as the **normal distribution,** or *normal curve,* which

TABLE A.3 _____
Calculating the Standard Deviation
The standard deviation of a set of scores reflects the average degree to which those scores differ from the mean of the set.

Raw Data	Difference from Mean = D		D^2
2	$2 - 4$	$= -2$	4
2	$2 - 4$	$= -2$	4
3	$3 - 4$	$= -1$	1
4	$4 - 4$	$= 0$	0
9	$9 - 4$	$= 5$	25
Mean $= 20/5 = 4$			$\Sigma D^2 = 34$

$$\text{Standard deviation} = \sqrt{\frac{\Sigma D^2}{N}} = \sqrt{\frac{34}{5}} = \sqrt{6.8} = 2.6$$

Note: Σ means "the sum of."

Normal distribution, showing the smoothed approximation to the frequency histogram.

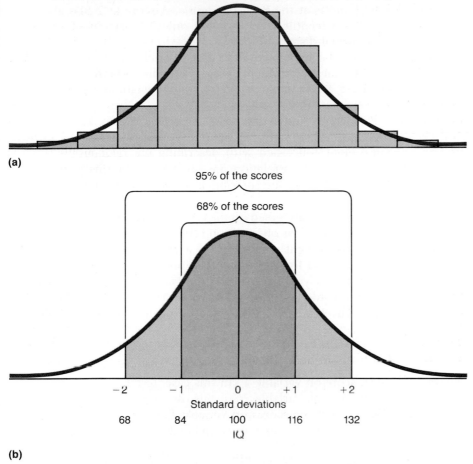

(a)

(b)

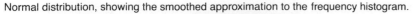

Figure A.2
The Normal Distribution
Many kinds of research data approximate the symmetrical shape of the normal curve, in which most scores fall toward the center of the range.

is shown in Figure A.2a. When a distribution of scores follows a truly normal curve, its mean, median, and mode all have the same value. Furthermore, if the curve is normal, we can use its standard deviation to describe how any particular score stands in relation to the rest of the distribution.

IQ scores provide an example. They are distributed in a normal curve, with a mean, median, and mode of 100 and an SD of 16 (see Figure A.2b). In such a distribution, half of the population will have an IQ above 100, and half will be below 100. The shape of the true normal curve is such that 68 percent of the area under it lies within one standard deviation in each direction. In terms of IQ, this means that 68 percent of the population has an IQ somewhere between 84 (100 minus 16) and 116 (100 plus 16). Of the remaining 32 percent of the population, half falls more than 1 SD above the mean, and half falls more than 1 SD below the mean. Thus, 16 percent of the population has an IQ above 116, and 16 percent scores below 84.

The normal curve is also the basis for percentiles. A **percentile score** indicates the percentage of people or observations that fall below a given score in a normal distribution. In Figure A.2b, for example, the mean score (which is also the median) lies at a point below which 50 percent of the scores fall. Thus, the mean of a normal distribution is at the 50th percentile. What does this mean for IQ? If you score 1 SD above the mean, your score is at a point above which only 16 percent of the population falls. This means that 84 percent of the population (100 percent minus 16 percent) must be below that score; so this IQ score is at the 84th percentile. A score at 2 SDs above the mean is at the 97.5 percentile level, because only 2.5 percent of the scores are above it in a normal distribution.

Scores may also be expressed in terms of their distance in standard deviations from the mean, producing what are called **standard scores.** A standard score of 1.5, for example, is 1.5 standard deviations from the mean.

Correlation   Histograms and measures of central tendency and variability describe certain characteristics of one dependent variable at a time. However, psychologists are often concerned with describing the *relationship* between two variables. Measures of correlation are often used for this purpose. We discussed the interpretation of the *correlation coefficient* in Chapter 1; here we describe how to calculate it.

Recall that correlations are based on the relationship between two numbers associated with each subject or observation. The numbers may represent, say, a person's height and weight or the IQ of a parent and child. Table A.4 contains this kind of data for four subjects from our incentives study who took the test twice. (As you may recall from Chapter 10, the correlation between their scores would be a measure of *test-retest reliability*.) The formula for computing the Pearson product-moment correlation, or *r,* is as follows:

$$r = \frac{\Sigma\,(x - M_x)\,(y - M_y)}{\sqrt{\Sigma\,(x - M_x)^2\,\Sigma\,(y - M_y)^2}}$$

where: x = each score on variable 1 (in this case, test 1)
    y = each score on variable 2 (in this case, test 2)
    M_x = the mean of the scores on variable 1
    M_y = the mean of the scores on variable 2

The main function of the denominator in this formula is to ensure that the coefficient ranges from +1.00 to −1.00, no matter how large or small the values of the variables being correlated. The "action element" of this formula is the numerator. It is the result of multiplying the amounts by which each of two observations (x and y) differ from the means of their respective distributions (M_x and M_y). Notice that, if the two variables "go together" (so that, if one is large, the other is also large, and if one is small, the other is also small), then either both will tend to be above the mean of their distribution or both will tend to be below the mean of their distribution. When this is the case, $x - M_x$ and $y - M_y$ will both be positive, or they will both be negative.

TABLE A.4
Calculating the Correlation Coefficient
Though it appears complex, calculation of the correlation coefficient is quite simple. The resulting r reflects the degree to which two sets of scores tend to be related, or to covary.

Subject	Test 1	Test 2	$(x - M_x)(y - M_y)$ [b]
A	1	3	$(1 - 3)(3 - 4) = (-2)(-1) = +2$
B	1	3	$(1 - 3)(3 - 4) = (-2)(-1) = +2$
C	4	5	$(4 - 3)(5 - 4) = (1)(1)\ \ \ \ = +1$
D	6	5	$(6 - 3)(5 - 4) = (3)(1)\ \ \ \ = +3$
	[a] $M_x = 3$	$M_y = 4$	$\Sigma(x - M_x)(y - M_y)\ \ \ \ \ \ \ \ \ \ = +8$

[c] $\Sigma(x - M_x)^2 = 4 + 4 + 1 + 9 = 18$

[d] $\Sigma(y - M_y)^2 = 1 + 1 + 1 + 1 = 4$

[e] $r = \dfrac{\Sigma(x - M_x)(y - M_y)}{\sqrt{\Sigma(x - M_x)^2\,\Sigma(y - M_y)^2}} = \dfrac{8}{\sqrt{18 \times 4}} = \dfrac{8}{\sqrt{72}} = \dfrac{8}{8.48} = +.94$

In either case, their product will always be positive, and the correlation coefficient will also be positive. If, on the other hand, the two variables go opposite to one another, such that, when one is large, the other is small, one of them is likely to be smaller than the mean of its distribution, so that either $x - M_x$ or $y - M_y$ will have a negative sign, and the other will have a positive sign. Multiplying these differences together will always result in a product with a negative sign, and r will be negative as well.

Now compute the correlation coefficient for the data presented in Table A.4. The first step (step a in the table) is to compute the mean (M) for each variable. M_x turns out to be 3 and M_y is 4. Next, calculate the numerator by finding the differences between each x and y value and its respective mean and by multiplying them (as in step b of Table A.4). Notice that, in this example, the differences in each pair have like signs, so the correlation coefficient will be positive. The next step is to calculate the terms in the denominator; in this case, as shown in steps c and d in Table A.4, they have values of 18 and 4. Finally, place all the terms in the formula and carry out the arithmetic (step e). The result in this case is an r of $+.94$, a high and positive correlation suggesting that performances on repeated tests are very closely related. A subject doing well the first time is likely to do well again; a person doing poorly at first will probably do no better the second time.

INFERENTIAL STATISTICS

The descriptive statistics from the incentives experiment tell the experimenter that the performances of the high- and low-incentive groups differ. But there is some uncertainty. Is the difference large enough to be important? Does it represent a stable effect or a fluke? The researcher would like to have some *measure of confidence* that the difference between groups is genuine and reflects the effect of incentive on mental tasks in the real world, rather than the effect of the particular subjects used, the phase of the moon, or other random or uncontrolled factors. One way of determining confidence would be to run the experiment again with a new group of subjects. Confidence that incentives produced differences in performance would grow stronger if the same or a larger between-group difference occurs again. In reality, psychologists rarely have the opportunity to repeat, or *replicate,* their experiments in exactly the same way three or four times. But **inferential statistics** provide a measure of how likely it was that results came about by chance. They put a precise mathematical value on the confidence or probability that rerunning the same experiment would yield similar (or even stronger) results.

Differences between means: The t test One of the most important tools of inferential statistics is the **t test.** It allows the researcher to ask how likely it is that the difference between two means occurred by chance rather than as a function of the effect of the independent variable. When the t test or other inferential statistic says that the probability of chance effects is small enough (usually less than 5 percent), the results are said to be *statistically significant.* Conducting a t test of statistical significance requires the use of three descriptive statistics.

The first component of the t test is the size of the observed effect, the difference between the means. In the example shown in Table A.2, the difference between the means is $7.23 - 5 = 2.23$.

Second, the standard deviation of scores in each group must be known. If the scores in a group are quite variable, the standard deviation will be large, indicating that chance may have played a large role in producing the results.

The next replication of the study might generate a very different set of group scores. If the scores in a group are all very similar, however, the standard deviation will be small, which suggests that the same result would probably occur for that group if the study were repeated. Thus, the *difference* between groups is more likely to be significant when each group's standard deviation is small.

Third, we need to take the sample size, N, into account. The larger the number of subjects or observations, the more likely it is that a given difference between means is significant. This is because, with larger samples, random factors within a group—the unusual performance of a few people who were sleepy or anxious or hostile, for example—are more likely to be canceled out by the majority, who better represent people in general. The same effect of sample size can be seen in coin tossing. If you toss a quarter five times, you might not be too surprised if heads comes up 80 percent of the time. If you get 80 percent heads after one hundred tosses, however, you might begin to suspect that this is probably not due to chance alone and that some other effect, perhaps some bias in the coin, is significant in producing the results.

To summarize, as the differences between the means get larger, as N increases, and as standard deviations get smaller, t increases. This increase in t raises the researcher's confidence in the significance of the difference between means.

Now we will calculate the t statistic and show how it is interpreted. The formula for t is:

$$t = \frac{M_1 - M_2}{\sqrt{\dfrac{(N_1 - 1)\, S_1^2 + (N_2 - 1)\, S_2^2}{N_1 + N_2 - 2}}}$$

where: M_1 = mean of group 1
  M_2 = mean of group 2
  N_1 = number of scores or observations for group 1
  N_2 = number of scores or observations for group 2
  S_1 = standard deviation of group 1 scores
  S_2 = standard deviation of group 2 scores

Despite appearances, this formula is quite simple. In the numerator is the difference between the two group means; t will get larger as this difference gets larger. The denominator contains an estimate of the standard deviation of the *differences* between group means; in other words, it suggests how much the difference between group means would vary if the experiment were repeated many times. Since this estimate is in the denominator, the value of t will get smaller as the standard deviation of group differences gets larger. For the data in Table A.2,

$$t = \frac{M_1 - M_2}{\sqrt{\dfrac{(N_1 - 1)\, S_1^2 + (N_2 - 1)\, S_2^2}{N_1 + N_2 - 2}}} = \frac{7.23 - 5}{\sqrt{\dfrac{(12)(5.09) + (12)(4.46)}{24}}}$$

$$= \frac{2.23}{\sqrt{4.78}} = 1.02 \text{ with 24 df}$$

To determine what a particular t means, we must use the value of N and a special statistical table called, appropriately enough, the *t table*. We have reproduced part of the t table in Table A.5.

	p Value		
df	.10 (10%)	.05 (5%)	.01 (1%)
4	1.53	2.13	3.75
9	1.38	1.83	2.82
14	1.34	1.76	2.62
19	1.33	1.73	2.54
22	1.32	1.71	2.50
24	1.32	1.71	2.49

TABLE A.5 _____

The _t_ Table
This table allows the researcher to determine whether an obtained t value is statistically significant. If the t value is larger than the one in the appropriate row in the .05 column, the difference between means that generated that t score is usually considered statistically significant.

First, find the computed value of *t* in the row corresponding to the **degrees of freedom,** or **df,** associated with the experiment. In this case, degrees of freedom are simply $N_1 + N_2 - 2$ (or two less than the total sample size or number of scores). Since our experiment had 13 subjects per group, df = $13 + 13 - 2 = 24$. In the row for 24 df in Table A.5, you will find increasing values of *t* in each column. These columns correspond to decreasing *p* values, the probabilities that the difference between means occurred by chance. If an obtained *t* value is equal to or larger than one of the values in the *t* table (on the correct df line), then the difference between means that generated that *t* is said to be significant at the .10, .05, or .01 level of probability. Suppose, for example, that an obtained *t* (with 19 df) was 2.00. Looking along the 19 df row, you find that 2.00 is larger than the value in the .05 column. This allows you to say that the probability that the difference between means occurred by chance was no greater than .05, or 5 in 100. If the *t* had been greater than the value in the .01 column, the probability of a chance result would have been only .01, or 1 in 100.

The *t* value from our experiment was only 1.02, with 24 df. Because 1.02 is smaller than all the values in the 24 df row, the difference between the high- and low-incentive groups could have occurred by chance more than 10 times in 100. As noted earlier, when an obtained *t* is not large enough to exceed *t* table values at the .05 level or less, it is not usually considered statistically significant. Perhaps the difference between our incentive groups was not large enough, the group Ns were not large enough, or the variance within the groups was too large.

Beyond the t test   Many experiments in psychology are considerably more complex than simple comparisons between two groups. They often involve three or more experimental and control groups. Some experiments also include more than one independent variable. For example, suppose we had been interested not only in the effect of incentive size on performance, but also in the effect of problem difficulty. We might then create six groups whose subjects would perform easy or difficult problems with low, high, or very high incentives.

In an experiment like this, the results might be due to the incentive, the problem difficulty, or the combined effects (known as the *interaction*) of the two. Analyzing the size and source of these effects is typically accomplished through procedures known as *analysis of variance*. The details of analysis of variance are beyond the scope of this book, but the statistical significance of each effect is influenced by differences between means, standard deviation, and sample size in much the same way as described for the *t* test.

For more detailed information about how analysis of variance and other inferential statistics are used to understand and interpret the results of psychological research, consider taking courses in research methods and statistical or quantitative methods.

KEY TERMS

Definitions of terms appear on the pages shown in parentheses.

central tendency (696)

data (695)

degrees of freedom (df) (703)

descriptive statistic (696)

frequency histogram (695)

inferential statistics (701)

mean (697)

median (696)

mode (696)

normal distribution (698)

null hypothesis (695)

percentile score (699)

range (697)

standard deviation (SD) (698)

standard score (700)

t test (701)

variability (697)

Answers to Questions in Linkages Diagrams

CHAPTER 2/HUMAN DEVELOPMENT

Question	Linkage to	Location of Answer
How can people inherit anything from their parents?	*Chapter 3* Biological Bases of Behavior	*Chapter 2* pp. 36–38
How does the world look and sound to a newborn baby?	*Chapter 4* Sensation	*Chapter 2* pp. 42–43
Do infants perceive the world as adults do?	*Chapter 5* Perception	*Chapter 5* pp. 198–199
How do boys learn to be men and girls learn to be women?	*Chapter 7* Learning	*Chapter 2* pp. 61–62
Are people born with an innate, unique ability to learn language?	*Chapter 9* Thought and Language	*Chapter 2* pp. 74–75
Why are some people smarter than others?	*Chapter 10* Mental Abilities	*Chapter 10* pp. 380–388
When does personality begin to develop?	*Chapter 14* Personality	*Chapter 2* pp. 49–50
When do mental disorders begin and develop?	*Chapter 15* Abnormal Psychology	*Chapter 15* pp. 578–579

CHAPTER 3/BIOLOGICAL BASES OF BEHAVIOR

Question	Linkage to	Location of Answer
How does the brain change as people develop throughout life, and how do these biological changes affect people?	*Chapter 2* Human Development	*Chapter 3* pp. 114–115
How do people learn what's out in the world? How is that information represented in the cortex?	*Chapter 4* Sensation	*Chapter 4* pp. 120–124
Where and how are memories stored?	*Chapter 8* Memory	*Chapter 8* pp. 314–315
What parts of the brain make thought and language possible?	*Chapter 9* Thought and Language	*Chapter 3* pp. 99–101
Do people have "two brains," one controlling verbal abilities and another for spatial abilities?	*Chapter 10* Mental Abilities	*Chapter 3* pp. 102–105
Do physical responses determine what people feel? What role does the brain play in emotion?	*Chapter 12* Emotion	*Chapter 12* pp. 446–460
Is schizophrenia caused by a chemical imbalance in the brain?	*Chapter 15* Abnormal Psychology	*Chapter 15* pp. 569–570
Does nature give people an instinctive urge to be aggressive?	*Chapter 18* Social Psychology (2)	*Chapter 18* pp. 690–691

CHAPTER 4/SENSATION

Question	Linkage to	Location of Answer
What does the world look and sound like to a newborn baby?	*Chapter 2* Human Development	*Chapter 2* pp. 42–43
How does the brain get information about the world?	*Chapter 3* Biological Bases of Behavior	*Chapter 4* pp. 120–124
What determines whether people sense a stimulus? How do sensations become perceptions?	*Chapter 5* Perception	*Chapter 5* pp. 162–168
How do drugs affect the senses?	*Chapter 6* Consciousness	*Chapter 6* pp. 228–238
Do people need a certain amount of sensory stimulation?	*Chapter 11* Motivation	*Chapter 4* pp. 156–157
How is the emotional response to pain different from the response to other sensations?	*Chapter 12* Emotion	*Chapter 4* pp. 152–154
What kinds of sensations are labeled "abnormal"?	*Chapter 15* Abnormal Psychology	*Chapter 15* pp. 546–548, 559–560

CHAPTER 5/PERCEPTION

Question	Linkage to	Location of Answer
Do infants perceive the world as adults do?	*Chapter 2* Human Development	*Chapter 5* pp. 198–199
What happens in the brain when people pay attention to a stimulus?	*Chapter 3* Biological Bases of Behavior	*Chapter 5* pp. 194–195
What determines whether people perceive a stimulus?	*Chapter 4* Sensation	*Chapter 5* pp. 168–171
Can people perceive stimuli without being aware of them?	*Chapter 6* Consciousness	*Chapter 6* pp. 209–211
Does language determine what people perceive?	*Chapter 9* Thought and Language	*Chapter 9* pp. 359–362
Do smarter people process information faster than other people?	*Chapter 10* Mental Abilities	*Chapter 10* pp. 390–391
How does stress affect the ability to pay attention to various stimuli?	*Chapter 13* Stress and Coping	*Chapter 5* pp. 193–194, 196
Do perceptions of people follow the same principles as perceptions of objects?	*Chapter 17* Social Psychology (1)	*Chapter 17* pp. 632, 640, 652–653

CHAPTER 6/CONSCIOUSNESS

Question	Linkage to	Location of Answer
How do drugs act in the nervous system to alter consciousness?	*Chapter 3* Biological Bases of Behavior	*Chapter 3* pp. 108–110
Can people perceive stimuli without being aware of them?	*Chapter 5* Perception	*Chapter 5* pp. 168–171
How can using drugs in unfamiliar surroundings make an overdose more likely?	*Chapter 7* Learning	*Chapter 7* pp. 252–253
Can expectations about a drug alter its effects on consciousness?	*Chapter 9* Thought and Language	*Chapter 6* pp. 236–237
Do forgotten memories remain at some subconscious level in the mind?	*Chapter 8* Memory	*Chapter 8* pp. 305–307
Can unconscious processes cause mental disorder?	*Chapter 15* Abnormal Psychology	*Chapter 15* pp. 549–550
What are the effects of meditation on stress and other psychological problems?	*Chapter 16* Treatment of Psychological Disorders	*Chapter 6* p. 228

CHAPTER 7/LEARNING

Question	Linkage to	Location of Answer
How do children learn a gender identity?	*Chapter 3* Human Development	*Chapter 7* pp. 276–277
How do people remember what they learn?	*Chapter 8* Memory	*Chapter 8* pp. 284–287
Can the principles of conditioning explain how people learn to speak?	*Chapter 9* Thought and Language	*Chapter 9* pp. 357–359
What events can produce learning by acting as rewards?	*Chapter 11* Motivation	*Chapter 11* p. 412
How can people learn to love what they once hated or to fear what they once loved?	*Chapter 12* Emotion	*Chapter 7* pp. 249–250, 254–255
Are people the sum of what they have learned?	*Chapter 14* Personality	*Chapter 14* pp. 527–531
How do therapists use knowledge about learning to help people with mental disorders?	*Chapter 16* Treatment of Psychological Disorders	*Chapter 16* pp. 600–605
Can television teach children to be aggressive? What determines whether children will imitate what they see, on television or elsewhere?	*Chapter 18* Social Psychology (2)	*Chapter 7* pp. 270–271

CHAPTER 8/MEMORY

Question	Linkage to	Location of Answer
Why do children's memories improve?	*Chapter 2* Human Development	*Chapter 8* pp. 310–311
Is there something physical that corresponds to each memory? Where and how are memories stored?	*Chapter 3* Biological Bases of Behavior	*Chapter 8* pp. 314–315
How can seemingly lost memories be brought into consciousness?	*Chapter 6* Consciousness	*Chapter 8* pp 305–307
How does memory shape problem solving and decision making? What makes experts different from laypeople?	*Chapter 9* Thought and Language	*Chapter 9* pp. 337, 341–342
Can mentally retarded people remember events as well as other people can?	*Chapter 10* Mental Abilities	*Chapter 8* p. 311
How do emotions affect what people remember?	*Chapter 12* Emotions	*Chapter 12* pp. 468–469
Can forgotten memories shape personality?	*Chapter 14* Personality	*Chapter 14* pp. 510–511

CHAPTER 9/THOUGHT AND LANGUAGE

Question	Linkage to	Location of Answer
How do children learn concepts? How do they learn to speak?	*Chapter 2* Human Development	*Chapter 9* p. 329–331
What parts of the brain make thought and language possible?	*Chapter 3* Biological Bases of Behavior	*Chapter 3* pp. 99–101
How do people perceive speech? Does language determine what people perceive?	*Chapter 5* Perception	*Chapter 9* pp. 354, 359–362
Can putting a problem out of consciousness help solve it?	*Chapter 6* Consciousness	*Chapter 9* p. 340
Can human learning be explained without considering cognitive processes?	*Chapter 7* Learning	*Chapter 7* pp. 271–275

CHAPTER 9/THOUGHT AND LANGUAGE (Continued)

Question	Linkage to	Location of Answer
How does memory affect problem solving and decision making? What makes experts different from laypeople?	*Chapter 8* Memory	*Chapter 9* pp. 337, 341–342
How does stress change the ability to solve problems and make decisions?	*Chapter 13* Stress and Coping	*Chapter 13* pp. 500–501
What is different about the thought and language of schizophrenics?	*Chapter 15* Abnormal Psychology	*Chapter 9* pp. 360–361

CHAPTER 10/MENTAL ABILITIES

Question	Linkage to	Location of Answer
How do mental abilities change over the lifespan?	*Chapter 2* Human Development	*Chapter 10* pp. 400–401
Are spatial and verbal abilities controlled by different parts of the brain?	*Chapter 3* Biological Bases of Behavior	*Chapter 3* pp. 102–105
Do smarter people process information faster than other people?	*Chapter 5* Perception	*Chapter 10* pp. 390–391
Can mentally retarded people remember events as well as other people can?	*Chapter 8* Memory	*Chapter 8* p. 311
What kinds of thought processes are associated with creativity?	*Chapter 9* Thought and Language	*Chapter 10* pp. 395–396
How does increased motivation influence performance on tasks that draw on mental abilities?	*Chapter 11* Motivation	*Chapter 11* pp. 411–412
Do creative geniuses have different personalities than other people?	*Chapter 14* Personality	*Chapter 10* p. 396
Are smart people less likely than others to change their minds?	*Chapter 17* Social Psychology (1)	*Chapter 17* p. 635

CHAPTER 11/MOTIVATION

Question	Linkage to	Location of Answer
How does the brain affect eating? How do hormones affect sexual behavior in humans?	*Chapter 3* Biological Bases of Behavior	*Chapter 11* pp. 416–418, 422–424
Do people need a certain amount of sensory stimulation?	*Chapter 4* Sensation	*Chapter 4* pp. 156–157
What events can act as reinforcers?	*Chapter 7* Learning	*Chapter 11* pp. 409–410
How are drives such as hunger different from emotions?	*Chapter 12* Emotion	*Chapter 12* pp. 444–445
What happens when motives are in conflict?	*Chapter 13* Stress and Coping	*Chapter 11* pp. 438–439
Can behavior be motivated by needs and drives of which people are unaware?	*Chapter 14* Personality	*Chapter 14* pp. 510–512, 522–523
Why do people kill themselves?	*Chapter 15* Abnormal Psychology	*Chapter 15* pp. 562–564
Why are people aggressive?	*Chapter 18* Social Psychology (2)	*Chapter 18* pp. 672–679

CHAPTER 12/EMOTION

Question	Linkage to	Location of Answer
Do physical responses determine what people feel? What role does the brain play in emotion?	*Chapter 3* Biological Bases of Behavior	*Chapter 12* pp. 446–460
How can people learn to like what they once loathed, or to fear what once seemed harmless?	*Chapter 7* Learning	*Chapter 7* pp. 249–250, 254–255
How do emotions affect what people remember?	*Chapter 8* Memory	*Chapter 12* pp. 468–469
How do cognitions affect emotions?	*Chapter 9* Thought and Language	*Chapter 12* pp. 456–460
Can emotions act as motivators of behavior?	*Chapter 11* Motivation	*Chapter 12* p. 467
What emotions are tied to stress? Can they harm one's health?	*Chapter 13* Stress and Coping	*Chapter 13* pp. 483–484, 492–493
Which mental disorders are disturbances of emotions?	*Chapter 15* Abnormal Psychology	*Chapter 15* pp. 561–566
Does fear produce aggression? Does empathy produce altruism?	*Chapter 18* Social Psychology (2)	*Chapter 18* pp. 675, 676, 679–680

CHAPTER 13/STRESS AND COPING

Question	Linkage to	Location of Answer
What are the physical consequences of stress?	*Chapter 3* Biological Bases of Behavior	*Chapter 13* pp. 479–483
How does stress affect the ability to pay attention to various stimuli?	*Chapter 5* Perception	*Chapter 5* pp. 193–194, 196
When people are under stress, how does their ability to solve problems and make decisions change?	*Chapter 9* Thought and Language	*Chapter 13* pp. 500–501
What are some common emotional responses to stress?	*Chapter 12* Emotion	*Chapter 13* pp. 483–484
Are there "stress-prone" personalities?	*Chapter 14* Personality	*Chapter 14* pp. 538–539
What role does stress play in the appearance of mental disorders?	*Chapter 15* Abnormal Psychology	*Chapter 15* pp. 551, 560–566, 571
Can people be helped to cope with stress more effectively?	*Chapter 16* Treatment of Psychological Disorders	*Chapter 13* pp. 494–500
Does social support help people cope with stress?	*Chapter 17* Social Psychology (1)	*Chapter 13* pp. 490–491, 493

CHAPTER 14/PERSONALITY

Question	Linkage to	Location of Answer
When does personality begin to develop?	*Chapter 2* Human Development	*Chapter 2* pp. 49–50
Are there biological predispositions that shape personality?	*Chapter 3* Biological Bases of Behavior	*Chapter 14* pp. 522–524
How might learning principles help explain personality?	*Chapter 7* Learning	*Chapter 14* pp. 527–531
Can behavior be motivated by needs and drives of which people are unaware?	*Chapter 11* Motivation	*Chapter 14* pp. 510–512, 522–523
Are there "stress-prone" personalities?	*Chapter 13* Stress and Coping	*Chapter 14* pp. 538–539

CHAPTER 14/PERSONALITY (Continued)

Question	Linkage to	Location of Answer
How do various theories of personality explain abnormal behavior?	*Chapter 15* Abnormal Psychology	*Chapter 15* pp. 548–551
Can personality be changed?	*Chapter 16* Treatment of Psychological Disorders	*Chapter 16* pp. 600–608
Is there one set of personality traits that makes a person a good leader?	*Chapter 18* Social Psychology (2)	*Chapter 18* p. 689

CHAPTER 15/ABNORMAL PSYCHOLOGY

Question	Linkage to	Location of Answer
What kinds of mental disorders appear in the early stages of life?	*Chapter 2* Human Development	*Chapter 15* pp. 578–579
What biological factors contribute to mental disorders?	*Chapter 3* Biological Bases of Behavior	*Chapter 15* pp. 565–566, 569–570, 571, 576–577
Can people learn to be abnormal?	*Chapter 7* Learning	*Chapter 15* pp. 550, 557–558, 560, 564–565, 570, 572–573
What is different about the thought and language of schizophrenics?	*Chapter 9* Thought and Language	*Chapter 9* pp. 360–361
What role does stress play in the appearance of abnormal behavior?	*Chapter 13* Stress and Coping	*Chapter 15* pp. 551, 557, 559, 565, 571, 572–573, 574
How do various theories of personality explain abnormal behavior?	*Chapter 14* Personality	*Chapter 15* pp. 548–551
What treatments are available to deal with abnormal behavior?	*Chapter 16* Treatment of Psychological Disorders	*Chapter 16* pp. 592–598, 597–600, 601–607, 611–614
Does the social environment define what behavior is normal and what is abnormal?	*Chapter 17* Social Psychology (1)	*Chapter 15* pp. 545–548

CHAPTER 16/TREATMENT OF PSYCHOLOGICAL DISORDERS

Question	Linkage to	Location of Answer
What are some of the pros and cons of using drugs to treat psychological disorders?	*Chapter 3* Biological Bases of Behavior	*Chapter 16* pp. 614–615
Can meditation help people deal with psychological problems?	*Chapter 6* Consciousness	*Chapter 6* pp. 226–227, 228
How can learning principles help clients develop better ways of thinking and acting?	*Chapter 7* Learning	*Chapter 16* pp. 600–605
How can therapists alter clients' maladaptive thought patterns?	*Chapter 9* Thought and Language	*Chapter 16* pp. 605–607
How does a person's motivation for treatment affect the outcome of therapy?	*Chapter 11* Motivation	*Chapter 16* pp. 620, 622
Can people be helped to cope with stress more effectively?	*Chapter 13* Stress and Coping	*Chapter 13* pp. 494–500
Are certain personality characteristics associated with successful psychotherapy?	*Chapter 14* Personality	*Chapter 16* pp. 620–622

CHAPTER 17/THE INDIVIDUAL IN THE SOCIAL WORLD

Question	Linkage to	Location of Answer
How does perception of objects relate to perception of people?	*Chapter 5* Perception	*Chapter 17* pp. 632, 640, 652–653
How are impressions of others represented and distorted in memory?	*Chapter 8* Memory	*Chapter 17* pp. 640–641, 653
Are smart people less likely than others to be persuaded to change their minds?	*Chapter 10* Mental Abilities	*Chapter 17* p. 635
What needs do other people fulfill?	*Chapter 11* Motivation	*Chapter 11* pp. 428–435
Why are people often unhappy after they move up in the world?	*Chapter 12* Emotion	*Chapter 17* pp. 627–628
How do other people affect one's experience of stress?	*Chapter 13* Stress and Coping	*Chapter 13* pp. 490–491, 493, 499–500
Does the social environment define what behavior is normal and what is abnormal?	*Chapter 15* Abnormal Psychology	*Chapter 15* pp. 545–548
What determines whether people conform and whether they obey someone else?	*Chapter 18* Social Psychology (2)	*Chapter 18* pp. 660–665, 668–670

CHAPTER 18/GROUP PROCESSES AND INTERPERSONAL BEHAVIOR

Question	Linkage to	Location of Answer
Does human aggression have biological sources?	*Chapter 3* Biological Bases of Behavior	*Chapter 18* pp. 690–691
When and how do the opinions of others affect what one perceives?	*Chapter 5* Perception	*Chapter 18* pp. 656–663, 665–671, 686–689
How do people learn from others?	*Chapter 7* Learning	*Chapter 7* pp. 269–271
Do problem-solving and decision-making strategies change when people work in groups?	*Chapter 9* Thought and Language	*Chapter 18* pp. 686–689
What role do emotional factors play in aggression?	*Chapter 12* Emotion	*Chapter 18* pp. 675–676
Is there one set of personality traits that makes a person a good leader?	*Chapter 14* Personality	*Chapter 18* p. 689
Does group psychotherapy offer advantages over individualized therapy?	*Chapter 16* Treatment of Psychological Disorders	*Chapter 16* pp. 595–596

Absolute threshold The minimum amount of stimulus energy that can be detected 50 percent of the time. (See also *internal noise* and *response bias*.)

Accessory structure A structure, such as the lens of the eye, that modifies a stimulus. In some sensory systems, this is the first step in sensation.

Accommodation (1) The lens's ability to change its shape and bend light rays so that objects are in focus. (2) The process of modifying schemes as the infant tries out familiar schemes on objects that do not fit them.

Acetylcholine The neurotransmitter used by cholinergic neurons in the peripheral nervous system to control muscle contractions and in the central nervous system to control movement and memory.

Achievement test A test that measures the current status of a person's knowledge of a specific subject.

Acoustic code A mental representation of information as a sequence of sounds.

Acquisition The process through which a conditioned stimulus begins to produce a conditioned response.

Action potential An impulse that travels down an axon when the neuron becomes depolarized and sodium rushes into the cell. This kind of nerve communication is "all or none": the cell either fires at full strength or does not fire at all.

Active sleep (also called *REM sleep*) A stage of sleep during which the EEG resembles that of someone who is active and awake; the heart rate, respiration, blood pressure, and other physiological patterns are also very much like those occurring during the day. At the same time, the sleeper begins rapid eye movements beneath closed lids, and muscle tone has decreased to the point of paralysis.

Acuity Visual resolution or clarity, which is greatest in the fovea because of its large concentration of photoreceptors.

Adaptive reading A skill in which a reader speeds up and slows down according to the information content of the material and the level of comprehension that it requires.

Addiction Development of a physical need for a psychoactive drug.

Adrenal gland A part of the sympathetic nervous system that affects target organs by releasing adrenaline and noradrenaline into the bloodstream. The adrenal medulla facilitates communication between the brain and various target organs; the adrenal cortex is involved in stress reactions. The release of adrenaline is responsible for the fight-or-flight syndrome. (See also *fight-or-flight syndrome*.)

Affective disorder See *mood disorder*.

Affirmation rule (also called *one-feature rule*) A rule which requires that an item must have one specific attribute to be classified as a member of a concept.

Age regression A phenomenon, displayed by some hypnotized people, that involves recalling and reenacting behaviors from childhood.

Aggression An act that is intended to cause harm or damage to another person.

Agonist A molecule, very similar to a neurotransmitter, that may occupy receptor sites for that neurotransmitter. Many drugs mimic neurotransmitters in this way. They fit snugly into the receptors and change a cell's membrane potential just as the neurotransmitter would.

Agoraphobia A strong fear of being alone or away from the security of home.

Alarm reaction The first stage in the general adaptation syndrome, which involves some version of the fight-or-flight response. In the face of mild stressors the reaction may simply involve changes in heart rate, respiration, and perspiration that help the body regulate itself. More severe stressors prompt more dramatic alarm reactions, rapidly mobilizing the body's adaptive energy. (See also *fight-or-flight syndrome, resistance,* and *exhaustion*.)

Alcoholism A pattern of continuous or intermittent drinking that may lead to addiction and almost always causes severe social, physical, and other problems.

Algorithm A systematic procedure that cannot fail to produce a solution to a problem. It is not usually the most efficient way to produce a solution. (See also *heuristic*.)

Alpha wave Very rhythmic brain waves that occur at a speed of about 8 to 12 cycles per second and are evident in stage 0, the stage preceding sleep, during which the person is relaxed, with eyes closed, but awake.

Altered state of consciousness (also called *alternate state of consciousness*) A condition that exists when quantitative and qualitative changes in mental processes are extensive enough that the person or objective observers notice significant differences in psychological and behavioral functioning.

Altruism A desire to help another person, rather than to benefit oneself.

Amplitude The difference between the peak and the trough of a waveform.

Analgesia The absence of pain sensation in the presence of a normally painful stimulus. The brain appears to use serotonin, endorphins, enkephalins, and dynorphins to block painful stimuli.

Anal stage The second of Freud's psychosexual stages, usually occurring during the second year of life, in which the focus of pleasure and conflict shifts from the mouth to the anus. The demand for toilet training conflicts with the child's instinctual pleasure in having bowel movements at will.

Anchoring heuristic A shortcut in the thought process that involves adding new information to existing information to reach a conclusion.

Androgen A masculine hormone that circulates in the blood-stream and regulates sexual motivation in both sexes. The principal androgen is testosterone and relatively more androgens circulate in men than in women. (See also *testosterone.*)

Anorexia nervosa An eating disorder characterized by self-starvation and dramatic weight loss.

ANS See *autonomic nervous system.*

Antagonist A drug that is similar enough to a neurotransmitter to occupy its receptor sites on nerve cells, but not similar enough to fit snugly and change the cells' membrane potential. While it remains attached to the receptors, the drug competes with and blocks neurotransmitters from occupying and acting on the receptors.

Anterograde amnesia A loss of memory for any event that occurs after a brain injury.

Antidepressant A drug that relieves depression.

Antipsychotic A drug that alleviates the symptoms of schizophrenia or other severe forms of psychological disorder.

Antisocial personality A personality disorder involving a long-term, persistent pattern of impulsive, selfish, unscrupulous, even criminal behavior.

Anxiety disorder A condition in which intense feelings of apprehension are long-standing or disruptive. (See also *phobia, generalized anxiety disorder, panic disorder,* and *obsessive-compulsive disorder.*

Archetype According to Jung, a classic image or concept that is part of the collective unconscious. One archetype is the idea of mother; everyone is born with a kind of predisposition to see and react to certain people as mother figures.

Arousal A general level of activation that is reflected in several physiological systems and can be measured by electrical activity in the brain, heart action, muscle tension, and the state of many other organ systems.

Arousal theory A theory of motivation stating that people are motivated to behave in ways that maintain what is, for them, an optimal level of arousal.

Artificial concept Concepts that can be clearly defined by a set of rules or properties, so that each member of the concept has all of the defining properties and no nonmember does. (See also *natural concept.*)

Artificial intelligence The field that studies how to program computers to imitate the products of human perception, understanding, and thought.

Assertiveness and social skills training A set of methods for teaching clients who are anxious or unproductive in social situations how to interact with others more comfortably and effectively.

Assimilation The process of taking in new information about objects by trying out existing schemes on objects that fit those schemes.

Association cortex Those parts of the cerebral cortex that receive information from more than one sense or combine sensory and motor information to perform such complex

cognitive tasks as associating words with images or abstract thought.

Attachment An affectionate, close, and enduring relationship with the single person with whom a baby has shared many experiences.

Attention The process of directing and focusing certain psychological resources, usually by voluntary control, to enhance information processing, performance, and mental experience.

Attitude A predisposition toward a particular cognitive, emotional, or behavioral reaction to an object, individual, group, situation, or action.

Attribution The process of explaining the causes of people's behavior, including one's own. (See also *attributional bias.*)

Attributional bias A tendency to distort one's view of behavior. (See also *egocentric bias, ego-defensive bias,* and *fundamental attribution error.*)

Auditory nerve The structure that carries stimuli from the cochlea's hair cells to the brain to facilitate hearing.

Authoritarian parent A firm, punitive, and unsympathetic parent, who values obedience from the child and authority for himself or herself, does not encourage independence, is detached, and seldom praises the child. The result of this parenting style is often an unfriendly, distrustful, and withdrawn child.

Authoritarian personality The traits exhibited by people who view the world as a strict social hierarchy and feel they have the right to demand deference and cooperation from all those who have lower status.

Authoritative parent A parent who reasons with the child, encourages give and take, is firm but understanding, and gives the child more responsibility as he or she gets older. Children of this type of parent are usually friendly, cooperative, self-reliant, and socially responsible.

Autokinetic effect An illusion, caused by an absence of reference points, in which a single point of light viewed in an otherwise dark environment appears to move.

Autonomic nervous system (ANS) A subsystem of the peripheral nervous system that carries messages between the central nervous system and the heart, lungs, and other organs and glands in the body. It regulates the activity of these organs and glands to meet varying demands placed upon the body and also provides information to the brain about that activity.

Availability heuristic A shortcut in the thought process that involves judging the frequency or probability of an event or hypothesis by how easily the hypothesis or examples of the event can be brought to mind. Thus people tend to choose the hypothesis or alternative that is most mentally "available."

Average evoked potential A series of evoked brain potentials made in response to the same stimuli. The recording reflects the firing of large groups of neurons, within different regions of the brain, at different times during the sequence of information processing. The pattern of peaks provides information about mental chronometry that is more precise than overall reaction time. (See also *evoked potential.*)

Aversive conditioning A method for reducing unwanted behaviors by using classical conditioning principles to create a negative response to some stimulus.

Avoidance conditioning A type of learning in which an

organism responds to a signal in a way that avoids exposure to an aversive stimulus.

Axon   The fiber that carries signals from the body of a neuron out to where communication occurs with other neurons. Each neuron generally has only one axon leaving the cell body but that one axon may have many branches.

Babblings   Repetitions of syllables; the first sounds infants make that resemble speech.

Base-rate frequency   An overall probability or frequency of occurrence for a phenomena.

Basilar membrane   The floor of the fluid-filled duct that runs through the cochlea. Waves passing through the fluid in the duct move the basilar membrane, and this movement deforms hair cells that touch the membrane. (See also *cochlea* and *hair cells.*)

Behavioral approach   Personality theories based on the assumption that human behavior is determined mainly by what a person has learned in life, especially by what a person has learned from interacting with other people. According to this approach, the consistency of people's learning histories, not an inner personality structure, produces characteristic behavior patterns.

Behavioral medicine   A broad-based movement focused on how behavior and illness are linked. Medical doctors, psychologists, dentists, nurses, health educators, social workers, and other health-related professionals work together to find ways to use behavioral science to aid in the prevention, detection, treatment, and cure of physical disease.

Behaviorism   An approach to consciousness and other aspects of human behavior that focuses on analyzing the relationship between behavior and its environment, how stimuli bring about responses.

Behavior modification   See *behavior therapy.*

Behavior therapy   (also called *behavior modification*) Treatments that use learning principles to change behavior by helping, often literally teaching, clients to act as well as think differently.

Biased sample   A group of research subjects selected from a population whose every member does *not* have an equal chance of being chosen for study.

Binocular disparity   A depth cue based on the difference between the two retinal images. It exists because each eye receives a slightly different view of the world. This difference, which decreases with distance, is measured by the brain, which combines the two images to create the perception of a single image located at a particular distance.

Biofeedback   A process through which some people can become aware of and may learn to control certain physiological processes at the nonconscious level.

Biological model   See *medical model.*

Biological psychologist   (also called *physiological psychologist*) A psychologist who analyzes the biological factors influencing behavior and mental processes.

Biological psychology   (also called *physiological psychology*) The psychological specialty that researches the physical and chemical changes that cause and occur in response to behavior and mental processes.

Bipolar cells   Cells through which a visual stimulus passes after going to the photoreceptor cells and before going to the ganglion cells.

Bipolar disorder   A condition in which a person alternates daily or even hourly between the two emotional extremes of depression and mania.

Bisexual   People who engage in sexual activities with partners of both sexes.

Blind spot   The point at which the axons from all of the ganglion cells converge and exit the eyeball. This exit point has no photoreceptors and is therefore insensitive to light.

Blocking   A phenomenon in which pairing a second conditioned stimulus with an unconditioned stimulus will not create a conditioned reponse to the new conditioned stimulus.

Bottom-up processing   Aspects of recognition that depend first on the information about the stimulus that comes up to the brain from the sensory receptors. (See also *top-down processing.*)

Brightness   The overall intensity of all of the wavelengths that make up light.

Brown-Peterson procedure   A method for determining how long unrehearsed information remains in short-term memory. It involves presenting a stimulus to individuals, preventing them from rehearsing it by having them perform a counting task, and then testing recall of the stimulus.

Bulimia   An eating disorder that involves eating massive quantities of food and then eliminating the food by self-induced vomiting or strong laxatives.

Burnout   A gradually intensifying pattern of physical, psychological, and behavioral dysfunctions in response to a continuous flow of stressors.

Cannon-Bard theory   A theory of the experience of emotion in which the brain interprets an emotional situation through the thalamus, which sends sensory signals simultaneously to the cerebral cortex and the autonomic nervous system. The emotion becomes conscious in the cerebral cortex and emotion is experienced with or without feedback about peripheral responses.

Case study   A research method involving the intensive examination of some phenomenon in a particular individual, group, or situation. It is especially useful for studying very complex or relatively rare phenomena.

Catastrophizing   Dwelling on and overemphasizing the consequences of negative events; one of the most common cognitive stress responses.

Catatonic schizophrenia   A type of schizophrenia characterized by a movement disorder in which the individual may alternate between total immobility or stupor (sometimes holding bizarre, uncomfortable poses for long periods) and wild excitement.

Catharsis   The release of pent-up aggressive impulses through socially acceptable activities; some theorists believe it can occur vicariously, as when people watch others display aggression.

Central nervous system (CNS)   The part of the nervous system encased in bone, including the brain and the spinal cord, whose primary function is to process information provided by the sensory systems and decide on an appropriate course of action for the motor system.

Central tendency The typical value in a set of data. (See also *mode, median,* and *mean.*)

Cerebellum A part of the hindbrain whose function is to control finely coordinated movements, and to store learned associations that involve movement, such as those movements required in dancing or athletics.

Cerebral cortex The outer surface of the cerebral hemispheres. It is physically divided into four areas called the frontal, parietal, occipital, and temporal lobes. It is divided functionally into the sensory cortex, the motor cortex, and the association cortex.

Cerebral hemisphere One-half, either right or left, of the round, almost spherical, outermost part of the cerebrum.

Cerebrum (also called the *telencephalon*) The largest part of the forebrain which is divided into the right and left cerebral hemispheres and contains the striatum and the limbic system.

Characteristic frequency The frequency to which any given neuron in the auditory nerve is most sensitive.

Chromosome In every biological cell, a long, thin structure that contains genetic information in the form of more than a thousand genes strung out like a chain.

Chunk Stimuli that are perceived as one unit or a meaningful grouping of information. Most people can hold five to nine (7 plus or minus 2) chunks of information in short-term memory.

Circadian rhythm A cycle, such as waking and sleeping, that repeats about once a day.

Classical conditioning A procedure in which a neutral stimulus is paired with a stimulus that elicits a reflex or other response until the neutral stimulus alone comes to elicit a similar response.

Client-centered therapy (also called *person-centered therapy*) A type of therapy in which the client decides what to talk about and when, without direction, judgment or interpretation from the therapist. This type of treatment is characterized by three important and interrelated therapist attitudes: unconditional positive regard, empathy, and congruence. (See also *empathy, congruence,* and *unconditional positive regard.*)

Clinical psychologist A psychologist who seeks to assess, understand, and correct abnormal behavior through methods such as tests, interviews, and observations.

Closure A Gestalt grouping principle stating that we tend to fill in missing contours to form a complete object.

CNS See *central nervous system.*

Cochlea A fluid-filled, spiral structure in the ear in which auditory transduction occurs.

Coding The process by which a stimulus's physical properties are translated into a pattern of neural activity that specifically identifies those physical properties and allows the brain to process the stimulus.

Cognitive behavior therapy Treatment methods that help clients change the way they think as well as the way they behave. Cognitive obstacles are brought to light and the therapist encourages the client to try new ways of thinking.

Cognitive complexity A set of abilities related to flexibility of thought; the ability to anticipate future events and to alter a chosen course of action based on unexpected happenings; the ability to interpret the consequences of actions in a variety of ways and appreciate several aspects of a problem.

Cognitive dissonance A state in which people's cognitions about themselves or the world are inconsistent with one another. Dissonance results in uneasiness and motivates people to take some action to make the cognitions consistent.

Cognitive map A mental representation, or picture, of the environment.

Cognitive psychologist A psychologist whose research focus is on analysis of the mental processes underlying judgment, decision making, problem solving, imagining, and other aspects of human thought or cognition.

Cognitive restructuring A therapy technique or process for coping with stress that involves replacing stress-provoking thoughts with more constructive thoughts in order to make stressors less threatening and disruptive.

Cognitive style The manner in which an individual performs cognitive tasks.

Collective unconscious According to Jung, a kind of memory bank in which are stored all the images and ideas the human race has accumulated since its evolution from lower forms of life.

Community psychology A movement whose goal is to minimize or prevent psychological disorders through promoting changes in social systems and through community mental health programs designed to make treatment methods more accessible to the poor and others who are unserved or underserved by mental health professionals.

Competition Any type of behavior in which individuals try to attain a goal for themselves while denying that goal to others.

Complementary colors Colors that result in gray when lights of those two colors are mixed. Complementary colors are roughly opposite each other on the color circle.

Compliance Adjusting one's behavior to match that of a group because of directly expressed social influence.

Components The information-processing capacities of perceiving stimuli, holding information in working memory, comparing values, retrieving information from memory, and calculating sums and differences.

Concept A class or category of objects, events, or ideas that have common properties. (See also *artificial concept* and *natural concept.*)

Concrete operations According to Piaget, the third stage of cognitive development, during which children can learn to count, measure, add, and subtract; their thinking is no longer dominated by visual appearances.

Conditioned stimulus (CS) In classical conditioning, the neutral stimulus that is paired with the unconditioned stimulus.

Conditioned response (CR) In classical conditioning, the reaction that the conditioned stimulus elicits.

Conditions of worth According to Rogers, the feelings an individual experiences when the entire person, instead of a specific behavior is evaluated. The person may feel that his or her worth as a person depends on displaying the right attitudes, behaviors, and values.

Cones Photoreceptors in the retina that use one of three varieties of iodopsin, a color-sensitive photopigment, to distinguish colors. (See also *rods.*)

Conformity Changing one's behavior or beliefs to match those of other group members, generally as a result of real or imagined, though unspoken, group pressure.

Confounding variable   In an experiment, any factor that affects the dependent variable along with or instead of the independent variable. Confounding variables include *random variables,* the *Hawthorne effect,* the *placebo effect,* and *experimenter bias,* among others.

Congruence   In client-centered therapy, a consistency between the way therapists feel and the way they act toward the client; therapists' unconditional positive regard and empathy are real, not manufactured.

Conjunctive rule   A classification rule based on two or more attributes which requires that an item must have all of the attributes for it to be classified as a member of a concept.

Conscious level   The level at which mental activities that we are aware of from moment to moment occur. (See also *preconscious level.*)

Consciousness   The awareness of external stimuli and our own mental activity; also mental processes of which we may be unaware.

Conservation   The ability to recognize that a substance's important properties, such as number, volume, or weight, remain constant despite changes in shape, length, or position.

Constructionist   A view of perception taken by those who argue that the perceptual system uses fragments of sensory information to construct an image of reality. (See also *ecological view.*)

Contact hypothesis   A hypothesis, based on learning theories of prejudice, which states that stereotypes and prejudices about a group should be reduced as contact (specifically, friendly contact, as equals) with that group increases.

Continuity   A Gestalt grouping principle stating that sensations that appear to create a continuous form are perceived as belonging together.

Continuous reinforcement schedule   In operant conditioning, a pattern in which a reinforcer is delivered every time a particular response occurs.

Control group   In an experiment, the group that receives no treatment or provides some other baseline against which to compare the performance or response of the experimental group.

Convergence   (1) The reception of information by one bipolar cell from many photoreceptors. This allows bipolar cells to compare the amount of light on larger regions of the retina and increases our sensation of contrast. (2) A depth cue involving the rotation of the eyes inward to project the image of an object on each retina. The closer an object is, the more cross-eyed the viewer must become to achieve a focused image of it.

Convergent thinking   The ability to apply the rules of logic and what one knows about the world in order to narrow down the number of possible solutions to a problem or perform some other complex cognitive task.

Conversion disorder   A somatoform disorder in which a person appears to be, but actually is not, blind, deaf, paralyzed, insensitive to pain in various parts of the body, or even pregnant. (See also *somatoform disorder.*)

Cooperation   Any type of behavior in which several people work together to attain a goal.

Cornea   The curved, transparent protective layer through which light rays enter the eye.

Corpus callosum   A massive bundle of fibers that connects the right and left cerebral hemispheres and allows them to communicate with each other. Severing the corpus callosum causes difficulty in performing tasks that require information from both hemispheres, such as recognizing and naming objects.

Correlation   In research, the degree to which one variable is related to another; the strength and direction of the relationship is measured by a *correlation coefficient.* Correlations do *not* guarantee causation.

Correlation coefficient   A statistic, *r,* that summarizes the strength and direction of a relationship between two variables. Correlation coefficients vary from 0.00 to ± 1.00 and include both an absolute value, which indicates the strength of a relationship between variables, and a sign (plus or minus), which indicates the direction, positive or negative, of a relationship. An *r* of $+1.00$ or -1.00 indicates a perfect correlation; knowing the value of one variable allows you to predict with certainty the value of the other variable.

Creativity   The capacity to produce original solutions or novel compositions.

Crisis of generativity   An event described by Erikson that occurs in people's thirties and is characterized by the desire to produce something lasting, usually through parenthood or job achievement.

Critical period   An interval during which certain kinds of growth must occur if development is to proceed normally. If it does not appear during the critical period, it never will.

Cross-sectional study   A research method in which data collected simultaneously from people of different ages are compared.

Crystallized intelligence   The specific knowledge gained as a result of applying fluid intelligence. It produces verbal comprehension and skill at manipulating numbers. (See also *fluid intelligence.*)

Culture-fair test   A test composed of items carefully chosen to limit the extent to which they depend on ideas and vocabulary that are tied to a specific culture.

Dark adaptation   The increasing ability to see in the dark as time passes, due to the synthesis of more photopigments by the photoreceptors.

Data   Numbers that represent research findings and provide the basis for research conclusions.

Daydream   An altered state of consciousness in which attention shifts away from external stimuli to dwell on internal events, sometimes in a fantasy-oriented, unrealistic way.

Decay theory   A theory of forgetting stating that if people do not use information in long-term memory, it gradually fades until it is lost completely.

Decomposition   A heuristic that consists of breaking a problem into smaller elements by working backward from the final goal.

Deep structure   An abstract representation of the relationships expressed in a sentence; the various underlying meanings of a given sentence.

Defense mechanism   A psychological response that helps protect a person from anxiety and the other negative emotions accompanying stress; it does little or nothing to eliminate the source of stress.

Deficiency orientation According to Maslow, a preoccupation with meeting perceived needs for material things a person does not have that can lead to perceiving life as a meaningless exercise in disappointment and boredom.

Degrees of freedom The total sample size or number of scores in a data set less the number of experimental groups.

Delayed conditioning In classical conditioning, the most effective method of producing a strong conditioned response, which involves presenting the conditioned stimulus, leaving it on while presenting the unconditioned stimulus, and then terminating both at the same time.

Delirium An organic mental disorder that involves a clouded state of consciousness. The person has trouble "thinking straight," may be unable to focus on a conversation or other environmental events, and may appear confused. Symptoms may also include delusions, hallucinations, and disruption of the normal sleep-waking cycle.

Delta wave The slow (0.5 to 0.3 cycles per second), high amplitude brain waves that usually first appear in stage 3 sleep. When delta waves occur more than 50 percent of the time, the person has entered stage 4, the deepest level of sleep and the one from which it is most difficult to be roused.

Delusion A false belief, such as those experienced by people suffering from schizophrenia or extreme major depression.

Dementia An organic mental disorder that involves a loss of intellectual functions. It may occur alone or in combination with delirium. The most common symptoms involve loss of memory-related functions. (See also *delirium.*)

Dendrite In a neuron, the fiber that receives signals from the axons of other neurons and carries that signal to the cell body. A neuron can have up to several thousand dendrites.

Denial In psychodynamic theory, the most primitive defense mechanism, which distorts reality by leading one to deny one's impulses or refuse to recognize unpleasant events.

Deoxyribonucleic acid (DNA) A gene's molecular structure that provides the genetic code. Each DNA molecule consists of two strands of sugar, phosphate, and nitrogen-containing molecules twisted around each other in a double spiral.

Dependent variable In an experiment, the factor affected by the independent variable.

Depth perception Perception of distance, one of the most important factors underlying size and shape constancy. It also allows us to experience the world in three-dimensional depth, not as a two-dimensional movie.

Descriptive statistics Numbers that summarize a pool of research data.

Developmental psychologist A psychologist who seeks to understand, describe, and explore how behavior and mental processes change over the course of a lifetime.

Developmental psychology The psychological specialty that documents the course of people's social, emotional, moral, and intellectual development over the life span and explores how development in different domains fits together, is affected by experience, and relates to other areas of psychology.

Diathesis An inherited predisposition that leaves a person vulnerable to problems.

Diathesis-stress model An integrative approach to psychological disorders that recognizes that each person inherits certain physical predispositions that leave him or her vulnerable to problems which may or may not appear, depending on what kinds of situations a person confronts. People who must deal with particular stressors may or may not develop psychopathologies, depending on their predisposition and ability to cope with those stressors.

Dichotic listening A task in which different messages are played into each ear. This type of task has been used to demonstrate the limitations on the capacity to divide attention.

Diffusion of responsibility The process through which a person tends not to take personal responsibility for helping someone in trouble when others are present.

Discrimination Differential treatment of various groups; the behavioral component of prejudice. (See also *prejudice.*)

Discriminative stimuli Stimuli that signal whether reinforcement is available if a certain response is made.

Disease of adaptation An illness that is caused or promoted by stressors.

Disjunctive rule A classification rule that requires members of a concept to have one feature or another.

Disorganized schizophrenia A rare type of schizophrenia characterized by a variety of jumbled and unrelated delusions and hallucinations. The person may display incoherent speech, strange facial grimaces, and meaningless ritual movements and may neglect personal hygiene and lose bowel and bladder control.

Displacement In psychodynamic theory, a defense mechanism in which unacceptable impulses are diverted toward alternative targets.

Dispositional approach A personality theory based on the assumptions that 1) each person has stable, long-lasting dispositions to display certain behaviors, attitudes, and emotions; 2) these dispositions are general in that they appear in diverse situations; and 3) each person has a different set of dispositions, or at least a set of dispositions that assume a unique pattern.

Dissociation theory A theory that defines hypnosis as a condition in which people relax central control of mental processes and share some of that control with the hypnotist, who is allowed to determine what the person will experience and do. According to this theory, hypnosis is a socially agreed-upon opportunity to display one's ability to let mental functions become dissociated. (See also *role theory* and *state theory.*)

Dissociative disorder A rare condition that involves a sudden and usually temporary disruption in a person's memory, consciousness, or identity.

Divergent thinking The ability to think along many alternative paths to generate many different solutions to a problem.

DNA See *deoxyribonucleic acid.*

Dominant gene A gene that is expressed in an individual's phenotype whenever it is present in the genotype; its expression in the phenotype does not depend on its pairing with a similar gene from the other parent.

Dopamine A neurotransmitter used by dopaminergic neurons. In the substantia nigra, these neurons control movement. In the midbrain, dopaminergic neurons extend into the cerebral cortex to control movement and complex cognitive abilities.

Double-blind design A research design in which neither the experimenter nor the subjects know which is the experimental group and which is the control group. This design helps prevent *experimenter bias* (a confounding variable) from occurring.

Down's syndrome A syndrome that severely limits intelligence and is caused by the presence of an extra chromosome. Children with Down's syndrome typically have IQ scores around 40 to 50, although their scores may be raised up to 10 points through careful education.

Dream A story-like sequence of images, sensations, and perception that lasts anywhere from several seconds to many minutes and occurs mainly during REM sleep (though it may take place at other times).

Drive In drive theory, a psychological state of arousal, created by an imbalance in homeostasis that prompts an organism to take action to restore the balance and, in the process, reduce the drive. (See also *need, primary drive,* and *secondary drive.*)

Drive theory A theory of motivation stating that much motivation arises from constant imbalances in homeostasis. (See also *drive* and *homeostasis.*)

Dyslexia A condition in which a person who shows normal intelligence and full comprehension of spoken words has difficulty understanding written words.

Dysthymia A pattern of depression in which the person shows the sad mood, lack of interest, and loss of pleasure associated with major depression, but to a lesser degree and for a shorter time. (See also *major depression.*)

Echo The mental representation of a sound in sensory memory.

Echoic memory The sensory register for auditory sensations.

Eclectic An approach to psychotherapy characterized by leaning toward one approach while borrowing methods from other approaches as appropriate; many contemporary psychotherapists use this approach.

Ecological view An approach to perception that states that humans and other species are so well adapted to their natural environment that many aspects of the world are perceived automatically and at the sensory level, without requiring higher-level analysis and inferences. (See also *constructionist.*)

ECT See *electroconvulsive therapy.*

EEG See *electroencephalogram.*

Ego In psychodynamic theory, that part of the personality that makes compromises between the unreasoning demands of the id and the demands of the real world; it operates according to the reality principle. (See also *id* and *reality principle.*)

Egocentric bias The tendency to assume that others act and believe just as you do.

Ego-defensive bias The tendency to take credit for success (attributing it to one's personal characteristics or efforts) but to blame external causes for failure.

Ego psychologist A psychodynamic theorist who views the ego as a creative, adaptive force in its own right, rather than just as a mediator in conflicts among id, superego, and environment.

Eidetic memory A type of memory (commonly called *photographic memory*) that involves automatic, long-term, detailed, and vivid images of virtually everything a person has seen. About 5 percent of all school-age children have eidetic imagery, but almost no adults have it.

Elaborative rehearsal A memorization method that involves thinking about how new information relates to information already stored in long-term memory.

Electroconvulsive therapy (ECT) A very brief electric shock administered to the brain, usually to reduce profound depression that does not respond to drug treatments.

Electroencephalogram (EEG) A recording of the electrical signals produced by the brain's nerve cells, obtained through electrodes attached to the skull's surface.

Embryo The developing individual from the fourteenth day after fertilization until the third month after fertilization.

Emotion An experience that is felt as happening to the self, is generated, in part, by the cognitive appraisal of a situation, and is accompanied by both learned and reflexive physical responses.

Empathy In client-centered therapy, the therapist's attempt to appreciate how the world looks from the client's point of view. It requires an internal perspective, a focus on what the client might be thinking and feeling.

Encoding The process of putting information into a form that the memory system can accept and use; the process of constructing mental representations of physical stimuli.

Encoding specificity principle A retrieval principle stating that the ability of a cue to effectively aid retrieval depends on the degree to which it taps into information that was encoded at the time of the original learning.

Endocrine system A class of cells that form organs called glands and communicate with each other by secreting chemicals called hormones.

Endorphin One of a class of neurotransmitters that can bind to the same receptors that opiates, such as morphine and heroin, bind to and that produces the same behavioral effects of pain relief, euphoria, and, in high doses, sleep.

Environmental psychology The study of the effects of the general physical environment on behavior and mental processes.

EP See *evoked potential.*

Episodic memory Recall of a specific event that happened while you were present.

Escape conditioning A type of learning in which an organism makes a particular response in order to terminate an aversive stimulus.

Estradiol A feminine hormone; the main estrogen.

Estrogen A feminine hormone that circulates in the bloodstream of both men and women; relatively more estrogens circulate in women. One of the main estrogens is estradiol. (See also *estradiol, progesterone,* and *progestin.*)

Ethologist A scientist who studies animals in their natural environment to observe how environmental cues affect behavior.

Evoked potential (EP) A small, temporary change in EEG voltage that is evoked by some stimulus. One such change is the P300, a positive swing in electrical voltage that occurs about 300 milliseconds after a stimulus. It can be used, for example, to determine if a stimulus distracts a person's attention from a given task.

Exhaustion The last stage in the general adaptation syndrome, which occurs when resistance has depleted the body's adaptive energy and the capacity to resist is gone. The typical result of this stage is signs of physical wear and tear, especially in organs that were weak initially or heavily involved in the resistance process. Extreme cases can result in death. (See also *alarm stage* and *resistance*.)

Expected utility In the rational decision-making process, the product of the probability that a given outcome will occur and the subjective value of that outcome.

Experiment A research method in which the researcher manipulates or controls one variable, the independent variable, and then observes its effect on another variable, the dependent variable.

Experimental group In an experiment, the group that receives the experimental treatment; its performance or response is compared with that of one or more control groups.

Experimental psychologist A psychologist who conducts experiments aimed at better understanding learning, memory, perception, and other basic behavioral and mental processes.

Experimenter bias A confounding variable that occurs when an experimenter unintentionally encourages subjects to respond in a way that supports the hypothesis.

Expert system A computer program that helps people solve problems in a fairly restricted, specific area, such as the diagnosis of diseases.

Extinction The gradual disappearance of a conditioned response or operant behavior by eliminating the association between conditioned and unconditioned stimuli or by ceasing to reward behaviors.

Facial-feedback hypothesis A view of the experience of emotion which suggests that facial movements provide information about what emotion is being felt. Facial movements are involuntary, and the feedback from those movements directs further emotional responses.

Factor analysis A statistical technique that involves computing correlations between large numbers of variables that is commonly used in the study of intelligence and intelligence tests.

Familial retardation Cases of mild retardation for which no environmental or genetic cause can be found. Most of the people in this group come from families in the lower socioeconomic classes and are more likely than those suffering from a genetic defect to have a relative who is also retarded.

Family therapy A type of treatment inspired by the psychodynamic theory that many psychological disorders are rooted in family conflicts. It involves two or more individuals from the same family, one of whose problems make him or her the initially identified client, although the family itself ultimately becomes the client.

Fear appeal A method of changing attitudes that involves instilling fear in the audience; it may produce lasting effects on the cognitive component of an attitude, but does not usually have a lasting influence on behavior.

Feature analysis A view of recognition based on evidence that brain cells respond to specific features of stimuli. It holds that any stimulus can be described as a combination of features.

Feature detector Cells in the cortex that respond to specific features of objects.

Fechner's law A law stating that the perceived magnitude of a stimulus is the product of K (a constant fraction of the intensity of a stimulus for the particular sensory system involved) and the logarithm of the stimulus intensity. (See also *Weber's law.* and *Steven's power law.*)

Fetal alcohol syndrome A pattern of defects found in babies born to alcoholic women that includes physical malformations of the face and mental retardation.

Fetus The developing individual from the third month after conception until birth.

FI See *fixed interval schedule.*

Fiber tract Axons that travel together in bundles. They are also known as *pathways* or *nerves*.

Field dependent The tendency to perceive individual objects in a way that is greatly influenced by the surrounding environment.

Fight-or-flight syndrome The physical reactions initiated by the sympathetic nervous system that prepare the body for combat or to run from a threatening situation. These reactions include increased heart rate and blood pressure, rapid or irregular breathing, dilated pupils, perspiration, dry mouth, increased blood sugar, decreased gastrointestinal motility, and other changes. (See also *adrenal gland, alarm reaction,* and *sympathetic nervous system.*)

Figure That part of the visual field which has meaning, stands in front of the rest, and always seems to include the contours or borders that separate it from the relatively meaningless background. (See also *ground.*)

Fixed interval (FI) schedule In operant conditioning, a type of partial reinforcement schedule that provides reinforcement for the first response that occurs after some fixed time has passed since the last reward.

Fixed ratio (FR) schedule In operant conditioning, a type of partial reinforcement schedule that provides reinforcement following a fixed number of responses.

Flooding A procedure for reducing anxiety which involves keeping a person in a feared, but harmless situation. Once deprived of his or her normally rewarding escape pattern, the client has no reason for continued anxiety.

Fluid intelligence The basic power of reasoning and problem solving. It produces induction, deduction, reasoning, and understanding of the relations between the meaning of different ideas. (See also *crystallized intelligence.*)

Forebrain The most highly developed part of the brain; it is responsible for the most complex aspects of behavior and mental life.

Formal operational period According to Piaget, the fourth stage in cognitive development, usually beginning around age eleven. It is characterized by the ability to engage in hypothetical thinking, including the imagining of logical consequences, and the ability to think and reason about abstract concepts.

Fovea A region in the center of the retina where cones are very concentrated.

FR See *fixed ratio schedule.*

Free association A psychoanalytic method that requires the client to report everything that comes to mind as soon as it occurs, no matter how trivial, senseless, or embarrassing it may seem.

Free-floating anxiety See *generalized anxiety disorder.*

Frequency The number of complete waveforms, or cycles,

that pass by a given point in space every second. For sound waves, the unit of measure is called a *hertz*; one hertz is one cycle per second.

Frequency histogram A graphic presentation of data that consists of a set of bars each of which represents how frequently different values of variables occur in a data set.

Frequency matching (also called the *volley theory*) A theory of hearing that explains how frequency is coded: the firing rate of a neuron matches the frequency of a sound wave. For example, one neuron might fire at every peak of a wave; so a 20 hertz sound could be coded by a neuron that fires twenty times per second.

Frustration-aggression hypothesis A proposition that the existence of frustration always leads to some form of aggressive behavior.

Functional analysis of behavior A method of understanding behavior (and thus the person) that involves analyzing exactly what responses occur under what conditions. This approach emphasizes the role of operant conditioning. (See also *operant conditioning*.)

Functional fixedness A tendency to think about familiar objects in familiar ways that may prevent using them in other, more creative ways.

Functionalism An approach to consciousness that focuses on how consciousness helps people adapt to their environment.

Fundamental attribution error The tendency to be more aware of the influence of situational factors on one's own behavior than on the behavior of others.

GABA An inhibitory neurotransmitter which reduces the likelihood that the postsynaptic neuron will fire an action potential. It is used by neurons in widespread regions of the brain.

Gambler's fallacy A false belief that events in a random process will correct themselves.

Ganglion cells The cells in the retina that generate action potentials. They are stimulated by bipolar cells and their axons extend out of the retina and travel to the brain.

GAS See *general adaptation syndrome*.

Gate theory An explanation of how the nervous sytem controls the amount of pain that reaches the brain. It holds that there is a functional "gate" in the spinal cord that either lets pain impulses travel to the brain or blocks their progress. Blocking occurs by either letting other sensations through instead of the pain impulses or sending signals down the spinal cord to close the gate. (See also *analgesia*.)

Gender role General patterns of work, appearance, and behavior that a society associates with being male or female.

Gene The biological instructions inherited from both parents and located on the chromosomes that provide the blueprint for physical development throughout the lifespan. (See also *DNA, dominant gene, genotype, phenotype,* and *recessive gene*.)

General adaptation syndrome (GAS) A consistent and very general pattern of responses triggered by the effort to adapt to any stressor. The syndrome consists of three stages: the alarm reaction, resistance, and exhaustion. (See also *alarm reaction, resistance,* and *exhaustion*.)

Generalized anxiety disorder A condition that involves relatively mild but long-lasting anxiety that is not focused on any particular object or situation.

Genital stage The fifth and last of Freud's psychosexual stages, which begins during adolescence when the person begins to mature physically and sexual impulses begin to appear at the conscious level. The young person begins to seek out relationships through which sexual impulses can be gratified. This stage spans the rest of life.

Genotype The full set of genes, inherited from both parents, contained in twenty-three pairs of chromosomes.

Gestalt psychologists A group of psychologists who suggested, among other things, that there are six principles or properties behind the grouping of stimuli that lead our perceptual system to "glue" raw sensations together in particular ways, organizing stimuli into a world of shapes and patterns. (See also *proximity, similarity, continuity, closure, orientation,* and *simplicity*.)

Gestalt therapy A form of treatment based on the assumption that clients' problems arise when people behave in accordance with other people's expectations rather than on their own true feelings. Gestalt therapy seeks to create conditions in which clients can become more unified, more self-aware and self-accepting.

Gradient A continuous change across the visual field. (See also *textural gradient* and *movement gradient*.)

Grammar A set of rules for combining the symbols, such as words, used in a given language. (See also *language*.)

Ground The meaningless, contourless part of the visual field, the background. (See also *figure*.)

Group polarization The tendency for groups to make decisions that are more extreme than the decision an individual group member would make.

Group therapy Psychotherapy involving five to ten individuals. Clients can be observed interacting with one another; they can feel relieved and less alone as they listen to others who have similar difficulties, which tends to raise each client's hope and expectations for improvement; and they can learn from each other.

Groupthink A pattern of thinking that, over time, renders group members unable to realistically evaluate the wisdom of various options and decisions.

Growth orientation According to Maslow, drawing satisfaction from what is available in a person's life, rather than focusing on what is missing.

Gustation The sense that detects chemicals in solutions that come into contact with receptors inside the mouth; the sense of taste.

Hawthorne effect A confounding variable in which the subjects' behavior occurs because they know that they are being observed, rather than because of the independent variable's effect.

Helping behavior Any act that is intended to benefit another person.

Heterosexual behavior Sexual activity between people of opposite sexes.

Heuristic A mental shortcut or rule of thumb that seems to be part of the thought process. (See also *anchoring heuristic, representativeness heuristic,* and *availability heuristic*.)

Hindbrain An extension of the spinal cord contained inside the skull. Nuclei in the hindbrain, especially in the medulla, control blood pressure, heart rate, breathing, and other vital functions.

Hippocampus   A limbic system structure that plays a major role in forming new memories.

Homeostasis   The tendency for organisms to keep their physiological systems at a stable, steady level by constantly adjusting themselves in response to change.

Homosexual   Sexual motivation that is focused on those of a person's own sex.

Hormone   A chemical that is secreted by a gland into the bloodstream, which carries it throughout the body, enabling the gland to stimulate remote cells to which it has no direct connection.

Hue   The essential "color," determined by the dominant wavelength of a light. Black, white, and gray are not considered hues because they have no predominant wavelength.

Hypersomnia   A sleeping problem characterized by sleeping longer than most people at night and by feeling tired and needing to take one or more naps during the daytime.

Hypnosis   An altered state of consciousness brought on by special induction techniques and characterized by varying degrees of responsiveness to suggestions for changes in experience and behavior.

Hypothalamus   A brain structure in the forebrain that regulates hunger, thirst, and sex drives; it has many connections to and from the autonomic nervous system and to other parts of the brain.

Hypothesis   In scientific research, a prediction stated as a specific, testable proposition about a phenomenon.

Icon   A mental representation of a visual image that is retained for a very brief time by the sensory register called *iconic memory*.

Id   In psychodynamic theory, a personality component containing a reservoir of unconscious psychic energy (sometimes called *libido*) that includes the basic instincts, desires, and impulses with which all people are born. The id operates according to the pleasure principle, seeking immediate satisfaction, regardless of society's rules or the rights or feelings of others. (See also *pleasure principle*.)

Identity crisis   An event during which an adolescent attempts to develop an integrated image of himself or herself as a unique person by pulling together self-knowledge acquired during childhood.

Idiots savants   Children who are retarded in most areas but amazingly proficient at some mental skill.

Immediate memory span   The maximum number of items a person can recall perfectly after one presentation of the items, usually six or seven items. (See also *chunk*.)

Immune system   The body's first line of defense against invading substances and microorganisms. The immune system includes T-cells, which attack virally infected cells; B-cells, which form antibodies against foreign substances; and natural killer cells, which kill invaders like tumor cells and virally infected cells.

Incentive theory   A theory of motivation stating that behavior is goal-directed; actions are directed toward attaining desirable stimuli, called *positive incentives*, and toward avoiding unwanted stimuli, called *negative incentives*.

Incubation   A problem-solving technique that involves putting the problem aside for a while and turning to some other mental activity while the problem "incubates," perhaps at a subconscious level. (See also *subconscious*.)

Independent variable   In an experiment, the controlled or manipulated factor whose effect on the dependent variable is observed.

Inferential statistics   A set of procedures that provides a measure of how likely it is that research results came about by chance. These procedures put a precise mathematical value on the confidence or probability that rerunning the same experiment would yield similar (or even stronger) results.

Information processing   The process of how information is taken in, remembered or forgotten, and used. It is one method for describing children's cognitive abilities.

Information-processing system   The procedures for receiving information, representing information with symbols, and manipulating those representations, so that the brain can interpret and respond to the information.

Ingroup   Any category of which people see themselves as a member. Characteristics such as age, sex, race, occupation, and other detectable distinctions form the basis of the categories. (See also *outgroup*.)

Insecure ambivalent attachment   A type of parent-child relationship in which the child is very upset when the mother leaves, but acts angry and rejects her efforts at contact when she returns.

Insecure avoidant attachment   A type of parent-child relationship in which the child ignores or avoids the mother after a brief separation and seems just as satisfied with comfort from another person.

Insight   A sudden understanding about what is required to produce a desired effect.

Insomnia   The most common sleeping problem, in which a person feels tired during the day because of trouble falling asleep or staying asleep at night.

Instinct   An innate, automatic disposition to respond in a particular way when confronted with a specific stimulus; instincts produce behavior over which an animal has no control.

Instrumental conditioning   (also called *operant conditioning*) A procedure in which responses are learned that help produce some rewarding or desired effect.

Intellectualization   In psychodynamic theory, a defense mechanism that minimizes anxiety by viewing threatening issues in cold, abstract terms.

Intelligence   Those attributes that center around reasoning skills, knowledge of one's culture, and the ability to arrive at innovative solutions to problems.

Interference theory   A theory stating that forgetting information in long-term memory is due to the influence of other learning. (See also *retroactive interference*.)

Intermittent reinforcement schedule   See *partial reinforcement schedule*.

Internal locus of control   A characteristic of people who think of themselves as generally capable of controlling what happens to them. They have a sense of personal control over stressors, making those stressors appear less threatening and more manageable.

Internal noise   The spontaneous, random firing of nerve cells that occurs because the nervous system is always active.

Variations in internal noise can cause absolute thresholds to vary.

Interposition A depth cue whereby closer objects block one's view of things farther away.

Intervening variable A variable that is not observed directly but that helps to account for a relationship between stimuli and responses.

Introjection In psychodynamic theory, the process of incorporating, or internalizing, parental and societal values into the personality.

Iris The part of the eye that gives it its color and adjusts the amount of light entering the eye by constricting to reduce the size of the pupil or relaxing to enlarge it.

James-Lange theory A theory of the experience of emotion in which automatic, peripheral responses precede the experience of emotion. The conscious aspect of emotion arises later, when the brain observes these responses.

JND See *just-noticeable difference.*

Just-noticeable difference (JND) The smallest detectable difference in stimulus energy. (See also *Weber's law.*)

Kinesthesia The sense that tells where the parts of your body are with respect to each other.

LAD See *language acquisition device.*

Language Symbols and a set of rules for combining them that provides a vehicle for the mind's communication with itself and the most important means of communicating with others.

Language acquisition device (LAD) A hypothesized innate ability to process speech and one that allows children to understand the regularities of speech and fundamental relationships among words.

Latency period The fourth of Freud's psychosexual stages, usually beginning during the fifth year of life, in which sexual impulses lie dormant and the child focuses attention on education and other matters.

Latent content A dream's unconscious meaning, which lies in the dream's symbolism.

Latent learning Learning that is not demonstrated at the time it occurs.

Lateral area A region of the hypothalamus that signals an animal to start eating and that also affects other motivated behaviors. (See also *ventromedial nucleus.*)

Lateral geniculate nucleus (LGN) A region of the thalamus in which the axons from most of the ganglion cells in the retina finally end and form synapses.

Lateral inhibition The visual process that occurs when greater activity in one cell suppresses the activity in one retinal cell. This process creates an exaggeration of the differences in light hitting the photoreceptors and enhances visual contrasts.

Lateralization The tendency for one cerebral hemisphere to excell at a particular function or skill compared to the other hemisphere.

Law of effect A law stating that if a response made in the presence of a particular stimulus is followed by a reward, that same response is more likely to be made the next time the stimulus is encountered. Responses that are not rewarded are less likely to be performed again.

Learned helplessness A phenomenon that occurs when an organism has or believes that it has no control over its environment. The typical result of this situation or belief is to stop trying to exert control.

Learning Any relatively permanent change in an organism that results from past experience.

Lens The part of the eye directly behind the pupil. Like the lens in a camera, the lens of the eye is curved so that it bends light rays, focusing them on the retina, at the back of the eye.

Level of processing model A view stating that differences in how well something is remembered reflect the degree or depth to which incoming information is mentally processed. How long the information stays in memory depends on how elaborate the mental processing and encoding becomes.

Levels of consciousness Varying segments of mental activity of which people may or may not be aware.

LGN See *lateral geniculate nucleus.*

LH See *luteinizing hormone.*

Libido See *Id.*

Light intensity A physical dimension of light waves that refers to how much energy the light contains; it determines the brightness of light. (See also *light wavelength.*)

Light wavelength A physical dimension of light waves that refers to their length. At a given intensity, different light wavelengths produce sensations of different colors. (See also *light intensity.*)

Limbic system A set of brain structures whose components have major interconnections and influence-related functions, such as emotion, memory, and some thought processes.

Linear perspective A depth cue whereby the closer together two converging lines are, the greater the perceived distance.

Lithium A mineral salt that helps relieve depression and reduces and even prevents both the depression and mania associated with bipolar disorder.

Logic The procedures that yield a valid conclusion during the reasoning process. (See also *reasoning.*)

Longitudinal study A research method in which a group of people are repeatedly tested as they grow older.

Looming A motion cue involving a rapid expansion in the size of an image so that it fills the available space on the retina. People tend to perceive a looming object as an approaching stimulus, not as an expanding object viewed at a constant distance.

Loudness A psychological dimension of sound determined by the amplitude of a sound wave; waves with greater amplitude produce sensations of louder sounds. Loudness is described in units called *decibels.*

Lucid dreaming The awareness that a dream is a dream while it is happening. This phenomenon is evidence that sleep does not involve a total loss of consciousness or mental functioning.

Luteinizing hormone (LH) A chemical released into the bloodstream by the pituitary gland that controls the rate at which the gonads secrete masculine or feminine hormones.

Maintenance rehearsal Repeating information over and over to keep it active in short-term memory. The method is very ineffective for encoding information into long-term memory. (See also *elaborative rehearsal.*)

Major depression A condition in which a person feels sad and hopeless for weeks or months, often losing interest in all activities and taking pleasure in nothing. Weight loss and lack of sleep or, in some cases, overeating and excessive sleeping are frequent accompaniments, as are problems in concentrating, making decisions, and thinking clearly.

Mania   An elated, very active emotional state.

Manifest content   A person's description of a dream, which often contains unimportant features and events from the person's day or reflects temporary needs.

Matching hypothesis   A hypothesis that people are most likely to be attracted to others who are similar to themselves in physical attractiveness.

Maturation   Natural growth or change, triggered by biological factors, that unfolds in a fixed sequence relatively independent of the environment.

Mean   A measure of central tendency that is the arithmetic average of the scores in a set of data; the sum of the values of all the scores divided by the total number of scores.

Median   A measure of central tendency that is the halfway point in a set of data: half the scores fall above the median, half fall below it.

Medical model   (also called *biological model*) A view in which behavior disorders are seen as the result of physical diseases whose causes are natural and related mainly to the brain.

Meditation   A set of techniques designed to create an altered state of consciousness characterized by inner peace, calmness, and tranquility.

Medulla   An area in the hindbrain that controls blood pressure, heart rate, breathing, and other vital functions through the use of reflexes and feedback systems.

Mental ability   A capacity to perform the higher mental processes of reasoning, understanding, problem solving, and decision making.

Mental chronometry   The timing of mental events that allows researchers to infer what stages exist during cognition. (See also *information-processing system, evoked brain potential,* and *average evoked brain potential.*)

Mental model   A large cluster of propositions that represents people's understanding of how things work and guides their interaction with those things.

Mental set   The tendency for old patterns of problem solving to persist, even when they might not be the most efficient method for solving a given problem.

Metacognition   The knowledge of what strategies to apply, when to apply them, and how to deploy them in new situations so that new specific knowledge can be gained and different problems mastered.

Metacomponents   The processes involved in organizing and setting up a problem.

Metamemory   Knowledge about how a person's own memory works. It involves understanding the abilities and weaknesses of one's own memory, knowing about different types of memory tasks, and knowing what types of strategies are most effective in remembering new information.

Midbrain   A small structure that lies between the hindbrain and the forebrain, relays information from the eyes, ears, and skin, and controls certain types of automatic behaviors in response to information received through those structures.

Mnemonics   Strategies for placing information in an organized context in order to remember it. Two powerful methods are the peg-word system, and the method of loci.

Mode   A measure of central tendency that is the value or score that occurs most frequently in a data set.

Modeling   A method of therapy in which desirable behaviors are demonstrated as a way of teaching them to clients.

Mood disorder   (also called *affective disorder*) A condition in which a person experiences extremes of mood for long periods, shifts from one mood extreme to another, and experiences moods that are inconsistent with the happy or sad events around them.

Morpheme   The smallest unit of language that has meaning. (See also *phoneme.*)

Motherese   A type of speech that adults use when talking to language-learning children. It parallels children's own speech and is characterized by short sentences and concrete, basic nouns and active verbs—not pronouns, adjectives, conjunctions, or past tenses. Grammatically correct utterances are exaggerated, repeated, and enunciated clearly.

Motivation   The influences that account for the initiation, direction, intensity, and persistence of behavior.

Motive   A reason or purpose for behavior.

Motor cortex   The part of the cerebral cortex whose neurons control voluntary movements in specific parts of the body, some controlling movement of the hand, others stimulating movement of the foot, the knee, the head, and so on.

Motor systems   The parts of the nervous system that influence muscles and other organs to respond to the environment in some way.

Movement gradient   The graduated difference in the apparent movement of objects across the visual field. Faster relative movement across the visual field indicates closer distance.

Multiple personality disorder   The most famous and least commonly seen dissociative disorder, in which a person reports having more than one identity, and sometimes several, each of which speaks, acts, and writes in a very different way. (See also *dissociative disorder.*)

Myelin   A fatty substance that wraps around some axons and increases the speed of action potentials.

Narcissistic personality disorder   A personality disorder characterized by an exaggerated sense of self-importance combined with self-doubt.

Narcolepsy   A daytime sleep disorder in which a person switches abruptly and without warning from an active, often emotional waking state into several minutes of REM sleep. In most cases the muscle paralysis associated with REM causes the person to collapse on the spot and to remain briefly immobilized even after awakening.

Narcotic   A psychoactive drug, such as opium, morphine, or heroin, that has the ability to produce both sleep-inducing and pain-relieving effects.

Natural concept   Concepts that have no fixed set of *defining* features but instead share a set of *characteristic* features. Members of a natural concept need not possess all of the characteristic features.

Need   In drive theory, a biological requirement for well-being that is created by an imbalance in homeostasis. (See also *drive, primary drive,* and *secondary drive.*)

Need achievement   A motive influenced by the degree to which a person establishes specific goals, cares about meeting those goals, and experiences feelings of satisfaction doing so; it is often measured by the Thematic Apperception Test.

Negative reinforcer An unpleasant stimulus, such as pain. The removal of a negative reinforcer following some response is likely to strengthen that response's probability of recurring. The process of strengthening behavior by following it with the removal of a negative reinforcer is called *negative reinforcement*. (See also *positive reinforcer*.)

Nervous system A complex combination of cells whose primary function is to allow an organism to gain information about what is going on inside and outside the body and to respond appropriately.

Neuron The fundamental unit of the nervous system; a nerve cell, which has the ability to communicate with other nerve cells.

Neurosis Conditions in which a person is uncomfortable (usually anxious) but can still function.

Neurotransmitter A type of chemical that assists in the transfer of signals from the axon of one neuron (presynaptic cell) across the synapse to the receptors on the dendrite of another neuron (postsynaptic cell).

Neurotransmitter system A group of neurons that communicates by using the same neurotransmitter, such as acetylcholine or dopamine.

Nightmare A frightening, sometimes recurring dream that takes place during REM sleep.

Night terrors A rapid shift from stage 4 to REM sleep, often accompanied by some horrific dream that causes the dreamer to sit up staring, let out a blood-curdling scream, and abruptly awaken into a state of intense fear that may last up to thirty minutes. This phenomenon is especially common in children, but milder versions occur among adults.

Noise A random sum of waveforms that are not related to one another in any regular way.

Nonconscious level A segment of mental activity devoted to those processes that are totally inaccessible to conscious awareness, such as blood rushing through veins and arteries, the removal of impurities from the blood, and the measuring of blood sugar by the hypothalamus.

Norepinephrine The neurotransmitter found in both the central and peripheral nervous systems that is used by neurons called adrenergic neurons to regulate sleep, learning, and mood.

Norm (1) A description of the frequency at which a particular score occurs, which allows scores to be compared statistically. (2) A learned, socially based rule that prescribes what people should or should not do in various situations.

Normal distribution A dispersion of scores such that the mean, median, and mode all have the same value. When a distribution has this property, the standard deviation can be used to describe how any particular score stands in relation to the rest of the distribution.

Nucleus The part of a neuron which carries the genetic information that determines whether the cell will be a brain cell, a liver cell, or whatever, and then acts to direct that cell's functioning.

Null hypothesis The assertion that the independent variable manipulated by the experimenter will have no effect on the dependent variable measured by the experimenter.

Obedience A form of compliance in which people comply with a demand, rather than with a request, because they think they must or should do so; it can be thought of as submissive compliance. (See also *compliance*.)

Obesity A condition in which a person is severely overweight, often by as much as one hundred pounds.

Objective test A paper-and-pencil form containing clear, specific questions, statements, or concepts to which the respondent is asked to give yes-no, true-false, or multiple-choice answers.

Object permanence The knowledge, resulting from an ability to form mental representations of objects, that objects exist even when they are not in view.

Object relations Personality theories that focus on the importance of the very early relationships between infants and their love objects. According to this theory, the nature of these object relations has a significant impact on personality development, including secure early attachment to the mother or other caregiver, gradual separation from the object of attachment, and finally the ability to relate to others as an independent individual.

Observational learning Learning how to perform new behaviors by watching the behavior of others.

Obsessive-compulsive disorder An anxiety disorder in which a person becomes obsessed with certain thoughts or images or feels a compulsion to do certain things. If the person tries to interrupt obsessive thinking or compulsions, severe agitation and anxiety usually result.

Oedipus complex According to psychodynamic theory, during the phallic stage, a boy's id impulses involve sexual desire for the mother and the desire to eliminate, even kill, the father, who is competition for the mother's affection. The hostile impulses create a fear of retaliation so strong that the ego represses the incestuous desires. Then the boy identifies with the father and begins to learn male sex-role behaviors. (See also *phallic stage*.)

Olfaction The sense that detects chemicals that are airborne, or volatile; the sense of smell.

Olfactory bulb The brain structure that receives messages regarding olfaction, or the sense of smell.

One feature rule See *affirmation rule*.

One-word stage A stage of language development during which children build their vocabularies one word at a time, tend to use one word at a time, and tend to overextend the use of a single word.

Operant A response that has some effect on the world; it is a response that operates on the environment in some way. (See also *operant conditioning*.)

Operant conditioning A synonym for *instrumental conditioning*, a procedure in which an organism learns to respond to the environment in a way that helps produce some desired effect. Skinner's primary aim was to analyze how behavior is changed by its consequences.

Opponent-process theory (1) A theory stating that the visual elements sensitive to color are grouped into three pairs: a red-green element, a blue-yellow element, and a black-white element. Each element signals one color or the other—red or green, for example—but never both. (2) A theory of motivation based on the assumptions that first, any reaction to a stimulus is automatically followed by an opposite reaction, called the *opponent process*; and that second, after repeated exposure to the same stimulus, the initial reaction weakens, and the opponent process becomes stronger.

Optic chiasm   Part of the bottom surface of the brain where half of the optic nerve fibers cross over to the opposite side of the brain; beyond the chiasm the fibers ascend into the brain itself.

Optic nerve   A bundle of fibers composed of axons from ganglion cells that carries visual information to the brain.

Oral stage   The first of Freud's psychosexual stages, occurring during the first year of life, in which the mouth is the center of pleasure.

Organic mental disorder   Forms of abnormal behavior that have a clearly biological basis. (See also *delirium* and *dementia*.)

Orientation   When basic features of stimuli have the same orientation (such as horizontal, vertical, or at an angle), we tend to group those stimuli together.

Osmoreceptor cell   A type of cell in the hypothalamus that detects when the salt level within cells becomes too high due to a lack of fluid in the body.

Outgroup   Any group of which people do not see themselves as a member. (See also *ingroup*.)

Panic disorder   Anxiety in the form of terrifying *panic attacks* that come without warning or obvious cause. These attacks last for a few minutes and are marked by heart palpitations, pressure or pain in the chest, dizziness or unsteadiness, sweating, and faintness. They may be accompanied by feeling detached from one's body or feeling that people and events are not real. The person may think he or she is about to die or "go crazy."

Papillae   Structures that contain groups of taste receptors, the taste buds.

Parallel search   A theoretical retrieval process in which information in short-term memory is examined all at once. (See also *serial search*.)

Paranoid schizophrenia   A type of schizophrenia characterized by delusions of persecution or grandeur accompanied by anxiety, anger, superiority, argumentativeness, or jealousy; these feelings sometimes lead to violence.

Paraphilia   A sexual disorder in which a person's sexual interest is directed toward stimuli that are culturally or legally defined as inappropriate.

Parasympathetic nervous system   The subsystem of the autonomic nervous system that typically influences activity related to the protection, nourishment, and growth of the body. (See also *autonomic nervous system*.)

Partial reinforcement extinction effect   A phenomenon in which behaviors learned under a partial reinforcement schedule are far more difficult to extinguish than those learned on a continuous reinforcement schedule. Individuals on a partial reinforcement schedule usually are not immediately sensitive to the fact that their behavior is no longer being reinforced; they are used to not being rewarded for every response. However, individuals on a continuous reinforcement schedule are accustomed to being reinforced for each response and are more sensitive to the fact that their responses are no longer being rewarded.

Partial reinforcement schedule   (also called *intermittent reinforcement schedule*) In operant conditioning, a pattern of reinforcement in which a reinforcer is administered only some of the time after a particular response occurs. (See also *fixed ratio schedule, variable ratio schedule, fixed interval schedule,* and *variable interval schedule*.)

Percentile score   The percentage of people or observations that fall below a given score in a normal distribution.

Perception   The process through which people take raw sensations from the environment and interpret them, using knowledge, experience, and understanding of the world, so that the sensations become meaningful experiences.

Perceptual constancy   The perception of objects as constant in size, shape, color, and other properties despite changes in their retinal image.

Perceptual set   A readiness or predisposition to perceive a stimulus in a certain way, which is influenced by past experience.

Performance scale   Five subtests in the Wechsler scales that include tasks that require spatial ability and the ability to manipulate materials; these subtests provide a performance IQ. (See also *verbal scale*.)

Peripheral nervous system   Includes all of the nervous system that is not housed in bone. It has two main subsystems: the somatic nervous system and the autonomic nervous system.

Permissive parent   A parent who gives the child complete freedom and whose discipline is lax. Children of this type of parent are often immature, dependent, and unhappy, lack self-reliance and self-control, and seek parental help for even the slightest problems.

Personal construct   According to Kelly's personal construct theory, a generalized way of anticipating the world that determines personality and guides behavior. When occurrences coincide with expectations based on personal constructs, the person feels comfortable and the constructs are validated. If not, the ability to accurately anticipate the world is diminished, and the result is discomfort or anxiety.

Personality   The pattern of psychological and behavioral characteristics by which each person can be compared and contrasted with other people; the unique pattern of characteristics that emerges from the blending of inherited and acquired tendencies to make each person an identifiable individual.

Personality disorder   Long-standing ways of behaving that are not so much severe mental disorders as styles of life, which, from childhood or adolescence, create problems, usually for others.

Personality psychologist   A psychologist who studies the characteristics that make people unique individuals and who explores the relationship between personality and a tendency to think, act, and feel in certain ways.

Person-centered therapy   See *client-centered therapy*.

Phallic stage   The third of Freud's psychosexual stages, lasting from approximately ages three to five, in which the focus of pleasure shifts to the genital area; the Oedipus complex occurs during this stage. (See also *Oedipus complex*.)

Phenomenological approach   A view of personality based on the assumption that each personality is created out of each person's unique way of perceiving and interpreting the world.

Proponents of this view believe that one's personal perception of reality shapes and controls behavior from moment to moment.

Phenotype How an individual looks and acts, which depends on how a person's inherited characteristics interact with the environment.

Pheromones Chemicals that are released by one animal, detected by another, and then shape that second animal's behavior or physiology. Often, though not always, the pheromone is detected by the olfactory system.

Phobia An anxiety disorder that involves a strong, irrational fear of an object or situation that does not objectively justify such a reaction. The phobic individual usually realizes that the fear makes no sense but cannot keep it from interfering with daily life.

Phoneme The smallest unit of sound that affects the meaning of speech. (See also *morpheme.*)

Photopigment A chemical contained in photoreceptors that responds to light and assists in changing light into neural activity.

Photoreceptor Nerve cell in the retina that codes light energy into neural activity. (See also *rods* and *cones.*)

Physiological psychologist See *biological psychologist.*

Physiological psychology See *biological psychology.*

Pitch How "high" or "low" a tone is; the psychological dimension determined by the frequency of sound waves. High-frequency waves are sensed as sounds of high pitch.

Placebo A physical or psychological treatment that contains no active ingredient but produces an effect because the person receiving it believes it will. In an experiment, the *placebo effect* (a confounding variable) occurs when the subject responds to the *belief* that the independent variable will have an effect, rather than to the independent variable's actual effect.

Place theory (also called the *traveling wave theory*) A theory of hearing stating that hair cells at a particular place on the basilar membrane respond most to a particular frequency of sound. High-frequency sounds produce a wave that peaks soon after it starts down the basilar membrane. Lower-frequency sounds produce a wave that peaks farther along the basilar membrane.

Pleasure principle In psychodynamic theory, the operating principle of the id, which guides people toward whatever feels good. (See also *id.*)

Polygenic Traits affected by more than one gene.

Positive reinforcer A stimulus that strengthens a response if it follows that response. It is roughly equivalent to a reward. (See also *negative reinforcer.*) Presenting a positive reinforcer after a response is called *positive reinforcement.*

Posthypnotic amnesia The inability of hypnotic subjects to recall what happened during hypnosis. For some, recall fails even when they are told what went on.

Posthypnotic suggestion Instructions about experiences or behavior to take place after hypnosis has been terminated.

Posttraumatic stress disorder A pattern of adverse and disruptive reactions following a traumatic event. One of its most common features is reexperiencing the original trauma through nightmares or vivid memories.

Preconscious level A segment of mental activity devoted to sensations and everything else that is not currently conscious, but of which people can easily become conscious at will. The amount of material at this level far surpasses what is present at the conscious level at any given moment. (See also *conscious level* and *nonconscious level.*)

Predictive value The ability of the conditioned stimulus to signal the unconditioned stimulus. Predictive value will be highest if the conditioned stimulus is presented *every* time the unconditioned stimulus is presented.

Prefrontal lobotomy A form of psychosurgery in which a sharp instrument is inserted into the brain and used to sever neural connections.

Prejudice A positive or negative attitude toward an entire group of people. (See also *discrimination.*)

Preoperational period According to Piaget, the second stage of cognitive development, during which children begin to understand, create, and use symbols to represent things that are not present.

Primacy effect A characteristic of recall in which recall for the first two or three items in a list is particularly good. (See also *recency effect.*)

Primary auditory cortex The first cells in the cortex to receive information about sounds. This area is in the temporal lobe and is connected to areas of the brain involved in language perception and production.

Primary drive A drive that arises from basic biological needs. (See also *drive, need,* and *secondary drive.*)

Primary reinforcer Something that meets an organism's most basic needs, such as food, water, air, and moderate temperatures. A primary reinforcer does not depend on learning to exert its influence.

Primary visual cortex An area in the occipital lobe, at the back of the brain, to which neurons in the lateral geniculate nucleus relay visual input.

Prisoner's dilemma game A research situation in which mutual cooperation guarantees the best mutual outcome; mixed cooperative and competitive responses by each person guarantee a favorable outcome for one person and an unfavorable outcome for the other; and mutual competition guarantees the worst mutual outcome.

Proactive interference A cause of forgetting in which previously learned information, now residing in long-term memory, interferes with the ability to remember new information. (See also *retroactive interference.*)

Procedural memory A type of memory that contains information about how to do things; it is also called *skill memory.*

Progesterone A feminine hormone; the main progestin.

Progestin A feminine hormone that circulates in the bloodstream of both men and women; relatively more progestins circulate in women. One of the main progestins is progesterone. (See also *estrogen, estradiol,* and *progesterone.*)

Programmed instruction A classroom application of instrumental conditioning to individualized instruction in which new material is presented in small, planned steps. Successful completion of each step brings positive reinforcement and the opportunity to go on to the next step.

Progressive relaxation training A procedure for learning to relax that involves tensing a group of muscles for a few seconds, then releasing that tension and focusing attention on the resulting feelings of relaxation; the procedure is repeated at least once for each of sixteen muscle groups throughout the body. It is a popular physiological method for coping with stress and an important part of systematic desensitization, a method for treating phobias.

Projection   In psychodynamic theory, a defense mechanism in which people see their own unacceptable desires in others instead of in themselves.

Projective test   Personality tests made up of relatively unstructured stimuli, such as inkblots, which can be perceived and responded to in many ways; particular responses reflect the individual's needs, fantasies, conflicts, thought patterns, and other aspects of personality.

Proposition   The smallest unit of knowledge that can stand as a separate assertion, may be true or false, and may represent a relationship between a concept and a property of that concept or between two or more concepts.

Proprioceptive   The sensory systems that allow us to know about where we are and what each part of our body is doing. (See also *kinesthesia* and *vestibular sense.*)

Prototype   A member of a natural concept that possesses all or most of the characteristic features.

Proximity   A Gestalt grouping principle stating that the closer objects are to one another, the more likely they are to be perceived as belonging together.

Pruning   Neurons generate an overabundance of dendrites during childhood. During adolescence, extra dendrites are "pruned" until they reach a level characteristic of the adult.

Psychedelic   Psychoactive drugs, such as LSD, PCP, and marijuana, that alter consciousness by producing a temporary loss of contact with reality and changes in emotion, perception, and thought.

Psychiatrist   A medical doctor who has completed special training in the treatment of mental disorder. Psychiatrists can prescribe drugs.

Psychoactive drug   A chemical substance that acts on the brain to create some psychological effect.

Psychoactive substance-use disorder   A problem that involves use of psychoactive drugs for months or years in ways that harm the user or others.

Psychoanalysis   A method of psychotherapy that seeks to help clients gain insight by recognizing, understanding, and dealing with unconscious thoughts and emotions presumed to cause their problems; and work through the many ways in which those unconscious causes appear in everyday behavior and social relationships.

Psychodynamic approach   A view developed by Freud that emphasizes the interplay of unconscious mental processes in determining human thought, feelings, and behavior.

Psychologist   (as therapist) A professional who has completed a graduate program in clinical or counseling psychology, often followed by additional specialty training.

Psychology   The science of behavior and mental processes.

Psychoneuroimmunology   The field that examines the interaction of psychological and physiological processes that affect the body's ability to defend itself against disease.

Psychopathology   Patterns of thinking and behaving that are maladaptive, disruptive, or uncomfortable for the person affected or for those with whom he or she comes in contact.

Psychopharmacology   The study of psychoactive drugs and their effects.

Psychophysics   An area of specialization that focuses on the relationship between the *physical* characteristics of environmental stimuli and the conscious *psychological* experience those stimuli produce. Psychophysical researchers seek to understand how people make contact with and become conscious of the world.

Psychosexual stage   In psychodynamic theory, a period of personality development in which internal and external conflicts focus on particular issues. There are five stages during which pleasure is derived from different areas of the body. (See also *oral stage, anal stage, phallic stage, latency period, and genital stage.*)

Psychosis   A condition involving a loss of contact with reality or an inability to function day to day.

Psychosocial stages   Eight stages of life-long personality development, proposed by Erikson, that emphasize social crises as the most important determinants of personality.

Psychosurgery   Procedures that destroy various regions of the brain in an effort to alleviate psychological disorders; this surgery is done infrequently and only as a last resort.

Psychotherapy   The treatment of psychological disorders through psychological methods, such as analyzing problems, talking about possible solutions, and encouraging more adaptive ways of thinking and acting.

Puberty   The condition of being able for the first time to reproduce; occurs during adolescence and is characterized by fuller breasts and rounder curves in females and by broad shoulders and narrow hips in males. Facial, underarm, and pubic hair grows. Voices deepen, and acne may appear.

Punishment   The presentation of an aversive stimulus or the removal of a pleasant stimulus; it *decreases* the frequency of the immediately preceding response.

Pupil   An opening in the eye, just behind the cornea, through which light passes (The pupil appears black because there is no light source inside the eyeball and very little light is reflected out of the eye.)

Pyramidal motor system   Part of the motor cortex; controls voluntary facial movements. Can also control extrapyramidal system, which controls involuntary facial movements and is primarily controlled by subcortical areas of brain.

Quantitative psychologist   A psychologist who develops and applies mathematical methods for summarizing and analyzing data from all subfields of psychology.

Quiet sleep   Sleep stages 1 through 4, which are accompanied by slow, deep breathing; a calm, regular heartbeat; and reduced blood pressure.

Random sample   A group of research subjects selected from a population whose every member had an equal chance of being chosen for study.

Random variable   In an experiment, a confounding variable in which an uncontrolled or uncontrollable factor affects the dependent variable along with or instead of the independent variable. This could include factors such as differences in the subjects' backgrounds, personalities, and physical health, as well as differences in experimental conditions.

Range   A measure of variability that is the difference between the highest and the lowest value in the data set.

Rational-emotive therapy (RET)   A treatment that involves identifying self-defeating, problem-causing thoughts that clients have learned and using modeling, encouragement, and logic to help the client replace these maladaptive thought patterns with more realistic and beneficial ones.

Rationalization   In psychodynamic theory, a defense mechanism in which one attempts to "explain away" unacceptable behavior.

Reactance   A state of psychological arousal that motivates people to restore a lost sense of freedom by resisting, opposing, or contradicting whatever they feel caused the loss.

Reaction formation   In psychodynamic theory, a defense mechanism in which one's behavior runs exactly opposite to one's true feelings.

Reaction time   The elapsed time between the presentation of a stimulus and an overt response to it.

Reality principle   According to psychodynamic theory, the operating principle of the ego that involves compromises between the unreasoning demands of the id to do whatever feels good and the demands of the real world to do what is acceptable. (See also *ego.*)

Reasoning   The process by which people evaluate and generate arguments and reach conclusions. (See also *logic.*)

Receiver operating characteristic (ROC) curve   In signal detection theory, a graphic representation of the results of measuring a subject's sensitivity to a stimulus.

Recency effect   A characteristic of recall in which recall is particularly good for the last few items on a list. (See also *primacy effect.*)

Receptive field   The portion of the world that affects a given neuron. For example, in the auditory system, one neuron might only respond to sounds of a particular pitch; that pitch is its receptive field.

Receptor   (1) A site on the surface of the postsynaptic cell which allows only one type of neurotransmitter to fit into it and thus trigger the chemical response that may lead to an action potential. (2) A cell that is specialized to detect certain types of energy and convert it into neural activity. This conversion process is called *transduction.*

Recessive gene   A gene that is expressed in an individual's phenotype only when paired with a similar gene from the other parent.

Reciprocal determinism   According to Bandura, the ways in which people's overt behaviors, cognitions, and the environment constantly influence one another.

Reconditioning   The relearning of a conditioned response following extinction. Because reconditioning takes much less time than the original conditioning, some change in the organism must persist even after extinction.

Reduced clarity   A depth cue whereby an object whose retinal image is unclear is perceived as being farther away.

Reference group   A category of people to which people compare themselves.

Reflection   Restating or paraphrasing what the client has said, which shows that the therapist is actively listening and helps make the client aware of the thoughts and feelings he or she is experiencing.

Reflexes   Involuntary, unlearned reactions in the form of swift, automatic, and finely coordinated movements in response to external stimuli. Reflexes are organized completely within the spinal cord.

Refractory period   A short rest period between action potentials; it is so short that a neuron can send action potentials down its axon at rates of up to one thousand per second.

Rehearsing   Repeating information to oneself, which allows the information to be maintained in short-term memory indefinitely, as long as rehearsing continues.

Reinforcer   A stimulus event that increases the probability that the response which immediately preceded it will occur again. (See also *positive reinforcer* and *negative reinforcer.*)

Relative deprivation   The sense that a person is not doing as well as others in the same reference group.

Relative size   A depth cue whereby larger objects are perceived as closer than smaller ones.

Releaser   An environmental stimulus that sets off a stereotyped pattern of behavior, usually in lower animals.

Reliability   The degree to which a test can be repeated with the same results. Tests with high reliability yield scores that are less susceptible to insignificant or random changes in the test taker or the testing environment.

REM sleep   See *active sleep.*

Representativeness heuristic   A shortcut in the thought process that involves judging the probability that a hypothesis is true or that an example belongs to a certain class of items by first focusing on the similarities between the example and a larger class of events or items, and then determining whether the particular example represents essential features of the larger class.

Repression   In psychodynamic theory, a defense mechanism that involves unconsciously forcing unacceptable impulses out of awareness, leaving the person unaware that he or she had the taboo desires in the first place.

Resistance   The second stage in the general adaptation syndrome, in which signs of the initial alarm reaction diminish while the body settles in to resist the stressor on a long-term basis. (See also *alarm reaction* and *exhaustion.*)

Response bias   A person's willingness or reluctance to respond to a stimulus, which reflects motivation and expectancies. Response bias is a source of variation in absolute threshold.

Response criterion   The amount of energy necessary for a person to justify reporting that a signal has occurred. It is the internal rule a person uses to decide whether or not to report a stimulus, and it reflects the person's motivation and expectations.

RET   See *rational-emotive therapy.*

Reticular formation   A network of nuclei and fibers threaded throughout the hindbrain and the midbrain that is composed of cells that are not arranged in a well-defined form. This network is very important in altering the activity of the rest of the brain.

Retina   The surface at the back of the eye onto which the lens focuses light rays.

Retrieval   The process of recalling information stored in memory and bringing it into consciousness.

Retrieval cues   Stimuli that allow people to recall things that were once forgotten and help them to recognize information stored in memory.

Retroactive interference   A cause of forgetting in which new information placed in memory interferes with the ability to recall information already in memory.

Retrograde amnesia   A loss of memory for events prior to some critical brain injury. Often, a person will be unable to remember anything that occurred in the months, or even years, before the injury. In most cases, the memories return gradually, but recovery is seldom complete.

ROC See *receiver operating curve*.

Rods Photoreceptors in the retina that allow us to see even in very dim light because their photopigment contains rhodopsin, a very light-sensitive chemical. Rods cannot discriminate colors. (See also *cones*.)

Role theory A theory that states that hypnotized subjects merely act in accordance with a special social role, which demands compliance, and do not enter an altered state of consciousness. According to this theory, the procedures for inducing hypnosis provide a socially acceptable reason to follow the hypnotist's suggestions. (See also *dissociation theory* and *state theory*.)

Saccadic movement The jump that a reader's eyes make from one point in text to another. How rapidly the reader can shift from one point to the next (usually about four times per second) and how much print the reader can take in at a single point, or fixation, are the two physical factors that determine how fast a person can read.

Sampling The process of selecting subjects who are members of the population that the researcher wishes to study.

Saturation The purity of a color. A color is more pure, more saturated, if a single wavelength is relatively more intense than other wavelengths.

Savings A method for measuring forgetting by computing the difference between the number of repetitions needed to learn, say, a list of words, and the number of repetitions needed to relearn it after some time has elapsed.

Schachter theory A theory of the experience of emotion in which the cognitive act of labeling an originally undifferentiated physiological arousal constitutes the core of emotion. People may attribute physiological arousal to different emotions depending on the information that is available about the situation. (See also *attribution*.)

Schema A coherent, organized set of beliefs and expectations that can influence the perception of others and objects.

Schema-plus-correction process An impression to which a change has been added. In social perception, the initial impression of a person is remembered better than is the change.

Scheme A basic unit of knowledge, which may be a pattern of action, an image of an object, or a complex idea. (See also *schema*.)

Schizophrenia A pattern of severely disturbed thinking, emotion, perception, and behavior that constitutes one of the most serious and disabling of all mental disorders.

SD See *standard deviation*.

Secondary drive A stimulus that acquires the motivational properties of a primary drive through classical conditioning or other learning mechanisms. (See also *drive, need*, and *primary drive*.)

Secondary reinforcer A reward that people or animals *learn* to like. Secondary reinforcers gain their reinforcing properties through association with primary reinforcers.

Secure attachment A type of parent-child relationship in which an infant's urge to be close to the parent for comfort,

contact, and conversation is balanced by an urge to explore the environment.

Self-actualization According to Rogers, an innate tendency toward growth that motivates all human behavior and results in the full realization of a person's highest potential.

Self-concept The way one thinks of oneself.

Self-efficacy According to Bandura, learned expectations about the probability of success in given situations; a person's expectation of success in a given situation may be enough to create that success and even to blunt the impact of minor failures.

Self-fulfilling prophecy An impression formation process in which an initial impression elicits behavior in another that confirms the impression.

Self-perception theory A theory which holds that when people are unsure of their attitude in a situation, they consider their behavior in light of the circumstances, and then infer what their attitude must have been.

Semantic code A mental representation of an experience by its general meaning.

Semantic memory A type of memory containing generalized knowledge of the world that does not involve memory of specific events.

Semantics In language, the rules that govern the meaning of words and sentences. (See also *syntax*.)

Sensation A message from a sense, which comprises the raw information that affects many kinds of behavior and mental processes.

Sense A system that translates data from outside the nervous system into neural activity, giving the nervous system, especially the brain, information about the world.

Sensitivity The ability to detect a stimulus; it is influenced by neural noise, by the intensity of the stimulus, and by the capacity of the sensory system.

Sensorimotor period The first in Piaget's stages of cognitive development, when the infant's mental activity is confined to sensory perception and motor skills.

Sensory cortex The part of the cerebral cortex located in the parietal, occipital, and temporal lobes which receives stimulus information from the skin, eyes, and ears, respectively.

Sensory memory A type of memory that is very primitive and very, very brief, but lasts long enough to connect one impression to the next, so that people experience a smooth flow of information. (See also *sensory register*.)

Sensory register A memory system that holds incoming information long enough for it to be processed further. (See also *sensory memory*.)

Sensory systems The part of the nervous system that provides information about the environment; the senses.

Septum A limbic system structure involved in regulating emotion, which also plays a role in memory and in some thought processes.

Serial search A theoretical retrieval process in which information in short-term memory is examined one piece at a time. (See also *parallel search*.)

Serotonin A neurotransmitter used by serotonergic neurons, which are located in the hindbrain and forebrain, to regulate sleep, mood, and pain sensation.

Set-point concept A theory of hunger and the regulation of eating based on studies of the hypothalamus. According to this theory, a homeostatic mechanism in the brain establishes a level, or set point, based on body weight, or some related metabolic signal. Normal animals eat until their set point is reached, then stop until their brain senses a drop in desirable intake, at which time they eat again.

Sexual disorder A sexual problem including sexual dysfunctions and paraphilias. (See also *sexual dysfunction* and *paraphilia*.)

Sexual dysfunction Problems with sex that involve sexual motivation, arousal, or orgasmic response regardless of sexual orientation, including low sexual desire, erectile dysfunction, infrequent orgasms, lack of orgasms, retarded ejaculation, and premature ejaculation.

Sexual response cycle The pattern of arousal during and after sexual activity.

Shaping In operant conditioning, a procedure that involves reinforcing responses that come successively closer to the desired response. (See also *successive approximation*.)

Short-term memory (also called *working memory*) A stage of memory in which information can last from one second to more than a minute.

Signal detection theory A formal mathematical model of what determines a person's report that a near-threshold stimulus has or has not occurred.

Similarity A Gestalt grouping principle stating that similar elements are perceived to be part of a group.

Simple phobia A strong irrational fear of specific things, such as heights, darkness, animals, or air travel.

Simplicity A Gestalt grouping principle stating that people tend to group stimulus features in a way that provides the simplest interpretation of the world.

Situational specificity The concept that in different situations, people are capable of many different behaviors, not all of which are necessarily compatible or consistent.

Sleepwalking A phenomenon that starts primarily in non-REM sleep, especially in stage 4, and involves walking while one is asleep. It is most common during childhood. In the morning sleepwalkers usually have no memory of their travels.

Social clock Particular age ranges during which certain milestones that mark a person's progress through life, such as completing school, leaving home, and getting married, are expected to occur.

Social comparison Using other people as a basis of comparison for evaluating oneself.

Social dilemma A situation in which the short-term decisions of individuals become irrational in combination and create long-term, clearly predictable damage for a group.

Social facilitation A phenomenon in which the mere presence of other people improves a person's performance on a given task.

Socialization The process by which parents, teachers, and other authority figures teach children the skills and social norms necessary to be well-functioning members of society.

Social learning Learning that occurs based on others' experiences, through processes known as *vicarious conditioning* and *observational learning*. (See also *vicarious conditioning* and *observational learning*.)

Social perception The way people perceive others and themselves.

Social phobia A strong, irrational fear relating to social situations. Common examples include fear of being negatively evaluated by others or publicly embarrassed by doing something impulsive, outrageous, or humiliating.

Social psychologist A psychologist who studies how people influence one another's behavior and attitudes, especially in groups of two or more.

Social psychology The psychological subfield that explores the effects of the social world on the behavior and mental processes of individuals, pairs, and groups.

Social referencing A phenomenon in which other people's facial expressions, tone of voice, and bodily gestures serve as guidelines for how to proceed in uncertain situations.

Social support network The friends and social contacts on whom one can depend for help and support.

Sociobiologist A proponent of the theory that human and animal social behaviors that increase the chances of species survival are genetically encoded and passed from generation to generation.

Socioemotional leadership A leadership style in which the leader provides loose supervision, asks for group members' ideas, and is generally concerned with subordinates' feelings.

Somatic nervous system The subsystem of the peripheral nervous system that transmits information from the senses to the central nervous system and carries signals from the CNS to the muscles that move the skeleton.

Somatic sense (also called *somatosensory system*) A sense that is spread throughout the body, not located in a specific organ. Somatic senses include touch, temperature, pain (the skin senses), and kinesthesia.

Somatoform disorder A psychological problem in which a person shows the symptoms of some physical (somatic) disorder, even though there is no physical cause. (See also *conversion disorder*.)

Somatosensory system See *somatic sense*.

Somatotopic organization The organization of information from the touch senses so that signals from neighboring points on the skin stay next to each other, even as they ascend from the skin through the spinal cord to the thalamus and on to the cortex.

Sound A repetitive fluctuation in the pressure of a medium like air.

Specific nerve energies A doctrine that states that stimulation of a particular sensory nerve provides codes for that one sense, no matter how the stimulation takes place.

Speech spectrograph A visual representation of the frequencies of speech as they unfold over time.

Spinal cord The part of the central nervous system contained within the spinal column that receives signals from peripheral senses (such as touch and pain) and relays them to the brain. It also conveys messages from the brain to the rest of the body.

Spontaneous recovery The reappearance of the conditioned response after extinction and without further pairings of the conditioned and unconditioned stimuli.

Standard deviation (SD) A measure of variability that is the average difference between each score and the mean of the data set.

Standard score A value that indicates the distance, in standard deviations, between a given score and the mean of all the scores in a data set.

Stanford-Binet A test for determining a person's intelligence quotient, or IQ.

State of consciousness The characteristics of consciousness at any particular moment—for example, what reaches awareness, what levels of mental activity are most prominent, and how efficiently a person is functioning.

State theory A theory that proposes that hypnosis does indeed create an altered state of consciousness. (See also *dissociation theory* and *role theory*.)

Statistical analysis The mathematical methods used to summarize and analyze research data. Some frequently used statistics include the mean, median, mode, standard deviation, correlation coefficient, and *t* test.

Statistically significant In statistical analysis, a term used to describe the results of an experiment when the outcome of a statistical test indicates that the probability of those results occurring by chance is small (less than 5 percent).

Stereotype An impression or schema of an entire group of people that involves the false assumption that all members of the group share the same characteristics.

Stevens's power law A law that generates accurate functions relating energy to subjective intensity for almost any kind of stimulus.

Stimulant A psychoactive drug that has the ability to increase behavioral activity. Amphetamines and cocaine do so primarily by augmenting the action of the neurotransmitter norepinephrine.

Stimulus discrimination A process through which individuals learn to differentiate among similar stimuli and respond appropriately to each one. (See also *stimulus generalization*.)

Stimulus generalization A phenomenon in which a conditioned response is elicited by stimuli that are similar but not identical to the conditioned stimulus. The greater the similarity between a stimulus and the conditioned stimulus, the stronger the conditioned response will be.

Storage The process of maintaining information in the memory system over time.

Stress The process of adjusting to circumstances that disrupt, or threaten to disrupt, a person's equilibrium.

Stress inoculation training A treatment method in which the therapist asks clients to imagine being in some stressful situation so that they can practice using new cognitive skills under controlled conditions.

Stressor An event or situation to which people must adjust.

Stress reaction The physical, psychological, and behavioral responses people display in the face of stressors.

Structuralism An approach to consciousness that proposes that conscious experience is constructed from basic sensations and other mental building blocks.

Style of life According to Adler, the ways in which each person goes about trying to reach personal and social fulfillment.

Subconscious level The term used by those who do not accept Freud's theory to designate the mental level at which important but normally inaccessible mental processes take place. (See also *unconscious level*.)

Sublimation In psychodynamic theory, a defense mechanism that involves converting repressed yearnings into socially approved action.

Substance-use disorder See *psychoactive substance-use disorder*.

Successive approximation In operant conditioning, responses that come successively closer to a desired response. (See also *shaping*.)

Superego According to psychodynamic theory, the component of personality that tells people what they should and should not do. Its two subdivisions are the conscience, which dictates what behaviors are wrong, and the ego ideal, which sets perfectionistic standards for desirable behaviors.

Surface structure The strings of words that people produce; the order in which words are arranged.

Survey A research method that involves giving people questionnaires or special interviews designed to obtain descriptions of their attitudes, beliefs, opinions, and intentions.

Susceptibility The degree to which people comply with and become involved in hypnosis and hypnotic suggestions. This can be measured by tests such as the Stanford Hypnotic Susceptibility Scales and the Harvard Group Scale of Hypnotic Susceptibility.

Syllogism In the reasoning process, an argument made up of two propositions, called *premises*, and a conclusion based on those premises. (See also *proposition*.)

Symbols-systems approach An approach to intelligence that focuses on how people learn and use various symbol systems, such as language, mathematics, music, and so on, rather than on the mathematical analysis of paper-and-pencil tests.

Sympathetic nervous system The subsystem of the autonomic nervous system that usually prepares the organism for vigorous activity, including the fight or flight syndrome. (See also *fight-or-flight syndrome* and *autonomic nervous system*.)

Syntax In language, the set of rules that govern the formation of phrases and sentences. (See also *semantics*.)

Task-oriented leadership A leadership style in which the leader provides very close supervision, leads by giving directives, and generally discourages group discussion.

Telegraphic speech Utterances that are brief and to the point and that leave out any word that is not absolutely essential to the meaning the speaker wishes to convey; children's first sentences, consisting of two-word utterances.

Temperament An individual's basic, natural disposition; the beginning of an individual's identity or personality, which is evident from infancy.

Test A systematic procedure for observing behavior in a standard situation and describing it with the help of a numerical scale or a category system.

Testosterone A masculine hormone, the principal androgen. (See also *androgen*.)

Textural gradient A graduated change in the texture or grain of the visual field, whereby changes in texture across the retinal image are perceived as changes in distance; objects with finer, less detailed textures are perceived as more distant.

Thalamus A brain structure in the forebrain that relays signals from the eyes and other sense organs to higher levels in the brain and plays an important role in processing and making sense out of this information.

Theory An integrated set of principles that can be used to explain, predict, and control certain phenomena (in psychology, these phenomena are behaviors and mental processes).

Thinking The manipulation of mental representations, performed in order to reason, understand a situation, solve a problem, make a decision, or reach some other goal. The manipulations can also be less goal-directed, such as when we daydream.

Timbre The quality of sound that identifies it, so that, for example, a middle C played on the piano is clearly distinguishable from a middle C played on a trumpet. The timbre depends on the mixture of frequencies and amplitudes that make up the sound.

Token economies A system for improving the behavior of severely disturbed or mentally retarded clients in institutions that involves rewarding desirable behaviors with tokens that can be exchanged for snacks, field trips, access to television, or other privileges.

Tonotopic organization A map of sound frequencies provided by neighboring cells in the auditory cortex that have similar preferred frequencies.

Top-down processing Those aspects of recognition that are guided by higher-level cognitive processes and psychological factors like expectations. (See also *bottom-up processing*.)

Topographical representation A map of each sense, contained in the primary cortex. Any two points that are next to each other in the stimulus will be represented next to each other in the brain.

Tranquilizer A drug that reduces feelings of tension and anxiety.

Transduction The second step in sensation, which is the process of converting incoming energy into neural activity through receptors.

Transference A phenomenon in which a client transfers to the therapist many of the feelings, attitudes, reactions, and conflicts experienced in childhood toward parents, siblings, and other significant people.

Transferred excitation The process of carrying over arousal from one experience to an independent situation, which is especially likely to occur when the arousal pattern from the nonemotional source is similar to the pattern associated with a particular emotion.

Trichromatic theory The theory postulated by Young and Helmholtz that there are three types of visual elements, each of which is most sensitive to different wavelengths, and that information from these three elements combines to produce the sensation of color.

t-test A tool of inferential statistics that allows the researcher to determine the probability that the difference between the means of sets of data occurred by chance.

Tympanic membrane A tightly stretched membrane (also known as the *eardrum*) in the middle ear which generates vibrations that match the sound waves striking it.

Type A A personality type characterized by nonstop working, intense competitiveness, aggressiveness, and impatience, accompanied by an especially strong need to control events. (See also *Type B*.)

Type B A personality type characterized by a more relaxed and easygoing attitude than that associated with a type A personality. (See also *Type A*.)

Unconditional positive regard In client-centered therapy, the therapist's attitude that expresses caring for and acceptance of the client as a valued person.

Unconditioned response (UCR) In classical conditioning, the automatic or unlearned reaction to a stimulus.

Unconditioned stimulus (UCS) In classical conditioning, the stimulus that elicits a response without conditioning. (See also *conditioned stimulus*.)

Unconscious level A segment of mental activity proposed by Freud which contains sexual, aggressive, and other impulses, as well as once-conscious but unacceptable thoughts and feelings of which an individual is completely unaware. (See also *subconscious level*.)

Utility In rational decision making, any subjective measure of value.

Validity The degree to which a test measures what it is supposed to measure.

Variability A measure of the dispersion of scores in a set of data. (See also *range* and *standard deviation*.)

Variable In an experiment, any specific factor or characteristic that can vary.

Variable interval (VI) schedule In operant conditioning, a type of partial reinforcement schedule that provides reinforcement for the first response after some varying period of time. For example, in a VI 60 schedule the first response to occur after an *average* of one minute would be reinforced, but the actual time between reinforcements could vary from, say, 1 second to 120 seconds.

Variable ratio (VR) schedule A type of partial reinforcement schedule that provides reinforcement after a varying number of responses. For example, on a VR 30 schedule, a rat might sometimes be reinforced after ten bar presses, sometimes after fifty bar presses; but an *average* of thirty responses would occur before reinforcement is given.

Ventromedial nucleus A region of the hypothalamus that signals an animal to stop eating and that also affects other motivated behaviors. (See also *lateral area*.)

Verbal scale Six subtests in the Wechsler scales that measure verbal skills as part of a measure of overall intelligence. (See also *performance scale*.)

Vestibular sense The proprioceptive sense that tells us about the position of the body in space and about its general movements. It is often thought of as the sense of balance.

VI See *variable interval schedule*.

Vicarious conditioning Learning the relationship between a response and its consequences (either reinforcement or punishment) or the association between a conditioned stimulus and a conditioned response by watching others.

Visible light Electromagnetic radiation that has a wavelength from about 400 nanometers to about 700 nanometers. (A nanometer is a billionth of a meter.)

Visual code A mental representation of stimuli as pictures.

Visual dominance A phenomenon that occurs when information received by the visual system conflicts with information coming from other sensory modalities; the sense of vision normally overrides other sensory information and is perceived as accurate. This is a major factor in people's ability to be fooled by certain illusions.

Volley theory   See *frequency matching.*

Volumetric receptor   A thirst mechanism in the heart and kidneys that monitors the volume and pressure of blood and other fluids outside the cells.

Vulnerability model   A view of schizophrenia which suggests that different people have differing degrees of vulnerability to schizophrenia; this vulnerability may not be entirely inherited; and it may involve psychological and biological components. (See also *diathesis* and *stress.*)

Waveform   A graphic representation of sound or other energy. For sound, a waveform represents in two dimensions the wave that moves through the air in three dimensions. The point where the air is compressed the most is the peak of the graph. The lowest point, or trough, is where the air pressure is least compressed.

Wavelength   The distance from one peak to the next in a *waveform.*

Weber's law   A law stating that the smallest detectable difference in stimulus energy, the just-noticeable difference (JND), is a constant fraction, K, of the intensity of the stimulus, I. The constant varies for each sensory system and for different aspects of sensation within those systems. In algebraic terms, Weber's law is JND = KI. (See also *just-noticeable difference.*)

Word   A unit of language composed of one or more morphemes. (See also *morpheme.*)

Working memory   See *short-term memory.*

Zygote   The cell that results from the merger of sperm and ovum.

Abbott, B. B., Schoen, L. S., & Badia, P. (1984). Predictable and unpredictable shock: Behavioral measures of aversion and physiological measures of stress. *Psychological Bulletin, 96,* 45–71.

Abel, G. G., Blanchard, E. B., & Becker, J. V. (1976). Psychological treatment of rapists. In M. Walker & S. Brodsky (Eds.), *Sexual assault: The victim and the rapist.* Lexington, MA: Lexington Books.

Abeles, N. (1985). Proceedings of the American Psychological Association, 1985. *American Psychologist, 41,* 633–663.

Abramovitz, C. V., Abramovitz, S. I., Rorback, H., & Jackson, C. (1974). Differential effectiveness of directive and nondirective group therapies as a function of client internal-external control. *Journal of Consulting and Clinical Psychology, 42,* 849–853.

Abrams, R., Taylor, M., Faber, R., Ts'o, T., Williams, R., & Almy, G. (1983). Bilateral vs. unilateral electroconvulsive therapy: Efficacy and melancholia. *American Journal of Psychiatry, 140,* 463–465.

Abramson, L. Y., Seligman, M. E. P., & Teasdale, J. D. (1978). Learned helplessness in humans: Critique and reformulation. *Journal of Abnormal Psychology, 87,* 49–74.

Achenbach, T. M. (1982). *Developmental psychopathology* (2nd ed.). New York: Wiley.

Adam, K. & Oswald, I. (1977). Sleep is for tissue restoration. *Journal of the Royal College of Physicians, 11,* 376–388.

Adams, G. R., & Jones, R. M. (1983). Female adolescents' identity development: Age comparisons and perceived child-rearing experience. *Developmental Psychology, 19,* 249–256.

Adams, H. E., & Chiodo, J. (1983). Sexual deviations. In H. E. Adams & P. B. Sutker (Eds.), *Comprehensive handbook of psychopathology.* New York: Plenum Press.

Adelson, E. H. (1983). What is iconic storage good for? *The Behavioral and Brain Sciences, 6,* 11–12.

Ader, R., & Cohen, N. (1985). CNS–immune system interactions: Conditioning phenomena. *Behavior and Brain Sciences, 8,* 379–394.

Adler, A. (1963). *The practice and theory of individual psychology.* Paterson, NJ: Littlefield Adams. (original work published 1927)

Adorno, T. W., Frenkel-Brunswik, E., Levinson, D. J., & Sanford, R. N. (1950). *The authoritarian personality.* New York: Harper & Row.

Ainsworth, M. D. S. (1973). The development of infant-mother attachment. In B. M. Caldwell & H. N. Ricciuti (Eds.), *Review of child development research: Vol. 3.* Chicago: University of Chicago Press.

Ainsworth, M. D. S., & Bell, S. M. (1977). Infant crying and maternal responsiveness: A rejoinder to Gewirtz and Boyd. *Child Development, 48,* 1208–1216.

Ainsworth, M. D. S., Blehar, M., Waters, E., & Wall, S. (1978). *Patterns of attachment: Observations in the strange situation and at home.* Hillsdale, NJ: Lawrence Erlbaum Associates.

Albee, G. (1968). Conceptual models and manpower requirements in psychology. *American Psychologist, 23,* 317–320.

Albee, G. (1985, February). The answer is prevention. *Psychology Today.*

Albert, D. J., & Walsh, M. L. (1984). Neural systems and the inhibitory modulation of agonistic behavior: A comparison of mammalian species. *Neuroscience and Biobehavioral Reviews, 8,* 5–24.

Alcohol and health: Report to the U.S. Congress. (1984). Rockville, MD: Department of Health and Human Services.

Alexander, F. M. (1963). *Fundamentals of psychoanalysis.* New York: W. W. Norton.

Allen, G. J. (1977). *Understanding psychotherapy.* Champaign, IL: Research Press.

Allen, K. E., Hart, B. M., Buell, J. S., Harris, F. R., & Wolf, M. M. (1964). Effects of social reinforcement on isolate behavior of a nursery school child. In L. P. Ullmann & L. Krasner (Eds.), *Case studies in behavior modification.* New York: Holt, Rinehart and Winston.

Allen, M. G. (1976). Twin studies of affective illness. *Archives of General Psychiatry, 33,* 1476–1478.

Allen, M. G., Cohen, S., & Pollin, W. (1972). Schizophrenia in veteran twins: A diagnostic review. *American Journal of Psychiatry, 128,* 939–947.

Allen, V. L., & Wilder, D. A. (1975). Categorization, belief similarity, and intergroup discrimination. *Journal of Personality and Social Psychology, 32,* 971–977.

Alloy, L. B., & Ahrens, A. H. (1987). Depression and pessimism for the future: Biased use of statistically relevant information in predictions for self versus others. *Journal of Personality and Social Psychology, 52,* 366–378.

Altman, I., & Taylor, D. A. (1973). *Social penetration: The development of interpersonal relationships.* New York: Holt, Rinehart and Winston.

American Law Institute. (1962). *Model penal code: Proposed offical draft.* Philadelphia: Author.

American Psychiatric Association. (1978). *Task force report 14: Electroconvulsive therapy.* Washington, DC: Author.

American Psychological Association. (1974). *Standards for educational and psychological test and manuals.* Washington, DC: Author.

American Psychological Association. (1981). Ethical principles of psychologists. *American Psychologist, 36,* 633–638.

Anastasi, A. (1971). Note on the concepts of creativity and intelligence. *Journal of Creative Behavior, 5,* 113–116.

Anastasi, A. (1982). *Psychological testing* (5th ed.). New York: Collier Macmillan.

Ancoli-Israel, S. (1981). Sleep apnea and nocturnal myocolonus in a senior population. *Sleep, 4,* 349–358.

Anderson, C. A., & Anderson, D. C. (1984). Ambient temperature and violent crime: Tests of the linear and curvilinear hypotheses. *Journal of Personality and Social Psychology, 46,* 91–97.

Anderson, C. R. (1977). Locus of control, coping behaviors and performance in a stress setting: A longitudinal study. *Journal of Applied Psychology, 62,* 446–451.

Anderson, J. R. (1979). *Cognitive psychology.* New York: Academic Press.

Anderson, J. R. (1976). *Language, memory, and thought.* Hillsdale, NJ: Lawrence Erlbaum Associates.

Anderson, R. C., Reynolds, R. E., Schallert, D. L., & Goetz, E. T. (1977). Frameworks for comprehending discourse. *American Educational Research Journal, 14,* 367–382.

Anderson, T. H. (1978). *Another look at the self-questioning study technique* (Technical Ed. Rep. No. 6). Champaign: University of Illinois, Center for the Study of Reading.

Andersson, B., & McCann, S. M. (1955). A further study of polydipsia evoked by hypothalamic stimulation in the goat. *Acta Physiologica Scandinavia, 33,* 333–346.

Andreasen, N. C., Olson, S. A., Dennert, J. W., & Smith, M. R. (1982). Ventricular enlargement in schizophrenia: Relationship to positive and negative symptoms. *American Journal of Psychiatry, 139,* 297–302.

Andrews, G., & Harvey, R. (1981). Does psychotherapy benefit neurotic patients? *Archives of General Psychiatry, 138,* 1203–1208.

Angell, J. R. (1907). The province of functional psychology. *Psychological Review, 14,* 61–91.

Angrist, B., Lee, H. K., & Gershon, S. (1974). The antagonism of amphetamine-induced symptomatology by a neuroleptic. *American Journal of Psychiatry, 131,* 817–819.

Archer, D., & Gartner, R. (1976). Violent acts and violent times: A comparative approach to postwar homicide rates. *American Sociological Review, 41,* 937–963.

Arend, R., Gove, F. L., & Sroufe, L. A. (1979). Continuity of individual adaptation from infancy to kindergarten: A predictive study of ego-resiliency and curiosity in preschoolers. *Child Development, 50,* 950–959.

Arkowitz, H., & Messer, S. B. (1984). *Psychoanalytic therapy and behavior therapy: Is integration possible?* New York: Plenum Press.

Arlin, P. K. (1980, June). *Adolescent and adult thought: A search for structures.* Paper presented at the meeting of the Jean Piaget Society, Philadelphia, PA.

Arndt, W. B., Jr., Foehl, J. C., & Good, F. E. (1985). Specific sexual fantasy themes: A multidimensional study. *Journal of Personality and Social Psychology, 48,* 472–480.

Aronson, E., Brewer, M., & Carlsmith, J. M. (1963). Experimentation in social psychology. In G. Lindzey & E. Aronson (Eds.), *The handbook of social psychology: Vol. 1* (3rd ed.). New York: Random House.

Aronson, E., & Cope, V. (1968). My enemy's enemy is my friend. *Journal of Personality and Social Psychology, 8,* 8–12.

Aronson, E., Turner, J. A., & Carlsmith, J. M. (1985). Communicator credibility and communication discrepancy as a determinant of opinion change. *Journal of Abnormal and Social Psychology, 67,* 31–36.

Asch, S. E. (1951). Effects of group pressure upon the modification and distortion of judgments. In H. Guetzkow (Ed.), *Groups, leadership, and men.* Pittsburgh: Carnegie Press.

Asch, S. E. (1955). Opinions and social pressure. *Scientific American, 193,* 31–35.

Asch, S. E. (1956). Studies of independence and conformity: A minority of one against a unanimous majority. *Psychological Monographs, 70,* 1–70.

Aserinsky, E., & Kleitman, N. (1953). Regularly occurring periods of eye motility and concomitant phenomena during sleep. *Science, 118,* 273.

Ash, P. (1949). The reliability of psychiatric diagnosis. *Journal of Abnormal and Social Psychology, 22,* 140–144.

Ashmead, D. H., & Perlmutter, M. (1980). Infant memory in everyday life. In M. Perlmutter (Ed.), *New directions in child development: Children's memory.* San Francisco: Jossey-Bass.

Associated Press. (1984). *Man sets wife afire after watching TV movie.*

Associated Press. (1986). *Media general poll.*

Atkinson, J. W., & Birch, D. (1978). *Introduction to motivation* (2nd ed.). New York: D. Van Nostrand.

Atkinson, J. W., & Raynor, J. O. (1974). *Personality, motivation, and achievement.* Washington, DC: Hemisphere.

Atkinson, R. C., & Shiffrin, R. M. (1968). Human memory: A proposed system and its control processes. In K. Spence (Ed.), *The psychology of learning and motivation: Vol. 2.* New York: Academic Press.

Averill, J. S. (1980). On the paucity of positive emotions. In K. R. Blankstein, P. Pliner, & J. Polivy (Eds.), *Advances in the study of communication and affect: Vol. 6. Assessment and modification of emotional behavior.* New York: Plenum Press.

Ayllon, T., & Azrin, N. H. (1968). *The token economy: A motivational system for therapy and rehabilitation.* New York: Appleton-Century-Crofts.

Bach, M. J., & Underwood, B. J. (1970). Developmental changes in memory attributes. *Journal of Educational Psychology, 61,* 292–296.

Bach, S., & Klein, G. S. (1957). The effects of prolonged subliminal exposure of words. *American Psychologist, 12,* 397–398.

Baddeley, A. (1982). *Your memory: A user's guide.* New York: Macmillan.

Badia, P., Suter, S., & Lewis, P. (1967). Preferences for warned shock: Information and/or preparation. *Psychological Reports, 20,* 271–274.

Bahrick, H. P., & Boucher, B. (1968). Retention of visual and verbal codes of the same stimuli. *Journal of Experimental Psychology, 78,* 417–422.

Baker, T. B., & Tiffany, S. T. (1985). Morphine tolerance as habituation. *Psychological Review, 92,* 78–108.

Bandura, A. (1965). Influence of a model's reinforcement contingencies on the acquisition of imitative responses. *Journal of Personality and Social Psychology, 1,* 589–595.

Bandura, A. (1969). *Principles of behavior modification.* New York: Holt, Rinehart and Winston.

Bandura, A. (1973). *Aggression: A social learning analysis.* Englewood Cliffs, NJ: Prentice-Hall.

Bandura, A. (1977). *Social learning theory.* Englewood Cliffs, NJ: Prentice-Hall. (original work published 1971)

Bandura, A. (1978). The self system in reciprocal determinism. *American Psychologist, 33,* 344–358.

Bandura, A., Blanchard, E. B., & Ritter, B. (1969). The relative efficacy of desensitization and modeling approaches for inducing behavioral, affective, and attitudinal changes. *Journal of Personality and Social Psychology, 13,* 173–199.

Bandura, A., & Huston, A. C. (1961). Identification as a process of incidental learning. *Journal of Abnormal and Social Psychology, 63,* 311–318.

Bandura, A., Ross, D., & Ross, S. A. (1963). Imitation of film-mediated aggressive models. *Journal of Abnormal and Social Psychology, 66,* 3–11.

Bank, S., & Kahn, M. D. (1975). Sisterhood-brotherhood is powerful: Sibling subsystems and family therapy. *Family Process, 14,* 311–337.

Banks, M. S., & Salapatek, P. (1983). Infant visual perception. In P. H. Mussen (Ed.), *Handbook of child psychology: Vol. 2. Infancy and developmental psychobiology.* New York: Wiley.

Barber, T. X. (1969). *Hypnosis: A scientific approach.* New York: Van Nostrand Reinhold.

Barclay, J. R., Bransford, J. D., Franks, J. J., McCarrell, N. S., & Nitsch, K. (1974). Comprehension and semantic flexibility. *Journal of Verbal Learning and Verbal Behavior, 13,* 471–481.

Barefoot, J. D., Dahlstrom, W. G., & Williams, R. B. (1983). Hostility, CHD incidence and total mortality: A 25-year follow-up study of 255 physicians. *Psychosomatic Medicine, 45(4),* 559–570.

Barenboim, C. (1981). The development of person perception in childhood and adolescence: From behavioral comparisons to psychological constructs to psychological comparisons. *Child Development, 52,* 129–144.

Bargh, J. A. (1982). Attention and automaticity in the processing of self-relevant information. *Journal of Personality and Social Psychology, 43,* 425–436.

Barlow, D. H., Vermilyea, J., Blanchard, E. B., Vermilyea, B. B., DiNardo, P. A., & Cerny, J. A. (1985). The phenomenon of panic. *Journal of Abnormal Psychology, 94,* 320–328.

Baron, R. A. (1977). *Human aggression.* New York: Plenum Press.

Barrett, C. J. (1978). Effectiveness of widows' groups in facilitating change. *Journal of Consulting and Clinical Psychology, 46,* 20–31.

Barrett, D. E., & Radke-Yarrow, M. (1977). Prosocial behavior, social inferential ability, and assertiveness in children. *Child Development, 48,* 475–481.

Barrett, J. E. (Ed.). (1979). *Stress and mental disorder.* New York: Raven.

Barron, F., & Harrington, D. M. (1981). Creativity, intelligence, and personality. *Annual Review of Psychology, 52,* 439–476.

Bartoshuk, L. M., Gentile, R. L., Moskowitz, H. R., & Meiselman, H. L. (1974). Sweet taste induced by miracle fruit (Synsephalum dulcificum). *Physiology and Behavior, 12,* 449–456.

Bartus, R. T., Dean, R. L., III, Beer, B., and Lippa, A. S. (1982). The cholinergic hypothesis of geriatric memory dysfunction. *Science, 217,* 408–417.

Bates, E. (1976). *Language and context: The acquisition of pragmatics.* New York: Academic Press.

Bates, J. E. (1980). The concept of difficult temperament. *Merrill-Palmer Quarterly, 25,* 299–319.

Batson, C. D., & Coke, J. S. (1981). Empathy: A source of altruistic motivation for helping? In J. P. Rushton & R. M. Sorrentino (Eds.), *Altruism and behavior: Social, personality, and developmental perspectives.* Hillsdale, NJ: Lawrence Erlbaum Associates.

Bauer, D. H. (1976). An exploratory study of developmental changes in children's fears. *Journal of Child Psychology and Psychiatry, 17,* 69–74.

Baum, A., & Valins, S. (1973). Residential environments, group size and crowding. *Proceedings of the 81st Annual Convention of the American Psychological Association.*

Baum, A., & Valins, S. (1977). *Architecture and social behavior: Psychological studies of social density.* Hillsdale, NJ: Lawrence Erlbaum Associates.

Bauman, E. (1971). Schizophrenic short-term memory: A deficit in subjective organization. *Canadian Journal of Behavioral Science, 3,* 55–65.

Baumeister, R. F. (1984). Choking under pressure: Self-consciousness and paradoxical effects of incentives on skillful performance. *Journal of Personality and Social Psychology, 46*(3), 610–620.

Baumeister, R. F., & Steinhilber, A. (1984). Paradoxical effects of supportive audiences on performance under pressure: The home field disadvantage in sports championships. *Journal of Personality and Social Psychology, 47,* 85–93.

Baumrind, D. (1971). Current patterns of parental authority. *Developmental Psychology Monographs, 4* (1, Pt. 2).

Baumrind, D. (1975). Early socialization and adolescent competence. In S. E. Dragastin & G. H. Elder (Eds.), *Adolescence in the life cycle.* New York: Wiley.

Baumrind, D. (1979, March). *Sex-related socialization effects.* Paper presented at the biennial meeting of the Society for Research in Child Development, San Francisco, CA.

Baumrind, D., & Black, A. E. (1967). Socialization practices associated with dimensions of competence in preschool boys and girls. *Child Development, 38,* 291–327.

Baxter, L.R., et al. (1985). *Archives of General Psychiatry, 42.*

Bayley, N. (1970). Development of mental abilities. In P. H. Mussen (Ed.), *Carmichael's manual of child psychology: Vol. 1* (3rd ed.). New York: Wiley.

Bayley, N., Rhodes, L., Gooch, B., & Marus, N. (1971). A comparison of the growth development of institutionalized and home reared mongoloids. In Hellnuth, R. (Ed.), *Exceptional infant: Vol. 2. Studies in abnormality.* New York: Brown-Mazel.

Beaman, A. L., Barnes, P. J., Klentz, B., & McQuirk, B. (1978). Increasing helping rates through information dissemination: Teaching pays. *Personality and Social Psychology Bulletin, 4,* 406–411.

Beaman, A. L., Cole, C. M., Preston, M., Klentz, B., & Steblay, N. M. (1983). Fifteen years of foot-in-the-door research: A meta-analysis. *Personality and Social Psychology Bulletin, 9,* 181–196.

Beck, A. (1984). Cognitive approaches to stress. In R. L. Woolfolk & P. M. Lehrer (Eds.), *Principles and practice of stress management.* New York: Guilford Press.

Beck, A. T. (1967). *Depression: Clinical, experimental and theoretical aspects.* New York: Harper & Row.

Beck, A. T. (1970). The core problem in depression: The cognitive triad. In J. Masserman (Ed.), *Depression: Theories and therapies.* New York: Grune & Stratton.

Beck, A. T., Rush, A. J., Shaw, B. F., & Emery, G. (1979). *Cognitive therapy of depression.* New York: Guilford Press.

Beck, J. (1966). Perceptual grouping produced by changes in orientation and shape. *Science, 154,* 538–563.

Becker, C., & Kronus, S. (1977). Sex and drinking patterns: An old relationship revisited in a new way. *Social Problems, 24,* 482–497.

Becker, W. C. (1971). *Parents are teachers.* Champaign, IL: Research Press.

Beckwith, L. (1972). Relationships between infants' social behavior and their mothers' behavior. *Child Development, 43,* 397–411.

Bell, A., & Weinberg, M. S. (1978). *Homosexualities: A study of diversities among men and women.* New York: Simon & Schuster.

Bell, A., Weinberg, M. S., & Hammersmith, S. K. (1983). *Sexual preference development in men and women.* Bloomington: Indiana University Press.

Bell, R. R., & Bell, P. L. (1972). Sexual satisfaction among married women. *Medical Aspects of Human Sexuality, 6,* 136–144.

Belmont, J. M., & Butterfield, E. C. (1971). Learning strategies as determinants of memory deficiencies. *Cognitive Psychology, 2,* 411–420.

Bem, D. J. (1967). Self-perception: An alternative interpretation of cognitive dissonance phenomena. *Psychological Review, 74,* 183–200.

Bem, D. J., & Allen, A. (1974). On predicting some of the people some of the time: The search for cross-situational consistencies in behavior. *Psychological Review, 81,* 506–520.

Bem, D. J., & Lord, C. G. (1979). Template matching: A proposal for probing the ecological validity of experimental settings in social psychology. *Journal of Personality and Social Psychology, 37,* 833–846.

Bemis, K. M. (1978). Current approaches to the etiology and treatment of anorexia nervosa. *Psychological Bulletin, 85,* 593–617.

Bennett, H. L. (1983). Remembering drink orders: The memory skills of cocktail waitresses. *Human Learning: Journal of Practical Research and Applications, 2,* 157–170.

Benson, H. (1975). *The relaxation response.* New York: Morrow.

Berger, P. A. (1978). Medical treatment of mental illness. *Science, 200,* 974–981.

Bergin, A. E. (1971). The evaluation of therapeutic outcomes. In A. E. Bergin & S. L. Garfield (Eds.), *Handbook of psychotherapy and behavior change.* New York: Wiley.

Bergin, A. E., & Lambert, M. J. (1978). The evaluation of therapeutic outcomes. In S. L. Garfield & A. E. Bergin (Eds.), *Handbook of psychotherapy and behavior change* (2nd ed.). New York: Wiley.

Berkman, L., & Syme, S. L. (1979). Social networks, host resistance, and mortality: A nine-year follow-up study of Alameda County residents. *American Journal of Epidemiology, 109,* 186–204.

Berkowitz, L. (1954). Group standards, cohesiveness and productivity. *Human Relations, 7,* 509–519.

Berkowitz, L. (1973). Reactance and the unwillingness to help others. *Psychological Bulletin, 79,* 310–317.

Berkowitz, L. (1980). *A survey of social psychology* (2nd ed.). New York: Holt, Rinehart and Winston.

Berkowitz, L. (1981). Aversive conditions as stimuli for aggression. In L. Berkowitz (Ed.), *Advances in experimental social psychology: Vol. 15.* New York: Academic Press.

Berkun, M. M. (1964). Performance decrement under psychological stress. *Human Factors, 6,* 21–30.

Berlyne, D. E. (1960). *Conflict, arousal, and curiosity.* New York: McGraw-Hill.

Berman, J. S., & Norton, N. C. (1985). Does professional training make a therapist more effective? *Psychological Bulletin, 98,* 401–407.

Berndt, T. J. (1978a, August). *Children's conceptions of friendship and the behavior expected of friends*. Paper presented at the annual meeting of the American Psychological Association, Toronto, Ontario.

Berndt, T. J. (1978b, August). *Developmental changes on conformity to parents and peers*. Paper presented at the annual meeting of the American Psychological Association, Toronto, Ontario.

Bernstein, D. A. (1970). The modification of smoking behavior: A search for effective variables. *Behaviour Research and Therapy, 8,* 133–146.

Bernstein, D. A., & Borkovec, T. D. (1973). *Progressive relaxation training: A manual for the helping professions*. Champaign, IL: Research Press.

Bernstein, I. L. (1978). Learned taste aversions in children receiving chemotherapy. *Science, 200,* 1302–1303.

Berscheid, E. (1966). Opinion change and communicator-communicatee similarity and dissimilarity. *Journal of Personality and Social Psychology, 4,* 670–680.

Berscheid, E., Dion, K., Walster, E., & Walster, G. W. (1971). Physical attractiveness and dating choice: A test of the matching hypothesis. *Journal of Experimental Social Psychology, 7,* 173–189.

Berscheid, E., & Walster, E. (1978). *Interpersonal attraction* (2nd ed.). Reading, MA: Addison-Wesley.

Best, P. J., Best, M. R., & Henggeler, S. (1977). The contribution of environmental non-ingestive cues in conditioning with aversive internal consequences. In L. M. Barker, M. R. Best, & M. Domjan (Eds.), *Learning mechanisms in food selection*. Waco, TX: Baylor University Press.

Bettelheim, B. (1967). *The empty fortress*. New York: Free Press.

Bexton, W. H. (1953). *Some effects of perceptual isolation in human beings*. Unpublished doctoral dissertation, McGill University, Montreal.

Bexton, W. H., Heron, W., & Scott, T. H. (1954). Effects of decreased variation in the sensory environment. *Canadian Journal of Psychology, 8,* 70–76.

Bharucha, J. J. (1984). Anchoring effects in music: The resolution of dissonance. *Cognitive Psychology, 16,* 485–518.

Biederman, I., Mezzanotte, R. J., Rabinowitz, J. C., Franeolin, C. M., & Plude, D. (1981). Detecting the unexpected in photo-interpretation. *Human Factors, 23,* 153–163.

Bierman, K. L., Miller, C. L., & Stabb, S. D. (1987). Improving the social behavior and peer acceptance of rejected boys: Effects of social skill training with instructions and prohibitions. *Journal of Consulting and Clinical Psychology, 55,* 194–200.

Bijou, S. W., & Baer, P. M. (1961). *Child development: Vol. 1. A systematic and empirical theory*. New York: Appleton-Century-Crofts.

Billings, A. G., & Moos, R. H. (1984). Coping, stress, and social resources among adults with unipolar depression. *Journal of Personality and Social Psychology, 46*(4), 877–891.

Billings, A. G., & Moos, R. H. (1985). Life stressors and social resources affect posttreatment outcomes among depressed patients. *Journal of Abnormal Psychology, 94*(2), 140–153.

Binet, A., & Simon, T. (1905). Methodes nouvelles pour le diagnostic du niveau intellectuel des anormaux. *L'Anneé Psychologique, 11,* 191–244.

Birch, H. G., & Gussow, M. (1970). *Disadvantaged children*. New York: Harcourt, Brace & World.

Birnbaum, M. H. (1973). Morality judgment: Test of an averaging model with differential weights. *Journal of Experimental Psychology, 99,* 395–399.

Bitterman, M. E. (1969). Thorndike and the problem of animal intelligence. *American Psychologist, 24,* 444–453.

Bjorklund, A., Stenevi, U., Dunnett, S. B., & Gage, F. H. (1982). Cross-species neural grafting in a rat model of Parkinson's disease. *Nature, 298,* 652–654.

Blakemore, C., & Van Sluyters, R. C. (1974). Reversal of the physio-logical effects of monocular deprivation in kittens: Further evidence for a sensitive period. *Journal of Physiology, 206,* 419–436.

Blass, E. M., & Epstein, A. N. (1971). A lateral preoptic osmosensitive zone for thirst. *Journal of Comparative and Physiological Psychology, 76,* 378–394.

Blatt, S. J., & Lerner, H. (1983). Psychodynamic perspectives on personality theory. In M. Hersen, A. E. Kazdin, & A. S. Bellack (Eds.), *The clinical psychology handbook* (pp. 61–86). New York: Pergamon Press.

Blazer, D. G., Bacher, J. R., & Manton, K. G. (1986). Suicide in late life: Review and commentary. *Journal of the American Geriatrics Society, 34,* 519–525.

Bloch, V., Hennevin, E., & LeConte, P. (1977). Interaction between post-trial reticular stimulation and subsequent paradoxical sleep in memory consolidation processes. In R. R. Drucker-Colin & J. L. McGlaugh (Eds.), *Neurobiology of sleep and memory*. New York: Academic Press.

Block, J. (1971). *Lives through time*. Berkeley: Bancroft Books.

Block, J. H. (1980). Another look at sex differentiation in the socialization behavior of mothers and fathers. In F. Denmark & J. Sherman (Eds.), *Psychology of women: Future directions of research*. New York: Psychological Dimensions.

Block, J. H. (1983). Differential premises arising from differential socialization of the sexes: Some conjectures. *Child Development, 54,* 1335–1354.

Bloom, F. E., Lazerson, A., & Hofstadter, L. (1985). *Brain, mind, and behavior*. New York: W. H. Freeman.

Blurton-Jones, N. (1972). Categories of child-child interaction. In N. Blurton-Jones (Ed.), *Ethological studies of child behaviour*. Cambridge: Cambridge University Press.

Bolles, R. C. (1975). *Theory of motivation* (2nd ed.). New York: Harper & Row.

Booth, D. A. (1980). Acquired behavior controlling energy intake and output. In A. J. Stunkard (Ed.), *Obesity*. Philadelphia: W. B. Saunders.

Bootzin, R. R., & Nicassio, P. M. (1978). Behavioral treatments for insomnia. In M. Herson, R. Eisler, & P. M. Miller (Eds.), *Progress in behavior modification: Vol. 6*. New York: Academic Press.

Boring, E. G. (1923). Intelligence as the tests test it. *New Republic, 35,* 35–37.

Boring, E. G. (1930). A new ambiguous figure. *American Journal of Psychology, 42,* 444–445.

Borke, H. (1971). Interpersonal perception of young children: Egocentrism or empathy? *Developmental Psychology, 5,* 263–269.

Borke, H. (1975). Piaget's mountains revisited: Changes in the egocentric landscape. *Developmental Psychology, 11,* 240–243.

Botwinick, J. (1966). Cautiousness in advanced age. *Journal of Gerontology, 21,* 347–353.

Botwinick, J. (1977). Intellectual abilities. In J. E. Birren & K. W. Schaie (Eds.), *Handbook of the psychology of aging*. New York: Van Nostrand Reinhold.

Bouchard, T. J., & McGue, M. (1981). Familial studies of intelligence: A review. *Science, 212,* 1055–1059.

Bourne, L. E. (1967). Learning and utilization of conceptual rules. In B. Kleinmuntz (Ed.), *Concepts and the structure of memory*. New York: Wiley.

Bower, G. H. (1970). Organizational factors in memory. *Cognitive Psychology, 1,* 18–46.

Bower, G. H. (1973). How to . . . uh . . . remember! *Psychology Today, 7,* 62–67.

Bower, G. H. (1975). Cognitive psychology: An introduction. In W. K. Estes (Ed.), *Handbook of learning and cognitive processes: Vol. 1*. Hillsdale, NJ: Lawrence Erlbaum Associates.

Bower, G. H. (1981). Mood and memory. *American Psychologist, 36,* 129–148.

Bower, G. H., & Cohen, P. R. (1982). Emotional influences in memory and thinking: Data and theory. In M. S. Clark & S. T. Fiske (Eds.), *Affect and cognition*. Hillsdale, NJ: Lawrence Erlbaum Associates.

Bower, G. H., Gilligan, S. G., & Monteiro, K. P. (1981). Selectivity of learning caused by affective states. *Journal of Experimental Psychology: General, 110,* 451–473.

Bower, T. G. R., & Wishart, J. G. (1972). The effects of motor skill on object permanence. *Cognition, 1,* 165–172.

Bowerman, C. E., & Kinch, J. W. (1956). Changes in family and peer orientation of children between the fourth and tenth grades. *Social Forces, 37,* 206–211.

Boyatzis, R. E. (1982). *The competent manager.* New York: Wiley.

Brackbill, Y. (1958). Extinction of the smiling response in infants as a function of reinforcement schedule. *Child Development, 29,* 115–124.

Brackbill, Y. (1979). Obstetrical medication and infant behavior. In J. D. Osofsky (Ed.), *Handbook of infant development.* New York: Wiley.

Braginsky, B. M., Grosse, M., & Ring, K. (1966). Controlling outcomes through impression management: An experimental study of the manipulative tactics of mental patients. *Journal of Consulting Psychology, 30,* 295–300.

Bransford, J. D., & Johnson, M. K. (1972). Contextual prerequisites for understanding: Some investigations of comprehension and recall. *Journal of Verbal Learning and Verbal Behavior, 11,* 717–726.

Bransford, J. D., Nitsch, K. E., & Franks, J. J. (1977). Schooling and the facilitation of knowing. In R. C. Anderson, R. J. Spiro, & W. E. Montague (Eds.), *Schooling and the acquisition of knowledge.* Hillsdale, NJ: Lawrence Erlbaum Associates.

Brantigan, T. A., Brantigan, C. O., & Joseph, N. H. (1978). Beta blockage and musical performance. *Lancet, 896,* ii.

Brazelton, T. B., & Tronick, E. (1983). Preverbal communication between mothers and infants. In W. Damon (Ed.), *Social and personality development.* New York: W. W. Norton.

Breggin, P. R. (1979). *Electroshock: Its brain-disabling effects.* New York: Halsted Press.

Brehm, J. (1966). *A theory of psychological reactance.* New York: Academic Press.

Brehm, J. (1972). *Responses to loss of freedom: A theory of psychological reactance.* Morristown, NJ: General Learning Press.

Brehmer, B. (1981). Models of diagnostic judgment. In J. Rasmussen & W. Rouse (Eds.), *Human detection and diagnosis of systems failures.* New York: Plenum Press.

Bremer, J. (1959). *Asexualization.* New York: Macmillan.

Brenner, C. (1974). *An elementary textbook of psychoanalysis.* New York: Anchor.

Breuer, J., & Freud, S. (1966). *Studies on hysteria.* New York: Avon. (original work published 1896)

Brewer, W. F., & Nakamura, G. V. (1984). The nature and functions of schemas. In R. S. Wyer & T. K. Srull (Eds.), *Handbook of social cognition: Vol. 1.* Hillsdale, NJ: Lawrence Erlbaum Associates.

Brewer, W. F., & Pani, J. R. (1984). The structure of human memory. In G. H. Bower (Ed.), *The psychology of learning and motivation: Vol. 17.* New York: Academic Press.

Brewer, W. F., & Treyens, J. C. (1981). Role of schemata in memory for places. *Cognitive Psychology, 13,* 207–230.

Brickman, P., Becker, L. J., & Castle, S. (1979). Making trust easier and harder through two forms of sequential interaction. *Journal of Personality and Social Psychology, 37,* 515–521.

Brigham, C. C. (1923). *A study of American intelligence.* Princeton, NJ: Princeton University Press.

British Psychological Society. (1986). Report of the working group on the use of the polygraph in criminal investigation and personnel screening. *Bulletin of the British Psychological Society, 39,* 81–94.

Broadhead, W. E., Kaplan, B. H., James, S. A., Wagner, E. H., Schoenbach, V. J., Grimson, R., Heyden, S., Tiblin, G., & Gehlbach, S. H. (1983). The epidemiologic evidence for a relationship between social support and health. *American Journal of Epidemiology, 117,* 521–537.

Brody, E. B., & Brody, N. (1976). *Intelligence: Nature, determinants, and consequences.* New York: Academic Press.

Bronson, W. C. (1975). Developments in behavior with age-mates during the second year of life. In M. Lewis & L. A. Rosenblum (Eds.), *Friendship and peer relations.* New York: Wiley-Interscience.

Brown, A., Campione, J. C., & Barclay, C. R. (1979). Training self-checking routines for estimating test readiness: Generalizations from list learning to prose recall. *Child Development, 50,* 501–512.

Brown, A. L. (1975). The development of memory: Knowing, knowing about knowing, and knowing how to know it. In H. W. Reese (Ed.), *Advances in child development and behavior: Vol. 10.* New York: Academic Press.

Brown, A. L. & Smiley, S. S. (1977). Rating the importance of structural units of prose passages: A problem of metacognitive development. *Child Development, 48,* 1–8.

Brown, J. (1958). Some tests of the decay theory of immediate memory. *Quarterly Journal of Experimental Psychology, 10,* 12–21.

Brown, J., & Cartwright, R. D. (1977). *Subject vs. experimenter elicited dream reports: Who knows best?* Paper presented at the meeting of the Association for the Psychophysiological Study of Sleep, Houston, TX.

Brown, J. S. (1981). In D. Gentner & A. Stevens (Eds.), *Mental models.* Hillsdale, NJ: Lawrence Erlbaum Associates.

Brown, P., & Elliott, R. (1965). Control of aggression in a nursery school class. *Journal of Experimental Child Psychology, 2,* 103–107.

Brown, R., & Kulik, J. (1977). Flashbulb memories. *Cognition, 5,* 73–99.

Brown, R., & McNeill, D. (1966). The "tip-of-the-tongue" phenomenon. *Journal of Verbal Learning and Verbal Behavior, 5,* 325–337.

Brown, R. A. (1973). *First language.* Cambridge: Harvard University Press.

Bruner, J. (1964). The course of cognitive growth. *American Psychologist, 19,* 1–55.

Bryan, J. H. (1975). Children's cooperation and helping behaviors. In E. M. Hetherington (Ed.), *Review of child development research: Vol. 5.* Chicago: University of Chicago Press.

Bryan, J. H., & Luria, Z. (1978). Sex-role learning: A test of the selective attention hypothesis. *Child Development, 49,* 13–23.

Bryan, J. H., & Walbek, N. H. (1970). Preaching and practicing generosity: Children's actions and reactions. *Child Development, 41,* 329–353.

Buchsbaum, M. S., Ingvar, D. H., Kessler, R., Waters, R. N., Cappelletti, J., van Kammen, D. P., King, A. C., Johnson, J. L., Manning, R. G., Flynn, R. W., Mann, L. S., Bunney, W. E., & Sokoloff, L. (1982). Cerebral glucography with positron tomography: Use in normal subjects and patients with schizophrenia. *Archives of General Psychiatry, 39,* 251–259.

Budzynski, T. H., & Stoyva, J. M. (1984). Biofeedback methods in the treatment of anxiety and stress. In R. L. Woolfolk & P. M. Lehrer (Eds.), *Principles and practice of stress management.* New York: Guilford Press.

Bunney, W. E., Jr., Goodwin, F. K., & Murphy, D. L. (1972). The "switch process" in manic-depressive illness: 3. Theoretical implications. *Archives of General Psychiatry, 27,* 312–317.

Burchfield, S. R. (1979). The stress response: A new perspective. *Psychosomatic Medicine, 41,* 661–672.

Burger, J. (1985). Desire for control and achievement-related behaviors. *Journal of Personality and Social Psychology, 48,* 1520–1533.

Burger, J. M., & Petty, R. E. (1981). The low-ball compliance technique: Task or person commitment? *Journal of Personality and Social Psychology, 40,* 492–500.

Burnstein, E., & Vinokur, A. (1977). Persuasive argumentation and social comparison as determinants of attitude polarization. *Journal of Experimental Social Psychology, 13,* 315–330.

Burnstein, E., Vinokur, A., & Trope, Y. (1973). Interpersonal comparison versus persuasive argumentation: A more direct test of alternative explanations for group-induced shifts in individual choice. *Journal of Experimental Social Psychology, 9*, 236–245.

Buss, A. H. (1966). *Psychopathology*. New York: Wiley.

Buss, A. H., Plomin, R., & Willerman, L. (1973). The inheritance of temperaments. *Journal of Personality, 41*, 513–524.

Buss, D. M. (1981). Predicting parent-child interactions from children's activity level. *Developmental Psychology, 17*, 59–65.

Butcher, J. N. (1979). Use of the MMPI in personnel selection. In J. N. Butcher (Ed.), *New developments in the use of the MMPI*. Minneapolis: University of Minnesota Press.

Butler, C. A. (1976). New data about female sexual response. *Journal of Sex and Marital Therapy, 2*, 40–46.

Butler, R. A., & Belendiuk, K. (1977). Spectral cues utilized in the location of sound in the median saggital plane. *Journal of the Acoustical Society of America, 61*, 1264–1269.

Butler, R. N. (1963). The life review: An interpretation of reminiscence in the aged. *Psychiatry, 26*, 65–76.

Butler, R. N. (1975). *Why survive? Being old in America*. New York: Harper & Row.

Butterfield, E. C., Wambold, C., & Belmont, J. M. (1973). On the theory and practice of improving short-term memory. *American Journal of Mental Deficiency, 77*, 654–669.

Byrne, D. (1964). Repression-sensitization as a dimension of personality. In B. Mayer (Ed.), *Progress in experimental personality research: Vol. 1.* New York: Academic Press.

Byrne, D., & Clore, G. L. (1970). A reinforcement model of evaluative responses. *Personality: An International Journal, 1*, 103–128.

Byrne, D., & Griffitt, W. B. (1966). A developmental investigation of the law of attraction. *Journal of Personality and Social Psychology, 4*, 699–702.

Byrne, D., London, O., & Reeves, K. (1968). The effects of physical attractiveness, sex, and attitude similarity on interpersonal attraction. *Journal of Personality, 36*, 259–271

Byrne, D., & Nelson, D. (1965). Attraction as a linear function of proportion of positive reinforcements. *Journal of Personality and Social Psychology, 1*, 659–663.

Cabanac, M. (1971). The physiological role of pleasure. *Science, 173*, 1103–1107.

Campbell, B. A., & Kraeling, D. (1953). Response strength as a function of drive level and amount of drive reduction. *Journal of Experimental Psychology, 45*, 97–101.

Campione, J. C., & Brown, A. L. (1977). Memory and metamemory development in educable retarded children. In R. V. Kail & J. W. Hagen (Eds.), *Perspectives on the development of memory and cognition*. Hillsdale, NJ: Lawrence Erlbaum Associates.

Campione, J. C., Brown, A. L., & Ferrara, R. A. (1982). Mental retardation and intelligence. In R. J. Sternberg (Ed.), *Handbook of human intelligence*. Cambridge: Cambridge University Press.

Campos, J., & Barrett, K. (1984). Towards a developmental theory of behavior. In C. Izard, J. Kagan, & R. Zajonc (Eds.), *Emotion, cognition, and behavior*. New York: Cambridge University Press.

Campos, J., Langer, A., & Krowitz, A. (1970). Cardiac responses on the visual cliff in prelocomotor human infants. *Science, 170*, 196–197.

Campos, J., & Stenberg, C. (1981). Perception, appraisal, and emotion: The onset of social referencing. In M. Lamb & L. Sherrod (Eds.), *Infant social cognition*. Hillsdale, NJ: Lawrence Erlbaum Associates.

Camras, L. A. (1977). Facial expressions used by children in a conflict situation. *Child Development, 48*, 1431–1435.

Cann, A., Sherman, S. J., & Elkes, R. (1975). Effects of initial request size and timing of a second request on compliance: The foot-in-the-door and the door-in-the-face. *Journal of Personality and Social Psychology, 32*, 774–782.

Cannabis: Report by the Advisory Committee on Drug Dependence. (1968). London: Her Majesty's Stationery Office.

Cannon, D. S., & Baker, T. B. (1981). Emetic and electric shock alcohol aversion therapy: Assessment of conditioning. *Journal of Consulting and Clinical Psychology, 49*, 20–33.

Cannon, W. B. (1927). The James-Lange theory of emotions: A critical examination and an alternative. *American Journal of Psychology, 39*, 106–124.

Cannon, W. B., & Washburn, A. L. (1912). An explanation of hunger. *American Journal of Physiology, 29*, 444–454.

Cantril, H. (1965). *The pattern of human concerns*. New Brunswick, NJ: Rutgers University Press.

Capaldi, E. J. (1967). A sequential hypothesis of instrumental learning. In K. W. Spence & J. T. Spence (Eds.), *The psychology of learning and motivation· Vol. 1*. New York: Academic Press.

Caplan, G. (1964). *Principles of preventive psychiatry*. New York: Basic Books.

Carey, T. (1982) User differences in interface design. *Computer, 15*, 14–20.

Carlsmith, J. M., & Anderson, C. A. (1979). Ambient temperature and the occurrence of collective violence: A new analysis. *Journal of Personality and Social Psychology, 37*, 337–344.

Carlson, J. S., Jensen, C. M., & Widaman, K. F. (1983). Reaction time, intelligence and attention. *Intelligence, 7*, 329–344.

Carlson, N. R. (1980). *Physiology of behavior* (2nd ed.). Boston: Allyn and Bacon.

Carmichael, L. L., Hogan, H. P., & Walter, A. A. (1932). An experimental study of the effect of language on the reproduction of visually perceived form *Journal of Experimental Psychology, 15*, 73–86.

Carrington, P. (1984). Modern forms of meditation. In R. L. Woolfolk & P. M. Lehrer (Eds.), *Principles and practice of stress management*. New York: Guilford Press.

Carroll, B. J., Feinberg, M., Greden, J. F., Tarika, J., Albala, A. A., Haskett, R. F, James, N. M., Kronfol, Z., Lohr, N., Steiner, M., De Vigne, J. P., & Young, E. (1981). A specific laboratory test for the diagnosis of melancholia—Standardization, validation and clinical utility. *Archives of General Psychiatry, 38*, 15–22.

Carroll, J. B. (1982). The measurement of intelligence. In R. J. Sternberg (Ed.), *Handbook of human intelligence*. Cambridge: Cambridge University Press.

Cartwright, R. D. (1978). *A primer on sleep and dreaming*. Reading, MA: Addison-Wesley.

Cartwright, R. D., Lloyd, S., Knight, S., & Trenholme, I. (1984). Broken dreams: A study of the effects of divorce and depression on dream content. *Psychiatry, 47*, 251–259.

Carver, R. P. (1972, August). Speed readers don't read; they skim. *Psychology Today*, pp. 23–30.

Casper, R. C., Eckhert, E. D., Halmi, K. A., Goldberg, S. C., & Davis, J. M. (1980). Bulimia: Its incidence and clinical importance in patients with anorexia nervosa. *Archives of General Psychiatry, 37*, 1030–1035.

Cassidy, J., & Main, M. (1984, April). *Quality of attachment from infancy to early childhood: Security is stable but behavior changes*. Paper presented at the International Conference on Infant Studies, New York, NY.

Cattell, R. B. (1971). *Abilities: Their structure, growth and action*. Boston: Houghton Mifflin.

Cavior, N., & Dokecki, P. R. (1969). *Physical attractiveness and popularity among fifth-grade boys*. Paper presented at the annual convention of the Southwestern Psychological Association.

Cerf, C. (1984). *The experts speak*. New York: Pantheon.

Chaiken, A. L., & Derlega, V. J. (1974). *Self-disclosure*. Morristown, NJ: General Learning Press.

Chaiken, A. L., Sigler, E., & Derlega, V. J. (1974). Nonverbal mediators of teacher expectancy effects. *Journal of Personality and Social Psychology, 30*, 144–149.

Chambliss, D., & Goldstein, A. (1980). The treatment of agoraphobia. In A. Goldstein & E. Foa (Eds.), *Handbook of behavioral interventions.* New York: Wiley.

Chapanis, A., & Lindenbaum, L. E. (1959). A reaction time study of control-display linkages. *Human Factors, 1,* 1–14.

Chapman, A. J. (1974). An electro-myographic study of social facilitation: A test of the "mere presence" hypothesis. *British Journal of Psychology, 65,* 123–128.

Charrow, R. P., & Charrow, V. R. (1979). Making legal language understandable: A psycholinguistic study of jury instructions. *Columbia Law Review, 79,* 1306–1374.

Chase, W. G., & Ericsson, K. A. (1979, November). *A mnemonic system for digit span: One year later.* Paper presented at the meeting of the Psychonomic Society, Phoenix, AZ.

Chase, W. G., & Ericsson, K. A. (1981). Skilled memory. In J. R. Anderson (Ed.), *Cognitive skills and their acquisition.* Hillsdale, NJ: Lawrence Erlbaum Associates.

Chemers, M. (1983). Leadership theory and research: A systems-process integration. In P. B. Paulus (Ed.), *Basic group processes.* New York: Springer-Verlag.

Chemers, M. M., Hays, R. B., Rhodewalt, F., & Wysocki, J. (1985). A person-environment analysis of job stress: A contingency model explanation. *Journal of Personality and Social Psychology, 49,* 628–639.

Chen, E., & Cobb, S. (1960). Family structure in relation to health and disease. *Journal of Chronic Diseases, 12,* 544–567.

Chen, S. C. (1937). Social modification of the activity of ants in nest-building. *Physiological Zoology, 10,* 420–436.

Cherry, C. (1953). Some experiments on the reception of speech with one and two ears. *Journal of the Acoustical Society of America, 25,* 975–979.

Chesnic, M., Menyuk, P., Liebergott, J., Ferrier, L., & Strand, K. (1983, April). *Who leads whom?* Paper presented at the meeting of the Society for Research in Child Development, Detroit, MI.

Chomsky, N. (1957). *Syntactic structures.* The Hague: Mouton.

Chorover, L. (1965). Discussion of the effects of electroconvulsive shock on performance and memory. In D. P. Kimble (Ed.), *The anatomy of memory.* Palo Alto, CA: Science & Behavior Books.

Christenssen-Szalanski, J. J., & Bushyhead, J. B. (1981). Physicians' use of probabilistic information in a real clinical setting. *Journal of Experimental Psychology: Human Perception and Performance, 7,* 928–936.

Christie, R., Gergen, K. J., & Marlowe, D. (1970). The ten-dollar caper. In R. Christie & F. L. Geis (Eds.), *Studies in Machiavellianism.* New York: Academic Press.

Chugani, H. T., & Phelps, M. E. (1986). Maturational changes in cerebral function in infants determined by 18FDG positron emission tomography. *Science, 231,* 840–843.

Cialdini, R. B. (1984). *Influence: The new psychology of modern persuasion.* New York: Quill.

Cialdini, R. B., Cacioppo, J. T., Bassett, R., & Miller, J. A. (1978). Low-ball procedure for producing compliance: Commitment then cost. *Journal of Personality and Social Psychology, 36,* 463–476.

Cialdini, R. B., Petty, R. E., & Cacioppo, J. T. (1981). Attitude and attitude change. *Annual Review of Psychology, 32,* 357–404.

Cialdini, R. B., Vincent, J. E., Lewis, S. K., Catalan, J., Wheeler, D., & Darby, B. L. (1975). Reciprocal concessions procedure for inducing compliance: The door-in-the-face technique. *Journal of Personality and Social Psychology, 31,* 206–215.

Clark, L. (1978). Strategies for communicating. *Child Development, 49,* 953–959.

Clark, H., & Clark, E. (1977). *Psychology and language: An introduction to psycholinguistics.* New York: Harcourt Brace Jovanovich.

Clark, M. S., & Isen, A. M. (1982). Toward understanding the relationship between feeling states and social behavior. In A. H.

Hastorf & A. M. Isen (Eds.), *Cognitive social psychology.* New York: Elsevier.

Clark, R. D., & Word, L. E. (1972). Why don't bystanders help? Because of ambiguity? *Journal of Personality and Social Psychology, 24,* 392–400.

Clark, R. D., & Word, L. E. (1974). Where is the apathetic bystander? Situational characteristics of the emergency. *Journal of Personality and Social Psychology, 29,* 279–287.

Clarke, A. M., & Clarke, A. D. B. (1976a). Some continued experiments. In A. M. Clarke & A. D. B. Clarke (Eds.), *Early experience: Myth and evidence.* New York: Free Press.

Clarke, A. M., & Clarke, A. D. B. (Eds.). (1976b). *Early experience: Myth and evidence.* London: Open Books.

Clarke-Stewart, K. A. (1973). Interactions between mothers and their young children: Characteristics and consequences. *Monographs of the Society for Research in Child Development, 38* (6–7, Serial No. 153).

Clarke-Stewart, K. A. (1978). And daddy makes three: The father's impact on mother and young child. *Child Development, 49,* 466–478.

Clarke-Stewart, K. A. (1980). The father's contribution to child development. In F. A. Pedersen (Ed.), *The father-infant relationship: Observational studies in a family context.* New York: Praeger Special Studies.

Clarke-Stewart, K. A., & Apfel, N. (1979). Evaluating parental effects on child development. In L. S. Shulman (Ed.), *Review of research in education: Vol. 6.* Itasca, IL: Peacock.

Clarke-Stewart, K. A., & Fein, G. G. (1983). Early childhood programs. In P. H. Mussen (Ed.), *Handbook of child psychology: Vol. 2. Infancy and developmental psychobiology.* New York: Wiley.

Clarke-Stewart, K. A., Friedman, F., & Koch, J. (1985). *Child development: A topical approach.* New York: Wiley.

Clarke-Stewart, K. A., & Hevey, C. M. (1981). Longitudinal relations in repeated observations of mother-child interaction from 1 to 2½ years. *Developmental Psychology, 17,* 127–145.

Clausen, J., Sersen, E., & Lidsky, A. (1974). Variability of sleep measures in normal subjects. *Psychophysiology, 11,* 509–516.

Cleary, T. A., Humphreys, L. G., Kendrick, S. A., & Wesman, A. (1975). Educational use of tests with disadvantaged students. *American Psychologist, 30,* 15–41.

Cleckley, H. (1976). *The mask of sanity* (5th ed.). St. Louis: Mosby.

Clement, U., & Pfafflin, F. (1980). Changes in personality scores among couples subsequent to sex therapy. *Archives of Sexual Behavior, 9,* 235–244.

Clifford, B. R., & Hollin, C. R. (1981). Effects of the type of incident and number of perpetrators on eyewitness testimony. *Journal of Applied Psychology, 67,* 364–370.

Cline, V. B., Croft, R. G., & Courrier, S. (1973). Desensitization of children to television violence. *Journal of Personality and Social Psychology, 27,* 360–365.

Clopton, J. R., Pallis, D. J., & Birtchnell, J. (1979). Minnesota Multiphasic Personality Inventory profile patterns of suicide attempters. *Journal of Consulting and Clinical Psychology, 47,* 135–139.

Coates, T. J., & Thoreson, C. E. (1977). *How to sleep better.* Englewood Cliffs, NJ: Prentice-Hall.

Cohen, F., & Lazarus, R. S. (1979). Coping with the stresses of illness. In G. C. Stone, F. Cohen, & N. E. Adler (Eds.), *Health psychology: A handbook.* San Francisco: Jossey-Bass.

Cohen, G., & Faulkner, D. (1981). Memory for discourse in old age. *Discourse Processes, 4,* 253–265.

Cohen, G., & Faulkner, D. (1983). Word recognition: Age differences in contextual facilitation effects. *British Journal of Psychology, 74,* 239–251.

Cohen, L. J., & Campos, J. J. (1974). Father, mother, and stranger as elicitors of attachment behaviors in infancy. *Developmental Psychology, 10,* 146–154.

Cohen, S. (1980). Aftereffects of stress on human performance and social behavior. A review of research and theory. *Psychological Bulletin, 88,* 82–108.

Cohen, S., & Hoberman, H. M. (1983). Positive events and social supports as buffers of life change stress. *Journal of Applied Social Psychology, 13,* 99–125.

Cohen, S., & Wills, T. A. (1985). Stress, social support, and the buffering hypothesis. *Psychological Bulletin, 98,* 310–357.

Cohn, J. F., & Tronick, E. Z. (1983). Three-month-old infants' reaction to simulated maternal depression. *Child Development, 54,* 185–193.

Coleman, J. C., Butcher, J. N., & Carson, R. C. (1984). *Abnormal psychology and modern life* (7th ed.). Glenview, IL: Scott, Foresman.

Colletta, N. D. (1979). Support systems after divorce: Incidence and impact. *Journal of Marriage and the Family, 41,* 837–846.

Collins, D. L., Baum, A., & Singer, J. E. (1983). Coping with chronic stress at Three Mile Island: Psychological and biochemical evidence. *Health Psychology, 2,* 149–166.

Colon, E. J. (1972). Quantitative cytoarchitectonics of the human cerebral cortex in schizophrenic dementia. *Acta Neuropathologica, 20,* 1–10.

Coltheart, M. (1980). Iconic memory and visual persistence. *Perception and Psychophysics, 27,* 183–228.

Coltheart, M. (1983). Ecological necessity of iconic memory. *The Behavioral and Brain Sciences, 6,* 17–18.

Commission of Inquiry into the Non-medical Use of Drugs. (1970, 1972, 1973). *Interim Report.* Ottawa: Queen's Printer for Canada.

Condry, J., & Condry, S. (1976). Sex differences: A study in the eye of the beholder. *Child Development, 47,* 812–819.

Condry, J., & Siman, M. L. (1974). Characteristics of peer adult-oriented children. *Journal of Marriage and the Family, 36,* 543–554.

Cone, J. D. (1977). The relevance of reliability and validity to behavioral assessment. *Behavior Therapy, 8,* 411–426.

Conger, J. J. (1951). The effects of alcohol on conflict behavior in the albino rat. *Quarterly Journal of Studies on Alcohol, 12,* 1–29.

Conley, J. J. (1984). Longitudinal consistency of adult personality: Self-reported psychological characteristics across 45 years. *Journal of Personality and Social Psychology, 47,* 1325–1333.

Conrad, R. (1964). Acoustic confusions in immediate memory. *British Journal of Psychology, 55,* 75–84.

Cook, E. W., III, Hodes, R. L., & Lang, P. J. (1986). Preparedness and phobia: Effects of stimulus content on human visceral conditioning. *Journal of Abnormal Psychology, 95,* 195–207.

Cooper, C. L. (1985). *Psychosocial stress and cancer.* New York: Wiley.

Cooper, H. (1979). Pygmalion grows up: A model for teacher expectation communication and performance influence. *Review of Educational Research, 49,* 389–410.

Cooper, J., & Croyle, R. T. (1984). Attitudes and attitude change. *Annual Review of Psychology, 35,* 395–426.

Coppen, A., Metcalf, M., & Wood, K. (1982). Lithium. In E. S. Paykel (Ed.), *Handbook of affective disorders.* New York: Guilford Press.

Corah, N. C., & Boffa, J. (1970). Perceived control, self-observation, and response to aversive stimulation. *Journal of Personality and Social Psychology, 16,* 1–4.

Cordes, C. (1985, April). A step back. *APA Monitor,* pp. 12–14.

Corsini, R. (Ed.). (1981). *Handbook of innovative psychology.* New York: Wiley.

Cowan, J. D. (1976). Implications of state dependent learning for drug abuse. *Problems of Drug Dependence, 38,* 888–921.

Cowan, W. M. (1979). The development of the brain. *Scientific American, 241,* 112–133.

Cowen, E. L. (1982). Help is where you find it: Four informal helping groups. *American Psychologist, 37,* 385–395.

Cowen, E. L. (1983). Primary prevention: Past, present, and future. In R. D. Felner, L. A. Jason, J. N. Moritsugu, & S. S. Faber (Eds.), *Preventive psychology: Theory, research and practice.* New York: Pergamon Press.

Cowles, J. T. (1937). Food-tokens as incentives for learning by chimpanzees. *Comparative Psychology Monographs* 14(5, Serial No. 71).

Cox, A., Rutter, M., Newman, S., & Bartak, L. (1975). A comparative study of infantile autism and specific developmental language disorders. II. Parental characteristics. *British Journal of Psychiatry, 126,* 146–159.

Coyle, J. T., Price, D. L., & DeLong, M. R. (1983). Alzheimer's disease: A disorder of cortical cholinergic innervation. *Science, 219,* 1184–1190.

Cozby, P. C. (1973). Self-disclosure: A literature review. *Psychological Bulletin, 79,* 73–91.

Craighead, L. W. (1984). Sequencing of behavior therapy and pharmacotherapy for obesity. *Journal of Consulting and Clinical Psychology, 52,* 190–199.

Craik, F. I. M. (1977). Age differences in human memory. In J. E. Birren & K. W. Schaie (Eds.), *Handbook of the psychology of aging.* New York: Van Nostrand Reinhold.

Craik, F. I. M., & Lockhart, R. S. (1972). Levels of processing: A framework for memory research. *Journal of Verbal Learning and Verbal Behavior, 11,* 671–684.

Craik, F. I. M., & Rabinowitz, J. C. (1984). Age differences in the acquisition and use of verbal information. In H. Bouma & D. G. Bouwhuis (Eds.), *Attention and performance: Vol. 10.* Hillsdale, NJ: Lawrence Erlbaum Associates.

Craik, K. H. (1986). Psychological perspectives on technology as societal option, source of hazard, and generator of environmental impacts. In V. Covello & J. Mumpower (Eds.), *Technology assessment, environmental impact assessment, and risk analysis.* New York: Springer-Verlag.

Crews, D., & Moore, M. C. (1986). Evolution of mechanisms controlling mating behavior. *Science, 231,* 121–125.

Crick, F., & Mitchison, G. (1983). The function of dream sleep. *Nature, 304,* 111–114.

Crisp, A. H., Palmer, R. L., & Klucy, R. S. (1976). How common is anorexia nervosa? A prevalence study. *British Journal of Psychiatry, 128,* 529–554.

Critchlow, B. (1986). The powers of John Barleycorn: Beliefs about the effects of alcohol on social behavior. *American Psychologist, 41,* 751–764.

Cronbach, L. J. (1970). *Essentials of psychological testing* (3rd ed.). New York: Harper & Row.

Cronbach, L. J. (1975). Five decades of public controversy over mental testing. *American Psychologist, 30,* 1–14.

Crosby, F. (1976). A model of egotistical relative deprivation. *Psychological Review, 83,* 85–113.

Crosby, F., & Gonzalez-Intal, A. M. (1982). Relative deprivation and equity theories: A comparative analysis of approaches to felt injustice. In R. Folger (Ed.), *The sense of injustice: Social psychological perspectives.* New York: Plenum Press.

Cross, D. G., Sheehan, O. W., & Kahn, J. A. (1982). Short- and long-term follow-up of clients receiving insight-oriented therapy and behavior therapy. *Journal of Consulting and Clinical Psychology, 50,* 103–112.

Crow, T. J. (1980). Molecular pathology of schizophrenia: More than one disease process? *British Medical Journal, 280,* 66–68.

Crow, T. J., Cross, A. J., Cooper, S. J., Deakin, J. F., Ferrier, I. N., Johnson, J. A., Joseph, M. H., Owen, F., Poulter, M., Lofthouse, R., et al. (1984). Neurotransmitter receptors and monoamine metabolites in the brains of patients with Alzheimer-type dementia and depression, and suicides. *Neuropharmacology, 12,* 1561–1569.

Croyle, R. T., & Cooper, J. (1983). Dissonance arousal: Physiological evidence. *Journal of Personality and Social Psychology, 45,* 782–791.

Csikszentmihalyi, M. (1975). *Beyond boredom and anxiety.* San Francisco: Jossey-Bass.

Csikszentmihalyi, M., & Larson, R. (1984). *Being adolescent: Conflict and growth in the teenage years.* New York: Basic Books.

Curran, J. P., & Lippold, S. (1975). The effects of physical attraction and attitude similarity on attraction in dating dyads. *Journal of Personality, 43,* 528–539.

Curran, J. P., & Monti, P. M. (1982). *Social skills training: A practical handbook for assessment and treatment.* New York: Guilford Press.

Curtis, R. C., & Miller, K. (1986). Believing another likes or dislikes you: Behaviors making the beliefs come true. *Journal of Personality and Social Psychology, 51,* 284–290.

Curtiss, S. (1977). *Genie: A psycholinguistic study of a modern-day wild child.* New York: Academic Press.

Czeisler, C. A., et al. (1986). Bright light resets the human circadian pacemaker independent of the timing of the sleep-wake cycle. *Science, 233,* 667–671.

Czeisler, C. A., Moore-Ede, M. C., & Coleman, R. M. (1982). Rotating shift work schedules that disrupt sleep are improved by applying circadian principles. *Science, 217,* 460–462.

Dale, N. (1983). *Early pretend play in the family.* Unpublished doctoral dissertation, University of Cambridge, Cambridge, ENG.

Dale, P. S. (1976). *Language and the development of structure and function.* New York: Holt, Rinehart and Winston.

Damon, W., & Hart, D. (1982). The development of self-understanding from infancy through adolescence. *Child Development, 53,* 841–864.

Daniel, W. F., & Crovitz, H. F. (1983). Acute memory impairment following electroconvulsive therapy: 1. Effects of electrical stimulus and number of treatments. *Acta Psychiatrica Scandinavica, 67,* 57–68.

Darley, C. F., Tinklenberg, J. R., Hollister, L. E., & Atkinson, R. C. (1973a). Marijuana and retrieval from short-term memory. *Psychopharmacologica, 29,* 231–238.

Darley, C. F., Tinklenberg, J. R., Roth, W. T., Hollister, L. E., & Atkinson, R. C. (1973b). Influence of marijuana on storage and retrieval processes in memory. *Memory and Cognition, 1,* 196–200.

Dashiell, J. F. (1930). An experimental analysis of some group effects. *Journal of Abnormal and Social Psychology, 25,* 190–199.

Dattore, P. J., Shontz, F. D., & Coyne, L. (1980). Premorbid personality differentiation of cancer and noncancer groups: A test of the hypothesis of cancer proneness. *Journal of Consulting and Clinical Psychology, 48,* 388–394.

Davanloo, J. (Ed.). (1978). *Basic principles and techniques in short-term dynamic psychotherapy.* New York: Spectrum.

Davidson, J. M., Kwan, M., & Greenleaf, W. J. (1982). Hormonal replacement and sexuality in men. *Clinics in Endocrinology and Metabolism, 11,* 599–623.

Davidson, R. J. (1984). Affect, cognition, and hemispheric specialization. In C. E. Izard, J. Kagan, & R. B. Zajonc (Eds.), *Emotions, cognition, and behavior.* Cambridge: Cambridge University Press.

Davis, J. H. (1980). Group decision and procedural justice. In M. Fishbein (Ed.), *Progress in social psychology: Vol.1.* Hillsdale, NJ: Lawrence Erlbaum Associates.

Davis, J. H., Spitzer, C. E., Nagao, D. H., & Stasser, G. (1978). Bias in social decisions by individuals and groups: An example from mock juries. In H. Brandstatter, J. H. Davis, & H. Schuler (Eds.), *Dynamics of group decisions.* Beverly Hills, CA: Sage.

Davis, J. M. (1978). Dopamine theory of schizophrenia: A two-factor theory. In L. C. Wynne, R. L. Cromwell, & S. Matthysse (Eds.), *The nature of schizophrenia: New approaches to research and treatment* (pp. 105–115). New York: Wiley.

Davis, K. B., (1929). *Factors in the sex life of twenty-two hundred women.* New York: Harper & Brothers.

Davis, R. (1986). Assessing the eating disorders. *The Clinical Psychologist, 39,* 33–36.

Davis, R. A., & Moore, C. C. (1935). Methods of measuring retention. *Journal of General Psychology, 12,* 144–155.

Davison, G. C., & Neale, J. M. (1982). *Abnormal psychology: An experimental clinical approach* (3rd ed.). New York: Wiley.

Davison, G. C., & Neale, J. M. (1986). *Abnormal psychology: An experimental clinical approach* (4th ed.). New York: Wiley.

Dawes, R. M., McTavish, J., & Shaklee, H. (1977). Behavior, communication, and assumptions about other people's behavior in a common dilemma situation. *Journal of Personality and Social Psychology, 35,* 1–11.

Deaux, K. (1976). Sex: A perspective on the attribution process. In J. H. Harvey, W. J. Ickes, & R. F. Kidd (Eds.), *New directions in attribution research: Vol. 1.* Hillsdale, NJ: Lawrence Erlbaum Associates.

DeCharms, R., Levy, J., & Wertheimer, M. (1954). A note on attempted evaluations of psychotherapy. *Journal of Clinical Psychology, 10,* 233–235.

DeCharms, R., & Moeller, G. H. (1962). Values expressed in American children's readers: 1800–1950. *Journal of Abnormal and Social Psychology, 64,* 136–142.

Deci, E. L. (1980). *The psychology of self-determination.* Lexington, MA: D. C. Heath.

Deci, E. L., Connell, J. P., & Ryan, M. (1987). *Self-determination in a work organization.* Unpublished manuscript, University of Rochester, Rochester, NY.

Defares, P. B., Grossman, P., & de Swart, H. C. G. (1983). Test anxiety, cognitive primitivation, and hyperventilation. In H. M. van der Ploeg, R. Schwarzer, & C. D. Sprilberger (Eds.), *Advances in test anxiety research: Vol. 2.* Hillsdale, NJ: Lawrence Erlbaum Associates.

Deikman, A. J. (1982). *The observing self.* Boston: Beacon Press.

Dellas, M., & Gaier, E. L. (1970). Identification of creativity: The individual. *Psychological Bulletin, 73,* 55–73.

DeLongis, A., Coyne, J. C., Dakof, G., Folkman, S., & Lazarus, R. S. (1982). Relationship of daily hassles, uplifts, and major life events to health status. *Health Psychology, 1,* 119–136.

Dember, W. N., Earl, R. W., & Paradise, N. (1957). Response by rats to differential stimulus complexity. *Journal of Comparative and Physiological Psychology, 50,* 514–518.

Dement, W. (1960). The effect of dream deprivation. *Science, 131,* 1705–1707.

Dement, W., & Kleitman, N. (1957). Cyclic variations in EEG during sleep and their relation to eye movements, body motility and dreaming. *Electroencephalography and Clinical Neurophysiology, 9,* 673–690.

Dennis, W. (1960). Causes of retardation among institutional children: Iran. *Journal of Genetic Psychology, 96,* 47–59.

Dennis, W. (1973). *Children of the creche.* New York: Appleton-Century-Crofts.

Derogatis, L. R., Meyer, J., & King, K. M. (1981). Psychopathology in individuals with sexual dysfunction. *American Journal of Psychiatry, 138,* 757–763.

De Silva, P., Rachman, S., & Seligman, M. E. P. (1977). Prepared phobias and obsessions: Therapeutic outcome. *Behaviour Research and Therapy, 15,* 65–77.

DeStefano, L. (1986). Personal communication. University of Illinois.

Deutsch, J. A., Young, W. G., & Kalogeris, T. J. (1978). The stomach signals satiety. *Science, 201,* 165–167.

Deutsch, M. (1975). Equity, equality, and need: What determines which value will be used as the basis of distributive justice? *Journal of Social Issues, 31,* 137–149.

Deutsch, M., & Gerard, H. B. (1955). A study of normative and informative social influences on individual judgments. *Journal of Abnormal and Social Psychology, 51,* 629–636.

DeVoge, J. T., & Sachs, L. B. (1973). The modification of hypnotic susceptibility through imitative behavior. *International Journal of Clinical and Experimental Hypnosis, 21,* 70–77.

Diamond, M. J. (1974). Modification of hypnotic susceptibility: A review. *Psychological Bulletin, 81,* 180–198.

Dickinson, A., & Mackintosh, N. J. (1978). Classical conditioning in animals. *Annual Review of Psychology, 29,* 587–612.

DiLollo, V., Hanson, D., & McIntyre, J. S. (1983). Initial stages of visual information processing in dyslexia. *Journal of Experimental Psychology: Human Perception and Performance, 9,* 923–935.

DiPietro, J. A. (1981). Rough and tumble play: A function of gender. *Developmental Psychology, 17,* 50–58.

Ditto, W. B. (1982). Daily activities of college students and the construct validity of the Jenkins Activity Survey. *Psychosomatic Medicine, 44,* 537–543.

Dixon, L. K., & Johnson, R. C. (1980). *The roots of individuality.* Monterey, CA: Brooks/Cole.

Doise, W., Csepeli, G., Cann, H. D., Gouge, C., Larson, K., & Ostell, A. (1972). An experimental investigation into the formation of intergroup representations. *European Journal of Social Psychology, 2,* 202–204.

Dollard, J., Doob, L., Miller, N., Mowrer, O. H., & Sears, R. R. (1939). *Frustration and aggression.* New Haven: Yale University Press.

Donahoe, C. P., Lin, D. H., Kirschenbaum, D. S., & Keesey, R. E. (1984). Metabolic consequences of dieting and exercises in the treatment of obesity. *Journal of Consulting and Clinical Psychology, 52,* 827–836.

Donaldson, M., & Balfour, G. (1968). Less is more: A study of language comprehension in children. *British Journal of Psychology, 59,* 461–471.

Donchin, E. (1981). Surprise! . . . Surprise? *Psychophysiology, 18,* 493–513.

Donchin, E., Kramer, A. F., & Wickens, C. D. (1986). Applications of brain event-related potentials to problems in engineering psychology. In M. G. H. Coles, E. Donchin, & S. Porges (Eds.), *Psychophysiology: Systems, processes, and applications* (702–718). New York: Guilford Press.

Donders, F. C. (1969). On the speed of mental processes (W. G. Koster, Trans.). *Acta Psychologica, 30,* 412–431.

Donnelly, J. (1978). The incidence of psychosurgery in the United States, 1971–1973. *American Journal of Psychiatry, 135,* 1476–1480.

Donnerstein, E. (1980). Aggressive-erotica and violence against women. *Journal of Personality and Social Psychology, 39,* 269–277.

Donnerstein, E. (1983). Erotica and human aggression. In R. Geen & E. Donnerstein (Eds.), *Aggression: Theoretical and empirical reviews.* New York: Academic Press.

Donnerstein, E. (1984). Aggression. In A. S. Kahn (Ed.), *Social psychology.* Dubuque, IA: William C. Brown.

Donnerstein, E., & Donnerstein, M. (1976). Research in the control of interracial aggression. In R. G. Geen & E. C. O'Neal (Eds.), *Perspectives on aggression.* New York: Academic Press.

Donnerstein, E. I., & Linz, D. G. (1986, December). The question of pornography. *Psychology Today.*

Donnerstein, E. I., & Wilson, D. W. (1976). Effects of noise and perceived control on ongoing and subsequent aggressive behavior. *Journal of Personality and Social Psychology, 34,* 774–781.

Donovan, W. L., Leavitt, L. A., & Balling, J. D. (1978). Maternal physiological response to infant signals. *Psychophysiology, 15,* 68–74.

Dore, J. (1978). Conditions for the acquisition of speech acts. In I. Markova (Ed.), *The social context of language.* New York: Wiley.

Doty, R. L. (1981). Olfactory communication in humans. *Chemical Senses, 6,* 351–376.

Drabman, R. S., & Thomas, M. H. (1974). Does media violence increase children's tolerance of real-life aggression? *Developmental Psychology, 10,* 418–421.

Dreben, E. K., Fiske, S. T., & Hastie, R. (1979). The independence of item and evaluative information: Impression and recall order effects in behavior-based impression formation. *Journal of Personality and Social Psychology, 37,* 1758–1768.

Dreyfus, H. (1979). *What computers can't do: A critique of artificial reason.* New York: Harper & Row.

Dreyfus, H., & Dreyfus, S. (1986). Why computers may never think like people. *Technology Review, 89,* 41–61.

Duke, P. M., Carlsmith, J. M., Jennings, D., Martin, J. A., Dornbusch, S. M., Gross, R. T., & Siegel-Gorelick, B. (1982). Educational correlates of early and late sexual maturation in adolescence. *Journal of Pediatrics, 100,* 633–637.

Dulewicz, V. (1984). *The use of the polygraph for personnel screening: A statement by the society issued by the Scientific Affairs Board.* Leicester: British Psychological Society.

Dunn, J., & Kendrick, C. (1982a). The speech of two- and three-year-olds to infant siblings: "Baby talk" and the context of communication. *Journal of Child Language, 9,* 579–595.

Dunn, J., & Kendrick, C. (1982b). *Siblings: Love, envy, and understanding.* Cambridge: Harvard University Press.

Durlak, J. A. (1979). Comparative effectiveness of paraprofessional and professional helpers. *Psychological Bulletin, 86,* 80–92.

Dusek, J. B., & Flaherty, J. F. (1981). The development of the self-concept during the adolescent years. *Monographs of the Society for Research in Child Development, 46* (4, Serial No. 191).

Dush, D. M., Hirt, M. L., & Schroeder, H. (1983). Self-statement modification with adults: A meta-analysis. *Psychological Bulletin, 94,* 408–422.

Dutton, D. G., & Aron, A. P. (1974). Some evidence for heightened sexual attraction under conditions of high anxiety. *Journal of Personality and Social Psychology, 30,* 510–517.

Dweck, C. S. (1986). Motivational processes affecting learning. *American Psychologist, 41,* 1040–1048.

Dweck, C. S., Davidson, W., Nelson, S., & Enna, B. (1978). Sex differences in learned helplessness: II. The contingencies of evaluative feedback in the classroom, and III. An experimental analysis. *Developmental Psychology, 14,* 268–276.

Dweck, C. S., & Gilliard, D. (1975). Expectancy statements as determinants of reactions to failure: Sex differences in persistence and expectancy change. *Journal of Personality and Social Psychology, 32,* 1077–1084.

Dweck, C. S., & Repucci, N. D. (1973). Learned helplessness and reinforcement responsibility in children. *Journal of Personality and Social Psychology, 25,* 109–116.

Easterbrook, J. A. (1959). The effect of emotion on cue utilization and the organization of behavior. *Psychological Review, 66,* 183–207.

Eaton, W. O., & Clore, G. L. (1975). Interracial imitation at a summer camp. *Journal of Personality and Social Psychology, 32,* 1099–1105.

Ebbinghaus, H. (1913). *Memory: A contribution to experimental psychology* (H. A. Roger & C. E. Bussenius, Trans.). New York: Columbia University Press. (original work published 1885)

Eberts, R., & MacMillan, A. C. (1985). Misperception of small cars. In R. Eberts & C. Eberts (Eds.), *Trends in ergonimics/human factors III.* Amsterdam: Elsevier.

Eckenrode, J. (1984). Impact of chronic and acute stressors on daily reports of mood. *Journal of Personality and Social Psychology, 46,* 907–918.

Eckert, E. D., Bouchard, T. J., Bohlen, J., & Heston, L. L. (1986). Homosexuality in monozygotic twins reared apart. *British Journal of Psychiatry, 148,* 421–425.

Edwards, A. E., & Acker, L. E. (1972). A demonstration of the long-term retention of a conditioned GSR. *Psychosomatic Science, 26,* 27–28.

Edwards, J. A., Wesnes, K., Warburton, D. M., & Gale, A. (1985). Evidence of more rapid stimulus evaluation following cigarette smoking. *Addictive Behaviors, 10,* 113–126.

Edwards, W. (1977). How to use multiattribute utility measurement for social decision making. *IEEE Transactions in Systems Man and Cybernetics, 17,* 326–340.

Edwards, W., Lindman, H., & Phillips, L. D. (1965). Emerging technologies for making decisions. In T. M. Newcomb (Ed.), *New directions in psychology II*. New York: Holt, Rinehart and Winston.

Egeland, B., & Sroufe, L. A. (1981). Attachment and early maltreatment. *Child Development, 52*, 44–52.

Egeland, J. A., Gerhard, D. S., Pauls, D. L., Sussex, J. N., Kidd, K. K., Allen, C. R., Hostetter, A. M., & Housman, D. E. (1987). Bipolar affective disorders linked to DNA markers on chromosome II. *Nature, 325*, 783–787.

Ehrlich, H. J. (1973). *The social psychology of prejudice*. New York: Wiley.

Eich, J. E. (1980). The cue dependent nature of state dependent retrieval. *Memory and Cognition, 8*, 157–173.

Eich, J. E., Weingartner, H., Stillman, R. C., & Gillin, J. C. (1975). State dependent accessibility of retrieval cues in the retention of a categorized list. *Journal of Verbal Learning and Verbal Behavior, 14*, 408–417.

Eichorn, D. H., Clausen, J. A., Haan, N., Honzik, M. P., & Mussen, P. H. (1981). *Present and past in middle life*. New York: Academic Press.

Eimas, P. D., Siqueland, E. R., Juzczyk, P., & Vigorito, J. (1971). Speech perception in early infancy. *Science, 171*, 303–306.

Einhorn, H., & Hogarth, R. M. (1981). Behavioral decision theory. *Annual Review of Psychology, 32*, 53–88.

Eisenberg, R. B. (1976). *Auditory competence in early life: The roots of communicative behavior*. Baltimore: University Park Press.

Eisner, J., Roberts, W., Heymsfield, S., & Yager, J. (1985). Anorexia nervosa and sudden death. *Annals of Internal Medicine, 102*, 49–52.

Ekman, P. (1964). Body position, facial expression, and verbal behavior during interviews. *Journal of Abnormal Psychology, 68*, 295–301.

Ekman, P. (1980). Biological and cultural contributions to body and facial movement in the expression of emotions. In A. Rorty (Ed.), *Explaining emotions*. Berkeley: University of California Press.

Ekman, P. (1984). Expression and the nature of emotion. In K. Sherer & P. Ekman (Eds.), *Approaches to emotion*. Hillsdale, NJ: Lawrence Erlbaum Associates.

Ekman, P. (1985, May 30). AP story by Paul Raeburn on AAAS meeting.

Ekman, P., & Friesen, W. V. (1986). A new pan-cultural facial expression of emotion. *Motivation and Emotion, 10*, 159–168.

Ekman, P., Friesen, W. V., & Ellsworth, P. (1972). *Emotion in the human face: Guidelines for research and a review of findings*. New York: Pergamon Press.

Ekman, P., Levenson, R. W., & Friesen, W. V. (1983). Autonomic nervous system activity distinguishes among emotions. *Science, 221*, 1208-1210.

Elashoff, J. D. (1979). Box scores are for baseball. *Brain and Behavioral Sciences, 3*, 392.

Ellis, A. (1962). *Reason and emotion in psychotherapy*. New York: Lyle Stuart.

Ellis, A. (1973). Rational-emotive therapy. In R. Corsini (Ed.), *Current psychotherapies*. Itasca, IL: Peacock.

Ellis, A., & Bernard, M. E. (1985). *Clinical applications of rational-emotive therapy*. New York: Plenum Press.

Ellis, L., & Ames, M. A. (1987). Neurohormonal functioning and sexual orientation: A theory of homosexuality-heterosexuality. *Psychological Bulletin, 101*, 233–258.

Ellison, K. W., & Buckhout, R. (1981). *Psychology and criminal justice*. New York: Harper & Row.

Elton, D., Burrows, G. D., & Stanley, G. V. (1980). Chronic pain and hypnosis. In G. D. Burrows & L. Dennerstein (Eds.), *Handbook of hypnosis and psychosomatic medicine*. Amsterdam: Elsevier.

Emmons, K. M., & Bernstein, D. A. (1987). *Spectral analysis as an assessment technique for identifying smoker subtypes*. Manuscript submitted for publication.

Emmons, R. A. (1986). Personal strivings: An approach to personality and subjective well-being. *Journal of Personality and Social Psychology, 51*, 1058–1068.

Epstein, S., & O'Brien, E. J. (1985). The person-situation debate in historical and current perspective. *Psychological Bulletin, 98*, 513–537.

Epstein, W. (1961). The influence of syntactical structure on learning. *American Journal of Psychology, 74*, 80–85.

Epstein, Y. M., Woolfolk, R. L., & Lehrer, P. M. (1981). Physiological, cognitive, and nonverbal responses to repeated experiences of crowding. *Journal of Applied Social Psychology, 11*, 1–13.

Erdelyi, M. H. (1985). *Psychoanalysis: Freud's cognitive psychology*. San Francisco: W. H. Freeman.

Erdelyi, M. H., & Goldberg, B. (1979). Let's not sweep repression under the rug: Toward a cognitive psychology of repression. In J. F. Kihlstrom & F. J. Evans (Eds.), *Functional disorders of memory*. Hillsdale, NJ: Lawrence Erlbaum Associates.

Ericsson, K. A., Chase, W. G., & Faloon, S. (1980). Acquisition of a memory skill. *Science, 208*, 1181–1182.

Eriksen, C. W., & Collins, J. F. (1967). Some temporal characteristics of visual pattern perception. *Journal of Experimental Psychology, 74*, 476–484.

Erikson, E. H. (1963). *Childhood and society*. New York: W. W. Norton.

Erikson, E. H. (1968). *Identity: youth and crisis*. New York: W. W. Norton.

Erlick, D. E. (1961). Judgments of the relative frequency of a sequential series of two events. *Journal of Experimental Psychology, 62*, 105–112.

Eron, L. D. (1980). Prescription for reduction of aggression. *American Psychologist, 35*, 244–252.

Eskew, R. T., & Riche, C. V. (1982). Pacing and locus of control in quality control inspection. *Human Factors, 24*, 411–415.

Evans, C. (1984). *Landscapes of the night: How and why we dream*. New York: Viking Press.

Exner, J. E. (1974). *The Rorschach: A comprehensive system*. New York: Wiley.

Eysenck, H. J. (1952). The effects of psychotherapy: An evaluation. *Journal of Consulting Psychology, 16*, 319–324.

Eysenck, H. J. (1960). *Behavior therapy and the neuroses*. London: Pergamon Press.

Eysenck, H. J. (1961). The effects of psychotherapy. In H. J. Eysenck (Ed.), *Handbook of abnormal psychology*. New York: Basic Books.

Eysenck, H. J. (1966). *The effects of psychotherapy*. New York: International Science Press.

Eysenck, H. J. (1970). *The structure of human personality* (3rd ed.). London: Methuen.

Eysenck, H. J. (1975a). A genetic model of anxiety. In L. G. Sarason & C. D. Spielberger (Eds.), *Stress and anxiety: Vol. 2*. New York: Wiley.

Eysenck, H. J. (1975b). *The inequality of man*. San Diego: Edits Publishers.

Eysenck, H. J. (Ed.). (1981). *A model for personality*. New York: Springer-Verlag.

Eysenck, M. W. (1977). *Human memory: Theory, research, and individual differences*. Oxford: Pergamon Press.

Fabricius, W. V., & Wellman, H. M. (1983). Children's understanding of retrieval cue utilization. *Developmental Psychology, 19*, 15–21.

Fairburn, C. (1981). A cognitive behavioral approach to the treatment of bulimia. *Psychological Medicine, 11*, 707–711.

Faraone, S. V., & Tsuang, M. T. (1985). Quantitative models of the genetic transmission of schizophrenia. *Psychological Bulletin, 98*, 41–66.

Farber, B. (Ed.). (1983). *Stress and burnout in human service professions*. New York: Pergamon Press.

Farberow, N. L., & Litman, R. E. (1958–1970). *A comprehensive suicide prevention program* (Unpublished final report DHEW NIMH Grants No. MH 14946 & MH 00128). Suicide Prevention Center, Los Angeles, CA.

Farberow, N. L., Shneidman, E. S., & Leonard, C. (1963, February 25). Suicide among general medical and surgical hospital patients with malignant neoplasms. (Medical Bulletin MB-9, pp. 1–11). Washington, DC: Veterans Administration, Department of Medicine and Surgery.

Farley, F. (1986, May). The big T in personality. *Psychology Today.*

Farley, J., & Alkon, D. L. (1985). Cellular mechanisms of learning, memory, and information storage. *Annual Review of Psychology, 36,* 419–494.

Faust, M. S. (1960). Developmental maturity as a determinant of prestige of adolescent girls. *Child Development, 31,* 173–184.

Feldman, S. (Ed.). (1966). *Cognitive consistency: Motivational antecedents and behavioral consequents.* New York: Academic Press.

Fellner, C. H., & Marshall, J. R. (1970). Kidney donors. In J. R. Macauley & L. Berkowitz (Eds.), *Altruism and helping behavior.* New York: Academic Press.

Felner, R. D., Aber, M. S., Primavera, J., & Cauce, A. M. (1985). Adaptation and vulnerability in high risk adolescents: An examination of environmental mediators. *American Journal of Community Psychology, 13,* 365–379.

Fenz, W. D. (1971). Heart rate responses to a stressor: A comparison between primary and secondary psychopaths and normal controls. *Journal of Experimental Research in Personality, 5,* 7–13.

Fernald, A. (1981, April). *Four-month-olds prefer to listen to "motherese."* Paper presented at the meeting of the Society for Research in Child Development, Boston, MA.

Ferster, C. B. (1961). Positive reinforcement and behavioral deficits of autistic children. *Child Development, 32,* 437–457.

Feshbach, N. D. (1967). Nonconformity to experimentally induced group norms of high-status versus low-status members. *Journal of Personality and Social Psychology, 6,* 55–63.

Festinger, L. (1954). A theory of social comparison processes. *Human Relations, 7,* 117–140.

Festinger, L. (1957). *A theory of cognitive dissonance.* Evanston, IL: Row, Petersen.

Festinger, L., & Carlsmith, J. M. (1959). Cognitive consequences of forced compliance. *Journal of Abnormal and Social Psychology, 58,* 203–210.

Feuerstein, R. (1980). *Instrumental enrichment: An intervention program for cognitive modifiability.* Baltimore: University Park Press.

Fillenbaum, S. (1974). Pragmatic normalization: Further results for some conjunctive and disjunctive sentences. *Journal of Experimental Psychology, 103,* 913–921.

Fillmore, K. M., & Caetano, R. (1980, May 22). *Epidemiology of occupational alcoholism.* Paper presented at the National Institute on Alcohol Abuse and Alcoholism's Workshop on Alcoholism in the Workplace, Reston, VA.

Fine, T. H., & Turner, J. W. (1982). The effect of brief restricted environmental stimulation therapy in the treatment of essential hypertension. *Behaviour Research and Therapy, 20,* 567–570.

Finer, B. (1980). Hypnosis and anaesthesia. In G. D. Burrows & L. Dennerstein (Eds.), *Handbook of hypnosis and psychosomatic medicine.* Amsterdam: Elsevier.

Fink, M. (1979). *Convulsive therapy: Therapy and practice.* New York: Raven.

Finke, R. A. (1983). Apparent motion and the icon. *The Behavioral and Brain Sciences, 6,* 20.

Finke, R. A., & Freyd, J. J. (1985). Transformations of visual memory induced by implied motions of pattern elements. *Journal of Experimental Psychology: Learning, Memory, and Cognition, 11,* 780–794.

Fischer, C. S., & Phillips, S. L. (1982). Who is alone? Characteristics of people with small networks. In L. A. Peplau & D. Perlman (Eds.), *Loneliness: A sourcebook of current theory, research, and therapy.* New York: Wiley.

Fischer, E., Haines, R., & Price, T. (1980). *Cognitive issues in head up displays.* (NASA Technical Paper 1711). Washington, DC: NASA.

Fischoff, B. (1977). Perceived informativeness of facts. *Journal of Experimental Psychology: Human perception and performance, 3,* 349–358.

Fischoff, B. (1982). Debiasing. In D. Kahneman, P. Slovic, & A. Tversky (Eds.), *Judgment under uncertainty: Heuristics and biases.* New York: Cambridge University Press.

Fischoff, B., & MacGregor, D. (1982). Subjective confidence in forecasts. *Journal of Forecasting, 1,* 155–172.

Fischoff, B., & Slovic, P. (1980). A little learning . . . Confidence in multicue judgment tasks. In R. Nickerson (Ed.), *Attention and performance: VIII.* Hillsdale, NJ: Lawrence Erlbaum Associates.

Fischoff, B., Slovic, P., & Lichtenstein, S. (1977). Knowing with certainty: The appropriateness of extreme confidence. *Journal of Experimental Psychology: Human Perception and Performance, 3,* 552–564.

Fisher, J. D., Bell, P. A., & Baum, A. (1984). *Environmental psychology* (2nd ed.). New York: Holt, Rinehart and Winston.

Fishman, S. M., & Sheehan, D. V. (1985, April). Anxiety and panic: Their cause and treatment. *Psychology Today,* pp. 26–32.

Fiske, D. W., & Maddi, S. R. (1961). *Functions of varied experience.* Homewood, IL: Dorsey Press.

Fiske, M. (1980). Tasks and crises of the second half of life: The interrelationship of commitment, coping, and adaptation. In J. E. Birren & R. B. Sloane (Eds.), *Handbook of mental health and aging.* Englewood Cliffs, NJ: Prentice-Hall.

Fiske, S. T., & Pavelchak, M. A. (1986). Category-based versus piecemeal-based affective responses: Developments in schema-triggered affect. In R. M. Sorrentino & E. T. Higgins (Eds.), *Handbook of motivation and cognition.* New York: Guilford Press.

Fiske, S. T., & Taylor, S. E. (1984). *Social cognition.* Reading, MA: Addison-Wesley.

Fixen, D. L., Phillips, E. L., Phillips, E. A., & Wolf, M. M. (1976). The teaching-family model of group home treatment. In W. E. Craighead, A. E. Kazdin, & M. J. Mahoney (Eds.), *Behavior modification: Principles, issues, and applications.* Boston: Houghton Mifflin.

Flaherty, C. F., Uzwiak, A. J., Levine, J., Smith, M., Hall, P., & Schuler, R. (1980). Apparent hyperglycemic and hypoglycemic conditional responses with exogenous insulin as the unconditioned stimulus. *Animal Learning and Behavior, 8,* 382–386.

Flavell, J. H. (1985). *Cognitive development* (2nd ed.). Englewood Cliffs, NJ: Prentice-Hall.

Flavell, J. H., Beach, D. H., & Chinsky, J. M. (1966). Spontaneous verbal rehearsal in a memory task as a function of age. *Child Development, 37,* 283–299.

Flavell, J. H., Friedrichs, A. G., & Hoyt, J. D. (1970). Developmental changes in memorization processes. *Cognitive Psychology, 1,* 324–340.

Flavell, J. H., & Wellman, H. M. (1977). Metamemory. In R. V. Kail & J. W. Hagen (Eds.), *Perspectives on the development of memory and cognition.* Hillsdale, NJ: Lawrence Erlbaum Associates.

Fleming, R., Baum, A., & Singer, J. E. (1984). Toward an integrative approach to the study of stress. *Journal of Personality and Social Psychology, 46*(4), 939–949.

Flynn, J., Vanegas, H., Foote, W., & Edwards, S. (1970). Neural mechanisms involved in a cat's attack on a rat. In M. Whelan, R. F. Thompson, M. Verzeano, & N. Weinberger (Eds.), *The neural control of behavior.* New York: Academic Press.

Fodor, J. A., Bever, T. G., & Garrett, M. F. (1974). *The Psychology of Language.* New York: McGraw-Hill.

Foenander, G., & Burrows, G. D. (1980). Phenomena of hypnosis: 1.

Age regression. In G. D. Burrows & L. Dennerstein (Eds.), *Handbook of hypnosis and psychosomatic medicine*. Amsterdam: Elsevier.

Folkman, S. (1984). Personal control and stress and coping processes: A theoretical analysis. *Journal of Personality and Social Psychology, 46,* 839–852.

Foreyt, J. P., & Kondo, A. T. (1984). Advances in behavioral treatment of obesity. In M. Hersen, R. M. Eisler, & P. M. Miller (Eds.), *Progress in behavior modification: Vol. 16*. New York: Academic Press.

Foulkes, D., & Fleisher, S. (1975). Mental activity in relaxed wakefulness. *Journal of Abnormal Psychology, 84,* 66–75.

Fozard, J. L. (1980). The time for remembering. In L. W. Poon (Ed.), *Aging in the 1980s: Psychological issues*. Washington, DC: American Psychological Association.

Fozard, J., Wolf, E., Bell, B., Farland, R., & Podolsky, S. (1977). Visual perception and communication. In J. Birren & K. Schaie (Eds.), *Handbook of the psychology of aging*. New York: Van Nostrand Reinhold.

Fraiberg, S. (1959). *The magic years*. New York: Scribners.

Frank, E., Anderson, C., & Rubenstein, D. (1978). Frequency of sexual dysfunction in normal couples. *New England Journal of Medicine, 299,* 111–115.

Frank, G. (1976). Measures of intelligence and critical thinking. In I. B. Weiner (Ed.), *Clinical methods in psychology*. New York: Wiley.

Frank, J. S. (1973). *Persuasion and healing* (rev. ed.). Baltimore: Johns Hopkins University Press.

Frank, J. S. (1978). *Psychotherapy and the human predicament*. New York: Schocken Books.

Frankel, B. G., & Whitehead, P. C. (1981). *Drinking and damage: Theoretical advantages and implications for prevention* (Monograph 14). New Brunswick, NJ: Rutgers Center of Alcohol Studies.

Frankel, F. H. (1984). Electroconvulsive therapies. In T. B. Karasu (Ed.), *The psychiatric therapies*. Washington, DC: American Psychological Association.

Frankenberg, W. K., & Dodds, J. B. (1967). The Denver developmental screening test. *Journal of Pediatrics, 71,* 181–191.

Frankenhaeuser, M., Nordheden, B., Myrsten, A., & Post, B. (1971). Psychophysiological reactions to understimulation and overstimulation. *Acta Psychologica, 35,* 298–308.

Frase, L. T. (1975). Prose processing. In G. H. Bower (Ed.), *The psychology of learning and motivation: Vol. 9*. New York: Academic Press.

Fredericksen, N. (1986). Toward a broader conception of human intelligence. *American Psychologist, 41,* 445–452.

Freed, E. X. (1971). Anxiety and conflict: Role of drug-dependent learning in the rat. *Quarterly Journal of Studies on Alcohol, 32,* 13–29.

Freed, W. J. (1983). Functional brain tissue transplantation: Reversal of lesion-induced rotation by intraventricular substantia nigra and adrenal medulla grafts, with a note on intracranial retinal grafts. *Biological Psychiatry, 18,* 1205–1267.

Freedman, J. L., & Fraser, S. C. (1966). Compliance without pressure: The foot-in-the-door technique. *Journal of Personality and Social Psychology, 4,* 195–202.

Freeman, N. H., Lloyd, S., & Sinha, C. G. (1980). Infant search tasks reveal early concepts of containment and canonical usage of objects. *Cognition, 8,* 243–262.

Freeman, W. (1959). Psychosurgery. In S. Arieti (Ed.), *American Handbook of Psychiatry, II*. New York: Basic Books.

Freeman, W., & Watts, J. W. (1942). *Psychosurgery*. Springfield, IL: Charles C. Thomas.

Fremgen, A., & Fay, D. (1980). Overextensions in production and comprehension: A methodological clarification. *Journal of Child Language, 7,* 205–211.

Freud, A. (1946). *The ego and the mechanisms of defense*. New York: International Universities Press.

Freud, S. (1900). *The interpretation of dreams*. In J. Strachey (Ed.), *The standard edition of the complete psychological works of Sigmund Freud: Vol. 8*. London: Hogarth Press.

Freud, S. (1914). *The psychopathology of everyday life*. New York: MacMillan.

Friedman, M., & Rosenman, R. H. (1959). Association of specific overt behavior patterns with blood and cardiovascular findings: Blood cholesterol level, blood clotting time, incidence of arcus senilis, and clinical coronary artery disease. *Journal of the American Medical Association, 169,* 1286–1296.

Friedman, M., & Rosenman, R. H. (1974). *Type A behavior and your heart*. New York: Knopf.

Friedman, M., Thoresen, C. E., Gill, J. J., Powell, L. H., Ulmer, D., Thompson, L., Price, V. A., Rabin, D. D., Breall, W. S., Dixon, T., Levy, R., & Bourg, E. (1984). Alteration of type A behavior and reduction in cardiac recurrences in postmyocardial infarction patients. *American Heart Journal, 108*(2), 237–248.

Friedman, M. I., & Stricker, E. M. (1976). The physiological psychology of hunger: A physiological perspective. *Psychological Review, 83,* 409–431.

Frisch, H. L. (1977). Sex stereotypes in adult-infant play. *Child Development, 48,* 1671–1675.

Frodi, A. M., Lamb, M. E., Leavitt, L. A., & Donovan, W. L. (1978). Fathers' and mothers' responses to infant smiles and cries. *Infant Behavior and Development, 1,* 187–198.

Fromm, E. (1941). *Escape from freedom*. New York: Rinehart.

Funder, D. C. (1983). Three issues in predicting more of the people: A reply to Mischel and Peake. *Psychological Review, 90,* 283–289.

Furth, H. (1964). Research with the deaf: Implications for language and cognition. *Psychological Bulletin, 62,* 145–164.

Gaddis, T. E., & Long, J. O. (1970). *Killer: A journal of murder*. New York: MacMillan.

Galin, D. (1974). Implications for psychiatry of left and right cerebral specialization. *Archives of General Psychiatry, 31,* 572–583.

Gallup, G. (1986, July). Poll on cigarette smoking.

Ganchrow, J. R., Steiner, J. E., & Daher, M. (1983). Neonatal facial expressions in response to different qualities and intensities of gustatory stimuli. *Infant Behavior and Development, 6,* 189–200.

Ganellen, R. J., & Blaney, P. H. (1984). Hardiness and social support as moderators of the effects of life stress. *Journal of Personality and Social Psychology, 47,* 156–163.

Ganong, W. F. (1984). The brain renin-angiotensin system. *Annual Review of Physiology, 46,* 17–31.

Garcia, J., Hankins, W. G., & Rusiniak, K. W. (1974). Behavioral regulation of the milieu interne in man and rat. *Science, 185,* 824–831.

Garcia, J., Kimeldorf, D. J., Hunt, E. L., & Davies, B. P. (1956). Food and water consumption of rats during exposure to gamma radiation. *Radiation Research, 4,* 33–41.

Garcia, J., & Koelling, R. A. (1966). Relation of cue to consequences in avoidance learning. *Psychonomic Science, 4,* 123–124.

Garcia, J., Rusiniak, K. W., & Brett, L. P. (1977). Conditioning food-illness aversions in wild animals: *Caveat Canonici*. In H. Davis & H. M. B. Hurwitz (Eds.), *Operant-Pavlovian interactions*. Hillsdale, NJ: Lawrence Erlbaum Associates.

Gardner, H. (1983). *Frames of mind: The theory of multiple intelligences*. New York: Basic Books.

Gardner, R. A., & Gardner, B. T. (1978). Comparative psychology and language acquisition. *Annals of the New York Academy of Science, 309,* 37–76.

Garfield, S. L. (1981). Psychotherapy: A 40-year appraisal. *American Psychologist, 36,* 174–183.

Garfield, S. L. (1986). Research on client variables in psychotherapy. In S. L. Garfield & A. E. Bergin (Eds.), *Handbook of psychotherapy and behavior change* (3rd ed.). New York: Wiley.

Garfield, S. L., & Kurtz, R. (1976). Clinical psychologists in the 1970s. *Journal of Consulting and Clinical Psychology, 45,* 78–83.

Garfinkel, P. E., Moldofsky, H., & Garner, D. M. (1980). The heterogeneity of anorexia nervosa. *Archives of General Psychiatry, 37,* 1036–1040.

Garrity, T. F. (1973). Vocational adjustment after first myocardial infarction: Comparative assessment of several variables suggested in the literature. *Social Science and Medicine, 7,* 705–717.

Garrity, T. F. (1975). Morbidity, mortality, and rehabilitation. In W. D. Gentry & R. B. Williams, Jr. (Eds.), *Psychological aspects of myocardial infarction and coronary care.* St. Louis: Mosby.

Garvey, C. (1975). Requests and responses in children's speech. *Journal of Child Language, 2,* 41–63.

Gastorf, J. W., & Teevan, R. C. (1980). Type A coronary-prone behavior pattern and fear of failure. *Motivation and Emotion, 4,* 71–76.

Gatchel, R. J., & Baum, A. (1983). *An introduction to health psychology.* Reading, MA: Addison-Wesley.

Gates, M. G., & Allee, W. C. (1933). Conditioned behavior of isolated and grouped cockroaches on a simple maze. *Journal of Comparative Psychology, 13,* 331–358.

Gazzaniga, M. S., & LeDoux, J. E. (1978). *The integrated mind.* New York: Plenum Press.

Geen, R. G. (1977). The effects of anticipation of positive and negative outcomes on audience anxiety. *Journal of Consulting and Clinical Psychology, 45,* 715–716.

Geen, R. G. (1985). Test anxiety and visual vigilance. *Journal of Personality and Social Psychology, 49,* 963–970.

Geen, R. G., Beatty, W. W., & Arkin, R. M. (1984). *Human motivation.* Boston: Allyn and Bacon.

Geen, R. G., & Donnerstein, E. I. (Eds.). (1983). *Aggression: Theoretical and empirical reviews.* New York: Academic Press.

Geen, R. G., & Stonner, D. (1971). Effects of aggressiveness habit strength on behavior in the presence of aggression-related stimuli. *Journal of Personality and Social Psychology, 17,* 149–153.

Geer, J. H., Davison, G. C., & Gatchel, R. I. (1970). Reduction of stress in humans through nonveridical perceived control of aversive stimulation. *Journal of Personality and Social Psychology, 16,* 731–738.

Geer, J. T., O'Donohue, W. T., & Schorman, R. H. (1986). Sexuality. In M. G. H. Coles, E. Donchin, & S. Porges (Eds.), *Psychophysiology: Systems, processes, and applications.* New York: Guilford Press.

Geller, A. M., & Atkins, A. (1978). Cognitive and personality factors in suicidal behavior. *Journal of Consulting and Clinical Psychology, 46,* 860–868.

Gellhorn, E., & Loofbourrow, G. N. (1963). *Emotions and emotional disorders.* New York: Harper & Row.

Gelman, R. (1969). Conservation acquisition: A problem of learning to attend to relevant attributes. *Journal of Experimental Child Psychology, 7,* 167–187.

Gentner, D., & Stevens, A. L. (1983). *Mental models.* Hillsdale, NJ: Lawrence Erlbaum Associates.

Gentry, W. D. (1970). Effects of frustration, attack, and prior aggressive training on overt aggression and vascular processes. *Journal of Personality and Social Psychology, 16,* 718–725.

Gerard, H. B., Wilhelmy, R. A., & Conolley, E. S. (1968). Conformity and group size. *Journal of Personality and Social Psychology, 8,* 79–82.

Gerbner, G. (1981, April). Television: The American school child's national curriculum day in and day out. *PTA Today,* pp. 3–5.

Gergen, K. J., & Bauer, R. A. (1967). Interactive effects of self-esteem and task difficulty on social conformity. *Journal of Personality and Social Psychology, 6,* 16–21.

Gergen, K. J., Gergen, M. M., & Meter, K. (1972). Individual orientations to prosocial behavior. *Journal of Social Issues, 8,* 105–130.

Gerschman, J. A., Reade, P. C., & Burrows, G. D. (1980). Hypnosis and dentistry. In G. D. Burrows & L. Dennerstein (Eds.), *Handbook of hypnosis and psychosomatic medicine.* Amsterdam: Elsevier.

Geschwind, N. (1979). Specializations of the human brain. *Scientific American, 241,* 180–199.

Getzels, J. W., & Jackson, P. W. (1962). *Creativity and intelligence.* New York: Wiley.

Gewirtz, J. L. (1972). *Attachment and dependency.* Washington, DC: Winston.

Gfeller, J. D., Lynn, S. J., & Pribble, W. E. (1987). Enhancing hypnotic susceptibility: Interpersonal and rapport factors. *Journal of Personality and Social Psychology, 52,* 595–596.

Gibb, C. (1969). Leadership. In G. Lindzey & E. Aronson (Eds.), *The handbook of social psychology: Vol. 4* (2nd ed.). Reading, MA: Addison-Wesley.

Gibson, E. J., & Walk, R. D. (1960). The visual cliff. *Scientific American, 202,* 64–71.

Gibson, J. J. (1966). *The senses considered as perceptual systems.* Boston: Houghton Mifflin.

Gibson, J. J. (1979). *The ecological approach to visual perception.* Boston: Houghton Mifflin.

Gil, D. G. (Ed.). (1979). *Child abuse and violence.* New York: AMS Press.

Gilbert, A. G., Goodman, L. S., & Gilman, A. (Eds.). (1980). *Goodman and Gilman's the pharmacological basis of therapeutics.* New York: MacMillan.

Gilbert, E., & DeBlassie, R. (1984). Anorexia nervosa: Adolescent starvation by choice. *Adolescence, 19,* 840–846.

Giles, T. R. (1983). Probable superiority of behavioral interventions: II. Empirical status of the equivalence of therapies hypothesis. *Journal of Behavior Therapy & Experimental Psychiatry, 14,* 189–196.

Gill, M. M., & Brenman, M. (1959). *Hypnosis and related states.* New York: International Universities Press.

Gilliam, D. M., & Schlesinger, K. (1985). Nicotine-produced relearning deficit in C57BL/6J and DBA/2J mice. *Psychopharmacology, 86,* 291–295.

Gilligan, C. (1982). *In a different voice: Psychological theory and women's development.* Cambridge: Harvard University Press.

Gladue, B. A., Green, R., & Hellman, R. E. (1984). Neuroendocrine response to estrogen and sexual orientation. *Science, 225,* 1496–1499.

Glanzer, M., & Cunitz, A. (1966). Two storage mechanisms in free recall. *Journal of Verbal Learning and Verbal Behavior, 5,* 351–360.

Glasgow, R. E., & Bernstein, D. A. (1981). Behavioral treatment of smoking behavior. In L. A. Bradley & C. K. Prokop (Eds.), *Medical Psychology: A New Perspective.* New York: Academic Press.

Glass, D. C. (1977). *Behavior patterns, stress, and coronary disease.* Hillsdale, NJ: Lawrence Erlbaum Associates.

Glass, D. C. (1977). Stress, behavior patterns and coronary disease. *American Scientist, 65,* 177–187.

Gleitman, H. (1981). *Psychology.* New York: W. W. Norton.

Gleitman, L. R., Newport, E. L., & Gleitman, H. (1984). The current status of the motherese hypothesis. *Journal of Child Language, 11,* 43–79.

Glenn, S. M., & Cunningham, C. C. (1983). What do babies listen to most? A developmental study of auditory preferences in nonhandicapped infants and infants with Down's syndrome. *Developmental Psychology, 19,* 332–337.

Gnepp, J. (1983). Children's social sensitivity: Inferring emotions from conflicting cues. *Developmental Psychology, 19,* 805–814.

Goddard, H. H. (1917). Mental tests and the immigrant. *Journal of Delinquency, 2,* 243–277.

Godden, D. R., & Baddeley, A. D. (1975). Context-dependent memory in two natural environments: On land and underwater. *British Journal of Psychology, 66,* 325–331.

Goelet, P., Castellucci, V. F., Schacher, S., & Kandel, E. R. (1986). The long and the short of long-term memory—A molecular framework. *Nature, 322,* 419–422.

Goldberger, L. (1982). Sensory deprivation and overload. In L. Goldberger & S. Breznitz (Eds.), *Handbook of stress: Theoretical and clinical aspects.* New York: Free Press.

Golden, C. J., Moses, J. A., Fishburne, F. J., Engum, E., Lewis, G. P., Wisniewski, A. M., Conley, F. K., Berg, R. A., & Graber, B. (1981). Cross-validation of the Luria-Nebraska Neuropsychological battery for the presence, lateralization, and location of brain damage. *Journal of Consulting Clinical Psychology, 50,* 87–95.

Goldenberg, I., & Goldenberg, H. (1980). *Family therapy: An overview.* Monterey, CA: Brooks/Cole.

Goldfried, M. R. (1982). On the history of therapeutic integration. *Behavior Therapy, 13,* 572–593.

Goldin-Meadow, S., & Feldman, H. (1977). The development of language-like communication without a language model. *Science, 197,* 401–403.

Goldman, R. D., & Widawski, M. H. (1976). A within subjects technique for comparing college grading standards. *Educational Psychology Measurement, 36,* 381–390.

Goldsmith, H. H. (1983). Genetic influences on personality from infancy to adulthood. *Child Development, 54,* 331–355.

Goleman, D. (1986, April 8). Studies point to the power of nonverbal signals. *New York Times.*

Goodenough, D. R. (1976). A review of individual differences in field dependence as a factor in auto safety. *Human Factors, 18,* 53–62.

Goodenough, F. L. (1932). Expression of the emotions in a blind-deaf child. *Journal of Abnormal and Social Psychology, 27,* 328–333.

Goodstein, L. P. (1981). Discriminative display support for process operators. In J. Rasmussen & W. Rouse (Eds.), *Human detection and diagnosis of system failures.* New York: Plenum Press.

Goodwin, D. W. (1979). Alcoholism and heredity: A review and hypothesis. *Archives of General Psychiatry, 36,* 57–61.

Goodwin, D. W., Crane, J. B., & Guze, S. B. (1973). Alcoholic "blackouts": A review and clinical study of 100 alcoholics. *American Journal of Psychiatry, 26,* 191–198.

Goolkasian, P., Terry, W. S., & Park, D. C. (1979). Memory for lectures: Effects of delay and distractor type. *Journal of Educational Psychology, 71,* 465–470.

Goplerud, E. N. (1980). Social support and stress during the first year of graduate school. *Professional Psychology, 11,* 283–290.

Gorassini, D. R., & Spanos, N. P. (1986). A social-cognitive skills approach to the successful modification of hypnotic susceptibility. *Journal of Personality and Social Psychology, 50,* 1004–1012.

Gordon, T. (1970). *Parent effectiveness training: The no-lose program for raising responsible children.* New York: Wyden.

Gore, S. (1978). The effect of social support in moderating the health consequences of unemployment. *Journal of Health and Social Behavior, 19,* 157–165.

Gore, W. V., & Taylor, D. M. (1973). The nature of the audience as it affects social inhibition. *Representative Research in Social Psychology, 4,* 18–27.

Gorney, R. (1976). Paper presented at the annual meeting of the American Psychiatric Association.

Gottesman, I. I. (1963). Heritability of personality. *Psychological Monographs, 77*(9, Whole No. 572).

Gottesman, I. I., & Shields, J. (1972). *Schizophrenia and genetics: A twin study vantage point.* New York: Academic Press.

Gottesman, I. I., & Shields, J. (1976). A critical review of recent adoption, twin, and family studies of schizophrenia: Behavioral genetics perspectives. *Schizophrenia Bulletin, 2,* 360–401.

Gottlieb, B. H. (Ed.). (1981). *Social networks and social support.* Beverly Hills, CA: Sage.

Gottman, J. M. (1979). *Marital interaction: Experimental investigation.* New York: Academic Press.

Gottman, J. M. (1981). *Time series analysis: A comprehensive introduction for social scientists.* New York: Cambridge University Press.

Gottman, J. M. (1987). The world of coordinated play: Same and cross-sex friendship in young children. In J. M. Gottman & J. Parker (Eds.), *Conversations of friends.* New York: Cambridge University Press.

Gough, H. G. (1965). Conceptual analysis of psychological test scores and other diagnostic variables. *Journal of Abnormal Psychology, 70,* 294–302.

Gould, S. J. (1983). *The mismeasure of man.* New York: W. W. Norton.

Graesser, A. C., & Nakamura, G. V. (1982). The impact of a schema on comprehension and memory. In G. H. Bower (Ed.), *The psychology of learning and motivation: Vol. 16.* New York: Academic Press.

Graesser, A. C., Woll, S. B., Kowalski, D. J., & Smith, D. A. (1980). Memory for typical and atypical actions in scripted activities. *Journal of Experimental Psychology: Human Learning and Memory, 6,* 503–515.

Graf, R. C., & Riddell, L. C. (1972). Helping behavior as a function of interpersonal perception. *Journal of Social Psychology, 86,* 227–231.

Graham, C., & Evans, F. J. (1977). Hypnotizability and the deployment of waking attention. *Journal of Abnormal Psychology, 86,* 631–638.

Granneman, J., & Friedman, M. J. (1980). Hepatic modulation of insulin-induced gastric acid secretion and EMG activity in rats. *American Journal of Physiology, 238,* 346–352.

Green, E. J., Greenough, W. T., & Schlumpf, B. E. (1983). Effects of complex or isolated environments on cortical dendrites of middle-aged rats. *Brain Research, 264* (2), 233–240.

Green, D. M., & Swets, J. A. (1965). *Signal detection theory and psychophysics.* New York: Wiley.

Green, R. (1987). *The 'sissy boy syndrome' and the development of homosexuality.* New Haven: Yale University Press.

Greene, B. (1985, January 15). Less violence would be a big hit on TV. *Chicago Tribune.*

Greeno, J. G., Riley, M. S., & Gelman, R. (1984). Conceptual competence and children's counting. *Cognitive Psychology, 16,* 94–143.

Greer, L. D. (1980). *Children's comprehension of formal features with masculine and feminine connotations.* Unpublished master's thesis, Department of Human Development, University of Kansas, Lawrence, KS.

Gregory, R. L. (1968). Visual illusions. *Scientific American, 219,* 66–67.

Gregory, R. L. (1973). *Eye and brain* (2nd ed.). New York: McGraw-Hill.

Greif, E. B., & Ulman, K. J. (1982). The psychological impact of menarche on early adolescent females: A review of the literature. *Child Development, 53,* 1413–1430.

Griffitt, W., Nelson, J., & Littlepage, G. (1972). Old age and responses to agreement-disagreement. *Journal of Gerontology, 27,* 269–274.

Griffitt, W., & Veitch, R. (1971). Hot and crowded: Influence of population density and temperature on interpersonal affective behavior. *Journal of Personality and Social Psychology, 17,* 92–98.

Griffitt, W. B., & Guay, P. (1969). "Object" evaluation and conditioned affect. *Journal of Experimental Research in Personality, 4,* 1–8.

Grobstein, C. (1979). External human fertilization. *Scientific American, 240*(6), 57–68.

Gross, W. B., & Colmano, G. (1969). The effect of social isolation on resistance to some infectious diseases. *Poultry Science, 48,* 514–520.

Grosz, H. I., & Zimmerman, J. (1970). A second detailed case study of functional blindness: Further demonstration of the contribution of objective psychological data. *Behavior Therapy, 1,* 115–123.

Gruder, C. L., & Duslak, R. J. (1973). Elicitation of cooperation by retaliatory and nonretaliatory strategies in a mixed motive game. *Journal of Conflict Resolution, 17,* 162–174.

Guilford, J. P. (1959). Traits of creativity. In H. H. Anderson (Ed.), *Creativity and its cultivation.* New York: Harper & Row.

Guilford, J. P., & Hoepfner, R. (1971). *The analysis of intelligence.* New York: McGraw-Hill.

Gunderson, J. G., & Mosher, L. R. (1975). The cost of schizophrenia. *American Journal of Psychiatry, 132,* 901–905.

Gurin, G., Veroff, J., & Feld, S. (1960). *Americans view their mental health: A nationwide survey.* New York: Basic Books.

Gurman, A. S., & Kniskern, D. P. (1978). Research on marital and family therapy. In S. L. Garfield & A. E. Bergin (Eds.), *Handbook of psychotherapy and behavior change* (2nd ed.). New York: Wiley.

Guroff, G. (1980). *Molecular neurobiology.* New York: Marcel Dekker.

Gustafson, D., & Thomas, W. (1970). A comparison of role differentiation in several situations. *Organizational Behavior and Human Performance, 5,* 299–312.

Gustavson, C. R., Garcia, J., Hawkins, W. G., & Rusiniak, K. W. (1974). Coyote predation control by aversive conditioning. *Science, 184,* 581–583.

Gwirtsman, H. E., & Germer, R. H. (1981). Abnormalities of dexamethasone suppression test and urinary MHPG in anorexia nervosa. *American Journal of Psychiatry, 138,* 650–653.

Haan, N., Aerts, E., & Cooper, B. A. B. (1985). *On moral grounds: The search for practical morality.* New York: New York University Press.

Haber, R. N. (1979). Twenty years of haunting eidetic imagery: Where's the ghost? *The Behavioral and Brain Sciences, 2,* 583–629.

Hales, D. J., Lozoff, B., Sosa, R., & Kennell, M. H. (1977). Defining the limits of the maternal sensitive period. *Developmental Medicine and Child Neurology, 19,* 454–461.

Haley, J. (1970). Family therapy. *International Journal of Psychiatry, 9,* 233–242.

Haley, J. (1971). *Family therapy: A radical change.* In J. Haley (Ed.), *Changing families: A family therapy reader.* New York: Grune & Stratton.

Hamberger, L. K., & Lohr, J. M. (1984). *Stress and stress management,* New York: Springer.

Hamilton, D. L., & Bishop, G. D. (1976). Attitudinal and behavioral effects of initial integration of white suburban neighborhoods. *Journal of Social Issues, 32,* 47–67.

Hamilton, D. L., & Zanna, M. P. (1972). Differential weighting of favorable and unfavorable attributes in impressions of personality. *Journal of Experimental Research in Personality, 6,* 204–212.

Hamilton, D. L., & Zanna, M. P. (1974). Context effects in impression formation: Changes in connotative meaning. *Journal of Personality and Social Psychology, 29,* 649–654.

Hammock, T., & Brehm, J. W. (1966). The attractiveness of choice alternatives when freedom to choose is eliminated by a social agent. *Journal of Personality, 34,* 546–554.

Hamner, W. C. (1974). Effects of a bargaining strategy and pressure to reach agreement in a stalemated negotiation. *Journal of Personality and Social Psychology, 30,* 458–467.

Hamner, W. C., & Yukl, G. A. (1977). The effectiveness of different offer strategies in bargaining. In D. Druckman (Ed.), *Negotiations: Social-psychological perspectives.* London: Sage.

Hanson, J. W. (1977). Unpublished manuscript.

Hardwick, D., McIntyre, A., & Pick, A. (1976). The content and manipulation of cognitive maps in children and adults. *Monographs of the Society for Research in Child Development, 41*(3, Serial No. 166).

Hare, R. D. (1970). *Psychopathy: Theory and research.* New York: Wiley.

Hariton, E. B., & Singer, J. L. (1974). Women's fantasies during marital intercourse: Normative and theoretical implications. *Journal of Consulting and Clinical Psychology, 42,* 313–322.

Harlow, H. F. (1958). The nature of love. *American Psychologist, 13,* 673–685.

Harlow, H. F., Harlow, M. K., & Suomi, S. J. (1971). From thought to therapy: Lessons from a private library. *American Scientist, 59,* 538–549.

Harrell, J. P. (1980). Psychological factors and hypertension. *Psychological Bulletin, 87,* 482–501.

Harris, P. L. (1974). Perseverative search at a visibly empty place by young infants. *Journal of Experimental Child Psychology, 18,* 535–542.

Harrison, A. A. (1976). *Individuals and groups.* Monterey, CA: Brooks/Cole.

Hart, J. T. (1965). Memory and the feeling-of-knowing experience. *Journal of Educational Psychology, 56,* 208–216.

Hart, J. T. (1967). Second-try recall, recognition, and the memory-monitoring process. *Journal of Educational Psychology, 58,* 193–197.

Harter, S., & Zigler, E. (1974). The assessment of effectance motivation in normal and retarded children. *Developmental Psychology, 10,* 169–180.

Hartman, B. K., Cozzari, C., Berod, A., Kalmbach, S. J., & Faris, P. L. (1986). Central cholinergic innervation of the locus coeruleus. *Society for Neuroscience Abstracts, 12,* 770.

Hartmann, E. (1982). From the biology of dreaming to the biology of the mind. *Psychoanalytic Study of the Child, 37,* 303–335.

Hartmann, E., Baekeland, F., & Zwilling, G. (1972). Psychological differences between long and short sleepers. *Archives of General Psychiatry, 26,* 463–468.

Hartmann, H. (1939). Psychoanalysis and the concept of health. *International Journal of Psychoanalysis, 20,* 308–321.

Hartmann, H. (1958). *Ego psychology and the problem of adaptation.* New York: International Universities Press.

Hartup, W. W., & Moore, S. G. (1963). Avoidance of inappropriate sex-typing by young children. *Journal of Consulting Psychology, 27,* 467–473.

Hastie, R., Penrod, S. D., & Pennington, N. (1983). *Inside the jury.* Cambridge: Harvard University Press.

Hattie, J. A., Sharply, C. F., & Rogers, H. J. (1984). *Psychological Bulletin, 95,* 534–541.

Hayes, J. R. M. (1952). *Memory span for several vocabularies as a function of vocabulary size.* Massachusetts Institute of Technology Acoustic Laboratory Progress Report. Cambridge: MIT.

Hayslip, B., & Sterns, H. L. (1979). Age differences in relationships between crystallized and fluid intelligences and problem solving. *Journal of Gerontology, 11,* 404–414.

Hebb, D. O. (1955). Drives and the C.N.S. (conceptual nervous system). *Psychological Review, 62,* 243–254.

Heffner, H. E., & Heffner, R. S. (1984). Temporal lobe lesions and perception of species-specific vocalizations by macaques. *Science, 226,* 75–76.

Heider, E. (1972). Universals of color naming and memory. *Journal of Experimental Psychology, 93,* 10–20.

Heinonen, O. P., Slone, D., & Shapiro, S. (1976). *Birth defects and drugs in pregnancy.* Littleton, MA. Publishing Sciences Group.

Hirsh-Pasek, K., Treiman, R., & Schneiderman, M. (1984). Brown and Hanlon revisited: Mothers' sensitivity to ungrammatical forms. *Journal of Child Language, 11,* 81–88.

Heitler, J. B. (1976). Preparatory techniques in initiating expressive psychotherapy with lower-class, unsophisticated patients. *Psychological Bulletin, 83,* 339–352.

Heller, K., & Monahan, J. (1977). *Psychology and community change.* Homewood, IL: Dorsey Press.

Heller, K., & Swindle, R. W. (1982). Social networks, perceived social support and coping with stress. In R. D. Felner, L. A. Jason, J. Moritsugu, & S. S. Farber (Eds.), *Preventive psychology: Theory, research, and practice in community intervention* (pp. 87–103). Elmsford, NY: Pergamon Press.

Helmsley, D. R., & Zawada, S. L. (1976). "Filtering" and the cognitive deficit in schizophrenia. *British Journal of Psychiatry, 128,* 456–461.

Henderson, N. D. (1982). Human behavior genetics. *Annual Review of Psychology, 33,* 403–440.

Hendlin, H. (1975). Student suicide: Death as a life-style. *Journal of Nervous and Mental Disease, 160,* 204–219.

Hendrick, C., & Hendrick, S. (1986). A theory and method of love. *Journal of Personality and Social Psychology, 50,* 392–402.

Hennessy, J. W., & Levine, S. (1979). Stress, arousal, and the pituitary-adrenal system: A psychoendocrine hypothesis. *Progress in Psychobiology and Physiological Psychology, 8,* 133–178.

Henry, G., Weingartner, H., & Murphy, D. L. (1973). Influence of affective states and psycho-active drugs on verbal learning and memory. *American Journal of Psychiatry, 130,* 966–971.

Herbert, M. (1982). Conduct disorders. In B. B. Lahey & A. E. Kazdin (Eds.), *Advances in clinical child psychology: Vol. 5.* New York: Plenum Press.

Herman, B. H., Hammock, M. K., Arthur-Smith, A., Egan, J., Chatoor, I., Zelnik, N., Carradine, M., Appelgate, K., Boecks, R., & Sharp, S. D. (1986, November). Role of opioid peptides in autism: Effects of acute administration of naltrexone. *Society for Neuroscience Abstracts, 12.*

Herman, C. P., & Polivy, J. (1975). Anxiety, restraint, and eating behavior. *Journal of Abnormal Psychology, 84,* 666–672.

Herman, J. H., & Roffwarg, H. P. (1983). Modifying oculomotor activity in awake subjects increases the amplitude of eye movement during REM sleep. *Science, 220,* 1074–1076.

Heron, W. (1957). The pathology of boredom. *Scientific American, 196,* 52–56.

Hersen, M., Bellack, A. S., Himmelhoch, J. M., & Thase, M. E. (1984). *Behavior Therapy, 15,* 21–40.

Herzberg, F. (1966). *Work and the nature of man.* New York: Crowell.

Herzberg, F. (1968). One more time: How do you motivate employees? *Harvard Business Review, 46,* 53–62.

Herzog, D. B. (1982). Bulimia: The secretive syndrome. *Psychosomatics, 22,* 481–487.

Heston, L. L. (1966). Psychiatric disorders in foster home reared children of schizophrenic mothers. *British Journal of Psychiatry, 112,* 819–825.

Higgins, E. T., & Rholes, W. S. (1976). Impression formation and role fulfillment: A "holistic reference" hypothesis. *Journal of Experimental Social Psychology, 12,* 422–435.

Hilgard, E. R. (1965). *Hypnotic susceptibility.* New York: Harcourt, Brace and World.

Hilgard, E. R. (1977). *Divided consciousness: Multiple controls in human thought and action.* New York: Wiley.

Hilgard, E. R. (1979). *Personality and hypnosis: A study of imaginative involvement.* Chicago: University of Chicago Press.

Hilgard, E. R. (1980). Consciousness in contemporary psychology. *Annual Review of Psychology, 31,* 1–26.

Hilgard, E. R. (1982). Hypnotic susceptibility and implications for measurement. *International Journal of Clinical and Experimental Hypnosis, 30,* 394–403.

Hilgard, E. R., Atkinson, R. L., & Atkinson, R. C. (1979). *Introduction to psychology* (7th ed.). New York: Harcourt Brace Jovanovich.

Hilgard, E. R., Morgan, A. H., & MacDonald, H. (1975). Pain and dissociation in the cold pressor test: A study of "hidden reports" through automatic key-pressing and automatic talking. *Journal of Abnormal Psychology, 84,* 280–289.

Hill, B. (1968). *Gates of horn and ivory.* New York: Taplinger.

Hill, W. F. (1982). *Principles of learning.* Palo Alto, CA: Mayfield.

Hillyard, S. A., Picton, R. W., & Regan, D. (1978). Sensation, perception and attention: Analysis using ERPs. In E. Calloway, P. Teuting, & S. H. Koslow (Eds.), *Evoked potentials.* New York: Academic Press.

Hiroto, D. S., & Seligman, M. E. P. (1975). Generality of learned helplessness in man. *Journal of Personality and Social Psychology, 31,* 311–327.

Hirsch, B. J. (1980). Natural support systems and coping with major life changes. *American Journal of Community Psychology, 8,* 159–172.

Hirsch, J., & Knittle, J. L. (1970). Cellularity of obese and nonobese human adipose tissue. *Federation of American Societies for Experimental Biology: Federation Proceedings, 29,* 1516–1521.

Hirsch-Pasek, K., Treiman, R., & Schneiderman, M. (1984). Brown and Hanlon revisited: Mothers' sensitivity to ungrammatical forms. *Journal of Child Language, 11,* 81–88.

Hirtle, S. C., & Jonides, J. (1985). Evidence of hierarchies in cognitive maps. *Memory and Cognition, 13,* 208–217.

Hobson, J. A., & McCarley, R. W. (1977). The brain as a dream state generator: An activation-synthesis hypothesis of the dream process. *American Journal of Psychiatry, 134,* 1335–1348.

Hochberg, J. E., & McAlister, E. (1955). Relative size versus familiar size in the perception of represented depth. *American Journal of Psychology, 68,* 294–296.

Hockey, G. R. (1984). Varieties of attentional state: The effects of environment. In R. Paraduraman & R. Davies (Eds.), *Varieties of attention.* New York: Academic Press.

Hoffman, L. R. (Ed.). (1979). *The group problem solving process: Studies of a valence model.* New York: Praeger.

Hoffman, L. R., Friend, K. E., & Bond, G. R. (1979). Problem differences and the process of adopting group solutions. In L. R. Hoffman (Ed.), *The group problem solving process: Studies of a valence model.* New York: Praeger.

Hoffman, L. R., & Maier, N. R. F. (1979). Valence in the adoption of solutions by problem-solving groups: Concept, method, and results. In L. R. Hoffman (Ed.), *The group problem solving process: Studies of a valence model.* New York: Praeger.

Hoffman, M. L. (1970). Moral development. In P. H. Mussen (Ed.), *Carmichael's manual of child psychology: Vol. 2.* New York: Wiley.

Hoffman, M. L. (1977). Sex differences in empathy and related behaviors. *Psychological Bulletin, 84,* 712–722.

Hoffman, M. L. (1982). Development of prosocial motivation: Empathy and guilt. In N. Eisenberg-Berg (Ed.), *Development of prosocial behavior.* New York: Academic Press.

Hogan, R., DeSoto, C. B., & Solano, C. (1977). Traits, tests, and personality research. *American Psychologist, 32,* 255–264.

Hogan, R., Mankin, D., Conway, J., & Fox, S. (1970). Personality correlates of undergraduate marijuana use. *Journal of Consulting and Clinical Psychology, 35,* 58–63.

Hohman, G. W. (1966). Some effects of spinal cord lesions on experienced emotional feelings. *Psychophysiology, 3,* 143-156.

Holden, C. (1985). A guarded endorsement for shock therapy. *Science, 228,* 1510–1511.

Holden, C. (1986). Researchers grapple with problems of updating classic psychological test. *Science, 233,* 1249–1251.

Hollander, E. P. (1985). Leadership and power. In G. Lindzey & E. Aronson (Eds.), *The handbook of social psychology: Vol. 2.* (3rd ed.). New York: Random House.

Holmes, D. S. (1984). Meditation and somatic arousal reduction: A review of the experimental evidence. *American Psychologist, 39,* 1–10.

Holmes, T. H., & Rahe, R. H. (1967). The social readjustment rating scale. *Journal of Psychosomatic Research, 11,* 213–218.

Holohan, C. J., & Moos, R. H. (1987). Risk, resistance, and psychological distress: A longitudinal analysis with adults and children. *Journal of Abnormal Psychology, 96,* 3–13.

Holway, A. H., & Boring, E. G. (1941). Determinants of apparent visual size with distance variant. *American Journal of Psychology, 54,* 21–37.

Honzik, M. P., MacFarlane, J., & Allen, L. (1948). The stability of mental test performance between 2 and 18 years. *Journal of Experimental Education, 4,* 309–324.

Horn, J. L., & Donaldson, G. (1976). On the myth of intellectual decline in adulthood. *American Psychologist, 31,* 701–719.

Horn, J. L., & Donaldson, G. (1980). Cognitive development in adulthood. In O. G. Brim & J. Kagan (Eds.), *Constancy and change in human development.* Cambridge: Harvard University Press.

Horn, J. M., Loehlin, J. C., & Willerman, L. (1979). Intellectual resemblance among adoptive and biological relatives: The Texas adoption project. *Behavior Genetics, 9,* 177–207.

Horney, K. (1937). *Neurotic personality of our times.* New York: W. W. Norton.

Horowitz, A. V., & Horowitz, V. A. (1975). *The effects of task-specific instructions on the picture memory of children in recall and recognition tasks.* Paper presented at the Society for Research in Child Development, Denver, CO.

Horowitz, I. A. (1980). Juror selection: A comparison of two methods in several criminal cases. *Journal of Applied Social Psychology, 10,* 86–99.

Hosch, H. M., & Cooper, D. S. (1982). Victimization as a determinant of eyewitness accuracy. *Journal of Applied Psychology, 67,* 649–652.

Houston, B. K., & Snyder, C. R. (Eds.). (1987). *Type A behavior pattern: Current trends and future directions.* New York: Wiley.

Hoversten, G. H., & Moncur, J. P. (1969). Stimuli and intensity factors in testing infants. *Journal of Speech and Hearing Research, 12,* 687–702.

Hovland, C. I., Janis, I. L., & Kelley, H. (1953). *Communication and persuasion.* New Haven: Yale University Press.

Howard, D. V. (1983). *Cognitive psychology.* New York: Macmillan.

Howard, K. I., Kopta, M., Krause, M. S., & Orlinsky, D. E. (1986). The dose-effect relationship in psychotherapy. *American Psychologist, 41,* 159–164.

Howe, M. J. A. (1970). Using students' notes to examine the role of the individual learner in acquiring meaningful subject matter. *Journal of Educational Research, 64,* 61–63.

Hoyer, W. J., & Plude, D. J. (1980). Attentional and perceptual processes in the study of cognitive aging. In L. W. Poon (Ed.), *Aging in the 1980s: Psychological issues.* Washington, DC: American Psychological Association.

Hsu, L. K. G. (1980). Outcome of anorexia nervosa: A review of the literature (1954 to 1978). *Archives of General Psychiatry, 37,* 1041–1046.

Hubel, D. H., & Wiesel, T. N. (1979). Brain mechanisms of vision. *Scientific American, 241,* 150–162.

Hudspeth, A. J. (1983). The hair cells of the inner ear. *Scientific American, 248,* 54–64.

Huesmann, L. R., Laperspetz, K., & Eron, L. D. (1984). Intervening variables in the TV violence-aggression relation: Evidence from two countries. *Developmental Psychology, 20,* 746–775.

Hull, C. L. (1943). *Principles of behavior.* New York: Appleton-Century-Crofts.

Hull, C. L. (1951). *Essentials of behavior.* New Haven: Yale University Press.

Humphreys, L. G. (1984). General intelligence. In C. R. Reynolds & R. T. Brown (Eds.), *Perspectives on bias in mental testing.* New York: Plenum Press.

Humphreys, L. G. (1986). Knowing the elephant. In R. J. Sternberg & D. Detterman (Eds.), *What is intelligence?* Norwood, NJ: Ablex.

Hunt, C. B. (1980). Intelligence as an information processing concept. *British Journal of Psychology, 71,* 449–474.

Hunt, E. (1983). On the nature of intelligence. *Science, 219,* 141–146.

Hunt, E., & Lansman, M. (1983). Individual differences in intelligence. In R. Sternberg (Ed.), *Advances in the psychology of human intelligence.* Hillsdale, NJ: Lawrence Erlbaum Associates.

Hunt, M. (1974). *Sexual behavior in the 1970s.* Chicago: Playboy Press.

Hunt, M. (1982). *The universe within.* New York: Simon & Schuster.

Hunt, R., & Rouse, W. B. (1981). Problem solving skills of maintenance trainees in diagnosing faults in simulated power plants. *Human Factors, 23,* 317–328.

Hunter, F. T., & Youniss, J. (1982). Changes in functions of three relations during adolescence. *Developmental Psychology, 18,* 806–811.

Hunter, J. E., & Hunter, R. F. (1984). Validity and utility of alternative predictors of job performance. *Psychological Bulletin, 96,* 72–98.

Hurst, R. (1984). *Pilot error.* London: Granada.

Hurvich, L. M. (1981). *Color vision.* Sunderland, MA: Sinauer.

Husband, R. W. (1940). Cooperative versus solitary problem solution. *Journal of Social Psychology, 11,* 405–409.

Huston, A. C. (1983). Sex-typing. In P. H. Mussen (Ed.), *Handbook of child psychology: Vol. 4* (4th ed.). New York: Wiley.

Huttenlocher, J. (1974). The origins of language comprehension. In R. L. Solso (Ed.), *Theories in cognitive psychology.* Hillsdale, NJ: Lawrence Erlbaum Associates.

Huttenlocher, P. R. (1979). Synaptic density in human frontal cortex: Developmental changes and effects of aging. *Brain Research, 163,* 195–205.

Hyde, J. S., & Phillis, D. E. (1979). Androgyny across the life span. *Developmental Psychology, 15,* 334–336.

Hyman, H., & Barnack, J. E. (1954). Special review: Sexual behavior in the human female. *Psychological Bulletin, 51,* 418–427.

Hyman, M. D. (1971). Disability and patients' perceptions of preferential treatment: Some preliminary findings. *Journal of Chronic Diseases, 24,* 329–342.

Ibuka, N., Inouye, S. T., & Kawamura, H. (1977). Analysis of sleep-wakefulness rhythms in male rats after suprachiasmatic nucleus lesions and ocular enucleation. *Brain Research, 122,* 33–47.

Ickes, W., & Earnes, R. D. (1978). Boys and girls together—and alienated: On enacting stereotyped sex roles in mixed-sex dyads. *Journal of Personality and Social Psychology, 36,* 669–683.

Illinois Criminal Justice Information Authority. (1985, November). Repeat offenders in Illinois. *Research Bulletin, 1.*

Insko, C. A., Smith, R. H., Alicke, M. D., Wade, J., & Taylor, S. (1985). Conformity and group size: The concern with being right and the concern with being liked. *Personality and Social Psychology Bulletin, 11,* 41–50.

Istomina, Z. M. (1975). The development of voluntary memory in pre-school age children. *Soviet Psychology, 13,* 5–64.

Izard, C. E. (1971). *The face of emotion.* New York: Appleton-Century-Crofts.

Izard, C. E. (1977). *Human emotions.* New York: Plenum Press.

Jacobs, T. J., & Charles, E. (1980). Life events and the occurrence of cancer in children. *Psychosomatic Medicine, 42,* 11–24.

Jacobson, A., Kales, J., & Kales, A. (1969). Clinical and electrophysiological correlates of sleep disorders in children. In A. Kales (Ed.), *Sleep: Physiology and pathology.* Philadelphia: J. B. Lippincott.

Jacobson, E. (1938). *Progressive relaxation.* Chicago: University of Chicago Press.

Jacobson, J., & Wille, D. (1986, April). *The influence of attachment pattern on peer interaction at 2 and 3 years.* Paper presented at the International Conference on Infant Studies, New York, NY.

Jaffe, J. H. (1975). Drug addiction and drug abuse. In L. S. Goodman & A. Gilman (Eds.), *The pharmacological basis of therapeutics* (5th ed.). New York: Macmillan.

James, W. (1890). *Principles of psychology.* New York: Holt.

James, W. (1892). *Psychology: Briefer course.* New York: Holt.

Janis, I. L. (1972). *Victims of groupthink.* Boston: Houghton Mifflin.

Janis, I. L. (1983). The role of social support in adherence to stressful decisions. *American Psychologist, 38,* 143–160.

Janis, I. L., & Field, P. B. (1956). A behavioral assessment of persuasibility: Consistency of individual differences. *Sociometry, 19,* 241–259.

Janowitz, H. D. (1967). Role of gastrointestinal tract in the regulation of food intake. In C. F. Code (Ed.), *Handbook of physiology: Alimentary canal 1.* Washington, DC: American Physiological Society.

Janowitz, H. D., & Grossman, M. I. (1949). Some factors affecting the food intake of normal dogs and dogs with esophagostomy and gastric fistula. *American Journal of Physiology, 159,* 143–148.

Janowitz, H. D., and Grossman, M. I. (1951). Effect of prefeeding, alcohol and bitters on food intake of dogs. *American Journal of Physiology, 164,* 182–186.

Jellinek, E. M. (1960). *The disease concept of alcoholism.* New Haven: Hillhouse Press.

Jemmott, J. B., & Locke, S. E. (1984). Psychosocial factors, immunologic mediation, and human susceptibility to infectious diseases: How much do we know? *Psychological Bulletin, 95,* 78–108.

Jenkins, J. G., & Dallenbach, K. M. (1924). Oblivescence during sleep and waking. *American Journal of Psychology, 35,* 605–612.

Jensen, A. R. (1969). How much can we boost IQ and scholastic achievement? *Harvard Educational Review, 39,* 1–123.

Jensen, A. R. (1983). The chronometry of intelligence. In R. Sternberg (Ed.)., *Advances in the psychology of human intelligence.* Hillsdale, NJ: Lawrence Erlbaum Associates.

Johansson, G., Hofsten, C. V., & Jansson, G. (1980). Event perception. *Annual Review of Psychology, 31,* 27–63.

Johnson, C. A., Ahern, F. M., & Johnson, R. C. (1976). Level of functioning of siblings and parents of probands of varying degrees of retardation. *Behavioral Genetics, 6,* 473–477.

Johnson, C. M., Bradley-Johnson, S., McCarthy, R., & Jamie, M. (1984). Token reinforcement during WISC-R. administration. *Applied Research on Mental Retardation, 5,* 43–52.

Johnson-Laird, P. N. (1983). *Mental models.* Cambridge: Harvard University Press.

Johnson-Laird, P. N., & Steedman, M. (1978). The psychology of syllogisms, *Cognitive Psychology, 10,* 64–99.

Jones, E. E. (1976). How do people perceive the causes of behavior? *American Scientist, 64,* 300–305.

Jones, E. E. (1985). Major developments in social psychology during the past five decades. In G. Lindzey & E. Aronson (Eds.), *The handbook of social psychology: Vol. 1* (3rd ed.). New York: Random House.

Jones, E. E., & Harris, V. A. (1967). The attribution of attitudes. *Journal of Experimental Social Psychology, 3,* 1–24.

Jones, J. W. (1978). Adverse emotional reactions of nonsmokers to secondary cigarette smoke. *Environmental Psychology and Nonverbal Behavior, 3,* 125–127.

Jones, K. L., Smith, D. W., Ulleland, C. N., & Streissguth, A. P. (1973). Pattern of malformation in offspring of chronic alcoholic mothers. *Lancet, 1,* 1267–1271.

Jones, M. C. (1957). The later careers of boys who were early or late maturing. *Child Development, 28,* 113–128.

Jones, M. C., & Bayley, N. (1950). Physical maturing among boys as related to behavior. *Journal of Educational Psychology, 41,* 129–148.

Jones, R. T. (1971). Marijuana-induced "high": Influence of expectation, setting, and previous drug experience. *Pharmacological Reviews, 23,* 359–369.

Jones, R. T. (1984). The pharmacology of cocaine. In J. Grabowski (Ed.), *Cocaine: Pharmacology, effects, and treatment of abuse.* Rockville, MD: National Institute on Drug Abuse.

Jordan, H. A. (1969). Voluntary intragastric feeding: Oral and gastric contributions to food intake and hunger in man. *Journal of Comparative and Physiological Psychology, 68,* 498–506.

Jordan, T. G., Grallo, R., Deutch, M., & Deutch, C. P. (1985). Long-term effects of enrichment: A 20-year perspective on persistence and change. *American Journal of Community Psychology, 13,* 393–414.

Julien, R. M. (1981). *A primer of drug action* (3rd ed.). San Francisco: W. H. Freeman.

Jung, C. G. (1916). *Analytical psychology.* New York: Moffat.

Jung, C. G. (1933). *Psychological types.* New York: Harcourt, Brace and World.

Justice, A. (1985). Review of the effects of stress on cancer in laboratory animals: Importance of time of stress application and type of tumor. *Psychological Bulletin, 98,* 108–138.

Kagan, J. (1966). Reflection-impulsivity: The generality and dynamics of conceptual tempo. *Journal of Abnormal Psychology, 71,* 17–24.

Kagan, J. (1984). *The nature of the child.* New York: Basic Books.

Kagan, J., Kearsley, R. B., & Zelazo, P. R. (1978). *Infancy: Its place in human development.* Cambridge: Harvard University Press.

Kagan, J., Reznick, J. S., & Snidman, N. (in press). The physiology and psychology of behavioral inhibition in children. *Child Development.*

Kahn, R. L., & French, J. R. P., Jr. (1970). Status and conflict: Two themes in the study of stress. In J. E. McGrath (Ed.), *Social and psychological factors in stress.* New York: Holt, Rinehart and Winston.

Kahneman, D., Beatty, J., & Pollack, I. (1967). Perceptual deficits during a mental task. *Science, 157,* 218–219.

Kahneman, D., Slovic, P., & Tversky, A. (Eds.). (1982). *Judgment under uncertainty: Heuristics and biases.* New York: Cambridge University Press.

Kalish, H. I. (1981). *From behavioral science to behavior modification.* New York: McGraw-Hill.

Kamin, L. J. (1969). Predictability, surprise, attention and conditioning. In B. A. Campbell & R. M. Church (Eds.), *Punishment and aversive behavior.* New York: Appleton-Century-Crofts.

Kanfer, F. H., & Goldstein, A. P. (1986). *Helping people change* (3rd ed.). New York: Pergamon Press.

Kanner, A. D., Coyne, J. C., Schaefer, C., & Lazarus, R. S. (1981). Comparison of two modes of stress measurement: Daily hassles and uplifts versus major life events. *Journal of Behavioral Medicine, 4,* 1–39.

Kanterowitz, D., & Cohen, B. D. (1977). Referent communication in chronic schizophrenia. *Journal of Abnormal Psychology, 86,* 1–9.

Kaplan, H. S. (1974). *The new sex therapy.* New York: Brunner/Mazel.

Karaz, V., & Perlman, D. (1975). Attribution at the wire: Consistency and outcome finish strong. *Journal of Experimental Social Psychology, 11,* 470–477.

Karlins, M., Coffman, T. L., & Walter, G. (1969). On the fading of social stereotypes: Studies in three generations of college students. *Journal of Personality and Social Psychology, 13,* 1–16.

Kastenbaum, R. (1965). Wine and fellowship in aging: An exploratory action program. *Journal of Human Relations, 13,* 266–275.

Kaufman, A. S., & Kaufman, N. L. (1983). *Kaufman assessment battery for children.* Circle Pines, MN: American Guidance Services.

Kaufman, L., & Rock, I. (1962). The moon illusion. *Science, 136,* 953–961.

Kaufman, R., Maland, J., & Yonas, A. (1981). Sensitivity of 5- and 7-month old infants to pictorial depth information. *Journal of Experimental Child Psychology, 32,* 162–168.

Kavanaugh, R. D., & Jirkovsky, A. M. (1982). Parental speech to young children: A longitudinal analysis. *Merrill-Palmer Quarterly, 28,* 297–311.

Kazdin, A. E. (1978). Evaluating the generality of findings in analogue therapy research. *Journal of Consulting and Clinical Psychology, 46,* 673–686.

Kazdin, A. E. (1984). *Behavior modification in applied settings* (3rd ed.). Homewood, IL: Dorsey Press.

Kazdin, A. E. (1985). The role of meta-analysis in the evaluation of psychotherapy. *Clinical Psychology Review, 5,* 49–61.

Kazdin, A. E., & Bootzin, R. R. (1972). The token economy: An evaluative review. *Journal of Applied Behavior Analysis, 5,* 343–372.

Kazdin, A. E., & Wilson, G. T. (1978). *Evaluation of behavior therapy: Issues, evidence, and research strategies.* Cambridge: Ballinger.

Keane, T. M., Lisman, S. A., & Kreutzer, J. (1980). Alcoholic beverages and their placebos: An empirical evaluation of expectancies. *Addictive Behavior, 4,* 313–328.

Keele, S. W. (1973). *Attention and human performance.* Pacific Palisades, CA: Goodyear.

Keeney, T. J., Cannizzo, S. R., & Flavell, J. H. (1967). Spontaneous and induced verbal rehearsal in a recall task. *Child Development, 38,* 953–966.

Keesey, R. E. (1980). A set-point analysis of the regulation of body weight. In A. J. Stunkard (Ed.), *Obesity.* Philadelphia: W. B. Saunders.

Keesey, R. E., & Powley, T. L. (1975). Hypothalamic regulation of body weight. *American Scientist, 63,* 558–565.

Keesey, R.E., & Powley, T. L. (1986). The regulation of body weight. *Annual Review of Psychology, 37,* 109–133.

Keinan, G. (1987). Decision-making under stress: Scanning of alternatives under controllable and uncontrollable threats. *Journal of Personality and Social Psychology, 52,* 639–644.

Keller, A., Ford, L. H., & Meacham, J. A. (1978). Dimensions of self-concept in preschool children. *Developmental Psychology, 14,* 483–489.

Kelley, H. H. (1973). The processes of causal attribution. *American Psychologist, 28,* 107–128.

Kelley, H. H., & Michela, J. L. (1980). Attribution theory and research. *Annual Review of Psychology, 31,* 457–501.

Kelley, H. H., & Stahelski, A. J. (1970). Social interaction basis of cooperators' and competitors' beliefs about others. *Journal of Personality and Social Psychology, 16,* 66–91.

Kelley, K. W. (1985). Immunological consequences of changing environmental stimuli. In G. P. Moberg (Ed.), *Animal stress.* Bethesda, MD: American Physiological Society.

Kellman, P. J., & Spelke, E. S. (1983). Perception of partly occluded objects in infancy. *Cognitive Psychology, 15,* 483–524.

Kelly, G. A. (1955). *The psychology of personal constructs.* New York: W. W. Norton.

Kelly, G. A. (1958). The theory and technique of assessment. In P. R. Farnsworth & Q. McNemar (Eds.), *Annual Review of Psychology, 9,* 323–352.

Kendall, P. C. (1982). Integration: Behavior therapy and other schools of thought. *Behavior Therapy, 13,* 559–571.

Kennell, J. H., Jerauld, R., Wolfe, H., Chesler, D., Kreger, N. C., McAlpine, W., Steffa, M., & Klaus, M. H. (1974). Maternal behavior one year after early and extended postpartum contact. *Developmental Medicine and Child Neurology, 16,* 172–179.

Kernberg, O. (1976). *Object relations theory and clinical psychoanalysis.* New York: Jason Aronson.

Kety, S. S., Rosenthal, D., Wender, P. H., Schulsinger, F., & Jacobson, B. (1975). Mental illness in the biological and adoptive families of adopted individuals who have become schizophrenic: A preliminary report based on psychiatric interviews. In R. R. Fieve, D. Rosenthal, & H. Brill (Eds.), *Genetic research in psychiatry.* Baltimore: Johns Hopkins University Press.

Keys, A., Brozek, J., Henschel, A., Mickelson, O., & Taylor, H. (1950). *The biology of human starvation.* Minneapolis: University of Minnesota Press.

Kiang, N. Y. S., Watanabe, T., Thomas, E. C., & Clark, L. F. (1962). Stimulus coding in the cat's auditory nerve. *Annals of Otology, Rhinology, and Laryngology, 71,* 1009–1026.

Kiecolt-Glaser, J. K., Garner, W., Speicher, C. E., Penn, G. M., Holliday, J., & Glaser, R. (1984). Psychosocial modifiers of immunocompetence in medical students. *Psychosomatic Medicine, 46,* 7–14.

Kiesler, C. A. (1982). Mental hospitals and alternative care: Noninstitutionalization as potential public policy for mental patients. *American Psychologist, 37,* 349–360.

Kiesler, C. A., & Kiesler, S. B. (1969). *Conformity.* Reading, MA: Addison-Wesley.

Kihlstrom, J. F., & Evans, F. J. (1976). Recovery of memory after posthypnotic amnesia. *Journal of Abnormal Psychology, 85,* 564–569.

Kinsey, A. C., Pomeroy, W. R., & Martin, C. E. (1948). *Sexual behavior in the human male.* Philadelphia: W. B. Saunders.

Kinsey, A. C., Pomeroy, W. R., Martin, C. E., & Gebhard, P. H. (1953). *Sexual behavior in the human female.* Philadelphia: W. B. Saunders.

Kintsch, W., & Bates, E. (1977). Recognition memory for statements from a classroom lecture. *Journal of Experimental Psychology: Human Learning and Memory, 3,* 150–159.

Kirigin, K. A., Braukmann, C. J., Atwater, J. D., & Wolf, M. M. (1982). An evaluation of teaching-family (Achievement Place) group homes for juvenile offenders. *Journal of Applied Behavior Analysis, 15,* 1–16.

Kirsch, I., & Henry, D. (1979). Self-desensitization and meditation in the reduction of public speaking anxiety. *Journal of Consulting and Clinical Psychology, 47,* 536–541.

Kitcher, P. (1985). *Vaulting ambition: Sociobiology and the quest for human nature.* Cambridge: MIT Press.

Klagsbrun, F. (1976). *Too young to die: Youth and suicide.* Boston: Houghton Mifflin.

Klatzky, R. L. (1980). *Human memory: Structures and processes* (2nd ed.). San Francisco: W. H. Freeman.

Klatzky, R. L. (1983). The icon is dead: Long live the icon. *The Behavioral and Brain Sciences, 6,* 27–28.

Klaus, M. H., & Kennell, J. H. (1976). *Maternal-infant bonding.* St. Louis: Mosby.

Klein, D. C., & Seligman, M. E. P. (1976). Reversal of performance deficits and perceptual deficits in learned helplessness and depression. *Journal of Abnormal Psychology, 85,* 11–26.

Klein, M. (1960). *The psychoanalysis of children.* New York: Grove Press.

Klein, M. (1975). *The writings of Melanie Klein: Vol. 3.* London: Hogarth Press.

Klerman, G. L. (1982). Practical issues in the treatment of depression and mania. In E. S. Paykel (Ed.), *Handbook of affective disorders.* New York: Guilford Press.

Klerman, G. L. (1983). The efficacy of psychotherapy as a basis for public policy. *American Psychologist, 38,* 929–934.

Kline, D. W., & Szafran, J. (1975). Age differences in backward monoptic masking. *Journal of Gerontology, 30,* 307–311.

Klinger, E., Barta, S. G., & Maxeiner, M. E. (1980). Motivational correlates of thought content frequency and commitment. *Journal of Personality and Social Psychology, 39,* 1222–1237.

Knittle, J. L., Tinners, K., Ginsberg-Fellner, F., Brown, R. E., & Katz, D. P. (1979). The growth of adipose tissue in children and adolescents. *Journal of Clinical Investigation, 63,* 239–241.

Knox, R. E., & Safford, R. K. (1976). Group caution at the racetrack. *Journal of Experimental Social Psychology, 12,* 317–324.

Kobasa, S. C. (1979). Stressful life events, personality, and health: An inquiry into hardiness. *Journal of Personality and Social Psychology, 37,* 1–11.

Kobasa, S. C., Maddi, S. R., & Courington, S. (1981). Personality and constitution as mediators in the stress-illness relationship. *Journal of Health and Social Behavior, 22,* 368–378.

Kobasa, S. C., Maddi, S. R., & Kahn, S. (1982). Hardiness and health: a prospective study. *Journal of Personality and Social Psychology, 42,* 168–177.

Kobasa, S. C., & Puccetti, M. C. (1983). Personality and social resources in stress-resistance. *Journal of Personality and Social Psychology, 45,* 839–850.

Kobasigawa, A., Arakaki, K., & Awiguni, A. (1966). Avoidance of feminine toys by kindergarten boys: The effects of adult presence or absence, and an adult's attitudes toward sex-typing. *Japanese Journal of Psychology, 37,* 96–103.

Koh, S. D., Kayton, L., & Berry, R. (1973). Mnemonic organization in young non-psychotic schizophrenics. *Journal of Abnormal Psychology, 81,* 299–310.

Kohlberg, L. (1966). A cognitive-developmental analysis of children's sex role concepts and attitudes. In E. E. Maccoby (Ed.), *The development of sex differences.* Stanford, CA: Stanford University Press.

Kohlberg, L., & Gilligan, C. (1971). The adolescent as a philosopher: The discovery of the self in a postconventional world. *Daedalus, 100,* 1051–1086.

Kohn, M. L. (1977). *Class and conformity: A study in values* (2nd ed.). Chicago: University of Chicago Press.

Kohut, H. (1984). Selected problems of self-psychological theory. In J. D. Lichtenberg & S. Kaplan (Eds.), *Reflections on self psychology* (pp. 387–416). Hillsdale, NJ: Lawrence Erlbaum Associates.

Kolata, G. (1985). Why do people get fat? *Science, 227,* 1327–1328.

Komorita, S. S. (1984). Coalition bargaining. In L. Berkowitz (Ed.),

Advances in experimental social psychology: Vol. 18. New York: Academic Press.

Komorita, S. S., Sweeney, J., & Kravitz, D. A. (1980). Cooperative choice in the N-person dilemma situation. *Journal of Personality and Social Psychology, 38,* 504–516.

Koriat, A., Lichtenstein, S., & Fischoff, B. (1980). Reasons for confidence. *Journal of Experimental Psychology: Human Learning and Memory, 6,* 107–118.

Korner, A. F. (1971). Individual differences at birth: Implications for early experience and later development. *American Journal of Orthopsychiatry, 41*(4).

Kosslyn, S. (1976). Can imagery be distinguished from other forms of internal representation? Evidence from studies of information retrieval times. *Memory and Cognition, 4,* 291–297.

Kotelchuck, M. (1976). The infant's relationship to the father: Experimental evidence. In M. E. Lamb (Ed.), *The role of the father in child development.* New York: Wiley.

Kozel, N. J., Grider, R. A., & Adams, E. H. (1982). National surveillance of cocaine use and related health consequences. *Morbidity and Mortality Weekly Report, 20,* 265–273.

Kraft, C. (1978). A psychophysical approach to air safety: Simulator studies of visual illusions in night approaches. In H. L. Pick, H. W. Leibowitz, J. E. Singer, A. Steinschneider, & H. W. Stevenson (Eds.), *Psychology: From research to practice.* New York: Plenum Press.

Krasner, L. (1978). The future and the past in the behaviorism-human dialogue. *American Psychologist, 33,* 799–804.

Krauss, R. M. (1966). Structural and attitudinal factors in interpersonal bargaining. *Journal of Experimental Social Psychology, 2,* 42–55.

Kravetz, D. F. (1974). Heart rate as a minimal cue for the occurrence of vicarious classical conditioning. *Journal of Personality and Social Psychology, 29,* 125–131.

Krebs, R. L. (1967). *Some relations between moral judgment, attention, and resistance to temptation.* Unpublished doctoral dissertation, University of Chicago, Chicago, IL.

Krebs, R. L., & Kohlberg, L. (1973). *Moral judgment and ego controls as determinants of resistance to cheating.* Unpublished manuscript, Center for Moral Education, Harvard University, Cambridge, MA.

Kriger, S. F., & Kroes, W. H. (1972). Child-rearing attitudes of Chinese, Jewish, and Protestant mothers. *Journal of Social Psychology, 86,* 205–210.

Kristeller, J. L., Schwartz, G. E., & Black, H. (1982). The use of restricted environmental stimulation therapy (REST) in the treatment of essential hypertension: Two case studies. *Behaviour Research and Therapy, 20,* 561–566.

Kroll, J. (1973). A reappraisal of psychiatry in the middle ages. *Archives of General Psychiatry, 26,* 276–283.

Krosnick, J. A., & Judd, C. M. (1982). Transitions in social influence at adolescence: Who induces cigarette smoking? *Developmental Psychology, 18,* 359–368.

Kryter, K. D. (1970). *The effects of noise on man.* New York: Academic Press.

Kuhlman, D. M., & Marsello, A. F. J. (1975). Individual differences in game motivation as moderators of preprogrammed strategy effects in prisoner's dilemma. *Journal of Personality and Social Psychology, 32,* 922–931.

Kuhn, D., Nash, S. C., & Brucken, L. (1978). Sex role concepts of two- and three-year-olds. *Child Development, 49,* 445–451.

Kunz, P. R., & Woolcott, M. (1976). Season's greetings: From my status to yours. *Social Science Research, 5,* 269–278.

Laberge, S. P., Nagel, L. E., Dement, W. C., & Zarcone, V. P. (1981). Lucid dreaming verified by volitional communication during REM sleep. *Perceptual and Motor Skills, 52,* 727–732.

Labouvie-Vief, G. (1982). Discontinuities in development from childhood. In T. M. Field, A. Huston, H. C. Quay, L. Troll, & G. E. Finley (Eds.), *Review of human development.* New York: Wiley.

Lachman, R., Lachman, J. L., & Butterfield, E. C. (1979). *Cognitive psychology and information processing: An introduction.* Hillsdale, NJ: Lawrence Erlbaum Associates.

Ladd, G. W., & Mize, J. (1983). A cognitive-social learning model of social-skill training. *Psychological Review, 90,* 127–157.

Laird, J. D. (1984). The real role of facial response in the experience of emotion: A reply to Tourangeau and Ellsworth, and others. *Journal of Personality and Social Psychology, 29,* 909–917.

Lamb, M. E. (1976). Parent-infant interaction in 8-month-olds. *Child Psychiatry and Human Development, 7,* 56–63.

Lamb, M. E. (1977). Father-infant and mother-infant interaction in the first year of life. *Child Development, 48,* 167–181.

Lambert, M. J., DeJulio, S. S., & Stein, D. M. (1978). Therapist interpersonal skills: Process, outcome, methodological considerations and recommendations for future research. *Psychological Bulletin, 85,* 467–489.

Lambert, M. J., Shapiro, D. A., & Bergin, A. E. (1986). The effectiveness of psychotherapy. In S. L. Garfield & A. E. Bergin (Eds.), *Handbook of psychotherapy and behavior change* (3rd ed.). New York: Wiley.

Lambert, W. W., Solomon, R. L. C., & Watson, P. D. (1949). Reinforcement and extinction as factors in size estimation. *Journal of Experimental Psychology, 39,* 637–641.

Landers, S. (1986a, November). DSM by APA? *APA Monitor, 17*(11).

Landers, S. (1986b, December). Judge reiterates IQ test ban. *APA Monitor, 17*(12), p. 18.

Landers, S. (1987, February). Debated DSM-III categories now official. *APA Monitor, 18*(2).

Landfield, P. W., Baskin, R. K., & Pitler, T. A. (1981). Brain aging correlates: retardation by hormonal-pharmacological treatments. *Science, 214,* 581–584.

Landman, J. T., & Dawes, R. M. (1982). Psychotherapy outcome: Smith and Glass' conclusions stand up under scrutiny. *American Psychologist, 36,* 937–952.

Lang, A. R., Goeckner, D. J., Adesso, V. J., & Marlatt, G. A. (1975). Effects of alcohol on aggression in male social drinkers. *Journal of Abnormal Behavior, 84,* 508–518.

Lang, P. J., & Melamed, B. G. (1969). Avoidance conditioning therapy of an infant with chronic ruminative vomiting. *Journal of Abnormal Psychology, 74,* 1–8.

Lange, A. J., & Jakubowski, P. (1976). *Responsible assertive training.* Champaign, IL: Research Press.

Langlois, J. H., & Downs, A. C. (1980). Mothers, fathers, and peers as socialization agents of sex-typed play behavior in young children. *Child Development, 51,* 1237–1247.

Larsen, K. S. (1976). *Aggression: Myths and models.* Chicago: Nelson-Hall.

Lashley, K. S. (1929). *Brain mechanisms and intelligence.* Chicago: University of Chicago Press.

Lashley, K. S. (1950). In search of the engram. *Symposium of the Society for Experimental Biology, 4,* 454–482.

Latané, B., & Darley, J. M. (1968). Group inhibition of bystander intervention in emergencies. *Journal of Personality and Social Psychology, 10,* 215–221.

Latané, B., & Darley, J. (1970). *The unresponsive bystander: Why doesn't he help?* New York: Appleton-Century-Crofts.

Latané, B., & Rodin, J. (1969). A lady in distress: Inhibiting effects of friends and strangers on bystander intervention. *Journal of Experimental Social Psychology, 5,* 189–202.

Latham, G. P., & Yukl, G. A. (1975). Assigned versus participative goal setting with educated and uneducated wood workers. *Journal of Applied Psychology, 60,* 299–302.

Latimer, P. R. (1983). Antidepressants and behavior therapy in agoraphobia and obsessive-compulsive disorders: A commentary. *Journal of Behavior Therapy and Experimental Psychiatry, 14,* 25–27.

Laudenslager, M. L., Ryan, S. M., Drugan, R. C., Hyson, R. L., & Maier, S. F. (1983). Coping and immunosuppression: Inescapable but not escapable shock suppresses lymphocyte proliferation. *Science, 221,* 568–570.

Lawson, A., & Ingleby, J. D. (1974). Daily routines of preschool children: Effects of age, birth order, sex and social class, and developmental correlates. *Psychological Medicine, 4,* 399–415.

Lawson, J. S., McGhie, A., & Chapman, J. (1964). Perception of speech in schizophrenia. *British Journal of Psychiatry, 110,* 375–380.

Lazar, I., Darlington, R. B., Murray, H., Royce, J., & Snipper, A. (1982). Lasting effects of early education: A report from the consortium for longitudinal studies. *Monographs of the Society for Research in Child Development, 47*(2–3, Serial No. 195).

Lazarus, A. A. (1971). *Behavior therapy and beyond.* New York: McGraw-Hill.

Lazarus, A. A. (1981). *The practice of multimodal therapy.* New York: McGraw-Hill.

Lazarus, R. S. (1966). *Psychological stress and the coping process.* New York: McGraw-Hill.

Lazarus, R. S. (1976). *Patterns of adjustment* (3rd ed.). New York: McGraw-Hill.

Lazarus, R. S., & Cohen, J. B. (1977). Environmental stress. In I. Attman & J. F. Wohlwill (Eds.), *Human behavior and the environment: Current theory and research: Vol. 2.* New York: Plenum Press.

Lazarus, R. S., & Folkman, S. (1984). *Stress, appraisal, and coping.* New York: Springer.

Lazarus, R. S., & Launier, R. (1978). Stress-related transactions between person and environment. In L. A. Pervin & M. Lewis (Eds.), *Perspectives in interactional psychology* (pp. 287–327). New York: Plenum Press.

Lazarus, R. S., Opton, E. M., Nomikos, M. S., & Rankin, M. O. (1965). The principle of short-circuiting of threat: Further evidence. *Journal of Personality, 33,* 622–635.

Leary, M. R., Robertson, R. B., Barnes, B. D., & Miller, R. S. (1986). Self-presentations of small group leaders: Effects of role requirements and leadership orientation. *Journal of Personality and Social Psychology, 51,* 742–748.

Leask, J., Haber, R. N., & Haber, R. B. (1969). Eidetic imagery in children: II. Longitudinal and experimental results. *Psychonomic Monograph Supplements, 3*(3, Whole No. 35).

Leavy, R. L. (1983). Social support and psychological disorder: A review. *Journal of Community Psychology, 11,* 3–21.

Leboyer, F. (1975). *Birth without violence.* New York: Knopf.

Lee, J. A. (1973). *The colors of love: An exploration of the ways of loving.* Don Mills, Ontario: New Press.

Leeper, R. (1935). A study of a neglected portion of the field of learning: The development of sensory organization. *Journal of Genetic Psychology, 46,* 41–75.

Lefcourt, H. M., Martin, R. A., & Saleh, W. E. (1984). Locus of control and social support: Interactive moderators of stress. *Journal of Personality and Social Psychology, 47,* 378–389.

Lehman, H. C. (1968). The creative production rates of present versus past generations of scientists. In B. L. Neugarten (Ed.), *Middle age and aging.* Chicago: University of Chicago Press.

Lehman, H. E. (1967). Schizophrenia: IV. Clinical features. In A. M. Freedman, H. I. Kaplan, & H. S. Kaplan (Eds.), *Comprehensive textbook of psychiatry.* Baltimore: Williams & Wilkins.

Leibowitz, H. W., Brislin, R., Perlmutter, L., & Hennessy, R. (1969). Ponzo perspective illusion as a manifestation of space perception. *Science, 166,* 1174–1176.

Leibowitz, H. W., & Owens, D. A. (1986). We drive by night. *Psychology Today, 20,* 54–58.

LeMagnen, J. (1971). Advances in studies on the physiological control and regulation of food intake. In E. Stellar & J. M. Sprague (Eds.), *Progress in physiological psychology: Vol. 4.* New York: Academic Press.

Lenneberg, E. H. (1967). *Biological foundations of language.* New York: Wiley.

Lerner, M. J. (1965). Evaluation of performance as a function of performer's reward and attractiveness. *Journal of Personality and Social Psychology, 1,* 355–361.

Lerner, R. M. (1984). *On the nature of human plasticity.* New York: Cambridge University Press.

Lesgold, A. M. (1984). Acquiring expertise. In J. R. Anderson & S. M. Kosslyn (Eds.), *Tutorials in learning and memory.* San Francisco: W. H. Freeman.

Lesgold, A. M., Feltovich, P. J., Glaser, R., & Wang, Y. (1981). *The acquisition of perceptual diagnostic skill in radiology* (Tech. Rep. PDS–1). Pittsburgh: University of Pittsburgh, Learning Research and Development Center.

Lester, B. M., Als, H., & Brazelton, T. B. (1982). Regional obstetric anesthesia and newborn behavior: A reanalysis toward synergistic effects. *Child Development, 53,* 687–692.

Levenkron, J. C., Cohen, J. D., Mueller, H. S., & Fisher, E. B. (1983). Modifying the Type A coronary-prone behavior pattern. *Journal of Consulting and Clinical Psychology, 51*(2), 192–204.

Levenson, A. H. (1981). *Basic psychopharmacology.* New York: Springer.

Leventhal, H. (1970). Findings and theory in the study of fear communications. In L. Berkowitz (Ed.), *Advances in experimental social psychology: Vol. 5.* New York: Academic Press.

Leventhal, H., & Tomarken, A. J. (1986). Emotion: Today's problems. *Annual Review of Psychology, 37,* 565–610.

Leventhal, H., Watts, J. C., & Pagano, F. (1967). Effects of fear and instructions on how to cope with danger. *Journal of Personality and Social Psychology, 6,* 313–321.

Levine, J. D., Gordon, N. C., & Fields, H. L. (1979). Naloxone dose dependently produces analgesia and hyperalgesia in postoperative pain. *Nature, 278,* 740–741.

Levine, J. L., Stoltz, J. A., & Lacks, P. (1983). Preparing psychotherapy clients: Rationale and suggestions. *Professional Psychology, 14,* 317–322.

Levine, M. (1966). Hypothesis behavior by humans during discrimination learning. *Journal of Experimental Psychology, 71,* 331–338.

Levine, M. W., & Schefner, J. M. (1981). *Fundamentals of sensation and perception.* Reading, MA: Addison-Wesley.

Levinger, G. (1974). A three-level approach to attraction: Toward an understanding of pair relatedness. In T. L. Houston (Ed.), *Foundations of interpersonal attraction.* New York: Academic Press.

Levinger, G., & Senn, D. J. (1967). Disclosure of feelings in marriage. *Merrill-Palmer Quarterly, 13*(3), 237–249.

Levinger, G., & Snoek, J. D. (1972). *Attraction in relationship. A new look at interpersonal attraction.* Morristown, NJ: General Learning Press.

Levinson, D. J., with Darrow, C. N., Klein, E. B., Levinson, M. H., & McKee, B. (1978). *The seasons of a man's life.* New York: Knopf.

Levitas, T. (1974). HOME—Hand over mouth exercise. *Journal of Dentistry for Children, 42,* 178–182.

Levy, J. (1985). Interhemispheric collaboration: Singlemindedness and the asymmetric brain. In C. Best (Ed.), *Hemispheric function and collaboration in the child.* New York: Academic Press.

Lewin, I. (1983). The psychological theory of dreams in the bible. *Journal of Psychology and Judaism, 7,* 73–88.

Lewin, I., & Glaubman, H. (1975). The effect of REM deprivation: Is it detrimental, beneficial, or neutral? *Psychophysiology, 12,* 349–353.

Lewinsohn, P. H. (1974). A behavioral approach to depression. In R. J. Friedman & M. M. Katz (Eds.), *The psychology of depression: Contemporary theory and research.* Washington, DC: Winston-Wiley.

Lewis, C. E. (1966). Factors influencing the return to work of men with congestive heart failure. *Journal of Chronic Diseases, 19,* 1193–1209.

Lewis, M., Feiring, C., McGuffog, C., & Jaskir, J. (1984). Predicting psychopathology in six-year-olds from early social relations. *Child Development, 55,* 123–136.

Leyens, J. P., Camino, L., Parke, R. D., & Berkowitz, L. (1975). The effects of movie violence on aggression in a field setting as a function of group dominance and cohesion. *Journal of Personality and Social Psychology, 32,* 346–360.

Licht, B. G., & Dweck, C. S. (1984). Determinants of academic achievement: The interaction of children's achievement orientations with skill area. *Developmental Psychology, 20,* 628–636.

Lichtenstein, E. (1980). *Psychotherapy: Approaches and applications.* Monterey, CA: Brooks/Cole.

Lichtenstein E., & Penner, M. P. (1977). Long-term effects of rapid smoking treatment for dependent cigarette smokers. *Addictive Behaviors, 2,* 109–112.

Liddell, H. (1950). Some specific factors that modify tolerance for environmental stress. In H. G. Wolff, S. G. Wolff, & C. C. Hare (Eds.), *Life stress and bodily disease.* Baltimore: Williams & Wilkins.

Lieberman, M. A., & Tobin, S. (1983). *The experience of old age.* New York: Basic Books.

Lieberman, P. (1967). *Intonation, perception, and language.* Cambridge: MIT Press.

Liebert, R. M., & Poulos, R. W. (1975). Television and personality development: The socializing effects of an entertainment medium. In A. Davids (Ed.), *Child personality and psychopathology: Current topics: Vol. 2.* New York: Wiley.

Lindsay, P. H., & Norman, D. A. (1977). *Human information processing* (2nd ed.). New York: Academic Press.

Lindsay, R. C., Wells, G. L., & Rumpel, C. M. (1981). Can people detect eyewitness identification accuracy within and across situations? *Journal of Applied Psychology, 67,* 79–89.

Linn, R. (1982). Ability testing: Individual differences, prediction and differential prediction. In A. Wigder & W. Gardner (Eds.), *Ability testing: Uses, consequences and controversies.* Washington, DC: National Academy Press.

Lipsitt, L. P., Reilly, B. M., Butcher, M. J., & Greenwood, M. M. (1976). The stability and interrelationships of newborn sucking and heart rate. *Developmental Psychobiology, 9,* 305–310.

Lipton, A. A., & Simon, F. S. (1985). Psychiatric diagnosis in a state hospital: Manhattan State revisited. *Hospital Community Psychiatry, 36,* 368–373.

Litwack, T. R. (1985, Fall). The prediction of violence. *The Clinical Psychologist,* 887–891.

Livesley, W. J., & Bromley, D. B. (1973). *Person perception in childhood and adolescence.* London: Wiley.

Loehlin, J. C., Horn, J. M., & Willerman, L. (1981). Personality resemblance in adoptive families. *Behavior Genetics, 11,* 309–330.

Loehlin, J. C., & Nichols, R. (1976). *Heredity, environment and personality: A study of 850 sets of twins.* Austin: University of Texas Press.

Loehlin, J. C., Willerman, L., & Horn, J. M. (1985). Personality resemblances in adoptive families when the children are late-adolescent or adult. *Journal of Personality and Social Psychology, 48,* 376–392.

Loftus, E. F. (1979). *Eyewitness testimony.* Cambridge: Harvard University Press.

Loftus, E. F., & Burns, T. E. (1982). Mental shock can produce retrograde amnesia. *Memory and Cognition, 10,* 318–323.

Loftus, E. F., & Loftus, G. R. (1980). On the permanence of stored information in the human brain. *American Psychologist, 35,* 409–420.

Loftus, G. R. (1983). The continuing persistence of the icon. *The Behavioral and Brain Sciences, 6,* 28.

Loftus, G. R., & Loftus, E. F. (1976). *Human memory: The processing of information.* Hillsdale, NJ: Lawrence Erlbaum Associates.

Logue, A. W. (1986). *The psychology of eating and drinking.* New York: W. H. Freeman.

London, P. (1970). The rescuers: Motivational hypothesis about Christians who saved Jews from the Nazis. In J. Macauley & L. Berkowitz (Eds.), *Altruism and helping behavior.* New York: Academic Press.

Long, G. M., & Beaton, R. J. (1982). The case for peripheral persistence: Effects of target and background luminance on a partial-report task. *Journal of Experimental Psychology: Human Perception and Performance, 8,* 383–391.

Long, P. (1986, January). Medical mesmerism. *Psychology Today.*

Loomis, A. L., Harvey, E. N., & Hobart, G. A. (1937). Cerebral states during sleep as studied by human brain potentials. *Journal of Experimental Psychology, 21,* 127–144.

Lopes, L. L. (1982). *Procedural debiasing* (Tech. Rep. WHIPP 15). Madison: University of Wisconsin, Human Information Processing Program.

Lorenz, K. (1966). *On aggression.* New York: Harcourt, Brace and World.

Lorenz, K. (1981). *Foundations of ethology.* New York: Springer-Verlag.

Lott, A. J., & Lott, B. E. (1972). The power of liking: Consequences of interpersonal attitudes derived from a liberalized view of secondary reinforcement. In L. Berkowitz (Ed.), *Advances in experimental social psychology: Vol. 6.* New York: Academic Press.

Lott, A. J., & Lott, B. E. (1974). The role of reward in the formation of positive interpersonal attitudes. In T. L. Houston (Ed.), *Foundations of interpersonal attraction.* New York: Academic Press.

Lovaas, O. I. (1987). Behavioral treatment and normal educational and intellectual functioning in young autistic children. *Journal of Consulting and Clinical Psychology, 55,* 3–9.

Low, W. C., Lewis, P. R., Bunch, S. T., Dunnett, S. B., Thomas, S. R., Iversen, S. D., Bjorklund, A., & Stenevi, U. (1982). Function recovery following neural transplantation of embryonic septal nuclei in adult rats with septohippocampal lesions. *Nature, 300,* 260–262.

Luborsky, L. (1954). A note on Eysenck's article, "The effects of psychotherapy: An evaluation." *British Journal of Psychology, 45,* 129–131.

Luborsky, L. (1972). Another reply to Eysenck. *Psychological Bulletin, 78,* 406–408.

Luborsky, L., Singer, B., & Luborsky, L. (1975). Comparative studies of psychotherapies: Is it true that everyone has won and all must have prizes? *Archives of General Psychiatry, 32,* 995–1008.

Lucas, R. (1975). The affective and medical aspects of different preoperative interventions with heart surgery patients. *Dissertation Abstracts International, 36,* 5763B.

Luce, G. G. (1971). *Body time.* New York: Random House.

Luce, R. D., & Raiffa, H. (1957). *Games and decisions.* New York: Wiley.

Luce, S., & Hoge, R. (1978). Relations among teacher ratings, pupil-teacher interactions, and academic achievement: A test of teacher expectancy hypothesis. *American Educational Research Journal, 15,* 489–500.

Luchins, A. S. (1942). Mechanization in problem solving: The effect of Einstellung. *Psychological Monographs, 54*(6, Whole No. 248).

Luchins, D. J., Pollin, W., & Wyatt, R. J. (1980). Laterality in monozygotic schizophrenic twins: An alternative hypothesis. *Biological Psychiatry, 15,* 87–93.

Ludwig, A. M. (1969). Altered states of consciousness. In C. T. Tart (Ed.), *Altered states of consciousness.* New York: Wiley.

Luria, Z., & Rubin, J. Z. (1974). The eye of the beholder: Parents' views on sex of newborns. *American Journal of Orthopsychiatry, 44,* 512–519.

Lutkenhaus, P. (1984, April). *Mother-infant attachment at 12 months and its relations to 3-year-olds' readiness to build up a new relationship.* Paper presented at the International Conference on Infant Studies, New York, NY.

Lykken, D. T. (1979). The detection of deception. *Psychological Bulletin, 86,* 47–53.

Lynch, J. G., & Cohen, J. L. (1978). The use of subjective expected utility theory as an aid to understanding variables that influence helping behavior. *Journal of Personality and Social Psychology, 36,* 1138–1151.

Lynn, D. B., & Cross, A. D. (1974). Parent preference of preschool children. *Journal of Marriage and the Family, 36,* 555–559.

Lynn, S. J., & Rhue, J. W. (1986). The fantasy-prone person: Hypnosis, imagination, and creativity. *Journal of Personality and Social Psychology, 51,* 404–408.

MacAndrew, C., & Edgerton, R. B. (1970). *Drunken comportment.* Chicago: Aldine.

Maccoby, E. E., & Feldman, S. S. (1972). Mother-attachment and stranger-reactions in the third year of life. *Monographs of the Society for Research in Child Development, 37*(1, Serial No. 146).

Maccoby, E. E., & Jacklin, C. N. (1974). *The psychology of sex differences.* Stanford, CA: Stanford University Press.

MacDonald, M., & Bernstein, D. A. (1974). Treatment of a spider phobia with *in vivo* and imaginal desensitization. *Journal of Behavior Therapy and Experimental Psychiatry, 5,* 47–52.

MacDonald, M. R., & Kuiper, N. A. (1983). Cognitive-behavioral preparations for surgery: Some theoretical and methodological concerns. *Clinical Psychology Review, 3,* 27–39.

Mace, W. M., & Turvey, M. T. (1983). The implications of occlusion for perceiving persistence. *The Behavioral and Brain Sciences, 6,* 29–31.

MacKenzie, B. (1984). Explaining race differences in IQ: The logic, the methodology, and the evidence. *American Psychologist, 39,* 1214–1233.

Madrazo, I., Drucker-Colin, R., Diaz, V., Martinez-Mata, J., Torres, C., & Becerril, J. J. (1987). Open microsurgical autograft of adrenal medulla to the right caudate nucleus in two patients with intractable Parkinson's disease. *New England Journal of Medicine, 316,* 831–834.

Mahler, M. S., Pine, F., & Bergman, A., (1975). *The psychological birth of the human infant.* New York: Basic Books

Maier, N. R. F. (1930). Reasoning in humans: I. On directions. *Journal of Comparative Psychology, 10,* 115–143.

Maier, S. F., Laudenslager, M. L., & Ryan, S. M. (1984). Stressor controllability, immune function, and endogenous opiates. In F. R. Brush & J. B. Overmier (Eds.), *Affect, conditioning, and cognition: Essays on the determinants of behavior.* Hillsdale, NJ: Lawrence Erlbaum Associates.

Malamuth, N. M., & Donnerstein, E. (1982). The effects of aggressive-pornographic mass media stimuli. In L. Berkowitz (Ed.), *Advances in experimental social psychology: Vol. 15.* New York: Academic Press.

Malamuth, N. M., & Donnerstein, E. (Eds.). (1984). *Pornography and sexual aggression.* New York: Academic Press.

Malamuth, N. M., Heim, M., & Feshbach, S. (1980). Sexual responsiveness of college students to rape depictions: Inhibitory and disinhibitory effects. *Journal of Personality and Social Psychology, 38,* 399–408.

Malamuth, N. M., & Spinner, B. A. (1980). A longitudinal content analysis of sexual violence in the best-selling erotic magazines. *Journal of Sex Research, 16,* 226–237.

Mandler, G. (1984). *Mind and body.* New York: W. W. Norton.

Manis, F., Keating, D. P., & Morrison, F. J. (1980). Developmental differences in the allocation of processing capacity. *Journal of Experimental Child Psychology, 29,* 156–159.

Marantz, S. A., & Mansfield, A. F. (1977). Maternal employment and the development of sex-role stereotyping in five- to eleven-year-old girls. *Child Development, 48,* 668–673.

Mark, V., & Ervin, F. (1970). *Violence and the brain.* New York: Harper & Row.

Marks, L. E., & Miller, G. A. (1964). The role of semantic and syntactic constraints in the memorization of English sentences. *Journal of Verbal Learning and Verbal Behavior, 3,* 1–5.

Marlatt, G. A., & Gordon, J. R. (1985). *Relapse prevention.* New York: Guilford Press.

Marlatt, G. A., & Rohsenow, D. J. (1980). Cognitive processes in alcohol use: Expectancy and the balanced placebo design. In N. K. Mello (Ed.), *Advances in substance abuse: Behavioral and biological research.* Greenwich, CT: JAI Press.

Marmor, J., & Woods, S. M. (Eds.). (1980). *The interface between psychodynamic and behavior therapies.* New York: Plenum Press.

Marsh, C. (1977). A framework for describing subjective states of consciousness. In N. E. Zinberg (Ed.), *Alternate states of consciousness.* New York: Free Press.

Marshall, G. D., & Zimbardo, P. G. (1979). Affective consequences of inadequately explained arousal. *Journal of Personality and Social Psychology, 37,* 970–985.

Martindale, C. (1981). *Cognition and consciousness.* Homewood, IL: Dorsey Press.

Maruyama, G., & Miller, N. (1975). *Physical attractiveness and classroom acceptance* (Research Report 75-2). Los Angeles: University of Southern California, Social Science Research Institute.

Marx, J. L. (1985, February 22). "Anxiety peptide" found in brain. *Science, 227.*

Maslach, C. (1979). Negative emotional biasing of unexplained arousal. *Journal of Personality and Social Psychology, 37,* 953–969.

Maslow, A. H. (1954). *Motivation and personality.* New York: Harper.

Maslow, A. H. (1962). *Toward a psychology of being.* Princeton, NJ: Van Nostrand.

Maslow, A. H. (1970). *Motivation and personality* (2nd ed.). New York: Harper & Row.

Maslow, A. H. (1971). *The farther reaches of human nature.* New York: McGraw-Hill.

Mason, J. W. (1971). A re-evaluation of the concept of "non-specificity" in stress theory. *Journal of Psychiatric Research, 8,* 323–333.

Mason, J. W. (1975). A historical view of the stress field. *Journal of Human Stress, I,* 22–36.

Masson, J. M. (1983). *Assault on the truth: Freud's suppression of the seduction theory.* New York: Farrar, Straus, & Giroux.

Masters, W. H., & Johnson, V. E. (1966). *Human sexual response.* Boston: Little, Brown.

Masters, W. H., & Johnson, V. E. (1970). *Human sexual inadequacy.* Boston: Little, Brown.

Matarazzo, J. D. (1983). The reliability of psychiatric and psychological diagnosis. *Clinical Psychology Review, 3,* 103–145.

Matlin, M., & Stang, D. (1978). *The Pollyanna principle: Selectivity in language, memory, and thought.* Cambridge: Schenkman.

Matthews, K. A. (1982). Psychological perspectives on the Type-A behavior pattern. *Psychological Bulletin, 91,* 293–323.

Matthews, K. A., Glass, D. C., Rosenman, R. H., & Bortner, R. W. (1977). Competitive drive, pattern A, and coronary heart disease: A further analysis of data from the Western Collaborative Group Study. *Journal of Chronic Disease, 30,* 489–498.

Matthews, K. A., & Haynes, S. G. (1986). Type-A behavior pattern and coronary disease risk: Update and critical evaluation. *American Journal of Epidemiology, 123,* 923–960.

Matthews, K. A., & Siegel, J. M. (1983). Type A behaviors for children, social comparison, and standards for self-evaluation. *Developmental Psychology, 19,* 135–140.

Maurer, D., & Vogel, V. H. (1973). *Narcotics and narcotic addiction.* Springfield, IL: Charles C. Thomas.

Mayer & Price. (1982). A physiological and psychological analysis of pain: A potential model of motivation. In D. W. Pfaff (Ed.), *The physiological mechanisms of motivation.*

Mayer, J. (1975). Obesity during childhood. In M. Winick (Ed.), *Childhood obesity.* New York: Wiley.

Mayer, R. E. (1983). *Thinking, problem solving, and cognition.* San Francisco: W. H. Freeman.

Mayer, W. (1983). Alcohol abuse and alcoholism: The psychologist's role in prevention, research, and treatment. *American Psychologist, 38,* 1116–1121.

Mayerson, N. H. (1984). Preparing clients for group therapy: A critical review and theoretical formulation. *Clinical Psychology Review, 4,* 191–214.

Mazis, M. B. (1975). Antipollution measures and psychological reactance: A field experiment. *Journal of Personality and Social Psychology, 31,* 654–660.

McArthur, L. A. (1972). The how and what of why: Some determinants and consequences of causal attribution. *Journal of Personality and Social Psychology, 22,* 171–193.

McCarthy, G., & Donchin, E. (1979). Event-related potentials: Manifestations of cognitive activity. In F. Hoffmeister & C. Muller (Eds.), *Bayer symposium: VIII. Brain function in old age.* New York: Springer.

McClelland, D. C. (1958). Risk-taking in children with high and low need for achievement. In J. W. Atkinson (Ed.), *Motives in fantasy, action, and society.* Princeton, NJ: Van Nostrand.

McClelland, D. C. (1978). Managing motivation to expand human freedom. *American Psychologist, 33,* 201–210.

McClelland, D. C. (1985). *Human motivation.* Glenview, IL: Scott, Foresman.

McClelland, D. C., & Winter, D. G. (1969). *Motivating economic achievement.* New York: Free Press.

McCloskey, D. I. (1978). Kinesthetic sensibility. *Physiological Reviews, 58,* 763.

McCollough, C. (1965). Color adaptation of edge-detectors in the human visual system. *Science, 149,* 1115–1116.

McCormick, D. A., & Thompson, R. F. (1984). Cerebellum essential involvement in the classically conditioned eyelid response. *Science, 223,* 296–299.

McCrae, R. R., & Costa, P. T., Jr. (1982). Aging, the life course, and models of personality. In T. M. Field, A. Huston, H. C. Quay, L. Troll, & G. E. Finley (Eds.), *Review of human development.* New York: Wiley-Interscience.

McDavid, J. W. (1959). Personality and situational determinants of conformity. *Journal of Abnormal and Social Psychology, 58,* 241–246.

McDougall, W. (1904). The sensations excited by a single momentary stimulation of the eye. *British Journal of Psychology, 1,* 78–113.

McDougall, W. (1908). *An introduction to social psychology.* London: Methuen.

McGeer, P. L., Eccles, J. C., & McGeer, E. G. (1978). *Molecular neurobiology of the mammalian brain.* New York: Plenum Press.

McGhie, A., & Chapman, J. (1961). Disorders of attention and perception in early schizophrenia. *British Journal of Psychiatry, 34,* 103–116.

McGuire, W. J. (1960). A syllogistic analysis of cognitive relationships. In C. I. Hovland & M. J. Rosenberg (Eds.), *Attitude organization and change.* New Haven: Yale University Press.

McGuire, W. J. (1968). Personality and susceptibility to social influence. In E. F. Borgatta & W. W. Lambert (Eds.), *Handbook of personality theory and research.* Chicago: Rand McNally.

McGuire, W. J. (1969). The nature of attitudes and attitude change. In G. Lindzey & E. Aronson (Eds.), *The handbook of social psychology: Vol. 3.* (2nd ed.). Reading, MA: Addison-Wesley.

McGuire, W. J. (1985). Attitudes and attitude change. In G. Linzey & E. Aronson (Eds.), *The handbook of social psychology: Vol. 2.* (3rd ed.). New York: Random House.

McKenna, R. J. (1972). Some effects of anxiety level and food cues on the eating behavior of obese and normal subjects: A comparison of the Schachterian and psychosomatic conceptions. *Journal of Personality and Social Psychology, 22,* 311–319.

McLeod-Morgan, C., & Lack, L. (1982). Hemispheric specificity: A physiological concomitant of hypnotizability. *Psychophysiology 19*(6), 687–690.

McNally, R. J. (1987). Preparedness and phobias: A review. *Psychological Bulletin, 101,* 283–303.

Mead, M. (1963). *Sex and temperament in three primitive societies.* New York: William Morrow.

Mednick, S. A. (1958). A learning theory approach to research in schizophrenia. *Psychological Bulletin, 55,* 316–327.

Mednick, S. A. (1970). Breakdown in individuals at high-risk for schizophrenia: Possible predispositional perinatal factors. *Mental Hygiene, 54,* 50–63.

Meehl, P. E. (1962). Schizotaxia, schizotypy, and schizophrenia. *American Psychologist, 17,* 827–838.

Megargee, E. I. (1976). The prediction of dangerous behavior. *Criminal Justice and Behavior, 3,* 3–22.

Mehle, T. (1982). Hypothesis generation in an automobile malfunction inference task. *Acta Psychologica, 52,* 87–116.

Meichenbaum, D. (1977). *Cognitive behavior modification: An integrative approach.* New York: Plenum Press.

Meichenbaum, D. (1985). *Stress-inoculation training.* New York: Pergamon Press.

Melamed, B. G., & Siegel, L. J. (1980). *Behavioral medicine.* New York: Springer.

Melton, A. W. (1963). Implications of short-term memory for a general theory of memory. *Journal of Verbal Learning and Verbal Behavior, 2,* 1–21.

Meltzer, D., & Brahlek, J. A. (1968). Quantity of reinforcement and fixed-interval performance. *Psychonomic Science, 12,* 207–208.

Meltzer, H. Y., & Stahl, S. M. (1976). The dopamine hypothesis of schizophrenia: A review. *Schizophrenia Bulletin, 2,* 19–76.

Meltzoff, J., & Kornreich, M. (1970). *Research on psychotherapy.* New York: Atherton.

Melzack, R., & Wall, P. D. (1965). Pain mechanisms: A new theory. *Science, 150,* 971–979.

Menaghen, E. (1983). Individual coping efforts: Moderators of the relationship between life stress and mental health outcomes. In H. B. Kaplan (Ed.), *Psychological stress: Trends in theory and research.* New York: Academic Press.

Merritt, J. O. (1979). None in a million: Results of mass screening for eidetic ability using objective tests published in newspapers and magazines. *The Behavioral and Brain Sciences, 2,* 612.

Merton, R. (1948). The self-fulfilling prophecy. *Antioch Review, 8,* 193–210.

Merzenich, M. M., & Kass, J. H. (1980). Principles of organization of sensory-perceptual systems in mammals. In J. M. Sprague & A. N. Epstein (Eds.), *Progress in psychobiology and physiological psychology: Vol. 9.* New York: Academic Press.

Messer, S. B. (1976). Reflection-impulsivity: A review. *Psychological Bulletin, 83,* 489–500.

Messick, S. (1980). *The effectiveness of coaching for the SAT: A review of and reanalysis of research from the fifties to the FTC.* Princeton, NJ: Educational Testing Services.

Messick, S., & Jungeblut, A. (1981). Time and method in coaching for the SAT. *Psychological Bulletin, 89,* 191–216.

Metalsky, G. I., Halberstadt, L. J., & Abramson, L. Y. (1987). Vulnerability to depressive mood reactions: Toward a more powerful test of the diathesis-stress and causal mediation components of the reformulated theory of depression. *Journal of Personality and Social Psychology, 52,* 386–393.

Metzner, R., Litwin, G., & Weil, G. M. (1965). The relation of expectation and mood to psilocybin reactions. *Psychedelic Review, 5,* 3–39.

Meyer, R. G. (1975). A behavioral treatment of sleepwalking associated with test anxiety. *Journal of Behavior Therapy and Experimental Psychiatry, 6,* 167–168.

Meyers, J. K., Weissman, M. M., Tischler, G. L., Holzer, C. E., Leaf, P. J., Orvaschel, H., Anthony, J. C., Boyd, J. H., Burke, J. D. Jr., Kramer, M., & Stoltzman, R. (1984). Six-month prevalence of psychiatric disorders in three communities. *Archives of General Psychiatry, 41,* 959–967.

Milgram, S. (1963). Behavioral study of obedience. *Journal of Abnormal and Social Psychology, 67,* 371–378.

Milgram, S. (1965). Some conditions of obedience and disobedience to authority. *Human Relations, 18,* 57–76.

Milgram, S. (1974). *Obedience to authority.* New York: Harper & Row.

Milgram, S. (1977). *The individual in a social world.* Reading, MA: Addison-Wesley.

Milgram, S., Bickman, L., & Berkowitz, L. (1969). Note on the drawing power of crowds of different size. *Journal of Personality and Social Psychology, 13,* 79–82.

Milgram, S., & Jodelet, D. (1976). Psychological maps of Paris. In H. M. Proshansky, W. H. Itelson, & L. G. Revlin (Eds.), *Environmental Psychology.* New York: Holt, Rinehart and Winston.

Miller, G. A. (1956). The magical number seven, plus or minus two: Some limits on our capacity to process information. *Psychological Review, 63,* 81–97.

Miller, G. A., Heise, G. A., & Lichten, W. (1951). The intelligibility of speech as a function of the text and the test materials. *Journal of Experimental Psychology,* 329–335.

Miller, I. W., & Norman, W. H. (1979). Learned helplessness in humans: A review and attribution model. *Psychological Bulletin, 86,* 93–118.

Miller, J. P. (1975). Suicide and adolescence. *Adolescence, 10*(37), 11–24.

Miller, N. E. (1959). Liberalization of basic S-R concepts: Extensions to conflict behavior, motivation, and social learning. In S. Koch (Ed.), *Psychology: A study of science: Vol. 2.* New York: McGraw-Hill.

Miller, R. C., & Berman, J. S. (1983). The efficacy of cognitive-behavior therapies: A quantitative review of the research evidence. *Psychological Bulletin, 94,* 39–53.

Miller, R. G., Palkes, H. S., & Stewart, M. A. (1973). Hyperactive children in suburban elementary schools. *Child Psychiatry and Human Development, 4,* 121–127.

Millon, T. (1981). *Disorders of personality. DSMIII: Axis II.* New York: Wiley.

Milner, B. R. (1966). Amnesia following operation on temporal lobes. In C. W. M. Whitty & O. L. Zangwill (Eds.), *Amnesia.* London: Butterworth.

Milner, B., Corkin, S., & Teuber, H. L. (1968). Further analysis of the hippocampal amnesic syndrome: 14-year follow-up study of H. M. *Neuropsychologia, 6,* 215–234.

Mineka, S., & Hendersen, R. W. (1985). Controllability and predictability in acquired motivation. *Annual Review of Psychology, 36,* 495–529.

Minimi, H., & Dallenbach, K. M. (1946). The effect of activity upon learning and retention in the cockroach. *American Journal of Psychology, 59,* 1–58.

Minshew, N. J., Payton, J. B., & Sclabassi, R. J. (1986). Cortical neurophysiologic abnormalities in autism. *Neurology, 36* (Suppl. 1), 194.

Minuchin, S., Rosman, B. L., & Baker, L. (1978). *Psychosomatic families: Anorexia nervosa in context.* Cambridge, MA: Harvard University Press.

Mischel, W. (1961). Delay of gratification, need for achievement and acquiescence in another culture. *Journal of Abnormal and Social Psychology, 62,* 543–552.

Mischel, W. (1965). Predicting the success of Peace Corps volunteers in Nigeria. *Journal of Personality and Social Psychology, 1,* 510–517.

Mischel, W. (1968). *Personality and assessment.* New York: Wiley.

Mischel, W. (1973). Toward a cognitive social learning theory reconceptualization of personality. *Psychological Review, 80,* 252–283.

Mischel, W. (1981). *Introduction to personality* (3rd ed.). New York: Holt, Rinehart & Winston.

Mischel, W. (1984). Convergences and challenges in the search for consistency. *American Psychologist, 39,* 351–364.

Mischel, W., & Peake, P. K. (1983). Some facets of consistency: Replies to Epstein, Funder, and Bem. *Psychological Review, 90,* 394–402.

Mishkin, M., & Appenzeller, T. (1987). The anatomy of memory. *Scientific American, 256,* 80–89.

Mogenson, G. J. (1976). Neural mechanisms of hunger: Current status and future prospects. In D. Novin, W. Wyrwicka, & G. Bray (Eds.), *Hunger: Basic mechanisms and clinical applications.* New York: Raven.

Monahan, J. (1981). *Predicting violent behavior: An assessment of clinical techniques.* Beverly Hills, CA: Sage.

Money, J. (1987). Sin, sickness, or status? Homosexuality, gender identity, and psychoneuroendocrinology. *American Psychologist, 42,* 384–399.

Monroe, S. M. (1983). Major and minor life events as predictors of psychological distress: Further issues and findings. *Journal of Behavioral Medicine, 6,* 189–205.

Montemayor, R. (1983). Parents and adolescents in conflict: All families some of the time and some families most of the time. *Journal of Early Adolescence, 3,* 83–103.

Montgomery, K. C. (1953). Exploratory behavior as a function of "similarity" of stimulation situations. *Journal of Comparative and Physiological Psychology, 46,* 129–133.

Montgomery, M. F. (1931). The role of the salivary glands in the thirst mechanism. *American Journal of Physiology, 96,* 221–227.

Moore, R. Y., & Bloom, F. E. (1979). Central catecholamine neuron systems: Anatomy and physiology of the norepinephrine and epinephrine systems. *Annual Review of Neuroscience, 2,* 113–168.

Moore-Ede, M. C., Sulzman, F. M., & Fuller, C. A. (1982). *The clocks that time us.* Cambridge: Harvard University Press.

Moos, R. H. (1980). *The environmental quality of residential care settings.* Paper presented at the annual convention of the Environmental Design Research Association.

Moos, R. H., & Lemke, S. (1980). Assessing the physical and architectural features of sheltered care settings. *Journal of Gerontology, 21,* 88–98.

Moos, R. H., & Schaefer, J. (1984). The crisis of physical illness: An overview and conceptual approach. In R. H. Moos (Ed.), *Coping with physical illness: New perspectives.* New York: Plenum Press.

Moray, N. (1960). Attention in dichotic listening: Affective cues and influence of instructions. *Quarterly Journal of Experimental Psychology, 11,* 56–60.

Morgan, C. D., & Murray, H. A. (1935). A method for investigating fantasy: The thematic apperception test. *Archives of Neurology and Psychiatry, 34,* 289–306.

Morgan, W. G. (1973). Situational specificity in altruistic behavior. *Representative Research in Social Psychology, 4,* 56–66.

Morrison, F., Holmes, D. L., & Haith, M. M. (1974). A developmental study of the effects of familiarity on short term visual memory. *Journal of Experimental Child Psychology, 18,* 412–425.

Moscovici, S. (1980). Toward a theory of conversion behavior. In L. Berkowitz (Ed.), *Advances in experimental social psychology: Vol. 13.* New York: Academic Press.

Moscovici, S. (1985). Social influence and conformity. In G. Lindzey & E. Aronson (Eds.), *The handbook of social psychology: Vol. 2.* (3rd ed.). New York: Random House.

Mountcastle, V. B. (1976). The world around us: Neural command functions for selective attention. *Neurosciences Research Program Bulletin, 14* (Suppl.), 1–47.

Moyer, K. E. (1983). The physiology of motivation: Aggression as a model. In C. J. Scheier & A. M. Rogers (Eds.), *G. Stanley Hall Lecture Series: Vol. 3.* Washington, D.C.: American Psychological Association.

Mueller, D., Edwards, D. W., & Yarvis, R. M. (1977). Stressful life events and psychiatric symptomatology: Change or undesirability? *Journal of Health and Social Behavior, 18,* 307–316.

Mueller, E. (1972). The maintenance of verbal exchanges between young children. *Child Development, 43,* 930–938.

Mueller, E., & Lucas, T. (1975). A developmental analysis of peer interaction among toddlers. In M. Lewis & L. A. Rosenblum (Eds.), *Friendship and peer relations.* New York: Wiley-Interscience.

Mueller, E., & Vandell, D. (1979). Infant-infant interaction. In J. D. Osofsky (Ed.), *Handbook of infant development.* New York: Wiley.

Muir, D., & Field, J. (1979). Newborn infants' orientation to sound. *Child Development, 50,* 431–436.

Mulvey, E. P., & Lidz, C. W. (1984). Clinical considerations in the prediction of dangerousness in mental patients. *Clinical Psychology Review, 4,* 379–401.

Murray, E. A., & Mishkin, M. (1985). Amygdalectomy impairs cross-modal association in monkeys. *Science, 228,* 604–606.

Murray, H. A. (1938). *Explorations in personality.* New York: Oxford University Press.

Murray, H. A. (1962). *Explorations in personality.* New York: Science Editions.

Murstein, B. I. (1972). Physical attractiveness and marital choice. *Journal of Personality and Social Psychology, 22,* 8–12.

Mussen, P. H., & Eisenberg-Berg, N. (1977). *The roots of caring.* New York: W. H. Freeman.

Mussen, P. H., & Jones, M. C. (1957). *Roots of caring, sharing, and helping.* San Francisco: W. H. Freeman.

Myers, A. K., & Miller, N. E. (1954). Failure to find a learned drive based on hunger: Evidence for learning motivated by "exploration." *Journal of Comparative and Physiological Psychology, 47,* 428–436.

Myers, D. G. (1975). Discussion–induced attitude polarization. *Human Relations, 28,* 699–714.

Myers, D. G., & Lamm, H. (1976). The group polarization phenomenon. *Psychological Bulletin, 83,* 602–627.

Myers, J. L., O'Brien, E. J., Balota, D. A., & Toyofuku, M. L. (1984). Memory search without interference: The role of integration. *Cognitive Psychology, 16,* 217–242.

Mynatt, C., & Sherman, S. J. (1975). Responsibility attribution in groups and individuals: A direct test of the diffusion of responsibility hypothesis. *Journal of Personality and Social Psychology, 32,* 1111–1118.

Nahemow, L., & Lawton, M. P. (1975). Similarity and propinquity in friendship formation. *Journal of Personality and Social Psychology, 32,* 205–213.

Nathan, P. E., Titler, N. A., Lowenstein, L. W., Solomon, P., & Rossi, A. M. (1970). Behavioral analysis of chronic alcoholism. *Archives of General Psychiatry, 22,* 419–430.

Nathans, J. E., Thomas, D., & Hogness, D. (1986). Molecular genetics of human color vision: The genes encoding blue, green, and red pigments. *Science, 232,* 193–202.

Nathans, J. E., et al. (1986). Molecular genetics of inherited variation in human color vision. *Science, 232,* 203–210.

National Academy of Sciences. (1982). *Marijuana and health.* Washington, DC: National Academy Press.

National Coalition on Television Violence. (1984). Shocking findings confirm TV violence causes adult crime. *NCTV Newsletter, 5,* 1.

National Commission on Marijuana and Drug Abuse, Raymond P. Shafer, Chair. (1972). *Marijuana: A signal of misunderstanding.* New York: New American Library.

Natsoulas, T. (1978). Consciousness. *American Psychologist, 33,* 906–914.

Natsoulas, T. (1983). Addendum to consciousness. *American Psychologist, 38,* 121–122.

Navon, D., & Gopher, D. (1979). On the economy of the human processing system. *Psychological Review, 86,* 254–255.

Neale, J. M., & Oltmanns, T. F. (1980). *Schizophrenia.* New York: Wiley.

Neale, J. M., Oltmanns, T. F., & Winters, K. C. (1983). Recent developments in the assessment and conceptualization of schizophrenia. *Behavioral Assessment, 5,* 33–54.

Neisser, U., & Becklan, K. (1975). Selective looking: Attention to visually specified events. *Cognitive Psychology, 7,* 480–494.

Nelson, K. E., Denninger, M. M., Bonvillian, J. D., Kaplan, B. J., & Baker, N. (1983). Maternal input adjustments and nonadjustments as related to children's linguistic advances and to language acquisition theories. In A. D. Pellegrini & T. D. Yawkey (Eds.), *The development of oral and written languages: Readings in developmental and applied linguistics.* Norwood, NJ: Ablex.

Nelson, T. O., Leonesio, R. J., Shimamura, A. P., Landwehr, R. F., & Narens, L. (1982). Overlearning and the feeling of knowing. *Journal of Experimental Psychology: Learning, Memory, and Cognition, 8,* 279–288.

Nelson, T. O., & Narens, L. (1980). A new technique for investigating the feeling of knowing. *Acta Psychologica, 46,* 69–80.

Nemeth, C. (1972). A critical analysis of research utilizing the prisoner's dilemma paradigm for the study of bargaining. In L. Berkowitz (Ed.), *Advances in experimental social psychology: Vol. 6.* New York: Academic Press.

Nemiah, J. C. (1975). Denial revisited: Reflections on psychosomatic theory. *Psychotherapy and Psychosomatics, 26,* 140–147.

Neugarten, B. L. (1968). Adult personality: Toward a psychology of the life cycle. In B. L. Neugarten (Ed.), *Middle age and aging.* Chicago: University of Chicago Press.

Neugarten, B. L. (1974). Age groups in American society and the rise of the young-old. *Annals of the American Academy of Political and Social Science, 415,* 187–198.

Neugarten, B. L. (1977). Personality and aging. In J. E. Birren & K. W. Schaie (Eds.), *Handbook of the psychology of aging.* New York: Van Nostrand Reinhold.

Neugarten, B. L. (1979). Time, age, and the life cycle. *American Journal of Psychiatry, 136,* 887–894.

Neugarten, B. L., & Hagestad, G. O. (1976). Age and the life course. In R. H. Binstock & E. Shanas (Eds.), *Handbook of aging and the social sciences.* New York: Van Nostrand Reinhold.

Neugarten, B. L., Havighurst, D. J., & Tobin, S. S. (1968). Personality and patterns of aging. In B. L. Neugarten (Ed.), *Middle age and aging.* Chicago: University of Chicago Press.

Newcomb, T. M. (1943). *Personality and social change.* New York: Dryden.

Newcomb, T. M. (1961). *The acquaintance process.* New York: Holt, Rinehart and Winston.

Newcomb, T. M. (1962). Persistence and regression of changed attitudes: The Kurt Lewin Memorial Address. *Journal of Social Issues, 19,* 3–14.

Newcomb, T. M. (1968). Interpersonal balance. In R. P. Abelson et al. (Eds.), *Theories of cognitive consistency: A source book.* Chicago: Rand McNally.

Newcomb, T. M., Koenig, K. E., Flacks, R., & Warwick, D. P. (1967). *Persistence and change: Bennington College and its students after twenty-five years.* New York: Wiley.

Newlin, D. B., Carpenter, B., & Golden, C. J. (1981). Hemispheric asymmetries in schizophrenia. *Biological Psychiatry, 16,* 561–582.

Newman, J. P., & Kosson, D. S. (1986). Passive avoidance learning in psychopathic and nonpsychopathic offenders. *Journal of Abnormal Psychology, 95,* 252–256.

Newson, J. (1977). An intersubjective approach to the systematic description of mother-infant interaction. In H. R. Schaffer (Ed.), *Studies in mother-infant interaction.* London: Academic Press.

Nicholls, J. G. (1984). Conceptions of ability and achievement motivation. In R. Ames & C. Ames (Eds.), *Research on motivation in education: Vol. 1.* New York: Academic Press.

Nichols, R. (1978). Twin studies of ability, personality, and interests. *Homo, 29,* 158–173.

Nickerson, R. A., & Adams, M. J. (1979). Long-term memory for a common object. *Cognitive Psychology, 11,* 287–307.

Nietzel, M. T., & Bernstein, D. A. (1987). *Introduction to clinical psychology* (2nd ed.). Englewood Cliffs, NJ: Prentice-Hall.

Nisbett, E. B. (1973). An escalator phobia overcome in one session of flooding in vivo. Journal of Behavior Therapy and Experimental Psychiatry, 4, 405–406.

Nisbett, R. E. (1972). Hunger, obesity, and the ventromedial hypothalamus. Psychological Review, 79, 433–453.

Nisbett, R. E. (1980). The trait construct in lay and professional psychology. In L. Festinger (Ed.), Retrospections on social psychology. New York: Oxford University Press.

Nisbett, R. E., & Gordon, A. (1967). Self-esteem and susceptibility to social influence. Journal of Personality and Social Psychology, 5, 268–276.

Nisbett, R. E., & Wilson, T. D. (1977). Telling more than we can know: Verbal reports on mental processes. Psychological Review, 84, 231–259.

Nottebohm, F. (1985). Neuronal replacement in adulthood. Annals of the New York Academy of Science, 457, 143–161.

Nurnberger, J. I., & Gershon, E. S. (1984). Genetics of affective disorders. In R. M. Post & J. C. Ballenger (Eds.), Neurobiology of mood disorders. Baltimore: Williams & Wilkins.

Oden, S. L., & Asher, S. R. (1977). Coaching children in social skills for friendship making. Child Development, 48, 495–506.

Offenbach, S. I. (1974). A developmental study of hypothesis testing and cue selection strategies. Developmental Psychology, 10, 484–490.

Ohman, A., Erixon, G., & Lofberg, I. (1975). Phobias and preparedness: Phobic versus neutral picture as conditioned stimuli for human autonomic responses. Journal of Abnormal Psychology, 84, 41–45.

Ollendick, T. H., Elliott, W., & Matson, J. L. (1980). Locus of control as related to effectiveness in a behavior modification program for juvenile delinquents. Journal of Behavior Therapy and Experimental Psychiatry, 11, 259–262.

Olpe, H. R., Steinmann, M. W., & Jones, R. S. G. (1985). Electrophysiological perspectives on locus coeruleus. Its role in cognitive versus vegetative functions. Physiological Psychology, 13, 179–187.

Olsen, K. M. (1969). Social class and age-group differences in the timing of family status changes: A study of age-norms in American society. Unpublished doctoral dissertation, University of Chicago, Chicago, IL.

Olson, G. M., & Sherman, T. (1983). Attention, learning, and memory in infants. In P. H. Mussen (Ed.), Handbook of child psychology: Vol. 2. Infancy and developmental psychobiology. New York: Wiley.

Olson, R. K., & Attneave, F. (1970). What variables produce stimulus grouping? American Psychologist, 83, 1–21.

Olson, R. P., Ganley, R., Devine, V. T., & Dorsey, G. C., Jr. (1981). Long-term effects of behavioral versus insight-oriented therapy with inpatient alcoholics. Journal of Consulting and Clinical Psychology, 49, 866–877.

Orne, M. T. (1970). Hypnosis, motivation and the ecological validity of the psychological experiment. In W. J. Arnold & M. M. Page (Eds.), Nebraska Symposium on Motivation. Lincoln: University of Nebraska Press.

Orne, M. T. (1977). The construct of hypnosis: Implications of definition for research and practice. In W. E. Edmonston, Jr. (Ed.), Conceptual and investigative approaches to hypnosis and hypnotic phenomena. Annals of the New York Academy of Sciences, 296, 14–33.

Orne, M. T. (1979). The use and misuse of hypnosis in court. International Journal of Clinical and Experimental Hypnosis, 14, 311–341.

Orne, M. T. (1980). On the construct of hypnosis: How its definition affects research and its clinical application. In G. D. Burrows & L. Dennerstein (Eds.), Handbook of hypnosis and psychosomatic medicine. Amsterdam: Elsevier.

Orne, M. T., & Evans, F. J. (1965). Social control in the psychological experiment: Antisocial behavior and hypnosis. Journal of Personality and Social Psychology, 1, 189–200.

Orne, M. T., & Holland, C. H. (1968). On the ecological validity of laboratory deceptions. International Journal of Psychiatry, 6, 282–293.

Orne, M. T., Sheehan, P. W., & Evans, F. J. (1968). Occurrence of posthypnotic behavior outside the experimental setting. Journal of Personality and Social Psychology, 9, 189–196.

Orne, M. T., & Wender, P. (1968). Anticipatory socialization for psychotherapy: Method and rationale. American Journal of Psychiatry, 124, 88–98.

Ornstein, R. E. (1977). The psychology of consciousness (2nd ed.). New York: Harcourt Brace Jovanovich.

Ornstein, R. E. (1985). Psychology: The study of human experience. San Diego: Harcourt Brace Jovanovich.

Ory, J. (1986). College, department, and course grade distribution for fall semester, 1985 (Research Memorandum No. 222). Champaign: University of Illinois, Office of Instructional Resources.

Oster, H. (1981). "Recognition" of emotional expression in infancy? In M. E. Lamb & L. R. Sherrod (Eds.), Infant social cognition. Hillsdale, NJ: Lawrence Erlbaum Associates.

Oster, H., & Ewy, R. (1980). Discrimination of sad vs. happy faces by 4-month-olds: When is a smile seen as a smile? Unpublished manuscript, University of Pennsylvania, Philadelphia.

O'Sullivan, C. S., & Durso, F. T. (1984). The effect of schema incongruent information on memory for stereotypical attributes. Journal of Personality and Social Psychology, 47, 55–70.

Otis, L. S. (1984). The adverse effects of meditation. In Shapiro, D. H., & Walsh, R. N. (Eds.), Meditation: Classical and contemporary perspectives. New York: Aldine.

Ouchi, W. (1981). Theory Z: How American business can meet the Japanese challenge. Reading, MA: Addison-Wesley.

Pachella, R. (1974). The use of reaction time measures in information processing research. In B. H. Kantowitz (Ed.), Human information processing. Hillsdale, NJ: Lawrence Erlbaum Associates.

Paine, W. S. (Ed.). (1982). Job stress and burnout: Research, theory, and intervention perspectives. Beverly Hills, CA: Sage.

Paivio, A. (1978). Dual coding: Theoretical issues and empirical evidence. In J. M. Scandura & C. J. Brainerd (Eds.), Structural process models of human behavior. Leiden: Nordhoff.

Palmer, F. H., & Anderson, L. W. (1979). Long term gains from early intervention: Findings from longitudinal studies. In E. Zigler & J. Valentine (Eds.), Project Head Start: A legacy of the war on poverty. New York: Free Press.

Palmer, S. E. (1975). The effects of contextual scenes on the identification of objects. Memory and Cognition, 3, 519–526.

Palys, T. S., & Little, B. R. (1983). Perceived life satisfaction and the organization of personal project systems. Journal of Personality and Social Psychology, 44, 1221–1230.

Panksepp, J. (1982). Toward a general psychobiological theory of emotions. The Behavioral and Brain Sciences, 5, 407–467:

Parke, R. D., Berkowitz, L., Leyens, J. P., West, S. G., & Sebastian, R. J. (1977). Some effects of violent and nonviolent movies on the behavior of juvenile delinquents. In L. Berkowitz (Ed.), Advances in experimental social psychology: Vol. 10. New York: Academic Press.

Parkes, C. M., & Brown, R. (1972). Health after bereavement: A controlled study of young Boston widows and widowers. Psychosomatic Medicine, 34, 449–461.

Parkes, K. R. (1984). Locus of control, cognitive appraisal, and coping in stressful episodes. Journal of Personality and Social Psychology, 46, (3), 655–668.

Parten, M. B. (1932). Social participation among preschool children. Journal of Abnormal and Social Psychology, 27, 243–269.

Parten, M. B. (1971). Social play among preschool children. In R. E. Herron & B. Sutton-Smith (Eds.), Child's play. New York: Wiley.

(Reprinted from *Journal of Abnormal and Social Psychology*, 1933, 28, 136–147)

Pascual-Leone, J. (1970). A mathematical model for the transition role in Piaget's developmental stages. *Acta Psychologica, 32,* 301–345.

Pastor, D. L. (1981). The quality of mother-infant attachment and its relationship to toddlers' initial sociability with peers. *Developmental Psychology, 17,* 326–335.

Patrick, C. J., Craig, K. D., & Prkachin, K. M. (1986). Observer judgments of pain: Facial action determinants. *Journal of Personality and Social Psychology, 50,* 1291–1298.

Patten, B. M. (1968). *Human embryology* (3rd ed.). New York: McGraw-Hill.

Patterson, F. G. (1978). The gestures of a gorilla: Language acquisition in another pongid. *Brain and Language, 5,* 72–97.

Patterson, G. R. (1976). *Living with children* (rev. ed.). Champaign, IL: Research Press.

Patterson, G. R. (1982). *Coercive family process.* Eugene, OR: Castalia Press.

Pattie, F. A. (1935). A report of attempts to produce uniocular blindness by hypnotic suggestion. *British Journal of Medical Psychiatry, 15,* 230–241.

Paul, G. L. (1969a). Behavior modification research: Design and tactics. In C. M. Franks (Ed.), *Behavior therapy: Appraisal and status* (pp. 29–62). New York: McGraw-Hill.

Paul, G. L. (1969b). Physiological effects of relaxation training and hypnotic suggestion. *Journal of Abnormal Psychology, 74,* 425–437.

Paul, G. L. (1986). Can pregnancy be a placebo effect?: Terminology, designs, and conclusions in the study of psychosocial and pharmacological treatments of behavior disorders. *Journal of Behavior Therapy and Experimental Psychiatry, 17,* 61–82.

Paul, G. L., & Lentz, R. J. (1977). *Psychosocial treatment of chronic mental patients: Milieu versus social learning programs.* Cambridge: Harvard University Press.

Pavlov, I. P. (1927). *Conditioned reflexes* (G. V. Anrep, Trans.). London: Oxford University Press.

Paykel, E. S., Prusoff, B. A., & Myers, J. K. (1975). Suicide attempts and recent life events. *Archives of General Psychiatry, 32,* 327–333.

Payne, R. W., Matussek, P., & George, E. I. (1959). An experimental study of schizophrenic thought disorder. *Journal of Mental Science, 105,* 627–652.

Peck, J. W. (1973). Discussion: Thirst(s) resulting from bodily water imbalances. In A. N. Epstein, H. R. Kissileff, & E. Stellar (Eds.), *The neuropsychology of thirst: New findings and advances in concepts.* Washington, DC: Winston.

Peck, J. W. (1978). Rats defend different body weights depending on palatability and accessibility of their food. *Journal of Comparative and Physiological Psychology, 92,* 555–570.

Peery, J. C., & Stern, D. (1976). Gaze duration frequency distributions during mother-infant interaction. *Journal of Genetic Psychology, 129,* 45–55.

Pekala, R. J., Wenger, C. F., & Levine, R. L. (1985). Individual differences in phenomenological experience: States of consciousness as a function of absorption. *Journal of Personality and Social Psychology, 48,* 125–132.

Pennebaker, J. W. (1985). Traumatic experience and psychosomatic disease: Exploring the roles of behavioural inhibition, obsession, and confiding. *Canadian Psychology, 26,* 82–95.

Pennebaker, J. W., & Chew, C. H. (1985). Deception, electrodermal activity, and inhibition of behavior. *Journal of Personality and Social Psychology, 49,* 1427–1433.

Pennebaker, J. W., & Hoover, C. W. (1986). Inhibition and cognition: Toward an understanding of trauma and disease. In R. J. Davidson, G. E. Schwartz, & D. Shapiro (Eds.), *Consciousness and self-regulation: Vol. 4.* New York: Plenum Press.

Pennebaker, J. W., & O'Heeron, R. C. (1984). Confiding in others and illness rate among spouses of suicide and accidental death victims. *Journal of Abnormal Psychology, 93,* 473–476.

Peper, R. J., & Mayer, R. E. (1978). Note taking as a generative activity. *Journal of Educational Psychology, 70,* 514–522.

Pepler, D., Corter, C., & Abramovitch, R. (1982). Social relations among children: Siblings and peers. In K. Rubin & H. Ross (Eds.), *Peer relationships and social skills in childhood.* New York: Springer-Verlag.

Perls, F. S. (1969). *Gestalt therapy verbatim.* Lafayette, CA: Real People Press.

Perls, F. S. (1970). Four lectures. In J. Fagan & I. L. Shepherd (Eds.), *Gestalt therapy now* (pp. 14–38). Palo Alto, CA: Science and Behavior Books.

Perls, F. S., Hefferline, R. F., & Goodman, P. (1951). *Gestalt therapy.* New York: Julian Press.

Pert, C. (1979). In *Keys to paradise* [NOVA film]. Boston: Public Broadcasting Service, WGBH.

Pessin, J. (1933). The comparative effects of social and mechanical stimulation on memorizing. *American Journal of Psychology, 45,* 263–270.

Peters, J. J. (1977). The Philadelphia rape victim project. In D. Chappell, R. Geiss, & G. Geis (Eds.), *Forcible rape: The crime, the victim, and the offenders.* New York: Columbia University Press.

Peters, T. J., & Waterman, R. H. (1983). *In search of excellence: Lessons from America's best-run companies.* New York: Warner.

Peterson, C., & Seligman, M. E. P. (1984a). Causal explanations as a risk factor for depression: Theory and evidence. *Psychological Review, 91,* 347–374.

Peterson, L. R., & Peterson, M. J. (1959). Short-term retention of individual verbal items. *Journal of Experimental Psychology, 58,* 193–198.

Peterson, J. L., & Zill, N. (1981). Television viewing in the United States and children's intellectual, social, and emotional development. *Television and Children, 2,* 21–28.

Petri, H. L. (1986). *Motivation: Theory and research* (2nd ed.). Belmont, CA: Wadsworth.

Petty, R. E., & Cacioppo, J. T. (1981). *Attitudes and persuasion: Classic and contemporary approaches.* Dubuque, IA: William C. Brown.

Phares, E. J. (1973). *Locus of control: A personality determinant of behavior.* Morristown, NJ: General Learning Press.

Phelps, M. E., & Mazziotta, J. C. (1985). Positron emission tomography: Human brain function and biochemistry. *Science, 228,* 799–809.

Piaget, J. (1932). *The moral judgment of the child.* Glencoe, IL: Free Press.

Piaget, J. (1952). *The origins of intelligence in children.* New York: International Universities Press.

Piaget, J. (1962). *Play, dreams and imitation.* New York: W. W. Norton. (Original work published 1951)

Piaget, J., & Inhelder, B. (1969). *The psychology of the child.* New York: Basic Books.

Piliavin, I. M., Piliavin, J. A., & Rodin, J. (1975). Costs, diffusion, and the stigmatized victim. *Journal of Personality and Social Psychology, 32,* 429–438.

Pilisuk, M., & Skolnick, P. (1968). Inducing trust: A test of the Osgood proposal. *Journal of Personality and Social Psychology, 8,* 121–133.

Plomin, R. (1981). Behavior genetics and personality. In R. M. Liebert & R. Wicks-Nelson, *Developmental psychology* (3rd ed.). Englewood Cliffs, NJ: Prentice-Hall.

Plomin, R., & Foch, T. T. (1980). A twin study of objectively assessed personality in childhood. *Journal of Personality and Social Psychology, 39,* 680–688.

Plomin, P., & Rowe, D. C. (1979). Genetic and environmental etiology of social behavior in infancy. *Developmental Psychology, 15,* 62–72.

Plutchik, R. (1980). *Emotions in humans and animals: A psychoevolutionary synthesis.* New York: Harper & Row.

Plutchik, R. (1984). A psychoevolutionary theory of emotions. *Social Science Information, 21,* 529–553.

Poeck, K. (1969). Pathophysiology of emotional disorders associated with brain damage. In P. J. Vinken & G. W. Bruyn (Eds.), *Handbook of clinical neurology: Vol. 3.* New York: American Elsevier.

Poincaré H. (1913). Mathematical creation. In G. H. Halstead (Trans.), *The foundations of science.* New York: Science Press.

Pollack, I. (1953). The assimilation of sequentially coded information. *American Journal of Psychology, 66,* 421–435.

Pollard-Gott, L. (1983). Emergence of thematic concepts in repeated listening to music. *Cognitive Psychology, 15,* 66–94.

Polya, G. (1957). *How to solve it.* Garden City, NY: Anchor.

Ponzetti, J. J., Cate, R. M., & Koval, J. E. (1982). Violence between couples: Profiling the male abuser. *The Personnel and Guidance Journal, 61,* 222–224.

Poon, L. W., & Fozard, J. L. (1978). Speed of retrieval from long-term memory in relation to age, familiarity, and datedness of information. *Journal of Gerontology, 33,* 711–717.

Pope H. G., & Lipinsky, J. F. (1978). Diagnosis in schizophrenia and manic-depressive illness: A reassessment of the specificity of schizophrenic symptoms in light of current research. *Archives of General Psychiatry, 35,* 811–828.

Porter, R. H., Cernich, J. M., & McLaughlin, F. J. (1983). Maternal recognition of neonates through olfactory cues. *Physiology and Behavior, 30,* 151–154.

Posner, M. I. (1978). *Chronometric explorations of the mind.* Hillsdale, NJ: Lawrence Erlbaum Associates.

Posner, M. I., Nissen, M. J., & Klein, R. (1976). Visual dominance: An information processing account of its origins and significance. *Psychological Review, 83,* 157–171.

Power, T. G., & Parke, R. D. (1983). Patterns of mother and father play with their 8-month-old infant: A multiple analysis approach. *Infant Behavior and Development, 6,* 453–459.

Powley, T. L., & Keesey, R. E. (1970). Relationship of body weight to the lateral hypothalamic syndrome. *Journal of Comparative and Physiological Psychology, 70,* 25–36.

Prager, R. A., & Garfield, S. L. (1972). Client initial disturbance and outcome in psychotherapy. *Journal of Consulting and Clinical Psychology, 38,* 112–117.

Premack, D. (1971). Language in chimpanzees? *Science, 172,* 808–822.

Prescott, S., & Letko, C. (1977). Battered women: A social psychological perspective. In M. Roy (Ed.), *Battered women: A psychological study of domestic violence.* New York: Van Nostrand Reinhold.

Pribram, K. H., & McGuiness, P. (1975). Arousal, activation and effort in the control of attention. *Psychological Review, 82,* 116–149.

Price, K. O., Harburg, E., & Newcomb, T. M. (1966). Psychological balance in situations of negative interpersonal attitudes. *Journal of Personality and Social Psychology, 3,* 255–270.

Pritchard, W. S. (1981). The psychophysiology of P300. *Psychological Bulletin, 89,* 506–540.

Prochaska, J. O., & Norcross, J. C. (1982). The future of psychotherapy: A Delphi poll. *Professional Psychology, 13,* 620–627.

Proshansky, H. M. (1976). Environmental psychology and the real world. *American Psychologist, 31,* 303–310.

Provence, S., & Lipton, R. C. (1962). *Infants in institutions.* New York: International Universities Press.

Putallaz, M. (1983). Predicting children's sociometric status from their behavior. *Child Development, 54,* 1417–1426.

Putallaz, M., & Gottman, J. (1981). An interactional model of children's entry into peer groups. *Child Development, 52,* 986–994.

Putallaz, M., & Gottman, J. (1983). Social relationship problems in children: An approach to intervention. In E. B. Lahey & A. E. Kazdin (Eds.), *Advances in clinical child psychology: Vol. 6.* New York: Plenum Press.

Pyle, R. L., Mitchell, J. E., & Eckert, E. D. (1981). Bulimia: A report of 34 cases. *Journal of Clinical Psychiatry, 42,* 60–64.

Quartermain, D., Kissileff, H., Shapiro, R., & Miller, N. E. (1971). Suppression of food intake with intragastric loading: Relation to natural feeding cycle. *Science, 173,* 941–943.

Raaijmakers, J. G. W., & Shiffrin, R. M. (1981). Search of associative memory. *Psychological Review, 88,* 93–134.

Rabbitt, P. (1977). Changes in problem solving ability in old age. In J. E. Birren & K. W. Schaie (Eds.), *Handbook of the psychology of aging.* New York: Van Nostrand Reinhold.

Rachman, S. (1973). The effects of psychotherapy. In H. J. Eysenck (Ed.), *Handbook of abnormal psychology.* San Diego, CA: Knapp.

Rachman, S. J., & Wilson, G. T. (1980). *The effects of psychological therapy* (2nd ed.). New York: Pergamon Press.

Rada, J. B., & Rogers, R. W. (1973). *Obedience to authority: Presence of authority and command strength.* Paper presented at the annual convention of the Southeastern Psychological Association.

Rader, N., Spiro, D. J., & Firestone, P. B. (1979). Performance on a stage IV object permanence task with standard and nonstandard covers. *Child Development, 50,* 908–910.

Radloff, L. (1975). Sex differences in depression: The effects of occupation and marital status. *Sex Roles, 1,* 249–265.

Rahe, R., Romo, M., Bennett, L., & Siltanen, P. (1974). Recent life changes, myocardial infarction, and abrupt coronary death: Studies in Helsinki. *Archives of Internal Medicine, 133,* 221–228.

Rakic, P., & Yaklovlev, P. I. (1968). Development of the corpus callosum and the cavum septi in man. *Journal of Comparative Neurology, 132,* 45–72.

Raloff, J. (1985). A sweet taste of success to drink in. *Science News, 127,* 262.

Ramey, C. T., & Haskins, R. (1981). The modification of intelligence through early experience. *Intelligence, 5,* 5–19.

Rangel-Guerra, R. A., Perez-Payan, H., Minkoff, L., & Todd, L. E. (1983). Nuclear magnetic resonance in bipolar affective disorders. *AJNR, 4,* 229–231.

Rapoport, A. (1973). *Experimental games and their uses in psychology.* Morristown, NJ: General Learning Press.

Rapoport, A. (Ed.). (1974). *Game theory as a theory of conflict resolution.* Dordrecht, Netherlands: D. Reidel.

Rappaport, J. (1977). *Community psychology: Values, research and action.* New York: Holt, Rinehart & Winston.

Raps, C. S., Peterson, C., Reinhard, K. E., Abramson, L. Y., & Seligman, M. E. P. (1982). Attributional style among depressed patients. *Journal of Abnormal Psychology, 91,* 102–103.

Raschke, H. J. (1977). The role of social participation in postseparation and postdivorce adjustment. *Journal of Divorce, 1,* 129–140.

Raskin, D. C., & Podlesny, J. A. (1979). Truth and deception: A reply to Lykken. *Psychological Bulletin, 86,* 54–59.

Rasmussen, J. (Ed.). (1973). *Man in isolation and confinement.* Hawthorne, NY: Aldine.

Rasmussen, J. (1981). Models of mental strategies in process control. In J. Rasmussen & W. Rouse (Eds.), *Human detection and diagnosis of system failures.* New York: Plenum Press.

Raven, J. C. (1948). The comparative assessment of intellectual ability. *British Journal of Psychology, 39,* 12–19.

Ray, D. W., Wandersman, A., Ellisor, J., & Huntington, D. E. (1982). The effects of high density in a juvenile correctional institution. *Basic and Applied Social Psychology, 3,* 95–108.

Raynor, J. O. (1970). Relationships between achievement-related motives, future orientation, and academic performance. *Journal of Personality and Social Psychology, 15,* 28–33.

Redd, W. H. (1984). Psychological intervention to control cancer chemotherapy side effects. *Postgraduate Medicine, 75,* 105–113.

Reder, L. M., & Anderson, J. R. (1980). A partial resolution of the paradox of interference: The role of integrating knowledge. *Cognitive Psychology, 12,* 447–472.

Reed, S. K. (1982). *Cognition.* Monterey, CA: Brooks/Cole.

Reed, T. (1980). Challenging some "common wisdom" on drug abuse. *International Journal of the Addictions, 15,* 359–373.

Reedy, M. N. (1983). Personality and aging. In D. S. Woodruff & J. E. Birren (Eds.), *Aging: Scientific perspectives and social issues* (2nd ed.). Monterey, CA: Brooks/Cole.

Reiman, E. M., Raichle, M. E., Butler, F. K., Herscovitch, P., & Robins, E. (1984). A focal brain abnormality in panic disorder, a severe form of anxiety. *Nature, 310,* 683–685.

Reiman, L. N., Helzer, J. E., Weissman, M. M., Orvaschel, H., Gruenberg, E., Burke, J. D., & Regier, D. A. (1984). Lifetime prevalence of specific psychiatric disorders in three sites. *Archives of General Psychiatry, 41,* 949–958.

Reinisch, J. M. (1981). Prenatal exposure to synthetic progestins increases potential for aggression in humans. *Science, 211,* 1171–1173.

Reisenzein, R. (1983). The Schachter theory of emotion: Two decades later. *Psychological Bulletin, 94,* 239–264.

Reisman, J. M. (1976). *A history of clinical psychology.* New York: Irvington.

Reitman, J. S. (1971). Mechanisms of forgetting in short-term memory. *Cognitive Psychology, 2,* 185–195.

Reitman, J. S. (1974). Without surreptitious rehearsal, information in short-term memory decays. *Journal of Verbal Learning and Verbal Behavior, 13,* 365–377.

Report of the British Advisory Committee on Drug Dependence, 1968.

Rescorla, L. A. (1981). Category development in early language. *Journal of Child Language, 8,* 225–238.

Rescorla, R. A. (1968). Probability of shock in the presence and absence of CS in fear conditioning. *Journal of Comparative and Physiological Psychology, 66,* 1–5.

Rescorla, R. A. (1978). Some implications of a cognitive perspective on Pavlovian conditioning. In S. H. Hulse, H. Fowler, & W. K. Honig (Eds.), *Cognitive processes in animal behavior.* Hillsdale, NJ: Lawrence Erlbaum Associates.

Resnick, L. B., & Glaser, R. (1976). Problem-solving and intelligence. In L. B. Resnick (Ed.), *The nature of intelligence.* Hillsdale, NJ: Lawrence Erlbaum Associates.

Restak, R. (1979, September 9). Male, female brains: Are they different? *Boston Globe,* p. A1.

Revusky, S. H. (1967). Hunger level during food consumption: Effects on subsequent preferences. *Psychonomic Science, 7,* 109–110.

Revusky, S. H. (1971). The role of interference in association over a delay. In W. K. Honig & P. H. R. James (Eds.), *Animal memory.* New York: Academic Press.

Revusky, S. H. (1977). The concurrent interference approach to delay learning. In L. M. Barker, M. R. Best, & M. Domjan (Eds.), *Learning mechanisms in food selection.* Waco, TX: Baylor University Press.

Reynolds, D. V. (1969). Surgery in the rat during electrical analgesia induced by focal brain stimulation. *Science, 164,* 444–445.

Rheingold, H. L., & Eckerman, C. O. (1971). Departures from the mother. In H. R. Schaffer (Ed.), *The origins of human social relations.* London: Academic Press.

Rhodewalt, F. (1984). Self-involvement, self-attribution, and the Type A coronary-prone behavior pattern. *Journal of Personality and Social Psychology, 47,* 662–670.

Rholes, W. S., & Ruble, D. N. (1984). Children's understanding of dispositional characteristics of others. *Child Development, 55,* 550–560.

Rickards, J. P. (1976). Interaction of position and conceptual level of adjunct questions in immediate and delayed retention of text. *Journal of Educational Psychology, 68,* 210–217.

Riegel, K. F. (1975). Toward a dialectical theory of development. *Human Development, 18,* 50–64.

Riggar, T. F. (1985). *Stress burnout: An annotated bibliography.* Carbondale: Southern Illinois University Press.

Rimm, D. C., & Masters, J. C. (1979). *Behavior therapy: Techniques and empirical findings* (2nd ed.). New York: Academic Press.

Rinn, W. E. (1984). The neuropsychology of facial expression: A review of the neurological and psychological mechanisms for producing facial expressions. *Psychological Bulletin, 95,* 52–77.

Riskey, D. R. (1979). Verbal memory processes in impression formation. *Journal of Experimental Psychology: Human Learning and Memory, 5,* 271–281.

Risley, T. R. (1968). The effects and side effects of punishing the autistic behaviors of a deviant child. *Journal of Applied Behavior Analysis, 1,* 21–34.

Robertson, J., & Robertson, J. (1971). Young children in brief separation: A fresh look. *Psychoanalytic Study of the Child, 26,* 264–315.

Robins, L. N., Helzer, J. E., Weissman, M. M., Orvaschel, H., Gruenberg, E., Burke, J. D., & Reigier, D. A. (1984). Lifetime prevalence of specific psychiatric disorders in three sites. *Archives of General Psychiatry, 41,* 949–958.

Rochester, S. R., Martin, J. R., & Thurston, S. (1977). Thought-process disorder in schizophrenia: The listener's task. *Brain and Language, 4,* 95–114.

Rock, I. (1978). *An introduction to perception.* New York: Macmillan.

Rock, M. A. (1978). Gorilla mothers need some help from their friends. *Smithsonian, 7,* 58–63.

Rockstein, M. J., & Sussman, M. (1979). *Biology of aging.* Belmont, CA: Wadsworth.

Rodin, J. (1973). Effects of distraction on the performance of obese and normal subjects. *Journal of Comparative and Physiological Psychology, 83,* 68–78.

Rodin, J. (1980). Current status of the internal-external hypothesis of obesity: What went wrong? *American Psychologist, 36,* 361–372.

Rodin, J. (1986). Aging and health: Effects of the sense of control. *Science, 233,* 1271–1276.

Rodin, J., & Langer, E. J. (1977). Long-term effects of a control-relevant intervention with the institutionalized aged. *Journal of Personality and Social Psychology, 35,* 879–902.

Roethlisberger, F. J., & Dickson, W. J. (1939). *Management and the worker.* Cambridge: Harvard University Press.

Roffwarg, H. P., Muzio, J. N., & Dement, W. C. (1966). Ontogenetic development of the human sleep-dream cycle. *Science, 152,* 604–619.

Rogers, C. R. (1942). *Counseling and psychotherapy.* Boston: Houghton Mifflin.

Rogers, C. R. (1951). *Client-centered therapy.* Boston: Houghton Mifflin.

Rogers, C. R. (1961). *On becoming a person.* Boston: Houghton Mifflin.

Rogers, C. R. (1970). *Carl Rogers on encounter groups.* New York: Harper & Row.

Rogers, C. R. (1980). *A way of being.* Boston: Houghton Mifflin.

Rook, K. S. (1987). Social support versus companionship: Effects on life stress, loneliness, and evaluations by others. *Journal of Personality and Social Psychology, 52,* 1132–1137.

Rosch, E. (1973). On the internal structure of perceptual and semantic categories. In T. E. Moore (Ed.), *Cognitive development and the acquisition of language.* New York: Academic Press.

Rosch, E. (1975). Cognitive representations of semantic categories. *Journal of Experimental Psychology: General, 104,* 192–223.

Rosch, E., Mervis, C. B., Gray, W. D., Johnson, D. M., & Boyes-Braem, P. (1976). Basic objects in natural categories. *Cognitive Psychology, 8,* 382–439.

Rosen, B. C., & D'Andrade, R. (1959). The psychosocial origins of achievement motivation. *Sociometry, 22,* 188–218.

Rosenberg, M. J. (1961). Group size, prior experience and conformity. *Journal of Abnormal and Social Psychology, 63,* 436–437.

Rosenhan, D. L. (1973). On being sane in insane places. *Science, 179,* 250–258.

Rosenhan, D. L., & Seligman, M. E. (1984). *Abnormal psychology.* New York: W. W. Norton.

Rosenman, R. H., Brand, R. J., Jenkins, D., Friedman, M., Straus, R., & Wurm, M. (1975). Coronary heart disease in the Western Collaborative Group study: Final follow-up experience of 8 1/2 years. *Journal of the American Medical Association, 233,* 872–877.

Rosenthal, D. (1977). Searches for the mode of genetic transmission in schizophrenia: Reflections and loose ends. *Schizophrenia Bulletin, 3,* 268–276.

Rosenthal, R. R. (1966). *Experimenter effects in behavioral research.* New York: Appleton-Century-Crofts.

Rosenthal, R. R., & Jacobson, L. (1968) *Pygmalion in the classroom.* New York: Holt, Rinehart & Winston.

Rosenzweig, M. R., Bennett, E. L., & Diamond, M. C. (1972). Brain changes in response to experiences. *Scientific American, 226,* 22–39.

Rosenzweig, M. R., & Leiman, A. L. (1982). *Physiological psychology.* Lexington, MA: D. C. Heath.

Roskies, E. (1980). Considerations in developing a treatment program for the coronary-prone (Type A) behavior pattern. In P. O. Davidson & S. Davidson (Eds.), *Behavioral medicine: Changing health life styles.* New York: Brunner/Mazel.

Ross, B. H. (1984). Remindings and their effects in learning a cognitive skill. *Cognitive Psychology, 16,* 371–416.

Ross, H. S., & Goldman, B. D. (1977). Establishing new social relations in infancy. In T. W. Alloway, P. Pliner, & L. Krames (Eds.), *Attachment behavior: Advances in the study of communication and affect. Vol. 3.* New York: Plenum Press.

Ross, L., Bierbrauer, G., & Hoffman, S. (1976). The role of attribution processes in conformity and dissent: Revisiting the Asch situation. *American Psychologist, 31,* 148–157.

Ross, L., Greene, D., & House, P. (1977). The "false consensus effect": An egocentric bias in social perception and attribution processes. *Journal of Experimental Social Psychology, 13,* 279–301.

Ross, M., & Sicoly, F. (1979). Egocentric biases in availability and attribution. *Journal of Personality and Social Psychology, 37,* 322–337.

Ross, R., & Glomset, J. A. (1976). The pathogenesis of atherosclerosis. *New England Journal of Medicine, 295,* 369–377, 420–425.

Ross, S. M., & Ross, L. E. (1971). Comparison of trace and delay classical eyelid conditioning as a function of interstimulus interval. *Journal of Experimental Psychology, 91,* 165–167.

Rossman, I. (1977). Anatomic and body composition changes with aging. In C. E. Finch & L. Hayflick (Eds.), *Handbook of the biology of aging.* New York: Van Nostrand Reinhold.

Rotter, J. B. (1954). *Social learning and clinical psychology.* Englewood Cliffs, NJ: Prentice-Hall.

Rotton, J., Frey, J., Barry, T., Mulligan, M., & Fitzpatrick, M. (1979). The air pollution experience and physical aggression. *Journal of Applied Social Psychology, 9,* 397–412.

Roueche, B. (1986, December 8) Cinnabar. *The New Yorker.*

Rowe, D. C., & Plomin, R. (1978). The Burt controversy: A comparison of Burt's data on IQ with data from other studies. *Behavioral Genetics, 8,* 81–84.

Rozin, P. (1982). "Taste-smell confusions" and the duality of the olfactory sense. *Perception and Psychophysics, 31,* 397–401.

Rozin, P., & Kalat, J. W. (1971). Specific hungers and poison avoidance as adaptive specializations of learning. *Psychological Review, 78,* 459–486.

Rubenstein, J., & Howes, C. (1976). The effects of peers on toddler interaction with mother and toys. *Child Development, 47,* 597–605.

Rubin, E. (1915). *Synsoplevede figure.* Copenhagen: Gyldendalske.

Rubin, J. Z., & Brown, B. R. (1975). *The social psychology of bargaining and negotiation.* New York: Academic Press.

Rubinstein, T., & Mason, A. F. (1979, November). The accident that shouldn't have happened: An analysis of Three Mile Island. *IEEE Spectrum,* 37–57.

Ruble, D. N., & Feldman, N. S. (1976). Order of consensus, distinctiveness, and consistency information and causal attribution. *Journal of Personality and Social Psychology, 34,* 930–937.

Rumbaugh, D. M. (Ed.). (1977). *Language learning by a chimpanzee: The Lana project.* New York: Academic Press.

Rumelhart, D. E. (1984). Schemata and the cognitive system. In R. S. Wyer & T. K. Srull (Eds.), *Handbook of social cognition: Vol. 1.* Hillsdale, NJ: Lawrence Erlbaum Associates.

Rundus, D. (1971). Analysis of rehearsal processes in free recall. *Journal of Experimental Psychology, 89,* 63–77.

Rushton, J., & Sorrentino, R. (Eds.). (1981). *Altruism and helping behavior.*

Rushton, J. P., Russell, R. J., & Wells, P. A. (1984). Genetic similarity theory: Beyond kin selection. *Behavior Genetics, 14,* 179–193.

Russek, M. (1971). Hepatic receptors and the neurophysiological mechanisms controlling feeding behavior. In S. Ehrenpreis (Ed.), *Neurosciences research: Vol. 4.* New York: Academic Press.

Russell, M. J. (1976). Human olfactory communication. *Nature, 260,* 520–522.

Russell, M. J., Dark, K. A., Cummins, R. W., Ellman, G., Callaway, E., & Peeke, H. V. S. (1984). Learned histamine release. *Science, 225,* 733–734.

Rutkowski, G. K., Gruder, C. L., & Romer, D. (1983). Group cohesiveness, social norms, and bystander intervention. *Journal of Personality and Social Psychology, 44,* 545–552.

Rutter, M. (1974). *The qualities of mothering: Maternal deprivation reassessed.* New York: Jason Aronson.

Sachs, J. (1967). Recognition memory for syntactic and semantic aspects of connected discourse. *Perception and Psychophysics, 2,* 437–442.

Sackeim, H. A. (1985, June). The case for ECT. *Psychology Today,* pp. 36–40.

Sackeim, H. A., Greenberg, M. S., Weiman, A. L., Gur, R. C., Hungerbuhler, J. P., & Geschwind, N. (1982). Hemispheric asymmetry in the expression of positive and negative emotions: Neurologic evidence. *Archives of Neurology, 39,* 210–218.

Sackeim, H. A., Gur, R. C. J., & Saucy, M. C. (1978). Emotions are expressed more intensely on the left side of the face. *Science 202,* 434–436.

Sacks, O. (1985). *The man who mistook his wife for a hat.* New York: Summit Books.

Saghir, M. T., & Robins, E. (1973). *Male and female homosexuality: A comprehensive investigation.* Baltimore: Williams & Wilkins.

Sajwaj, T., Libet, J., & Agras, S. (1974). Lemon-juice therapy: The control of life-threatening rumination in a six-month infant. *Journal of Applied Behavioral Analysis, 7,* 557–563.

Sakitt, B., & Long, G. M. (1979). Spare the rod and spoil the icon. *Journal of Experimental Psychology: Human Perception and Performance, 5,* 19–30.

Saks, M. (1976). The limits of scientific jury selection. *Jurimetrics Journal, 17,* 3–22.

Salthouse, J. A. (1985). *A theory of cognitive aging.* Amsterdam: North Holland.

Sampson, H. A., & Jolie, P. L. (1984). Increased plasma histamine concentrations after food challenges in children with atopic dermatitis. *The New England Journal of Medicine, 311,* 372–376.

Sanders, G. S., & Baron, R. S. (1977). Is social comparison irrelevant for producing choice shifts? *Journal of Experimental Social Psychology, 13,* 303–314.

Sapolsky, R. M., Krey, L. C., & McEwen, B. S. (1985). Prolonged glucocorticoid exposure reduces hippocampal neurin number: Implications for aging. *Journal of Neuroscience, 5,* 1222–1227.

Sarason, I. G. (1978). The test anxiety scale concept and research. In C. D. Spielberger & I. G. Sarason (Eds.), *Stress and anxiety: Vol. 5,* (pp. 193–216). Washington, DC: Hemisphere.

Sarason, I. G. (1984). Stress, anxiety, and cognitive interference: Reactions to tests. *Journal of Personality and Social Psychology, 46*(4), 929–938.

Sarason, I. G., & Sarason, B. R. (Eds.). (1985). *Social support: Theory, research and applications.* The Hague: Martinus Nijhof.

Sarason, I. G., Sarason, B. R., Keefe, D. E., Hayes, B. E., & Shearin, E. N. (1986). Cognitive interference: Situational determinants and traitlike characteristics. *Journal of Personality and Social Psychology, 51,* 215–226.

Sarbin, T. R. (1950). Contributions to role-taking theory: I. Hypnotic behavior. *Psychological Review, 57,* 255–270.

Sartorius, N., Shapiro, R., & Jablensky, A. (1974). The international pilot study of schizophrenia. *Schizophrenia Bulletin, 1,* 21–35.

Sasfy, J., & Okun, M. (1974). Form of evaluation and audience expertness as joint determinants of audience effects. *Journal of Experimental Social Psychology, 10,* 461–467.

Saufley, W. H., Otaka, S. R., & Bavaresco, J. L. (1985). Context effects: Classroom tests and context independence. *Memory and Cognition, 13,* 522–528.

Savin-Williams, R. C., & Demo, D. H. (1984). Developmental change and stability in adolescent self-concept. *Developmental Psychology, 20,* 1100–1110.

Scarr, S., Webber, P. L., Weinberg, R. A., & Wittig, M. A. (1981). Personality resemblance among adolescents and their parents in biologically related and adoptive families. *Journal of Personality and Social Psychology, 40,* 885–898.

Scarr, S., & Carter-Saltzman, L. (1982). Genetics and intelligence. In R. Sternberg (Ed.), *Handbook of human intelligence.* Cambridge: Cambridge University Press.

Scarr, S., & Weinberg, R. A. (1976). IQ test performance of black children adopted by white families. *American Psychologist, 31,* 726–739.

Scarr, S., & Weinberg, R. A. (1977). Intellectual similarities within families of both adopted and biological children. *Intelligence, 1,* 170–191.

Schachter, S. (1959). *The psychology of affiliation.* Stanford, CA: Stanford University Press.

Schachter, S. (1971). Some extraordinary facts about obese humans and rats. *American Psychologist, 26,* 129–144.

Schachter, S., & Friedman, L. N. (1974). The effects of work and cue prominence on eating behavior. In S. Schachter & J. Rodin (Eds.), *Obese humans and rats.* Potomac, MD: Lawrence Erlbaum Associates.

Schachter, S., & Rodin, J. (Eds.). (1974). *Obese humans and rats.* Potomac, MD: Lawrence Erlbaum Associates.

Schachter, S., & Singer, J. (1962). Cognitive, social and physiological determinants of emotional state. *Psychological Review, 69,* 379–399.

Schaefer, C., Coyne, J. C., & Lazarus, R. S. (1982). The health-related functions of social support. *Journal of Behavioral Medicine, 4,* 381–406.

Schafer, R., & Murphy, G. (1943). The role of autism in a figure-ground relationship. *Journal of Experimental Psychology, 32,* 335–343.

Schaffer, C. E., Davidson, R. J., & Saron, C. (1983). Frontal and parietal EEG asymmetry in depressed and non-depressed subjects. *Biological Psychiatry, 18,* 753–762.

Schaie, K. W. (1979). The primary mental abilities in adulthood: An exploration in the development of psychometric intelligence. In P. B. Baltes & O. G. Brim, Jr. (Eds.), *Life-span development and behavior: Vol. 2.* New York: Academic Press.

Schaie, K. W., & Labouvie-Vief, G. (1974). Generational versus ontogenetic components of change in adult cognitive behavior. *Developmental Psychology, 10,* 305–320.

Scheerer, M., Rothmann, R., & Goldstein, K. (1945). A case of "idiot savant": An experimental study of personality organization. *Psychol. Monognomics, 58,* (4).

Scheier, M. F., Weintraub, J. K., & Carver, C. S. (1986). Coping with stress: Divergent strategies of optimists and pessimists. *Journal of Personality and Social Psychology, 51,* 1257–1264.

Scherwitz, L., Graham, L. E., II, & Ornish, D. (1985). Self-involvement and the risk factors for coronary heart disease. *Advances, 2,* 6–18.

Schick, R. R., Yaksh, T. L., & Go, V. L. W. (1986). An intragastric meal releases the putative satiety factor cholecystokinin from hypothalamic neurons in cats. *Brain Research, 370,* 349–353.

Schiff, M., Duyme, M., Dumaret, A., Stewart, J., Tomkiewicz, S., & Feingold, J. (1978). Intellectual status of working class children adopted early into upper-middle class families. *Science, 200,* 1503–1504.

Schiffman, H. R. (1982). *Sensation and perception: An integrated approach.* New York: Wiley.

Schleidt, M., Hold, B., & Attili, G. (1981). A cross-cultural study on the attitude towards personal odours. *J. Chem. Ecol., 7,* 19–31.

Schleifer, S. J., Keller, S. E., Camerino, M., Thornton, J. C., & Stein, M. (1983). Suppression of lymphocyte stimulation following bereavement. *Journal of the American Medical Association, 250,* 374–377.

Schlesier-Stroop, B. (1984). Bulimia: A review of the literature. *Psychological Bulletin, 95,* 247–257.

Schmale, A. H., & Iker, H. P. (1966). The effect of hopelessness and the development of cancer. *Psychosomatic Medicine, 28,* 714–721.

Schmidt, H. O., & Fonda, C. P. (1956). The reliability of psychiatric diagnosis: A new look. *Journal of Abnormal and Social Psychology, 52,* 262–267.

Schneider, D. J., Hastorf, A. H., & Ellsworth, P. C. (1979). *Person perception* (2nd ed.). Reading, MA: Addison-Wesley.

Schneider, D. J., & Miller, R. S. (1975). The effects of enthusiasm and quality of arguments on attitude attribution. *Journal of Personality, 43,* 693–708.

Schneider, W., & Shiffrin, R. (1977). Controlled and automatic human information processing. *Psychological Review, 84,* 1–66.

Schneider-Rosen, K., & Cicchetti, D. (1984). The relationship between affect and cognition in maltreated infants: Quality of attachment and the development of visual self-recognition. *Child Development, 55,* 648–658.

Schoenfeld, H. H. (1979). Explicit heuristic training as a variable in problem solving performance. *Journal for Research in Mathematical Education, 10,* 173–187.

Schofield, W. (1964). *Psychotherapy: The purchase of friendship.* Englewood Cliffs, NJ: Prentice-Hall.

Schuckit, M. A. (1983). The genetics of alcoholism. In B. Tabakoff, P. B. Sutker, & C. L. Randall (Eds.), *Medical and social aspects of alcohol use.* New York: Plenum Press.

Schulman-Galambos, C., & Galambos, R. (1979). Brain stem auditory evoked audiometry in newborn hearing screening. *Archives of Otolaryngology, 105,* 86–90.

Schulz, R. (1978). *The psychology of death, dying, and bereavement.* Reading, MA: Addison-Wesley.

Schum, D. (1975). The weighing of testimony of judicial proceedings from sources having reduced credibility. *Human Factors, 17,* 172–203.

Schwartz, G. E. (1982). Testing the biopsychocial model: The ultimate challenge facing behavioral medicine. *Journal of Consulting and Clinical Psychology, 50,* 6.

Schwartz, G. E., & Weiss, S. M. (1978). Behavioral medicine revisited: An amended definition. *Journal of Behavioral Medicine, 1,* 249–252.

Schwartz, P. (1983). Length of day-care attendance and attachment behavior in eighteen-month-old infants. *Child Development, 54,* 1073–1078.

Schwartz, R. M. (1982). Cognitive-behavior modification: A conceptual review. *Clinical Psychology Review, 2,* 267–293.

Schwarzwald, J., Bizman, A., & Raz, M. (1983). The foot-in-the-door paradigm: Effects of second request size on donation probability and donor generosity. *Personality and Social Psychology Bulletin, 9,* 443–450.

Schwitzgebel, R. L., & Schwitzgebel, R. K. (1980). *Law and psychological practice.* New York: Wiley.

Scovern, A. W., & Kilmann, P. R. (1980). Status of electroconvulsive therapy: Review of the outcome literature. *Psychological Bulletin, 87,* 260–303.

Searles, J. S. (1985). A methodological and empirical critique of psychotherapy outcome meta-analysis. *Behaviour Research and Therapy, 23,* 453–463.

Sears, D. O. (1986a). College sophomores in the laboratory: Influences of a narrow data base on social psychology's view of human nature. *Journal of Personality and Social Psychology, 51,* 515–530.

Sears, D. O. (1986b). *Positivity biases in evaluations of public figures.* Paper presented at the annual convention of the American Psychological Association.

Sears, R. R. (1972). Attachment, dependency, and frustration. In J. L. Gewirtz (Ed.), *Attachment and dependency.* Washington, DC: Winston.

Secord, D., & Peevers, B. (1974). The development and attribution of person concepts. In T. Mischel (Ed.), *Understanding other persons.* Oxford: Blackwell.

Secretary of Health, Education, and Welfare. (1980). *Marijuana and health.* Washington, DC: U.S. Government Printing Office.

Seeman, P., & Lee, T. (1975). Antipsychotic drugs: Direct correlation between clinical potency and presynaptic action on dopamine neurons. *Science, 188,* 1217–1219.

Segal, M., & Bloom, F. E. (1976). The action of norepinephrine in the rat hippocampus: III. Hippocampal cellular responses to locus coeruleus stimulation in the awake rat. *Brain Research, 107,* 499–511.

Segal, M. W. (1974). Alphabet and attraction: An unobtrusive measure of the effect of propinquity in a field setting. *Journal of Personality and Social Psychology, 30,* 654–657.

Segall, M. H., Campbell, D. T., & Herskovitz, M. J. (1963). Cultural differences in the perception of geometric illusions. *Science, 139,* 769–771.

Seidman, L. J. (1983). Schizophrenia and brain dysfunction: An integration of recent neurodiagnostic findings. *Psychological Bulletin, 94,* 195–238.

Seitz, V., Apfel, N. H., & Rosenbaum, L. (1981). Projects Head Start and Follow Through: A longitudinal evaluation of adolescents. In M. J. Begam, H. Garber, & H. C. Haywood (Eds.), *Prevention of retarded development in psychosocially disadvantaged children.* Baltimore: University Park Press.

Seligman, M. E. P. (1970). On the generality of the laws of learning. *Psychological Review, 77,* 406–418.

Seligman, M. E. P. (1971). Phobias and preparedness. *Behavior Therapy, 2,* 307–320.

Seligman, M. E. P. (1975). *Helplessness: On depression, development, and death.* San Francisco: W. H. Freeman.

Seligman, M. E. P., Klein, D. C., & Miller, W. R. (1976). Depression. In H. Leitenberg (Ed.), *Handbook of behavior modification and behavior therapy.* Englewood Cliffs, NJ: Prentice-Hall.

Seligman, M. E. P., & Maier, S. F. (1967). Failure to escape traumatic shock. *Journal of Experimental Psychology, 74,* 1–9.

Selman, R. L. (1980). *The growth of interpersonal understanding: Developmental and clinical analyses.* New York: Academic Press.

Selman, R. L. (1981). The child as a friendship philosopher. In S. R. Asher & J. M. Gottman (Eds.), *The development of children's friendships.* New York: Cambridge University Press.

Selman, R. L., Schorin, M. Z., Stone, C. R., & Phelps, E. (1983). A naturalistic study of children's social understanding. *Developmental Psychology, 19,* 82–102.

Selye, H. (1956). *The stress of life.* New York: McGraw-Hill.

Selye, H. (1976). *The stress of life* (2nd ed.). New York: McGraw-Hill.

Serber, M. (1972). Shame aversion therapy with and without heterosexual retraining. In R. D. Rubin, H. Fensterheim, J. D. Henderson, & L. P. Ullmann (Eds.), *Advances in behavior therapy.* New York: Academic Press.

Shaffer, L. H. (1975). Multiple attention in continuous verbal tasks. In S. Dornic (Ed.), *Attention and performance: Vol. V.* New York: Academic Press.

Shapiro, A. K., & Morris, L. A. (1978). Placebo effects in medical and psychological therapies. In S. L. Garfield & A. E. Bergin (Eds.), *Handbook of psychotherapy and behavior change* (2nd ed.). New York: Wiley.

Shapiro, D. A., & Shapiro, D. (1983). Comparative therapy outcome research: Methodological implications of meta-analysis. *Journal of Consulting and Clinical Psychology, 51,* 42–53.

Shapiro, D. H. (1980). *Meditation: Self regulation strategy and altered state of consciousness.* New York: Aldine.

Shapiro, D. H. (1984). Overview: Clinical and physiological comparison of meditation with other self-control strategies. In D. H. Shapiro & R. N. Walsh (Eds.), *Meditation: Classical and contemporary perspectives.* New York: Aldine.

Shapiro, D. H., & Giber, D. (1978). Meditation and psychotherapeutic effects: Self regulation strategy and altered states of consciousness. *Archives of General Psychiatry, 35,* 294–302.

Shapiro, D. H., & Walsh, R. N. (Eds.). (1984). *Meditation: Classical and contemporary perspectives.* New York: Aldine.

Shapiro, S., Skinner, E. A., Kessler, L. G., Von Korff, M., German, P. S., Tischler, G. L., Leaf, P. J., Beham, L., Cottler, L., & Legler, D. A. (1984). Utilization of health and mental health services. *Archives of General Psychiatry, 41,* 971–978.

Shaw, M. E. (1981). *Group dynamics: The psychology of small group behavior* (3rd ed.). New York: McGraw-Hill.

Shaw, M. E., Rothschild, G. H., & Strickland, J. F. (1957). Decision processes in communication nets. *Journal of Abnormal and Social Psychology, 54,* 323–330.

Shekelle, R. B., et. al. (1985). The MRFIT behavior pattern study: Type A behavior and the incidence of coronary heart disease. *American Journal of Epidemiology, 122,* 559–570.

Shepard, R. & Metzler, J. (1971). Mental rotation of three dimensional objects. *Science, 171,* 701–703.

Shepherd-Look, D. L. (1982). Sex differentiation and the development of sex roles. In B. B. Wolman & G. Stricker (Eds.), *Handbook of developmental psychology.* Englewood Cliffs, NJ: Prentice-Hall.

Sher, K. J., & Levenson, R. W. (1982). Risk for alcoholism and individual differences in the stress-response-dampening effects of alcohol. *Journal of Abnormal Psychology, 91,* 350–367.

Sherif, M. (1937). An experimental approach to the study of attitudes. *Sociometry, 1,* 90–98.

Sherwin, B. B., Gelfand, M. M., & Brender, W. (1985). Androgen enhances sexual motivation in females: A prospective crossover study of sex steroid administration in the surgical menopause. *Psychosomatic Medicine, 47,* 339–351.

Sherwin, R., & Sherry, C. (1985). Campus sexual norms and dating relationships: A trend analysis. *Journal of Sex Research, 21,* 258–274.

Shiffrin, R. M. (1973). Information persistence in short-term memory. *Journal of Experimental Psychology, 100,* 39–49.

Shneidman, E. S. (1973). Suicide. In *Encyclopedia Britannica.* Chicago: Encyclopedia Britannica.

Shneidman, E. S. (1985). *Definition of suicide.* New York: Harper & Row.

Shneidman, E. S. (1987, March). At the point of no return. *Psychology Today.*

Shor, R. E., & Orne, M. T. (1963). Norms on the Harvard group scale of hypnotic susceptibility, Form A. *International Journal of Clinical and Experimental Hypnosis, 11,* 39–47.

Shortliffe, E. H. (1983). Medical consultation systems: Designing for doctors. In M. E. Sime & M. J. Coombs (Eds.), *Designing for human computer communication*. New York: Academic Press.

Shrom, S. H., Lief, H. I., & Wein, A. J. (1979). Clinical profile of experience with 130 consecutive cases of impotent men. *Urology, 13*, 511–515.

Shugan, S. M. (1980). The cost of thinking. *Journal of Consumer Research, 7*, 99–111.

Siegel, L. S., McCabe, A. E., Brand, J., & Matthews, J. (1978). Evidence for the understanding of class inclusion in preschool children: Linguistic factors and training effects. *Child Development, 49*, 688–693.

Siegel, S. (1984). Pavlovian conditioning and heroin overdose: Reports by overdose victims. *Bulletin of the Psychonomic Society, 22*, 428–430.

Siegel, S., & Ellsworth, D. W. (1986). Pavlovian conditioning and death from apparent overdose of medically prescribed morphine: A case report. *Bulletin of the Psychonomic Society, 24*, 278–280.

Siegelman, M. (1974). Parental background of male homosexuals and heterosexuals. *Archives of Sexual Behavior, 3*, 3–18.

Siever, L. J., & Davis, K. L. (1985). Overview: Toward a dysregulation hypothesis of depression. *American Journal of Psychiatry, 142*, 1017–1031.

Sifneos, P. (1979). *Short-term dynamic psychotherapy: Evaluating and technique*. New York: Plenum Press.

Silver, R. L., & Wortman, C. B. (1980). Coping with undesirable life events. In J. Garber & M. E. P. Seligman (Eds.), *Human helplessness: Theory and applications* (pp. 279–340). New York: Academic Press.

Silverman, I. W., & Stone, J. M. (1972). Modifying cognitive functioning through participation in a problem solving group. *Journal of Educational Psychology, 63*, 603–608.

Silverman, L. H. (1976). Psychoanalytic theory: Reports of my death are greatly exaggerated. *American Psychologist, 31*, 621–637.

Silviera, J. M. (1971). *Incubation: The effect of interruption timing and length on problem solution and quality of problem processing*. Unpublished doctoral dissertation. University of Oregon, Eugene.

Sime, W. E. (1984). Psychological benefits of exercise training in the healthy individual. In J. D. Matarazzo, S. M. Weiss, J. A. Herd, N. Miller, & S. M. Weiss (Eds.), *Behavioral health: A handbook of health enhancement and disease prevention*. New York: Wiley.

Simmons, R. G., Rosenberg, F., & Rosenberg, M. (1973). Disturbance in the self-image at adolescence. *American Sociological Review, 38*, 553–568.

Simon, H. A. (1974). How big is a chunk? *Science, 183*, 482–488.

Simons, H. W., Berkowitz, N. N., & Moyer, R. J. (1970). Similarity, credibility and attitude change: A review and a theory. *Psychological Bulletin, 73*, 1–16.

Simonton, O. C., & Simonton, S. (1975). Belief systems and management of the emotional aspects of malignancy. *Journal of Transpersonal Psychology, 7*, 29–48.

Singer, J. (1976). *The inner world of daydreaming*. New York: Harper & Row.

Singer, J. L., & Singer, D. G. (1981). *Television, imagination, and aggression*. Hillsdale, NJ: Lawrence Erlbaum Associates.

Sizemore, C. C., & Pittillo, E. S. (1970). *I'm Eve*. New York: Doubleday.

Skeels, H. M. (1938). Mental development in children in foster homes. *Journal of Consulting Psychology, 2*, 33–43.

Skeels, H. M. (1966). Adult status of children with contrasting early life experiences. *Monographs of the Society for Research in Child Development, 31*(3, Serial No. 105).

Skinner, B. F. (1950). Are theories of learning necessary? *Psychological Review, 57*, 193–216.

Skinner, B. F. (1953). *Science and human behavior*. New York: Macmillan.

Skinner, B. F. (1961). *Cumulative record* (3rd ed.). Englewood Cliffs, NJ: Prentice-Hall.

Skodak, M., & Skeels, H. M. (1949). A final follow up study of one hundred adopted children. *Journal of Genetic Psychology, 75*, 85–125.

Slaby, R. G., & Frey, K. S. (1975). Development of gender constancy and selective attention to same-sex models. *Child Development, 46*, 849–856.

Slamecka, N. J., & McElree, B. (1983). Normal forgetting of verbal lists as a function of their degree of learning. *Journal of Experimental Psychology: Learning, Memory, and Cognition, 9*, 384–397.

Slater, J., & Depue, R. A. (1981). The contribution of environmental events and social support to serious suicide attempts in primary depressive disorder. *Journal of Abnormal Psychology, 90*, 17–35.

Sloane, R. B., Staples, F. R., Cristol, A. H., Yorkston, N. J., & Whipple, K. (1975). *Psychotherapy versus behavior therapy*. Cambridge: Harvard University Press.

Slovic, P. (1984). *Facts versus fears: Understanding perceived risk*. In science and public policy seminar sponsored by the Federation of Behavioral and Psychological and Cognitive Sciences, Washington, DC.

Smith, D. (1982). Trends in counseling and psychotherapy. *American Psychologist, 37*, 802–809.

Smith, E. E., Adams, N., & Schorr, D. (1978). Fact retrieval and the paradox of interference. *Cognitive Psychology, 10*, 438–464.

Smith, E. E., Shoben, E. J., & Rips, L. R. (1974). Structure and process in semantic memory: A featural model for semantic decisions. *Psychological Review, 81*, 214–241.

Smith, G. F., & Dorfman, D. D. (1975). The effect of stimulus uncertainty on the relationship between frequency of exposure and liking. *Journal of Personality and Social Psychology, 31*, 150–155.

Smith, J. C. (1975). Meditation as psychotherapy: A review of the literature. *Psychological Bulletin, 82*, 558–564.

Smith, J. M., & Smith, D. E. P. (1976). *Child management*. Champaign, IL: Research Press.

Smith, M. L., Glass, G. V., & Miller, T. I. (1980). *The benefits of psychotherapy*. Baltimore, MD: Johns Hopkins University Press.

Smith, P. K., & Connolly, K. (1972). Patterns of play and social interaction in preschool children. In N. Blurton Jones (Ed.), *Ethological studies of child behaviour*. Cambridge: Cambridge University Press.

Smith, R. C., Calderon, M., Baumgartner, R., Ravichandran, G. K., & Schoolar, J. C. (1984). NMR studies of schizophrenia. *Society for Neuroscience Abstracts, 10*, 814.

Smith, S., & Freedman, D. G. (1983, April). *Mother-toddler interaction and maternal perception of child temperament in two ethnic groups: Chinese-American and European-American*. Paper presented at the meeting of the Society for Research in Child Development, Detroit, MI.

Smith, S. M., Brown, H. O., Toman, J. E. P., & Goodman, L. S. (1947). The lack of cerebral effects of d-tubocurarine. *Anesthesiology, 8*, 1–14.

Smith, S. M., Glenberg, A. M., & Bjork, R. A. (1978). Environmental context and human memory. *Memory and Cognition, 6*, 342–355.

Smith, W. P., & Anderson, A. J. (1975). Threats, communication and bargaining. *Journal of Personality and Social Psychology, 32*, 76–82.

Snow, R. E., & Yallow, E. (1982). Education and intelligence. In R. Sternberg (Ed.), *Handbook of human intelligence*. Cambridge: Cambridge University Press.

Snowdon, C. T. (1969). Motivation, regulation, and the control of meal parameters with oral and intragastric feeding. *Journal of Comparative and Physiological Psychology, 69*, 91–100.

Snyder, M. (1981). Seek, and ye shall find: Testing hypotheses about other people. In E. T. Higgins, C. P. Herman, & M. P. Zanna (Eds.), *Social cognition: The Ontario symposium*. Hillsdale, NJ: Lawrence Erlbaum Associates.

Snyder, M., & Gangestad, S. (1981). Hypothesis-testing processes. In J. H. Harvey, W. Ickes, & R. F. Kidd (Eds.), *New directions in attribution research: Vol. 3.* Hillsdale, NJ: Lawrence Erlbaum Associates.

Snyder, M., Tanke, E. D., & Berscheid, E. (1977). Social perception and interpersonal behavior: On the self-fulfilling nature of social stereotypes. *Journal of Personality and Social Psychology, 35,* 656–666.

Snyder, S. H. (1978). Dopamine and schizophrenia. In L. C. Wynne, R. L. Cromwell, & S. Matthysse (Eds.), *The nature of schizophrenia: New approaches to research and treatment* (pp. 87–94). New York: Wiley.

Snyder, S. H., & Childers, S. R. (1979). Opiate receptors and opiod peptides. *Annual Review of Neuroscience, 2,* 35–64.

Solomon, R. L. (1980). The opponent-process theory of acquired motivation: The costs of pleasure and the benefits of pain. *American Psychologist, 35,* 691–712.

Solomon, R. L., & Corbit, J. D. (1974). An opponent-process theory of motivation: I. Temporal dynamics of affect. *Psychological Review, 81,* 119–145.

Solomon, R. L., Kamin, L. J., & Wynne, L. C. (1953). Traumatic avoidance learning: The outcomes of several extinction procedures with dogs. *Journal of Abnormal and Social Psychology, 48,* 291–302.

Solso, R. L. (1979). *Cognitive psychology.* New York: Harcourt Brace Jovanovich.

Sorce, J., Emde, R., Campos, J., & Klinnert, M. (1981, April). *Maternal emotional signaling: Its effect on the visual cliff behavior of one-year-olds.* Paper presented at the meetings of the Society for Research in Child Development, Boston, MA.

Sorce, J., Emde, R., & Frank, M. (1982). Maternal referencing in normal and Down's syndrome infants: A longitudinal study. In R. Emde & R. Harmon (Eds.), *The development of attachment and affiliative systems.* New York: Plenum Press.

Sorrells-Jones, J. (1983). *A comparison of the effects of Leboyer delivery and modern "routine" childbirth in a randomized sample.* Unpublished doctoral dissertation, University of Chicago, Chicago IL.

Spanos, N. P., & Bodorik, H. L. (1977). Suggested amnesia and disorganized recall in hypnotic and task-motivated subjects. *Journal of Abnormal Psychology, 86,* 295–305.

Spanos, N. P., Gwynn, M. L., & Stam, H. J. (1983). Instructional demands and ratings of overt and hidden pain during hypnotic analgesia. *Journal of Abnormal Psychology, 92,* 479–488.

Spanos, N. P., & Hewitt, E. C. (1980). The hidden observer in hypnotic analgesia: Discovery or experimental creation? *Journal of Personality and Social Psychology, 39,* 1201–1214.

Spanos, N. P., Radtke, H. L., & Bertrand, L. D. (1985). Hypnotic amnesia as a strategic enactment: Breaching amnesia in highly susceptible subjects. *Journal of Personality and Social Psychology, 47,* 1155–1169.

Spark, R. F., White, R. A., & Connolly, P. B. (1980). Impotence is not always psychogenic: Newer insights into hypothalamic-pituitary-gonadal dysfunction. *Journal of the American Medical Association, 243,* 750–755.

Spearman, C. (1927). *The abilities of man.* London: Macmillan.

Spelt, D. K. (1948). The conditioning of the human fetus in utero. *Journal of Experimental Psychology, 38,* 338–346.

Speltz, M. L., & Bernstein, D. A. (1979). The use of participant modeling for claustrophobia: A case report. *Journal of Behavior Therapy and Experimental Psychiatry, 10,* 251–255.

Spence, M. J., & DeCasper, A. J. (1982, March). *Human fetuses perceive maternal speech.* Paper presented at the meeting of the International Conference on Infant Studies, Austin, TX.

Sperling, G. (1960). The information available in brief visual presentations. *Psychological Monographs, 74,* 1–29.

Sperry, R. W. (1968). Hemisphere deconnection and unity in conscious awareness. *American Psychologist, 23,* 723–733.

Sperry, R. W. (1974). Lateral specialization in the surgically separated hemispheres. In F. O. Schmitt & F. G. Wordon (Eds.), *The neurosciences third study program.* Cambridge: MIT Press.

Spiegel, D., Cutcomb, S., Ren, C., & Pribram, K. (1985). Hypnotic hallucination alters evoked potentials. *Journal of Abnormal Psychology, 94,* 249–255.

Spiegler, M. D. (1983). *Contemporary behavioral therapy.* Palo Alto, CA: Mayfield.

Spielberger, C. (1979). *Understanding stress and anxiety.* New York: Harper & Row.

Spitzer, R. L., Forman, J. B. W., & Nee, J. (1979). DSM-III field trials: I. Initial interrater diagnostic reliability. *American Journal of Psychiatry, 136,* 815–817.

Spitzer, R. L., Skodol, A. E., Gibbon, M., & Williams, J. B. W. (1983). *Psychopathology: A casebook.* New York: McGraw-Hill.

Spring, B., Maller, W., Wurtman, J., Digman, L., & Cozolino, L. (1982–1983). Effects of protein and carbohydrate meals on mood and performance: Interactions with sex and age. *Journal of Psychiatric Research, 17,* 155–167.

Springer, S. P., & Deutsch, G. (1985). *Left brain, right brain.* San Francisco: W. H. Freeman.

Squire, L. R. (1986). Mechanisms of memory. *Science, 232,* 1612–1619.

Squires, K. C., Donchin, E., Herning, R. I., & McCarthy, G. (1977). On the influence of task relevance and stimulus probability on event-related-potential components. *Electroencephalography and Clinical Neurophysiology, 42,* 1–14.

Srull, T. K., & Gaelick, L. (1983). General principles and individual differences in the self as a habitual reference point: An examination of self-other judgements of similarity. *Social Cognition, 2,* 108–121.

Srull, T. K., & Wyer, R. S. (1980). Category accessibility and social perception: Some implications for the study of person memory and interpersonal judgement. *Journal of Personality and Social Psychology, 38,* 841–856.

Srull, T. K., & Wyer, R. S. (1983). The role of control processes and structural constraints in models of memory and social judgement. *Journal of Experimental Social Psychology, 19,* 497–521.

Srull, T. K., & Wyer, R. S. (1986). The role of chronic and temporary goals in social information processing. In R. M. Sorrentino & E. T. Higgins (Eds.), *Handbook of motivation and cognition.* New York: Guilford Press.

Standing, L., Conezio, J., & Haber, R. N. (1970). Perception and memory for pictures: Single-trial learning of 2500 visual stimuli. *Psychonomic Science, 19,* 73–74.

Stang, D. J. (1972). Conformity, ability and self-esteem. *Representative Research in Social Psychology, 3,* 97–103.

Stankov, L. (1983). Attention and intelligence. *Journal of Educational Psychology, 75,* 471–490.

Stanley, G., & Hall, R. (1973). Short term visual information processing in dyslexics. *Child Development, 44,* 841–844.

Starr, A., Amlie, R. N., Martin, W. H., & Saunders, S. (1977). Development of auditory function in newborn infants revealed by auditory brainstem potentials. *Pediatrics, 60,* 831–839.

Steele, C. M. (1986, January). What happens when you drink too much? *Psychology Today.*

Steers, R. M., & Porter, L. W. (1979). *Motivation and work behavior* (2nd ed.). New York: McGraw-Hill.

Steggerda, F. R. (1941). Observations on the water intake in an adult man with dysfunctioning salivary glands. *American Journal of Physiology, 132,* 517–521.

Stein, A. H. (1967). Imitation of resistance to temptation. *Child Development, 38,* 157–169.

Stephens, J. H., & Kamp, M. (1962). On some aspects of hysteria: A clinical study. *Journal of Nervous and Mental Disease, 134,* 305–315.

Stern, R. (1983). Antidepressant drugs in the treatment of obsessive-compulsive disorders. *Journal of Behavior Therapy and Experimental Psychiatry, 14,* 19–23.

Sternberg, R. J. (1977). *Intelligence, information processing and analogical reasoning: The componential analysis of human abilities.* Hillsdale, NJ: Lawrence Erlbaum Associates.

Sternberg, R. J. (1982). Reasoning, problem solving and intelligence. In R. J. Sternberg (Ed.), *Handbook of human intelligence.* Cambridge: Cambridge University Press.

Sternberg, R. J. (1984). Toward a triarchical theory of human intelligence. *Brain and Behavioral Sciences, 7,* 269–315.

Sternberg, R. J. (1985). *Beyond IQ: A triarchical theory of human intelligence.* New York: Cambridge University Press.

Sternberg, R. J., & Barnes, M. (1985). Real and ideal others in romantic relationships: Is four a crowd? *Journal of Personality and Social Psychology, 49,* 1586–1608.

Sternberg, R. J., & Detterman, D. (1986). *What is intelligence?* Norwood, NJ: Ablex.

Sternberg, R. J., & Grajek, S. (1984). The nature of love. *Journal of Personality and Social Psychology, 47,* 312–329.

Sternberg, S. (1966). High-speed scanning in human memory. *Science, 153,* 652–654.

Sternberg, S. (1969). Mental processes revealed by reaction time experiments. *American Scientist, 57,* 421–457.

Sternglanz, S. H., & Serbin, L. A. (1974). Sex-role stereotyping in children's television programs. *Developmental Psychology, 10,* 710–715.

Stevens, A., & Coupe, P. (1978). Distortions in judged spatial relations. *Cognitive Psychology, 10,* 422–437.

Stevens, J. C., (1984, June). Perception and psychophysics. *Time.*

Stevens, S. S. (1957). On the psychophysical law. *Psychological Review, 64,* 153–181.

Stewart, A. L., & Brook, R. H. (1983). Effects of being overweight. *American Journal of Public Health, 73,* 171–178.

Stigler, J. W. (1984). "Mental abacus": The effect of abacus training on Chinese children's mental calculation. *Cognitive Psychology, 16,* 145–176.

Stiles, W. B., Shapiro, D. A., & Elliott, R. (1986). "Are all psychotherapies equivalent?" *American Psychologist, 41,* 165–180.

Stokes, J. P. (1983). Predicting satisfaction with social support from social network structure. *American Journal of Community Psychology, 11,* 141-152.

Stokes, J. P. (1985). The relation of social network and individual difference variables to loneliness. *Journal of Personality and Social Psychology, 48,* 981–990.

Stokols, D. (1983). *Scientific and policy challenges of a contextually–oriented psychology.* Paper presented at the annual convention of the American Psychological Association.

Stokols, D., & Novaco, R. W. (1980). Transportation and well-being: An ecological perspective. In I. Altman, J. Wohlwill, & P. Everett (Eds.), *Human behavior and environment: Vol. 5.* New York: Plenum Press.

Stone, A. R., Frank, J. D., Nash, E. H., & Imber, S. D. (1961). An intensive five-year follow-up study of treated psychiatric outpatients. *Journal of Nervous and Mental Disease, 133,* 410–422.

Strayer, D. L., Wickens, C. D., & Braune, R. (1987). Adult age differences in the speed and capacity of information processing: 2. An electrophysiological approach. *Psychology and Aging, 2,* 99–110.

Stretch, J. D. (1985). Posttraumatic stress disorder among U.S. Army Reserve Vietnam and Vietnam-era veterans. *Journal of Consulting and Clinical Psychology, 53,* 935.

Streufert, S. (1986). *Complexity, managers and organizations.* Orlando, FL: Academic Press.

Strickland, B. R. (1978). Internal-external expectancies and health-related behaviors. *Journal of Consulting and Clinical Psychology, 46,* 1192–1211.

Stroop, J. R. (1935). Studies of interference in serial verbal reactions. *Journal of Experimental Psychology, 18,* 643–662.

Strube, M. J., Gardner, W., & Hartmann, D. P. (1985). Limitations, liabilities, and obstacles in reviews of the literature: The current status of meta-analysis. *Clinical Psychology Review, 5,* 63–78.

Strupp, A. R., & Bloxom, A. (1973). Preparing lower-class patients for group psychotherapy: Development and evaluation of a role induction film. *Journal of Consulting and Clinical Psychology, 41,* 373–384.

Strupp, H. H., Sandell, J. A., Waterhouse, G. J., O'Malley, S. S., Anderson, J. L. (1982). Short term dynamic therapies for depression: Theory and research. In A. John Ruch (Ed.), *Short term psychotherapies for the depressed patient* (pp. 215–250). New York: Guilford Press.

Suberi, M., & McKeever, W. F. (1977). Differential right hemispheric memory storage of emotional and non-emotional faces. *Neuropsychologia, 15,* 757–768.

Sue, D. (1979). Erotic fantasies of college students during coitus. *Journal of Sex Research, 15,* 299–305.

Suedfeld, P. (1980). *Restricted environmental stimulation: Research and clinical applications.* New York: Wiley.

Suedfeld, P., Roy, C., & Landon, P. B. (1982). Restricted environmental stimulation therapy in the treatment of essential hypertension. *Behaviour Research and Therapy, 20,* 553–560.

Suggs, D., & Sales, B. D. (1978). The art and science of conducting voir dire. *Professional Psychology, 9,* 367–388.

Suggs, D., & Sales, B. D. (1979). Using communication cues to evaluate prospective jurors during voir dire. *Arizona Law Review, 20,* 629–642.

Suinn, R. M. (1982). Intervention with Type A behaviors. *Journal of Consulting and Clinical Psychology, 50,* 6.

Sulin, R. A., & Dooling, D. J. (1974). Intrusion of a thematic idea in retention of prose. *Journal of Experimental Psychology, 103,* 255–262.

Sullivan, H. S. (1953). *The interpersonal theory of psychiatry.* New York: W. W. Norton.

Sullivan, H. S. (1954). *The psychiatric interview.* New York: W. W. Norton.

Sullivan, J. W., & Horowitz, F. D. (1983). The effects of intonation on infant attention: The role of the rising intonation contour. *Journal of Child Language, 10,* 521–534.

Suls, J., & Miller, R. L. (Eds.). (1977). *Social comparison processes.* Washington, DC: Hemisphere.

Suls, J., & Mullen, B. (1981, June). Life events, perceived control, and illness: The role of uncertainty. *Journal of Human Stress,* pp. 30–34.

Svejda, M., Pannabecker, B., & Emde, R. N. (1982). Parent-to-infant attachment: A critique of the early "bonding" model. In R. N. Emde & R. J. Harmon (Eds.), *The development of attachment and affiliative systems: Psychological aspects.* New York: Plenum Press.

Swann, W. B. (1984). Quest for accuracy in person perception: A matter of pragmatics. *Psychological Review, 91,* 457–477.

Swanson, L. W. (1976). The locus coeruleus: A cytoarchitectonic, Golgi, and immunohistochemical study in the albino rat. *Brain Research, 110,* 39–56.

Sweeney, P. D., Shaeffer, D. E., & Golin, S. (1982). Pleasant events, unpleasant events, and depression. *Journal of Personality and Social Psychology, 43,* 136–144.

Sweller, J., & Gee, W. (1978). Einstellung: The sequence effect and hypothesis theory. *Journal of Experimental Psychology: Human Learning and Memory, 4,* 513–526.

Symington, T., Currie, A. R., Curran, R. S., & Davidson, J. N. (1955). The reaction of the adrenal cortex in conditions of stress. In *Ciba Foundations Colloquia on Endocrinology: Vol. 8.* Boston: Little, Brown.

Szasz, T. S. (1960). The myth of mental illness. *American Psychologist, 15,* 113–118.

Szilagyi, A. D., & Wallace, M. J. (1980). *Organizational behavior and performance.* Santa Monica, CA: Goodyear.

Tanck, R. H., & Robbins, P. R. (1979). Assertiveness, locus of control, and coping behaviours used to diminish tension. *Journal of Personality Assessment, 43,* 396–400.

Tarler-Benlolo, L. (1978). The role of relaxation in biofeedback training: A critical review of the literature. *Psychological Bulletin, 85,* 727–755.

Tarpy, R. M., & Sawabini, F. L. (1974). Reinforcement delay: A selective review of the last decade. *Psychological Bulletin, 81,* 984–987.

Tart, C. T. (1969). *Altered states of consciousness: A book of readings.* New York: Wiley.

Tavris, C. (1984). On the wisdom of counting to ten: Personal and social dangers of anger expression. In P. Shaver (Ed.), *Review of personality and social psychology: Vol. 5.* Beverly Hills, CA: Sage.

Taylor, D. M., & Jaggi, V. (1974). Ethnocentrism and causal attribution in a South Indian context. *Journal of Cross-Cultural Psychology, 5,* 162–171.

Taylor, G. R. (1981). *The natural history of the mind.* New York: Penguin.

Taylor, S. E., & Crocker, J. (1981). Schematic bases of social information processing. In E. T. Higgins, C. P. Herman, & M. P. Zanna (Eds.), *Social cognition: The Ontario symposium.* Hillsdale, NJ: Lawrence Erlbaum Associates.

Taylor, S. E., & Fiske, S. T. (1978). Salience, attention, and attribution: Top of the head phenomena. In L. Berkowitz (Ed.), *Advances in experimental social psychology: Vol. 11.* New York: Academic Press.

Taylor, S. E., & Koivumaki, J. H. (1976). The perception of self and others: Acquaintanceship, affect, and actor-observer differences. *Journal of Personality and Social Psychology, 33,* 403–408.

Teasdale, J. (1983). Negative thinking in depression: Cause, effect, or reciprocal relationship? *Advances in Behaviour Research and Therapy, 5,* 3–25.

Tecoma, E. S., & Huey, L. Y. (1985). Psychic distress and the immune response. *Life Sciences, 36,* 1799–1812.

Teitelbaum, P. (1957). Random and food-directed activity in hyperphagic and normal rats. *Journal of Comparative and Physiological Psychology, 50,* 486–490.

Teitelbaum, P. (1961). Disturbances in feeding and drinking behavior after hypothalamic lesions. In M. R. Jones (Ed.), *Nebraska symposium on motivation.* Lincoln: University of Nebraska Press.

Tellegen, A., Lykken, D. T., Bouchard, T. J., Jr., Wilcox, K., Segal, N., & Rich, S. (in press). Personality similarity in twins reared apart and together. *Journal of Personality and Social Psychology.*

Tellegen, A., & Atkinson, G. (1974). Openness to absorbing and self-altering experiences ("absorption"), a trait related to hypnosis. *Journal of Abnormal Psychology, 83,* 268–277.

Terestman, N., Miller, J., & Webber, J. (1974). Blue-collar patients at a psychoanalytic clinic. *American Journal of Psychiatry, 131,* 261–266.

Terkel, J., & Rosenblatt, J. S. (1972). Humoral factors underlying maternal behavior of parturition: Cross transfusion between freely moving rats. *Journal of Comparative and Physiological Psychology, 80,* 365–371.

Terman, L. M. (1916). *The measurement of intelligence.* Boston: Houghton Mifflin.

Terman, L. M. (1948). Kinsey's "Sexual behavior in the human male": Some comments and criticisms. *Psychological Bulletin, 45,* 443–459.

Terman, L. M., & Oden, M. H. (1947). *The gifted child grows up: Volume 4. Genetic studies of genius.* Stanford, CA: Stanford University Press.

Terman, L. M., & Oden, M. (1959). *The gifted group at midlife.* Stanford, CA: Stanford University Press.

Terrace, et al. (1979)

Thoits, P. A. (1986). Social support as coping assistance. *Journal of Personality and Social Psychology, 54,* 416–423.

Thomae, H. (1980). Personality and adjustment to aging. In J. E. Birren & R. B. Sloane (Eds.), *Handbook of mental health and aging.* Englewood Cliffs, NJ: Prentice-Hall.

Thomas, A., & Chess, S. (1977). *Temperament and development.* New York: Brunner/Mazel.

Thomas, A., Chess, S., & Korn, S. J. (1982). The reality of difficult temperament. *Merrill-Palmer Quarterly, 28,* 1–20.

Thomas, E. L., & Robinson, H. A. (1972). *Improving reading in every class: A sourcebook for teachers.* Boston: Allyn & Bacon.

Thompson, C. P., & Cowan, T. (1986). Flashbulb memories: A nicer interpretation of a Neisser recollection. *Cognition, 22,* 199–200.

Thompson, R. A., & Lamb, M. E. (1983). Security of attachment and stranger sociability in infancy. *Developmental Psychology, 19,* 184–191.

Thompson, R. F. (1986). The neurobiology of learning and memory. *Science, 233,* 941–947.

Thompson, S. K. (1975). Gender labels and early sex role development. *Child Development, 46,* 339–347.

Thompson, T., & Grabowski, J. (Eds.). (1972). *Behavior modification of the mentally retarded.* New York: Oxford University Press.

Thorndike, E. L. (1898). Animal intelligence: An experimental study of the associative processes in animals. *Psychological Monographs, 2*(Whole No. 8).

Thorndike, R. L., Hagan, E., & Sattler, J. (1986). *Stanford-Binet* (4th ed.). Chicago: Riverside.

Thorne, F. C. (1950). *Principles of personality counseling.* Brandon, VT: Journal of Clinical Psychology.

Tinbergen, N. (1953). *The study of instinct.* New York: Oxford University Press.

Tolman, E. C., & Honzik, C. H. (1930). Introduction and removal of reward and maze performance in rats. *University of California Publication in Psychology, 4,* 257–275.

Trabasso, T., & Bower, G. H. (1968). *Attention in learning.* New York: Wiley.

Tracor, Inc. (1971). *Community reaction to aircraft noise: Vol. 1* (NASA Report CR-1761). Washington, DC: National Aeronautics and Space Administration.

Tranel, D., & Damasio, A. R. (1985). Knowledge without awareness: An autonomic index of facial recognition by prosopagnosics. *Science, 228,* 1453–1454.

Travis, L. E. (1925). The effect of a small audience upon eye hand coordination. *Journal of Abnormal and Social Psychology, 20,* 142–146.

Trevarthen, C. (1977). Descriptive analyses of infant communicative behavior. In H. R. Schaffer (Ed.), *Studies in mother-infant interaction.* London: Academic Press.

Triplett, N. (1897). The dynamogenic factors in pacemaking and competition. *American Journal of Psychology, 9,* 507–533.

Trujillo, C. M. (1986). A comparative evaluation of classroom interactions between professors and minority and non-minority college students. *American Educational Research Journal, 23,* 629–642.

Tudiver, J. (1979). *Parental influences on the sex role development of the preschool child.* Unpublished manuscript, University of Western Ontario, London, Ontario.

Tulving, E. (1972). Episodic and semantic memory. In E. Tulving & W. Donaldson (Eds.), *Organization of memory.* New York: Academic Press.

Tulving, E. (1974). Cue-dependent forgetting. *American Scientist, 62,* 74–82.

Tulving, E. (1979). Relation between encoding specificity and levels of processing. In L. S. Cermak & F. I. M. Craik (Eds.), *Levels of processing in human memory.* Hillsdale, NJ: Lawrence Erlbaum Associates.

Tulving, E. (1982). *Elements of episodic memory.* New York: Oxford University Press.

Tulving, E. (1985). How many memory systems are there? *American Psychologist, 40,* 385–398.

Tulving, E., & Psotka, J. (1971). Retroactive inhibition in free recall: Inaccessibility of information available in the memory store. *Journal of Experimental Psychology, 87,* 1–8.

Tulving, E., & Thomson, D. M. (1973). Encoding specificity and retrieval processes in episodic memory. *Psychological Review, 80,* 352–373.

Turek, F. W., & Losee-Olson, S. (1986). Benzodiazepine used in the treatment of insomnia phase-shifts the mammalian circadian clock. *Nature, 321,* 167–168.

Turk, D. C. (1978). Cognitive behavioral techniques in the management of pain. In P. J. Foreyt & D. P. Pathjen (Eds.), *Cognitive behavior therapy: Research and applications.* New York: Plenum Press.

Turkington, C. (1984, April). Parents found to ignore sex stereotypes. *APA Monitor,* p. 12.

Turner, A. M., & Greenough, W. T. (1985). Differential rearing effects on rat visual cortex synapses: I. Synaptic and neuronal density and synapses per neuron. *Brain Research, 329,* 195–203.

Turnure, C. (1971). Response to voice of mother and stranger by babies in the first year. *Developmental Psychology, 4,* 182–190.

Tversky, A. (1977). Elimination by aspects: A theory of choice. *Psychological Review, 79,* 281–299.

Tversky, A., & Kahneman, D. (1974). Judgment under uncertainty: Heuristics and biases. *Science, 185,* 1124–1131.

Tversky, A., & Kahneman, D. (1981). The framing of decisions and the psychology of choice. *Science, 211,* 453–458.

Ullmann, L., & Krasner, L. (1969). *A psychological approach to abnormal behavior.* Englewood Cliffs, NJ: Prentice-Hall.

Ullmann, L., & Krasner, L. (1975). *A psychological approach to abnormal behavior* (2nd ed.). Englewood Cliffs, NJ: Prentice-Hall.

Ulrich, R. E., Stachnik, T. J., & Stainton, N. R. (1963). Student acceptance of generalized personality interpretations. *Psychological Reports, 13,* 831–834.

U. S. Congress. (1983). Scientific validity of polygraph testing: A research review and evaluation (Technical Memorandum OTA-TM-H-15). Washington, DC: U. S. Congress, Office of Technology Assessment.

U. S. Department of Commerce. (1986). *Statistical Abstract* (106th ed.). Washington, DC: U. S. Government Printing Office.

Vaillant, G. E. (1977). *Adaptation to life: How the best and brightest came of age.* Boston: Little, Brown.

Valenstein, E. S. (Ed.). (1980). *The psychosurgery debate.* San Francisco: W. H. Freeman.

Van Buskirk, R. L., & Erickson, R. P. (1977). Odorant responses in taste neurons of the rat NTS. *Brain Research, 135,* 287–303.

Vander Zanden, J. W. (1981). *Human development* (2nd ed.). New York: Knopf.

Vane, J. (1972). Intelligence and achievement test results of kindergarten children in England, Ireland and the United States. *Journal of Clinical Psychology, 29,* 191–193.

Vaughn, B., Joffe, L., Egeland, B., Dienard, A., & Waters, E. (1979, March). *Relationships between neonatal behavioral organization and infant-mother attachment in an economically disadvantaged sample.* Paper presented at the meeting of the Society for Research in Child Development, San Francisco, CA.

Venn, J. R., & Short, J. G. (1973). Vicarious classical conditioning of emotional responses in nursery school children. *Journal of Personality and Social Psychology, 28,* 249–255.

Vernon, P. A. (1983). Speed of information processing and general intelligence. *Intelligence, 7,* 53–70.

Vokey, J. R., & Read, J. D. (1985). Subliminal messages: Between the devil and the media. *American Psychologist, 40,* 1231–1239.

Volkmar, F. R., & Greenough, W. T. (1972). Rearing complexity affects branching of dendrites in the visual cortex of the rat. *Science, 176,* 1445–1447.

Von Wright, J. M., Anderson, K., & Stenman, U. (1975). Generalization of conditioned GSRs in dichotic listening.

Vuchinich, R. E., & Sobell, M. B. (1978). Empirical separation of physiological and expected effects of alcohol on complex perceptual motor performance. *Psychopharmacology, 60,* 81–85.

Vuchinich, R. E., Tucker, J. A., & Sobell, M. B. (1979). Alcohol, expectancy, cognitive labeling, and mirth. *Journal of Abnormal Psychology, 88,* 641–651.

Wachs, T. D., & Gruen, C. E. (1982). *Early experience and human development.* New York: Plenum Press.

Wachtel, P. L. (1967). Conceptions of broad and narrow attention. *Psychological Bulletin, 68,* 417–419.

Wachtel, P. L. (1977). *Psychoanalysis and behavior therapy.* New York: Basic Books.

Wachtel, P. L. (1982). *Psychoanalysis and behavior therapy.* New York: Basic Books.

Wagner, H. L., MacDonald, C. J., & Manstead, A. S. R. (1986). Communication of individual emotions by spontaneous facial expressions. *Journal of Personality and Social Psychology, 50,* 737–743.

Waid, W. M., & Orne, M. T. (1981). Cognitive, social, and personality processes in the physiological detection of deception. In L. Berkowitz (Ed.), *Advances in experimental social psychology: Vol. 14.* New York: Academic Press.

Waldrop, M. M. (1984). Computer vision. *Science, 224,* 1225–1227.

Wall, P. D., & Cronly-Dillon, J. R. (1960). Pain, itch and vibration. *AMA Archives of Neurology, 2,* 365–375.

Wallace, R. K., & Benson, H. (1972). The physiology of meditation. *Scientific American, 226,* 84–90.

Wallander, J. L., & Hubert, N. C. (1985). Long-term prognosis for children with attention deficit disorder with hyperactivity (ADD/H). In B. B. Lahey & A. E. Kazdin (Eds.), *Advances in child clinical psychology: Vol. 8.* New York: Plenum Press.

Walster, E., Aronson, V., Abrahams, D., & Rottman, L. (1966). Importance of physical attractiveness in dating behavior. *Journal of Personality and Social Psychology, 4,* 508–516.

Walster, E., & Festinger, L. (1962). The effectiveness of "overheard" persuasive communications. *Journal of Abnormal and Social Psychology, 65,* 395–402.

Walster, E., & Walster, G. W. (1978). *Love.* Reading, MA: Addison-Wesley.

Wandersman, A., Poppen, P., & Ricks, D. (1976). *Humanism and behaviorism: Dialogue and growth.* New York: Pergamon Press.

Ward, C. H., Beck, A. T., Mendelson, M., Mock, J. E., & Erbaugh, J. K. (1962). The psychiatric nomenclature: Reasons for diagnostic disagreement. *Archives of General Psychiatry, 7,* 645–650.

Ward, W. D. (1974). *Proceedings of the international congress on noise as a public health problem.* Washington, DC: U. S. Government Printing Office.

Warden, C. J. (1931). *Animal motivation: Experimental studies on the albino rat.* New York: Columbia University Press.

Warm, J. S. (Ed.). (1984). *Sustained attention in human performance.* London: Wiley.

Warner, R. A., & Sugarman, D. B. (1986). Attributions of personality based on physical appearance, speech, and handwriting. *Journal of Personality and Social Psychology, 50,* 792–799.

Waterman, A. S. (1982). Identity development from adolescence to adulthood: An extension of theory and a review of research. *Developmental Psychology, 18,* 341–358.

Waterman, G., Geary, P., & Waterman, C. (1974). Longitudinal study of changes in ego identity status from the freshman to the senior year at college. *Developmental Psychology, 10,* 387–392.

Waters, E., Wippman, J., & Sroufe, L. A. (1979). Attachment, positive affect, and competence in the peer group: Two studies in construct validation. *Child Development, 50,* 821–829.

Watkins, L. R., & Mayer, D. J. (1982). Organization of endogenous opiate and nonopiate pain control systems. *Science, 216,* 1185–1192.

Watson, D. (1976). *Molecular biology of the gene* (3rd ed.). Menlo Park, CA: Benjamin Cummings.

Watson, J. B. (1924). *Behaviorism.* New York: W. W. Norton.

Watson, J. B. (1930). *Behaviorism* (rev. ed.). New York: Norton.

Watson, J. B., & Rayner, R. (1920). Conditioned emotional reactions. *Journal of Experimental Psychology, 3,* 1–14.

Watson, M. W. (1981). The devlopment of social roles: A sequence of social-cognitive development. *New Directions for Child Development, 12,* 33–41.

Webb, W. B. (1968). *Sleep: An experimental approach.* New York: Macmillan.

Webb, W. B. (1975). *Sleep: The gentle tyrant.* Englewood Cliffs, NJ: Prentice-Hall.

Wechsler, D. (1949). *The Wechsler Intelligence Scale for children.* New York: Psychological Corporation.

Wechsler, D. (1975). Intelligence defined and undefined: A relativistic appraisal. *American Psychologist, 30,* 136–139.

Wehr, T. A., Sack, D., Rosenthal, N., Duncan, W., & Gillian, J. C. (1983). Circadian rhythm disturbances in manic-depressive illness. *Federation Prac., 42,* 2809–2814.

Weinberger, D. A., Schwartz, G. E., & Davidson, R. J. (1979). Low anxious, high anxious and repressive coping styles: Psychometric patterns and behavioral and physiological responses to stress. *Journal of Abnormal Psychology, 88,* 369–380.

Weiner, B. (1972). *Theories of motivation.* Chicago: Rand McNally.

Weiner, B. (1980). *Human motivation.* New York: Holt, Rinehart & Winston.

Weiner, R. D. (1984). Does electroconvulsive therapy cause brain damage? *The Behavioral and Brain Sciences, 7,* 1–53.

Weir, C. (1979). Auditory frequency sensitivity of human newborns: Some data with improved acoustic and behavioral controls. *Perception and Psychophysics, 26,* 287–294.

Weiss, J. M. (1970) Somatic effects of predictable and unpredictable shock. *Psychosomatic Medicine, 32,* 397–409.

Weissenberg, P., & Kavanagh, M. J. (1972). The independence of initiating structure and consideration: A review of the evidence. *Personnel Psychology, 25,* 119–130.

Weissman, M. M., Fox, K., & Klerman, G. I. (1973). Hostility and depression associated with suicide attempts. *American Journal of Psychiatry, 103,* 450–455.

Weisz, J. R. (1986). Contingency and control beliefs as predictors of psychotherapy outcomes among children and adolescents. *Journal of Consulting and Clinical Psychology, 54,* 789–795.

Weitzenhoffer, A. M., & Hilgard, E. R. (1959). *Stanford hypnotic susceptibility scale, Forms A and B.* Palo Alto, CA: Consulting Psychologists Press.

Weitzenhoffer, A. M., & Hilgard, E. R. (1962). *Stanford hypnotic susceptibility scale, Form C.* Palo Alto, CA: Consulting Psychologists Press.

Wekstein, L. (1979). *Handbook of suicidology: Principles, problems, and practice.* New York: Brunner/Mazel.

Wells, C. F., & Stuart, I. R. (Eds.). (1981). *Self-destructive behavior in children and adolescents.* New York: Van Nostrand Reinhold.

Wells, G. L., & Leippe, M. R. (1981). How do triers of fact infer the accuracy of eyewitness identification? *Journal of Applied Psychology, 67,* 682–687.

Wener, R., Frazier, W., & Farbstein, J. (1987, June). Building better jails. *Psychology Today.*

Werner, P. D., Rose, T. L., & Yesavage, J. A. (1983). Reliability, accuracy, and decision-making strategy in clinical predictions of imminent dangerousness. *Journal of Consulting and Clinical Psychology, 51,* 815–825.

West, S. G., & Brown, T. J. (1975). Physical attractiveness, the severity of the emergency and helping: A field experiment and interpersonal simulation. *Journal of Experimental Social Psychology, 11,* 531–538.

Weston, D. R., & Richardson, E. (1985, April). *Children's world views: Working models and quality of attachment.* Poster presented at the biennial meeting of the Society for Research in Child Development, Toronto, Ontario.

Wexley, K. N., & Yukl, G. A. (1984). *Organizational behavior and personnel psychology.* Homewood, IL: Richard D. Irwin.

Whalen, R., & Simon, N. G. (1984). Biological motivation. *Annual Review of Psychology, 35,* 257–276.

Whimbey, A. (1976). *Intelligence can be taught.* New York: Bantam.

White, F. J., & Wang, R. Y. (1986). Electrophysiological evidence for the existence of both D-1 and D-2 dopamine receptors in the rat nucleus accumbens. *Journal of Neuroscience, 6,* 274–280.

White, G. L., Fishbein, S., & Rutstein, J. (1981). Passionate love and the misattribution of arousal. *Journal of Personality and Social Psychology, 41,* 56–62.

Whitehouse, P. J., Struble, R. G., Hedreen, J. C., Clark, A. W., White, C. L., Parhad, I. M., & Price, D. L. (1983). Neuroanatomical evidence for a cholinergic deficit in Alzheimer's disease. *Psychopharmacology Bulletin, 19,* 437–440.

Whorf, B. L. (1956). *Language, thought and reality.* Cambridge and New York: MIT Press and Wiley.

Wichman, H. (1970). Effects of isolation and communication on cooperation in a two-person game. *Journal of Personality and Social Psychology, 16,* 114–120.

Wickelgren, W. (1979). *Cognitive psychology.* Englewood Cliffs, NJ: Prentice-Hall.

Wickens, C. D. (1984a). *Engineering psychology and human performance.* Columbus, OH: Charles Merrill.

Wickens, C. D. (1984b). Processing resources in attention. In R. Parasuraman & R. Davies (Eds.), *Varieties of attention* New York: Academic Press.

Wickens, C. D., Heffley, E., Kramer, A., & Donchin, E. (1980). The event related brain potential as an index of attention allocation in visual displays. In *Proceedings, 24th Annual Meeting of the Human Factors Society.* Santa Monica: Human Factors.

Wickens, C. D., & Kramer, A. (1985). Engineering psychology. *Annual Review of Psychology, 36,* 307–348.

Wickens, C. D., Sandry, D. L., & Vidulich, M. (1983). Compatibility and resource competition between modalities of input, output and central processing: Testing a model of complex task performance. *Human Factors, 25,* 227–248.

Wickens, D. D. (1938). Transference of conditioned excitation and conditioned inhibition from one muscle group to the antagonistic muscle group. *Journal of Experimental Psychology, 22,* 101–123.

Wickens, D. D. (1972). Characteristics of word encoding. In A. W. Melton & E. Martin (Eds.), *Coding processes in human memory.* Washington, DC: Winston.

Wickens, D. D. (1973). Some characteristics of word encoding. *Memory and Cognition, 1,* 485–490.

Wiener, E. L. (1977). Controlled flight into terrain accidents. *Human Factors, 19,* 171–180.

Wiesenfeld, A. R., & Klorman, R. (1978). The mother's psychophysiological reactions to contrasting affective expressions by her own and an unfamiliar infant. *Developmental Psychology, 14,* 294–304.

Wilder, D. A. (1977). Perception in groups, size of opposition, and social influence. *Journal of Experimental Social Psychology, 13,* 253–268.

Wiley, J. A., & Camacho, T. C. (1980). Life-style and future health: Evidence from the Alameda County study. *Preventive Medicine, 9,* 1–21.

Wilkinson, A. C. (1984). Children's partial knowledge of the cognitive skill of counting. *Cognitive Psychology, 16,* 28–64.

Williams, B. W., Jr., Haney, T. L., Lee, K. L., Yi-Hong Kong, Y. Blumenthal, J. A., & Whalen, R. E. (1980). Type A behavior, hostility, and coronary atherosclerosis. *Psychosomatic Medicine, 42,* 539–549.

Williams, C. D. (1959). Elimination of tantrum behavior by extinction procedures. *Journal of Personality and Social Psychology, 59,* 269.

Williams, R. C. (1985). *College, department, and course grade distribution for fall semester, 1984 (Research Memorandum No. 222)*. Champaign: University of Illinois, Office of Instructional Resources.

Williams, R. J. (1967). The biological approach to the study of personality. In T. Million (Ed.), *Theories of psychopathology*. Philadelphia: W. B. Saunders.

Willis, C. (1984, June 11). Unlocking pain's secrets. *Time*, pp. 58–66.

Willis, S. L., & Baltes, P. B. (1980). Intelligence in adulthood and aging: Contemporary issues. In L. Poon (Ed.), *Aging in the 1980s*. Washington, DC: American Psychological Association.

Wilson, E. O. (1975). *Sociobiology: The new synthesis*. Cambridge, MA: Harvard University Press.

Wilson, G. T. (1984). Weight control treatments. In J. D. Matarazzo, S. M. Weiss, J. H. Herd, N. E. Miller, & S. M. Weiss (Eds.), *Behavioral health: A handbook of health enhancement and disease prevention*. New York: Wiley.

Wilson, G. T. (1985). Limitations of meta-analysis in the evaluation of the effects of psychological therapy. *Clinical Psychology Review, 5*, 35–47.

Wilson, G. T., & Rachman, S. J. (1983). Meta-analysis and the evaluation of psychotherapy outcome: Limitations and liabilities. *Journal of Consulting and Clinical Psychology, 51*, 54–64.

Wilson, J. F. (1981). Behavioral preparation for surgery: Benefit or harm? *Journal of Behavioral Medicine, 4*, 79–102.

Wilson, L., & Kihlstrom, J. F. (1986). Subjective and categorical organization of recall during posthypnotic amnesia. *Journal of Abnormal Psychology, 95*, 264–273.

Wilson, L., & Rogers, R. W. (1975). The fire this time: Effects of race of target, insult and potential retaliation on black aggression. *Journal of Personality and Social Psychology, 32*, 857–864.

Wilson, S. C., & Barber, T. X. (1978). The creative imagination scale as a measure of hypnotic responsiveness: Applications to experimental and clinical hypnosis. *The American Journal of Clinical Hypnosis, 20*, 235–249.

Winder, P. H., Kety, S. S., Rosenthal, D., Schulsinger, F., Ortmann, J., & Lunde, I. (1986). Psychiatric disorders in biological and adoptive families of adopted individuals with affective disorders. *Archives of General Psychiatry, 43*, 923–929.

Winterbottom, M. R. (1953). *The relation of childhood training in independence to achievement motivation*. Unpublished doctoral dissertation, University of Michigan, Ann Arbor.

Wise, R. A. (1978). Catecholamine theories of reward: A critical review. *Brain Research, 152*, 215–247.

Wise, R. A., & Bozarth, M. A. (1984). Brain reward circuitry: Four circuit elements "wired" in apparent series. *Brain Research Bulletin, 12*, 203–208.

Wish, M., Deutsch, M., & Kaplan, S. J. (1976). Perceived dimensions of interpersonal relations. *Journal of Personality and Social Psychology, 33*, 409–420.

Wissler, C. (1901). The correlation of mental and physical traits. *Psychological Monographs, 3*, 1–62.

Witkin, H. A., Dyke, R. B., Faterson, H. F., Goodenough, D. R., & Karp, S. A. (1962). *Psychological differentiation*. New York: Wiley.

Wolfgang, M. (1978). *An overview of research into violent behavior*. Testimony before the U. S. House of Representatives, Committee on Science and Technology.

Wolpe, J. (1958). *Psychotherapy by reciprocal inhibition*. Stanford, CA: Stanford University Press.

Wolpe, J. (1982). *The practice of behavior therapy* (3rd ed.). New York: Pergamon Press.

Woodworth, R. S., & Schlosberg, H. (1954). *Experimental psychology*. New York: Holt.

Woody, E. Z., Costanzo, P. R., Liefer, H., & Conger, J. (1981). The effects of taste and caloric perceptions on the eating behavior of restrained and unrestrained subjects. *Cognitive Therapy and Research, 5*, 381–390.

Woolfolk, R. L., & McNulty, T. F. (1983). Relaxation treatment for insomnia: A component analysis. *Journal of Consulting and Clinical Psychology, 4*, 495–503.

Worchel, S., & Brehm, J. W. (1970). Effects of threats to attitudinal freedom as a function of agreement with the communicator. *Journal of Personality and Social Psychology, 14*, 18–22.

Wortman, C. B., & Dunkel-Schetter, C. (1979). Interpersonal relationships and cancer: A theoretical analysis. *Journal of Social Issues, 35*, 120–155.

Wyer, R. S., & Srull, T. K. (1986). Human cognition in its social context. *Psychological Review, 93*, 322–359.

Yaffe, M., & Nelson, E. C. (Eds.). (1982). *The influence of pornography on behavior*. New York: Academic Press.

Yakimovich, D., & Saltz, E. (1971). Helping behavior: The cry for help. *Psychonomic Science, 23*, 427–428.

Yalom, I. D. (1985). *The theory and practice of group psychotherapy* (3rd ed.). New York: Basic Books.

Yonas, A., & Arterberry, M. E. (in press). Space perception in infancy. In R. Vasta (Ed.), *Annals of Child Development: Vol. 4*.

Young, M. (1966). Problem solving performance in two age groups. *Journal of Gerontology, 21*, 505–509.

Young, M. (1971). Age and sex differences in problem solving. *Journal of Gerontology, 26*, 331–336.

Yukl, G. (1981). *Leadership in organizations*. Englewood Cliffs, NJ: Prentice-Hall.

Zafiropoulou, M., & McPherson, F. M. (1986). "Preparedness" and the severity and outcome of clinical phobias. *Behavior Research and Therapy, 24*, 221–222.

Zahn-Waxler, C., Friedman, F. L., & Cummings, E. M. (1983). Children's emotions and behaviors in response to infants' cries. *Child Development, 54*, 1522–1528.

Zahn-Waxler, C., Iannotti, R., & Chapman, M. (1982). Peers and prosocial development. In K. H. Rubin & H. S. Ross (Eds.), *Peer Relationships and Social Skills in Childhood*. New York: Springer-Verlag.

Zahn-Waxler, C., & Radke-Yarrow, M. (1979). *A developmental analysis of children's responses to emotions in others*. Paper presented at the biennial meeting of the Society for Research in Child Development, San Francisco, CA.

Zajonc, R. B. (1965). Social facilitation. *Science, 149*, 269–274.

Zajonc, R. B. (1980). Feeling and thinking: Preferences need no inferences. *American Psychologist, 35*, 151–175.

Zajonc, R. B. (1985). Emotion and facial efference: A theory reclaimed. *Science, 228*, 15–21.

Zaleska, M. (1978). Some experimental results: Majority influence on group decisions. In H. Brandstatter, J. H. Davis, & H. Schuler (Eds.), *Dynamics of group decisions*. Beverly Hills, CA: Sage.

Zax, M., & Stricker, G. (1963). *Patterns of psychopathology*. New York: Macmillan.

Zellner, M. (1970). Self-esteem, reception, and influenceability. *Journal of Personality and Social Psychology, 15*, 87–93.

Zentall, S. S., & Zentall, T. R. (1983). Optimal stimulation: A model of disordered activity and performance in normal and deviant children. *Psychological Bulletin, 94*, 446–471.

Zigler, E., & Phillips, L. (1961). Psychiatric diagnosis and symptomatology. *Journal of Abnormal and Social Pathology, 63*, 69–75.

Zigler, E., & Seitz, V. (1982). Social policy and intelligence. In R. J. Sternberg (Ed.), *Handbook of human intelligence*. Cambridge: Cambridge University Press.

Zigler, E., & Valentine, J. (Eds.). (1979). *Project Head Start: A legacy of the war on poverty*. New York: Free Press.

Zilboorg, G., & Henry, G. W. (1941). *A history of medical psychology*. New York: W. W. Norton.

Zillmann, D. (1971). Excitation transfer in communication-mediated aggressive behavior. *Journal of Experimental Social Psychology, 7,* 419–434.

Zillmann, D. (1978a). Attribution and misattribution of excitatory reactions. In J. H. Harvey, W. J. Ickes, & R. F. Kidd (Eds.), *New directions in attribution research: Vol. 2.* Hillsdale, NJ: Lawrence Erlbaum Associates.

Zillmann, D. (1978b). *Hostility and aggression.* Hillsdale, NJ: Lawrence Erlbaum Associates.

Zillmann, D. (1983). Arousal and aggression. In R. Geen & E. Donnerstein (Eds.), *Aggression: Theoretical and empirical reviews.* New York: Academic Press.

Zillmann, D. (1984). *Connections between sex and aggression.* Hillsdale, NJ: Lawrence Erlbaum Associates.

Zillmann, D., Baron, R. A., & Tamborini, R. (1981). Social costs of smoking: Effects of tobacco smoke on hostile behavior. *Journal of Applied Social Psychology, 11,* 548–561.

Zillmann, D., Katcher, A. H., & Milavsky, B. (1972). Excitation transfer from physical exercise to subsequent aggressive behavior. *Journal of Experimental Social Psychology, 8,* 247–259.

Zimbardo, P. G., Weisenberg, M., Firestone, I., & Levy, B. (1965). Communicator effectiveness in producing public conformity and private attitude change. *Journal of Personality, 33,* 233–255.

Zinberg, N. E. (1974). *High states: A beginning study.* Washington, DC: Drug Abuse Council.

Zitrin, C. M. (1983). Differential treatment of phobias: Use of imipramine for panic attacks. *Journal of Behavior Therapy and Experimental Psychiatry, 14,* 11–18.

Zubek, J. P. (Ed.). (1969). *Sensory deprivation: Fifteen years of research.* New York: Appleton-Century-Crofts.

Zubin, J., & Spring, B. (1977). Vulnerability—A new view of schizophrenia. *Journal of Abnormal Psychology, 86,* 103–126.

Zuckerman, M. (1979). *Sensation seeking: Beyond the optimal level of arousal.* Hillsdale, NJ: Lawrence Erlbaum Associates.

Zuckerman, M. (1984). Sensation seeking: A comparative approach to a human approach. *The Behavioral and Brain Sciences, 7,* 413–471.

Chapter 1: **p. 3 (Opener):** © Kent Hanson/DOT. **p. 5**: © Yoav/Phototake. **p. 6**: © M. Philippot/Sygma. **p. 7**: © Jerry Irwin/Photo Researchers, Inc. **p. 8**: © Mark Antman/The Image Works. **p. 10**: © M. Serraillier/Photo Researchers, Inc. **p. 11**: © Jerry Howard/Positive Images. **p. 12**: © Bill Bernstein/Phototake. **p. 18**: © Billy E. Barnes/Click Chicago. **p. 20**: © Thomas McAvoy, Life Magazine, © 1955 Time Inc. **p. 22**: © Jim Pickerell/Click Chicago.

Chapter 2: **p. 29 (Opener):** © Jane Art Ltd./The Image Bank. **p. 32**: © Elizabeth Crews. **p. 35**: © Michael Weisbrot and Family. **p. 40**: © Camera M. D. Studios. **p. 43**: © Elizabeth Crews. **p. 47**: © Elizabeth Crews. **p. 49**: © Andrew Brilliant. **p. 57**: © Michael Weisbrot and Family. **p. 58**: © Michael Weisbrot and Family. **p. 61**: © Wanstall/The Image Works. **p. 65**: © James Carroll. **p. 69**: © J. P. Laffont/Sygma. **p. 72**: © Eastcott/Momatiuk/The Image Works. **p. 73**: © Andrew Brilliant. **p. 76**: © Michael Weisbrot and Family.

Chapter 3: **p. 81 (Opener):** Science Photo Library/Photo Researchers, Inc. **p. 91**: By permission of the Brain Tissue Resource Center, Ralph Lowell Laboratories, McLean Hospital. **p. 92**: Courtesy of Wright State University, Dayton, Ohio. **p. 95**: © Michael Brohm/Nawrocki Stock Photo. **p. 105**: top: © Harvey Stein 1986 from *Artists Observed*; bottom: © Karsh/Ottawa/Woodfin Camp & Associates. **p. 107**: © Ira Wyman/Sygma.

Chapter 4: **p. 119 (Opener):** © David Hughes/The Picture Cube. **p. 125**: © Tannenbaum/Sygma. **p. 129**: Scanning electron micrographs by Robert E. Preston, Courtesy of Professor J. E. Hawkins, Kresge Hearing Research Institute, University of Michigan. **p. 131**: © Alex Webb/Magnum Photos. **p. 134**: © Joel Gordon 1980. **p. 138**: © Lionel Atwill/Peter Arnold, Inc. **p. 140**: © Peter L. Chapman. **p. 148**: © Andrew Brilliant. **p. 150**: © Peter L. Chapman. **p. 151**: © Karsh/Ottawa/Woodfin Camp & Associates. **p. 157**: © Rancinan/Sygma.

Chapter 5: **p. 163 (Opener):** © Norm Francoeur. **p. 173**: © Alan Carey/The Image Works. **p. 176**: © Will Barnet, Collection Mr. & Mrs. Lee M. Oser Jr. **p. 178**: © Jim Anderson/Woodfin Camp & Associates. **p. 180**: © Chuck O'Rear/Woodfin Camp & Associates. **p. 196**: © Michael Brohm/Nawrocki Stock Photo.

Chapter 6: **p. 205 (Opener):** © Don Landwehrle/The Image Bank. **p. 208**: top: © The Bettmann Archive; bottom: © The Bettmann Archive. **p. 209**: © Alan Carey/The Image Works. **p. 210**: top: © 1986, Washington Post Writers Group, reprinted with permission; bottom: Reproduced with permission of the American Association of Advertising Agencies. **p. 213**: © Michael Nichols/Magnum Photos. **p. 222**: National Library of Medicine. **p. 223**: © John Running/Stock Boston. **p. 227**: © H. Angelo-Castrillo/Black Star. **p. 229**: © Joel Gordon, 1986. **p. 233**: © Jeff Rotman/Peter Arnold, Inc. **p. 238**: © Richard Hutchings/Photo Researchers, Inc.

Chapter 7: **p. 243 (Opener):** © Walter Booth/National Audubon Society/Photo Researchers, Inc. **p. 247**: © Jerry Howard/Positive Images. **p. 256**: © Abigail Heyman/Archive Pictures, Inc. **p. 259**: © Carol Palmer. **p. 261**: © Carlos Vergara/Nawrocki Stock Photo. **p. 264**: © Frank Siteman/EKM-Nepenthe. **p. 271**: © Michael Weisbrot and Family. **p. 276**: © Eastcott/Momatiuk/The Image Works.

Chapter 8: **p. 281 (Opener):** © Cosimo/The Image Bank. **p. 284**: © Carol Palmer. **p. 285**: © Elizabeth Crews. **p. 290**: © Michael Weisbrot and Family. **p. 299**: top; © Ira Wyman/Sygma; bottom: © Robert W. Ginn/EKM-Nepenthe. **p. 300**: © Andrew Brilliant. **p. 304**: © Michael Weisbrot and Family. **p. 309**: © 1986, G. B. Trudeau, Reprinted with permission of Universal Press Syndicate. All rights reserved. **p. 313**: © Jeff Cadge/The Image Bank.

Chapter 9: **p. 321 (Opener):** © David W. Hamilton/The Image Bank. **p. 325**: © Brian Drake/EKM-Nepenthe. **p. 329**: left: © Wide World Photos; right: © Robert Eckert/EKM-Nepenthe. **p. 334**: © Arthur Grace/Sygma. **p. 340**: © Jill Cannefax/EKM-Nepenthe. **p. 345**: © David Welcher/Sygma. **p. 349**: © Ken Regan/Camera 5. **p. 351**: © Jerry Howard/Positive Images. **p. 352**: © Bob Adelman/Magnum. **p. 357**: © Jerry Howard/Positive Images.

Chapter 10: **p. 367 (Opener):** © Will McIntyre/Photo Researchers, Inc. **p. 373**: © Michael Weisbrot and Family. **p. 375**: © Carol Palmer. **p. 377**: © Michal Thompson/EKM-Nepenthe. **p. 379**: © Karsh/Ottawa/Woodfin Camp & Associates. **p. 380**: © Leo Cullum, 1987. **p. 381**: © Brent Jones. **p. 383**: © Elizabeth Crews. **p. 387**: © Elizabeth Crews. **p. 393**: © Alan Carey/The Image Works. **p. 394**: © Rick Friedman/Black Star. **p. 396**: top: Courtesy of the Harvard University Art Museums (Fogg Art Museum) Bequest-Collection of Maurice Wertheim, Class of 1906; bottom © Four by Five.

Chapter 11: **p. 405 (Opener):** © Bob Krist. **p. 412**: © Jill Cannefax/EKM-Nepenthe. **p. 417**: Courtesy Neal E. Miller, Rockefeller and Yale Universities. **p. 419**: From "The Control of Eating Behavior in an Anorexia by Operant Techniques," by Arthur J. Bachrach, William J. Erwin, and Jay P. Mohr, in *Case Studies in Behavior Modification,* edited by Leonard P. Ullman and Leonard Krasner. Copyright 1965 by Holt, Rinehart, and Winston, Inc. **p. 421**: © Mike Mazzaschi/Stock Boston. **p. 425**: © Steven Baratz/The Picture Cube. **p. 428**: © Peter L. Chapman. **p. 430**: © Roy Roper/EKM-Nepenthe. **p. 431**: © Michael Weisbrot and Family. **p. 432**: © James Carroll. **p. 434**: © J. Guichard/Sygma. **p. 437**: © Michael Nichols/Magnum Photos.

Chapter 12: **p. 443 (Opener):** © Jeff Jacobson/Archive Pictures, Inc. **p. 449**: © John Eastcott/Yva Momatiuk/The Image Works. **p. 456**: © Rick Mansfield/The Image Works. **p. 459**: © Jeb Bladine/EKM-Nepenthe. **p. 461**: left: © Kurt Thorson/EKM-Nepenthe; middle: © Andrew Brilliant; right: © R. Darolle/Sygma. **p. 462**: © Copyright Paul Ekman, 1972 P. Ekman "Universals and cultural differences in facial expressions of emotion," in J. Cole (Ed.), *Nebraska Symposium on Motivation,* 1971, vol. 19, Lincoln: University of Nebraska Press, 1972. **p. 464**: © Carol Palmer. **p. 466**: © Jerry Howard/Positive Images.

Chapter 13: **p. 473 (Opener):** © Matthew Naythons/Stock Boston. **p. 476**: © Wide World Photo. **p. 478**: © Hans Wolf/The Image Bank. **p. 483**: © Michael Weisbrot and Family. **p. 486**: © 1984, Washington Post Writers Group, reprinted with permission. **p. 487**: © James Carroll. **p. 488**: © E. Hartmann/Magnum Photos. **p. 489**: © Owen Franken/Sygma. **p. 491**: © Michael Weisbrot and Family. **p. 492**: © Tom Grill/Comstock Inc. **p. 497**: © John Griffin/The Image Works. **p. 499**: © Yoav/Phototake.

Chapter 14: **p. 505 (Opener):** © Cary Wolinsky/Stock Boston. **p. 507**: © Michael Weisbrot and Family. **p. 510**: © The Bettmann Archive. **p. 511**: © Historical Pictures Service, Inc. **p. 514**: © Robert Cushman Hayes. **p. 519**: © Carol Palmer. **p. 523**: Drawing by Chas. Addams; © 1981 The New Yorker Magazine, Inc. **p. 524**: © Jeff Persons/Stock Boston. **p. 528**: © David Grossman **p. 533**: © Patrick L. Pfister/Stock Boston. **p. 536**: © John Maher/EKM-Nepenthe.

Chapter 15: **p. 543 (Opener):** © Denley Karlson/Stock Boston. **p. 547**: © Randy Taylor/Sygma. **p. 549**: © Culver Pictures. **p. 556**: © 1985, Universal Press Syndicate. Reprinted with permission. **p. 560**: *I'm Eve* by Chris Sizemore and Ellen Sain Pittillo. Copyright © 1977 by Chris Costner Sizemore. Reprinted by permission of Doubleday & Company, Inc. **p. 561**: © Joel Gordon 1978. **p. 563**: Courtesy Samariteens. **p. 567**: Prinzhorn Collection, Photograph by I. L. Klinger. **p. 568**: © Grunnitus/Monkmeyer Press. **p. 573**: © Michael